SOCIOLOGY: HUMAN SOCIETY

SECOND EDITION

CRITICAL READERS

Harold J. Abramson, University of Connecticut
Carl W. Backman, University of Nevada at Reno
Robert Blauner, University of California at Berkeley
Lynn Brody, Michigan State University
Donald R. Brown, University of Michigan
Carol Ehrlich, University of Maryland
Howard J. Ehrlich, Research Group One, Baltimore
Doris R. Entwisle, Johns Hopkins University
Myron F. Erickson, Mount San Antonio College
David A. Goslin, National Research Council
Edward Gross, University of Washington
Jeffrey K. Hadden, University of Virginia
Bill J. Harrell, University of Connecticut
Joan Huber, University of Illinois
Dorothea Hubin, Fairleigh Dickinson University
Charlene Knuckman, The City of Chicago
Kurt Lang, State University of New York at Stony Brook
Richard F. Larson, California State University at Hayward
David T. Lewis, University of Maryland
Stanley Lieberson, University of Arizona
William H. Martineau, George Washington University
Leon H. Mayhew, University of California at Davis
Kenneth Neubeck, University of Connecticut
Kenneth Polk, University of Oregon
Ira L. Reiss, University of Minnesota
Leonard Reissman, Cornell University
Joseph W. Scott, University of Notre Dame
David R. Segal, University of Maryland
James F. Short, Jr., Washington State University
Curt Tausky, University of Massachusetts
Arthur M. Vener, Michigan State University
Glenn M. Vernon, University of Utah
Lyle G. Warner University of Nevada at Reno
Charles R. Wright, University of Pennsylvania

SOCIOLOGY: HUMAN SOCIETY

SECOND EDITION

Melvin L. DeFleur
Professor of Sociology, Washington State University

William V. D'Antonio
Chairman, Department of Sociology, University of Connecticut

Lois B. DeFleur
Professor of Sociology, Washington State University

With the assistance of
Cynthia H. Adamic

Scott, Foresman and Company   Glenview, Illinois
Dallas, Tex.   Oakland, N.J.   Palo Alto, Cal.   Tucker, Ga.   Brighton, England

Library of Congress Cataloging in Publication Data

DeFleur, Melvin Lawrence, 1923–
    Sociology

    Includes bibliographical references and indexes.
    1. Sociology. I. D'Antonio, William V., joint
author. II. DeFleur, Lois B., 1936–   joint
author. III. Title.
HM51.D39 1976   301   75-28466
ISBN 0-673-07927-9

1 2 3 4 5 6 7 8 9 10–WAK–82 81 80 79 78 77 76 75

ACKNOWLEDGMENTS

Chapter 1

American Sociological Association: "Why I Wanted to Become a Sociologist" by Stuart A. Rice, *The American Sociologist*, November 1968, p. 285.

Chapter 2

The University of Chicago Press: selections from *Street-Corner Society* by William F. Whyte, 1955. Reprinted by permission of the publisher.

Chapter 4

Social Forces: selection from "The Structure of the Brazilian Family" by Emilio Willems, August 1953; reprinted by permission.

Chapter 5

Kingsley Davis: selection from "Final Note on a Case of Extreme Isolation," from *The American Journal of Sociology*, 52 (March 1947). Reprinted by permission.

The Free Press: table reprinted with permission of Macmillan Publishing Co., Inc., from *The Nature of Human Values* by Milton Rokeach. Copyright © 1973 by The Free Press, a Division of Macmillan Publishing Co., Inc.

Saturday Review: from "A Conversation With Jerome Kagan." First appeared in *Saturday Review of Education*, April 1973. Copyright © 1973 by Saturday Review Company. Used with permission.

Chapter 6

Ms. Magazine: from "Down With Sexist Upbringing" by Letty Cottin Pogrebin in *Ms.*, Spring, 1972. Reprinted by permission.

The New York Review of Books: selection from "Teaching the Unteachable" by Herbert R. Kohl. Reprinted with permission from *The New York Review of Books*. Copyright © 1967 Herbert R. Kohl.

Chapter 7

America: selection from "The Morality of Punishment" by Robert M. Byrn from *America*, January 15, 1972. Reprinted with permission of *America*, 1972. All Rights Reserved. © 1972 by America Press, 106 West 56th Street, New York, N.Y., 10019.

American Sociological Association: table on "How People View the Seriousness of Crimes" by Peter H. Rossi, Emily Waite, Christine E. Bose, and Richard E. Berk, from *American Sociological Review*, Vol. 39, No. 2, April 1974, pp. 228–229. Reprinted by permission.

The Free Press: table reprinted with permission of Macmillan Publishing Co., Inc., from *Social Theory and Social Structure* by Robert K. Merton. Copyright © 1957 by The Free Press, a Corporation.

Newsweek: table from "Crime in the Nation's Cities," U.S. Department of Justice (Law Enforcement Assistance Administration), April 29, 1974. Copyright Newsweek, Inc., 1974, reprinted by permission.

Chapter 8

Chapter 9

Chapter 10

Chapter 11

PREFACE

This second edition of *Sociology: Human Society* not only builds on the strengths that made the first edition a widely popular text but also incorporates many substantial improvements. In preparing the revision, we have systematically sought advice from specialists in the major subfields of sociology, from colleagues teaching introductory sociology in a variety of academic settings, and—equally important—from students who have used the book. Our goal has been to make the text increasingly effective as a teaching and learning tool as well as to bring its content up to date with recent developments in the discipline.

It is impossible to enumerate all the changes made in this edition, but a few examples will suggest the broad scope of the revision. The discussion of culture (Chapter 4) has been expanded to include a detailed consideration of subcultures, highlighted by an extended example drawn from the occupational world of the carnival. New material on perception and cognition has been incorporated into the chapter on personal organization (Chapter 5), which now focuses more specifically on the importance of social experience in shaping individual personality. The discussion of deviance (Chapter 7) has been substantially revised and moved forward to follow the chapter on socialization, to which it logically relates. Similarly, the discussion of minority groups (Chapter 9) has been revised and repositioned so that it builds on the ideas developed in the analysis of social stratification (Chapter 8). Throughout the text, a consistent effort has been made not only to clarify the basic concepts of sociology but also to show the relationships between them.

Major additions to later chapters of the book include: a look at rural life in urban America in Chapter 12; an extended analysis of social movements, illustrated by the current women's movement, in Chapter 13; a consideration of media violence and its possible effects in Chapter 14; a discussion of the Chinese family system in Chapter 15; and new materials on the military-industrial complex, the civil bureaucracy, and multinational corporations in the political and economic chapters. The largest single block of new material appears in Chapter 19, which now includes a major section on the American welfare system as a social institution. The final chapter of the text contains a new section on the ethics of sociological research, built around a discussion of Laud Humphreys's controversial study of the "tearoom trade."

Every chapter of the text has been rewritten not only to clarify central ideas but also to avoid language constructions, such as the use of masculine pronouns in referring to both sexes, that seem to suggest less than equal status for women. An effort has been made throughout to provide a more balanced consideration of male and female sex roles and to show how they have been changing.

More generally, the objectives guiding us in the preparation of this revision of *Sociology: Human Society* have been the ones that guided us in developing the original edition. First, we have attempted to integrate the important theoretical concepts of classic and contemporary sociology with the discipline's accumulation of empirical studies. Instead of trying to catalogue every aspect of modern sociology, the text thoroughly discusses the concepts, theories, and research that are basic to the discipline. While clearly selective, this coverage includes a broad spectrum of specialized interests and methodological approaches. Throughout the book, examples are integrated with the textual discussion of concepts. These illustrations are drawn from many sources, ranging from quantitative research reports to eyewitness accounts of riots, mass hallucinations, and deviant behavior. We have also evaluated the validity of sociological formulations, distinguishing those that have solid research support from more tentative theories and from sociological speculation.

Second, we have attempted to develop our sociological framework within a context of significant social issues. The text emphasizes that an understanding of modern society requires an analysis of the processes underlying not only social equilibrium but also social conflict. It maintains that sociology is as much concerned with rock festivals, urban riots, and class conflict as it is with the small-group laboratory, the large-scale bureaucratic organization, and the foundations of social order.

Finally, we have tried to present a comprehensive picture of sociology as a discipline, treating its ethical issues, controversies, and shortcomings along with its contributions and accomplishments. Rather than emphasizing a particular theoretical perspective to the exclusion of other points of view, the text discusses the competing orientations of modern sociology.

The second edition of *Sociology: Human Society* retains two special features that have proved particularly significant for the introductory student: the essays on research methods, now called *Tools of Sociology*, and the contrasting *Viewpoints* on particular issues of social concern. The twenty-nine Tools of Sociology included in this edition have been prepared with the help of a number of our colleagues to introduce the student to the research techniques and procedures commonly used by sociologists. Each essay is set off in a special format and positioned near related textual discussion. While these essays will by no means equip students to do research on their own, they should give them a feeling for the working tools of the sociologist. They should also help students understand the difficulty of studying social phenomena and some of the practical problems that sociologists encounter in attempting to assemble valid and reliable data.

The Viewpoints, a second special feature of the text, are intended to promote sociological discussion of specific issues and to illustrate the need for careful inquiry in unraveling complex problems. Each Viewpoints page presents two brief interpretations of a particular issue. One pair of Viewpoints in Chapter 9, for example, contrasts the ideas of two important American Indian leaders on tactics for achieving Indian objectives. Dennis Banks, who has played a key role in the events at Wounded Knee, advocates a militant stand by Indians to redress their grievances, whereas Vine Deloria, Jr., author of *Custer Died for Your Sins*, advocates outwitting whites by superior intellectual strategies. Other Viewpoints, most of them new to this edition, examine such issues as sex roles, equality and inequality, the social responsibility of business, and shortages of natural resources.

Sociology: Human Society provides maximum flexibility for the instructor and adjusts easily to courses of different lengths. The first ten chapters of the book are central to any introductory course since they present the most basic concepts and theories of sociology. But beyond that, instructors can pick and choose the chapters they want to cover, depending not only on the time available but also on their special interests. The "institutional" chapters are grouped conveniently at the end of the text and can be used selectively or omitted entirely. If it appears desirable, instructors can also bypass some or all of the Viewpoints and Tools of Sociology. The Epilogue is recommended even for a short course, especially among students who are interested in the problems and challenges facing sociology as a discipline. Supplementary items available for use with the text include a study guide, a recently prepared personalized system of instruction, test items, and an instructor's manual.

Individual contributions to a book of this type are cumulative and therefore all but impossible to unravel. The critical readers, who are listed opposite the title page, made innumerable suggestions for improving the manuscript. We would like to thank them for their valuable assistance while emphasizing that they are in no way responsible for any shortcomings in the book. Many students, both undergraduates and graduates, helped us sharpen our ideas, and many colleagues and friends provided helpful information and references, both in this revision and in the original edition. To everyone who has given us a helping hand along the way, we express our collective gratitude.

Colleagues who provided help and suggestions specific to this edition include Irving Allen, Bonnie Baker, Sandra Ball-Rokeach, Arnold Dashefsky, Fabio Dasilva, James Davidson, Riley Dunlap, Michael Gordon, Jerold Heiss, Jeff Hubbard, Joan Huber, Richard Kurtz, Otto Larsen, Luis Leñero, Roger W. Little, John Maiolo, Armand Mauss, Ron Miller, Milton Rokeach, Herbert Roll, Vickie Rose, James F. Short, Jr., and Andrew Weigert. We would also like to thank Stanley Anderson; Linda Copp; Albert, Carla, and Nancy D'Antonio; Marilyn Horton; Susan Miller; Ronald Petruzello; Jo Anne D. Placona; Carol Rediske; Nancy Reiff; and Elizabeth Scotta, who aided in typing, tracking down census data, footnote references, tables, and other basic information and helped develop the Glossary.

The staff of Scott, Foresman's College Division kept us going through many rounds of writing, rewriting, revising, and plain hard work. John Nolan, Barbara Forlenza, Mary Helfrich, John Reuter-Pacyna, and Veronica Ward all worked behind the scenes to produce this book. We are especially appreciative of the many contributions made by Sybil Sosin, who not only provided irreplaceable editorial work on the manuscript but also coordinated the seemingly endless tasks that made this edition a reality.

Melvin L. DeFleur
William V. D'Antonio
Lois B. DeFleur
Cynthia H. Adamic

CONTENTS (Brief)

CONTENTS (Complete)

Tools of Sociology

SOCIOLOGY: HUMAN SOCIETY

SECOND EDITION

PROLOGUE
THE SCIENCE
OF SOCIETY

1
The Science
of Society

At a midwestern university, a student protest against U.S. foreign policy ends tragically as National Guardsmen fire a volley of shots that leave fifteen students wounded or dead.[1] In a suburb of Boston, a middle-aged woman spends the afternoon drinking herself into oblivion behind closed curtains. In San Francisco, a sixty-two-year-old man shuts the door of his garage, settles into the front seat of his car, starts the engine, and waits for death. Sociologists are concerned with explaining all these tragic events. Why does orderly group conflict sometimes erupt into violent confrontation or mob action? What leads to alcoholism and what impact does it have on people's lives? Under what personal and social circumstances do 24,000 Americans—young and old, black and white, rich and poor—deliberately end their lives each year?

In their efforts to understand the fundamental nature of human society, sociologists study *all* aspects of social behavior—the usual as well as the unusual, the conforming as well as the deviant, the impersonal as well as the personal. As this text will make clear, many of the issues that concern them as social scientists are issues that concern us all as citizens. Why, in a society committed to ideals of equality, are some Americans continuously kept down because of race, sex, religion, or some other characteristic that has nothing to do with their abilities? What factors in family life or in society make one marriage in every three end in divorce within ten years? Why do millions of workers in the United States find their jobs agonizingly dull, and what does this do to them? What will be the long-range effects of our present rate of population growth? Does television viewing encourage violence in children? What influence is the women's movement having on our society? Why did such groups as the Jesus People emerge? What is happening to our cities, and what is likely to be their future?

1. In May 1970, Ohio National Guardsmen opened fire on students at Kent State University, who were demonstrating against the invasion of Cambodia by United States troops.

But though sociologists devote a great deal of research to contemporary issues and social problems, their overall concern is much broader. They are attempting to develop a body of concepts, principles, theories, and methods of study that will lead to an increasingly precise understanding of *basic social processes*. Sociologists differ from one another in their theoretical orientations as well as in their areas of special interest, but probably most would agree to a definition of sociology as an attempt to examine society *systematically* within the scientific perspective. Their long-range goals are to understand human social behavior, to predict it, and, in some cases, to apply their knowledge toward changing it.

Many students turn to sociology hoping to find answers that will help them understand and cope with their immediate social world. Others look to sociology for guides to improving society as a whole. While much of the knowledge sociologists have accumulated is relevant to these practical goals, it is a mistake to assume that sociology offers a blueprint for utopia or even for the solution of specific social problems. Indeed, for the thoughtful student this introduction to the discipline may raise as many questions as it answers. What sociology *can* do is provide us with a better understanding of the underlying principles that shape social life and thus give us new insights into our particular social worlds.

THE PRESCIENTIFIC ORIGINS OF SOCIOLOGY

Although sociology as an organized field of research and teaching dates back only a few generations, people have been seeking to understand and improve social life for many centuries. Indeed, contemporary sociology can be viewed as a modern extension of the age-old efforts of philosophers and other scholars to determine how society worked and how its problems might be solved. A brief discussion of several high

points in the history of social thought will help place sociology in perspective.

THE QUEST FOR AN IDEAL SOCIAL ORDER

Some of the earliest attempts to stabilize the social order and make it work more justly are found in ancient systems of law such as the Code of Hammurabi in ancient Babylonia, the Hindu Laws of Manu, and the Mosaic Code of the Old Testament. Each of these documents sets forth rules that were intended to ensure harmony in society as a whole and also to provide fair treatment for individuals. Hammurabi, a powerful king of Babylonia more than four thousand years ago, had 282 laws inscribed on great stone tablets. These laws included provisions for regulating commerce, the practice of medicine, military and political affairs, the treatment of children, and many other kinds of social relationships, like troublesome neighbors and unhappy marriages:

If any one be too lazy to keep his dam in proper condition, and does not keep it; if then the dam break and all the fields be flooded, then shall he in whose dam the break occurred be sold for money, and the money shall replace the corn which he has caused to be ruined. . . .

If a man's wife, who lives in his house, wishes to leave it, plunges into debt, tries to ruin her house, neglects her husband, and is judicially convicted; if her husband offers her release, she may go on her way, and he gives her nothing as a gift on release. If her husband does not wish to release her, and if he take another wife, she shall remain as servant in her husband's house.[2]

Like modern legal codes, Hammurabi's laws were based to a large extent upon the customs of his society, established by tradition long before they were written down. But—again like modern laws—they also represented a determined effort to achieve social reform. As Hammurabi stated in the prologue to his code, he was exercising his divine authority as king of Babylonia "to cause justice to prevail in the land, to destroy the wicked and the evil, to prevent the strong from oppressing the weak . . . to

2. In Lewis Browne, ed., *The World's Great Scriptures* (New York: The Macmillan Company, 1946).

The Code of Hammurabi, which was inscribed on stone tablets, was one of the earliest and most systematic attempts to improve social life.

enlighten the land and to further the welfare of the people.'' If these phrases sound like the preelection promises of a twentieth-century politician, it is because the goal of an ideal social order has continued to intrigue humankind.

Many philosophers have tried to design a perfect society. Plato, for example, spent much of his life working out a blueprint for the organization of a utopian society in which justice could be maximized. His *Republic,* written in the fourth century B.C., is the first really extensive and systematic social analysis produced in the Western world.[3] The society described by Plato was modeled upon the relatively small *polis,* the Greek city-state with which he was familiar. He believed that his ideal society could serve as a guide for those who wanted to ensure just treatment for all citizens. Plato described in detail his plans for government, family life, economic organization, class structure, and education, all designed to promote harmonious social relationships. No known society has ever tried to put his

social system into practice, however, and despite Plato's continued influence on Western thought, his ideas for improving society have remained unproven speculations of unknown practical utility.

THE BEGINNINGS OF SOCIAL THEORY
Throughout most of history, the great stumbling block for social theorists has been that they lacked a reliable method for verifying their conclusions—for testing them against empirical evidence. During the Middle Ages, for example, explanations of both physical and social phenomena were evaluated by comparing them with the teachings of ancient authorities (e.g., Plato and Aristotle). They were accepted as valid only if they seemed consistent with Christian dogma. A new way of assessing the validity of cause-effect generalizations—the *scientific method*—finally became available as part of the intellectual revolution of the seventeenth and eighteenth centuries.

The Foundations for a Science of Society
The logical foundations for today's scientific method were established early in the seventeenth century by such people as Francis Bacon and René Descartes. They argued that scientists must rid themselves of preconceived notions about the nature of things in the world and seek new understandings through three processes: observation, experiment, and reason. *Observation* meant that a systematic effort must be made to obtain all the relevant facts concerning the phenomenon under study. *Experiment* referred to the need for making observations under controlled conditions that would minimize the influence of irrelevant factors. *Reason* meant that observed facts must be interpreted in an objective and logical way in order to arrive at sound conclusions. These processes represent the foundations of the scientific method, and by the eighteenth century their application was producing impressive advances in the physical and biological sciences. The groundwork was thus laid for developing a reliable method of analyzing social phenomena.

3. *The Republic of Plato,* trans. Francis P. Cornford (New York: Oxford University Press, 1961).

The Social Contract Theorists

While the foundations of the scientific method were being developed within the context of the physical and biological sciences, ideas about society continued to accumulate, and the basis of a new approach to the study of society began to emerge. An important contributor was the English political philosopher Thomas Hobbes (1588–1679), who sought a rational justification of political authority that would be consistent with the facts of history and with his own dark view of human nature. Hobbes believed that since the individual in a state of nature was "as a wolf to his fellow man," absolute government was essential to prevent social conflict and to maintain an ordered society. In *Leviathan* (1651), he pictured the state as a great artificial man, "in which the sovereignty is the artificial soul, as giving life and motion to the whole body."[4]

Hobbes believed that in the distant past people had willingly surrendered their rights to an absolute government in order to protect themselves from each other and so create a workable society. He thus provided one of the earliest statements of the social contract theory of government, which sees the origins of the state as an agreement among society's members to submit voluntarily to rule in order to stabilize social relationships. Later writers such as John Locke (1632–1704) and Jean Jacques Rousseau (1712–1778) developed important variations of the social contract theory. Unlike Hobbes, however, both Locke and Rousseau used the concept to challenge authoritarian rule and to demonstrate the people's right to overthrow an unjust government and establish a more equitable "contract."[5]

Here we see the social theorist's perennial concern with the relationship of social stability to social conflict. The contract theorists were concerned mainly with ways to eliminate, or at least minimize, conflict. In more modern times, by contrast, conflict has come to be viewed as probably inescapable in society and sometimes as an important beginning point for social change. These issues will be addressed more fully in a later section (pages 16–17).

THE EMERGENCE OF MODERN SOCIOLOGY

Between the beginning of the eighteenth century and the first quarter of the nineteenth, the social sciences had their formal beginnings. As the scientific method began to be applied to the study of social phenomena, social philosophy gradually was divided into more specialized fields such as anthropology, economics, political science, sociology, and psychology. It was a time of intellectual excitement, stimulated by the enticing vision of a "social physics" that would provide for students of society what the natural sciences were providing for students of the physical world.

AUGUSTE COMTE AND THE POSITIVE PHILOSOPHY

As the nineteenth century began, philosophers were trying to understand science better, to classify the knowledge it was generating, and to apply its methods of study to new fields. The French social philosopher Henri de Rouvroy, Comte de Saint-Simon (1760–1825), for example, proposed a *science politique* that would draw on the methods of the physical sciences.[6] A more famous name is that of Auguste Comte (1798–1857). Comte developed the first truly systematic proposal for the application of science to the study of human society, and he is now widely regarded as one of the principal founders of sociology. Indeed, it was Comte who gave the discipline its name.[7]

4. Thomas Hobbes, *Leviathan* (Oxford: James Thornton, 1881).

5. See John Locke, *Two Treatises of Government* (1690), and Jean Jacques Rousseau, *A Treatise on the Social Compact* (1762).

6. Henri de Rouvroy, Comte de Saint-Simon, *Social Organization: The Science of Man*, trans. and ed. Felix Markham (New York: Harper & Row, Inc., 1964).

7. Auguste Comte, *The Positive Philosophy*, trans. and ed. Harriet Martineau (London: George Bell and Sons, 1915).

Comte's Law of Three Stages

In several important works written between 1830 and 1834, Comte traced the evolution of human knowledge from earliest times through his own day, arguing that the scientific revolution would reach its culmination with the development of a new "science of society." After reviewing and classifying all the scientific knowledge that had been accumulated to date, Comte analyzed the course of human intellectual development in terms of his famous *Law of Three Stages*. He maintained that knowledge in a given field of study is at first based on *theological* concepts. In astronomy, for example, movements of the heavenly bodies were explained in early societies as the work of gods, demons, or other supernatural beings. As knowledge develops, Comte said, theological concepts are gradually replaced with *metaphysical* explanations—based on reasoning, but divorced from observable facts. During the Middle Ages, for example, elaborate formulations were worked out to explain the nature of the stars, the planets, the moon, and so on, but these explanations were rooted in intellectual and religious tradition rather than empirical study. Finally, according to Comte, a given field of study moves into the *positive* stage, in which knowledge is derived from controlled, objective observations coupled with carefully reasoned interpretation. In other words, explanations are tested against reality by application of the scientific method.

The "Queen" of the Sciences

Comte asserted that the time had come for a positive approach to the study of society. The new science was to be called "sociology." According to Comte, it would be the last science to emerge and was therefore dependent upon all the sciences that had already been developed. In the hierarchy of the sciences (an order of complexity and dependence, not prestige) sociology was to be the "queen"—the most complex and in many ways the most important for human welfare. The major divisions of the new science were to be *social statics*, concerned with the organization or structure of society, and *social dynamics*, concerned with societal evolution and change.

While few of his ideas still serve as day-to-day guides for social researchers, Comte gave the field a direction and a commitment to science that it retains today. Although he did little research himself and did not try to analyze in detail the nature of the social order, he did outline what sociologists call an organic view of society. Society, Comte noted, shares many of the observable characteristics of living organisms: it has a *structure*, its parts *function interdependently*, and it has *evolved* from simpler to more complex forms. The particular organizational characteristics of society led Comte to classify it as a *collective* organism, as distinct from an individual animal or plant.

The Priesthood of Positivism

Comte was a product not only of the scientific revolution but also of the social unrest of his time. The old order had just given way before the French Revolution, and the Industrial Revolution was beginning to have far-reaching social effects. It was Comte's deep dissatisfaction with society as he saw it that led him to stress the need for applying science to the task of "social reconstruction." He firmly believed that positivism would eventually yield the knowledge necessary for rebuilding society on a rational basis. This belief led him to suggest that the direction of society should be turned over to a "priesthood of positivism"—a new class of leaders selected for their ability to apply the scientific method and sociological principles to the task of developing effective social policies.

Comte's emphasis on social reform forecast the direction that much sociological research would take in years to come. His scheme for establishing sociologists as the scientific directors of society did not win wide acceptance, but it opened the question of the sociologist's proper role in societal leadership—a question still being debated today. In terms of sociological analysis, Comte's ideas about the organizational nature of society directed the attention of sociologists who followed him to order, consensus, and social integration. For Comte as for many other early theorists, social conflict and change were only the means to a desired utopia, not an inevitable part of the social process itself.

EVOLUTION VERSUS REVOLUTION AS MECHANISMS OF SOCIAL CHANGE

After its initial outlines had been established in the writings of Comte, sociology became heavily influenced by the social impact of the Industrial Revolution. As the problems accompanying the move toward an urban-industrial society became increasingly apparent, social theorists began to analyze them. Why did they occur? Were they inevitable?

Of the many nineteenth-century writers who proposed answers to the problems generated by the Industrial Revolution, no two offer a sharper contrast than Herbert Spencer (1820–1903), who believed that social progress would come inevitably through *evolution,* and Karl Marx (1818–1883), who advocated reform through *revolution.* Both men have had a continuing influence on sociological thought, especially on theories of social change.

Herbert Spencer

Spencer had an unbounded faith in the natural development of society through evolutionary processes that would lead to "the survival of the fittest" and thus ultimately to social progress. He strongly opposed legislation as a means of solving social problems. The government, he argued, should adopt a policy of laissez-faire, so as not to interfere with the "natural selection" of those persons and social forms most fit to survive. He argued against free public education, for example, on the grounds that a person who really wanted to learn would somehow find the means.

Spencer's approach to societal development did not recognize planned change as a means of achieving more adequate societal integration. He considered as pathological anything that disturbed the orderly evolution of what he was sure were increasingly improved social forms. Spencer didn't oppose change; indeed, he saw it as part of the life process, in the very

nature of things. Nor was he necessarily opposed to conflict, as the phrase "survival of the fittest" makes clear. But he viewed conflict itself as part of an orderly process: what *was* at any time *ought* to be! Those who had wealth, power, and property proved by that very fact that they were the fittest and thus deserved what they had. Most contemporary social theorists have recognized this pronounced conservative bias in Spencer's work.

Spencer's interpretation of society in terms of evolution and natural selection — sometimes called Social Darwinism — was related to the elaborate analogy he developed between society and a biological organism. Although this analogy had also been made by Comte and ultimately had roots in the writings of ancient philosophers, Spencer was the first to work out a systematic theory of the structure and functioning of society and of the processes through which it changed.[8] While his organic theory is now mainly of historical interest, modern social theorists who adopt the *functional* approach to the analysis of social systems (page 48) make use of somewhat analogous concepts.

Karl Marx

An analysis totally different from Spencer's was that of Karl Marx, who observed the early form of industrial capitalism in England and concluded that total political revolution was the only realistic means by which social betterment could be achieved. The major points of the Marxian interpretation of society are outlined in the *Communist Manifesto,* which he prepared with Friedrich Engels in 1848, and are further elaborated in his *Das Kapital.*[9] Basically, Marx's theory of society was one of economic determinism; it attempted to account for social structure and social change in terms of the relationships between people and the means of production. Marx saw the social classes as corporate bodies pitted against one another and developing within themselves a strong feeling of solidarity. He believed that the social injustices of this struggle, in which the owners exploited

8. Herbert Spencer, *The Principles of Sociology* (New York: D. Appleton and Co., 1898).

9. Karl Marx and Friedrich Engels, *The Communist Manifesto,* ed. Samuel H. Beer (New York: Appleton-Century-Crofts, Inc., 1955); and Karl Marx, *Capital,* ed. Friedrich Engels (New York: International Publishers, 1967).

the workers, could end only when the working class overthrew the capitalist class and established a dictatorship of the proletariat. This, he maintained, would eventually lead to a classless and collectivistic society, where each would labor according to ability and each would receive according to need.

Marx has had an important influence on social theory no less than on political thought.[10] He was the first to develop a systematic theory about one segment of the societal structure—the economic—and to show what its consequences might be for the society as a whole. He was also one of the first proponents of a conflict theory of social change. It may be noted, however, that Marx did not see conflict as an intrinsic part of the human condition; rather, it was only the consequence of certain kinds of social structures. In a sense, Marx was an evolutionist no less than Spencer, for he saw society inevitably moving toward a utopia in which conflict would finally cease.

THE BEGINNINGS OF SOCIAL RESEARCH

It was only toward the end of the nineteenth century that an international corps of scholars came to think of themselves specifically as sociologists and to write works labeled "sociology." Such pioneers as William Graham Sumner, Lester Ward, Georg Simmel, Ferdinand Tönnies, Émile Durkheim, and Max Weber addressed themselves to the task of understanding society as it actually *was*, not as it "ought to be," and they began to work out methods for studying it objectively.

Social thought ever since Plato had approached the study of society on a broad scale, seeking generalizations about such matters as the origins of the state, the moral bases of society, its overall structure, its political functioning, and the direction of its change or development. Working from these same broad concerns, the early sociologists sought to give their new discipline a sharper focus.

Émile Durkheim's now famous monograph on suicide, published in 1897, has a special historical significance for two reasons. It showed that sociology could make a unique contribution to our understanding of a social problem and established a crude model for much subsequent sociological research.[11]

By collecting and analyzing the raw data of suicide statistics in various European countries over a period of years, Durkheim was able to place the act of self-destruction in an entirely new perspective. Specifically, he demonstrated a relationship between (1) the degree to which individuals are integrated into cohesive groups and (2) their inclination to various *types* of suicide. Durkheim found, for example, that the suicide rate for unmarried individuals was higher than for married ones, and he explained these statistics in terms of his belief that the unmarried are likely to have a lower level of social integration and group involvement. Since the emotional attachment of single persons to a meaningful family group is less than that of married persons, he said, they experience a less strong barrier to suicide in times of personal stress.

Durkheim referred to this type of suicide as *egoistic* suicide. He accounted for differences in suicide rates of Protestant and Catholic countries with the same concept, suggesting that suicide rates were higher among Protestants than among Catholics (though both religions condemned suicide) because the Catholic church integrated the individual more strongly into group life. For Protestants, a central concept was that individuals stood alone before their Maker; for Catholics, a hierarchical order of clergy intervened. Thus, according to Durkheim, Protestants were more susceptible to egoistic suicide than Catholics because the former were required by their religion to be more dependent on their own resources.

10. See, for example, Irving M. Zeitlin, *Ideology and the Development of Sociological Theory* (Englewood Cliffs, N.J.: Prentice-Hall, Inc., 1968).

11. Émile Durkheim, *Suicide: A Study in Sociology*, trans. John A. Spaulding and George Simpson, ed. George Simpson (New York: The Free Press, 1951).

TOOLS OF SOCIOLOGY
THEORY-BUILDING

The methods employed by Durkheim in his classic study of suicide were primitive indeed by today's standards. The statistical records available at the time were scattered and incomplete, and he lacked even the most rudimentary of modern methods for data analysis. Social scientists now command an array of sophisticated techniques for determining how variables are related and for assessing the probability that their findings might be due to chance factors. Moreover, today's computers can perform in an instant work that would have overwhelmed thousands of clerks in the 1890s. Why is it, then, that Durkheim's *Suicide* continues to hold the interest of sociologists?

Aside from its historical importance, the significance of the work is twofold. First, it is still a convincing demonstration that social variables can be of great importance in the causation of an act that on the surface seems explainable only in terms of personal or psychological variables. Second, Durkheim's systematic effort to assemble and interpret relevant data represents an impressive start toward theory-building.

Durkheim's guiding hypothesis was that there are several types of suicide, each of which can be explained in terms of the individual's social involvement. As a first step in his study, Durkheim examined the various hypotheses attributing suicide to such extra-social factors as mental illness, racial characteristics, hereditary factors, and "imitation." Eliminating each of these explanations in turn, on the grounds that they failed to account for variations in suicide rates, he then went on to assemble data showing a probable relationship between suicide and certain social variables.

In demonstrating the pattern of suicide that he termed *egoistic,* Durkheim prepared tables and density maps which showed the rates of suicide per million inhabitants for areas of Europe in which there were heavy concentrations of people belonging to particular religious groups. The data showed that suicide rates were related in a regular way to the proportion of individuals affiliated with a given religion in a given population: rates among Protestants were proportionately higher than those among Catholics, and rates among the nonreligious were highest of all. In another comparison, Durkheim found that married persons had relatively low suicide rates, single persons had higher rates, and the widowed had very high rates. On the basis of these statistics, he concluded that the social constraints of religious and family groups served as a deterrent to suicide.

Durkheim demonstrated the *anomic* pattern of suicide by much the same method, using comparisons of suicide rates and indices of social change to show that conditions such as economic crisis and war were accompanied by a significant increase in suicides. Crises in smaller groups—for example, divorce in a family—seemed to have much the same effect, increasing the likelihood that a member would take his or her own life. Thus Durkheim concluded that a disruption of group stability and the consequent loss of social constraints increased the probability of self-destruction.

As evidence of an *altruistic* pattern of suicide, Durkheim cited accounts and descriptions of primitive tribes and other groups to show that in certain settings individuals have committed socially approved suicide because of old age, serious illness, the death of a spouse, or the loss of a leader. In such instances, they saw it as their *duty* to take their own lives; failure to do so would have been considered an act of dishonor. Durkheim supplemented these illustrations with data showing differences in suicide rates among military personnel and civilians in various European countries during times of war. On the basis of both historical and statistical evidence, then, he concluded that intense loyalty to a group, with the reduced individuality this implied, might predispose individuals to take their own lives if the welfare of the group seemed to require it.

Durkheim's methodology was considerably more elaborate than this brief summary can suggest, and his *Suicide* still stands as an impressive example of painstaking social research. In terms of theory-building, however, Durkheim's effort was far from complete—he only induced a theory; he did not test it. Subsequent scholars have picked up the task where Durkheim left off, following his leads and testing and refining his hypotheses.

Durkheim identified a second type as *anomic* suicide, and again he saw the structure and characteristics of the individual's group life as providing an important key. If a society or other group was characterized by a high degree of confusion and contradiction in its basic social rules—a condition that Durkheim termed *anomie*—a higher than usual rate of suicide could be predicted. Under conditions of anomie, it is difficult for individuals to know what is expected of them or to feel a sense of close identity with the group. Durkheim demonstrated that rates of suicide rose sharply in a society when established standards and expectations no longer seemed to apply, as during periods of economic depression or inflation, during political disturbances, after defeat in war, or under frontier conditions.

The third type that Durkheim identified, *altruistic* suicide, was also seen as related to the individual's social integration, but in quite a different way. In this case, it was not lack of integration with a group that reduced the barriers to suicide, but rather a close sense of identity with a group. People may feel such strong ties to a group, Durkheim maintained, that they will place its welfare above their own and willingly accept self-destruction in its behalf. Durkheim illustrated altruistic suicide by noting the different suicide rates among civilians, ordinary enlisted soldiers, and noncommissioned officers. Enlisted soldiers had higher rates than civilians, and noncommissioned officers—who presumably felt the greatest sense of commitment to military norms and goals—had the highest rates of all. In general, Durkheim believed that altruistic suicide was more characteristic of folk and traditional societies, where group life is highly integrated, than of urban-industrial societies, which tend to be more individualistic and competitive.

Although the more sophisticated research techniques of today make it possible to criticize Durkheim's study on many grounds, it was nevertheless a classic demonstration that the sociologist could shed new light on human behavior by making a systematic analysis of social phenom-ena. In relating the different suicide rates of different categories of people to the variable of social integration, Durkheim cast doubt upon the "common-sense" assumption that all suicides could be adequately explained in terms of mental or emotional disturbances. Subsequent studies of suicide have refined both Durkheim's methods (see Tools of Sociology, page 9) and his conclusions, but all owe an ultimate debt to his early model of sociological research.

THE "AMERICANIZATION" OF SOCIOLOGY

For the first sociologists in Europe, humanitarian motives were far more urgent than the goal of developing a science of societal phenomena for its own sake. A scientific approach to the study of society was widely sought, but at this stage of sociology's development it was for the purpose of correcting social ills rather than that of acquiring knowledge per se. Thus the term *sociology* came to be understood as practically synonymous with social reform.

Sociology and Social Problems

Sociology retained its reformist image as it became established in the United States during the final decades of the nineteenth century. In fact, it appears to have been this very aspect of the new discipline which made it especially attractive to Americans and ultimately caused it to flourish in this country as nowhere else.

American society during the late nineteenth and early twentieth centuries was characterized by a number of social displacements and severe social problems. The South had yet to recover from the collapse of its economy following the Civil War. Industrialization in the North was proceeding very rapidly, and large numbers of people from rural areas were leaving their farms for urban centers in search of a better life. Some of them were southern blacks, whose northward migration would continue for decades. The growing cities were also being flooded by foreign immigrants, whose diverse values, cultures, and beliefs sometimes conflicted with established ways.

Large segments of the American population were unable to cope effectively with the many impersonal, seemingly intractable, social and economic difficulties that these changes were generating. Racial, religious, and ethnic preju- dices, periodic unemployment, boom-or-bust business cycles, political corruption, the rising incidence of crime, spreading slums, increasing rates of family disorganization, juvenile delin- quency, problems of congestion, exploitation, pollution, and a variety of other unsettling fea- tures of the new urban-industrial society were blighting the lives of millions of its citizens.

The scientific study of society seemed to many American intellectuals, as it had earlier to many Europeans, to be potentially capable of coming to grips with these problems. If achiev- able, an accumulation of scientifically verified principles of the functioning of society would perhaps be able to provide a rational basis for bringing about needed social change. Thus early sociologists in the United States "directed their interest to the conditions or issues associated with the urban poor: pauperism, charity, scien- tific philanthropy, private and public relief, unemployment, migratory labor, child labor, women wage earners, the labor movement, dependent children, insanity, illness, crime, juvenile delinquency, family instability, temper- ance, immigration, and race relations."[12] In- deed, sociology began in the United States al- most as a social movement, with many of its leaders bent on doing away with the evils inher- ent in the new urban-industrial society.

The Growth of Sociology in the United States
Although the transformation from social philoso- phy to social science was initially the work of European sociologists, the rapid growth of soci- ology in the United States greatly accelerated that change. Publications dealing with the sub- ject matter of sociology began to appear in this country late in the 1880s, and during the follow- ing decade courses in sociology were estab- lished in a few colleges and universities. The new discipline found most ready acceptance on the campuses of the Middle West. Unlike the

older schools along the eastern seaboard, the newly established land-grant colleges, with their technical and problem-solving orientations, and new privately endowed schools such as the University of Chicago were relatively unham- pered by tradition. They found sociology an ex- citing young discipline.

Between World War I and World War II the science of sociology became an established part of the curriculum of almost every college and university in the United States, and since then the discipline has grown at an astonishing rate. Membership in the American Sociological Asso- ciation, for example, was only 1300 in 1945; by 1975 the number of professional sociologists in the United States had increased tenfold. More significant than mere numbers, however, is the fact that as sociology became firmly established on American campuses, it began to shift its fo- cus from social problems and to develop a new identity as a basic science of society, aimed at developing explanatory theories concerning so- cial phenomena of every conceivable type.[13]

THE FOCUS OF SOCIOLOGY
Sociology shares its scientific interest in social behavior with other social sciences such as an- thropology, economics, history, and political science. In some of its specific areas of concern, it also has much in common with psychology. However, the central focus of sociology remains distinct from that of related disciplines.

Sociology and the Other Social Sciences
Each of the social sciences began with some specialized area of study, such as preliterate so- ciety and culture (anthropology); systems of production, distribution, and exchange (eco- nomics); the structure and functioning of gov- ernment (political science); and so on. Sociolo- gy, as we have seen, took as its area of study the broad organizational properties of groups and societies and the manner in which they change. Historically, it has also had a special concern with the *problem* aspects of society.

12. Roscoe C. Hinkle, Sr., and Gisela J. Hinkle, *The De- velopment of Modern Sociology* (New York: Random House, Inc., 1963), p. 4.
13. For a good review of the circumstances responsible for the development of scientific sociology in the United States, see Talcott Parsons, "The Development of Sociology as a Discipline," *American Sociological Review*, 24 (1959): 547–559.

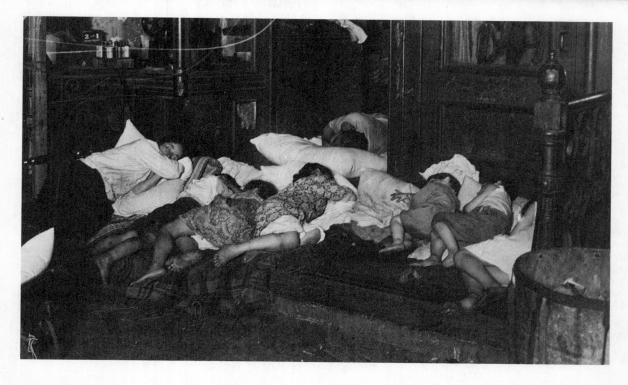

Lewis Hine, International Museum of Photography at George Eastman House.

During the late nineteenth and early twentieth centuries, life in the United States was characterized by severe social problems. Industrialization and immigration (opposite, far left) caused the cities to grow rapidly after the Civil War, resulting in urban congestion, as seen in this view of Hester Street in New York City (opposite, left). Although the cities represented opportunity, newcomers found in them a host of new problems. In New York City and elsewhere, recent arrivals lived in tenements (above left), finding relief from overcrowding and hot weather only in the streets (opposite, bottom). In cotton and steel mills and in coal mines (above right), children worked long hours for pitifully small wages. Non-English-speaking immigrants with few marketable skills lived on the small amount of money they could earn as factory workers or street vendors (bottom). These and other problems spawned by industrialization and urbanization led early sociologists to focus their attention on understanding and improving social conditions.

Each of the social sciences, including sociology, has gradually extended its area of concern until today it is difficult to draw exact lines between them. For example, the interests of the sociologist parallel those of the anthropologist at many points in the study of culture and its relationship to human personality. Political behavior and the forces that shape it concern both the sociologist and the political scientist. Sociologists share with economists the study of work patterns and a concern with the consequences of differential distribution of income within a society.

All the social sciences, in short, are in some way concerned with discovering the nature of social relationships and their varied influence on human behavior. But whereas most of the social sciences are concerned only with particular facets of social life, such as political or economic behavior, sociology is concerned more broadly with "those social elements and relationships found among human beings, whether they are acting as familial groups, say, or as political groups, or in economic pursuits. . . . Sociologists, then, study human interaction *as such*. They try to learn the likenesses and differences among people in groups, no matter what the particular orientation of the group may be."[14]

Although sociologists are ultimately concerned with understanding the structure and functioning of society as a whole, much of their research focuses upon more limited areas of study represented by such established subfields as criminology, urban sociology, marriage and the family, population, intergroup relations, religion, mass communications, and so on. Specialization in sociology, as in the other sciences, helps define a particular field of observation and enables the scientist to discern regular patterns of behavior that might otherwise go unnoticed. The new knowledge thus gained can often be applied in other areas of behavior and often can be synthesized into general principles about human societies. By studying in detail a wide range of both deviant and conforming behavior, sociologists work toward their ultimate task of explaining the fundamental nature of society.

Sociology and Psychology

Sociology and psychology are concerned with many of the same phenomena. Both have a special interest, for example, in the process of socialization (Chapter 6), by which individuals learn the values, beliefs, and behavior patterns expected of them as group members. Sociologists and psychologists have together developed the interdisciplinary field of social psychology, which focuses specifically on individual-group relationships.

But despite their areas of common interest, sociology and psychology have quite different orientations. Psychology observes the actions of people as they respond to their environment and infers the mental processes, motivational patterns, habit structures, and so forth that account for *individual behavior*. Sociology, on the other hand, observes the interaction that takes place *between* people and infers the interpersonal processes and patterns of group structure that account for *social behavior*. Thus, even when psychologists and sociologists study the same phenomena, they tend to do so from different perspectives. For example, psychologists are interested in the organizational patterns of groups not because they are interested in social structure as such, but rather because groups constitute important sources of reward and punishment that influence individual behavior. Similarly, sociologists try to understand the motives that people have for participating in particular groups not because they are especially interested in motivation as an area of research, but rather because the motives of individual members help shape the behavior of groups.

For the most part in this book, we will simply assume that individuals participate in groups in order to satisfy their personal needs. Our central concern will be to determine what happens when two or more people coordinate their activities and attempt to achieve shared or interrelated goals by interacting as members of a group.

14. Pitirim A. Sorokin, as cited in *A Career in Sociology* (Washington, D.C.: The American Sociological Association, n.d.), p. 5.

ISSUES IN CONTEMPORARY SOCIOLOGY

A body of tested information in any science is very difficult to obtain, and this is especially true in sociology and the other social sciences because of the great complexity of social life and the difficulties involved in trying to study it under controlled conditions. Possible explanations have to be invented and repeatedly tried out against observed facts. Hypotheses have to be proposed, exhaustively tested, and often abandoned. And inevitably, debates arise about what issues to study, what methods to use, what facts to assemble, and how to interpret findings.

As this book will make clear, sociology is not a completely unified discipline; it never has been and probably never will be. For the inquiring student, this may well be one of its most attractive as well as one of its most frustrating features. In this section we shall consider three issues that are the subject of continuing debate among contemporary sociologists. The first centers around the differing orientations involved in the study of human behavior. The second concerns differing views about the importance of stability and conflict in group life. The third concerns the relationship between social science and social reform.

DIFFERING ORIENTATIONS TO THE STUDY OF HUMAN BEHAVIOR

As sociology developed into a social science during the nineteenth century, two major contrasting approaches to the study of human behavior also developed. One was the *Verstehen* approach, first advocated by Max Weber; the other, based on the ideas of Émile Durkheim and Auguste Comte, is known as the neopositivistic approach.

The Verstehen Approach

Max Weber defined *social action* as all human behavior oriented toward other people in which *the actors attach a subjective meaning to what they do.*[15] According to this view, which has many adherents among contemporary sociologists, the concept of social behavior refers not only to what the interacting parties do, but to what they think, feel, and otherwise experience while they are doing it. The observer of social behavior, therefore, must note and record the subjective experiences of interacting persons as well as their overt actions. This, of course, is no easy task.

The method Weber suggested for analyzing the subjective elements of social interaction was called *Verstehen* (a German word meaning *understanding* or *insight*), in which observers try to see the interaction from the point of view of the interacting parties. Weber believed that by searching through their own experiences, thoughts, and emotions, observers should be able to gain an interpretive understanding *(Verstehen)* of what such interaction would mean to them, the observers, if they were in fact one or both of the interacting parties.

The *Verstehen* approach is particularly relevant to social scientists who use the method of participant observation as a major tool for gathering data. This technique often requires that the researcher spend considerable time establishing rapport with the group under study and becoming immersed in their total pattern of living. In the late 1930s, for example, William Foote Whyte spent three and a half years living among the members of an Italian slum community in Boston, gathering data for his classic study, *Street-Corner Society.* (See Tools of Sociology, page 49.) Elliot Liebow used a similar approach in his more recent study of black streetcorner men in Washington, D.C., adopting the men's manner of dress and something of their speech patterns in order to interact with them more freely and thus gain insight into their patterns of social behavior.[16] (See page 65.)

15. Max Weber, *The Theory of Social and Economic Organization,* trans. A. M. Henderson and Talcott Parsons (New York: The Free Press, 1957), pp. 88, 112–123; originally published in 1925.

16. Elliot Liebow, *Tally's Corner: A Study of Negro Streetcorner Men* (Boston: Little, Brown and Company, 1967). For a more recent study which in some ways parallels Whyte's, see Gerald Suttles, *The Social Order of the Slum: Ethnicity and Territory in the Inner City* (Chicago: The University of Chicago Press, 1968).

Some sociologists object that the *Verstehen* approach provides evidence primarily on the subjective experiences of the observer rather than on those of the people being observed: there is no way to know if they themselves had the same thoughts and emotions as they carried out their activities. Such critics point out that no other science depends on private data that cannot be verified by other researchers. In reply to this objection, those sociologists who favor the approach argue that the data are not really private. Through their own participation in many kinds of groups, sociologists come to share with other members of society the beliefs, thoughts, and emotions that give meaning to social interaction. One of the researcher's jobs as a scientist, then, is to be able to distinguish more accurately than the ordinary citizen the significance of an act to the individuals involved.

The Neopositivistic Approach

The neopositivists have a different approach to the study of interaction. Building on the ideas of Auguste Comte and more particularly Émile Durkheim, they maintain that interaction should be defined as behavior that can be seen and recorded by objective techniques. Sociologists should limit themselves to the observable facts and avoid subjective interpretations of what the actors might be thinking or feeling. The neopositivists do not rule out such subjective meanings as a legitimate focus of concern, but they insist that they be studied through controlled experiments, tests, scales, and other techniques that remove the need for introspection and insight on the part of the observer. (Sociometry, described in Tools of Sociology on page 46, is but one of many objective techniques for studying interpersonal behavior.)

Those who object to the neopositivistic approach argue that insistence on a strict empiricism ignores many nuances of meaning important to the interacting parties. They maintain that if sociologists restrict their study to behavior that can be measured precisely, their data will be incomplete. Since complicated psychological processes undoubtedly guide the behavior of individuals as they interact with others, why not take these processes fully into account, even though they must be reconstructed through introspection?

Both the *Verstehen* approach and the neopositivistic approach obviously have strong arguments in their favor. The one provides for a more sensitive and complete interpretation of the causes and meaning of interaction; the other lends itself more easily to quantitative assessment and reproducible observations. Progress in sociology actually depends on the careful application of both. The *Verstehen* approach, for example, is often used to explore research areas that cannot realistically be studied by means of questionnaires, surveys, sociometric devices, attitude scales, and the like. It can also provide the insight that leads to the development of new theories and hypotheses, which can then be studied more systematically by objective and quantitative means.

SOCIAL EQUILIBRIUM VERSUS SOCIAL CONFLICT

Following the early lead of Auguste Comte (pages 5–6), many sociologists seek to describe social life primarily in terms of social *equilibrium*. That is, they tend to see all human groups, including societies, within an organic perspective—as systems made up of interdependent parts and tending toward stability. If conflict arises, it is seen either as "abnormal" or as a means by which temporary strains between elements are being reduced in a move toward greater equilibrium. Other sociologists, however, see *conflict* as an inevitable part of social life and as the principal means by which groups achieve change. An early proponent of this perspective was Karl Marx (pages 7–8), who believed that conflict between classes was the basic mechanism by which society would perfect itself.

The relationship between conflict and equilibrium in human groups defies any easy analysis.[17] Every group requires some degree of stability and predictability so that members can coordinate their activities and work toward their

17. See Chapter 2, pages 58–60.

individual and collective goals. On the other hand, conflict is an obvious, seemingly inevitable element of group life. Is it necessarily bad, or can it have desirable effects under some circumstances? We may also ask: Under what conditions does either conflict or stability become the dominating tendency in a society?

The answers that individual sociologists give to these questions almost always reflect their value judgments as well as their theoretical orientations. It is seldom possible to think about stability or change in the abstract. When conflict leads to change, is the change "better" or "worse"? Does stability necessarily imply a "healthy" group in "social harmony," or can equilibrium sometimes mean the maintenance of an objectionable status quo? Such questions cannot be answered by applying the scientific method. They are answerable only from the viewpoint of a given set of values or ideological premises. Yet they are the kinds of issues that often confront the sociologist.

SOCIAL SCIENCE VERSUS SOCIAL AMELIORATION

Probably most sociologists today think of themselves as *basic* scientists, seeking knowledge about social life through systematic study. Like researchers in other scientific fields, they attempt to describe and explain what they discover by formulating generalizations, hypotheses, and theories. They also seek to evaluate the validity of their explanations by applying the criteria of scientific analyses.[18]

But sociology is not merely an abstract study without practical applications. On the contrary, its findings have proved of immense value to numerous professions that deal with problems of people—medicine, law, social welfare, law enforcement, prison work, education, and industry, to mention only a few. The results of sociological research have been applied in reshaping our nation's schools, in developing new systems for delivering various kinds of social services, in reforming penal systems, in designing hospitals, and in hundreds of other ways. When the information it generates is thus put to practical use, sociology can be considered an *applied* science.

In sociology, as in physics or chemistry, the line that distinguishes basic science from applied science is seldom clear-cut. It is difficult to anticipate either the practical consequences of basic research or the theoretical implications of applied studies. The distinction is further complicated by the question of how sociology can best make its contribution as a science. Social problems press in on all sides, urgently demanding solution, and it may be argued that the "science of society" has a special obligation to concern itself directly with societal needs.

The real object of science is to benefit man. A science which fails to do this, however agreeable its study, is lifeless. Sociology, which of all sciences should benefit man most, is in danger of falling into the class of polite amusements, or dead sciences.

This statement was made not by a modern-day critic of American sociology but rather by one of its founders, Lester Frank Ward.[19] Writing in 1911, Ward was warning his colleagues to spend less time on esoteric debates and to get on with the task of developing knowledge that would meet societal needs.

Most contemporary sociologists would agree with Ward that their science should concern itself with matters that have relevance for contemporary society—that it should benefit people now—but they disagree as to where the sociologist's responsibilities lie. Do sociologists have a special obligation to *do* something with their knowledge? After studying a given problem, should they, as citizen-members of a troubled society, take an active role in trying to bring about changes in social behavior? Or are they obliged, as scientists, to remain ethically neutral and to concentrate their energies on the pursuit of knowledge about how society works? Indeed, it has often been argued that knowledge per se is the only relevant goal in any of the sciences.

18. The final two sections of this chapter will discuss the basic "rules" of sociological inquiry, which follow the methods and logic of science in general. See also George C. Homans, *The Nature of Social Science* (New York: Harcourt Brace Jovanovich, Inc., 1967), p. 4.

19. Lester Frank Ward, *Dynamic Sociology*, 2nd ed. (New York: D. Appleton & Co., 1911), 1:xxvii.

Poverty, racism, alienation, the urban crisis—these are some of the dilemmas Americans face in the 1970s. Since solutions to such problems will require reliable data on many facets of social life, sociological knowledge will increasingly play a part in attempts to improve society.

VIEWPOINTS   TAKING SIDES IN SCIENCE

■ To have values or not to have values: the question is always with us. When sociologists undertake to study problems that have relevance to the world we live in, they find themselves caught in a crossfire. Some urge them not to take sides, to be neutral and do research that is technically correct and value free. Others tell them that their work is shallow and useless if it does not express a deep commitment to a value position.

This dilemma, which seems so painful to so many, actually does not exist, for one of its horns is imaginary. For it to exist, one would have to assume, as some apparently do, that it is indeed possible to do research that is uncontaminated by personal and political sympathies. I propose . . . that it is not possible. . . .

The scientist who proposes to understand society must, as Mead long ago pointed out, get into the situation enough to have a perspective on it. And it is likely that his perspective will be greatly affected by whatever positions are taken by any or all of the other participants in that varied situation. Even if his participation is limited to reading in the field, he will necessarily read the arguments of partisans of one or another side to a relationship and will thus be affected, at least, by having suggested to him what the relevant arguments and issues are. . . . Almost all the topics that sociologists study, at least those that have some relation to the real world around us, are seen by society as morality plays and we shall find ourselves, willy-nilly, taking part in those plays on one side or the other. . . .

We can never avoid taking sides. So we are left with the question of whether taking sides means that some distortion is introduced into our work so great as to make it useless. Or, less drastically, whether some distortion is introduced that must be taken into account before the results of our work can be used. . . . Our problem is to make sure that, whatever point of view we take, our research meets the standards of good scientific work, that our unavoidable sympathies do not render our results invalid.

Howard S. Becker
"Whose Side Are We On?"

● In my opinion sociologists are obligated, to the best of their abilities as scientists, to analyze and interpret problems affecting society; and to reach and make known the conclusions from their studies, with the data behind them. As citizens they should participate in public affairs. They may express opinions on issues regarding which evidence is partial or nonexistent. But they should not allow such opinions to be understood by others as professional—as expressions of scientific judgment. . . .

When Charles Francis Murphy, sachem of Tammany Hall, was interviewed by New York reporters during John Purroy Mitchel's reform campaign for the mayoralty in 1913, they reported him as saying, "Sure, boys, I'm for the Uplift too, if that's the word." Now, like Murphy, I'm for reform—of many aspects of life and society. My views regarding some social issues derive from evidence and analysis; but respecting a larger number of others they are doubtless emotional and uninhibited by rational examination. Therein is a potential disservice. I may injure both the profession with which you are identifying me and the wider society if my romantic or unreflective support of debatable "causes" is assumed to be an expression of sociology. . . .

There is much to be done. The social stresses are severe. If we, as sociologists, can divorce ourselves from prejudices, wishful thinking and partisanship, creating a true science of society, I believe we can help to relieve stress and further peaceful human relationships. The "heroic task," to quote Manning Nash's review of Gunnar Myrdal's recent *Asian Drama,* is "an understanding of human affairs that will help men intervene in their own destinies with knowledge and deliberation."

Stuart A. Rice
"Why I Wanted to Become a Sociologist"

I propose to define science as knowledge of reality because "truth" is used in such a variety of senses. I do not know whether it is possible for us ever to arrive at a knowledge of "truth" in regard to any important matters. I doubt if it is possible. It is not important. It is the pursuit of truth which gives us life, and it is to that pursuit that our loyalty is due.

The author of this statement, William Graham Sumner, stands with Ward as one of the important early contributors to the development of sociology in the United States. The title of the essay from which the quotation is taken — "The Absurd Effort to Make the World Over" — clearly removes Sumner from the ranks of the social activists.[20] Is his position defensible today?

As we have seen, efforts to make sociology contribute to the solution of social problems are as old as the discipline itself, but the societal crises of recent times have given such efforts a new urgency. Some contemporary sociologists argue that we can no longer afford the luxury of pursuing knowledge for its own sake — that sociologists must actively apply their findings, however incomplete, to the solution of society's ills. But is it possible to become a social activist and still remain effective as a social scientist? The many who doubt that it is maintain that sociologists can make the greatest contribution by remaining objective and building up a store of verified knowledge about how society really works. But again the rejoinder comes back: Is objectivity really possible when the subject matter is the society in which one lives? And must a sociologist abandon a critical area of research if it doesn't wholly lend itself to the scientific method? These are some of the questions being hotly debated by sociologists today.

Meanwhile, the field of sociology continues to accumulate basic and practical knowledge. We now understand far better a long list of social phenomena that have troubled people for ages. We have acquired an impressive amount of information concerning the basic nature of human culture, social organization, and social change,

and we have gained considerable insight into causal sequences behind a long list of social problems. In the remaining sections of this chapter we will review the general procedures sociologists follow in their attempt to systematically unravel the complexities of human society.

THE FORMULATION OF SOCIOLOGICAL KNOWLEDGE

Like other sciences, sociology organizes its accumulated knowledge in the form of concepts, generalizations, and theories. We will discuss each of these forms of knowledge in turn, with special reference to their uses in sociological research.

CONCEPTS

Ideally, scientific analysis always begins with concepts. A concept in sociology, as in other sciences, is a miniature *system of meaning* — that is, a symbol, such as a word or letter, which stands in an agreed-upon relationship to a particular phenomenon that the scientist is studying. By giving a name or label to a class of events on the basis of those properties which distinguish all members of the class, a concept becomes a kind of "map" of a particular segment of reality. In sociological analysis, the segments of reality identified by concepts are typically qualities, attributes, or properties of social phenomena. Concepts may be concrete and readily recognizable to the lay person (*Catholic, Jew, suicide*), somewhat abstract but still relatively common (*class, power*), or very abstract and difficult for the student to recognize (*anomie*, Verstehen).

Variables

Concepts whose properties can vary — that is, come in different amounts, either simply or subtly — are called *variable concepts* or, more commonly, *variables*. To illustrate, sociologists use the term *social cohesion* to describe the degree to which group members share common

---

20. Quotation reprinted from Maurice Davie, *William Graham Sumner: An Essay of Commentary and Selections* (New York: Thomas Y. Crowell Company, 1963), p. 10.

beliefs, practices, and values and thus act "like one." A group can be more or less cohesive; thus *cohesion* is a variable concept. Some sociologists feel that at this early stage in the development of the discipline, many sociological concepts must be treated *qualitatively* without attempting to measure them precisely. Other sociologists are convinced of the scientific need for assessing and describing all variables in quantitative terms through the use of such measuring techniques as indices and scales.

Problems in Choosing Terms

Regardless of whether sociologists approach a concept quantitatively or not, it serves as a kind of window through which they view whatever phenomenon they have chosen to study. For example, Durkheim viewed the phenomenon of suicide through the concepts of *egoistic, anomic,* and *altruistic suicide* in order to focus on its relationships with other social factors. Because the particular concepts scientists use will inevitably affect what they "see," they must construct their concepts in such a way that they will distort reality as little as possible. This is an especially difficult task for sociologists, who are concerned with the elusive reality of social acts rather than the more stable properties of things. They must be careful not only to identify the specific attributes a concept will represent but also to choose a name for the concept that will introduce as few unwanted connotations as possible. For example, an attempt to study interracial attitudes today must take into account the different connotations of the labels *Negro, black, Afro-American,* and *colored.*

Developing an adequate terminology for sociological concepts is an exacting—and sometimes exasperating—task. It is complicated not only by the fact that almost all of the concepts in the field are undergoing continuous revision and refinement but also by the fact that many of them deal with aspects of social behavior already understood in part by the lay person. Often a new name must be invented to symbolize some newly discovered property of a familiar societal phenomenon, or a term already in popular use must be assigned a new meaning so that it can be used to signify properties of social events which have not previously been studied. Thus, in their search for adequate tools of conceptualization, social scientists often find it necessary to manipulate language in ways that are puzzling or even irritating to members of the general public, some of whom charge that sociological terminology is a hopeless jargon that obscures communication instead of clarifying it. Sociologists are aware of this difficulty, but they rightly insist on the need for using the symbols of language in whatever way is necessary to define the concepts they need as tools for systematically exploring the nature of social reality.

GENERALIZATIONS

A generalization is formed by combining concepts into a statement that sets forth some meaningful relationship between them. Usually a generalization states a *quantitative* relationship, predicting that if one variable changes in some regular fashion, predictable changes will take place in another. To illustrate, it can be stated as a generalization that *the birth rate of a society regularly declines as the level of industrialization in that society increases.* Here we have two variable concepts (birth rate and level of industrialization) and a statement of inverse quantitative relationship between them.

This particular generalization was formulated on the basis of numerous studies of the birth rates and levels of industrialization in modern countries, which have actually demonstrated the relationship stated. A generalization that summarizes factual evidence, as this one does, can be called an *empirical generalization.* It is assumed to be valid insofar as it corresponds with observed realities.

Now let us suppose, for the moment, that extensive data on birth rates and levels of industrialization had not yet been gathered. In such case, the generalization would simply be posing a possible or potential relationship between the two concepts. Only a careful scientific investigation aimed at gathering the relevant evidence would then enable us to evaluate the validity of the stated relationship. <u>Generalizations that have not yet been adequately confirmed by empirical evidence are called</u> *hypotheses*. This type of generalization is important because it helps define the further research problems that must be studied to clarify the relationship between the concepts.

THEORIES

Generalizations take on increasing importance if they can be combined into *theories*. <u>A theory is a set of interrelated generalizations, combined in such a way that they form a logical system of explanation in which one generalization does not contradict another.</u> Theories not only provide explanations of observed realities but also serve as important sources of new hypotheses.

To illustrate, let us refer to our earlier generalization concerning declining birth rates in societies undergoing industrialization. If we now add the generalization that in such societies a *decline in the death rate regularly precedes a decline in the birth rate,* we can take the two propositions as a related set and logically derive a hypothesis: *The population of a society undergoing industrialization will grow rapidly at first and then level off as a result of successive reductions in death rates and birth rates.* These relationships are illustrated schematically in Figure 1.1.

The proposition we have stated here serves to illustrate how a logically related set of generalizations is capable of yielding a more comprehensive generalization in the form of a theory. To substantiate the proposition, it would be necessary to check the factual evidence through appropriate research on populations undergoing industrialization. (In fact, many such studies have already been made. The complex relationships between industrialization and population growth are discussed in detail in Chapter 11, ''Demographic Change.'')

Explanation

The great importance of theories is that they provide comprehensive explanations of social phenomena. A single generalization may accurately describe how classes of events are related;

a theory adds to our understanding by accounting for the antecedent conditions which *lead to* particular events. (Thus rapid population growth can be explained by changes in birth and death rates resulting from increasing industrialization.) All of the many kinds of sociological theories attempt to show that some repetitive social event occurs as an effect of some prior set of circumstances. In other words, theories outline the causes of whatever phenomena they attempt to explain.

Theories, like generalizations, have more than an explanatory or predictive value, however. <u>Equally important to the scientist, they suggest lines of further inquiry.</u> The old notion that scientific discoveries are made accidentally or through flashes of genius does not fit very well with reality. For the most part, scientific progress is built upon painstaking research directed toward testing hypotheses that have been derived in some way from systematic theory.

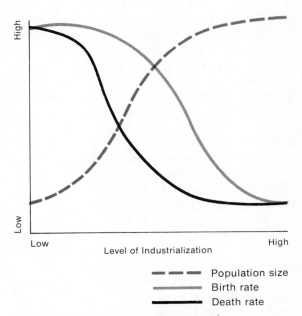

Figure 1.1. SCHEMATIC DIAGRAM OF GENERALIZATIONS CONCERNING BIRTH RATES, DEATH RATES, AND POPULATION SIZE IN AN INDUSTRIALIZING SOCIETY

Validation

The formulation and verification of an explanatory theory is a task of tremendous difficulty in any science. Most theories remain in a state of partial validation for substantial periods of time, as scientists continue to test them against empirical data. Strictly speaking, no theory or hypothesis is ever finally proved; it is valid only in the sense that it has been supported by a substantial amount of empirical evidence. The continued testing and refining of theoretical formulations is basic to the scientific method, and it is made especially necessary in sociology because patterns of social relationship change. A contemporary sociologist must ask, for example, if the relationship Durkheim found between social cohesion and suicide rates still holds in a highly secularized and diversified society.

Most generalizations in sociology state a *probable* relationship between variables, indicating that there is a tendency for them to be related in a statistically meaningful way. Seldom is the relationship one that permits no exceptions. For example, after reviewing a large number of research studies, sociologists have concluded that *certain categories of children who are heavily exposed to televised portrayals of violence are somewhat more likely to exhibit aggressive behavior, in certain kinds of situations, than those less exposed.* Thus, just as heavy cigarette smoking increases the likelihood of contracting heart and lung diseases, heavy television viewing increases the likelihood of aggressive behavior in some types of children. These are probabilistic relationships. That is, not all smokers get lung cancer or emphysema; nor do all members of juvenile television audiences behave aggressively. The probabilities are clear, however. Heavy smokers *tend* to have certain definable health problems. Heavy viewers *tend* to be influenced by TV violence. Critics of such findings often attempt to discredit them by citing the case of X, who lived to be ninety-eight while smoking five packs a day, or the case of Y, who watches TV twelve hours a day and sings in the children's choir for recreation. But in spite of such exceptions, the tendencies remain *for most people in the relevant population.*

Even in the most highly developed sciences, one seldom finds generalizations in the form of invariant laws. Most sciences accumulate their knowledge in the form of probabilistic statements, or hypotheses, concerning the relationship between variables. The continuing task is to refine such generalizations so that they permit fewer and fewer exceptions.

THE LOGIC OF SCIENTIFIC INQUIRY

Although each science has its own particular subject matter and research techniques, all adhere to the same general logic of inquiry. This system of inquiry, commonly termed the *scientific method,* is a set of rules for ensuring that research will lead to valid generalizations and theories. Every science shares a concern that the data it gathers will accurately reflect the properties of the phenomena it studies. The scientific method has evolved, then, as a basic safeguard against the possibility of arriving at false conclusions or of accepting generalizations that have not adequately been supported by evidence.[21]

In outlining the scientific method and showing its applicability to the social sciences, we do not mean to suggest that contemporary sociologists always abide by its rigorous rules. On the contrary, most social research continues to fall far short of the ideal that any description of the method implies.[22] But the practical difficulties that a researcher may encounter in following the scientific method do not detract from

21. For a sociologist's rejoinder to criticisms commonly leveled at the discipline, see Robert K. Merton, "The Case for Sociology," in *Life in Society,* Thomas E. Lasswell, John H. Burma, and Sidney Aronson, eds. (Glenview, Ill.: Scott, Foresman and Company, 1965), pp. 26–29.

22. For a recent discussion of the special problems of methodology in the social sciences, see Gideon Sjoberg and Roger Nett, *A Methodology for Social Research* (New York: Harper & Row, Inc., 1968); see also Philip E. Hammond, ed., *Sociologists at Work: Essays on the Craft of Social Research* (New York: Basic Books, Inc., 1964).

The Social Psychology of G. H. Mead

The human individual is born into a society characterized by symbolic inter-action. The use of significant symbols by those around him enables him to pass from the conversation of gestures--which involves direct, unmeaningful response to the overt acts of other--to the occasional taking of the roles of others. This role-taking enables him to share the perspectives of others. Concurrent with role-taking, the self develops, i.e., the capacity to act toward oneself. Action toward oneself comes to take the form of viewing oneself from the standpoint, or perspective, of the generalized other (the composite representative of others, of society, within the individual), which implies defining one's behavior in terms of the expectations of others. In the process of such viewing of oneself, the indivi-dual must carry on symbolic interaction with himself, involving an internal conver-sation between his impulsive aspect (the "I") and the incorporated perspectives of others (The "Me"). The mind, or mental activity, is present in behavior whenever such symbolic interaction goes on--whether the individual is merely "thinking" (in the everyday sense of the word) or is also interacting with another individual. (In both cases the individual must indicate things to himself.) Mental activity necessarily involves meanings, which usually attach to, and define, objects. The meaning of an object or event is simply an image of the pattern of action which de-fines the object or event. That is, the completion in one's imagination of an act, or the mental picture of the actions and experiences symbolized by an object, de-fines the act or the object. In the unit of study the Mead calls "the act," all of the foregoing processes are usually entailed. The concluding point to be made in this summary is the same

twine and mutually imply one another. To drive home this important point, I must emphasize that human society (characterized by symbolic interaction) both preceded the rise of individual selves and minds, and is maintained by the rise of individual selves and minds. This means, then, that symbolic interaction is both the medium for the development of human beings and the process by which human beings associate as human beings.

Extracted from Symbolic Interaction, Jerome G. Manis and Bernard N. Meltzer (eds), p. 19

new born has no patterned behavior.
it begins to have patterned beh.
- eventually becomes goal oriented
- begins to take the role of the other - child.
- child becomes an object to himself and before
a subject.
- self only develops in a social relationship -
- social psychology

its usefulness as a model. In sociology as in other sciences, it provides not only the guidelines to be followed in building a research design but also a means for evaluating research results.

FORMULATING RESEARCH QUESTIONS

The scientific method requires that a researcher begin with a clearly formulated question about some specific problem. Although this sounds like a relatively simple task, formulating testable hypotheses is actually one of the most difficult chores scientists face. It is not enough to identify a problem that needs study, though even this may be difficult, especially during the early period of a science's development. But how does one start to investigate anything so complicated as human society? To isolate a problem capable of being studied systematically, the social researcher must first have the insight to see that a possible relationship exists between two or more aspects of some complex societal phenomenon. Durkheim, for example, noted that suicide rates rose or dropped sharply in particular countries during certain periods, and he believed such fluctuations in rates could not be wholly explained by family troubles, mental illness, remorse, or any of the other reasons that were listed in the official records on suicide. Rejecting the usual explanations of suicide, he then went on to formulate a research problem, investigating suicide in terms of the individual's involvement in social relationships. (See Tools of Sociology, page 9.)

Arriving at new concepts, insights, and inferences is one vital aspect of scientific inquiry.

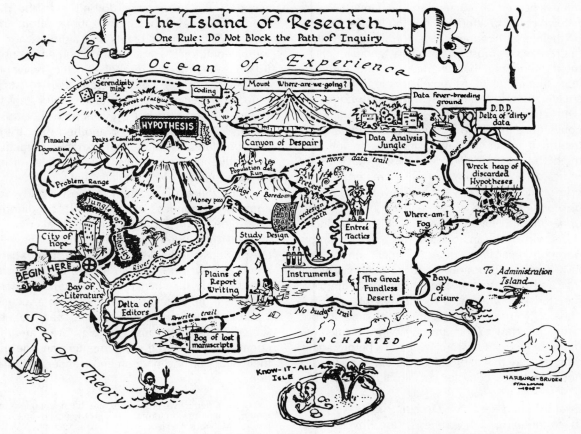

The course of social research, like that of true love, seldom runs smooth. Here is one sociologist's humorous yet realistic view of the obstacles scientists may encounter in their research.

As a science matures, however, investigators find it increasingly possible to derive research problems from theories developed by earlier researchers. Indeed, as we have already suggested, one of the basic values of a scientific theory is that it suggests new lines of inquiry. Often, for example, it is possible to *deduce* from a theory various logical propositions that can be stated as hypotheses and tested.[23] If such derived hypotheses are supported by subsequent research, they lend weight to the theory. Negative results can be equally important, showing that the theory probably needs revision.

Framing a Testable Hypothesis

A careful distinction must be made between a research *problem,* which merely identifies an area of concern, and a research *hypothesis* that lends itself to systematic investigation. For example, let us say that the problem is to determine whether all citizens in the United States receive equal treatment under the law regardless of their socioeconomic position. To study this the researcher must first frame a tentative statement predicting that changes in one variable (e.g., income level, as a measurable indicator of socioeconomic position) will regularly correlate with changes in another (e.g., percentage of convictions in criminal courts, as an indicator of treatment under the law). Thus, the hypothesis might be: *Among individuals who have been indicted for criminal offenses, a greater proportion of those from low-income levels is likely to be convicted than of those from middle- and upper-income levels.* Although this proposition deals with only an isolated facet of the larger question regarding equal treatment under the law, it may still be too broad for adequate testing, and the researcher might decide to narrow the study by limiting it to indictments for one class of offense, such as burglary or rape, in the cities of New York and Chicago. Typically, many related studies are necessary before sociologists can make broad empirical generalizations about any complex social phenomenon.

Establishing a Research Design

In formulating a hypothesis, the investigator must always think in terms of a *research design.*

What are the variables being studied? How can they be measured? What other variables might intervene to cause misleading results? How can the influence of such variables be controlled or discounted? And since researchers can study only a selection of the relevant data, how can they make sure that those cases selected for study are adequately representative of the whole? All of these questions and many others must be answered in the course of defining a research hypothesis that will yield trustworthy results.

GATHERING THE DATA

Once the hypothesis has been clearly formulated, the researcher is ready to subject it to empirical test. Although all of the sciences follow the same general rules for gathering evidence, each has developed devices and techniques appropriate to its own subject matter. The radio telescope of the astronomer doesn't help the paleontologist develop generalizations about the fossilized remains of plants and animals, nor is the paleontologist's system of carbon dating useful in studying the motion of the heavenly bodies. No matter how different their research tools, however, all scientists take careful steps to ensure that the evidence they gather will be trustworthy. By one method or another, they try to rule out the possibility that extraneous factors will influence their results and lead to a misinterpretation of the accumulated data.

Controlled observation is most readily accomplished under experimental conditions, where *ideally* all variables are rigidly accounted for. Having hypothesized a relationship between the particular variables under study, the experimenter allows one of them (called the *independent* variable) to change in some regular manner. Then, the effect of such change on a second variable (the *dependent* variable) can be observed. All extraneous variables are carefully controlled so that the experimenter can rule out their effect on the phenomenon under observation.

23. Such deductive procedures are often complex and require familiarity with formal systems of logic. For an example, see Melvin L. DeFleur and Richard E. Quinney, "A Reformulation of Sutherland's Differential Association Theory and a Strategy for Empirical Verification," *Journal of Research in Crime and Delinquency,* 3 (January 1966): 1–22.

TOOLS OF SOCIOLOGY
INTERPRETING STATISTICAL TABLES   David Dodge

Modern sociological research makes considerable use of statistical tables, both as sources of data and as a means of summarizing research results. Thus the ability to read tables is an essential skill for the student of sociology.

Before trying to interpret the figures in a table, examine its *title* carefully; it should indicate specifically what data the table presents. The titles of the two tables opposite, for example, indicate that both give suicide rates in the United States for different subpopulations in 1970 (as indicated in the headnote to the table). After determining what data a table includes, examine the *source* (or sources) from which the data were obtained. The source information at the bottom of the table will help you judge the reliability of the data being presented; it also gives you the option, if you have a question, of checking the original data.

Look at the *labels* not only at the top of the various columns but also along the left-hand side of the table. The data in a table must usually be interpreted with both sets of labels in mind. In Tables 1.A and 1.B the column headings show, in each case, that suicide rates are given for two race groupings and, within each of these categories, for subgroupings based on sex. But note that the row labels in 1.A indicate regional groupings, whereas those in 1.B indicate age groupings. The two tables show quite different information, even though both are derived from the same basic data—data on the size, composition, and distribution of the U.S. population in 1970 as reported by the Bureau of the Census and the latest available data on suicides in the U.S. as reported by the Office of Vital Statistics.

Finally, in order to interpret a table you must understand what *units* are being used— if the figures represent thousands or millions, for instance, or if they express percentages or rates. In each of the tables shown here, the figures are suicide *rates,* and the rates indicate the number of suicides *for each 100,000* of population. Standardized rates of this sort make possible direct comparisons of the rates for groups (populations or subpopulations) of different sizes.

Table 1.A. SUICIDE RATES FOR REGIONS OF THE U.S. BY COLOR AND SEX

Rates per 100,000 of 1970 population

Region	White			Nonwhite		
	Male	Female	Total	Male	Female	Total
North	14.3	5.2	9.6	6.8	2.0	4.3
South	18.3	6.0	12.0	6.3	1.7	3.9
West	21.7	9.9	15.8	10.4	5.0	7.7
U.S.	16.7	6.3	11.4	7.0	2.3	4.6

Table 1.B. SUICIDE RATES FOR AGE GROUPS IN THE U.S. BY COLOR AND SEX

Rates per 100,000 of 1970 population

Age	White			Nonwhite		
	Male	Female	Total	Male	Female	Total
20–24	13.8	4.4	9.0	11.8	3.8	7.5
25–29	15.5	6.6	11.0	14.6	3.9	8.9
30–34	17.8	7.9	12.8	14.5	4.3	9.0
35–39	22.6	10.9	16.6	11.5	4.5	7.6
40–44	24.9	12.7	18.6	12.8	4.0	8.0
45–49	26.9	13.0	19.7	11.6	3.7	7.4
50–54	30.3	13.5	21.6	12.0	3.2	7.3
55–59	35.1	12.0	23.1	12.5	2.9	7.4
60–64	35.0	10.2	21.8	10.3	2.1	5.9

SOURCE: *United States Census of Population, 1970: United States Summary, General Population Characteristics* (Washington, D.C.: Bureau of the Census), pp. 255, 269–274, and 286; *Vital Statistics of the United States, 1968,* Vol. II, *Mortality* (Washington, D.C.: Office of Vital Statistics), pp. 124–125 and 129–434.

The comparisons shown in Tables 1.A and 1.B raise many sociological questions. For example, why does the West have higher suicide rates than either the North or the South? Why is there a strong tendency for suicide rates to increase with age, especially for whites? Why do whites have much higher rates than nonwhites? And why are male rates higher than female rates, regardless of color? Note also the striking influence of *combinations* of characteristics (e.g., the rate for white males in the West versus that for nonwhite females in the South). Such variations need to be explained. Would Durkheim's theory help here?

For some recent attempts to explain variations in suicide rates in terms of social variables, see Louis I. Dublin, *Suicide: A Sociological and Statistical Study* (New York: The Ronald Press, 1963); Jack P. Gibbs and Walter T. Martin, *Status Integration and Suicide: A Sociological Study* (Eugene, Ore.: University of Oregon Press, 1964); Andrew F. Henry and James F. Short, *Suicide and Homicide* (New York: The Free Press, 1954); and R. W. Maris, *Social Forces in Urban Suicide* (Homewood, Ill.: Dorsey Press, 1969).

Although the classic laboratory experiment is still held up as a scientific ideal, there are today many alternative methods for making controlled observations. Sophisticated statistical and mathematical techniques are now widely used in all the sciences, either to hold constant extraneous factors or to measure them so that they can be taken into account in interpreting results. Statistical controls are especially valuable in sociology, which can make only very limited use of the classic laboratory experiment in studying social phenomena. (The varied research methods used by sociologists will be introduced at relevant points in the text. See the listing of Tools of Sociology following the Table of Contents.)

ANALYZING THE RESULTS

After the relevant observations have been made under appropriate conditions, research data must be summarized and interpreted. In sociology as in other sciences, this is frequently done today through the use of statistics. On the basis of probability theory, statistical tests tell researchers how far they can trust their evidence and how great the likelihood is that chance or extraneous factors might have yielded similar results.

Sociologists seldom try to predict what specific individuals will do, any more than agronomists try to predict which specific stalks of grain in a field will contribute to a high or a low yield. However, different levels of probability can be assigned to different *categories* of persons concerning the likelihood that they will engage in particular forms of behavior in given circumstances. Statistical inference need not be the final court of appeal in all cases, especially for generalizations that do not lend themselves readily to quantitative form. Nevertheless, at some point a discipline must submit its explanations to a process of verification capable of demonstrating that they are valid according to logically sound standards of proof.

Even those sociological explanations that must be regarded as tentative are based upon some degree of empirical analysis and are thus more trustworthy than speculations dictated simply by "common sense." For example, common sense suggests that capital punishment should serve as an effective deterrent to serious crimes such as murder. But what is the evidence? One comprehensive study compared the homicide rates of Michigan, Indiana, and Ohio—three adjacent states that are more or less homogeneous culturally—over a period of almost forty years.[24] The homicide rate in Michigan, which had no death penalty, closely paralleled and was often lower than the homicide rate in the neighboring states which *did* have capital punishment. Similar studies made in other states have invariably produced similar findings.[25] Thus, the argument that the death penalty is an effective deterrent to murder runs counter to the evidence from empirical studies.

In everyday conversation the term *theory* is frequently used as a synonym for *hunch* or *guess*. Friends say, "I don't care about your theories, only about the facts," or "That may be all right in theory, but it won't work in practice." In science, however, theories that have been adequately verified by research *are* "the facts." In other words, they are the most accurate explanations of reality that scientists have been able to formulate. Furthermore, valid theories *do* "work in practice," providing objective and reliable guides for predicting relationships between phenomena.

Sociologists are not yet able to make precise predictions in all areas of their concern, but they have been able to demonstrate that social behavior follows remarkably stable patterns, despite the fact that much human conduct may seem unpredictable or a matter of individual choice. For example, it can be safely predicted within small margins of error that during a given year a certain proportion of people in our society will take their own lives, change jobs, commit armed robbery, get divorced, become addicted to drugs, go to college, move from one city to another, have a child, vote Republican, violate their paroles, or engage in numerous other specific forms of behavior. Taken as a

24. Thorsten Sellin, "Capital Punishment," *Federal Probation,* 15 (September 1961): 3–11.

25. See, for example, Walter C. Reckless, "The Use of the Death Penalty—A Factual Statement," *Crime and Delinquency,* 15, No. 1 (January 1969): 43–56; and Charles R. Tittle and Charles H. Logan, "Sanctions and Deviance: Evidence and Remaining Questions," *Law and Society Review* (Spring 1973): 371–374.

whole, human social behavior seems to follow predictable regularities, and sociology has assumed the task of identifying them as precisely as possible.

SUMMARY

Although sociology as an organized field of teaching and research dates back just over a century, thinkers have been concerned with understanding and improving society since very early times. Ancient rulers and philosophers sought ways of designing a social order so as to minimize deviance, maximize social stability, and promote just treatment for all. Numerous plans were developed over the ages, but early social analysts lacked a method by which they could test their ideas against empirical evidence.

Development of the scientific method began to yield important results in the physical and biological sciences in the late seventeenth and the eighteenth centuries. By the beginning of the nineteenth century, proposals were being made for the scientific study of various aspects of social life. It was Auguste Comte who advanced the most thorough and extensive analysis of this new field of study, which he called *sociology*. Comte did little in the way of actual fact-gathering, but he mapped out in great detail many of the methods, concepts, and theories of sociology that would be followed later.

A modern approach to sociological analysis began to develop at the turn of the century through the efforts of European scholars such as Émile Durkheim. Durkheim's theories about different types of suicide and the underlying conditions of social cohesion that brought them about showed how sociological analysis could reveal understandings of a significant human act that were unobtainable from other disciplines. It was about this time that sociology was taken up by American scholars. The field had a special appeal to a new society with numerous problems and highly practical orientations. Sociology grew rapidly in the United States, and currently it is a more fully developed discipline in this country than anywhere else.

The goals of sociology today are not basically different from those of social philosophers in ancient times. It seeks to understand social organization and social processes. It attempts to describe and explain social stability, social change, and the effects of various kinds of social conditions. And in so doing, it attempts to accumulate knowledge that will be useful in the development of a more adequate social order. Sociologists approach such tasks with differing theoretical and methodological orientations; they also hold differing views of the role sociology should play in developing a more adequate social order.

Sociological knowledge is accumulated through the development of concepts, generalizations, and theories which are tested against the world of reality by numerous techniques of controlled observation. Concepts identify specific classes of social phenomena. Generalizations state relationships between two or more concepts. When verified reasonably well by factual evidence, generalizations can often be combined to form theories. Theories provide explanations of how consequences follow from antecedents—how certain prior social conditions lead to specific social effects. They also suggest directions for further research.

The analysis of concepts, generalizations, theories, and the various steps involved in the application of scientific logic to sociology can at times seem divorced from the concrete realities of human groups. Yet, if sociologists are to understand the underlying processes of human groups and society, they need to go beyond the superficial level of mere description to understand why people behave as they do. Thus sociologists formulate their research questions precisely into hypotheses—generalizations stated in such a way that they may be tested by empirical research. They establish designs for controlling observations and eliminating unwanted influences on those observations. They assemble factual data, analyze their evidence, often with the aid of probability-based statistics, and make careful inferences about results. It has been mainly through the systematic application of the logic of scientific inquiry that modern sociology has developed.

Part I
THE SOCIAL ORDER

2
Social Organization

A sociology instructor drew this diagram on the blackboard, asking the class what it represented and how it related to sociology:

```
            0   0      0
    0    0    0            0
      0    0   0     0
    X    X X X X       X
               X
      X    X   X
```

For anyone knowledgeable about football, the answer to the first part of the instructor's question is obvious: the diagram represents a T-formation attack countered by a 4-4-3 defense. The Xs and 0s show the position of each player on the two teams and indicate the specialized role each is expected to perform. The football fan who recognizes the pattern of the play can predict, within limits, what the individual members of each team will do and can see how their various actions interrelate.

What does this diagram have to do with sociology? It illustrates that the behavior of a given group becomes more understandable if we can relate it to underlying patterns of group organization—to the members' shared understandings about how "the game" is to be played. One of the basic tasks of sociological research is to analyze the recurring patterns of interaction in groups of all types.

Like the football teams in our example, all kinds of human groups—families, faculty committees, social clubs, business organizations, legislative assemblies, and so on through an endless list—function within a framework of general rules that every member is expected to follow. And again, as in football and other team sports, they also have specific expectations for individual members, depending on the specialized part each plays within the group. When individual members violate the general rules or fail to play their parts in expected ways, someone "blows the whistle" and a penalty is assessed. Carrying the analogy to team sports one step further, groups of every type have a system for ranking members differentially on the basis of criteria recognized by the members. "Players" whose positions are deemed critical to the group's success and those who perform especially well are rated higher than others and receive higher rewards in the form of more prestige, a larger salary, greater authority and influence, or some combination of all three. In short, the "rules of the game"—mutually understood patterns of interaction—shape the behavior of people as group members in everyday life as truly as they do in football or any team sport.

In this chapter we will examine the fundamental nature of group activity. After analyzing the various elements of social organization that govern interaction among group members, we will discuss the group as an on-going system that changes in response to changing circumstances and demands. We will also consider some of the causes and consequences of tension and conflict in group life.

As we noted in the preceding chapter, the study of social organization and social processes does not guarantee that solutions will be found for specific societal ills, any more than the study of human physiology guarantees cures for specific diseases. But unless we increase our understanding of the way human groups form, are maintained, undergo change, and sometimes collapse, we stand little chance of learning how social systems generate problems or satisfactions for the people who compose them. The study of organized social interaction also helps us recognize the power of groups—not only how they are able to accomplish tasks that would be impossible for individuals acting alone, but also how strongly they influence the behavior of their members.

GROUP AS A SOCIOLOGICAL CONCEPT

Any inclusive definition of the concept *group* must be equally applicable to an amazing variety of interacting human aggregates. It must cover, for example, such diverse phenomena as a Bantu family, a New York street gang, the board of directors for IBM, the International Red Cross, the U.S. Army, the British House of Commons, and even whole communities and societies. Even when we consider only one type of group, such as the family, the range of variation is great. Each group has its own special behavior patterns, and each is composed of individuals, none of whom are exactly alike or will interact with others in exactly the same way.

Despite great differences in size, complexity, and orientation, however, all human groups fit this general definition: *a group is a number of individuals who interact recurrently according to some pattern of social organization.* Although the pattern may vary dramatically from group to group, the basic components of social organization are always the same. Sociologists identify these as a system of *norms* that defines appropriate behavior for group members; a system of *roles* that coordinates their activities; a system of sanctions that maintains *social control*; and a *ranking system* that assigns different degrees of importance to particular roles. As we will illustrate in this chapter and in Chapter 3, "Types of Groups," these elements of social organization are common to all groups, ranging from those that include only two persons to heterogeneous societies made up of hundreds of millions of members. Even in groups that are not formally organized, social interaction is patterned around "rules" and expectations that are understood by the members.

Sociologists make a clear distinction between groups and social categories. A *social category* may be defined as a number of individuals who are classified together simply because they share a common characteristic or, in some cases, a cluster of characteristics. There is an almost unlimited number of ways in which people can thus be classified: for example, men under thirty-five, people with incomes above $10,000, people with a common national origin, blue-eyed blonds, salesmen, and women might all be considered social categories. The individuals are alike in some specified way. However, they do not constitute groups in a sociological sense unless they recurrently interact in some organized way.

Although social categories, by definition, are unstructured, they are often a factor in the structuring of organized groups. A group may recruit or exclude certain categories of people (e.g., a business may hire only college graduates), or it may use membership in a particular social category as a basis for allocating roles, regardless of the qualifications of the particular individuals involved (e.g., in most companies, women have been excluded from top executive positions). In addition, social categories sometimes provide the basis for the development of new groups. College students, for example, can be classified as a social category; but because of their common problems, interests, and goals, they develop patterns of social interaction among themselves and form groups of many kinds. Occupational, ethnic, and age categories have similarly provided a basis for the development of many organized groups.

INTERACTION: THE BASIS OF GROUP LIFE

Although sociologists seldom have an opportunity to observe the actual development of groups, it is helpful in trying to understand social organization to think of a group in the process of being formed. Stated in the simplest terms, the conditions necessary for the formation of a group are (1) the existence of *potential members* (2) who begin to engage in *recurrent interaction* (3) in order to achieve *similar goals* or satisfactions. As they begin to interact with each other on a repeated basis, they gradually develop regularized patterns of interpersonal behavior—a system of social organization that enables them to function as a unit. Through repetitive interaction, in short, they coordinate their individual activities into group activity.

The study of group behavior begins with the observation of interaction among members. On the basis of such observations, sociologists attempt to understand how groups create and organize rules of behavior, how these rules become stabilized, and how they undergo change.

With such knowledge it becomes possible to understand better the meanings that shared expectations have for the members of groups and how they are capable of shaping the conduct of individuals.

TYPES OF INTERACTION

Strictly speaking, social interaction includes every human act that somehow influences another individual. But not all types of interaction lead to the formation of groups. The policeman who handcuffs a suspected criminal is certainly engaging in an act that influences another person. The mugger who beats up his victim is doing the same. However, interaction of this sort, consisting mainly of physical contact, is unlikely to lead to a continuing social relationship between the parties. The interaction out of which groups develop is much more commonly based on the exchange of mutually meaningful symbols, especially the symbols of everyday language. Human groups are in a very real sense *systems of communication,* in which the members relate to each other primarily through the use of words, gestures, and other kinds of symbols that are understandable to all. Without some system of shared symbols—some form of mutually understood language—group behavior as we know it would be all but impossible.[1]

Transitory Versus Recurrent Interaction

In differentiating between group behavior and other forms of interpersonal activity, sociologists often make a distinction between transitory and recurrent interaction. Transitory interaction typifies the behavior of such human aggregates as crowds, publics, and audiences, whose members interact only briefly—though often with great intensity—and then go their separate ways. Such aggregates are not truly groups. Many kinds of nongroup behavior have a loose pattern of their own, however, for as people move in

---

1. Communication based on the exchange of meaningful symbols is equally critical to the development of human culture (see pages 97–98) and to the development of individual personality (see page 138).

and out of similar situations, they develop standard ways of responding to them. The kind of transitory interaction that takes place among members of a theater audience or among strangers at a cocktail party is nonrecurrent only in the sense that the same individuals do not interact on a repeated basis.[2] The *situation* is repetitive; the participants change.

Although interpersonal behavior based on transitory interaction is of considerable interest to sociologists, their central concern is with the coordinated, recurrent interaction patterns characteristic of organized groups. A simple example will illustrate the distinction between group and nongroup interaction. Imagine that a number of individuals, all from the same town but most of them strangers to one another, are waiting for a commuter train in a small railway station. Suddenly a fire breaks out. Most of the waiting commuters rush to escape the burning building, pushing and shoving in their effort to get out unharmed. They then stand around as a loose crowd of spectators to watch the fire. This is clearly an example of unstructured interaction; it does not constitute group behavior.

Now let us assume that one individual suddenly takes charge. This person directs some of the people to work as a bucket brigade, others to remove valuables from the building, and still others to administer first aid. Interaction thus becomes coordinated.

If the commuters disperse after the fire and never again work together, their interaction still cannot be classified as group behavior. But suppose that the experience of the fire makes the community aware of the need for some kind of organized fire-fighting force and that the individuals who cooperated earlier decide to join together as a volunteer fire department to achieve that goal. Their subsequent meetings, drills, planning sessions, and actual fire fighting would constitute a pattern of recurrent, goal-oriented interaction. They would have formed a group in the sociological meaning of the term. A sociologist could now attempt to discover the group's pattern of social organization.

Informal Versus Formal Interaction

Group organization may be based on either formal or informal patterns. *Informal* interaction is typical among family members, friends, and members of other groups whose activities are not governed by a body of "official" rules. This does not mean that informal interaction follows no rules—only that the rules are implicit, unwritten, loosely formulated, and relatively flexible. The members share a general understanding about the kinds of behavior that are appropriate and acceptable, and they tend to tolerate any behavior that falls within this rather broad range. This informal type of social organization—or *informal structure*, as it is sometimes called—is characteristic of many kinds of groups.

At the other end of the scale, *formal* interaction proceeds on the basis of rules that are clearly specified, usually in a written document. They may be spelled out in a handbook, as in the bylaws of a corporation, or, even more inflexibly, in legal or quasi-legal contracts that specify in detail the behavior each party will tolerate and expect of the other.

Many kinds of social relationships have elements of both formal and informal interaction. For example, the Squire Agency of New York City and the Rent-A-Bird Agency of Miami, Florida, are in the business of providing escorts for an evening's companionship to people who wish to pay for such services. After an interview, the customer selects his or her companion from a photo album and signs a formal contract, promising good conduct and agreeing that no other services (e.g., prostitution) are to be provided. The young man or woman who serves as the escort gets about half the fee, plus a free evening on the town. After these formal arrangements have been made, the "date" proceeds, presumably through the usual forms of informal interaction.

While such a social relationship is unlikely to lead to the formation of a group, the example illustrates the principle that elements of both formal and informal interaction are found in social behavior. This generalization is particularly true in the case of large-scale groups with formal rules of procedure. Even the most formal group

2. For a provocative analysis of transitory and related forms of interaction, see Erving Goffman, *Encounters: Two Studies in the Sociology of Interaction* (Indianapolis: The Bobbs-Merrill Co., Inc., 1961).

tends to spawn a variety of spontaneous *sub-groups* in which interaction proceeds according to informal rules. As we shall have occasion to note, these rules sometimes conflict with those of the formal structure.

The Stabilization of Interaction

As the members of a group interact over a period of time, their interpersonal exchanges follow increasingly predictable patterns. Members come to know more clearly what is expected of them and what they can expect of others. Even such two-person relationships as those between physician and patient or teacher and student are based on interactional patterns that have the important characteristic of predictability.

The process of developing orderly, stable, and increasingly predictable forms of recurrent interaction is called *institutionalization*. Once patterns of interaction have become institutionalized, they come to be thought of as binding by group members. Schools, businesses, military units, communities, and societies all have institutionalized patterns of interaction which members feel they "ought" to follow. The institutionalization of behavioral rules serves to maintain the stability of the group by providing standard ways for coping with needs and achieving group goals.

THE FOCUS OF INTERACTION: GROUP GOALS

We have postulated that groups are formed so that their members, through coordinated effort, can together achieve satisfactions they could not achieve singly. In other words, one of the necessary conditions for the formation of a group is the existence of *goals* that are valued individually and collectively by the members-to-be. Such goals may be related to money, religion, emotional satisfaction, the control of social deviants, the acquisition of political power, the preservation of historical sites, the military defeat of enemies, the prevention of strip mining, the restructuring of a social system, or any one of thousands of other purposes. In general, the satisfaction of individual members and the continued existence of the group are dependent on the group's success in attaining its goals.

Manifest and Formal Goals

Sometimes when groups are formed, the members have in mind certain clearly specified goals that they can state in explicit terms. A group of political leaders meeting to draft a constitution for a new government may formally state in an official document that their purpose is "to form a more perfect union." A new sorority may note in its charter that its purpose is "to foster a spirit of sisterhood among the members." Those gathered to participate in a wedding may be told ritualistically that they are gathered "to join this man and this woman . . . ." In such cases, the goals to be obtained by coordinated activity are both manifest (that is, clearly understood by the members) and formal. The members willingly submit to the "rules of the game" so that the mutually desired outcome can be effectively achieved.

Latent and Informal Goals

Sometimes groups form for reasons that the members understand only vaguely, if at all. For example, several boys may begin to engage in acts of delinquency together because they find it more satisfying to steal or commit acts of vandalism together than to do these same things alone.[3] Similarly, several college students may begin playing bridge, studying, and going out together, always including one another in their plans. Individually, the students may think of their friends as a group only vaguely, and they would probably be at a loss to explain their common goals.

The goals of such groups are *informal,* in that they are not officially specified by the group or its leaders, and *latent,* in that they are not consciously recognized by the members. Typically, they are closely related to the members' desire for approval, acceptance, and companionship. Without the relatively stable pattern of relationships found even in informal groups, individual members could not achieve these basic satisfactions. The meshing of individual goals, then, is an important factor in establishing and maintaining even the most informal groups.

3 See, for example, Albert K. Cohen, *Delinquent Boys* (New York: The Free Press, 1955).

Mixed Goals

Sometimes the manifest goals of a formally organized group are only loosely related to the motivating goals of individual members. An illustration of a group with mixed goals is provided by Hans Toch's analysis of a popular chain of learn-to-dance studios.[4] For the owners and operators, the principal goal of the group is profit. For the clients, a manifest goal is learning to waltz, to tango, or to do the latest popular dance. For many participants, however, learning to dance is not the only goal or even the most important one. Most of the clients are relatively lonely, socially isolated people who participate in the dance lessons and in the parties that the studio arranges (for a price) because these activities provide an opportunity for companionship. As a commercially available group, the staff of the dance studio provides satisfying social relationships for people who are unable, for various reasons, to establish such relationships in other ways.

A young person who drops out of the drug scene to join a fundamentalist religious movement with a membership composed largely of former drug users may have as a manifest purpose the achievement of personal religious salvation. A latent goal may be to find acceptance and companionship among others with similar backgrounds.

THE PRINCIPAL COMPONENTS OF SOCIAL ORGANIZATION

As the members of a group interact to achieve their individual and collective goals, they develop shared understandings about what behavior patterns are appropriate within the group: individuals come to know what is expected of them as group members, and also what they can expect of others. Without such common definitions regarding "the rules of the game," coordinated interaction—group behavior—would be

4. Hans Toch, *The Social Psychology of Social Movements* (Indianapolis: The Bobbs-Merrill Co., Inc., 1965), pp. 91–93.

impossible. *Groups can exist only if their members behave in somewhat predictable ways.*

The patterns of expectation that regulate group behavior fall into four general categories. Stated briefly, groups establish general rules, or *norms,* which apply more or less uniformly to all members of the group. To achieve a necessary division of labor, groups also develop a system of *roles.* Roles are configurations of specialized rights, duties, and obligations allocated to particular members of the group. To ensure that members will behave according to both the general rules and the specialized role expectations, groups institute techniques of *social control.* And, finally, groups develop a *ranking system,* by means of which members are accorded different levels of prestige, power, and privilege. Norms, roles, social control, and ranking are the principal components of social organization, and they can be found in the organizational pattern of every human group. We will examine each of these important concepts in turn.

NORMS: SHARED RULES FOR INTERACTION

Norms are regularities of behavior that arise from interaction as members of a group stabilize their interpersonal conduct. They are the rules people use to define what they expect of one another. Once institutionalized, such regularities define what conduct is appropriate and what conduct is inappropriate for the members of the group. Norms are a very important aspect of social organization. They account for a large part of the patterning of daily conduct of individuals as they relate to each other in human groups.

Norms as Behavior Versus Expectation

One way to define the norms of a group is to observe the overt behavior of its members. If a given form of interaction frequently occurs, it can be inferred that such a behavioral regularity constitutes a norm. For example, among groups of good friends in Latin-American societies, males often greet each other with a vigorous *abrazo,* a mutual embrace. Women in similar circumstances often kiss each other's cheeks. Because these forms of greeting are regularly used in these particular societies, we can define them as norms of behavior.

To be effective, both formal and informal norms must be supported by group consensus.

A second view of norms defines them in terms of the expectations of group members. Seen in this light, norms are shared convictions about the patterns of behavior that are appropriate or inappropriate for members of the group. They are the more or less uniformly understood "rules of the game" that define what group members may, ought, must, cannot, or should not do in varying circumstances. If all the members hold reasonably similar convictions, the norm serves as a guide to conduct. For example, male friends in Latin America *expect* to be greeted with an embrace, female friends with a kiss on the cheek. If either party were to behave in a way substantially different from what was expected, the other would be uncertain how to react; thus interaction would be difficult. In this sense, norms serve as formulas for social behavior: they define what is anticipated and approved, permitting members to know in advance how to interact in specific circumstances.

Universal Versus Specialized Norms

Some norms are universal in their application.

They apply to all members of the group, no matter how important or unimportant a particular member may be. The rule specifying monogamy, for example, is a universal norm in our society; the expectation of loyalty to other members is a universal norm in most close-knit groups. At the societal level, universal norms are sometimes called *folkways* or *mores* (pages 87, 88).

Many norms, on the other hand, have only specialized applications. They apply to certain categories of members but not to others. The wearing of lipstick by women in our society is more or less normative. At present, wearing lipstick is considered a violation of norms for men. Sometimes the norms of a group provide great flexibility and many *alternate* forms of behavior. A hostess giving a dinner can serve her guests a main course of meat, fish, or poultry prepared in any of thousands of ways and still conform to the norms of what is appropriate when company comes. She may not, however, serve them cornflakes, peanut-butter sandwiches, or jelly beans as the main dish, even though these are widely used foods in our society.

Formal Versus Informal Norms

Formal norms are those that are consciously or rationally designed to govern behavior within a deliberately organized group. Examples of formal norms are regulations governing behavior in the armed forces, legal statutes such as criminal and civil codes, traffic regulations, and the official rules of colleges, clubs, businesses, and other groups. The distinguishing characteristics of formal norms are their origin in deliberate planning, the conviction of members that they are "official," and usually their explicit statement in written form.

Informal norms have less clear-cut origins. Some emerge spontaneously, without deliberate design, from the informal interaction of group members. For example. a group of college students occasionally frequents a local pub. As the semester wears on, they develop the practice of meeting there regularly on Friday nights to drink beer, talk, and play pool. The loser at pool is expected to buy a pizza for the whole group. Informal norms have been established.

Other informal norms are adaptations of more general norms in the society. For example, in a play group of younger children, one youngster is discovered to have tattled to the teacher concerning the misdeeds of some of the other members. Because of this the child is rejected by the group. Informal norms against being a "tattletale" are widespread in our society, and they become part of the informal expectations of many kinds of groups.

Informal norms are often as compelling as formal norms. They are not deliberately designed, "official," or written down, but insofar as they are mutually understood by group members, they provide clear guides as to what is considered conforming and what is considered deviant. Thus, when an informal norm becomes institutionalized, it constitutes an important element in the social organization of the group in which it exists.

To be effective, both formal and informal norms must be supported by group *consensus:* the great majority of members must regard the norm as appropriate and sufficiently important to demand conformity. In the absence of such consensus, a norm loses its compelling quality and ceases to be a norm in the behavioral sense. In the United States, for example, widespread support of the norm forbidding any kind of work on the Sabbath has long since been lost; and though some states still have "blue laws" prohibiting most kinds of business activity on Sunday, they are seldom stringently enforced.

The Differential Importance of Norms

The extent to which a group demands conformity to a norm depends on how much the norm contributes to the group's purposes and how deeply it is rooted in sentiment and tradition. Some norms are only vaguely formulated and loosely adhered to; others are precisely spelled out and rigidly enforced. The hostess inviting friends to a cocktail party may specify the hours as from five o'clock to seven; but she knows that many guests will not arrive before six, and she can only hope that all of them will leave before midnight. Yet the next day in her role as college

professor, the same person may insist that her students be on hand promptly at nine o'clock for the beginning of a class and that they stay until she dismisses them.

Many norms, such as the custom of saying "I'm glad to meet you" after being introduced to someone or "Excuse me" after stepping on someone's toe, are established rituals for making social relationships simple, pleasant, and predictable. People may be offended by the violation of such norms, but they are likely to shrug off their annoyance or disappointment without reprimanding the offender. Other norms, however, such as the army's prohibition against desertion, are deemed critical to the achievement of group goals, and their violation may be severely punished.

The total number of norms to which a given individual is expected to conform is immense. Most people belong to a great many groups, each of which imposes a number of formal and informal norms that control behavior in a wide variety of ways.[5] But if norms reduce the freedom of the individual, they also make life less complicated and confusing by making social relationships more predictable. In most interpersonal dealings, people know what they can expect of others as well as what others will expect of them. One of life's unsettling circumstances is to be in a social setting where the norms are unclear—going through registration at a large university for the first time, meeting one's prospective in-laws, being a guest in the home of people much richer (or poorer) than oneself. Most people feel nervous in such situations, fearing that they may embarrass themselves by doing "the wrong thing."

SOCIAL ROLES: INTERLOCKING SPECIALIZATIONS

Group action is often far more effective than individual action in achieving desired goals because groups can call on the varied resources of all their members and assign them different activities. *Specialization* is a key concept here. If a group can somehow get each member to carry out certain specific activities consistently and

5. Norms do not control people rigidly; norms modify people's behavior according to the situation they are in and in the presence of specific others. See Ervin Staub, "Instigation to Goodness: The Role of Social Norms and Interpersonal Influence," *The Journal of Social Issues,* 28, No. 4 (1972): 131–150.

not engage in other activities, the behavior of all members can be coordinated to attain the group's goals. The development of specialized expectations for different members is called *role allocation*. The interlocking web of specialized role activities resulting from this allocation is referred to as the group's *division of labor*.

A social role defines the rights, duties, and obligations of any group member who performs a specialized function. In formal groups, most key roles are explicitly defined, perhaps in a series of job descriptions or a manual of procedure. In informal groups, they are more likely to be "understood." Whether formal or informal, however, the roles of a given group are interpreted in much the same way by all the members. For example, all members of a family understand the general rights, duties, and obligations of the father, mother, and offspring. Thus, all share more or less common expectations of how these roles will be performed and how family members will interact. It is in this sense that roles are sometimes viewed as *configurations of norms*. They not only differentiate the behavior of individual group members into specialized activities but also organize the behavior and expectations of the group as a whole.

The Allocation of Specialized Roles

Every group either deliberately or unwittingly allocates roles in terms of distinctive expectations for different members. Although role specialization is most easily recognized in formal organizations, it is also characteristic of informal groups. On the surface, most girls in a teen-age clique might seem to behave in essentially similar ways, but extended observation of any such group would probably reveal that one girl is the unofficial leader, that one or two others take over the direction of particular activities, and that even the followers fit into the group in different ways.

When spontaneously formed groups continue to exist, informal role specialization tends to become increasingly pronounced. If one member of the teen-age clique repeatedly smooths over quarrels, for example, the other members may learn to turn to her whenever strife occurs. Another member may take the role of the joker.[6]

Many groups also have an opinion leader, a person who is more closely in contact with outside sources of information than the other members. Opinion leaders relay information, ideas, and rumors they pick up from various sources and help interpret this material for the rest of the group.[7]

Ascribed and Achieved Criteria

Sociologists make a distinction between the ascribed and the achieved criteria groups use to allocate certain roles to specific members. Ascribed criteria are those about which the individual can do little or nothing. Almost every society, for example, allocates some roles on the basis of age, with youngsters (and often oldsters) barred from a number of roles. Sex is another widely used ascribed criterion. Although some occupations that were traditionally all-male or all-female now have practitioners of the other sex—for example, women jockeys and men telephone operators—there is still a strong tendency to exclude one sex or the other from many roles in our society.

Achieved criteria are those about which people can do something. They can successfully undergo costly or difficult training or otherwise demonstrate the ability to assume the responsibilities a given role demands. Formal groups with elaborate divisions of labor, like those typically found in modern business, education, and government, make extensive use of achieved criteria. In fact, it is a basic principle of American society that roles should be allocated on the basis of ability to perform. However, the fact that we need laws to guarantee equal employment practices for minority-group members, women, and older workers indicates that ascribed criteria continue to be used in many cases.

The Coordination of Roles

The allocation of specialized roles provides one major element of a group's social organization; the coordination of these roles into an overall

6. Jacqueline D. Goodchilds, "The Effects of Being Witty on Position in the Social Structure of a Small Group," *Sociometry*, 22 (1959): 261–272.
7. Paul F. Lazarsfeld, Bernard R. Berelson, and Helen Gaudet, *The People's Choice*, 2nd ed. (New York: Columbia University Press, 1948).

system of reciprocal relationships provides another. The role of borrower has no meaning unless it is linked with the *complementary role* of lender. The same is true of father and child, buyer and seller, lawyer and client, and so on. All social roles can be viewed as complementary to other roles. There can be no physician without a patient, no teacher without a student, and no friend without someone to be friendly with. Thus the activities or expectations relevant to a given role are reciprocally linked with other roles in an interdependent system.

In small, spontaneously formed groups the pattern of role coordination and interdependency is usually quite simple and only vaguely defined. The members seldom need formal direction in working together. A more clear-cut division of labor is usually found in formally organized groups, even if they are relatively small. In a restaurant, for example, the cooks, waiters and waitresses, busboys, cashiers, dishwashers, and manager are linked in a coordinated pattern of specialized roles in such a way that the customers are served and the goals of the group are achieved.

In large organizations the division of labor often becomes highly elaborate. The managers of a corporation employing hundreds or thousands of people must give detailed attention to both the allocation and the coordination of interdependent roles. Often they rely on detailed job descriptions to give formal definitions of the various occupational roles within the organization, from clerk-typist to section manager. They may use time-and-motion studies to determine the most efficient pattern of movement for workers on an assembly line. And always they create an organizational chart, showing lines of communication and responsibility from the head of the organization on down through lower levels of management.

Essentially, it is the need for coordinating roles that is responsible for development of *leadership*. As we have already noted, spontaneous leaders develop in informal groups when members repeatedly turn to the same person for advice, for suggestions, or for direction in achieving group goals. In formally organized groups that require more definite leadership, authority is specifically delegated: certain individuals have a clearly defined right to coordinate the activities of others. Very different criteria and procedures are used to select leaders in different types of groups, but always the basic reason for the existence of a leader is the need for coordinating the members' specialized activities.

Role Expectation and Role Behavior
As the preceding discussion has suggested, a social role can be thought of either as a set of expectations shared by members of a group concerning the activities appropriate to a given position or as the actual behavior of the role incumbent—of the group member who carries out the role. Although the concepts of role *expectations* and role *behavior* are closely related, the distinction between them is important. If the way a group member acts out a role is fairly consistent with the group's expectations of the role, group interaction will proceed harmoniously; but if an incumbent's performance does *not* match the group's expectations, conflict is likely. This is especially true when the gap between role expectations and role performance widens to a point where achievement of the group's goals seems threatened. Thus most groups develop a system of social control so that members will behave according to expected patterns.

SOCIAL CONTROL: LIMITING DEVIATION
Groups of all types attempt to maintain stability by developing techniques of social control. *Social control* can be defined as the application of sanctions to ensure that members will (1) abide by the group's norms, (2) perform required roles in a prescribed manner, and (3) coordinate their activities in such a way that group goals can be achieved. *Negative sanctions* are punishment of, or threats of punishment to, members who violate norms or fail to perform their roles adequately; the purpose is to check deviation. *Positive sanctions*, on the other hand, are used to reward members who meet or exceed the group's normative and role expectations; they

serve to reinforce approved patterns of behavior.[8] Both kinds of sanctions are considered necessary to maintain the organization of a group and to increase the probability that its goals will be attained.

Tolerance Limits

Although some groups are much stricter than others in demanding conformity from their members, most of the rules in any group provide for a *range* of tolerable behavior. Except when norms are deemed critical, such as the societal norm prohibiting murder, some degree of deviation from them is permitted before negative sanctions are invoked.

Although tolerance limits are seldom precisely defined, members of a group soon learn from experience how much leeway they have in interpreting particular norms and roles. For example, some motorists regularly drive slightly faster than the posted limit on the assumption that speeds up to five miles beyond the limit will usually be tolerated by the police. They have conceived a tolerance limit that defines the point beyond which negative sanctions will be invoked.

Sometimes strict enforcement of a group's rules arouses considerable hostility among the members, especially if the rules seem relatively unimportant. In military establishments located in combat zones or other hardship areas, for example, traditional discipline and rituals are often greatly relaxed. A newly arrived officer who insists on strict adherence to the norms associated with formal military protocol will be cordially hated by those under his or her command.

The Administration of Sanctions

The negative sanctions used by various groups range from subtle gestures like raising an eyebrow when a member has committed a social error to such drastic acts as executing a member who has violated a major taboo. In small, intimate groups sanctions are usually verbal, but occasionally they involve the administration of physical punishment under the guise of a game. In a classic study of a group of factory workers, Roethlisberger and Dickson noted that under a piecework incentive plan, workers had developed an informal norm specifying the number of units that each member of the group should produce as a fair day's work. If a given member greatly exceeded this norm, producing so many units that the others might appear to be loafing, sanctions were employed to bring the deviant back into line. The member was called a rate-buster and other less flattering names, all in a semi-humorous vein but not entirely in fun. A really serious violation was punished through the game of "binging," a form of horseplay in which the workers exchanged blows to the upper arm, with the rate-buster always getting the worst of it.[9]

Similar sanctions are sometimes used by students who resent an individual whose grades are "too high." Although superior students may receive positive sanctions from their professors in the form of praise and good grades, they may be subjected to negative sanctions from their fellow students. Joking references to the person as a "curve breaker," "brown nose," or "grind" are actually techniques of control aimed at lowering performance to a level where it will not longer pose "unfair" competition.

In most small groups, sanctions are devised spontaneously and can generally be administered by any member. In large groups, social control is likely to be much more formal, and sanctions are usually meted out according to official policies. Most formal organizations have a wide variety of positive and negative sanctions. An obvious example from business is the practice of awarding or withholding promotions and pay increases on the basis of merit—that is, for adequate or inadequate role performance. Many groups also use symbolic sanctions. College students are given grades; military cadets are given

8. For a very early discussion of social control, see Edward A. Ross, *Social Control: A Survey of the Foundations of Order* (New York: Macmillan, 1901). See also A. R. Radcliffe-Brown, "Sanction, social," *Encyclopedia of the Social Sciences*, Vol. 13 (London: Macmillan, 1934), pp. 531–534.

9. Fritz J. Roethlisberger and William J. Dickson, *Management and the Worker* (Cambridge, Mass.: Harvard University Press, 1939), Part 4.

decorations or demerits; successful corporate managers are given a more prestigious title, a rug on the floor, a private secretary, a reserved parking space, or a key to the executive washroom.

The authority to apply formal sanctions is an important basis of control for those charged with the task of coordinating the organizational machinery of a corporation or other large group. The heads of formal organizations are respected — and sometimes feared — largely because they have been vested with the final authority to give or withhold official rewards.

The Interplay of Formal and Informal Sanctions

Since most large groups incorporate a variety of spontaneous subgroups, individual members are subject to both formal and informal social controls. If an official norm conflicts with one supported by a subgroup, individuals must make a choice. Often they will decide to violate a norm of the larger group rather than one upheld by people with whom they more closely identify.

An effective dovetailing of formal and informal controls can produce a tenacious adherence to norms and an outstanding performance of roles, as has often been demonstrated by the performance of small military units in combat. In a study seeking to explain the extraordinary effectiveness of the German army on several fronts during most of World War II, Shils and Janowitz tested the hypothesis that the key factor motivating the average German soldier was "the steady satisfaction of certain primary personality demands afforded by the social organization of the army" rather than the competence of the German high command or the ideological strength of National Socialism. The data obtained supported the hypothesis by showing that as long as the soldier felt a special loyalty to his squad or platoon and identified himself emotionally with other squad members, his morale remained high and he was extremely effective. The researchers found further that the effectiveness of the army as a whole seemed to be en-

hanced, not endangered, by the fact that smaller units focused their attention and their loyalty on their own members.[10]

SOCIAL RANKING: HIERARCHIES OF ROLES

As a group's pattern of social organization is becoming institutionalized, the various roles that have been delineated tend to become ranked into a hierarchy. The term *social ranking* refers to the higher or lower evaluation of a role with respect to some criterion that a group's members deem important. For example, a specific role may be accorded high rank because of the higher degree of responsibility, power, or authority it carries relative to other roles in the structure of the group. Or a given role may be ranked high because it presupposes a talent that few possess. Other high-ranking roles may be associated with unusual wealth or require long and demanding periods of training. Conversely, some roles in a group may be ranked low because they carry little power, few privileges, or limited responsibility. Whatever the criteria, the shared judgments of the members form some evaluative system for ranking the group's roles.

Social Ranking, Status, and Esteem

In the present text a distinction will be maintained between the concepts of status, esteem, and social ranking. The term *social ranking* will be used, as in the section above, to refer to the differential evaluation of roles in a group. The term *status* will be used to designate the level of prestige that is accorded to group members by virtue of the particular role they play. Status (prestige) is thus seen as a *consequence* of social ranking; it is a characteristic attributed to individuals because of the roles allocated to them. Thus a woman who is the president of a company has high status because of the high social ranking of the role she plays; a male vice-president in the company has lower status because of the lower ranking of his role.

10. Edward A. Shils and Morris Janowitz, "Cohesion and Disintegration in the Wehrmacht in World War II," *The Public Opinion Quarterly*, 12 (1948): 280–315.

Groups use a wide range of techniques to encourage approved patterns of behavior and to check deviation. A hug serves as a positive sanction, as does the formal presentation of the Stanley Cup to a victorious hockey team. Techniques used to discourage disapproved behavior can range all the way from a disapproving look to the exercise of legal force.

TOOLS OF SOCIOLOGY
SOCIOMETRY

Sociometry is an objective technique for assessing patterns of attraction, indifference, or even rejection among the members of a specific group, such as a class in school, the occupants of a college dormitory, a factory subgroup, or even the residents of a small village. These patterns provide indices of friendship, influence, and power among the people being studied, thus demonstrating how the feelings of group members may influence the group's pattern of social organization.

One approach to gathering sociometric data is to observe a group's behavior directly over a period of time and infer the regular patterns of interaction among members. This is difficult to do, however, and can lead to misinterpretation unless all interaction can be adequately sampled. A more common technique involves the use of a questionnaire, in which members of the group are asked to name the individuals with whom they would most like to engage in some specific form of activity. In some cases, they are asked to make several choices, ranking members according to their first preference, second preference, and so on.

A variety of social relationships can be studied—eat with, sit next to, go camping with, live next to, have as a close friend, etc. The people making selections are assured that their choices will never be revealed to the other members of the group—an important ethical consideration.

The data obtained are often represented in the form of a *sociogram,* which indicates symbolically the patterns of choice existing between the members at the time the data were gathered. The figure below shows several of the choice patterns that are commonly found. For example, the lines between persons 01 and 05 show a pair who are *mutually attracted,* at least with respect to the kind of interaction being studied. Individual 12 was heavily chosen by other members of the group and can be characterized as a *star.* Person 10 was chosen only once, but since that choice was by the star, this individual can be characterized as a potential *power behind the throne.* Person 02, who chose others but was not chosen by others, can be termed an *isolate.* Individuals 03, 14, 07, and 16 form an interesting *nonreciprocated chain.* Finally, the trio 13, 15, and 09 have mutually chosen each other but are relatively isolated from the remainder of the group; these three form a *clique.*

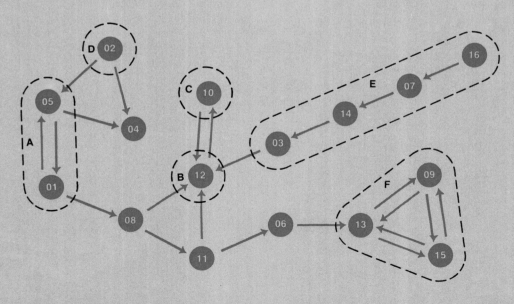

A   Mutually attracted pair
B   Star
C   Power behind the throne
D   Isolate
E   Nonreciprocated chain
F   Clique

The level of status accorded to an individual as the result of a given role is independent of the level of *esteem* accorded to him or her as a person. The distinction between status and esteem can be simply illustrated by analyzing the criteria we might use in rating the personnel in a dentist's office—typically, the dentist, a dental technician, and a receptionist. Patients seeking the professional services of this group could easily distinguish the three roles in terms of the status they carried, and their ranking would be the same regardless of the individuals involved. The hierarchy might be quite different, however, if patients were to rate the role incumbents in terms of their personal qualities. The dentist might be a grouch, and the technician might be cold and officious. The receptionist, on the other hand, might be a pleasant person who made the patients' visits less of an ordeal. Thus the patients' rating of the three individuals in terms of their personal qualities might be just the reverse of the way they would view their relative status.

The Human Significance of Social Ranking

Social ranking—with its attendant implications of personal evaluation, power, privilege, and authority—is especially important because it is the social rank of the roles we play that determines whether or not we receive many of the rewards that our society deems important. The ability to obtain such rewards often provides an important basis upon which others judge us and upon which we judge ourselves. Also, in a society in which "success" is a dominant theme, status and other rewards derived from given social roles can provide strong motivations toward conformity within the group or powerful pressure toward movement from lower ranks to higher. Certainly not all persons are affected by such motivations and pressures, but the inability to improve one's rank appears to be one of the major factors producing discontent and "alienation" among those in blue-collar work roles in the United States.[11]

11. A large-scale study of worker discontent in American industry is Harold Sheppard and Neal Q. Herrick, *Where Have All the Robots Gone?* (New York: The Free Press, 1972).

Injustice in social ranking may occur when those whose aspirations to enter specific roles are blocked by ascribed criteria (page 40). To possess the requisite ability to play a given role and be denied it because of race, sex, or age is an extremely frustrating, embittering experience. In our society, attempts are being made—not always successfully—to provide equal opportunity for everyone. Sociologically, this means minimizing the use of ascribed criteria, stressing achieved criteria, and letting all comers compete for the status and rewards available in a system of differentially ranked roles.

THE GROUP AS A SOCIAL SYSTEM

In the preceding sections we have examined norms, roles, sanctions, and ranking systems in terms of their importance to group *structure*. This is essentially a static view of the human group. To continue our analysis of social organization, we must bring the time variable into the picture and consider the group as an ongoing system.

The concept of *system* is used in sociology much as it is in the physical and biological sciences: it defines a configuration of parts that are in a dynamic relationship of interdependency. Thus we can speak of the sun and the heavenly bodies that revolve around it as the *solar system;* of the human body with its interrelated parts and functions as a *biological system;* of a group with its integrated pattern of social organization and behavior as a *social system*. Each system, whether living or nonliving, has a characteristic structure and a characteristic pattern of functioning. Finally, each is composed of subsystems and is itself part of a larger system, or *field*.

The analysis of a group as a social system requires two stages. First, it is necessary to observe the interaction of group members over a period of time in order to infer the group's structure—the specific norms, roles, systems of ranking, and techniques of social control that make up its pattern of social organization. Second, it is necessary to define the ways in which these structural elements are *interrelated* and *interdependent*—how they function together as an ongoing whole.[12]

An analysis of this type is made difficult by the fact that no group exists in a social vacuum. Each has transactions with, or is part of, other groups. Thus the Smith children are a subgroup of the Smith family and perhaps of a playground group. The family as a whole is a subgroup of the neighborhood, which is a subgroup of the community. The community itself is one of countless subgroups of the society. Individually or as a family, the Smiths also belong to a variety of educational, occupational, recreational, religious, and political groups—all of which are also community and societal subgroups. The *internal system* of any particular group, then, must be analyzed in the context of the *external system,* or total environmental field, of which it is a part.

The task of actually unraveling every pattern of interdependency within a group, and between a group and its social environment, is nearly impossible. The patterns are almost infinitely complex, and they are continuously changing. Nevertheless, the social systems perspective can be very useful in sociological analysis, leading to the discovery of cause-and-effect relationships that might otherwise go unnoticed.[13]

STABILITY AND CHANGE
In sociology as in other disciplines, a systems perspective generally assumes not only that the various components of a system are interrelated but also that every component makes some contribution toward maintaining the system as a whole. In the human biological system, for example, inborn drives propel the organism to seek the food, water, sleep, and oxygen it needs in order to survive. If the organism is invaded by disease-causing microorganisms, it forms antibodies to fight the invaders. If physical danger threatens, automatic changes in body chemistry help the individual cope with the emergency. A similar tendency toward self-maintenance and equilibrium has been observed in human social systems.[14] A group's system of sanctions, for example, serves not only to discourage deviation from established norms but also to bring deviators back into line.

Sociologists utilizing the social systems perspective have, for the most part, stressed stability and equilibrium as the normal conditions of group life. They recognize that stable groups change over time, just as stable individuals do, but they assume that change usually comes gradually, without altering the basic nature of the system. From this perspective, social conflict is viewed to some extent as a "disease" that must be "cured" in order to bring the social system back into harmony.

Conflict theorists do not accept this view. They agree that the various elements of a social system are interrelated, but as we noted in Chapter 1 (pages 16 – 17), they believe that conflict is inherent in group life and see it as the principal mechanism by which groups change and improve. We will consider both the positive and negative aspects of social conflict in a later section of this chapter.

FUNCTIONAL ANALYSIS
An important corollary to the assumption that social systems tend toward equilibrium is that every element of a group's social organization plays some part in enabling it to operate effectively.[15] Research aimed at discovering such relationships is known as *functional analysis.*

12. See, for example, Talcott Parsons, *The Social System* (New York: The Free Press, 1951).
13. George C. Homans, *The Human Group* (New York: Harcourt Brace Jovanovich, Inc., 1950).
14. Charles P. Loomis, *Social Systems: Essays on Their Persistence and Change* (Princeton, N.J.: D. Van Nostrand Co., Inc., 1960). See also Walter Buckley, *Sociology and Modern Systems Theory* (Englewood Cliffs, N.J.: Prentice-Hall, Inc., 1967).
15. This view was once very popular in anthropology. See A. R. Radcliffe-Brown, *The Andaman Islanders* (New York: The Free Press, 1948), p. 397.

TOOLS OF SOCIOLOGY
PARTICIPANT OBSERVATION

Participant observation is a method that can be used to obtain an intimate view of the social organization and orientations of a specific group of people. It is also valuable for the exploratory phases of research. Participant observation is exactly what the name implies: the sociologist becomes a group member and observes group processes from the "inside."

Although the exact steps used in this method are not rigorously codified, William F. Whyte's classic work, *Street-Corner Society,* illustrates the necessary procedures. Whyte used participant observation to study young men in an Italian slum neighborhood. Essentially, he followed the steps indicated below.

1. *Initial Formulation of Research Objectives.* Whyte questioned the widely held belief that slum neighborhoods are socially disorganized; he suspected that informal and subtle social organization characterized such areas. His research objective was to study slum society for the purpose of determining its organization and its relationship to the larger community.

2. *Initial Contact.* Whyte lived with an Italian family in a particular neighborhood for eighteen months, but later rented a nearby apartment. He made his first contacts with the Nortons—a corner gang he studied intensively—through the local settlement house.

3. *Learning to "Fit In."* He learned to speak Italian and began to participate in neighborhood activities. He identified himself as a writer studying Italian customs and the history of that area of the city. Later, Whyte revealed his purposes to some of the informal leaders of the group. (In some cases, the researcher may not wish to do this.)

4. *Gaining Full Acceptance.* Gradually, Whyte became accepted as a good fellow and was able to participate fully in the activities of the group. He bowled, dated, played cards, shot pool, and ate and drank with the young men. They trusted and accepted him as a friend.

5. *Systematic Observation.* As their acceptance of him increased, Whyte began to make systematic notes on the group's patterns of interaction, social structure, and way of life. He trained himself to remember details of their social relations in order to make accurate notes later. He accumulated a mass of detailed data.

6. *Avoiding Influence on the Group.* A major problem with any method is to avoid altering the process under investigation by the act of observing. Whyte attempted, not always successfully, to avoid influencing the activities of the group. Above all, he avoided making moral evaluations of their activities. He was there to learn about life in the neighborhood and not to pass judgment on it.

7. *Forming Generalizations.* Whyte used his mass of recorded observations in preparing sociological generalizations about the neighborhood. He organized his material around the components of a social system, describing social control techniques, shared values, and sets of interlocking roles among corner gangs, rackets, the police, political clubs, and numerous other groups. He set forth details on normative systems prevailing in the area. For example, the young men had various ways of designating which females could be exploited sexually and which should not. Clear codes prevailed concerning the obligations of friendship and relationships with other gangs, social workers, school, and the larger community. Whyte mapped patterns of leadership and determined the position of each member of the corner gang in its social structure.

In general, Whyte found that it was possible to portray the organizational characteristics of the slum as a complex social system having a latent and informal structure. In this study, participant observation yielded much data on the nature and basis of social organization. While not suitable for some kinds of sociological research, the method is ideal for the type of investigation Whyte conducted.

William Foote Whyte, *Street-Corner Society: The Social Structure of an Italian Slum* (Chicago: The University of Chicago Press, 1948; rev. ed., 1955).

Latent and Manifest Functions

Functionally oriented sociologists usually distinguish between the latent functions and the manifest functions of an established pattern of social relationships.[16] *Manifest* functions are those that are built into a social system by design; like manifest goals, they are well understood by a group's members. *Latent* functions, by contrast, are unintentional and often unrecognized. They are the unanticipated consequences of a system that has been set up to achieve other ends. The system of free public education in the United States, for example, has the manifest function of opening educational opportunity to all citizens and thereby increasing their ability to participate equally in a democratic society. In practice, however, the system has had the unintended effect of opening opportunity for some and closing it for others (see pages 569–577).

Almost every pattern of social organization has similarly unexpected effects. In a corporation, management may establish a tight system of control in an attempt to increase productivity, only to make the employees resentful and perhaps *less* productive. In a family, the parents may try to let a daughter develop as much independence as possible, only to have her think they don't care what she does. In making a functional analysis of any group, the sociologist tries to determine both the latent and the manifest functions of each aspect of social organization and to show how they interrelate. Tools of Sociology on page 76 describes the application of functional analysis to the study of bureaucratic organizations.

Function and Dysfunction

The equilibrium assumption, more than any other aspect of the functionalist perspective on social systems, can have an important influence on the direction of social research, for it orients the sociologist who accepts the assumption to search for the effects of particular organizational patterns *on the stability of the system as a whole*. Some functionally oriented sociologists maintain, for example, that the unequal distribution of wealth, status, and power in a society is necessary for motivating individuals to fill difficult societal roles and to perform them ade-

quately. Seen in this light, social stratification is integrative rather than divisive: it may penalize some individuals and groups, but it has a positive function for society as a whole. In Chapter 8, "Social Stratification," we will weigh this theory against the arguments of Karl Marx and others who have related social stratification to theories of social conflict.

In making a functional analysis of any social arrangement, a main objective is to distinguish the consequences for different parts of the system. Functionally oriented sociologists say that a given practice is <u>dysfunctional if it somehow hampers the achievement of group goals or disrupts the group's equilibrium.</u> Thus the practice of retaining firemen on diesel trains, which have no practical need for firemen, can be viewed as dysfunctional from the point of view of a company that is trying to operate a railroad for profit. The practice may be functional, however, from the point of view of the railroad workers, in that it retains jobs for those who might otherwise be displaced. In short, application of the terms *functional* and *dysfunctional* depends upon the particular group that is being analyzed.

GROUP TENSION AND CONFLICT

Thus far we have emphasized the relatively stable and predictable patterns that develop in groups as their members engage in coordinated interaction over a period of time. In a sense, we have constructed an idealized model of a smooth-functioning, stable group.

In the world of social reality, of course, few groups remain completely harmonious and stable over long periods of time. Even in the absence of conflict, a group changes as its members change and as new goals command their attention. Much more dramatic are the disruptions that occur when conflict develops within a group—or between constituent groups in a larger setting, such as a community or society. The episode described below, drawn from the recent

16. Robert K. Merton, *Social Theory and Social Structure* (New York: The Free Press, 1957), pp. 19–84.

history of our own society, serves to illustrate the sociological implications of both *intra*group and *inter*group conflict.

AN INCIDENT OF SOCIAL DISORDER

In August 1968 the Democratic party held its national convention in Chicago. The attention of the nation, and indeed of the world, was concentrated on this group as it sought to achieve its goals. The news media had made elaborate preparations: television cameras, reporters, and newspaper photographers covered the convention hall, the headquarters of the contenders for the nomination, and the gathering places of the thousands of young dissidents who had descended on Chicago.

Prior to the convention, a number of groups had made it known that they would come to Chicago in strength to demonstrate their dissatisfaction with the Johnson administration's handling of the war in Vietnam and other issues.[17] Some of the dissenters were enthusiastic young supporters of Eugene McCarthy, who had challenged President Johnson and the Democratic party organization in seeking the presidential nomination. Others included socialists, anarchists, New Leftists, Yippies, Communists, and a variety of moderate liberals. These groups were by no means united in philosophy or goals; in fact, they represented almost every possible position on the political spectrum from the middle through the far left. But they shared one goal: they wanted to make their dissatisfaction known.

Representatives of some of the more extreme elements among these groups maintained that one of their purposes in coming to the city was to provoke the Chicago police into over-retaliation so that, as they put it, "the worst aspects of establishment fascism would be re-

Whether an activity is seen as functional or dysfunctional is often a matter of perspective. A teachers' strike is likely to be regarded as dysfunctional by school authorities, since it disrupts the normal operations of the schools. From the perspective of the teachers, however, the strike may be viewed as a necessary step toward making the schools function more effectively.

vealed." A few protest leaders threatened to disrupt the city as well as the convention itself. As *Time* magazine later noted:

Chicago's newspapers repeatedly listed diabolical threats aimed at the city, ranging from burning Chicago down by flooding the sewers with gasoline, to dumping LSD in the water supply, to having 10,000 nude bodies float on Lake Michigan. Also widely accepted was the boast that from 100,000 to 200,000 demonstrators would descend on the city.[18]

In the face of these threats, city authorities mobilized twelve thousand policemen and six thousand Illinois National Guardsmen to maintain order during convention week. Additional

17. This description of the convention week disturbances in Chicago is drawn from the Walker Report to the National Commission on the Causes and Prevention of Violence, *Rights in Conflict* (New York: Bantam Books, 1968). The study team directed by Daniel Walker was composed of 212 investigators who interviewed over three thousand witnesses and reviewed countless films and photographs taken by the news media, police photographers, and private citizens.

18. *Time,* December 6, 1968, p. 34. Actually, according to reliable estimates, only about five thousand protesters arrived from out of town. Other thousands came from the city itself.

military units were brought into the Chicago area from out of state to be ready if reinforcements were needed.

Protesters, members of the news media, and the police readied themselves for the week of the convention against an emotionally charged background of tension, suspicion, and mutual distrust. From the start, the more radical demonstrators were openly antagonistic to the police, whom they referred to individually and collectively as "pigs." Moderates and radicals alike protested the city's refusal to grant them permits for parades and rallies. The police, mobilized for the possibility of a serious disturbance, regarded the protesters as the potential enemy. Police officials were also critical of the news media, charging that the reporters had sometimes staged incidents to create news and that, for some demonstrators, their very presence would be an invitation to start trouble. The police also maintained that the cumbersome television equipment and the popping of the news photographers' flashbulbs interfered with the policemen's ability to pursue their duties. For their part, members of the media insisted on their right to be present wherever news might be expected to break. They spoke of their obligation to keep the public informed and complained of harassment by the police and convention officials.

The public, looking on, was apprehensive. People had mixed feelings about the demonstrators. Some were concerned that the elaborate police preparations would unnecessarily provoke violent countermeasures. Others warned that if the police were allowed to suppress the demonstrators' activities, the right of Americans to dissent publicly would be seriously endangered. Most Chicagoans, however, were not particularly sympathetic toward the protesters, whom they lumped together as draft-dodging, pot-smoking, radical, foul-mouthed young punks—a threat to decent, hard-working citizens. At best, they were "irresponsible kids who needed to grow up"; at worst, they were perpetrators of "a Communist plot." Chicago's mayor, Richard J. Daley, was not alone in insisting that the demonstrators should be kept in line by whatever means became necessary. The police were very much aware of these sentiments.

As the week of the convention approached, thousands of demonstrators gathered in the city's Lincoln and Grant parks. On Sunday night, the eve of the convention's opening, the police were ordered to enforce an ordinance specifying that Lincoln Park be cleared of people by 11:00 P.M. As the police swept through the park, where several groups of demonstrators had established their headquarters, they met unexpectedly strong resistance. Soon rocks, bottles, and other debris were being hurled at them. They were taunted and jeered in vile terms.

For a time the police took these provocations in stride. They arrested numerous demonstrators and continued their sweep of the area. But resistance grew increasingly intense. Some demonstrators hurled plastic bags filled with excrement. There were unverified reports that other demonstrators sprayed officers with cans of oven cleaner, threw potatoes in which razor blades were embedded, and used sharpened sticks as spears. The constant barrage of verbal obscenity was said to have exceeded anything previously encountered by an American police force.

The melee on Sunday night turned out to be only a prelude to the violence that marked convention week. As the resistance of the demonstrators grew, the countermeasures used by the police became increasingly rough. Soon, policemen were making few distinctions between the different types of people they encountered in the areas where trouble occurred. Bystanders, reporters, peaceful demonstrators, and rioters alike were subjected to police attack. As the demonstrators and some onlookers struck back, police discipline sometimes collapsed completely. Ignoring the orders of their superior officers, policemen flung themselves into the crowds, beating their tormenters with clubs, shouting obscenities of their own, kicking and striking anyone who came in their way. Some demonstrators were repeatedly beaten even after they had fallen and ceased to resist.[19]

The confrontation between police and protesters reached its climax on the night of

---

19. The Walker Report documents numerous incidents of violence on the part of both police and demonstrators; see especially pp. 235–285.

Wednesday, August 28. Americans who had turned on their television sets to watch the convention proceedings were startled at the scene they witnessed in front of convention headquarters in downtown Chicago. They saw policemen clubbing and kicking young men and women while shoving them into waiting vans. They saw reporters and photographers with bloodied heads and smashed equipment. (More than sixty out of three hundred media representatives covering the events had their equipment damaged, suffered physical injury, or were arrested.) The Walker Report to the National Commission on the Causes and Prevention of Violence later termed the breakdown of police discipline a police riot. An official observer from the Los Angeles Police Department said about the events of Wednesday night:

There is no question but that many officers acted without restraint and exerted force beyond that necessary under the circumstances. The leadership at the point of conflict did little to prevent such conduct and the direct control of officers by first-line supervisors was virtually nonexistent.[20]

The violence of convention week touched off an intense debate over the moral, legal, and political implications of what had happened. No one was without an opinion, and emotions ran high. There were loud denunciations of the Chicago police and equally loud denunciations of the demonstrators. Moderate views on either side were in the minority.

Whatever the final interpretation of this episode, it provides a dramatic example not only of the kinds of social conflict that can be generated between groups but also of the kinds of disruptions that can occur within a group, even one so firmly committed to the principles of order and discipline as a major metropolitan police force. In the following section we will examine the sources of such conflict in terms of what we have already learned about social organization.

Goal conflicts, normative confusion, and breakdowns in communication all helped set the stage for the violence that erupted in Chicago during the Democratic Convention in August 1968.

SOURCES OF SOCIAL DISORDER

Social instability and disorder can stem from a variety of causes, many of them related to group structure. A conflict in goals, a breakdown in the usual channels of interaction and communication, normative confusion, role conflict and strain, the ineffectiveness of available sanctions, and disturbances in status relations are but a few of the possible sources of tension and disharmony within groups and between groups. Such breakdowns in social organization can help explain the violent events that occurred in Chicago as well as the less dramatic forms of conflict that occur in all human groups.[21]

Conflicts in Group Goals

Groups often devote their efforts toward the attainment of more than one goal. Universities, for example, usually proclaim officially that they are dedicated to excellence in teaching, scientific research, and public service. In many universities such goals are simultaneously pursued with few problems, and when this is the case,

20. *Rights in Conflict,* p. 2.

21. Sociologists recognize that breakdowns in group patterns sometimes occur because members are mentally disturbed or temporarily overwhelmed by strong emotion. But social conflict more often involves clinically normal people and can be traced to problems in social organization. The present section, therefore, focuses upon *structural* sources of instability and conflict.

there is little basis for conflict. But if administrative policy requires faculty members to "publish or perish" (produce scholarly articles, monographs, and books or be denied promotion and perhaps reappointment), it can be confidently predicted that some professors will make themselves less available to students and spend less time on course preparation in order to complete more research for publication. Under such circumstances, students may become dissatisfied, faculty members cynical, and administrators frustrated by continuing complaints. A basis for potential conflict is clearly present.

Other forms of goal conflict are present when the formal goals of the organization and the informal goals of its members sharply diverge. In the Chicago incident there was an obvious conflict between the manifest and formal goals of the police force and the informal goals of some of its members. The official purpose in bringing large numbers of policemen to confront the demonstrators was to maintain order. However, as the Walker Report indicates, an individual goal of some policemen during the incident was to punish rather than to control. Even more significant was the polarity of the goals of the two groups — the demonstrators and the police — and the potential for conflict between them. Although such goal conflicts did not in themselves directly cause the confrontation and the breakdown of police discipline, they were clearly contributing factors.

Problems of Communication

During the Chicago convention disturbances, communication became confused at every level — between the demonstrators and the authorities, among the demonstrators themselves, and within the police force. The Walker Report describes the conflicting reactions of the demonstrators on Sunday night after the police announced that Lincoln Park must be cleared:

Confusion followed. Some [demonstrators] urged avoidance of conflict, others urged active resistance to the curfew. Two other recommendations were dispersal in small groups and street demonstrations. . . .

In the middle of a large group, one youth suddenly got up and yelled, referring to the marshalls [from one of the more organized protesting groups, the National Mobilization Committee to End the War in Vietnam], "Fuck the marshalls! Down with the leaders!" Someone else was giving instructions to a crowd of demonstrators who did not wish to receive them. "Daley gives orders," someone yelled, "don't you give us orders, you fascist." There were other objections in the same vein, and one witness says he was afraid that violence would break out within the demonstrating group itself. . . .

. . . Mobilization marshalls were yelling: "This is suicide! Suicide!" They urged people to flee the park and told them they could sleep on the grounds of the McCormick Theological Seminary, apparently unaware that seminary officials had already denied such use.[22]

Earlier we noted the importance of communication in the formation and maintenance of human groups. Through the exchange of gestures, words, and other kinds of symbols, interacting parties can respond with meaning to each other. While communication is critical to the group process, it can also be an important basis for group disruption. It all depends upon what kinds of meanings are directed toward whom by what individuals. We have already noted in our summary of the events at Chicago that intense efforts were made by the demonstrators to provoke the police through the use of obscenities and insults. While the police were able to ignore such symbols at first, the vile invective increased anger and resentment as the rioting progressed. When tensions rose to a certain point, the insults and obscenities began to produce the reactions they were designed to produce. The cops got mad! Such emotional responses do not provide a sound basis for cool professional teamwork to control crowds with a minimum of force.

During the height of the violence, other problems of communications were apparent. As individual officers became increasingly angry at the demonstrators, communications between police officials and their men began to deteriorate. Those in charge repeatedly ordered their men to avoid unnecessary force, only to have

22. *Rights in Conflict*, p. 148.

their orders ignored by officers angrily wanting to get back at their tormenters. Thus an incessant barrage of verbal abuse directed against the police by the mob, plus a consequent erosion of communication between police officials and the rank and file, contributed to the collapse of police discipline.

Normative Confusion

Émile Durkheim developed the concept of *anomie* (page 10) to describe a social situation in which rules of conduct are so weakened or confused that they no longer provide effective behavioral guides. Certainly normative confusion was a contributing factor in the police-protester confrontations that occurred in Chicago during the Democratic convention. The title of the Walker Report, *Rights in Conflict,* suggests a fundamental difference between the norms of the conflicting groups. The demonstrators were exercising their right to dissent; the police were acting on the city's acknowledged right to protect its citizens and its property. Thus, normative behavior for one group was, in the eyes of the other, deviant and potentially disruptive.

As previously suggested, there was also a great deal of normative confusion among the demonstrators themselves. Many of the protesting groups had no unified program, and the differences between one group and another were often greater, initially at least, than differences with the police. Many demonstrators were determined to act within the law; others were equally determined to flout it.

Finally, there was a confusion of norms even within the police force itself. A few months before the convention, Mayor Daley had publicly rebuked the Chicago police for showing too much restraint in dealing with arsonists and looters during the riots that had followed the assassination of Martin Luther King, Jr.[23] By some policemen, this was interpreted as an official "green light" to handle rioters roughly—despite police regulations that clearly forbade the use of force except as a last resort. Furthermore, there was a discrepancy between official police norms, which define the officer's task as that of maintaining order, and the informal norms of particular policemen who felt that people looking for trouble deserved rough treatment.

Such normative confusion undoubtedly contributed to the eventual breakdown of order within the police department, just as normative differences between police and protesters established the basis for a confrontation between the two groups. During the violence of convention week, relatively few people knew clearly what to expect of others or what was expected of them.

Normative confusion can similarly disrupt a family, a peer group, a business office, or any other group. Parents who are inconsistent in enforcing the rules they set down for their children often find that the children become a problem: not knowing what is expected of them, the young don't know how to behave in order to avoid friction with their parents. Employees who make their own rules can disrupt the smooth operation of a business and cause dissension among their own informal group of co-workers. A dating couple with conflicting norms of sexual behavior soon fights or breaks up.

Role Conflict

Role conflict, like a conflict in norms, is a cause of disruption in all kinds of groups, both large and small.[24] Sometimes conflict is actually built into a role definition. For example, the role of college professor, as we have already noted, often involves conflicting expectations for scholar and teacher. Similarly, the role of supervisor in a business group typically involves one set of role expectations from management and quite different expectations from those being supervised. Even the general sex roles in our society involve some built-in contradictions.[25] Parents may remind a daughter in college that she is expected to study hard, make good grades, and prepare herself for a career; at the same time they may

23. The mayor's widely publicized remark, which he later modified, was that the police should "shoot to kill arsonists and shoot to maim looters."

24. See, for example, Jack J. Preiss and Howard J. Ehrlich, *An Examination of Role Theory: The Case of the State Police* (Lincoln, Neb.: University of Nebraska Press, 1966), especially pp. 94–121.

25. See Mirra Komarovsky, "Cultural Contradictions and Sex Roles," *American Journal of Sociology,* 52 (November 1946): 184–189.

For a system of social control to be effective, group members must accept as legitimate the authority of those empowered to administer formal sanctions.

anxiously inquire whether she has met "any nice young men," clearly implying that they envision her first "career" choice to be that of a wife and mother and that they think of college mainly as a good place for her to find a suitable husband.

Role conflicts of this type are sometimes referred to as *internal* role conflicts, since conflicting expectations are inherent in the roles themselves. *External* role conflicts, by contrast, are generated by the incompatible demands of two or more different roles. A man's role as husband and father requires that he devote himself

to his family, whereas his role as employee may require that he spend most of his time and energy on his job. A young woman whose friend asks for help in cheating on an examination also faces an external role conflict: her role as a member of an academic community requires that she refuse the request; her role as friend includes the expectation that she will provide the requested aid.[26]

In the breakdown of police discipline during the Chicago convention, the role of law enforcement officer was clearly incompatible with the role of outraged private citizen. The one role called upon the individual policeman to maintain a professional calm and to use only the force necessary to control the demonstrators. The more general role of private citizen defined the appropriate response to extreme provocation in a different way: striking back was the "natural" reaction, at least by definition of those policemen whose discipline collapsed.[27] Some of the demonstrators faced a similar conflict between their role as law-abiding citizens respecting the city's need to maintain order and their role as political activists expressing their dissatisfaction with the status quo.

Ineffectiveness of Social Control

A group's system of social control can be effective only to the extent that sanctions are considered meaningful and that most members support the authority of those empowered to administer them.[28] For reasons we have already cited, members of the Chicago police force had reason to doubt that they would be punished for violating the department's official rules of conduct when called upon to handle a riot. They apparently had the support of city officials and also of

26. Rose K. Goldsen, Morris Rosenberg, and Robin M. Williams, *What College Students Think* (Princeton, N.J.: D. Van Nostrand Co., Inc., 1960).

27. Dennis Wenger also points to another form of role conflict. When a police department responds to a large-scale civil disorder, it shifts from small-unit organization with roles of great autonomy for individual officers to large-unit, military-type organization. This sharply changes the role of the officer, making him less autonomous and more responsible to a tight chain of command. Some officers find this adjustment difficult to make. See Dennis Wenger, "The Reluctant Army: The Functioning of Police Departments During Civil Disturbances," *American Behavioral Scientist*, 16 (January–February 1973): 326–342.

28. See Ralph H. Turner, "Unresponsiveness as a Social Sanction," *Sociometry*, 36 (March 1973): 1–19.

most citizens. The fact that there were relatively few suspensions or dismissals after the convention disturbances tended to support their conviction and caused critics to ask whether the department's internal system of controls could be effective under similar circumstances in the future.

The confrontation itself, of course, provides an even more dramatic instance of the breakdown of social controls. Many of the more radical demonstrators denied the authority of the police altogether; the officers were defined as pigs doing the dirty work of a corrupt society. Even those demonstrators who were initially intent on an orderly protest soon came to feel that the police had seriously overstepped their authority. Social controls became progressively weakened as more and more protesters came to feel that the police had lost all right to be obeyed.

In his classic study of a maximum security prison as a social system, Sykes has shown that similar factors work to undermine the effectiveness of a prison's system of internal controls.[29] At first glance, a maximum security prison would seem to be a social system in which control is absolute: guards and prison officials are given complete authority by the state and can effectively enforce whatever rules are needed to govern a population of captives. In fact, however, rule violations are frequent and the guards are relatively powerless to prevent them.

One reason that prisoners misbehave despite the near certainty of punishment is that the sanctions used as punishment are often relatively meaningless to inmates. For minor violations of rules, prisoners may lose certain privileges. They may be barred from their prison jobs and forced to remain idle; but since most prison jobs are boring and unpleasant, this does not provide much of a deterrent. They may be restricted in their movements—not allowed to leave the cell block except for meals—but since they really can't go anywhere except within the prison walls, and usually in a group under guard, this doesn't seem very important either. Punishments such as the cancellation of visiting privileges and the restriction of mail are similarly meaningless because even well-behaved inmates are allowed little mail and few visitors. Even more severe punishments, such as being placed in solitary confinement on a diet of bread and water, are not especially dreaded by inmates accustomed to the harsh environment and unappetizing food that are a regular part of prison life.

A really effective system of social control is one where those controlled subscribe to the legitimacy of the authority of those who exercise the sanctions and to the necessity of the norms that govern the group. Although prison officials, supervisors, and guards are committed to the necessity and rationality of the regulations they impose, prisoners are not. The inmates readily admit that prison officials have the legal right to control them, but they are not committed to the rules in such a way that they willingly enforce them on themselves. In most groups, as we noted earlier in this chapter, members readily control their own behavior because they don't want to violate the rules that are important to their group. In "the society of captives," self-enforcement of the norms is weak at best, and compliance to the authority of the guards is grudging. It is nearly impossible to exercise social control within such a setting, and those in power are faced with a continuous repetition of violations.

Disturbances in Social Ranking

If anything is clear about the conflict between police and protesters in Chicago, it is that the role of policeman was ranked quite differently by most demonstrators than by the officers themselves or the public as a whole. Even before their initial efforts to clear Lincoln Park, the police were taunted with obscenities and cries of "fascist pig" and "oink." Not all of the demonstrators joined in the name-calling, but most were at least skeptical of police motives and concerned about the issue of police brutality. Whatever prestige the police had in the eyes of the protesters was almost completely eroded during the course of the confrontation.

The same was true in reverse. The police, by and large, regarded the demonstrators not as

29. Gresham M. Sykes, *The Society of Captives: A Study of a Maximum Security Prison* (Princeton, N.J.: Princeton University Press, 1958).

citizens exercising their right to dissent but as radicals intent on disrupting the convention, the city, and the country. After the first violence of Sunday night, distaste for the protesters grew. A tape of the police department's radio log gives this sampling of police attitudes:

Police Operator: "1814, get a wagon over at 1436 North Wells. We've got an injured hippie."
Voice: "1436 North Wells?"
Operator: "North Wells."
In quick sequence, there are the following remarks from five other police cars:
"That's no emergency."
"Let him take a bus."
"Kick the fucker."
"Knock his teeth out."
"Throw him in a wastepaper basket."[30]

The negative evaluation of the police by the demonstrators and of the demonstrators by the police made the behavior of each toward the other unpredictable. The police could not expect that their orders would be obeyed; the demonstrators could not expect that their rights would be respected. The established relationship between the law and the citizen broke down.

The disruption of an established ranking system is a frequent source of conflict within groups as well as between groups. Sometimes the source of instability is excessive competition, as in a business group where managerial personnel vie with each other for positions of greater power and prestige.

Other kinds of disruptions occur when status relationships are unclear or when they seem unfair to individual members. In formally organized groups the clouding of role distinctions often becomes a source of friction. The manager who is a "good guy" and develops personal ties with the people under him is in some ways an ideal boss; but the reduction of social distance between a supervisor and subordinates can create jealousies among co-workers and also make it difficult for the manager to maintain the "company perspective" required by his role. In informal groups, by contrast, the deemphasis of status distinctions is expected; friends in a peer group are supposed to be equal, and those who get "uppity" soon find themselves on the outside.

Ranking systems, perhaps more than any other aspect of social organization, touch closely upon the emotional and psychological needs of individual members. Not every member can be or wants to be at the top of every system, but all people need the feeling that they are respected. As one police officer asked after an encounter with some of the demonstrators, "Why do you call us pigs?" His question is not wholly unlike the one that black children have often asked their parents: "Why do they call us niggers?"

In summary, it can be suggested that the Chicago convention disorders occurred, at least in part, because the various elements of social organization broke down. Some degree of conflict between the police and the demonstrators was inevitable, since they had opposing goals and were equally determined to stand fast in trying to attain them. But it seems likely that intergroup conflict would not have erupted into widespread violence if there had not been an almost total collapse of communication and if the members of either or both factions had held more closely shared definitions of what behavior was appropriate in coping with the demands of the situation.

CONSEQUENCES OF CONFLICT

Sociologists have long recognized that disruption and conflict are normal aspects of group life. But what of their consequences? In the short term, conflict is disturbing to the individuals involved and disruptive of the group in which it occurs. Sometimes, indeed, it can result in a group's dissolution. But the effects of conflict are not necessarily negative in every respect, even for a group in danger of being destroyed.[31]

30. *Rights in Conflict*, p. 183.
31. A large literature on the nature and effects of social conflict has accumulated over many decades. For an assessment of the current state of theory in this area, see Robin M. Williams, Jr., "Conflict and Social Order: A Research Strategy for Complex Propositions," *Journal of Social Issues*, 28, No. 1 (1972): 11–26.

VIEWPOINTS   SOCIAL CONFLICT AND SOCIAL REFORM

■   World history yields plenty of cases in which some historical logjam seems to have been broken up by an eruption of violence, which is then followed by a period of peaceful, gradualist improvement. It is always possible in such cases to argue (though difficult to prove) that the violence was a necessary precondition of the peaceful change that followed. . . .

Violence can succeed in a political environment like that of the United States under certain conditions. Those who use it must be able to localize it and limit its duration. They must use it under circumstances in which the public is either indifferent or uninformed, or in which the accessible and relevant public opinion . . . is heavily biased in their favor. If violence is accompanied by exceptional brutality . . . it must be kept a local matter, and one must hope that it can somehow be screened from the attention of the larger polity. . . .

Most of the social reforms in American history have been brought about without violence, or with only a marginal and inessential use of it, by reformers who were prepared to carry on a long-term campaign of education and propaganda. . . . Ours, however, is an age that cannot wait. . . . The activists, according to their temperaments, will argue either that earlier reforms, being props to the Establishment, were of little or no value, or that they were all a generation overdue when they came. The first response is simply inhumane, but the second has much truth in it: such reforms were indeed long overdue. . . . Under some conditions the fear or threat of violence may hasten social reforms, yet if actual outbreaks of violence were the primary force in bringing reform, one might have expected social-welfare laws to come in the United States before they came to such countries as Great Britain and Germany where there was less industrial violence. The important element seems to have been not the resort to violence but the presence of powerful labor movements with a socialist commitment and the threat of sustained action through normal political channels.

Richard Hofstadter
American Violence: A Documentary History

●   What is nonviolent action? One thing that surely ought to be clear is that nonviolence does not simply refer to the mere absence of violence. . . . Nonviolence is not to be equated with passive yielding to superior force or with working only through established channels. It is a positive, active, and in fact militant strategy, designed to produce thoroughgoing changes in social patterns.

Though it respects the adversary as a human being and attempts to mobilize his conscience, nonviolent action is not just a moral appeal and a petition to the other that he do the right thing. It is very definitely and deliberately an exercise of power. . . . Indeed, a nonviolent confrontation presents real threats to the adversary. By dramatically exposing his unjust practices, by refusing continued cooperation with them, and by replacing them with new patterns, it may threaten him with embarrassment and adverse publicity, with reduction in his economic or political power, and with disruption of the orderly processes he cherishes. It does not, however, threaten to destroy him, and thus leaves open the way for reappraisal, for negotiation, and for rebuilding. . . .

I am convinced that nonviolent means are far more likely to be effective in producing real changes than the violence now being elevated into a positive value in the romantic mystique and the revolutionary rhetoric. . . . What is wrong with the cult of violence is not that it is too radical, but that it is not radical enough. It relies on the slogans, the methods, and the ways of thinking that have characterized all of the old nationalisms, and, in advocating violence, it is — to use [Martin Luther] King's words — "imitating the worst, the most brutal and the most uncivilized values of American life." The advocacy of violence may be radical in the sense of using an aggressive style and calling for "extreme" actions. The advocacy of nonviolence, however, is truly radical in its insistence on an analysis that goes to the roots, on a redefinition of ends and means, and on a search for innovative approaches.

Herbert C. Kelman
A Time to Speak: On Human Values and Social Research

Conflict Can Clarify Issues

Whether they sided with the demonstrators or with the police, few Americans would regard the convention week violence in Chicago as anything but deplorable. Yet it is possible that the widespread public discussion precipitated by the incident contributed to a clarification of basic issues. What are the rights of the dissenting citizen, and what are the limitations on those rights? Where should the line be drawn between the legitimate and the excessive use of force in controlling civil disorder?

The riots that erupted in the black ghettos of many American cities during the 1960s and recent confrontations between Indians and white officials (for example at "the second battle of Wounded Knee" in 1973) have served to focus attention on a critical social issue, that of injustice toward racial minorities. Both Indian and black militancy has had mixed effects on the attitudes of white Americans, but at least general indifference to the problems of minorities has given way to greater awareness that some citizens in our democracy are less equal in a *de facto* sense than others.[32] Problems affecting the members of a group or a nation cannot be solved until they are seen and examined. Conflict is one means whereby attention can be focused on such issues.

Conflict Can Integrate a Group

The nineteenth-century German sociologist Georg Simmel was among the first to write about how intergroup conflict could reduce tensions within a group by providing an external target for resentments and hostilities.[33] The way in which conflict with outsiders tends to draw the members of a group more closely together can be observed in many contexts. The confrontation between police and protesters in Chicago had a divisive effect on the community and the society, but it solidified group feeling within the police department and also served to unify the protesting factions. A religious sect that breaks away from an established church to initiate some type of reform is likely to become increasingly close-knit as conflict develops with the larger group. A society fighting for its very existence against a common enemy, as Great Britain did during World War II, often exhibits a powerful sense of determination and will to resist as individuals subordinate their personal interests to the welfare of their country. The motivation to work together for common goals typically weakens after the external threat has been met or the conflict resolved.

Conflict Can Stimulate Change

Conflict theorists (page 16) have stressed the importance of conflict as a stimulus to social change. Clearly, the conflict between the ruling and working classes in pre-Communist China, Cuba, and the Soviet Union resulted in new social structures in those countries. Conflict has also been a mechanism of social change in the United States. Management-labor conflict has helped improve working conditions, raise the standard of living for most Americans, and create the machinery for settling disputes that might disrupt the economy. Racial conflicts in recent years have led to the passage of new laws and the reinforcement of old laws aimed at eliminating racial discrimination, particularly in voting, housing, education, and employment. Technological change has been stimulated by an institutionalized form of conflict known as business competition.

The effects of intragroup and intergroup conflict, then, are generally mixed.[34] The question for the student of social behavior is not whether conflict can be avoided but rather how much and what kind of conflict a particular group can accommodate while still maintaining enough

32. There is also the question as to whether attention by mass media to such issues contributes to or even causes conflict. See Gladys Engel Lang and Kurt Lang, "Some Pertinent Questions on Collective Violence and the News Media," *Journal of Social Issues,* 28, No. 1 (1972): 93–110.

33. Georg Simmel, *Conflict and the Web of Group Affiliations,* trans. Reinhardt Bendix (New York: The Free Press, 1955), pp. 92–93.

34. In his study of fifteen American cities that have experienced civil disorders in recent years, Gary Kreps has noted extensive changes in police organization, policy, planning, training, and resources. In large part these represent improvements over earlier situations. See Gary A. Kreps, "Change in Crisis-Relevant Organizations: Police Departments and Civil Disturbances," *American Behavioral Scientist,* 16 (January–February 1973): 356–367. See also Robert E. McGarrah, "The Peaceful Uses of Conflict," *Vista,* 8, No. 4 (February 1973): 22–25.

order and stability to resist disintegration. The student must also be ready to evaluate the significance of disintegration itself. There is no basis for assuming that the dissolution of a group always has negative consequences.

SUMMARY

For the sociologist, the starting point for scientific analysis is the organizational structure of the human group. The sociological perspective focuses on interaction — the behavioral events that take place *between* people. The prerequisites for the development of a group in the sociological meaning of the term are the existence of potential members who seek similar satisfactions or purposes and who undertake coordinated, recurrent interaction to achieve their goals. Group behavior is distinguished from other kinds of interpersonal activity by the fact that it is based upon some relatively stable pattern of social organization.

Although the pattern may vary greatly from group to group, the basic components of social organization are always the same. Sociologists identify these as a set of regulative norms; an interlocking pattern of specialized roles; a variety of sanctions for maintaining social control; and hierarchies of social ranking based upon various types of criteria. The components of social organization serve to coordinate the activities of members, making their behavior predictable and understandable to one another. Social organization makes possible the achievement of goals through a coordinated division of labor that would not be possible to attain by an equal number of individuals acting independently.

A human group must be understood not only in terms of its structural components but also as an ongoing system. The social systems perspective emphasizes the integrated functioning of groups as they persist over time. It generally assumes that groups have a basic tendency to maintain equilibrium — that they resist both internal and external disruptions and tend to restore stability after disruptions occur. Functional analysis is aimed at understanding the manifest and latent functions of norms, roles, sanctions, etc., in maintaining the equilibrium of a given group.

In the world of social reality, no group remains completely harmonious or stable over long periods of time. Groups change as members come and go, as goals change, and as external circumstances alter. Conflict typically results, both within and between groups, when contradictory goals develop, when communication collapses, when norms become confused or inapplicable, when conflicting role demands are placed on members, when sanctions are meaningless and social control is ineffective, when social ranking and status relationships are confused or unacceptable to the interacting parties, or when some combination of these conditions occurs.

Although people usually view social conflict as something to be avoided, if at all possible, because of its immediate costs in frustration or suffering, its effects are sometimes beneficial to a group over the long run. For example, conflict can help clarify issues that need to be resolved if the group is to continue to function effectively; it can integrate group members around a common purpose and make them more determined to achieve their goals; and it can stimulate change that ultimately leads to improved social or material conditions. In most groups, and particularly in complex modern societies, tendencies toward dissent and conflict are no less observable than tendencies toward stability and equilibrium. An important task of sociological analysis is to understand and interpret the interplay of the circumstances that generate these contrasting characteristics of group life.

3
Types of Groups

Barbara thought about how much she looked forward to bowling on Friday night. It wasn't so much that she enjoyed the game; the main thing was being with people she liked. Sue and Pat had been her best friends in school, and she still felt more comfortable with them than she did with anyone she'd met at work. And Joan could always be counted on to make her laugh even when she was in a bad mood. Over Labor Day weekend the four of them had gone to a bowling tournament together and had more fun than they'd had in ages. Friday night they were going to talk about arranging their vacations so they could go on a trip to the West and Canada next summer.

Barbara hoped her boss would let her take her vacation when she wanted to. For some reason the company always seemed to make a big deal out of little things, whether it was arranging the vacation schedule or using the right forms for reports. Why did they always have to go by the book? Processing insurance claims according to fixed rules wasn't much fun. She'd be a lot happier in her job, and would probably accomplish a lot more, if they'd let her exercise a little initiative once in a while. Following the same routine day after day could drive you up the wall.

Barbara was experiencing on a personal level the differences between a small group composed of close friends and a large bureaucratically organized group. The analysis of characteristic differences between various types of groups is of fundamental concern to sociologists and provides the focus of this chapter.

Scientists in every field, from astronomy to zoology, classify the phenomena they study into various categories. Biologists, for example, classify living forms into phylum, class, order, genus, and species; chemists use the periodic table to classify elements on the basis of their inferred atomic properties. In all sciences, the reason for classification is essentially the same: it provides a framework for the orderly accumulation of knowledge about similarities and differences among the things or events being studied.

Over the last century sociologists have attempted to classify groups by a number of systems, most of them based on relatively simple divisions representing the ends of some kind of continuum.[1] One of the earliest systems of classification, and still one of the most important, was that developed at the turn of the century by Charles H. Cooley, an American sociologist who noted the distinction between *primary* and *secondary* groups.[2] Primary groups are small, intimate groups composed of close friends or family members; they are especially important as sources of emotional satisfaction. Secondary groups are relatively formal and impersonal organizations such as schools, business concerns, and political groups. Cooley's concept of the primary group has had a central importance in many sociological theories, and it will be examined in the next section (page 65).

A second early system of classification was that of William Graham Sumner, another pioneer American sociologist. Sumner drew a distinction between *in-groups* and *out-groups* in order to account for the strong feelings of ethnocentrism (page 103) that many groups develop, which leads them to reject certain categories of people simply because they are "different." The term *in-group* refers broadly to any social unit with which you personally identify. An *out-group*, by contrast, is any social unit whose members you regard as outsiders—with whom you feel no "consciousness of kind."[3] Toward an in-group you have feelings best described by the term *we;* toward an out-group you have feelings of *they.* This system for classifying groups is based wholly on subjective criteria.

A more recent system of classification, which retains some elements of subjective orientation but adds new dimensions, distinguishes between *membership* and *reference* groups.[4] A membership group is one to which you belong, whether or not you share its attitudes and values. A reference group, on the other hand, is one whose attitudes and values are important to you even though you may not be a member. To illustrate, an undergraduate student who hopes to be admitted to medical school may adopt the official positions of the American Medical Association on social issues relating to the practice of medicine, such as how best to provide medical care for the poor. Although not a member of the AMA, the student is nevertheless using it as a reference group in forming personal opinions. A practicing doctor who actually belongs to the AMA, on the other hand, may wholly disagree with its official stand on social and political issues. For this individual, the AMA would be a membership group but not a reference group.

Groups can also be contrasted and compared with respect to variations in their *goals,* their characteristic patterns of *interaction,* and their systems of *norms, roles, social control,* and *social ranking.* Analyzing the patterns of variation in these basic facets of social organization helps us understand the significance of different kinds of groups for both individuals and societies. The sections that follow will examine some of the differences in organizational patterns that typify groups ranging from the small and intimate to the huge and impersonal.

SMALL GROUPS

Two very different types of small groups can readily be observed in most societies: the *primary group,* made up of family members or close friends, and the *decision-making group*—the committee, the advisory panel, the board of directors, the council of tribal elders. The primary group has always had a central place in sociological analysis because of its key importance in shaping the individual's basic attitudes and values. The formal decision-making group

1. In recent years some sociologists have attempted to develop much more elaborate systems based on abstract properties that usually can be identified only through the use of sophisticated statistical techniques or computer applications. See James S. Coleman, "Mathematical Models and Computer Simulation," in *Handbook of Modern Sociology,* ed. Robert E. L. Faris (Chicago: Rand McNally & Co., 1964), pp. 1027–1059.

2. Charles H. Cooley, *Social Organization* (New York: Charles Scribner's Sons, 1929). Originally published in 1907.

3. William Graham Sumner, *Folkways* (New York: The New American Library, Inc., 1960), p. 27. Originally published in 1906.

4. Developed by Robert K. Merton about the time of World War II, this classification has proved useful in many kinds of sociological theories. See Robert K. Merton (in collaboration with Alice S. Rossi), "Contributions to the Theory of Reference Group Behavior," in *Social Theory and Social Structure* (Glencoe, Ill.: The Free Press, 1957), pp. 225–280.

From childhood to old age, primary groups are especially important as sources of emotional satisfaction.

has become increasingly important in urban industrial societies as the tasks of business, government, education, and other societal institutions have grown in size and complexity.

PRIMARY GROUPS

Of special significance to all of us are the many small groups we form for the personal satisfactions they afford. Charles Horton Cooley, who first formulated the concept of primary groups, defined them thus:

By primary groups I mean those characterized by intimate face-to-face association and cooperation. They are primary in several senses, but chiefly in that they are fundamental in forming the social nature and ideals of the individual. The result of intimate association, psychologically, is a certain fusion of individualities in a common whole, so that one's very self, for many purposes at least, is the common life and purpose of the group. Perhaps the simplest way of describing this wholeness is by saying that it is a "we"; it involves the sort of sympathy and mutual identification for which "we" is the natural expression.[5]

The formation of primary groups outside the family begins early in life when children find playmates whose company they particularly enjoy, and it continues throughout life. People's need for informal interaction with others who are like them in age and interests is so strong that *peer-group* activity never ends; even the very old maintain these and other primary ties. This was well-illustrated in Elliott Liebow's study of Tally's Corner. Using the method of participant observation (see page 49), Liebow assembled information on the friendship networks, patterns of work, and male-female relationships of black street-corner men in an urban neighborhood in Washington, D.C. He found that primary groups were of great importance to his subjects:

So important a part of daily life are these relationships that it seems like no life at all without them. Old Mr. Jenkins climbed out of his sickbed to take up a seat on the Coca-Cola case at the Carry-out [a small restaurant serving as a neighborhood social center] for a couple of hours. "I can't stay home and play dead," he explained, "I got to get out and see my friends."[6]

The family (Chapter 15) is a special kind of primary group, so essential both to individuals and to society that its formation is usually legitimized by the community through religious and legal rituals. The rights, duties, obligations, and privileges that make up family roles are deeply embedded in societal traditions and are surrounded by formal norms and legal sanctions. Dissolution of a family by divorce can be accomplished only through institutionalized means, usually prescribed by law.

How is it possible to distinguish primary groups as a type from other small groups whose members associate on a friendly basis? The answer lies in their distinctive pattern of social organization. A group can be classified as primary to the extent that its goals, interaction patterns, norms, role structure, methods of social control, and ranking system fall into the characteristic pattern described below.

Primary Group Goals

People engage in primary interaction because they enjoy the interaction itself—the group is maintained more for its own sake than for the purpose of accomplishing specified goals. Being with others and interacting on a close, personal basis is fulfilling regardless of the particular activities the group may engage in—whether playing cards, washing dishes, going to church, or smoking marijuana.

To the extent that interaction is *not* an end in itself, the group is less a primary one. In some families the members dislike each other and act out their roles ritualistically, without enjoyment. Although such families may remain intact, they have ceased to be primary groups in the fullest sense once the members fail to derive personal satisfaction from the interaction.

Primary Interaction and Communication

For a primary group to survive, channels of communication must remain open. Although primary interaction can be carried on for long

5. Cooley, *Social Organization*, pp. 23–24.
6. Elliott Liebow, *Tally's Corner: A Study of Negro Street-corner Men* (Boston: Little, Brown and Company, 1967), p. 164.

periods of time without face-to-face communication, physical nearness is normally an important condition for holding a primary group together. The fate of the average high-school clique after graduation day can be partly explained by the fact that regular communication cannot be maintained. Even when members of the group remain in the same community, marriage, jobs, and changing interests prevent the closeness of school days. Members communicate less frequently and less openly until finally the group loses its identity. From time to time there may be attempts to reestablish old ties, but relationships are never quite the same. Though by no means solely responsible, the disruption of the original patterns of interaction and open communication have clearly contributed to the group's dissolution.

In a true primary group the level of self-disclosure is high: members let down their guards and talk openly about their feelings and ideas. Thus they come to know each other intimately and to be genuinely concerned about each other as individuals. Group members respond to each other in terms of their complete personalities rather than merely their role performances. For example, a man may be a terrible gardener, an inept driver, and an unskilled host, but his wife can ignore these failings or even find them endearing: she responds to her husband as a *whole* person rather than as a set of specific skills.

Primary Group Norms
Many of the norms of a given primary group are *unique* in that they pertain only to the members of that particular group and are not shared by outsiders. Indeed, they may not even make sense to nonmembers. The normative use of language in ways that nonmembers do not understand is a common practice; for example, every family has its own inside jokes, its special nicknames or terms of endearment, its use of phrases carried over from courtship or from the children's early years.

But though primary groups have many norms that are unique, they are also principal agencies for transmitting and interpreting cultural and subcultural norms. This is particularly true of the family, where the children generally acquire the normative orientations of their parents toward politics, minority groups, religious beliefs, status striving, and many other broad issues. An almost equally strong influence is exerted by other primary groups. The teen-age peer group, for example, transmits norms concerning hairstyles, dance forms, modes of dress, sexual conduct, smoking, drinking, and other aspects of behavior. Comparable influences could be cited among adult peer groups.

Primary groups not only help *teach* cultural and subcultural norms but also help *enforce* them. For example, a wife may criticize her husband for exceeding the speed limit or failing to keep the front yard looking nice; a husband may criticize his wife for failing to vote or for letting the children skip school. Although such sanctioning has taken place within the family unit, it is directly related to the goals of the community and society. Countless other examples could be cited of how primary groups serve to teach and help enforce the norms of larger groups.

Primary group norms are especially significant in shaping our overall behavior because of the importance we attach to them. The normative attitudes, beliefs, and guides to conduct that we acquire from our family and peer groups are not easily displaced or altered. This is an important aspect of socialization (Chapter 6).

Primary Group Roles
Role expectations in a primary group are based upon the strong "we" feeling noted by Cooley. Members are bound together by their feeling of sameness and common identity rather than by the fact that their roles create a division of labor. This does not mean that the members of primary groups do not develop some specialized roles; as we have already noted (page 40), they turn to particular individuals for leadership, for help in smoothing over quarrels, for help in clarifying issues, and so forth. But the roles are usually informal, and the way they interlock is less important in binding the members together than are the reciprocal bonds of affection that lead, in

Cooley's words, to a "certain fusion of individualities in a common whole."

Many of the essential characteristics of primary group roles as a basis of mutual support are illustrated in Liebow's study of *Tally's Corner* (page 65):

[*Each of the men centers his life around*] *those persons he knows and likes best, those with whom he is "up tight": his "walking buddies," "good" or "best" friends, girl friends, and sometimes real or putative kinsmen. These are the people with whom he is in more or less daily face-to-face contact, and whom he turns to for emergency aid, comfort or support in time of need or crisis. He gives them and receives from them goods and services in the name of friendship, ostensibly keeping no reckoning. Routinely, he seeks them out and is sought out by them. They serve his need to be with others of his kind, and to be recognized as a discrete, distinctive personality, and he, in turn, serves them the same way. They are both his audience and his fellow actors.*[7]

Primary groups constitute a subtle but real web of interdependency, not only in terms of exchanges of "goods and services" or help in emergencies but in a more personal sense. Primary role systems allow each person to be recognized and valued as a unique personality and at the same time bind members to each other.

Informal Social Control

Members of a primary group enforce the norms and roles of the group informally, using a great variety of techniques to apply positive and negative sanctions. For example, the fisherman who presents a friend with some of his catch is reinforcing social bonds by the application of a positive sanction. And in showing his appreciation by inviting the fisherman in for a beer, the friend is similarly reinforcing exemplary primary-group role performance by a reciprocal application of positive sanctions. When a young woman invites her male friend to dinner and he reciprocates by taking her to the theater, both are engaging in the application of positive sanctions.

7. Liebow, *Tally's Corner*, p. 163. See also William Foote Whyte, *Street-Corner Society: The Social Structure of an Italian Slum*, rev. ed. (Chicago: The University of Chicago Press, 1955), especially pp. 106–108.

Although none of the individuals in such exchanges is likely to think of the behavior in such terms, from a sociological perspective this is precisely what is happening. Close examination of primary group interaction reveals a continuous stream of informal sanctioning behavior. Such simple gestures as laughing at the jokes of a fellow member or smiling in approval can be used as positive sanctions. Negative sanctions can be exercised by yawning, frowning, or simply looking blank when some other form of response is hoped for.

Much of the control that maintains the social organization of a primary group is self-generated and self-administered: anticipation of disapproval or rejection is usually sufficient to deter a member who contemplates some act that would upset the other members. If a person has in fact already offended the other members, feelings of guilt or anxiety may serve as more severe negative sanctions than open criticism from the others.

Reduction of Social Distance

Although ranking systems develop within primary groups as the members work out an informal system of roles with accompanying distinctions in rank, primary interaction tends to minimize distinctions among members—especially distinctions originating in other contexts, such as economic, educational, or occupational roles. Among many military units, for example, small teams, such as flight crews or demolition squads, are often made up of personnel representing several different levels of status in the military hierarchy. Working together day after day, often under dangerous conditions, these teams frequently develop into close-knit primary groups despite military norms proscribing personal friendships between officers and those under their command. Similarly, college students from quite different social backgrounds often join together in primary groups that minimize differences in wealth or social standing. One of the important consequences of primary interaction, then, is the *reduction of social distance* between people from dissimilar backgrounds.

FORMAL DECISION-MAKING GROUPS

Increasingly important in modern society are small groups such as committees, commissions, councils, juries, boards of supervisors, and other appointed or elected bodies that are formed for the specific purpose of making decisions and formulating policies within larger organizational structures. Much of the available information about the dynamics of such groups has been obtained from experimental studies of "artificial" groups in laboratory settings, since it is difficult to observe "natural" decision-making groups in actual operation. Legal proscriptions forbid the presence of outsiders in jury rooms, and the demands of security prohibit the presence of observers at many kinds of industrial and governmental policy-making conferences. But in spite of these obstacles, social scientists have learned much about the patterns of interaction that are characteristic of small, task-oriented groups.[8]

Manifest and Latent Goals

The goals of a decision-making group are typically related to policy allocating resources, distributing rewards, approving proposals, or similar issues. Since the decision may affect positively or negatively the interests of individuals and factions both within the group and outside it—the employees and stockholders of a corporation, for example—meetings of the decision makers often involve power struggles and competitive maneuvering.[9]

Interaction in such a setting can be extremely subtle, as members attempt to influence each other and to promote decisions that will favor their special interests. Often there is a "hidden agenda": members have a variety of goals they hope to attain—some manifest, some latent, some formal, some informal, and often some that remain unrevealed as the group goes about completing its formal assignments.

Stages of Interaction

As noted in a classic study by Bales and Strodtbeck,[10] interaction in decision-making groups seems to develop in stages. At the start, the individual members are essentially concerned with *collecting information:* they ask for orientation, exchange facts, and analyze the problem. The second phase is primarily devoted to *evaluating the information.* Members offer their own opinions on the issue and react positively or negatively to the views of other members. In the third phase the group concentrates on *reaching a decision.* Emotional strains are most likely to develop at this stage, as members become more open in their criticisms, form or resist coalitions, and support some individuals and reject others.[11]

Once the group has arrived at a decision or agreed on the formulation of a policy, the pattern of interaction typically shifts to an attempt at *restoring equilibrium.* Rates of negative reaction fall off and positive reactions increase. The members joke and laugh, releasing tension and emphasizing group solidarity. These successive patterns of interaction can be observed in almost every small decision-making group, whatever the nature of its task.

Formal and Informal Roles

Titles such as "foreman of the jury," "chairman of the board," or "executive secretary of the commission" refer to rather well-defined roles in particular kinds of decision-making groups. These formally designated roles, however, allow for considerable variation in performance. Some leaders are authoritarian; others are democratic. The harmony or strain within the group as it proceeds with its task can be closely related to the role performance of the designated leader.

In groups that meet repeatedly, particular members are likely to assume informal leadership roles. Someone other than the formal leader often emerges as the "best idea" person—the one who gives guidance to the group, contributes suggestions for solving its problems, and generally offers the most effective ideas for reaching its goals. And a social-emotional leader often emerges—the one who serves to minimize

8. A. Paul Hare, "Bibliography of Small Group Research 1959–1969," *Sociometry* 35, No. 1 (March 1972): 6.

9. Marvin E. Shaw, *Group Dynamics: The Psychology of Small Group Behavior* (New York: McGraw-Hill Book Company, 1971), pp. 260–266.

10. Robert F. Bales and Fred L. Strodtbeck, "Phases in Group Problem Solving," *Journal of Abnormal and Social Psychology,* 46 (1951): 485–495.

11. Shaw, *Group Dynamics*, pp. 101–112.

friction in the group. Studies have shown that the person who assumes the "best idea" role frequently becomes the least liked member of the group, while the social-emotional leader is the best liked.[12]

Social Control

When a decision-making group operates within the context of some larger group, as is usually the case, the formal controls of the larger group carry over into the smaller one. In addition, decision-making groups rely heavily on informal controls similar to those of primary groups. Positive and negative sanctions are exercised by means of words and gestures indicating approval and disapproval. Generally an effort is made to keep the interaction pleasant and polite. Eventually, of course, a decision-making group reaches the stage where members must vote on the issue or otherwise formally declare their positions. As already noted, criticism of individual members is likely to become much more open at this point than during the earlier stages of collecting and evaluating information.

Criteria of Rank

Investigators have found that the status individuals have outside a small decision-making group helps determine the prestige and power they enjoy within the group. For example, business and professional people appear to have greater influence on jury decisions than individuals from occupational roles of lesser prestige. In groups that include members of both sexes, the designated leader is apt to be a man and the person appointed secretary is almost invariably a woman. Men seem to emerge as task leaders more often than do women, whereas women are more likely than men to become social-emotional leaders. Thus both role-playing and relative rank within a small decision-making group are heavily influenced by the status and roles that members have *outside* the group.[13]

Members of a small formal decision-making group may hope to attain a variety of goals—latent and informal as well as manifest and formal.

Sometimes the informal hierarchy that eventually emerges in a decision-making group is the product of a struggle for position in the early meetings. Until the informal ranking system has been worked out, the members are generally less effective in moving forward with their task than they are after the hierarchy has settled into a stable pattern. The pattern that evolves may represent a complex of several different ranking systems, each based on different criteria. For example, groups typically develop a *hierarchy of relative popularity,* in which members are ranked by their colleagues on the basis of personal attractiveness. As we have already noted, the popularity of members within the group is often related to the type of informal role they assume. They may have quite different rankings in the *hierarchy of relative power,* which emerges as some individuals prove more able than others to influence the decisions of the group.[14]

Neither of these informal hierarchies is necessarily related to the system of formal ranking, where designated leaders are supposed to have the greatest prestige. The formal leader may actually have less influence on group decisions than the "best idea" person or some other informal leader. As in all formally organized groups, the informal structure is a significant aspect of social organization.

12. Robert F. Bales, "The Equilibrium Problem in Small Groups," in *Working Papers in the Theory of Action,* Talcott Parsons, Robert Bales, and Edward Shils, eds. (New York: The Free Press, 1954), pp. 111–161.

13. Fred L. Strodtbeck and R. D. Mann, "Sex Role Differentiation in Jury Deliberations," *Sociometry,* 19 (1956): 3–11.

14. Shaw, *Group Dynamics,* p. 261.

TOOLS OF SOCIOLOGY
IDEAL TYPES   John Maiolo

Sociology, during its formative years, was characterized by many attempts to create typologies that would give direction to research and theory-building. Comte developed three basic typologies to explain human intellectual development (page 6); Durkheim attempted to explain social change in terms of mechanical and organic types of social solidarity (see page 90), and Tönnies formulated contrasting types of social relationships that he termed *Gemeinschaft* and *Gesellschaft* (page 84). It was Max Weber, however, who systematically developed the concept of the *ideal type*.

As methodological tools, Weber intended ideal types to be mental constructs—precise concepts developed from scientific observations—that could be used in making a comparative analysis of two or more social phenomena. Thus, a sociologist can compare the distribution of authority, say, in organizations A and B by comparing the pattern in *each* organization with that in Weber's model of bureaucracy.

Weber proposed three criteria for the construction of ideal types. First, they are to *accentuate*, even exaggerate, reality rather than to describe it accurately. Thus, when Weber characterized bureaucratic organization (pages 71–75), he was abstracting characteristics that could be observed, in some form or other, in a variety of existing organizations, such as corporations and government bureaus. Ideal types, as such, *do not exist in reality.*

The second criterion for ideal types is related to the first: they are not ready-made constructs but rather must be *contrived* by the social scientist. Their purpose is to help us conceptualize social phenomena, much as our systems of weights and measures help us to conceptualize and observe the physical world. When physicists conceptualize one horsepower in terms of raising 33,000 pounds one foot per minute or 550 pounds one foot per second, they are using a completely arbitrary abstraction as an aid in relating themselves to the phenomena they study. Ideal types serve a parallel purpose for the sociologist.

The third criterion of ideal types is that they should generate hypotheses and give direction to empirical research. Thus, in studying the dynamics of bureaucracy, Peter Blau (page 76) used Weber's ideal type of bureaucracy as a starting point and derived the hypothesis that adherence to well-defined bureaucratic procedures leads to more efficient and productive behavior. The fact that Blau's research did not confirm this hypothesis does not mean that Weber's ideal type is incorrect or useless. Since ideal types are abstractions, their accuracy is less relevant than their usefulness as a framework for examining reality and for building tested generalizations and theories.

Weber was careful to point out that ideal types are not "ideal" in the sense of representing a desired state of affairs. Nevertheless, many contemporary sociologists have abandoned Weber's original term in favor of *pure type, constructed type,* or *model,* which are free of the value connotations associated with the word *ideal.* Few sociologists, however, question the continuing utility of Weber's basic conceptions. The ideal types he constructed have generated a great deal of fruitful research and led to a refinement of his early theories about such phenomena as bureaucracy, social action, authority, and political power. More important perhaps, his development of the ideal type as a methodological tool has provided modern sociologists with one means for opening new areas of research and theory-building. Studies of urban-rural differences, the culture of poverty, the professionalization of work roles, the anatomy of confrontation and conflict—all these and many other areas of contemporary research have been influenced by Weber's early contribution.

For further reading on ideal types, see H. H. Gerth and C. Wright Mills, *From Max Weber. Essays in Sociology* (New York: Oxford University Press, 1958), pp. 59 ff., and Don Martindale, *The Nature and Types of Sociological Theory* (Boston: Houghton Mifflin Company, 1960), pp. 381–383. Martindale also has compared Weber's views with those of recent works; see "Sociological Theory and the Ideal Type" in *Symposium on Sociological Theory*, ed. Llewellyn Gross (Evanston, Ill.: Harper & Row, Inc., 1959), pp. 57–91.

ASSOCIATIONS: BUREAUCRATIC ORGANIZATION

Much of the activity of modern urban-industrial societies is carried out through large, formally organized groups called *associations,* in which the prevailing pattern of social organization is *bureaucracy.* In terms of Cooley's classification (page 63), associations are *secondary* groups. However, their overall effects on our lives are much more significant than "secondary" might suggest. Blau and Scott state the matter thus:

If the most dramatic fact that sets our age apart from earlier ones is that we live today under the shadow of nuclear destruction, the most pervasive feature that distinguishes contemporary life is that it is dominated by large, complex, and formal organizations. Our ability to organize thousands and even millions of men in order to accomplish large-scale tasks—be they economic, political, or military—is one of our greatest strengths. That free men might become mere cogs in the bureaucratic machineries we set up for this purpose is one of the greatest threats to our liberty.[15]

Bureaucracy is not a modern invention; political and military endeavors were organized bureaucratically as far back as ancient Egypt and ancient Rome. But bureaucracy did not become a pervasive pattern of social organization until after the Industrial Revolution, which led to an increasing division of labor and a shift of population from farms to cities. Today, elements of bureaucratic structure can be observed not only in economic, political, and military organizations but in almost all large groups, whatever their particular goals.

In analyzing *associations* as a distinct type of group, we will begin by examining the formal elements of bureaucratic organization. Then we will consider the impact of individuals and informal subgroups in modifying the formal structure.

15. Peter M. Blau and W. Richard Scott, *Formal Organizations* (San Francisco: Chandler Publishing Co., 1961), p. ix.
16. Max Weber, *Theory of Social and Economic Organization,* trans. A. M. Henderson and Talcott Parsons (New York: The Free Press, 1957), p. 334. Originally published in 1925.

FORMAL BUREAUCRATIC STRUCTURE

Our understanding of bureaucratic organization owes much to the early work of Max Weber, who was the first to analyze bureaucracy as an abstract model, or *ideal type.*[16] It should be noted that Weber did not intend his model of bureaucracy to be an accurate description of reality, nor did he consider it "ideal" in any evaluative sense. Rather, his purpose was to isolate and accentuate the characteristics that distinguish bureaucracy from other patterns of social organization. (The uses of *ideal types* in research and theory-building are discussed in Tools of Sociology, opposite.)

According to Weber, the basic principles underlying bureaucratic organization are *rationality* and *efficiency.* Bureaucracies are designed to accomplish specific goals quickly, smoothly, and economically, with a minimum of interpersonal friction. The duties and responsibilities of individuals are intended to be highly specialized and clearly defined, with all roles intermeshed in a complex organizational structure that is stable and self-perpetuating. An effort is made to design the total operation so that its efficiency will not be appreciably affected by changes in personnel. Interpersonal relations are supposed to be formal and impersonal. Weber insisted, indeed, that bureaucratic efficiency is achieved in direct proportion as interpersonal relationships are kept free of emotional involvement.

The Formal Definition of Goals

If a bureaucratic association is to function efficiently and rationally, its goals must be specifically and formally defined. Ideally, the definition of goals determines the structure of a bureaucracy and the resources it needs:

The nature of the goal provides the criteria to be used in the recruitment of personnel and determines what resources are required and the priorities for their acquisition. It also furnishes a basis (relative contribution to the attainment of the objectives) for determining the amount of compensation participants receive and, in part, for allocating authority among them. It should be apparent, then, that to the extent that organizational goals are diffuse or lacking in clarity and to the extent that multiple, possibly conflicting goals are being pursued, the organization will lack the rational basis for making these critical decisions.[17]

Multiple goals do not necessarily create a problem unless the pursuit of one goal interferes with the pursuit of another. In organizations as large and complex as those in government, such conflicts are not uncommon. One section of the Department of the Interior, for example, may be working to create more dams to reduce flood damage and to better utilize the available water supply, while another section may be working to preserve areas of natural beauty that the dams would destroy. Requirements for military and defense spending often seriously interfere with the government's ability to pursue programs aimed at correcting serious social problems.

Whatever the purposes of an association, the pursuit of conflicting goals is clearly inconsistent with the principle of rationality upon which the efficiency of bureaucracy depends. The principle of rationality also breaks down when the individual members of an association are unaware of its goals or are misinformed about them. Although it seems obvious that participants must know what is expected of them if they are to do their jobs well, studies in various countries have shown that members of large-scale organizations are often poorly informed about group goals.[18]

Generally, the effectiveness of bureaucracy also suffers if the association fails to consider the personal goals of its members. A truly rational system is one in which individuals can achieve their own goals effectively by fulfilling their formal roles and working for organizational objectives. In business associations, for example, formal incentives such as salary, title, and job security may satisfy the personal goals of individual participants and at the same time encourage them to carry out the purposes of the company for which they work. A little later in this chapter, we will use an actual case study to show how the goals and interests of individuals work to modify the formal structure of a bureaucratic association.

Channeled Communication as a Basis of Interaction

In marked contrast to the open communication of primary groups, communication in a bureaucratically organized association proceeds through clearly defined channels. Reports, requests, orders, and policy decisions are all passed from one level in the hierarchy to another, and almost everything must be put in writing. Probably no feature of bureaucratic organization is more subject to criticism from insiders and outsiders alike than the quantity of paper work required to accomplish a seemingly simple task, yet formal patterns of communication are necessary to maintain the interactive machinery and the effective operation of bureaucratic organization. When subordinates bypass their immediate supervisors and communicate directly with superiors several steps removed, lines of authority and responsibility break down.

Official Norms

Like channeled communication, the application of *general rules* to *particular cases* is one of the most characteristic features of bureaucracy. Rules of procedure are formally standardized so that particular tasks can supposedly be performed uniformly, regardless of who is performing them. In addition to defining standard operating procedure (in bureaucratic jargon, SOP), the formal norms of a bureaucracy typically prescribe such matters as the type of clothing that is appropriate (in some cases the wearing of uniforms and insignia), the hours of work, and the proper use of tools and materials. Sometimes there are even norms defining the kind of behavior that is expected of members in their life outside the organization. A church board may specify that its members should not smoke or drink alcohol in public; a corporation may insist that its executives take an active role in community affairs. "The Teacher Role" on page 73 is an older example of such formal norms.

17. W. Richard Scott, "Theory of Organizations," in *Handbook of Modern Sociology,* p. 492.
18. Ibid., pp. 492–493.

THE TEACHER ROLE

Schools today are radically different from those of the 1920s, but most still require some form of "professional behavior" on the part of teachers. The following requirements from a 1923 teachers' contract in Cook County, Illinois, illustrate the official norms that then defined the teacher role.

1. Do not get married. (This contract becomes null and void immediately if the teacher marries.)
2. Do not keep company with men.
3. Be home between the hours of 8 p.m. and 6 a.m. unless in attendance at a school function.
4. Do not loiter downtown in ice cream stores.
5. Do not leave town at any time without permission of the chairman of the board.
6. Do not smoke cigarettes. (This contract becomes null and void immediately if the teacher is found smoking.)
7. Do not drink beer, wine, or whiskey. (This contract becomes null and void if the teacher
is found drinking beer, wine, or whiskey.)
8. Do not get in a carriage or automobile with any man except your brother or father.
9. Do not dress in bright colors.
10. Do not dye your hair.
11. Do not wear dresses more than two inches above the ankles.
12. Wear at least two petticoats.
13. Keep the schoolroom neat and clean: (a) Sweep the floor at least once daily. (b) Scrub the floor at least once weekly with hot water and soap. (c) Clean the blackboards at least once daily. (d) Start the fire at 7 a.m., so the room will be warm by 8 a.m.

Thus the formal norms of bureaucratic organizations range from simple rules for writing memoranda to procedures governing a wide range of behaviors. But their purposes are in every case the same — to bring order and efficiency to procedures so that every problem handled by the association becomes a simple matter of bureaucratic routine, and to ensure that the whole structure operates predictably.

Fixed Allocation of Interlocking Roles

The allocation of roles in a bureaucratic structure is intended to create a clear-cut and relatively fixed division of labor. The sphere of responsibility associated with each role is often defined in an official job description. Individuals are expected to perform their duties in a specified way and to refrain from assuming the obligations of others.

The division of labor in a bureaucratic organization is based on the assumption that job specialization will lead to increased competence in a limited sphere of activity. It also has

the effect of freeing the organization from unnecessary dependence on the unique skills of individuals. The maxim that "no one is irreplaceable" is true to the extent that a given role is clearly defined and calls only for performance that meets that definition.

The formalization of roles is also supposed to minimize the possibility that friction between individuals will interfere with overall operating efficiency. With responsibilities clearly fixed, two members in interlocking roles can, in theory at least, carry out their assigned tasks even if they thoroughly dislike each other. The dehumanization of roles, which Max Weber saw as an essential of bureaucratic efficiency, has appeared to many as a threat to human dignity and freedom.[19] As we shall see shortly, however, the impersonality of bureaucratic organizations is often more apparent than real.

Social Control by Consent and Contract

Bureaucratic roles are organized into a strict hierarchy, with the roles at each level coming under the supervision of another level of roles

19. Jerome H. Skolnick, *The Politics of Protest* (New York: Simon & Schuster, Inc., 1969), p. 12.

The contractual basis of bureaucratic organization is the basis not only for control by consent but also for the group's solidarity. Individuals are bound to the organization by what it gives them in return for being members and not necessarily by loyalty, sentiment. or other personal ties that hold members together in many other types of groups.

Most associations use both positive and negative sanctions to reinforce control by consent. The gold star awarded to schoolchildren for not being late and the gold watch presented to the faithful employee for twenty-five years of service are positive sanctions that reinforce well-understood norms. Low performance ratings, unfavorable work assignments, withheld raises and promotions, and firing are typical negative sanctions in groups relying mainly on control by consent.

Ranking Based on Competence

In principle at least, all roles in a bureaucratic organization call for different skills; this is the basis of the division of labor. Not all roles are equally easy to fill, however, nor equally crucial to the attainment of basic group goals. Differences in the kinds of skills required by particular roles and differences in the amount of responsibility and authority the roles carry are the criteria for developing a ranking system.

In many associations the ranking system consists of three general levels based on the kinds of competence required to fill the roles within each stratum. At the bottom of the pyramid are the *workers* or *followers,* the rank and file who do the routine work of the association according to established procedural norms. The roles at this level call for specialized competence, but the skills are not difficult to acquire; the workers can be easily replaced.

The *functionaries*—supervisors and middle managers—are essentially administrators: their task is to implement the policies and directives they receive from above. Thus, their skills usually relate to the handling of people rather than things, and the ability to interact smoothly with others—superiors, subordinates, and equals—becomes crucial The most capable administrators are those who can best coordinate the activities of their subordinates so that assigned goals

The allocation of roles in a bureaucratic structure creates a clear-cut and relatively fixed division of labor. Individuals are expected to perform their duties in a specified way, to avoid ad-libbing, and to refrain from assuming the obligations of others.

higher in the structure. Authority—the right to give commands and expect them to be obeyed—is clearly delimited and is vested in the role, not in the individual. Most associations have organizational charts that designate lines of authority as well as channels of communication and areas of responsibility.

In most associations, social control is based on voluntary submission to authority. Individuals consent to follow the orders of their superiors because they realize that in joining the organization they have, in effect, accepted a *contract* that obligates them to follow the rules. In return for their services they can expect a secure place in the organization and other appropriate compensation, such as a guaranteed salary and a chance of promotion. Whether or not a legal contract is involved, the arrangement is essentially legalistic in that it formally specifies what each party can legitimately expect of the other.

are achieved with maximum harmony and minimum interpersonal conflict. The special skill of the successful functionary is to see that the job is done efficiently and well without relying on negative sanctions injurious to morale.

At the top level of the pyramid are the *policy makers*. Their roles require them to generate ideas which, when implemented, will move the association toward its goals. Generally, the skills necessary at this level depend upon accumulated years of experience and a substantial degree of creative talent.

The prestige associated with different levels within a bureaucracy is made evident not only through the differential distribution of rewards but also through the use of visible status symbols. In a fancy restaurant the different ranks of busboy, waiter, wine steward, and headwaiter are easily recognized by their distinctive uniforms. The blue collar and the white collar in an industrial association signify widely understood status differentials. In a corporation upper-status levels are made apparent by special titles, office decor, the privilege of having a private secretary, a reserved parking place, a key to the executive washroom, and other symbols of prestige.

THE INFORMAL STRUCTURE

While the principles of rationality and efficiency that underlie the design of a bureaucratic association are intended to produce a social system that works flawlessly, the system is unlikely to do so in reality.[20] Once people are "plugged into" the roles of the association, it becomes something other than the formal structure its designers intended. The *informal structure* is defined by the ways people actually work toward goals and develop systems of norms, roles, social control, and ranking. These are almost always different from those prescribed in the formal plan.

Sources of Informal Organization

On paper, various individuals may appear to have the same qualifications for a particular role in an organization. In fact, however, no two people will carry out the role in exactly the same way or with exactly the same effect. All employees bring to a bureaucratic association their own attitudes, prejudices, and other personality characteristics, which lead them to play their assigned roles in ways not prescribed by the designers. As a result of recurrent interaction, people develop feelings of affection or hostility, of trust or distrust, toward other members of the group organization. And primary-group loyalties and personal goals may be more important to them than the goals of the association.

Sometimes the formal bureaucratic structure is informally modified simply because it is inadequate for getting a job done. When the rules fail to provide for particular problems that come up, individuals are forced to invent their own solutions or to follow unofficial procedures that other workers have made standard. In other cases, the formal structure, though well-designed in terms of organizational goals, may fail to account for the goals and needs of the people who must carry policy into effect. Thus an association designed to utilize volunteers in rank-and-file positions may have difficulty in recruiting individuals because the work is not personally rewarding. Similarly, a carefully designed wage-incentive plan may not do much to motivate workers whose jobs are routine and boring.

Consequences of Informal Structure

In general, the development of an informal structure in an association injects new and unofficial goals into the group; it redefines channels of communication and interaction in ways that are not part of the official plan; it redefines formal norms or invents new ones to meet changing problems that are not covered by the existing rules; it results in the reinterpretation of roles that are theoretically fixed; it supplements official techniques of social control with informal sanctions; and it leads to informal ranking systems that alter the formal hierarchy in subtle ways.

20. Peter M. Blau, *Dynamics of Bureaucracy: A Study of Interpersonal Relationships in Two Government Agencies,* 2nd ed., rev. (Chicago: The University of Chicago Press, 1963). Originally published in 1955.

TOOLS OF SOCIOLOGY
THEORY AND RESEARCH

Blau's study *Dynamics of Bureaucracy* provides an excellent example of the interplay of theory and research in sociology. This is an analysis of two bureaucratic organizations, a federal enforcement agency and a state employment agency. The basic concepts that Blau used came from Weber, but the theoretical orientation that guided his research was functional analysis (page 50). Thus the study focused on the consequences of particular interaction patterns and organizational arrangements for the functioning of the agency as a whole.

Blau relied on three basic research techniques: participant observation (page 49), use of statistical records, and interviews (page 398). Participant observation went on daily in each departmental office for three months. During the same time office operational records were carefully examined. Following the observation period in each case, all members of the departments that had been studied — a total of eighty-five persons — were interviewed in their homes.

Blau himself has pointed out the limitations of his study. In the first place, the findings for the organizations studied may not be representative of other bureaucratic organizations. The two agencies that granted Blau permission to carry out his research were relatively new ones; a number of private agencies and older public ones refused to participate. Blau acknowledged that this process of self-selection might bias his findings: the agencies that were willing to be studied showed by that fact alone that they were more flexible than the organizations that would not participate. A further limitation was that only single departments of the two agencies were studied, representing but a small segment of their total social structure. Thus, there is some question about the significance of the observed practices for the functioning of either agency as a whole.

But if selectivity had disadvantages, it also had some important advantages, especially in enabling Blau to use a variety of research techniques and to study the functioning of the departments in depth. For example, through participant observation he gained the impression that competitive practices set up in the employment agency interfered with productivity. An analysis of office records confirmed this impression: the more competitive a group was, the lower its productivity. Blau then hypothesized that a group's productivity was affected by its degree of social cohesion. He tested and confirmed this hypothesis by observation and interviews, using a specially created index of social cohesion.

The multiple techniques Blau used also allowed him to test the reliability of his conclusions. For some social-interaction situations, the responses obtained in interviews with departmental personnel proved to be unreliable when compared with the findings obtained through observation and the analysis of office records. By checking one research technique against another, Blau was able to develop more thorough and accurate explanations for his research questions, even if the range of generalization was limited.

Blau's study shows the almost inevitable discrepancy between a research plan worked out in advance and actual research procedures. Blau maintained a flexible approach and periodically revised his research design to fit the circumstances and new research needs. Blau sums up the challenge:

"The researcher who compulsively insists on following his predesigned plan will miss [some] rare opportunities. Conversely, the one who is seduced by every new lead will find he has failed to collect information on the theoretical problems that had prompted his research. A research schedule that is recurrently revised but that is quite closely followed guards against these dangers. . . . At the very least my research schedule prevented me from inadvertently forgetting to obtain some information that was essential in terms of my theoretical framework."

Peter M. Blau, *Dynamics of Bureaucracy: A Study of Interpersonal Relationships in Two Government Agencies,* 2nd ed., rev. (Chicago: The University of Chicago Press, 1963); quotation from p. 274.

Sometimes the informal structure contributes to the achievement of organizational goals. Individuals may create new procedures to get a job done more efficiently or may feel so committed to the organization that they go beyond the simple requirements of their roles. In other cases, the informal structure that emerges is clearly at cross-purposes with the large-scale goals of the organization, as when workers develop their own norms concerning the length of coffee breaks and lunch periods, what constitutes a fair day's work, or the legitimacy of pilfering company supplies. Regardless of whether the informal structure subverts or supports the formal structure, however, *it is an integral part of the group's social organization*.

THE DYNAMICS OF BUREAUCRACY

The interplay of formal and informal structure in directing the ongoing activity of an association has been demonstrated by Peter Blau, who has done continuing research on the manner in which bureaucratic organizations actually attempt to achieve their goals. In one well-known study, Blau examined the operation of a state employment agency serving the clothing industry of a large city. Using the research techniques described in Tools of Sociology on page 76, he made a detailed analysis of the agency's organization with respect to both its internal functioning and its relationship with the public.[21]

Blau observed a clear-cut difference between what the interviewers in the employment office were trained to do and what they actually did on the job. For example, they were taught to fill out all job requests for workers in detail, to find the best client for a given vacancy, and to provide counseling for clients who needed it. But these procedures did not fit the reality of their office situation. Employers needed workers at once or not at all, and the level of skills required was usually so low that there was little apparent need to try to find the best-qualified workers. As a result, the interviewers usually selected the first available client who met the minimum qualifications. In doing so, they were able to satisfy the needs of the employers and to some extent the needs of the clients.

The interviewers also adjusted to the reality of how they were being evaluated. The employment agency was dependent on appropriations from the state legislature, which judged its performance on the basis of the number of job placements it made. In this situation, the counseling of clients, especially of unskilled workers looking for unskilled jobs, seemed a questionable use of time. Thus the interviewers eliminated counseling for the great majority of clients in order to make the greatest possible number of placements.

Even the receptionists tended to modify their prescribed roles. Their task was the seemingly routine one of assigning potential clients their first appointment with an interviewer. Because jobs were scarce at certain times, the regulations called for delays in appointments of from thirty to sixty days. But often the receptionists faced clients who were desperate for work, and if they knew that job openings had just come in, they would arbitrarily schedule appointments to fit the job needs. Although this had the effect of improving their relations with the clients, it often led to overcrowding in the office, with too many applicants for the few jobs available. It also meant that applicants were not treated equally, though equal treatment was a basic premise of the employment agency. Again, however, the major organizational goal of maximizing placements was achieved.

Blau found that the system for rating an interviewer's performance had the effect of improving supervisor-interviewer relationships while increasing tensions between interviewers. Performance ratings were based to a considerable degree on objective criteria (e.g., number of referrals made). This meant that the supervisor could place the onus for criticism on the record, without having to make a subjective evaluation or criticize the interviewer as a person.

Blau also studied the importance of impersonality to the agency. He found that interviewers were not satisfied with their work when they had to follow strictly bureaucratic procedures. The pressures to maximize referrals and find

21. Ibid.

clients for low-skill jobs in a hurry led to a work routine that many found boring. The interviewers' most satisfying experiences came when they were "doing something more than was called for." They particularly liked to help clients who were "very personable and very anxious to work." On balance, these clients tended to be middle-class, white-collar workers, who represented only a small percentage of the whole.

Blau found that the agency was continually adjusting internally to try to achieve efficiency of operation and that many of the adjustments were brought about by actions taken by personnel at all levels of the hierarchy. Furthermore, adjustments were often deemed necessary because of pressures brought to bear by elements outside the bureaucratic organization, such as the state legislature, clients, and employers. Overall the findings of this study supported Blau's thesis that bureaucracies contain the seeds, not necessarily of their own destruction, but of their continuous transformation. The conditions that Blau found to be crucial to the self-adjustment process and thus to the maintenance of efficient operation were:

(1) at least some security in employment; (2) the absence of basic conflict between work group and top management; (3) a professional orientation toward the performance of duties; (4) established work groups that command the allegiance of their members; (5) organizational needs that are experienced as disturbing.[22]

The first three characteristics listed by Blau are consistent with the principles of formal bureaucratic structure, but the last two clearly fall outside Weber's typology of an "ideal" bureaucracy. Whereas efficiency theoretically requires that work relationships be kept impersonal, Blau found that such personal interaction patterns as joking and complaining were in fact helpful in creating and maintaining social cohesion. This, in turn, became the basis for the establishment of informal work groups which, by developing their own unofficial norms, were able to adjust to the practical, ongoing needs of the organization. In some ways, Blau's findings parallel those of Shils and Janowitz (page 43), who determined that primary-group relationships were essential in maintaining the effectiveness of the German army.

Judging from the research of Blau and others, the effectiveness of a bureaucracy is not necessarily dependent on impersonality. Though increasingly hemmed in by rules and regulations, people today apparently remain very much individuals, capable of having an impact on the large bureaucratic organizations around which contemporary life revolves.

VOLUNTARY ASSOCIATIONS

The Swiftwater Flycasters of Bergerville is a group of some sixty-two fishing enthusiasts. The members meet monthly at the Downtown Restaurant to have drinks, exchange fishing stories, eat dinner, and enjoy a program (usually a speaker or a film) related to flycasting. In addition to such meetings, plus an occasional field trip to nearby fishing waters, the club participates in regional efforts aimed at improving the quality of angling in the state and at conservation generally. The club is also affiliated with regional and national coalitions of fishing clubs. Though small, the group is often taken into account by policy-makers in the State Department of Fisheries in reaching decisions related to the Bergerville area, mainly because the members can swing a lot of votes if the need arises.

The Swiftwater Flycasters is a *voluntary association* with a president, a secretary, and a board of directors, all elected by popular vote. Like other types of bureaucratic associations, it has a formal and an informal structure.

Voluntary associations range in size from small groups of this kind to organizations with thousands of members, like the American Legion, the Grange, the American Medical Association, the American Civil Liberties Union, and the Ku Klux Klan. There are groups formed for almost every conceivable purpose, to which people devote their time, energies, and other resources. Although some of the larger groups may have a paid staff to provide continuity and leadership, many depend entirely upon voluntary participation.

As early as 1835 the French observer Alexis de Tocqueville noted that one of the most striking features of American society was the way

22. Ibid., p. 256.

people banded together to form voluntary associations to meet specific needs or solve problems.[23] Although American life has changed greatly since Tocqueville wrote, we are still very much a nation of joiners. Arnold Rose has estimated that there are at least 100,000 voluntary associations in the United States.[24]

The orientation of voluntary associations may be primarily community service, like the Rotary and the Lions Clubs; civic-political, like the NAACP and the League of Women Voters; commercial, like the Chamber of Commerce; or socioreligious, like some churches. Or the orientation may be primarily social, as in the case of many clubs formed by ethnic and racial minorities. Often the formation of social and ethnic clubs has provided the first step toward political power.

Over the past two decades, members of minority groups have turned increasingly to voluntary association as a means for achieving equal rights. And growing numbers of employees who previously felt little kinship with organized labor have begun to organize on their own. Associations of policemen, firemen, public school teachers, and other city employees have become unions in order to have a stronger voice in decisions affecting the lives of their members. Meanwhile, throughout urban and suburban America, the residents of neighborhoods and even the families living in a single block have banded together to solve local problems — perhaps a temporary one, like the encroachment of a new superhighway, perhaps a long-term one, like the spread of vandalism and blight.

As masses of previously unorganized people discover that, through coordinated effort, they can help control the course of their lives, voluntary associations proliferate. As Daniel Bell has suggested:

It is the extended network of voluntary associations which has been the source of so much independent initiative, in politics and social life, in the United States. One might argue that with our increasing urbanization such civic consciousness would diminish and that in this decline one could find the source of the dis-orientation that individuals feel in the large, urban environment. And yet I would argue to the contrary. In American life today there is probably more voluntary association, more local community and suburban newspapers and more participation in a variety of organizations, professional, hobby and civic, than at any previous period in American history.[25]

Voluntary associations, then, use a specific type of social organization, bureaucracy, to achieve a great variety of distinct goals. It is important to understand both the sociological nature of such groups and the part they play in the life of our society.

COMMUNITIES AS GROUPS

The term *community* is derived from the Latin word for "fellowship" and was used at one time to refer to the warm, affective relationships that could be expected among closely knit groups of people. Gradually, its meaning broadened to refer to an aggregate of people living together in a particular geographical area and bound together politically and economically. We will use the term *community* in this rather broad sense, as roughly synonymous with village, town, or city.

Like the other groups we have examined, the community has a distinctive pattern of social organization. Every village, town, and city has goals, typical patterns of interaction, role structures defining a division of labor, norms for regulating behavior, techniques of social control, and a system of social ranking. Because of these organizational features, communities are groups in every important respect.

Unlike most types of groups, however, communities usually have distinct *spatial patterns*. Not only is the community itself defined in terms of a fixed geographic area (nomadic communities are a rare exception to this rule),

23. Alexis de Tocqueville, *Democracy in America,* 2 vols. (New York: Vintage Books, 1954). Originally published in 1835 (Vol. I) and 1840 (Vol. II).

24. Arnold M. Rose, *The Power Structure* (New York: Oxford University Press, 1967), p. 218.

25. Daniel Bell, "Toward a Communal Society," *Life,* May 12, 1967.

but even the specialized groups within it, such as schools, businesses, families, and churches, have characteristic spatial locations. This is not meant to suggest that a community is simply a complex of buildings, streets, and people—or, as one wag put it, a lot of families connected by a common set of sewer pipes. It is an *integrative social system* that ties together the activities of the various groups of which it is composed. By interacting together, its families, business enterprises, religious organizations, schools, civic groups, political parties, and other constituent groups create a complex behavioral system.

PRIMARY AND SECONDARY GOALS

The primary goals of communities have always been basically economic. In earlier times they were also defensive. Primitive food-gathering communities, for example, were probably formed as early hunters and gatherers discovered that by banding together they could ensure themselves a more adequate food supply and defend themselves more effectively against their enemies.

Similar goals are basic to the agricultural village, a form of community organization that has been common in most parts of the world from earliest times to the present, although it is rarely found in the United States. In this pattern, family dwellings cluster together in a village surrounded by the fields and pastures of the residents. Agricultural workers leave the village every day to go out and cultivate their fields, returning to the village at night. This pattern of community organization was developed to provide groups of families with a means of defense as well as a system for producing food and exchanging goods.

The growth and decline of particular communities is closely related to economic factors. Typically, individuals are first attracted to a specific location because it offers some kind of economic resource. Soon others come along to service those involved in the primary economic activity, and the nucleus of a community is established. Silent yet dramatic testimony for the importance of a firm economic base in maintaining a community is provided by the ghost towns of the American West. (See also the case study of "Caliente," a railroad town, pages 297–298.)

Once its economic base seems assured a community typically diverts an increasing amount of attention and effort to such secondary goals as improving the educational system, providing recreational facilities, beautifying the surroundings, and promoting the arts. Though of secondary importance in maintaining the community, these goals are closely related to the basic need of every individual to interact with other human beings and to feel a sense of common purpose.

VARIATIONS IN PATTERNS OF INTERACTION

Interaction in a small town is likely to involve close and frequent contact between friends, relatives, and acquaintances. Residents of a big city have proportionately more communication with people they do *not* know on a personal basis. The clerk who waits on them in a department store, the bus driver who gets them to work, and the teller who handles their bank deposits may all be strangers with whom they interact only in impersonal role-playing situations. Even the friendships they form at work do not necessarily carry over to their leisure hours, since their homes are likely to be widely separated.

It should not be assumed, however, that everyone in an urban area lives a socially isolated existence.[26] In middle-class suburbs, close interpersonal ties develop in a relatively short time. A chief complaint of many suburbanites, in fact, is lack of privacy. And even within the city, many residential areas are stable neighborhoods where families interact on a regular basis.[27]

Nevertheless, social interaction among urban dwellers is, *on the whole,* less primary than that among residents of small towns. In a few areas of the city, particularly those close to the central business district, anonymity and social

26. John D. Kasarda and Morris Janowitz, "Community Attachment in Mass Society," *American Sociological Review,* 39 (June 1974): 328–339.
27. See Gerald Suttles, *The Social Order of the Slum* (Chicago: The University of Chicago Press, 1968). A classic study is Whyte, *Street-Corner Society.*

isolation are undeniable realities for some people. Here indigent and impoverished persons may feel almost wholly lacking in community ties. But even the inner city, which seems to many middle-class observers to epitomize social isolation, turns out, on close inspection, to be an area where primary groups give meaning and focus to life.[28] In Chapter 12, "The Urban Transition," we will consider in detail both the real and the imagined differences between patterns of interaction in urban communities and small towns.

NORMS AT THE COMMUNITY LEVEL

An urban community is likely to bring together people from a wide variety of ethnic, religious, racial, regional, educational, and occupational groups, each with its own conceptions of proper behavior. Most will agree on certain fundamental rules of conduct, such as respect for a person's life and property; but there is less agreement on informal norms governing many aspects of behavior. And since high population density creates many problems unknown in low density areas, a large city must rely on formal norms to regulate conduct much more than a small community does. In addition to the usual criminal codes, the statutes of a city may include rules for everything from parking one's car to wrapping one's garbage.

At the same time, the largeness of a city and the relative anonymity of its residents make it possible for many minor deviations in behavior to go unnoticed. There is also greater acceptance of varying behavioral norms. People expect their families, friends, and business associates to behave in a particular way, but they tend to accept or at least to tolerate some nonconformity in the behavior of others. A middle-class businessman, for example, may be amused at the city's hippie community or charmed by its ethnic neighborhoods, feeling that both add "character" to the city. Yet in matters that concern him more closely, he expects adherence to his own set of norms: the hippie may no longer seem amusing when he becomes a prospective

28. Ibid., pp. 175–194.

son-in-law, and old-world customs may no longer seem quaint when practiced by the neighbors next door.

The smaller the community and the greater its physical isolation, the more unchanging its norms are likely to be. In many areas of the world, isolated villages still retain a structure of norms that shapes life much as it was in the nineteenth century. The greater the degree of contact with the outside world, the less likely it is that traditional patterns survive. If a small town is located on good highways, is served by a bus line, and receives a newspaper and a television signal from an urban area, its norms tend to become increasingly like those of larger communities. In the United States today, most small towns are thus linked to the larger society. Increasingly, therefore, urbanism is "a state of mind," only loosely related to place of residence.

THE COMMUNITY AS A SYSTEM OF ROLES

Communities of every type have a role structure based on a division of labor. In traditional communities, the roles people play in the occupational system of the community and in its political, recreational, and religious life tend to be rather closely integrated with their roles in the family. Where the principal economic activity is farming, for example, the family is likely to have a distribution of roles whereby each member has not only a family role but a corresponding role in the operation of the farm. Even the young children have economic roles, such as feeding the small animals and gathering the eggs. Religious activities in traditional communities are similarly interwoven with family life, with an older member of the family usually taking the role of religious leader and teacher of the young. The integration of different roles within the family setting is less often found in the United States today than in earlier times or in other parts of the world, but some aspects of the pattern can still be observed in many small American communities.

In urban-industrial communities, by contrast, there is relatively little integration between family and community roles. Economic roles vary widely among persons of the same age,

Life in an urban community tends to be more impersonal than that in a small town. But even the largest city is a web of interdependent interaction, and near chaos can result when basic services are interrupted for a few days. Here garbage is piled high on the sidewalk in front of an automat in New York City, where a recent strike of sanitation workers created a city-wide health emergency.

sex, and general educational background, and it is relatively uncommon to find a family in which children are trained systematically to take over the economic roles of their parents. On the contrary, most children have only a vague idea of what a working parent actually does on the job. Even in a very large city, however, community roles interlock. Anyone doubting that cities are webs of interdependency need only observe the near-chaos that can result when basic services (police, transportation, fuel delivery, garbage disposal, electricity) are disrupted for even a short time.

MECHANISMS OF SOCIAL CONTROL

Informal techniques of social control are especially effective in the small community, where most people have rather similar values, attitudes, and standards of conduct. Furthermore, residents know that any misconduct is likely to become a matter of general concern among their fellow townspeople. As in larger communities, the police and the courts are authorized to use formal sanctions when necessary, but the fear of gossip and of social rejection keeps much potential deviation in check.

In the large city, where norms are less uniform, social control is somewhat more likely to require the threat and the occasional use of force. The vast majority of city residents, of course, voluntarily obey the many regulations and laws. Through interaction with family, school, and other agents of socialization, they have developed internalized controls much like those of small-town residents. And although potential wrongdoers are less subject to community pressure, they nonetheless fear rejection by their family and friends. To the extent that their reference groups support the official norms of the community, they are likely to behave in a generally approved way.

The problem of social control may be most difficult in economically deprived areas of a city. The residents of poorer areas often represent a mixture of backgrounds and have conflicting loyalties and norms. Some are cut off from the mainstream of community life not only by ethnic or racial differences but also by poverty and lack of economic opportunity. Many are transients who feel no identity with the neighborhood, its residents, or the community as a whole. Schools may be substandard, and there may be few other community associations and groups. Under these conditions there is little opportunity for people to internalize the community's system of norms, and some degree of social conflict therefore becomes almost inevitable.

SOCIAL RANKING

At the community level, the system of social ranking is based largely on occupational roles. Ordinarily, a number of roles carry the same general social rank and thus constitute a relatively homogeneous stratum. In a typical community in the United States, for example, people who work at unskilled jobs make up a single stratum of relatively low rank, regardless of their particular occupations. Those who have white-collar jobs constitute a stratum that is ranked somewhat higher, and professional people make up a still higher rank. Usually members are ranked as *families:* the husband, the wife, and the children are accorded the same general rank collectively, even if there is some basis for ranking them differently.

In Western societies, most communities rank their families according to wealth, prestige, and power. Even in a very small town, where the variation or distinction between those at the top and those at the bottom is relatively small, rank is important and residents are sensitive to those differences that do exist—differences outsiders may not notice. Such communities seem almost classless, however, in comparison to large metropolitan areas, where members of the highest and lowest socioeconomic classes have such totally different life-styles that they might well be living in different societies.

The criteria used as bases for social stratification usually are related to the community's economic structure and its system of values. In a primitive community where food must be taken from the wild, a man's social rank is likely to be based on his skill and courage as a hunter. These are qualities necessary to the community's survival and thus tend to be valued highly. In an agricultural community, the stratification system is more likely to be based upon ownership of land or livestock. As communities grow in size and their economies become more complex, the criteria by which an individual or a family are ranked become more and more varied. In a large urban-industrial community, education, income, occupational role, life-style, material possessions, and purchasing power are commonly used bases for social stratification, with occupation being probably the single most important criterion.

Few facets of organized social life have received more attention from sociologists than the complex phenomenon of social ranking at the community and societal levels. The large body of research and theory that has been accumulated will be examined in detail in Chapter 8, ''Social Stratification.''

SOCIETIES

Despite their large size, the great complexity of their organizational structures, and the indirectness of the ties between members, societies nevertheless meet our broad definition of a group as ''a number of individuals who interact recurrently according to some pattern of social organization'' (page 33). Like a community, a society is an integrative system that coordinates and binds together the great many smaller groups of which it is composed. It is the largest group with which most people can feel a sense of personal identity, and in some ways it is the most important in its effects on the life of the individual. A society is the only group, for example, that can legitimately claim the power of life and death over its members. It also plays a very significant role in determining the kinds of interaction that take place within its constituent groups and in shaping their norms, roles, sanctions, and ranking. A society, in short, can be analyzed as an enormously complex pattern of social organization that interrelates its members in patterns of mutual dependency and provides them with guidelines for all areas of social behavior.

SOCIETAL GOALS

Like many other kinds of groups, societies often have formally stated goals. The Preamble to our own Constitution, for example, states the people's intent ''to form a more perfect Union, establish Justice, insure domestic Tranquility, provide for the common defense, promote the general Welfare, and secure the Blessings of Liberty to ourselves and our Posterity." Other basic goals of our society—also important and sometimes conflicting—can be inferred from the choices we make as a nation (e.g., build nuclear warheads, go to the moon, reduce poverty, clean up the environment). A societal goal—whether military, political, economic, or social—can be achieved only if it is accepted as a legitimate goal by a majority of the society's members.

The shared values of a society's members help shape the basic social institutions through which individual and collective goals are pursued. For example, the emphasis on individual freedom and achievement in the American value system finds expression not only in the average American's search for personal satisfaction and material success but also in our form of government (representative democracy), economic system (competitive capitalism), and dominant religious orientation (Protestantism). A potential source of conflict in all societies is that, once established, patterns of social organization tend to resist change, whether or not they continue to be effective means for achieving individual and societal goals. In the long run, however, the institutions of a society must accommodate themselves to the values and expectations shared by most members, even if these change from time to time. (The importance of consensus in maintaining systems of government will be analyzed in Chapter 17, "The Political Institution.")

PATTERNS OF SOCIETAL INTERACTION

In some societies relationships between people tend to be relatively informal and intimate, regardless of the group context in which interaction takes place, while in other societies interaction tends to be more formal, ritualistic, and impersonal. Sociologists have long been concerned with analyzing such differences and with studying the changing patterns of interaction that have characterized Western societies.[29]

The Trend Toward Contractual Relationships

One of the early students of societal interaction was Sir Henry Maine, the British legal scholar whose *Ancient Law* was first published in 1861.[30] Although Maine was principally interested in tracing the development of law as an index of societal development, one aspect of his work pointed to an important change that was occurring in the interaction patterns of Western societies.

Maine noted that the "tie between man and man" (mutual obligations) had for centuries been shifting away from relationships in which individuals' rights and duties were defined by family tradition and fealty, to a new form in which individuals were increasingly free to choose the relationships they entered into. Maine called attention to the growing use of the *contract* as a vehicle for specifying obligations between persons. Although most of his writing is primarily of legal-historical interest, the changing pattern of interaction he noted has been a central focus of sociological concern.

Gemeinschaft and Gesellschaft

The industrialization of Western societies has been accompanied by a move toward increasingly impersonal forms of interaction. An early analysis of this trend was Ferdinand Tönnies' *Gemeinschaft und Gesellschaft,* first published in Germany in 1887 and still considered a classic.[31] The words *Gemeinschaft* and *Gesellschaft,* defining two quite different kinds of social relationship, do not translate easily into English. The former is sometimes translated as *community* and the latter as *society,* but Tönnies' concepts imply more than the meanings we usually attach to those words.

Essentially, the term *Gemeinschaft* implies a binding interactional relationship based on feelings of common interest and mutual trust.

29. For an analysis of cross-cultural differences see Delbert C. Miller, "Measuring Cross-National Norms," *International Journal of Comparative Sociology*, 13, Nos. 3–4 (September–December 1972): 201–216.
30. Sir Henry Maine, *Ancient Law*, 5th ed. (New York: Henry Holt Co., 1885); see especially pp. 163–165.
31. Ferdinand Tönnies, *Community and Society (Gemeinschaft und Gesellschaft)*, trans. Charles P. Loomis (East Lansing, Mich.: Michigan State University Press, 1957).

VIEWPOINTS   THE LOSS OF COMMUNITY

■ It seems to me that, though we are finding that we can adjust to a rootless style of life, we must not become a society that has learned to be rootless.

Rootlessness seems clearly to be associated with a decline in companionship, a decline in satisfying group activities, a decline in mutual trust, and a decline in psychological security. It encourages a shallowness in personal relationships and a relative indifference to community problems. It produces a loss in one's sense of personal well-being along with an increase in both personal and social malaise. And it contributes to a personal sense of powerlessness and insignificance. Whether for better or worse — and I think worse — it encourages hedonism as a life style.

Under the flag of technological progress — with its unthinking demands for giant institutions, environmental turbulence, urban sprawl, and high mobility — we have been pursuing a depersonalizing course that is dangerously radical for man as a social animal. . . .

Man needs a community; he needs continuity. Being a full-fledged card-carrying member of a community is not incompatible — as some assume — with being a free full-fledged individual. It can be, since the community functions through cooperation, consensus and regulations, but it need not be. The community, by encouraging interaction between people, can contribute greatly to the individual's sense of self-respect and can provide opportunities for self-fulfillment. Both contribute to an individual's sense of identity. . . .

We need to focus our most creative thinking on developing ways to rediscover the natural human community. And we must work out — invent if necessary — patterns of living that permit us to enjoy some sense of continuity in our lives, so that we can feel clearly that we have a place in the ongoing stream of life.

Vance Packard
A Nation of Strangers

● Today we talk about our "loss of community" in city and suburb. Often we discuss it intellectually while sipping scotch. Sometimes mystically, passing a joint. Or nostalgically over beer. . . .

A *sense* of community is what we find among the people who know us, with whom we feel safe. That rarely includes the neighbors.

It wasn't always so. For most of history man found his sense of community where he lived, with the people among whom he was born and with whom he died. For some that remains true today. But most of us in city and suburb live one place and find "community" in another. Or nowhere. . . .

It's not that we don't want more community. We do. We crave community. We lust after it. "Community" is a national obsession. But we want other things more. . . . Not getting involved with the neighbors is worth more to us than "community."

It's this confusion, this ambivalence, that confounds our quest for community. We yearn for a simpler, more communal life; we sincerely want more sense of community. But not at the sacrifice of any advantages that mass society has brought us, even ones we presumably scorn.

We didn't lose community. We bought it off. And rediscovering community isn't a matter of finding "the solution." We know how to do it. It's a question of how much we're willing to trade in. . . .

Even as we hate being unknown to each other, we crave anonymity. And rather than take paths that might lead us back together, we pursue the very things that keep us cut off from each other. There are three things we cherish in particular — mobility, privacy and convenience — which are the very sources of our lack of community. . . .

We do seek community. There's no question about it. But also we're scared of it. So we seek a safe community, one in which we needn't be fully known. We want to preserve as much as we can of our privacy, our conveniences, as well as the freedom to pick up and move on.

Ralph Keyes
We, The Lonely People

Since relationships among people in large cities are often characterized by individualism, isolation, and mutual distrust, sociologists have labelled such relationships Gesellschaft. *But even in the center of a crowded metropolis,* Gemeinschaft *relationships (like the one occurring at the left end of the bench) can be observed.*

Tönnies identified several types of social relationships as being primarily *Gemeinschaft* in character. Those who are united by kinship usually form a *Gemeinschaft,* as do those who live in a particular locality over a long period of time. People who band together because they are like-minded and wish to pursue a common goal, such as a religious brotherhood, may similarly form a *Gemeinschaft.*

The *Gemeinschaft* relationship is an intimate one, not unlike that found in primary groups. The close interpersonal ties that bind lifelong friends and neighbors in a rural village provide one familiar example. The members of the community are concerned with each other's welfare; they stand ready to lend a helping hand; they may do things for each other without thought of repayment or personal gain. The *Gemeinschaft* relationship is one of mutual trust and concern and willing cooperation for common goals. The actors feel a reciprocal and binding sentiment toward each other. The *Gemeinschaft,* in short, welds people into a "common unity"; it is in this sense that the term means *community.*

The *Gesellschaft,* on the other hand, is an interactional system characterized by *individualism* and *mutual distrust.* As Tönnies put it:

Here everybody is by himself and isolated, and there exists a condition of tension against all others. Their spheres of activity and power are sharply separated, so that everybody refuses to everyone else contacts with and admittance to his sphere, i.e., intrusions are regarded as hostile acts.[32]

In the *Gesellschaft,* interpersonal relationships are basically competitive. People struggle with each other to gain a personal advantage. There is no mutual sentiment that generates trust and reciprocal concern. A formal or informal *contract* becomes the principal instrument for defining reciprocal obligations: "For everything pleasant which someone does for someone else,

32. Ibid., p. 65.

he expects, even demands, at least an equivalent."[33] Tönnies saw the urbanization of society, even in his time, as leading to an increase in *Gesellschaft* relationships.

In reality, of course, no society is based exclusively upon the interactional model of either the *Gemeinschaft* or the *Gesellschaft:* all societies are some blend of the two. Tönnies constructed these concepts as "ideal types" — that is, as abstractions to aid in understanding basic organizational trends in Western society. (See Tools of Sociology, page 70.) He did not imply that there was a simple evolutionary development of society from a predominance of one to a predominance of the other, but he did point out that rural society is based much more on *Gemeinschaft* interaction, while urban society has a higher frequency of *Gesellschaft* relationships.

Communal and Associative Relationships

Max Weber elaborated Tönnies' theme about forty years later. In *Theory of Social and Economic Organization,* published in 1925, Weber suggested the terms *communal* and *associative* to describe two types of social relationship corresponding closely to *Gemeinschaft* and *Gesellschaft.* A social relationship of the communal type is based upon a "subjective feeling of the parties . . . that they belong together." The associative relationship, on the other hand, is "one resting upon a rational motivated adjustment of interests or a similarly motivated agreement [arranged] by mutual consent."[34] As we noted in our analysis of bureaucratic organization, this kind of interaction typifies most large formally organized groups — hence their classification as *associations.*

SOCIETAL NORMS

Societal norms determine the ways in which most groups within a society are organized and operate. They also provide individuals with guides to conduct that are above and beyond the norms of the particular groups to which they belong. Without some core norms shared by

33. Ibid., p. 78.
34. Weber, *Theory of Social and Economic Organization,* pp. 136–137.

most members of society, social life would be almost wholly unpredictable.

Most people bring to each of their groups a number of ideas about how they should play their roles in that group. For example, newlyweds begin their family life with a great many preconceptions about what the relationships should be between husband and wife, between parents and children, and between the family and the community. They share the *common core* of mutual expectations concerning the rules of conduct in the family relationship that prevails in their society. While it is true that each family group will modify these societal norms or perhaps work out private norms that pertain only to itself, family members will generally follow the institutionalized expectations of their society.

Precisely these same observations can be made of other kinds of groups. The business corporation, the peer group, the religious congregation, and the school all derive their particular systems of norms from a common core of behavioral expectations current in the society. The individual normative systems of elementary schools in the United States, for example, resemble each other to a striking degree, even though they may vary considerably from community to community and from state to state.

Folkways

Every society has a number of norms that do not specifically apply to any particular group but are institutionalized expectations about social conduct generally. Americans, for example, disapprove of the person who refuses to bathe regularly; the customary expectation is that an individual will bathe often enough to avoid smelling bad. Other general rules specify that lawns should be mowed, that belching in public is not "polite," that bathing suits should not be worn to the theater, and that slurping one's soup at a dinner party is not good form. These are not norms of a specific group, such as the PTA, the Moose lodge, or the local supermarket, but *general* norms endorsed by most members of society.

The classic statement on general societal norms is that of William Graham Sumner. In *Folkways,* published in 1906, Sumner outlined several categories of societal norms and illustrated them profusely with examples drawn from a great many societies in different historical periods.[35] A society's folkways specify modes of dress, etiquette, language usage, and other routine matters not regarded as having much moral significance. Whether, on being introduced, people shake hands, press their palms together, or bow and suck in their breath is determined by their society's folkways.

No one knows precisely how the particular practices of a given society begin or how they become institutionalized. As Sumner put it, "The operation by which the folkways are produced consists in the frequent repetition of petty acts, often by great numbers acting in concert or, at least, acting in the same way when face to face with the same need."[36] Many long-established folkways probably once had an adaptive or functional origin, but it is generally impossible to trace them back to their exact beginnings. The custom of hand-shaking, for example, may have originated as a gesture to show that the individual carried no weapon.

In societies undergoing rapid change, new folkways are constantly created and old ones abandoned. As technical innovations, such as the telephone, the automobile, and the television set, have become integral parts of modern life, each society has developed its own norms to govern their use. No one knows why Americans answer the phone with "Hello" while the British identify themselves with "Smith here," or why the Mexicans say "Bueno" (good) while the Spaniards say "Habla" (talk); but each custom serves its purpose. Like these formulas for telephone usage, many of the established folkways of a society provide convenient techniques for handling routine situations.

A basic characteristic of a folkway is that the intensity of feeling associated with it is relatively low. If individuals choose to reject folkways by dressing in an unconventional manner,

answering the telephone in a unique way, eating odd combinations of food, or displaying strange table manners, they may be regarded as eccentrics or persons to be avoided, but they will usually be allowed to go their own way. Violations of the folkways do not generally provoke strong reactions. But the very existence of alternative or competing folkways may in some cases constitute a beginning point for social conflict. In our own society, immigrants with "foreign ways" or young people who adopt nonconforming patterns may be viewed with hostility by the majority simply on the basis of their distinctive folkways, whether they deviate from society's more fundamental norms or not.

Mores

Unlike folkways, mores are associated with intense feelings of right and wrong. They define rules of conduct that are simply not to be violated. If they are, the violator is rejected by society and punished severely. In some societies the penalty for violation of particular mores is death. All the mores of a society concern acts that threaten critical values. Cannibalism, incest, and infanticide, for example, arouse almost universal feelings of disgust and condemnation among members of Western societies.

Of particular significance are mores governing sexual conduct. Since the family is such a significant group for the survival of society, it is not difficult to understand why strong norms have developed in various parts of the world to ensure its stability. Societies differ considerably in their sex codes, but whatever their particular rules, they are apt to take strong measures against individuals who deviate conspicuously from accepted practices. In our own society today, sexual mores are undergoing change and new rules are emerging (see Chapter 15, "Marriage and the Family," pages 440–469).

Folkways and mores are the two extremes on a continuum of societal norms. Folkways govern routine behavior and do not carry strong sanctions for violators; mores regulate more critical forms of behavior, and deviants are subject to severe disapproval and punishment for transgressions. Many societal norms fall somewhere

35. Sumner, *Folkways.*
36. Ibid., pp. 18–19.

Societal norms that specify general expectations for behavior in routine matters—as when two acquaintances meet on the street—are known as folkways.

between these two extremes. Public drunkenness, for example, is not such a serious transgression that offending individuals are forever banished from the company of their neighbors, yet in some segments of society such activity causes a considerable amount of gossip and a degree of social rejection. Similarly, gambling and cursing are accepted as normal in some groups but regarded as serious affronts by others.

Laws

Laws are formalized codes of conduct. For illegal acts they provide negative sanctions in the form of fixed punishments promulgated by an official body of leaders within the society. As with folkways and mores, the intensity of feeling and emotional reaction associated with the norms represented by laws varies considerably. Unlike folkways and mores, however, laws have a clear-cut origin.

Some laws concern matters of only limited public concern. Nearly every community has statutes that prohibit jaywalking and parking in certain areas, but violators of such norms are seldom sent to jail. These are regulative statutes, designed to eliminate confusion and inconvenience in routine situations. Many are simply formalized folkways. Other laws concern such serious matters as homicide, robbery, and assault. For the most part, these are adequately regulated by the mores, but experience has shown that self-applied sanctions alone are not adequate to control the behavior of all individuals.

The laws most consistently enforced are those with strong support in the mores. Others, for which an adequate basis in the mores has faded away or for which no basis ever really existed, are difficult to enforce and likely to be ineffective. The notorious failure of Prohibition is a dramatic illustration that laws not rooted in the informal norms of all the major groups in a society are largely unenforceable.

ROLES AND ROLE COMPLEXES

General Roles

Society as a whole defines a number of general roles which cut across particular groups. Such characteristics as age, sex, race, and occupation provide bases for general role patterns to which individuals are expected to conform in all their interactions with other societal members. For example, the rights, duties, and obligations associated with the role of child are much more restricted than those ascribed to the role of adult. Some societies develop fairly elaborate role patterns associated with age. In our own society, the role of child is somewhat distinct from the role of teen-ager; young adulthood entails a different set of expectations than middle age; and still different expectations are associated with old age.

Male and female roles provide another example of general roles at the societal level. Because of traditional sex-role differentiation we often unconsciously begin training boys and girls for different roles at a very early age. If little Johnny scrapes his knee and runs howling to his mother or father, he will likely be told that "big boys don't cry." If a similar accident befalls little Suzie, she will likely be cuddled and told to "go ahead and cry."

For centuries, societal roles for males and females have included not only different patterns of emotional expression but also different clusters of interests, distinctive modes of dress and adornment, distinctive speech mannerisms, and even distinctive ways of moving the body that are identified as "masculine" or "feminine." Specific expectations vary from society to society, and they also vary with the age of the individual. In American society, many aspects of sex roles are now changing rather rapidly, but numerous expectations remain that define "masculinity" and "femininity" in terms of general role behavior.

Some societies also prescribe general roles on the basis of race. In the United States, black people have until recently been expected to be subservient: a black male was supposed to doff his hat in the presence of a white person, blacks routinely went to the back door at the homes of white families, and so on. This was a general role in that *every* black was expected to behave in this manner in contacts with whites. It mattered little if the black person were more highly educated, wealthier, or more law-abiding than the white individuals with whom he or she was interacting.

The Division of Labor and Social Solidarity

The division of labor in an urban-industrial society is a tremendously complex system that coordinates not only general societal roles but also the roles developed in various specialized groups. One of the most significant analyses of this aspect of social organization is that of Émile Durkheim, who compared the role structure and division of labor in small traditional societies with that of industrial societies. His *Division of Labor in Society,* published in 1893, remains one of the most important theoretical statements concerning the society as a special type of group.[37] Durkheim's central thesis was that the division of labor in a society determines the type of *solidarity* that binds its members and welds the society into a cohesive whole.

In small agricultural societies, the division of labor is relatively simple and restricted. Every adult male plays roughly the same roles as every other adult male in the society, and he plays them in about the same way. The same thing is true of females. Largely by virtue of their role *similarities,* people tend to identify with each other and to subscribe wholeheartedly to the values and beliefs of the society as a whole. Durkheim called the type of social solidarity based upon common sentiments *mechanical solidarity,* because he considered the attraction patterns between like individuals to be somewhat analogous to the attraction patterns between similar molecules in a chemical compound.

By contrast, urban-industrial societies have an extended division of labor characterized by a high degree of *specialization.* Occupational roles, for example, become increasingly dissimilar as systems of mass production are de-

---

37. Émile Durkheim, *The Division of Labor in Society,* trans. George Simpson (New York: The Free Press, 1947).

veloped, as more and more goods of different types are produced, and as more and more specialized services are needed. Individuals find their way into these specialized roles and pursue occupations that may be totally different from those of their neighbors. More and more functions that had traditionally been the family's are taken over by outside groups. Medical facilities, school systems, government agencies, labor unions, and many other groups assume responsibility for different tasks in the society and provide additional role specialization for the individuals who participate in them.

Durkheim maintained that an extended division of labor increases the differences among people and thus eliminates the basis for mechanical solidarity. But the members of a complex industrial society are nevertheless linked to each other in one very important way: the very specialization that separates them makes them *mutually dependent.* Durkheim referred to this type of social cohesiveness as *organic solidarity,* because it is based on an interdependence of specialized functions like that in an organic system. Even in the absence of common sentiments, the members of an industrial society are effectively bound together by their need for each other's services. Indeed, the members of such societies are in many ways *more* dependent on each other than the members of simpler societies, who are economically self-sufficient to a much greater degree.

Durkheim's analysis of the social significance of the division of labor generally supports the assumption that there are tendencies toward equilibrium in society (page 48). In both traditional and industrial societies, according to this view, the lives of individuals are linked together in such a way as to ensure the stability of the group as a whole.

SOCIAL ORDER AND SOCIAL CONTROL
In a society as in other types of groups, the most effective type of social control is essentially *voluntary*—that is, most people willingly submit to the rules and regulations that society imposes on them. But there is a minority in every society that does not conform. These two facts demand sociological explanation. What produces willing conformity in some people, and what explains the conspicuous deviation of others?

Voluntary control and conformity are closely related to the kinds of training a society's members receive as children and even as adults. Through the process of *socialization* (Chapter 6), individuals internalize the attitudes, values, beliefs, and patterns of behavior supported by those with whom they associate, particularly their families, teachers, and friends. The shared definitions of right and wrong, of acceptable and unacceptable behavior, become the individual's definitions almost automatically. To the extent that such standards reflect societal norms, the person is likely to conform willingly to society's rules.

What, then, is the explanation for deviant behavior? Why does a particular individual or group fail to accept society's norms and to follow its rules? In general, sociologists search for the causes of deviant behavior through the analysis of social and cultural systems. They look to the social and social-psychological conditions that shape people's values and define their life possibilities. When individuals have different goals from those supported by societal consensus, or when they find society's goals outside their personal reach, they are unlikely to internalize society's norms or to follow its rules voluntarily. If the goals and institutions of a society are meaningless to substantial segments of the population—if the social system does not provide for their needs—voluntary social control is unlikely to check behavior that deviates from conventional norms. Sociological perspectives on deviant behavior will be discussed in detail in Chapter 7, "Deviance."

RANKING: SOCIETAL STRATIFICATION
Social stratification has been studied most often at the community level, where patterns of selective interaction between the members of different strata can most readily be observed. A community's system of social ranking, however, reflects the ranking system of the society as a whole.

The implications of stratification for determining the distribution of power, wealth, and prestige have been recognized ever since people first became concerned with the systematic study of society. Both Plato and Aristotle wrote extensively on social stratification, not only as it existed in the societies they knew but as they thought it ought to be. Aristotle, for example, distinguished three basic classes: the rich, the poor, and the middle class. But though class to Aristotle was clearly an economic concept, it had significant social and political consequences. Political stability, he said, depended on the existence of a large middle class.

Aristotle was certain that the best legislators would come from this middle class, whose members were the least likely either to shrink from rule or to be overly ambitious for it. He felt that the rich were spoiled by their wealth and would never be able to submit to authority. If allowed to rule, they would become despots. The poor, on the other hand, were too accustomed to exploitation. They were too subservient to rule, knowing only how to obey. Thus that state would be most secure which had a large middle class, with the rich and the poor on either side not too numerous. Only in this way, he maintained, could stratification be an integrative force in society.

In the eighteenth and nineteenth centuries, changes brought about by the Industrial Revolution generated new interest in this aspect of social organization, particularly in the significance of the economic system in dividing the population into classes. Industrialization gave prominence to an upper class based not upon such criteria as nobility of birth, inherited position, or ownership of land but upon the individual's relationship to the means of production and ability to accumulate wealth through business pursuits. The older social order had long been regarded as natural and just, but new political philosophies challenged the assumption that any group had a natural right to dominate others.

One of the most significant nineteenth-century theories of societal stratification was that outlined by Karl Marx (pages 214–216), who maintained that the relationship between social classes had been one of continuous exploitation of the weak by the strong. Marx linked the class struggle closely to both the political process and the economic system, proclaiming the latter to be the determining force for change. He believed that class struggle would eventually culminate in the establishment of a classless society. Marxian theory is a clear example of a social theory that attempts to account for the emergence of new social forms through conflict.

SOCIAL INSTITUTIONS

We have noted that societies are not only groups in their own right but also *integrative systems:* they bring families, bureaucratic associations, communities, and other social elements together in larger patterns or configurations. Probably the most important integrative configurations in any society are its basic *social institutions.*

Basic Social Institutions

A social institution may be defined as all the "institutionalized" social forms—organizational patterns, folkways, mores, laws, customs, traditions, shared attitudes, values, etc.—that pertain to some important goal-oriented activity within a given society.[38] For example, within every society there are a number of specific group structures with particular kinds of norms, roles, social controls, etc., that are oriented toward the task of producing and distributing goods. Taken together, these constitute the society's means of achieving its economic goals. Sociologists refer to such a configuration as the society's *economic institution.* Another configuration of elements in a society will focus upon the goal of governing. This is referred to as the *political institution.* (Obviously the term *social institution* as used by sociologists differs from everyday usages, such as referring to a prison or an orphanage as a "social institution.")

38. For representative definitions and discussions of social institutions see Lester F. Ward, *Pure Sociology* (New York: Macmillan, 1907); and Charles H. Cooley, *Social Organization* (New York: Charles Scribner's Sons, 1929).

In the United States people who have felt that established religious institutions were not meeting their needs have sometimes created communal societies. In the early nineteenth century, the Shaker sect established a number of utopian communities in which members could engage in their own mode of worship and more closely approximate the simple life of Christ. Lama, a commune in New Mexico, is one of many communities that offer today's young people freedom to experiment with new religious life-styles.

Several basic social institutions—the *economic, political, familial, educational,* and *religious*—are present in some form in all known societies, and modern industrial societies usually have many more (e.g., scientific, legal, recreational, welfare, health, military). The social institutions of a society are not always mutually exclusive categories; their elements and functions sometimes overlap (e.g., the legal institution overlaps with the political, the welfare with the economic). Nevertheless, an analysis of particular institutions provides a convenient framework for viewing the web of interrelationships by which societies accomplish their goals.

Without social institutions that effectively meet the needs of its members, a society cannot long continue as a viable social system. History provides many examples of societies that did not survive because one or more of their social institutions were inadequate to meet new challenges. The great empires of the Inca and the Aztec, for example, collapsed before a handful of Spaniards. These societies were conquered not only because the Spanish had superior military weapons and techniques, but also because they brought with them their own political and religious institutions, which proved stronger than those of the Indians. The study of social institutions is an important part of understanding the way societies survive or decline. Chapters 15 through 19 will be devoted to a detailed analysis of six key institutions with special attention to the forms they have taken in American society.

New Designs for Social Institutions

At various times in the past people have become dissatisfied with the established social institutions of existing societies and have banded together to design new ways of life. During the nineteenth century literally scores of self-sufficient societies-in-miniature were established in the United States because of this country's emphasis on freedom and local autonomy. For the most part, the participants were people who were dissatisfied with existing religious institutions in one country or another.[39] Many of these groups are no longer in existence because their social institutions did not function according to their designers' hopes. While they often achieved the religious goals they sought, these miniature societies usually foundered because of domestic, financial, or administrative problems. Other groups, such as the Quakers, Amish, and Mormons, survived very well.

Almost every conceivable form of communal living has been tried in various parts of the world, some with considerable success. The People's Republic of China organized numerous communes, with distinctive social institutions, as part of its New Social Order. In Israel, the *kibbutzim* were originally established as pioneering colonies that permitted escape from the pressures of intolerance imposed by an outside world.[40] More recently, in the United States, young people alienated from the established social institutions of their society have experimented with new ones. Some seek new forms of religious expression; some, freedom from the controls of the economic institution; others, escape from the political system; and still others, new ways for men and women to live together and raise children.[41] Communes have been set up, both in relatively isolated locations and in big cities. Such experimental societies-in-miniature continue to provide interesting sociological perspectives on the nature of social institutions.

SUMMARY

In this chapter we have differentiated among several basic types of groups in terms of their distinctive patterns of social organization—their characteristic goals, patterns of interaction,

39. Charles Nordhoff, *The Communistic Societies of the United States* (New York: Schocken Books, Inc., 1965). Originally published in 1875.

40. Muki Tsur, "Between the Kibbutz and the Havura," in *Countercultures: Israel and the United States* (New York: American Histadrut Cultural Exchange Institute, 1972), Histadrut Round Table 9, pp. 26–32.

41. Ron E. Roberts, *The New Communes: Coming Together in America* (Englewood Cliffs, N.J.: Prentice-Hall, Inc., 1971), p. 2.

norms, roles, sanctions, and systems of social ranking. Like other systems of classification in sociology, this one is intended as an aid in the orderly accumulation of knowledge about human social behavior.

Of special significance both to the individual and to the various social systems of which he or she is a part are *primary groups* such as family and peer groups. The cohesion of such groups depends less on formal organization than on the mutual bonds of affection between members, on their sense of oneness. Primary groups are of central importance in shaping the attitudes, values, and goals of individuals. They are often people's most important reference groups.

Decision-making groups, though also small, are much more formally organized than primary groups; interaction in decision-making groups is task-oriented. Sociological research has shown that the decision-making process in groups such as committees, councils, and juries typically proceeds through several stages, as the members collect information, evaluate it, reach a decision, and then dissipate the interpersonal tensions that have developed. Although interaction in such groups follows a formal pattern, an informal organizational structure usually emerges that helps give direction to the decision-making process.

Another type of formal group that has assumed increasing prominence in modern society is the large, bureaucratically organized *association*. Associations are organized around structural forms that stress the principles of rationality and efficiency. But no matter how careful the design, when people are brought in to carry out the plan, an association becomes something other than its designers intended. An informal structure develops that injects new and unofficial goals into the group and redefines channels of communication and interaction; new norms emerge, and people act out roles in creative ways. This leads to unofficial techniques of social control and social ranking. The informal structure may either support or subvert the official design; in either case, it is an integral part of the group's social organization.

Social organization at the *community* level is complex, but communities nevertheless have all the structural characteristics necessary to classify them as groups. Although there are many types of communities, differing in size, complexity, and purpose, all are integrative social systems that link together the activities of their various constituent subgroups.

The most comprehensive human group is the *society*. The components of social organization are the same in societies as in smaller groups, but they take distinctive forms. Societal norms can be identified as folkways, mores, and laws. General roles are defined in a society in terms of characteristic patterns of expectation for members of different ages and for males and females. Roles in a society are linked together in a division of labor that has significant implications for social solidarity. A restricted division of labor, such as that in an agricultural society, fosters cohesiveness based on common interests, values, and attitudes (mechanical solidarity). An extended division of labor leads to interdependency based on specialized but interlocking roles (organic solidarity).

Much classic sociological theory has been devoted to describing and analyzing societal organization and its direction of change over time. Such concepts as *Gemeinschaft* and *Gesellschaft,* and *communal* and *associative* relationships, and *mechanical* and *organic* solidarity illustrate the range of sociological formulations that have been developed to aid us in understanding how societies are organized and the effects of their organization on individual lives.

Societies bring together many constituent groups and elements of social structure into configurations oriented toward major societal goals. Among the most important of such configurations are the basic *social institutions* found in every society: economic, political, familial, educational, and religious. Urban-industrial societies have many other social institutions, such as those oriented toward legal, scientific, or military activities. The analysis of social institutions is important in helping us understand how societies function and why they sometimes decline.

4
Culture and Subculture

The previous two chapters have emphasized the significance of social organization as a sociological concept. *Culture* is a second broad concept that is essential in analyzing the ways human beings relate to one another. Social scientists use the term quite differently from most people, who associate culture with sophisticated appreciation of the arts. For the sociologist, *culture* refers to the total of all material, social, and symbolic creations that a society's members have incorporated into their overall design for living. Thus a comic book and a tin whistle are as much a part of our society's culture as are a book of poetry and a bassoon.

Culture is often referred to as the social heritage of a society. Because each generation passes on to its offspring the design for living it acquired from its forebears, individuals are relieved of the necessity of working out all over again the solutions to innumerable recurring problems. We Americans living today did not have to invent the wheel, learn to control fire or harness steam, create a spoken and a written language, discover metallurgy, devise ways for growing, harvesting, and storing food, or develop a system of laws. Earlier generations left us an elaborate cultural heritage, which we will transmit, along with many modifications and additions, to our children.

Culture may also be viewed as a people's *solutions to problems,* accumulated over time. The members of every society face a number of identical problems simply because they share certain fundamental biological characteristics. We all get uncomfortably hot or cold; techniques for cooling, warming, and sheltering the body must be provided. Food and water are necessary for individual survival; procreation and child rearing are essential for societal survival; death is inescapable.

All people share these problems, but the solutions they arrive at are astonishingly varied. The diversity of the habits of dress, architectural forms, dietary practices, family structures, and burial rites that have been devised by different peoples at different times in history is almost incredible. Nevertheless, each society's solutions "work": cultural forms that at first glance seem merely colorful or exotic generally prove upon closer analysis to be very practical solutions to particular problems. Take, for example, the problem of shelter. Working with minimal resources, Eskimos created the snug igloo. Dwellers in hot and humid rain forests on islands in the South Pacific developed a cool, airy type of shelter that withstands monsoons but permits the lightest breezes to circulate at night. The American Plains Indians found that the tepee, constructed of poles and hides, was easy to take down and set up again as the tribes followed the buffalo. It furnished shade during the scorching summers and turned aside the coldest winds of sub-zero winters. Its ventilating flaps and hole at the top let fresh air in and smoke out, while its double wall held in the fire's warmth in chilly weather.[1]

The culture of every society includes workable solutions not only to practical problems but to abstract problems as well. A people's presence on earth and relationship to the cosmos are matters for speculation, and the members of every society devise legends, myths, folk tales, religions, and philosophies to explain them. These, too, have great variety, yet each explanation more or less satisfies the society in which it develops.

Because of the extensive borrowing of cultural elements that has taken place throughout history, societies often have many cultural parallels.[2] But even when two societies have similar elements, they are likely to organize them into unique patterns or configurations. Thus we tend to think of each society as having its own distinctive culture. In addition, most societies are likely to have a number of distinctive *subcultures*—specialized patterns of norms, values, beliefs, language, and other culture traits that have been developed by people who confront similar life circumstances because of some shared attribute such as occupation, social class, or ethnic background. The study of subcultures, as we shall see, is becoming increasingly important in sociological analysis.

1. George P. Murdock, *Our Primitive Contemporaries* (New York: The Macmillan Company, 1934), pp. 268–269.
2. For a detailed discussion of cultural borrowing and cultural diffusion, see Chapter 10, "Social and Cultural Change," pages 274–303.

This painting from the Cave of Altamira in Spain is among the oldest examples of pictorial art. It tells us that prehistoric people used symbols to communicate with each other about the necessities of life—the hunt, the community, and so on. But as culture developed over time so also did the means of expression. Today our symbolic development has reached the point where an elaborate system of symbols enables us to express highly complex abstractions.

CULTURE AND SOCIAL LIFE

From the biological standpoint, human beings are little more than middle-sized, rather weak, terrestrial bipeds.[3] They lack the fangs, claws, and strength of most large carnivores, and their relatively hairless hide offers little protection from the elements or from enemies. How is it that such a poorly equipped species has been able to gain dominion over all other animal species and achieve extraordinary control over the physical environment? The answer lies in the human being's enormous learning ability as compared to that of other creatures. With the growth of this capacity, in the course of the evolutionary process, humans eventually became distinctly separate from all other animals and were able to develop languages and cultures.[4]

HUMAN EVOLUTION AND THE DEVELOPMENT OF CULTURE

The biological evolution of human beings over eons of time need not concern us here, and we will note only two of the basic steps in the development of their material culture. The first was the creation of simple tools and weapons. Once they taught themselves to make sharp edges and points on stones by striking one stone against another, they could greatly expand their food supply; increasingly they became hunters rather than the hunted. There is evidence to suggest that there was a substantial growth and spread of human population as a result, for the new technology gave humans an important advantage over competing species in the struggle for survival.[5] A second cultural spurt occurred when people mastered techniques for producing their own food. This advance led to another considerable growth of population and a great many cultural changes. In particular, the development of agriculture and animal husbandry made it possible for people to begin forming stable communities.

Even more significant to human history than the development of tools and farming techniques has been the development of language.

We do not know how language originated, but we are beginning to understand its essential place in human life.[6] Without it, the development and elaboration of culture could never have taken place. As early human beings interacted, they gradually became able to assign agreed-upon meaning to verbal *symbols*—utterances at first and, long afterward, written marks.[7] Through the use of these symbols, one individual was able to convey meaning to another, and communication as we know it began. Language has made it possible for people to share what they have learned both about things—spears, horses, shoes, transistors—and about abstractions—evil, loyalty, holiness, democracy. Through the use of symbols, people have been able to record their ideas and transmit them to others.[8]

If the manipulation of verbal symbols went no further than the everyday use of language for interpersonal communication, human culture would never have developed to its present elaborate state. Human progress has depended largely on the application of reason—on people's ability to think in consistent, orderly steps from premises to conclusions. Various formal systems of reasoning have been developed, from the syllogisms of Aristotle in ancient Greece to the most abstract modern mathematics. Today we are embarked on an era in which machines—computers—perform some of the more laborious systematic manipulations of symbols, but it is human beings who provide the sets of symbols that program the computers.

CULTURE, SOCIAL ORGANIZATION, AND SOCIETY

The concept *culture* needs to be distinguished from the concepts *social organization* and *society*. A convenient way to begin is to provide an

---

3. Ralph Linton, *The Tree of Culture* (New York: Alfred A. Knopf, Inc., 1955), p. 7.

4. Ibid., p. 8.

5. Edward S. Deevey, Jr., "The Human Population," *Scientific American*, September 1960, pp. 195–203.

6. Ibid., p. 53. See also Edward Sapir, "Communication," *Encyclopedia of the Social Sciences*, 4 (1942), p. 78.

7. Alfred R. Lindesmith and Anselm L. Strauss, *Social Psychology*, 3rd ed. (New York: Holt, Rinehart and Winston, Inc., 1968).

8. As noted in the next chapter, pages 137–138, the ability to communicate through symbols is a prerequisite not only of cultural development but also of individual development.

example of social organization without culture in a nonhuman society:

Termites, like bees and ants, are social insects living in colonies. Like bees and ants they work together, performing special tasks for the good of the colony, but, unlike them, they live together continuously, instead of interruptedly, in the nests or burrows. This colonial habit has given rise to different kinds of individuals . . . fitted structurally to perform definite functions in the life of the colony: soldiers for defense, a king and queen for reproduction, often replaced or supplemented by the supplemental reproductives; and usually . . . workers for the collection of food, the care of the king, queen, soldiers and young. . . .[9]

By stretching things a bit, we might interpret such insect phenomena within a framework of social organization, as evidenced by behavioral regularities (norms), a division of labor (specialized roles), group goals, social ranking, etc. But the termite colony operates on very different behavioral principles than those of human groups. The role specializations are genetically *built into* the individual members of the colony, and learning has little bearing on the way they carry on their collective life. We do not presume that termites and other social insects such as bees and ants have the ability to modify their own shared solutions to the problems of living in their environment; they cannot mutually adopt new ways.

Thus the social insects do not have culture in any accepted sense of the term. Although their life is *organized* in that it follows predictable patterns and *social* in that it is based on interrelated and mutually dependent forms of interaction, the colonies have no accumulated social heritage that each new generation must learn. They have social organization, but they have no culture.

In human societies, by contrast, culture provides the broad base from which particular groups derive their particular patterns of social organization. Thus the system of norms, roles, sanctions, and so forth developed by the John Smith family of Center Town, Iowa, will be in

9. Charles A. Kofoid, ed., *Termites and Termite Control* (Berkeley: University of California Press, 1934), p. 8.

The proliferation of chain stores and franchise operations has helped increase the number of cultural definitions Americans share, making it possible for people to "feel at home" in most parts of the United States

some ways unique to that specific group; but it will also reflect one part of our society's culture—namely, our shared definitions of what an American family is supposed to be like.

The same is true of other kinds of groups. If we were to visit Center Town, we would discover that we and the residents there share cultural conceptions of the nature of patterns of interaction found in a supermarket, a department store, a cocktail lounge, and hundreds of other specific kinds of groups, both formal and informal. We not only share collective definitions of the patterns of social organization that would probably be encountered in particular groups, but we can imagine—with greater or lesser accuracy—the attitudes, beliefs, and values that would characterize their members. We can even predict the nature of the material objects that would be associated with a given group, such as Center Town's bank, funeral parlor, or local Methodist church. Our shared cultural definitions, therefore, enable us to walk into a given place of business, to accept an invitation to dinner, to go to a cocktail party, or to attend a wedding—even though we are unfamiliar with the people involved—and know in advance, within limits, how behavior will proceed, what people will say, and what objects they will use. Thus, the concept *culture* is far more inclusive than *social organization*.

Culture is also conceptually distinct from *society*. We have already defined society as a relatively large number of individuals engaging in repetitive interaction according to a pattern of social organization. Culture can be thought of as the *products* of such interaction. Collectively the members of a society devise and share beliefs, symbols, codes, rituals, traditions, customs, attitudes, values, objects of art, technology, and numerous other products of human inventiveness or adaptation. Taken together, in a specific configuration, these constitute the culture of that particular society.

In a sense the distinction between society and culture is an artificial one, since a culture clearly requires a society to create and maintain it. Nevertheless, cultural phenomena can be analyzed independently of the societies with which they are associated. Thus we can compare the cultural patterns of one society with those of another in cross-cultural studies, some of which may involve different historical periods. We can examine the content and structure of a given culture and its processes of continuity and change over time. And we can reach conclusions about the functions of any item in a culture and about the degree to which it is integrated into cultural patterns.

From a societal perspective, the importance of culture is that it gives direction to and sets limits on the patterns of social organization that will be worked out within the society. A group cannot easily be formed in a society for the pursuit of goals that its culture does not tolerate; it cannot easily utilize sanctions that violate basic cultural values; it cannot easily prescribe roles that are outside cultural limits. Thus culture sets the broad limits for the development of specific patterns of social organization by particular groups within the society.

COMPARATIVE CHARACTERISTICS OF CULTURE

As one examines the life-styles found in different societies around the world, three general characteristics of culture stand out. First, cultural solutions to basic life problems are immensely *variable*. Second, the merits of given solutions are culturally *relative*—that is, their utility, morality, beauty, or propriety is evaluated in terms of how they "work" in the particular society that has adopted them. Finally, the various elements of a culture tend to be somewhat *consistent* with each other; beliefs, practices, values, etc., form a more-or-less integrated pattern. As we shall see, the tendency toward cultural consistency is more apparent in small, relatively isolated societies than it is in urban-industrial societies.

CULTURAL VARIABILITY
Endless differences exist not only in the forms of technology different people use to satisfy basic needs such as those for food and shelter, but also in their systems of courtship, family organization, kinship structures, inheritance rules, value commitments, religious concepts, health practices, political processes, and all other forms of organized social activity. Yet as we pointed out earlier, in spite of these innumerable variations, all cultures seem to "work." They provide the means by which the members of a society can cope with their environment and coordinate their lives.

Descriptive anthropologists, or ethnographers, have studied the cultural patterns of hundreds of societies in all parts of the globe, and their reports have made possible a great many cross-cultural comparisons (see Tools of Sociology on page 101). Such comparisons raise a number of questions. Why is it that some people have developed very complex forms of art, social organization, technology, and religion while others have retained simpler forms? Are there variations in inherited ability that have brought some groups to the space age while others continue to use stone implements? And to what extent are the cultures of "primitive" or "traditional" societies really less complex than those of urban-industrial societies?

TOOLS OF SOCIOLOGY
THE COMPARATIVE APPROACH

The idea of comparing groups or societies in order to study the effects of different cultural patterns and social structures is as old as sociology itself. Auguste Comte described several variations of the comparative approach as early as 1840. Émile Durkheim included three basic designs for comparative studies in *Rules of the Sociological Method* (1895); his classic work on suicide (page 9) clearly demonstrated the value of comparative research in explaining a given kind of behavior.

The comparative approach is not a specific method of research but rather employs a wide range of sociological techniques. Some comparative studies, for example, involve direct observation of the groups being compared. Others, like Durkheim's study of suicide, are based largely on an analysis of statistical and historical records. One of the richest sources of secondary data for intersocietal comparisons is the Human Relations Area Files (HRAF) developed by George Murdock and Associates. Essentially a system for accumulating and storing retrievable information on societies around the world, the files contain about eight hundred categories of information on more than four hundred different societies.

An intriguing example of a comparative study based on direct observation is David Sudnow's *Passing On: The Social Organization of Dying*. Using the research techniques of the *ethnomethodologist* (a sociologist who studies "everyday" behaviors and the meanings ordinary people attach to their routine activities), Sudnow spent fourteen months closely observing what happened in two very different modern hospital settings when a patient was perceived by medical personnel as "dying," and what happened after a death actually occurred. One of the hospitals was a large urban institution operated by the local county; most of its patients were charity cases. The other was a large private hospital with a religious affiliation serving a more affluent clientele. Sudnow observed in detail such matters as "how dead bodies are handled in hospitals, how care is given 'dying' patients, how members of deceased patients' families are informed of the death of their relatives, how the social organization of the hospital is affected by and affects the occurrence of deaths within its confines." (p. 3)

Sudnow found great differences between the two institutions, "not only with respect to the treatment of 'dying' patients, but with respect to a wide range of aspects of medical care." (p. 5) In the county hospital, the amount of effort that was made to attempt revival when "clinical death signs" were detected was rather strongly correlated with the age, social background, and perceived moral characteristics of patients. Generally speaking, people whose "social value" was judged to be low by the staff received less consideration than those with a higher "social value" before being pronounced "dead." As Sudnow puts it: "Among other categories of persons whose deaths will be more quickly adjudged, and whose 'dying' more readily noticed and used as a rationale for palliative care, are . . . those persons whose moral characters are considered reproachable." (p. 105) At the private hospital, in contrast, intensive efforts were made to revive any patient who appeared to be approaching death.

Sudnow's rather grim research also uncovered many variations between the two hospitals in such matters as relationships between medical staff and the families of patients, the methods of disposal of stillborn fetuses in different stages of development, and even in the manner in which news of death was presented to survivors. Overall, Sudnow concluded that, from a sociological point of view, the terms "dying" and "death" have meanings far beyond their clinical implications — meanings rooted in the social structures and the institutionalized cultural practices of the settings within which they occur.

In this study, the comparative approach provided the investigator with a perspective that enabled him to check the observations he made in one sociocultural setting against those he made in another. It also permitted him to discover important differences in the medical care received by terminal patients of different social origins in our society. Such findings have obvious policy implications for those concerned with improving medical care for the poor.

David Sudnow, *Passing On: The Social Organization of Dying* (Englewood Cliffs, N.J.: Prentice-Hall, Inc., 1967). A good treatment of the comparative approach is Robert M. Marsh, *Comparative Sociology* (New York: Harcourt Brace Jovanovich, Inc., 1967). See also George P. Murdock, *Outline of World Cultures*, 4th rev. ed. (New Haven, Conn.: HRAF Press, 1963).

In some cases cultural variability may be due to factors that are quite apparent. It is not surprising that the Arabic language has terms for camels of every size, age, shape, color, odor, state of health, and degree of strength[10] or that Eskimo languages have a very large number of words for snow in various forms, densities, etc. But the causes of many other cultural variations are by no means obvious. For example, why do some societies have religious beliefs that keep them in a state of terror, while others have a comfortable, comforting faith in benevolent, undemanding deities? One problem in identifying the origins of cultural forms is that preliterate peoples leave no record of the beliefs and values around which they have organized their social lives. While historians can frequently discover the reasons for particular cultural developments in literate societies by examining their literature and other written records, explanations of cultural choices by the preliterate must usually be far more tentative.

The available evidence suggests that cultural differences are not due to variations in native learning capacity. Although comparative testing is difficult, the members of all human societies appear to have about the same average level of native intelligence. Aldous Huxley argues, indeed, that human intellectual capacity has changed very little over the last twenty or thirty thousand years:

The native or genetic capacities of today's bright city child are no better than the native capacities of a bright child born into a family of Upper Paleolithic cave-dwellers. But whereas the contemporary bright baby may grow up to become almost anything—a Presbyterian engineer, for example, a piano-playing Marxist, a professor of biochemistry who is a mystical agnostic and likes to paint in watercolours—the paleolithic baby could not possibly have grown into anything except a hunter or food-gatherer, using the crudest of stone tools and thinking about his narrow world of trees and swamps in terms of some hazy system of magic.[11]

As Huxley's statement implies, some of the important variables contributing to cultural differences are the kind of *environment* within which the society exists, the kinds of *materials* available within this environment, the amount of *contact* the society has with other people from whom they can borrow ideas, and, of course, the richness of their own *cultural heritage* from the past. Some societies, because of their geographical location, are well endowed with natural resources and have been able to profit from contact with others, enriching their culture by absorbing borrowed solutions. Others, located in particularly harsh environments or in isolated parts of the world, have few resources and have been involved in little cultural cross-fertilization.

In comparing the cultural achievements of different societies, it is well to remember that "progress" is not all of one kind. Societies, like individuals, direct their energies according to their goals, which reflect their basic beliefs and values. The medieval European was guided by religious convictions that directed attention away from things of this world. The Chinese, after making remarkable progress in science and technology, became more concerned with the maintenance of tradition. The failure of some peoples to invent steam engines, electric dynamos, or penicillin may be because they lacked the appropriate background and resources, but it may also be simply because their cultural values placed no great merit on working toward such goals.

CULTURAL RELATIVITY

Societies use very different standards in making judgments and evaluations concerning truth, beauty, morality, and the "correctness" of particular patterns of behavior. The women of one society starve their way to beauty while the women of another gorge their way to the same goal. Our society finds dogs lovable; some other societies find them delicious. Muslims and Jews think it wrong to eat pork; Hindus have religious scruples against slaughtering cattle; most West-

10. Otto Klineberg, *Social Psychology*, rev. ed. (New York: Holt, Rinehart and Winston, Inc., 1954), p. 50.

11. Aldous Huxley, "Human Potentialities," in *Science and Human Affairs*, ed. R. E. Farson (Palo Alto, Calif.: Science & Behavior Books, 1965), p. 69.

ern peoples, including Americans, are repelled at the thought of eating lizards, grasshoppers, locusts, ants, and termites, although millions of other people eat them regularly.[12] Condemnation of cannibalism is by no means universal. Societies may revere youth or age, music or money, wisdom or war.

Validity of Standards

Are the many differing norms concerning morality, beauty, and truth equally valid, or is there one universal moral code, one correct logic, one ultimate criterion of truth, one true standard of beauty? This question becomes particularly perplexing when posed in the context of religion. Is there one true form of religious belief, or do all the world's religious faiths have equal validity?

Although many attempts have been made to establish universal standards of right and wrong, they have never been accepted by all people at any point in history. Human societies have been as varied in their standards of morality, esthetics, rationality, and religious conviction as they have been in such matters as hairstyles, food tastes, clothing, and bodily adornment. Standards differ greatly not only from one society to the next but also *within* a given society as it undergoes cultural change. Such change often takes place as rapidly as from one generation to the next. Early in the present century, for example, American women wore dresses that concealed them from neckline to shoe top, and the sight of a woman's calf was a strong erotic stimulus for males. Little more than a half century later, the same society was experimenting with see-through garments, see-all films, and nude theater. In between, hems had risen and fallen, and censorship, too, had had its ups and downs.

But granting all this variation both among and within cultures, is there no behavior that should be condemned no matter where and when it occurs? The sociologist would say that it is possible to speak of conduct as wrong when individuals or groups violate standards of which they are aware and to which their society has generally given approval. Thus the murder of

millions of helpless people by the Nazis was a calculated act in violation of moral principles of which Hitler and his subordinates were very much aware and to which the German people as a whole subscribed. Such forms of behavior cannot simply be dismissed as illustrations of cultural relativity. On the other hand, the killing of infants by a primitive people who have long subscribed to the practice of infanticide and regard it as morally correct within their own system must obviously be looked at differently.

Sociologists do not suggest that students try to assume some impossible kind of Olympian objectivity. They do suggest, however, that people try to learn about other cultures and try to understand the meaning of a given belief, practice, and so on from the perspective of other cultures. Thus a specific form of behavior may be seen as objectionable within one's own society but normal in another. To impose our own standards arbitrarily on societies that do not subscribe to them requires that we assume that ours is the best of all possible cultures, that ours are the most wisely developed rules for behavior, and that the ways of others are by definition inferior. Such an assumption is an example of *ethnocentrism*.

Ethnocentrism

Stated simply, ethnocentrism is the tendency of a group to regard its own ways as superior and to look down upon the ways of others. All known societies are to some degree ethnocentric, and almost all groups within a given society are ethnocentric with respect to one another. Ethnocentrism fosters a feeling of superiority on the part of the members of a group as they judge nonmembers. This attitude finds expression in the labels the group applies. To the ancient Greeks, for example, all non-Greeks were "barbarians." The ancient Hebrews believed themselves to be the "chosen people," their god to be the only god. Christian Europe viewed non-Christians as "pagans," "infidels," or "heathens," and Islam returned the compliment. A number of peoples, including some American Indian tribes, have called themselves "the People"—a supreme example of ethnocentrism.

12. Marston Bates, *Gluttons and Libertines* (New York: Random House, Inc. 1968).

Ethnocentrism carried to extremes can be ultimately self-destructive, closing the door to innovation and to peaceful interaction with other groups.

Our own language is replete with negative epithets — wops, broads, Polacks, pigs, Chinks, Japs, kikes, whiteys, greasers, niggers, honkies — that downgrade "outsiders" of one sort or another. They are all part of the language of chauvinistic ethnocentrism.

Ethnocentrism is an obvious source of tension and conflict within societies. Thus in the United States the antiblack attitudes characteristic of white ethnocentrism led eventually to the formation of the black power movement with its own strongly ethnocentric ideology. Whether ethnocentrism is seen as socially disruptive, however, is partly a matter of perspective, for while causing disharmony *between* groups, it also serves as a source of unity and stability *within* groups. By maintaining attitudes of superiority toward outsiders, a society or other group promotes its own solidarity, maintains loyalty, and builds morale. Patriotism, nationalism, and attitudes of cultural superiority serve to reinforce the norms of a people and preserve the stability of their culture and social organization. But even from the perspective of a smooth-functioning, unified group, ethnocentrism carried to extremes can be ultimately self-destructive, closing the door to innovation and to constructive interaction with others.

CULTURAL CONSISTENCY

Cultures differ significantly in the extent to which they are internally consistent in their patterns of value, belief, and behavior. If the principles to which people commit themselves while acting as family members, say, or in practicing their religion, are inconsistent with what they do and believe while engaging in economic or political behavior, we can say that their culture is poorly integrated, that it incorporates built-in strains. A fully integrated culture is one in which there are no significant contradictions between people's beliefs and their actions, or between one set of actions or beliefs and another. To illustrate differences in cultural consistency, we can compare the culture of the Zuñi, an Indian group that has lived for centuries in the Rio Grande Valley of New Mexico, with the culture of the United States as a whole.

Zuñi Culture

The Zuñi, like the Acoma, the Hopi, and several other nearby groups, are contemporary survivors of the pre-Columbian Pueblo Indians who formerly occupied northwestern New Mexico.[13] The Zuñi live in one of the most desertlike environments in the United States. Rainfall is scanty, and the summers are searingly hot. The Indians are farmers. They learned many centuries ago to grow corn, which became their basic food, as well as other minor crops. Spanish explorers found the Zuñi grouped in seven villages (which the Spaniards referred to as the Seven Cities of Cibola), but most of them are now concentrated in a single large pueblo.

The Zuñi have been well aware of their precarious dependence upon the whims of nature. In their desert environment, agriculture is a risky venture at best, but the Zuñi long ago invented ingenious techniques for growing their food under adverse conditions. In addition to planting, tending, and harvesting the corn, they have always devoted much of their lives to learning and performing the intricate ceremonies and rituals that make up an important part of their religious institution. These observances are intimately associated with the traditional agricultural techniques of their economic institution—that is, they represent attempts to control the environment by pleasing the gods and spirits that the Zuñi feel are responsible for fertility and rain. The central theme that threads through all the elaborate seasonal observances, the rain dances, and the other religious rituals is water. The activities of the priests, the succession of dances, and the sacred objects are all in some way intended to assure a sufficient supply of moisture. Much of this old culture remains intact today.

The Zuñi live an intensely social life. The physical structure of their pueblo is such that families are in close contact with each other. But though close physical proximity and scarce resources are conditions that might lead to interpersonal and interfamilial conflict, the Zuñi culture actively discourages such disruption. Individualism, emotion, and personal striving are not approved of, and conflict is kept to a minimum.

The Zuñi family institution reflects the fact that the principal social system is the village, or pueblo, itself. Marriages are rather casually arranged and are not occasions for great public ceremony.[14] Divorce is relatively simple and causes neither social upheaval nor public censure. The Zuñi have a means of preserving familial continuity and order in the face of changes in marital partnership. One of the many organizational structures that help integrate the society is the matrilineal family. It is the women who own and inherit the house, the sacred objects, the family lands, and the supplies of stored corn. The husband comes to his wife's house and lives there with her mother and her husband and the other married daughters and their husbands. This group is also the major economic unit in the production of corn. If divorce occurs, the husband returns to the home of his own mother with little more than his spare moccasins and a few of his personal religious objects. The wife arranges for a new marriage, and another male enters the household. In spite of the relative ease of divorce, however, most Zuñi marriages are enduring ones.

According to the anthropologist Ruth Benedict, in the traditional culture of the Zuñi there is no struggle for power in political affairs. Indeed, one who seeks a position of authority or leadership is strongly disapproved of; offices of any kind are avoided and will be undertaken only with great reluctance and at the insistence of others. Personal competitiveness is considered an unwholesome trait; if individuals give evidence of it, they will be discouraged by the rest.

The ideal man in Zuñi is a person of dignity and affability who has never tried to lead, and who has never called forth any comment from his neighbours. Any conflict, even though all right is on his side, is held against him. Even in contests of skill like their foot-races, if a man wins habitually he is debarred from running. They are interested in a game that a number can play with even chances, and an outstanding runner spoils the game: they will have none of him.[15]

13. Carl C. Seltzer, "Racial Prehistory in the Southwest and the Hawikuh Zuñis," *Papers of the Peabody Museum of American Archaeology and Ethnology,* 23, 1.

14. Ruth Benedict, *Patterns of Culture* (Boston: Houghton Mifflin Co., 1961), pp. 74–75.

15. Ibid., p. 99.

VIEWPOINTS THE INCONSISTENT AMERICAN

■ We [Americans] expect too much of the world. Our expectations are extravagant. . . .

When we pick up our newspapers at breakfast, we expect — we even demand — that it bring us momentous events since the night before. We turn on the car radio as we drive to work and expect "news" to have occurred since the morning newspaper went to press. Returning in the evening, we expect our house not only to shelter us, to keep us warm in winter and cool in summer, but to relax us, to dignify us, to encompass us with soft music and interesting hobbies, to be a playground, a theater, and a bar. We expect our two-week vacation to be romantic, exotic, cheap, and effortless. We expect a faraway atmosphere if we go to a nearby place; and we expect everything to be relaxing, sanitary, and Americanized if we go to a faraway place. We expect new heroes every season, a literary masterpiece every month, a dramatic spectacular every week, a rare sensation every night. We expect everybody to feel free to disagree, yet we expect everybody to be loyal, not to rock the boat or take the Fifth Amendment. . . . We expect our nation to be strong and great and vast and varied and prepared for every challenge; yet we expect our "national purpose" to be clear and simple, something that gives direction to the lives of nearly two hundred million people and yet can be bought in a paperback at the corner drugstore for a dollar.

. . . We expect the contradictory and the impossible. . . . We expect to be rich and charitable, powerful and merciful, active and reflective, kind and competitive. We expect to be inspired by mediocre appeals for "excellence," to be made literate by illiterate appeals for literacy. We expect to eat and stay thin, to be constantly on the move and ever more neighborly, to go to a "church of our choice" and yet feel its guiding power over us, to revere God and to be God.

Never have people been more the masters of their environment. Yet never has a people felt more deceived and disappointed. For never has a people expected so much more than the world could offer.

Daniel J. Boorstin
The Image: A Guide to Pseudo-Events in America

● Since you will arrive [in the United States] in September I had better give you a warning. You will see [Americans] first during a curious male festival which is very ancient and deep-seated. At that time the shops exhibit pictures of dead animals and surround them with clusters of guns and saw-edged knives. In the skirts of the woods you will find groups of young men and boys, armed with every sort of weapon from air guns to antique muzzle-loaders. The countryside resounds with a crash of boughs brought down by the fusillade. This is very exciting and male. . . .

But September is a thing apart. Americans are not like that. . . . With a gun out of his hand, the hunter becomes an amiable gas-station attendant, a student, a banker, perhaps, and just as human as you are.

For the Americans are not at all what anyone thinks who has only seen them outside their own country, or on films, or listened to propaganda about them. Sometimes [in Europe] their political image seems too like saber-rattling. At home they have none of the truculence nor the world outlook that their politicians are fashioning into an image for them. For one thing that really hurts them bitterly is the fact that they are not — or their image is not — universally loved; for they do not yet understand that power is not loved, but feared and hated. The acid of this is seeping slowly into the American consciousness.

At home they are the mildest and gentlest of people. Approach them as a stranger in their country and they will go to endless trouble to help you. . . . Out of hundreds of ordinary Americans I met from one end of the country to the other, there was not one who did not want to explain and show, to guide, advise, and help. Their principal desire, as I conceive it, is to be left, each one in his own landscape, troubling no one and being troubled by nobody. He is neither a warmonger nor a conscious exploiter. He cares far less about the world outside America than his political spokesmen would have us believe. He is friendly and parochial, not so much a man of his state, as a man of his country.

William Golding
Advice to a Nervous Visitor

Viewed as a whole, the Zuñi culture is a remarkably integrated one. Religious values and beliefs are closely tied to the economic system. Zuñi family customs aid in preserving the stability of the society and in maintaining the orderly succession of inheritance and property ownership. Zuñi attitudes toward competitiveness and rivalry limit political conflict and strain even though the people live in a physically concentrated village. What the Zuñi do, what they believe, and what they hold in high value form an integrated configuration. This does not mean that there is never any conflict or that every single aspect of their culture is closely and perfectly linked with every other one. But compared with most other societies, the Zuñi have developed a very harmonious culture.

American Culture

In our society cultural orientations often are the source of much conflict. Changes in these orientations disrupt families, making it difficult for parents to understand their children and for children to listen to their parents. Our society is split by conflict between groups with conflicting ideologies and interests: management and labor, haves and have-nots, whites and nonwhites, Protestants and Catholics, Christians and Jews, producers and consumers, liberals and conservatives, federal, state, and local political bureaucracies—the list is almost endless.

Americans lack the long history of continual cultural evolution in a single locality that has permitted the Zuñi and many Asian, African, and European peoples to develop unified sets of traditions, customs, and values. American society has been formed within a relatively short period by immigrants from many different homelands who brought with them a great diversity of attitudes and practices. Nor do Americans live under a single set of environmental conditions. Differences in climate, terrain, and natural resources have led to different economic

activities in the Northeast, the South, the Midwest, the Southwest, and the Far West. And the different ways of life in these areas have helped develop differences in beliefs and philosophies.

For all this diversity, however, American culture has its mainstream, and a major element in that mainstream is the conviction that every individual should struggle to rise in the status system, to "get ahead," to succeed. As a result, the acquisition of material goods, economic independence, and symbols of prestige is a goal that we as a people hold very high.[16] This emphasis on individual material success has been attributed to the Puritan heritage, the capitalist ethic, and the frontier spirit, which are sometimes combined under a single label like the "Protestant Ethic" or the "work ethic." In any case, the drive to succeed is bound to be a source of conflict, since it involves competition: getting ahead means getting ahead of someone else.

Conflict and competition, then, characterize American society as both individuals and groups strive to achieve a greater share of the available rewards. While our expanded division of labor increases the functional dependency of one occupational group upon the next and thus is a source of unity, it also tends to produce feelings of "we" versus "they" as the various groups seek their goals. Psychological unity among Americans is further weakened by the class structure, with some people enjoying material abundance while others are in greater or lesser degree deprived, sometimes to the point of destitution. Economic inequality is less marked in the United States than in many other societies, but it is nevertheless a significant cause of disharmony, partly because of our culture's emphasis on the importance of success and increased consumption for all.

Religious disunity has also weakened cultural integration. The various major religions practiced in the United States did not grow out of attempts to cope with the native environment in any immediate sense, as did the religion of the Zuñi, but in most cases were brought here

16. Richard Weiss, *The American Myth of Success* (New York: Basic Books, Inc., 1969). The author points out that the Puritan divines who offered guidance to colonial New Englanders always treated material success "in the context of a larger framework of values." But in the Puritan heritage these other values are not always visible.

A major element in the mainstream of American culture is the drive to succeed—that is, to acquire material goods, economic independence, and symbols of prestige.

from the Old World. Nor is religion in our culture closely integrated with other areas of life, as it is in the culture of the Zuñi. Divided into many competing churches, denominations, and sects, religion in America has often been a focus of division.

Although the fundamental teachings of all our major faiths stress much the same values, religious ideals are largely ignored in the competitive struggle of everyday life. The same is true of our political ideals. From our early years we are taught that all people are God's children and that we should love our neighbors as ourselves. In school, from the lowest grades, we pledge allegiance to a nation based on the principle that all people are created equal and offering liberty and justice to all. We profess belief in these great ideals. Yet we regularly deny opportunity to some members of our society on the basis of skin color and sex; we discriminate

among our fellow citizens on the basis of regional or foreign accent, place of birth, education, occupation, and income; and we rank all foreigners as more or less inferior, depending upon how much their ways differ from ours. This practice of flouting the very ideals and values that we proclaim to be the basis of our democracy and that are fundamental to the teachings of our religious faiths involves serious cultural contradictions, stressful for the individual as well as for the society.[17]

It should be noted, however, that even though American culture embodies many sources of conflict, the result is not chaos. For the most part the struggles that take place in our society follow the established "rules of the

17. Gunnar Myrdal, *An American Dilemma: The Negro Problem and American Democracy*, rev. ed. (New York: Harper & Row, Inc., 1962).

game." If conflict exceeds acceptable bounds, the society invokes both formal and informal mechanisms of control. Internal conflicts usually are tolerated only if they occur within the limits of an established cultural framework.

Even so, our culture (like the cultures of most other rapidly changing industrial societies) is much less consistent than that of the Zuñi. This does not mean that one culture is "good" and the other "bad," nor does it mean that one will endure and the other will decline. History makes it clear that societies can function adequately without a high degree of cultural integration. Indeed, as we have noted, there are social theorists who argue that conflict can be a creative force that stimulates change.[18] Without making value judgments, then, we can say only that the Zuñi and American cultures are very different. We have our configuration, often characterized by conflict; the Zuñi have theirs, usually characterized by harmony. For many of us, life among the Zuñi might be downright boring. For them, life in the general American society might be a nightmare.

THE CONTENT AND STRUCTURE OF CULTURE

Over the years social scientists have developed a number of theoretical tools to aid them in the study of culture. In general, they use either one of two broad strategies. The *analytic* approach focuses on small units of culture; the *synthetic,* on broad cultural patterns.

Much of what we know about culture represents the work of anthropologists, who until recently have directed their efforts primarily to the study of preliterate societies. Thus their research has paralleled and complemented that of sociologists, whose interests have focused for the most part on urban, industrial societies. These two fields now share a large number of perspectives that together have proved useful in interpreting, classifying, and comparing cultures.

18. Lewis A. Coser, *The Functions of Social Conflict* (New York: The Free Press, 1956), p. 153.

THE ANALYTIC STUDY OF CULTURE

The *analytic* approach to the study of culture seeks to identify, describe, and classify individual culture *traits*—the smallest meaningful units of cultural content. For example, the bow and arrow is often cited as an example of a culture trait. One may note immediately that this weapon involves a combination of several parts: the arrow shaft, the arrowhead, the fletching or feathers, the bow itself, and the bowstring. Physically, the apparatus can readily be reduced to these separate parts. Behaviorally, however, it cannot. Only when the parts are assembled as a unit do they provide a workable cultural solution to the problem of killing game at a distance. Our electronic computers, automobiles, and atomic bombs represent solutions to problems that other societies solve with such units as the abacus, the horse, and the war club; and in the sense that they would be behaviorally meaningless if disassembled into a heap of unconnected parts, each is a trait—an elementary unit of our fantastically complex mechanical culture.

Culture traits are by no means limited to weapons and machines. A specific hairstyle can be a trait. So can a type of dance, a particular superstition, or a given attitude toward marrying one's cousin. The entire culture of a society is made up of traits, which fall into different categories. Mechanical objects such as fish spears, guns, and movie cameras might form one class, for example, and nonmaterial traits such as folk tales, puberty rites, beliefs, and values might form another. There is no standard system for classifying culture traits, but most social scientists recognize the usefulness of the general categories described below.

Material Culture

The material traits in a culture include all the artifacts a society makes and uses: weapons of war, articles of clothing, agricultural implements, jewelry, industrial machines, household furnishings, transportation devices, and scientific apparatus. Some social scientists would also include the various techniques required to use the physical objects, on the theory that the technology of a society comprises not only its devices but the skill patterns and lore that their human users must have in order to apply them to the solution of problems.

Regulative Culture

The regulative traits of a society make up a major category of its nonmaterial culture. They include all the institutionalized expectations the members of the society follow in their dealings with each other, such as the assumption by restaurant operators that customers will pay for their food. The society's folkways, mores, and laws are included in this category, together with institutionalized role patterns common in the society and any other rules of conduct that serve to make interaction more predictable.

It is at this point that the concepts of culture and social organization most closely parallel each other. Norms, roles, and other institutionalized expectations are given specific direction, limitation, and definition by culture. They also constitute the basis for the organization of behavior within the society. Thus the regulative category of culture traits holds special significance for sociologists. In searching for the causes of some particular form of behavior in a group, whether crime, divorce, combat effectiveness, suicide, or acceptance of innovation, it is to the regulative culture—that is, to the basis of social organization—that they often turn first for clues.

Symbolic Culture

A third broad category of culture traits is made up of the language practices and other symbols used in a society plus all the shared understandings made possible by a people's ability to communicate. Obviously this is an enormously complex and inclusive category of traits, since language plays some part in virtually every aspect of culture. It is clearly paramount, however, in developing beliefs about the nature of reality—scientific and philosophical theories, religious concepts, political beliefs, myths and legends. Other cultural forms heavily dependent on the use of symbols are literature, music, and the various visual arts.

Evaluative Culture

A fourth major category of culture traits is made up of the values and other deep-seated sentiments the members of a society share—a people's emotionally held orientations of approval-disapproval. These basic sentiments determine what a society interprets as sacred or sordid, as meritorious or monstrous, as honorable or heinous. They determine its goals and its ideals. In some ways this aspect of nonmaterial culture is the most difficult category of all to separate clearly from the others: the values people hold are closely linked to their beliefs about the nature of reality and also to their cultural norms. But for purposes of cultural analysis it is often convenient to make a distinction between values and other aspects of culture. The identification of the basic values and sentiments held by a group can provide considerable insight into the reasons for their behavior.

SYNTHESIZING CULTURAL CONFIGURATIONS

The classification of traits into rough categories sheds light on the structure of culture and also provides a tool for studying specific traits. But in reality, the categories are closely intertwined. In American culture the automobile may be classified as a material trait, but it also represents a whole way of life. Similarly, any one of the mores of our society is not only a regulative rule prohibiting some act such as murder or incest but also a set of beliefs and sentiments defining that act's importance and its moral significance. The study of individual traits, then, must be supplemented by the study of *cultural configurations*—patterns of interrelated traits that together account for some broad pattern of behavior. Among the patterns that have been identified through the synthetic approach are the cultural complex, the cultural ethic, and the cultural ethos.

Cultural Complexes

A cultural complex is a cluster of related traits around which people organize some aspect of their lives. A good example from a primitive society is the hunting-fishing complex of the traditional polar Eskimo. This complex includes a number of material traits: the kayak, the harpoon and various other fishing devices, specialized clothing, and other artifacts. It also includes a considerable body of technical lore. There are norms differentiating the roles of men and women and other norms governing the types of animals to be hunted at various times. The tales, legends, and myths about hunting and animals that abound in this culture are a part of the complex. Values and sentiments are also included: some types of animals are sacred; others are highly prized as food or for other uses. Various religious concepts, technical skills, material objects, and sets of beliefs, then, form an identifiable and meaningful configuration within the culture, and this complex constitutes a major component of its overall structure.[19]

In our own society we organize our lives around a great number of culture complexes. From the standpoint of the culture as a whole, for example, basketball is a configuration including backboards, nets, balls, whistles, uniforms, a court, seats for spectators, and a host of other material objects. The norms surrounding it include standards of appropriate dress for players, officials, and members of the audience. Rules of conduct define the roles of each member of the team, the general manner in which the game is played, appropriate behavior by spectators, recruitment of players by management, and much more. Stories of earlier teams, outstanding coaches, and memorable games are retold. The basketball traditions of high schools and colleges and their records of wins and losses are recounted. Details of the lives and past performances of star players are discussed avidly by the fans. Values are also prominent. The supporters of a team place high importance on victory. Spectators often travel hundreds of miles at considerable inconvenience and expense to watch their favorites play. There are general values pertaining to the presumed sportsmanship of players and character-building virtues of the game. A similar summary could be made for every other spectator sport in American society.

Illustrations of such complexes can be drawn from many areas of culture. Concerning relationships between the sexes, Emilio Willems has described a set of complexes that help structure upper- and middle-class culture in Brazil:

The female role is centered around a cluster of values which may be characterized as virginity complex. The belief that the virginity of unmarried females ought to be preserved at any cost has so far tenaciously resisted change. Such institutional arrangements as segregation of the sexes, chaperonage and family-controlled courtship, which are to be regarded as component traits of the virginity complex, have undergone so many changes, at least in the larger cities of Brazil, that the original pattern is hardly recognizable. However, under the somewhat deceiving appearance of changing intersexual relationships and vanishing family controls, the old rule that females should abstain from premarital sexual experiences has been rigidly maintained. Carefully conducted interviews carried out over a period of nearly twelve years showed that even the most liberal-minded men were apt to become suddenly intransigent if asked how they envisaged the prospect of marrying somebody with premarital sexual experience. Most men feel they would make fools of themselves if they married a girl who had been deflowered by somebody else.

The male role is centered around a set of values which may properly be called virility complex. A young Brazilian is expected to get actively interested in sex at the age of puberty. Even before puberty the average boy becomes used to the sexual bravado of older companions. He learns that regular sexual intercourse is not only believed to be physically healthy, but above all an essential attribute of manhood. There is a generally accepted opinion that early and frequent sexual intercourse is stimulated by peculiar racial qualities and the physiological effects of a tropical climate. This point of view, which is presumed to be scientific, entitles men to feel irresponsible in sex affairs. Marriage is not expected to channelize or to restrict his sexual activities. Normally a male feels free to have intercourse with as many different women as may be available.[20]

Cultural Ethic
Broadly speaking, certain values, regulative traits, goal orientations, and moral definitions cluster together to define people's shared orientations toward some significant activity. Thus sociologists and others sometimes use such terms as "work ethic," "Puritan ethic," and

19. Murdock, *Our Primitive Contemporaries*, pp. 192–220.
20. Emilio Willems, "The Structure of the Brazilian Family," *Social Forces* 31, No. 4 (August 1953): 340–341.

"frontier ethic." The classic study of such configurations is that of Max Weber, who effectively synthesized two such major cultural trait clusters in *The Protestant Ethic and the Spirit of Capitalism* (page 282).[24] Based on an ambitious comparative study of religious and economic institutions in both Western and non-Western societies, this classic work advanced the thesis that capitalism developed in western Europe as an outgrowth of Puritanism. Weber abstracted the value orientations associated with Calvinism — individualism, hard work, frugality, rationality — and showed how they were readily translated into economic activity. Thus the configuration of attitudes and values associated with a new religious orientation became the guiding spirit behind the growth of entrepreneurial capitalism. The Puritan ethic continues as a basic orientation in most Western cultures today, though it has long since lost most of its religious meaning.

Cultural Ethos

In another classic work, first published at the turn of the century, William Graham Sumner revived the ancient Greek term *ethos* to mean "the sum of the characteristic usages, ideas, standards and codes by which a group was differentiated and *individualized in character* from other groups." Thus the ethos of a society is a synthesis of the guiding beliefs that give the people of that society a distinctive makeup.[22] While difficult to measure and define, this attribute of a people is not difficult to note through observation. The general character of Mexican culture or German culture stands in clear contrast to the culture prevailing in the United States.

Formulations of this type are necessarily imprecise, and most efforts to abstract and synthesize the configurations distinguishing particular cultures have been highly controversial.[23] But despite their limitations, such constructs can provide the sociologist with new insights into why a society's members tend to behave as they do. In general, the synthesis of trait configurations permits a more meaningful description of a culture than an analysis of individual traits out of context.

SUBCULTURES

Distinctive patterns of traits and cultural configurations that characterize a particular group, type of group, or subsegment of a society are called *subcultures*. Some societies produce many differentiated subcultures while others do not. The organizational characteristic most closely related to subcultural diversity in a society is its degree of social differentiation.

The populations of small, traditional societies are not highly differentiated. There are, of course, differences among the members of such societies in age, sex, and social rank, but typically all families will be farmers, hunter-gatherers, tenders of livestock, or more or less uniformly engaged in some other pursuit that constitutes their chief means of livelihood. Thus there are few problems for one family that are not shared by all families, and the techniques by which problems are handled will normally be part of the general culture of the society. Under such circumstances, most of the people share the same level of material life and the same basic values, beliefs, folkways, mores, and so on. There are few bases for the development of cultural differences that set off one group or segment of the society from others.

Modern urban-industrial societies, by contrast, tend to have a high degree of social differentiation. Their occupational structures are extremely complicated; they are likely to be highly stratified; they often show much regional variation in folkways and mores; their populations may include people from diverse racial, religious, and ethnic backgrounds. These and other kinds of social differentiations serve as the bases for the development of *subcultures*.

21. Max Weber, *The Protestant Ethic and the Spirit of Capitalism,* trans. Talcott Parsons (London: George Allen and Unwin, Ltd., 1930); originally published in 1920.

22. William Graham Sumner, *Folkways* (New York: The New American Library, Inc., 1960), p. 48; originally published in 1906.

23. For a controversial analysis of the general value orientations in American society, see Robin M. Williams, Jr., *American Society: A Sociological Interpretation,* 2nd ed. (New York: Alfred A. Knopf, Inc., 1960).

While people in every social category share the general culture to some degree, it is their particular subcultures that enable them to cope with their unique life situations. For example, young people entering college face new experiences and new problems that they are not fully prepared to handle. However, they soon become oriented to a student subculture that provides them with the perspectives and know-how they need for dealing with their new situation.[24] It is in this sense that subcultures are "problem solving."

Like more general cultures, subcultures have both content and structure. They include the several categories of traits we have previously mentioned—material, regulative, symbolic, and evaluative—and these traits are integrated into distinctive patterns that people experience as a *unit,* as a total way of life. For example, a child of immigrant parents growing up in a poor ethnic neighborhood feels the impact of the local subculture as a configuration. As Milton Gordon puts it, such a child

is not a person who is simultaneously affected by separable items consisting of ethnic background, low economic status, and a highly urbanized residential situation. He is a person whose environmental background is an interwoven and variegated combination of all these factors. Each of the elements has been somewhat transformed by virtue of its combination with the others.[25]

The concept of subculture has become increasingly important in sociology in recent years as researchers have sought to understand how people in various positions in the complex social structure have invented ways of dealing with the special problems that confront them.[26] In the section that follows we will examine in detail an American subculture with which few people are familiar, that of the carnival. Then we will briefly consider some of the more common types of subcultures in American society.

THE CARNIVAL AS A WAY OF LIFE

The American carnival is a distinctive physical and social world. Unlike the circus, which is largely a theaterlike display of animal and human performers, the carnival is a collection of rides, games, shows, exhibits, refreshment concessions, and gambling devices. While the circus appeals to a passive audience that assembles to view its attractions, the carnival seeks to involve the customer as an active participant in its various kinds of concessions.

The American carnival appears to have emerged from the World's Columbian Exposition in Chicago in 1893.[27] The exposition was being poorly attended and the concessionaires wanted to pique public interest. They induced a prominent local clergyman to denounce a suggestive dance being performed on the midway. Attendance figures began to soar as people flocked to see the controversial "Little Egypt" and stayed for further entertainment. Having become financially successful, the assembled concessions moved on to other communities. The idea of a traveling conglomeration of games, rides, exhibits, gambling devices, and shows caught on. The American carnival became a part of our cultural heritage.

For those who pursue it as a vocation, the carnival is a total way of life. It is effectively separated from the more general society because carnival people have developed a specialized subculture that creates a "consciousness of kind," identifies members of the "in-group," and meets their special needs. "The carnival is a unique and fascinating subculture. It is also a complex work organization, a significant part of the country's outdoor amusement industry, a multi-million dollar business, and a rich segment of America's past and present culture. . . ."[28]

24. Burton R. Clark and Martin Trow, "The Organizational Context," in *College Peer Groups: Problems and Prospects for Research,* Theodore Newcomb and Everett Wilson, eds. (Chicago: Aldine Publishing Co., 1966), pp. 17–70.

25. Milton M. Gordon, "The Concept of Sub-Culture and Its Application," *Social Forces,* 26 (October 1947): 41.

26. Ibid., pp. 40–44. See also Albert K. Cohen, "A General Theory of Subcultures," in *Delinquent Boys* (Beverly Hills: Glencoe Press, 1955), pp. 50–52; and David O. Arnold, *The Sociology of Subcultures* (Berkeley: The Glendessary Press, 1970).

27. Billboard Publications 75th Anniversary Issue of *Amusement Business,* 81 (December 31, 1969).

28. Theodore M. Dembroski, "Hanky Panks and Group Games versus Alibis and Flats: The Legitimate and Illegitimate of the Carnival's Front End," *Journal of Popular Culture,* 4, No. 3 (Spring 1973): 567.

The American carnival is composed of shows, rides, games, exhibits, gambling devices, and refeshment stands, which are arranged along the "midway." The carnival has its own system of ranking: the owners of shows and rides are ranked higher than the freaks and other performers, and those who are hired to operate the rides are near the bottom of the social ladder. The customers are called "marks" and constitute an out-group allowed to watch—but not mingle with—the "carnies."

Two contemporary social scientists—Marcello Truzzi and Patrick C. Easto—were carnival people before they entered academic life. In the following sections, we draw upon their fascinating analyses of the subculture of the carnival.[29] We will look briefly at the carnival as a physical entity, review selective aspects of the carnival's social organization, particularly in terms of its ranking system and some of its major roles, and, finally, examine some of the ways in which specialized values and communications patterns separate carnival people from the outside world.

Punk Rides and Hanky-Panks: Physical Characteristics

Carnivals range in size and sophistication from small, poorly equipped "rag bags" and "forty-milers" (so named because of the usual distance from one stopover to the next) to huge shows with hundreds of members who move great distances on fleets of special trucks and flatcars. In terms of physical plan the carnival consists of a horseshoe-shaped "midway," along which are arranged a variety of rides, games, shows, exhibits, refreshment concessions, and gambling booths. About 50 percent of the concessions in the "line-up" (outer perimeter of the midway) are games of skill or chance called *hanky-panks*. These require the "mark" (customer) to knock over iron milk bottles with a baseball, burst balloons with darts, or perform some other difficult, but not impossible, task in order to win one of the prizes on the "flash" (display of merchandise). Most prizes are very cheap items called "slum" by those who operate the concessions. Naturally, slum predominates when every player is a "winner"—as in hanky-panks like "pitch-till-you-win" and the "duck-pond." In the duck-pond, the mark pays to select a toy duck from the flock that perpetually moves around an elongated tank. A number on the bottom of each duck corresponds to the number on a prize exhibited on the flash. The mark usually wins a small trinket. Occasionally, the mark wins a "piece of plush" (a stuffed animal) or some other attractive prize. Such games are popular with children.

Located between the line-up and the rides are *center joints* and *group games*. Together with the hanky-panks, these make up from 70 to 80 percent of the games along the midway. A typical center joint is the "bear pitch," in which the mark pitches coins into dishes. With skill and luck the player can win a teddy bear. In group games several marks can play simultaneously. For example, in the "rat game" the players bet on which of several holes a rat will choose to run through when released. Since the average take from a group of marks exceeds the value of the prize, these games are seldom "gaffed" (rigged against the mark).

Flat stores are gambling devices that permit wagering on the outcome of turning a "wheel of fortune," spinning an arrow, dumping marbles on a perforated board, or throwing hoops over an array of clothespins. In the past, these were often gaffed and marks could lose heavily.

The financial success of a given game is largely dependent upon the skill of the operator in attracting the attention of marks, persuading them to "spring" (play), and getting them successively more and more involved. Elaborate verbal techniques are used to keep marks enthusiastic. Often they are allowed to win so they will continue playing.

The number of gaffed joints appears to be on the decline; many modern carnivals are mainly "Sunday-school shows" (completely legitimate). Gaffed joints are more typical of "rag bags."

Every carnival includes a number of *punk rides*—the familiar merry-go-round, Ferris wheel, tilt-a-whirl, boats, miniature trains, and other mechanical conveyances that appeal to children. Normally, they are aligned down the middle of the midway. Also present are freak shows, animal exhibits, girl shows, refreshment stands, and straight sale concessions.

Carnival people refer to the "front end" and the "back end" of the midway. This is in part a physical description, but it has status overtones as well. Those whose concessions are located

29. See *Circuses, Carnivals and Fairs*, Marcello Truzzi, ed., special issue of the *Journal of Popular Culture*, 4, No. 3 (Spring 1973). The present section is based upon articles presented in this special issue.

on the "front end" often feel superior to those located at the back. Concessions that have joined the show more recently are usually assigned to the back end until they have shown their worth and have been with the carnival for a period of time.

Social Organization

At the top of the carnival's ranking structure are the owner of the show, who is unquestionably in the highest position, and the administrative staff. Typical of the latter are the "lot man," the "ride superintendent," and the "patch." The lot man's task is to go ahead of the carnival and assign locations for each of its various attractions. This is a difficult role that requires an intimate knowledge of the space requirements of every ride, show, and concession. Competition for favorable locations along the midway is keen, and elaborate norms are used in deciding what should be where. In some cases, it is necessary to "grease" (bribe) the lot man to obtain a good spot. Mainly, however, the choice spots are rotated on an equitable basis.

The ride superintendent is responsible for the mechanical operation of the rolling stock and the rides. The machinery is often complicated and sometimes antiquated; keeping the rides working properly and the trucks, trailers, and other vehicles in good order requires a high level of skill. If a ride breaks down, the ride superintendent is expected to get it back into operation as quickly as possible.

The special responsibility of the "patch" is solving problems with people. In particular, he is expected to handle all complaints or other difficulties that relate to strained relations between the carnival and the community in which it is operating. His services are essential, for example, when a mark concludes that he has been cheated by a gambling concession:

Cooling the mark out, especially after a big score, is often difficult to accomplish. The mark may take the heat and threaten physical and legal retaliation in an effort to secure the return of his money. If the agent

30. Dembroski, "Hanky Panks and Group Games," p. 581.

[of the concession] cannot cool the mark out, . . . the patch . . . is called in. In addition to his many other duties such as bribing or fixing legal authorities, the patch deals with exceptionally disgruntled marks. He is likely to cool the mark out by refunding all or part of his losses and/or giving him some merchandise, or he might "bull" the mark (e.g., advise him that he, as well as the agent, is guilty of breaking the law since both were gambling). The patch is usually quite proficient at appraising the mark and the situation and employing appropriate tactics to cope with the problem.[30]

The next level in the ranking system is occupied by the owners of rides, shows, and concessions that contract to join the carnival. Few owners of carnivals also own all the attractions. Instead these are often family owned and operated businesses that sign up for a given season, paying either a flat rate or a percentage of their gross. When concessionaires own and operate a "string of joints," their status varies with the number of attractions they own.

Performers occupy a position slightly lower in status than that of the owners of independent concessions. They include the girls who perform in strip shows, the freaks, illusion specialists, and the like. There are numerous gradations of ranking among the people in this stratum, as in the others. Freaks are not universally looked down upon. While seldom envied, they are accepted as persons. In fact, marriages between freaks and normal persons are fairly common (although some carnival people do not approve of such marriages).

Near the bottom of the social ladder are the employees who help operate rides, hanky-panks, flat stores, and other components of the carnival. The lowest level in the ranking structure is assigned to blacks and gypsies. Gypsies are tolerated because they often operate "mitt camps" (fortune-telling concessions) that are a traditional part of the carnival. However, they are by no means treated as social equals:

Gypsies represent a special problem for the carnival. Their identification is primarily with the gypsy world rather than with the carnival subculture. Whereas carnival people feel great loyalty and a sense of honor towards one another, gypsies see non-

gypsy carnival workers as outsiders, too. Thus it is not at all uncommon to see carnival advertisements for personnel saying "no rag-heads" (gypsies).[31]

While clear differences in status exist within the carnival world, "carnies" regard themselves as a special "in-group." They maintain sharp boundaries between themselves and the people of the towns in which they stop. Marks are not allowed to visit the areas off the general midway. Carnival children are discouraged from interacting with local youngsters. Unmarried women from the carnival are expected to have nothing to do with males from town. The maintenance of social distance between carnies and "others" sometimes takes curious forms. For example, because some of the women in the girl shows usually are the wives of carnival men, it is a norm that men from the carnival are not allowed to see the performances. The attitude is that it is all right for the marks to ogle the bodies of the women—the marks, after all, are just "suckers"—but that it is quite a different matter for other carnival men to ogle one's wife. Thus marks are defined as lesser human beings, and the boundaries between the carnival social system and the larger community are maintained.

Argot and Cant: Specialized Communications

A significant part of the carnival subculture, and one that separates it rather sharply from the American culture in general, is its *argot,* its specialized vocabulary and idiom. We have already introduced a number of terms from carnival argot—"mark," "hanky-pank," "patch," "mitt-camp," "rag-head," "gaff"—and there are hundreds more. Easto and Truzzi examined almost two hundred terms that had been listed as carnival argot by another social scientist in 1931; some forty years later the majority were still in use.[32] A number of terms that apparently originated in the carnival have entered the common slang of the general culture (e.g., the term "G," meaning a thousand dollars, was in use by New York carnival pitchmen as early as 1906).[33]

Carnival people have also developed their own *cant*—a manner of speech that is virtually unintelligible to anyone but members of the in-group. The cant used by carnival people, Z-Latin, is created by inserting additional sounds in ordinary words; the result superficially resembles the pig latin of childhood. Here are some common words and their Z-Latin modifications:[34]

The	thee-a-zuh
Cat	kee-a-zat
Would	wee-a-zood
Like	lee-a-zike
Name	nee-a-zame

When carnies mix their argot and their Z-Latin, the result is an in-group language that effectively shuts out any listening mark.

While the carnival subculture is more distinctive and exotic than many, all subcultures have the same general features, including a specialized technology and distinctive values, communication patterns, beliefs, and attitudes.

MAJOR TYPES OF SUBCULTURES

In a complex society like ours, there are countless subcultures organized around specific interests and needs. Teen-agers, college students, and military personnel all support subcultures. So do the devotees of camping, photography, horse racing, dog breeding, sailing, and hot rodding. We can even speak of a male subculture and a female subculture insofar as distinctive norms, attitudes, interests, activities, clothing styles, language, and material possessions are associated with each of the sexes.

To some extent, every specific group has elements of a subculture. A local school, department store, or Elk's Lodge may have unique regulations, argot, and so on. However, a given subculture may be shared by numerous specific groups. For example, Bruce D. Johnson has noted that drug subcultures developed by groups in various locations and regions are remarkably

---

31. Patrick C. Easto and Marcello Truzzi, "Towards an Ethnography of the Carnival Social System," *Journal of Popular Culture,* 4, No. 3 (Spring 1973): 556.

32. Ibid., p. 561.

33. Jack Dadswell, *Hey There Sucker* (Boston: Bruce Humphries, 1946).

34. Easto and Truzzi, "Towards an Ethnography of the Carnival," p. 563.

similar, even though there may be no contact whatever between their members:

If for some strange reason a midwestern high school student who [regularly] smokes marijuana found himself with a Harlem street-corner group in which a "joint" was being passed around, the student would know what to do without being told. He could recognize the joint as a marijuana cigarette, realize that he is expected to smoke it, know how to inhale, recognize the effects, comment on the quality of the drug, and espouse beliefs that would be familiar to the blacks.[35]

Several major types of subcultures in American society have been extensively studied by sociologists and are particularly important for understanding American life. Since many will be illustrated in more detail in later chapters, we need only mention them at this point.

Ethnicity

Because of the relatively recent pattern of immigration from other countries, American society incorporates people of many cultural backgrounds. Incoming segments of the population have perpetuated elements of their parent cultures that have not been uniformly adopted by the majority. Specialized foods, forms of worship, orientations toward the family, in-group sentiments, language forms, and value differences tend to differentiate one ethnic subculture from another.

Race

Because of historical circumstances, American society has brought together various nonwhite people—not only those with origins in Africa and Asia but Native Americans who had established their own cultures here long before Europeans arrived. Insofar as each racial minority has had unique problems and experiences, each has developed its own ways of dealing with the majority society. It can be difficult to distinguish "racial" from "ethnic" subcultures (e.g., Chinese and Japanese Americans are both of the

Oriental race, but their subcultures are very different). In Chapter 9, "Intergroup Relations," we will discuss such issues in detail.

Occupations

No one can really say how many distinct occupational specialties exist in the United States. More than 25,000 are listed in the Department of Labor's *Dictionary of Occupation Codes and Titles.* The life circumstances confronting a steel worker in northern Indiana differ greatly from those faced by a ranch hand in southern Utah. Although they share many elements of the general American culture, each has a way of life with a number of traits and complexes that are unique.

The medical profession provides a good illustration of an occupational subculture: physicians share a common background of extensive training, a common set of goals in the healing of the sick, a professional association that tends to unify their orientations and attitudes, a complex technical jargon, a vast number of specialized material traits, and a set of values pertaining to the practice of their profession.

Regions

The varied geographic regions of a society are likely to have had very different histories of development and to have drawn their populations from different sources. The result is a blending of traits into regional subcultures. In the United States, for example, people from the Deep South or from New England can be easily identified from their speech patterns. Regional subcultures are likely to involve special folkways, tastes in food, styles of architecture, and even political orientations.

Religion

Religious differences can also lead to the development of subcultures. In our society Jews, Catholics, and members of some Protestant denominations have distinctive traits that often form the basis of a religious subculture, especially among individuals who also share a common national origin.[36] A few religious groups like the Amish have highly integrated

35. Bruce D. Johnson, *Marijuana Users and Drug Subcultures* (New York: John Wiley & Sons, Inc., 1973), p. 10.
36. See, for example, Nathan Glazer and Daniel P. Moynihan, *Beyond the Melting Pot* (Cambridge, Mass.: The M.I.T. Press, 1963).

subcultures that include not only distinctive religious practices but modes of dress, vehicles, farming methods, attitudes toward schooling, and many other traits that set them quite apart from the larger society.

Social Class

Of particular significance in most societies are the subcultures associated with differences in social ranking. In a highly stratified society each broad stratum develops particular attitudes, practices, norms, values, and beliefs not uniformly shared by the members of other classes. Most middle-class Americans, for example, place great value on upward mobility, individual responsibility, resourcefulness, and personal initiative. They share norms concerning dress, etiquette, and "manners" that persons higher or lower in the socioeconomic hierarchy do not always subscribe to. The analysis of "class" subcultures has been very useful in explaining the wide range of behavior patterns found in many modern societies.

Deviance

Most subcultures exist harmoniously within the cultural complex supported by society as a whole. Deviant subcultures, by contrast, are configurations of behavioral practices, attitudes, values, and other traits that are widely disapproved. Some deviant subcultures are grudgingly tolerated by the society (e.g., certain communal subcultures composed of young people), but the practices of others, such as the subcultures of drug addicts and professional criminals, so seriously transgress the general societal norms that vigorous attempts are made to eliminate them. (See Chapter 7, pages 174–203.)

Sociologists find the concept of subculture extremely useful as a theoretical tool. It can be applied not only in analyzing the structure and content of a particular society's culture but also in explaining patterns of individual and group conduct that fall outside the range of generally approved behavior. In a large society such as ours, individuals obtain many of their behavioral definitions from the various subcultures in which they participate. Although they share in the culture supported by society as a whole, their own particular social milieus provide them with the basic attitudes, norms, and values around which they organize their lives. In the remaining chapters of this text, we will examine many examples of both conforming and deviant subcultures.

SUMMARY

Culture refers to the total of all material, social, and symbolic creations that members of a society incorporate into their design for living. Culture is the social heritage of a society that represents a people's accumulated solutions to the problems of living.

Although human beings are not particularly well equipped for survival from a purely physical standpoint, the tools, technology, language, social organization, and other cultural products they have developed have enabled them to dominate other species. Among these products of human life, none is more important than language. It is through the use of symbols—written and spoken, verbal and mathematical—that culture has been developed to its most complex forms.

The concepts *culture, society,* and *social organization,* though closely related, are distinguishable for purposes of analysis. Society consists of human beings acting within a complex pattern of social organization. Culture consists of the regulative, material, symbolic, and evaluative products of that interaction accumulated over time. Specific patterns of social organization found in local groups derive their definitions of norms, roles, and other components from cultural definitions prevailing broadly in the society.

The general characteristics of culture can be analyzed in terms of cultural *variability,* cultural *relativity,* and cultural *consistency.* The diversity of cultural elements in different societies has been extensively documented by ethnographers who have studied both primitive and modern societies the world over. In spite of their variability, all cultures seem to "work" for the people who adopt them. Thus, the merits of particular cultural patterns are relative. There appear to be no universal standards that all peoples accept. To assume that one's own group has definitions of morality, beauty, logic, or truth that all others should follow is ethnocentric, expressing an attitude of in-group superiority that can promote group solidarity but can also lead to tension and conflict. Finally, cultures differ significantly in the extent to which they are internally consistent in their patterns of value, belief, and behavior. The Zuñi provide an example of a highly integrated way of life. Their economic, political, and family institutions fit together in a way that limits strain. The general American culture, by contrast, is varied by region, differentiated by historical developments, and productive of numerous sources of conflict and tension.

Social scientists take two basic approaches to the study of culture—the *analytic* and the *synthetic.* The analytic study of culture focuses on small, meaningful units called culture traits. Such traits may be invented within a culture or borrowed from other cultures. The analytic approach permits the classification of traits into categories, such as material, regulative, symbolic, or evaluative culture.

The synthetic approach to the study of culture focuses on meaningful configurations or clusters of traits. Examples are cultural complexes, such as the hunting-fishing complex of the Eskimo; cultural ethics, such as those studied by Weber; and cultural ethos, by which societies are given distinctive characteristics and identities.

Subcultures are distinctive patterns of traits and configurations worked out by people who share given social circumstances. Small, traditional societies have fewer subcultures than complex urban-industrial societies, in which there is a great deal of social differentiation. Students, the police, religious bodies, deviants, farmers, motorcycle enthusiasts, and many other categories of people share somewhat unique problems, orientations, and circumstances. Subcultures develop as products of interaction within such categories. Subcultures have content and structure and can be viewed analytically or synthetically.

Of the many types of subcultures in the United States, the way of life found in the carnival provides a colorful illustration. Subcultures used extensively in sociological analysis are those related to ethnicity, race, occupations, regions, religion, social class, and deviance. Overall, both culture and subculture are important tools of sociological analysis.

Part II
SOCIETY AND THE INDIVIDUAL

5
Personal Organization and Group Experience

THE STRUCTURE AND DYNAMICS OF PERSONAL ORGANIZATION

Motivation   Habit Patterns   Acquired Predispositions
Perception and Cognition   Personal Organization as System

THE BIOLOGICAL BACKGROUND OF INDIVIDUALITY

The Absence of Human Instincts   Limiting and Facilitating Factors

THE SOCIAL SOURCES OF INDIVIDUALITY

The "Looking-Glass Self"   Mind, Self, and Society

THE DENIAL OF GROUP EXPERIENCE

Isolation in Early Life   Social Isolation and Adult Personality

In preceding chapters we have deliberately deemphasized the individual to show that social and cultural phenomena can be studied and understood in their own terms. But sociologists are interested in individuals as well as in the organizational and cultural patterns of the groups they form. They look at the relationship between personal and social phenomena from two complementary perspectives. First, the motives, sentiments, attitudes, and other personal characteristics of individuals help determine the kinds of groups they form and how they behave as group members—how they interpret norms, act out roles, and so on. Second, group experience is of key importance in shaping the personality, or personal organization, of individuals.

The interdependency of individuals and groups provides the focus of this chapter. We shall begin by examining briefly the principal concepts that behavioral scientists use in analyzing the structure and functioning of personal organization. Next, we will consider the role of biological and constitutional factors in shaping individual differences. Finally, we will analyze the importance of group experience and symbolic interaction in the development and maintenance of personal organization.

THE STRUCTURE AND DYNAMICS OF PERSONAL ORGANIZATION

The study of personal organization is a concern of both psychologists and sociologists, who have jointly developed the field of social psychology over the last three-quarters of a century. It also draws on the work of anthropologists, who have long been concerned with the ways in which distinctive cultures tend to produce distinctive personality types.[1] Because of the many points

1. The study of the ways in which distinctive cultures produce such phenomena as "modal personality," "national character," and "basic personality structure" has a long tradition in anthropology. The first two books on social psychology were Edward A. Ross, *Social Psychology* (New York: Macmillan) and William McDougal, *Introduction to Social Psychology* (London:Methuen), both published in 1908. Ross was a sociologist, McDougal a psychologist. The field has been jointly developed ever since.

of view brought to the field by scholars with different theoretical orientations, no single definition of personality has been universally accepted.[2] The one we will use as a general guide was originally formulated by T. W. Adorno and his associates, who defined *personality* as "a more or less enduring organization of forces within the individual."

These persisting forces of personality help to determine response in various situations, and it is thus largely to them that consistency of behavior—whether verbal or physical—is attributable. But, behavior, however consistent, is not the same thing as personality; personality lies behind behavior and within the individual. The forces of personality are not responses but readiness for response.[3]

To help in understanding such "forces," we will consider some facets of personal organization concerning which there is considerable consensus. These include motivational patterns, habit patterns, acquired predispositions, perception, and cognition.

MOTIVATION

Certain fundamental sources of individual motivation appear to be built into the human organism. Biological needs for food, water, and air must be satisfied if a person is to survive, and even temporary deprival of one of these needs causes serious disequilibrium in the functioning of the organic system. Other imbalances may be caused by inadequate diet, lack of salt, changes in bodily temperature, etc.[4] When organic imbalance occurs, the individual typically experiences an *urge* to obtain whatever will restore equilibrium. Such urges constitute basic motivational processes and are usually referred to as *biological drives.*[5]

Other kinds of human motivations are acquired through learning. From habitual exposure to particular kinds of gratifying experiences, the individual may develop an *acquired need* for the same or similar experiences.[6] For example, anyone who regularly enjoys hearing music of a given type, eating certain foods, or interacting with particular friends may become uncomfortable when deprived of these pleasures and feel an urge to reexperience them. The needs people acquire through their participation in social and cultural processes can range from a specific need for pizza to a broad need for social approval.

Acquired needs are not necessarily less "basic" than organic ones in terms of their motivational consequences. Indeed, they are perhaps even more important than the biological drives in explaining the great variety and complexity of human behavior.

HABIT PATTERNS

The term *habit* can refer to almost any regularly patterned way of acting, feeling, or thinking that an individual has acquired through learning. Indeed, the concept of habit is so broad and inclusive that it becomes difficult to identify any form of learned behavior that is *not* a habit in some sense. The individual develops literally thousands of routine patterns of everyday behavior that are consistent with societal folkways and cultural definitions—habits governing such matters as eating, bathing, dressing, using mechanical devices like can openers and cars, and behaving with "propriety." Of more central importance to personal organization, however, are people's learned patterns of emotion, their characteristic ways of responding to particular kinds of events, and their habits of language use.

Emotions and Sentiments

Personal emotional experience depends on social learning as well as on involuntary physiological processes. People of different cultures often respond to similar situations in quite different ways. For example, in the traditional society of the Polar Eskimos, it was considered a gesture of hospitality to invite a male guest to sleep with the host's wife, and all three parties experienced pleasure at the arrangement. But in

2. Victor Barnouw, *Culture and Personality* (Homewood, Illinois: Dorsey Press, 1973), pp. 7–10.
3. T. W. Adorno, Else Frenkel-Brunswik, D. J. Levinson, and R. Nevitt Sanford, *The Authoritarian Personality* (New York: Harper & Row, Inc., 1950), p. 5.
4. David Krech, Richard S. Crutchfield, and Egerton L. Ballachey, *Individual in Society* (New York: McGraw-Hill Book Company, 1962), pp. 71–73.
5. S. Stansfeld Sargent and Robert C. Williamson, *Social Psychology*, 3rd ed. (New York: The Ronald Press Company, 1966), pp. 191–192.
6. Ibid.

our society, a man who offered his wife to a visitor would probably evoke emotional reactions of shock and disgust.

Occupational and other subcultural differences often lead individuals to form emotional habits that are distinct from those of other people within the same society. For example, morticians learn emotional orientations to death and human remains that are not characteristic of most people. Similarly, young people learn to enjoy listening to rock records played at peak volume, whereas most older people find the experience nerve-wracking. In short, individuals acquire personal habits of internal response that reflect the cultural norms of both their society and their particular subcultures.

Character Traits

Social learning also helps shape the habitual response tendencies known as character traits. In the analysis of personality, *trait* refers to a relatively fixed aspect of personal organization that makes an individual's behavior in given situations relatively predictable.[7] For example, in everyday conversations we often refer to particular individuals as being good-natured or grouchy, stingy or generous, honest or untrustworthy, optimistic or pessimistic, hardworking or lazy. Our language includes literally thousands of terms to characterize various aspects of a person's social behavior.[8] To this long list the social and behavioral sciences have added such terms as *introverted, masochistic, inner-directed,* and *peer-oriented*—each used to identify as precisely as possible some organized pattern of response to a particular class of events. Such a pattern is a *character trait,* a cluster of habitual forms of response which constitute the characteristic way a person relates to a given recurring situation.

The concept of character traits is an elusive one, and behavioral scientists do not wholly agree on how to identify, classify, or study them. It seems clear, however, that every individual tends to develop some relatively complex profile of traits. These profiles reflect variations in personality that make each individual a distinctive psychological entity.

Habits of Language Use

To participate in the social process, individuals must associate linguistic symbols with specific meanings according to the established language conventions of their particular society. Only by acquiring such habits of language use can they bridge some of the gap between their own inner worlds of experience and the experience systems of other people. The habitual use of linguistic symbols is basic not only to interpersonal communication but to *internal* communication as well (see page 137). It underlies the abilities to think and remember as well as the abilities to talk, write, and read.

ACQUIRED PREDISPOSITIONS

An acquired predisposition is a response pattern involving the tendency to accept or reject some type of object, situation, or event. Most predispositions can be classified as preferences, attitudes, and values.

Preferences

A preference is a tendency to accept or reject a rather specific object. We all have specific tastes in food and are attracted to or repelled by certain types of automobiles, styles of clothing and furniture, architectural forms, color schemes, and so forth. Any one preference, such as liking blue better than green, is insignificant. But all of a person's preferences together determine much of what is patterned and predictable in his or her behavior.

There are no grounds for assuming that preferences are inherited. They appear to be acquired from others with whom the individual interacts. The role of culture in the acquisition of individual preferences is often quite clear. Armenians, Americans, and Argentinians, for example, would normally prefer different art forms, foods, and styles of dress because of their respective cultures.

7. For a thorough discussion of trait theory see Gordon W. Allport, *Pattern and Growth in Personality* (New York: Holt, Rinehart and Winston, Inc., 1961).

8. *Webster's Second New International Dictionary* has been found to include almost eighteen thousand trait names; see Gordon W. Allport and H. S. Odbert, "Trait Names: A Psycho-Lexical Study," *Psychological Monographs,* 47, No. 211 (1936). See also N. H. Anderson, "Likableness Ratings of 555 Personality-trait Words," *Journal of Personality and Social Psychology,* 9 (1968): 272–279.

Attitudes

An attitude is a set of evaluative beliefs concerning the acceptability of certain broad classes of objects, situations, or events.[9] Attitudes are often focused on "objects" such as minority groups, economic policies, religions, and so on. Like preferences, these predispositions are products of social learning.

Attitudes help simplify life in that they provide the individual with ready-made modes of response to rather broad categories of stimuli. For example, the person with a set of emotionally charged negative beliefs about some particular category of people does not have to decide how to respond to every member of that category but instead can reject them collectively. Since attitudes provide simple "formulas" for responding to a complex environment, they tend to be rather resistant to change. (For one method of measuring attitudes, see Tools of Sociology on page 266.)

Values

The values a person holds are one of the most basic features of personality. Values are enduring beliefs that define certain modes of conduct or states of existence as personally and socially preferable. Milton Rokeach has identified two important kinds of values: *instrumental* values and *terminal* values.[10] Terminal values define end-states of existence that the individual would like to reach, whereas instrumental values define the preferred patterns of behavior for working toward those end-states. Table 5.1 lists eighteen terminal values and eighteen instrumental values held by people in many parts of the world. Rokeach has identified these by using quantitative procedures to measure the values of thousands of people in different societies and different walks of life. His measurement of values has been found to be valid and reliable (see Tools of Sociology, page 129).

According to the Rokeach theory, each of us develops a personal system of instrumental and terminal values, ranked in importance according to our beliefs as to what is personally and socially preferable. Values play a significant part in shaping the kinds of orientations individuals habitually assume toward a great many aspects of the social environment. Decisions in areas such as civil rights, religion, politics, and education are heavily influenced by value systems. Since people sharing the same ethnic background, social class, or occupation tend to show characteristic patterns of values, it appears clear that subcultural norms can be very important in determining individual values.

Table 5.1. TERMINAL AND INSTRUMENTAL VALUES FROM THE ROKEACH VALUE SURVEY

TERMINAL VALUES

A comfortable life (a prosperous life)	Inner harmony (freedom from inner conflict)
An exciting life (a stimulating, active life)	Mature love (sexual and spiritual intimacy)
A sense of accomplishment (lasting contribution)	National security (protection from attack)
A world at peace (free of war and conflict)	Pleasure (an enjoyable, leisurely life)
A world of beauty (beauty of nature and the arts)	Salvation (saved, eternal life)
Equality (brotherhood, equal opportunity for all)	Self-respect (self-esteem)
Family security (taking care of loved ones)	Social recognition (respect, admiration)
Freedom (independence, free choice)	True friendship (close companionship)
Happiness (contentedness)	Wisdom (a mature understanding of life)

INSTRUMENTAL VALUES

Ambitious (hard-working, aspiring)	Imaginative (daring, creative)
Broadminded (open-minded)	Independent (self-reliant, self-sufficient)
Capable (competent, effective)	Intellectual (intelligent, reflective)
Cheerful (lighthearted, joyful)	Logical (consistent, rational)
Clean (neat, tidy)	Loving (affectionate, tender)
Courageous (standing up for your beliefs)	Obedient (dutiful, respectful)
Forgiving (willing to pardon others)	Polite (courteous, well-mannered)
Helpful (working for the welfare of others)	Responsible (dependable, reliable)
Honest (sincere, truthful)	Self-controlled (restrained, self-disciplined)

NOTE: The terminal and instrumental values are listed here in alphabetical order, not in the order of their importance to the individuals surveyed.

SOURCE: Milton Rokeach, *The Nature of Human Values* (New York: The Free Press, 1973), p. 28.

9. The most complete contemporary statement on the nature and functions of attitudes as they relate to human personality is Theodore M. Newcomb, Ralph H. Turner, and Phillip E. Converse, *Social Psychology* (New York: Holt, Rinehart and Winston, Inc., 1965), pp. 17–153.

10. Milton Rokeach, *The Nature of Human Values* (New York: The Free Press, 1973).

Attitudes provide the individual with ready-made modes of response to rather broad classes of stimuli. The prejudiced person, one with an emotionally charged attitude toward some social category, can reject all members of that category without bothering to consider them as individuals.

PERCEPTION AND COGNITION

How do people attribute meaning to the objects, events, and social situations they apprehend with their senses, and what does this have to do with the groups they belong to? How do people deal with the many inconsistencies they encounter in their social environment? In this section we will consider the processes of perception and cognition that enable human beings to impose order or balance on their social worlds.

Perception of Meaning

The process through which the individual assigns meaning to sensory data is called *perception*. The particular meaning assigned to a particular set of stimuli depends greatly upon what the individual has learned from past social experience. For example, an American dinner guest who is served a slice of rare roast beef would probably "see" a delicious entrée. In similar circumstances, a Hindu, to whom cattle are sacred, would "see" a horrifying violation of a sacred taboo. Much of what a person perceives is dependent upon habitual, socially derived modes of attributing meaning to sensory phenomena.

Historically, studies of perception in psychology have focused on the processes involved in interpreting the physical environment—in identifying objects, for example, and in perceiving spatial relationships, motion, and the passage of time. But sociologists and social psychologists are primarily interested in *social perception*—the processes involved in perceiving the characteristics, actions, and intentions of other people. Research has shown that there is usually less correspondence between the objective properties of social events and the way they are perceived than there is between the properties of physical events and the way they are perceived.[11]

The way individuals "see" their social environment is an important key to understanding their behavior in groups. A classic study of the stratification system of an American community by Davis, Gardner, and Gardner shows that people's habits of perception in interpreting social phenomena are greatly influenced by their own patterns of social experience. These investigators found by sociological analysis that the community had six rather well-defined social classes. But they also discovered that the members of each of these classes perceived the stratification system differently. For example, those at the bottom thought that there were only two social levels above them, whereas those at the top believed that there were four levels below them. The process of social perception led the members of each level to interpret the community stratification system in different ways.[12]

More generally, no member of a given group experiences that group in exactly the same way as another. Each person brings to a group perceptual habits that provide a unique perspective on the group's patterns of interaction. Nevertheless, all members must share a sufficient number of perceptual interpretations so that they are able to interact with each other.

11. Robert B. Zajonc, "Cognitive Theories in Social Psychology," in *The Handbook of Social Psychology*, Vol. I, Gardner Lindzey and Elliot Aronson, eds. (Reading, Mass.: Addison-Wesley Publishing Company, 1968).

12. Allison Davis, Burleigh B. Gardner, and Mary R. Gardner, *Deep South: A Social Anthropology Study of Caste and Class* (Chicago: The University of Chicago Press, 1941).

TOOLS OF SOCIOLOGY
VALIDITY AND RELIABILITY   Jeffrey C. Hubbard

In order to measure such personal variables as preferences, attitudes, and values, sociologists use a variety of measurement procedures, including scales, indices, and questionnaires. A good measurement procedure must be both *valid*—measure what it was designed to measure—and *reliable*—produce similar results when repeatedly applied to the same people. Problems of validity and reliability arise not only in the measurement of personal characteristics, but also in assessing social rates and indices of all kinds.

A measuring procedure, instrument, or index that is unreliable cannot be thought of as valid, since it is obviously assessing something different each time it is used rather than measuring what it was designed to measure. But even if a procedure or instrument has been found to be reliable, it still may be invalid. For example, if a measure of the crime rate of a city based on official police records produces the same numerical data each time it is studied, it is reliable. But if the police records do not adequately reflect the actual amount of crime in the city, the measurement procedure has low validity. Similarly, a scale designed to assess attitudes toward a racial minority may in fact be found to measure attitudes toward poor people in general; therefore it would not be valid.

There are several methods for determining the reliability of such measurement instruments as tests, scales, and questionnaires. One is the *test-retest* method. For example, a researcher administered a scale designed to assess black people's attitudes toward whites to a sample of black citizens. Later the same attitude scale was readministered to the same subjects, and the results were compared person-by-person and in the aggregate. Since the results were quite similar, the scale was shown to be reliable.

Another procedure is the *equivalent-forms* method, which calls for the application of different but presumably equivalent forms of the same scale or test to the same people. If the instrument is reliable, the parallel forms will produce comparable results. Make-up examinations used by college instructors are examples of alternative but (presumably) parallel forms. If properly constructed, the two forms measure in an equivalent way students' understanding of the content of the course.

In measuring reliability, the degree of similarity between equivalent forms is usually expressed in terms of a *coefficient of correlation* (see "Statistical Analysis," page 570). When scores on both forms of the scale or test are identical, the coefficient for each person is 1.00 and the coefficient for the aggregate is also 1.00. When performance on the two forms is unrelated, such coefficients are 0.00.

A common technique for assessing validity is the *predictive* method, in which the researcher uses the measurement instrument to predict a specific form of behavior. The measurement instrument is valid to the degree to which such predictions are correct. For example, many colleges and universities use aptitude tests to predict the academic performance of applicants. A test is valid if students who score low on it have difficulty in their school work and students who score high do well in their courses.

Validity, like reliability, is expressed in terms of a correlation coefficient. A perfectly valid test has a coefficient of 1.00, indicating complete correspondence between test scores and predicted behavior. A test with no validity has a coefficient of 0.00.

Cognitive Structure

The term *cognitive structure* refers to a rather complex system of psychological components that aid the individual in consciously apprehending, interpreting, and coping with the physical and social environment.[13] We will examine cognition in terms of *attributes, concepts,* and *social schemata.*

Attributes. In interpreting an object or event in our environment, we relate it to our prior experience and identify its essential *attributes* — the characteristics or qualities that enable us to assign it a meaning. The saying "Beauty is in the eye of the beholder" serves to indicate an important fact about perception and cognition — namely, that different individuals may interpret given stimuli in quite different ways, depending on the particular configuration of attributes they "see."

The meaning a perceiver assigns to a given object, person, or event is a product not of any single attribute it may have but rather of its *combined* attributes. Thus any alteration in an existing configuration of attributes can substantially alter the meaning of a stimulus situation for the individual. To illustrate, the attributes "bright," "ambitious," and "experienced" could provide an employer who is interviewing a job applicant with one basis for perception and response. However, if the attribute "alcoholic" is added to form a new configuration, both perception and response may be considerably altered. Research on cognitive processes has focused considerable attention on the importance of attributes and the way they are linked in configurations.[14]

Concepts. A *concept* is a miniature system of meaning that places a given event, object, or idea in a recognizable *class.* It invokes all the attributes necessary for identifying a member of that class. Meaning can thus be assigned to a perceived event by referring it to a class that past experience has shown to be identifiable in terms of a given set of attributes.

To illustrate, if you are in the woods and note the approach of a small group of people carrying guns, it is important for you to be able to classify them in order to respond appropriately. If you recognize a sufficient number of attributes so that the group can be classified as a hunting party (field clothing, shotguns, type of dogs, etc.), an appropriate response might be simply a cheery wave of the hand. If, however, you classify them as escaped convicts (prison dress, handguns as well as shotguns), the appropriate behavior would be of a quite different order. The problem of classifying the perceived characteristics and intentions of persons with whom one interacts is very complex, involving a continuous input and processing of information.

Social schemata. The term *social schemata* refers to the ability people have to make relatively accurate predictions about various aspects of their social environment in the course of their daily lives. Every person is a "practicing sociologist" in the sense of having some implicit understanding of the way groups work. This understanding includes knowing something about the requirements of norms, the nature of roles, the consequences of social control, and the implications of social ranking. Social schemata, in other words, are the subjective "theories" of social behavior we use every day to predict how other people will behave under a variety of conditions. Social scientists have become increasingly interested in studying social schemata, trying to determine through empirical research how they evolve and how they influence interpersonal relationships.

Closely related to the study of social schemata is a branch of social research known as *ethnomethodology* (see Tools of Sociology, page 101), in which the principal focus is upon the meanings of social interaction for the persons involved. *Ethnomethodology* does not connote "methods" in the sense of special research pro-

13. James P. Spradley, ed., *Culture and Cognition: Rules, Maps and Plans* (San Francisco: Chandler Publishing Co., 1972).

14. E. E. Jones and K. E. Davis, "From Acts to Dispositions: The Attribution Process in Person Perception," in *Advances in Experimental Social Psychology,* Vol. 2, L. Berkowitz, ed. (New York: Academic Press, Inc., 1965).

cedures but refers to the "methods" by which individuals perceive, interpret, and relate to their particular social world.[15] Thus the social psychologist studying social schemata and the sociologist interested in ethnomethodology are focusing their attention on approximately the same thing, but from somewhat different perspectives.

Cognitive Dynamics

The individual's cognitive structure is never at rest; it is continuously responding to the surrounding physical and social environment. The way people use attributes, concepts, and social schemata to interpret and cope with changing environmental conditions is called *cognitive dynamics.*

Balance theory. Prominent among the major approaches to the study of cognitive dynamics is *balance theory,* originally proposed by Fritz Heider in 1946.[16] One important idea in Heider's thesis is that individuals seek to develop an orderly and coherent interpretation of their environment; they try to understand both physical and social phenomena in terms of *invariant properties* that underlie changing surface conditions. Thus in social interaction they seek to attribute invariant properties to the behavior of others by looking beneath surface behavior and trying to understand predictable motives and attitudes.[17]

The central thesis of Heider's analysis is that individuals seek consistency or *balance* in interpreting the interrelationship of elements in their social environment. For example, assume that young Jerry has two friends, Ted and Dick, whom he likes very much and who like him. Then he discovers that Ted and Dick hate each other and perceives that the relationships among the three of them are no longer in a state of balance. Heider's theory predicts that psychological pressures will arise to change Jerry's perception of the interrelationships so as to bring

Our perceptions of people are based on their combined attributes. At the Democratic National Convention in 1972 Thomas Eagleton was perceived as a "young, attractive, popular politician"—the ideal running mate for presidential candidate George McGovern. But when it was discovered that Eagleton had undergone shock treatment for a nervous breakdown, the attribute "former mental patient" was added to the configuration, and he was no longer considered a "viable" candidate. As a result, Eagleton was forced to resign from the ticket.

harmony into his cognitive structure. Jerry might change his opinion of either Ted or Dick, deciding that one wasn't worth his friendship, or he might redefine his interpretation of the relationship between them, convincing himself that they didn't really dislike each other after all. The example oversimplifies the theory, but it illustrates the basic principle that in the face of cognitive imbalance, cognitive changes tend to occur in such a way as to produce congruence and harmony in a person's perceptual field.[18]

Dissonance theory. The theory of cognitive dissonance elaborates balance theory by stressing the dynamic relationship between cognition and overt behavior. It is for the most part the work of Leon Festinger, who formalized its basic princi-

15. Harold Garfinkel, *Studies in Ethnomethodology* (Englewood Cliffs, N.J.: Prentice-Hall, Inc., 1967).
16. Fritz Heider, *The Psychology of Interpersonal Relations* (New York: John Wiley & Sons, Inc., 1958).
17. Ibid.
18. Morton Deutsch and Robert M. Krauss, *Theories in Social Psychology* (New York: Basic Books, Inc., 1965), pp. 29–35.

ples in 1957.[19] The central thesis of dissonance theory can be illustrated by the story of ''The Fox and the Grapes'' in *Aesop's Fables*. Dating back to the sixth century B.C., it suggests how long people have been thinking about the need for harmony between thought and action:

The Fox was very hungry, for he had eaten neither breakfast nor dinner. Finding himself in a vineyard, he saw a particularly delicious looking bunch of grapes hanging just overhead. His mouth watering, the Fox jumped up to get the grapes but found he couldn't reach them. He jumped again and again, but he was unable to get the grapes no matter how hard he tried. Finally, exhausted, he left, saying to himself, ''I guess I'm not really hungry. Anyway, those grapes are probably sour.''

Like the Fox in this fable, people try to interpret their environment in such a way that their own behavior ''makes sense.'' Balance theory and dissonance theory both stress our need to eliminate or at least reduce contradictions in perception and cognition; but dissonance theory goes a step further by relating the need for perceptual and cognitive consistency to subsequent action. It assumes that lack of harmony between the way we interpret our environment and the way we behave is distressful and thus motivates us to change either our interpretations or our actions.[20]

PERSONAL ORGANIZATION AS SYSTEM

The components of personal organization discussed in the foregoing sections are not isolated entities but rather are linked together into a *system* that is more than the sum of its parts. An individual's personal organization has continuity over time, but it is also constantly changing in response to both the internal and external environment.

The Interdependence of Personality Components

The close linkage between the various facets of personal organization has been documented by a considerable body of research. A classic experiment by Bruner and Goodman, for example, demonstrated how need and value can sometimes influence the perception of a physical object. The subjects were thirty ten-year-old boys,

half from relatively rich families and half from poor families. The boys were asked to estimate the size of coins (socially valued objects) by adjusting the size of a circle of light so that its diameter would match that of a given coin. The light circle was projected on a screen, and the subjects could make it larger or smaller simply by turning a knob. A separate control group was similarly tested, but with cardboard discs of various sizes (nonvalued objects) rather than actual coins. The boys in the experimental group all tended to overestimate the size of the coins, whereas those in the control group did not overestimate the size of the discs. And as the experimenters had predicted, the poor boys overestimated the coin sizes to a considerably greater degree than did the rich boys.[21] Subsequent research has tended to confirm the conclusion that perception is influenced by value and need as well as other personality variables.

An interesting experiment by Hastorf and Cantril provides evidence that attitudes play an important part in shaping what a person ''sees'' in complex social situations. The situation chosen for study was a football game between rival colleges; after the game, each school had publicly accused the other's players of deliberate and unnecessary roughness. The researchers showed films of the controversial game to a sample of students at each of the institutions involved, and in each case the students ''saw'' about twice as many infractions committed by their opponents as by their own team.[22] In the chapter on Intergroup Relations (page 267), we shall consider how attitudes lead to stereotyped perceptions of minority group members and thus help perpetuate discrimination.

Equilibrium and Conflict Perspectives

Although behavioral scientists widely agree that needs, values, attitudes, emotional response pat-

19. Leon Festinger, *A Theory of Cognitive Dissonance* (Stanford, Cal.: Stanford University Press, 1957).

20. For an excellent summary of the theory and modifications of the original formulation, see Marvin E. Shaw and Philip R. Costanzo, *Theories of Social Psychology* (New York: McGraw-Hill Book Company, 1970), pp. 207–217.

21. Jerome S. Bruner and C. C. Goodman, ''Value and Need as Organizing Factors in Perception,'' *Journal of Abnormal and Social Psychology*, 42 (1947): 33–44.

22. Albert H. Hastorf and Hadley Cantril, ''They Saw a Game: A Case Study,'' *Journal of Abnormal and Social Psychology*, 49 (1954): 129–134.

terns, perceptual processes, and so forth are closely interlinked in an ongoing system, there is still much debate about the nature of that system.[23] Most researchers see personality as a system tending toward harmony and equilibrium. Balance theory and cognitive dissonance theory clearly illustrate this orientation.[24] Other theorists, mainly building on the ideas of Freud, see personality as a system characterized by internal conflict.

Freud analyzed the structure of human personality in terms of three major components, id, ego, and superego, which he believed to be constantly competing for control of the individual's behavior.[25] The *id,* according to Freudian theory, is an inborn force that continuously motivates the individual to seek physical gratification. The *superego* develops through social learning and represents society's norms of morality. The *ego* is the conscious and directive part of personality. Balanced between id and superego, it tries to satisfy both—for example, by redirecting the energy of the id toward activities that are socially acceptable.

Much has been learned about personality since Freud developed his theory, and his followers have modified or discarded many of his original ideas. However, they continue to find his conceptions of competing personality forces and unconscious motivations extremely useful in explaining human behavior.

THE BIOLOGICAL BACKGROUND OF INDIVIDUALITY

It was once assumed that the structure of personality was present at birth and emerged as the individual matured. However, we now know that personal development is shaped by a complex interplay between inherited potentialities and sociocultural influences. In this section we

will examine some conclusions about the nature of biological influences on personal organization.

THE ABSENCE OF HUMAN INSTINCTS

Although there is still some debate about the exact role of genetic factors in shaping personality, the biological and behavioral sciences have abandoned instinct theories as general explanations of human behavior. Instincts can be defined as behavior patterns that are (1) *unlearned*—inherited through genetic transmission in some manner—(2) *universal*—found in every member of the species in much the same form—and (3) *complex*—requiring the coordination of various specific behaviors. Animals seem to have many blind inherited patterns connected with such complex activities as mating, rearing offspring, and migrating, but modern science places no credence in the instinct idea as applied to human beings. For every proposed instinct, too many exceptions can be found.

Even something as seemingly fundamental as self-preservation can scarcely be universal when thousands of people who are not insane take their own lives every year in most major societies. Similarly, a motherhood instinct is difficult to defend when abortion is a regular and expected practice in some societies. Although people do inherit many reflexes and other unlearned behavior patterns of a relatively simple nature, there is no scientific basis for assuming that complex behavior patterns of any sort are genetically determined.

LIMITING AND FACILITATING FACTORS

Although there is no evidence that personality as such is inherited, biological factors play both a direct and an indirect part in shaping personal organization. Intelligence, aptitudes, temperament, and energy level, for example, are all determined in part by heredity; and all influence the kinds of experiences individuals will have and the kinds of persons they will become. The term *constitutional factor* is used broadly to refer to any organic or physical characteristic—whether a product of inheritance, diet, disease, plastic surgery, or physical fitness program—that limits or facilitates the individual's ability to develop in particular directions.

23. Salvatore R. Maddi, *Personality Theories: A Comparative Analysis* (Homewood, Ill.: Dorsey Press, 1968).
24. Barnouw, *Culture and Personality,* pp. 16–17.
25. Sigmund Freud, *An Outline of Psychoanalysis,* trans. James Strachey (New York: W. W. Norton & Co., Inc., 1949).

VIEWPOINTS THE NATURE OF HUMAN NATURE

■ The human species has exhibited for at least 100,000 years certain traits which are uniquely and pleasantly human and which are more interesting than those that account for its bestiality. . . . The human species has the power to choose among the conflicting traits which constitute its complex nature, and it has made the right choices often enough to have kept civilization so far on a forward and upward course. The unique place of our species in the order of things is determined, not by its animality, but by its humanity. . . .

The uniqueness of humankind comes indeed from its potential ability to escape from the tyranny of its biological heritage. Instead of being slaves to their genes and hormones, as animals are, human beings have the kind of freedom which comes from possessing free will and moral judgment. We can repress our animality if we will. . . .

To understand the human species as part of the animal kingdom requires only knowledge of its genetic structure and organic reactions to environmental stimuli. But to understand its humanity, it is essential to know why so much of human life is devoted to tasks that have no immediate utilitarian application — the arts, the sciences, the ceremonies, the innumerable forms of self-sacrifice. Human beings derive their most profound satisfactions — true happiness — from those activities which are furthest removed from animality. . . . It is not sufficient to know that *Homo sapiens* evolved from a certain kind of primate. A more important question is what he would like, or should try, to become. . . .

We are human to the extent that we are able and willing to make choices that enable us to transcend genetic and environmental determinism, and thus to participate in the continuous process of self-creation which seems to be the task and the reward of humankind.
René Dubos
Beast or Angel?

● The picture which emerges from a scientific analysis is not of a body with a person inside, but of a body which *is* a person in the sense that it displays a complex repertoire of behavior. The picture is, of course, unfamiliar. The man thus portrayed is a stranger, and from the traditional point of view he may not seem to be a man at all. . . .

We are told that what is threatened is "man *qua* man," or "man in his humanity," or "man as Thou not It," or "man as a person not a thing." . . . What is being abolished is autonomous man — the inner man, the homunculus, the possessing demon, the man defended by the literatures of freedom and dignity.

His abolition has been long overdue. Autonomous man is a device used to explain what we cannot explain in any other way. He has been constructed from our ignorance, and as our understanding increases, the very stuff of which he is composed vanishes. Science does not dehumanize man, it de-homunculizes him, and it must do so if it is to prevent the abolition of the human species. To man *qua* man we readily say good riddance. . . .

Science has probably never demanded a more sweeping change in a traditional way of thinking about a subject, nor has there ever been a more important subject. In the traditional picture a person perceives the world around him, selects features to be perceived, discriminates among them, judges them good or bad, changes them to make them better (or, if he is careless, worse), and may be held responsible for his action and justly rewarded or punished for its consequences. In the scientific picture a person is a member of a species shaped by evolutionary contingencies of survival, displaying behavioral processes which bring him under the control of the environment in which he lives, and largely under the control of a social environment which he and millions of others like him have constructed and maintained during the evolution of a culture. The direction of the controlling relation is reversed: a person does not act upon the world, the world acts upon him.
B. F. Skinner
Beyond Freedom and Dignity

Intelligence and Learning Capacity

An individual's learning capacity seems to be limited by heredity, though exactly how is by no means clear. Certainly the intelligence level the individual eventually develops is not a simple product of genetic transmission; it is heavily influenced by the learning environment he or she is exposed to. But most people could never develop into geniuses, regardless of how rich their sociocultural environment might be. By the same token, there is no assurance that inherited high potentials will be developed, especially if the individual is in a limiting sociocultural environment.

Aptitudes

Like intelligence, aptitudes have long been thought to be partly determined by inheritance. The evidence on this issue is not entirely conclusive, but aptitudes seem to set an upper limit on the development of certain complex skills. For example, some people simply do not have the prerequisite quickness and coordination to develop into highly skilled athletes, though such skills can certainly be improved through training. The importance of aptitudes in the development of linguistic and social skills is much less clear.

Temperament and Energy Level

Some persons are nervous, quick-moving, and responsive while others are much slower to react and are more calm and deliberate in coping with their environment. We do not know just why this is the case, though there is a good possibility that inheritance plays some part. There is also reason to suspect that genetic factors play a part in a person's general *energy* level. The metabolic processes differ from person to person, and these appear to place limits on the individual's general rate of activity. But it is difficult to sort out the influence of such factors as nutrition or even the influence of cultural norms concerning the value placed on hard work, self-discipline, and high levels of activity.

Categories Based on Race and Sex

Some constitutional factors have an indirect but obvious influence on the kind of social experiences and general sociocultural environment a person will be exposed to. Physical criteria place individuals in certain significant social categories with important ascribed statuses that sharply structure their sociocultural experiences. The female child, for example, experiences different expectations and training than the male child in most societies. A black child born into a predominantly white society that ranks this racial category low in status encounters a very different sociocultural environment than does a black child in an all-black society.

Many other subtle influences operate on the individual because of constitutional factors. For example, each society holds to some set of standards concerning physical attractiveness. If the tall, muscular, blond male with a symmetrical profile is the ideal, a short, fat, dark man with irregular features may find reason to regret his physiological inheritance. Beauty may be only skin-deep, but the fact that norms concerning its attributes are shared can have important consequences for personality development.

THE SOCIAL SOURCES OF INDIVIDUALITY

It is through meaningful communication with other people that the infant gradually develops a personality, an ability to function as a conscious, thinking human being. Modern sociological thinking concerning the relationship between individual human nature and symbolic interaction stems from the pioneering work of Charles Horton Cooley and George Herbert Mead. Subsequent research has strongly supported the theoretical insights of these men.

THE "LOOKING-GLASS SELF"

Shortly after the turn of the century, Charles Horton Cooley formulated a theory concerning the emergence of the *self* through a process of social interaction. Cooley maintained that the development of a social self began very early in life. He stressed the importance of the primary group, which in the earliest years means the family, in providing the experiences necessary for the emergence of the infant's self-image. Later, peer groups and other associates provide additional social contexts within which the individual can continue to develop as a social being.

Distinguishing Self from Others

As Cooley observed the developmental process in his own children, he noted that the voices, facial expressions, and bodily movements of surrounding adults are, at the beginning, much like any other phenomena in the young infant's environment. Slowly, however, through an accumulation of interactive experience, the child begins to attach special meaning to other human beings. Gradually, it begins to perceive the limits of its own body and to define itself as an object that is different from the physical environment and distinct from other human beings. This first crude differentiation of self from others is aided by the very words we use to make such distinctions. The social nature of self-realization is implied by the word *I*, which automatically indicates the existence of non-I's — that is, of other people who must be taken into account.

As children come to distinguish between self and others, they gradually become aware that other individuals are evaluating them, that their appearance and conduct are being judged according to rules and standards. These standards and rules must be understood before individuals can begin to evaluate *themselves* as social objects. They are certainly not born with such an ability, and they can acquire it only through involvement in a complex and subtle interaction within groups where these rules and standards prevail. As children begin to learn these evaluative criteria, they can make more and more sophisticated judgments about their own appearance and behavior. A *self-image*, in other words, emerges as a product of group involvement and communication with others.

Seeing Oneself Through the Eyes of Others

Cooley's phrase "the looking-glass self" makes clear the process by which we arrive at self-evaluation. As Cooley himself stated it in 1902:

Each to each a looking glass
Reflects the other that doth pass.

As we see our face, figure and dress in the [mirror], and are interested in them because they are ours, and pleased or otherwise with them according as they do or do not answer to what we should like them to be; so in our imagination we perceive in another's mind some thought of our appearance, manners, aims, deeds, character, friends, and so on, and are variously affected by it.

A self idea of this sort seems to have three principal elements: the imagination of our appearance to the other person; the imagination of his judgment of that appearance; and some sort of self-feeling, such as pride or mortification.[26]

It is thus that people build sets of beliefs and evaluations about themselves as individual human beings. Each person's self-image is a socially derived understanding of personal qualities, attributes, and characteristics, as these are evaluated by other members of society.

In identifying the origins of this important aspect of human nature and in tying it to the social process, Cooley made a radical departure from earlier traditions, which strictly held either that mind and self were God-given or that they were wholly dependent on biological factors. For Cooley, it was the "imaginations which people have of one another" that constituted the "solid facts of society." These "facts" enable us to interact in groups and to develop images of self.[27]

Although Cooley emphasized the childhood years as the most crucial for the development of the looking-glass self, it should be obvious that the process continues through life. As we move successively from infancy into old age, through childhood, adolescence, young adulthood, and middle age, the social mirror around us responds in ever changing ways. We learn to read these successive looking glasses and to redefine ourselves in realistic and appropriate terms as each new stage is reached. At some point we stop thinking of ourselves as (or behav-

26. Charles Horton Cooley, *Human Nature and the Social Order* (New York: Schocken Books, Inc., 1964), p. 184; first published in 1909.
27. Ibid., p. 121.

ing as) young and vigorous persons. We find that we have to face the fact that we are middle-aged and, eventually, old men and women, whose lives are nearly over. These successive self-images may not come easily, but they are an important aspect of personal organization at each life stage.

MIND, SELF, AND SOCIETY

Cooley's ideas suggested to others the importance of social interaction in the shaping of individual development. Of particular significance was the work of George Herbert Mead, whose theories, formulated in the early 1900s, added a great deal to our understanding of the communicative act and of its significance both to the individual and to society.

Significant Symbols and the Sharing of Meaning

The basis of human communication is the *symbol*—an arbitrary and conventional sign, such as a word, that stands for something else, such as an object or an idea. Symbols are called *arbitrary* signs because people can use almost any kind of sign as a substitute stimulus for something else. They can use bodily gestures or any of the astounding variety of grunts, pops, whistles, hums, and whines the human voice is capable of producing. Or they can scratch characters in clay, form tokens of metal, and imprint designs with dark liquid on a light surface. However, an arbitrarily selected stimulus can communicate meaning only after it has become *conventional*—that is, only when other people accept it as the sign for a particular referent. The distinguishing characteristic of human language as opposed to the languages of other species is that its signs are both arbitrary and conventional and therefore a part of shared culture.

28. This is the central thesis of the symbolic interactionists. See George Herbert Mead, *Mind, Self and Society: From the Standpoint of a Social Behaviorist,* ed. Charles W. Morris (Chicago: The University of Chicago Press, 1934).
29. Anselm Strauss, ed., *George Herbert Mead on Social Psychology: Selected Papers* (Chicago: The University of Chicago Press, 1964), p. 195.

Mead was among the first to analyze these relationships, and he coined the term *significant symbol* to describe the essence of the communicative act. A word is a significant symbol if, when it is used, the interacting individuals understand it in much the same way—that is, if their internal responses and experiences *parallel each other rather closely.*[28] Once a given symbol has become conventionalized within a group, each individual in that group can experience approximately the same general meaning when confronted with either the symbol or its referent. Mead recognized that only through the use of significant symbols can human beings participate in the social process. Through such participation the individual derives an ability to engage in thought, a concept of self, and guidelines for personal behavior—unique aspects of human nature.

The Social Nature of Mind

Mead's theory of communication clarified the act of thinking, which he explained as an internal response to self-directed symbols. People respond to these internal communications in the same way they respond to symbols directed toward them by others. Mead believed that mind and self emerged jointly from the individual's experience in the social order:

Mind arises in the social process [when that process enters into] the experience of . . . the given individuals involved in that process. When this occurs the individual becomes self-conscious and has a mind; he becomes aware of his relations to that process as a whole, and to other individuals participating in it with him. . . .[29]

Thus, as Mead delineated the process, individuals become social persons (acquire human natures) as they acquire the response abilities called *mind.* It is important to recognize that the acquisition of mind and of self takes place at the same time. Although we can discuss and analyze these aspects of personal organization separately, they are interlocking parts of an ongoing system.

Genesis of the Self

Self, like mind, has its genesis in communication, the basis for interaction with other people. It is through this social interaction that we define ourselves as individuals. The process begins, according to Mead, in the interplay between the newborn infant and its parents, especially the mother. The infant's crying and other behavior are a constant source of stimuli. We do not assume that the child is consciously trying to convey specific meanings, such as the fact of being hungry, cold, or wet, but the mother responds to the stimuli by providing a bottle or her breast, cuddling or a blanket, a fresh diaper, or other forms of relief. From the point of view of the infant, the process of communication has begun. The child's cries become patterned, and the mother begins to distinguish between the pain cry, the hunger cry, and so on.

As the areas of communication expand, the child learns to elicit appropriate behaviors from the mother by particular kinds of cries and noises. The child, in other words, learns to stimulate its mother and to respond to her in a variety of patterned ways. What began as a conversation of gestures from the infant's point of view becomes communication with significant symbols as the child anticipates the mother's response. The child's symbols are calling out the responses it anticipates in the other.

Play and the Game

As children develop skill in communicating through the use of significant symbols, they gradually become able to take the roles of other people. For example, children pretend to be mother, who scolds them for a naughty act. Thus they begin to understand the point of view of another person and to exercise the attitudes and orientations of that other toward themselves. Mead called this phase in the development of role understanding the *play* stage. Children play at being teachers, police officers, doctors, or fathers. Such imaginary role taking is, at first, limited to one role at a time, but gradually children's role-taking skills expand into what Mead called the *game*. Even in a game as simple as hide-and-seek, children must simultaneously grasp not only their own individual roles but also the roles of all the other players as they fit together in an organized system. Every human group is a game in the sense that it is a system of roles that must be understood by the members. Mead maintained that only through a simultaneous grasp of the roles of all others in a group can individuals effectively see and understand their own behavior.

Once such simultaneous role systems are grasped, Mead claimed, they become a kind of *generalized other*. That is, they "organize into a sort of unit, and it is that organization which controls the responses of the individual."[30] Thus learning the "rules" of group life, plus the general predispositions of others, provides not only a basis for the development of a self-image but an effective foundation for guiding one's behavior in social settings. Mead's concept of the generalized other is closely related to the concept of social schemata (page 130).

The I and the Me

Although Mead postulated that the self develops in the fullest sense only as it mirrors the expectations of others, he also recognized a creative and spontaneous aspect of self. He labeled these two complementary aspects of personality the *I* and the *Me*.

The *I* is unfettered by the generalized other; it encompasses that which is personal, distinct, and unique about the individual, that which permits the person to be creative and nonconforming. The *Me*, on the other hand, is the predictable reflection of the social group; it is the product of socialization (Chapter 6). If our selves had only the *I* aspect, social behavior would be unpredictable, and organized group activity would be impossible. If, on the other hand, our selves had only the *Me* aspect, there would be no creativity or innovation.

30. Ibid., p. 218.

Gestures encompass a wide range of human behavior—from the simple to the very complex. A fist raised in anger, the "power to the people" sign, and a salute are gestures that have general meanings for most Americans. But some gestures, when used by formal groups, become standardized to ensure that very specific meanings are being communicated. The members of the Board of Trade, for example, use an out-turned palm to signal an offer to sell and a palm turned inward to indicate an offer to buy. Fingers indicate the price.

In playing school, these children are learning to understand the roles of teacher and student and thus to see and understand their own behavior.

THE DENIAL OF GROUP EXPERIENCE

If, as we have suggested, personal organization depends on group experience and symbolic interaction, a simple prediction can be made: the personal organization of human beings who are *denied* normal participation in group life will show noticeable deficiencies or impairment. The sections that follow summarize the impact of social isolation on both infants and adults.

ISOLATION IN EARLY LIFE

Herodotus, the Greek historian of the fifth century B.C., reports that Psammetichus, king of Egypt, had several children raised by nurses who were forbidden to speak to them, in order to find out if the children would first utter the Egyptian tongue or some other. According to the story, when the children tired of the goat's milk they were being fed, they asked for bread in the more ancient Phrygian tongue! When Emperor Frederick II attempted to repeat the experiment in the thirteenth century, the children died, thereby confirming the existing belief that children raised without speech would have no souls and therefore lack vitality. King James IV of Scotland, investigating the belief that children raised in isolation would speak Hebrew, the language of Adam, arranged for two children to be placed on an island in the care of a woman who could not speak. And according to the reports of the experiment, when the children came to the age of speech, "they spak guid Hebrew."[31] Not surprisingly, contemporary observations fail to support the idea that children come into the world naturally predisposed to speak one language or another.

The absence of communicative contact with other human beings in early life appears to have very drastic consequences for the developing infant. Jerome Kagan studied children in Guatemala who were isolated from language in their early years and, as a result, appeared to be retarded:

31. Robert Briffault, *The Mothers: A Study of the Origins of Sentiments and Institutions* (London: George Allen and Unwin, Ltd., 1927), pp. 23–24.

I found myself in a thirteenth-century, pre-Columbian village, located on the shores of Lake Atitlán. I saw 850 Indians, poor, exploited, alienated, bitter, sick. I saw infants in the first years of their lives completely isolated in their homes, because parents believe that sun and dust and air or the gazes of either pregnant women or men fresh with perspiration from the field will cause illness. It's the evil-eye belief. So the infants are kept in bamboo huts. There are no windows in these huts, so the light level at high noon on a perfectly clear day is what it should be at dusk. Very dark. Although parents love their children — mothers nurse on demand and hold their infants close to their bodies — they don't talk or interact with them. And there are no toys. So at one-and-one-half years of age, you will have a very retarded child.[32]

Later, when the children began to participate more fully in the language community, they recovered from the earlier effects:

The 11-year-olds in the Guatemalan village are beautiful. They're gay, alert, active, affective, just like 11-year-olds in the United States. They're more impressive than the Americans in a set of "culture-fair" tests — where the words and the materials are familiar. For example, we asked them, "What is brown, hard and found near the shore of the lake?" And they'd say, "a wharf." They have no problem with this. In reasoning, memory, inference, deduction and perception, these children at 11 — who, we must assume, were "ghosts" as infants — had recovered.[33]

Information on the effects of isolation from groups in early age is also available from case studies of children who, for one reason or another, were raised under conditions of substantial isolation from group life.[34] Two specific cases can be cited where extended, controlled observations were made on the development of such children when they were placed in a so-

cially stimulating environment after their discovery. (See page 386 for a discussion of the case study as a research tool.)

The Case of Anna

Anna was the second illegitimate child of a sturdy young woman who lived on and operated her grandfather's farm. The grandfather, a man of stern morals, strongly disapproved of this new evidence of his granddaughter's indiscretions. But after efforts to have the infant adopted failed, the mother was forced to take Anna home in spite of the grandfather's wrath. To avoid trouble, the child was confined on the second floor in an atticlike room. Kingsley Davis, who studied Anna's case, reported:

Anna was left almost without attention. Ordinarily, it seems, Anna received only enough care to keep her barely alive. She appears to have been seldom moved from one position to another. Her clothing and bedding were filthy. She apparently had no instruction, no friendly attention.

It is little wonder that, when finally found and removed from the room in the grandfather's house at the age of nearly six years, the child could not talk, walk, or do anything that showed intelligence. She was in an extremely emaciated and undernourished condition, with skeleton-like legs and a bloated abdomen. She had been fed on virtually nothing except cow's milk during the years under her mother's care.[35]

After she was discovered, Anna spent about a year and a half in a county home. She learned to walk, to feed herself, to understand simple commands, to be more or less neat, to remember people, etc. She made little progress toward speech; she could only babble like a normal child of about one year of age. At this time, she was placed in a private home for retarded children where she received more adequate training. Approximately four years after discovery, the school reported on her condition: She could play with a ball, eat with a spoon, dress herself (except for buttoning up), and use the toilet. She had begun to develop speech. She could use a few complete sentences, call people by name, and generally talk at about the level of a two-year-old.[36]

32. From an interview with Jerome Kagan, published as "What Children Can Do," *Saturday Review of Education*, April 1973, pp. 79–80.

33. Ibid.

34. In an earlier era, much was made of reports of so-called *feral* children, who supposedly were raised by animals. These reports have been largely discredited as failing to meet adequate scientific standards of reporting. For this reason, they will be ignored in this discussion, even though their conclusions are entirely consistent with those we present.

35. Kingsley Davis, "Final Note on a Case of Extreme Isolation," *The American Journal of Sociology*, 52 (March 1947): 433.

36. Ibid., p. 434.

The motion picture, The Wild Child, *portrays the real-life attempt of Jean-Marc Itard to train a ten- or twelve-year-old boy, Victor, to become a normal human being. Abandoned in a forest in France at about age two, Victor progressed rapidly during the first year of training (1800–1801), but though he lived to be about forty, he never advanced beyond the achievements of the first year. It is not known if Victor was brain-damaged or psychotic or, simply, so deprived of human contact when young that he could never become truly human.*

In the year following this report, Anna made additional progress: she could string beads, identify colors, play lovingly with a doll, wash her hands, brush her teeth, and help other children. Unfortunately, she died at the age of ten. There is little doubt that Anna was seriously retarded as compared to normal children of her own age, but considering that when found she was an apathetic, animallike creature, her psychological development at the time of her death provides a striking contrast. She was unmistakably acquiring a human nature, including the ability to use language.

Anna's retardation appears to have been a product of both the impoverished social environment of her early life and inherited limitations on her capacities for development. (Although the latter cannot be fully confirmed, her mother's IQ of 50 was considerably below normal.) In spite of the possibility of genetically linked limitations on her potentialities, Anna's progress after being removed from social isolation provides a dramatic demonstration of the significance of social interaction for the development of personal organization.

The Case of Isabelle

Only nine months after the plight of Anna first came to light, another child of almost identical age was discovered living under isolated conditions.[37] In this case, the child was not completely alone during her isolation. Isabelle was the illegitimate offspring of a deaf-mute mother, who had been confined with her. This young mother was not feebleminded. She had suffered severe brain damage at the age of two, which limited her sight to one eye, and as a result of the injury she could neither talk, hear, read, nor write, although she was able to communicate with her family with crude gestures. When she became pregnant at the age of twenty-two, her family locked her up in a darkened room. After Isabelle's birth, both remained involuntarily confined in this room for six and a half years. Finally, the mother escaped with her child in her arms; the two were immediately brought to the attention of authorities, who placed them both in a children's hospital.

Since the mother was unable to communicate verbally, Isabelle's environment during her confinement had been one entirely without speech and normal human social interaction. At first, in her new environment, she could make only strange croaking sounds. She was as terrified by strangers as is a wild animal just after capture. She was, from the point of view of human personality development, about as bad off as Anna. Her physical condition was somewhat better, but she was a wan, thin child with legs badly bowed from a rachitic condition caused by improper nourishment and lack of sunshine. The soles of her feet came nearly flat together so that she could not walk.

At first the authorities thought her to be feebleminded. She was completely unable to respond to human speech. When it was finally

37. Marie K. Mason, "Learning to Speak After Six and One-Half Years of Silence," *Journal of Speech Disorders,* 7 (1942): 303.

established that she was neither deaf nor feeble-minded, an expert in speech undertook to give her language training. Isabelle's progress under this tutelage was remarkable. Within two weeks she was making her first attempts to identify toys by name when they were presented to her (ball, car, etc.). Within two months, the child knew dozens of words and could volunteer simple sentences. After a year of effort Isabelle could write, count up to twenty, add up to ten, and give a simple summary of a story that had been read to her. After a year and a half of training, she had a vocabulary of between 1500 and 2000 words.[38]

In short, by the age of eight Isabelle had progressed to a point where she was becoming like a normal child of her age. After six and a half years of silence and isolation, she was an energetic, rapidly progressing, and happy youngster. She had passed through all the stages of learning that other children experience, but in a much shorter time. Eventually, she entered a regular school and made entirely satisfactory progress.

The conclusions from these two cases parallel those of the limited number of other cases of young children found living under severely isolated conditions.[39] When denied interaction with others, children fail to develop human personality structure in anything like the normal pattern.

SOCIAL ISOLATION AND ADULT PERSONALITY

Scientists believe that social interaction is necessary for *maintaining* as well as for developing personal organization. Again, reliable data are meager, since experiments involving lengthy isolation would be unthinkable. However, explorers, people lost in the wilderness, and others cut off from human associations almost uniformly report serious effects on their personal organi-

Prolonged social isolation can have serious effects on the personal organization of adults.

zation. The experiences under severe isolation of the famous Antarctic explorer, Admiral Richard E. Byrd, have been summarized by the social psychologist Robert E. L. Faris in the following terms:

His first reaction after being left by his men at the lonely outpost on March 28th, was a general feeling of peacefulness. Within about ten days he noted a fear of boredom, then of loneliness. By the end of the first month it took some moments after awakening in the morning to collect his wits, and he found himself wondering where he was and what he was doing there. The silence depressed him, and he became irritable and reported that he had difficulty in concentrating. A month and a half after being alone he reported that his table manners had deteriorated to the point where they were atrocious. He also wrote on May 11th, after about forty-four days of solitude, that he found it hard to think in words.[40]

The effects of prolonged isolation on personal organization have also been observed in prison settings. During the early part of the nineteenth century, for example, the states of Penn-

38. Ibid.
39. René Spitz, "Hospitalism," in R. S. Eissler et al., *The Psychoanalytic Study of the Child,* Vol. I (New York: International Universities Press, 1945), pp. 53–72.
40. Robert E. L. Faris, *Social Psychology* (New York: The Ronald Press Company, 1952), pp. 342–343. This summary is taken from Richard E. Byrd, *Alone* (New York: G. P. Putnam's Sons, 1938).

sylvania and New York established men's prisons where inmates were held in complete solitary confinement during their entire sentence. Each prisoner was provided with a Bible, work, and ample time for him to pray and meditate upon his sins. The hope was that he would undergo inner reformation and find the determination to return to the ways of the Lord. But instead, the prisoners became eccentric, apathetic, and reclusive as a result of their isolation. Many developed severe mental disorders, and suicide attempts appear to have been quite common. The system was eventually abandoned.[41]

Overall, the effects of social isolation seem to be reasonably clear, even though the evidence is unsystematic. Human beings can neither develop nor maintain an adequate level of personal organization in the absence of meaningful interaction with other people.

SUMMARY

Just as people shape groups, so do groups shape people. On the one hand, the personal characteristics of individuals greatly influence the kinds of groups they form and the ways they behave as group members. On the other, group experience greatly influences the personality, or personal organization, of individuals.

We have examined the structure and functioning of personal organization in terms of motivational patterns, habit patterns, acquired predispositions, perceptual processes, cognitive structure, and cognitive dynamics. Each of these facets of personal organization is influenced to a greater or lesser extent by social experience. *Motivational patterns* can be either a product of biology or a product of learning. *Habit patterns* include not only people's learned routines for coping with everyday life but also their learned ways of expressing emotion, their characteristic ways of responding to particular kinds

of situations, and their habits of language use and thought. *Acquired predispositions* range from specific preferences to more general attitudes to very comprehensive values. All predispositions serve to orient individuals positively or negatively toward various objects, situations, events, or forms of action. *Perception* and *cognition* are processes by which people assign meaning to stimuli received through the senses and thus interpret the demands of their environment. Cognition can be analyzed in terms of the attributes, concepts, and social schemata people use in determining the meaning of particular stimuli and thus in deciding how they should react.

Behavioral scientists agree that the components of personal organization are linked together in systematic configurations, but controversy exists over whether the personality system tends toward internal equilibrium or internal conflict. The *equilibrium perspective* is illustrated by balance and dissonance-reduction theories, which attempt to describe the ways people reduce inconsistency in their interpretations of, or in their responses to, their surrounding milieus. Freudian and neo-Freudian personality theories provide examples of the *conflict perspective*.

Biological factors play a significant role in *facilitating* and *limiting* the development of personal organization. Scientists no longer believe that specific behavior forms in humans are products of inherited factors. However, such general aspects of individuality as learning capacity, aptitudes, and temperament appear to be considerably influenced by inheritance. In addition, biological characteristics such as race and sex place individuals into social categories that have profound influences on their sociocultural experiences.

In the development of biological potential, social interaction plays a critical role. It is through participation in the communicative processes of group life that individuals develop a human nature. Unlike lower forms of life, human beings communicate through the exchange

41. Donald R. Taft and Ralph W. England, *Criminology* (New York: Macmillan, Inc., 1964), pp. 404–407.

of *significant symbols* — arbitrary signs, such as words, that have become conventionally associated with given meanings.

Our understanding of the relationship between social interaction and personal organization owes much to the work of two early theorists. Both placed special emphasis on the importance of language. Charles Horton Cooley developed the concept of the "looking-glass self" to explain how an individual's self-image emerges from group involvement and communicative interaction. George Herbert Mead elaborated the importance of symbolic interaction in enabling the developing individual to differentiate "self" from "other" and, subsequently, to relate his or her own behavior to that of other group members.

Further insight into the importance of social interaction can be gained by noting what happens when human beings are cut off for extended periods of time from communication with other people. Children raised in social isolation fail to develop adequate patterns of personal organization, but tend to "catch up" if they are later exposed to language and normal group life. The negative effects of social isolation can also be observed in adults who spend long periods of time alone. The available evidence indicates that prolonged isolation from social interaction impairs personal organization for persons at any age level.

6
Socialization

Monday through Friday, three hundred children aged three to seven live at the Pei Hai kindergarten in Peking, China. Weekends they spend with their parents, who work during the week. A park surrounds the kindergarten, and the rooms are bright and sunny. Unlike adults in China, the children are colorfully dressed. As the headmistress explains, "They are dressed in colors because they are children and we love to see them look bright and happy. Isn't the same true in America?"

But the school differs from American kindergartens in many respects. The children eat and sleep there, as well as sing songs, play games, and begin to learn the three R's. And according to the headmistress, they are also taught to dress themselves, to set a table properly, and "to love the great leader Chairman Mao, communism, and the motherland" so that they may, when they are grown, "produce many successes for the cause."[1]

To the Chinese, it seems appropriate to board young children in a government-operated institution with hundreds of other children during the week and to provide a good deal of political indoctrination along with lessons on how to eat, dress, read, and do arithmetic. To most Americans, such an approach to early child rearing seems overly regimented and lacking in parental affection. American and Chinese views on what young children should learn, where, and from whom are different in many respects.

As this example illustrates, child-training practices may differ substantially from one society to another. But in spite of cultural variations, all societies provide some institutionalized means by which the young are taught the norms, values, and skills that will be expected of them as they grow up. This is the essence of *socialization*—a complex process of social learning by which individuals come to internalize, or accept as their own, cultural and subcultural patterns.

We will begin our analysis of the socialization process by examining the relationship between the personal organization of individuals and the social organization and cultural patterns of the groups in which they participate. Next we

1. William O. Johnson, "For the Chinese Woman and Child: A New Life Style," *The Smithsonian*, August 1974, p. 45.

will single out particular agents of socialization—such as the family, peer groups, the school, and the mass media—and examine the special parts they play in shaping individual personality. And finally we will consider the socialization process as it affects individuals during various stages in the life cycle. For, as our discussion will make clear, socialization does not end with childhood or adolescence; it is a continuing process of adjustment to changing expectations and demands.[2]

SOCIALIZATION AS PERSONAL AND SOCIAL PROCESS

For the individual, socialization is the process by which personal organization is developed and maintained. For society, it is the process upon which social order and societal continuity depend. Through socialization, individuals learn to think and act somewhat like other people who share the same culture. However, the product of such learning is never thoroughgoing conformity. As we shall see, socialization helps explain the differences among a society's members as well as the similarities, and it allows for social change.

SOCIALIZATION AND THE INDIVIDUAL
The personal aspect of socialization has been viewed by social and behavioral scientists from at least three complementary perspectives.[3] Each of them focuses on somewhat distinct aspects of

individuals in their relationships to the surrounding sociocultural order.

First, socialization can be viewed as preparing individuals for participation in group life. The emphasis here is upon trying to understand how individuals are "trained"—both formally and informally—to accept the normative and role expectations of the groups to which they belong. The study of socialization as social preparation focuses on the way various facets of social organization are internalized by the young and adjusted to after childhood. This perspective is the one that has been most fully developed by sociologists, and it will provide the main focus of the present chapter.

A second perspective is to view socialization as *enculturation*. As Ruth Benedict has put it:

By the time [a child] can talk, he is the little creature of his culture, and by the time he is grown and able to take part in its activities, its habits are his habits, its beliefs are his beliefs, its impossibilities his impossibilities.[4]

This tradition of viewing personality as internalized culture has been most closely followed by anthropologists. Insofar as every culture is to some degree a self-contained or integrated system, the enculturation experiences of persons within it will be more or less similar. While individual differences are clearly recognized, the student of socialization who adopts this perspective looks for *central tendencies*—that is, for similarities among the personalities of people who have been raised within a given cultural setting.[5]

A third scholarly orientation toward socialization sees it as a process geared to controlling disruptive drives. According to this view, socially unacceptable impulses are "tamed" by training within the context of a social system. The psychoanalytic theory of Sigmund Freud is an obvious example of this orientation. As we have already noted (page 133), Freud theorized that the inborn psychic energy of the libido manifests itself through the pleasure-seeking id. It is the task of civilization, said Freud, to "cage the beast within." Society must encourage the

2. For an extensive review of the sociological implications of socialization, see John A. Clausen, ed., *Socialization and Society* (Boston: Little, Brown and Company, 1968).

3. Robert A. Levine, *Culture, Behavior and Personality* (Chicago: Aldine Publishing Co., 1973). See esp. pp. 61–68 from which much of the present subsection has been drawn.

4. Ruth Benedict, *Patterns of Culture* (Boston: Houghton Mifflin Co., 1934), pp. 2–3.

5. Social scientists have been no less fascinated than travelers with the observation that different cultures seem to produce distinct personality types. See, for example, Abraham Kardiner, *The Psychological Frontiers of Society* (New York: Columbia University Press, 1945); Margaret Mead, *Soviet Attitudes Toward Authority* (New York: McGraw-Hill Book Co., 1951); Ruth Benedict, *The Chrysanthemum and the Sword* (Boston: Houghton Mifflin Co., 1946); Ralph Linton, *Cultural Background of Personality* (New York: Appleton-Century-Crofts, 1945); and R. Lynn, *Personality and National Character* (Elmsford, N.Y.: Pergamon Press, 1971).

individual to develop a superego of internalized rules of socially acceptable behavior to hold the id in check. Modern theories reflecting a similar perspective place less emphasis upon unconscious forces and discuss socialization in terms of positive and negative reinforcements that encourage the acquisition of socially approved patterns and habits of behavior.[6]

SOCIALIZATION AND SOCIETY

One of the most remarkable features of any society is that it can survive as an organized, viable system despite the constant change of its membership through birth and death. It is the transmission of culture and social organization through socialization that makes this continuity possible. The socialization process explains not only the continuation of societies through successive generations but also the ability of the members of a society to interact meaningfully. A common language, a body of common knowledge and beliefs, shared norms and values, common ways of handling routine situations, a common technology and material culture, and shared social institutions all provide the basis for purposeful interaction. If socialization did not work to make all members of a society take many of the same things for granted and to make them in some ways alike, group behavior would be impossible.

Because socialization is basic to societal continuity and stability, there may be a tendency to think of it simply as indoctrination to produce social conformity. However, socialization is accomplished through many different agents—family, peer groups, school, church, occupations, the mass media, and various other formal and informal "teachers"—and no two individuals are exposed to precisely the same pattern of experiences. Thus none of us is shaped into exactly the same mold.

Furthermore, as we noted in reviewing Mead's theory of the "I" and the "Me" (page 138), there is a creative and spontaneous aspect of self that remains unfettered by social expectations. Each human being responds to the environment with behavioral tendencies that are personally typical. These tendencies seem to be the product not only of previous experience but also, as we have pointed out, of constitutional factors such as aptitude and temperament. Because each individual learns from every situation in his or her own way, socialization can result in an almost unlimited variety of personalities while still producing sufficient uniformity so that meaningful interaction can take place.

In short, the societal goal of teaching new members to participate in a shared social process leaves ample room for individuality and thus for social and cultural change. Indeed, most societies provide some kinds of socialization to *encourage* change. The fact that scientists, engineers, artists, and others are deliberately trained to be creative suggests that societal goals usually include more than mere efforts to maintain stability.

INTERNALIZING SOCIAL ORGANIZATION

The same elements of social organization that give stability and direction to *groups* serve also to help shape the personal organization of the *individuals* who participate in them. It is by interacting repeatedly with others in group situations that individuals develop personal standards of conduct and the distinctive pattern of habits, attitudes, beliefs, and values that we refer to as "personality."

THE INTERNALIZATION OF NORMS

Anyone who has observed young children learning to guide their own personal conduct according to accepted standards has seen the socialization process at first hand. As children mature, they learn how to feed and dress themselves, develop habits of cleanliness, learn how to play with other children, and gradually master thousands of other aspects of "appropriate" behavior. When individuals of any age come to accept as their own a behavioral norm of their group, they are said to have internalized that norm. *Internalization,* then, is a consequence or product of socialization. It explains the individual's tendency to behave in relatively predictable ways even in the absence of formal group pressures.

6. Neal E. Miller and John Dollard, *Social Learning and Imitation* (New Haven: Yale University Press, 1941).

TOOLS OF SOCIOLOGY
THE LABORATORY EXPERIMENT

In recent decades the *small-group laboratory experiment* has become a convenient sociological research tool. In such studies, investigators attempt to reproduce certain fundamental social processes in the laboratory setting. Key advantages of the laboratory study are its simplicity, the close observations that it permits, and the high degree of control that can be exercised. Experimenters can select the members of the group; they can dictate the rules of the interaction among the members; and they can eliminate behaviors that would confound the interpretation of the results.

The basic purpose of a laboratory experiment is to study the cause-effect relationship between two variables: the experimenter systematically changes one of them (called the *independent variable*) in order to calculate its effect on another (called the *dependent variable*). Extraneous factors that might affect the dependent variable are held constant or else measured so that their influence can be taken into account; these are called *control variables.* Usually the researcher begins by preparing an *experimental design,* a formal statement in which the variables are defined, the conditions under which observations are to be made are described, and the procedures for measuring and recording results are specified.

One commonly used type of design for assessing the influence of extraneous variables involves a *control group.* The experimental conditions for the control group are identical to those for the experimental group *except* that the independent variable is not introduced.

A classic example of a small-group laboratory experiment with a control group is that reported by Solomon Asch on the effects of group pressure (the independent variable) on individual judgment (the dependent variable). Several experimental groups were used, each consisting of eight "confederates" of the researcher and one naive subject who knew nothing of the true purpose of the experiment. The groups were shown a series of eighteen panels, each of which contained three horizontal lines of slightly different lengths, rang-

ing from two to ten inches. With each panel, the group was also shown a separate "comparison" line. Members were asked to judge which of the three panel lines most closely matched the length of the comparison line. Things were arranged so that the actual subject was always the last to state an opinion.

In six of the eighteen trials, all the confederates gave uniformly *correct* answers by choosing a line from the panel that exactly matched the comparison line in length. In such trials, the subject experienced nothing unusual. However, in twelve of the trials the confederates uniformly chose a line from the panel that did not match the comparison line. The "errors" made by the eight confederates were large, ranging from .5 to 1.75 inches. In these error trials, the subject had to choose between going along with the majority and making an independent judgment. Many subjects simply went along with the majority. Those who made independent judgments reported experiencing emotional stress.

Numerous trials were run and the results were repeatedly confirmed. A control group without confederates showed very different results: there was no evidence of conformity or emotional stress. Overall, the experiment illustrated the powerful influence of group norms on individual behavior.

Critics of small-group laboratory research point out that the situations created by the experimenter are artificial: people in "real life" might behave differently. This could be true. But the same argument could be made concerning experiments in the physical sciences; numerous phenomena are studied under conditions that would never be found in nature. The advantage is that all laboratory experiments—physical, biological, and social—permit variables to be manipulated, controlled, and observed in simple and flexible ways. Such procedures may seldom duplicate nature, but they yield important insights into the characteristics of the phenomena under study.

Solomon E. Asch, "Effects of Group Pressure Upon the Modification and Distortion of Judgments," in *Readings in Social Psychology,* eds. Eleanor E. Maccoby, Theodore M. Newcomb, and Eugene L. Hartley (New York: Holt, Rinehart and Winston, Inc., 1958), pp. 174–183.

Group Norms and Individual Behavior

The compelling influence of group norms on individual behavior has been demonstrated in controlled laboratory experiments (see page 149). In a classic study by Muzafer Sherif, for example, subjects were asked to judge the apparent movement of a pinpoint of light some distance away from them in a totally dark room. The light was actually stationary, but under such conditions a light appears to move (the so-called *autokinetic effect*). When subjects were asked to make judgments in small groups, their responses over a number of trials tended to *converge* on a common average distance of perceived movement. Thus a norm was established. When these same individuals were later tested in isolation, one by one, they continued to confine their reports of perceived movement within the limits established earlier by their group. By contrast, the judgments of individuals who were tested without the prior experience of establishing a group norm were much more variable and erratic.[7]

Everyday observations of human behavior confirm the experimental findings of Sherif, Asch, and others regarding the compelling influence of group-established norms. People continue to behave as social beings even when they are home alone. Although they may not bother to conform to all the standards they use in public, they are not likely to gobble their food like animals, cease to bathe, or go naked. Nor do they abandon somewhat less obvious norms, such as cultural standards of logic, morality, artistic beauty, and humor which, through socialization, have become part of their personalities. Only after prolonged isolation from social interaction does personal organization tend to break down (see Chapter 5, pages 140–144).

Selective Internalization

The norms an individual internalizes reflect the totality of his or her social experience, which is in some ways unique. Even within a given group, no two members encounter precisely the same norms in precisely the same way. More significant for the socialization process, however, is the fact that almost every person belongs not just to one group but to many, each with its own set of "rules." When the norms of one group conflict with those of another, as often happens, the individual must choose one set or the other. Typically, individuals internalize *some* norms from *each* of their membership and reference groups, but the influence of primary groups—of family and peers—is usually greater than that of more impersonal groups.

The effects of differential association have been clearly illustrated in studies of deviant groups in which members are regularly exposed to norms quite different from those of society as a whole.[8] In an intensive study of lower-class delinquent boys Kvaraceus and Miller found, for example, that the appearance of "toughness" was paramount.[9]

The street-corner boy will say, "Man, I ain't been home or ain't slept for two nights. I've been on the prowl." Or: "They grilled me and beat me with a hose but I didn't admit nothing." Similarly: "My old man and me had one helluva fight. Man, he beat me up good."

Another quality embodied in the norms of the streets and alleys is the ability to outsmart others:

Skill in duping and outsmarting the other guy as well as the ability to avoid being duped by others indicate a lower-class concern with "smartness." . . . The models of estimable achievement in the area of "smartness" are the con man, the fast-man-with-a-buck, the bunco operator, whose victims are seen as suckers and dupes.

7. Muzafer Sherif, *The Psychology of Social Norms* (New York: Harper and Brothers, 1936). See also Robert C. Jacobs and Donald T. Campbell, "The Perpetuation of an Arbitrary Tradition through Several Generations of a Laboratory Microculture," *Journal of Abnormal and Social Psychology*, 62, No. 3 (1961): 649–658.

8. The principle of differential association is central to a well-known theory of criminality developed some years ago by Edwin H. Sutherland (see Chapter 7, "Deviance," pp. 186–187). See also Edwin H. Sutherland and Donald R. Cressey, *Principles of Criminology*, 5th ed. (New York: J. B. Lippincott Co., 1955), pp. 77–80.

9. William C. Kvaraceus and Walter B. Miller, "Norm Violating Behavior and Lower Class Culture," in *Readings in Juvenile Delinquency*, 2nd ed., Ruth Shonle Cavan, ed. (New York: J. B. Lippincott Co., 1969), pp. 37–47; quotations from pp. 40–41. See also James F. Short, Jr., and Frank L. Strodtbeck, *Group Process and Gang Delinquency* (Chicago: The University of Chicago Press, 1965).

When the norms of one group conflict with those of another, an individual who belongs to both groups must at times choose one set of norms at the expense of the other. In the United States, participants in the Hare Krishna religious movement have chosen Krishna norms regarding dress and other matters over those of the general society.

The normative culture of lower-class delinquents also stresses the excitement to be found in taking risks and in flouting the norms of the community as a whole:

The desire for excitement is reflected in prevalent patterns involving drinking, gambling and playing the numbers, goading ("testing") official authorities such as teachers and policemen, picking up girls, going out on the town, participating in a "rumble," destroying public property, stealing a car and joy riding.

In some cases the standards of the larger society seem all but irrelevant to the member of a deviant group. As Clifford Shaw noted some years ago, "The cultural standards of his group may be such as not to tolerate socially approved forms of expression; they may represent a complete reversal of the standards and norms of conventional society."[10] For the most part, however, an individual can scarcely avoid internalizing at least some conventional norms. The school, television, the movies, and usually the family expose even those who participate in deviant subcultures to the standards of behavior considered acceptable by society as a whole.

For both the "conformist" and the "deviant," socialization involves the selective internalization of norms from a great many different groups. The conflict faced by those who participate in a deviant group is different in degree, but not basically different in kind, from the conflict experienced by a member of the middle class who must choose, consciously or unconsciously, between the norms of parents, spouse, church, peer groups, and business associates.

10. Clifford Shaw, "Juvenile Delinquency: A Group Tradition," in *Gang Delinquency and Delinquent Subcultures*, James F. Short, Jr., ed. (New York: Harper & Row, Inc., 1968), p. 83.

Through anticipatory socialization, children begin to learn the skills and attitudes that are associated with adult roles. Developing an interest in fashions and beauty has been a part of traditional sex-role socialization for girls.

THE ORGANIZING INFLUENCE OF ROLES

The view that human social activity is organized into systems of roles is sometimes called the "dramaturgical" theory of behavior. Social roles are the parts we play in the dramas of everyday life, and like roles in the theater they must be learned.

Role Socialization

Groups can function smoothly only if the individuals who fill particular roles "learn their lines" and perform more or less as expected, so that their behavior can be coordinated with that of other "actors" in the cast. Learning to play a real-life role generally requires the acquisition not only of specialized skills but also of supportive attitudes, values, and emotions. Learning the role of "mother," for example, involves much more than acquiring the skills taught in a child-care course; it also means acquiring the attitudes and motivations that make caring for one's children seem an important and gratifying task.

Preparation for many adult roles begins with *anticipatory socialization* in childhood.[11] Girls undergoing traditional sex-role socialization begin learning the attitudes and skills they will need as mothers by watching and helping their own mothers keep house, by playing with dolls, and by reading books and watching films that portray the joys and responsibilities of motherhood. Parallel experiences prepare individuals for other family roles such as father, brother, sister, grandparent, aunt, or uncle and also for many roles outside the family, including occupational roles.

General and Segmental Roles

General societal roles such as those based on age, sex, or occupation (page 40) are perhaps the most significant ones in the socialization process, for they organize many facets of personality and behavior.[12] A woman who thinks of herself primarily in terms of being a wife and mother, for example, will have a configuration of attitudes and behavior patterns generally consistent with societal expectations for this traditional adult role. By contrast, the orientation of a woman who is primarily interested in a career will, like that of her male counterpart, be shaped largely around the demands of her job. Because caring for a home and family and pursuing a career require such different configurations of values, goals, and dedications, to say nothing of different day-to-day activities, and because there is societal pressure to give the

11. The phrase *anticipatory socialization* came originally from studies related to promotion in rank in military groups, but the concept has been broadened to include any type of socialization that rehearses in advance the assumption of future roles, either overtly or in fantasy. See Robert K. Merton and Alice S. Kitt, "Contributions to the Theory of Reference Group Behavior," in *Continuities in Social Research: Studies in the Scope and Method of "The American Soldier,"* Robert K. Merton and Paul F. Lazarsfeld, eds., (New York: The Free Press, 1950).

12. Talcott Parsons, "Age and Sex in the Social Structure of the United States," *American Sociological Review,* 7 (1942): 604–616.

former priority over the latter, women who combine these two general roles often experience considerable conflict.

The various segmental roles a person plays from time to time — as a motorist, member of the PTA, golf partner, airline passenger, voter, or customer at the supermarket — have a less pervasive influence on personality organization than general roles, but they too are part of the socialization process. Individually and collectively, they involve patterns of expectation that help shape the "inner person" as well as the individual's behavior in specialized situations.

Roles are not straitjackets that rigidly determine how people behave. We all play our roles in individualized ways, and however much the roles may change over a period of time, we remain distinctively "ourselves." Yet once we learn a new role, we are never quite the same people we were before. Each role we assume generally has the effect of somewhat altering our behavior patterns, including our ways of looking at life.

Adjusting to New Roles

Often the assumption of some new role requires *unlearning* older orientations as well as acquiring new ones. Such "resocialization" is required, for example, when a young woman decides to dedicate herself to a career after being socialized since early childhood to think that being a good wife and mother was every woman's chief goal in life. Resocialization is likely to be particularly difficult if the occupation she chooses is one not traditionally pursued by females, such as that of carpenter or engineer. Similar difficulties are experienced by a young man who decides to become a secretary or a nurse.

Any significant change from one general role to another is likely to involve some degree of resocialization. When couples marry, for example, each partner helps resocialize the other. Only if each participant can adjust to new role expectations is the marriage likely to be a satisfying one. The arrival of a child requires further adjustments. Suddenly, family roles are not what they were before. The child serves as a focus for the resocialization of both husband and wife as they adjust their behavior patterns

and attitudes to the requirements of new roles as father and mother. Changes in societal definitions of general sex roles can make these adjustments particularly difficult. We have already noted the conflict that women may experience in trying to reconcile an occupational role with the traditional wife-mother role. By the same token, men who have grown up in traditional homes where the roles of the parents were clearly distinct may have considerable difficulty in adjusting to the idea of being expected to share the duties of homemaking and child rearing.

The experiences of Jan Morris, a well-known British journalist who changed sex identity in mid-life, illustrate both the nature of resocialization and the significance of general sex roles in organizing attitudes and behavior. Jan Morris began life as James Morris and lived as a male for over forty years, serving in the army, marrying and fathering five children, and building a successful career as a writer. But Morris became increasingly uncomfortable with a male identity and, after a long period of self-searching and debate, eventually reached the difficult decision to undergo a sex-change operation. In describing her resocialization as a woman, Jan Morris offers considerable insight into how sex roles are assigned and learned.

We are told that the social gap between the sexes is narrowing, but I can only report that having, in the second half of the 20th century, experienced life in both roles, there seems to me no aspect of existence, no moment of the day, no contact, no arrangement, no response, which is not different for men and for women. The very tone of voice in which I was now addressed, the very posture of the person next in the queue, the very feel in the air when I entered a room or sat at a restaurant table, constantly emphasized my change of status.

And if others' responses shifted, so did my own. The more I was treated as a woman, the more woman I became. I adapted willy-nilly. If I was assumed to be incompetent at reversing cars, or opening bottles, oddly incompetent I found myself becoming. If a case was thought too heavy for me, inexplicably I found it so myself. Thrust as I now found myself far more into the company of women than of men, I began to find women's conversation in general more congenial. . . . Men treated me more and more as a junior — my lawyer, in an unguarded moment one morning, even called me "my child"; and so, addressed every day of my life as an inferior, involuntarily, month by month I accepted the condition. I discovered that even now men prefer women to be less informed, less able, less talkative, and certainly less self-centered than they are themselves; so I generally obliged them.[13]

Jan Morris's experiences provide a dramatic example of resocialization, showing how personal organization changes in response to new roles. Although her life story is unusual, the processes of relearning she underwent are not. In later sections of this chapter we will discuss some kinds of resocialization that are typically required of all of us as we move through the life cycle and adjust to changing role expectations and demands.

THE INTERNALIZATION OF SOCIAL CONTROLS

From a group perspective, positive and negative sanctions are techniques to encourage adherence to established norms and to discourage deviation. They are directed primarily toward the *actions* of individuals and not toward the individuals as persons. But from the perspective of the group member whose behavior is rewarded or punished, sanctions are experienced very personally. They cause either pleasure or distress. It is through experiencing social control that individuals learn personal control.[14]

A behavior pattern is acquired, modified, or eliminated as a consequence of the rewards or punishments it elicits from other people. Rewards are pleasurable experiences that *reinforce* the connection between the behavior pattern and the conditions that aroused it. Thus rewards increase the probability that the individual will behave in a similar way the next time he or she is confronted with similar circumstances. On the other hand, if unpleasant experiences follow the performance of the behavior pattern, the likelihood that it will be repeated in similar circumstances is reduced. Although learning theory is more complicated than this brief summary of it suggests, the essential idea is that behavior patterns that are repeatedly rewarded tend to become more firmly established over time (reinforced), whereas those that are associated with punishment—such as disapproval or even the withholding of previously established rewards—tend to be eliminated (extinguished).[15]

Ordinarily, the members of a group do not monitor each other's behavior so thoroughly that *every* approved act is rewarded and *every* nonconforming act is punished. As Doby has noted, reward and punishment are likely to occur only intermittently:

A child does not always get rewarded or punished for a given type of response. The rewards and punishments sometimes follow a given response and sometimes they do not. This is true all through life. An investor does not make a profit on every investment. Nor does a fisherman catch a fish every time he goes fishing, but he keeps on going fishing.[16]

Experimental studies of learning in animals have demonstrated that behavioral responses rewarded on an intermittent basis are particularly resistant to extinction. This raises the possibility that socialization may actually be facilitated by the fact that positive and negative sanctions are administered somewhat irregularly.[17] In any case, reward in socializing situations apparently occurs often enough, and in patterns sufficiently related to group-supported norms and roles, so that individuals come to organize their behavior around group expectations. Gradually they begin to apply to *themselves* the same standards that other people have used in judging them.

The effects of sanctioning on personality formation are most readily observed in early childhood, when parents use rewards and punishment as deliberate techniques for teaching the child approved forms of behavior. As the individual matures and begins to participate

13. Jan Morris, *Conundrum* (New York: Harcourt Brace Jovanovich, Inc., 1974).

14. Ernest R. Hilgard and Gordon H. Bower, *Theories of Learning*, 3rd ed. (New York: Appleton-Century-Crofts, Inc., 1966), p. 26.

15. For a more detailed discussion of theories of social learning, see Marvin E. Shaw and Phillip R. Costanzo, *Theories of Social Psychology* (New York: McGraw-Hill Book Company, 1970), esp. pp. 23–113.

16. John T. Doby, *Introduction to Social Psychology* (New York: Appleton-Century-Crofts, Inc., 1966), pp. 172–173.

17. See Albert Bandura and Richard H. Walters, *Social Learning and Personality Development* (New York: Holt, Rinehart and Winston, Inc., 1963), p. 5.

more fully in social life, sanctioning becomes increasingly complex. For example, many of the sanctions commonly used by groups depend for their effectiveness on prior experience. Unlike the food and electric shocks used in animal experiments, the rewards and punishments used in everyday life by human beings to encourage adherence to group expectations often have no inherent ability to gratify the human organism or to cause it distress. People must *learn* to be rewarded by such symbols of approval as diplomas, titles, praise, and applause. Among the most significant symbolic sanctions are those that are applied informally, often without conscious intent. The intense loyalty that most people reserve for their primary groups attests to the effectiveness of informal rewards—a smile, a word, a spontaneous gesture of friendship—in encouraging adherence to group norms.

Social control in most human groups seldom requires physical punishment or other strong sanctions. Through the socialization process, individuals internalize the standards of the groups that are important to them and thus monitor their own behavior. The feelings of "pride" that come with self-approval have much the same effect as rewards given by others; the feelings of distress and anxiety that we commonly term "bad conscience" can be every bit as painful as punishment administered by a group. Often social norms are internalized so completely that the mere contemplation of some act of deviation will result in self-recrimination and private embarrassment. In extreme cases self-sanctioning may be so severe that individuals will commit suicide rather than suffer their own self-imposed feelings of guilt.

GROUP RANKING SYSTEMS AND SOCIALIZATION

The impact of ranking systems on the socialization process becomes dramatically clear at the community level, where position in the class structure narrowly channels an individual's exposure to cultural norms. Because interaction

between members of different social classes is limited, each class tends to develop and maintain a distinctive pattern of subcultural traits and thus to transmit distinctive values and forms of conduct to new members. In a study of families in the San Francisco Bay area, Cohen and Hodges found a number of striking differences between the lower working class and the middle class. First, lower-class persons tend to interact mainly with relatives and to live in clusters near their kin. This closeness with relatives occurs despite a relatively unstable and strife-ridden family pattern. Insofar as such persons have any social contacts other than with their kin, these contacts are with neighbors, not (as in the middle class) with persons met at work or in the outside community. People who are very low in the social hierarchy seem to prefer the familiar and tend to avoid contacts like those in community organizations where they might show up at a disadvantage. As Cohen and Hodges say, the person of very low social status "cares greatly what others think of him; he lacks confidence in his ability to say and do 'the right things' in encounters with strangers; he is therefore anxious and uncomfortable in such encounters."[18]

Persistent patterns of belief, interest, motivation, and attitude that distinguish lower-class and middle-class Americans have been summarized by a number of writers.[19] For example, it has often been noted that children in middle-class families are exposed to a set of values representing a kind of tempered version of the Protestant Ethic (page 282), an orientation to which lower-class families are much less deeply committed. The central value in this orientation is *achievement*. Middle-class norms define "getting ahead" as a kind of moral obligation. Individuals without ambition to improve their position in society are seen as somehow lacking in character. Members of the middle class have great faith in "rationality"—in what can be accomplished by planning ahead and by allocating time, money, and energy efficiently. Children are taught the value of forgoing immediate gratification and rewards in the interest of attaining long-range goals.

The value orientations of most lower-class people place much less emphasis on future

18. A. Cohen and H. Hodges, "Characteristics of the Lower Blue Collar Class," *Social Problems,* 10 (1963): 312.
19. See, for example, Melvin Kohn, *Class and Conformity* (Homewood, Ill.: Dorsey Press, 1969). See also Albert K. Cohen, *Delinquent Boys* (New York: The Free Press, 1955), pp. 84–87.

Middle-class American parents generally believe that children should make use of leisure time rather than "just fritter it away." For many middle-class children, this means that their free time is spent in such regimented activities as taking dance lessons.

achievement. Although ambition is by no means deplored, economic security is generally stressed more than upward mobility or long-range goals. Lower-class people are far less likely than middle-class people to put much faith in careful, long-range planning. Life over the short term seems unpredictable enough; enjoyment should be taken when it can. If a lower-class family receives an unexpected financial windfall, it is likely to spend the money right away for something that can be enjoyed then and there. A middle-class family, by contrast, is more inclined to invest the money or save it for a rainy day.

Middle-class families stress the value of self-reliance and self-improvement. When children are old enough to start thinking about work, they are taught that the most desirable job is one in which they can exercise ability and initiative to get ahead. Lower-class children, by contrast, are oriented more toward valuing a job that offers security and immediate rewards.

Different orientations to achievement are reflected even in attitudes toward recreation. Middle-class parents believe firmly that children should spend their leisure time doing something that is "worthwhile," such as learning to play a musical instrument, participating in sports, or pursuing a hobby. Lower-class parents are much more tolerant of youngsters who spend their free time doing "nothing" or just hanging around with their friends.

Middle-class ways of life have been challenged in recent years, but middle-class children are still taught that manners, courtesy, and proper appearance are important in building and maintaining pleasant social relationships. Lower-class families are less concerned with teaching their children to behave with what middle-class people consider "propriety." The two classes also have different attitudes about the appropriateness of physical violence as a means for settling disputes. If a middle-class boy comes home with a bloody nose or a black eye, his parents are likely to lecture him about fighting and to encourage him to make friends with his opponent. A lower-class boy, on the other hand, may be told that he'd better learn how to use his fists so that people won't push him around.

American society is run, for the most part, by the middle class, and despite recent challenges to middle-class standards by some social critics and by young people who have "dropped out," they remain a kind of measuring rod for assessing behavior and values in a number of important areas of life. Thus an individual who has internalized standards the middle class does not accept may find it difficult to fit in—much less to excel—in school, in business, and in many other activities. For such an individual, the net result of socialization may be to limit opportunities.

AGENTS OF SOCIALIZATION

As we pointed out earlier, certain types of groups and social institutions can be singled out for the special part they play in the socialization process. Some of the principal agents of socialization, such as the family and the school, have a clear mandate from society to "train" new generations of members — to transmit the society's cultural heritage and to teach its accepted ways of acting, thinking, and feeling. Agents such as peer groups and the mass media, by contrast, do most of their teaching unwittingly or incidentally, influencing how the individual perceives and responds to the social world. Other more specialized agents of socialization are the various formal groups an individual joins. To a greater or lesser extent, each one of them molds or remolds the individual's attitudes, beliefs, and motivations in the process of developing effective group members.

There is currently considerable confusion about which agents of socialization should do what. Is it the school's task or the family's task to teach the young about sex or drug abuse? How much job training should the school provide? Until about a century ago the United States was largely an agrarian society. Most occupations were learned by the "watch and do" method; girls learned cooking, sewing, housekeeping, and gardening from their mothers; boys learned their fathers' trades or professions or were apprenticed to a local merchant, artisan, doctor, or lawyer. Today, very few children learn the skills of an occupation directly from parents, and many families do not feel responsible for providing anything in the form of vocational training. They leave this to the schools, which often do very little to prepare the young for jobs or for adulthood generally.[20] Frequently, young people's ideas about the norms, roles, and other ex-

pectations of the adult world are largely the product of chance learning from adults, peers, and the communication media.

THE FAMILY
The family has been central to every theory of personality formation, socialization, and child rearing that has been formulated within the behavioral sciences. It is the family that has always borne the major responsibility for teaching children the essentials of social order and culture and for guiding their personal development. We will review briefly two perspectives on family socialization.

Psychoanalytic Interpretations
Freud's theories of personality (page 147) have greatly influenced psychological interpretations of the family's role in the socialization process. In Freudian theory it is specifically the task of the family to develop the child's superego — that is, to instill in the child the moral values and norms of the society so that he or she obtains effective guides for controlling behavior according to culturally approved patterns. The Freudian viewpoint also emphasizes that the family acts as the major societal agent for establishing sex-role identity. Talcott Parsons, drawing heavily from Freudian sources, points out that family roles are divided mainly by sex (mothers versus fathers, sisters versus brothers). Boys begin life with a strong identification with the mother. They must then face the problem of breaking down this cross-sex identification and learning to identify with males as they move toward maturity. Girls who move on into traditional female roles have less difficulty with sex identification because their early identification with their mother is more likely to continue in adult life.[21]

Sociological Interpretations
In primitive and traditional societies the family is the principal agent of socialization throughout childhood and even adolescence. This has become much less true in urban-industrial societies such as the United States, where nuclear

20. Lois B. DeFleur and Ben A. Menke, "Learning About the Labor Force," *Sociology of Education,* Winter 1975.
21. Talcott Parsons and Robert F. Bales, *Family Socialization and Interaction Process* (New York: The Free Press, 1955), esp. Chapters 1 and 2.

family units (mother, father, and their children) usually live apart from other relatives and where the father is typically away from home for a large part of the day. Partly for this reason, more and more outside groups are performing tasks of child rearing and socialization that were formerly carried out by the family. There has been much debate about what effect this may have on the emotional security of children.[22] If their mothers work, even preschoolers may spend most of their day away from home. Upon entering school, the child encounters not only a formal system of socialization but also informal systems among peers. Activity directors such as athletic coaches and scout leaders may also act as important agents of socialization for the school-age child.

Among the very poor in our society, the care and training of children is often left largely to chance. In some families there is lively interchange when parents return from work, but in others the father and mother seldom talk to the children at all. Preschool children may be left alone all day, or until an older sibling returns from school. Often slum children spend much of their time in the streets with peers, living on snacks and not even sharing mealtime with their parents.

In all socioeconomic levels of society, the father takes a less active role in socializing the children than was usual in former times. In a middle-class home with a traditional role structure, the mother still provides the girl with an adult female role model, but the boy has much less experience with the adult male role. The result for the male child of having no steadily present adult male to model himself after may be what Parsons has called "sex-role blurring."[23] With the mother as the main socializing agent, the boy may take on many of the attitudes, values, and behaviors that have traditionally been considered "feminine."

Girls or boys raised in families where an opposite sex sibling is present seem to take on different traits than do those in families where the children are all of the same sex. Brim found

that girls with brothers have more traits that have traditionally been considered "masculine" than do girls without brothers.[24] At the same time, they did not evidence fewer so-called feminine traits; rather, they seemed to have a broader behavioral repertoire. The pattern with boys was similar, except that the boys seemed to displace some "masculine" patterns with "feminine" ones.

Today a number of people feel that children should not be socialized into "masculine" and "feminine" sex roles. Some parents are trying to socialize their sons and daughters as similarly as possible—giving dolls, cooking sets, sports equipment, and tools to both boys and girls. While this kind of socialization may not be adopted on a widespread basis, there is less consensus today than previously about what trait differences, if any, are desirable for males and females.

Overall, the socialization experiences of the child and the role of the family as an agent in this process depend upon a host of factors, such as the occupational activities of the parents and their individual attitudes toward child rearing, the family's position in the social-class structure, the presence or absence of either parent, and the presence or absence of brothers and sisters.

THE PEER GROUP

Next to the family, the peer group (page 65) is probably the most influential agent of socialization in the life of the individual. Jean Piaget, the eminent Swiss psychologist, has maintained that peer-group interaction is essential if children are to become fully developed morally.[25]

22. Alex Inkeles, "Society, Social Structure and Child Socialization," in Clausen, *Socialization and Society*, pp. 121–122. See also Eleanor E. Maccoby, "Attachment and Dependency," in P. H. Mussen, ed., *Carmichael's Manual of Child Psychology*, vol. 2 (New York: John Wiley & Sons, Inc., 1970), pp. 73–151.

23. Parsons, "Age and Sex."

24. Orville G. Brim, Jr., "Family Structure and Sex Role Learning by Children: A Further Analysis of Helen Koch's Data," in *Selected Studies in Marriage and the Family*, rev. ed., Robert F. Winch, Robert McGinnis, and Herbert R. Barringer, eds. (New York: Holt, Rinehart and Winston, Inc., 1962), pp. 275–290. This article was adapted from *Sociometry*, 21 (1958): 1–16.

25. Jean Piaget, *The Moral Judgment of the Child* (London: Routledge & Kegan Paul, 1932).

VIEWPOINTS   ARE SEX ROLES INEVITABLE?

■ Even if the boy is more aggressive than the girl only because the society allows him to be, the boy's socialization still flows from society's acknowledging biological reality. . . . If society did not teach young girls that beating boys at competitions was unfeminine (behavior inappropriate for a woman), if it did not socialize them away from the political and economic areas in which aggression leads to attainment, these girls would grow into adulthood with self-images based not on succeeding in areas for which biology has left them better prepared than men, but on competitions that most women could not win. If women did not develop feminine qualities as girls (assuming that such qualities do not spring automatically from female biology) then they would be forced to deal with the world in the aggressive terms of men. They would lose every source of power their feminine abilities now give them and they would gain nothing. (Likewise, if there is a physiological difference between men and women . . . social values and socialization will conform to this fact. They will conform both because observation by the population of men and women will preclude the development of values which ignore the physiological difference and because, even if such values could develop, they would make life intolerable for the vast majority of males, who would feel the tension between social expectation and the dearth of maternal feelings, and the vast majority of females, whose physiologically generated feelings toward the infant would be frustrated.)

Steven Goldberg
The Inevitability of Patriarchy

● Home environments tend to set the stage for sex-role stereotypes. We've all seen little girls' rooms that are so organdied, pink and pippy-poo one would never dream of besmirching them with Play-Doh or cartwheels. We've seen little boys living in nautical decors or in cell-like rooms heavy on athletic equipment but lacking a cozy place to read a book. We've seen little boys scolded for parading in their sisters' ballet tutus; girls enjoined from getting soiled; boys forbidden to play with dolls; girls forbidden to wrestle. . . .

In school books, the Dick and Jane syndrome reinforced our emerging attitudes. The arithmetic books posed appropriate conundrums: "Ann has three pies . . . Dan has three rockets. . ." We read the nuances between the lines: Ann keeps her eye on the oven; Dan sets his sights on the moon.

Put it all together, it spells conform. Be beautiful, feminine, alluring, passive, supportive. Subvert your energies, dear. Conceal your brains, young lady. Spunky girls finish last on the way to the prom. Tomboys must convert. Boys don't make passes at female smart-asses. We all got the message—finally. . . .

The boy reading the same material is victimized by the reverse effects. If she's all dainty and diaphanous, he has to be strong and assertive. If she faints for love for a fullback then he'd better try out for the team. If Mom and the kiddies are at home all day, then who but Dad must work to keep starvation from the door? The pressure is on. . . .

How can you raise your kids to be free when they're so systematically shackled within the schools? The answer is, you can't. Emancipation from sex-stereotypes is not possible unless all institutions affecting a child's development are brought into harmonious accord. . . .

Human liberation is the prize. Our daughters and sons gain the freedom to develop as persons, not role-players.

Letty Cottin Pogrebin
"Down With Sexist Upbringing"

Unlike the family and the school, a peer group does not deliberately try to socialize its members. Its major purpose is to provide enjoyment. Nevertheless, cliques and gangs unintentionally exert a great amount of pressure on their members to acquire particular values, orientations, and outlooks. The same is true of adult peer groups. Because primary interaction with close friends is emotionally satisfying, the codes and expectations of peer groups are usually strongly internalized by individual members.

Peer Groups and Other-Directedness

David Riesman, who maintains that the peer group is becoming the single most important agent of socialization in modern society, has described three very different types of general personality structure that result from distinctive patterns of socialization.[26] In primitive and traditional societies, the coherent culture and stable patterns of social organization provide an adequate basis for behavioral definition. Socialization in such societies usually results in a "tradition-directed" person, one who looks to the accepted ways of society for guidance in matters of personal conduct. Conversely, the "inner-directed" person is most often found in a society undergoing rapid normative change. Since external codes do not provide stable guides for personal conduct under such circumstances, guidance must come from within. The socialization processes in this type of society (as, for example, in nineteenth-century America) emphasize the development of strong personal ideals and inner moral convictions to give adequate direction to personal behavior.

In modern society, Riesman says, people tend to be "other-directed." They look to their peers for ideas as to how they should behave. There is considerable need for social approval and great fear of social rejection. "Other-directed" individuals have neither a strong social order with stable, deeply institutionalized behavioral norms to serve as a guide to conduct nor an independent set of internal convictions about what constitutes proper conduct. Instead, they follow those courses of action that seem most likely to win peer approval.

The "Generation Gap"

In many contemporary societies, the importance of the peer group can be seen in the disparity between the norms of young people and their parents. By the time the individual is a teenager, the peer group is demanding that he or she think, act, and feel in ways that are often in sharp contrast to the norms of older generations. Modern youth cultures have emphasized modes of dress, hairstyles, art forms, sexual mores, diets and drugs, exotic and occult religions and philosophies, and political activities that often deviate sharply from the practices and beliefs of adults.

On the other hand, the extent of the schism between the generations has often been exaggerated. As adolescents, today's parents had their styles, their art forms, their fads and cults. They also had their articulate minority of political, moral, and social rebels. Furthermore, careful analyses of high-school students have shown that in arriving at many important decisions, adolescents are actually influenced more strongly by family and background variables than by peers. For example, in deciding on plans to go to college, it is usually the adolescent's parents, not friends, who exert the most influence.[27] A study by Floyd and South suggests that the use of peers as reference groups tends to level off or decline after about the tenth grade. The same study showed that teen-age boys are somewhat more likely than girls to choose peers over family.[28]

The present fast rate of social change in the United States and other urban-industrial societies inevitably emphasizes differences between generations. Where change is less rapid the differences seem less extreme. In the traditional society of the Hopi Indians, for example, adolescence has been a period for gradually assuming adult roles.

26. David Riesman, in collaboration with Reuel Denney and Nathan Glazer, *The Lonely Crowd* (New Haven, Conn.: Yale University Press, 1950).

27. E. L. McDill and L. Rigsby, *Structure and Process in Secondary Education: The Impact of Educational Climates* (Baltimore, Md.: The Johns Hopkins University Press, 1973), esp. Chapter 1.

28. H. Hugh Floyd, Jr., and Donald R. South, "Dilemma of Youth: The Choice of Parents or Peers as a Frame of Reference for Behavior," *Journal of Marriage and the Family*, 34, No. 4 (November 1972): 627–634.

As the Hopi boy approaches adolescence his economic responsibilities increase. He now accompanies his father or grandfather to the fields or grazing areas. By the age of fourteen he is expected to have mastered most agricultural skills and to be able to take charge of his own herd and his mother's fields. In winter he accompanies his elders into the kiva [men's ceremonial chamber] where the men's handcrafts, including weaving and moccasin making, are taught him. Here also he is expected to learn tribal lore and master the rituals of . . . the wider Hopi society.[29]

Until recently, at least, adolescence among the Hopi has been a period in which young people have greatly increased their interaction with adults. By contrast, in contemporary Western urban society the generations tend to become compartmentalized, with young people during adolescence *decreasing* their involvement with adults. This is partly a consequence of shifting the responsibility for socialization from the family to other agencies.

THE SCHOOL

In its formal structure, the school is a rationally organized bureaucracy—a social machine designed to "process" batches of human beings who are fed into the system at the bottom and who are expected to emerge some years later with useful and socially approved modifications in their knowledge, skills, values, attitudes, and general orientations to society. As the statistics on dropouts and delinquency make clear, however, the school does not always succeed in its task. To understand some of the reasons for its failures, we need to look beyond the formal structure of the school and examine the ways in which it is linked to other groups and to social processes over which it has little control. Of special significance are the values and loyalties that individual teachers and learners bring to the school situation.

Values and Value Conflict

Most of the teachers in our schools are recruited from the middle class. This background, plus their own "processing" in teacher-training insti-

tutions, results in special viewpoints and outlooks. Normally, teachers are very strongly committed to the set of norms and orientations that we previously described as "the middle-class value system." At the same time, many schools draw large proportions of their students from lower-class homes. As we have indicated, such children are seldom very strongly committed to the middle-class ideals and values that teachers use to evaluate them. As a consequence, lower-class children are likely to be perceived as poor performers and as having little potential.

Compare these two poems by sixth-grade children:

> SHOP WITH MOM
> I love to shop with mom
> And talk to the friendly grocer
> And help her make the list
> Seems to make us closer.
> —Nellie, age 11

> THE JUNKIES
> When they are
> in the street
> they pass it
> along to each
> other but when
> they see the
> police they would
> run some would
> just stand still
> and be beat
> so pity ful
> that they want
> to cry
> —Mary, age 11

The poems appear in a book by a teacher, Herbert R. Kohl, who uses them to describe a clash between middle- and lower-class culture in the elementary school where he taught.

Nellie's poem received high praise. Her teacher liked the rhyme "closer" and "grocer," and thought she said a great deal in four lines. Most of all the teacher was pleased that Nellie expressed such a pleasant and healthy thought. . . . I was moved and excited by Mary's poem and made the mistake of showing it to

29. Stuart A. Queen, Robert W. Habenstein, and John B. Adams, *The Family in Various Cultures*, rev. ed. (New York: J. B. Lippincott Co., 1961), p. 60.

the teacher who edited the school newspaper. She was horrified. First of all, she informed me, Mary couldn't possibly know what 'junkies were, and, moreover, the other children wouldn't be interested in such a poem. There weren't any rhymes or clearly discernible meter. The word "pityful" was split up incorrectly, "be beat" wasn't proper English and, finally, it wasn't really poetry but just the ramblings of a disturbed girl.[30]

As this example points out, conflict between the middle-class expectations of teachers and the lower-class orientations of many students can seriously subvert the best intentioned efforts of the educational system to train all young people equally for adult roles and responsibilities.

Subcultures and Informal Structure

Also important in the informal structure of the school are the subcultures that are fostered and maintained by students themselves. Much lore is perpetuated about particular teachers, other students, courses of study, sex, and ways to beat the system. Modes of dress, dance forms, and speech mannerisms peculiar to the age group are introduced, disseminated, and adopted as part of these ever changing subcultures.[31] Student subcultures may or may not be directly subversive to the formal goals of the school; but even at best, they are not likely to be particularly supportive.

In addition to school-wide subcultural patterns, the informal structure of the school includes a system of social ranking among the students.[32] Generally, there are elite groups at the top of the status system, outcasts at the bottom, and various kinds of groups in between. In many ways, these informal structures modify the efforts of the formal system to transmit and instill community-approved values, motivations, and skills. In some cases they actually subvert socially approved goals and values, providing alternate ways for obtaining social approval, a positive self-image, and personal esteem through outright delinquency and vandalism.[33] In other cases they may link the individual quite directly with the values of Main Street in ways the school cannot accomplish.[34]

THE MASS MEDIA

The average American today spends a substantial portion of each day with the mass media, particularly television.[35] Recent census figures show television ownership approaches saturation in families with young children—99 percent. Wilbur Schramm has estimated that from ages three through sixteen the child spends more time on television than on school.[36]

What does all this mean in terms of socialization? Heavy exposure to television and other media is easy to document, but unraveling the influence of such exposure is not a simple task. Research has focused on (1) the effects of the media in defining cultural norms, (2) the kinds of incidental learning that may result from exposure to the media, and (3) the effectiveness of deliberate efforts to employ the media, especially television, to foster learning and social change.[37]

The Media and Cultural Norms

According to one view, by emphasizing certain topics, stressing particular interpretations, and repeating specific themes, the media may create a distorted impression of societal realities. For example, if television and movies regularly portray sexual promiscuity as widely practiced, viewers may accept such conduct as normative. When they must define their own sexual behavior, standards internalized from media sources may guide their conduct. This same type of re-

30. Herbert R. Kohl, *Teaching the "Unteachable"* (New York: The New York Review, 1967), p. 15.
31. James S. Coleman, *The Adolescent Society* (New York: The Free Press, 1961), p. 3.
32. Robert S. and Helen M. Lynd, *Middletown: A Study in American Culture* (New York: Harcourt Brace Jovanovich, Inc., 1929); August B. Hollingshead, *Elmtown's Youth* (New York: John Wiley & Sons, Inc., 1949); Patricia C. Sexton, *The American School: A Sociological Analysis* (Englewood Cliffs, N.J.: Prentice-Hall, Inc., 1967).
33. Cohen, *Delinquent Boys*, pp. 121–179.
34. Sexton, *The American School*, p. 93.
35. John P. Murray, "Television and Violence," *American Psychologist*, 28 (1973): 472–478.
36. Wilbur Schramm, *Television in the Lives of Our Children* (Stanford, Calif.: Stanford University Press, 1961), p. 30.
37. Although television and the other media have been charged with everything from causing juvenile delinquency to ruining the cultural tastes of the nation, research has thus far failed to turn up any convincing evidence of immediate and direct causal links between the media and particular patterns of social behavior. For a detailed discussion of this issue, see Chapter 14, "Mass Communication."

lationship may prevail with respect to such matters as the use of alcohol, tobacco, drugs, and even violence. If violence is depicted repeatedly (by movies, television, comics, etc.) as a socially acceptable means of settling differences, the individual may follow this model when confronted with a situation where violence is an option.

The life-styles depicted on television and in popular magazines are often noticeably on the affluent side. Young women with beautiful hair and impeccable clothes demonstrate new products in homes that look like mansions. Television teen-agers have attractive friends and often own expensive sport cars. In most television programs about contemporary life in America, the settings imply a kind of wealth and security actually available in this country to only a few. Viewers, of course, are not warned of this. In fact, they may conclude, like fourth- and fifth-graders studied in Ohio, that such programs depict "life the way it really is."[38] Low-income children were more likely to feel this way than children from more affluent homes.

The selective emphasis given by television, magazine, and newspaper ads to cars, fancy appliances, cosmetics, instant foods, and expensive sports equipment has contributed to our defining these things as *needs* rather than luxuries. Even people with comfortable incomes are subject to feelings of relative deprivation. Middle-class Americans with two cars and a house in the suburbs may grumble that they can't afford a boat or a swimming pool. For the poor, the contrast between life as it *is* and life as it seemingly *should* be is made much more striking. Here as elsewhere, it is difficult to isolate the precise effects of the media, but it can be hypothesized that they have played a significant part in motivating the disadvantaged in our society to press for a more equal share of society's "good things."

The norm-defining role of the media should not be overestimated. Sociologists who are con-

cerned with the effects of the media on cultural norms recognize the importance of differential association. That is, most people are exposed to many sources of norms other than the mass media, some of which reject such things as sexual promiscuity, violence, and all-out consumption. But for individuals who lack counter associations, the media may play a rather decisive role in providing behavioral definitions.

The Media and Incidental Learning

Through television, the movies, and other media, children are exposed to portrayals of an adult world of which they are not yet a part but which holds great fascination for them. In this way, they acquire conceptions of people's values, numerous social roles, and other kinds of social knowledge without really seeking it. This is incidental learning, an unplanned by-product of entertainment.

A study exploring the potential role of the mass media in fostering accurate or incorrect conceptions about society monitored six months of television broadcasts as they appeared on the screens of a small midwestern community in order to see how occupational roles were portrayed in ordinary television fare.[39] The televised occupational distribution departed from reality in a number of significant ways. For example, no factory worker appeared among the 450 occupations portrayed in the samples of television time reviewed, though such workers constituted more than one fifth of the actual labor force in the state where the study was made. About a third of the workers portrayed on television were professionals, though in fact professionals made up only about one tenth of the labor force. A full third of the televised workers were engaged in occupations associated with the law.

The real issue raised by such research is the impact of television on the young audience: Do children actually develop badly distorted ideas about the world of work from watching television? To study this question, a second research project was designed to follow up the analysis of

38. Bradley S. Greenberg, "Summary of Findings and Future Research Directions," in *Mass Media and the Urban Poor,* ed. B. Derwin, et al. (New York: Praeger, Inc., 1970), pp. 73–86.

39. Melvin L. DeFleur, "Occupational Roles as Portrayed on Television," *Public Opinion Quarterly,* 28 (Spring 1964): 57–74.

occupational portrayals on TV. Special questionnaires were devised for interviewing a sample of 237 schoolchildren in the community where the original study had been conducted. The purpose was to measure how much they knew about the roles and requirements of particular jobs and how well they could rank the jobs into a socioeconomic hierarchy that would correspond to adult rankings of the same occupations. Three types of jobs were studied: those with which the child had extensive personal contact; those encountered mainly on television; and those present in the community but not particularly visible to the child either directly or through TV.

As might be expected, the study revealed that the children were most familiar with those occupations with which they had had some form of personal contact. But occupational roles that had been frequently portrayed on TV were understood almost as well. The children had a poor understanding of jobs that were present in the community but not visible to them in life or on screen. Overall, this study showed that television can be a rich source for incidental learning about occupations. Children of all social levels were able to describe the duties, modes of dress, and relative social rank of such roles as butler and head waiter, even though they had never encountered them in person. At the same time, the findings indicated that there were numerous distortions and stereotypes in the ideas the children entertained about the occupational roles studied.[40]

The findings of such research help us understand the interplay of influences from the mass media and other agents of socialization. Modern society expects that young people will gradually prepare themselves to assume roles in the labor force. Yet neither the family nor the school nor any other agent of deliberate socialization provides systematic information about the varied world of work. Thus in this area as in many others, television and other mass media become teachers by default. In providing incidental information about the social world, some of which is inaccurate, they help shape children's ideas about what life as an adult should be like.

In recent years there has been growing concern about the incidental learning children may acquire through exposure to televised violence. From animated cartoons aimed directly at juvenile audiences to Westerns and shows dealing with urban crime, beatings and shootings are daily entertainment fare for television audiences. There is mounting evidence that excessive portrayals of violence on television and in movies, comic books, and magazines may lead to significant increases in violent behavior among certain kinds of children.[41] We will discuss this issue further in Chapter 14, "Mass Communication."

Television and Deliberate Socialization

Although most of what children learn from television is "taught" without intent, many people have recognized TV's potential as a direct teaching tool. Particularly noteworthy has been the effort to help children overcome cultural disadvantages through television programs like *Sesame Street, The Electric Company,* and *Zoom.* The effectiveness of *Sesame Street* has been assessed by Samuel Ball and Gerry Bogatz, who studied 943 preschool children, including 741 disadvantaged children (urban and rural, Spanish-speaking as well as English-speaking). These researchers found that viewing the program led to gains in many kinds of knowledge. Children who watched it improved their skills at recognizing letters and numbers, reading words, and the like. They also manifested gains in such skills as sorting and classifying. Regular viewers far surpassed infrequent viewers on these gains. Spanish-speaking children in particular were very low in attainment before they started viewing; if they watched frequently, they gained more than any other group.[42] Further evaluations need to be made, but thus far the evidence suggests

40. Melvin L. DeFleur and Lois B. DeFleur, "The Relative Contribution of Television as a Learning Source for Children's Occupational Knowledge," *American Sociological Review* 32, No. 5 (October 1967): 777–789.

41. The Surgeon General's Scientific Advisory Committee on Television and Social Behavior, *Television and Growing Up: The Impact of Televised Violence* (Washington, D.C.: U.S. Government Printing Office, 1972).

42. Samuel Ball and Gerry Bogatz, *The First Year of Sesame Street: An Evaluation* (Princeton, N.J.: Educational Testing Service, 1970).

that television programs like *Sesame Street* may effectively implement traditional methods of education.

AGENTS OF SPECIALIZED SOCIALIZATION

Churches, corporations, the military services, labor unions, and other associations of all kinds provide specialized socialization for particular segments of society. We will look at the corporation and the military services, both of which attempt to reshape their recruits so that they will behave more effectively as group members.

The Corporation

In the mid-1950s William H. Whyte, Jr., analyzed corporate processes for recruiting, evaluating, and utilizing "executive material." He placed particular emphasis upon the way a corporation may shape and influence the values and activities of those it retains and moves up the ladder.[43] Whyte contended that the organization serves as a powerful agency for suppressing the creative innovator, the driving, self-motivated individualist identified in popular thought as a potential captain of industry. While in the rough-and-tumble days of American industry such two-fisted types were destined to drive quickly to the top, modern corporations, according to Whyte, quickly channel them out of their management systems as unorthodox and even dangerous.

In most large corporations the team-oriented person is the one most likely to move upward through the administrative hierarchy, fitting in smoothly with the committee approach to management. Such a person "does not think up ideas himself, but mediates other people's ideas, and so democratically that he never lets his own judgment override the decisions of the group."[44] In dealings with subordinates the team-oriented person is concerned primarily with "human relations" and with the techniques of welding employees into a loyal and smoothly running team. Whyte saw the modern corporation as demanding this type of personality configuration.

Corporations differ in the degree to which they approximate Whyte's model, and everyone can cite examples of individuals who have risen in a corporate hierarchy primarily because they were hard-driving innovators. It seems generally true, nevertheless, that a successful business organization modifies the prior socialization of its recruits, reshaping their attitudes and loyalties so that they function more effectively as team members.

The Military Services

An extreme example of specialized socialization is provided by the Marine Corps, the most conservative unit in the armed services of the United States. The following is a brief sociological description of the traditional process of training Marine recruits.

A Marine-to-be arrives at the training base psychologically structured as a civilian. His past socialization, self-image, and general orientations tend to support his identity with his former life. The Corps systematically suppresses this identity in order to transform the recruit into a Marine.

First, his physical body is transformed. His head is shaved. His civilian clothes are replaced by shapeless dungarees. Like every other "boot," he is issued a specific number of identical undershirts, socks, shoelaces, belts, etc. The last external vestiges of individuality have been removed; he is as much like the others as it is possible to be.

The recruit is restricted to his immediate barracks or camp area, and, lest he retreat vicariously into his former identity, his communication with his past is temporarily restricted. He is permitted to write to his immediate family but, for the moment, to no one else.

To hasten the systematic suppression of his civilian self-image, his new drill instructor and his assistants demand a degree of physical performance that the recruit cannot meet. Complex commands confuse him. Official policies to the contrary, he is degraded by kicks in the rump, by raps on the helmet, and by vile name-calling and general verbal abuse. Those in charge have traditionally taken great delight in inventing humiliating punishments for trivial infractions.

43. William H. Whyte, Jr., *The Organization Man* (New York: Simon & Schuster, Inc., 1956).

44. Ibid., p. 150.

The purpose of the specialized socialization of the Marine Corps is to transform civilians into team-oriented combat soldiers. When recruits first arrive at the training camp, their heads are shaved and they are given identical uniforms. Gradually extensive physical training and harsh punishment weld the recruits together into a combat group.

After many days of this treatment, the individual comes to the conclusion that he is, in fact, a disgrace to himself, his family, his country, and most of all to the Marine Corps, just as he has been told over and over.

But meanwhile, other things have been happening. The shared punishment and the shared pride in each individual's ability to "take all that can be dished out" welds the trainees together into a brotherhood that becomes an effective substitute for former "significant others" and reference groups. This is the germ of the *esprit de corps* that the whole process is designed to foster. Second, constant exercise, good diet, and regular hours provide the basis for a physical transformation that gives the recruit a great boost in morale. Finally, the sergeant in charge tells the group, somewhat grudgingly, that maybe they aren't such a bad bunch after all. As the group increases in proficiency, there is additional praise—almost always for the group rather than for specific persons, so as to reinforce the group identity of the individual.

Gradually, the new Marine is given more freedom, snappier uniforms, and increased praise. The rewards for conformity are sweet. Systematically, his self-concept has been rebuilt as a member of the Corps, and he has intense pride in his new status. At the end of the training period, when there is a "graduation ceremony" for his platoon, he feels that he has made the grade and thinks of himself as a Marine. His new value system follows a profile carefully designed to make him a reliable and effective combat soldier.

SOCIALIZATION AND THE LIFE CYCLE

While experiences in infancy and childhood are especially crucial in shaping personality, the socialization process never ends. We have already noted that new occupational roles typically require resocialization. So also do changes in

age. As we move through the life cycle, we assume a progression of general roles, such as adolescent, spouse, parent, widower, and retired person. Finally, as the end of the life span nears, we face the unpleasant reality of being a dying person. Each of these broad roles involves special demands and expectations. So, too, do the hundreds of limited or specialized roles that an individual occupies in a lifetime. As we noted in introducing this chapter, socialization is a continuing process of adjustment to changing expectations and demands.

SOCIALIZATION IN ADOLESCENCE

In American society the meaning of *adolescence* has changed. Once young people assumed adult roles when they graduated from high school or even earlier. Now it is estimated that over 60 percent of young people who finish high school in the United States go on to some form of advanced or specialized education. The increase in the average age at leaving school, plus the unwillingness of firms to hire persons without college training, means that a sizable proportion of young people are in a kind of social limbo, functionally dependent upon support from others. Today social adolescence—in the sense of dependent status beyond childhood—stretches for many individuals from age ten or eleven until the time that they leave college or graduate school and take their first adult jobs. Some may be functionally dependent upon support from others into their early thirties. Perhaps it is necessary to propose a new life stage called "studenthood" that is separate from the older meanings of *childhood, adolescence,* and *adulthood.*

In contemporary society, at least two distinct patterns of adolescence are discernible, each with its special problems of socialization. At the bottom of the socioeconomic scale, the school dropout rate is high. Those young people who leave school before graduating from high school are barred from being a part of the "adolescent society" that continues on in the schools, yet they cannot effectively enter the conventional adult world.

Even for those who go to college, the transition to adulthood can be a major problem. As they approach graduation, young people are expected to make decisions about such matters as careers, marriage, and starting a family—major role changes for which they often feel unprepared. Graduate school may seem an attractive alternative to joining the larger society. The Peace Corps, VISTA, and similar programs have also served as vehicles for helping those just out of school achieve an adult self-identity without immediate commitment to adult roles.

SOCIALIZATION IN ADULT LIFE

For both males and females there are a number of significant transitions during adulthood that require continuing socialization—not only the learning of new behavior patterns but also the acquiring of new orientations.

The Adult Female

Although the socialization of most female children stresses the learning of attitudes, values, and skills they are likely to need someday as wives and mothers, getting married and having children are major adjustments even for young women who are oriented toward assuming the traditional wife/mother role. The dating and courtship period does little to prepare the female (or the male) for such realities of married life as keeping house, stretching limited financial resources, and staying home to care for young children. A well-educated young woman who has perhaps worked for a time may find it particularly difficult to adjust to a full-time domestic routine.

There has been little research on the relationship between the adolescent female's viewpoint and her later role performance. One study shows that while middle-class adolescent boys dislike the idea of women pursuing career goals traditionally seen as "male," this conservatism is not shared by middle-class girls. There may be clashes or compromises later when, as mates, young men and women try to accommodate to each other's conceptions of the female work role.[45]

Attitudes toward the woman who remains unmarried (whether or not she is a career-wom-

Traditional socialization does little to prepare women for the realities of married life.

an) and toward the career-woman (whether married or single) have recently been undergoing change. Nevertheless, major adjustments are still required of a woman in her late twenties who has remained single. As she nears the end of the period when she is considered "young," she must develop orientations that will enable her to maintain a positive self-image in a society where the category of "single woman" is still negatively defined by many. To a degree, the same adjustments must be made by a married woman who elects to remain in the labor force on a full-time, career-oriented basis rather than to have a family. Surrounded by people who consider it "normal" for married women to want to stay home and raise children, she must seek experiences that provide a basis for positive self-definitions in her "deviant" role.

For those women who choose the traditional wife/mother role, the need to adjust to the full-time responsibilities of mothering young children is inevitably followed by the need to adjust to the *loss* of those responsibilities. Today the average woman will have borne all her children within six or eight years after marriage, and

45. Doris R. Entwisle and Ellen Greenberger, "Adolescent's Views of Women's Work Role," *American Journal of Orthopsychiatry,* 42 (1972): 648–656.

by the time she reaches her middle or late thirties the scope of her domestic responsibilities will have been sharply reduced. With average life expectancy into the seventies, she thus has more than half of her adult years ahead of her. Yet she has no demanding role responsibilities comparable to those of her contemporaries who are in the labor force. To avoid "social death" at midlife, some women attempt to recapture the glamour and gaiety of their youth. Others channel their talents and energy into civic affairs or social clubs. Many women (more than 40 percent) enter or re-enter the labor force, and increasing numbers are resuming their formal education. Fortunately, adult role choices for females have broadened greatly in recent years, and it seems likely that they will become broader still in the future.

The Adult Male
With his traditional roles as wage-earner, husband, and father, the adult male faces a combination of changing role expectations at least as complex as those of the female. Almost every adult male in our society is expected to enter the labor force in some capacity and, if married, to be the major breadwinner for his family. Even if

his wife works, the husband is still usually regarded as the chief economic provider, and traditionally he lacks the choice his wife may have of whether to work or not.

Continuing resocialization is necessary for the male throughout his working years, as he moves from job to job, wins or fails to win promotion, achieves increasing satisfaction in his work or finds himself trapped in a job he dislikes. And if married he must integrate the changing demands of his occupational role with the changing demands of being a husband and father.

Because the occupational role is such a significant one for males in our society, many men come to equate self-worth with upward mobility in the world of work. As he moves up the ladder of success, a man may translate his ability to accumulate wealth or to provide his family with material possessions into an increasingly favorable self-image. A man who fails to get ahead in his occupational role, on the other hand, is likely to suffer self-devaluation unless he is able to find compensating satisfaction in other areas of his life.

Many of the adjustment problems requiring resocialization are very similar for males and females. Women are not alone, for example, in

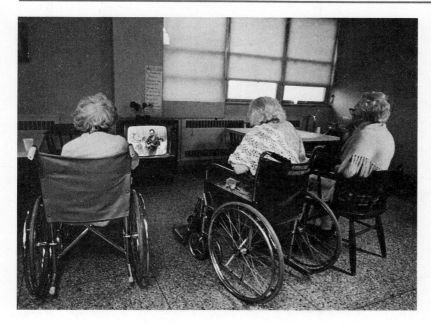

Today there are few meaningful social roles for the elderly. While some may become involved in the lives of their children and grandchildren, many others must patiently bide their remaining time in nursing homes. Currently, some elderly people have formed associations to try to persuade society to allow them to be useful.

being reluctant to accept the loss of youth. More than a few middle-aged men die of heart attacks every year trying to prove they have not lost the strength and endurance necessary to perform some physically demanding task or sport. In a society that venerates youth, such symptoms of aging as baldness, an expanding waistline, and a decline in sexual ability all pose the need for acquiring new attitudes and orientations that will enable the individual to live comfortably with the idea of "getting older."

SOCIALIZATION AND THE ELDERLY

It is doubtful that becoming old was ever very easy, but it has been made more and more difficult in modern society for two reasons. First, as noted above, our society venerates youth, not old age. Second, old age is marked by the loss of significant roles that in younger years serve as important sources of personality maintenance.

The Decline of Group Involvement

In old age, group ties that formerly linked the individual with significant others gradually fade

away. As friends die and health fails, the individual is likely to become increasingly isolated from meaningful interaction with other people. For many older people, more and more time is spent doing nothing at all—or in activities designed to conceal the fact that there is nothing to do:

Q. What did you do after supper?
A. I filled out my diary and my mail book. . . .
Q. What mail book?
A. Oh, I notice generally the mail I get and send.
Q. You keep track of it in a book?
A. Everything.
Q. The mail you receive. . . .
A. And the mail I send. . . .
Q. And that's what you did after supper?
A. Yes. It takes only a little while. And then I rest a while again, with the window open to get some wind and look at the trees, and I'm glad that I can look at them.
Q. How long did you look at the trees?
A. Oh, I can't tell you. Then I look at the television program. . . . At 10:00 generally I retire to bed with a whole lot of books.
Q. Did anybody come to the door?
A. No.[46]

46. From an interview in Edgar May, *The Wasted Americans: Cost of Our Welfare Dilemma* (New York: Harper & Row, Inc., 1964), p. 104.

We saw earlier that social isolation can have a very serious impact on the maintenance of personality in adulthood. Thus what often seems to be physical decline in ability among the aged may in part be a result of progressive disengagement from group life. As long as individuals are under the pressure of complex role expectations from others, they have every prospect of maintaining alertness into advanced years. In fact, numerous diplomats, musicians, jurists, and educators have produced some of their most important work in their old age.

The Role of Elder

In our society, the question "Who am I?" is generally answered in terms of occupational role. Consequently, retirement from the labor force, which usually comes as a sharp and sudden break, creates an identity problem for the older person. By contrast, traditional societies usually increased the responsibility and general status of elders. Because they had lived longer, the old people knew more and thus had very important roles to play. There was no rapid explosion of new scientific knowledge to displace their patiently accumulated lore. An illustration is provided by the role of elder in the Chinese family under the traditional clan system:

Retirement did not mean loss of authority in decision-making. The elders were always consulted, and theirs was the final "yes" or "no," if they chose to take part in family councils. Withdrawal from such activities did not mean complete loss of other functions, such as scholarly pursuits and religious duties, art and hobbies, or the care and education of grandchildren. Certainly it meant no loss of position or status in the household, for the place of the elder was at the top of the hierarchy.[47]

Throughout most of human history, the elderly have had a scarcity value; only a handful of people survived to old age. The intergenerational continuity of the society guaranteed them a role in the socialization of younger generations. They retained a sense of being useful and important all during the time they were being slowly phased out of communal life.

The Aged in Contemporary Society

In our society, there is little dignity in being among the elderly. The scientific accomplishments of industrialized society have prolonged the lives of our aged until most people over sixty-five now have a life expectancy of between ten and fifteen years. But the technical revolution has also brought marked changes in the structure of the family and in the role of the aged in community life. Like adolescents, the elderly are not needed in the contemporary labor market. The information explosion in all fields has made their knowledge obsolete, and rapid changes in cultural definitions have even made their morals and manners out of date. The "golden years" of senior citizenship may mean taking it easy in a warm climate and staying out of the hair of the rest of society. More often, they mean poverty, boredom, and loneliness. There is a crucial need to locate more meaningful roles for the elderly members of our society and to provide adequate socialization to prepare them to play these roles.

SUMMARY

Socialization may be viewed, as preparation for participation in group life, as enculturation, or as training to gain control over socially unacceptable drives. Sociologists are primarily interested in socialization as social preparation.

Socialization provides for continuity in society by training new members to play established roles. It produces sufficient conformity so that people can interact within a framework of mutual expectations. But socialization also allows great variation in individual personality; no two people have exactly the same socializing experiences, and they always bring their personal predispositions and creativity to the socialization process. The result is a changing society composed of individuals who are in many ways

47. Dorothy R. Blitsten, *The World of the Family* (New York: Random House, Inc., 1963), p. 121.

unique but who are able to conform to social and cultural expectations sufficiently to act together in predictable ways.

Socialization as training for group life involves learning norms, acquiring roles, and internalizing controls. Ranking systems narrow the range of contact between society's members and thus lead to the development of subcultural traits. Socialization prepares the individual for participation in a particular social milieu through the internalization of subcultural norms and values.

Every group in which an individual participates serves as an agent of socialization, but some have a greater influence than others. The family and the school, for example, have a special mandate from society to train new generations of members—to teach the knowledge, skills, attitudes, values, and general orientations that are needed to function effectively as an individual and group member. But not all the learning that takes place in these settings is intended, and some of it may run counter to the norms and values that the society formally supports.

Peer groups have a special importance as agents of socialization during all stages of life, simply because the individual values them so highly as sources of emotional support. Desire for the esteem of one's close friends exerts a strong pressure for conformity to their standards. The mass media can at times portray society in ways that misrepresent reality and that create erroneous impressions of the adult world among children. The mass media act as agents of socialization through the incidental learning process. Groups with specialized goals, such as business organizations and the armed services, are often important agents of socialization in adulthood, remolding the attitudes and behavior patterns of individuals so that they will function effectively in specified roles. What individuals learn in any of these contexts depends on the total pattern of their socializing experiences.

Socialization proceeds throughout the entire life span as individuals assume changing roles and encounter changing needs and demands. Although anticipatory socialization helps people prepare for some of their future roles, often there is relatively little continuity between one stage of life and the next. Adolescents, for example, are effectively isolated from adult society by various conditions of modern life.

Adult socialization almost always involves a degree of discontinuity and conflict, for the individual must move quickly into changing role relationships of fundamental importance. Job requirements, marital relationship, parenthood, and so on necessitate major adjustments in orientation. In old age, the loss of many former roles creates an identity crisis and again requires the formation of new habits and attitudes.

7
Deviance

At the age of fifteen, Mike Richards (a pseudonym) has been in trouble with the law for two years—for burglary, larceny, malicious mischief, shoplifting, assault. He has repeatedly run away from his comfortable Southern California home, and he ran away from the vocational school to which he was sent after being expelled from regular school.

During his many confinements in Juvenile Hall, social workers, psychologists, and probation officers have tried to find out why he acts as he does and how he can be helped.

"Mike volunteers no information about his parents. None. They celebrate their silver wedding anniversary this year. Mr. Richards is an electrical engineer. Mrs. Richards, with little formal education, is a voracious reader. They have seven children. They have lived in Escondido for years.

"Mike talks willingly only about one person, his brother Ron, 21. Ron has gotten into scrapes with the law, but nothing serious. 'He's stopped getting in trouble. One time after he got in trouble, my Mom started crying and he couldn't face it.' . . .

"Mike has no real explanation for his behavior. 'My brother and I did the same things. I just started younger,' he says. Pressed for an explanation, he switches off. He gets lost. . . . Mr. and Mrs. Richards have no real explanation for their son's behavior either."

At the reform school to which he has been committed by the juvenile court, Mike is a popular boy, easily identifiable by the Homburg hat he wears on all occasions.[1]

In attempting to understand deviance such as Mike's, sociologists look to the social and cultural factors that shape individual behavior. Whereas psychological explanations of deviance stress personality disturbances and maladjustments that lead to deviant acts, sociological explanations focus on the social structure and on patterns of interaction between the individual and other members of the society. In preceding chapters we have examined a number of concepts, generalizations, and theories about group organization, culture and subculture, personal organization, and socialization. These not only help us explain conforming behavior in society, but they also provide a foundation for the sociological study of deviance. To understand such phenomena as crime, delinquency,

1. Peter Koenig, "Boy in Trouble," *Psychology Today,* September 1973, pp. 50–51.

sexual deviance, alcoholism, and drug abuse (to mention only a few of the more common forms of deviant behavior), it is necessary to examine the social systems in which such acts occur as well as the personal characteristics of the individuals who commit them.

The first section of this chapter will consider deviance from a broad perspective, focusing first on the social factors that shape our definitions of deviant behavior and then on the problem of evaluating the social consequences of deviance. Later sections will review a number of sociological explanations of how and why some people engage in deviant activities. Such explanations provide a better basis for understanding not only Mike Richards's delinquency but many other patterns of deviance as well.

DEVIANCE AS SOCIAL BEHAVIOR

A variety of behaviors have been regarded as deviant or conforming in different cultures and during different periods in history. Sometimes the same act is defined as deviant in one group but not in another or deviant when engaged in by some types of people but conforming when performed by others. The following situation illustrates the fine line that sometimes differentiates deviant and conforming behavior.

Mississippi was a "dry" state from 1908 until 1966, when the state legislature legalized the sale of alcoholic beverages. In spite of this prohibition, few people in the state went without liquor if they wanted it. It was estimated that $40 million worth of illegal spirits, mostly from neighboring states, was sold yearly in Mississippi. Bootleggers were so prosperous and so well protected by local law enforcement personnel that they were able to offer curb service and home delivery. In spite of constant pressure by groups of ministers and other advocates of prohibition, the laws forbidding the sale of liquor were seldom enforced. For many years it was

said that Mississippi legislators drank wet and voted dry. They defended their stand with the wry remark that "the wets have their liquor and the drys have their laws."

Under these circumstances, was the purchase of liquor in Mississippi a deviant act? If so, then a large proportion of state residents would have to be classified as criminally deviant. Many comparable situations exist in American society. It is therefore important that the sociocultural environment in which acts of deviance take place be carefully considered.

DEFINING DEVIANT BEHAVIOR

In a general sense, *deviant behavior* can be defined as any kind of conduct that in some way fails to meet the shared behavioral expectations of the particular group in which it occurs. Specifically, it involves an actor, a norm, an act, and an audience that defines that act as nonconforming to a degree exceeding the *tolerance* limits of some segment of society.

Theoretically, the tolerance limits associated with a particular norm can be exceeded either positively or negatively. Roles and rules can be so meticulously fulfilled and observed as to irritate the very group that supports the expectation. The individual who is "too good" or "too much a conformist" is seldom well liked. But though on occasion positive deviance may be annoying, it is seldom regarded as a serious threat by group members. Violations of institutionalized expectations in a negative direction, on the other hand, often cause great concern. This is the type of behavior that the present chapter will focus on.

Several factors are important in determining whether a nonconforming act will be defined as deviant. They include the significance attached to the norm being violated, the particular situation in which the nonconforming act takes place, and the personal and social characteristics of the individual committing the nonconforming act. Each of these variables will be briefly examined.

Differential Importance of Norms

In all groups, distinctions are made concerning the relative importance of norms. At the societal level, as we noted in Chapter 3, folkways are norms of relatively minor significance, and deviations from them are seldom regarded as a serious matter. For example, in our society, belching loudly after a meal is regarded as uncouth but not as a major threat to societal values. Of greater significance are mores, which are usually considered crucial for preserving the social order. Because of the importance of mores, laws are often passed to reinforce them.

In general, the less important a norm is to a group, the greater the degree of nonconformity that will be tolerated, and vice versa. For norms of major significance, tolerance limits are narrow indeed. Legal penalties for violations of formal norms reflect society's evaluation of their importance. Thus penalties for driving infractions are much less severe than those for such crimes as robbery and rape. A recent study by Peter Rossi and his associates indicates that most

people in our society—blacks and whites, males and females, rich and poor—largely agree on the relative seriousness of particular crimes.[2] The crimes regarded as most serious include murder, pushing of hard drugs, and rape; those regarded as least serious include such activities as public drunkenness and loitering (see Table 7.1). In general, the tolerance levels associated with various crimes correspond with such rankings.

Situation of the Act

Another factor that affects the degree to which departures from group norms are tolerated is the situation in which the deviating behavior occurs. We know that in most communities exces-

2. Peter H. Rossi, et al., "The Seriousness of Crimes," *American Sociological Review*, 39, No. 2 (April 1974): 224–237.

Table 7.1. HOW PEOPLE VIEW THE SERIOUSNESS OF CRIMES

MOST SERIOUS	LEAST SERIOUS
Planned killing of a policeman	Shoplifting a dress from a department store
Planned killing of a person for a fee	Beating up an acquaintance
Selling heroin	Driving while license is suspended
Forcible rape after breaking into a home	Pouring paint over someone's car
Impulsive killing of a policeman	Shoplifting a pair of shoes from a shoe store
Planned killing of a spouse	Overcharging for credit in selling goods
Planned killing of an acquaintance	Shoplifting a carton of cigarettes from a supermarket
Hijacking an airplane	Smuggling goods to avoid paying import duties
Armed robbery of a bank	Killing a suspected burglar in home
Selling LSD	False claims of dependents on income tax return
Assault with a gun on a policeman	Knowingly using inaccurate scales in weighing meat
Kidnapping for ransom	for sale
Forcible rape of a stranger in a park	Refusal to make essential repairs to rental property
Killing someone after an argument over a business transaction	Engaging in male homosexual acts with consenting adults
Assassination of a public official	Engaging in female homosexual acts with consenting adults
Killing someone during a serious argument	Breaking a plate glass window in a shop
Making sexual advances to young children	Fixing prices of a consumer product like gasoline
Assault with a gun on a stranger	Fixing prices of machines sold to businesses
Impulsive killing of a spouse	Selling pornographic magazines
Impulsive killing of a stranger	Shoplifting a book in a bookstore
Forcible rape of a neighbor	Repeated refusal to obey parents
Impulsive killing of an acquaintance	Joining a prohibited demonstration
Deliberately starting a fire which results in a death	False advertising of headache remedy
Assault with a gun on a stranger	Refusal to pay alimony
Manufacturing and selling drugs known to be harmful to users	Refusal to pay parking fines
Knowingly selling contaminated food which results in a death	Disturbing the peace
Armed robbery of a company payroll	Repeated truancy
Using heroin	Repeated running away from home
Assault with a gun on an acquaintance	Loitering in public places
Armed holdup of a taxi driver	Refusal to answer census taker
	Being drunk in public places

SOURCE: Peter H. Rossi et al., "The Seriousness of Crimes," *American Sociological Review*, 39, No. 2 (April 1974): 228–229.
NOTE: In this study, 140 crimes were rated by 200 Baltimore residents. This table shows the 30 crimes considered by the respondents to be most serious and the 30 crimes considered least serious. In both columns the crimes are listed in descending order of seriousness—from most to least serious.

Deviant behavior is more likely to be tolerated when the norm being violated is considered of minor importance. Transvestism — dressing in clothes of the opposite sex — generally does not result in the application of legal penalties.

sive drinking is viewed with greater tolerance on New Year's Eve than it is ordinarily. On Halloween, some acts that would be classified as vandalism on other occasions are considered mere mischief. In wartime, killing is acceptable; indeed, we may even give the killer a medal. These examples suggest only a few of the situational factors that affect the tolerance limits surrounding a given departure from group norms.

Characteristics of the Violator

A small child who grabs a candy bar in a supermarket or destroys someone's flower bed will probably receive no harsher punishment than a slapped hand or a scolding, but an adult who does the same things is likely to be reported for shoplifting or vandalism. Various other individual characteristics may similarly affect tolerance for nonconforming behavior. Certain forms of mischief committed by college students are apt to be treated as harmless pranks, whereas the same acts are generally punished when they are committed by nonstudents of the same age. The college professor who dresses oddly or forgets appointments may be looked on with amused affection, but similar behavior by a diplomat would evoke a quite different reaction. Distinctions are also made between the sexes, often following typical stereotypes. For example, in most states, female criminal offenders are less often sent to prison than male offenders, on the assumption that women are unlikely to be as dangerous.

The social rank of the violator is often an important factor in determining tolerance limits for nonconforming behavior. Physicians, bankers, and others of high socioeconomic rank are often able to avoid being arrested or punished for breaking the law. The same violations may get janitors or laborers prison sentences. Racial characteristics also provide a basis for differential tolerance in our society. For example, black men who have raped white women are generally treated much more harshly than white men who have raped black women, and also more harshly than either black men or white men convicted of raping women of their own race.

CULTURAL RELATIVITY OF DEVIANCE

In Chapter 4 we pointed out the need for interpreting a given act, belief, or norm within the framework of the particular cultural system of which it is a part. Concepts of conforming and deviant behavior vary greatly from group to group and from time to time.

Societal Variation

Activities that one society regards as offensive may seem normative in another. In traditional China, female infants were often killed because they were regarded as an "expense" that the family could not afford. Among the polar Eskimos, older people who had ceased to be useful were put on an ice floe to die. Among some tribes in New Guinea, cannibalism is practiced not only as a means of vengeance against enemies, but also as a means of supplementing an inadequate diet.[3] Viewed from our own perspective, such practices represent extreme forms of deviance, but within the context of particular cultures they may be regarded as conforming behavior.

Among modern industrial societies, there are substantial similarities in definitions of deviant behavior, but there are also significant differences. For example, Walter Connor examined the nature and extent of crime in Soviet society and found that many of the offenses covered in the criminal codes of the Soviet Union are similar to those defined in American codes.[4] Crimes against persons, such as homicide or assault, are regarded as deviant in both systems. But in Russia theft, crimes against property, mismanagement, and the like are regarded as "crimes against the state," while in American criminal codes most of these offenses are regarded as crimes against specific individuals or businesses.

The Soviet criminal codes list a rather large number of political offenses. Many Russian intellectuals who have publicly spoken out or written against the Soviet political system have been found guilty of engaging in political crimes against the Soviet state. Some Soviet artists have even been accused of such crimes as "unauthorized creative activities." The cultural perspectives of most Americans make it difficult for them to define such activities as "crimes."

Another example of differences in definition and interpretation of deviance can be seen in varying societal attitudes toward mental illness. In our society and most other contemporary Western societies, individuals with mental disorders are generally regarded with compassion as sick people in need of help. But at other times and in other societies, the mentally ill have been regarded quite differently. In seventeenth-century England, for example, people regularly paid admission fees to enter Bedlam Hospital in order to be amused by the "lunatics." And in numerous primitive societies, people whom we would define as mentally ill were regarded with profound reverence; their words were listened to with awe for signs of "revelation" from the spirits. In order to adequately understand varying definitions of deviance, it is necessary to examine them within the social and cultural framework of which they are a part.

Time Period Variations

Definitions of deviance vary not only from society to society but also within given societies at different points in history. In the United States a few generations ago, women who smoked cigarettes or wore lipstick were not acceptable in "decent" society, and the norms associated with styles of dress required that the body be fully clothed, even at the beach. Definitions of these activities are very different today. Smoking, cosmetics, and exposure of most of the body at the beach are no longer regarded as deviant in most groups. In fact, some communities now tolerate complete nudity on a few designated beaches.

In order to understand changing definitions of deviance within a society, it is necessary to examine the sociocultural background of given historical periods. For example, during colonial times in New England there was an apparent outbreak of witchcraft. Believing in and fearing the Devil, the Puritans regarded the possibility of a witchcraft "crime wave" as particularly menacing and went to great lengths to try to stamp it out. Kai Erikson has studied historical records of the period and has analyzed the development of this strong reaction to "deviance" from a sociological perspective.[5]

The outbreak of witchcraft occurred after some young Puritan girls in Salem learned about

3. Mark D. Dorstreich and George E. B. Morren, "Does New Guinea Cannibalism Have Nutritional Value?" *Human Ecology*, 2, No. 1 (January 1974): 1–10.

4. Walter D. Connor, *Deviance in Soviet Society* (New York: Columbia University Press, 1972), pp. 148–149.

5. Kai Erikson, *Wayward Puritans* (New York: John Wiley & Sons, Inc., 1966), pp. 137–159.

At the Salem witch trials, young girls who had been "bedeviled" accused people they did not know of being witches. The accusation of deviance was considered evidence enough for the application of legal sanctions.

the art of magic from a local slave woman. Two of the girls began to behave strangely. A local physician, unable to alleviate their seizures and erratic behaviors, concluded that they were bewitched by the Devil. The people prevailed upon the girls to identify the "witches" in the community who were responsible for their condition. The girls identified three initial suspects, who were immediately subjected to a public hearing. These proceedings only stirred up more concern, and more "witches" were identified. Panic spread. Erikson has described the culmination of these events as follows:

Salem jail was choked with people awaiting trial. We know nothing about conditions of life in prison, but it is easy to imagine the tensions which must have echoed within those grey walls. Some of the prisoners

had cried out against their relatives and friends in a desperate effort to divert attention from themselves, others were witless persons with scarcely a clue as to what had happened to them; and a few (very few, as it turned out) were accepting their lot with quiet dignity. . . . As [the hysteria] grew in scope, so did the appetites of the young girls. They now began to accuse persons they had never seen from places they had never visited, yet their word was so little questioned that it was ordinarily warrant enough to put respected people in chains. . . . Judges worked hard to keep pace with their young representatives in the field. In early August five persons went to the gallows in Salem. A month later fifteen more were tried and condemned, of which eight were hung promptly and the others spared because they were presumably ready to confess their sins and turn state's evidence. Nineteen people had been executed, seven more condemned, and one pressed to death under a pile of rocks for standing mute at his trial. At least two more persons had died in prison, bringing the number of deaths to twenty-two. And in all that time, not one suspect brought before the court had been acquitted.[6]

Thus, simply by being accused of witchcraft and labeled as witches, individuals were suddenly defined as deviant, and many suffered the consequences of that definition. To understand these events today, it is necessary to assume a historical perspective and examine the sociocultural conditions in which they occurred. Erikson maintains that seventeenth-century New England was characterized by a great deal of social disruption and change. The Puritan settlements were lonely outposts in a vast wilderness. Their norms and sense of solidarity were not well defined. In such a situation, the threats of such menacing deviance as witchcraft served to clarify norms and increase solidarity. With Erikson's explanation in mind, we can ask: Who are the "witches" of contemporary America, and how do they and their deviant acts reflect the sociocultural conditions of our own time?

SOCIAL CONSEQUENCES OF DEVIANCE

From the standpoint of the society within which it occurs, deviant behavior is usually considered undesirable, since it threatens shared values, but the social consequences of deviance are not always uniformly negative. As Erikson has point-

6. Ibid., pp. 145–149.

ed out, deviance can even contribute to the stability of a group by helping it define its own identity and thus increase its sense of cohesiveness:

As a trespasser against the group norms, [the deviant] represents those forces which lie outside the group's boundaries: he informs us, as it were, what evil looks like, what shape the devil can assume. And in doing so, he shows us the difference between the inside of the group and the outside. It may well be that without this ongoing drama at the outer edges of group space, the community would have no inner sense of identity and cohesion, no sense of the contrasts which set it off as a special place in the larger world.

Thus deviance cannot be dismissed simply as behavior which disrupts stability in society, but may itself be, in controlled quantities, an important condition for preserving stability.[7]

Some types of deviance are tolerated and even applauded. The innovator who introduces some new item of culture, some new belief or behavioral practice, is usually departing from the norms of the group and society, but without this type of deviance there could be little social change. The politician who succeeds in cutting red tape to better serve constituents is also engaging in deviant behavior, but this deviance is positively valued, at least by those who are served. Furthermore, if everyone were a thoroughgoing conformist in all things, life would be impossibly dull.

Even when deviance disrupts a group, the consequences may not be uniformly bad. The Watergate scandal provides a case in point. The disclosure that high-placed government officials had committed or condoned illegal acts shook many people's faith in our political leadership and in our political system itself. Yet it seems likely that Watergate will yield at least some positive effects in terms of political reforms.

SOCIOLOGICAL EXPLANATIONS OF DEVIANCE

The following incident was reported by a nineteen-year-old inmate in a Philadelphia prison:

On Tuesday morning, the first week of June at about 9:30 A.M., I was in my cell 412 on D block and I had started to clean up. A tall, heavy-set fella came into the cell and asked for a mirror and shaving brush and a comb, and that my cell partner said he could borrow.

He then said that he heard something about me concerning homosexual acts. I told him what he had heard was not true. He then started to threaten me and if I didn't submit to him. Then I hit him with my fist in his face before he could hit me. Then about three more men came into my cell, and they started to beat me up, too. I fought back the best I could and then I fell on the floor and I got kicked in the ribs. Three guys were holding me while the other one tore my pants off; I continued to fight until one of the guys knocked me out.[8]

How can we explain this incident of sodomous rape? Perhaps our first reaction is to assume that the individuals involved were not normal. In our culture there is a clear "psychologizing" tendency, and it is particularly evident in attempts to understand deviance. In everyday discourse, deviant behavior is often attributed to "poor adjustment" or even "mental illness." There is an implication that there has to be something wrong with a person who commits some conspicuous act of nonconformity.

There is considerable evidence, however, that most deviant behavior in our society is committed by individuals who would be classified as normal.[9] This does not mean that psychological factors such as individual needs, attitudes, motivations, habits, tensions, and stresses can be ignored; they are important for understanding both conforming and deviant behavior. But the sociological approach is also needed if we are to understand the patterns and distribu-

7. Kai T. Erikson, "Notes on the Sociology of Deviance," in The Other Side: Perspectives on Deviance, ed. Howard S. Becker (New York: The Free Press, 1964), p. 15. See also Robert A. Dentler and Kai T. Erikson, "The Functions of Deviance in Groups," Social Problems, 7 (Fall 1959): 98–107.
8. Allan J. Davis, "Sexual Assaults in the Philadelphia Prison Systems, and Sheriff's Vans," Trans-action, 6, No. 2 (December 1968): 10. Investigations of various local and county institutions in other sections of the country—e.g., Chicago and Cook County—have revealed the widespread occurrence of similar incidents.
9. Karl F. Schuessler and Donald R. Cressey, "Personality Characteristics of Criminals," American Journal of Sociology, 55 (March 1950): 476.

tion of various types of deviance and the ways in which these behaviors develop.

We can illustrate this point by returning to the example of homosexual behavior in prisons. Studies have shown that homosexual activities are more common in certain types of penal institutions than others and that prisoners who commit sodomous rape consider their victims to be "homosexuals" but think of themselves as "he-men." We cannot explain homosexual behavior in the prisons until we understand the significance of these findings.

Whether or not the rate of sexual deviance is unusually high in a given institution seems to depend in large part upon the role characteristics, norms, stratification patterns, systems of social control, and other organizational characteristics of that institution. A recent survey of United States prisons showed that a much higher level of homosexual behavior was reported in institutions characterized by "custodial" features than in institutions that were "treatment-oriented."[10]

Of importance, too, is the way individual inmates relate to the social system of the prison. For example, if previously learned sexual orientations make homosexual behavior among inmates seem acceptable, then prisoners may be more receptive to it. Also, since the prisoner role provides few other avenues for "proving" one's masculinity, aggressive men may attempt to establish dominance and protect their feelings of adequacy by sexually using younger and weaker men. In some prisons the inmate subculture equates physical-sexual prowess with prestige and self-esteem. Individuals who become more integrated into the inmate subculture than others are often more motivated to strive for prestige by engaging in homosexual activity. All these factors are important in the generation of homosexual behavior in penal institutions.

Deviant behavior in such instances can thus be seen as the product of a complex interplay between the characteristics of the social system and the personal characteristics and learned orientations of the human beings within it. It is this interplay that sociologists seek to explain in their study of deviance. In the sections that follow, several major sociological explanations of deviance will be examined.

ANOMIE THEORY

In a well-known attempt to formulate a rather general theory of deviant behavior, Robert Merton observed that there were significant variations in rates of deviance in different groups in our society.[11] The starting point for understanding Merton's analysis is to make note of the relationship between the *cultural* goals that our society stresses and the *institutionalized means* that are culturally defined as legitimate in our society for working toward those goals. One major goal in our culture, for example, is the acquisition of wealth. Yet many Americans lack access to culturally approved means by which to achieve that goal. Since they remain under pressure to "succeed," they may lose interest in the legitimacy of the means; what counts for them is the end result. Such lack of integration between culturally approved ends and means, Merton maintained, leads to the strains associated with *anomie* or normlessness.

Given the conditions of anomie, what are the principal ways by which individuals at different points in the social structure can deal with the conflict between cultural goals and institutionalized means? In an attempt to answer this question, Merton devised a typology of *modes of adaptation* (Table 7.2) that has contributed to a better understanding of certain kinds of conforming and deviant behavior.

---

10. Ronald L. Akers, Norman S. Hayner, and Werner Gruninger, "Homosexual and Drug Behavior in Prisons: A Test of the Functional and Importation Models of the Inmate System," *Social Problems*, 21, No. 3 (1974): 410–422.

11. Robert K. Merton, *Social Theory and Social Structure* (New York: The Free Press, 1956), p. 140.

Table 7.2. MERTON'S TYPOLOGY OF MODES OF INDIVIDUAL ADAPTATION

Modes of adaptation	Culture goals	Institutionalized means
I. Conformity	+	+
II. Innovation	+	−
III. Ritualism	−	+
IV. Retreatism	−	−
V. Rebellion	±	±

SOURCE: Robert K. Merton, *Social Theory and Social Structure* (New York: The Free Press, 1956), p. 140.

Conformity

First, individuals can accept both the cultural goals and the culturally approved means for reaching them. This is the response selected by most members of American society. Obviously, the conformist must have access to legitimate means for achieving cultural goals or else be willing to accept the fact that they are out of reach.

Innovation

Second, individuals can subscribe to a cultural goal (e.g., accumulation of wealth) without accepting the institutionalized means for attaining it. This type of adaptation Merton calls *innovation*. The individual uses methods other than those that are culturally approved and engages in some form of norm violation. This type of adaptation is evident in certain strata of our society, where there is an emphasis on monetary success but where access to the conventional and legitimate channels for achieving such success may be limited. Thus we find that innovative but illegitimate means are frequently used in order to get money and be "successful." This familiar pattern of behavior has led Merton to hypothesize the following:

It is only when a system of cultural values extols, virtually above all else, certain common success-goals for the population at large while the social structure rigorously restricts or completely closes access to approved modes of reaching these goals for a considerable part of the same population, that deviant behavior ensues on a large scale.[12]

The innovation mode of adaptation to the squeeze between goals and means has received substantial attention in the sociological literature on crime and delinquency.[13]

Ritualism

The third type of adaptation Merton discusses is *ritualism*, which involves a rigid adherence to rules prescribing the "proper" way of doing things. In this case, however, the cultural goals have been abandoned or rejected. This mode of adaptation is illustrated by those bureaucrats whose main mission in life is to enforce petty rules and by others who persist in ritualistic conformity almost as an end in itself. The terms *over-conformity* and *over-compliance* are used in describing such behavior. Merton points out that ritualism is not usually regarded as seriously deviant behavior; though it can be annoying, ordinarily it does not exceed the tolerance limits of the community or society.

Retreatism

The fourth type of adjustment to conflict between cultural goals and accepted means is *retreatism*, which entails abandoning both cultural goals and the institutionalized means for attaining them. Merton describes retreatist individuals as "in the society but not of it" and as constituting the "true aliens." The retreatist adaptation is characteristic of tramps, alcoholics, drug addicts, and some psychotics.

According to Howard Bahr, who recently completed a study of skid row and homelessness in New York, homeless people and those who live on skid row are detached from society and have no social ties to groups and institutions.[14] They suffer from a variety of social, physical, and mental problems; they neither perform common social roles nor live in normal social contexts.

One of the homeless women Bahr studied provides a vivid example of retreatism. Carrie was born of immigrant parents from Russia and had led an uneventful early life in Brooklyn. She left school at an early age and worked in a factory, continuing to live with her family. Later she married a German immigrant who died of cancer within ten years of their marriage. She was very distraught at the loss and returned to live with her parents. Soon afterward, when Carrie was twenty-nine, both her mother and father died. She never again had a permanent home. She never worked and never received public aid or financial assistance from friends or relatives.

12. Ibid., p. 146.
13. See, for example, James F. Short, Jr., "Gang Delinquency and Anomie," in *Anomie and Deviant Behavior,* ed. Marshall B. Clinard (New York: The Free Press, 1964).
14. Howard M. Bahr, *Skid Row* (New York: Oxford University Press, 1973).

In the following account, Carrie describes her social isolation:

Since my husband died twenty-five years ago I've kept to myself. I don't talk to people. I want to be left alone; I enjoy being alone; I'm individualistic. I just don't like people. . . . They make demands on you, so I stay away from them. . . . The only person I ever [saw was] my sister. I lost her last June. She was the only person I knew, the only one who understood me, who cared about me . . . I don't have any friends; I don't want any friends. . . . I don't like to work. Last job I held was when I was eighteen. I get by; I have for 25 years and not on welfare, either. People give me money. I'll be walking around Canal Street or on Times Square and people just give me money. I don't know why. . . . Sometimes I find money. Oh, occasionally, when my luck is down, I'll ask somebody on the street for a dime or something. I get by.[15]

Since Carrie had neither home nor job, she had spent recent years living in New York subways, public parks, restrooms, condemned buildings, and warehouses. She had a number of techniques for maintaining herself in the city:

You've got to have ingenuity. You've got to know New York, its people, how to get around. I sleep in the subways nowadays. It works out fine. . . . You can't sleep there when an officer's on duty. That's from 8 (P.M.) to 4 (A.M.). So, I go there about 10 (minutes) till 4; sleep to noon, usually. . . . I like the Eighth Avenue line. Less stops. I sleep on one of the front or back cars; never the middle. Too many disturbances. Works out just fine, just fine. I get a good night's rest.[16]

At the time Carrie was interviewed, she was continuing her wandering, homelessness, and isolation. Her life-style provides sharp contrast to the extensive social involvements of most individuals in our society.

Rebellion
The fifth form of deviant adaptation identified by Merton is rebellion, which involves not only the rejection of culturally approved goals and norms

15. Ibid., pp. 215–216. (Gerald R. Garrett is coauthor of the chapter from which this example is taken.)
16. Ibid., p. 216.

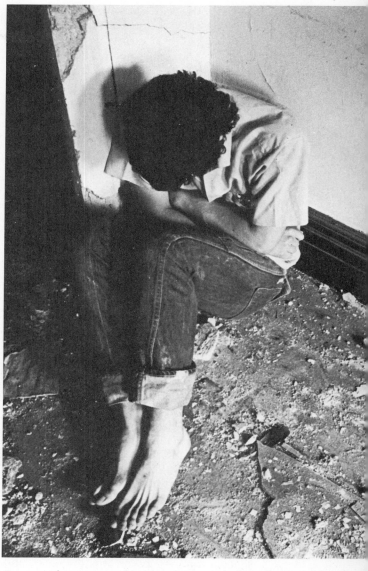

Persons who cannot achieve society's goals through legitimate means may retreat from society altogether —abandoning the goals as well as the institutionalized means for attaining them. Retreatism is characteristic of drug addicts. As Merton has put it, these individuals are "in the society but not of it"; they constitute the "true aliens."

but also an attempt to develop new or modified goals and new means of reaching them. This kind of adjustment is characteristic of individuals who start social movements. Dissident groups in the United States and western Europe in the late 1960s often attacked the existing social and political structure by means of mass demonstrations, the occupation of buildings, and the destruction of property. Some formed communal living groups in attempts to substitute new goals and norms for the dominant ones in the society.

Because the anomie theory of deviance is relatively simple and quite general, it has provoked considerable debate. There have been numerous reformulations of the theory since Merton first introduced it.[17] Most contemporary studies of deviance focus on variables other than those emphasized in anomie theory.

LABELING THEORY

Labeling theory does not attempt to explain the characteristics of deviants, nor is it much concerned with distinctive patterns of deviant behavior. Rather, it seeks to understand how definitions of deviance are formulated by society, how such definitions or labels are applied to individuals, and what the consequences of such application are for those individuals' future behavior.[18]

Societal Reaction

How do individuals become defined and differentiated as deviant? In American society, the classifying of individuals as deviant increasingly takes place in bureaucratically organized social control agencies such as police departments, the courts, mental hospitals, or youth service bureaus. An example of the process is found in Thomas J. Scheff's study of mental illness.[19]

Scheff examined psychiatrists' ratings and court records, interviewed court officials and psychiatrists, and observed court proceedings concerning patients who had been involuntarily committed to mental hospitals in a midwestern state. His study showed that the decision to institutionalize given individuals was often influenced by factors other than those usually thought to be relevant in assessing a person's mental state. Institutionalization was generally based upon a "presumption of illness" rather than on thorough psychiatric examination.

From our observations of the medical examinations and other commitment procedures, we formed a very strong impression that the [psychiatric] doctrines of danger to self or others, early treatment, and the avoidance of stigma were invoked partly because the officials believed them to be true, and partly because they provided convenient justification for a preexisting policy of summary action, minimal investigation, avoidance of responsibility, and, after the patient is in the hospital, indecisiveness and delay.

The policy of presuming illness is probably both cause and effect of political pressure on the court from the community. The judge, an elected official, runs the risk of being more heavily penalized for erroneously releasing than for erroneously retaining patients. Since the judge personally appoints the panel of psychiatrists to serve as examiners, he can easily transmit the community pressure to them, by failing to reappoint a psychiatrist whose examinations were inconveniently thorough.[20]

The implications of such findings are that it is essential for sociologists to try to unravel the processes of interaction between individuals and agencies of social control that result in a particular behavior or a particular individual being labeled "deviant." To a considerable degree, data on the extent and distribution of deviance are reflections of official definitions and policies. (For further discussion of this issue, see pages 191–197.)

Impact of Labels

How do group members change their responses to individuals once the latter have been defined as deviant, and what are the consequences for the future behavior of these labeled individuals? Being labeled as deviant is tantamount to being assigned a new role that will determine the nature of one's future social interactions. Becker comments on the effects of being labeled a criminal:

17. Marshall B. Clinard, ed., *Anomie and Deviant Behavior* (New York: The Free Press, 1964).
18. See Chapter 10, "Labelling Theory Reconsidered," in Howard S. Becker, *Outsiders: Studies in the Sociology of Deviance*, 2nd ed. (New York: The Free Press, 1973), and Jack P. Gibbs, "Conceptions of Deviant Behavior: The Old and the New," *Pacific Sociological Review*, 9 (Spring 1966): 9–14.
19. Thomas J. Scheff, *Being Mentally Ill* (Chicago: Aldine Publishing Co., 1966).
20. Ibid., p. 153.

To be labeled as a criminal one need only to commit a single criminal offense, and this is all the term formally refers to. Yet the word carries a number of connotations specifying auxiliary traits characteristic of anyone bearing this label. A man who has been convicted of housebreaking and thereby labeled criminal is presumed to be a person likely to break into other houses; the police, in rounding up known offenders for investigation after a crime has been committed, operate on this premise. Furthermore, he is considered likely to commit other crimes as well, because he has shown himself to be a person without "respect for the law."[21]

Various studies have investigated the impact of being officially labeled a criminal or suspected criminal. The results of a field experiment by Schwartz and Skolnick point to the consequences of criminal records for unskilled workers seeking jobs.

Various types of legal records are systematically related to job opportunities. It seems fair to infer also that the trend of job losses corresponds with the apparent punitive intent of the authorities. Where the man is convicted, that intent is presumably greatest. It is less where he is accused but acquitted and still less where the court makes an effort to emphasize the absence of a finding of guilt. Nevertheless, where the difference in punitive intent is ideally greatest, between conviction and acquittal, the difference in occupational harm is very slight.[22]

Numerous examples could be cited with respect to other forms of deviance. If individuals become known as homosexuals, alcoholics, users of narcotics, cheats, or simply liars, people's expectations of them change. With the label goes a new role, and the imputation of "auxiliary traits" may follow. Thus, the alcoholic may be thought to be sexually promiscuous and the user of narcotics untrustworthy in money matters, whether or not there is factual evidence to support the suspicions.

There seems little doubt that labeling leads to redefinitions of the relationships between the person labeled and the general community. In some ways the process resembles the categorical treatment accorded to members of minority groups in our society and the imputation of cultural stereotypes. (These issues are reviewed in Chapter 9, "Intergroup Relations.")

One additional issue concerning labeling theory merits comment. In Chapter 5 we examined the theory that individuals' evaluations of self are basically reflections of other people's reactions to their conduct (see pages 135–138). If this theory of the "looking-glass self" is sound, we might expect that people whose social relationships have been restructured by a particular deviant role-assignment would come to think of themselves as members of that deviant group and develop stable patterns of behavior along the lines of these new social and self definitions. Some theorists believe that this does indeed happen:

Take the case, for example, of a woman who is rather casual about sexual contacts. Over a period of years, she engages in sex relations more or less promiscuously. If one day she should suggest or hint at receiving a gift for her sexual favors or if one of her friends presents her a gift or some money shortly after the sex act, her status has been redefined. Hereafter, other people may come to think of her as a prostitute and she may, reciprocally, come to think of herself in these same terms. When this happens, casual sex promiscuity has become transmuted into a deviant occupational role.[23]

Although many specific points in labeling theory remain controversial, it clearly has broadened our understanding of deviant behavior. It includes an important emphasis on definitional and reactive factors, processes, and situations that is absent in other theories.

THE SOCIAL BONDS PERSPECTIVE

According to another approach to deviance, the lack or loss of effective social bonds makes individuals more susceptible to deviant acts or roles. Important social bonds include attachments and commitments to conventional groups such as parents, schools, occupations, and other agents of socialization.

21. Becker, *Outsiders*, p. 33.
22. Richard D. Schwartz and Jerome H. Skolnick, "Two Studies of Legal Stigma," in *The Other Side*, Becker, ed., pp. 103–118.
23. Earl Rubington and Martin Weinberg, *Deviance: The Interactionist Perspective*, 2nd ed. (New York: Macmillan, Inc., 1973), p. 5.

Delinquency and Social Bonds

An illustration of the social bonds approach is found in Travis Hirschi's study of California high school students. Comparing delinquent and nondelinquent students, Hirschi found that relationships between parents and children were less developed among the delinquents and that they had fewer friends who were committed to conventional life styles. In addition, delinquent youth had less involvement with non-deviant adults who could serve both as role models and links to community groups. In general, the delinquents' social bonds to conventional institutions were limited.[24]

The social bonds theory appears to have application not only to American adolescents but to delinquents in other societies as well. In a study of juvenile delinquents in Cordoba, Argentina, it was found that social ties through family, school, church, and economic activities were substantially less developed among delinquent youngsters than among comparative groups of conforming youngsters.[25]

The School

Although the educational institution has been cited as a vital link to conventional society for adolescents, some researchers have found that school experiences are not always favorable for the development of social bonds. This is particularly true for youths who are not in the socioeconomic mainstream.

In fact, the school has been identified as a possible factor in the *development* of delinquency. Polk and Schafer have studied some of the features that contribute to school failures and therefore appear to be important in the development of delinquent youth. They have called attention to various problems in school authority systems, decision-making processes, and basic teaching-learning structures in the secondary schools—specifically, to situations that most frequently affect lower-income and nonwhite pupils and contribute to their high rate of school failure. These include irrelevant school materials and teaching methods, as well as ineffective school responses to misbehavior. Polk and

Schafer maintain that such situations contribute to the disengagement and eventual delinquency of many lower-class and nonwhite youth.[26]

SOCIOCULTURAL LEARNING THEORIES

Sociocultural learning theories stress the processes by which deviant behavior is learned and the specific conditions in which this learning takes place. By and large, these conditions are the same as those involved in learning other forms of social behavior. Thus many of the same concepts and generalizations that have been examined in the chapters on personal organization and socialization (Chapters 5 and 6) are relevant here.

Differential Association

Edwin Sutherland's differential association theory of criminal behavior, formulated in the late 1930s, was an application of the ideas of earlier sociologists such as Cooley and Mead and stressed the importance of learning in primary groups.[27] According to this theory, criminal behavior is learned in the same way other forms of behavior are learned—through a process of symbolic interaction with others, particularly in primary groups. Through such groups, an individual is exposed to both criminal and anticriminal norms, motivations, attitudes, and skills. The result is an uneven balance of criminal and anticriminal orientations. If the balance is favorable to the law and to conforming norms, the outcome is conformity. But if procriminal definitions and orientations exceed anticriminal ones, deviant behavior results. As in all learning situations, this balance of conforming and deviating

24. Travis Hirschi, *Causes of Delinquency* (Berkeley: University of California Press, 1969), Chapters 6–10.
25. Lois B. DeFleur, *Delinquency in Argentina* (Pullman, Wash.: Washington State University Press, 1970), pp. 156–161.
26. Kenneth Polk and Walter E. Schafer, eds., *Schools and Delinquency* (Englewood Cliffs, N.J.: Prentice-Hall, Inc., 1972), Chapters 3 and 4.
27. See Albert K. Cohen, Alfred Lindesmith, and Karl Schuessler, eds., *The Sutherland Papers* (Bloomington, Ind.: Indiana University Press, 1956), pp. 13–29. Sutherland's differential association theory has recently been restated and reformulated as a mathematical model; see Melvin L. DeFleur and Richard Quinney, "A Reformulation of Sutherland's Differential Association Theory and a Strategy for Empirical Verification," *Journal of Research in Crime and Delinquency*, 3, No. 1 (January 1966): 1–26.

orientations is based on the frequency, duration, priority, and intensity of exposures to either type of socializing experiences.

Many studies of juvenile delinquency have emphasized the importance of sociocultural learning in the development and continuation of delinquent activity. Differential association has also been used to explain the commission of crimes by middle-class people in their occupations. These are often called "white-collar" crimes because of the offenders' relatively high socioeconomic status.[28] Persons who commit these offenses are apparently living respectable law-abiding lives, but frequently, through associates on the job, they become exposed to norms favoring such illegal acts as tax evasion, the manipulation of accounts, and employee theft.

One of the distinguishing features of white-collar crime is that violators do not think of themselves as criminals, nor are they usually regarded as such by the public. White-collar criminals typically develop elaborate rationalizations to justify their behavior, and usually they receive differential treatment in the hands of the police, the courts, and other agencies. Indeed, because of status considerations and the lack of strong societal reaction to these behaviors, most of the acts of white-collar criminals never become part of the official crime statistics.

Differential Reinforcement

Ronald Akers has further developed many of the ideas of differential association by incorporating additional principles of learning.[29] He places particular emphasis on the ways deviant behavior is reinforced.

Akers illustrates the reinforcement process in terms of learning excessive drinking. Social interaction with others often involves a great deal of ambivalence: individuals are attracted to others but fear rejection or negative responses. Alcohol is frequently used as a social lubricant to reduce this anxiety. When individuals reduce their anxiety through the use of alcohol, their relief increases their enjoyment of the situation, and they tend to drink more. Research has shown that the more individuals use alcohol to reduce social anxiety, the more likely they are to become problem drinkers.[30]

As drinking becomes heavier, family, friends, and others begin to exercise some negative sanctions in attempts to reduce the problem. When criticism becomes unpleasant, the heavy drinker seeks more congenial groups that are tolerant of drinking and associated behaviors. The individual may later move on to groups of increasingly heavy drinkers, tying his or her life-style more and more closely to excessive drinking while gradually severing ties to more conventional groups.

At this point societal reactions and labeling begin to operate. The person is often arrested and is labeled by police and treatment agencies as "alcoholic." Returning to sobriety and conventional behavior becomes more and more difficult. Finally, the individual may retreat from society, perhaps developing new social roles and self-definitions—as an alcoholic housewife, a drunken executive, or even a resident of skid row.

As these various theories and examples illustrate, sociological perspectives on the causes of deviant behavior coincide at various points. Each perspective—anomic, labeling, social bonds, and sociocultural learning—focuses on somewhat different aspects of the ways in which deviant behavior is generated in society. Each perspective seeks to explain deviance in terms of interactions between the nonconforming individual and others within a social and cultural context. Such perspectives have moved social scientists away from explanations that rely solely on the psychological or biological makeup of the individual.

28. See Edwin H. Sutherland, *White Collar Crime* (New York: Holt, Rinehart and Winston, Inc., 1961); Gilbert Geis, ed., *White-Collar Criminal* (New York: Atherton Press, 1968); and Richard Quinney, "The Study of White Collar Crime: Toward a Reorientation in Theory and Research," *Journal of Criminal Law, Criminology, and Police Science*, 55 (June 1964): 208–214.

29. Ronald L. Akers, *Deviant Behavior: A Social Learning Approach* (Belmont, Calif.: Wadsworth Publishing Co., 1973), pp. 46–61.

30. Don Cahalan, *Problem Drinkers: A National Survey* (San Francisco: Jossey-Bass, Inc., 1970).

DEVIANT SUBCULTURES

As indicated in Chapter 4, subcultural norms, beliefs, values, activities, and even language are distinct from those of the more general culture. This creates few problems as long as the requirements of the larger society and the subculture are not contradictory; but when the norms, beliefs, and values of a subculture clash head-on with those of the general culture, the individual must make a choice.

Individuals subscribing to deviant subcultures and sharing the orientations of deviant groups are deviants from the perspective of the larger society, but they are conformists by the definition of their own subcultures. This point becomes clear in Leznoff and Westley's study of the homosexual community:

Since the homosexual group provides the only social context in which homosexuality is normal, deviant practices moral, and homosexual responses rewarded, the homosexual develops a deep emotional involvement with his group, tending toward a ready acceptance of its norms and dictates, and subjection to its behavior patterns.[31]

It would be erroneous, however, to assume that all individuals involved in deviant acts subscribe to subcultures or participate in such groups.

FUNCTIONS OF DEVIANT SUBCULTURES

Groups that subscribe to deviant subcultures function as agents of socialization and social support for their members. Both functions will be discussed in the following sections.

Socialization

Deviant subcultures are "problem solving" for those who subscribe to them.[32] In subcultural settings a variety of socializing experiences take place that may help individuals adjust to their particular life circumstances. The following account of a young man who had experienced some homosexual encounters, but had not previously participated in a homosexual group, illustrates these processes.

Tom entered one of San Francisco's approximately 40 gay bars. He had never been there before but had heard about it from some of his friends with whom he played poker regularly on Wednesday nights. One of them had gone into the bar by mistake a couple of weeks before and the subject was mentioned as a sort of joke around the poker table; no one suspected that Tom might have been interested in finding out about the bar. No one would have had any idea at all that Tom had any homosexual interests. He was 27, fairly good-looking, married, and the father of four children. He worked as a truck driver for a bakery in one of the suburbs of San Francisco. . . .

Walking into a gay bar is a momentous act in the life history of a homosexual, because in many cases it is the first time he publicly identifies himself as a homosexual. Of equal importance is the fact that it brings home to him the realization that there are many other young men like himself and, thus, that he is a member of a community and not the isolate he had previously felt himself to be. . . .

By the time Tom had finished his martini, he had developed enough courage to walk over to David, to whom he was attracted, and make a conversational opener. Tom began . . . by asking David about the bar, and David's quite friendly response led him to believe that he might have some chance of getting him to go to bed with him. . . . They exchanged some more biographical information and then David asked Tom about his homosexual interests, for although Tom was the older, David was much more experienced in the practices of the gay world and was able to take the lead in this conversation. Tom asked David a lot of questions about gay life and found out about other bars and about the baths, the parks, and the gay sections of the beach.[33]

Through this experience Tom learned a number of things about the homosexual subculture. By means of such contacts, potential members (such as Tom) become resocialized and are often integrated into the deviant community or group.

31. Maurice Leznoff and William A. Westley, "The Homosexual Community," *Social Problems*, 3 (April 1956): 257–263.
32. Albert K. Cohen, *Delinquent Boys: The Culture of the Gang* (New York: The Free Press, 1955), p. 59.
33. Martin Hoffman, *The Gay World* (New York: Basic Books, Inc., 1968), pp. 15–19.

Many individuals support subcultures whose basic values and norms run counter to those of the majority of the society. Members of street gangs, "winos," and homosexuals, for example, are deviants from the perspective of the larger society, but they are conformists by the definitions of their own subcultures.

Social Support

For individuals who have been repeatedly rejected and have become increasingly isolated from others, participation in and acceptance by groups with specialized subcultures is very important. This is called the *social-support function* of subcultures. Such social support has both positive and negative functions. The more individuals participate in and become integral members of groups sharing deviant subcultures, the more difficult it is for them to participate in conforming groups. For example, when Tom, the young homosexual, encountered the gay subculture and realized that there were many other young men like himself—that he was a member of a "community"—he no longer felt like a social isolate. But he experienced other feelings as well: "Standing in a room with over a hundred men who shared the same sexual orientation he did, he felt the stigma of public identification for the first time in his life."[34] While deviant subcultures lessen feelings of isolation, participation in such groups results in additional stigma and societal reactions.

SOME TYPES OF DEVIANT SUBCULTURES

Research has shown that teen-age gangs and groups composed of homosexuals, drug users, criminals, and other deviants support values, beliefs, attitudes, and practices that are quite different from those incorporated in the general norms.[35] The following examples illustrate many of the distinctive features of these groups and how they function to provide learning experiences and meaningful interaction for their members.

Drug Subcultures

The use of different types of drugs often involves participation in deviant groups.[36] A recent study has provided an outline of the drug subculture among white college students. Bruce Johnson collected data from several thousand students at twenty-one colleges in the New York metropolitan area.[37] The results of his study showed that many peer groups have incorporated occasional marijuana use as a legitimate activity in much the same way that sex, drinking, and smoking

were incorporated in the past. But some young people become heavily involved in marijuana use and progressively more integrated into a specialized drug subculture.

Johnson found that participants in drug groups were expected to interact with marijuana users and to use marijuana or hashish regularly. They also were expected to sell marijuana or hashish if they had a large enough supply. In addition, they were expected to accept and befriend users of other drugs and, if called upon, be willing to try these drugs (e.g., hallucinogens, amphetamines, sedatives, etc.).

The shared beliefs, values, and attitudes of the subculture revolved around *justification* of drug use and sale. For example, members believed that they were among the more independent, thoughtful, and creative college students and that drugs aided them in socializing and communicating with others. Such beliefs and norms provided social support for this pervasive and persistent deviant behavior.

Professional Crime

Quite distinctive subcultures are found among different types of professional criminals. Professional criminals are engaged in activities such as pickpocketing, shoplifting, confidence games, check forgery, and counterfeiting.[38] They perform their illegal work with great skill, arrived at through training, internship, and practice.

Professional criminals regard themselves as the elite of the criminal world and view with disdain the bumbling, often violent amateur who frequently gets caught. Other distinctive attitudes, values, perceptions, and even speech patterns are shared by different types of professional criminals. Their way of life is strongly

34. Ibid., p. 17.
35. See "Deviant Subcultures," Part Three in Rubington and Weinberg, *Deviance*, p. 5.
36. See, for example, Richard H. Blum et al., *Utopiates: The Use and Users of LSD-25* (New York: Atherton Press, 1964); and Erich Goode, *The Marijuana Smokers* (New York: Basic Books, Inc., 1970).
37. Bruce D. Johnson, *Marijuana Users and Drug Subcultures* (New York: John Wiley & Sons, Inc., 1973), pp. 194–200.
38. See, for example, Mary Owen Cameron, *The Booster and the Snitch* (New York: The Free Press, 1964); Edwin M. Lemert, "The Behavior of the Systematic Check Forger," *Social Problems*, 6 (Fall 1958): 141–149; and Edwin H. Sutherland, ed., *The Professional Thief* (Chicago: The University of Chicago Press, 1937).

reinforced by high involvement with other professionals and by very little involvement with noncriminal segments of society. Maurer has described the lure of the "big-con" profession:

There is a thrill about big-con work which no other branch of the grift [theft] can duplicate. The confidence man extends himself fully while he works; all his faculties and abilities are called into play; each mark [victim] is a new challenge to his ingenuity; and, perhaps most important, the stakes for which he plays are very high. "Once a heavy gee [safeblower], always a heavy," said the Postal Kid [a famous conman]. "And it's the same with the con. When the mark is being played for a big chunk, there is a kick in it just like there is to the heavy when a big peter [safe] is being knocked off."[39]

Given the strong tie to their careers and their supportive subcultures, it isn't surprising that most professional criminals find it difficult to quit their work and dissolve their interactions with other professional criminals.

Organized Crime

Like professional criminals, members of organized criminal groups share a distinctive subculture. They develop distinctive attitudes and values and often a special vocabulary. In general, organized crime is defined as "any crime committed by a person occupying a position in an established division of labor designed for the commission of crime."[40] Through various sources, such as informants and government investigations, some information about this type of crime has emerged.

Organized crime depends on a highly structured group, which is often described as having a very clear-cut hierarchy of participants, with those at the top holding much personal power.

Usually these organizations operate over rather large, well-defined, protected geographical areas, which they think of as their "territory."

Basically, these groups are in business, and their goal is extensive profit. Many of their activities are illegal and monopolistic in character. It is reported that organized criminal groups control most of the illegal gambling in the United States. They are heavily involved in usury (illegal money lending at extremely high interest rates). They are reported to be the principal importers and wholesalers of narcotics. Organized criminal groups have also infiltrated and obtained control of a number of legitimate businesses and organizations, including labor unions, jukebox companies, restaurants and bars, linen-supply companies, and even some factories. The operation of many of these enterprises is facilitated by payoffs to local, state, and federal government officials.[41]

Many of the values and norms of organized criminal groups are vital to their activities. A number of the norms revolve around mutual trust and loyalty among group members. For example, members are expected to be completely honest and trustworthy with each other. They would not cheat one of their own. Members are also expected to be intensely loyal to the group. One of the most serious norm violations is to give information to outsiders about the group and its activities. Informing to the police is regarded as "deadly." These values and norms have enabled organized criminal groups to carry out their business very effectively and have made it very difficult to obtain complete information about organized crime.

EXTENT AND DISTRIBUTION OF DEVIANCE

Almost daily the mass media carry stories about crime, drug use, problem drinking, and other incidents of deviance in American society. There is a perennial concern with the extent of deviance. What are the bases for this concern, and what estimates can be made of the rates of deviant behavior?

39. David W. Maurer, *The Big Con* (New York: Signet Books, 1962), p. 145.

40. Donald R. Cressey, *Theft of the Nation* (New York: Harper & Row, Inc., 1969), p. 313. See also Francis A. J. Ianni, *A Family Business: Kinship and Social Control in Organized Crime* (New York: Russell Sage Foundation, 1972); Thorsten Sellin, "Organized Crime: A Business Enterprise," *The Annals of the American Academy of Political and Social Science*, 347 (May 1963): 12–19; and The President's Commission on Law Enforcement and the Administration of Justice, *The Challenge of Crime in a Free Society* (Washington, D.C.: U.S. Government Printing Office, 1967).

41. Cressey, *Theft of the Nation*, p. xi.

TOOLS OF SOCIOLOGY
RESEARCH USE OF OFFICIAL RECORDS

An important aspect of the culture of contemporary urban societies is their preoccupation with record keeping for official purposes. Every significant event in peoples' lives is usually noted in some fashion in public documents. Records are made of births, education, employment, marriages, divorces, arrests, court convictions, organizational memberships, political participation, and deaths. If present trends continue, the Age of the Computer will probably make record keeping even more elaborate, accurate, and detailed.

Although official records are rich sources of data for sociologists, they are by no means ideal for research purposes. They consist largely of observations made by nonsociologists, who usually work within the framework of complex legal and administrative regulations. Also, the observations are recorded for purposes of the organization and not for research. For example, a number of states prohibit by law the recording of the racial characteristics of individuals involved in many public transactions, ranging from obtaining a marriage license to applying for employment. While these proscriptions protect individual rights to privacy and may reduce certain forms of discrimination, they limit the relevance of official files to the sociologist studying racial issues.

Even such seemingly accurate data as records of births and deaths are not without error. Some births are never registered, and some deaths remain unreported. Furthermore, the social and cultural circumstances surrounding such events can lead to distorted records. For example, because of sympathy for family members in a case of suicide, some physicians or coroners list a more "acceptable" cause of death in the public records. Similarly, some states prohibit recording a birth as illegitimate on the assumption (probably correct) that the child might be stigmatized later. For the sociologist attempting to assess suicide rates or the incidence of illegitimate births in a given area, such practices can introduce errors of unknown proportions. The researcher who intends to use official records needs to examine the personnel and processes involved in the generation of these records—recognizing that many potential biases exist.

For example, one source of secondary data for the criminologist is police records on specific types of crimes. Police files on a serious crime, in particular, contain detailed reports of investigating officers, statements of witnesses, comprehensive descriptions of the crime, and a wealth of detail about the situation in which it occurred. Such files often contain photographs, diagrams, ballistic reports, medical data, personal histories, and various other documents and facts about both offenders and their victims. Since the police normally assemble this information for a specific purpose—the apprehension and conviction of criminals—the sociologist who uses such information must examine it very critically.

Marvin Wolfgang's investigation of criminal homicide illustrates the way official records have been used in social research. Using the complete records of the Homicide Squad of the Philadelphia Police Department over a five-year period, during which time files were developed on 588 criminal homicides, Wolfgang found that most of the homicides recorded by the police in Philadelphia were unplanned acts involving stabbing or shooting. Homicides were committed disproportionately by black offenders against black victims. They were generally of male aggressors against male victims. The vast majority of participants knew each other. The age group 20–24 years showed the highest rate of incidence. Homicide was found to vary seasonally and to be related to both days of the week and hours of the day. The weekends had the highest rates, and especially high concentrations appeared during the late hours of Saturday night. Alcohol was prominently present in a large number of the crimes studied. Nearly two-thirds of the offenders and one-half of the victims had prior criminal records.

This was a descriptive study that summarized the patterns of criminal homicide reported to the police. It has provided many new insights into the patterns of circumstance that may lead to criminal homicide.

Marvin E. Wolfgang. *Patterns in Criminal Homicide* (New York: John Wiley & Sons, Inc., 1966); first published in 1958.

EXTENT OF DEVIANCE

Almost all record-keeping agencies warn that various problems need to be carefully considered before their data are used as the basis for authoritative pronouncements about the extent of deviance. Many of the problems in interpreting such statistics stem from the lack of precise, uniform definitions of the particular acts to be counted as deviant. Different political jurisdictions have varying systems of norms and laws, and these undergo frequent change, as do the day-to-day policies and practices of formal control agencies. Such changes make it particularly difficult to compare deviance from one period to another or from one locale to another. Some critics have suggested that official statistics may more accurately reflect changes in the operations of social control agencies than actual changes in the incidence of deviance.[42]

A study of drug-related arrests in Chicago from the 1940s through the 1960s showed clearly how crime statistics can be affected by changes in enforcement policy. During the late 1960s, for example, growing public concern about drug use among young people led to police surveillance of school populations and to a marked increase in arrests involving white youth and marijuana. In discussions with the investigator, police administrators indicated that they were making the kinds of arrests that the public was demanding.

Individual officers also consistently mentioned pressures from the community, organizations, parents, etc. Thus, during the late 1960's, they were bringing in pot and pills, while earlier they had largely ignored these drugs. "We always worked out south before—with the Mau Mau's (blacks in general)—it was mostly heroin and coke . . . the pot and stuff went down the stool (toilet) since nobody gave a damn about it and we didn't want to inventory the stuff . . . now we bring in every seed and joint." In recent years, the officers have felt that arrests for these drugs were acceptable

and that the courts would convict at least some of the offenders. Thus, community pressures and police perception of public demand influenced their enforcement activities. Specifically, they changed who was arrested, where, for what, and in what manner.[43]

Sociologists have become increasingly concerned with identifying such problems of bias and distortion in statistics on crime and other forms of deviance.

Criminal Statistics

National statistics on the extent of criminal behavior have been maintained by the Federal Bureau of Investigation since the 1930s. Data on specific types of crimes are collected from reports prepared by police departments throughout the United States, covering approximately 95 percent of the population. Each year the FBI summarizes the various data it has collected in its *Uniform Crime Reports for the United States.* These reports contain a number of indices on various types of crime for different cities and sections of the country. For the most part, the data are expressed as rates in terms of the number of crimes of a given type for each 100,000 persons in the population.

The FBI also uses such indices as "crimes known to the police" and "arrests" in an attempt to obtain an accurate estimate of the extent of crime. To record trends related to serious crime in the United States, specific "index crimes" are used (murder, forcible rape, robbery, aggravated assault, burglary, larceny, and auto theft). The arrest trends for these index crimes and other types of crimes are shown in Table 7.3.

Recent *Uniform Crime Reports* indicate that crime in the United States has been increasing at a much faster rate than the population. It was estimated in 1973 that the total national crime rate (total number of offenses per 100,000 population) had risen 24 percent since 1968 (see Figure 7.1). But though the amount of crime has clearly been increasing, it may be that official statistics have somewhat exaggerated the *extent* of increase.

42. John I. Kitsuse and Aaron V. Cicourel, "A Note on the Uses of Official Statistics," *Social Problems,* 11 (Fall 1963): 131–139.

43. See, for example, Lois B. DeFleur, "Biasing Influences on Drug Arrest Statistics: Implications for Deviance Research," *American Sociological Review,* 40 (February 1975): 88–103; quotation from p. 98.

One of the factors contributing to some of the increases in the rates derived from such records (both in crimes reported *to* the police and *by* the police) is that the police are keeping records better than they did in the past and thus reporting crimes more accurately. In addition, changes in the definition and classification of offenses have often resulted in statistical increases in crime.[44]

Other factors may also be contributing to statistical increases in crime. Since more people have insurance against theft, more citizens are reporting crimes to the police in the hope that this will aid them in collecting their insurance.

44. NIMH Center for Studies of Crime and Delinquency, *Criminal Statistics* (Washington, D.C.: U.S. Government Printing Office, 1972).

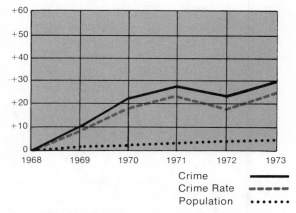

Crime —
Crime Rate — — —
Population • • • • • •

SOURCE: FBI, *Uniform Crime Reports*, 1973, p. 3. Crime-Crime Index Offenses; Crime Rate-Number of Offenses per 100,000 Inhabitants.

Figure 7.1. CRIME AND POPULATION, 1968–1973, PERCENT CHANGE OVER 1968

Table 7.3. TOTAL ARREST TRENDS, 1960–1973

Offense charged	Total number of persons arrested, all ages		Percent change, 1960–1973		
	1960	1973	Total, all ages	Under 18 years of age	18 years of age and over
Total	3,242,574	4,381,968	**+35.1**	**+144.1**	**+16.8**
Criminal homicide:					
(a) Murder and nonnegligent manslaughter	4,541	10,629	**+134.1**	+255.2	+124.4
(b) Manslaughter by negligence	1,766	1,660	**−6.0**	+63.6	−11.6
Forcible rape	6,857	13,823	**+101.6**	+132.3	+95.2
Robbery	31,197	83,012	**+166.1**	+299.0	+125.1
Aggravated assault	50,402	108,076	**+114.4**	+206.2	+101.3
Burglary—breaking or entering	117,084	211,029	**+80.2**	+104.2	+58.9
Larceny—theft	190,443	431,506	**+126.6**	+124.3	+128.7
Auto theft	54,202	87,975	**+62.3**	+51.0	+79.8
Subtotal for above offenses	456,492	947,710	**+107.6**	+115.7	+101.6
Other assaults	115,156	182,985	**+58.9**	+204.0	+42.1
Forgery and counterfeiting	21,329	28,175	**+32.1**	+105.1	+26.6
Fraud and embezzlement⟩	30,551	56,208	**+84.0**	+205.0	+80.8
Stolen property; buying, receiving, possessing	9,147	48,141	**+426.3**	+529.2	+386.9
Weapons; carrying, possessing, etc.	30,865	85,749	**+177.8**	+119.6	+192.2
Prostitution and commercialized vice	24,331	40,354	**+65.9**	+286.2	+62.0
Sex offenses (except forcible rape and prostitution)	39,582	35,693	**−9.8**	−19.0	−7.2
Narcotic drug laws	29,889	328,670	**+999.6**	+4673.3	+774.6
Gambling	105,607	43,983	**−58.4**	+.7	−59.0
Offenses against family and children	35,906	24,063	**−33.0**	−25.0	−33.1
Driving under the influence	142,698	413,837	**+190.0**	+401.3	+188.3
Liquor laws	81,735	109,392	**+33.8**	+151.8	+2.4
Drunkenness	1,215,555	837,551	**−31.1**	+88.0	−32.3
Disorderly conduct	364,289	317,531	**−12.8**	+51.0	−22.1
Vagrancy	127,643	40,508	**−68.3**	−42.8	−69.8
All other offenses (except traffic)	411,799	841,418	**+104.3**	+169.1	+66.6
Suspicion (not included in totals)	123,196	30,876	**−74.9**	−58.4	−78.7

SOURCE: FBI, *Uniform Crime Reports*, 1973, p. 124. Based on comparable reports from 1854 cities representing 79,540,000 population and 524 counties representing 14,711,000 population.

TOOLS OF SOCIOLOGY
THE SURVEY TECHNIQUE   Charles W. Thomas

The survey technique is applicable to a broad variety of issues, and surveys are used by a large number of individuals and organizations as well as by sociologists. Broadcast networks continue or cancel programs on the basis of listener and viewer surveys; manufacturers use consumer surveys to help them decide what products to market and where to market them; and builders and developers examine government census surveys for information on where to initiate housing projects.

All surveys seek to gather reliable and valid information about the goals, expectations, behavior, or values of well-defined sets of individuals, groups, or organizations. Although the techniques employed are frequently complex and sophisticated, the underlying logic of the method is simple. First, researchers carefully specify the issues to be addressed in the research and define the population to be studied. Second, they develop a sample design, which specifies the means by which sample elements (the individuals, groups, or organizations to be studied) are to be selected. The sample design ensures that bias in selecting sample elements will be minimized (page 365). Third, they decide how to contact each of the elements in the sample. For example, when individuals are being surveyed, each person could be interviewed in a face-to-face setting or by telephone or could be asked to fill out a questionnaire. Finally, the researchers prepare a form for recording the sought-after information, such as a questionnaire or an interview schedule. This form must be appropriate for the research problem, the type of population under study, and the means used to survey the population. It can be structured or relatively unstructured (page 398), depending on whether members of the sample must explain their answers or can simply select them from a list.

An illustration of the use of the survey technique can be seen in recent efforts of the Law Enforcement Assistance Administration (LEAA) of the United States Department of Justice to gain a more accurate measure of the extent of crime in the United States. For years both law enforcement agencies and researchers have had to rely on official records compiled by such agencies as the Federal Bureau of Investigation in order to measure the amount of crime. Unfortunately, such reports contain many inaccuracies because of the way in which their original data are gathered (see pages 193–196). Many criminologists have suggested that officially recorded crime statistics are a far better indicator of police activity than they are of criminal activity.

LEAA has attempted to overcome the problems of accuracy in official records by using sophisticated victimization surveys. In one of these surveys information was obtained from several thousand randomly selected households and businesses in a number of large metropolitan areas in order to determine the actual incidence of criminal victimization, the impact of victimization on the victims, and the extent to which official data provide an accurate index of the volume of crime in the cities studied. Not surprisingly, this victimization survey and others have documented significant biases in the official records.

The LEAA could get the information they wanted only by surveying representative samples of citizens and business organizations. Since similar situations are common in other areas of social science, the survey technique is generally viewed as a fundamental methodological tool in contemporary sociological research.

Law Enforcement Assistance Administration, *Criminal Victimization in the United States: A National Crime Panel Survey Report* (Washington, D.C.: United States Department of Justice, November 1974). For a criminologist's view of official reports on crime, see Donald J. Black, "Production of Crime Rates," *American Sociological Review,* 35 (August 1970): 733–747.

Increased anxiety about crime and being victimized may make people somewhat more willing to report criminal acts to official agencies. However, victimization studies show that a great many crimes still go unreported.

Victimization Studies

Sociologists have taken several innovative steps to try to obtain more reliable indicators of the incidence of crime. The President's Commission on Law Enforcement and the Administration of Justice initiated a national survey that focused on household members and their experiences as victims of crimes.[45] When victimization was claimed, respondents were asked if the offense had been reported to the police. Over ten thousand households were questioned in this manner, and the criminal offenses claimed by victims were compared with those reported in police statistics. In general, the survey found a significant number of crimes that had not been reported to the police.

Additional victimization surveys in a number of large cities have focused on crimes incurred by both residents and commercial establish-ments. As Table 7.4 shows, there are significant variations in victimization rates from city to city, and in most of them at least two out of every three crimes still go unreported to the police. Such surveys appear to offer an important technique for assessing the actual extent of crime, though they still must be interpreted with caution (see Tools of Sociology, page 195).

Other Statistics

Most data on noncriminal types of deviance are compiled and reported by various social agencies. These agencies have varying degrees of contact with the relevant deviant population, and some devote more resources than others to record keeping. Before relying on such data, a researcher should find out as much as possible about the agency and how it gathers its information. For example, statistical data on suicides have been regularly compiled and reported for approximately a hundred years (see Table 7.5).

45. The President's Commission on Law Enforcement and the Administration of Justice, *Criminal Victimization in the United States: A Report of a National Survey* (Washington, D.C.: U.S. Government Printing Office, 1967).

Table 7.4. CRIMES REPORTED BY VICTIMS

Rates per 1000 urban residents

| City | Types of Crimes | | | Total crimes of violence | Victim reports per crime in official records |
	Rape and attempted rape	Robbery	Assault		
Detroit	3	32	33	68	2.7
Denver	3	17	46	67	2.9
Philadelphia	1	28	34	63	5.1
Portland, Ore.	3	17	40	59	2.6
Baltimore	1	26	28	56	2.2
Chicago	3	26	27	56	2.8
Cleveland	2	24	28	54	2.4
Los Angeles	2	16	35	53	2.9
Atlanta	2	16	30	48	2.3
Dallas	2	10	31	43	2.6
Newark	1	29	12	42	1.4
St. Louis	1	16	25	42	1.5
New York	1	24	11	36	2.1

NOTE: Detailed breakdown of figures may not equal totals because of rounding.
SOURCE: "Crime in the Nation's Cities," U.S. Department of Justice (Law Enforcement Assistance Administration), April 1974.

Such data come primarily from coroners and other officials who determine causes of death. The bases for deciding whether death is suicidal, accidental, homicidal, or natural often varies greatly from place to place, and frequently the exact definitions of "cause of death" are vague and flexible. Also, officials sometimes allow the socioeconomic status of the victim to influence their decisions as to cause of death: a skid row bum is more likely to be called a suicide than an upper-middle-class executive. Thus it is very difficult to adequately evaluate the accuracy of such statistics.[46]

For some types of deviance, such as homosexuality or bisexuality, accurate information on incidence is virtually impossible to obtain from official records. Some data have been obtained through surveys on sexual behavior, such as those made by Kinsey and his associates in the 1940s and 1950s and the more recent survey funded by the Playboy Foundation.[47] Kinsey esti-

mated that 25 percent of American males and 20 percent of American females had experienced some type of homosexual activity, and the Playboy study concludes that there is no indication of an increase in these behaviors. However, all these surveys suffer from difficulties in obtaining adequate, reliable data.

DISTRIBUTION OF DEVIANCE
Official statistics on deviance give some indications of how it is distributed among different types of individuals in our society, and the variations are rather striking. They result from many factors, including differences in tolerance limits and differential detection and reporting. The rates vary among different age and racial groups and social classes and between men and women.

Age and Sex
Males have been arrested by police approximately six times as frequently as females, though this ratio has been decreasing in recent years. Some writers have attempted to link the greater incidence of male crime to biological or psychological factors, but most criminologists stress the importance of social and cultural factors that

46. Jack Douglas, *The Social Meanings of Suicide* (Princeton, N.J.: Princeton University Press, 1967).
47. Alfred Kinsey et al., *Sexual Behavior in the Human Male* (Philadelphia and London: W. B. Saunders, 1948); Alfred Kinsey et al., *Sexual Behavior in the Human Female* (Philadelphia and London: W. B. Saunders, 1953); and Morton Hunt, *Sexual Behavior in the 1970's* (New York: Playboy Press, 1974).

Table 7.5. SUICIDE MORTALITY RATES, BY RACE, SEX, AND AGE GROUPS, 1940–1969

Sex and age	1940 White	1940 Negro and other races	1950 White	1950 Negro and other races	1960 White	1960 Negro and other races	1969 White	1969 Negro and other races
Total	**15.5**	**4.6**	**12.2**	**4.3**	**11.4**	**4.5**	**11.9**	**5.3**
Male	**23.5**	**7.2**	**19.0**	**7.0**	**17.6**	**7.2**	**17.2**	**8.1**
5–14	0.4	0.4	0.3	0.1	0.5	0.1	0.5	0.2
15–24	8.8	5.1	6.6	5.3	8.6	5.3	12.6	9.9
25–34	19.9	11.5	13.8	10.1	14.9	12.9	18.3	17.8
35–44	30.1	10.6	22.4	11.3	21.9	13.5	22.4	15.8
45–54	44.1	14.8	34.1	11.7	33.7	12.8	28.6	12.1
55–64	58.8	12.6	45.9	16.8	40.2	16.9	34.9	10.6
65 and over	60.2	12.0	55.8	13.3	46.7	12.4	40.8	14.8
Female	**7.3**	**2.1**	**5.5**	**1.7**	**5.3**	**2.0**	**6.8**	**2.8**
5–14	0.1	0.0	0.1	0.1	0.1	0.0	0.2	0.2
15–24	3.9	3.3	2.7	1.7	2.3	1.5	3.8	4.1
25–34	8.6	3.5	5.2	2.8	5.8	3.5	8.1	6.1
35–44	11.5	3.0	8.2	2.2	8.1	3.7	12.7	4.8
45–54	14.0	3.2	10.5	4.0	10.9	3.2	13.3	3.7
55–64	13.1	1.4	10.7	1.2	10.9	3.4	11.8	2.3
65 and over	11.6	2.4	9.9	2.4	8.8	3.9	8.6	2.8

SOURCE: *Statistical Abstract of the United States, 1973*. Based on unpublished data from U.S. National Center for Health Statistics. Rate per 100,000 population.

have different influences on the two sexes. Actually, relatively little is known about female deviance because most studies have concentrated on males.[48] This situation is gradually changing, and new information is being assembled that may help us understand both the similarities and the differences between the sexes in deviant behavior.

Age distributions vary according to the type of deviance. For example, the incidence of problem drinking and suicide is greatest among older people. In contrast, criminal statistics show a disproportionately high incidence of serious crime among the young: by far the largest proportion of those arrested for serious crimes is under twenty-five years of age. This is particularly true for drug offenses.

Social Class
Official statistics indicate that the largest proportion of criminals in this country comes from the lower socioeconomic levels. For example, from two thirds to three quarters of prison inmates are members of the lower strata. The crimes they commit most frequently are crimes against property—usually some form of theft.

These statistics have been used to show that low socioeconomic position is linked to crime, but they are somewhat distorted. Crimes committed by persons of higher socioeconomic position are less likely to be detected, reported, or processed in the courts. For example, we do not know how much embezzlement, graft, tax fraud, and other white-collar crimes are committed by "respectable" people—in business and government—in the course of doing their jobs. Nor do we know how many corporate executives commit crimes against the public for their companies.

Based upon evidence from investigative committees, consumer groups, and others, it appears that white-collar crime is very prevalent in our society and may be more costly than the usual "index crimes" reported in the *Uniform Crime Reports*. The President's Commission on Law Enforcement and the Administration of Justice estimated that annual losses to the government from tax fraud total $25 to $40 billion; that securities frauds total $500 million to $1 billion; that medical and drug frauds total $500 million;

and that frauds in home and auto repair total from $500 million to $1 billion.[49] Undoubtedly there are many other unrecognized and unpunished crimes against the public. If more reliable data on such activities could be obtained, they might alter the assumption that crime is related to low social class.

Widespread concern has been voiced over the differential legal treatment received by people at different socioeconomic levels.[50] Substantial numbers of the poor have been unable to obtain pretrial release and have faced courts with no legal counsel. White-collar and professional lawbreakers not only receive better treatment before and during the trial; they also have a much better chance of receiving light punishment or none at all. Most of those convicted in the Watergate cases, for example, spent very little time in jail. Such class-linked differentials in the administration of justice are matters of continuing concern.

Race
Official statistics indicate that there is more crime among blacks than among whites. Blacks are arrested approximately four times more frequently than whites, and although blacks make up only 11 to 12 percent of the population, they represent 30 to 40 percent of prison inmates.

Like the statistics on social class, the data on race and crime are deceptive. A high proportion of minorities are in the lower levels of our class structure, and all lower-class populations—black and white—tend to have higher involvements in street crime, or at least tend to get caught more often, than upper-class populations. Also, there is clear evidence that racial minorities are discriminated against by the police and in the courts.[51] Thus, much of the official data showing concentrations of deviance among minorities must be interpreted with care.

48. Dorie Klein, "The Etiology of Female Crime: A Review of the Literature," *Issues in Criminology*, 8, No. 2 (Fall 1973): 3–30.

49. The President's Commission on Law Enforcement and the Administration of Justice, *Crime and Its Impact: An Assessment* (Washington, D.C.: U.S. Government Printing Office, 1967), pp. 102–103.

50. Jacobus Tenbroek et al., *The Law of the Poor* (San Francisco, Calif.: Chandler Publishing Co., 1966).

51. Charles E. Reasons and Jack L. Kuykendall, *Race, Crime and Justice* (Pacific Palisades, Calif.: Goodyear Publishing Co., Inc. 1972).

SOCIAL CONTROL OF DEVIANCE

In the small homogeneous society, extensive behavioral conformity is ensured by the fact that socializing experiences are very much the same for all members. Societal norms tend to be consistent with each other and to be strongly supported by tradition. Social control, then, is primarily dependent on self-sanctioning. Even on those occasions when external sanctions are required, they seldom involve formal punishment. Deviants can usually be brought back to conformity through the use of gossip, ridicule, or humiliation.

Even in a heterogeneous society such as ours, social control rests largely on the internalization of shared norms. Most people behave in socially acceptable ways because they seldom conceive of behaving otherwise. And as in simpler societies, fear of disapproval from family, friends, and neighbors is usually adequate to keep potential deviators in check. Nevertheless, the great diversity of the population, the lack of direct communication between various segments, and the competitive struggles between groups with different interests have all led to an increasing need for formal mechanisms of social control.

In the United States, public response to deviant acts and individuals has resulted in more and more laws, larger police forces, increasingly complex legal processing, and a variety of programs aimed at "rehabilitating" various types of deviants. An additional concern has been to find effective ways of controlling deviance without infringing upon individual rights and freedoms. The issue is one of maintaining social order and at the same time protecting basic values.

GENERAL STRATEGIES OF CONTROL

Reduction of crime, delinquency, drug abuse, alcoholism, and other major forms of deviance is generally considered one of the major problems of contemporary American society. But although there is widespread agreement that our present techniques for controlling deviance have not been very effective, there is little agreement about how the system should be changed. Current strategies for controlling various forms of deviance include punishment, the diversion of some offenders into special rehabilitation programs, and the decriminalization of "victimless" offenses.

Punishment

Most people believe that imprisonment and other forms of punishment administered by official agencies of the state are the most appropriate devices for reducing deviance and inducing conformity. The reason most frequently cited for the use of punishment is that it acts as a *deterrent*. It is widely assumed that punishing people for violating societal standards will not only discourage them from repeating their actions but also deter other people who might be similarly tempted. It is an open question, however, whether punishment is actually an effective deterrent to deviance. Research on the issue to date has dealt mainly with the efficacy of specific penalties (e.g., the death penalty) in deterring specific criminal behaviors (e.g., homicide). The results of such studies have been mixed, but there is general agreement that punishment and other formal sanctions will not be effective in preventing deviance unless supported by informal sanctions.[52]

Imprisonment, the most widely used sanction for criminal deviance, has been justified in terms of *rehabilitation* as well as deterrence. Besides punishing offenders most modern correctional facilities attempt to help them develop attitudes and skills that will facilitate their reentry into society. The emphasis on reform and rehabilitation has greatly increased among penologists, but the general public still holds strongly to the more traditional concept of punishment. In fact, concern over rising rates of crime and delinquency has in recent years led many people to argue for a more punitive approach.

---

52. Franklin E. Zimring and Gordon Hawkins, *Deterrence: The Legal Threat in Crime Control* (Chicago: The University of Chicago Press, 1973).

VIEWPOINTS   REFORMING THE PRISONS

■   What a large part of the public really wants is, not brutality toward convicts, but a re-recognition that the offender's conduct is immoral. . . . These Americans feel that the removal of moral guilt from crime has placed us on a slippery slope of accelerating violence where any anti-social act can be rationalized either as a protest or as a product of one's environment. . . . When the legal order excises moral guilt from crime, it undermines the law as a moral deterrent.

Recognition of the moral element in crime does not mandate a jail sentence in every case of a serious criminal conviction. Probation is appropriate where the offender realizes his moral guilt, evidences remorse, and seeks help in a genuine effort to reform which has some prospect of success, and where the circumstances in the community are such that release of the offender will not produce an anomic reaction. . *norm lessness*

Further, while morality-in-law may necessitate pervasive discipline in jails, it cannot justify brutality, inhuman living conditions or the "doing time" atmosphere of many prisons. Nor are institutionalized vocational training and education to moral responsibility inconsistent. . . .

Everyone agrees that something must be done about our correctional system. . . . The public, already concerned that the amoralization of crime has become an invitation to accelerated violence and rationalized recidivism, is hardly likely to embrace a general jail delivery under the guise of reform.

Somewhere between behavioral rehabilitationism and irrational retributionism, at a place where the criminal sanction serves to reaffirm community moral norms while at the same time attempting to educate the offender to social productivity, as well as to an awareness of moral guilt and personal responsibility, there lies the starting point for a new approach to punishment for crime that is both just and human. Until we remoralize punishment, all of us—prisoner and public, governor and guard—will remain trapped in the crossfire of extremists.
Robert M. Byrn
"The Morality of Punishment"

●   In correction, as in much of our lives, we have substituted the auspices of science for the auspices of religion. The problem is that science, like religion, has proven inexact and frequently unpersuasive in the correction business. And the scientists in correction, like the religionists, have not hesitated to lace their rehabilitative techniques with heavy doses of imprisonment and deprivation. The Quaker called it "penitence"; the psychologists call it "negative reinforcement." My concern is that we will give the scientists more power than the religionists ever had and more than their theories warrant. . . .

The theories of both these well-intentioned groups are fundamentally akin. Both make a man his own prison. The intention is to help the offender become happy and whole again, but in practice these theories put too much power over inmates in the hands of fallible prison administrators. I believe the only power society should have in forcing an individual to change his behavior is to require each criminal to pay for what he has done wrong. That is why I favor a program that would require a thief to pay back what he steals; to force a mugger to make adequate restitution to the person he assaults. In many cases this can be done outside prison; in most cases, it cannot be done inside prison. Thus, prisons really are useful only for the small minority who need to be sequestered from society. Even treatment-oriented prisons create more behavior problems than they cure. . . .

Now, when the public seems ready for correctional reform, it is especially important to move carefully. Neither the get-tough approach nor the treatment-in-prison approach will make our correctional system work. For all the fear that it generates, for all the difficulties that it presents, I still believe we should seriously consider tearing down most prison walls, and deinstitutionalizing our whole correctional system.
Ronald L. Goldfarb
"American Prisons: Self-Defeating Concrete"

Diversion

Currently, various techniques are being used by law enforcement agencies to place some offenders into special diversion programs rather than letting the law run its full course. For example, in some states police may refer drug offenders to a treatment agency rather than holding them for prosecution.

Technically, diversion can take place at any stage of legal processing—at the police station, in the courts, or at the penal institution. Familiar posttrial examples are probation and suspended sentences. Newer diversion programs include pretrial release, in which the court places the individual on a type of probation instead of bringing him or her to trial.[53] If at the end of a specified period the person has a satisfactory record, all charges are dismissed.

Some of the pressures for diversionary measures have developed because of the tremendous overloading of our courts and overcrowding of our jails. More and more the judicial system has been operating less and less as it was designed to operate. As a result, diversions have become an essential aspect of that system, though they are just beginning to be recognized as such.[54] Objective research evaluations have been few, but diversion programs are often justified on the basis of lower costs for the state as well as more humane treatment for offenders.

Decriminalization

Our society outlaws certain kinds of "morally objectionable" behavior, such as gambling, homosexuality, prostitution, and public drunkenness, and defines these behaviors as crimes even though they are "victimless."[55] That is, there are no "victims" of these behaviors in the usual sense, and formal legal complaints are generally made by the police rather than by members of the general public.

A number of objections have been raised against using the system of criminal law to prosecute victimless crimes. Critics claim that it represents an attempt to legislate private morality and note that enforcement requires the diversion of resources that could otherwise be devoted to the arrest and prosecution of perpetrators of crimes that do have victims. Also, labeling theorists have argued that arresting, trying, and punishing these offenders does little to preserve "morality." It simply adds to the problems of the offenders: no longer do they just have a drinking problem, for example, they are also "public nuisances" or even "criminals."

In recent years there has been a trend toward removing victimless offenses from the criminal justice system—in other words, *decriminalizing* them. For example, a number of states have abolished arrests for public drunkenness. This policy has reduced the number of people crowding the jails and has raised hopes that problem drinkers will be treated rather than punished, if the proper social programs can be established.

CORRECTIONAL SERVICES

The basic outlines and directions of the correctional system in the United States were developed in 1870 at the National Prison Association Congress in Cincinnati, Ohio.[56] This meeting raised the issue of rehabilitating rather than merely punishing convicted offenders. A century later there is a real question whether the initial goals outlined in Cincinnati have been accomplished.

Correctional institutions and programs have always received very limited financial support. Their needs are given low priority when cities, counties, and states make up their budgets. Although there have been some significant reforms in a few states and at the federal level within recent years, most local and county institutions are extremely overcrowded and essentially punitively oriented. Riots by inmates and administrative scandals have drawn public attention to conditions in these institutions, bringing some pressure for change.

53. Elizabeth W. Vorenberg and James Vorenberg, "Early Diversion from the Criminal Justice System," in *Prisoners in America,* ed. Lloyd E. Ohlin (Englewood Cliffs, N.J.: Prentice-Hall, Inc., 1973).

54. Clarence Schrag, *Crime and Justice: American Style,* NIMH Center for Studies of Crime and Delinquency (Washington, D.C.: U.S. Government Printing Office, 1971).

55. Edwin M. Schur, *Crimes Without Victims* (Englewood Cliffs, N.J.: Prentice-Hall, Inc., 1965).

56. R. M. Carter, D. Glaser, and L. Wilkins, eds., *Correctional Institutions* (New York: J. B. Lippincott Co., 1972).

Most prisons still have a basically punitive atmosphere, and there is probably some justice to the charge that they serve more as training grounds for criminals than as effective rehabilitation centers. An estimated two-thirds of all inmates return to prison at least once.

Changing Nature of Institutions

Prisons and jails were initially established for the purpose of punishment, and most of our correctional institutions are still primarily punitive. But as rehabilitative orientations have become increasingly prevalent, new correctional policies and programs are being developed. Some programs are little more than token efforts at reform, but others represent a dramatic change. Kassebaum and his associates have described a modern prison in one state:

The cells in the medium security prison where this study took place are painted in a variety of pastel colors. Each inmate has a key to his own "room." Recreational activities include outdoor bowling, tennis, handball, and shuffleboard. . . . Major components of the treatment program included: group counseling, "community living" (a version of the therapeutic community approach), alcoholics anonymous, formal education through high school, and vocational training. Limited individual psychotherapy was available from the prison's clinical staff. An effort was made in one of the prison's four separate 600-man living units to address inmates as "Mr. _____." . . . But multicolored rooms are still cells, inmate keys do not work when the master cell lock switch is thrown,

one cannot go home when the bowling match is over, full participation in all aspects of the treatment program does not guarantee release, and the violation of any of a detailed list of inmate regulations may be punished by up to 29 days in an isolation cell (not "room").[57]

In its efforts to treat prisoners as individuals and to help them develop socially approved attitudes and skills, this modern institution stands in marked contrast to traditional prisons and jails. Yet, as in older institutions, an emphasis on punishment remains. It is questionable whether rehabilitation programs can be successfully combined with a punitive system. This is a persistent dilemma, and many recent correctional innovations represent new attempts to resolve it.

Community-Based Programs

There is mounting evidence that confinement in prison or jail often leads to *increased* criminality. Most correctional institutions tend to be schools for crime rather than effective rehabilitation centers. For this reason, there has been significant growth in recent years of decentralized, community-based programs designed to rehabilitate convicted offenders. An additional argument for such programs is that their cost per individual is generally less than that of institutional confinement.

Two community-based programs, probation and parole, have been in use for many years. Probation entails the suspension of sentence with provisions for supervision and guidance in the community. Parole is a procedure through which the offender is released from prison after having served part of his or her sentence; after release, the parolee is subject to the supervision of a parole officer for a specified period of time.

Newer community-based programs use a wide variety of approaches.[58] Many of them involve release for work or education; prisoners go out into the community daily for jobs or schooling and return to the correctional institution at night. In some states furlough programs allow prisoners to stay in the community, usu-

57. Gene Kassebaum, David A. Ward, and Daniel M. Wilner, *Prison Treatment and Parole Survival: An Empirical Assessment* (New York: John Wiley & Sons, Inc., 1971), p. 1.
58. Daniel Glaser, "Correction of Adult Offenders in the Community," in *Prisoners in America,* Ohlin, ed.

ally with their families, for varying periods of time. Other types of community programs make use of halfway houses and guidance centers that help convicted offenders make their way back into society.

Community-based programs have proved more successful than traditional, punitively oriented correctional facilities in rehabilitating some types of offenders, but they by no means provide a complete answer to the problem of controlling deviance. In addition, they have met with considerable opposition from members of the general public, who feel that law-abiding citizens are unnecessarily threatened by having convicted offenders "set loose" in their midst.

Recent trends in social control — diversion, decriminalization, community-based programs, etc. — are all aimed at overcoming recognized flaws in our traditional correctional system, but obviously other innovations are needed. None of the programs devised thus far shows promise of coping effectively with the overall problem of deviance, either from an individual point of view or from the perspective of society. This gives increased urgency to the sociological study of deviance. Those aspects of the social system that contribute to deviance must be better understood before there can be effective responses to it.

SUMMARY

Deviant behavior is any behavior that exceeds the tolerance limits associated with some normative expectation. Tolerance limits are influenced by the importance of the violated norm, by the situation in which the deviant behavior occurs, and by the characteristics of the violator. Conformity and deviation are culturally relative. Behavior that is considered deviant in one group or at one time may not be so defined in another group or at another time. And individuals who are defined as deviants by the larger society may be defined as conformists by specific subcultures within that society.

Sociological theories of the causes of deviance focus on the social structure and on patterns of interaction between the individual and other members of society. Anomie theory, labeling theory, the social bonds perspective, and sociocultural learning theories represent different but complementary approaches to understanding the generation of deviant behavior.

Individuals who are rejected by the larger society for disapproved activities often find social acceptance in groups sharing deviant subcultures. Deviant subcultures also provide socialization for their participants, thus helping deviants adjust to societal disapproval.

Public agencies, at both local and federal levels, collect data on the incidence of some categories of deviance, but for a variety of reasons such public records do not provide accurate assessments of deviance rates. The best available evidence suggests that certain types of deviance are more common among certain age, sex, racial, and socioeconomic categories than others. A variety of factors contributes to these variations.

The control of deviance is a major concern to all societies, but the problem of control is likely to be most difficult in large heterogeneous societies. The most effective control is the voluntary control that most individuals impose on themselves by virtue of having internalized, through socialization, the shared norms of their society. Self-sanctioning and informal controls are usually sufficient to ensure extensive behavioral conformity in small homogeneous societies, but heterogeneous societies such as ours have found an increasing need for formal sanctions administered through official agencies.

A society's usual response to deviance is to punish the offender, often by imprisonment. But there have been attempts to deemphasize punitive measures through such steps as decriminalization and diversion. At the same time, most institutions have been giving increased emphasis to programs aimed at treatment and rehabilitation. There has also been a growth of community-based programs designed to prepare inmates for life outside prison walls. We lack sufficient research to evaluate these various innovations, but none of them promises to be a complete answer to the problem of effectively reducing deviant behavior.

Part III
SOCIAL DIFFERENTIATION

8
Social Stratification

DIMENSIONS OF STRATIFICATION

Status   Class   Power

OPPOSING THEORIES OF STRATIFICATION

Conflict Theory   Functional Theory

AGENTS OF STRATIFICATION

The Family   The Educational System   The Economic
System   The Government

SOCIAL MOBILITY

Causal Factors in Mobility   Mobility and Societal Values
Mobility in International Perspective

As we noted in Chapters 2 and 3, social ranking
is a basic component of social organization
found in all human groups. In this chapter we
will take a closer look at the phenomenon of
social ranking as it operates in the community
and society—the ranking of individuals and families into strata that share unequally in the distribution of prestige, wealth, and power. Ranking
of this type is referred to as *social stratification*.[1]

Although stratification systems show great
variety, all societies throughout history have been
found to be stratified on one basis or another. In
modern industrial societies, the prime criterion
of social ranking is occupation. Members of the
various professions are ranked higher than clerical workers and manual laborers, for example,
regardless of individual role performance. *Within* the various occupational categories, those
individuals who do the best job are likely to be
most highly rewarded, but this is not the major
criterion in the stratification system. A first-rate
file clerk cannot hope to make as much money
as a second-rate doctor or lawyer.

As we shall see, social stratification tends to
be transmitted from one generation to the next.
A family is ranked as a whole, and its position in
the social hierarchy goes far to determine the
range of opportunities available to all family
members. This is not to say that factory workers'
children cannot become doctors—only that their
chances of doing so are much inferior to those
of doctors' children. So too are their chances of
marrying a doctor's son or daughter.

We will begin the chapter by examining the
three dimensions of social stratification—status,
class, and power—and then discuss two opposing theories of why social inequalities occur.
Next, we will examine the part played by various social institutions in both maintaining and
altering stratification patterns. Finally, we shall
consider patterns of social mobility, both in the
United States and in other countries.

1. For an introduction to the concept of stratification, see
pages 83 and 91–92.

DIMENSIONS OF STRATIFICATION

Social scientists generally agree with Max Weber that an individual's position in the social hierarchy is measured in terms of three separate but interrelated dimensions of stratification: status, class, and power.[2] *Status* is the degree of prestige, or social honor, accorded to individuals by other members of a society. A *class* is made up of people who have roughly the same economic position by virtue of their occupations and/or their inherited wealth. *Power* is the ability to initiate policies and see that they are implemented, even in the face of opposition.[3]

These three dimensions of stratification generally intertwine. High status may stem from the possession of wealth; so also may political power. Similarly, power may provide access to wealth or to prestige or to both. But as we shall see, the phenomenon of social stratification is highly complex, and class, status, and power do not always go neatly hand-in-hand. Wealth, for example, does not automatically confer high status or even political power. And status derived from the possession of wealth or power may be maintained for a time even if wealth or power is lost. We shall examine these and other relationships in the sections that follow.

STATUS
Status is the amount of prestige that accrues to individuals in their social roles. It provides them with self-respect, with a sense of worth. Desire for these feelings is built into the individual early in the socialization process. As was pointed out in earlier chapters on individual development, we derive self-respect from the groups that are most significant to us. In our so-

ciety these are usually our family, our peer groups, and—in adulthood—our occupational groups.

Acquisition of Prestige
One of the most common ways to acquire high status has been to be born into a family that has long held an honored position in the community. Historically, valor in battle and the accumulation of wealth have been ways in which people who were not born with high status could acquire it. Daniel Defoe, in a poem called "What Makes a Peer?" noted how well the English had managed to develop their nobility, despite the fact that the ancestors of the peers were mainly foreign and of questionable background:[4]

> *Wealth, howsoever got, in England makes*
> *Lords of mechanics, Gentlemen of rakes.*
> *Antiquity and birth are needless here;*
> *'Tis impudence and money makes a peer.*

Defoe's poem, written in the seventeenth century, touches on the relationship between wealth and prestige that Weber later noted. Wealth may make the difference in the first place, but with the passing of generations status often becomes more important. William Thackeray, a nineteenth-century English novelist, noted the following status differences—as reflected in speech, manners, tastes, and education—among the people of his time:

> *They [the lower strata] are not like you, indeed. They have not your tastes and feeling: your education and refinements. They would not understand a hundred things which seem perfectly simple to you. They would shock you a hundred times a day by as many deficiencies of politeness, or by outrages upon the Queen's English—by practices entirely harmless, and yet in your eyes actually worse than crimes—they have large hard hands and clumsy feet.*[5]

In American society the people who made enormous fortunes in the nineteenth century were often crudely spoken, bad mannered, and uneducated by upper-class standards. But their grandchildren—if not their children—were able

---

2. Max Weber, "Class, Status and Party," in *Max Weber: Essays in Sociology,* ed. Hans Gerth and C. Wright Mills (New York: Oxford University Press, 1946), pp. 180–195.

3. Weber used the term *party* to denote political dominance and the ability to control decision making. In American sociology, this dimension of the stratification system is usually called *power,* and we shall follow this usage.

4. Reprinted in Lewis A. Coser, ed., *Sociology Through Literature* (Englewood Cliffs, N.J.: Prentice-Hall, Inc., 1963), p. 131.

5. William Makepeace Thackeray, *Sketches and Travels in London,* reprinted in Coser, *Sociology Through Literature,* pp. 138–139.

Although the traditional caste system of India has been abolished by law, it has not totally disappeared. Members of the lowest stratum, known as the untouchables, are still often denied educational and occupational opportunities.

to qualify as "old" families of established position and to snub the "new rich" as vulgar social climbers. Meanwhile, families that had reached America in the seventeenth and eighteenth centuries looked down on both of the newer generations of wealth in the smug conviction that lineage, not money, was the only sound basis of prestige.

For most of us, prestige is a reward to be ardently sought and ferociously defended. Lenski points out that the quest for prestige "influences almost every kind of decision from the choice of a car to the choice of a spouse. Fear of the loss of status, or honor, is one of the few motives that can make men lay down their lives on the field of battle."[6]

Closed Status Systems

In numerous societies throughout history differences in prestige have become so pronounced as to create more or less closed status systems. The most extreme form of a closed status system is the *caste* system, in which people are born into

a particular stratum of society and must remain in that stratum until they die, regardless of their abilities. Their occupational and marital opportunities are rigidly prescribed by the fact of caste, as indeed are nearly all forms of social interaction. India provides the classic example of stratification built around a closed status system. Although the caste system has now been abolished by law in India, the traditional castes of Hinduism continue to limit the opportunities of millions of citizens.

In the United States the structure of relationships between whites and blacks has had many characteristics of a caste system. Being black has automatically put individuals into a low status position and limited their access to wealth and political power. The persistence of these patterns of discrimination for more than a hundred years after the signing of the Emancipation Proclamation illustrates the strength of status systems strongly supported by institutionalized customs and beliefs.

Elements of a closed status system permeate many other sectors of American life. Ascribed characteristics such as sex, religious background, ethnicity, and lineage have all been used as criteria of social rank.[7] Jews may still have difficulty getting jobs or being promoted in New York banks, and names of southern and eastern European origin have only recently begun to appear with any frequency in the lists of top corporate executives. Women are still not accepted in many occupations on an equal basis with men, and opportunities are probably still better for graduates of Yale, Harvard, and Princeton than for graduates of less prestigious schools.

Open Status Systems

In most Western nations the Protestant Reformation, the Industrial Revolution, and the gradual development of political democracy have com-

6. Gerhard Lenski, *Power and Privilege: A Theory of Stratification* (New York: McGraw-Hill Book Company, 1966), p. 37.

7. The most elaborate attempts to measure the impact of status groups on the American community have been made by W. Lloyd Warner and his associates (page 211). See, for example, W. Lloyd Warner and Paul S. Lunt, *The Status System of a Modern Community* (New Haven, Conn.: Yale University Press, 1942) and W. Lloyd Warner and Leo Srole, *The Social Systems of American Ethnic Groups* (New Haven, Conn.: Yale University Press, 1945).

Throughout most of history, status symbols have been used to indicate the prestige associated with various social roles. In early twentieth-century England, for example, one could determine the different degrees of "social honor" by scanning the hats worn at the Ascot races. Those of wealth and lineage wore top hats and took the top position. Straw hats and bowlers indicated the success of the nouveaux riches, while members of the lower strata, who had the poorest view of the race, wore cloth caps.

bined to disrupt traditional systems of assigning prestige almost solely on the basis of ascribed characteristics. The trend has been toward the development of more open status systems in which people move up or down on the status scale depending on their level of achievement, especially in occupational roles.

American society, like other industrialized societies, has a relatively open status system. Social prestige is not the exclusive possession of "a chosen few" as it often has been in traditional societies. Yet status differences continue to exist and are often a source of conflict. Although American ideology minimizes the importance of status, most Americans are very conscious of

what their position is and are very anxious to protect or improve it—by moving to a "better" neighborhood, by buying a "better" car, by keeping up with the Joneses. And the social position of one's family has an important effect on job opportunities as well as on patterns of friendship, dating, and marriage.

Status Distinctions in Communist Societies

It is difficult to conceive of a society without status distinctions of some kind. Clearly such distinctions have not wholly disappeared in Communist societies, despite an ideological insistence on total equality. Recent research indicates that the level of prestige associated with various occupations in the Soviet Union, for example, closely parallels the pattern found in Western capitalist societies.[8] But there are also some interesting differences. The Soviet government

8. See Seymour M. Lipset and Richard B. Dobson, "Social Stratification and Sociology in the Soviet Union," *Survey*, 88, No. 3 (Summer 1973): 141–142.

confers high status and special economic privileges not only on scientists but also on poets, dancers, composers, writers, and all kinds of international competitors, from athletes to chess players, because these gifted individuals contribute to the prestige of the society as a whole.

CLASS

The concept of class refers to a stratum or aggregate of persons who share more or less the same economic position in a society. Class position derives largely but not exclusively from the occupational role or roles of the household breadwinner(s). Inherited wealth may also be a factor.

Economic Mobility

Even in a relatively open stratification system, social prestige can usually be increased only very gradually. Economic position, by contrast, can change quite rapidly—either for better or for worse.

The concept of economic mobility is meaningful only in an industrial society where changing technologies are continually creating new kinds of specialized jobs to be filled. Unlike traditional societies, where future occupation as well as status may be determined at birth, industrialized societies provide an ever changing variety of occupational roles that are open to at least some degree of competition. Although ability and initiative are by no means the only criteria determining who will get ahead and how far, they are clearly important. Even minority group members, who are overtly or subtly denied the opportunity to compete on an equal basis, generally find it relatively less difficult to improve their economic position than their position in the status hierarchy.

An increasingly significant phenomenon in industrial societies is that of the wife working for wages outside the home. In 1950 about 24 percent of married women in the United States were part of the labor force; by the mid-1970s the figure had risen to about 45 percent.[9] The overall effect of this trend may be to ensure an even greater openness of social classes, for the additional income from a second breadwinner may radically alter a family's economic advantages.

Measuring Class and Class Consciousness

Contemporary sociological interest in class differences is due in part to the community research carried out in the thirties and forties by W. Lloyd Warner and his associates (see Tools of Sociology, page 211).[10] The fact that people with no knowledge of sociology readily classify families as being "lower-middle" class or "upper-middle" class, "upper-lower" class or "lower-upper" class, is direct testimony to the impact of the Warner studies on American thinking about stratification.

Warner's approach to measuring class has been widely criticized for its failure to distinguish between class and status and its tendency to assume that power is largely a function of wealth. But these criticisms should not obscure the importance of Warner's contribution. He and his colleagues provided both a set of concepts for dealing with class differences and a means for measuring such differences systematically.

Studies of the stratification patterns in American communities have used both objective and subjective measures of class. In the objective approach, variables such as income, occupation, education, and place and type of residence are used as indices of class. In the subjective approach, individuals may simply be asked to assess their own class position. Studies of both types have consistently shown the existence of some three to six classes in American communities. An additional distinction is sometimes made between "blue-collar" and "white-collar" workers. These popular terms do not identify economic classes as such but rather imply differences in status between manual workers and those wage earners employed in offices.

9. *Work in America*, Report of a Special Task Force to the Secretary of Health, Education and Welfare (Cambridge, Mass.: The M.I.T. Press, 1973), pp. 57–59.
10. Among the best-known studies are those of "Yankee City" (Newburyport, Massachusetts): W. L. Warner and L. Srole, *The Social Systems of American Ethnic Groups* (1945); and W. L. Warner and J. O. Low, *The Social System of a Modern Factory* (1947), all published by Yale University Press. Another influential group of studies was the series on "Jonesville" (Morris, Illinois, also called "Elmtown," "Hometown," and "Prairie City"): W. L. Warner, R. J. Havighurst, and M. B. Loeb, *Who Shall Be Educated?* (New York: Harper & Row, Inc., 1949); W. L. Warner, M. Meeker, and K. Eels, *Social Class in America* (Chicago: Science Research Associates, Inc., 1949); and A. B. Hollingshead, *Elmtown's Youth* (New York: John Wiley & Sons, Inc., 1949).

TOOLS OF SOCIOLOGY
MEASURING CLASS AND STATUS   Joan Huber

Although *social class* is one of the most widely used terms in sociology, sociologists have difficulty in measuring it as distinct from other dimensions of stratification, especially status. Some sociologists follow Marx, who divided the world into those who own the means of production (the capitalist class) and those who do not (the workers). Most contend that this dichotomy disappeared as wages rose, the white-collar work force expanded, and giant corporations became controlled more by salaried managers than by their owners, the stockholders.

Today most sociologists rank people on the basis of a combination of class, status, and power, measuring such economically related attributes as community prestige, income, education, and occupational prestige. One measurement technique ranks individuals in communities; another ranks occupations on a national basis.

Methods to rank people in small towns were developed more than forty years ago by W. Lloyd Warner. Assuming that people were aware of the ranking system in their community, the researchers asked informants to identify and rank social classes, placing people they knew in these ranks. This method required too much interviewing time, so Warner developed a less expensive method based on occupation, source of income (inherited wealth, salary, wages, welfare payments), house type, and dwelling area. Warner identified six classes: upper-upper, lower-upper, upper-middle, lower-middle, upper-lower, and lower-lower. Sociologists agree that Warner's "classes" are actually status groupings, but they continue to use the terms.

At the national level, measurement focuses on occupations, the main source of rewards in industrial societies. More than sixty years ago, Alba Edwards, at the Bureau of the Census, devised the most widely used hierarchy of occupations. On the basis of the amount of training needed and the prestige of the job, Edwards ranked occupations as headwork (professionals, managers, clerical, and sales) and handwork (craftsmen, operatives, service, and common labor). A major problem with this approach is the lack of homogeneity within the categories: for example, nurses and corporation lawyers, who differ markedly in earnings and prestige, are both ranked as professionals.

About a decade ago, Charles Nam, also at the Bureau of the Census, assigned scores to a large number of occupations based on the average education and income levels of men in these occupations. Physicians were ranked highest, with a score of 99, followed by architects and lawyers (98), chiropractors (89), funeral directors (83), clergymen (67), auto mechanics (46), janitors (19), and lumbermen (04).

In 1947 the National Opinion Research Center (NORC) published the first national measure of occupational prestige based on evaluation of 90 occupations (see Table 8.3, page 225). The average score was 70, and the highest ranked occupation was that of Supreme Court Justice (96), followed by physician (93). Some below-average occupations were garage mechanic (62), lumberjack (53), and janitor (44).

Marie Haug has criticized these and other occupational measurement techniques for ignoring women, especially married women. While men are ranked by their own occupations, women—even if they are divorced or widowed—are ranked only by their husbands' occupations. Since only one-fifth of working wives hold jobs in the same Census Bureau categories as the jobs held by their husbands, assigning the wife her husband's rank is misleading, for her occupation may be crucial in determining such matters as whether the children will attend college. Furthermore, assigning women their husbands' rank conceals the fact that women's occupational attainment is much lower than men's in relation to educational level. No widely accepted measure of women's occupational rank has yet appeared.

For Warner's discussion of his methods, see W. Lloyd Warner, Marchia Meeker, and Kenneth Eels, *Social Class in America* (Chicago: Science Research Associates, 1949). For a discussion of the other methods discussed above, see U.S. Bureau of the Census, *Methodology and Scores of Socioeconomic Status,* Working Paper No. 15 (Washington, D.C., 1963); National Opinion Research Center, "Jobs and Occupations: A Popular Evaluation," *Opinion News,* 9 (September 1, 1947): 3–13; and Marie R. Haug, "Social Class Measurement and Women's Occupational Roles," *Social Forces,* 52 (September 1973): 86–98. A good general discussion is Robert W. Hodge and Paul M. Siegel, "The Measurement of Social Class," in *The International Encyclopedia of Social Science,* ed. David Sills (New York: Macmillan, Inc., 1968), pp. 316–325.

Research over the last quarter century has shown that most Americans are aware of the existence of a class structure and that there is a strong tendency toward self-identification with the middle class.[11] In one study nearly three-quarters of the adults in a national sample identified themselves as being "average" or as falling somewhere within the broad range of the middle class when asked to identify their own class in their own words.[12] Only 11 percent acknowledged being in the working class or lower class. In the same study a five-option question brought forth somewhat different responses but showed the same basic pattern. The class options offered were upper, upper-middle, middle, working, and lower. In this situation 61 percent of the sample identified themselves as middle or upper-middle class and 34 percent as working class. Overall, the study revealed not only that wealth and prestige mingle in the minds of Americans but that most of them feel they belong to a relatively open, more or less middle-class society.

Class Distinctions in Communist Societies

The ideology of the United States and of most other Western democracies stresses the importance of class mobility rather than the elimination of class differences. By contrast, the ideology of the Communist societies emphasizes the disappearance of classes. In both cases, the reality is somewhat different than the ideology: classes are not fully open in democratic societies, nor have they been eliminated in Communist societies. In the Soviet Union during the 1960s, several thousand people had incomes of more than 1000 rubles a month, while as many as 30 percent of the people subsisted on incomes of less than 60 rubles a month. Soviet researchers during the 1960s put the per capita poverty line at 51 rubles per month.[13]

In China, which has an economic level much lower than the Soviet Union's and which has often charged the Russian leaders with reverting to capitalism, the government has established a guaranteed minimum standard of living.

Nevertheless, it has been reported that incomes at the top are as much as 15 to 20 times as high as those at the bottom.[14] The Chinese government believes that as productivity increases the wages of low-paid factory workers will rise. In China, as in Russia, low rents, free education, and inexpensive health care, as well as some food and clothing allowances, lessen, but have not eliminated, class differences.

POWER

Max Weber defined power as "the probability that one actor within a social relationship will be in a position to carry out his own will despite resistance."[15] Power, in other words, is the ability to make and implement decisions, with or without the consent of those who will be affected. Control of decision making is an important measure of rank in all human groups, but it is especially significant at the level of community and society, where those with power can control those without it. Power, thus conceived, is not only a reward of the stratification system in itself but also a means for determining the distribution of other rewards.

In traditional societies the rewards of power, wealth, and status have generally gone hand in hand. It has been accepted as "natural" that the rich should rule, that the powerful should be rich, and that all others should serve and obey. These principles are only now being challenged in the developing countries, where an unequal power distribution has been strongly supported by tradition and religious belief. When power struggles have occurred in these countries, they have been primarily among those already in the top stratum; whatever the outcome, power has remained concentrated in

11. A pioneer study of class consciousness was that of Richard Centers, *The Psychology of Social Classes* (Princeton, N.J.: Princeton University Press, 1949).

12. Robert W. Hodge and Donald J. Treiman, "Class Identification in the United States," *American Journal of Sociology*, 73, No. 5 (March 1968): 535–547.

13. Lipset and Dobson, "Social Stratification and Sociology in the Soviet Union," pp. 126–127.

14. "China's Guaranteed Wage Impresses Yale Teacher," an interview with Yale Economics Professor Lloyd Reynolds, as reported in the *Hartford Courant*, November 13, 1973, p. 33.

15. Max Weber, *The Theory of Social and Economic Organization* (New York: The Free Press, 1957), p. 152.

the hands of a few. Many Latin American "revolutions," for example, have meant little more than a changing of the palace guard.

In the industrialized societies of the West, the trend over the last several centuries has been toward some diffusion of power. Traditional systems of authority have gradually given way to legal-rational systems in which power is vested not in a class of individuals but in a system of offices with clearly defined rights and responsibilities. Political power is distributed to citizens through the vote and through access to public office.

Despite this trend toward the diffusion of power, it would be naive to believe that wealth and power are no longer linked. The wealthiest industrialists and financiers cannot operate today with the freedom of their predecessors a century ago—John D. Rockefeller, Andrew Carnegie, J. P. Morgan, and lesser monopolists and entrepreneurs. Nor can big business ignore the interests of its employees, or of the public, to the extent that it once did. But many of the individuals with the largest incomes still make decisions that affect thousands of workers, millions of consumers, and sometimes the national economy itself. And even if they did not contribute large sums to congressional and presidential candidates (sometimes of both major parties), they would be listened to in the nation's capital, and their wishes would not be rejected lightly. The fact that the people appointed to ambassadorships have frequently made large political contributions is only one relatively minor indication of the continuing relationship between wealth and political influence in the United States.

Power and Class

The complexities of social stratification become clear when we try to analyze the extent to which competition for political power in a democratic society reflects competition between classes. In some of the European democracies, political parties—Britain's Labour party, for example—reflect class interests more strongly

than they do in the United States. The value-orientations of American society support an open class system as being morally right, and political leaders have for the most part avoided making an all-out appeal to class differences. Still, the generalization is often made that the Democrats represent the interests of the working class, whereas the Republicans represent the interests of business and property. A review of the voting records of the members of the United States House and Senate lends some support to this contention, though not to the point of establishing class divisions. Overall, Democrats have supported legislation aimed at reducing social and economic inequalities much more strongly than have Republicans, while Republicans have given stronger support to legislation favorable to corporate interests, on the theory that a prosperous business community benefits the whole society. Democrats have been more likely to support organized labor and Republicans to place restrictions on it.

This view of the differences between the two political parties is challenged by those who believe that both work within an extremely narrow ideological range, support the status quo, and are subservient to the interests of big business. And it is true that competition for power *within* the parties seems to be weighted in favor of those who have inherited or achieved a favored position in society. In theory, any native-born American has an equal chance of growing up to become President, but those actually selected as presidential candidates have hardly represented a complete cross section of American society. All have been middle- or upper-class males; almost all have been professional men, particularly lawyers; and all have enjoyed some degree of high status before nomination.[16] Furthermore, though possession of wealth is not in itself a guarantee of political power, access to wealth has increasingly become a necessary condition for winning—or even running for—political office.

The problem of campaign financing is severalfold: Not only have skyrocketing costs made it difficult if not impossible for the average citizen to consider campaigning for high office,

16. For an analysis of the backgrounds of presidential candidates since 1831, see Ralph M. Goldman, *The Democratic Party in the United States* (New York: Macmillan, Inc., 1966), p. 129.

thus in effect restricting access to office to a relatively small pool of people, but large money donations by individuals and organizations support the hypothesis of the close linkage between class and power. It remains to be seen whether the class factor in power can be reduced by legal restraints on contributions to political campaigns or eliminated through the process of financing all campaigns through taxation.

Power Distinctions in Communist Societies

The Communist societies are by no means free of the linkages of class and status to power. It is part of Communist ideology that every worker should have a hand in decision making affecting the work situation, but research by students of Soviet society suggests that such a situation has not yet come to pass, at least not for a majority of the workers. One study showed that a majority of rural workers believed that they did not exercise influence over the affairs of their collective farms, though workers with higher education and more professional occupations felt that they exerted some control over decision making. Lipset and Dobson argue that these findings "point up the extent to which social status influences an individual's sense that he is able to determine his life conditions."[17]

Another way in which status relates to power in the Soviet Union is through membership in the Communist party. The party controls the government at all levels, and party membership is narrowly restricted. According to Lipset and Dobson, the data show that

> the proportion of the population who are Party members jumps considerably with indicators of higher occupational status or education. Thus, as of 1967, over fifty per cent of all candidates for, and holders of, academic doctorates were Party members, as were 33 per cent of all engineers and 25 per cent of managers and specialists. At the other extreme, only 9 per cent of the workers and 5 per cent of the peasantry belonged to the party.[18]

The evidence suggests that the three dimensions of stratification—class, status, and power—are closely interrelated in every society, and that in every society they continue to limit or enhance the opportunities of individuals.

OPPOSING THEORIES OF STRATIFICATION

It is one thing to point out that all societies are stratified; it is another to try to explain why. Most of the explanations cluster around two general theories. The equilibrium, or *functional*, theory focuses on integration, order, and equilibrium. According to this view, stratification is a system of rewards that helps maintain social stability; it is an integral part of every society, undergirded by a broadly accepted system of values and beliefs. *Conflict* theory, on the other hand, focuses on class cleavage and social change. It implies that stratification is basically a result of coercion: those in a position of control impose it on the rest of society's members. In the following section we will examine each of these views in turn.

CONFLICT THEORY

The writings of Karl Marx and his associate Friedrich Engels are generally recognized as among the most basic in the study of conflict theory, especially with respect to social stratification. Marx's theory of *dialectical materialism* centered on the propositions that (1) societal life is characterized by tension and conflict between opposing forces and interests and (2) society is being propelled by this "struggle of opposites" along an inevitable path of change.[19] In his writings Marx emphasized that the crucial area of conflict was in the economic sphere—in the struggle between those who controlled the means of production (capital and land) and those who did not. This, for Marx, was the essence of social stratification. His emphasis on economic relationships stemmed from his belief that economic patterns are of crucial importance in shaping other social institutions. He maintained that those who control production exploit

17. Lipset and Dobson, "Social Stratification and Sociology in the Soviet Union," p. 134.
18. Ibid., pp. 132–134.
19. Karl Marx and Friedrich Engels, *The Communist Manifesto*, ed. Samuel H. Beer (New York: Appleton-Century-Crofts, Inc., 1955).

the working class and reward themselves with wealth and power, building a system of stratification that is reinforced through such institutions as the family and the government. The state came into being, in Marx's view, to mediate the conflicting interests that emerged in society as property began to accumulate. But as capitalism developed, the state itself became involved in the conflict and the economic rulers generally controlled the political ones.

Marx argued that the capitalistic system contained the seeds of its own destruction: the exploitation of the workers would inevitably lead to conflict that would finally result in the overthrow of the old ruling class and the emergence of a new one. Essential to this process was the development of class consciousness. Marx believed that by concentrating large masses of workers in factories and making available improved methods of communication, industrial capitalism made possible a fuller and more complete development of class consciousness than could have existed under earlier economic systems. And more than any previous economic system, capitalism set those in control of production apart from those whose energy produced the goods.

When the workers finally perceived the extent of the exploitation under which they suffered, Marx believed, they would gradually unite to free themselves from bondage. In fact, both classes would be locked into the struggle as each became more aware of its own class interests. Polarization would be followed by increasing conflict; finally, the masses of workers would overthrow their capitalist masters.

Marx theorized that this revolution would lead to a temporary dictatorship of the proletariat (workers), followed by the establishment of a classless society in which the state would maintain control of banking, industry, and agriculture. Political power, along with class distinctions, would ultimately disappear because "political power, properly so called, is merely the organized power of one class for oppressing another."[20] At this point, according to Marx, "In place of the old bourgeois society, with its classes and class antagonisms, we shall have an association in which the free development of each is the condition for the free development of all."[21] For Marx, then, social stratification was both an instrument by which one class oppressed another and also a mechanism for stimulating the eventual development of a classless society.

Critics of Marx regularly point out that the "Marxist" revolutions of the twentieth century did not, in fact, develop according to his theory—that they took place in countries that were predominantly agricultural rather than industrial and were dependent primarily on leadership rather than on a well-developed class consciousness. Critics have also noted that in the industrialized countries a broad middle class of white-collar workers has emerged and that this class has tended to identify its interests more with the capitalists than with the labor movement. And in the United States, as Wilensky notes, organized labor itself has been relatively conservative.

Compared to European labor, it shows a low degree of class consciousness. Its leaders have become integrated into the power and status structure of a private-enterprise economy and a pressure group polity. The mass of unorganized wage and salaried workers is similarly integrated into the mainstream of community life.[22]

Other critics have attacked the very foundation of Marx's theory. Martindale, for example, questions the contention that Marxian theory is scientific just because it considers all phenomena to be economic in nature. He asserts that Marx treated his theory of dialectical materialism "not as a hypothesis to be tested, but as a foregone conclusion to be illustrated."[23]

Objective appraisal of Marx is made more difficult by the fact that his writings represent not only a grand-scale social theory but also a call to social action ("The workers have nothing to lose but their chains. They have a world to

20. Ibid., p. 32.
21. Ibid.
22. Harold L. Wilensky, "Class, Class Consciousness, and American Workers," in *American Society Inc.*, ed. Maurice Zeitlin (Chicago: Markham Publishing Co., 1970), p. 436.
23. Don Martindale, *The Nature and Types of Sociological Theory* (Boston: Houghton Mifflin Co., 1960), p. 160.

In the United States, organized labor has tended to be somewhat conservative, working within the system and, in general, accepting its "rules" and values. It is hard to imagine American workers overthrowing their "capitalist masters" and establishing a dictatorship of the proletariat.

win. Workers of the world, unite!"). The acceptance or rejection of Marxian ideology has often clouded efforts to evaluate Marx's contributions to our understanding of social processes. Increasingly, however, social scientists have come to recognize the extent of Marx's influence on the study of social stratification.

In recent years conflict theorists have adapted various aspects of Marxian theory and applied them to an analysis of contemporary social relationships. Ralf Dahrendorf, for example, argues that social structures are naturally coercive and that the basic antagonisms between the "rulers" and the "ruled" can be found in the differential distribution of authority in *all* social organizations, not just those in the economic sphere. He suggests that the patterns of domination and subjugation built into organizational arrangements lead to "social conflicts of a type that are germane to class conflicts in the traditional (Marxian) sense of this term."[24]

Nor has Marx's influence on social theory and social research been limited to conflict theorists. Max Weber's early analysis of social stratification in terms of the separable dimensions of class, status, and power (page 207) was developed in direct reaction to Marx's view that stratification could be explained wholly in economic terms. Social scientists ever since Weber have continued both to challenge Marx's work and to draw on it. After examining in detail the ways in which Marx has influenced theory and research over the years, Bottomore concludes:

A great deal of Marx's work is a permanent acquisition of sociological thought; the definition of the field of study, the analysis of the economic structure and its relations with other parts of the social structure, the theory of social classes, and the theory of ideology. But this incorporation of Marx's ideas entails the disappearance of a "Marxist" sociology.[25]

FUNCTIONAL THEORY

Out of the writings of Comte, Durkheim, and others has come the view that people adhere to an orderly system of social relationships because they are goal-oriented and because they accept certain values and beliefs as fundamental to the achievement of their goals. From this perspective, stratification is an integral part of every society, both reflecting and reinforcing the value-belief system.

Kingsley Davis and Wilbert Moore have stated this general view of stratification most clearly.[26] As they see it, stratification is universal because every society must distribute its members in the different positions that make up its division of labor. And every society must also ensure that the individuals who fill particular

24. Ralf Dahrendorf, *Class and Class Conflict in Industrial Society* (Stanford, Calif.: Stanford University Press, 1959), p. 165. See also Celia Heller, "Unresolved Issues in Stratification Theory," in *Structured Social Inequality: A Reader in Social Stratification,* ed. Celia Heller (New York: Macmillan, Inc., 1969), pp. 479–531. Heller notes that recent events in Europe (e.g., the general strike in France in 1968) and in the United States (e.g., the Poor People's Campaign and the strikes led by Cesar Chavez and the American Farm Workers) support the theory of continuing class conflict in modern industrial societies.
25. T. B. Bottomore, ed., *Karl Marx: Selected Writings in Sociology and Social Philosophy* (New York: McGraw-Hill Book Company, 1964), p. 48.
26. Kingsley Davis and Wilbert Moore, "Some Principles of Stratification," *American Sociological Review,* 10 (April 1945): 242–249.

roles will be motivated to meet the expectations associated with them. Not all roles are of equal difficulty: it takes less skill to be a bat boy than a pitcher, less skill to be a hospital orderly than a surgeon. And some difficult roles entail unattractive labor. A medical doctor must spend many years in specialized training, much of it far more exhausting than inspiring. In some ways, the work is "dirty," dealing as it does with diseases, infections, foul odors, and the like. But human life is valued highly, and so are those who can help save it. To outweigh the difficulties connected with playing such a role, significant rewards must be offered, and these are built into the system.

The central argument of the Davis-Moore position is that unless roles are rewarded unequally, some jobs won't get done. In general, the greatest rewards are associated with those roles that (1) have the greatest importance for the society and (2) require the greatest training or talent. As Davis and Moore note, however, societies do not overreward positions that are easy to fill (e.g., teaching positions), even if they are important.

According to functional theory, social stratification is basically integrative. It ensures that the jobs a society rates as most important will get done, and it may even provide a certain amount of pyschological security to individuals: they know their place; they have the respect of their peers; they do their jobs and are rewarded accordingly. The city councilman doesn't believe that he should have as much power as the mayor, nor does the bat boy expect to receive as much money or applause as the star pitcher. Satisfaction is a highly relative matter. In the perspective of this theory of stratification, it means that people accept differential rewards because they accept the value system and rules of their society.

It is possible to glance quickly at American society and say, "Yes, this is how the system works." We value entertainment, for instance, and we reward those who provide it. Barbra Streisand, Billie Jean King, and Kareem Abdul Jabbar might serve as examples of the open-class system that permits the talented to find their way to the top and to be rewarded accordingly. But if we analyze the system more carefully, we find it necessary to question at least parts of the theory. Do the professions—including politics—really attract the most talented people? Are top business positions filled by giving everyone equal access to valued roles, or are there biases along the way favoring certain people over others? Can the theory account for the fact that those with Spanish surnames, blacks, and women are grossly underrepresented in the middle and upper levels of the occupational ladder? Furthermore, how does the theory explain the fact that almost 20 percent of American medical doctors are children of medical doctors? This more-than-chance pattern of succession is evident throughout business and the professions.[27]

Acknowledging that many more people have the capacity to become medical doctors than actually do, Davis and Moore assert that most potential doctors are discouraged by the prospect of the long training process. Hence it is necessary to offer high prestige and wealth to attract enough people to meet the need. But do the medical schools in fact lack applicants, or is it true instead that they have many more qualified applicants than they can, or will, accept? Clearly, functional theory does not wholly explain the patterns of inequality in American society. And it seems even less applicable to those traditional societies stressing the belief that "God created the rich and the poor"—unless one assumes that God also made the rich uniformly more talented than the poor. History, of course, suggests otherwise.

As we examine the evidence regarding social stratification and social mobility patterns in the United States and elsewhere, we shall find that both conflict and functional theory fit some, but not all, of the facts. Functional theory best fits those patterns found in the middle strata of a relatively open society. It assumes that roles are filled largely on the basis of achieved rather than ascribed criteria, and it also assumes that education is readily available to help people prepare for the roles to which they aspire.

27. See Charles F. Schumacher, "The 1960 Medical School Graduate: His Biographical History," *Journal of Medical Education,* 36 (May 1961): 398–406; see also Clifford Kirkpatrick and Melvin DeFleur, "Influence of Professors on the Flow of Talent to the Academic Profession," *Social Forces,* 38, No. 4 (May 1960): 296–302.

AGENTS OF STRATIFICATION

The social institutions having the greatest impact on the stratification system in American society are the family, the school, the economic system, and the government. The family, for example, is the primary agent for perpetuating class, status, and probably power differences, despite the fact that most families strive to improve their own position. The school, designed as the great social equalizer, also tends to sort out society's members and give some of them better opportunities than others. The economic system offers money, prestige, and upward mobility, but neither job opportunities nor opportunities for advancement are open to everyone on an equal basis. The government has played a part in altering some aspects of the stratification system, but a middle- or upper-class bias remains. In the sections that follow, we will examine the influences of each of these institutions with respect to the distribution of prestige, wealth, and power. The focus of our discussion will be primarily, but not exclusively, on American society.

THE FAMILY

The functional theory of stratification seems to ignore the fact that people are literally born into different social strata. As William J. Goode has noted, the family is "the keystone of the stratification system, the social mechanism by which it is maintained."[28] The class, status, and power of our families help determine not only our educational and job opportunities but also our opportunities for social interaction. For the most part, people go to school with, become friends with, work with, and spend their leisure time with other people at the same general social level. Thus, when it comes to choosing a marriage partner, the choice is pretty well limited to someone of the same class, status, and power position.

Many observers have noted that a pattern of intraclass marriage tends to maintain the stability of the family. Similar backgrounds enhance the probability that husbands and wives will share a wide range of interests, attitudes, and values and be better able to rear their children with a minimum of conflict. In turn, the children

learn the values and attitudes of their own family, come to see them as right, and seek out other young people of similar viewpoint. As the saying goes, they feel comfortable with "their own kind." But this very pattern of like seeking out like tends to perpetuate the inequalities between the classes.

Whatever criteria a society uses for determining social rank—whether lineage and landed wealth or education and occupational achievement—the upper classes have the most resources at their disposal, and the futures of their children are most assured. As Goode notes, "in all family systems, upper class children obtain unearned advantages, entirely irrelevant to their skills or intelligence."[29] Because they are often able to bypass open competition in the job market, they limit the opportunities of others.

Goode offers a comforting thought to families waiting their turn on the ladder. His historical analysis shows that the uppers as a general class aggregate have never had long-term insurance against loss of position. In most societies ineptness, plain stupidity, low fertility, and unexpected disasters have resulted in some measure of downward mobility from the upper class.[30] Still if families at the top may be unable to stay there forever, most families will never get there at all.

Within the family itself, societal definitions of husband-wife and mother-father roles have led to an unequal distribution of class, status, and power between the sexes. Until recently in most societies, a woman's place has been in the home. With women thus effectively closed off from outside occupations and activities, men became not only the breadwinners who determined the family's class but also the holders of status and power. Even in an agricultural economy, power and status were located primarily in the male role. (For a discussion of a major exception to this pattern, see the section on the Hopi in Chapter 15, pages (445–449.) For a majority of married women in American society today, class, status, and power are still derived primarily from the husband's occupational role.

28. William J. Goode, *The Family* (Englewood Cliffs, N.J.: Prentice-Hall, Inc., 1964), p. 80.
29. Ibid., p. 84.
30. Ibid., pp. 85–86.

THE EDUCATIONAL SYSTEM

Until the last century, formal education beyond the rudimentary level was pretty much limited in all societies to the sons of the wealthy. They were educated to be gentlemen, and a small number of elite schools served their needs. Barber, after reviewing the evidence from the United States and western Europe, states: "On the whole, schools formerly served primarily to help the upper classes maintain their established position, only secondarily to permit some mobility within the bourgeois middle classes and from the bourgeoisie into the nobility."[31]

The question is whether, despite all that has been written and said about the school as the great equalizer in American society, the school operates in a substantially different manner today. Considerable evidence suggests that American schools have been inadvertently separating out an intellectual elite at one extreme and, at the other, an alienated class of "failures" cut off from higher education and most decent employment opportunities.[32] In a landmark critique of American education at the start of the 1960s, James B. Conant asserted that "The contrast in money available to the schools in a wealthy suburb and to the schools in a large city jolts one's notions of the meaning of equality of opportunity."[33] As Conant went on to point out, though the "pedagogic tasks" in slum schools are much more difficult than those in wealthy suburban schools, the expenditure per pupil is generally much less. Programs of federal and state aid have somewhat reduced these inequalities over the last ten or fifteen years, but they have by no means eliminated them. Nor is it at all clear that equality in terms of physical facilities and teacher-pupil ratios can alone bring true equality of educational opportunity. The children of the poor are not generally expected to do well in school—by their families, by their peers, by their teachers, or by society as a whole. There is increasing recognition that these patterns of negative expectation must be overcome before our public schools can become the equalizers they are intended to be.

Our educational system helps perpetuate stratification patterns even at the post-high-school level. It makes a difference in terms of income and prestige not only whether people get to college but also what kind of college they get to. Though many of the best schools have made real efforts to increase their enrollment of students from lower-class families, both white and nonwhite, family background and income continue to have great influence on what schools young people attend. And the schools they attend continue to exert an influence on the level of income, power, and prestige they will have later in life.

Lenski seems to be correct when he says that "educational status has become increasingly important as a resource in the struggle for power and privilege."[34] But the fact remains that this resource is not equally available to all. The educational system functions in such a way as to allow some individual mobility from one social stratum to another while at the same time ensuring that no major changes in prevailing stratification patterns will occur.

Education appears to be similarly related to stratification and mobility in other industrial societies, including the Soviet Union. There, too, education has become the stepping stone to individual success. Although schooling at all levels is free in the USSR, the opportunity for advanced study is limited to a relative few. Barber and others report that "since the thirties children of the new middle and upper classes have had various differential advantages."[35] Not the least of these has been to be brought up in families that recognize the importance of the school in the stratification system. The school in the Soviet Union, as in the United States and probably in all societies, supports the political and social ideology of the nation-state and thereby reinforces existing arrangements for distributing income, status, and power.

31. Bernard Barber, *Social Stratification: A Comparative Analysis of Structure and Process* (New York: Harcourt Brace Jovanovich, Inc., 1957), p. 391.

32. See, for example, Patricia Sexton, *Education and Income* (New York: Compass Books, 1964); and Christopher Jencks et al., *Inequality: A Reassessment of the Effect of Family and Schooling in America* (New York: Basic Books, Inc., 1972).

33. James B. Conant, *Slums and Suburbs* (New York: McGraw-Hill Book Company, 1961), pp. 2–3.

34. Lenski, *Power and Privilege*, p. 392.

35. Barber, *Social Stratification*, p. 403.

The social ranking of one's family is probably the most important indicator of one's own social position. Since most Americans identify themselves as being somewhere in the broad category of "middle class," we might assume that most children begin life with equal opportunities for advancement. But, in fact, even among so-called middle-class families, there are economic, status, and power differences that affect the futures of the children.

Table 8.1. SELECTED PROFESSIONS AND OCCUPATIONS OF MALES RANKED BY MEDIAN INCOME, 1969 AND 1959

	1969			1959
Rank	Median Income		Rank	Median Income
1	$25,000+	Physicians	1	$15,392
2	22,682	Dentists	2	12,567
3	20,139	Lawyers & judges	3	10,829
4	18,446	Airplane pilots	4	10,514
5	16,520	Physicists & astronomers	5	9,345
6	16,144	Mathematicians	11	8,337
7	15,765	Engineers	6	9,301
8	14,327	Social scientists	12	8,066
9	14,129	Geologists	9	8,731
10	13,989	Mechanical engineers	10	8,602
11	13,908	Electrical & electronic engineers	8	8,787
12	13,734	Sales engineers	7	8,895
13	13,421	Teachers (coll. & univ.)	15	7,571
14	13,333	Civil engineers	13	7,930
15	13,107	Statisticians & actuaries	16	7,506
16	13,018	Life & physical scientists	14	7,762
17	12,595	Chemists	17	7,495
18	12,210	Editors & reporters	18	7,331
19	12,142	Real estate agents & brokers	25	6,411
20	12,101	Managers & administrators (except farm)	20	6,855
21	11,969	Accountants	21	6,821
22	11,774	Biological scientists	23	6,598
23	10,837	Agricultural scientists	26	6,233
24	10,578	Sales managers & department heads	19	7,029
25	10,483	Foremen	22	6,711
26	10,093	Sales workers	32	5,747
27	10,026	Electricians	29	6,106
28	9,933	Draftsmen	24	6,496
29	9,886	Secondary teachers	30	5,989
30	9,819	Linemen & servicemen (telephone & power)	27	6,167
31	9,693	Plumbers	31	5,765
32	9,663	Firemen	34	5,549
33	9,393	Policemen & detectives	37	5,364
34	9,284	Elementary teachers	35	5,379
35	8,964	Musicians & composers	36	5,377
36	8,901	Machinists	33	5,607
37	8,872	Health technicians	39	4,940
38	8,395	Mechanics & repairmen	38	4,980
39	8,257	Carpenters	44	4,393
40	8,067	Truck drivers	42	4,424
41	8,023	Mine operatives	43	4,402
42	8,014	Bus drivers	41	4,560
43	7,858	Automobile mechanics	28	6,028
44	7,704	Painters (construction & maintenance)	47	3,986
45	7,089	Bank tellers	40	4,753
46	6,671	Clergymen	45	4,187
47	6,430	Barbers	46	3,990

SOURCE: *United States Census of Population, 1960: Occupation by Earnings and Education* [PC(2)–7B], Table 1; *United States Census of Population, 1970: Occupation by Earnings and Education* [PC(2)–8B], Table 1.

THE ECONOMIC SYSTEM

We have previously noted that the occupational system is the prime agent of stratification in industrialized societies. In this section we will examine more specifically the ways in which income, prestige, and power are differentially distributed within the occupational structure.

Work and Income

We are all aware that professional people and business executives earn more than filing clerks and manual laborers. The usual explanations for such differences are that they reflect society's evaluation of the importance of given occupations; that they depend on the ease or difficulty of filling particular jobs; and/or that they have developed in response to organized pressure from various occupational groups. But Tables 8.1 and 8.2 present data that raise questions about these explanations. For example, how does a society determine that a clergyman deserves only about half the income of a real estate agent? Why do airline pilots, who have so many lives to protect each day, earn a third less than physicians, most of whose patients are likely to survive regardless of the quality of the medical care they receive? And are such enormous earnings as those of the "top brass" (Table 8.2) truly functional for society? What would be the gain for all wage earners if this 8 percent of the total income was divided more or less equally among all workers? And how would the psychological gains or losses affect the system as a whole? Would large differences in earnings seem objectionable if they occurred in a society in which the basic needs of all people were adequately met? Such questions have no easy answers.

Some twenty to twenty-five million Americans today are living at an income level defined by the government as inadequate to provide the basic necessities of life. A large percentage of poverty-level people hold jobs, but their incomes don't provide them with enough money to rise above the poverty level. Sobin reports that "special surveys of 51 urban areas in the 1970 Census revealed that 60 percent of all workers there did not earn enough for a decent standard of living for their families, while 30 percent could not even earn a poverty level income."[36] It is small consolation to such people to be reminded that they are "better off," at least in terms of material advantages, than 80 percent of the world's population.

Only the contributions of working wives and working children make it possible for America to claim that most of its families enjoy a comfortable life. If we accept functional theory's proposition that the salary a job pays is determined by the importance of the job to society, then we must conclude that a great many jobs in American society are defined as not being important enough to provide an income sufficient to allow a family of four to live in modest comfort.

Work and Prestige

It is now generally recognized that income alone is not reward enough for working; most people also look to their job for the sense of worth that they receive as a result of holding it. Having a job that carries prestige helps people establish their sense of identity and provides them with psychic rewards. Conversely, having

36. Dennis P. Sobin, *The Working Poor* (Port Washington, N.Y.: The Kennikat Press, 1973), p. 3.
37. Studs Terkel, *Working* (New York: Pantheon Books, 1974), p. 108.

a job that most people don't want can cause psychic wounds. Champions of the work ethic insist that workers who give their best can take pride in even the most menial job, but it is difficult to feel good about a job that many other people regard with contempt. As Louis Hayward, a sixty-two-year-old washroom attendant, puts it:

I'm not particularly proud of what I'm doing. The shine man and I discuss it quite freely. In my own habitat I don't go around saying I'm a washroom attendant at the Palmer House. Outside of my immediate family, very few people know what I do. They do know I work at the Palmer House and let that suffice. You say Palmer House, they automatically assume you're a waiter.

This man shining shoes, he's had several offers—he's a very good bootblack—where he could make more money. But he wouldn't take 'em because the jobs were too open. He didn't want to be seen shining shoes. . . .

No, I'm not proud of this work. I can't do anything heavy. It would be hard to do anything else, so I'm stuck.[37]

By contrast, a high-level position that attracts widespread admiration, envy, and respect gives the one who holds it a sense of being important. W. H. Whyte reports:

Table 8.2. WHAT THE TOP BRASS EARN

	Company Sales of			
	$200 million	$500 million	$1 billion	$2 billion
Airlines		$203,000	$226,000	$252,000
Aircraft and parts	$193,000	$210,000	$223,000	$238,000
Building products	$126,000	$189,000	$257,000	
Chemicals		$193,000	$242,000	$303,000
Electrical and electronic equipment	$150,000	$193,000	$233,000	$282,000
Household appliances	$137,000	$176,000	$213,000	
Machinery and equipment	$125,000	$181,000	$241,000	
Nonferrous metals		$196,000	$261,000	$346,000
Office machines	$117,000	$167,000	$219,000	$287,000
Petroleum			$230,000	$283,000
Pharmaceuticals		$222,000	$316,000	$451,000
Steel	$137,000	$174,000	$208,000	$249,000
Tobacco	$184,000	$227,000	$266,000	$311,000
Utilities		$132,000	$171,000	$223,000

SOURCE: *The McKinsey Quarterly*, Autumn 1974, p. 22. The money earned by chief executives varies both by size of company and by industry. The table above is based on the salaries and fringe benefits paid to top officers in 1973 and shows what top executives would earn while working for comparable companies in comparable industries.

Although most Americans subscribe to the belief that ability and initiative should be the only criteria for achieving a fair share of wealth, prestige, and power, the fact remains that ascribed criteria can greatly limit—or enhance—an individual's life chances.

Many management aspirants have the mistaken idea that status and "all that stuff" is an extremely minor incentive for executives. In actual fact executives love it, and they have no pious reluctance to admit the fact. "When I walk out of the building," the head of one of America's largest corporations . . . told a friend, "a lot of people turn and stare at me, and whisper that there goes Mr. Big. My friends think this probably annoys and embarrasses me. Frankly, I thoroughly enjoy it. Why shouldn't I?"[38]

The American public's ranking of occupations in terms of prestige does not seem to change significantly with changes in the structure of the labor market. Extensive studies conducted in 1947 and 1963 by the National Opinion Research Center (NORC) found that the ratings over this fifteen-year period were remarkably stable (Table 8.3). Indeed, when the ratings from these surveys were compared with findings from earlier research, it was found that the prestige of occupations had changed very little since 1925. No comparable surveys have been made in recent years, but it would appear that occupational prestige ratings today are not dramatically different from what they were fifteen or even fifty years ago.

The data on income and prestige levels associated with various occupations (Tables 8.1 and 8.3) cannot be directly compared, but they suggest that income and prestige are closely related. One of the few major deviations occurs with the occupation of clergyman, which is rela-

38. William H. Whyte, "How Hard Do Executives Work?" in *Class and Conflict in American Society*, ed. Robert Lejeune (Chicago: Rand McNally & Co., 1972), pp. 62–63.

tively high in prestige but low in income. Traditionally, this occupation has been perceived as nonmaterialistic; but today many clergymen are demanding—and in some instances receiving— higher salaries.

In a classic study published in 1956, Inkeles and Rossi compared the ranking of occupations in six industrialized countries—the United States, Great Britain, the Soviet Union, Japan, New Zealand, and Germany—and found remarkable similarities. They concluded on the basis of their data that "there is a relatively invariable hierarchy of prestige associated with the industrial system, even when it is placed in the

Table 8.3. OCCUPATIONAL PRESTIGE RATINGS, 1963 AND 1947

Occupation	1963 Score	1947 Score	Occupation	1963 Score	1947 Score
U.S. Supreme Court Justice	94	96	Newspaper columnist	73	74
Physician	93	93	Policeman	72	67
Nuclear physicist	92	86	Reporter on a daily newspaper	71	71
Scientist	92	89	Radio announcer	70	75
Government scientist	91	88	Bookkeeper	70	68
State governor	91	93	Tenant farmer—one who owns livestock and machinery and manages the farm	69	68
Cabinet member in the Federal Gov't.	90	92	Insurance agent	69	68
College professor	90	89	Carpenter	68	65
U.S. Representative in Congress	90	89	Manager of a small store in a city	67	69
Chemist	89	86	A local official of a labor union	67	62
Lawyer	89	86	Mail carrier	66	66
Diplomat in U.S. Foreign Service	89	92	Railroad conductor	66	67
Dentist	88	86	Traveling salesman for a wholesale concern	66	68
Architect	88	86	Plumber	65	63
County judge	88	87	Automobile repairman	64	63
Psychologist	87	85	Playground director	63	67
Minister	87	87	Barber	63	59
Member of the board of directors of a large corporation	87	86	Machine operator in a factory	63	60
Mayor of a large city	87	90	Owner-operator of a lunch stand	63	62
Priest	86	86	Corporal in the regular army	62	60
Head of a dept. in state government	86	87	Garage mechanic	62	62
Civil engineer	86	84	Truck driver	59	54
Airline pilot	86	83	Fisherman who owns his own boat	58	58
Banker	85	88	Clerk in a store	56	58
Biologist	85	81	Milk route man	56	54
Sociologist	83	82	Streetcar motorman	56	58
Instructor in public schools	82	79	Lumberjack	55	53
Captain in the regular army	82	80	Restaurant cook	55	54
Accountant for a large business	81	81	Singer in a nightclub	54	52
Public school teacher	81	78	Filling station attendant	51	52
Owner of a factory that employs about 100 people	80	82	Dockworker	50	47
Building contractor	80	79	Railroad section hand	50	48
Artist who paints pictures that are exhibited in galleries	78	83	Night watchman	50	47
Musician in a symphony orchestra	78	81	Coal miner	50	49
Author of novels	78	80	Restaurant waiter	49	48
Economist	78	79	Taxi driver	49	49
Official of an international labor union	77	75	Farm hand	48	50
Railroad engineer	76	76	Janitor	48	44
Electrician	76	73	Bartender	48	44
County agricultural agent	76	77	Clothes presser in a laundry	45	46
Owner-operator of a printing shop	75	74	Soda fountain clerk	44	45
Trained machinist	75	73	Share-cropper—one who owns no livestock or equipment and does not manage farm	42	40
Farm owner and operator	74	76	Garbage collector	39	35
Undertaker	74	72	Street sweeper	36	34
Welfare worker for a city government	74	73	Shoe shiner	34	33
			Average	**71**	**70**

SOURCE: Robert W. Hodge, Paul M. Siegel, and Peter H. Rossi, "Occupational Prestige in the United States: 1925–1963," *American Journal of Sociology*, 70 (November 1964): 286–302.

context of larger social systems which are otherwise differentiated in important respects."[39] Follow-up research by R. W. Hodge and his associates has shown that even developing countries have occupational prestige hierarchies similar to those of the industrialized societies. In an effort to explain why this should be so, these researchers speculate that

acquisition of a "modern" system of occupational evaluation would seem to be a necessary precondition to rapid industrialization, insofar as such an evaluation of occupations insures that resources and personnel in sufficient numbers and of sufficient quality are allocated to those occupational positions most crucial to the industrial development of a nation.[40]

The accumulated data on occupational prestige hierarchies have led Hodge, Siegel, and Rossi to conclude that rankings are not only "similar from country to country but also from subgroup to subgroup within a country."[41] Such consensus can best be explained, these researchers believe, within the context of functional theory:

The prestige position of an occupation is apparently a characteristic of that occupation, generated by the way in which it is articulated into the division of labor, by the amount of power and influence implied in the activities of the occupation, by the characteristics of incumbents, and by the amount of resources society places at the disposal of incumbents.[42]

But although functional theory may go far to explain the different levels of prestige associated with different occupations, it fails to come to grips with class antagonisms or with the problems created, on an individual level, by the many jobs that offer little prestige and little opportunity for self-satisfaction. American society today includes a stratum of workers who have become increasingly well paid but many of whom are also bored and rebellious. For some, particularly those who lived through the Great Depression of the 1930s, good pay and security largely compensate for meaningless routine. But for many other workers, particularly younger ones, they do not.

Work and Power

Power, like income and prestige, is unequally distributed among occupations. However, power is much less generalized than the other two dimensions of stratification. The power individuals derive from their occupational roles does not necessarily carry over to the roles they have outside their jobs, and, unlike economic privilege and social status, it is not readily transferred to other members of their families. Nor is power all of one kind. A surgeon, a building contractor, a corporation president, a shop owner, a judge, an army major, and the President of the United States all have the power to make and implement decisions in their respective occupational spheres, but the power of one cannot readily be equated with the power of another.

Some social theorists have maintained that people at the top in certain occupations—primarily top military officers, corporate executives, and leaders in the executive branch of government—form a power elite that effectively controls most of the important decisions in American society.[43] But although the special position of those at the top is clearly a factor to be reckoned with, power does not seem to be their exclusive prerogative. The people who run big business are not always unified in their interests, nor do they always get their way. Labor legislation of the late 1920s and the 1930s provided labor unions with the means of countering to some extent the power of business leaders within the political as well as the economic system. Through organized effort, workers whose jobs rank relatively low in the occupational hier-

39. Alex Inkeles and Peter H. Rossi, "National Comparisons of Occupational Prestige," American Journal of Sociology, 61 (1956): 329–339; quotation from p. 339.

40. Robert W. Hodge, Donald J. Treiman, and Peter H. Rossi, "A Comparative Study of Occupational Prestige," in Class, Status, and Power: Social Stratification in Comparative Perspective, ed. Reinhard Bendix and Seymour M. Lipset, 2nd ed. (New York: The Free Press, 1966), pp. 309–321.

41. Robert W. Hodge, Paul M. Siegel, and Peter H. Rossi, "Occupational Prestige in the United States: 1925–1963," American Journal of Sociology, 70 (November 1964): 286–302.

42. Ibid.

43. C. Wright Mills, The Power Elite (New York: Oxford University Press, 1966); and Arnold M. Rose, The Power Structure: Political Process in American Society (New York: Oxford University Press, 1967). For a discussion of the power elite, see Chapter 17, pages 521–523.

archy have gained considerable ability to influence decision making.

The degree of power inherent in occupational roles as such is most clearly delineated in bureaucratic organizations: the closer a role is to the top of the bureaucratic structure, the more authority—and hence power—is generally attached to it. The power enjoyed by job incumbents depends not on their authority alone, however, but also on the amount of influence they can wield. Whereas authority is rather specifically delimited by the job, influence varies according to the incumbent's ability to persuade or manipulate people.

The informal work norms that all work groups seem to develop are a manifestation of the influence workers can exercise in their occupational roles even if they are at the lower end of the occupational hierarchy. In his study of two bureaucratic government agencies (page 76), Blau found that employees developed work patterns significantly at variance with established rules and authority in order not only to get the job done but also to improve their own position. Although Blau's concern was more with the dynamics of bureaucracy than with

power per se, we should not overlook this evidence of individual influence even at the lower levels of bureaucratic organization.

We have previously noted the research on occupational status and power done in the Soviet Union. The Soviet scientist Arutiunian concludes that "The higher people's skill grade, the more they involve themselves in modern complex production, the higher is their responsibility for the fate of the collective, and the more active is their social role."[44] It would appear that occupations act as agents of power stratification as they do of income and wealth, regardless of official government policies or prevailing ideologies.

THE GOVERNMENT

Some observers have maintained that the law is written by people of middle-class and middle-status background to be applied against people of lower class and status. The strong antilabor posture of the United States government during the nineteenth and early twentieth centuries lends support to this argument,[45] as do the inequities in our present tax structure (Figure 8.1). It remains true, furthermore, that those occupying the most important positions in government are drawn almost exclusively from the middle and upper classes.

44. Quoted in Lipset and Dobson, "Social Stratification and Sociology in the Soviet Union," p. 132.

45. For a detailed discussion of the long struggle between labor unions and government, see Joseph Shister, *Economics of the Labor Market* (New York: J. B. Lippincott Co., 1949), esp. pp. 277–310.

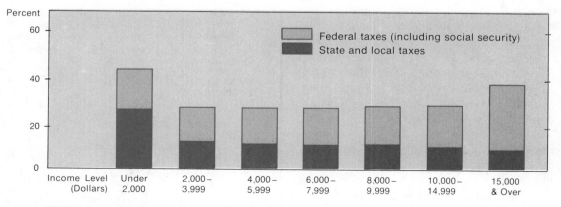

SOURCE: *Economic Report of the President*, U.S. Government Printing Office, 1969, p. 161.

Figure 8.1. TAXES AS PERCENT OF INCOME, BY INCOME LEVEL

But it is difficult to maintain that government in the United States has acted solely as an agent of the status quo. Like governments in many other societies, it has taken an active role in initiating and directing social change; and in doing so, it has on at least some occasions acted on behalf of the people in the lower strata. Today business, as well as labor, is regulated to some extent. And if government has continued to protect the interests of the upper and middle classes, it has at the same time encouraged more and more members of the society to work their way into these classes. Land-grant colleges, Federal Housing Administration mortgages, the GI Bill, minimum-wage laws, federal aid to college students, and school desegregation are examples of government action that has been an impetus to social mobility if not a direct causal factor. Civil rights legislation in the 1960s was designed to affect the power of blacks vis à vis whites through better voting guarantees and, more generally, to make possible a more equitable distribution of societal rewards.

So far as improving the position of women is concerned, the record of the federal government has been mixed. During the Civil War it opened a major occupational role for women by hiring large numbers of female office workers. The United States lagged behind a number of other Western nations in granting women the vote, however, and legislative support for equal employment opportunities was achieved only through organized pressure after long delay.

Overall, government has played a mixed role with regard to stratification patterns in the United States, serving in some ways to modify them and in other ways to maintain them. It taxes those with large incomes at a higher rate than those with low incomes, but at the same time it provides tax loopholes that benefit only the rich. It has taken steps toward diffusing political power (for example, by enacting and enforcing voting-right laws), while at the same time concentrating more and more power in the hands of a relatively few top officials (most notably, those in the executive branch of federal and state government). It has restricted the power of corporations, and it has also restricted the power of labor unions. The fact that both the "haves" and "have-nots" in American society alternately criticize and praise governmental policy is perhaps the best evidence that government has not exclusively served the interests of either one.

SOCIAL MOBILITY

The United States was founded on an ideology of "equal opportunity for all," and over the course of its history most of its citizens have professed the belief that individual ability and initiative should be the only requirements for achieving a fair share of wealth, prestige, and power. The fact that these societal rewards have been to some extent separable in American society has helped make upward mobility possible for successive aggregates of people.[46] The businessmen-entrepreneurs of the nineteenth century gained wealth and then power. The sons and grandsons of European immigrants gained power in the political organizations of the cities and thus gradually won access to wealth and prestige. Meanwhile, the old established families retained prestige but often lost power and sometimes wealth as well.

Table 8.4. PERCENT OF FAMILIES, WHITE AND NONWHITE, AT VARIOUS INCOME LEVELS, 1950 AND 1970 (IN 1970 DOLLARS)

	1950		1970	
	White	Nonwhite	White	Nonwhite
Under $3,000	20.3%	49.7%	7.5%	20.1%
$3,000–$4,999	21.4	28.8	9.5	17.0
$5,000–$6,999	24.6	13.7	11.3	16.4
$7,000–$9,999	19.5	4.6	20.1	18.2
$10,000–$14,999 }	14.1	3.1	27.9	17.3
$15,000 and over }			23.7	10.9
Median Income	$5,601	$3,014	$10,236	$6,516

SOURCE: *Statistical Abstract of the United States, 1972*, Table 524, p. 322. NOTE: The figures in the table compare 1950 and 1970 family income levels in terms of "constant" 1970 dollars—that is, figures for 1950 have been adjusted to compensate for the depreciation of the dollar between 1950 and 1970. For example, the median incomes for white and nonwhite families were actually (in 1950 dollars) $3,445 and $1,869 respectively; the equivalents of these figures in terms of 1970 dollars, as shown in the table, are $5,601 and $3,014.

46. Robert A. Dahl, *Who Governs? Democracy and Power in an American City* (New Haven, Conn.: Yale University Press, 1961).

One of the thorniest questions in social research today is whether the process of reducing and dispersing inequalities in American society still continues, or whether new forms of cumulative inequality have developed. Statistics on changes in family income over the last few decades suggest that the American system continues to enable the majority of people to improve their economic position. The percentage of families at the bottom of the income scale dropped by more than half between 1950 and 1970, while the percentage of those in the top levels rose dramatically—more than threefold for white families and ninefold for nonwhite families (see Table 8.4). On the basis of both objective and subjective criteria, the majority of Americans today can be classified as part of a broad middle class.

But the very fact that most Americans now are middle class also highlights the persisting patterns of inequality. Even though the median income of nonwhite families increased by 119 percent between 1950 and 1970 (Table 8.4) compared with an increase of only 83 percent for white families, nonwhites in 1970 were still earning less than two thirds as much as whites, and almost three times as many of them had incomes below $3000. It should be noted, too, that there has been practically no change since World War II in the proportions of the nation's total income distributed to those at the top and those at the bottom of the economic ladder.[47] The top fifth continues to earn about 42 percent of the total while the bottom fifth earns only about 5 percent (Figure 8.2).

Of special concern is the plight of those who now seem trapped at the bottom level of society, the urban and rural poor. The very fact that American society has preached upward mobility so loudly and so long increases the bitterness and frustration of those who find themselves cut off from the material benefits upward mobility can bring (though not from advertisements of these things) and thus contributes to alienation and conflict.

But discontent is by no means limited to the very poor; many Americans now seem much less certain than they did previously that they can attain wealth and power. In 1973 a nationwide Harris poll taken for a Senate subcommittee found that the percentage of those who believed that "The rich get richer and the poor get poorer" had increased from about 45 percent in 1966 to over 75 percent, and that 45 percent thought that the quality of life had declined over the past decade, as compared with only 35 percent who saw improvement.[48] As this poll and others indicate, many Americans are denying that the American system is working well for them.

Clearly, there is ample evidence of both the successes and failures of the American system. How social scientists interpret the evidence is influenced by both their theoretical positions and their ideological commitments. Because the majority of Americans now live comfortably,

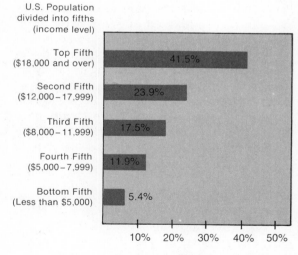

U.S. Population divided into fifths (income level)

Top Fifth ($18,000 and over) — 41.5%
Second Fifth ($12,000–17,999) — 23.9%
Third Fifth ($8,000–11,999) — 17.5%
Fourth Fifth ($5,000–7,999) — 11.9%
Bottom Fifth (Less than $5,000) — 5.4%

Share of Total U.S. Income, in Percent

SOURCE: *Economic Report of the President*, U.S. Government Printing Office, 1974, pp. 139–141. It should be noted that the top 5 percent of the population have incomes over $27,837 and receive 15.9 percent of the total U.S. income.

Figure 8.2. DISTRIBUTION OF INCOME IN THE UNITED STATES

47. Peter Henle, "Exploring the Distribution of Earned Income," *Monthly Labor Review,* December 1972, pp. 16–27.

48. Reported in *Newsweek,* December 10, 1973, pp. 40–48.

enjoy some prestige, and can participate in the political process through the vote, it is possible to argue that the system does indeed guarantee everyone an opportunity to get ahead. Because some others enjoy a disproportionately large share of these societal rewards, it is also possible to argue that the system guarantees the prerogatives of the "haves" at the expense of the "have-nots." Even if a scholar takes a middle position (the system is basically functional but has built-in conflicts and inequalities), the analysis is almost inevitably biased by personal experiences with the system and feelings about how it *should* work. No matter how hard they strive for objectivity, it makes a difference, in the end, that social scientists are part of the system and analyze it from that perspective. It is important to keep these limitations in mind as we examine the evidence regarding mobility patterns in the United States and compare them with those in other societies.

CAUSAL FACTORS IN MOBILITY

Patterns of social mobility in the United States and other industrialized societies have been closely tied to the changes that have accompanied industrial development—an expanded and altered labor market, the increasing tendency for workers to change jobs and geographical locations, changing fertility patterns, and a growing emphasis on education. All these factors have interacted in complex ways not only to facilitate upward mobility but also to change "the rules of the game."

Changes in the Labor Market

An important measure of mobility in a society is the degree to which children succeed their parents in their occupations. Perfect succession would imply not only a closed stratification system but also a stable occupational structure, in which the available jobs changed little from one generation to the next. In industrial societies the trend has been in the other direction: stratification systems have become relatively more open, and both the number and the variety of jobs have steadily increased.

In 1900 almost 40 percent of all those in the labor force were in agriculture, whereas today farm workers constitute only about 4 percent of the work force. An industrial economy involving thousands of occupations requiring varying levels of skill is bound to offer far more opportunities for mobility than an agricultural economy. Thus the industrial-agricultural revolution has been a stimulus to upward mobility in at least two ways: first, in the increase in the absolute number of jobs; second, in the change in the job structure—the dramatic shift away from farming and unskilled jobs toward clerical, service, business, and professional jobs (Table 8.5).

But while in some respects economic expansion and a changing job structure have clearly stimulated mobility, in other respects they have also restricted it, especially over the last fifty years. Mechanization, specialization, and the trend toward "bigness" have made it much more difficult and costly for individuals to get ahead by setting up their own businesses. These technological trends have also raised the educational requirements for most jobs and created many more steps to climb in the move from bottom to top. Empirical research since the 1920s has consistently produced evidence challenging the reality of the American Dream that able and ambitious people can raise themselves from rags to riches. An early study by Sorokin, for example, showed that most men entered the occupational world at about the same level as their fathers and that only a very small proportion moved up more than a step or two.[49] Robert and Helen Lynd's studies of "Middletown" (Muncie, Indiana) showed a similar pattern: although "anyone" might theoretically work up to the job of foreman in the factory, the probabilities that anyone would were extremely low.[50] Subsequent research by Warner and others points to the conclusion that for most people upward mobility is a slow, gradual process at

49. Pitirim Sorokin, *Social Mobility* (New York: Harper & Row, Inc., 1927).
50. Robert and Helen Lynd, *Middletown* (New York: Harcourt Brace Jovanovich, Inc., 1929) and *Middletown in Transition* (New York: Harcourt Brace Jovanovich, Inc., 1937). See also Warner and Low, *The Social System of a Modern Factory,* and Eli Chinoy, *The Automobile Worker and the American Dream* (Garden City, N.Y.: Doubleday & Company, Inc., 1955).

best.[51] More recently Sennett and Cobb have argued that many of the occupational changes do not represent upward mobility—that much of the growth in white-collar jobs is in dull, monotonous, poorly paid work like filing that does not increase the workers' prestige, income, or power over their previous blue-collar jobs.[52]

As the structure of the job market has changed and education has become increasingly important, intragenerational mobility has largely given way to mobility from one generation to the next. Kahl has estimated that between 1920 and 1950 total intergenerational mobility was about 67 percent; that is, 67 percent of the sons were mobile relative to their fathers. Industrial and economic expansion—the creation of new jobs—accounted for almost one third of this mobility, most of which was moderately rather than dramatically upward (e.g., from clerks and salesmen to semiprofessionals).[53] But individual success stories are not wholly a thing of the past. Kahl's study showed that in 1952 some 69 percent of American business leaders had managed to rise to their positions, rather than simply succeeding their fathers, and 18 percent of this business elite had come from blue-collar families.[54] More recent research points to education as the key factor in determining an individual's chances for occupational advancement but suggests that educational opportunity, in turn, depends to a considerable degree on the class position of one's family.[55] Upward mobility, obviously, is not equally available to all.

Horizontal and Geographical Mobility

The term *horizontal mobility* refers to movement from one job to another that results in little or no change in rank. Typically a horizontal move is from company to company or from business to business. Although horizontal mobility is often overlooked in discussions of stratification, it may be a vital precondition for achieving upward mobility. A person cut off from hope of advancement in a small, family-owned company may take a similar job in a larger company where there is a

51. For example, Blau and Duncan report that only about eight in every thousand males from a working-class background become self-employed professionals. See Peter H. Blau and Otis Dudley Duncan, *The American Occupational Structure* (New York: John Wiley & Sons, Inc., 1967).
52. Richard Sennett and Jonathan Cobb, *The Hidden Injuries of Class* (New York: Alfred A. Knopf, Inc., 1972).
53. Joseph Kahl, *The American Class Structure* (New York: Holt, Rinehart and Winston, Inc., 1961), p. 257–262.
54. Ibid., pp. 267–268.
55. See Robert M. Hauser and David L. Featherman, "Trends in Occupational Mobility of U.S. Men, 1962–1970," *American Sociological Review*, 38 (June 1973): 302–310; also Peter M. Blau and Otis D. Duncan, "Occupational Mobility in the United States," in Heller, *Structured Social Inequality*, pp. 340–352.

Table 8.5.   PERCENT OF AMERICAN WORKERS IN MAJOR OCCUPATIONAL GROUPS, 1900 TO 1970

	1900	1910	1920	1930	1940	1950	1960	1970
Total labor force (in 1000's)	29,030	37,291	42,206	48,686	51,742	59,648	66,681	78,627
White-collar workers	**17.6**	**21.3**	**24.9**	**29.4**	**31.1**	**37.5**	**43.1**	**48.3**
Professional & technical workers	4.2	4.7	5.4	6.8	7.4	7.5	11.2	14.2
Managers, officials, & proprietors	5.8	6.6	6.6	7.4	7.3	10.8	10.5	10.5
Clerical workers	3.0	5.3	8.0	9.1	9.6	12.8	14.7	17.4
Sales workers	4.5	4.7	4.9	6.3	6.7	6.4	6.6	6.2
Blue-collar workers	**35.8**	**38.2**	**40.2**	**39.6**	**39.8**	**39.1**	**36.3**	**35.3**
Craftsmen & foremen	10.5	11.6	13.0	12.8	12.0	12.8	12.8	12.9
Operatives	12.8	14.6	15.6	15.8	18.4	20.4	18.0	17.7
Non-farm laborers	12.5	12.0	11.6	11.0	9.4	5.9	5.5	4.7
Service workers	**9.0**	**9.5**	**7.8**	**9.8**	**11.7**	**10.9**	**12.5**	**12.1**
Private household workers	5.4	5.0	3.3	4.1	4.7	3.1	3.3	
Other service workers	3.6	4.6	4.5	5.7	7.1	7.8	9.2	
Farmworkers	**37.5**	**30.9**	**27.0**	**21.2**	**17.4**	**12.4**	**8.1**	**4.0**

SOURCE: Bureau of the Census, *Historical Statistics of the United States, Colonial Times to 1957*, p. 74 (for data before 1950); *Statistical Abstract of the United States, 1972*, p. 230. Data beginning 1950 not strictly comparable with earlier years due to reclassification of occupations.

better chance of moving up. One who has become lost in the shuffle in a particular company may move to a different company that offers the new employee an opportunity to make a fresh impression on the management and/or make better use of his or her skills. Lateral movement of this sort has become increasingly typical of white-collar and professional workers, many of whom see job changes as necessary for occupational advancement, especially early in their careers.

Striving for upward mobility often involves *geographical* moves from one place of residence to another as well as horizontal moves from job to job. The major population shifts in the United States over the past hundred years—the movements from farm to city, from East to West, from South to North, from North to South, and from city to suburb (see page 341 ff.)—have all been stimulated by the search for greater opportunity and a more satisfying way of life. The nineteenth-century adage "Go West, young man" reflected the recognition that *there* lay opportunity, not only in the open lands but even more in the booming new cities. In the present century, economic and technological change has increasingly moved the locus of opportunity to the cities, making urban or suburban residence an important condition for upward mobility.

Differential Fertility

Demographic evidence shows that beginning in the nineteenth century members of the middle and upper classes began to restrict their family size and produce fewer children on the average than did members of the lower class. Kahl has estimated that at least 7 percent of the intergenerational mobility that took place in the labor force between 1920 and 1950 could be attributed to differential fertility rates between those with blue-collar occupations (including farmers) and those with white-collar occupations.[56] He found that professional men, for example, had less than one son each on the average—not enough even to replace themselves—whereas farmers had between one and two sons each on

the average. Thus the farmers and urban working class became the source of the population needed to fill the new white-collar jobs being created by an expanding economy.

The evidence today suggests, however, that high fertility is more likely to impede than to facilitate upward mobility for members of the lower class, especially for the very poor. The pattern of early marriage and lack of family planning makes it difficult if not impossible for many lower-class parents to finish their educations and thus to compete for good jobs. The children of such families, in turn, are cut off by their parents' poverty from educational and other opportunities necessary for their own advancement. Thus low socioeconomic position either perpetuates or intensifies itself. With the growing national consensus in favor of family planning, class differences in fertility can be expected to become less significant in determining patterns of mobility. (For a more detailed discussion of these issues, see Chapter 11, "Demographic Change," especially pages 327–330.)

Differential Socialization

Whereas the schools and other agents of socialization tend to open opportunities for the children of the middle and upper classes, they often have the effect of curtailing chances for the children of the poor. Research since the 1920s has shown that children from lower-class families are much more likely than those from middle- and upper-class families to drop out of school. Dropping out seems to be related to a lack of emphasis on education by parents and a conviction on the part of lower-class students that doing well won't change their futures anyway. The school is also the focus for a clash between the norms and general behavior patterns learned in the homes of the poor and the middle-class norms and behavior demanded in the classroom, where teachers and administrators frequently display a sometimes unconscious bias against the children of the poor by giving them less encouragement and help.

56. Kahl, *The American Class Structure*, pp. 257–262.

The importance of socialization in determining mobility patterns can also be illustrated by the changing role of women in contemporary society. There has been little research on female mobility, primarily because the status and class positions of all family members have traditionally been heavily dependent on the husband and father. This pattern has tended to persist despite the continuing movement of married women into the labor market. The limited research available indicates that, for an increasing percentage of females, high school and college education improves their preparation for a career that will enable them to become upwardly mobile whether they marry or not. In addition, by improving their overall status, education has increased to some extent women's chances for political power.[57]

But at the same time, socialization continues to limit women's opportunities to move upward on their own. The middle- or upper-class daughter who rises to the top is no less unusual in most fields (including those in which women predominate, such as professional education) than is the working-class son who becomes a captain of industry. Despite changes, we are still a long way from establishing a societal consensus for egalitarian socialization patterns for males and females.

MOBILITY AND SOCIETAL VALUES

Some observers believe that opportunities for achieving significant upward mobility have decreased in recent years. There is considerable movement within the blue-collar and white-collar ranks, but those at the top and at the bottom tend to stay there. Efforts to alter the pattern for those now at the bottom have lacked consistent governmental or public support, and there seems to be little in the value system to urge a significant change at the top.

Belief in the openness of American society can create serious problems of self-devaluation for individuals who have not succeeded. The Puritan ethic stresses individual responsibility and holds that people who do not get ahead have only themselves to blame. A recent nationwide survey shows that this attitude toward the poor remains firmly entrenched in the American value-belief system.[58] The respondents, randomly selected to represent a demographic cross section, were asked to evaluate the relative importance of eleven "reasons some people give to explain why there are poor people in this country." Results of the survey, summarized in Table 8.6, page 234, showed that a majority of Americans continue to believe that individual characteristics of the poor—e.g., lack of thrift, lack of initiative, weak character—are primarily responsible for their poverty. Structural explanations, blaming poverty on social and economic forces, received the most support from minority group members, people under thirty, and the poor. But even among respondents with family incomes below $4000 a year, 51 percent emphasized individual faults as the most important explanations for poverty. Only 8 percent of all respondents stressed the fatalistic explanation of "just bad luck."

Belief in the Puritan ethic may lead individuals to blame themselves even for setbacks caused by factors clearly beyond their control. Sennett and Cobb cite research on auto workers which showed that, in one plant, only six foreman's positions became available over a period of several years. Yet over half of the three thousand workers applied for these jobs. Although the selection process may well have been arbitrary, those who were not chosen had been trained by the system to accept the fact that management knew what it was doing and that therefore the failure was their own.[59] Similarly,

57. For recent discussions of stratification and mobility patterns as they relate to women, see Joan Huber, ed., *Changing Women in a Changing Society* (Chicago: The University of Chicago Press, 1973), pp. 174–183; and Ruth B. Kundsin, ed., *Women and Success* (New York: William Morrow & Co., Inc., 1974).
58. Joe R. Feagin, "God Helps Those Who Help Themselves," *Psychology Today,* November 1972, pp. 101–110, 129.
59. Sennett and Cobb, *The Hidden Injuries of Class,* pp. 153–154.

women and members of racial and ethnic minorities often blame themselves for failing to receive a job or promotion when in fact they were disqualified by discriminatory hiring practices. The belief is implanted in us through socialization that the top jobs go to the "best people."

Ironically, belief in the importance of getting ahead may lead to dissatisfaction and unhappiness even for those who succeed. Urged on by ambitious parents and by teachers and counselors, young people may choose a prestigious profession and work hard to become a scientist or a lawyer or a corporate executive only to discover that the job they have strived for doesn't suit them. Now and then we read of someone who, at forty, walks out of a supposedly successful career in order to pursue a much less prestigious, less lucrative, but more personally appealing vocation. And there are some young people today who are deliberately turning their backs on prestige jobs and seeking personal satisfaction as farmers, carpenters, or potters. Some go further. Convinced that one's job should not be one's life—convinced, in fact, that one's life and one's job should be kept separate—they choose work that will earn them a living wage while making minimal demands on either their muscles or their minds. The attitudes and actions of this very small minority represent a complete rejection of the Puritan ethic.

MOBILITY IN INTERNATIONAL PERSPECTIVE

One way to define the "revolution of rising expectations" now taking place in the developing societies around the world is to say that it is a drive for upward mobility—in fact, for a transformation in the structure of stratification. To the extent that governments are now acting as agents to stimulate social change, they are also acting as agents of mobility. For example, land reform programs in Latin America and elsewhere are designed not only to change farming practices and patterns of land ownership but also to make new sources of wealth available and to create new patterns of distribution. The evidence from Mexico shows that such objectives can be achieved; but even there, after more than forty years of sustained government activity, the results, while encouraging, are still spotty.[60]

60. Patterns of social and economic change in modern Mexico are analyzed at length in Chapter 11, pages 315–318.

Table 8.6. AMERICAN ATTITUDES TOWARD POVERTY

Reasons selected by Americans in national survey	Very important	Somewhat important	Not important
Lack of thrift and proper money management by poor people	58%	30%	11%
Lack of effort by the poor themselves	55	33	9
Lack of ability and talent among poor people	52	33	12
Loose morals and drunkenness	48	31	17
Sickness and physical handicaps	46	39	14
Low wages in some businesses and industries	42	35	20
Failure of society to provide good schools for many Americans	36	25	34
Prejudice and discrimination against Negroes	33	37	26
Failure of private industry to provide enough jobs	27	36	31
Being taken advantage of by rich people	18	30	45
Just bad luck	8	27	60

SOURCE: Joe R. Feagin, "God Helps Those Who Help Themselves," *Psychology Today*, November 1972, p. 104. The survey was designed by Joe R. Feagin and conducted by the Opinion Research Corporation of Princeton, N.J. Interviews averaged 45 minutes each. The respondents were 1017 adults randomly selected to represent a cross section of the population in terms of socioreligious background, race, geographical region, age, family income level, and educational level.

VIEWPOINTS   EQUALITY AND INEQUALITY

■ Of several kinds of equality, America has traditionally stood for equality of opportunity, giving everyone a chance to become affluent on the basis of his or her abilities without regard to race, sex or socioeconomic origin. But in America today income, wealth and other resources are still as unequally distributed as ever. . . .

The history of America is a history of people striving for more resources, and our economy and political institutions have always encouraged this tendency. Because of this ingrained tradition, many people may look upon equality as a denial of their desire to achieve more than their fellow men. While nearly everyone may favor more equality in the abstract, no one wants to give up income, wealth, or power. Even the people who would benefit from egalitarian policies often want more than mere equality. . . .

In an individualistic America, egalitarian policies must also be individualistic; public ownership of all resources will not work for us. . . . Some resources, such as health care, must be nationalized so that no one will suffer from poor health or huge medical bills. But an individualistic egalitarianism should concentrate on the greater equalization of income and wealth, and then let everyone decide how to spend their income in whatever way they please. . . .

America is quickly becoming what sociologist Daniel Bell has called a postindustrial society, in which huge private corporations and public agencies are amassing the capital, technology, knowledge and political power they need to function effectively. Whether they intend to or not, these huge bodies are also obtaining greater control over society and over our lives. At the same time, many Americans are also demanding more control over their lives than ever before. Eventually, these two tendencies must clash. In the end, a postindustrial society can only hold together if it deals constructively with that conflict. More equality may therefore be the key not only to making America a better and more democratic society, but also to our very survival as a society.

Herbert J. Gans
More Equality

● In America, so powerful is the democratic rhetoric of equality that few people ever risk saying a good word for inequality. They simply live by it. Though American politics proclaims a belief in equality, Americans sort themselves out by the differences in where they live and how they live. The inequality that Americans feel most comfortable with is, accordingly, economic. Inequality by professional specialization is also accepted, but any other kind is condemned. Assertion of social superiority, for example, is often considered snobbery, and intellectual superiority damned as elitist. . . .

The worst form of inequality, Aristotle argued, is to try to make unequal things equal. He held instead that "equals ought to have equality" and recalled the retort of the lions, in the fable of Antisthenes, when in the council of the beasts the hares began haranguing for equality for all. "Where," asked the lions, "are your claws and teeth?" Still, more than claws and teeth are presumed to be estimable in civilized society. This is why the undue emphasis on economic inequality in American life, which puts such a premium on acquisitiveness, is an erratic measure of individual worth.

It is not simply that thousands of Americans, as teachers, nurses or lab workers, find more gratification in their work than they might have found in opportunities that would have paid them better. . . . Such essential qualities as character, honor, decency, intelligence, lovableness, dependability, common sense, humor and perception are randomly dispersed in the population and do not necessarily ascend on a parallel curve with a man's economic status. Nor do such qualities depend upon the amount of his schooling or "brains"; IQ tests do not measure character. . . .

The stubborn American belief in equality does not depend on a false claim of similarity among men when their differences are real. Instead, it argues for a broader test in judging each person's qualities. By deploying his own range of qualities as best he can, each man frames his own dignity and asserts his right to look any other man squarely in the face.

Thomas Griffith
"The Delicate Subject of Inequality"

We have already observed that studies of occupational prestige show a rather consistent pattern of similarity among societies, including some of the less developed ones. The findings of cross-cultural studies of mobility, while still far from conclusive, seem to point in the same direction; that is, there seems to be no great difference between the amount of mobility in the United States and the amount in the other highly industrialized societies of the Western world.

Lenski has attempted to systematize and analyze a variety of research findings on mobility in different societies.[61] In the more industrialized societies, intergenerational mobility averaged about 30 percent in jobs not involving movement in or out of agricultural occupations, with the United States at the top with 34 percent and Italy at the bottom with 22 percent. There was also a range in total mobility, with the United States showing a distinct but not a great lead over the other societies studied. And the net general drift, after deducting for rates of downward mobility, was upward in all societies. This is not surprising since all these societies are undergoing similar changes in their economies, toward occupations demanding increasingly complex skills.

At the present time, the most accurate generalization about mobility in international perspective would seem to be that the rate for the United States is somewhat higher than the rate for other countries but that there is a tendency toward convergence based on the level of industrialization of any particular society. Future trends in mobility and perhaps in stratification itself will depend on such factors as political policies, growth of the economy, fertility trends, educational opportunities, and socialization.

SUMMARY

Stratification refers to established patterns of interaction that result in inequalities of status (prestige), class (wealth), and power. The unequal distribution of these societal rewards leads to the development in community and society of social strata; within each stratum people share more or less the same opportunities. In modern industrial societies, occupation is the primary criterion by which people are assigned to different social strata.

Status refers to the level of prestige that accrues to people by the mere fact of birth or because of the positions they occupy in the societal structure. Status systems may be relatively open (people can move from one stratum to another over time on the basis of achievement), or they may be rigidly closed (as in the Hindu caste system). *Class* is essentially an economic concept. It refers to the material advantages a stratum of people share because of their income level and sometimes because of inherited wealth. *Power,* in the study of stratification, refers not only to political dominance but also to the unequal control of decision making found in all social organizations.

Social stratification may be explained by both conflict theory and functional theory. *Conflict* theory, deriving largely from the thinking of Karl Marx, sees stratification as a system imposed on the society by those at the top of the ladder and conducive to dissension and change. Marx's political philosophy was built around an economic interpretation of history in which class conflict was seen as fundamental. In the Marxian view, the concept of class focuses less on the material advantages that accrue from income than on the power that accrues from control over the means of production. Marx saw

---

61. Lenski, *Power and Privilege,* pp. 410 ff. A more recent study that reached the same general conclusions is Lawrence E. Hazelrigg, "Cross-National Comparisons of Father-to-Son Occupational Mobility," in *Social Stratification: A Reader,* ed. Joseph Lopreato and Lionel S. Lewis (New York: Harper & Row, Inc., 1974), pp. 469–493.

stratification not only as a system of class oppression but also as a mechanism for stimulating the eventual development of a classless society.

Whereas conflict theory stresses social dissension and social change, *functional* theory sees stratification as an established system of differential rewards that is supported by societal consensus. It helps integrate the society and maintain social equilibrium by ensuring that the jobs considered most important to the society's welfare will get done. Our analysis of stratification and mobility patterns in the United States and other societies have shown that both functional and conflict theory explain some, but not all, of the facts.

The family, the educational system, the economic system, and the government are the social institutions that seem to have the greatest effect in maintaining or altering stratification patterns. In the United States all four have exerted both liberalizing influences that encourage upward mobility and conservative influences that restrict the number of those who can move into a higher stratum.

The United States has always claimed to offer equal opportunity for all, and it is true that social mobility has brought the majority of the population into the middle class. Patterns of serious inequality persist, however, and there is evidence that Americans' faith in progress up the economic ladder is waning. Currently, there is continuing movement within the ranks of blue-collar and white-collar workers, but those at the top and bottom of the stratification system seem to stay put. Cross-cultural studies suggest that the amount of mobility in the United States is not greatly different from that in other highly industrialized countries.

9
Intergroup Relations

THE SOCIAL DEFINITION OF MINORITIES

Ascribed Low Status   Relative Powerlessness   Economic Disadvantage

CULTURAL CRITERIA FOR IDENTIFYING MINORITIES

Race   Ethnicity   Visibility   Relative Size

THE HISTORY OF AMERICAN MINORITIES

Blacks   Jews   Spanish-Surnamed Minorities
Orientals   Native Americans

PATTERNS OF CONFLICT AND ACCOMMODATION

Aggression   Exclusion and Avoidance   Assimilation
Pluralism

PREJUDICE

The Origins of Prejudicial Norms   Social Distance
Hierarchies   Stereotypes   The Language of Prejudice
Prejudice and Discrimination

In the last chapter we examined the general nature of social stratification—the ranking of a society's members in different social strata that share unequally in the distribution of status, wealth, and power. We noted that the trend in the United States and other western urban-industrial societies has been to minimize the relative importance of ascribed characteristics as criteria of social rank and to emphasize instead the importance of individual achievement. But no society can honestly claim that access to societal rewards is determined by talent or accomplishment alone. Patterns of inequality based on ascription rather than achievement are especially apparent in relations between dominant and minority groups.

Almost every society can provide examples of tension and conflict between its dominant group and those groups that have been relegated to a subordinate position by virtue of racial, religious, ethnic, or other characteristics. In recent years intergroup relations deteriorated into a bloody civil war between the Ibo and the Hausa in Nigeria, led to renewed restrictions on the movements of Jews, Lithuanians, and other ethnic minorities in the Soviet Union, caused savage guerilla warfare between Protestants and Catholics in Northern Ireland, brought about the expulsion of nonblack groups from Uganda, and stimulated renewed movements of ethnic assertion among French Canadians and Greek and Turkish Cypriots. Although this chapter will focus primarily on problems of intergroup relations in the United States, such problems are clearly of worldwide concern.

After examining the social consequences of minority group membership, we will consider the various criteria societies use in identifying certain categories of people as minorities. Then we will proceed to a historical overview of intergroup relations in the United States, noting the various patterns of social interaction in dominant-minority relations. And finally, we will investigate the nature of prejudice and consider its consequences for both dominant and minority group members.

THE SOCIAL DEFINITION OF MINORITIES

The term *minority group* has long been used by sociologists and others, not in its literal sense, to indicate numerical inferiority, but to designate a segment of a society that is subordinate—that is, that occupies a low level in the society's system of social stratification.[1] There is no simple way to describe the basis people use in designating—and treating—a segment of the population as a minority. Each part of the society that is thought of as a minority has shared a unique set of historical experiences and thereby has acquired a somewhat distinctive place in the general social structure. Each has its own general position in the system of stratification, and each faces its own particular situation with respect to prejudice and discrimination.

In the United States race, religion, and national origin have all been commonly used as bases for identifying minorities. Thus minority groups in our society include black Americans (a racial group), Jewish Americans (a religiocultural group), and Mexican Americans (a nationality group). Other criteria for minority designation are socioeconomic class (the poor), sex (women), and age (the elderly).

In all societies, to be labeled a minority group member is to be denied equal access to social prestige, power, and wealth. Let us now briefly examine these three dimensions of social stratification as they relate to minority group life.

ASCRIBED LOW STATUS

Perhaps the most significant consequence of minority group membership is ascribed low status: to be born into a minority is to be identified categorically as a "second-class citizen." Even the most favorably treated minority groups are usually cut off from some significant forms of interaction with the dominant group. Patterns of

In the United States all minority groups have been excluded from some significant forms of interaction with the majority. Jews, for example, have been excluded from numerous occupations, kept out of certain residential areas, and denied access to some hotels and restaurants. Such exclusions identify the member of the minority group as a "second-class citizen" and are thus an important basis for intergroup hostility.

exclusion may range from ostracism that forces a minority to live on an isolated reservation or in an urban ghetto to more subtle forms such as avoidance by the dominant group of close personal interaction with members of the minority. Such exclusions, whether severe or seemingly inconsequential, limit the life opportunities of minority group members, regardless of individual ability, and may greatly challenge their sense of personal worth.

Because a dominant group automatically assigns low status to those born into a minority, the relatively low status of minorities tends to carry over from one generation to the next. In-group marriage, or *endogamy*, is strongly encouraged by members of dominant groups as a means of maintaining and reinforcing existing stratification patterns. Indeed, societies have sometimes passed laws to prevent particular minorities from marrying into a dominant group.

---

1. The meaning of *group* as used in this context departs somewhat from our earlier definition of a group as a number of individuals who interact on a regular basis according to some pattern of social organization (page 33). But the term *minority group* has been used for a long time, and we will follow the traditional usage in this chapter. For a fuller discussion of *minority group,* see William M. Newman, *American Pluralism* (New York: Harper & Row, Inc., 1973), Chapter 2.

VIEWPOINTS   WASPS AND WHITE ETHNICS

■ I am born of PIGS—those Poles, Italians, Greeks, and Slavs, non-English-speaking immigrants, numbered so heavily among the workingmen of this nation. Not particularly liberal, nor radical, born into a history not white Anglo-Saxon and not Jewish—born outside what in America is considered the intellectual mainstream. And thus privy to neither power nor status nor intellectual voice. . . .

Nowhere in my schooling do I recall an attempt to put me in touch with my own history. The strategy was clearly to make an American of me. English literature, American literature; and even the history books, as I recall them, were peopled mainly by Anglo-Saxons from Boston . . . .

The fact that I was born a Catholic also complicated life. What is a Catholic but what everybody else is in reaction against? . . . It is hard to grow up Catholic in America without becoming defensive, perhaps a little paranoid, feeling forced to divide the world between "us" and "them." . . .

Since earliest childhood, I have known about a "power elite" that runs America: the boys from the Ivy League in the State Department, as opposed to the Catholic boys in Hoover's FBI who, as Daniel Moynihan once put it, keep watch on them. . . .

The ethnics erred in attempting to Americanize themselves, before clearing the project with the educated classes. They learned to wave the flag and to send their sons to war. . . . They learned to support their President. . . .

At no little sacrifice, one . . . apologized for foods that smelled too strong for Anglo-Saxon noses, moderated the wide swings of Slavic and Italian emotion, learned decorum, given oneself to education American style, tried to learn tolerance and assimilation. . . . And now when the process appears near completion, when a generation appears that speaks without accent and goes to college, still you are considered pigs, fascists, and racists.

Michael Novak
The Rise of the Unmeltable Ethnics

● Over the past few years, American pop culture has acquired a new folk antihero: the Wasp. . . . The Wasps, in fact, are rapidly becoming the one minority that every other ethnic group . . . feels absolutely free to dump on. . . .

As a Wasp, the mildest thing I can say about the stereotype emerging from the current wave of anti-Wasp chic is that I don't recognize myself. As regards emotional uptightness and sexual inhibition, modesty forbids comment. . . . I will admit to enjoying work—because I am lucky enough to be able to work at what I enjoy—but not, I think, to the point of compulsiveness. And so far as ruling America, or even New York, is concerned, I can say flatly that (a) it's a damn lie because (b) if I *did* rule them, both would be in better shape than they are. . . .

Admittedly, both corporate and (to a lesser extent) political America are dominated by Wasps. . . . But to conclude from this that The Wasps are the American elite is as silly as to say that The Jews are cloak-and-suiters or The Italians are gangsters. Wasps, like other ethnics, come in all varieties, including criminals—political, corporate and otherwise. . . .

We Wasps, like other people, don't always live up to our own principles, and those of us who don't, if occupying positions of power, can pose formidable problems to the rest of us. Time after time, in the name of anti-Communism, peace with honor or some other slippery shibboleth, we have been conned or bullied into tolerating government interference with our liberties and privacy in all sorts of covert—and sometimes overt—ways; time after time we have had to relearn the lesson that eternal vigilance is the price of liberty.

It was a Wasp who uttered that last thought. And it was a congress of Wasps who, about the same time, denounced the executive privileges of George III and committed to the cause of liberty their lives, their fortunes and . . . their sacred honor.

Robert Claiborne
"A Wasp Stings Back"

A minority group may inadvertently help perpetuate its disadvantaged position by drawing into itself and developing strong feelings of "we" versus "they." Minority groups, no less than dominant groups, encourage their members to marry "someone of their own kind." Although the practice of in-group marriage is an important means by which a minority group maintains social cohesion and a sense of identity and pride, it also facilitates the transmission of ascribed low status to successive generations of members.

RELATIVE POWERLESSNESS

A minority group, by definition, is dominated by other segments of society. In the United States the patterning of dominant-minority relations varies as one considers each specific minority. Collectively, for example, blacks have been dominated by whites (including those who are themselves minorities), and the same has been generally true for Indians. Jews and Catholics, on the other hand, have not been dominated by all who were not Jewish or Catholic. Nationality factors complicate the picture; it would be difficult to specify the exact composition of the dominating segment of society for each minority group. In general, however, it can be said that native-born, white, Anglo-Saxon Protestants—the so-called WASPs—are dominant over other categories of people in American society.

Dominance over minority groups may take many forms, the most extreme being slavery. Peonage and debt servitude fall just short of slavery. Less obvious are forms of dominance that seem to permit total political and economic freedom but subtly deny equal access to education, employment, or advancement. All possible forms of dominance, including slavery, military subjugation, peonage, economic suppression, and various kinds of discrimination—from the most blatant to the most subtle—have been

practiced at one time or another in American society.

The importance of political subjugation in maintaining patterns of dominance is clearly illustrated by the current political structure in the Union of South Africa. The white Afrikaners, constituting only 20 percent of the population, are legally entitled to 80 percent of the seats in parliament. Nonwhites, though an overwhelming majority of the population, are limited to the remaining 20 percent of the seats. Thus, they are prevented by law from developing sufficient political power to improve their status or their economic position.

As the example of South Africa illustrates, numerical strength is not always enough in itself to ensure a group's political strength. In a number of major American cities, blacks constitute a majority or near majority of the population, yet they have been largely excluded from important policy-making positions, both public and private.[2] Similarly, Mexican Americans in Texas, though numerically strong, have for the most part been effectively discouraged from trying to gain access to political office and using local government to meet their needs. A study by D'Antonio and Form has documented the manner in which the dominant white "Anglos" long managed to prevent any Mexican American from becoming mayor of El Paso, despite the fact that nearly half the city's population was of Mexican descent.[3] A great organizing effort was needed to persuade Mexican Americans to pay the then constitutional poll tax, to find Anglos who would support and run on the ticket with a Mexican American for mayor, and to rally support for such a ticket. The campaign in El Paso in which a Mexican American ran for the first time—and won—was similar to more recent campaigns by black candidates in cities such as Gary, Indiana, and Newark, New Jersey. It also mirrored earlier campaigns by Irish Americans and Italian Americans to gain political strength in the northeastern cities where they had settled in large numbers.[4] Although white ethnic groups in the United States continue to be victims of subtle and not-so-subtle discrimination, many

2. See, for example, Harold M. Baron, "Black Powerlessness in Chicago," *Trans-action*, 6, No. 1 (November 1968): 27–33.
3. William V. D'Antonio and William H. Form, *Influentials in Two Border Cities* (South Bend, Ind.: University of Notre Dame Press, 1965), esp. pp. 130–144.
4. For an excellent study of white ethnic politics, see Robert A. Dahl, *Who Governs? Democracy and Power in an American City* (New Haven, Conn.: Yale University Press, 1961).

white ethnics have largely overcome minority status and the powerlessness that goes with it.

ECONOMIC DISADVANTAGE

Ascribed low status and relative powerlessness bring in their wake the third major consequence of minority group membership: economic disadvantage. The dominant group owns and controls most of the society's productive facilities and other economic resources, and it tends to use them to its own advantage. Minority group members are usually excluded from important policy-making positions not only in government but also in business. A recent study of top management and business directorships in Chicago, for example, revealed that 0.1 percent were Spanish-surnamed, 0.3 percent were of Polish descent, 0.4 percent were black, and 1.9 percent were Italian American. These minority groups comprise 34 percent of the Chicago metropolitan population, yet together they hold less than 3 percent of the top jobs.[5]

The economic disadvantages stemming from lack of economic control are compounded by patterns of discrimination that deter individual minority group members from being able to get ahead on the basis of ability. The economic disadvantages of blacks in American society have been well documented. Very similar disadvantages are suffered by Americans of Spanish surname (see Table 9.1). The Hispanos of the Southwest, who occupied this territory long before the arrival of Anglos, were systematically deprived of their lands during the late nineteenth and early twentieth centuries. The imposition of Anglo laws, taxes, and customs made the Spanish-surnamed peoples relatively easy victims of the dominant group.[6] (In an earlier period, the Hispanos used similar means to establish their own dominance over Indians native to the area.)

Occasionally a minority group is able to establish a position of economic strength without substantially improving its prestige or its position in the overall power structure. Jews provide the classic illustration of this pattern. Throughout the centuries European Jews were often able to accumulate considerable wealth as money lenders and merchants. But a strong economic position provided them with neither high status nor security, as was made evident by their expulsion from Spain in the sixteenth century and efforts to exterminate them in Hitler's Germany. In American society, the economic position of Jews is again much stronger than their position in the hierarchies of status and power. It seems clear not only from the history of Jews but from the history of dominant-minority relations more generally that equality of treatment in any society depends on equality with respect to *all three* dimensions of social stratification.

Table 9.1. FAMILY INCOME RELATED TO RACE AND ETHNICITY

	Median Income	Percent of Families with Incomes	
		Under $5000	$15,000 or more
All U.S. families	$10,285	18.5	24.8
White families	10,672	16.2	26.4
Black families	6,440	38.6	10.6
Families of			
Spanish surname	7,548	30.4	10.3
Mexican	7,486	31.2	9.1
Puerto Rican	6,185	38.5	5.3
Cuban	9,371	22.4	21.4
Other	8,494	24.5	13.0

SOURCE: *Manpower Report of the President*, March 1973, p. 100.

CULTURAL CRITERIA FOR IDENTIFYING MINORITIES

The major criteria used to designate categories of people as minority groups are race and ethnicity. In the following section we will discuss each of these concepts in turn and then consider the

5. Data compiled by the Institute for Urban Affairs, 820 North Michigan Avenue, Chicago, Ill., and reprinted in Institute for Urban Life and National Center for Urban Ethnic Affairs, *Minority Report* (Washington, D.C., November 1973).

6. William V. D'Antonio and Irwin Press, "Fabens, Texas: A Community Study," (South Bend, Ind.: University of Notre Dame Press, unpublished ms., 1970), pp. 3ff.; and John S. Shockley, *Chicano Revolt in a Texas Town* (South Bend, Ind.: University of Notre Dame Press, 1974), esp. pp. 3–14.

importance of visible differences in establishing and maintaining minority group identification. We will also consider the significance of group size, which may or may not be a key factor in dominant-minority relations.

RACE

Scientists — mainly physical anthropologists and geneticists — have worked long to develop precise criteria by which to define the concept *race*. Their proposed systems of classification provide anywhere from three to thirty racial categories, generally based on such physical characteristics as skin color, nose shape, hair texture, eye color, blood type, gene frequency, head measurement, and facial structure. Whatever particular system of classification they use, most scientists agree on a general definition of *race* as an aggregate of people who are biologically distinguishable. They also agree that there is no evidence of racial differences in intelligence, character, ability to play social roles effectively, or the like — in other words, no evidence of "superior" and "inferior" races.

But scientific conclusions do not necessarily shape cultural beliefs; and in the area of intergroup relations, *cultural definitions* of race, not scientific ones, are what determine patterns of social interaction. As Westie puts it, "Race relations are relations between people who are biologically different or *believed to be biologically different,* who are aware of these differences, and whose relations to one another are affected by this awareness."[7] In terms of sociocultural consequences, it makes little difference that there is no scientific basis for thinking of Jews, Germans, and various other religious and nationality groups as "races." Nor does it make much difference that neither "blacks" nor "whites" nor "browns" nor "yellows" are biologically superior or inferior if people believe — and act — to the contrary.

7. Frank R. Westie, "Race and Ethnic Relations," in *Handbook of Modern Sociology*, ed. R. E. L. Faris (Chicago: Rand McNally & Co., 1964), p. 580.
8. George E. Simpson and J. Milton Yinger, *Racial and Cultural Minorities*, 3rd ed. (New York: Harper & Row, Inc., 1965).
9. The present policy of the Bureau of the Census is to allow individuals to determine their own racial and ethnic identification.
10. Milton M. Gordon, *Assimilation in American Life* (New York: Oxford University Press, 1964), p. 24.

In designating a category of people as a racial minority, the dominant group uses biological differences — real or imagined — as justification for making *sociocultural* distinctions between "we" and "they." Often members of the dominant group employ what Simpson and Yinger have called an "administrative concept of race," using official acts and established practices as bases for an institutionalized system of "racial" classification.[8] In the United States, for example, the Bureau of the Census until quite recently classified as "Negro" any person of known black ancestry, even though the individual might be more Caucasian in appearance than many "whites." Similarly, people who were regarded in their community as "Indian" were so classified in the official records. The roots of these practices reach back to the days of slavery and the frontier.[9]

The administrative concept of race has been used in many societies. In the Union of South Africa, an extensive *apartheid* system maintains elaborate segregation policies for the four major population groups: Africans, Coloureds (of racially mixed ancestry), Indians, and Whites. In Nazi Germany, not only Jews but members of various other religious and ethnic groups (including Jehovah's Witnesses, gypsies, and Slavic peoples) were officially classified as "non-Aryan" and thus made candidates for extermination.

ETHNICITY

Most of us think of ethnic groups as double-named fellow citizens — Greek Americans, Italian Americans, Polish Americans, and the like. However, a shared foreign origin is by no means the only basis for the development of ethnicity. Religion, language, and racial identification provide focuses for the feelings of allegiance and common identity that help create ethnic groups.

In sociological terms, an ethnic group is one whose members are bound together by common cultural ties. Such people have a sense of common identity; they feel a "consciousness of kind," an in-group loyalty and "we-ness," "a shared feeling of peoplehood."[10] Generally, ethnic groups live by folkways, mores, and customs that are distinct from those of the general culture. Members have their own group legends, myths, and traditions. Their particular beliefs and values distinguish them from others around them, link them to the past, and influence their future. Ethnicity and race often converge because physical differences, if used as a basis for segregation within a society, generate cultural differences. Thus blacks in the United States are both a racial group and an ethnic group.

Ethnicity is especially apparent in large industrial societies that have drawn together peoples of diverse backgrounds. The United States has many population groups that maintain identifiable ethnic subcultures (Figure 9.1). The Soviet Union includes more than a hundred ethnic groups distinguished by language, custom, and religion. But ethnic groups also exist in smaller, more homogeneous countries like Ireland and Uganda. An ethnic group may or may not suffer minority status. Indeed, the dominant segment of a society may itself be considered an ethnic group.

VISIBILITY

Minorities vary greatly in the degree to which they are "visible" within a society. Religious and cultural practices other than language use are less easily "seen" by the casual observer than skin color, for example, but use of a different language, a foreign accent, or even a distinctive body movement, like the low bow of the Japanese, can create high visibility. Visibility may also be imposed upon minorities, as was the case when Jews in Nazi Germany were forced to wear identifying arm bands.

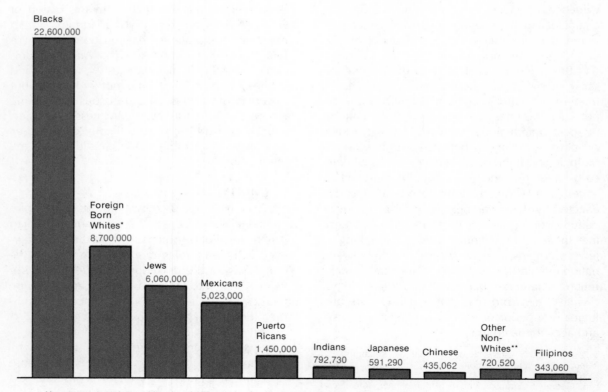

*A more accurate picture of the size of white ethnic minorities would include the millions of second- and third-generation persons who still identify themselves or are identified as ethnics.

**Includes Asiatic Indians, Koreans, Polynesians, Indonesians, Hawaiians, and Eskimos.

SOURCE: *Statistical Abstract of the United States, 1972.*

Figure 9.1. PRINCIPAL RACIAL AND ETHNIC MINORITIES IN THE UNITED STATES

When there are serious tensions and strains between dominant and minority groups or between different minorities, differences that may not be apparent to an outsider are highly visible to those involved. Thus, under conditions of tension and conflict in Northern Ireland, Catholics are as highly visible to their Protestant neighbors as the blacks in some American towns and cities are to the local whites. A recent study quotes a middle-class Protestant in Belfast who maintained, "You can tell a Catholic by the way he walks."[11]

If members of a minority group choose to minimize the differences between themselves and those in the dominant group, they can often cast off minority status. This has happened with some members of minorities identified in the United States in terms of national origin. Immigrants of Italian, Polish, Scandinavian, and other European origins were assigned minority positions in American society because of language, religion, and other cultural differences. By abandoning their cultural ties and sometimes their social ties with their ethnic group, by marrying outside the group, sometimes by "Americanizing" their names, many members merged with the dominant population.

But nationality groups persist in the United States after three or more generations, and today some of them are becoming more visible as they strive for power and recognition in their own right. Indeed, one of the most significant social phenomena of recent years has been the resistance of minority groups in the United States to assimilation on the one hand and to subordination on the other. Both racial and ethnic groups are now increasingly insistent on their right to maintain separate identities without suffering prejudice and discrimination. This trend will be discussed in more detail later in the chapter (pages 263–264).

11. Leif Skoogfors, John Cooney, and Lenore Cooney, *The Most Natural Thing in the World* (New York: Harper & Row, Inc., 1974).

12. Gunnar Myrdal, *An American Dilemma: The Negro Problem and American Democracy*, rev. ed. (New York: Harper & Row, Inc., 1962); and Frank R. Westie, "The American Dilemma: An Empirical Test," *American Sociological Review*, 30, No. 4 (August 1965): 527–538.

RELATIVE SIZE

Usually a minority is considerably smaller than the dominant segment of the society. This simple numerical fact has significant implications for the members of the minority because it tends to place them at a disadvantage in both political and economic activities. This has certainly been true for racial and ethnic minorities in the United States, though it is by no means the only reason for the disadvantages they have suffered.

Nor does numerical inferiority always bring minority status. In the Union of South Africa, as we have seen, the numerically inferior whites are dominant both politically and economically. By no stretch of the imagination could they be considered a minority group in the sociological sense of the term. In the United States, where they slightly outnumber men, women have shared several of the attributes of minority groups, including ascribed low status, relative powerlessness, and lower pay for the same work.

THE HISTORY OF AMERICAN MINORITIES

While Americans of almost every persuasion endorse the general principles of democracy, they vary sharply in the degree to which they are willing to apply those principles in their relationships with members of minority groups. This is the great "American Dilemma"—the continuing struggle between our ideal of equality for all and the harsh realities of prejudice and discrimination toward minority groups.[12] While much change has occurred in some areas of our intergroup relations, the hierarchy of dominance still exists, and complete social equality remains a distant goal.

Like our language and our basic social institutions, the orientations and values defining intergroup relationships in the United States today have in large part been handed down to us from earlier generations. While this does not justify existing practices, it helps explain the difficulties encountered in trying to change them. In the sections that follow we will briefly trace the history of several minority groups in American society, noting the social and cultural processes by which dominant-minority relations have been altered or maintained.

BLACKS

In 1619 the influx of black Africans into the southern region of colonial America began.[13] Since that time, the destiny of the black minority has been inextricably interwoven with that of the society as a whole. American history is black as well as white, though most American history books have failed to make this clear.

Slavery by custom preceded slavery by statute. Many of the blacks who arrived during the early period were technically classified as servants. But when the several colonies began to clarify their laws and make clear distinctions between indentured servitude and slavery, the latter became the category reserved for blacks, and the fate of the black people in America was sealed for many generations to come.

The Culture of Slavery

By the end of the seventeenth century, slavery had been given legal status in all the American colonies. Even after the African slave trade was outlawed by the United States and the major European powers in the early nineteenth century, the slave population in America continued to grow. In 1800 there were a million slaves in the United States; by 1860 the number had increased to nearly four and a half million. The slave population was concentrated primarily in the southern states, where the vast agricultural land and the major crops—cotton, sugarcane, tobacco—required quantities of cheap, unskilled labor. In the northern states, a relatively small number of slaves served primarily as domestics.

The institution of slavery developed an elaborate system of rituals to govern relationships between blacks and whites. This system called for blacks to give overt and symbolic indications of humility and inferiority in the presence of whites, and it required whites to treat blacks in a condescending and patronizing manner. Surviving elements of this system are apparent even today.

More significantly, the system of slavery demanded that blacks be defined as biologically, morally, and intellectually inferior. Religious arguments based upon isolated biblical references were often used to justify these views. In many states it was forbidden to teach blacks to read and write. Laws were passed giving slaveholders life-and-death control over their "property." Cultural definitions of blacks as "naturally inferior" made it far easier to justify such treatment both morally and legally. The ideological foundation for the system of slavery was developed so thoroughly that it continues to influence relationships between blacks and whites more than a century after emancipation.

The Civil War and Its Aftermath

During the Civil War, the issue of emancipation was a thorny one. Slaveholding border states had remained loyal to the Union, and President Lincoln was anxious not to lose their support. The Emancipation Proclamation he issued in 1862 freed *some* slaves but not others; it declared free only "those slaves residing in territory in rebellion against the Federal government" (over which the Union actually had no control). Slavery was at last completely abolished by the Thirteenth Amendment in December 1865.

By the war's end, the economic system founded on slavery had been largely destroyed. But the ideology of black inferiority, which had been refined over two centuries to justify slavery, continued in full force. Emancipation changed the legal status of blacks, but little else.

In the South there was a clear determination to suppress the attempts of blacks to escape their "place" at the bottom of the social struc-

13. This section is based on Leslie H. Fishel, Jr., and Benjamin Quarles, *The Black American: A Documentary History* (Glenview, Ill.: Scott, Foresman and Company, 1970); Benjamin Brawley, *A Social History of the American Negro* (New York: Macmillan, Inc., 1921), p. 9; and Lorenzo J. Greene, *The Negro in Colonial New England* (Port Washington, N.Y.: The Kennikat Press, 1942), pp. 20–21.

ture. And even in the North, there was no cultural basis upon which to establish equality for blacks. Although many northerners had strongly opposed slavery, few were ready to treat blacks as equals or to accept them as competitors for employment. The black sociologist W. E. B. DuBois, who devoted much of his life to the study of his people, concluded: "To the northern masses, the Negro was a curiosity, a subhuman minstrel, willingly and naturally a slave, and treated as well as he deserved to be."[14]

Few blacks left the South after the war. Most simply returned to the fields that they had always known, now as free people but in fact little better off than they had been in slavery. The old paternalistic relationships between planters and field hands had scarcely been disturbed. A system of peonage based upon debt servitude and sharecropping began to spread. The net of economic bondage replaced the chains of slavery.

Gradually, legislative changes in the southern states disenfranchised the blacks, and by the beginning of the twentieth century the policy of "white supremacy" had been firmly established. Poll taxes, literacy tests, property ownership requirements, and other restrictions effectively denied blacks the vote. "Jim Crow" laws sanctioned a rigid pattern of segregation in public and private facilities of all kinds; education of blacks was all but blocked. In general, blacks were assigned a place in the social structure that made them, in effect, a subordinate caste.

One of the most terrifying techniques employed to keep blacks "in their place" was lynching. Blacks were also beaten to death and even burned at the stake. These acts were usually justified by the claim that the black had raped a white woman or killed someone, but typically little care was taken as to whether the person chosen to be punished had actually done the deed. The number of lynchings increased sharply in the South in the 1890s, during the period when most of the laws legalizing white supremacy were passed. There was another flare-up in the 1920s, associated with Ku Klux Klan activity.

The Great Migrations to the "Black Metropolis"

Prior to the First World War, the large northern city held little attraction for black field hands, but the war found northern industries caught in a severe labor shortage, and recruiting agents descended upon the South, urging blacks northward by the tens of thousands. Blacks moved to the industrial centers of the North; those who came early sent for their families and relatives. Even though conditions in these cities were far from ideal, they offered hope of improvement over the grinding toil, social humiliation, and abject poverty the blacks had experienced in the South.

But though black workers were hired in the North, they were not welcomed as neighbors. Black ghettos were established and became desperately crowded. Rents skyrocketed; families doubled up. Pressures to enlarge the "black belts" were resisted, and a new kind of conflict emerged between black and white, exacerbated by the frictions and frustrations of urban life. Minor incidents of violence became increasingly common. Then, as war industries closed and the returning soldiers arrived home, the labor shortage became a labor surplus. As blacks would find repeatedly in the years to come, they were "last hired and first fired."

But blacks were in the northern cities to stay. An educated business and professional stratum emerged, while the flow of the unskilled and poorly educated from the rural South continued. The "Black Metropolis" had become a social reality of American urban life.

During World War II labor shortages in northern industries swelled the stream of black migrants from the South and intensified the race problems in metropolitan areas. Overcrowding, segregation, job ceilings (only lower-status jobs for blacks), discrimination in the armed services, white resentment, and a host of other factors stretched tempers to the breaking point; and race riots flared in northern industrial communities.

14. William E. B. DuBois, *Black Reconstruction in America* (New York: Harcourt Brace Jovanovich, Inc., 1935), p. 60.

The civil rights movement of the late 1950s and early 1960s was based on a philosophy of passive resistance and was aimed primarily at eliminating legal injustices in the South. Marches and demonstrations—like those in 1963 in Selma (top left) and Birmingham (above), Alabama—often met with resistance from whites, but they effectively dramatized the goals of the movement and helped speed the desegregation of public facilities. Later, civil rights workers turned their attention to the cities of the North. In the late 1960s the "black power" movement emphasized economic and political independence and racial pride—though it was taken by some as a call to violence. Despite the numerous successes of the civil rights movement, prejudice and discrimination have not been eradicated. Today the integration of urban schools by "busing" students is a highly controversial issue, and in some northern cities—like Boston (opposite)—it has led to racial violence.

The postwar period saw a great increase in mechanization on southern farms. Machines replaced black field hands in the planting, cultivating, and harvesting of crops. Government agricultural programs and the economic squeeze on farmers created a national trend toward larger and larger farm units. Thus, many rural southern blacks were forced out, and additional thousands of black families migrated to the industrial cities of the North, hoping for good jobs but seldom finding them. As the numbers of urban blacks increased, so too did their frustration and their demands for more jobs, better housing, and a place in the society that economists and advertisers called "affluent."

Civil Rights and Passive Resistance

The initial thrust of the civil rights movement came not from the Black Metropolis in the North but from the South itself. In 1955 a massive boycott by blacks effectively eliminated segregation on city buses in Montgomery, Alabama. From such confrontations emerged the Reverend Martin Luther King, Jr., and other black leaders who sought to achieve rapid social change by nonviolent means. Blacks and sympathetic whites undertook to challenge the system by which public facilities of all kinds were operated on a two-caste basis. Finally, as increasing pressures were applied, the old patterns slowly began to give way. By the mid-1960s the drive for full civil rights for blacks reached national proportions. The Civil Rights Act of 1964 meant that Jim Crow in a formal legal sense was all but dead so far as the voting booth, public facilities, and educational institutions were concerned. Even old laws against interracial marriage were eventually abandoned.

The cost of progress was high. Some civil rights workers were murdered; many more were beaten and abused. At Little Rock, the University of Mississippi, and Birmingham, southern white resentment flared into open aggression. But the civil rights movement itself stuck for the most part to its philosophy of passive resistance and the concept of social justice within the structure of law.

Urban Riots and Black Militancy

The civil rights movement in the South achieved significant legal and social changes. But it did little or nothing to alter the daily struggle for existence of blacks in northern ghettos. It was economic as well as social oppression that triggered the explosion in the Black Metropolis.

Faced with continued poverty, closed opportunity, neighborhood segregation resulting in *de facto* school segregation, substandard housing, and numerous other indignities, the blacks in northern ghettos provided ready audiences for leaders advocating forceful action. Young blacks especially began to reject such ideas as "working within the system," "nonviolent means," "gradualism," and even the concept of "integration." In order to win "freedom now," they argued, black people must separate themselves from the white community and build an independent position of power.

The new "black power" movement was essentially a separatist movement, directed toward such goals as economic and political independence and the reestablishment of racial pride. In this respect it followed the lead of the Black Muslim religious group. But to some it was a call for militant retaliation against the "honkeys." In the mid-1960s the Black Metropolis blew up in the face of incredulous whites. By the end of the decade fire-bombing, looting, and rioting had broken out for short periods in most major cities in the United States, including the nation's capital. Some of the worst violence was set off by the assassination of Martin Luther King, Jr., in 1968.

The urban disorders of the sixties were significantly different from the "race riots" of earlier years. For one thing, they were not primarily physical clashes between particular groups of blacks and whites but rather widespread disorders aimed at the most visible symbols of white society—property, the police, local merchants, and public officials. Black leaders advocating nonviolent approaches to the solution of black problems were sometimes castigated as much as whites.

By the beginning of the 1970s, black violence seemed to have burned itself out. It had called attention to the desperation of the urban black; but it had also destroyed black neighborhoods, and it had stirred up fear and resentment among whites. Congress had gone as far as it was willing to go for the time being. A period of "benign neglect" began. Equality was still a long way off.

The Outlook

The conditions underlying contemporary racial strains have been created by three centuries of racial injustice and by far-reaching economic, political, and demographic change. They are imbedded in a complex of deeply institutionalized and deeply emotional norms among both whites and blacks, norms so complex and so difficult to manipulate that prospects for immediate and complete solution are virtually nonexistent, even assuming improved goodwill on the part of both whites and blacks.

The demographic trends for urban populations are clear: as many as twenty of our principal urban centers may have black majorities by the end of the seventies. As the proportion of black citizens increases in these cities, black public officials will undoubtedly come to play a major role in urban administration. Indeed, during the 1970s politics has become perhaps the major strategy of the civil rights movement. Although political power in the United States is still predominantly a white prerogative, blacks have made significant political gains over the past few years. This has occurred not only in northern cities but also in the "old South," where the black vote has grown enough since the Voting Rights Act of 1965 so that white candidates in increasing numbers are seeking the support of their black constituents. In this respect, black power is slowly becoming a reality.

JEWS

There are more Jews in the United States than in any other country in the world (see Table 9.2), though they account for only about 3 percent of our total population. Historically, the Jews are people of Mediterranean Caucasian origin who have mixed with various ethnic stocks. They have been distinguished from other groups in our society primarily on the basis of religious beliefs, cultural practices, and a strong sense of community with other Jews, both here and abroad.

Jews have been a part of American society since colonial times. The story of their experiences as a minority group in the United States is in many ways unique.

The Immigrant Jew

The history of Jews on the North American continent began in 1654 with the arrival in New Amsterdam (New York) of twenty-three Jewish refugees from Brazil. These first immigrants were Sephardic Jews, whose ancestors had lived in Spain and Portugal and who followed the Spanish Jewish rites. There was a trickle of Jewish immigration from Europe throughout the colonial period, and by the time the United States was created, there were approximately 2500 Jews in the new nation, most of them living in towns and cities along the Atlantic seaboard. Fifty years later their number had swelled to perhaps fifteen thousand.

The first large influx began in the 1840s, as a part of the wave of immigration caused by political and economic difficulties in Europe and the promise of freedom and opportunity in the

Table 9.2. ESTIMATED JEWISH POPULATION BY COUNTRIES

Country	Jewish Population
United States	6,115,000
Israel	2,723,000
Soviet Union	2,648,000
France	550,000
Argentina	500,000
England	410,000
Canada	305,000
Brazil	150,000
Republic of South Africa	117,990
Rumania	90,000
Hungary	80,000
Iran	80,000
Morocco	31,000
All other countries	570,750
Total	14,370,740

SOURCE: *The American Jewish Year Book*, Vol. 74, 1973.

United States. The vast majority of Jewish immigrants were from Germany, especially from southern German towns and villages. By 1880 American Jews numbered a quarter of a million.

The new immigrants took part in America's westward movement, often as traders and peddlers. A considerable number established themselves as pioneer merchants and bankers in the new towns and cities. Many of those who settled in the older urban centers opened stores and factories. Jews played a major role in developing America's ready-made clothing industry. By the late nineteenth century there was hardly a form of business or professional activity in which Jews were not represented.

Then, around 1880, there began the torrent of immigration that was to bring more than two million Jews to the United States within forty years. Again the cause was both positive — America's promise — and negative — Europe's pain. In eastern Europe, particularly in Russia, Poland, and Rumania, persecution of the Jews had reached new heights: entire Jewish communities had to flee for their lives. Unlike earlier Jewish immigrants, these Jews had been isolated from western European culture. American Jews, who felt socially superior to these new arrivals, were concerned that their "foreignness" would cause an increase in anti-Semitism.

Yiddish-speaking and mostly poor, the eastern European Jews settled in ghettolike concentrations in New York and other big eastern cities, often taking menial jobs in firms and factories established by Jews who had come before them.[15] Their settlement patterns tended to perpetuate the cultural traits they had brought from the Old World. They were determined that their children would rise in the New World, and they were convinced that education was the ladder. No American minority has placed greater stress on schooling or benefited more from it.

A fourth and much smaller wave of Jewish immigration occurred from 1936 to 1946 as a result of the Nazi program of Jewish extermination. The social characteristics of the Jews who immigrated at this time tended to be very different from those in the third wave. Most were middle class and well educated; they had fewer problems in adjusting to the new society; and they had less tendency to form neighborhood concentrations within the urban community.

American Jews Today

Although about two-fifths of all the Jews in the United States live in New York City, Jews live in communities both large and small in all parts of the country. Today Jews are distinguishable from other American citizens of the same social rank mainly by their ancient religious and cultural heritage and by very little else.[16]

In the process of assimilation, there has been a de-emphasis of traditional and orthodox religious forms that once were an important basis of Jewish unity and that preserved a sense of apartness from the general society. Increasingly, the daily lives of most Jews have become secularized. But most still retain an active psychological identification with their religious and ethnic origins.[17]

American Jews tend to feel a strong bond of sympathy, identification, and kinship with their coreligionists abroad. The horrors of the Nazi exterminations greatly reinforced these feelings and created among many Jews a special emotional frame of reference concerning the state of Israel. As the first national homeland for Jews since they were dispersed from the ancient land of Canaan (roughly the site of modern Israel) by the Romans in the first century A.D., it is regarded as a haven that must be preserved.

There have been periods of virulent anti-Semitism in the United States. The 1920s saw a wave of prejudice and discrimination develop, in part as a reflection of the anti-Jewish feeling being generated in Europe during a period of political and economic crisis. In some parts of the United States, restrictive covenants in real estate contracts were used to keep Jews out of certain residential areas. Jews were also denied access to hotels and restaurants in some parts of the country, and a number of colleges and universities had quotas for Jews. They were system-

15. Gordon, *Assimilation in American Life,* p. 185.
16. Ibid., p. 190; see also Marshall Sklare, ed., *The Jews: Social Patterns of an American Group* (New York: The Free Press, 1958).
17. Herbert J. Gans, "American Jewry: Present and Future," *Commentary,* 21, No. 5 (May 1956): 422–430.

atically excluded from numerous organizations and occupations.

For the most part, the more open forms of discrimination have disappeared. Aiding in the fight against discrimination have been such organizations as the American Jewish Committee, the American Jewish Congress, and the Anti-Defamation League of B'nai B'rith, all of which have been aggressive in forcing an end to restrictive covenants, quotas, and other formal systems of exclusion. Today, both prejudice and discrimination against Jews appear to be declining, thanks in part to legal reforms, such as the outlawing of restrictive covenants. The dropping of quotas and the lessening of job discrimination have been accompanied by an increasing assimilation of Jews into the cultural, social, and economic mainstreams of American society, even though undeniable forms of discrimination remain in some areas (e.g., in the "executive suites" of the banking and insurance industries) and latent hostilities are still widespread.

SPANISH-SURNAMED MINORITIES

The United States has over six million Spanish-surnamed people within its borders. These Americans are not a single cultural group but rather several distinct minorities who came to this country at different times from different places under widely varying conditions. There are substantial individual differences in class, status, and power within the various Spanish-surnamed minorities, but the majority share at least some of the disadvantages of structured inequality.

18. Carey McWilliams, *North from Mexico* (Philadelphia: J. B. Lippincott Co., 1949); for a more recent exposition of the problem of the Mexican Americans in the Southwest, see Julian Samora, ed., *La Raza: The Forgotten Americans* (South Bend, Ind.: University of Notre Dame Press, 1966).

19. The term *Chicano* apparently developed as a shortened form of *Mexicano*. Originally a derogatory term used primarily by Anglos, it has been adopted as a symbol of pride by Mexican Americans in their struggle to escape minority status. See Renato Rosaldo, Gustav L. Seligmann, and Robert A. Calvert, eds., *Chicano: The Beginnings of Bronze Power* (New York: William Morrow & Co., Inc., 1974).

20. Helen Rowan, "A Minority Nobody Knows," *The Atlantic,* June 1967, p. 47. See also John H. Burma, *Spanish-Speaking Groups in the United States* (Durham, N.C.: Duke University Press, 1954); and Burma, ed., *Mexican Americans in the United States* (Cambridge, Mass.: Schenkman Publishing Co., 1970).

Hispanos

The oldest segment of Spanish-surnamed people in the United States is made up of the so-called Hispanos of the Southwest—descendants of the Spaniards who occupied that region before New England was first settled.[18] In 1848, following the Mexican War, Mexico ceded a vast area to the United States, including what are now the states of California, Nevada, and Utah, most of Arizona and New Mexico, and parts of Colorado and Wyoming. Under the terms of the Treaty of Guadalupe Hidalgo, American citizenship was granted to those in the area who wished to remain on their land. Most elected to stay, and their descendants now constitute about half a million people. The largest proportion resides in New Mexico and until recently has tended to remain in somewhat isolated rural villages.

As a result of their way of life, most of the Hispanos of the Southwest have not undergone the assimilation that might have been expected, considering that they were the earliest of the Spanish-surnamed groups to become citizens. Their isolation has also meant that they have encountered little formal discrimination.

Chicanos

The largest group of Spanish-surnamed Americans is composed of citizens of Mexican birth or descent. There are almost five million Chicanos now living in this country, most of them in the states along the Mexican border, in Colorado, and in California.[19] The great majority are unskilled or semiskilled workers, and the group as a whole suffers serious discrimination. According to one writer, Mexican Americans in the Southwest are "worse off in every respect than the nonwhites (Negroes, Indians, and Orientals), not to mention the dominant Anglos (everybody else)."[20]

Today, there is growing impatience and militance among Chicanos. On the one hand, there is the desire to merge with the dominant group. Some studies indicate that second- and third-generation Mexican Americans are undergoing rapid assimilation. In Los Angeles, for example, Mexican Americans are marrying out of their ethnic community to a much greater extent than ever before.[21] At the same time, there are movements to unite the Chicanos, to teach them pride in their own culture and family organization, and to win them a better position in American society.

The Chicano cause was highlighted in the 1960s by the struggle of Cesar Chavez to organize the migrant workers of the Southwest and California. He gathered considerable support from religious leaders and some of the major labor unions, as well as from a surprising number of middle Americans.[22] Chavez's farm-labor movement was an important catalyst for improving the condition of the Chicanos and making society more sensitive to their problems.

Puerto Ricans

A third Spanish-surnamed minority has come from the island of Puerto Rico, which the United States acquired at the close of the Spanish American War in 1898. Puerto Ricans have been American citizens since 1917 and may come to the mainland as they wish. Following World War II, migration to the United States from Puerto Rico rose sharply as Puerto Ricans took the jobs formerly filled by European immigrants in New York and New England factories. According to the 1970 census, there were about 1,500,000 persons of Puerto Rican birth or parentage on the mainland. The largest numbers remain concentrated in New York City, but many have now settled in other areas. For those Puerto Ricans who are darkskinned (some are blue-eyed blondes), acceptance in the United States has been complicated by the traditionally strong patterns of prejudice and discrimination against blacks.[23]

Puerto Ricans tend to come to the mainland in good times and return to the island in times of recession.[24] With their mixed racial characteristics and their continuing close ties to their homeland added to the barrier of language, the Puerto Ricans have had a particularly difficult time finding a place in the dominant society.

Heavy concentration in urban ghettos has created many problems in education, employment, and cultural contact both for them and for their communities. Though a few Puerto Ricans have managed to escape the ghetto, the institutionalized structures of poor housing, poor schools, poor health care, and low-skill, poor-paying jobs make it likely that change will be slow.

Cubans

Changes in the political and socioeconomic structure of Cuba following Castro's take-over in 1959 have produced a steady influx of Cuban refugees into the United States. The 1970 census reported more than half a million Cubans in this country, and the number has continued to grow. Many Cuban immigrants consider themselves exiles and retain hope that they will some day return to their own country. In recent years, however, increasing numbers have become American citizens.

The experiences of this new American minority group have been in many ways unique. Unlike most immigrants to the United States, the great majority of Cuban refugees enjoyed middle- or upper-class positions in their native land. Almost all of them have been well educated. But like other immigrants, Cubans newly arrived in the United States found themselves relegated to the lower ranks of the socioeconomic hierarchy. Many were forced to accept low-level jobs, and practically all suffered a loss of status—despite the fact that Americans tended to be very sympathetic to their anti-Castro cause.

In less than two decades, the situation of the Cuban minority in the United States has changed dramatically. About 400,000 Cubans have settled in Miami and surrounding areas of

21. Frank G. Mittelbach, Joan W. Moore, and Ronald McDaniel, "Intermarriage of Mexican-Americans," Advance Report 6, Division of Research, Graduate School of Business Administration, University of California at Los Angeles (November 1966); and Leo Grebler, Joan W. Moore, and Ralph C. Guzman, *The Mexican American People* (New York: The Free Press, 1970).

22. John Howard, "Mexican-Americans: The Road to Huelga," in John Howard, ed., *Awakening Minorities* (New Brunswick, N.J.: Transaction Books, 1972), pp. 89ff.

23. C. Wright Mills, Clarence Senior, and Rose Goldsen, *The Puerto Rican Journey* (New York: Harper & Row, Inc., 1950).

24. John Howard, "Puerto Ricans: The Making of a Minority Group," in Howard, ed., *Awakening Minorities*, pp. 123ff.

As Cuban refugees have begun to attain economic success, they have turned Miami into a bilingual city. Miami will be a testing ground for cultural pluralism as Cuban and Anglo residents try to work out the intergroup tensions created in part by their cultural differences.

Dade County, where they now make up more than a third of the total population; in Miami itself, they have become a slight numerical majority. These Cuban immigrants have succeeded in transplanting the culture of their homeland to Florida almost intact, establishing a large and prosperous ethnic enclave in downtown Miami known as Little Havana. And they have also succeeded in "making it" on American terms. Over 8000 businesses in Dade County are owned by Cubans; several banks have Cuban presidents; and about a fourth of Cuban families have incomes of over $15,000 a year.[25] In 1974 the Dade County Commission proclaimed metropolitan Miami to be officially bilingual and bicultural.

But success has brought problems of its own, causing resentment among many longtime Anglo residents. As one Cuban leader expressed it, "Before, the Cubans were competing for low-level jobs. Now they're competing for the job of bank president, corporation executive, even mayor. We are starting to step on toes."[26] Some Anglo residents of the Miami area are less distressed by the economic competition Cubans pose than by cultural differences. A white Miamian expressed the feelings of many Anglos

in complaining, "I don't even know what the store signs say, and the people refuse to speak anything but Spanish. This is *our* country. Why should I have to learn Spanish?"[27]

A growing number of Americans have come to believe that cultural pluralism should replace assimilation as the preferred pattern of intergroup relations in the United States—that racial and ethnic groups should be allowed an equal chance in American society without being expected to submerge their separate identities. Largely through historical accident, Miami has become a testing ground for this ideal.

ORIENTALS

Of the various Oriental minority groups in the United States, the Chinese and the Japanese are most well known. The largest concentrations of both Chinese and Japanese are along the Pacific Coast and in Hawaii. Their histories are dissimilar except in one respect: both have suffered severe persecutions at the hands of white Americans.

The Chinese

The Chinese began to arrive in large numbers in the middle of the last century, during the gold rush boom on the West Coast. Later, Chinese "coolie" labor was imported to help build the

25. "La Saguesera: Miami's Little Havana," *Time*, October 14, 1974, p. 24.
26. "Backlash in Miami," *Newsweek*, March 17, 1975, pp. 29, 32.
27. Ibid., p. 32.

During the late 1800s San Francisco was the scene of bitter anti-Chinese feelings as white laborers found themselves in economic competition with Chinese workers.

first transcontinental railroads.[28] Because there were few women in the West, the Chinese also took over such tasks as washing and cooking; the Chinese laundry and the Chinese restaurant, so familiar in urban America, resulted from this adaptation.

After construction of the railroads was complete, many white workers on the West Coast found themselves competing directly with cheap Chinese labor. The result was a wave of bitter anti-Chinese feeling. During the late 1800s the Chinese were beaten, burned out, stoned, kicked in the streets, and otherwise harassed until many returned to China. Eighteen were lynched in a single race riot in Los Angeles in 1871. Most of the Chinese who remained in this country withdrew to enclaves in urban centers where they could insulate themselves from American society and retain their own cultural patterns.[29]

The Chinese Exclusion Act of 1882 ended Chinese immigration for ten years, and it was not allowed to resume. California enacted numerous laws that denied the Chinese access to schools, jobs, and property. Only since World War II have these discriminatory laws been declared unconstitutional. Today the Chinese are increasingly respected for their achievements in business, the sciences, and the arts. Until the recent revival of Chinese immigration gave them new life,[30] the old "Chinatowns" were tending to disappear.

The Japanese

Japanese immigration into the United States reached substantial numbers only around the beginning of the present century. Just prior to World War II about 90 percent of the Japanese in the United States were concentrated along the Pacific Coast, with the majority in California.[31] From the start, they felt the impact of the same prejudices that had been directed against the Chinese. Legislation and many informal practices were quickly established to exclude the new group from schools, the labor force, and other areas of social life. President Theodore Roosevelt was able to persuade San Francisco to admit Japanese children to white schools only by securing a "Gentlemen's Agreement" whereby Japan agreed to block the emigration of unskilled workers. Japanese immigration was stopped by federal law in 1924. With other Orientals, the Japanese were regarded by the white majority as a "yellow peril" that somehow threatened the American way of life. In fact, the cultural values the Japanese brought to America made them a frugal, hard-working people who established family farms and businesses and who were upwardly mobile in the manner strongly approved by the American value system.

When Pearl Harbor was bombed in 1941, a wave of anti-Japanese hysteria overwhelmed the

28. B. Schrieke, *Alien Americans* (New York: The Viking Press, Inc., 1936), pp. 8–10.

29. David Te-chao Cheng, *Acculturation of the Chinese in the United States* (Philadelphia: University of Pennsylvania Press, 1948).

30. Between 1960 and 1970 the Chinese-American population increased by 90 percent, from 230,000 to 435,000, largely as a result of immigration.

31. James W. Vander Zanden, *American Minority Relations*, 2nd ed. (New York: The Ronald Press Company, 1966), p. 259.

During World War II the Japanese experienced an extreme form of segregation in the United States; more than 100,000 persons were evacuated from their homes and forced to live in war relocation camps.

United States. Americans of Japanese ancestry, most of whom lived along the West Coast, were suddenly considered security risks and potential traitors. Early in 1942 it was decided to evacuate all Japanese Americans from the Coast and place them in internment camps in the interior. Over 100,000 people of Japanese extraction, about two-thirds of whom were American citizens, were forced to sell—or abandon—their

homes, farms, and businesses and live in government-controlled camps for the duration of the war or else leave the country.[32] After the war, Japanese Americans could not easily pick up their former pursuits, and many never returned to the West Coast. Their dispersion to various other parts of the country has perhaps hastened their assimilation into the mainstream of American society. In any case, Japanese Americans have enjoyed an increasing measure of acceptance in recent years.

32. Leonard Broom and Ruth Reimer, *Removal and Return* (Berkeley: University of California Press, 1949), pp. 202–204.

VIEWPOINTS INDIAN VIEWS ON INDIAN MILITANCY

■ The great danger in the gathering Indian movement is that urban Indians will allow themselves to be betrayed by reservation entanglements. Because of the pressure on reservation communities by terminationists in the Senate, reservation people have been on the defensive for a decade and a half. Their first inclination is to view a proposal in terms of its possible detrimental effect on their communities.

There is an added danger to urban Indians from their involvement with the militants of other minority groups, particularly the black power people. . . . Young Indians are talking like black militants and beginning to ape their ideas and techniques. Participation in the Poor People's March gave additional impetus toward development of red power movements.

By and large, blacks have rioted and marched for undefined objectives. Cries of "Freedom now!" have provided very little understanding of problems or solutions. Indians who copy blacks simply because they are attracted by the chance to make their names household words are embarking on a disastrous course of action.

For Indians to walk the steps of the black militants would be a disaster. The problems of Indians have always been ideological rather than social, political, or economic. Simply to invite violence upon oneself for the sake of temporary concessions seems ridiculous and stupid.

It would be fairly easy, however, with a sufficient number of articulate young Indians and well-organized community support, to greatly influence the thinking of the nation within a few years. The white man asks only the opportunity to chase the almighty dollar. Whoever can take the burden of thinking from him is worshipped and praised beyond belief.

So, it is vitally important that the Indian people pick the intellectual arena as the one in which to wage war. Past events have shown that the Indian people have always been fooled about the intentions of the white man. Always we have discussed irrelevant issues while he has taken the land. Never have we taken the time to examine the premises upon which he operates so that we could manipulate him as he has us.

Vine Deloria, Jr.
Custer Died for Your Sins

● History will record for us one simple fact— that the longest undeclared war is not Vietnam (where we have lost loved ones), but the longest undeclared war has been against the American Indian. Since 1492, we have been at war. . . . We have suffered a casualty figure of over two and one-half million men, women, and children. Actual declared wars in the United States against Indian tribes have cost one and one-half million lives. Another form of war—hunger, suicide, poverty, disease, the Trail of Tears, Wounded Knee, Sand Creek—we have lost another million. Officially, the Indian wars are over. But, unofficially, the casualties continue to mount. We suffer today from the highest infant mortality rate. You know it. You know these figures. For every non-Indian baby born that lives, three Indian babies die. We suffer from the highest unemployment figure ever. Not the 40 or 50 percent that some people believe, but a figure approaching 65 percent. Suicide and malnutrition still exist in some areas. But this war against us cannot and must not be allowed to continue. . . . Today it is us who must now declare the war, war against the conditions that are caused by poverty, racial discrimination, malnutrition, hunger, and alcoholism, but most importantly, the national anti-Indian attitudes and laws that promote these conditions. These are the laws and conditions that we must attack. This is the war that we've got to get involved in. Let it be known today that those same thoughts which ran through Chief Joseph, Sitting Bull, Crazy Horse, Geronimo, are with us today. Let every non-Indian institution know, let every state in the union know, let every non-Indian government know, whether they are friend or enemy, that today a cooperative effort was born, that this union of Indian tribes and Indian people will never, never again take a back seat to anyone, regardless of their race, color, or creed. Let America know that its racist exploitation of Indian people and Indian lands must cease and efforts to rectify past injustices must commence immediately. We are the original people. We are the landlords of this country and America must be put on notice that it's the first of the month and the American Indian is coming for the rent.

Dennis Banks
Speech to National Congress of American Indians

NATIVE AMERICANS

Historically, no minority in the United States has suffered greater injustice than American Indians, whose ancestors had been established on this continent for many centuries before whites came. The Indians encountered by the invading whites did not share a single culture. The various tribes had their own distinctive life-styles, well adapted to their particular needs and to the particular areas in which they lived. These Native Americans were little attracted to European culture with its monotheistic religion and its seeming obsession with private property and technology. But the culture of the invaders enveloped and overwhelmed them nonetheless.

Today there are some 800,000 Native Americans in the United States, most of them living under conditions of poverty which, because of geographical isolation, have gone largely unnoticed. The majority are still faced with the dilemma of how best to relate to the society of their conquerors.[33] This dilemma has been compounded by the fact that white America has held widely divergent—and frequently changing—views concerning Indian-white relations. Opinion became divided almost as soon as exploration and settlement of the New World began. Some whites wanted to educate and "civilize" the Indians according to European standards; others wanted to leave them alone; and still others demanded that they be wiped out. Official policies of the federal government since our nation's founding have at one time or another reflected variations on all these views.[34]

The first government policy was to move Indians off lands wanted by white settlers, which often involved killing them off. Then Indians were concentrated on restricted hunting grounds, and finally they were forced onto reservations—again, with bloodshed as the alternative. As the Indians, now wards of the government, settled

American Indians have long been the victims of extreme forms of discrimination, and the indications of their suffering are still appalling. The life expectancy of an Indian, for example, is twenty-seven years less than that of a white American, and an Indian family living on a reservation—as many do—has an annual income far below the government-designated poverty limit.

33. Daisnke Kitagawa, "The American Indian," in Arnold M. Rose and Caroline B. Rose, eds., *Minority Problems: A Textbook of Readings in Intergroup Relations* (New York: Harper & Row, Inc., 1965), p. 26.

34. For the Indian version of an important chapter in American history, see Dee Brown, *Bury My Heart at Wounded Knee* (New York: Holt, Rinehart and Winston, Inc., 1971), which describes westward expansion through the eyes of its victims. See also Brewton Berry, *Race and Ethnic Relations*, 3rd ed. (Boston: Houghton Mifflin Co., 1965), pp. 233–241.

down within the confines established by the whites, attempts were made to break up tribal organizations and to bring about "Americanization" through schooling of the young and suppression of tribal customs.

Government policy over the last hundred years has reflected a continuing uncertainty as to how the problem of Indian-white relations can best be resolved. In the late 1880s the government attempted to promote assimilation by adopting a policy that encouraged the breaking up of tribal lands into individual holdings; then, in the 1930s, efforts were made to restore communal holdings so that Indians could maintain their traditional cultures. During the 1950s assimilation was promoted; in the 1970s, partly because of the heightened sense of self-determination of Native Americans, government policy is marked by ambivalence and confusion.

Today there are more than two hundred reservations in the United States, established for various tribes through special treaties with the federal government. Among those individuals who have left their reservations and moved to cities, some have given up their traditional culture, whereas others have sought to maintain at least a semblance of tribal customs and organization in their new surroundings. Some Indian groups, particularly in the Southwest, still retain many elements of their ancient heritage. But a great many Indians feel divorced both from their own cultural roots and from the dominant culture of contemporary American society.

In recent years Indians have joined other minority groups in the United States in demanding that the structure of intergroup relations be changed. But though change is in the wind, the direction it will take remains unclear. Whites concerned with eliminating patronizing and discriminatory policies toward Indians cannot seem to agree on either goals or means. Nor is there a consensus among Indians themselves. Is assimilation or pluralism the preferred pattern, and how can either pattern be achieved? Indians are divided into traditionalists, conservatives, gradualists, and militants — each favoring somewhat different programs and strategies for achieving the ultimate goal of acceptance on equal terms.

PATTERNS OF CONFLICT AND ACCOMMODATION

The history of American minorities makes clear that there are many possible patterns of relationship between dominant and minority groups, and that relationships are likely to change over time. At one point tensions may flare into open conflict; at another, some new mode of accommodation may evolve.

Initially at least, the structure of intergroup relations is shaped mainly by the dominant group — that is, what happens to the minority is in many respects a result of policies adopted, either formally or informally, by those in political, economic, and social control. The relationship initiated by a dominant group can range all the way from an attempt to exterminate a minority to a policy of "live and let live." In American society, the dominant group has usually taken a position somewhere between these extremes — discriminating against minorities while also encouraging them to shed cultural differences in order to become "more acceptable."

Whatever the policy of the dominant group, the structure of intergroup relations becomes fully established only with the minority's response. The members of a minority group may resign themselves to discriminatory treatment or may employ various active strategies for improving their relative position in the society. Similarly, they may either welcome or reject opportunities for becoming assimilated into the dominant group.

When particular members of a minority group band together in an organization, their behavior becomes truly *group* behavior, and in this context their response to minority position may become more clearly defined. Some of the organizations formed by minority-group members are primarily defensive: the NAACP and the Urban League, for example, are collective efforts to protect blacks from injustice. Other organizations, like the Raza Unida party of the Chicanos, are basically political, seeking the election of candidates who will work for the interests of the minority. Still others may develop as separatist movements, like the Black Muslims. All such organizations may play some part in shaping the complex structure of intergroup relations. At the very least, they give focus to feelings of "we" and "they."

In the following sections we will examine four characteristic patterns of relationship between dominant and minority groups: aggression, exclusion, assimilation, and pluralism.

AGGRESSION

In its most extreme form, aggression by a dominant group may be directed toward wiping out a minority. At the end of the nineteenth century, for example, thousands of Armenians were slaughtered by the Turks. In the history of European colonial expansion, aboriginal peoples often were simply annihilated. The Spanish slaughtered the Indians of southern Argentina in systematic military campaigns; the English in Tasmania hunted the aborigines for sport and for dog food;[35] whites in North America wiped out a number of important Indian tribes, particularly along the Atlantic seaboard.

Except during the Indian wars, American minority groups have seldom employed the strategy of open aggression. Although rebellious slaves were numerous in the antebellum South, only a few slave revolts involved significant numbers. But in the 1960s some American blacks became convinced that they had to fight for their rights. Indeed, some came to believe that blacks faced annihilation unless they fought back—that they had to fight to survive.

More typically, however, aggression by either a dominant or minority group is not fully open or direct. For example, intergroup antagonisms are often expressed through *symbolic* aggression: the dominant group maintains a culture of jokes, epithets, and other symbolic devices that perpetuate its prejudices against the minority; the minority develops its own jokes, epithets, and other verbal means of ridiculing or denigrating the dominant group. An old example is the black's use of "ofay" to refer to a white.

Another way of acting out one's hostilities is through *covert* aggression. In the United States members of the dominant group have used it to circumvent civil rights legislation. For example, whites may obey the letter of the law by serving black customers but provide such slow, reluctant, rude, or inferior service that the customers are made perfectly aware that they are unwelcome. On the other side, members of the minority may use covert aggression to avoid overt retaliation. As employees of the dominant group, they may deliberately do poor work and do it in such a way that they can be accused of no more than clumsiness or stupidity. During the period of slavery, blacks sometimes mutilated themselves so that they could neither work for their white masters nor be sold.

EXCLUSION AND AVOIDANCE

As noted earlier in this chapter, policies of exclusion can range from imposition of rigid spatial limits on the movements of a minority (as in ghettos, reservations, concentration camps, or other special areas) to the use of discriminatory practices that exclude the minority group from full participation in societal life. In the United States, all the principal minorities have been excluded to a greater or lesser degree from equal access to employment, education, housing, and political life. Some have been refused admission to trains and buses, restaurants, swimming pools, theaters, parks, and even churches. While many overt forms of discrimination have been declared illegal in recent years, many other types of exclusion continue to be practiced, particularly those that result from informal policies and are not subject to regulation by the law. A comparison of the white and nonwhite populations in the United States with respect to housing, income, and other indices of stratification makes it clear that, despite progress, we have not come close to realizing the American ideal of equal opportunity for all citizens (Table 9.3, page 262).

Policies of segregation practiced by the dominant group may result in efforts by minority groups to avoid contact with those who treat them as inferiors. While intergroup contacts are extremely difficult to avoid completely in a society like ours, many individual members of mi-

35. George P. Murdock, *Our Primitive Contemporaries* (New York: Macmillan, Inc., 1934), pp. 16–18.

nority groups attempt to minimize them. This may mean choosing not to enter a restaurant or store where there is any possibility of being rebuffed. Or it may mean general avoidance, such as choosing to live and work in a neighborhood inhabited chiefly by members of one's own group.

Efforts toward insulation may also take the form of collective avoidance, through migration or through separatist social movements. From the end of the nineteenth century, for example, many European and American Jews participated in the Zionist movement; their goal was to establish a nation of Israel, where all Jews would be free of persecution. A little-known example of a collective attempt at separatism was that of former planters and plantation owners of the Confederacy who emigrated to the Belem region of Brazil after the Civil War in an attempt to reestablish the kind of society they had had in the antebellum South. Among American blacks, "back-to-Africa" movements have had relatively little support, but a significant number of writers, artists, and musicians avoid American forms of discrimination by living in Europe. Other examples of separatism among American minorities include the Black Muslims, who preach and practice separation, some Indian tribes that try to keep contacts with whites to a minimum, and a number of white religious sects—for example, the Amish—that avoid "worldly" society.

ASSIMILATION

Our national motto *E Pluribus Unum* ("one out of many") expresses not only the concept of a federal union forged out of separate states but also the ideal of American society as a "melting pot"—a society in which people from different origins gradually blend their differences, forming in the process a new people. Until fairly recently it was widely assumed that this was, in fact, how the American system worked. Successive waves of immigrants have become assimilated into American society, while that society has adopted foods, words, musical forms, art styles, and other cultural elements brought from other lands.

But there has been a growing recognition that assimilation is largely a one-way street. Although it is premised on a commitment to equality for all people, it works only if minorities are willing to accept the values, beliefs, and norms of the dominant group as somehow superior to their own. Those minority group members who have merged into the mainstream of American life have done so by shedding cultural

Table 9.3. COMPARISON OF SOCIAL AND ECONOMIC CONDITIONS OF WHITES AND NONWHITES IN THE UNITED STATES, 1960 AND 1970

Index of stratification	1960 White	1960 Nonwhite	1970 White	1970 Nonwhite
Place of residence				
Percent living in central cities	30	51	28	56
Percent lacking some or all plumbing facilities	12	41	5	17
Education				
Percent of males 25–29 years old having completed 4 or more years of high school	63	36	79	54
Employment				
Unemployment rate	4.9	10.2	4.5	8.2
Percent of male workers with white-collar jobs	39.1	12.7	43.1	21.7
Income				
Median family income of nonwhites as percent of median family income of whites	—	55	—	64

*In 1970 dollars
SOURCES: *Social and Economic Status of the Black Population in the United States, 1971,* Current Population Reports, Series P–23, No. 42, U.S. Department of Commerce; *Handbook of Labor Statistics, 1971,* U.S. Department of Labor, p. 57; *Statistical Abstract of the United States, 1972,* p. 322.

Many minority group members have attempted to become assimilated into American society; they have met with varying degrees of success.

differences and learning the rules of the game as Anglo-America has defined them. Usually the process of assimilation has taken two or three generations to complete.

Minority group members in the United States have had mixed feelings about cultural assimilation. For some, assimilation has represented an opportunity to escape prejudice and discrimination and to "get ahead." A great many white ethnics have changed their difficult "foreign" names or ceased to profess the "foreign" faith of their forebears. Similarly, some "nonwhite" Americans have chosen to deny their racial heritage.

But while complete assimilation has been the goal of many minority group members, others have been fiercely opposed to the idea of losing their racial or ethnic identity. Furthermore, as we have attempted to show throughout this chapter, American society is not fully open to minority group members even if they are willing to play by the dominant group's rules. It is true that millions of individuals have become assimilated and merged with the dominant group, but it is equally true that millions of others have not. The latter category includes not only persons with "black," "brown," "red," and "yellow" skins but also a great many whites, including Jews, Italians, Polish, Irish, and members of more than fifty other identifiable ethnic groups now residing in the United States. Many of these people have desired assimilation and failed to achieve it. Others have remained apart by choice.[36]

PLURALISM

Although the various minority groups in the United States have always maintained distinctive subcultures, these subcultures have been

36. The traditional concept of the United States as a melting pot was first challenged in Nathan Glazer and Daniel P. Moynihan, *Beyond the Melting Pot,* (Cambridge, Mass.: The M.I.T. Press, 1963; 2nd ed., 1970). See also Andrew M. Greeley, *Why Can't They Be Like Us?* (New York: E. P. Dutton & Co., Inc., 1971); Harold J. Abramson, *Ethnic Diversity in Catholic America* (New York: John Wiley & Sons, Inc., 1973); Newman, *American Pluralism;* and Michael Novak *The Rise of the Unmeltable Ethnics* (New York: Macmillan, Inc., 1971).

In recent years numerous ethnic groups have rejected the idea of a "melting pot" society and have expressed renewed interest in their own cultures. Among the many manifestations of this renewed consciousness has been an increase in ethnic celebrations in cities across the United States, including Greek-American (left) and Polish-American (right) parades.

largely ignored by the dominant segment of society. And when not ignored, they usually have been negatively valued. But the movements of racial and ethnic assertion that began in the late 1960s have forced Americans to take a more realistic look at their "melting pot" society and their habits of penalizing people who don't fit the dominant mold. More and more people have come to argue that pluralism, not assimilation, is the ideal—that minority group members should be able to enjoy full access to the benefits of American society without having to merge into the cultural mainstream.

As ideology, pluralism has gained broad support: cultural diversity is now increasingly seen as a positive value, not something to be "melted away." But it remains to be demonstrated whether the ideology can be translated into social reality, and if so, by what means. An important challenge to social scientists will be helping to identify the conditions under which peoples with differing cultural orientations can coexist on equal terms in the same community or society.

PREJUDICE

Individuals acquire attitudes of prejudice and habits of discrimination in much the same way that they acquire tastes in music and habits of eating and dressing. All are products of socialization, and all reflect cultural and subcultural norms. No one is "born prejudiced," and no one is prejudiced "in general." We internalize the particular patterns of prejudice that are normative in our own social environment.[37]

Viewing individual prejudice as a reflection of cultural and subcultural norms helps us understand how people sometimes become prejudiced against the members of given minority groups even though they have little or no direct contact with them. And it also helps us understand how members of different minority groups become prejudiced against each other. As participants in American society, Orientals may learn

37. See Howard J. Ehrlich, *The Social Psychology of Prejudice* (New York: John Wiley & Sons, Inc., 1973), pp. 5–8.

to become prejudiced against blacks, blacks may learn to become prejudiced against Jews, and Jews may learn to become prejudiced against Italians and Poles. Exposure to cultural norms may even cause minority group members to become prejudiced against themselves. Research has indicated that black children of pre-school age are already aware that their color and racial characteristics are negatively evaluated by most people in their society.[38] The black power movement has done much to reduce self-devaluation among blacks, but it is doubtful that a feeling of in-group pride can fully counter the effects of being reminded every day in countless ways that much of society considers you inferior.

THE ORIGINS OF PREJUDICIAL NORMS

Cultural norms related to racial and ethnic minorities develop as other kinds of norms develop. In some cases it is possible to trace their specific point of invention; in other cases they seem to have been borrowed from other societies; in still other cases their origins are obscure.

A society in which people with different racial and ethnic identities must compete with each other for scarce resources offers a fertile site for the development of prejudices. In fact, some social scientists maintain that groups ''invent'' prejudices explicitly for the purpose of gaining or maintaining economic or political dominance. Over time, such prejudices tend to become institutionalized as a part of the general culture and begin to play a part in the socialization of the next generation.

In our discussion of the Chinese minority in American society, we reviewed a specific instance of prejudice rising out of competition. During a time of economic crisis, substantial segments of the white population of the Pacific Coast found themselves in direct competition for jobs with immigrants from the Orient. In the struggle the Chinese became the objects of intense prejudice and discrimination. Economic

Typically, parents and peers indoctrinate children in the prevailing prejudices and patterns of discrimination that exist in their community. Thus individuals can easily learn to be prejudiced against the members of a minority group even though they have little or no actual contact with them.

competition also helps explain hostilities between working-class whites and blacks in contemporary American society.

The hypothesis that intergroup competition may stimulate the development of prejudice receives indirect support from evidence that, in the absence of competition, unlike groups have often lived together without developing mutual antipathies. Ralph Linton has described the historical situation of the Puyallup Indians of the Puget Sound region of the present state of Washington.

38. Kenneth B. Clark and Mamie P. Clark, ''Racial Identification and Preference in Negro Children,'' in *Readings in Social Psychology*, 3rd ed., ed. Eleanor Maccoby, Theodore Newcomb, and Eugene Hartley (New York: Holt, Rinehart and Winston, Inc., 1958), pp. 602–611.

TOOLS OF SOCIOLOGY
MEASURING ATTITUDES　Alan C. Acock

An important part of studying attitudes is measuring them. One of the methods used is a procedure first developed by Rensis Likert, called a Likert scale.

In using a Likert scale, the researcher first defines the *attitude object.* For example, if we wish to measure people's attitudes toward interracial marriage, we might define the attitude object as marriage between a black and a white. Then we must define the *target population,* the group or category whose attitudes will be studied—for example, unmarried, white college students in the United States. An attitude scale developed for a specific population cannot be applied to a different population, for members of the second group might not understand the questions in exactly the same way as did members of the original group.

The purpose of the scale is to locate people on a *continuum* of very favorable to very unfavorable attitudes toward the attitude object. Such a continuum might look like this:

Jane	Bill	Dick	Tom	Sue
↓	↓	↓	↓	↓
Very Unfavorable	Unfavorable	Neutral or Don't Know	Favorable	Very Favorable

Here, Sue has the most favorable attitudes and Jane the least, while the others fall in between.

People are located on the continuum on the basis of their answers to a series of questions. Many researchers develop three kinds of questions: *cognitive* questions, those concerning what people think or know about the attitude object, even though their ideas may reflect biases; *behavioral* questions, which concern predispositions to act favorably or unfavorably toward the attitude object; and *affective* questions, which concern emotional reactions to the attitude object—liking, hating, and so on.

In Likert scales, people are asked to indicate the *strength* of their agreement or disagreement with each statement by circling the response that best indicates how they feel: Strongly Agree, Agree, Neutral or Don't Know, Disagree, Strongly Disagree:

Cognitive: I think interracial marriage
　causes a lot of problems for the chidren.
　SA　A　NDK　D　SD
Behavioral: I would invite an interracial
　married couple to dinner.
　SA　A　NDK　D　SD
Affective: I am repulsed by a married couple
　that are not of the same race.
　SA　A　NDK　D　SD

A response of SD for the first question indicates a favorable attitude, as does a response of SA for the second question and SD for the third.

In constructing a Likert scale, researchers avoid questions that all members of the target population would answer in the same way; such questions would not differentiate among people on the attitude continuum. They ask as many questions as possible—without making the questionnaire overly long. Researchers also *pretest* the questionnaire in order to find out how respondents interpret each question and to see if they agree that the answers (SA, SD, etc.) indicate positive or negative attitudes.

Often, some questions can be interpreted in a different way than is intended. To overcome this problem, researchers include a number of cognitive, behavioral, and affective questions, so that ambiguities about individual questions are cancelled out.

After the questionnaire is administered to the target population, the answers to each question are scored, with a one (1) being given to the most negative response category and a five (5) to the most positive. Each respondent's attitude score is obtained by adding up the points earned on each question. The higher the total, the more favorable the attitude. This method has been proven very reliable in ordering the respondents along an attitude continuum.

For more information on Likert's procedure, see Nigel Lemon, *Attitudes and Their Measurement* (New York: John Wiley & Sons, Inc., 1973), esp. pp. 177–182.

When whites first began to settle the region in small numbers, the settlers and the Indians developed a harmonious and mutually advantageous relationship. Indians worked for the whites and were treated fairly. There was mutual respect. In the absence of white women, many settlers legally married Indian women. These unions provoked no social stigma. The two groups worked together, traded together, and adopted numerous customs from each other. Then, following the Civil War and the more general opening of the West, large numbers of whites came into the area. The culture of the whites was more vigorously established. The partially assimilated and cooperative society of an earlier time was overwhelmed.[39]

Norms of prejudice are sometimes rooted in historical conflicts that go back many centuries. And often they are carried from country to country as part of an immigrant's baggage. When successive waves of Europeans came to settle in this country, they brought with them the cultures of prejudice that they had shared in their countries of origin. Thus anti-Semitism crossed the Atlantic, along with anti-Catholicism and the innumerable cross-border animosities caused by ethnocentrism and long-term group conflict overseas.

SOCIAL DISTANCE HIERARCHIES

One of the most stable aspects of the culture of prejudice has been revealed by accumulated behavioral research on *social distance*.[40] These investigations probe the degree to which people are willing to admit members of racial and ethnic categories to varying degrees of intimacy in social relationships—for example, as work partners, neighbors, or marriage partners.[41]

One interesting finding of research on social distance hierarchies is that members of minority groups appear to share the views of the dominant group. Blacks, for example, will place their own group at the top of the scale of preference, but in all other respects their rankings are almost identical to those of whites.[42] This phenomenon has been studied among such diverse classes of respondents as college students, businessmen, children, Jews and other religious groups, and American Orientals. Minor shifts appear in the relative position of one group or another, but, overall, social distance hierarchies are very consistent (see Table 9.4, page 268).

STEREOTYPES

History shows that groups of people have always had a tendency to differentiate themselves from other groups and, in the process, to judge themselves superior. Such images of self and others provide the basis for *stereotypes*, the caricatures we carry in our heads of what we and other people are like.[43] A stereotype reflects shared beliefs and feelings about the distinctive characteristics of the group in question, and it is applied categorically to all the group's members. The accuracy of stereotypes ranges along a continuum from minor oversimplification to extreme distortion of reality.

Stereotypes play an important part in the development and maintenance of prejudice. Where intergroup conflict exists, they are used to justify feelings of hostility on both sides. A Protestant housewife in Northern Ireland explains that Catholics cause a problem because they "don't keep a nice little house and their children—oh, all those children—always seem to be dirty. Why can't they just fix up their houses like decent people do?" One of her Catholic countrymen notes, "We always lived within a stone's throw of Protestants, but neither me nor my brothers ever knew any. They always seemed different from the rest of us. They didn't laugh or joke like we always did."[44]

Once formed, stereotypes are highly resistant to change. By repeating a stereotype, peo-

39. Ralph Linton, *Acculturation in Seven American Indian Tribes* (New York: Appleton-Century-Crofts, Inc., 1940), p. 37.

40. Emory S. Bogardus, *Social Distance* (Yellow Springs, Ohio: The Antioch Press, 1959).

41. For a very different approach to the study of social distance between black and white, see Frank R. Westie and Margaret Westie, "The Social Distance Pyramid: The Relationship Between Caste and Class," *American Journal of Sociology*, 63, No. 2 (September 1957): 190–196.

42. See Emory S. Bogardus, "Comparing Racial Distance in Ethiopia, South Africa, and the United States," *Sociology and Social Research*, 52 (1968): 149–156; and Ehrlich, *Social Psychology of Prejudice*, pp. 61ff.

43. For an understanding of the origin of the concept *stereotype*, see Walter Lippmann, *Public Opinion* (New York: Harcourt Brace Jovanovich, Inc., 1922), esp. pp. 29 and 79; for a recent critical review of the concept, see Ehrlich, *Social Psychology of Prejudice*, pp. 20ff.

44. Skoogfors, Cooney, and Cooney, *The Most Natural Thing in the World*.

ple strengthen their belief in its accuracy. Indeed, they may insist that the stereotype wouldn't exist if it weren't based on established fact. That the ignorant and uninformed have no monopoly on stereotypes can be demonstrated by the remark of the Chairman of the Joint Chiefs of Staff of the United States Armed Forces that Jews "own, you know, the banks in this country."[45] Undoubtedly millions of people believe this statement. But to what extent is it true?

During the 1960s American Jewish leaders themselves were concerned about the extent to which Jews did in fact exert control over banks, especially in New York City, the financial capital of the nation and the city with the largest proportion of the nation's Jews. Studies were carried out in several large cities, as well as nationally, with similar results.[46] Among the nation's fifty largest commercial banks, forty-five had no Jewish senior officers at all. The other

five banks had a total of eight senior executives who were Jewish, four of them in one bank. Thus Jews made up a total of 1.3 percent of the senior officers in the nation's leading commercial banks. At the middle management level in these banks, Jews comprised only 1 percent of the 3438 executives and 4 percent of the members of the boards of directors. Jews fared no better in New York City banks than in those of other cities, despite the fact that Jews comprise about a fourth of the city's population and half of its college graduates.

45. Quoted in *Time*, November 25, 1974, p. 16.
46. See the following reports: *Patterns of Exclusion from the Executive Suite: Corporate Banking* (New York: The American Jewish Committee, Institute of Human Relations, August 1966); *The Mutual Savings Banks of New York City* (New York: The American Jewish Committee, Institute of Human Relations, October 1965); and *The Mutual Savings Banks of New York City: A Follow-up Report* (New York: The American Jewish Committee, Institute of Human Relations, November 1966).

Table 9.4. RACIAL AND ETHNIC DISTANCE IN THE UNITED STATES IN 1926, 1946, AND 1966

Group	Rank 1926	Group	Rank 1946	Group	Rank 1966
English	1	Amer. (nat. white)	1	Amer. (nat. white)	1
Amer. (nat. white)	2	Canadians	2	English	2
Canadians	3	English	3	Canadians	3
Scotch	4	Irish	4	French	4
Irish	5	Scotch	5	Irish	5
French	6	French	6	Swedes	6
Germans	7	Norwegians	7	Norwegians	7
Swedes	8	Hollanders	8	Italians	8
Hollanders	9	Swedes	9	Scotch	9
Norwegians	10	Germans	10	Germans	10
Spanish	11	Finns	11	Hollanders	11
Finns	12	Czechs	12	Finns	12
Russians	13	Russians	13	Greeks	13
Italians	14	Poles	14	Spanish	14
Poles	15	Spanish	15	Jews	15
Armenians	16	Italians	16	Poles	16
Czechs	17	Armenians	17	Czechs	17
Indians (Amer.)	18	Greeks	18	Indians (Amer.)	18
Jews	19	Jews	19	Japanese Amer.	19
Greeks	20	Indians (Amer.)	20	Armenians	20
Mexicans	21	Chinese	21	Filipinos	21
Mexican Amer.	22	Mexican Amer.	22	Chinese	22
Japanese	23	Filipinos	23	Mexican Amer.	23
Japanese Amer.	24	Mexicans	24	Russians	24
Filipinos	25	Turks	25	Japanese	25
Negroes	26	Japanese Amer.	26	Turks	26
Turks	27	Koreans	27	Koreans	27
Chinese	28	Indians (East)	28	Mexicans	28
Koreans	29	Negroes	29	Negroes	29
Indians (East)	30	Japanese	30	Indians (East)	30

SOURCE: Emory S. Bogardus, "Comparing Racial Distance in Ethiopia, South Africa, and the United States," *Sociology and Social Research*, 52 (1968): 149–156. Bogardus observed that while there have been only moderate changes in the rankings over time—e.g., Jews and Italians have moved up while Mexicans and Negroes have moved down—there has been a measurable decrease in social distance between the groups during this forty-year period. He interpreted this decrease to mean that people were gradually becoming aware of their similarities.

American life provides many examples of stereotypes. In this "Hill-Billy Village" in Tennessee, stereotypes of two minority groups—Appalachian whites and American Indians—predominate. While such caricatures may seem harmless, they have the unintended effect of maintaining and justifying prejudice and discrimination.

The studies revealed interesting explanations for the absence of Jews in key banking positions by bank officials who were interviewed. Two quotes are representative: "The slow progress of a banking career does not appeal to people who are aggressive." "Banking does not appeal to Jews because they are too anxious to get ahead and make substantial money."[47]

Thus we come full circle. The Jews' supposed control of banks—an element in the established stereotype—is used to help explain their supposedly inordinate influence in American society. When it is discovered that they do not own or control the banks, an explanation drawn from the same stereotype is used to account for that fact.

Research has shown that status-equal contacts between differing peoples helps reduce negative stereotyping. In an early study of interracial housing, for example, Deutsch and Collins found that blacks and whites required to live in integrated apartment buildings in New York City because of public housing codes got to know each other and even became good friends, whereas blacks and whites in segregated public housing in Newark kept their distance and tended to be mutually antagonistic.[48] Status-equal contacts in school and on the job can be similarly effective in modifying negative stereotypes.

47. *Patterns of Exclusion*, p. 5.
48. Morton Deutsch and Mary F. Collins, *Interracial Housing* (Minneapolis: University of Minnesota Press, 1951).

NATIONAL BROTHERHOOD WEEK

Oh, the white folks hate the black folks,
And the black folks hate the white folks,
To hate all but the right folks
Is an old established rule.

But during National Brotherhood Week, National
   Brotherhood Week,
Lena Horne and Sheriff Clark are dancing cheek
   to cheek.
It's fun to eulogize the people you despise,
As long as you don't let 'em in your school.

Oh, the poor folks hate the rich folks,
And the rich folks hate the poor folks,
All of my folks hate all of your folks,
It's American as apple pie.

But during National Brotherhood Week, National
   Brotherhood Week,
New Yorkers love the Puerto Ricans, 'cause it's
   very chic.
Step up and shake the hand of someone you
   can't stand,
You can tolerate him if you try.

Oh, the Protestants hate the Catholics,
And the Catholics hate the Protestants,
And the Hindus hate the Moslems,
And everybody hates the Jews.

But during National Brotherhood Week, National
   Brotherhood Week,
It's national everyone-smile-at-one-anotherhood
   week.
Be nice to people who are inferior to you,
It's only for a week, so have no fear,
Be grateful that it doesn't last all year.

"National Brotherhood Week," words and music by Tom
Lehrer (ASCAP).

THE LANGUAGE OF PREJUDICE

The culture of prejudice is reflected not only in negative stereotypes but also in the use of unflattering epithets. These epithets connote negative images and are deeply resented by those to whom they refer. "Nigger," "wop," "spic," "Kraut," "gook," and "kike" are emotional terms that connote undesirability and social rejection. Similarly, such phrases as "jew him down" and "working like a nigger" reinforce negative stereotypes and perpetuate prejudicial norms.

Racial and ethnic jokes provide yet another example of the language of prejudice. Jokes that characterize members of a racial, religious, or ethnic group as stupid, lazy, dirty, greedy, thieving, or otherwise inferior or undesirable have the effect of perpetuating stereotypes and reinforcing existing patterns of stratification. For centuries people have used ridicule as a means of putting down those over whom they wished to retain dominance.

Epithets, clichés, and jokes based on stereotypes represent widely shared, habitual ways of thinking about and characterizing minority group members and are thus part of the culture of prejudice. They are also techniques for maintaining prejudice at the personal level. Although members of the dominant group use the language of prejudice casually, their words are often stinging insults to the minority groups that are the targets of the antipathies they express.

PREJUDICE AND DISCRIMINATION

Until recently, efforts to improve intergroup relations have focused largely on attempts to eliminate or at least reduce prejudice on an individual level. But as Tom Lehrer reminds us in his satirical song "National Brotherhood Week," intergroup hostilities are not easily eliminated. As norms of prejudice are transmitted from one generation to the next, they become part of a society's culture and are built into its institutions. Elliot Liebow has provided a striking example of how the culture of prejudice expresses itself in institutionalized patterns of discrimination:

The 6-year-old son of a woman on welfare was struck and killed by an automobile as he tried to run across the street. The insurance company's initial offer of $800 to settle out of court was rejected. In consulta-

tion with her lawyer, the mother accepted the second and final offer of $2000. When I learned of the settlement, I called the lawyer to protest, arguing that the sum was far less than what I assumed to be the usual settlement in such cases, even if the child was mainly at fault. "You've got to face the facts," he said. "Insurance companies and juries just don't pay as much for a Negro child." Especially, he might have added, a Negro child on welfare.

If the relative worth of human life must be measured in dollars and cents, why should the cash surrender value of a black child's life be less than that for a white child's life? The answer clearly has nothing to do with private prejudice and discrimination. Insurance companies and our legal system take an actuarial perspective. Damage awards are based primarily on the projected life-time earnings of the individual; they are statements about his probable productivity, not about his skin color.

But this child, this Anthony Davis, was only 6 years old. On what basis do they make lowered projections of earnings for a 6-year-old child, before he has acquired or rejected an education, before he has demonstrated any talents or lack of them, before he has selected an occupation or, indeed, before he has made a single life choice of his own?

. . . What is most important for us to know and admit is this: the insurance company was absolutely right. Anthony was more likely than his white, middle-class counterpart to go to an inferior school, to get an inferior job, to be last hired and first fired, to be passed over for promotion, and to live a shorter life. And we are a racist society because we know this to be true before the fact, when Anthony is only 6 years old.[19]

In recent years blacks and other minority groups in American society have increasingly turned their attention from the problem of overcoming individual prejudice to the problem of rooting out discriminatory practices that have become deeply embedded in the social system. The struggle for equal rights has brought clear gains, but glaring inequalities still exist. It remains to be seen whether racial and ethnic minorities in the United States are in fact on their way toward achieving equality or whether we have been witnessing only token changes in the stratification system.

49. Elliot Liebow, "No Man Can Live With the Terrible Knowledge That He Is Not Needed," in Class and Conflict in American Society, Robert Le Jeune, ed. (Chicago: Rand McNally & Co., 1972), pp. 62–63.

SUMMARY

The term *minority group* applies to any category of people who are relegated to a low position in a society's stratification system, being denied equal access to status, wealth, and power. The most commonly used criteria for categorizing groups as minorities are race and ethnicity.

In reviewing the history of intergroup relations in American society, we have outlined in some detail the experiences of blacks, Jews, Indians, Orientals, and Spanish-surnamed peoples in order to show how the present structure of our dominant-minority relationships has emerged over the years. As the history of American minorities makes clear, intergroup relations do not follow a single pattern and seldom are completely stable. The structure of relationships that prevails between a dominant group and a particular minority at any given time is a product of historical circumstance as well as of the posture each group assumes toward the other. Common patterns of dominant-minority relationship are aggression, exclusion, assimilation, and pluralism. Although the dominant group is primarily responsible for defining the broad structure of intergroup relations, the pattern that emerges also depends on the response of the minority group.

Discrimination against minority groups is rooted in prejudice, a negative emotional bias toward members of another group. Prejudice is usually thought of as an individual characteristic, but it must also be viewed as a collective phenomenon, part of the culture that is passed on from generation to generation through the socialization process. The culture of prejudice includes not only a relatively stable set of social distance relationships between various groups but also beliefs and verbal habits that support prejudice, such as negative stereotypes, epithets, and clichés. The view of prejudice as a cultural phenomenon does much to explain the persistence of discriminatory practices in a society that formally avows the equality of all its members.

Part IV
PROCESSES OF CHANGE

10
Social and Cultural Change

To realize how rapidly social and cultural changes have occurred in the United States and other industrialized societies, we need only look back to a few indicators of what our society was like a century ago. During the 1870s nearly three fourths of America's 40 million people lived in rural areas. The greatest waves of European immigration and the rapid growth of our cities were yet to come.

In its material and technological culture the United States in the 1870s more closely resembled colonial America than the America of today. No one had ever driven a car, put food in a refrigerator, turned down a thermostat, traveled in an airplane, gone to a movie, listened to a radio, opened a beer can, or worn synthetic fabrics. Industry relied on the steam engine for power, and the principal source of energy available to most families was the horse. The division of labor was elementary by comparison to what it is today. Most Americans worked on their own farms, where responsibilities were allocated largely on the basis of age and sex.

The average American had never been to high school, and few had even seen a college. At the beginning of the decade higher learning in the United States was not very high: faculties were often undistinguished, and course offerings were scanty. Advanced education for women was still widely regarded as a dangerous experiment.[1]

The moral norms of society disapproved of outspoken women and of children who did not unquestioningly obey their parents. Any public mention of sexual matters was an outrageous breach of etiquette. Many husbands and wives never saw each other nude. There was little sense of public responsibility for social welfare. Although private charities and philanthropies were common, and private citizens struggled to help the less fortunate, there were no old-age pensions and no retirement plans, no minimum-wage laws, and no federal laws against child labor. In short, life in "the good old days" was very different from life as we know it today. The number of changes that have occurred in the last ten decades is almost beyond belief.

1. Eleanor Flexner, *Century of Struggle: The Women's Rights Movement in the United States* (New York: Atheneum, 1972), pp. 113–130.

Whether or not all these changes have meant "progress," in the sense of improving the quality of life for the majority of Americans, is a subject of continuing debate. The primary interest of sociologists is in analyzing change as an integral aspect of societal life. What factors in the physical and social environment seem to stimulate or impede change? What are the processes by which change is initiated, and how does it spread? How do particular changes in one part of a social system alter the system as a whole? And what part have our various social institutions played in modifying our patterns of life? These are some of the questions we will consider in the present chapter.

BASIC TYPES OF CHANGE

In analyzing the complex phenomenon of change, sociologists often use the terms *social change* and *cultural change* synonymously. In fact, however, the two terms reflect important conceptual distinctions—the distinctions we have already noted (page 98) between social organization and culture. Thus *social* change refers to alterations in the patterns of social organization of specific groups within a society or even of the society itself. *Cultural* change, on the other hand, refers to the emergence of new traits and trait complexes—that is, to changes in a culture's content or structure.

Usually, of course, it is very difficult to isolate a particular change and to classify it as clearly cultural or social. We may ask, for example, whether the widespread adoption of the automobile as an item of material culture was a contributing *cause* or only an *effect* of the changing structure of American society early in the present century. It clearly made possible the expansion of the suburbs; it contributed to changes in the norms concerning contacts between the sexes; it helped reduce differences between urban and rural ways of life. But these trends were already well under way at the time the automobile was introduced, and perhaps it

Changes occurring in one component of a system are generally felt in the other components. The discovery and exploitation of oil in Arab countries has already led to societal change. What effect will the increased income due to higher oil prices have on these nations? Will the rich get richer? Or will the standard of living of all citizens rise?

was widely adopted because it fitted the emerging patterns of social change. Because a clear-cut distinction between social and cultural change is often impossible, we will sometimes refer simply to the basic phenomenon of change.

CHANGES IN SOCIAL ORGANIZATION

Alterations in the social organization of a group or society can mean the development of new norms, the modification of role expectations, a shift to new types of sanctions, or the development of different criteria of ranking. Usually changes in one component of social organization are accompanied by changes in at least some of the other components.[2] Perhaps the most obvious form of social change is the modification of group norms. For example, colleges and universities, which traditionally have sought to take the place of parents in guiding the behavior of students, have recently adopted a policy of laissez-faire in all but academic matters. Rigid curfews for dormitory residents, prohibitions against drinking, and regulations concerning cross-sex visiting have been disappearing rapidly.

Typically, changes in informal norms lead to broader tolerance limits for the violation of laws and other formal norms even before the "rules" are officially changed. When the use of marijuana, once lumped together with the use of hard narcotics and treated as a major criminal offense, became widespread, for example, public sentiment no longer supported vigorous prosecution. Now some states have greatly reduced their legal sanctions. In some cases, however, formal norms are modified while public opinion is still widely divided, as in the case of the Supreme Court decisions on school desegregation (1954) and abortion (1973).

One of the most obvious kinds of social change in American society has been a long-term change in forms of legal sanctions. Until relatively recent times physical punishment was common. Although shaming those guilty of minor crimes by exhibiting them in stocks did not survive the colonial period, whipping continued in some states into the twentieth century.

Public hangings, both official and unofficial, had a long history in this country. Gradually, corporal punishment, including capital punishment, was replaced by imprisonment, and in recent years the emphasis on rehabilitation rather than punishment has led to efforts to find substitutes for incarceration.

In the discussion of groups as *social systems* on pages 47–50, we pointed out that changes occurring in one component in a system are likely to be felt in other components. To illustrate, recent modifications of traditional norms regarding premarital sexual activity are reflected in new patterns of relationship between young people who live together without marrying, a lessening of family and community pressures to make them "conform," and an increased willingness among community members to accept them as social equals. Changes in informal norms, in short, have been accompanied by related changes in society's role structure and in its systems of sanctioning and social ranking.

CHANGING PATTERNS OF CULTURE

Cultures as well as patterns of social organization undergo change. New traits are acquired; old ones become obsolete. New cultural configurations develop; existing ones are modified.

Perhaps the most obvious cultural change is in material and technological culture. Homemakers are constantly confronted with new gadgets that supposedly make work easier. Advertisers bombard us with messages that their pills, powders, and other products are NEW, NEW, NEW! Technological devices for the solution of every conceivable kind of problem—including many we did not know we had—are constantly added to our growing base of material and technological culture traits.

Our symbolic culture also changes. For example, Glock and Stark have noted that established religious groups in American society have become more secular, while at the same time new mystical, evangelical, and fundamentalist movements have emerged[3] (see pages 491–

2. See Bryce F. Ryan, "Processes of Change in Social Systems," in *Social and Cultural Change*, ed. Bryce F. Ryan (New York: The Ronald Press Company, 1969), pp. 77–288.
3. Charles Y. Glock and Rodney Stark, *Religion and Society in Tension* (Chicago: Rand McNally & Co., 1965).

496). American values have also undergone continual modification. Many of the choices we make and the priorities we set today are radically different from what they were in the past. During the 1950s, for example, relatively little was heard of environmental impact, food shortages, or energy problems. At that time it seemed acceptable to build larger and more powerful cars, develop more and more freeways, reduce agricultural production, expand suburbs, invent stronger DDT, dam up more rivers, and explode larger atom bombs. There is little doubt that the 1980s will see the development of values and emphases in our society different from those of the present decade.

One of the most significant kinds of change is the emergence of new subcultures. The 1960s, for example, saw widespread dissatisfaction with the status quo in American society give rise to a variety of different ways of life, as represented by the hippies, the drug-users, the political activists, the violent revolutionaries, and the followers of Eastern religions. Women began a new crusade for liberation from inequality and injustice. Racial and ethnic minorities adopted more militant ideologies. Even subcultures that are short-lived may leave modifications of the society's general culture in their wake.

FACTORS STIMULATING CHANGE

People often speculate on why there should be more creative activity in some societies than in others and among only a few rather than a majority of individuals. We may agree with Ralph Linton that change is a result of "the restless energy of the human mind."[4] But why are people in some societies seemingly more "restless" than those in other societies? And why is social and cultural ferment so much more characteristic of some periods of history, such as our own, than of others?

In trying to answer these questions, social scientists have identified a number of factors that have helped stimulate social and cultural change in the past. Here we will consider the potential importance of physical resources, population growth, ideology, and individual leadership. It should be recognized from the start, however, that changes in a group's living patterns can never be explained in terms of simple cause and effect. As Parsons warns,

no claim that social change is "determined" by economic interests, ideas, personalities of particular individuals, geographical conditions, and so on, is acceptable. All such single-factor theories belong to the kindergarten stage of social science's development. Any single factor is always interdependent with several others.[5]

The analysis that follows can only suggest the complexity of factors influencing the direction and pattern of change. An interplay of forces is always at work, and change in one part of a system invariably affects other parts as well— often, as we shall see, with wholly unforeseen results.

AVAILABLE PHYSICAL RESOURCES

The physical resources available to a people help shape their way of life and influence the direction of social and cultural change. There is no way of predicting how available resources will be used or what social and cultural conditions will develop through their use. But history makes clear that the discovery or exhaustion of particular resources can significantly affect patterns of social life.

Exploitable Resources

Certain categories of resources seem to have led to change more frequently than others. One of the most important resources is arable land. In ancient times great civilizations developed close to fertile agricultural land. In the Middle East along the Tigris and Euphrates, in Egypt along the Nile, and in China along the great rivers, nomadic peoples settled and changed their way

4. Ralph Linton, *The Study of Man: An Introduction* (New York: Appleton-Century-Crofts, Inc., 1936), pp. 326–327.

5. Talcott Parsons, *Societies: Evolutionary and Comparative Perspectives* (Englewood Cliffs, N. J.: Prentice-Hall, Inc., 1966), p. 113.

During the 1970s changes in weather patterns caused a serious drought in the Sahel region of West Africa. When their cattle died from lack of water, the people of the Sahel were faced with famine. Relief efforts organized by other countries kept many people alive in temporary camps, but the effect was to destroy the traditional tribal organization of the Sahel.

of life from hunting and gathering to farming. Eventually they developed towns and cities.

Not land but the lure of gold and silver brought the Spanish conquistadores to Mexico and Peru during the early sixteenth century. Their expeditions altered the course of history for both the New World and the Old. Three centuries later, when the discovery of gold in California attracted thousands of gold seekers, the forty-niners who traveled overland by wagon train opened up mid-America for settlement. Much of the social and cultural history of the United States can be related to the presence, location, and perceived utility of exploitable resources—arable land, timber, fish and furs, ores and fossil fuels, rivers and harbors.

Energy

The amounts and types of energy available to a society condition its way of life materially and set limits on what people can do and how their

society will be organized.[6] Prehistoric peoples knew how to use only the energy that could be delivered by their own muscles. However, a number of important energy discoveries took place in very ancient times. People learned how to control fire. With fire, they could split rocks, clear areas for agriculture, cook food, keep dangerous animals at bay, and survive in cold climates.

The domestication of draft animals was a most important development because it greatly increased the energy our early ancestors could put to use. Possession of animals like the horse and the ox permitted agrarian societies to raise more food, to increase the complexity of their division of labor, and to grow larger; ultimately it led to the development of towns and cities.

6. Linton, *Study of Man*, pp. 87 ff. See also Fred Cottrell, *Energy and Society* (New York: McGraw-Hill Book Company, 1955), p. vii.

VIEWPOINTS   SCARCITY AND CHANGE

■ When did some economists become persuaded that the future could be permanently prosperous, more so with each passing year? When did they become convinced by their own mathematical models that mankind no longer depended for his well-being upon a fixed store of natural resources but on the amount of printed money in circulation? . . .

Think of it this way: A lot of people in the U.S. are paid to ponder the future and describe it for the rest of us. . . . They have developed a sort of poetry of the age that begins like this:

"If present trends continue, and we see no reasons why they should not, then. . . ."

And the electric utility vice president finished the line this way:

". . . then the demand for electricity will continue to double every ten years for the rest of the century and in order to meet the demand we must build at least 1,200 nuclear power plants each with a capacity of one million kilowatts, or one new plant every ten days." . . .

And the oil company planner said, sometimes right out in the open:

"Then the demand for petroleum will grow from 4 to 6% a year and that means we must drill offshore for oil, build the Alaskan pipeline or we must be friends always with the Persian Gulf people." . . .

But the skeptic said, mostly to himself:

"Lead us not into absurdity. Those trendlines on your nicely drawn graphs are not engraved in stone. They are not the road to the future. And do not forget this basic law of physics: 'Thou shalt not stuff ten pounds of potatoes into a sack made for five.' "

But few people listened to the skeptic as they all drove confidently up . . . trendline freeways into the exhilarating heights of the future.

Until 1974, when everyone suddenly looked ahead and found the roads bending over and dropping off and the vision of the future that had been drawn brightly for them recede into a dense fog.

Paul G. Hayes
"The Unknown Lies Just Ahead"

● Many people fear that the disappearance of fossil fuels will doom civilization. They envision tractors paralyzed in the fields, highways choked with derelict cars and factories ground to a halt. They pity our descendants who, they imagine, will face everlasting drudgery. But history does not support such apocalyptic predictions. When "energy crises" occurred in the past and the main sources of power dwindled, society found alternative power sources.

The first "energy" shortage occurred during Paleolithic times, the result of man's too heavy reliance on a hunting and gathering economy that exploited resources without conserving or replacing them. Faced with a shortage of animal food, man had to move on or die off or change the basis of his economy. Those who followed the last course developed agriculture. Anthropologists believe that the scarcity of food animals precipitated the Neolithic revolution.

Thousands of years later, ancient Rome met an energy crisis—a manpower shortage—by developing her waterpower. . . .

Twelve hundred years later, a shortage of wood laid the foundation for the Industrial Revolution. . . .

Perhaps we are now on the brink of yet another technological revolution. The historical shortages of animal food, of manpower and of wood proved beneficial in the long run. To secure alternative sources of power, people had to come to grips with their environment. The discoveries they made in the process of adapting the new power sources to society's needs bred a host of technological refinements. The energy shortage that we face also bids fair to stimulate new inventions and discoveries as well as a new social order.

Andrew Hardy
"Man's Age-Old Struggle for Power"

For nomadic peoples, dogs and camels also carried and dragged loads, greatly increasing the range a family could cover in hunting and gathering food. In some societies horses, camels, and elephants were ridden as well as used as beasts of burden.

Moving water provided preindustrial societies with still another source of energy. Water wheels can turn grinding machinery and operate sawmills, weaving machines, and simple irrigation devices. Each of these applications implies an economic base that leads to changing patterns of social organization and culture.

Harnessing the energy of the wind can have a similar impact. Windmills, for example, can often be located more conveniently than water wheels. But perhaps the most important use of wind power was with sailing vessels. In ancient times, numerous societies were able to use this energy source to create new modes of life. The ships of the great trading nations of the Mediterranean depended upon wind; the creation of the Roman Empire and the far-flung expeditions of the Vikings would have been impossible without this application of energy.

The harnessing of steam in the eighteenth century represented a great leap forward. Burning wood and coal as fuel, steam engines were used to drive railroads and ships, to pump water, and to operate the machinery in factories and mills. The effects of steam power on transportation and manufacturing had a profound impact on Western societies.

The pace of energy development increased with the use of petroleum—first as an illuminant (kerosene), then as a power source (gasoline) in the internal-combustion engine. After some years of competition, gasoline won out over steam and electricity as the fuel for the automobile, and petroleum products became sources of energy for the airplane and for diesel-powered ships and locomotives. All of these greatly increased the industrial capacity and transportation efficiency of the societies in which they were used.

Like other industrial societies, American society today is largely dependent upon fossil fuels—coal, petroleum, and natural gas. Unfortunately, these resources are finite in amount and renewable only over periods of millions of years. In addition, our society has already reached its maximum production of petroleum products by conventional means.[7]

The early 1960s marked a kind of crossover point at which the rate of production and use of petroleum products began to exceed the rate at which new sources were being discovered. Thus the United States had to turn to foreign sources for petroleum energy; and when the oil-producing Arab states declared an embargo in 1973, Americans suddenly became aware that they faced an "energy crisis." The embargo was lifted, but the problem remained.

Energy shortages have already caused economic, social, and cultural readjustments and unless new sources can be found, the organization and culture of American society will undergo many more changes.[8] (Among the "new" sources under consideration are the most ancient—the sun, the wind, and the ocean tides.)

POPULATION GROWTH

History shows that famines, plagues, and warfare have periodically checked population growth and even depleted populations. The Black Death that swept through western Europe during the fourteenth century sharply reduced a population that had been increasing steadily for several centuries (see Table 10.1). We may speculate that such changes in population size would lead to changes in marriage and family patterns. For example, in a society whose numbers had been depleted, we might expect an increased emphasis on early marriage and a high birth rate. During periods of sustained population growth, on the other hand, delayed marriage or enforced bachelorhood might be the preferred patterns. Records of feudal Europe do in fact indicate that many men and women did not marry. Limited resources made marriage impractical for large numbers of people. Laws of

7. Committee on Resources and Man, National Academy of Sciences and National Research Council, *Resources and Man: A Study and Recommendations* (San Francisco: W. H. Freeman and Company, 1969).

8. Howard T. Odum, *Environment, Power, and Society* (New York: John Wiley & Sons, Inc., 1971), p. 308.

primogeniture, specifying that a family's entire property should pass to the eldest son, had the indirect effect of encouraging celibacy, for younger sons had few options open to them other than military service or a life in the Church.[9]

In our own time, the population explosion that took on such critical overtones after World War II has clearly altered patterns of social behavior. Cities have mushroomed. Housing is often in short supply. Environmental pollution has become a widespread reality. In the developing nations, where population growth generally far outstrips economic growth, increasing numbers of people go jobless and hungry. These problems have spurred the development and distribution of more effective contraceptive devices, while also increasing the frequency with which sterilization and abortion are practiced. Today governments, religious groups, population experts, and individual married couples all have their own perspectives on the issue of population growth, but there is a general movement in the direction of family planning. And in the process, traditional values and beliefs are being questioned. What is the real meaning of sexual

9. For historical detail on these points, see John T. Noonan, Jr., *Contraception: A History of Its Treatment in the Catholic Theologians and Canonists* (Cambridge, Mass.: Harvard University Press, 1965), pp. 228–230.

morality? What are the primary obligations of parents? What role should a woman have in the family and in society?

The relationship between population trends and social change defies any simple analysis. In the Western world, the improvements in agriculture, sanitation, and medicine that accompanied the Industrial Revolution served to lower death rates and thus to increase population growth. But population growth then combined with other variables to promote new patterns of social organization and to complete the transformation to urban-industrial society. And this transformation in turn led to changes in family structure and a gradual reduction in birth rates. Whether this cycle will repeat itself in the developing countries, however, is debatable. (See Chapter 11, "Demographic Change.")

IDEOLOGY

In all human groups, beliefs and values—manifested in norms and goals—are important guides to behavior. A complex of beliefs and values providing an overall rationale for a society is termed an *ideology*. Ideologies obviously help sustain societies. But do they also act to stimulate change? And, if they do, how, and to what extent?

Table 10.1. POPULATION OF THE WORLD, IN MILLIONS, 1000–1980

Year	Europe and Russia	India and Southwest Asia	China, Japan and Southeast Asia	Africa	The Americas	World
1000	47	80	85	50	13	275
1100	54	83	97	55	17	306
1200	68	85	111	61	23	348
1300	81	83	125	67	28	384
1400	54	73	142	74	30	373
1500	80	83	160	82	41	446
1600	102	98	181	90	15	486
1700	130	131	256	90	10	617
1800	205	190	405	90	29	919
1900	421	325	545	120	144	1,555
1980	456	1,001	1,427	449	635	4,268

SOURCE: Adapted from Merrill Kelley Bennett, *The World's Food* (New York: Harper & Brothers, 1954), p. 9. Projected 1980 figures from the United Nations, *Provisional Report on World Population Prospects* (New York, 1964).
NOTE: In addition to pointing up the dramatic growth of world population in the last two centuries, this chart reflects some interesting historical developments in various regions. Between 1300 and 1400 the population in Europe and Russia declined drastically, mainly as the result of the Black Death; in 1500 the population was still slightly below that of 1300. By 1600, while the population of Europe had again risen significantly, that of the New World has been all but destroyed as a result of the European conquest. In 1800 the population of North and South America was still less than those continents had possessed four hundred years earlier. Africa experienced a slow, even growth from 1000 to 1600, but during the following two centuries the population remained stationary because of the slave trade and an almost static balance between high birth rates and high death rates.

The Protestant Ethic and the Development of Capitalism

Max Weber's study of the development of modern capitalism represents one of the most thoroughgoing efforts yet made in the social sciences to establish a relationship between ideology and sociocultural change. Weber wanted to establish the principle that *ideas* as well as technological developments and the economic structure could be determining factors in bringing about change. To do this, he set out to identify the major factors responsible for the rise of capitalism as it had developed in Western societies—the type of capitalism characterized by double-entry bookkeeping, uniform pricing, systematic planning, and bureaucratic social organization.[10]

Weber acknowledged that the development of industrial technology, increased agricultural productivity, improvements in sanitation and preventive medicine, and better methods of transportation had all been necessary to the development of capitalism. But he found the determining factor not in science or technology but in what he called the "Protestant Ethic" (page 112). Calvinism, Weber maintained, made possible the emergence of capitalism by providing people in Western societies with a new "this-worldly" orientation. In focusing their attention on such values as individualism, hard work, and frugality, it paved the way for a major restructuring of economic life.

Through a wide-ranging historical analysis, Weber attempted to show that the attitudes engendered by the religions of Eastern societies were in various ways hostile to the development of modern capitalism. In China, India, and ancient Israel, adherence to tradition, stereotyping, otherworldly orientations, and closed-class or caste systems of stratification all acted to impede the development of the capitalistic spirit upon which the modern Western economy was eventually built.

In the years since Weber wrote *The Protestant Ethic and the Spirit of Capitalism,* his theory has been both defended and denounced by other scholars.[11] But the thesis he advanced was substantially strengthened by his careful comparative studies, and though it cannot be proved, it is nonetheless plausible. Whether they accept Weber's thesis or not, most social scientists today would agree that values and beliefs must be recognized as potential forces of change and also of resistance to change.

Marxist Ideology as a Stimulus to Change

As we noted in the chapter on Social Stratification (page 214), Marx was convinced that the economic structure of a society, not the beliefs and values of its members, provide the impetus for social conflict and change: "It is not the consciousness of men that determines their existence, but rather it is their social existence which determines their consciousness."[12] Yet Marxism itself became an ideology. Millions of people believe and act on at least some parts of Marxian theory, and it seems likely that their *belief* has been at least as much a force for social change as have the economic forces that Marx saw at work.

The influence of Marx's ideas as ideology illustrates one of the basic principles of sociology: If people define situations as real, they are real in their consequences.[13] People who have believed in Marx's theory have worked to bring about the changes he considered inevitable. They have carried out the revolutions that Marx predicted, even though the conditions he saw as essential to revolution were sometimes lacking.

10. Weber's best-known work, published in 1920, is *The Protestant Ethic and the Spirit of Capitalism* (New York: Charles Scribner's Sons, 1958), but the full scope of Weber's thesis cannot be appreciated without reference to several other works, notably *Ancient Judaism* (New York: The Free Press, 1952); *The Religion of China* (New York: The Free Press, 1951); *The Religion of India* (New York: The Free Press, 1958); and *General Economic History* (New York: Macmillan, Inc., 1961).

11. For a recent critique, see Kurt Samuelsson, *Religion and Economic Action* (New York: Harper & Row, Inc., 1961).

12. Karl Marx, *A Contribution to the Critique of Political Economy* (New York: International Publishers, 1969); see also Karl Marx and Friedrich Engels, *The German Ideology* (New York: International Publishers, 1947), esp. pp. 7–25.

13. The principle of the "self-fulfilling prophecy" was first developed by W. I. Thomas in *The Child in America: Behavior Problems and Programs* (New York: Alfred A. Knopf, Inc., 1928), p. 81. For a further elaboration of this principle, see Robert K. Merton, *Social Theory and Social Structure,* rev. ed. (New York: The Free Press, 1957), pp. 421–434.

LEADERSHIP AND SOCIAL MOVEMENTS

Leaders succeed in bringing about sociocultural change to the extent that they can persuade their followers to believe in their cause and act accordingly. Often the success of leaders depends on personal charisma. In the biblical tradition, the term *charisma* means a "gift of grace," divinely given. Weber used the term to describe "a certain quality of an individual personality by virtue of which he is set apart from ordinary men and treated as endowed with supernatural, superhuman or at least specifically exceptional powers or qualities."[14] Old Testament prophets such as Isaiah and Jeremiah are historical examples of leaders with charismatic qualities. They spoke out against the rulers of the day, warned of doom, and in the name of their God, Yahweh, urged a return to the old ways. In a strictly historical sense, Christ may be seen as the great charismatic leader whose teachings changed the history of the Western world, much as Muhammad changed the history of parts of Asia and Africa. But inspiring leadership is not limited to religious leaders. In modern times the term *charisma* has been applied to leaders as different as Gandhi, Pope John XXIII, Franklin D. Roosevelt, Adolf Hitler, John F. Kennedy, Martin Luther King, Jr., Fidel Castro, and Cesar Chavez. All have spoken for a cause and helped lead people to significant social and cultural changes.

Attempts to reorder a social system seldom succeed unless there are severe stresses and strains in the current system. However, the mere existence of such conditions does not in itself guarantee that marked change will take place. People must be ready to seek alternatives, and usually they must be led toward finding them. For example, living conditions are much worse in many countries of the Western Hemisphere, such as Haiti and Paraguay, than they were in Cuba in 1958; but a revolution began in Cuba because new values, beliefs, and norms were developing there, and because a charismatic leader emerged to help shape the vision of a new social order. In times of conflict and stress,

charismatic leadership can be the crucial factor in determining the direction of change.

A social movement for change must itself undergo change if it is to have a lasting effect. Ideas must be put to work, and sometimes they have to be modified. Often this creates a conflict within the movement between bureaucrats and ideologists. The former become increasingly concerned with developing, and then with strengthening and maintaining, social and cultural complexes that reflect the movement's basic tenets. The ideologists, on the other hand, try to keep the founder's "message" intact and protect its principles from compromise. Such differences in viewpoint sometimes erupt into severe conflict, as happened in Red China during the mid-1960s. The Cultural Revolution of Mao's Red Guards was an attempt to restore ideological purity to the process of constructing a new China. The technical experts who had been directing China's program of economic development were charged with corrupting the revolutionary movement. The real answer to China's future, the ideologists argued, lay in absorbing the "thought" of Chairman Mao Tsetung, which would bring inevitable improvement in all areas of personal and social endeavor.

Relatively few leaders are innovators in the sense of articulating a new vision for their people. More typically, individuals come to be accepted as leaders because they provide focus for existing or emerging values and beliefs. Leaders usually share their followers' aspirations and adhere closely to the norms their followers accept. Because they are so closely identified with their followers, they are able to give direction to the felt needs of the group and to count on its support.

PROCESSES OF CHANGE

Among the concepts traditionally used in analyzing social and cultural change are *evolution, borrowing and diffusion, invention,* and *guided*

14. Max Weber, *Theory of Social and Economic Organization,* trans. A. M. Henderson and Talcott Parsons (New York: The Free Press, 1957), p. 358.

change. We will examine each of these concepts in turn, concluding with a brief discussion of the kinds of problems that develop when some facets of a social or cultural system change more slowly than others.

EVOLUTION

In the latter half of the nineteenth century the concept of evolution assumed a central place in explanations of all forms of human development, in the social sciences as well as in the biological sciences. Most influential among the evolutionists were Charles Darwin, whose theory of natural selection provided a solid base for the hypothesis of biological evolution, and Herbert Spencer (page 7), who systematized a theory of societal evolution.[15] Spencer saw evolution as a *unilinear* development—that is, as a steadily continuing, accumulative process by which everything in the cosmos was continuously being synthesized at ever higher levels of complexity. He maintained that human society had followed a course of natural development from relatively simple patterns of organization to more complex structures characterized by an increasing specialization of parts.

Spencer held that the process of societal evolution followed inexorable laws of nature, and that it led inevitably toward *progress*— toward the development of increasingly desirable and just forms of society. Although a particular stage of societal evolution might seem oppressive or undesirable, it was folly, said Spencer, to believe that society could be improved by legislation. The state should play the smallest possible role in the regulation of society in order not to interfere with natural evolutionary processes.

Spencer's ideas had a strong influence on the young science of sociology. For example, in the United States at the turn of the century, William Graham Sumner became an outspoken theorist of social evolution.[16] In a famous dictum he argued that *stateways could not change folkways*—that social improvement could only come about through the natural evolution of society and not by legislation. His arguments are echoed today by those who oppose laws providing for more equitable treatment of minorities on the ground that morality cannot be legislated.

Other pioneers of American sociology accepted parts of the evolutionary theory of societal change, while rejecting the notion that society could not be improved by deliberate effort. Lester Frank Ward, for example, believed that both human beings and human society had developed through eons of evolution. But he maintained that once intellect had evolved in humans, they gained the ability to help shape the subsequent evolution of social forms. Through the application of intelligence, people could effect desired change in society.[17] In this respect Ward was following in the tradition of Auguste Comte, the founder of sociology, who maintained that human intelligence had reached the point where society could be reconstructed through application of the scientific method.

Another important figure in the development of evolutionary theories of social change was Karl Marx. As we have seen (page 214), Marx believed that the continuing struggle of opposing interests propelled societies along an inevitable path of social change. He maintained that societal evolution would proceed through successive stages, with new social orders emerging each time opposing segments of society clashed, until the final stage—a classless and stateless society—had been reached. At this point, the evolutionary process would cease. Marx, like Spencer and Sumner, believed in the inevitability of the changes he foresaw. But he also believed that the evolutionary process could be hastened by the involvement of individuals in class conflict.[18]

Although few social scientists today view societal change as the "inevitable outcome of inexorable laws," most acknowledge the contribution of Spencer, Marx, and other evolutionary theorists in calling attention to the process of social differentiation—the tendency of changing societies to become increasingly complex in

15. Herbert Spencer, *The Principles of Sociology* (New York: D. Appleton and Co., 1898).
16. William Graham Sumner, *Folkways* (Boston: Ginn and Company, 1906), pp. 87–88.
17. Lester Frank Ward, *Dynamic Sociology*, 2nd ed., Vol. 1 (New York: D. Appleton and Co., 1911), p. 451.
18. Karl Marx, *Capital*, ed. Friedrich Engels (New York: International Publishers, 1967).

social organization and culture.[19] An additional contribution of the evolutionists has been to make social scientists more keenly aware that a change in any one part of a social system, such as the economic or political structure, is likely to bring about related changes throughout the whole system. Several specific illustrations of this phenomenon are examined elsewhere in this chapter.

BORROWING AND DIFFUSION

Anthropologists are continually reminding us that we are great culture borrowers. Writing in the 1930s, Ralph Linton made the point well:

Our solid American citizen awakens in a bed built on a pattern which originated in the Near East but which was modified in northern Europe before it was transmitted to America. He throws back covers made from cotton, domesticated in India, or linen, domesticated in the Near East, or wool from sheep, also domesticated in the Near East, or silk, the use of which was discovered in China. All of these materials have been spun and woven by processes invented in the Near East. He slips into his moccasins, invented by the Indians of the Eastern woodlands, and goes to the bathroom, whose fixtures are a mixture of European and American inventions, both of recent date. He takes off his pajamas, a garment invented in India, and washes with soap invented by the ancient Gauls. He then shaves, a masochistic rite which seems to have been derived from either Sumer or ancient Egypt.

Returning to the bedroom, he removes his clothes from a chair of southern European type and proceeds to dress. He puts on garments whose form originally derived from the skin clothing of the nomads of the Asiatic steppes, puts on shoes made from skins tanned by a process invented in ancient Egypt and cut to a pattern derived from the classical civilizations of the Mediterranean, and ties around his neck a strip of bright-colored cloth which is a vestigial survival of the shoulder shawls worn by the seventeenth-century Croatians. Before going out for breakfast he glances through the window, made of glass invented in Egypt, and if it is raining puts on overshoes made of rubber discovered by the Central American Indians and takes an umbrella, invented in southeastern Asia. Upon his

head he puts a hat made of felt, a material invented in the Asiatic steppes.

On his way to breakfast he stops to buy a paper, paying for it with coins, an ancient Lydian invention. At the restaurant a whole new series of borrowed elements confronts him. His plate is made of a form of pottery invented in China. His knife is of steel, an alloy first made in southern India, his fork a medieval Italian invention, and his spoon a derivative of a Roman original. He begins breakfast with an orange, from the eastern Mediterranean, a canteloupe from Persia, or perhaps a piece of African watermelon. With this he has coffee, an Abyssinian plant, with cream and sugar. Both the domestication of cows and the idea of milking them originated in the Near East, while sugar was first made in India. After his fruit and first coffee he goes on to waffles, cakes made by a Scandinavian technique from wheat domesticated in Asia Minor. Over these he pours maple syrup, invented by the Indians of the Eastern woodlands. As a side dish he may have the egg of a species of bird domesticated in Indo-China, or thin strips of the flesh of an animal domesticated in Eastern Asia which have been salted and smoked by a process developed in northern Europe.

When our friend has finished eating he settles back to smoke, an American Indian habit, consuming a plant domesticated in Brazil in either a pipe, derived from the Indians of Virginia, or a cigarette, derived from Mexico. If he is hardy enough he may even attempt a cigar, transmitted to us from the Antilles by way of Spain. While smoking he reads the news of the day, imprinted in characters invented by the ancient Semites upon a material invented in China by a process invented in Germany. As he absorbs the accounts of foreign troubles he will, if he is a good conservative citizen, thank a Hebrew deity in an Indo-European language that he is 100 percent American.[20]

American culture, of course, is not the only one with widespread origins. Anthropologist George Murdock estimates that about 90 percent of every culture known to history has acquired its elements from other peoples.[21] There are very clear reasons for this. One important function of culture traits is that they help people solve problems. A society facing a problem for which it has developed no adequate solutions is generally willing to borrow an approach that has proved effective elsewhere.

19. For a recent discussion of the process of differentiation, see Parsons, *Societies: Evolutionary and Comparative Perspectives*, esp. pp. 20–25 and 113–115.
20. Linton, *Study of Man*, pp. 326–327.
21. George P. Murdock, *Our Primitive Contemporaries* (New York: Macmillan, Inc., 1934).

The Tasaday, a Stone-Age tribe living in a mountain rain forest in the southern Philippines, were geographically isolated for centuries. Resources were plentiful, and until the early 1970s, when the Tasaday were "discovered," their culture remained unchanged. Today the tribe, composed of less than thirty members, is protected by the Philippine government. But despite this protection, Tasaday culture is slowly changing. Among the culture traits they have borrowed from those who have come to study them are the bow and arrow, the knife, and headache pills.

The Process of Diffusion

A considerable amount of culture borrowing is very indirect; that is, the culture in which a given trait originated may be far removed in space or time (or both) from a people who have more recently acquired that trait. The spread of smoking tobacco provides one interesting illustration of indirect intersocietal diffusion. The habit of smoking originated in tropical America, where the tobacco plant is indigenous. Over centuries it was acquired and cultivated by one neighboring Indian group after another until it traveled up Central America and spread out north, east, and west across the North American continent. Sometimes the tobacco was rolled into a crude cigar, and sometimes it was crushed and stuffed into a reed. Every conceivable variation on the pipe has been found in ancient Indian sites, with the stem and bowl put together in different ways and with carvings and art forms characteristic of the people who used it.

Among the Eskimos, on the other hand, no ancient remains of the pipe have been found. These people did not smoke, for their climate prohibited the growing of tobacco and they were too far removed from its sources to have acquired it by trade. In recent centuries, however, the Alaskan Eskimo acquired both the pipe and tobacco along with the word *tawak,* a corruption of the Spanish word *tabaco* with which this plant seems to be identified nearly the world over. The Eskimos borrowed this culture trait from traders coming across the Bering Strait from Siberia. The traders, in turn, had tobacco because it had earlier spread across Europe and Asia from Spain, whose explorers got it from the Indians of tropical America. Thus tobacco reached the Eskimos of Alaska by a journey of diffusion around the entire world.[22] Although not every cultural form that moves from one society to another travels this far, the concept of intersocietal diffusion provides an important perspective on the process of cultural borrowing and on the accumulation of traits in a given culture.

The concept of diffusion also applies to exchanges of culture traits between subgroups *within* a complex society. Many cultural forms that originate within specialized groups of a society, as part of a specific subculture, are later taken on by other groups. For example, jazz was developed by American Negro musicians in the South; but as blacks moved north to Chicago and other urban centers, they took their music along, with the result that jazz became part of the social heritage of the nation as a whole. Many traits of our popular culture — hair styles, clothing styles, dance forms, and slang — similarly spread from distinct subcultures to society as a whole.

Patterns of Diffusion

When a new culture trait or complex is introduced to a group and eventually becomes widely adopted, it follows a characteristic pattern as it spreads through the population. A few individuals may see what they believe to be the advantages of the new trait — perhaps a material item, perhaps a belief or idea — as soon as it is introduced, and they adopt it almost immediately. After these innovators have accepted the trait, it begins to spread gradually to growing numbers of people. Usually it is only after a substantial number of early adopters have made it a standard form among themselves that the majority of the group or society begin to adopt it. Some late adopters may not accept the trait until long after the majority have made it part of their culture, and a few very conservative individuals may never take it up at all.[23]

A *diffusion curve* can often be plotted for a given innovation by noting its spread through a specific population. Figure 10.1, for example, shows the spread of television in the United States between 1946 and 1970 in terms of the number of sets owned per family. It should be noted that in studying the diffusion of a material trait, such as television or tobacco, it is the population's *behavior* in relation to the new item, and not the item itself, that most interests the student of social change.

22. This account is summarized from Alfred L. Kroeber, *Anthropology: Culture Patterns and Processes* (New York: Harcourt Brace Jovanovich, Inc., 1923), pp. 211–214.
23. Everett Rogers, *Diffusion of Innovations* (New York: The Free Press, 1962).

If a new pattern of behavior becomes widely diffused through a society, it is a potential folkway. However, to qualify as a folkway, it must become firmly established. As was suggested in Chapter 3 (page 87), two important characteristics of folkways are that they are widely practiced (have diffused through the entire society) and that they have become an accepted element of the culture (have become *institutionalized*). Diffusion and institutionalization are key aspects of a society's mores as well. The additional element identifying the mores is the great intensity of feelings associated with them.

Even when a particular cultural element is widely adopted by the members of a society, there is no guarantee that it will remain forever a part of their culture. Our vocabulary makes note of this by labeling as *fashions* those cultural forms that become generally accepted but are periodically subject to change. Clothing styles obviously fall in this category. So too do our changing preferences for certain styles of furniture, certain sports, certain breeds of dog, and certain expressions.

The behavior patterns we label as *fads* and *crazes* appear and disappear even more quickly than fashions. Often they involve limited segments of society and are regarded by the majority as examples of pure foolishness, or worse. Whereas fashions are likely to be cyclical (witness the ups and downs of hemlines and the recurrent appearance and disappearance of shoulder pads), particular fads and crazes seldom become popular again once they have been abandoned. And usually they are abandoned just as quickly as they are adopted.

Obsolescence and Displacement

A pattern of declining usage identifies *obsolescence,* which we may define as the abandoning of previously established modes of conduct toward some cultural item. Thus diffusion and obsolescence are natural counterparts. One indicates the phase of increasing acceptance of a new cultural element, and the other indicates its decline.

The diffusion of a new culture trait sometimes causes another trait to become obsolescent. The neighborhood movie, for example, has been to a considerable degree displaced by the increasing diffusion of television in American society. *Displacement,* then, refers to the de-

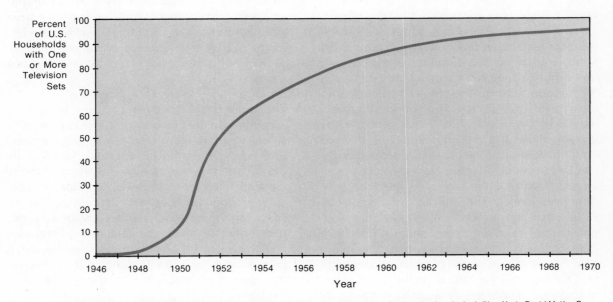

SOURCE: For years 1946–1949, 1951, and 1953, Melvin L. DeFleur, *Theories of Mass Communication,* 2nd ed. (New York: David McKay Co., Inc., 1970), p. 72. For other years, except where data are not available (1952, 1954, 1963, and 1968), U.S. Bureau of the Census, *Current Housing Reports,* Series H-21; *1970 Census of Housing, Final Report, Housing Characteristics,* HC(1)-B1; and U.S. Bureau of the Census, *Statistical Abstract of the United States, 1972.*

FIGURE 10.1. THE DIFFUSION CURVE FOR TELEVISION, 1946–1970

cline of one cultural form brought about by the increasing adoption of a *functional alternative* — that is, a cultural item that performs essentially the same function as the displaced item but that comes to be preferred.

Some Implications of Diffusion

Although people ordinarily adopt new traits because there seems to be some advantage in doing so, the diffusion of a social or cultural trait is not necessarily beneficial, either in the short run or in the long run. A classic example of the mixed results of diffusion involves the American Indians and their contacts with whites. The Plains Indians, for instance, incorporated the horse into their own way of life and suddenly found their social patterns radically altered. The horse increased their mobility and vastly improved their hunting ability. The buffalo became their staple of life, and their meager agricultural economy was generally abandoned. As a result, the Plains Indians became more prosperous. But when the buffalo was effectively eliminated by the white man, the culture of the Plains Indians was disastrously disrupted. Adoption of the horse, initially an advantage, had led them to exchange their long-established style of life for a new one that could not be maintained.

In considering the implications of diffusion we must remember, finally, that it is not limited to material items like furniture and guns and music; in the long run the most important kind of diffusion may be the spread of beliefs and ideas between societies. Thus during the nineteenth century, the political ideals generated by the American and French revolutions diffused not only across Europe but also slowly throughout Latin America, where some societies even adopted constitutions based on the French or American model. The diffusion of democratic values in Latin American societies was very uneven, however, and met with great resistance from entrenched leaders who wished to maintain the status quo. Most of these societies still find themselves in a state of political and social turmoil, faced with the increasing probability of revolutionary convulsions in the decades ahead. Not only in Latin America but in the world as a whole, the diffusion of opposing ideologies has become a major source of conflict both within societies and between them.

INVENTION

Much cultural and social change is a product of the human ability to invent, to create something that has not previously been part of the culture or society. We tend to think of inventions as mechanical devices and technical artifacts, but they may also be new songs, art forms, religious beliefs, games, political philosophies, or other nonmaterial products of the creative mind. Or they may be new forms of social organization such as bureaucracy or the voluntary association.

Invention becomes possible because individuals are capable of taking existing ideas and structural patterns and casting them in a new light. For example, until a young man named Hank Luisetti began to play basketball, the only way to try for a basket was to use both hands in shooting the ball. Luisetti introduced the one-handed shot in 1938 and revolutionized the game. The new shot not only challenged traditional beliefs and norms about how the game should be played but it also radically altered the structural patterns of offensive and defensive play. Yet these changes did not destroy the original game. Typically there is continuity in a pattern of social behavior even as it undergoes change.

The Exponential Principle

Many inventions involve much more than a simple new grouping of a few traits, and often they are not the product of a single inventor. In every case, however, they represent new forms that individuals or groups of individuals have devised from the existing culture base. Many significant inventions involve grasping some new principle about the relationship between known concepts. Classic examples are Newton's gravitational laws, the periodic table of chemistry, and Harvey's discovery of the circulation of the blood.

The possibilities for invention in a society are closely related to its existing cultural content. A society that lacks a technology for working with glass and a knowledge of optical principles can scarcely be expected to invent a microscope. By contrast, a society that has the technology for working in various metals to reasonably close tolerances, that has available the wheel, the piston, and the connecting rod, and that understands something of the expansive power of confined steam is one in which some reasonably bright tinkerer is likely to come up with the idea of a steam engine. This would be especially true if there were a number of ready applications for a source of cheap and dependable power.

The relationship between the number of traits making up the culture base of a particular society and the number of inventions that can potentially be made from them forms an exponential curve (Figure 10.2). The exponential principle is based on the elementary mathematics of combinations. If, for example, a hypothetical culture contained only 100 traits, there would be 4950 possible ways in which these could be paired together as potential inventions. (The formula for the number of pairs in n objects is $N(n - 1)/2$. Where $n = 100$, the number of possible pairs is 4950). If the number of traits in the culture base were merely to double to 200, the number of pairs that could be made would increase to a startling 19,900. The possibilities for invention increase even more dramatically when we consider the additional combinations that could be made by using three, four, or more traits.

The exponential principle helps explain why the flow of inventions in our society has reached such astounding proportions. It is not so much that we are an especially clever or inventive people as it is that we have accumulated an enormous culture base. Because each new invention stimulates others, we may expect the technologically advanced societies of the world to experience cultural accumulation at an ever increasing pace.

Invention and Social Change

History has been written in large part around invention and technological advancement—the

increasingly sophisticated control of heat energy; the invention of the wheel, the steel plow, and gunpowder; progress in medicine and sanitation; the development of the printing press, radio, and television; the invention of the automobile and the airplane. How did it all begin? We can only speculate with Hagen, Linton, and other students of change that early inventions were due in part to the random discoveries of intelligent individuals and in part to people's dissatisfaction with existing solutions to their problems.[24]

More important are the questions of why technological advance has proceeded unevenly over time and why it has brought more significant change to some societies than to others. History reveals periods of little change interspersed with periods of great innovation.

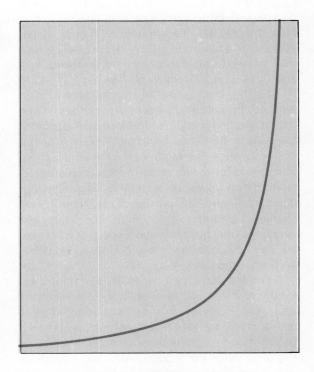

Figure 10.2. THE EXPONENTIAL PRINCIPLE

The potential for technological advance follows an exponential curve. As the culture base grows larger, the number of conceivable inventions increases at an ever more rapid rate.

24. See Everett E. Hagen, *On the Theory of Social Change: How Economic Growth Begins* (Homewood, Ill.: Dorsey Press, 1962), pp. 13 ff.; and Linton, *Study of Man*, pp. 306 ff.

Throughout the Middle Ages, for example, trade routes between societies were opened, closed, and then reopened. Hagen asserts that reopening them seemed to stimulate change but not necessarily initiate it. The pattern of developments leading to the Industrial Revolution is similarly lacking in simple cause-effect relationships. The number of scientific inventions doubled from the fourteenth to the fifteenth century and then tripled in the sixteenth century. But not all societies participated on an equal basis in the growth of science, not even those that contributed significant scientific inventions. Scholars are still seeking a full explanation of why the Industrial Revolution should have reached its culmination in England rather than somewhere else. It was certainly not because all the great inventions had occurred there. Max Weber may have provided a partial explanation with his theory on the economic significance of the Protestant Ethic (page 282). Technological change in England was accompanied by ideological change that stressed the importance of individualism and "this-worldly" accomplishment.

Changes in culture and social organization tend to stimulate and feed on each other. When technological inventions are accepted as part of the culture, they may bring on the development of new groups (the factory and the corporation) that require new role relationships (bureaucratic authority and specialists such as engineers, accountants, and advertising personnel). Such changes, in turn, alter family life-styles and structures (the husband and even the wife may be removed from the home during a significant portion of the day).

For the most part, at least, inventions are simply new combinations of existing ideas. Many disappear without leaving a trace, whereas others stimulate significant changes in societal life. Although it is impossible to anticipate all the long-range consequences of any invention, either positive or negative, Western societies have traditionally proceeded on the optimistic assumption that invention means progress.

GUIDED CHANGE

Today we see an increasing tendency for governments and other organized groups to initiate sociocultural change and attempt to control its direction. The reclamation of the Columbia basin—an area in eastern Washington state—illustrates one effective program of guided change. Because dams brought not only electricity but also water for irrigation, the whole economic, social, and cultural life of a region was altered. What had formerly been a desert is now richly productive crop land. A similar example on a much larger scale was the creation of the Tennessee Valley Authority (TVA), a complex program of flood control, rural electrification, and agricultural development that radically altered the way of life for people in the several states of the TVA region.

Governmental programs to achieve urban renewal, implement the goals of the civil rights movement, reduce environmental pollution, combat poverty, and gain equal rights for women all represent ambitious efforts to guide the direction of change in American society. Though some conservatives cling to the view that social and economic problems tend to work themselves out and that government "interference" helps nothing, the trend has clearly been in the opposite direction: it is now widely accepted that government has an impelling responsibility to initiate and implement programs aimed at social amelioration. Sumner's philosophy has given way to Ward's.

Ideally, a program of guided change involves "(1) a clear and unambiguous definition of a problem that demands solution; (2) careful study of the nature, meaning, and implications of the problem; (3) a decision regarding ultimate solutions; and (4) action on the solution agreed upon."[25] But though social planning can only proceed on the assumption that workable solutions are available, the actual course of planned change seldom if ever runs smoothly. The funds necessary for implementing a program of guided change may not be forthcoming. The people whose cooperation is needed often fail to cooperate. Efforts to improve one area of social life

25. Murray G. Ross and B. W. Lappin, *Community Organization: Theory and Principles*, 2nd ed. (New York: Harper & Row, Inc., 1967), p. 139.

have the unanticipated effect of creating new strains and stresses in other areas. And the more encompassing the goals of a program, the more difficult it is for the planners to see all the variables involved, much less control them.

Demographic Change

Efforts to introduce preventive medicine and improved sanitation to the underdeveloped areas of the world illustrate some of the complexities of social planning. Such programs have had pronounced success since World War II, but the resulting increase in life expectancy and the reduction of infant mortality have enormously accelerated population growth, creating severe social and economic problems. (See Chapter 11, "Demographic Change.")

One by-product of the population explosion has been an increased emphasis on family planning. Indeed, programs to control population growth can be seen as a worldwide effort at planned change, an effort that now officially involves the United Nations. A review of the literature on the subject reveals a pattern of continuing evaluation of existing programs, attempts to coordinate programs at the national and international levels, an effort to define the problem more clearly and to anticipate the ramifications of various possible solutions, and an increasing awareness of the necessity to motivate those most important to any program's success, the people involved—in this case, individual husbands and wives. There is also an increasing tendency to tie family planning in with agricultural and industrial development and to attempt to allocate available funds according to some overall plans.[26]

Urban Planning

Population growth and population movement have put tremendous pressures on cities in all parts of the world and have led to an increasing awareness of the need for urban planning. One of the most remarkable examples of this kind of social planning has been the attempt to halt the physical growth of London. Great Britain's planners actually stopped this growth at the point it had reached in the summer of 1939, and a Green Belt five miles wide has been maintained around London ever since. Strategically placed around the outer rim of the Green Belt are eight New Towns, each planned for low-density population and traditional British housing patterns, with few multistory buildings. To minimize commuting problems, the British have attempted to relocate industry and to situate shopping centers for maximum accessibility.

Critics acknowledge that the planned communities around London's Green Belt have been unusually successful; in fact, community planners have come from all over the world to study them for the lessons they offer. But new problems were in the making even as old ones were being solved. Chief among the factors that worked to lessen the success of this experiment was the unexpected population growth in England after World War II. Added to this, an economic boom in the 1950s attracted new people to the London area, raising the population density and threatening the housing patterns that were so highly valued.[27] The planners simply did not foresee these possibilities.

Perhaps the chief lessons to be learned from the London example are that social systems are dynamic and that change, whether planned or not, may introduce new problems that in turn will create new pressures for change. This principle seems to be valid whether the unit of analysis is a school system, a city, or a whole society.

CULTURAL AND SOCIAL LAG

In considering the process of *diffusion* we noted that new cultural and social patterns spread through a society at different rates and reach different proportions of the population. Some patterns become institutionalized while others become obsolescent and are abandoned. In the short run, at least, neither cultures nor societies change in a steady and coordinated way.

26. See, for example, Bernard Berelson et al., *Family Planning and Population Programs: A Review of World Developments* (Chicago: The University of Chicago Press, 1966).

27. Peter Hall, *The World Cities* (New York: McGraw-Hill Book Company, 1966), pp. 48–52.

TOOLS OF SOCIOLOGY
HISTORICAL-STATISTICAL ANALYSIS   William Martineau

In studying social and cultural change, researchers are often unable to be on the spot to control the circumstances and to record observations and measurements of what is changing. Indeed, they may not even be aware that any change is taking place until it is completed. Thus, in order to study change, sociologists often turn to a general procedure known as *historical-statistical analysis,* in which data is assembled to describe and measure the item being studied as it existed at previous times and as it exists now. By comparing such measurements, researchers can ascertain if change has taken place and can draw conclusions about the direction, permanence, and determinants and agents of the change. Frequently, this procedure is used in conjunction with comparative studies (page 101). The main limitation of historical-statistical analysis is that data for the time periods under study may not be available.

Sociologists have used historical-statistical analysis to study the emergence of the city as a new form of community organization and, particularly, the changing structure of the large metropolitan city. The use of this approach is illustrated by Leo Schnore's study of the timing of the decentralization (suburbanization) of American cities.

Although decentralization is still continuing, much of the change has already taken place. The problem facing Schnore was one of gathering information about cities at earlier historical dates so that he could identify when decentralization began. Schnore defined the beginning of decentralization as that time when population growth in the rings around the city exceeded the growth of the city itself. He was able to get statistical information on the population of the cities and their rings from the United States Census of Popula-

tion, which has been taken every ten years since 1790 (see page 324).

For his unit of analysis, Schnore selected the "metropolitan unit of population data" (which is similar to the SMSA, see page 342) as it was defined in the 1950 census; he also recategorized population data from earlier censuses to conform to this standard definition. Schnore prepared statistical data for 99 metropolitan central cities with populations of at least 100,000. By reviewing the historical profiles for each city, he was able to determine the earliest decade of decentralization for each. Since ring growth may exceed city growth for reasons other than the occurrence of decentralization (e.g., it may result from some unique events that have created a momentary population change), Schnore's criterion was that each city had to show the excess of ring growth over city growth for three successive decades before it could be classified as experiencing decentralization.

Analysis of the statistical profiles enabled Schnore to draw some interesting conclusions. For example, he found that the suburbanization or decentralization process is not new. New York City began decentralizing as early as 1850, and nine other cities did so before 1900. The rush of decentralization, popularly known as the "flight to the suburbs," began as early as 1920–1940, when as many as sixty cities started decentralizing.

Schnore was able to combine data on the timing of decentralization with other historical-statistical information in order to determine the causes of decentralization. His study is only one of numerous efforts to study complex social and cultural changes through the use of historical-statistical analysis.

Leo Schnore, "The Timing of Metropolitan Decentralization: A Contribution to the Debate," *Journal of the American Institute of Planners,* 25 (November 1959): 200–206.

Some years ago William Ogburn noted that material or technological aspects of culture tend to soar ahead in their rate of change, while norms, beliefs, values, and patterns of social organization change much more slowly. The result of such differing rates of change is a phenomenon he termed *cultural lag*. Several sociologists have expanded Ogburn's idea and provided insights into the problem of cultural lag in American society. Hauser gives the following illustration:

The right to bear arms, important in 1790, is today a fine example of cultural lag. With almost three fourths of the American people urban and about 65 percent metropolitan, a gun is certainly not needed to obtain food or for protection from wild animals or hostile Indians. The widespread prevalence of guns throughout urban and metropolitan America gives the United States the highest gunshot death rate of any nation in the world. We kill or maim tens of thousands of people a year compared with dozens in other comparable populations in which the gun is prohibited to the private citizen. In the United Kingdom, a society not too dissimilar from our own in many respects, not even the police force, except under special conditions, is permitted to bear arms. The right to bear arms in contemporary America is a cultural atavism—a survival from the past which works much mischief in contemporary society.[28]

As Hauser points out, while some cultural "lags" may pose a threat to society, others are insignificant. "In the trivial category is the persistence of the string designed to keep collars closed against inclement weather before the advent of the pin and the button. The string has become the necktie, a relatively harmless if not always esthetic vestige which has acquired a new function, decoration."[29] In a later section (page 300) we will discuss some of the factors that may cause people to resist change—a tendency that often cannot be overcome by the mere accumulation of facts or logical arguments.

28. Philip M. Hauser, "Population and Social Problems," in *Contemporary Civilization: Issue 5*, ed. James Findlay (Glenview, Ill.: Scott, Foresman and Company, 1971), p. 181.
29. Ibid., p. 184.

AGENTS OF CHANGE

To some extent, all institutional sectors of a society are instruments both for changing and maintaining the status quo. But certain social institutions seem more central than others in initiating and directing change. In modern society these are the economic, political, and educational systems. The mass media contribute to the rapid diffusion of cultural change and may also influence its direction.

THE ECONOMY

The worlds of business, industry, and finance seem to most Americans to be great founts of change and progress in this society. In fact, patriotic literature on how an economic system based on free enterprise made this society great continues to wax strong. We are encouraged to believe that economic growth and progress are synonymous.

Unplanned Effects of Economic Change

In some respects, change has been built into daily life as a part of our economic system. Automobiles, the great backbone of the American economy, are a case in point. Properly looked after, a new car can provide adequate transportation for many years; but each year the auto makers launch multimillion-dollar advertising campaigns extolling the improvements available in their new models, the dealer warns that the trade-in value of the present car is diminishing, and the owner, if not troubled by shame at driving an "old" car, at least is led to worry about how much he or she may be missing by not buying a new one. On the surface, most of the change initiated by the automotive industry is technical rather than social. In fact, however, the automobile manufacturers have encouraged us to accept the car as part of our status-ranking system.

Enthusiasm for economic and technological progress tends to obscure the fact that such change is seldom free of disruptive consequences. The growth of the automobile industry may again be cited as an example:

Courtesy Chicago Historical Society.

As long ago as the 1850s some of America's cities were experiencing the positive and negative consequences of technological change. Prior to the Civil War, Galena and Chicago were two of the most prosperous cities in Illinois. Galena, in fact, was the state's wealthiest city, the lead mining capital of the world, and the major commercial port on the upper Mississippi. Today, however, Galena is often described as the "town that time forgot." In 1853 the leaders of Galena rejected an opportunity for the city to become a railroad center, and from that time on, Galena's commerce and industry became smaller and smaller. No longer the bustling community of a past century (bottom left), the town now has a population of only 4500. Having changed very little since the days of its decline, Galena today (bottom right) attracts visitors because of its historical significance. Chicago, on the other hand, made the more progressive move of adopting the railroad, and the economic consequences have been obvious. Above are two views of Chicago's Water Tower on Michigan Avenue. A comparison between the drawing at the left, which was done more than a century ago, and the recent photograph at the right indicates the development of what is now America's second largest city.

Suppose that in 1914, Henry Ford had told the American people that he was offering them a revolutionary technology which had certain undeniably attractive features, but which would in the course of the next 60 years lead directly to the deaths of about two million people and the maiming of tens of millions of others in collisions; which would increase the incidence of deaths from heart attacks by reducing the opportunity for proper exercise; which would destroy our cities by making possible a mass exodus into the countryside which would then be scarred by inefficient land use; which would clog our judicial system with suits and countersuits resulting from damage and injury associated with the automobile; which would require the sacrifice of thousands of square miles of forests and fields for road construction; which would generate such pollution of the atmosphere that cities would at times become uninhabitable; which would consume vast amounts of irreplaceable mineral resources and would burn up in a century all the oil stored in the earth during the previous few hundred million years—what price should have been set on the internal combustion engine automobile, the agent of this technology?[30]

The Industrial Revolution created vital social and cultural changes that in turn triggered other changes throughout the whole social system. Industrial growth was marked by a change from small, locally owned enterprises to giant corporations with plants in many different areas. The entrepreneurs of the nineteenth century had their roots in the towns where they developed their factories; they identified with the towns and had a commitment to them. But the growth of the corporation brought with it the replacement of the owner-boss by professional managers, salaried executives whose primary job was to make money for the corporation and its stockholders. Seldom did they remain in one town with one factory during the whole course of their careers. They moved at the direction of their corporation, which often found it more profitable to close an old plant and start a new one in a more desirable location. New England is full of towns that time has passed by, their abandoned factories testifying to the fact that

progress for the textile industry meant relocation in the South, where labor was cheaper and raw materials were closer at hand.

The Case of Caliente

The problems caused by such relocations led W. F. Cottrell to study the sociological implications of economic change. In his now classic study, "Death by Dieselization," Cottrell examined a community faced with radical change in its economic structure in order to observe the effect of economic change throughout the social structure.[31] He selected a one-industry town, where other economic factors did not enter in to complicate the case.

Caliente, as Cottrell called the town of his study, was located in the American Southwest. It had come into existence in order to service the steam locomotive, which in the beginning required frequent stops. Long before Caliente finally came to grief, many other railroad towns felt the negative effects of engineering progress, for with improvements in locomotive construction during the early part of the twentieth century, trains were able to travel longer and longer distances without needing to be serviced. Because Caliente was midway between terminals six hundred miles apart, however, these technical improvements actually represented a gain for the town. Trains still stopped at Caliente, and they now needed more servicing.

Thus Caliente grew and prospered with the railroad, and the people built homes, put in a water system in cast-iron pipes, established businesses, and built a twenty-seven-bed hospital, school buildings, a theater, and even a park. They also established a Chamber of Commerce, a Masonic Lodge, a Rotary Club, and other civic organizations. Caliente was a community with a solid social structure, growing and optimistic.

Caliente was suddenly threatened with extinction in the mid-1940s when the railroad announced that it would no longer maintain its facilities in the town. In Cottrell's words, "The location of Caliente was a function of boiler temperature and pressure and the resultant service requirements of the locomotive." World War II, which had originally brought increased

30. Joseph J. Loferski, "While Fantastic Technological Marvels Have Occurred, Our Cities Have Been Technologically Asleep," *Brown Alumni Monthly,* November 1972.

31. W. F. Cottrell, "Death by Dieselization," *American Sociological Review,* 16 (June 1951): 358–365.

prosperity to Caliente, had also hurried the de-mise of the steam locomotive. The war effort used up the old steam engine, and the govern-ment helped to underwrite the costs of their re-placement with diesels. The new diesel engines were more efficient and required fewer stops for servicing. Thus Caliente, a division point essen-tial to the steam engine, rapidly became obso-lete. A change that benefited most of American society sealed the fate of a one-industry town.

Nearly everyone in Caliente experienced some loss. The railroad had owned thirty-nine homes, a clubhouse, and a hotel in town. These became virtually worthless, but at least the company could write them off. The workers, who had seniority only in the local union, lost a great deal more. For many, technical advance meant that their old skills and talents were obso-lete. A boilermaker might be reduced to an un-skilled laborer. Moreover, three out of every four men had to look for new jobs, since the diesel engine reduced overall labor needs. The local merchants also lost badly. The younger ones could move out, but even they lost, for their property became worthless. The bondholders and the homeowners both lost; it was hard to foreclose on a dead town, and 135 homeowners had no one to sell to.

Cottrell observed that those people who had been the most "moral" in the American sense—that is, had lived by the values, goals, and norms of American culture—had suffered the most. Friendships rapidly cooled and the community structure, built on a seemingly solid foundation, began to disintegrate. The local owners who had assumed family and commu-nity responsibility lost the most; the nomads who ran national chain stores lost the least.

The early reaction of the people was to band together to save the town; they saw the community as a real, meaningful entity, and they tried to attract new industry. But no one wanted to come to Caliente. As hope for new industry faded, the people developed a feeling of bitterness against the railroad. They acknowl-edged that nobody wanted to stand in the way of progress, but they could not believe that true progress would penalize loyal employees and their families or destroy a community that had

developed in the American way through de-cades of service and good citizenship. They found it difficult to justify cold-blooded profit-motive decisions. The workers tried to get union backing to set up new rules that might aid them in retaining their jobs. They argued for "make-work" rules. They fought for "justice," for the things they had a "right to expect." But Caliente was dead, the victim of collective forces beyond the control of community leaders, forces that have their source in the vast systematic networks of social interdependence.

Calientes of the Future

During the years ahead, the United States and other industrial societies will see the birth and death of many Calientes. Technological changes related to new and old energy sources, altera-tions of manufacturing processes, and changing patterns of agriculture will have repercussions throughout all sectors of the social system. Changes that may be beneficial to some people will bring hardship to others. While our federal government and the society at large have be-come increasingly concerned about dislocations caused by technological change, it is difficult even to anticipate them and more difficult still to counteract them. Economic change, like changes in other areas of social life, will contin-ue to have unforeseen and often far-reaching effects.

GOVERNMENT

American government is organized on three lev-els—federal, state, and local—each consisting of executive, legislative, and judicial branches. At a given time any branch of government at any level may be actively seeking to maintain stabili-ty or to foster change in particular areas of American life.

The federal government has done more than government at the state and local levels to stimulate change, not only because it has the financial resources and power to initiate and implement far-reaching programs but also be-cause it provides a focal point for the debating of national issues. It is at the federal level of government, too, that competition between the two major political parties is most intense, stimulating the development of programs designed to attract voter support.

Thomas Jefferson, one of the chief architects of the Republic and in many ways a conservative, was well aware that government plays a role in fostering change:

I am not an advocate for frequent changes in laws and institutions. But laws and institutions must go hand in hand with the progress of the human mind as that becomes more developed, more enlightened, as new discoveries are made, new truths discovered and manners and opinions change with the change of circumstances. Institutions must advance also to keep pace with the times.

For much of the country's history, government efforts to alter societal patterns had very specific goals, and often the goals were those being pressed by local or regional interests. They involved among other things land acquisition and suppression of the Indians, the building of roads, canals, and railroads, and the development of land-grant colleges. In contemporary times the federal government has fostered change in ever expanding areas, including many that closely affect the lives of millions of citizens. It has attempted to provide financial security for the elderly and adequate health care for all. It has attempted to alter long-existing patterns of inequality between whites and blacks and between males and females. It has attempted to stimulate the economy and to stabilize prices. And it has attempted to wipe out poverty.

Government efforts to initiate and guide change have met with mixed success. Some programs have achieved their goals well enough to win widespread popular support, whereas others have turned out to be such dismal failures that they have lost whatever support they originally had. There is a growing recognition, too, that the society has been changed at least as much by governmental expansion per se as it has by government efforts to foster particular types of social change. The federal government has become by all odds the nation's largest single employer. When it alters its programs or reallocates funds, the jobs of countless individuals are affected. In areas where large-scale government programs or facilities open or close, booms or busts occur. A further effect of government "bigness" has been the impact of federal spending on individual tax bills and purchasing power, on particular industries, and on the economy of the country as a whole. In recent years these side effects of governmental expansion have become matters of increasing public concern.

EDUCATION

Although education has often been championed as the best hope for improving American society, in fact our formal system of education is primarily an agent of socialization rather than of change. This is especially true at the elementary and secondary levels. But even today's "multiversity" serves the socializing functions of putting a polish on young adults, preparing them to enter the labor force, helping them find marriage partners, and passing on the accepted knowledge of the past that will enable them to get along in various social roles.

Despite the widely held assumption that going to college changes attitudes and values, the evidence does not support this belief. On the basis of data gathered a number of years ago from some thirty colleges and universities, Philip Jacobs concluded that students' values did *not* generally change in college, that higher education tended to refine values already instilled, and that only a few small colleges, known for the high quality of their liberal education, seemed to have any major impact in changing values.[32] Despite many criticisms of the Jacobs study, more recent research has generally supported his conclusions, suggesting that college serves mainly to bring out tendencies already within students, to sharpen their attitudes and norms, and to make them more conscious of the general cultural milieu.

32. Philip E. Jacobs, *Changing Values in College* (New York: Harper & Row, Inc., 1957).

THE MASS MEDIA

The influence of the mass media in fostering changes in attitudes and values has been a subject of continuing debate. Studies to date indicate that the media probably have a less powerful effect than is commonly supposed; people do not readily change their views on particular subjects in response to media messages. But as we noted in the chapter on socialization (page 164), there has been growing concern about the possible effects of television—and to a lesser extent films, magazines, and newspapers—in stimulating violence and other types of deviation from societal norms. Much additional research is needed before we can draw firm conclusions on these issues.

Whatever the effects of the mass media on societal values and standards of conduct, they have clearly been responsible for many kinds of social and cultural change. The development of television, for example, created a large new industry and many new occupations, and it brought changes in other industries as well—witness the decline of the neighborhood movie theater and subsequent changes in the film industry, the marked growth of advertising budgets, and the increasing professionalization of sports. There has been little empirical research dealing with the impact of television on lifestyles, but few doubt that it has had some effect. In many American homes, television scheduling helps determine mealtimes and bedtimes. New Year's Day has become a day for watching three football games. Morning programs for preschool children are translated into a chance for their mothers to "get something done."

Television can stimulate interest in possibilities for change by providing a close-up view, if usually a somewhat distorted one, of the world beyond our immediate experience. Through television, we come to see political leaders as personalities, and whether we like them or not may affect our attitudes toward the policies they represent. The fact that crime, civil strife, and war are brought into our living rooms may influence our beliefs and judgments about these issues. On a more personal level, we see that new fashions are catching on and may decide that we need to replenish our wardrobes. Or we may become convinced by commercials that expensively furnished homes equipped with a microwave oven, a garbage compactor, a TV and telephone in almost every room, and two late-model cars in the garage are now the rule in American society. Many people go into debt in an attempt to achieve the standard of material comfort that advertisers present as normative.

The part played by the mass media, and particularly by television, in stimulating and fostering change is of great interest to sociologists, who are trying to assess more accurately the influence of the media in altering and diffusing beliefs, ideas, knowledge, technology, and other aspects of culture. The significance of mass communication in modern societies will be examined more fully in Chapter 14.

RESISTANCE TO CHANGE

Even within rapidly changing societies, there may be considerable resistance to new ideas, new scientific and technical developments, and new patterns of social life. Often change is resisted because it conflicts with traditional values and beliefs. Or a particular change may simply cost too much money. And sometimes people resist change because it interferes with their habits or makes them feel frightened or threatened.

SOCIAL AND CULTURAL BASES OF RESISTANCE

Resistance to change is usually most pronounced when traditional values and beliefs are involved. In India, much of the population is ill fed or even starving, yet over 200 million cows, sacred to the Hindus, are not only exempt from being slaughtered for food but are also allowed to roam through villages and farmlands, often causing extensive damage to crops. It is unlikely that the raising of cattle for food will become acceptable in India in the near future, since the eating of beef runs counter to long-held religious beliefs.

Throughout history, new ideas have often met with entrenched resistance. The astronomical theories of Copernicus and Galileo were long suppressed because they challenged beliefs about the central position of human beings in the universe. When Darwin proposed his theories of the origin of the species and the evolution of biological forms, this new scientific "truth" also clashed head-on with existing religious beliefs, touching off controversies that are not dead even today.

ECONOMIC COSTS

Sometimes the cost of an innovation can prevent its adoption, at least for a time. A society of limited economic means cannot afford to initiate programs involving nuclear energy, nor can the majority of its citizens afford to adopt such modern appliances and conveniences as refrigerators, central heating, and a family automobile. Even in the most affluent societies, limited economic resources constitute a barrier to changes that might otherwise be readily adopted. In the United States most people accept the desirability of more effective controls on pollution, cheaper and more convenient systems of public transportation, and adequate health care for all; the fact that improvement in these areas comes very slowly is a matter not only of priorities but also of cost.

In many cases, too, vested interests work to forestall changes. The automotive industry regularly introduces styling and engineering changes to stimulate sales, but it just as regularly resists consumer-oriented and ecology-oriented changes (smaller cars, safety devices, pollution controls) that threaten profits. The beverage industry has fought vigorously against the adoption of state laws banning nonreturnable bottles and cans, even though Oregon's experiment in banning nonreturnables has significantly reduced the

problem of highway litter. Labor unions, to protect the jobs of their members, have resisted not only the automated factory but also the diesel engine (the fireman's union), the unbreakable plastic window (the glazer's union), and even the paint roller (the painter's union).

INDIVIDUAL FACTORS

Personal habits, attitudes, and other predispositions can limit the extent to which individuals are willing to accept given innovations. There are many examples of products and procedures that failed to be adopted by people for whom they would seemingly have been beneficial. For example, in a rural village in Peru an effort was made to reduce the incidence of typhoid and other water-borne diseases by introducing the hygenic measure of boiling contaminated water. But in spite of efforts to convince the residents of the advantages of the innovation and the great benefits to their health, most refused to take it up. Their beliefs about the origins of disease and their association of boiled water with illness prevented them from accepting this new kind of behavior.[33]

Another example involves the attempt by an American firm to market a new product called Analoze, a combination pain killer and stomach sweetener in the form of a lozenge. Since Americans annually ingest billions of headache pills and aids to acid indigestion, it was felt that a lozenge combining the benefits of both would be a natural winner. But Americans have a deeply established habit of swallowing headache pills with water rather than dissolving them in their mouth or chewing them, and this habit apparently prevented Analoze from becoming a success. After extensive and very expensive efforts to market this pill, the company withdrew it from the market, a total failure.[34]

Sometimes fear plays an important part in individual resistance to innovation. For example, many people in our society are still afraid of air travel. Although carefully gathered government statistics indicate that flying is many times safer than traveling by automobile, these indi-

33. Edward Wellin, "Water Boiling in a Peruvian Town," in *Health, Culture, and Community*, ed. Benjamin D. Paul (New York: Russell Sage Foundation, 1955), pp. 71–103.

34. Everett M. Rogers and F. Floyd Shoemaker, *Communication of Innovations: A Cross Cultural Approach*, 2nd ed. (New York: The Free Press, 1971), pp. 136–137.

Sometimes people resist change out of fear. Some Americans have resisted the influx of "outsiders" — people of a different racial or ethnic group — into their neighborhoods because they have felt that the outsiders posed a threat to their safety or to their way of life.

viduals are petrified by the idea of getting into an airplane and taking off. Fear is also involved in resistance to changes that threaten people with a loss of status, income, or power. Individual opposition to both the civil rights movement and the women's movement has often reflected the fear of dominant group members — whites on the one hand, males on the other — that gains for a minority would mean losses for them. In such cases stereotyped thinking (page 267) is likely to act as a further barrier to acceptance of change.

People's habitual ways of thinking, acting, and believing are not easily displaced. Such individual habits can effectively block the adoption or diffusion of change.

SUMMARY

The term *social change* refers to alterations in norms, role expectations, sanctions, or ranking. Because groups constitute social systems, modifications in one component of their structures lead to modifications in other components. *Cultural change* occurs through the acquisition of new traits and the abandonment of obsolete ones or through the synthesis of new cultural configurations. Typically, social and cultural change are closely interrelated and not easily distinguishable from each other.

Societal change is often stimulated by the discovery or exhaustion of exploitable natural resources. Energy resources in particular have a profound impact on both direction and degree of change.

Population growth, ideology, and leadership also can stimulate change. Rapid population growth places pressure on resources; ideology channels change along lines determined by political or religious convictions; leaders help articulate group goals and the routes for achieving them. Charismatic leadership often plays a key part in the development of social movements.

Various types of processes are involved in the development and diffusion of change. Nineteenth-century theorists tended to see societal change as an evolutionary process leading to progressively more desirable social patterns. The wisdom of attempting to intervene in this process became the subject of considerable debate. The view of societal change as proceeding along an inevitable path according to inexorable laws has now been largely discounted.

Anthropological studies of cultural change have focused on intersocietal borrowing, whereas sociological research has centered more on the diffusion of changes *within* societies. The significance of invention as a source of change increases as a society's culture base broadens, creating the possibility of more and more new trait combinations.

Efforts to initiate sociocultural change and guide its course have ranged from reclamation of land resources to antipoverty programs and large-scale energy research. The mixed success of such efforts reflects the difficulty of foresee-ing, much less controlling, all the variables involved. Changes in material and technological culture usually occur more rapidly than changes in attitudes and values. The unevenness of change results in various forms of social and cultural lag.

Of the various social institutions that stimulate change in the United States, one of the most important is the economic system, with its emphases on developing new consumer goods and improving industrial technology. Another important agent of change is government—particularly the federal government—which has been the source of far-reaching programs in such areas as social security, health, welfare, and civil rights. The educational system and the mass media also stimulate change, though the extent of their influence is less clear.

Resistance to change is caused by many factors—some social and cultural, some personal and individual. Stable patterns of social organization that meet the needs of group members constitute barriers to social change. Cultural values and beliefs may also be a basis for resistance to change. Another factor is economic: change may be too expensive or threaten vested interests. On an individual level, people tend to resist changes that are inconsistent with their habitual ways of thinking, acting, and believing or that somehow threaten their personal security.

11
Demographic Change

POPULATION GROWTH—THE LESSONS OF HISTORY

Malthus's Gloomy Prophecy   The Demographic Transition in the Industrialized World   Demographic Changes in the Developing World   Population Growth and Economic Development

MEXICO—THE PROBLEMS OF A NEIGHBOR

Background of the Problem   Progress and Poverty   Birth Control: The Current Situation

THE PEOPLE'S REPUBLIC OF CHINA

The Restructuring of a Society   Marx Against Malthus   The Lessons of China and Mexico

THE UNITED STATES

Is There a Population Problem?   Changing Orientations Toward Birth Control

POPULATION CONTROL IN THE DEVELOPING WORLD

Latin America   Asia and Africa

In the last three decades the world has been rocked by two great explosions—the literal explosion of the atomic bomb and the figurative explosion of the world's population. Indeed, during the last decade the mass media have focused attention increasingly on the population explosion as the more serious of the two threats. Why? Simply because the world's societies have responded even less successfully to the challenge of controlling their own runaway growth than to the challenge of controlling nuclear weapons. If the current rate of growth continues, the population of the world will double by the time most readers of this text are fifty years old. What kind of society, what kinds of group life will this mean—for you readers and your children, and for the billions of other human beings who may never have a chance to learn to read?

No social problem is more closely tied to questions of human values than the problem of checking population growth. If there is a universal human value, then surely it is the value of "being alive." To be born is good and to die is bad—it is as simple as that. Until recently most people have not even considered the question of whether a conscious effort should be made to limit births.

We will begin this chapter with a historical overview of the growth of human populations, to show the background and dimensions of the so-called population explosion. Then, through case studies of Mexico, China, and the United States, we will point up some of the implications of current population trends for societies in different stages of economic development and population growth. Finally, we will consider differences in attitudes toward family planning in various parts of the world, together with prospects for change.

Throughout the chapter we will try to make clear the differences between the industrially advanced, urban societies that have already undergone a demographic transition from high to relatively low rates of population growth (for example, the United States, the countries of western Europe, Canada, Australia, and Japan) and the technologically underdeveloped or developing nations that have yet to experience this transition and are currently growing in population very rapidly (the countries of Latin America and Africa and some Asian countries, especially India, Ceylon, Pakistan, and the Philippines). As we will see, the patterns and problems of population growth vary markedly in these different parts of the world.

POPULATION GROWTH—THE LESSONS OF HISTORY

For a generation, world population has been growing at the rate of about 2 percent a year, faster than ever before in history. With total population now having reached 4 billion, this means an increase of 75 to 80 million people each year—more than the current population of Great Britain.

The limited evidence available suggests that the total population of the world at the beginning of the Christian era was about 250 million people. It took roughly 1650 years for that figure

1. Thomas R. Malthus, *An Essay on the Principle of Population* (Homewood, Ill.: Richard D. Irwin, Inc., 1963).

to double to half a billion, but in the next three hundred years it doubled and redoubled, reaching two billion by 1930 (Figure 11.1, below). If present trends continue, world population will continue to double about every thirty-five years.

MALTHUS'S GLOOMY PROPHECY

Thomas Robert Malthus (1766–1834), an English clergyman, mathematician, and economist, was the first to write systematically about the possible dire consequences of unchecked population growth. In his *Essay on the Principle of Population,* first published in 1798, he set forth the theory that human populations could—and under the right circumstances *would*—grow by geometrical progression (2, 4, 8, 16, 32, 64, 128), whereas food production could increase only arithmetically (1, 2, 3, 4, 5, 6, 7) and would reach some ultimate limit. He predicted that whenever a population grew to the point where it could no longer be supported by the available food supply, the death rate would inevitably rise to bring the two forces again into balance.[1]

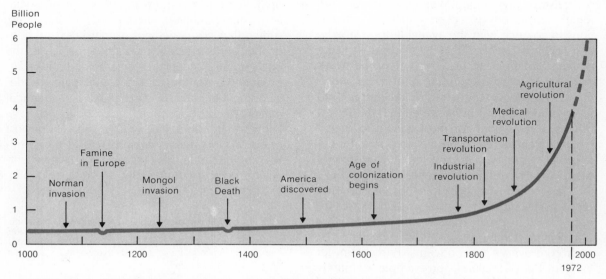

SOURCE: Data for 1300, Ralph Thomlinson, *Population Dynamics* (New York: Random House, Inc., 1965); for 1650–1900, A. M. Carr-Saunders, *World Population: Past Growth and Present Trends* (New York: International Scholarly Book Service, 1964); for 1950–2000, United Nations data; other estimates by Social and Economic Statistics Administration, U.S. Bureau of the Census. Chart from *Population Program Assistance* (Washington, D.C.: Agency for International Development, Office of Population, December 1972), p. 60.

Figure 11.1. TEN CENTURIES OF WORLD POPULATION GROWTH

As this German portrayal of the danse macabre *suggests, death was an ever present specter in medieval Europe. According to Malthus, high death rates due to famines, plagues, and wars were "divinely ordained" to keep population in balance with the available food supply. Writing in 1798 that "the power of population is indefinitely greater than the power in the earth to produce subsistence for man," he predicted that the death rate would rise again if population was not controlled.*

Malthus believed that the biological drive for sexual gratification was essentially incompatible with the biological need for food. It is a law of nature, he said, that "the power of population is indefinitely greater than the power in the earth to produce subsistence" for people. Malthus predicted that all of a society's efforts to improve its standards of living were in the long run destined to fail. Any increase in the food supply would only further stimulate population growth, so that the benefits would be quickly wiped out.

Historically, famine, plagues, and wars had functioned as *positive checks* to keep populations in balance with the available food supply, and Malthus believed that these disasters were divinely ordained. In his later writing he urged that people try to avert future disaster by applying the *preventive check* of "moral restraint" to limit reproduction. But he feared that the sexual drive was too strong for most people to accept what he considered to be the only morally defensible means of reducing fertility—postponement of marriage and continence in marriage.

The Malthusian principle became synonymous with a gloomy prophecy that living standards for the great masses of people were doomed to remain low, and as such it stirred both controversy and concern.[2] Prime Minister William Pitt of England, for example, withdrew proposed legislation that would have provided relief payments in direct relation to family size, for Malthus's theory had led him to fear that such a law would only encourage more rapid population growth and thus lead to increased poverty. Fifty years later Karl Marx denounced the Malthusian doctrine as just another defense of the status quo. Poverty, he claimed, resulted not from a shortage of resources but rather from the capitalist system of production and distribution.

In retrospect, we can see that Malthus's theory failed to account for the possibility of social and cultural change. In the first place, it assumed that postponement of marriage and continence in marriage would continue to be the only morally acceptable means for limiting reproduction. Malthus did not anticipate the development of effective mechanical and chemical means of contraception, nor could he have known that within 150 years of his death most of the world's major religious bodies—and millions of individual families—would have accepted the need for some form of family planning and birth control.

2. For critical commentary, see Judy K. Morris, "Malthus in Retrospect," *Population Bulletin* of the Population Reference Bureau, 22, No. 1 (February 1966): 28 ff.; and William Petersen, *Population*, 2nd ed. (New York: Macmillan, Inc., 1969), pp. 141 ff.

Perhaps even more important in upsetting Malthus's formula have been the revolutionary changes in agricultural methods and technology. In Malthus's time, it was the practice in farming to leave one third of the land fallow each year so that the soil could recover its fertility. If this system had continued and there had been no other changes in agricultural techniques, Malthus's dire forecast might indeed have come true already. But the introduction of crop rotation in the mid-nineteenth century increased land utilization by 50 percent. Shortly after Malthus's death, too, came the important discovery of chemical fertilizer. This development and subsequent improvements in farming techniques—irrigation, hybridization of seed, pest and weed control, better drainage systems, more efficient tools—have helped increase agricultural yields in the developed world ten times over those of Malthus's day. World population in the same period has increased less than four times. Thus the Malthusian day of reckoning has at least been temporarily postponed, and there is hope that further changes in agriculture and economic planning will prolong the postponement.

THE DEMOGRAPHIC TRANSITION IN THE INDUSTRIALIZED WORLD

Concern over today's population explosion tends to obscure the fact that throughout most of human history rates of population growth were little more than enough for couples to replace themselves. Probably never before 1800 did the world's population growth rate reach 0.5 percent, or a fourth of its present level. (See the definitions of demographic terms, opposite.) Birth rates were generally much higher than now, but high fertility only compensated for high rates of mortality, especially among infants and children. As noted in the preceding chapter (page 280), the ravages of war, famine, and disease periodically brought actual *declines* in population on both a regional and a world scale.

BASIC DEMOGRAPHIC TERMS

Demography is the statistical study of populations, their size, distribution, and composition. It is concerned with such matters as the changes over time in fertility, mortality, and migration and with factors related to these changes. In this chapter we will focus primarily on four basic demographic concepts and their implications: population growth rate, death rate, birth rate, and fertility rate.

The term *population growth rate* refers to the rate, usually given as an annual percentage, by which a population is changing in size, either growing or declining. For the world as a whole, the growth rate depends on the relationship between births and deaths in a given year: it is obtained by subtracting the total number of deaths from the total number of births and then calculating what percentage the remainder is of the world population for that year. Thus, if there are as many infants born to the world in a year as there are people dying, the population remains stable; any excess of births or of deaths leads respectively to growth or to decline. For a given nation or community, the population growth rate for any year must include not only the net difference between births and deaths *(natural growth)* but also the net difference, if any, between in-migration and out-migration. During the late nineteenth and early twentieth centuries, for example, in-migration was a significant factor in boosting annual growth rates in the United States.

Birth rates and *death rates* are generally figured on the basis of every 1000 persons in a given population for a given year. Thus a birth rate (or death rate) of 20 means that there were twenty births (or deaths), on the average, for every 1000 persons in the total population. Often specific death (mortality) rates are calculated on the basis of some variable such as age, occupation, race, or sex. The *infant mortality rate*, for example, indicates the number of children per 1000 live births who die during the first year of life.

Finally, the term *fertility rate* refers to the number of births in a particular population relative to every 1000 women of childbearing age (usually defined as women from fifteen to forty-five). Fertility relates only to actual births and should thus be distinguished from *fecundity*, which refers to the biological capacity for producing offspring.

The Industrial Revolution

In western Europe in the nineteenth century, industrial growth and progress in agriculture were accompanied by a gradual reduction in death rates. Since 1800, when Malthus wrote, improvements in sanitation and successive advances in medicine have lowered death rates in most of the industrialized nations from levels of 25 to 30 per 1000 population to current levels ranging from 7 to 11 per 1000. In the United States, mortality rates in the last two decades have stabilized, at least temporarily, in the area of 9 or 10 per 1000.

As death rates began to drop in the Western world, rates of population growth accelerated accordingly, causing many people to fear that Malthus's prophecy would soon be fulfilled. By the middle of the nineteenth century, it was apparent that more rapid population growth was both a spur to and a result of such phenomena as urbanization, industrialization, migration, and some improvements in standards of living. The agricultural revolution was slowly providing an increasingly adequate food supply, and industrial expansion was bringing jobs to growing numbers of people. Population growth, in fact, came to be seen as a necessary stimulant for economic development: if the economy was to grow, more people were needed to produce — and, in turn, consume — more goods. As we shall see, the same argument is sometimes used today to defend unchecked population growth in the developing countries.

Declining Growth Rates

By the middle of the nineteenth century, per capita income in western Europe and the United States was already much higher than it is today in the developing areas of the world, and the population base was much smaller. Furthermore, changes in the rate of population growth occurred more slowly and were closely tied to an overall pattern of technical, economic, and social change.[3] Death rates, for example, declined only gradually during the nineteenth and early twentieth centuries, as medical science slowly improved; and by the time they had dropped significantly, birth rates had also begun to decline. Birth rates in the industrialized countries have continued to fall during the present century, while death rates have tended to level out.

The lowering of birth rates in the industrialized countries has been related to a number of factors. In the first place, the marked reduction in infant and child mortality meant that parents no longer needed to have eight or ten children to be sure that some would survive to adulthood. Equally important, industrialization and urbanization were gradually changing the character of the family from a producing to a consuming unit. In an agricultural economy, children contribute to the family income, farming along with their parents. Industrialization took work away from the family setting and shifted economic responsibility primarily to the father. Children ceased to be economically productive members of the family unit and became instead a family expense. At the same time, the changing structure of the labor force and the extension of the educational system, especially in the United States, led to new job opportunities outside the home for women. A wife who was not kept at home by a succession of pregnancies and births could often find work that would appreciably increase the family income. These various changes have worked together in the industrialized nations to create favorable attitudes toward the conscious limitation of family size. And these attitudes, even more than the development of effective contraceptives, have been responsible for gradually decreasing birth and fertility rates and thus for holding population growth rates, over the long term, to fairly moderate levels.

Over a period of two hundred years, then, the now industrialized nations have experienced what demographers call a *demographic transition,* moving from high mortality rates and high fertility rates to low mortality and low fertility. Death rates started to drop before birth rates did, causing population growth rates to rise rapidly

3. See George J. Stolnitz, "The Demographic Transition," and J. J. Spengler, "Population and Economic Growth," in *Population: The Vital Revolution,* ed. R. Freedman (New York: Doubleday & Company, Inc., 1964). See also E. A. Wrigley, *Population and History* (New York: McGraw-Hill Book Company, 1969).

This family, like thousands of others in India, has no home but the open sidewalk. Conditions are equally grim for those families living in tiny, windowless, rat-infested houses in the slums. With a population of well over 500 million, India is in no position to meet even the most basic needs of a large number of its citizens.

for a time. Gradually, however, birth rates also began to fall, and rates of growth in most of the industrialized nations now seem to be stabilizing at relatively low levels. During the 1960s in the United States and the Soviet Union, for example, annual growth rates declined from a high of 1.65 percent to a low of less than 1 percent. Japan and most countries of western Europe had even lower growth rates, ranging from 0.2 to 0.75 percent. Because of the large population base in most of the industrialized nations, even moderate growth can be expected to worsen many existing problems—crowded housing, jammed highways, air and water pollution, the energy shortage—at least if people continue their present life-styles. But it seems unlikely that population growth will itself greatly affect societal prosperity one way or the other.

DEMOGRAPHIC CHANGES IN THE DEVELOPING WORLD

Birth and death rates in the industrialized countries gradually arrived at their present levels as a result of modifications that took place over two centuries. By contrast, the developing nations in Asia, Africa, and Latin America have experienced a precipitous drop in their death rates over a period of only twenty to thirty years, while their birth rates have remained close to their previous high levels, averaging about 40 per 1000 as compared to about 17 per 1000 in the industrial countries (Figure 11.2, page 310). As Dorn states the matter, "It is the combination of a medieval birth rate with a twentieth-century death rate that is responsible for the current high rate of population increase."[4]

4. Harold F. Dorn, "World Population Growth," in *The Population Dilemma*, ed. Philip M. Hauser (Englewood Cliffs N.J.: Prentice-Hall, Inc., 1963), p. 16.

The Revolution in Mortality Control

Since World War II, public health programs involving the widespread use of antibiotics, vaccines, and insecticides—all imported from the industrialized nations—have caused death rates in the developing world to plummet from 35 to 40 per 1000 population to averages between 10 and 20 per 1000. In a few countries, death rates are now comparable to those in the industrialized world. Although life expectancy has improved somewhat for all age groups, the marked drop in death rates has been caused primarily by dramatic reductions in infant and child mortality. This is the fact that gives substance to the phrase "population explosion." It is not that couples are having more children than they did before, but rather that more of their offspring are surviving and eventually becoming parents themselves. Even if the young people already born were to produce only enough children to replace themselves, world population could

be expected to increase almost 60 percent before becoming stabilized around the year 2050.[5] With birth and death rates at their present levels, world population could double twice in that period, growing from 4 to 16 billion.

According to United Nations projections, more than 90 percent of the world population increase that can be expected by the end of this century will be generated by the less developed nations, which are currently doubling their populations more than twice as fast as countries in the industrialized world.[6] Already the developing countries account for about 70 percent of the world's total population. The changing dis-

5. Thomas Frejka, "The Prospects for Stationary World Population," *Scientific American*, March 1973.
6. Ansley J. Coale, "The History of the Human Population," *Scientific American*, September 1974, p. 51. Coale's article is one of eleven in a special issue of *Scientific American* devoted to an examination of demographic processes and the problems posed by current rates of population growth.

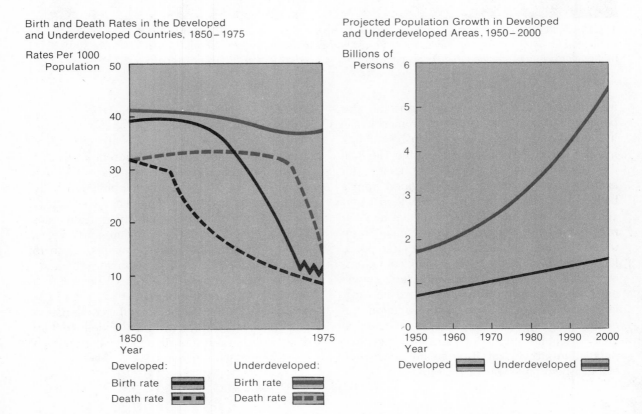

Figure 11.2. POPULATION TRENDS IN THE DEVELOPED AND UNDERDEVELOPED COUNTRIES

tribution of the world's population becomes dramatically clear in the case of Latin America: in 1900 only one out of every thirty-seven persons in the world was a Latin American, but by 1980 the figure is expected to be one in twelve.

Traditionalism Versus Change

In the developing nations, Western technology is being imported by societies which, for the most part, are still traditional in orientation. It has been relatively simple and inexpensive to lower death rates dramatically over a very short period of time; in Ceylon, for example, the death rate dropped 40 percent in a single year following the widespread use of residual insecticides to combat malaria. But it has proved very difficult to implement programs of birth control, which depend for their ultimate success not on technical knowledge and government support but on the development of norms favorable to the limitation of family size.

The complexity of social and cultural change is nowhere more apparent than in the area of population dynamics, for here the values, beliefs, and behavior patterns of traditional or folk societies stand in marked contrast to those that have now evolved in urban, industrialized societies. In most of the developing countries, for example, almost everyone marries—and marries young—which means that the wives have a long reproductive period. In addition, the desire for male heirs continues to be strong. Sons carry on the family name, provide the hard labor still so necessary for economic survival, perform key roles at religious ceremonials, and often are considered proof of the father's masculinity. Not least important, sons are a form of social security: if parents should survive to old age, they must, under present circumstances, rely on their sons to take care of them.

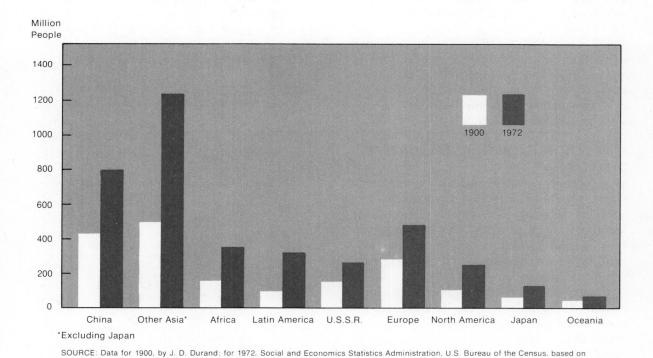

SOURCE: Data for 1900, by J. D. Durand; for 1972, Social and Economics Statistics Administration, U.S. Bureau of the Census, based on United Nations data. Chart from *Population Program Assistance*, p. 61.

Figure 11.3. POPULATION BY AREAS, 1900 AND 1972

Studies in many countries of the developing world consistently show that between 60 and 80 percent of both men and women say they want to limit their family size. Yet the fact is that most do not.[7] A partial explanation is that many people in these societies continue to assume that some of their children will probably die in infancy or childhood. Thus when they say that they want only three or four children, they seem to mean three or four who will survive to adulthood.

Another factor that helps account for the continued high birth rates in these societies is the strong force of tradition. Children aspire to be what their parents were, a value orientation that tends to discourage individual motivation for change.

Even among the upper classes, there is no clear-cut pattern of family planning that would provide a model for others to adopt. As long as traditional patterns are maintained, those who try to plan their families may feel like, and be perceived as, outsiders. Yet evidence supports the hypothesis that unchecked population growth threatens to preclude the achievement of social and economic goals in the developing nations. Indeed, where food supplies are already inadequate, as they are in most parts of Asia, the challenge of checking this rapid growth may soon be a matter of survival.[8]

POPULATION GROWTH AND ECONOMIC DEVELOPMENT

Most societies and their leaders proclaim themselves in favor of higher living standards, more adequate food supplies, technical innovation, and economic growth. But how can such aspirations be achieved, and what relationship, if any, exists between socioeconomic development and population growth?

Some leaders of the developing countries, pointing to the history of the industrialized nations, assert that rapid population growth is a necessary stimulant to economic expansion. Eugene Black sums up their thinking as follows:

Some people argue that a big population implies a good market for the businessman's product: he can use mass production techniques and charge low prices. They insist, too, that with a growing population, the businessman constantly finds demand exceeding his estimates. Optimism and production run high; new products win ready acceptance, while obsolete industries die painlessly; the incentive to invest is strong and social mobility and change are encouraged. The burden of social costs is spread widely. By contrast, they suggest, a declining or even stationary population brings pessimism and economic stagnation; there is insufficient reward for private enterprise, and the state is thereby forced to intervene increasingly in fields better left to the private citizen.[9]

In Latin America, many people point to the vast expanses of empty space to demonstrate the need for more people. Bolivia, for example, has as much land area as East and West Germany combined but only about five million people, less than one-tenth the population of West Germany alone; hence the conclusion that Bolivia is not threatened by its current high rate of population growth but actually needs more people to stimulate economic development. It is argued that population control will follow naturally, as it did in western Europe and the United States, once economic development has taken place. But are these in fact the lessons from history?

Parallels and Contrasts

It is true that the current rate of population growth in Latin America is no greater than that of the United States between 1790 and 1860, but different patterns of settlement and of social

7. For a critical summary of the research on attitudes toward family size, see Bernard Berelson, "KAP Studies on Fertility," in *Family Planning and Population Programs: A Review of World Developments*, ed. B. Berelson et al. (Chicago: The University of Chicago Press, 1966); and Bernard Berelson, "World Population: Status Report 1974," *Reports on Population/Family Planning*, No. 15 (1974): 47.

8. For discussions of the relation between agricultural and population growth, see Roger Revelle, "Food and Population," *Scientific American*, September 1974, pp. 160 ff.; William and Paul Paddock, *Famine 1975!* (Boston: Little, Brown and Company, 1968); and Paul R. Ehrlich, *The Population Bomb* (New York: Ballantine Books, 1968). See also *The Population Crisis: Implications and Plans for Action*, eds. Larry K. Y. Ng and Stuart Mudd (Bloomington, Ind.: Indiana University Press, 1965); and *Science*, May 9, 1975 (see entire issue).

9. Eugene R. Black, "Address to the Economic and Social Council of the United Nations," in Ng and Mudd, *Population Crisis*, p. 41. From a different but related perspective, David Heer argues that "large governmental expenditures on health and education will enhance the reduction in fertility obtainable from an increase in national economic level alone." See David M. Heer, "Economic Development and Fertility," *Demography*, 3, No. 2 (1966): 423–444.

and economic change seem to be leading to quite different consequences. Like the United States during its frontier days, Latin America has considerable land-use potential that remains untapped, even allowing for its extensive mountainous areas and impenetrable jungles; but rather than spreading out to develop virgin lands, its peoples are swarming to the already crowded cities.

The phenomenon of urban growth in Latin America—which has parallels in the developing countries of Asia and Africa—cannot be compared to the urbanization of the Western world, for it has not been stimulated by the need for industrial workers. Some of the most spectacular population growth, in fact, has occurred in cities where job opportunities are conspicuously lacking. (See Chapter 12, "The Urban Transition," pages 347–348.) In most cases the central administration is finding it increasingly difficult to provide a rapidly growing population with even the basic necessities—water, sewage disposal, lighting, and roads—to say nothing of schools and hospitals.

As Black and others point out, the theory that rapid population growth will automatically stimulate economic development simply does not apply in most of the developing world, where there are already too many unskilled hands without prospects for productive employment. Brazil's labor force, for example, is expected to grow from its present level of about 40 million to more than 160 million within sixty years if population continues to grow at the present rate of about 3 percent a year. It is doubtful that any economy can expand fast enough to create jobs for so many new workers.

Economists estimate that to keep per capita income from declining, the amount of national income allocated to capital investment—to the creation of new factories and other productive facilities, including the means for training and retraining workers—must increase annually at a percentage three times greater than the annual percentage increase of the labor force. Thus, if the number of workers increases by 3 percent a year, as in Brazil at the present time, the rate of investment increase must be about 9 percent just to maintain per capita income. A further increase in capital investment would be necessary to effect a net gain in per capita income. Yet most of the developing countries have been unable to expand their economies at a sustained rate of even 5 percent a year. If present trends continue, therefore, economic "growth" may mean little more than growth in the number of people *available* for employment. Standards of living will improve very little and may even deteriorate.

As Coale has noted, the problems created by the lack of adequate productive facilities are "compounded by the lack of education and training on the part of the labor force itself."[10] Efforts to improve education and job training create a significant drain on national income, reducing the amount of capital available for other purposes. The problem is particularly severe in the developing countries, where rapid population growth has greatly increased the proportion of young people relative to other age groups: close to 50 percent of the population in these countries is under fifteen years of age, as compared to 20 to 30 percent in the industrialized nations (see Figure 11.4, page 314). The task of educating these children and of providing for their needs puts an unusually heavy strain on the economy.

The Prospects for Change

In the industrialized nations, as we have noted, the decline in birth rates was a *consequence* of the sociocultural changes that accompanied economic growth. In the developing nations, by contrast, a reduction of birth and fertility rates may be a *prerequisite* for accelerating economic growth. A country that can reduce its rate of population growth to about 1 percent a year seems to have much better prospects for raising the living standards of its people than one whose growth rate remains at 2 or 3 percent a year. While the differences in life opportunities for the two populations will be relatively small for the first generation, they should become progressively greater as the number of workers

10. Ansley Coale, "Population and Economic Development," in Hauser, *Population Dilemma*, p. 66.

competing for jobs begins to level off. Coale estimates, for example, that a 50 percent reduction in fertility, accomplished over a period of twenty-five years, might lead to a 40 percent gain in per capita income at the end of thirty years, a 100 percent gain in sixty years, and a 500 percent gain in 150 years.[11] These economic changes would presumably lead to changes in other patterns of social behavior, including probably an upgrading of education and new roles and higher status for women and children.

11. Coale, "Population and Economic Development," pp. 68-69. Coale's theoretical model is highly rationalized, and no society currently operates on such a basis. Two factors should be kept in mind: (1) a population control policy such as the one Coale suggested costs money to set up and operate, and as yet we have no cost-benefit studies that would show the socioeconomic consequences of such a policy; (2) as we saw in Chapter 10, the values, beliefs, and attitudes of people influence political and economic issues and thus affect economic growth independent of population pressures. For a recent critique of Coale's theoretical model, see B. Maxwell Stamper, "Population Policy in Development Planning," *Reports on Population/Family Planning*, No. 13 (1973): 1–30.

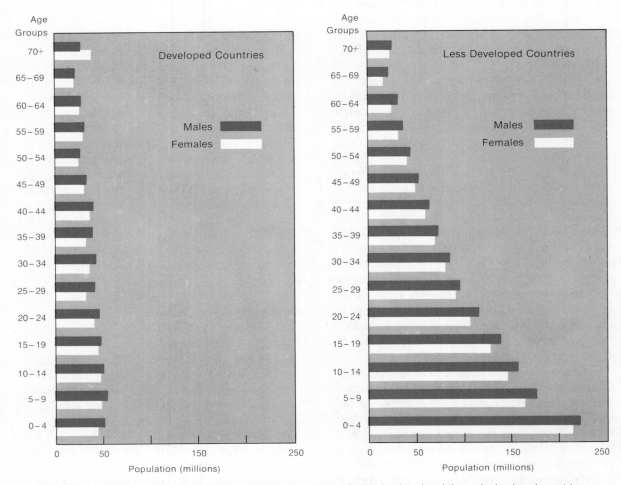

These population graphs portray the population by age groups in the developed and the underdeveloped countries In the developed countries, where population is growing slowly, people are distributed more or less evenly throughout all age groups—there are about as many old people as young people. In the underdeveloped countries, on the other hand, population is growing rapidly and almost half the people are young.

SOURCE: Data from United Nations. Chart from *Population Program Assistance*, p. 61.

Figure 11.4. POPULATION BY AGE GROUPS, 1970

Such sociocultural developments would be likely to further depress fertility rates, as they have in nations that have already experienced industrialization.

Although there is clearly a need to better understand the complex relationship between population growth and economic development, a major hypothesis is that the current population explosion is impeding, not helping, the process of modernization in the developing countries. That this explosion has created a crisis of worldwide proportions is amply demonstrated by recent efforts of the United Nations to deal effectively with population growth through programs aimed both at decreasing fertility and at increasing agricultural and industrial productivity. Technology has provided the means for making such programs successful, but how well they will succeed hinges largely on questions of attitude and belief. As we shall see, the "problem of people"—that is, rapid population growth and its consequences—takes on different dimensions in different societies.

MEXICO—THE PROBLEMS OF A NEIGHBOR

Among the nations of the world that we label underdeveloped or developing, Mexico is often cited as one that has made remarkable progress toward achieving its social and economic goals.[12] In the aftermath of a political revolution dating back to 1910, Mexico has fostered an ideology of social progress that is only now beginning to emerge in most other countries of the developing world. The ideals of the Mexican Revolution—now broadly accepted by all major political factions—included agrarian and labor reform, the extension of educational opportunity, the assimilation of isolated Indian villages into national life, the improvement of living standards, and the development of a political democracy.

During the past few decades Mexico's political structure has been the most stable in Latin America. The *Partido Revolucionario Institucional* (PRI) has firmly dominated most aspects of national life, steering Mexico between the economic orientations of socialism on the one hand and twentieth-century capitalism on the other. Under the land reform program, 27 percent of Mexico's farmland, formerly concentrated in large private holdings and operated under a system of peonage, has been confiscated by the government and redistributed to the peasants as *ejidos* (literally, *common lands*). These lands are owned collectively by the agricultural workers *(ejidatarios)* who farm them.[13] Currently, some 45 percent of all agricultural workers in Mexico farm *ejidos*. Geared primarily to the production of subsistence foods, the Mexican land reform program has helped increase agricultural output as well as improve the lot of the peasant.

Government in Mexico has been similarly responsible for accelerating industrial growth, for modernizing communication and transportation facilities, and for improving public education and public health. In the forty years between 1930 and 1970, real wages per capita more than tripled in Mexico. Compared with most of its Latin-American neighbors, then, Mexico has made an enviable record of social and economic progress over the last several decades. It is against this setting that we will examine the difficulties this nation is experiencing as a result of rapid population growth.

BACKGROUND OF THE PROBLEM

Until late in the nineteenth century, disease, warfare, internal strife, economic exploitation, and the extreme poverty of the masses all helped keep Mexico's population at fewer than 10 million. By 1900 it had grown only to 13.6 million—several million less than the current

12. The following discussion is based largely on "Mexico: The Problem of People," *Population Bulletin* of the Population Reference Bureau, 20, No. 7 (November 1964); Luis Leñero Otero, "The Mexican Urbanization Process and Its Implications," in *Demography*, 5, No. 2 (1968): 866–873; and James W. Wilke, *The Mexican Revolution*, 2nd ed. (Berkeley: University of California Press, 1970).

13. For a discussion of the *ejido* system, see Eyler N. Simpson, *The Ejido: Mexico's Way Out* (Chapel Hill, N. C.: University of North Carolina Press, 1937); and Nathan L. Whetten, *Rural Mexico* (Chicago: The University of Chicago Press, 1948), esp. pp. 114–124.

population of New York State. Since then, however, it has more than quadrupled. Mexico's 1970 census reported a population of approximately 51 million, and this figure has been growing by over 1.5 million each year.

Net in-migration has been inconsequential in accounting for Mexico's rapid growth during the last several decades. As elsewhere in the developing world, the primary factor has been a sharp decline in the death rate, which began earlier in Mexico than in most of the developing countries because of public health measures instituted by the government. In 1930 the mortality rate in Mexico was 26.6 per 1000 population; by 1970 it had fallen to 9.9. The birth rate, in the meanwhile, increased slightly, from 43 per 1000 in 1930 to 47 per 1000 in 1970.

The combination of a high birth rate and a low death rate has boosted Mexico's rate of population growth to over 3.5 percent a year, among the highest in the world. Since there is little chance that this will be significantly reduced in the immediate future, we can project that the population of Mexico will increase 30 to 40 percent over the course of the present decade—from 51 million in 1970 to somewhere between 65 and 70 million by 1980. How will this affect the nation and its people?

PROGRESS AND POVERTY

Mexico has established an enviable record of economic development over the past several decades. The country's gross national product (the total value of goods and services produced in a given year) tripled between 1940 and 1960 and then tripled again between 1960 and 1970. Agricultural productivity has also increased dramatically in recent years, with the result that Mexico is now self-sufficient in wheat and corn. Unlike many of the developing countries, especially those in Asia, Mexico has the potential for producing all the food it will need for the foreseeable future.

But the statistics showing Mexico's progress are somewhat misleading, for gains have been distributed among the population very unevenly. Only 16 percent of national income goes to the bottom half of the population; almost 40 percent

goes to the 5 percent at the top.[14] Of approximately 12 million people who reported an income in Mexico's 1970 census, nearly three-fourths said they earned less than $80 a month. The census also showed that one-third of Mexico's people live in one-room dwellings with dirt floors and that almost one-fourth are illiterate. And though Mexico is one of the few developing nations in which the average diet meets the minimum daily nutritional requirement of 2500 calories, millions of Mexicans still suffer from malnutrition. A fifth of the population never eat meat, eggs, or bread made with wheat; a third never drink milk; over half never eat fish.[15]

The problem of wide-scale poverty in Mexico began long before the recent population explosion. It has deep roots in the country's traditional stratification system, which has remained strong despite industrialization and despite government efforts to reduce gross inequalities. But as we shall see, rapid population growth now appears to be making solution of the problem more difficult. At the very least, it has increased the number of those who are poor: more Mexicans are living at a subsistence level today than were alive in 1940.

Industrialization

Among the developing nations, Mexico is one of the world leaders in industrialization, but it faces great pressures. Its task is not merely to match the developed nations in industrial efficiency and productive capacity but, perhaps more importantly, to create enough new jobs for its expanding labor force. The rapid population growth of recent years means that about 400,000 persons will be entering the Mexican labor market *each year* between now and 1980. Yet new jobs are being created at less than half that rate, because capital is being invested in automated industries that require relatively few workers.

Economists remind us that making jobs has become an expensive process. In the United

14. Stanley Meisler, "Mexico," *The Atlantic,* February 1975, pp. 14–24. For comparable figures on income distribution in the United States, see Figure 8.2.
15. Ibid., p. 15. See also "Mexico: The Problem of People," p. 181; and "Mexico," *The World Almanac* (New York: Newspaper Enterprise Association, 1973), p. 585.

States, where the costs of productive facilities and job training run unusually high, between $50,000 and $100,000 must be invested to create a job not previously available in the marketplace. The cost per job is usually less in developing economies, but it is still high relative to the amount of capital available for investment, especially considering the number of new jobs needed to achieve and maintain full employment. Even if it cost only $10,000 to capitalize a new job, Mexico would still have to spend $4 billion *annually* to create jobs for the 400,000 people joining the labor force each year. In fact, the problem is much more serious than that, for Mexico is actually capitalizing new jobs at a cost near $40,000 each. The figure is so high because of the automated nature of the new plants, which, relative to cost and productive capacity, provide fewer jobs than older plants. In the cotton textile industry, employment actually dropped about 29 percent during the 1950s, while the value of production increased 177 percent.[16]

Automation is probably necessary if Mexico wishes to compete on equal terms with the already advanced industrial nations, but it greatly complicates the economic problems of a developing nation with a surfeit of labor. Thus, while the *percentage* of Mexicans with good jobs has greatly increased in the last half century, many millions of workers are either unemployed or employed at such low levels of skill and income as to preclude their being able to attain a decent standard of living. Certainly they are unable to stimulate demand for the goods being produced in Mexico's factories: after modernizing their productive facilities, many industries are operating at only 25 to 50 percent of capacity simply because too few people can afford their products. If Mexico's population continues to grow at the present rate, the economic and social problems created by a glutted labor market may well become increasingly severe.

16. "Mexico: The Problem of People," p. 195; and K. Ruddle and M. Hamour, eds., *Statistical Abstract of Latin America, 1970* (Los Angeles: University of California, Latin American Center, 1972), p. 7.

Education

In Mexico as in other developing countries, rapid population growth has created a heavy burden of child dependency. Between 40 and 50 percent of Mexico's population is under fifteen years of age. This large proportion of young people puts a heavy strain on Mexico's resources.

Although the government has been committed since the Revolution to wiping out illiteracy and providing at least a primary education for every child, rapid population growth and limited capital have thus far kept the goal out of reach. Today about 75 percent of Mexico's people can read and write, but the population has grown so rapidly that there are still almost as many illiterate Mexicans as there were twenty years ago. And despite the vast sums of money that have gone into building new schools and hiring more teachers, government officials estimate that almost 5 million children aged five to fourteen were not enrolled in school in 1970—a slightly larger number than in 1960.

Looking ahead to 1980, the problem is staggering, for if the current rate of population growth continues, the number of children between five and fourteen will by then reach 19 million—a number almost equal to Mexico's total population in 1940. Even though the federal government (which largely finances the public schools) is allocating some 15 to 20 percent of its total budget to education, there is no guarantee that it will be able to provide even the rudiments of education for that many youngsters. And the real challenge is to do much more, for educational requirements become increasingly great as industry is automated and the economy grows more complex. A lowering of the birth rate would begin to reduce the need for additional elementary facilities and thus make more capital available for developing new secondary and technical schools.

BIRTH CONTROL: THE CURRENT SITUATION

Only recently have Mexico's leaders acknowledged that family planning and a lowering of the birth rate may be necessary if the country is to achieve its social and economic goals. Pope Paul's 1968 encyclical "On Human Life," reaffirming the traditional stand of the Roman Catholic Church against the use of contraceptives, received the formal support of the Mexican Catholic hierarchy and apparently reinforced the government's do-nothing policy on the question of population control.

The Mexican government took no action until 1972, when the regime headed by President Luis Echeverría announced its intention "to carry out programs furthering a sound family planning in the noblest human, social, and ethical sense of that concept." The announcement stated further that "each couple should be encouraged to decide on the number of children it wishes to raise, so as to provide security for them and assure them the dignity, love, and respect that human procreation deserves." Even more unexpected was a pastoral letter issued by the Mexican bishops in support of the government's program. Addressed to clergy and laity alike, it carefully reiterated traditional Church teachings, but it also emphasized the right of couples to decide on the number of children they should have and readily acknowledged that the rhythm method of birth control might not be possible for many couples. The pastoral letter clearly conveyed the idea that each couple could be expected to choose the means for controlling family size that best suited its own life situation.[17]

In view of these developments, it seems likely that the decade of the 1970s will see the start of a decline in Mexico's high growth rate, although the large proportion of young people in the population means that population will probably increase rapidly for some time to come. The most crucial requirement for slowing population growth over the long term will be achieving a norm of two children per family instead of the current four or five.

THE PEOPLE'S REPUBLIC OF CHINA

Since its founding after World War II, the People's Republic of China has probably added some 250 million to its population—more than the present population of the United States. Although accurate census figures are lacking, the population of China is now estimated at approximately 800 million, making it by far the most populous country in the world. How does this developing giant—a "young" nation built on one of the great civilizations of the ancient world—react to the "problem of people"?[18]

THE RESTRUCTURING OF A SOCIETY

When the Chinese Communists formally assumed power in October 1949, they inherited a country impoverished and disorganized, the victim of years of warfare, colonial exploitation, government corruption, and internal strife. It took 85 percent of the work force to produce the food supply (at that time the proportion for Mexico was a little more than 50 percent and for the United States about 12 percent). The Communists came to power confident of their ability to bring about a radical social revolution—to remodel an agrarian, family-oriented society into a prosperous industrial society built on the theories of Marx and Lenin as interpreted by Mao Tse-tung.

The Communists were able to achieve some things rapidly, such as ridding the streets of prostitutes, thieves, beggars, and filth, putting an end to government corruption, and halting inflation. They pushed land reform relentlessly, destroying the class of large landowners and giving small plots to the peasants. Even more basic, perhaps, was the Communists' attack on China's

17. Data for this discussion, including the quotations from the Mexican government's statement, are taken from the *Bulletin* of the Latin American Documentation Center, III (January 1973): 1–12.

18. Much of the following discussion is taken from John S. Aird, "Population Policy and Demographic Prospects in the People's Republic of China," in *People's Republic of China: An Economic Assessment* (Washington, D.C.: U.S. Department of Health, Education, and Welfare, 1972), pp. 230–331. See also, Aird, "China: A Demographic Crisis," *Population Bulletin* of the Population Reference Bureau, 19, No. 5 (August 1963).

traditional family system, which diverted loyalty from the state to the clan.

Clan structure, long considered the heart of the Chinese family system, dates back to the eleventh century.[19] The clan is literally an association of families sharing a common ancestry through the male line. Over the centuries, the clan assumed a variety of socioreligious functions — maintenance of clan genealogies and ancestral shrines, promotion of ancestor worship, provision of clan schools that stressed filial duty and disseminated Confucian ethics. Great emphasis was placed on father-son loyalty, and marriages were arranged by the clan in order to ensure its continued stability. Individuals were encouraged to put the welfare of the clan before other considerations and to focus their efforts on building its wealth and prestige. Traditional clan structure was obviously inimical to Communist ideology and to the goals of the Revolution.

Although the beginnings of industrialism had put considerable strains on the clan system long before the Communists came to power, Communist pressures greatly accelerated the disruption of traditional family patterns. Under a new marriage law enacted in 1950 (see page 450), young people were declared free to choose their own marriage partners, and women were given equal rights with men in all things, including occupational choice and divorce. In order to increase production and to free more hands for work, the Communists also established communal work forces, communal dining halls, and communal day-care centers, which effectively separated the members of the family during much of the day. Some of these programs met with resistance, but family patterns in China have undoubtedly changed. For the urban Chinese, at least, the family's main functions are now seen as the procreation of children and the sharing of leisure time. Thus one effect of the Communist effort to shift the focus of family life from the clan to the community has been to make Chinese family patterns in some ways more congruent with those in the industrialized West.[20]

MARX AGAINST MALTHUS

The close relationship between population size and food needs was officially recognized in China six hundred years ago:

T'ai Tsu, the first Ming emperor, decreed that a sacred Yellow Register be compiled every 10 years, giving the number of households in each district and the number of "mouths" to be fed in each household. A placard, called Hu T'ieh, was posted on the household gate, and the family was obliged to mark on it the number of mouths inside the gate. The census takers then simply counted the mouths recorded on the placards, enabling the emperor's men to estimate the amount of food required for each district.[21]

Accurate statistics on China's population were lacking when the Communists took power in 1949; the last official census had been taken in 1928, and there was no effective administrative organization for gathering and recording population data. One of the new government's first moves was to establish a State Statistical Bureau to coordinate all government statistical work. A national census was planned to provide basic information for the first Five-Year Economic Development Plan, to be launched in 1953, and also for the registration of voters for the first national elections, to be held in that same year. For ideological reasons, the Census Bureau was not allowed to seek help from the West; it received limited help from the Soviet Union.[22]

19. Ping-ti Ho, "An Historian's View of the Chinese Family System," in *Man and Civilization: The Family's Search for Survival*, eds. Seymour M. Farber et al. (New York: McGraw-Hill Book Company, 1965), pp. 15–30.

20. For more information on the changes in family life in China, see Chapter 15, pp. 449–451.

21. Revelle, "Food and Population," p. 161.

22. See, for example, Aird, "China: A Demographic Crisis," and Leo A. Orleans, "The Population of Communist China," in Freedman, *Population: The Vital Revolution*, pp. 228 ff.

In the People's Republic of China, as in most parts of the world, ideological beliefs and values largely determine the way population growth is viewed and what, if anything, is done about it. Chinese leaders have advocated the Marxist position that poverty is caused by the capitalist system of production and distribution rather than by a large population. Economic policies and current efforts to control population growth are expressions of a political philosophy that places communal good before individual freedom. The Chinese have attempted to eradicate poverty and increase productivity by the formation of agricultural communes (top left) and factories—like the textile mill (top, middle)—where health-care and day-care services are provided for workers and their children. The Chinese government has also encouraged late marriages, so that young people will continue their education. Since 1969 an increasingly well-organized family limitation program has been under way in China, and there is reason to believe that traditional attitudes will not seriously impede this program.

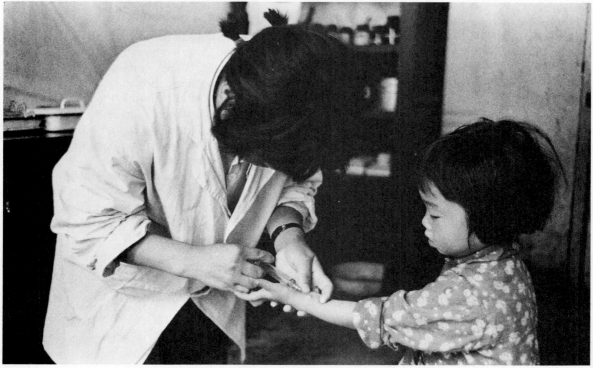

In 1953 the Chinese government reported a population of 583 million people. The urban population was said to be only 13 percent of the total, or 77 million people, though no clear-cut criteria were set forth to define what was meant by "urban." Census figures showed a birth rate of 37 per 1000 population and a death rate of 17 per 1000. This would mean a growth rate of 2 percent, or an increase of between 12 and 17 million a year.[23] The Chinese appeared to be satisfied with their census and declared that the growing size of their population meant more hands for production.

China's new leadership firmly rejected the Malthusian argument that rapid population growth would prevent the people from ever satisfying their needs. In the Communist view, the problem was not one of numbers per se but of how the economic system was organized. China's large population and rapid rate of growth had been a danger, the Communists maintained, only under the old clan-capitalist-landlord system, which wasted human labor. Under a restructured political and economic system, China's huge population would no longer be a liability. Through the rational use of human labor as a valuable resource, productivity could quickly be raised, "and the living conditions of the people — even the living conditions of a population that was rapidly expanding — could be steadily improved. It was possible, now, to abolish unemployment, poverty, vagrancy, hunger, pestilence, war and untimely death."[24]

The First Five-Year Plan
Under the first five-year plan, 1953–1958, the small farms that had been given to peasants were collectivized — that is, organized into communes where property and tools were held in common and labor was centrally managed. Reportedly, peasant resentment was widespread. Farm production did not meet expected quotas. Throughout the 1950s millions of peasants attempted to enter the cities, with counter attempts by the government to force them back to collectivized farms in order to improve agricultural production. As a result of government efforts to stem urbanization, China has avoided a problem that plagues most of the developing nations — the flooding of the cities with many more people than can be accommodated in terms of jobs and decent living conditions. The current urban population of China is less than 20 percent of the total.

Disappointing food crops in 1954 and again in 1956 probably played some part in encouraging the government to modify its stand on population control. At the Eighth Congress of the Chinese Communist Party in 1956, Premier Chou En-lai declared: "To protect women and children and bring up and educate our younger generation in a way conducive to the health and prosperity of the nation, we agree that a due measure of birth control is desirable."[25] However, the Chinese leaders continued to reject the Malthusian argument that unchecked population growth would outstrip economic growth regardless of economic policies, insisting that their program was designed simply to protect the health of mother and child and to provide women with adequate time for work and study.

The Great Leap Forward
In 1958 ideological fervor in China reached new heights, and the government launched its "Great Leap Forward." The immediate goal was to double overall production in a single year. Great Britain's industrial production was to be matched within fifteen years. At the same time, the party reverted to its original position against birth control and proclaimed again that population growth was a creative force. Several reasons have been suggested for this change in attitude: the conflict between population control and Marxist ideology; a possible shortage of factory workers; a lack of cheap, effective contracep-

---

23. In 1959 the Chinese announced that the death rate had been reduced to 11 per 1000, quite comparable to the rates in the most advanced nations of the world. As far as can be ascertained, some 40 percent of China's population is now under fifteen years of age.
24. As quoted in Robert C. North, "Communist China and the Population Problem," in Ng and Mudd, *Population Crisis*, p. 91.
25. As quoted by Aird, "China: A Demographic Crisis," p. 125.

tives; and the continued strength of the traditional ways among the overwhelmingly rural population.

But the "Great Leap" soon bogged down. Despite attempts to inflate the statistics, nothing could hide the fact that efforts to spur industrial expansion ran into countless snags or that agricultural growth between 1958 and 1961 failed to keep up with, much less surpass, population growth.

One of the casualties of the "Great Leap" was the Chinese Census Bureau. The ideological fervor of 1958–1959 included denunciation of bourgeois statistics on birth and death. At the same time, the statisticians were forced to produce figures to support Mao's propaganda claims, and the result was total disruption of the Census Bureau. By the early 1960s the government still lacked trained and reliable personnel to handle vital statistics, which are generally deemed essential for effective planning in a complex society. Nevertheless, some Western scholars believe that the regime probably knows enough about its urban population, its labor force, and its educated people and skilled laborers to get by. In fact, Orleans doubts that a difference of 25 or even 50 million people above or below the figures the Chinese leaders are currently using would alter their goals and policies.[26]

Birth Control: The Current Situation

In recent years, the government has moved slowly but steadily toward programs of family limitation. As early as 1964, Premier Chou En-lai declared:

26. Orleans, "The Population of Communist China," p. 238.
27. Edgar Snow, "Population Control in China: An Interview with Chou En-lai," in Ng and Mudd, *Population Crisis*, pp. 101–102. See also H. Yuan Tien, "China's Experience in Population Control: The Illusive Model," *Sociological Focus*, 8, No. 2 (April 1975): 191–196.
28. Carl Djerassi, "Fertility Limitation Through Contraceptive Steroids in the People's Republic of China," *Studies in Family Planning*, No. 1 (1974): 13–29.
29. A notable characteristic distinguishing between modern and archaic census enumerations is accessibility. The modern census dates from the second half of the eighteenth century. Prior to that time, information on the number and characteristics of population was kept secret because it indicated strengths or weaknesses of interest to possible military foes.

We do believe in planned parenthood, but it is not easy to introduce all at once in China and it is more difficult to achieve in the rural areas, where most of our people live, than in the cities. The first thing is to encourage late marriages. The years 20 to 30 are very important to mental and physical development—years when scientific and artistic growth often occur most rapidly. Among various means of deferred parenthood, sterilization is only the last, and only applies to those already burdened by too many children.[27]

All methods of birth control are now available to the Chinese people, including abortion and sterilization.[28] The Chinese themselves originated a method of abortion called the Vacuum Apparatus Technique that is becoming widely used throughout the world. The birth-control pill, sterilization, and intrauterine devices (IUDs) are the most widely used forms of contraception. Studies show that one-third of the relevant Chinese population (33 million women in the fertile age grouping) are currently using some form of contraception, with almost half using the pill. Efforts to encourage late marriages have been somewhat successful.

It is difficult to estimate the population growth rate for China because of the lack of vital statistics for the country as a whole. Statistics are available for cities and a few rural communes, but there is doubt as to whether these are representative of the nation as a whole. Many observers believe, however, that despite the decline in the death rate brought about by improved health care and the virtual abolition of starvation, the population growth rate of China is now less than 2 percent and is much lower in urban than in rural areas. With the advances that have recently been made in family planning and birth control, it seems possible that Chou En-lai's goal of a 1 percent population growth rate by the year 2000—which would give China a population in excess of 1.3 billion—may be attained.

THE LESSONS OF CHINA AND MEXICO

China and Mexico are not fully comparable for several fairly obvious reasons. In the first place, China not only lacks solid statistical information like that collected by the Mexican census bureau but closely guards the data it does have.[29]

TOOLS OF SOCIOLOGY
A NOTE ON THE CENSUS

Although governments have always been interested in knowing facts about their citizens, for military, tax, and other purposes, information has been sporadically gathered and often has provided only rough estimates. The United States has the world's oldest regular census of population, the first one dating back to 1790. A major reason for this is the nature of the composition of the House of Representatives, as established by the Constitution. The number of representatives from each state is based on the population of that state relative to the population of the other states.

As our society has grown more complex, our census taking has gone far beyond mere head counts. We have censuses of manufacturing, farming, and business every five years. In addition, we have added a great array of questions to our decennial census, dealing with such matters as housing, education, occupation, income, migration, and commuting. In a census year, some 180,000 persons are hired to handle the various phases of work. Because of the amount and variety of data that must be obtained, the Bureau of the Census uses *samples* as a basis for much of its information (see Tools of Sociology, "Sampling," page 365).

By law citizens are required to answer all the questions asked of them by the census taker. This requirement holds for all societies that take regular censuses. Government officials argue that a reliable census could not be obtained otherwise, and the individual citizen as well as the society would suffer from the lack of accurate information.

Actually, in the 1970 census about 80 percent of all United States families had to answer only some twenty-two to twenty-four questions. Only a minority of families had to fill in longer forms. Thus sampling procedures have reduced the amount of work and number of families involved while still making it possible to accumulate important information. And to those who worry about the confidentiality of the census procedures, the Bureau of the Census proudly claims that there is no known case in which a census employee violated the oath of confidentiality.

The census-taking process, like so many activities in and out of government, has been a stimulant to technological change. For example, by 1890 it had become literally impossible to handle the desired data by existing methods. Herman Hollerith of the Bureau of the Census invented a procedure by which he was able to record the data about each person on special cards by a key-punch process. Thus came into being the cards that are so much a part of our lives today, and with these cards came the counter-sorter machines, forerunners of the computers.

The decennial census provides data on some 18,000 incorporated places in the United States, some 35,000 townships, and 31,000 counties. For the big cities, data are also available on areas known as *census tracts* and even city blocks. Census tracts are geographical areas of a city, usually set off by streets or other natural boundaries, which are more or less homogeneous with regard to physiographic land use, demographic characteristics, socioeconomic status, and indices of social disorganization. The population size of a census tract is relatively small, varying between one thousand and fourteen thousand persons, with the average around three thousand.

Almost every governmental agency at federal, state, and local levels uses census data to project such needs as schools and water supplies. Business and industry are also major users, for they must project their production and sales according to the expected size and needs of varying age groups. Finally, the census data provide social scientists with crucial facts about society—facts that raise many questions about education, income, marriage patterns, and earning power. For example, why should income be distributed as it is? What is happening to social mobility in the society? Why are people having only two, three, or four children? These and other questions raised by census data form the basis for much sociological research and theory-building.

This discussion of the census is based on Conrad Taeuber, "Taking an Inventory of 180 Million People," in *Population: The Vital Revolution,* ed. Ronald Freedman (Chicago: Aldine Publishing Co., 1965), pp. 84–99; and Estie Stoll, "Census or Nonsense," *The Sciences,* 9, No. 11 (November 1969), 24–29. Summaries of the statistics obtained by the Bureau of the Census include *Current Population Reports, Historical Statistics of the United States (Colonial Times to 1957),* and the *Statistical Abstract of the United States.*

More fundamental are the differences between the two governments and the two societies. The Mexican Revolution is now more than fifty years old, and party control—though tight in some ways—is orderly and not without some semblance of democratic process. Opposition to the ruling party is legal, and there is a somewhat free interchange of ideas. Government programs have evolved into a mixture of state control and free enterprise, of socialist ideology and pragmatism. Mexico is influenced by cultural patterns from the industrialized countries of the West, which support norms generally favorable to family planning and population control while fostering an economic policy oriented to individual consumption. In China, where the Revolution is less than half as old, government programs closely follow the Marxist-Leninist line; both the economic policies and the increasing efforts to control population growth are expressions of a political philosophy that places communal good before individual freedom as it is conceived of in the West.

Despite these differences, the case studies of Mexico and China indicate some of the ways in which population growth relates to other facets of societal life. Political, religious, and familial beliefs and values largely determine the way population growth is viewed and greatly influence what, if anything, will be done about regulating it. In Mexico both government and church ignored or denied the problem of population growth until recently. Postrevolutionary China has vacillated on the issue, but given the popular support the government has earned by improving the lot of the people, there is reason to believe that its recent policy of encouraging birth control will not be seriously impeded by traditional attitudes, many of which have already undergone fundamental change.

30. *Population Report* of the Sierra Club, No. 6, April 15, 1975.

THE UNITED STATES

The United States may be taken as representative of the developed Western societies (see Table 11.1, page 326, for data on these societies). It provides us with the most up-to-date statistics on population trends and their implications for industry, education, government, welfare, recreation, and the like. These statistics reveal that its more than 200 million citizens live in a highly industrialized society geared until recently to steadily increasing affluence. Birth control is practiced effectively by the majority of married couples and is broadly supported by family, religious, and governmental norms.

IS THERE A POPULATION PROBLEM?

During the 1950s and early 1960s the United States experienced a moderate overall growth rate of about 1.65 percent per year, very similar to that of the Soviet Union. Early in the 1970s, however, after a decade of steady decline, the birth rate reached a new low of 15 per 1000 population and the growth rate appeared to be stabilizing at less than 1 percent a year. Within one generation the United States had produced headlines proclaiming a population explosion— the "baby boom" following World War II—and then new headlines proclaiming a "baby bust."

This leveling off of the growth rates does not tell the whole story, however, for the number of women in the most fertile years—ages 20 to 29—will double between 1970 and 1990. Thus, without a further drop in the fertility rate, the number of births per year in the United States will continue to increase over the next few decades, with the country's population reaching a projected 260-270 million by the year 2000. If the three-child family should again become normative, the figure would go much higher (see Figure 11.5, page 327). Furthermore, the population of the United States continues to increase through immigration—both legal and illegal. In 1974, for example, it was estimated that the population increased by more than 2 million, of which nearly half was due to immigration.[30]

Does even moderate growth constitute a problem? Many think that it does. In the following sections, we will consider the possible effects of population growth with respect to education, the economy, the problems of minority groups and the poor, and the environment.[31]

Education

The baby boom that followed World War II placed great strains on all levels of our educational system. High-school enrollment, for example, increased by 50 percent between 1960 and 1970, from 10 to 15 million students. In the early 1970s, total school enrollment reached a record high of 60.1 million. Expansion of the educational system has required constant increases in taxes and school bond issues — occasioning, in a few communities, taxpayer revolts that forced the temporary closing of schools.

Overcrowded classrooms and a lack of qualified teachers during the 1950s and 1960s drew attention to a societal need that the schools did not seem to be meeting — that of providing a meaningful education, one that would equip students for life in a complex technological society. While the United States may no longer have to face the problem of providing

enough schools and teachers — if the number of births does not begin to climb once again — the educational system is still being criticized for its seeming inability to provide a meaningful learning experience.

Many people feel that the schools should do more toward helping students understand societal problems, including the problems posed by population growth. The Commission on Population and the American Future has recommended that schools develop programs on demographic processes and on the implications of population change with respect to quality of life, the economic system, male-female sex roles, and so on. Knowledge of how such variables interrelate should make it more possible for individuals to help shape the future rather than be its victims.

The Economy

As the children born during the baby boom of the 1950s have come of age, they have begun to

31. The following discussion is based in large part on *Population and the American Future,* The Report of the Commission on Population and the American Future (Washington, D.C.: U.S. Government Printing Office, 1972).

Table 11.1. POPULATION DATA AND PROJECTIONS, WESTERN EUROPE AND NORTH AMERICA

Country	Population estimates mid-1975 (millions)	Annual rate of population growth (percent)	Number of years to double population	Population projections to 1985 (millions)
Austria	7.5	0.2	347	8.1
Belgium	9.8	0.4	173	10.8
Albania	2.5	2.7	26	4.3
Denmark	5.0	0.4	173	5.4
Finland	4.7	0.2	347	4.7
France	52.9	0.9	77	62.1
Germany (Federal Republic of)	61.9	0.3	231	66.2
Greece	8.9	0.3	231	9.6
Iceland	0.2	1.2	58	0.3
Ireland	3.1	1.2	58	4.0
Italy	55.0	0.5	139	60.9
Luxembourg	0.3	0.2	347	0.4
Malta	0.3	0.2	347	0.3
Netherlands	13.6	0.8	87	16.0
Norway	4.0	0.7	99	4.5
Portugal	8.8	0.3	231	9.9
Spain	35.4	1.0	69	44.9
Sweden	8.3	0.6	116	9.4
Switzerland	6.5	0.8	87	7.4
United Kingdom	56.4	0.3	231	62.8
Yugoslavia	21.3	0.9	77	25.7
Canada	22.8	1.3	53	31.6
United States	213.9	0.9	77	264.4

SOURCE: "1975 World Population Data Sheet," published by the Population Reference Bureau, Washington, D.C.

look for jobs. The labor force is expected to grow by some 35 million workers during the 1970s, with an additional 35 million added during the 1980s. The creation of new jobs can be expected to put considerable pressure on the economic system.

Declining birth rates over recent years make it probable that the number of people entering the American labor force will gradually level off. Were population to stabilize, the number could conceivably begin to decline. However, this is unlikely. Only about half of the women of working age are currently in the labor force, and the percentage would probably rise rapidly with lower fertility rates.

A slowly growing or even stationary population would not necessarily be the disaster for business that many people fear. The Commission on Population studied eighteen major businesses in the United States and found that demand would not be reduced below current levels for any one of them if population leveled off. On the basis of such evidence the Commission concluded: "We find no convincing economic argument for continued national population growth."[32]

Although periods of rapid economic growth have in the past also been periods of rapid population growth, economic growth does not depend on more *people* per se but rather on increases in the amount of *disposable income* available. By the year 2000, U.S. family income in constant dollars—that is, adjusted to compensate for any changes in purchasing power—is expected to be at least double what it is today. If the fertility rate is kept at an average of two children per couple, per capita income at the end of this century could be as much as 15 percent higher than if couples had three children. It seems likely that any reduction in spending for the care and education of children would be countered by *increased* spending for other types of goods and services. The Commission Report argues, for example, that stabilization of the population would facilitate capital formation for such things as improving the quality of the environment and providing new educational opportunities for adults. In short, there seems to be no reason to believe that slower population growth would, of itself, necessarily hurt the American economy.

The Problems of Minorities and the Poor

Although fertility rates among minority groups in American society are higher than the national average, this fact has not had much effect on the recent growth of the country's population. The Commission on Population makes the point that if blacks and people with Spanish surnames had not borne any children at all during the 1960s, the population would be only 4 percent smaller than it is now. Insofar as there may be a problem of high fertility among minorities, it is much the same problem that affects the poor more generally. The Commission found "a strong relationship between high fertility and the economic and social problems that afflict the 13 percent of our people who are poor."[33]

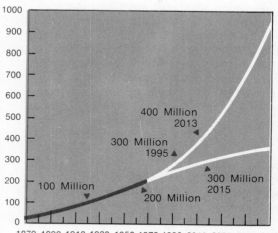

This graph projects the future population of the United States if the average family size remains at two children per family or rises to three children per family.

SOURCE: Data from *Population and the American Future*, Report of the Presidential Commission on Population and the American Future, 1972; and *Vital Statistics Report*, Vol. 21, No. 12 (March 1973). Chart from *Population Problems and Policies in Economically Advanced Countries*, Population Crisis Committee and American Pitchley Foundation, 1973. p. 36.

Figure 11.5. UNITED STATES POPULATION PROJECTIONS, TWO- VERSUS THREE-CHILD FAMILY

32. Ibid., pp. 40–41.
33. Ibid., p. 72.

TOOLS OF SOCIOLOGY
USING THE COMPUTER   C. E. Noll

In almost every area of our lives, the computer has revolutionized the way things are done. Computers are used to schedule college classes, manage traffic, and process income tax forms, among other things. Needless to say, the social sciences have been influenced by the computer revolution.

According to Hugh Cline, social scientists have in the past used computers for controlled experimentation, simulation, and data processing and statistical analysis. The newest use of the computer is managing data files—for example, choosing one representative person out of a thousand for census sampling (see page 365). Data processing and statistical analysis are the most common use of the computer by social scientists, while computer simulation has been done less often. Controlled experimentation by computer has been done mainly by psychologists.

In almost every use of the computer, one begins with raw data—the census or survey results, for example, or data recorded in observing a small group. These data are in numerical form or in other forms of symbolic representation, such as letters. The first step in using the computer is to make the material machine-readable, that is, to make it ready for transfer to the computer. Usually this is done by keypunching the information onto cards. Data can also be put on special forms; the data are then transferred to cards or to magnetic tape by a machine called an optical scanner.

The second step is machine editing, or "cleaning" errors. Machine editing gives the researcher a chance to get rid of errors that may have been introduced in collecting the data or in transferring them to machine-readable form.

Once the editing process has been completed, the investigator has a choice of procedures. In data processing and statistical analysis, researchers generally prepare a "system file," which involves merging the data with descriptive information so that they can be used with a packaged statistical program. The computer then can provide an initial summary of the data. For instance, in the case of census, the computer groups the data by region, state, sex, age groups, and so on. The initial summary may also include such descriptive statistics as means, medians, and modes (see page 570).

After the initial summary is done, data are combined and recorded into scales, indices, and the like. For example, one might build an index of socioeconomic status by combining or recording each individual's responses to questions on occupation, education, and income.

Most universities now have data centers, in which data files are kept. In some instances, data are "on-line," that is, directly accessible through the use of a computer terminal. The availability of data files means that researchers have easy access to vast amounts of information at a high level of reliability and validity.

It is likely that computers will be used more in the future for simulation and model building. Social scientists are gradually attaining the mathematical sophistication needed for simulation and model building, and more schools have access to the machinery, or "hardware," that is necessary.

The computer has made it possible for social scientists to handle very large files, to merge and gain access to multiple files, and to explore or test hypotheses using more than one set of respondents. With the computer, data are available to nearly everyone and are of increasingly better quality than ever before.

Hugh F. Cline, "Social Science Computing, 1962–1972," a speech presented at the Joint Computer Conference, Spring 1972, and reprinted in *AFIPS Conference Proceedings,* Vol. 40.

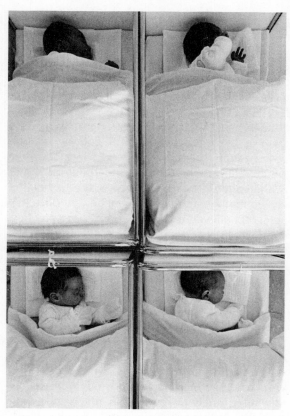

In the early 1970s the growth rate in the United States appeared to be stabilizing at less than 1 percent a year. But even if the fertility rate does not increase, the U.S. population will probably reach 260–270 million by 2000.

Apparently one key variable is education. Among both whites and nonwhites, couples who marry young and without having completed high school have significantly larger families—and significantly lower incomes—than those who marry later and after having finished more schooling. The procreative patterns of minority group members who are not educationally disadvantaged closely parallel those of American society as a whole. The Commission study showed, for example, that blacks with a high-school education have about the same

34. Ibid.

number of children as whites of the same educational level, and that college-educated blacks tend to have even smaller families than their white counterparts.[34]

Many minority group members have been openly suspicious of society's efforts to reduce fertility through family-planning clinics and the like. They believe that the only chance minorities have to achieve equal rights is to grow so large in numbers that they cannot be ignored. But as we noted in Chapter 9, numerical strength in itself is not enough to guarantee a group's political or economic strength. The close correlation of high fertility with low educational and income levels suggests that a reduction in fertility might help rather than hinder minorities in their struggle for social equality.

Resources and the Environment

In recent years it has become increasingly difficult for any citizen of the United States to remain unaware of the fact that our resources are limited. We have been faced with meat shortages, wheat shortages, paper and lumber shortages, steel shortages, fuel shortages, even "space" shortages—not only in our cities and suburbs but on our beaches and in our national parks. A leveling off of population growth would by no means solve such problems, but it might at least cut down the rate at which irreplaceable resources such as iron, copper, lead, and petroleum are consumed and thus give us a little more time to consider and develop alternatives. The need apparently will be not only for new technologies but also for new patterns of life.

America's present use of energy is enormous. We are already facing serious fuel shortages, and further population growth is likely to exacerbate them. More than that, energy consumed by most present means causes one of our gravest problems—air pollution. A stable population would ensure that as progress is made in reducing the amount of pollution per unit of energy consumed (for example, by producing automobiles that caused less pollution), the resultant gains would not be negated by increasing numbers of users.

Other resources in short supply range from water (most of the Midwest is expected to be deficient in water by 2020) to recreation lands, which are already overtaxed by vacationing families. Some of the shortages—of pure air and water, for example—threaten the very lives of future generations. Others threaten our ways of living; but since some of our living patterns contribute to waste and pollution, changing them may ultimately be of benefit to us all. As the Commission on Population Growth states: "Much of the damage we do results from efforts to satisfy fairly trivial preferences—for unblemished fruit, detergents, rapidly accelerating cars, and brightly colored paper products."[35]

Gaining time through slower population growth will enable us to decide what sacrifices we are willing to make to protect our remaining resources. That sacrifice will be necessary seems undeniable.

CHANGING ORIENTATIONS TOWARD BIRTH CONTROL

As late as 1965 the government of the United States declined to pass legislation that would support family-planning clinics at home or abroad. Less than ten years later, not only was the government funding such programs in amounts exceeding $400 million, but discussion had gone beyond contraception to the more controversial issue of abortion. In January 1973 the Supreme Court outlawed as unconstitutional all restrictive laws against abortion during the first three months of pregnancy. Although many individuals and groups continue to oppose abortion and even contraception, attitudes and public policy toward family planning in general have changed dramatically in a relatively few years.

The 1960s were a decade of dissent, of challenge to traditional authority and conventional wisdom in all areas of social life. Changing attitudes toward birth control seem to have been part of a broad move toward social and cultural change. Scientists and popularizers used the mass media to voice their concern over

population growth and its effect on the environment and the quality of individual life. The women's liberation movement voiced the concern of many women that they should have control over the number and spacing of their children and the right to choose not to have a child. In 1968 Pope Paul released the encyclical "On Human Life," which took a strong stand against the use of contraceptive birth control (as opposed to the "rhythm method" of birth control, which relies on the timing of intercourse). Shortly thereafter a Gallup Poll was taken that revealed that a majority of American Catholics (65 percent) believed that it was possible to practice contraception and still remain a "good Catholic."[36] Other polls taken at about the same time revealed that even larger percentages of Protestants and Jews were in favor of using contraceptives.

Family planning became easier during the 1960s with the introduction and wide availability of dependable contraceptives: the birth-control pill and intrauterine devices (IUDs). Unlike older types of contraceptives, which had to be worn during intercourse or used immediately thereafter, an IUD remains in place over long periods, and the pill is taken on a regular schedule. Both are less trouble to use and have a lower rate of failure than traditional devices. By 1970 34 percent of all married women of reproductive age were using the pill, with little difference in frequency of use between whites and nonwhites or between Protestants and Catholics. More recently, the use of the pill has leveled off, and there has been an increase in voluntary sterilization, particularly among married men who, with their wives, feel that they do not want any more children.

The growing acceptance of birth control has encouraged the government to institute broad family-planning programs. Today birth-control services are available not only to the middle and upper classes but also to the poor and even to the young and unmarried. American norms, which for a generation favored three-

35. Ibid., p. 51.
36. As reported in an Associated Press article by George Cornell, *The New York Times*, September 27, 1968.

Traditionally in Latin America, the good family has been the large family, and both men and women have found a sense of self-fulfillment in having many children. Unless traditional attitudes change rapidly, population growth in Latin America will remain high.

and four-children families, have apparently changed to the point where Zero Population Growth may become a reality in the United States.

POPULATION CONTROL IN THE DEVELOPING WORLD

A significant lowering of birth rates in the developing countries will ultimately depend, as it has in the United States and other industrialized countries, on changes in societal attitudes and beliefs. Public concern about rapid population growth and its effects has already led some of the developing countries of Latin America, Asia, and Africa to institute family-planning programs. But in many other countries traditional attitudes

and values retain their strength, making it unlikely that population will be stabilized in these areas in the near future.

LATIN AMERICA

Nowhere is the question of population control more complicated than in Latin America, which until recently was considered underpopulated. Many Latin-American leaders complained that the slow economic growth of their countries was due to a lack of people, and several countries (notably Brazil, Chile, and Argentina) encouraged immigration. But, as we have seen, it becomes daily more difficult to maintain the thesis that social and economic development in Latin America is being hampered by lack of people. While educated people, highly skilled workers, and experienced managers are in short supply, there is a surplus of the illiterate and unskilled, many of them permanently weakened by malnutrition and ill health.

VIEWPOINTS   POPULATION CONTROL: VOLUNTARY OR INVOLUNTARY?

■ The tragedy of the commons develops in this way. Picture a pasture open to all. It is to be expected that each herdsman will try to keep as many cattle as possible on the commons. Such an arrangement may work reasonably satisfactorily for centuries because tribal wars, poaching, and disease keep the numbers of both man and beast well below the carrying capacity of the land. Finally, however, . . . the inherent logic of the commons remorselessly generates tragedy. . . . The rational herdsman concludes that the only sensible course for him to pursue is to add another animal to his herd. And another; and another. . . . But this is the conclusion reached by each and every rational herdsman sharing the commons. Therein is the tragedy. Each man is locked into a system that compels him to increase his herd without limit—in a world that is limited. . . . Freedom in a commons brings ruin to all. . . .

The most important aspect of necessity that we must now recognize, is the necessity of abandoning the commons in breeding. No technical solution can rescue us from the misery of overpopulation. Freedom to breed will bring ruin to all. At the moment, to avoid hard decisions many of us are tempted to propagandize for conscience and responsible parenthood. The temptation must be resisted, because an appeal to independently acting consciences selects for the disappearance of all conscience in the long run, and an increase in anxiety in the short.

The only way we can preserve and nurture other and more precious freedoms is by relinquishing the freedom to breed, and that very soon. "Freedom is the recognition of necessity"—and it is the role of education to reveal to all the necessity of abandoning the freedom to breed. Only so, can we put an end to this aspect of the tragedy of the commons.

Garrett Hardin
"The Tragedy of the Commons"

● The specter, unseen by some and ignored by others, . . . is the continuing rapid population growth of the world's poor countries. Some scientists and publicists have seriously advocated a "lifeboat ethic," saying that nations which do not *compel* human fertility control (by what means is never stated) are endangering the survival of our species—hence they should be starved out of the human race by denying them food aid. This obscene doctrine assumes that men and women will not voluntarily limit their own fertility when they have good reasons and the knowledge and means to do so.

The sharp decline in birthrates during the past decade in a dozen developing countries belies the assumption. But one thing is clear from this experience: environmental changes can bring down birthrates only if they affect the people who have the children—the great mass of the poor who now have little hope for a better life.

In the past, much foreign assistance has benefited elite groups; it has contributed little to the welfare of poor people in poor countries. In future aid programs, the rich nations would be morally justified in insisting that the major part of capital and technical assistance be directed toward improving the living conditions and raising the aspirations of poor people, through bringing about higher levels of literacy and employment opportunities for women, improved health of both children and adults, better communications, greater opportunities for socioeconomic mobility, rational urbanization, agricultural modernization that benefits small farmers and landless laborers, and family planning services that give poor families freedom to choose the numbers of their children. Some or all of these conditions characterize the developing nations which have already markedly reduced their birthrates.

Roger Reville
"The Ghost at the Feast"

The beginnings of the population explosion in Latin America can be traced back to 1920. Its growth rate was not affected by either World War, nor was it greatly affected by the depression of the 1930s. At the present time the population is increasing by about 9 million people per year.

The Forces of Traditionalism

Well over 90 percent of Latin Americans are at least nominally Catholic—that is, have been baptized in the Catholic Church. Whatever else their Catholicism means depends on the criteria used. Formal liturgical worship is most likely to be found in the cities and to be practiced by the middle and upper classes, which make up only a small segment of the total population. Probably no more than a fourth of Latin-American Catholics attend church more than once a month. Among the poor, particularly among the Indians, there is a folk Catholicism that is only loosely related to the formal structure of the Catholic Church. The great majority of the poor see a priest or other functionary once a year at most. Nevertheless, these people identify themselves as Catholics and adhere to many of the traditional teachings of the Catholic Church, including the belief that children are a gift of God and therefore to be welcomed without question.

Church teachings about the blessings of a large family have found reflection and support in familism—the configuration of values and behavior patterns associated with family life in Latin America. Traditionally, the good family has been the large family. The ideal for the male has been that he should be *macho*—brave, virile, and able to produce children. Premarital sexual activity has been expected of males, and in some parts of Latin America extramarital sex has also been normative for men. The Latin-American woman has found her identity in motherhood. If she has not always been well loved as a wife, as a mother she has been worshiped. Large families, then, have traditionally been a means of fulfillment for both men and women.

In most Latin-American countries, government itself has been a force for traditionalism, at least until recently. Political regimes have typically been allied with the Church hierarchy in efforts to maintain the status quo; in several countries such alliances still exist, working against the possibility of government action in the area of fertility control. In any case, most Latin-American leaders either have not been interested in population questions or else have believed that their countries were underpopulated.

Social Ferment

Today the traditional patterns of Church, family, and government in Latin America are in a state of flux. The situation is not everywhere the same, however, and it is by no means clear what new patterns will eventually emerge. Certainly there is no basis for the easy generalization that change will be in the direction of the dominant Western pattern as exemplified by Europe or the United States. Nor is it clear that this pattern is necessarily the desirable one for Latin America.

Traditional family patterns in Latin America have been greatly disrupted by the phenomenon of rural-urban migration—the flood of humanity pouring into the older cities and making new cities out of small towns. Extended kinship ties are subject to increasing strain in this new kind of urban life. Lack of housing and lack of jobs force people to keep on the move. And industrialization requires new work patterns and challenges many of the values and attitudes that have long undergirded familism. The traditional role of women is being questioned increasingly by both sexes.

In many parts of Latin America, the ferment for change within the Catholic Church acts as a further stimulus in altering traditional family patterns. In the 1965 Schema on the Church in the Modern World, Church leaders formally recognized the right of husband and wife to decide how many children they would have and when they would have them. Furthermore, the statements on conjugal love as a fundamental good of married life placed Catholic teaching very much in line with that of other Western religious groups. Now that women are formally recognized by the Church as equal partners in the marriage enterprise, it can be expected that women's status will gradually rise.

Government Policy

Government leaders, too, have started to take a fresh look at the status quo. Most Latin-American governments have now instituted formal demographic studies that will give them more precise information about the nature of their own populations, and some have even given support to the establishment of family-planning programs. One outstanding example is that of Chile.

Under the leadership of President Eduardo Frei, himself a practicing Catholic, the Christian Democratic party in the 1960s permitted the development of experimental family-planning programs using national health facilities. This move reflected a grave concern over rising rates of illegal abortion. A series of studies on induced abortion carried out by Chilean physicians had shown that 25 to 30 percent of the women questioned had had at least one induced abortion; that some middle-class women were resorting to sterilization to prevent further conceptions; and that in some cases churchgoing Catholic women had higher rates of induced abortion than did Protestant Evangelicals.[37] These findings, together with the results of attitude studies showing that a majority of women (around 75 percent) and their partners felt that birth control should be made universal and that the Church had no right to interfere in such matters, led the government to institute an aggressive campaign to decrease abortions through effective family planning and the use of such contraceptives as the IUD and the pill. The results became noticeable within a decade, and age-specific fertility rates declined between 1960 and 1968. Family-planning programs have continued in Chile in the 1970s.

In Latin America generally, studies show that increasing percentages of adults want small families but that people are generally ignorant about modern methods of fertility control and are hesistant to use any methods other than rhythm until leaders of the Catholic Church give their permission. This uncertainty is reflected in a 1972 study of the twenty-three Latin-American nations, which showed that only seven had programs geared specifically to population limitation, while ten others supported family-planning programs for reasons other than population control per se—primarily, as in Chile, as a public health service aimed at reducing the number of abortions.[38] These seventeen countries account for only about half of the total population of Latin America. Thus it is likely that population growth in Latin America, which now boasts the highest rate in the world, will remain high for at least another decade.

ASIA AND AFRICA

India and China, which together have almost a third of the world's population, were among the first countries in the world to develop government-sponsored family-planning and birth-limitation programs. Increasingly throughout Asia, and to a lesser extent in Africa, governments are beginning to recognize that planning for economic development, to which they are all committed, must take into account the consequences of population growth. There has been a growing recognition, too, that millions of people will starve if population growth goes unchecked. But as in Latin America, traditional values and norms continue to work against effective family planning.

The Religious Factor

Islam has become an increasingly vital religious force throughout Asia and parts of Africa. Generally the birth rate among Muslims has been higher than that of any other major religious group—in excess of 40 per 1000 and ranging as high as 62 per 1000 in Pakistan.[39] For the most part, Muslims still live in folk-peasant conditions, with high mortality. Sons are considered necessary to continue the family line, to guarantee land ownership and an adequate labor supply, to give support to parents in old age, and to offer prayers for them after death.

37. Herman Romero, "Chile," in Berelson et al., *Family Planning and Population Programs*, pp. 235–247.

38. Stamper, "Population Policy in Development Planning," pp. 4–7.

39. Petersen, *Population*, pp. 591–602. The following discussion of the Muslim countries is based on Dudley Kirk, "Factors Affecting Moslem Natality," in Berelson et al., *Family Planning and Population Programs*, pp. 561–579.

Faced with a population explosion which threatens to wipe out economic gains, many governments have given high priority to massive family-planning programs. At the Family-Planning Association of Pakistan, a doctor explains the stages of pregnancy to housewives.

For the Muslims as for no other major religious group, religion and family life are completely intertwined. The Koran (the holy book of the Muslims) allows men to have more than one wife, supports male dominance patterns, and gives sexual pleasure a positive emphasis unknown in traditional Christian teachings. Custom encourages early marriage: in ten Muslim countries for which data are available, 70 to 86 percent of all females aged fifteen to forty-four are married, and less than 3 percent of Muslim women remain unmarried at forty-five. Almost all widows and divorcees remarry. In most of the Muslim countries less than 30 percent of the women have had any formal education.

Continued strong anti-Western, anti-Christian, and anti-Jewish feelings among the Muslims have made them hostile to Western ways, Western medicine, and Western urban patterns—and to birth control as a Western means to diminish their numbers. Malnutrition, disease, and high infant mortality have tended to keep the rate of population growth in Muslim countries below that in most other parts of the developing world, but the acceptance of modern health measures could bring a dramatic change.

40. Berelson, "World Population: Status Report 1974," p. 24.
41. Kirk, "Factors Affecting Moslem Natality," pp. 561–579.
42. Ibid.

Changing Public Opinion

It now appears that "some 87 percent of the population of the developing world is covered within a policy to make family planning available," but the policy itself has been implemented effectively for only a minority of the people.[40] Because of geographical and social isolation, the majority are still not aware of modern methods of birth control. Such knowledge continues to be found predominantly among educated urbanites.

Fertility studies in Muslim countries show that most couples have wanted only three children, especially if one or two of the children already born were male. However, actual family size has been considerably larger. In Turkey, for example, women past childbearing age (over 45) reported an average of 6.3 pregnancies, 5.8 live births, and 4.1 living children.[41] But despite such statistics, fertility patterns seem to be slowly changing. A study in Beirut showed that 60 percent of the less educated women and 83 percent of the more educated women were making at least some attempt to limit the size of their families.[42] Berelson reports that surveys throughout Asia and Africa have shown that 70 percent of married people in the areas studied claim to want no more than four children.[43] It remains to be seen whether this ideal will be realized and whether average family size can then be further lowered. If three or four children become normative, rapid population growth will continue despite family planning.

Government Policy

In Asia more than in any of the other developing areas, governments have started to recognize the impact of such demographic factors as age structure, fertility rates, and the like on needs for food, housing, education, employment, and health services. As a result, by the mid-1970s ten Asian nations had incorporated demographic data into their national development programs and launched ambitious programs of family limitation, some of which seem to be succeeding. These ten nations contain 90 percent of Asia's population and thus constitute a significant model for the other developing nations.

The Indian government has made family planning a top priority in its fourth five-year plan and in the past decade has trained 80,000 medical personnel and auxiliary staff to integrate child and maternal health care with family-planning services. It is estimated that 13 percent of India's 100 million fertile couples are now using contraceptives. A major objective is to reduce the birth rate from 40 to 25 per 1000. In Pakistan the objective is to reduce the birth rate from 55 to 45 per 1000.

Six African nations have established family-planning programs in order to limit population growth, while another eight have developed programs geared to helping individual citizens determine the size of their families. These fourteen nations include most of the African states with the largest populations—for example, Egypt, Nigeria, South Africa, and Morocco. Most of the family-planning policies emphasize that the public must be educated about the need for and desirability of family planning. Some countries have specified concrete objectives; for example, Morocco hopes to decrease its birth rate from 50 to 45 per 1000 during the course of

its five-year plan, and Uganda hopes to reduce its growth rate to about 3 percent by 1979.[44] It must be emphasized again that even if such goals are realized, they will be only first steps in stemming runaway population growth.

As Coale notes, the current rate of world population growth must inevitably decline, simply because the world cannot sustain it. But it remains to be seen whether population growth will be checked by a reduction in birth rates, an increase in death rates, or some combination of both:

Arithmetic makes a return of a growth rate near zero inevitable before many generations have passed. What is uncertain is not that the future rate of growth will be about zero but how large the future population will be and what combination of fertility and mortality will sustain it. The possibilities range from more than eight children per woman and a life that lasts an average of 15 years, to slightly more than two children per woman and a life span that surpasses 75 years.[45]

Reasoning from the perspective of the late eighteenth century, Malthus would argue that the current population explosion must ultimately be stemmed by such "positive checks" as war, famine, and disease. Today, changing attitudes and technologies provide the basis for reasonable hope that wide-scale disaster can somehow be averted.

43. Berelson, "World Population: Status Report 1974," p. 300.
44. Stamper, "Population Policy in Development Planning," pp. 9–12.
45. Coale, "The History of the Human Population," p. 41.

SUMMARY

The population of the world is increasing at a rate unprecedented in history, with the overwhelming preponderance of growth occurring in the underdeveloped and developing nations. This growth is largely the result of the precipitous drop in death rates in these areas. And herein lies one of the important differences between the "two worlds." It took more than a century and a half for the death rates to drop to their current low levels in the industrialized areas of the world. In the developing areas the drop has occurred in less than thirty years. One of the most significant immediate consequences of these demographic changes has been a radical alteration in the age structure of many societies, leading to a fantastic increase in the percentage of population under twenty years of age.

The recent development of simple and effective methods of contraception has brought the countries of the developing world within reach of fertility control, which, if accomplished, could restore the balance between birth and death rates and perhaps make it possible for the first time for the great majority of human beings to share a life of material well-being. The evidence shows that governments, which have been largely responsible for the rapid reduction of mortality rates in the developing countries, have now begun to take an active role in reducing birth rates. As Ryder notes, "It seems that the future fertility of modern nations will depend primarily on the relative success with which their respective governments can bring individual decisions about childbearing into correspondence with demographic requirements of the society."[46] Thus there is a new awareness of the mutual dependence of society's most basic social unit, the family, and its largest and in some ways most pervasive unit, the government.

46. Norman B. Ryder, "The Character of Modern Fertility," *Annals of the American Academy of Political and Social Science,* 369 (January 1967): 36.

12
The Urban Transition

The establishment of permanent settlements began thousands of years ago, but urbanization—the extensive movement of people from rural areas to cities—is essentially a phenomenon of the nineteenth and twentieth centuries. Scientific and technological advances in industry, agriculture, transportation, commerce, and sanitation have together made possible the development of cities as we know them today. In 1800 less than 3 percent of the world's population lived in cities of 20,000 or more inhabitants; by 1990, over 50 percent are likely to be living in cities of 100,000 or more.

Although the growth of cities has been closely associated with the idea of progress, even the most casual observer knows that urbanization has caused numerous problems. Indeed, anti-urban attitudes have accompanied urbanization.[1] Balzac painted Paris in the first half of the nineteenth century as a city of feverish activity whose inhabitants, driven by the desire for money and pleasure, ignored the destruction of beauty and wisdom. Long before automobile exhausts poisoned the urban atmosphere, Balzac was complaining that "half of Paris sleeps amidst the putrid exhalations of courts and streets and sewers."[2] On the other hand, Thomas De Quincey described his first visit to London in 1800 as a heavenly occurrence and likened the city to the wonders of nature—a "mighty wilderness," "some vast magnetic range of Alps," "a Norwegian maelstrom," "the roar of Niagara."[3] And Benjamin Franklin, very much an urbanite, saw the culture of the city, with its library, university, and other amenities, as the key to enlightenment.

In this chapter we will examine some of the factors that have propelled the growth of cities over the past two hundred years and also some of the social and cultural changes that have

1. For a critical review of antiurban attitudes, see Morton and Lucia White, *The Intellectual Versus the City* (Cambridge, Mass.: Harvard University Press and The M.I.T. Press, 1962).

2. Honoré de Balzac, "The Anatomy of Paris," in *Sociology Through Literature*, 2nd ed., Lewis Coser, ed. (Englewood Cliffs, N.J.: Prentice-Hall, Inc., 1972), p. 326.

3. Thomas De Quincey, "The Powers and Rhythms of London," in *Sociology Through Literature*, pp. 311–313.

accompanied such growth. We will attempt to understand how urban life differs from rural life and to assess the kinds of social organization that are both cause and consequence of contemporary urban life.

THE CITY IN HISTORICAL PERSPECTIVE

A city may be defined as an area of dense population set off by clear-cut political boundaries and a name. Cities are also characterized by the fact that a majority of their residents earn a livelihood in non-farming work. As a distinct form of social organization the city is at least six thousand years old.[4]

THE DEVELOPMENT OF THE PREINDUSTRIAL CITY

Urban life is ultimately dependent on the existence of food surpluses. Thus it is not surprising that the earliest cities emerged in environments where the soil was especially fertile and where there was sufficient water available for crops and livestock as well as for concentrations of people. The emergence of the preindustrial city also depended on the existence of relatively large populations in outlying areas on which the city could draw. Historically, disease and famine kept death rates higher in urban areas than elsewhere, so that cities were barely able to maintain their size without a constant influx of people from outside.

The first known cities emerged in the fertile valleys of the Tigris and Euphrates rivers, regions where agriculture was well developed and where there was much contact among peoples of diverse cultures. Evidence of other very early cities has been found in the Nile River Valley,

the Indus Valley of present-day Pakistan, the Yellow River Valley of China, and several parts of Mesoamerica. In all these areas, the ability to produce larger and larger surpluses of food gave people increasing freedom to pursue nonagricultural activities and led to a gradual specialization of arts and crafts. Archeological finds in the valleys of the Tigris and Euphrates show that even the earliest cities supported skilled artisans. They also supported a literate elite.

As preindustrial cities evolved, they developed characteristic organizational forms. (1) Political control was usually theocratic—the king and the high priest were one. (2) The center of the city was the area of highest prestige, and the elite lived there. The poorest people lived on the fringes of the city and had the least protection from attack by enemies. (3) Artisans established themselves in special quarters or streets, further sharpening differences in social ranking.

In many ways the organizational structure of the preindustrial city worked to maintain a rigid system of social stratification. Wealthy families controlled the government and religious activities. The fact that they lived close together in the center of the city made it easy for them to communicate among themselves and helped maintain their distinctive patterns of life. Religious orthodoxy stressed the moral rightness of the established social order, as did formal education, which was available only to the elite.

Even while supporting the status quo, however, the preindustrial city stimulated many kinds of social and cultural change. As a center of trade, the city was also a center for the exchange of new ideas and inventions, which then diffused from the city to outlying areas. The concentration of artisans served to stimulate technological innovation. And not least important, new forms of social organization were developed to accommodate the increasing numbers of people living close together and to coordinate their specialized activities. Organizational problems concerned especially the distribution of goods—not only within the city but also between city and countryside—and the protection of the city from outside enemies. Thus the preindustrial city brought about the gradual

4. The following discussion draws heavily on Gideon Sjoberg, "The Origin and Evolution of Cities," Philip M. Hauser, "Urbanization: An Overview," and R. M. Adams, "The Origin of the City," all in *Metropolis in Crisis*, ed. Jeffrey K. Hadden, Louis H. Masotti, and Calvin J. Larson (Itasca, Ill.: F. E. Peacock Publishers, Inc., 1967); Max Weber, *The City*, trans. and ed. Don Martindale and Gertrude Neuwirth (New York: Collier Books, 1962); and Amos Hawley, *Urban Society* (New York: The Ronald Press Company, 1971).

This engraving, done in 1799, shows the junction of Second Street and High Street in the heart of Philadelphia. Like other cities that were developed in colonial times, Philadelphia was a center of trade and commerce, serving as a major port during the eighteenth century.

development of new forms of political, military, and economic organization. Its dependence on trade made necessary the establishment of common standards of weights and measures and of rules governing trade and civility among peoples who were otherwise strangers.

THE CITY IN COLONIAL AMERICA

The earliest cities in the Western hemisphere were the creations of Indian peoples, chiefly in Central and South America. Before the arrival of the British and French, Spanish colonists both built upon the ruins of these Indian cities and established new settlements.[5]

The cities that evolved somewhat later in the North American colonies served much the same functions as preindustrial cities in Europe: they provided protection for their residents and facilitated trade and commerce. They also served as bases for the movement of populations into undeveloped territories. To a great extent, their growth depended on their location, and especially on accessibility to navigable waterways and agricultural support.

Although the British colonies offered social mobility for many, the colonial city was not without class distinctions. The old aristocracy did not come to America, but a new aristocracy— composed of wealthy merchants and landowners—emerged. Below this class were artisans

and clerks and, at the bottom of the hierarchy, unskilled laborers, servants, and, finally, slaves.[6]

Although the colonial city was free of some of the problems that beset modern American cities, it had problems enough of its own. Chitwood describes it as follows:

In none of the cities was there running water in the houses, and there was probably not a bathtub in any American home before the Revolution. Water was obtained from surface wells and was always liable to pollution by disease germs. . . .

None of the colonial cities had any arrangement for disposing of garbage, and New York was the only one that attempted to clean the streets. Ashes and garbage were thrown into unsanitary heaps in the alleys and on vacant lots. In some cities and towns hogs were allowed to roam through the streets and act as scavengers by eating up the scraps of meat and vegetables that had been thrown out by the housewives. . . . These unsanitary conditions persisted long after colonial times and are matters of comment by travelers in the middle of the nineteenth century.[7]

5. For an account of one of the earliest settlements in North America, see Frank Waters, *Book of the Hopi* (New York: Ballantine Books, 1963), esp. pp. 132 ff.

6. For an account of the history of the American city see Charles N. Glaab, *The American City: A Documentary History* (Homewood, Ill.: Dorsey Press, 1963). For an analysis of stratification in the preindustrial American city, see Robert A. Dahl, *Who Governs?* (New Haven, Conn.: Yale University Press, 1961), Book 1.

7. Oliver P. Chitwood, *A History of Colonial America* (New York: Harper and Brothers, 1931), p. 580.

URBANIZATION AND INDUSTRIALIZATION

The term *urbanization* refers to the movement of population from farmlands to towns and cities. Historically, rural areas have produced people and cities have consumed them. Only recently have urban death rates been lowered to the point where city populations can grow rapidly without an influx of people from outside.

As we discussed in Chapter 11, "Demographic Change," population in western Europe and the United States increased dramatically during the Industrial Revolution as a result of improved sanitation and medical advances. At the same time, more efficient farming techniques and machinery improved productivity, and fewer farmers were needed to produce food for the growing population. Lack of employment opportunities in rural areas led many farmers and their families to move to towns and cities, where mills and factories were increasing in size and number and thus creating many new jobs.

In the following section we shall discuss urbanization in the United States, noting the important part that economic factors have played in stimulating the movement of people from farm to city and, more recently, from city to suburb. Then we shall look briefly at the recent experience with urbanization in the developing countries, where the growth of cities is generally proceeding more rapidly than the capacity of the cities to provide jobs and essential services.

THE AMERICAN EXPERIENCE

The United States was well set for urbanization by 1800. It had a gradually developing industrial and agricultural technology, rich farmlands capable of yielding an abundance of food, and a system of waterways that could be used for transporting goods. If anything was lacking it was experience in the practical arts of building and governing cities, which were bringing together ever increasing numbers of people from a wide variety of cultural backgrounds. But whether the cities were ready for them or not, the people flocked in, presumably in the hope of improving their lives.

From Farm to Metropolis

Rural-to-urban migration during the nineteenth and twentieth centuries has reflected the accelerating course of industrialization. The first official United States census in 1790 showed a total of only twenty-four communities with populations in excess of 2500, just two of which were larger than 25,000. Altogether, residents of these "urban places" made up less than 3.5 percent of the country's total population. A hundred years later, there were 160 cities with over 25,000 people, including three with populations of over a million. The total urban population—defined by the Bureau of the Census as those living in incorporated areas of 2500 or more—had increased to almost 30 percent of the total.

The pace of urbanization has further quickened during the twentieth century. Today there are more than 800 cities in the United States with populations in excess of 25,000, and an estimated 75 percent of Americans live in places officially defined as *urban*. About 40 percent of the population is concentrated in Standard Metropolitan Statistical Areas of a million or more people. (See "Defining Urban Populations," page 342.)

Although urbanization has been primarily the consequence of a flight from the farm, the values and virtues of rural life have continued to be celebrated in American ideology. Lewis Mumford has drawn this critical portrait of New York City in the 1870s:

Within the span of a generation, the open spaces and the natural vistas began to disappear. . . . Vanishing from the consciousness of most Manhattanites were the open markets that had once brought the touch of the sea and the country to its streets, connecting farmstead and city home . . . .

DEFINING URBAN POPULATIONS

The United States Bureau of the Census has continued its original practice of defining any locality with a population of 2500 or more persons as an *urban place.* Thus the urban population, as officially defined, includes the residents of many places that we would normally think of today as small towns rather than as cities. Other countries tend to restrict the term *urban* to localities in which the population is 20,000 or more persons. Whatever cutoff point is used, however, the objective is essentially the same: to locate areas in which economic activities are predominantly *nonagricultural.*

In earlier eras, persons who earned their livelihood within a city usually lived within its political boundaries. Today, however, the formal boundaries of a city are much less likely to delimit activity. Millions of people who work in the city live in "dormitory suburbs" or nearby small towns. Increasingly, daily life focuses in and on the *metropolis* — a central city and the area immediately surrounding it, including many communities that were once largely self-sufficient.

In order to deal with this complex phenomenon, the United States Bureau of the Census has developed three special concepts to identify and analyze units of population that are functionally integrated even though they may be broken up by various political boundaries. The most general concept, *urbanized area,* was adopted in 1950 to provide a meaningful separation of rural and urban populations in areas surrounding large cities. An urbanized area includes at least one city of 50,000 or more inhabitants, plus all closely settled territory surrounding it. Everyone who lives within an urbanized area is counted as part of the urban population, even though some may live in communities of less than 2500 people or in unincorporated places.

A *Standard Metropolitan Statistical Area* (SMSA) is defined somewhat more specifically as an integrated unit. According to the Bureau of the Census, an SMSA is "a county or group of contiguous counties which contains at least one city of 50,000 inhabitants or more or 'twin cities' with a combined population of at least 50,000. In addition to the county or counties containing such a city or cities, contiguous counties are included in an SMSA if, according to certain criteria, they are essentially metropolitan in character and are socially and economically integrated with the central city." The Bureau of the Census delineated 243 SMSAs on the basis of the 1970 census. In addition, it delineated two unique complexes of SMSAs as *Standard Consolidated Areas:* New York-Northeastern New Jersey and Chicago-Northwestern Indiana. These large metropolitan complexes are functionally unified in many ways, but they do not meet all the criteria of social and economic integration that would be necessary to classify them as single SMSAs.

A broader and more inclusive term that has come into wide use is *urban region.* An urban region is characterized as having a population of one million or more in a continuous zone of metropolitan areas and contiguous counties. The urban region provides a variety of residential settings, from rural to cosmopolitan, within a metropolitan economy that includes much decentralization of commercial and industrial activity. The Commission on Population Growth and the American Future has described it as "a constellation of urban centers dispersing outward" (p. 119). By 1980 the United States is expected to have twenty-three such regions, and by 2000 it is expected that one super-urban region, stretching along the Atlantic coast and westward to Chicago, will contain 41 percent of the total population.

The United Nations has been working, so far unsuccessfully, to develop a standard set of concepts for identifying urban populations and delimiting urban boundaries. For a fuller discussion of this point and an elaboration of the concepts used by the U.S. Bureau of the Census, see Jack P. Gibbs, ed., *Urban Research Methods* (New York: D. Van Nostrand Co., Inc., 1961). See also *Population and the American Future,* The Report of the Commission on Population Growth and the American Future (Washington, D.C.: U.S. Government Printing Office, 1972), pp. 35–37 and 119–120.

As the premier urban center of the United States, New York City has symbolized the best and the worst in urban living. With approximately eight million residents, New York can be said to have too many people and too much noise, congestion, crime, pollution, and poverty. Here we see a mountain of garbage representing the amount collected in a single day in the city.

Meanwhile, the city as a whole became progressively more foul. In the late seventies the new model tenement design, that for the so-called dumbbell apartment, standardized the habitations of the workers on the lowest possible level, encouraging for twenty years the erection of tenements in which only two rooms in six or seven got direct sunlight or a modicum of air. Even the best residences were grim, dreary, genteelly fusty. If something better was at last achieved for the rich in the 1890's, on Riverside Drive and West End Avenue, it remained in existence scarcely twenty years and was replaced by mass congestion.[8]

Today New York City is America's premiere urban center. In terms of noise, congestion, crime, air pollution, and housing conditions, it has continued in the direction that Mumford

deplored, becoming "progressively more foul." For many people, these disadvantages are counterbalanced by the fact that the city offers them a wide choice of employment opportunities, cultural stimulation, and freedom to develop their own individual life-styles. But for others the modern city has provided little of value; for many minority group members, it has meant entrapment in a ghetto with little hope of escape. We will take a closer look at the ghetto and other realities of contemporary urban life later in this chapter.

Other Population Trends

As Kingsley Davis has noted, the period of rural-to-urban migration in the United States has been accompanied by several other major patterns of population movement: (1) a movement from East to West, (2) a movement from South to

8. Lewis Mumford, *City Development* (New York: Harcourt Brace Jovanovich, Inc., 1945), pp. 34–35.

North, and more recently from North to South, and (3) a movement out from the central city to the suburbs.[9]

East to West Both rural-to-urban and East-to-West migration are reflected in Table 12.1 (below), which shows the ten largest American cities in 1820, 1900, and 1970. The first area of the country to be settled, the east coast, continues to be the most densely populated, but it now includes only four of the ten largest cities. Census Bureau figures show that the center of population gravity has been shifting steadily westward ever since the nation's founding.[10] At the time of the first census in 1790, it was just east of Baltimore, Maryland. By 1970 it had moved about seven hundred miles west and was located just east of St. Louis, Missouri. California, which had a population of less than 100,000 when it was admitted to statehood in 1850, now is home to over 20 million people—almost 10 percent of the country's total population.

The steady movement of population from East to West in the United States has been stimulated by new economic opportunities on the country's changing frontier. It has also reflected the fact that immigration to the United States has always been primarily from Europe rather than from Asia. Many of the millions of people who have come to this country from Europe have settled permanently in New York, Boston, and other cities of the East, but many others have joined the growing stream of Americans moving westward.

South to North and North to South Migration from South to North began as a trickle in the late nineteenth century but was greatly accelerated by the need for industrial workers during World Wars I and II. Although this pattern of migration has involved whites as well as blacks, the exodus of the black population from the South has been particularly marked (see Chapter 9, pages 247–250). Whereas the vast majority of the black population at one time lived in the southern states, the percentage has now dropped to about half (Table 12.2). Most of the migration has been to the large cities of the North, in some of which black minorities are rapidly becoming majorities. This is true despite the fact that the movement northward has slowed somewhat: the black population in the cities is now experiencing natural growth, while the white population dwindles as a result of a steady exodus to the suburbs.

The years since World War II have also seen a considerable movement of population from North to South. For the most part, those who have moved South are white-collar and

9. See Kingsley Davis, "The Urbanization of the Human Population," *Scientific American*, September 1965, pp. 41–53. See also Davis, "Urbanization—Changing Patterns of Living," in *The Changing American Population; A Report of the Arden House Conference*, ed. Hoke S. Simpson (New York: Columbia University Press, 1962), pp. 59–68.
10. The Bureau of the Census defines the center of population gravity as "that point upon which the United States would balance if it were a rigid plane without weight and the population distributed thereon with each individual being assumed to have equal weight and to exert an influence on a central point proportional to his distance from that point."

Table 12.1. TEN LARGEST CITIES IN THE UNITED STATES, 1820, 1900, AND 1970

1820		1900		1970	
New York, N.Y.	123,706	New York, N.Y.	3,437,202	New York, N.Y.	7,771,730
Philadelphia, Pa.	63,802	Chicago, Ill.	1,698,575	Chicago, Ill.	3,325,263
Baltimore, Md.	62,738	Philadelphia, Pa.	1,293,697	Los Angeles, Cal.	2,782,400
Boston, Mass.	42,541	St. Louis, Mo.	575,238	Philadelphia, Pa.	1,926,529
New Orleans, La.	27,176	Boston, Mass.	560,892	Detroit, Mich.	1,492,914
Charleston, S.C.	24,780	Baltimore, Md.	508,957	Houston, Texas	1,213,064
Washington, D.C.	13,247	Cleveland, Ohio	381,768	Baltimore, Md.	895,222
Albany City, N.Y.	12,630	Buffalo, N.Y.	352,387	Dallas, Texas	836,121
Providence, R.I.	11,767	San Francisco, Cal.	342,782	Washington, D.C. (est.)	764,000
Salem, Mass.	11,346	Cincinnati, Ohio	325,902	Indianapolis, Ind.	742,613

SOURCE: Bureau of the Census.

professional people, some of them moving to take new jobs and others to enjoy retirement in a warm climate.

City to Suburbs Now that the urbanization of American society is virtually complete, perhaps the significant demographic distinction is not between rural and urban but rather between city and suburbs. A dramatic change is taking place in the nature of the population of major cities, as the poor become concentrated there and the middle and upper classes move out. The 1970 Census showed, for the first time, that more Americans lived in the suburbs of big cities (74.2 million) than in the cities themselves (62.2 million).

The movement toward suburbia is not new, but it has vastly accelerated over the last two decades and has been tied to patterns of racial segregation. (See, for example, Table 12.3 and Table 12.4.) Whites are leaving the large cities in increasing numbers: in 1970, 40 percent of whites lived in the suburbs, as compared to only 16 percent of blacks.[11]

This population trend has created not only a personal crisis for those who are trapped in the slums but a crisis for the city as a whole. Racial segregation has increased despite federal programs aimed at desegregation. And though suburbanites continue to depend on the city for their livelihood, they contribute disproportionately little to its maintenance and to the provision of crucial public services. Since the poor who are left behind cannot pay for such services themselves, a downward spiral sets in, with further deterioration of already deteriorated housing, inadequate educational opportunities, and high rates of unemployment and welfare dependency. These are the conditions that give meaning to the phrase, "the crisis of the cities." We will examine them more closely elsewhere in this chapter.

11. Reynolds Farley and Karl E. Taeuber, "Population Trends and Residential Segregation Since 1960," *Science,* 159 (March 1, 1968): 953–956; and E. J. Kahn, Jr., "Who, What, Where, How Much, How Many?" *New Yorker,* October 15, 1973, pp. 141–142.

Table 12.2. PERCENT DISTRIBUTION OF BLACKS IN THE UNITED STATES, BY REGION, 1940–1970

	1940	1950	1960	1970
South	77	68	60	53
Northeast	11	13	16	19
North Central	11	15	18	20
West	1	4	6	8

SOURCE: Bureau of the Census, *General Population Characteristics,* PC(1)–B1, United States Summary, p. 293. By the standard Census definition, the South includes Delaware, the District of Columbia, Kentucky, Maryland, Oklahoma, and West Virginia as well as the states of the Confederacy.

Table 12.3. PERCENTAGE OF WHITES IN CENTRAL CITIES OF TWELVE LARGEST SMSAS, 1940–1970

SMSA	1940	1950	1960	1970
New York	93.6	90.2	85.3	73.2
Los Angeles–Long Beach	94.0	90.2	84.7	79.0
Chicago	91.7	85.9	76.4	65.4
Philadelphia	86.9	81.7	73.3	65.6
Detroit	90.7	83.6	70.8	55.7
San Francisco–Oakland	95.1	88.2	78.9	67.4
Boston	96.7	94.7	90.2	82.1
Pittsburgh	90.7	87.7	83.2	79.1
St. Louis	86.6	82.0	71.2	58.7
Washington, D.C.	71.5	64.6	45.2	27.7
Cleveland	90.3	83.7	71.1	60.9
Baltimore	80.6	76.2	65.0	52.9

Table 12.4. PERCENTAGE OF NONWHITES IN SUBURBS OF TWELVE LARGEST SMSAS, 1940–1970

SMSA	1940	1950	1960	1970
New York	4.6	4.5	4.8	13.1
Los Angeles–Long Beach	2.3	2.7	4.1	9.4
Chicago	2.2	2.9	3.1	4.0
Philadelphia	6.6	6.6	6.3	7.1
Detroit	2.9	5.0	3.8	3.9
San Francisco–Oakland	3.6	6.8	6.8	7.6
Boston	0.9	0.8	1.0	1.3
Pittsburgh	3.6	3.5	3.4	3.9
St. Louis	6.7	7.3	6.3	7.6
Washington, D.C.	13.7	8.7	6.4	8.7
Cleveland	0.9	0.8	0.8	3.5
Baltimore	11.9	10.2	6.9	6.5

SOURCE: Harry Sharp and Leo F. Schnore, "The Changing Color Composition of Metropolitan Areas," *Land Economics,* 38 (May 1962), 169–185, reproduced with permission; also *Census of Population and Housing, 1970* (for each of the above SMSAs), U.S. Government Printing Office, 1972.

These photographs, which were taken from the same spot forty-four years apart, point up the fact that the west coast has experienced a more dramatic growth than any other section of the country. In 1922 (left) Los Angeles was a relatively small city with about half a million inhabitants, but today (right) it has a population of about three million and ranks as one of the largest cities in the United States.

URBANIZATION IN THE DEVELOPING WORLD

Urbanization in the developing countries of Asia, Africa, and Latin America is proceeding much more rapidly than it did in the United States and other industrialized nations. Furthermore, it is being impelled less by the development of new economic opportunities in the cities than it is by the pressures created by rapid population growth in outlying areas. In general, it represents a very uneven and unstable kind of social and cultural change. The lack of industry to support the growing urban population and the retention of traditional systems of stratification mean that most people who have abandoned rural life for "the promise of the cities" are condemned to desperate poverty. The problems associated with inner-city slums in the United States extend throughout most of the urban areas in these countries, often in exaggerated form.

Rural-to-urban migration in the developing countries has been primarily to key cities—generally the capital cities. Typically, the capital is the main point of contact with other parts of the world and thus a symbol of modernization. As it continually increases its importance as the center of influence and authority, the capital city also acts as a special agent for implementing and diffusing change in the society, becoming in the process the point of concentration for the nation's talent and labor force.[12] This concentration of wealth and power in one city tends to make it especially attractive to the migrant seeking escape from rural poverty. From a distance the prime city seems full of promise; in fact, it is usually unprepared to offer even marginal support to new arrivals.

In most cities of the developing world housing, sanitation, and transportation are wholly inadequate to serve the needs of a growing, highly concentrated population. Most of the new immigrants who crowd to the cities live in squalor, with grossly inferior housing, inadequate diets, and none of the basic facilities most Americans take for granted. And they seem to have little chance of improving their lot—economically, politically, or otherwise.

Poverty, of course, is not new to history, nor is it confined to the cities of the developing nations. What *is* new in this pattern of urbanization is that such vast numbers of human beings live under conditions barely capable of sustaining life. The following excerpts from the diary of a woman living in one of Brazil's worst slums tell more than statistics do.

May 20: . . . At 8:30 that night I was in the favela [slum area] breathing the smell of excrement mixed with the rotten earth. When I am in the city I have the impression that I am in a living room with crystal chandeliers, rugs of velvet, and satin cushions. And when I'm in the favela I have the impression that I'm a useless object, destined to be forever in a garbage dump.

Sometimes families move into the favela with children. In the beginning they are educated, friendly. Days later they use foul language, are mean and quarrelsome. They are diamonds turned to lead. They are transformed from objects that were in the living room to objects banished to the garbage dump.

How horrible it is to see a child eat and ask: "Is there more?" This word "more" keeps ringing in the mother's head as she looks in the pot and doesn't have any more.

May 21: . . . Yesterday I ate that macaroni from the garbage with fear of death, because in [the past] I sold scrap over there in Zinho. There was a pretty black boy. He also went to sell scrap in Zinho. He was young and said that those who should look for paper were the old. One day I was collecting scrap when I stopped at Bom Jardim Avenue. Someone had thrown meat into the garbage, and he was picking out the pieces. He told me:

"Take some, Carolina. It's still fit to eat."

He gave me some, and so as not to hurt his feelings, I accepted. I tried to convince him not to eat the meat, or the hard bread gnawed by the rats. He told me no, because it was two days since he had eaten. He made a fire and roasted the meat. His hunger was so great that he couldn't wait for the meat to cook. He heated it and ate. So as not to remember that scene, I left thinking: I'm going to pretend I wasn't there. This can't be real in a rich country like mine. I was disgusted with that Social Service that had been created to readjust the maladjusted, but took no notice of we marginal people. I sold the scrap at Zinho and returned to Sao Paulo's back yard, the favela.

12. Gerald Breese, *Urbanization in Newly Developing Countries* (Englewood Cliffs, N.J.: Prentice-Hall, Inc., 1966), Ch. 2.

In the favelas of Rio, one of Brazil's worst slums, vast numbers of human beings live under conditions barely capable of sustaining life. As one resident has put it, "I was in the favela breathing the smell of excrement mixed with the rotten earth. . . . I have the impression that I'm a useless object, destined to be forever in a garbage dump."

The next day I found that little black boy dead. His toes were spread apart. The space must have been eight inches between them. He had blown up as if made out of rubber. His toes looked like a fan. He had no documents. He was buried like any other "Joe." Nobody tried to find out his name. The marginal people don't have names.[13]

In the developing societies, the preindustrial pattern of organizing urban space persists. The central city is the area of highest prestige and still the residential area of choice for most members of the middle and upper classes; slums have appeared as expanding rings around this central core. A quite different pattern has emerged in the United States and, to a somewhat lesser extent, in the industrialized societies of Europe. People financially able to do so have moved to the outskirts, while the center of the city has been relegated largely to the poor and the powerless.

THEORIES OF URBAN LIFE

Because the dramatic move toward urbanization in the nineteenth and twentieth centuries has closely paralleled the growth of sociology as a discipline, sociologists have taken a special interest in studying urban life and its problems. The establishment of such subfields as delinquency, ecology, and collective behavior reflects this orientation. During the first half of the present century the sociology department at the University of Chicago pioneered in literally using the city as a sociological laboratory, analyzing Chicago's ghettos, Gold Coast, and gangs in an effort to understand the effects of urbanization on social interaction, social organization, and culture. The term "Chicago School" came to denote not only a specific group of scholars but also an empirical orientation to the study of urban life.

13. *Child of the Dark: The Diary of Carolina Maria de Jesus,* trans. David St. Clair (New York: Signet Books, 1962), pp. 38–41.

THE RURAL-URBAN CONTINUUM

Sociologists have long been concerned with defining the nature of *urbanism*—the patterns of social organization and culture that characterize life in the city. Until recently, most theorists of urban life have tried to explain the sociocultural consequences of urbanization by contrasting the differing lifeways in urban and traditional communities. Following the lead of Tönnies, Weber, and Durkheim (pages 84–87, 90–91), they have suggested that the patterns of social interaction characteristic of traditional communities, based on feelings of shared identity and purpose, have been largely replaced in the urban-industrial community by more formal and competitive relationships. As the division of labor has become more complex, the locus of social action has become increasingly centered around large, bureaucratic organizations and the qualities of affection, trust, and loyalty have presumably disappeared from most interpersonal relations.

The theories of urban life developed during the 1930s and 1940s by Robert Redfield and Louis Wirth reflect these themes. Working respectively in the fields of anthropology and sociology at the University of Chicago, both scholars were concerned with identifying and analyzing the essential differences between traditional and urban communities; and although they did not directly collaborate, their efforts complemented each other in important ways. As we shall see, a growing body of empirical evidence shows that the theories of Redfield and Wirth exaggerated the differences between urban and rural life, but they were landmark achievements nevertheless, illuminating many aspects of urbanism and paving the way for continued research and theory-building.

14. See Tools of Sociology, p. 70, on the uses of the "ideal type" as a theoretical and research tool.
15. Robert Redfield, "The Folk Society," *American Journal of Sociology*, 52 (January 1947): 293–308. In later writings Redfield delineated another ideal type, the "peasant community," which combined characteristics of both the folk and the urban communities.
16. Introduction to Horace Miner's *St. Denis: A French-Canadian Parish* (Chicago: The University of Chicago Press, 1939).

Redfield's "Folk Society"

According to Redfield, the folk society as an "ideal type"[14] is small, isolated, preliterate, and homogeneous—both culturally and physically. Communication is face-to-face, and there is a high degree of group solidarity. Isolation necessitates economic independence in the form of a subsistence economy. The technology is very simple, and the division of labor exists primarily along sex and age lines. Family and community ties make mutual assistance obligatory.[15]

In the "ideal" folk society, patterns of belief and behavior are systematized into a coherent and consistent culture. Tradition is sacred: there is no tendency to reevaluate the past and no tendency to criticize the present. Behavior follows long-established folkways: "That is the way to do it because that is the way it has always been done." Life is an all-inclusive web of activity from which nothing can be separated without affecting the rest. In Redfield's words, "Life is like a wheel turning."[16]

Status in the folk society is largely fixed at birth. On those rare occasions when an individual does rise to a higher level of status, there is a norm that declares the change to be in the natural order of things. One simply accepts what *is* as what *ought* to be. The folk society, as delineated by Redfield, is a functionally integrated system, a system in equilibrium.

Redfield suggested that much could be learned about the identifying characteristics of the modern urban community by contrasting it to the folk society. For example, the solidarity built on uninterrupted face-to-face relationships so characteristic of the folk society is lacking in the urban community. Because it is too large to permit close ties among any large number of citizens, impersonal relationships become the norm. Furthermore, the urban system is so complex and differentiated that socialization experiences are likely to be quite different for different segments of the population. Diversity of beliefs and norms leads to greater tolerance of deviant behavior and also to critical scrutiny of existing ways. Change becomes an important part of everyday life.

Redfield noted that when a folk society comes into contact with an urban society, the former tends to adopt the characteristics of the latter. He also emphasized that the effects of such contact are likely to be far-reaching, since change in one element of social organization tends to bring about change in others.

Wirth's Theory of Urbanism

In 1938, even before Redfield had completely worked out his typology, Louis Wirth published his influential essay, "Urbanism as a Way of Life."[17] In a sense the culmination of many years of research and writing by the scholars of the Chicago school, it became the point of departure for urban sociologists during the following generation. Wirth defined the city as "a relatively large, permanent, dense settlement of socially heterogeneous individuals." His primary concern was with analyzing the ways in which population size and density affect various characteristics of community life.

According to Wirth, an inevitable consequence of large population size is social heterogeneity: the greater the number of people in a community, the greater the possible range of ideas, cultural patterns, occupations, and personal traits. The growth of cities through immigration continually reinforces heterogeneity as a basic characteristic of urban life.

Wirth also believed that there is a direct relationship between the size of a community's population and its quality of social interaction. He maintained that as the number of potential interactors in a community *increases,* the intensity of interaction *decreases.* Whereas people in a small town see and interact with each other in a variety of social settings, city dwellers are likely to "know" each other only in terms of segmentalized roles. Thus social relationships in an urban setting are relatively more formal, superficial, and transitory than in a smaller community or folk society. Individuals tend to be reserved in their dealings with others, protecting themselves from the personal claims and expectations of people with whom they feel no common bond.

Another characteristic distinguishing urban from rural life, according to Wirth, is a greater tolerance for individual differences. Such tolerance is in part an inevitable by-product of greater heterogeneity in the population, but it also

stems from the fact that the complex organization of urban life often requires people to interact in terms of their roles regardless of personal likes and dislikes—as coworkers, for example, or as salespersons and customers.

Wirth maintained that primary relationships learned in the family do not serve in the larger milieu of the city. As a result, kinship bonds weaken, the family declines in importance relative to other social groups, and the neighborhood loses much of its significance. The consequence of these changes is an undermining of the traditional bases of social solidarity. Faced with these losses, individuals have to turn to new forms of social organization in order to fulfill their needs.

THE ECOLOGICAL APPROACH

Much of the material on which Wirth based his ideas was drawn from the work of other sociologists at the University of Chicago during the 1920s and 1930s, some of whom emphasized the importance of ecological processes—especially of competition for land—in determining the spatial patterning of the city. These sociologists argued that natural forces operate in human communities, as they do in plant and animal communities, to create areas that are clearly differentiated in terms of use.[18] Thus some segments of the city are allocated to business or industry and others to different patterns of housing. The various areas tend to be more or less isolated and self-sufficient and to resist the intrusion of other types of land use. When such intrusion can no longer be resisted successfully, *succession* occurs: a different pattern of land use becomes predominant, and the displaced pattern re-creates itself in a different (usually adjoining) locality. Thus as a city grows, its spatial organization is continually being modified.

17. Louis Wirth, "Urbanism as a Way of Life," *American Journal of Sociology,* 44 (July 1938): 1–24.
18. See Robert E. Park, Ernest W. Burgess, R. C. McKenzie, and Louis Wirth, *The City* (Chicago: The University of Chicago Press, 1925).

One member of the Chicago group, Ernest W. Burgess, hypothesized that the impersonal process of land-use competition led to the development of a series of concentric zones spreading out from the city's center, each reserved for particular activities and for occupancy by particular segments of the population (Figure 12.1, A). At the heart of the city is the central business district, an area of intensive land use that plays host to throngs of workers and shoppers by day but whose nighttime population is largely limited to transient hotel residents. Immediately surrounding the business district is a zone in transition, which is continually threatened by the invasion of commercial activities from the expanding city center. Generally a blighted area, it is associated with cheap housing, residential instability, and high rates of crime, delinquency, and vice. Its population consists for the most part of racial and ethnic minorities, migrants from rural areas, social outcasts, and others who for one reason or another cannot move to more desirable residential areas. Ringing this transitional area is a zone of working-class homes, surrounded in turn by middle- and upper-class residential areas in the zones farther out.

While Burgess apparently intended his scheme of concentric zones as a hypothesis to be tested, it became popularized almost as a general theory. Subsequent research has shown that the zonal pattern exists, at least to a degree, in a number of American cities, especially those that developed rapidly (as Chicago did) during the period of heavy European immigration in the nineteenth century. However, the zonal theory does not apply nearly so well to cities built before the Industrial Revolution (e.g., Boston and New Haven) or to cities built after the coming of the automobile. Peculiarities of topography, such as the presence of hills, rivers, and lakes, can also have important effects on the course of a city's development. Even Chicago, which Burgess used as his model, developed not as a series of concentric circles but rather as a series of half-circles, cut off on one side by Lake Michigan. Land use along Chicago's lake shore, furthermore, follows quite a different pattern than it does elsewhere in the various zones.

The impersonality of city buildings seems to symbolize the social isolation of city residents. Empirical studies have shown, however, that social isolation and anonymity are not necessary characteristics of urban life. Much human activity in the city continues to be focused in primary groups, where social relationships are essentially Gemeinschaft in character.

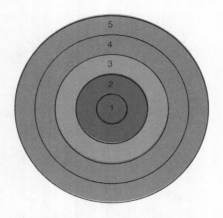

A. Concentric Zone Hypothesis

1. Central business district
2. Zone in transition
3. Zone of workingmen's homes
4. Residential zone
5. Commuter zone

SOURCE: Adapted from Ernest W. Burgess, "The Growth of the City," in *The City*, ed. R. E. Park, E. W. Burgess, R. D. McKenzie, and L. Wirth (Chicago: The University of Chicago Press, 1925.)

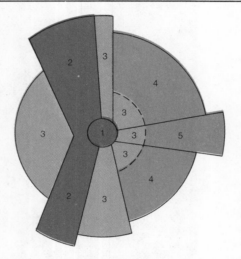

B. Sector Hypothesis

1. Central business district
2. Wholesale, light manufacturing
3. Low-class residential
4. Medium-class residential
5. High-class residential

SOURCE: Homer Hoyt, *The Structure and Growth of Residential Neighborhoods in American Cities* (Washington, D.C.: Federal Housing Administration, 1939); drawing adapted from Chauncy D. Harris and Edward L. Ullman, "The Nature of Cities," *Annals of the American Academy of Political and Social Science*, 242 (November 1945)

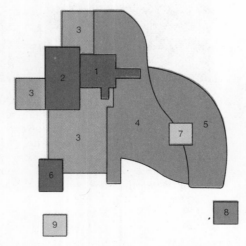

C. Multiple Nuclei Hypothesis

1. Central business district
2. Wholesale, light manufacturing
3. Low-class residential
4. Medium-class residential
5. High-class residential
6. Heavy manufacturing
7. Outlying business district
8. Residential suburb
9. Industrial suburb

SOURCE: Adapted from Chauncy D. Harris and Edward L. Ullman, "The Nature of Cities," *Annals of the American Academy of Political and Social Science*, 242 (November, 1945).

Figure 12.1. HYPOTHESES OF URBAN ECOLOGY

A modification of Burgess's scheme was developed in the 1930s by Homer Hoyt, who envisioned the structure of the city in terms of *sectors* or quadrants (Figure 12.1, B). Hoyt stressed the importance of transportation arteries (main streets, rail lines, and waterways) in determining the spatial organization of the city and the direction of its growth. Concentrating his study primarily on rental values and residential patterns, he found that high-rent areas tend to move out toward the periphery of the city but to stay within their original sectors. The expansion of low-rent residential areas generally follows a similar pattern, as does that of industrial sections. Thus according to Hoyt's theory, a land-use map of a city would look more like a series of unequal spokes radiating from the center than a series of concentric circles.

Still another theory of ecological patterning is the *multiple nuclei* theory developed by Chauncy D. Harris and Edward L. Ullman (Figure 12.1, C). These ecologists argued that land use within a city is organized around a number of nuclei, each distinguished by its own special functions and requirements. The differentiation of these areas, they believed, resulted from the interplay of four main factors. (1) Certain activities require specialized facilities (manufacturing, for example, requires large blocks of land and good shipping facilities). (2) Certain related activities, such as retail stores, tend to group together because they benefit from each other's presence. (3) Certain dissimilar activities, such as residential development and industrial development, are detrimental to each other and thus tend to locate in separate areas. (4) Certain activities cannot afford to locate where property values are high (bulk wholesaling, for example, and low-income housing). Harris and Ullman

argued that as a city grew in size, its nuclei would increase in number and become more specialized in their activities.

Taking a somewhat different approach, Amos Hawley has hypothesized that both centrifugal and centripetal forces are at work in the current growth of metropolitan and urban areas. According to Hawley:

The centrifugal movement scatters people, residences, churches, schools, establishments retailing goods and services, and industries more and more widely over the area lying within a sixty-minute commuting radius of the central city core.

The centripetal movement has concentrated administrative offices and institutions, the services that cater to administrative tasks, and the retailing of expensive and fashionable commodities in the central business district of the central city.[19]

The organization of people in urban space reflects the interplay of many factors and cannot be accounted for simply by competitive economic processes. Nor can the behavior of urban populations be explained solely in terms of such variables as size, density, and heterogeneity. As we shall see, cultural factors continue as independent variables, and traditional patterns of social organization may be influential in the larger urban milieu as well as in the small town.

URBAN THEORY RE-EVALUATED

Gideon Sjoberg, Leo Schnore, Herbert Gans, and others have argued that Wirth overstated the impersonality of urban life.[20] They point out that there is insufficient data to prove that size, density, and heterogeneity are the only independent variables operating or that they have severely diminished the importance of primary relationships. Anonymity, impersonal interaction, and segmentation of roles may all be parts of urbanism, but they have not totally replaced the patterns implied by Tönnies's term *Gemeinschaft* or Redfield's "folk society."

Gans has pointed out that Wirth's formulation was largely derived from and supported by research in the central part of the city, especially the transient areas bordering the main business district. Here the heterogeneity of the population is indeed associated with anonymity, impersonality, and superficiality. But hetero-

19. Hawley, *Urban Society*, pp. 172–174.
20. For a detailed critique of the Chicago school and Wirth in particular, see Gideon Sjoberg, "Comparative Urban Sociology," in *Sociology Today*, ed. Robert K. Merton et al. (New York: Basic Books, Inc., 1959), pp. 334–359; Leo Schnore, "Community," in *Sociology: An Introduction*, ed. Neil Smelser (New York: John Wiley & Sons, Inc., 1967), esp. pp. 105 ff.; and Herbert J. Gans, "Urbanism and Suburbanism as Ways of Life: A Re-evaluation of Definitions," in *Human Behavior and Social Processes*, ed. Arnold Rose (New York: Houghton Mifflin Co., 1962), pp. 306–323.

geneity may be less their cause, Gans concludes, than *residential instability*. In fact, he
says,

> *heterogeneity is itself an effect of residential insta-*
> *bility, resulting when the influx of transients causes*
> *landlords and realtors to stop acting as gatekeepers—*
> *that is, wardens of neighborhood homogeneity. Resi-*
> *dential instability is found in all types of settlements,*
> *and, presumably, its social consequences are every-*
> *where similar.*[21]

Gans next questions whether the outer city,
the area of working-class and middle-class residences, accurately mirrors Wirth's theory. Gans
hypothesizes from the little evidence available that these neighborhoods might best be
described as "quasi-primary"—that is, "the interaction is more intimate than a secondary contact, but more guarded than a primary one."
Sociability rather than formality is the keynote in
neighborhood groups, in social clubs, and in
voluntary associations such as PTAs and civic
associations.

THE REALITIES OF URBAN LIFE

On the basis of empirical research conducted
after Wirth formulated his thesis, Gans developed three propositions:

> *1. As concerns ways of life, the inner city must be*
> *distinguished from the outer city and the suburbs; and*
> *the latter two exhibit a way of life bearing little re-*
> *semblance to Wirth's urbanism.*
> *2. Even in the inner city, ways of life resemble*
> *Wirth's description only to a limited extent. Moreover,*
> *economic condition, cultural characteristics, life-*
> *cycle stage [of the families], and residential instability*
> *explain ways of life more satisfactorily than number,*
> *density, or heterogeneity.*
> *3. Physical and other differences between city and*
> *suburb are often spurious or without much meaning*
> *for ways of life.*[22]

It will be useful to keep these three propositions
in mind as we examine the accumulated research about various facets of urban life.

THE INNER-CITY SLUMS

We have already indicated that it is *perhaps* in
the slums that Wirth's theory of urbanism comes
closest to portraying reality. It is here that heterogeneity may combine with residential instability
to keep people from developing strong interpersonal ties and to create conditions of normlessness, or anomie. But are these necessary features
of urban life, even in the inner-city?

Street-Corner Society

At the time Wirth and his colleagues were examining urban life in Chicago, William Foote
Whyte was making his community study of an
Italian subcommunity of Boston, which he described in his book *Street-Corner Society* (1943).
Whyte's introductory comments to this classic
work are instructive:

> *In the heart of "Eastern City," there is a slum district*
> *known as Cornerville, which is inhabited almost ex-*
> *clusively by Italian immigrants and their children. To*
> *the rest of the city it is a mysterious, dangerous, and*
> *depressing area. . . .*
> *Respectable people have access to a limited body*
> *of information upon Cornerville. They may learn that*
> *it is one of the most congested areas in the United*
> *States . . . that children overrun the narrow and*
> *neglected streets, that the juvenile delinquency rate*
> *is high, that crime is prevalent among adults, and that*
> *a large proportion of the population was on home re-*
> *lief or W.P.A. during the depression.*
> *In this view, Cornerville people appear as social*
> *work clients, as defendants in criminal cases, or as*
> *undifferentiated members of "the masses." . . .*
> *. . . The middle-class person looks upon the slum*
> *district as a formidable mass of confusion, a social*
> *chaos. The insider finds in Cornerville a highly orga-*
> *nized and integrated social system.*[23]

In his study of Cornerville, Whyte contrasted the organizational patterns of Doc's streetcorner gang with those of Chick's club. Chick and
his friends were college students learning to orient themselves to the structural patterns of the
larger American society. Doc and his gang were
oriented inward toward the slum in which they
lived. The two groups knew each other well.

21. Gans, "Urbanism and Suburbanism," p. 311.
22. Ibid., p. 315.
23. William F. Whyte, *Street-Corner Society: The Social
Structure of an Italian Slum*, rev. ed. (Chicago: The University of Chicago Press, 1955), pp. xv – xvi.

Doc's relationship with "his boys" belies the theory that life in the slums is devoid of primary-group ties. As Doc told Whyte:

Bill, I owe money now, but if I was paid all the money owed me, I would have a gang of money. I never saved. I never had a bank account. . . . If the boys are going to a show and this man can't go because he is batted out, I say to myself, "Why should he be deprived of that luxury?" And I give him the money. . . . And I never talk about it.

Interestingly enough, ties of loyalty and affection were much less characteristic of Chick's group, whose members aspired to merge with the middle class. In discussing the difference between Chick's club and his own gang, Doc said:

Chick says that self-preservation is the first law of nature. Now that's right to a certain extent. You have to look out for yourself first. But Chick would step on the neck of his best friend if he could get a better job by doing it. . . . We were talking one night on the corner about that, and I was sucking him in. I got him to admit it—that he would turn against his best friend if he could profit by it. . . . I would never do that, Bill. . . . None of my boys would do that.

Nor would Doc advance himself socially if he had the chance to live life over:

I suppose my boys have kept me from getting ahead . . . . But if I were to start over again—if God said to me, "Look, here, Doc, you're going to start over again, and you can pick out your friends in advance," still, I would make sure that my boys were among them— even if I could pick Rockefeller and Carnegie. . . .

24. Whyte, *Street-Corner Society*, pp. 106–108. For other studies on patterns of social organization in the inner city, see Gerald D. Suttles, *The Social Order of the Slum: Ethnicity and Territoriality in the Inner City* (Chicago: The University of Chicago Press, 1968), and Elliot Liebow, *Tally's Corner: A Study of Negro Street-Corner Men* (Boston: Little, Brown and Company, 1967).

25. Gans, "Urbanism and Suburbanism," p. 309.

26. Ibid., pp. 309–310.

27. See, for example, Ronald H. Bayor, "The Darker Side of Urban Life: Slums in the City," in *Cities in Transition*, ed. Frank J. Coppa and Philip C. Dolce (Chicago: Nelson-Hall Co., 1974), pp. 128–137; Byrl Boyce and Sidney Turoff, eds., *Minority Groups and Housing* (Morristown, N.J.: Silver Burdett Company, 1972); and Peter H. Rossi, ed., *Ghetto Revolts*, 2nd ed. (New Brunswick, N.J.: Transaction Books, 1973).

[People] have said to me, "Why do you hang around those fellows?" I would tell them, "Why not? They're my friends."[24]

The "Deprived" and the "Trapped"

Gans identifies five different types of inner-city residents: (1) the "cosmopolites," chiefly intellectuals and professionals who want to live near the city's cultural facilities; (2) the "unmarried or childless," who also live in the inner city by choice and are generally middle class in their orientations; (3) the "ethnic villagers," who maintain close kinship and in-group ties and have little contact with other people except in their occupational pursuits; (4) the "deprived"; and (5) the "trapped."[25] The last two have become increasingly predominant in the inner city and are of special concern to us here.

As Gans notes, the "deprived" and the "trapped" are distinguished from the other groups who live in the central city in that they lack residential choice. They live in the inner city by necessity, whether they want to or not. The "deprived" population includes

the very poor; the emotionally disturbed or otherwise handicapped; broken families; and, most important, the non-white population. These urban dwellers must take the dilapidated housing and blighted neighborhoods to which the housing market relegates them, although among them are some for whom the slum is a hiding place, or a temporary stopover to save money for a house in the outer city or the suburbs.

The "trapped" are the people who stay behind when a neighborhood is invaded by non-residential land uses or low-status immigrants, because they cannot afford to move, or are otherwise bound to their present location.[26]

The "deprived" and "trapped" who make up so much of the inner city's population today are different in many ways from the "ethnic villagers" who predominated two or three generations ago and who can still be found there in lesser numbers. Undoubtedly the most significant difference is that they find it so much harder to move out.[27] For those who are nonwhite, problems of poverty are vastly compounded by problems of racial discrimination.

Most urban sociologists agree that the story of "life in the big city" is not one of alienation and impersonalization. People in large metropolitan areas enjoy a considerable amount of primary-group interaction, and they can—and do—have fun. Children usually make use of whatever is available to them—such as a mountain of old cars to climb—while older urban dwellers take advantage of the many facilities for culture and amusement. Some may take their families ice skating or to museums; others get together with neighbors to chat; and still others join their cronies for a chess game in the park.

For the "deprived" and the "trapped," life in the city often means isolation, poverty, and alienation. Crime is prevalent in the inner-city slums, and people may fear to "get involved" or may become so inured to it that they do nothing. Here a man is being robbed on the street, while a workman goes about his job—unconcerned.

Studies of the urban riots that occurred during the late sixties have suggested that it was not blacks who were newcomers to the ghettos but second- and third-generation slum dwellers who showed the most despair and participated most actively in the destruction.[28]

Urban Renewal—Help for Whom?

At least part of the explanation for the continuing plight of so many people—whites as well as blacks—in the central cities can be found in the housing and urban renewal programs sponsored by the federal government. The idea of improving living conditions for the urban poor can be traced back to the latter part of the nineteenth century when urban slums were already a reality. But most early efforts were of a private, sporadic nature geared primarily to helping needy individuals, as in the settlement house movement.

The federal government became involved in housing programs during the 1930s. The first

National Housing Act of 1934 established the Federal Housing Administration (FHA) to provide home-loan mortgage guarantees and thus encourage private home building. This legislation gave help primarily to the middle and working classes, and one of its effects was to stimulate their move to the suburbs.[29] A second National Housing Act in 1937 created the U.S. Housing Authority and provided the first federal support for slum clearance and the development of low-cost rental housing. However, urban renewal as such did not become a focus of national concern until after World War II. Legislation in 1949 gave the first real impetus to urban land redevelopment by providing loans for the construction of low-cost homes and apartments.

28. *Report of the National Advisory Commission on Civil Disorders* (New York: Bantam Books, 1968), pp. 110–111. See also Nathan S. Caplan and Jeffrey M. Paige, "A Study of Ghetto Rioters," *Scientific American*, August 1968, pp. 15–21.
29. See Leonard S. Rubinowitz, "A Question of Choice: Access of the Poor and the Black to Suburban Housing," in *The Urbanization of the Suburbs*, ed. Louis H. Masotti and Jeffrey K. Hadden (Beverly Hills, Calif.: Sage Publications, Inc., 1973), pp. 329–366; see esp. pp. 330–333.

During the 1950s, a series of major housing bills gave increasing federal support both to slum clearance and to the building of public housing projects. The "model cities" program launched in the 1960s recognized the problems inherent in public housing programs and focused instead on encouraging the restoration of low-income urban neighborhoods.

From the beginning, urban-renewal programs have involved basically conflicting goals. On the one hand, they have been seen as a way to improve housing conditions for the urban poor; on the other, as a way to revitalize cities by developing new commercial centers and new housing to attract middle- and upper-income residents. By and large, the interests of those with power and money have taken precedence over the needs of the poor. A distinguished professor of urban planning describes the "economics" of slum clearance as follows:

[A city] may acquire a slum area under eminent domain, clear it of its buildings and sell it to a developer. No one today can afford to build for the poor without subsidy. On expensive central land, it is nearly impossible to build at all except for the rich, and even that must be done at high density by means of apartment towers. On central land, the city can be quite certain that it is exchanging the poor slum dwellers for wealthy apartment dwellers. . . . The profits to the city will be increased tax revenue resulting from newer and more expensive property plus the savings in city services.[30]

30. William Alonso, "Cities and City Planners," in *Taming Megalopolis,* ed. H. W. Eldridge (New York: Doubleday & Company, Inc., 1967), pp. 580–596; quotation from pp. 589-590. See also Lawrence M. Friedman, *Government and Slum Housing* (Chicago: Rand McNally & Co., 1968); and "Urban Renewal: One Tool Among Many," *The Report of the President's Task Force on Urban Renewal* (Washington, D.C.: U.S. Government Printing Office, May 1970).

31. Peter Hall, *The World Cities* (New York: McGraw-Hill Book Company, 1966), pp. 193–194.

32. Gans, "Urbanism and Suburbanism," p. 311. For a challenging analysis of the effects of this life on black family structure see Lee Rainwater and William K. Yancey, eds., *The Moynihan Report and the Politics of Controversy* (Cambridge, Mass.: The M.I.T. Press, 1967). See also Michael Harrington, *The Other America* (New York: Macmillan, Inc., 1962), which stimulated public concern about the deprived and the trapped in the early 1960s.

While the creation of attractive shopping complexes and high-rise, high-rent apartments may be necessary to keep the cities economically alive, the poor receive little or no benefit from this type of planning. In general, urban renewal projects have increased social disorganization among the urban poor by breaking up their traditional neighborhoods and forcing them to crowd into whatever other housing is available for their income level. Hall describes the effects of urban renewal on the black population of New York City:

Urban renewal, initiated under the 1949 Housing Act, has been carried out through private developers on a commercial basis. In many cases it has exacerbated the problem [of insufficient housing]: between 1950 and 1957, fully half the residents of demolished dwelling units in the city were Negro, while only 5 per cent of the new construction was taken up by non-whites. . . .

The Negroes thus find themselves under almost impossible pressure. The white areas are closed to them, and give way slowly and reluctantly if at all. Any dispersion is apt to be into the immediately neighboring blocks, which rapidly lose their white populations.[31]

The Growing Crisis of the Cities

The black ghettos of the modern metropolis are the areas in which a heavy density of population seems to contribute most directly to personal and social disorganization. Heterogeneity is also a contributing factor, insofar as blacks with differing backgrounds and values have been forced together in the central city. But as Gans points out, these conditions are a consequence of racial discrimination and poverty, not inevitable concomitants of urban life. Lack of residential choice forces the deprived "to live amid neighbors not of their own choosing, with ways of life different and even contradictory to their own. If familial defenses against the neighborhood climate are weak, as is the case among broken families and downward mobile people, parents may lose their children to the culture of 'the street.'"[32]

VIEWPOINTS THE URBAN CRISIS

■ In a few more years, lacking effective public action, this is how [our] cities will likely look:

Central business districts in the heart of the city, surrounded by mixed areas of accelerating deterioration, will be partially protected by large numbers of people shopping or working in commercial buildings during daytime hours, plus a substantial police presence, and will be largely deserted except for police patrols during night-time hours.

High-rise apartment buildings and residential compounds protected by private guards and security devices will be fortified cells for upper-middle and high-income populations living at prime locations in the city.

Suburban neighborhoods . . . will be protected mainly by economic homogeneity and by distance from population groups with the highest propensities to commit crimes. . . .

Ownership of guns will be almost universal in the suburbs, homes will be fortified by an array of devices from window grills to electronic surveillance equipment. . . .

High-speed, patrolled expressways will be sanitized corridors connecting safe areas, and . . . vehicles will be routinely equipped with . . . security features. . . .

Streets and residential neighborhoods in the central city will be unsafe in differing degrees, and the ghetto slum neighborhoods will be places of terror with widespread crime, perhaps entirely out of police control during night-time hours. Armed guards will protect all public facilities such as schools, libraries, and playgrounds in these areas.

Between the unsafe, deteriorating central city on the one hand and the network of safe, prosperous areas and sanitized corridors on the other, there will be, not unnaturally, intensifying hatred and deepening division. Violence will increase further, and the defensive response of the affluent will become still more elaborate.
Final Report of the National Commission on the Causes and Prevention of Violence

● Serious problems are to be found in all large cities and in most small ones. But they affect only parts of these cities (and only a minority of the city populations). . . .

In many important respects, conditions in the large cities have been getting better. There is less poverty in the cities now than there has ever been. Housing, including that of the poor, is improving rapidly. . . . [M]ost children finish high school. The treatment of racial and other minority groups is conspicuously better than it was. . . .

If the situation is improving, why, it may be asked, is there so much talk of an urban crisis? The answer is that the improvements in performance, great as they have been, have not kept pace with rising expectations. . . .

To a large extent, then, our urban problems are like the mechanical rabbit at the racetrack, which is set to keep just ahead of the dogs no matter how fast they may run. Our performance is better and better, but because we set our standards and expectations to keep ahead of performance, the problems are never any nearer to solution. Indeed, if standards and expectations rise *faster* than performance, the problems may get (relatively) worse as they get (absolutely) better.

Some may say that since almost everything about the city can stand improvement (to put it mildly), this mechanical rabbit effect is a good thing in that it spurs us on to make constant progress. No doubt this is true to some extent. On the other hand, there is danger that we may mistake failure to progress as fast as we would like for failure to progress at all and, in panic, rush into ill-considered measures that will only make matters worse. After all, an "urban crisis" that results largely from rising standards and expectations is not the sort of crisis that, unless something drastic is done, is bound to lead to disaster. To treat it as if it were might be a very serious mistake.
Edward C. Banfield
The Unheavenly City

The social disorganization and sense of alienation that seem typical of inner-city life today are not the inevitable by-products of urbanization, as Wirth's theory might suggest. They are problems with cultural roots that trace back to the nation's beginning. The movement to suburbia by those who can afford it reflects a long-standing value preference among Americans for "open space" and for owning one's own home and a piece of land. It also reflects the American emphasis on individual achievement and the importance of getting ahead—on building a more comfortable life for oneself and one's family. The hemming in of blacks and other minorities in the central city reflects another cultural theme that predates urbanization: the belief that white people and Anglo-Saxon culture are "best."

Whatever the cultural and economic causes of the "crisis of the cities," a crisis of major proportions clearly exists. In 1968 the Kerner Commission sounded the warning that urban America has been rapidly "moving toward two societies":

The future of [the] cities, and of their burgeoning Negro populations, is grim. Most new employment opportunities are being created in suburbs and outlying areas. This trend will continue unless important changes in public policy are made. . . .

To continue present policies is to make permanent the division of our country into two societies; one, largely Negro and poor, located in the central cities; the other, predominantly white and affluent, located in the suburbs and in outlying areas.[33]

The situation remains essentially unchanged today. Indeed, a recent study concluded that black residential segregation had increased between 1960 and 1970. In a study of major metropolitan areas of the United States, segregation decreased in only seven areas and actually increased in thirty-six areas.[34] Similar findings were reported by the Commission on Population Growth and the American Future in 1972.

THE SUBURBS

Contrary to popular belief, suburbs are not entirely a twentieth-century phenomenon. Glaab reports that as early as 1823 New York City realtors were advertising "country" lots that were within fifteen to twenty-five minutes of the central business district by foot.[35] And so it was with other American cities during the nineteenth century. The suburbs grew and flourished as improved transportation made it possible to move easily over ever greater distances. Their growth was determined by the amount of time it took to travel to and from the central business district. By the 1870s Chicago had become one of the most suburban-oriented cities in the world, with more than one hundred trains daily moving people in and out of nearly one hundred outlying communities, housing an estimated fifty thousand people. Suburbs were widely praised for combining the advantages of urban and rural life:

The controversy which is sometimes brought, as to which offers the greater advantage, the country or the city, finds a happy answer in the suburban idea which says, both—the combination of the two—the city brought to the country. . . . The city has its advantages and conveniences, the country has its charm and health; the union of the two (a modern result of the railway) gives to man all he could ask in this respect.[36]

What is new about the suburbs today is the rapid rate at which they have been attracting not only residents but also jobs and business away from the city. As a result, city revenues from personal and corporate taxes have been seriously eroded. Suburbanites may indeed have the best of both worlds, but where does this leave the cities on which they depend?

33. *Report of the National Advisory Commission on Civil Disorders*, pp. 21–22.

34. David W. Sears and David L. Faytell "Black Residential Segregation in American Metropolitan Regions: Some Changes During the 1960–70 Decade," paper presented at the Annual Meeting of the American Sociological Association, Montreal, abstract printed in the *1974 Annual Proceedings*, p. 197; see also *Population and the American Future*, The Report of the Commission on Population Growth and the American Future (Washington, D.C.: U.S. Government Printing Office, 1972), p. 123.

35. Glaab, *American City*, p. 229.

36. Ibid., p. 233.

Another characteristic of modern suburbs is that they are decreasing in density. The New York suburbs geared to subway transportation and built between the two World Wars had densities of ten to fifty dwellings on each acre. The post-World War II suburbs like Levittown on Long Island averaged seven houses per acre. Suburbs have continued to move farther and farther out, and many of the newest ones are zoned in single-dwelling lots of from one-half to two-thirds of an acre each.[37]

There is no reason to believe that the movement to suburbia will abate in the near future, unless fuel shortages drastically curtail the use of automobiles. With the reduction in the official work week to forty hours or less, employees can now spend eight to ten hours a week commuting without increasing their total time away from home. And they will be encouraged to do so as long as suburbs offer more pleasant living conditions than the city.

Life-Style

In what significant ways, if any, do the life-styles of suburbanites differ from the life-styles of families who live in middle- and upper-class neighborhoods in the city? There is not enough empirical evidence to support any theory, but the differences are probably less than is commonly supposed. As Gans remarks, "Such differences as walking to the corner drug store and driving to its suburban equivalent seem . . . of little emotional, social, or cultural import."[38]

We may ask how, if at all, do husband-wife patterns in the middle-class neighborhoods of the city differ from those in middle-class suburbs? If peer groups dominate the lives of teen-agers in the suburbs, do they not also dominate the lives of teen-agers in the city? How, if at all, are suburban do-it-yourselfers different from their city counterparts? A study by Ross compared the life-styles of upper-middle-class whites in two New York City neighborhoods, one in the central city and one on the periphery. In both cases, those surveyed were apartment-house dwellers. Ross could find no important differences between the two groupings. He suggested that "city-suburban differences in life

style are primarily the product of underlying differences in class, ethnicity and family status."[39]

Although the point is sometimes made that suburbanites are "all alike," the evidence suggests that today's suburban neighborhoods are no more homogeneous than the city neighborhoods of yesterday. The difference, rather, may be that neighborhood homogeneity centering around ethnic and religious identification has been replaced for most suburbanites (and many city residents) by homogeneity of occupational and educational level. Summarizing research on occupational and residential distribution, Schnore concluded that "social distance" is generally a good predictor of spatial distance, since people "who are like each other in occupational terms tend to reside in the same areas."[40] A study of New England communities showed varying degrees of heterogeneity regarding income, education, occupation, and ethnic identification, with no significant differences discernible between urban and suburban residential areas.[41]

In their reader on the suburbs, Masotti and Hadden present a wide range of studies and analyses which support the thesis that differences in class, status, and power determine the differences in life-style within the metropolitan area, and that these differences may be found as readily within and among suburbs as within the city itself. Masotti maintains that the process of suburban urbanization since World War II "has resulted in an 'outer city' that is rapidly becoming more like the inner city in social structure, economy, problems and life style."[42]

Planning for the Future

Growing concern over the problems associated with metropolitan sprawl in the United States has led to a consideration of new types of com-

37. Hall, *World Cities*, esp. pp. 196–199.
38. Gans, "Urbanism and Suburbanism," p. 313.
39. H. Laurence Ross, "Uptown and Downtown: A Study of Middle Class Residential Areas," *American Sociological Review* (April 1965): 255–259; quotation from p. 256.
40. Schnore, "Community," p. 125.
41. See Mary G. Powers, "Socio-Economic Heterogeneity of Urban Residential Areas," *Canadian Review of Sociology and Anthropology*, 1, No. 2 (August 1964): 129–137.
42. Louis Masotti, "Epilogue: Suburbia in the Seventies . . . and Beyond," in Masotti and Hadden, eds., *Urbanization of the Suburbs*, p. 533.

munity planning. In an analysis of a proposal that the federal government encourage the growth of small towns and cities, the Commission on Population Growth and the American Future projected growth patterns for 121 towns and cities ranging in size in 1970 from 10,000 to 350,000 people. They found that if these towns and cities were to grow at the rate of about 30 percent per decade over the next twenty-five years, they would absorb about 10 million people who might otherwise add to the population of existing metropolitan areas. However, such growth would soon turn these small towns and cities themselves into big cities and metropolitan areas.[43] And so far there is neither legislation nor any proposals for legislation that would direct the growth of these communities so that they could avoid the problems plaguing today's big cities.

A recent evaluation of new planned communities in the United States—e.g., Reston, Virginia, and Columbia, Maryland—raises interesting questions. The researchers compared fifteen new communities with twenty-one older suburbs and small towns. First, they wanted to determine if the planned communities provided a significantly different type of environment from the older, unplanned ones. And, second, they wanted to find out how successful the new communities were, as compared with the old, in meeting the needs of such special groups as blacks, low- and moderate-income families, and the elderly. Their conclusion was that "with the exception of superior recreation facilities, new communities do not differ greatly from less planned suburban communities at either the level of the immediate neighborhood or the overall community." However, the study found that these new communities did provide improved environments for blacks and those of low and moderate income.[44]

The finding that these new planned communities could improve the lot of the disadvantaged raises an important question: What makes

Reston, Virginia, a planned community, has been seen as a solution to the problems of disadvantaged urban dwellers. While Reston seems to be working in some ways, it has not been an unqualified success. Disadvantaged residents have complained that they are unable to take advantage of recreational facilities because of the high membership fees. And some Reston residents feel that residential segregation is creating racist attitudes among young people.

these new communities better than older ones for blacks and people of limited income? Is it the creation of new patterns of community organization? Or is it a belief on the part of those who move into them that new suburbs and towns demand new forms of intergroup relations?

A question must be raised, too, about the costs and benefits of building new communities as compared with rehabilitating older ones. Weissbourd argues that ample land is available near all existing metropolitan areas for the building of new planned communities, that these metropolitan areas contain the great majority of black and other minority populations, and that it is less costly to develop new communities than to try to provide new integrated housing in established communities. He estimates that it would now cost about $2.5 billion to purchase some 800,000 acres of open land on which

43. *Population and the American Future,* pp. 34 ff.
44. Robert B. Zehner, Raymond J. Burby, III, and Shirley F. Weiss, "Evaluation of New Communities in the United States," paper presented at the Annual Meeting of the American Sociological Association, Montreal, 1974, pp. 22–23, quote from p. 23.

housing could be built for some 20 million people. The federal government's current annual expenditure on housing, both direct and indirect, amounts to about $10 billion. According to Weissbourd:

New communities offer options for living in black, white, or mixed neighborhoods; they can provide an integrated school system; they open up opportunities for employment in the new suburban industrial plants; they reduce automobile traffic by allowing people to live near their work, thus lessening air pollution and the drain on our diminishing oil resources.

Certainly, new satellite communities provide an organizing idea which permits the planning needed to rationalize our transportation systems as well as our land use. Furthermore, only in new satellite communities will it be possible to aggregate the housing market efficiently in order to make industrialized housing feasible, while their higher density would permit us to protect the environment by saving land and preserving open space.[45]

Here, then, is one possible solution to the urban-suburban problem. But obstacles to its realization are many. Do most people really want to become divorced from established cities? New towns offer the advantages of "pleasant living," including superior recreational facilities and a relative lack of crowding; but older cities offer their own advantages, including a variety of cultural attractions, a wide range of jobs, and relative freedom from pressures to conform. And whether people favor the creation of new planned communities or the rehabilitation of older cities, how much are they willing and able to pay in order to implement programs of development? Equally important, what measure of government and community control will they accept? Government can stimulate new directions in urban planning and encourage the development of new norms, but the direction of change will be determined by developments in the cities and, to a large extent, by the choices individual families make in trying to better their own living conditions.

PRIMARY AND SECONDARY RELATIONSHIPS IN URBAN LIFE

Most theories of urban life have stressed the theme that urbanization has diminished the importance of family and kin relations and of primary relationships generally. To an extent, this generalization is valid: urbanization has clearly brought a decline, overall, in social interaction based on feeling—love, affection, trust, loyalty, respect—and a corresponding increase in formalized relationships. But much human activity in the city continues to be focused in primary groups, where social relationships are essentially *Gemeinschaft* in character. Even bureaucracies, as we noted in Chapter 3, are not nearly so depersonalized as they would seem to be. In the following sections we shall examine some of the empirical evidence regarding primary and secondary relationships in urban life.

The Urban Family

Empirical studies of urban life show that industrialization and urbanization have indeed brought changes in family structure and function, but they do not support the hypothesis of some urban theorists that the family has lost its central importance to the individual. Examining family and kin relationships among a sample of middle-class and working-class families in Cleveland, Ohio, Sussman found that practically all the families in the sample were actively engaged in interfamily help patterns.[46] About 70 percent of the working-class families and 45 percent of the middle-class families had relatives living in their neighborhood, and the automobile and other modes of transportation made it possible for relatives not living in the same neighborhood to help each other. Among the most common forms of assistance to family members were help during illness (reported by 76 percent), financial aid (53 percent), care of children (47 percent), personal or business advice (31 percent), and valuable gifts (22 percent). In view of these findings and similar ones by other researchers, Sussman questioned why sociological theory has given so much emphasis to the decline of primary relationships in the urban milieu. His conclusion is worth noting:

45. Bernard Weissbourd, "The Satellite Community as Suburb," in Masotti and Hadden, eds., *Urbanization of the Suburbs,* p. 508.
46. Marvin B. Sussman, "The Isolated Nuclear Family: Fact or Fiction," *Social Problems,* 6, No. 4 (1959): 333–340.

TOOLS OF SOCIOLOGY
SAMPLING

A preliminary step in most social research is making decisions about what units among those available are to be studied. Often this involves defining a population and selecting a sample of its units for actual observation. A *population* may include all members of a society, but in most research it is considerably more specific—e.g., the residents of "Springdale" or Chicago, the non-white population of New York City, middle-class families in Cleveland. But the population to be studied is seldom so small that researchers can observe every member. Rather, they must select a representative *sample* of the population and use it in making inferences about the whole.

A sample is said to be *representative* (or *unbiased*) if it accurately reflects the characteristics of the entire population being studied, or at least those characteristics that may be relevant to the research problem. For example, if the population being studied is 55 percent male and 45 percent female, the sample should include males and females in these proportions. The same is true for any population characteristic that may have some influence on research results (e.g., age, income level, level of educational attainment, racial or ethnic background). Although the distribution of relevant characteristics is not always known, the composition of a well-designed sample is likely to resemble closely that of the whole population.

In sociology as in other kinds of scientific research, samples are drawn from populations according to carefully specified procedures based on probability theory. In selecting particular cases for study, researchers use a *sampling design* that exactly specifies the method for choosing cases that will yield an unbiased estimate of how a given variable is distributed in the population as a whole. An estimate is judged to be *unbiased* if repeated samples produce almost identical results; this indicates that similar results would probably be obtained by studying the entire population. Even if researchers use only one sample in a given study, the use of a standard sampling design creates a high probability that their estimates will closely approximate population values. The sample is likely to contain some error, but the error probably will not be large.

Of the various sampling designs used in social research, the one most readily understood is the *simple random design.* The use of this design depends upon the availability of a *sampling frame* which correctly lists all members of the population. Cases are then selected from this list by any procedure that gives each member an equal probability of being included in the final sample. For instance, a name card for every person may be placed in a drum that is rotated thoroughly before the first name is drawn and also between subsequent drawings. After a name card has been selected, it is usually returned to the drum to equalize probabilities, but no name can be included in the sample more than once. The drawing of names continues until a sample of the desired size has been selected.

Because a simple random sample of an entire population is seldom practical, various logical substitutes are frequently used. One of these is the *area sample,* in which the units selected are city blocks, census tracts, counties, or other spacial configurations. Those living (or working) in the selected area units then become the subjects for study. If it is impossible to interview or otherwise study all relevant members of these units, further sampling becomes necessary. In a typical *multistage sample,* a random selection of area units is followed by a random selection of households within each unit. Sometimes the precise person to be interviewed in a given household is also determined by random means. Complex designs provide for substituting alternate subjects in place of those "not at home."

Sampling theory and procedures have become highly sophisticated. There are sampling designs to take care of almost any conceivable problem, and elaborate computations may be required to compute estimates of population values from sample data. Essentially, however, all sampling designs are systematic procedures for selecting representative cases for study and for making unbiased estimates about the way in which given variables are distributed in a particular population.

For a discussion of sampling theory as applied to social research, see Bernard Lazerwitz, "Sampling Theory and Procedures," in *Methodology in Social Research,* ed. Hubert M. Blalock, Jr., and Ann B. Blalock (New York: McGraw-Hill Book Company, 1968), pp. 279–328.

The urbanite is said to be dependent upon secondary rather than primary group relationships. This view may exist because of a time lag between urban and family theory and research. It may also reflect a cultural lag between what was believed to be a generation ago (or may actually have been) and what exists today. The writings of such men as Durkheim, Simmel, Tönnies, and Mannheim contain early twentieth-century views of family and social life in a growing urban industrial society. Durkheim's research on suicide indicated weaknesses in family structure and the effects of isolation upon the individual. In no way did he indicate the basic features of family structure which did, do today, and will tomorrow sustain its continuity on through time. In other words, a theoretical view tinted towards the ills of social and family life was implanted and subsequent research sought to ferret out the disorganizing features of social life.[47]

Sussman's conclusions have been generally supported by subsequent research. One of the most detailed studies of kinship in an urban setting was done by Adams in Greensboro, North Carolina, a middle-sized industrial city which grew rapidly after World War II. Adams found that young adults in Greensboro had extremely frequent contacts with their parents and that these contacts were "primary" in the sense of "including intimate communication and relationship for its own sake [and] focusing in a basic concern for each other's welfare."[48] Among adult siblings, mutual aid was infrequent, but fairly frequent contact was maintained, even though it was somewhat restrained because of divergent interests. Only a small minority of respondents reported extensive contact with uncles, aunts, and cousins.

Adams's findings can be summarized as follows.[49]

1. Aging parents link their children together after they leave the parental home. To a lesser extent, parents also link their children to aunts and uncles—the parents' own siblings. The frequency of contact between family members is an expression both of feelings of affection and of a sense of obligation.

2. Family life in an urban setting remains strong and meaningful, but not in the traditional pattern of the extended family.

3. Physical distance tends to limit family contacts, but not to prevent them or eliminate their importance.

4. Females and the elderly provide the focus of kin affairs in urban areas as they do in rural ones.

5. The efforts of grown children to "get ahead" does not appear to have a negative effect on family contacts. On the contrary, parents and parents-in-law often help young adults in their strivings for upward mobility, and this aid is recognized and appreciated.

Studies of urban life in the developing nations suggest that family and kinship ties continue to be just as important to the new urbanites in Asia, Africa, and Latin America as they are to the residents of American cities. On the basis of a study of West African cities, for example, Aldous has concluded that "the extended family is indeed functional. Besides filling recreational, religious, legal or economic needs of urbanites, it substitutes for a nonexistent public social welfare program. Kinsmen provide for the elderly and support the sick, the jobless and the destitute."[50]

Family patterns differ in urban and rural settings, and they differ also from society to society. But in all types of communities and societies, and during all periods of history, the family has had a central importance both to the society and to the individual.

Bureaucracy in Urban Life

With urbanization, societies increasingly become complexes of bureaucratic organizations. Today an estimated 85 percent of all employed Americans work for some type of bureaucratic organization. Whether an urbanite's occupation be that of machine toolist or college professor, priest or surgeon, department store clerk or

47. Ibid., p. 339. Litwak and Szeleny have provided more recent support of Sussman's argument. See Eugene Litwak and Ivan Szeleny, "Primary Group Structures and Their Functions," *American Sociological Review* (August 1969): 465–481.

48. Bert N. Adams, *Kinship in an Urban Setting* (Chicago: Markham Publishing Co., 1968), p. 164.

49. Ibid., pp. 165 ff.

50. Joan Aldous, "Urbanization, the Extended Family, and Kinship Ties in West Africa," in *Urbanism in World Perspective*, ed. Sylvia Fava (New York: Thomas Y. Crowell Company, 1968), pp. 297–305.

accountant, corporation president or assistant personnel director, the role is defined to some extent by bureaucratic rules and regulations. In addition, urbanites must spend a good part of their nonworking hours interacting with others in bureaucratic roles as they attempt to take care of personal and family affairs.

Impersonality and formality have traditionally been considered the hallmarks of bureaucracy. Indeed, in analyzing bureaucracy as a distinct form of social organization, Max Weber theorized that bureaucratic efficiency was directly dependent on the depersonalization of interaction within the organization. But as we noted in our earlier discussion of bureaucratic organization (pages 71–79), there are forces at work within bureaucracies that Weber did not take into account. Just as research on the city and on residential patterns has failed to support the urbanism thesis of Louis Wirth, so studies of actual bureaucracies have failed to show that primary-group relationships disappear in bureaucratic organizations or that such relationships lessen bureaucratic efficiency.[51] Indeed, Blau's analysis of the operation of a state employment agency (page 77) showed that one condition *necessary* to the efficient operation of the agency was the establishment of informal work groups that commanded the allegiance of their members.

Although the problems associated with bureaucracies are real, bureaucratic organization is nonetheless one of society's most important inventions, since it enables people to achieve complex goals that would otherwise be out of reach. The available evidence suggests, furthermore, that the danger to individuality posed by society's bureaucratization has been exaggerated. Patterns of primary relations learned through socialization in the family and peer groups are carried by urbanites into their job situations. These tend to modify in some degree the formal structure of the job environment, but without necessarily endangering the achievement of bureaucratic goals. However rigid and impersonal a bureaucracy may be in the abstract, individuals can find ways to modify the structure so that it satisfies their basic psychological needs.

The Voluntary Association in Urban Life

Urbanization has led to the growth of voluntary associations (page 79) not only in the United States and other industrialized societies but also in the developing countries. Kenneth Little, for example, reports the existence of a wide variety of voluntary associations in the urbanized areas of West Africa.[52] Some are urban extensions of traditional tribes that provide food, clothing, and shelter to their own poor. Some are mixtures of traditional and modern organization. They help newcomers understand city ways, act as credit unions, and help tribal members find jobs. Some are primarily social, but with a strong religious orientation derived from small Christian congregations like the Pentacostals.

Little found special associations for men and for women and also some that served both sexes. The latter, he pointed out, provided a means whereby males and females could meet socially under the new conditions of urban life.

In the United States, voluntary associations had an important place in societal life even before extensive urbanization: as Tocqueville noted early in the nineteenth century, we seem to be a nation of joiners. But voluntary associations have proliferated as American society and American communities have become larger and more complex.

Surveys show that today about half the adults in the United States belong to at least one voluntary association. People from medium-sized cities (20,000–50,000) are more likely to belong than people from either small towns or large metropolises. Participation in voluntary associations also varies with income and educational level: people with some college education are the most likely of all to belong to at least one such group (80 percent).[53]

51. For an extensive discussion of this and related problems of bureaucracy, see Robert K. Merton et al., eds., *Reader in Bureaucracy*, rev. ed. (New York: The Free Press, 1965); and Peter M. Blau and W. Richard Scott, *Formal Organizations* (San Francisco, Calif.: Chandler Publishing Co., 1962).

52. Kenneth Little, "The Role of Voluntary Associations in West African Urbanization," in *The Substance of Sociology,* ed. Ephraim H. Mizruchi (New York: Appleton-Century-Crofts, Inc., 1967), pp. 362–378.

53. James Curtis, "Voluntary Association Joining: A Cross-National Comparative Note," *American Sociological Review* (October 1971): 872–880.

Overall, minority group members are less active than middle-class Anglo-Americans in voluntary associations. However, sometimes minority group members are *more* active. A study in Austin, Texas, found that Mexican Americans had the lowest rates of participation in voluntary associations and that blacks had the highest, with Anglos in between.[54] Other recent studies have shown similar differences in voluntary-group membership among blacks and Mexican Americans. Blacks have apparently been increasing their participation in voluntary associations of various types, whereas participation among Mexican Americans has remained relatively low.[55] Degree of ethnic consciousness may be an important factor in explaining such differences. The struggle by blacks for equality and justice during the 1960s and 1970s has heightened their sense of ethnic identity and has led to their becoming more active in all kinds of social and political organizations. It may be hypothesized that as Mexican Americans and other minorities become further involved in their own movements of assertion, they too will look toward voluntary associations as an important means for achieving their goals.[56]

Figures on voluntary-group membership do not, of course, tell the whole story with regard to their significance in urban life. Not all members are active, nor are all nonmembers social isolates. In a detailed study of the Detroit metropolitan area, Axelrod found that although a majority of the population were members of at least one formal group, less than half of this majority considered themselves active members. In contrast, *informal* group association was found to be almost universal. A majority of those surveyed—regardless of income or education level—reported relatives as the people they associated with most frequently.[57]

Accumulated research makes it clear that voluntary associations have not significantly diminished the importance of primary groups in urban life. Rather, they seem to supplement primary groups and to provide yet another setting in which people can interact, both formally and informally, in order to achieve a variety of goals.

RURAL LIFE IN URBAN AMERICA

In the United States, as in other highly urbanized nations, rural life-styles have been inevitably influenced by "city ways." Rural families watch the same television programs and read the same magazines that their urban counterparts do; they may also shop at outlets of the same national chains and make regular visits to a major city. And they must cope, just as city people do, with bureaucratic rules and regulations. Whether they like it or not, the rural population has been markedly affected by the phenomenon of urbanization.

THE RURAL POPULATION

While the population of rural areas of the United States has remained fairly stable for decades, the farm segment of the rural population has continued the steady decline that began in the nineteenth century.[58] Today less than 5 percent of the total population—only 20 percent of the rural population itself—is still in farming. These 9.7 million Americans work some 3 million farms, which not only feed more than 200 million of their fellow citizens but also produce surpluses for export to the rest of the world.

54. J. Allen Williams, Jr., Nicholas Babchuk, and David R. Johnson, "Voluntary Associations and Minority Status: A Comparative Analysis of Anglo, Black and Mexican-Americans," *American Sociological Review* (October 1973): 637–646.

55. See, for example, J. F. Barbosa-Dasilva, "Participation of Mexican-Americans in Voluntary Associations," *Research Reports in the Social Sciences*, 2 (Spring 1968): 33–43; Mario Renzi, "Negroes and Voluntary Associations: An Open Question," in *Research Reports in the Social Sciences*, pp. 63–71; Herbert H. Hyman and Charles R. Wright, "Trends in Voluntary Association Memberships of American Adults: Replication Based on Secondary Analysis of National Sample Survey," *American Sociological Review* (April 1971): 205.

56. For discussions of ethnic consciousness as a factor in voluntary-group participation, see Williams, Babchuk, and Johnson, "Voluntary Associations and Minority Status"; and Marvin E. Olsen, "Social and Political Participation of Blacks," *American Sociological Review* (August 1970): 682–697.

57. Morris Axelrod, "Urban Structure and Social Participation," *American Sociological Review* (February 1956): 13–18.

58. This discussion of the rural population is based on *Farm Population Estimates, 1910–1970* (U.S. Department of Agriculture, Statistical Bulletin No. 523, July 1973); Lee Taylor, *Urban-Rural Problems* (Belmont, Calif.: Dickenson Publishing Co., 1968); and *Keeping Up with Change in Rural Society* (U.S. Department of Agriculture, Federal Extension Service, January 1970).

Though rural areas are today influenced by city ways, the image of rural life as the ideal way to live remains a part of American culture.

Obviously the rapid decrease in size of the farm population has been more than matched by increases in farm productivity. A single farmer produced enough food in 1910 for seven persons, in 1950 for fifteen persons, and in 1970 for thirty-five persons. At the same time, it has become increasingly difficult for the individual farmer to make a good living on a family owned farm. Most of the high-income farms are corporate operations that bear little resemblance to the farms idealized in the popular image of rural life.

Independent farmers, like small businessmen, have had a difficult time surviving in the industrial economy. They must compete with the enormous operations of farming corporations that have acreages, machinery, and capital small farmers can never hope to match. Some of these corporations own processing plants and marketing outlets and thus represent not simply farming but agribusiness.

Although 95 percent of all active farms are still family owned and operated, and although families do three-fourths of all farm labor, these operations yield only about a quarter of the annual farm product. As a result, many farm families must look for outside sources of income. The average family operating a farm today earns about as much from nonfarm sources as from farming itself.

Almost one-third of the United States farm population is made up of the rural poor—Southern blacks, Appalachian whites, Mexican Americans, owners of marginal farms, sharecroppers, and migrant and nonmigrant farm laborers. It is from this sector that some of the most significant out-migration of recent years has taken place. For example, with the collapse of the tenant farming system of the South during the 1960s, the black farm population decreased by more than 50 percent.

By federal government standards there are more rural poor than urban poor, and many of the rural poor lack basic amenities that even their very poor urban counterparts take for granted. For example, some 6 percent of rural families are without electricity, and more than 25 percent lack telephones.[59] In addition, many of the same problems that now plague the inner city also plague depressed rural areas: ill health, high mortality rates, low educational levels, the plight of people who are prevented by age and/or lack of funds from moving to better surroundings, and the inability of local governments to raise funds for providing needed services.

RURAL VERSUS URBAN VALUE SYSTEMS

The tendency to see rural life as promoting an integrated social order and hence "good," and to see urbanism by contrast as promoting personal and social disorganization and therefore "bad," has been a popular way to read folk-urban theory. This tendency is especially pronounced among those Americans who have continued to live on farms and in small towns. Nesius has found seven basic suppositions deeply embedded in American farm culture:

1. The farmer is the most noble and independent man in our society.

2. Agriculture is the fundamental employment of man because the rest of our economy depends upon it.

3. Agricultural life is the ideal life because it is concerned with nature and it is the natural way. . . .

4. The family-owned farm is the foundation of our democracy.

5. Hard work is morally good and doing nothing is sinful.

6. Cities breed corruption. They do not provide a wholesome environment in which to raise children because they affect their morals adversely.

7. City politicians and labor leaders are corrupt and undemocratic.[60]

Similarly, in their study of a small country town called "Springdale" during the late 1950s, Vidich and Bensman found that most of the three thousand residents were still strongly tied to Jeffersonian agrarianism. They seemed to pity the poor city people, who lived in what Springdalers thought of as a bustling, jostling, nerve-racking, impersonal environment. Here is how the authors summarized the average Springdaler's belief:

1. The basic traditions of American society — "grassroots democracy, free and open expression, individualism — are more firmly located in rural society. The American heritage is better preserved in the small town because it can resist bad city influences and thereby preserve the best of the past."

2. The future hope of American society lies in rural life because it has resisted all "isms" and constitutes the only major bulwark against them.

3. Much of the progress of society is the result of rural talent which has migrated to the cities. In this way rural society has a positive influence on urban life; rural migrants account for the virtues of city life. "Everyone knows that most of the outstanding men in the country were raised in small towns."

4. "When you live in a small town you can take or leave the big cities — go there when you want to and always come back without having to live as they do." There is the belief that "if more people lived in small towns, you wouldn't have all those problems."[61]

Table 12.5. RESIDENTIAL PREFERENCES OF THE AMERICAN PEOPLE

	Percent who now live in	Percent who would prefer to live in
Open country	12	34
Small town or city	33	30
Medium-size city or suburb	28	22
Larger city or suburb	27	14

SOURCE: *Population and the American Future*, The Report of the Commission on Population Growth and the American Future (Washington, D.C.: U.S. Government Printing Office, 1972), p. 34. This table shows the results of a poll taken in 1971 in which people were asked where they lived and where they would prefer to live. Less than half of the respondents lived in small towns and open country, but 64 percent stated that they would prefer to.

59. Taylor, *Urban-Rural Problems*, pp. 10–12.

60. Ernest J. Nesius, *The Rural Society in Transition* (Morgantown, W. Va.: University of West Virginia Bulletin, Series 66, No. 10-4, April 1966), pp. 3–4.

61. Arthur Vidich and Joseph Bensman, *Small Town in Mass Society* (Princeton, N.J.: Princeton University Press, 1958); as summarized in Dennis Wrong and Harry Gracey, eds., *Readings in Introductory Sociology* (New York: Macmillan, Inc., 1967), p. 365.

While the Springdalers spoke eloquently about the virtues of rural life, the researchers found that clear-cut status distinctions prevailed there no less than in the city and that most people could and did rank each other on the basis of their economic worth. Perhaps ironically, those town folk who were most strongly linked to the city were in the best position to improve themselves socially, economically, and politically in Springdale. And information—e.g., national news—reached them through the urban-based mass media, particularly television. The question of whether Springdalers could "take or leave" the big city was perhaps not so simple as they wanted to believe.

As a further sidelight on these studies, we may note that people living in rural areas must share responsibility for the urban problems they deplore. Political scientists have pointed out that the residents of small towns have long had a disproportionate influence on urban places through their control of state legislatures. Furthermore, many residents of small towns—like most residents of suburbs—earn their living in the city and take their money back to their own community. In doing so, they are contributing at least indirectly to the "crisis of the cities."

In any event, the days of the traditional small rural community seem to be all but over. As urban areas have grown, they have not only altered rural life-styles but have also encroached on rural land. Small towns have become suburbs and many suburbs have become medium-sized cities. Industrial plants and business offices have increasingly moved out of older cities and into surrounding areas, bringing valued jobs to small communities but also changing their character. As stated by the Department of Agriculture, "The fact is that throughout America the small, autonomous community types of yesteryear are gradually melding into single rural-urban communities of tomorrow."[62]

62. *Keeping Up with Change in Rural Society*, p. 19.

SUMMARY

In this chapter we have briefly traced the historical development of the city and some of the efforts to explain its impact on society and the individual. The preindustrial cities of Europe and the colonial cities of the United States served the purpose of providing protection for the residents and facilitating trade and commerce. The various social and cultural changes that accompanied the Industrial Revolution made possible the urbanization of Western nations.

In the developing countries urbanization is related more to rapid population growth than to industrialization and has been proceeding more rapidly than in the West. Poverty and squalor have become facts of life for the majority of urban dwellers in these countries.

Sociologists have developed many theories regarding urbanism and city growth. Some of these theories see urban life as creating feelings of alienation and isolation. Theorists have contrasted traditional agricultural societies, in which primary relationships are said to predominate, with urban-industrial societies, in which more formal and impersonal relationships are seen as most common. Sociologists who take the ecological approach see the development of cities as related to land-use competition.

Empirical research on the theories of urban life has indicated that primary relationships are most common in suburbs and residential neighborhoods and that, even in slums, social disorganization is not always characteristic. The family continues to play a major role in the life of urban dwellers. Urbanization has been accompanied by the growth of voluntary associations.

Urban renewal programs that operate mainly in the interests of the affluent have only worsened the "crisis of the cities." The suburbs continue to attract middle-class people and jobs from the city. Planned communities may be a potential solution to the problems of the cities.

Today most rural people are not involved in farming at all, and those that are usually supplement their income from nonfarm sources. But the belief that farm life is "better" than urban life is deeply embedded in our culture, as is the corresponding belief of small-town residents that city life is "bad."

Part V
BEHAVIOR IN MASS SOCIETY

13
Collective Behavior and Social Movements

From time to time throughout history people have been swept up in spontaneous forms of behavior that follow neither logic nor past experience nor the established conventions of society. They have participated in riots, lynchings, ecstatic religious revivals, wild outbursts of financial speculation, migrations, manias, and crazes. Sociologists use the term *collective behavior* as a rather loose label for such events. The term is somewhat misleading since all kinds of social interaction are in a sense "collective." But its use has become traditional in referring to social behavior that does not follow an organized pattern of conventions and expectations.

Essentially, collective behavior differs from group behavior in that it is relatively unstructured and therefore relatively unpredictable. Those involved do not know what they can expect of others or what is expected of them. As a result, their behavior often takes unusual turns. The most dramatic forms of collective behavior usually occur when people are confronted with a situation to which they feel compelled to respond but for which they have no previously acquired guides to action. For example, the thousands of Americans who were convinced by a radio play in 1938 that the country was being invaded by Martians felt they had to do *something:*

Long before the broadcast had ended, people all over the United States were praying, crying, fleeing frantically to escape death from the Martians. Some ran to rescue loved ones. Others telephoned farewells or warnings, hurried to inform neighbors, sought information from newspapers or radio stations, summoned ambulances and police cars. At least six million people heard the broadcast. At least a million of them were frightened or disturbed.[1]

Even though collectivities lack an established pattern of social organization, collective behavior is seldom if ever *completely* unstructured. Probably only the most extreme danger could lead to an instance where individuals in

1. Hadley Cantril, "The Invasion from Mars," in Eleanor Maccoby et al., *Readings in Social Psychology* (New York: Holt, Rinehart and Winston, Inc., 1958), pp. 291–292.

an aggregate might act wholly on their own, completely oblivious to the influence of others. Most types of collective action are quite clearly combinations of structured and unstructured behavior.

Sociologists are interested in collective behavior not only because it is a fascinating phenomenon in its own right but also because it frequently is a stimulant of sociocultural change. The Paris mob was instrumental in destroying the monarchy in France during the French Revolution. Crowd reaction to the speeches of Adolf Hitler opened the way to Nazi control of Germany in the 1930s. In the United States, urban riots in the 1960s stimulated the creation of new social programs and at the same time brought increased demands for stronger law enforcement.

The tulip mania that occurred in Holland in the seventeenth century shows how collective behavior can take strange turns with unpredictable results.[2] The tulip, said to have been introduced from Turkey in 1559, was at first a rarity in Holland, prized only by a few horticultural enthusiasts. Before long, however, every wealthy person had a collection of the plants, and soon the enthusiasm spread to the middle class. Bulbs were scarce, and their prices rose rapidly as demand increased. People became less and less interested in the flowers as such and more and more interested in the profit to be made from buying and selling bulbs. In the 1630s a rage for tulip bulbs swept through the whole country. Some bulbs sold for the equivalent of thousands of dollars—many times the value of their weight in gold. Then, mysteriously, prices began to level off. The shrewder speculators quietly disposed of their holdings. As prices slipped, public confidence melted away. Thousands were ruined when they were unable to sell bulbs for which they had paid enormous sums. The price of tulips fell to almost nothing.

This widely documented case of a mania provides an interesting example not only of spontaneous collective behavior but also of the lasting impact such an incident can have. To this day, Holland remains the world center of

tulip growing. Thus the society as a whole was altered by an instance of collective behavior.

In the opening sections of this chapter we will analyze the organizational characteristics of crowds and the general psychology of crowd behavior. We will then consider the dynamics of collective behavior—the processes by which crowds and other aggregates of people are sometimes stimulated to dramatic forms of action. These theoretical formulations will be used to study an actual instance of collective behavior, an urban riot. Finally, we will examine the nature of social movements, which share some of the characteristics of collective behavior but are relatively more structured. The women's movement will be used to illustrate this special type of social behavior.

THEORETICAL APPROACHES TO THE STUDY OF CROWDS

All of us are familiar with crowds, from small clusters of street-corner gawkers to huge gatherings of spectators at scheduled events. Casual crowds that form spontaneously and audiences that come together purposefully share many characteristics. Under certain circumstances both can be transformed into highly expressive aggregations within which dramatic forms of collective behavior occur.

Traditionally crowds have been studied in terms of their impact on the individual. But crowds must also be understood within a theoretical framework derived from concepts of social organization. In the sections that follow, several types of crowds will be analyzed from these two distinct perspectives.

ORGANIZATIONAL CHARACTERISTICS OF CROWDS

We may classify crowds on the basis of such criteria as whether the participants have gathered spontaneously or for a scheduled event, whether they are behaving peacefully or violently, and

2. Charles McKay, *Extraordinary Popular Delusions and the Madness of Crowds* (New York: L. C. Page, 1932), pp. 89–97. (Reprint of the original 1841 edition.)

whether they are preoccupied mainly with personal, subjective experiences or with events external to themselves. In addition, we may analyze crowds in terms of their organizational characteristics. In some instances of crowd behavior, certain components of social organization may be present in elementary form, while in others the situation is almost wholly unstructured.

Some years ago, Herbert Blumer proposed a relatively simple classification of crowds, using the terms *casual, conventionalized, active,* and *expressive* to identify distinct types of collectivities.[3] In the following discussion we will examine these four major crowd forms and note their varying organizational characteristics.

The Casual Crowd

In a casual crowd, onlookers come together spontaneously for brief periods when their attention is drawn to some commonly perceived event. They do very little but view that event and are thus mainly a passive and fleeting aggregate of persons. As sociologists have pointed out, the members of a casual crowd share no collective goal and do not interact in any organized way. Although they define their behavior in terms of norms, roles, social controls, etc., these derive from general social experience rather than from conventions established within the crowd itself. In this sense, the casual crowd is one of the least structured of all human collectivities. It lacks completely any form of social organization generated within itself.

The Conventionalized Crowd

Several of the elements of group structure discussed in Chapter 2 can be observed in conventionalized crowds such as audiences. In the first place, the participants have a common goal—e.g., the enjoyment of attending a particular performance or spectacle. In addition, the conventionalized crowd normally imposes simple norms and roles on its members. For example,

the person who laughs when silence is more appropriate or who makes an unnecessary commotion is deviating from expected and approved patterns of audience behavior. The expectations for participants vary in different types of conventionalized crowds: the behavior permitted and even expected of an enthusiastic fan at a hockey game would certainly be regarded as conspicuously deviant at a chess match. When individuals deviate from norm and role expectations, attempts at informal social control are likely to be forthcoming. In the case of conspicuous nonconformity, other members of the audience may first ask offenders to desist and then, if they fail to do so, demand that they leave.

While these elements of social organization are generally observable in conventionalized crowds, other important elements are usually absent. There is no allocation of specialized roles forming a coordinated division of labor. Consequently, there is no system of differentially rewarded and differentially ranked positions. The conventionalized crowd, in other words, lacks important elements of social organization, and whatever structure it does have is extremely unstable and relatively useless in the face of crisis.

The Active Crowd

The members of both casual and conventionalized crowds are primarily observers; normally, they do not become directly involved in the event that has brought them together. Members of an active crowd, by contrast, become participants in the event, engaging in unpredictable and sometimes violent forms of behavior. Damage to property or injuries to persons often result from the behavior of an active crowd, such as a mob participating in a riot. On occasion, a conventionalized crowd that is faced with an unexpected turn of events becomes an active crowd. A theater audience may stampede at the cry of "Fire," and sports fans enraged by a series of "bad calls" may swarm the playing field in protest.

3. Herbert Blumer, "Elementary Collective Groupings," in *New Outline of the Principles of Sociology,* ed. Alfred McClung Lee (New York: Barnes & Noble, Inc., 1951), pp. 178–179.

The active crowd is almost wholly lacking in structure. As Blumer describes it:

It has no heritage or accumulation of tradition to guide its activity; it has no conventions, established expectations, or rules. It lacks other important marks of a society, such as an established social organization, an established division of labor, a structure of established roles, a recognized leadership, a set of norms, a set of moral regulations, an awareness of its own identity, or a recognized "we-consciousness."[4]

The Expressive Crowd

In the expressive crowd, the subjective experiences of the members themselves are the principal feature of attention. A highly emotional religious revival meeting is an example. In the context of such a crowd, exaltation, grief, joy, fear, and other emotions can be generated in ways unlikely to be experienced by individual members in isolation. Another example is the rock music festival, where members of the audience react in a wide variety of ways not only to the emotional impact of the music but also to the excitement of those around them.

The expressive crowd may develop initially as a conventionalized crowd, in which there are norms of expected behavior. But as emotions become more intense, conventional expectations no longer apply. People in expressive crowds lose the restraints on emotional expression that operate under ordinary circumstances. Caught up in the intensity of their feelings, they seldom try to control their own behavior, much less the behavior of others. Thus norms in the usual sense of institutionalized expectations cease to be relevant in such settings. Indeed, "losing control" may temporarily become normative itself.

THE SOCIAL PSYCHOLOGY OF CROWD BEHAVIOR

Individuals often behave quite differently in a crowd than they would if they were acting alone or as participants in a conventional group. Both sociologists and social psychologists have tried to understand why this is so.

Classic Theory

Gustave LeBon's *Psychology of Crowds,* first published in Paris in 1895, provided the first systematic analysis of the social psychology of crowd behavior.[5] LeBon was interested in the role of crowds in the new type of urban-industrial society that had emerged in Europe in the nineteenth century. "The age we are about to enter," he said, "will in truth be the *era of crowds.*"

LeBon was centrally concerned with the psychological impact of the crowd on its individual members. He concluded that persons forming a crowd underwent marked changes that led them to behave in new ways:

Whoever be the individuals that compose it, however like or unlike be their modes of life, the fact that they have been transformed into a crowd puts them in possession of a sort of collective mind which makes them feel, think and act in a manner quite different than that in which each individual of them would feel, think and act were he in a state of isolation.[6]

While the concept "collective mind" has been abandoned by most behavioral scientists, the idea that a crowd can produce profound changes in the psychological functioning of its individual members is still widely accepted. At exciting sports events spectators jump and scream in emotional displays that could scarcely be generated in solitude. Under the stress of warfare, persons who would not individually think of themselves as killers can collectively commit acts of extreme violence.

Key Concepts

LeBon's attempts to account for the behavior of individuals in crowd situations were much influenced by the new emphasis on psychiatry, which had come into vogue in his time. LeBon felt that the *anonymity* the crowd provides somehow strips away the checks on behavior that are operative under ordinary circumstances.

4. Ibid., p. 180.
5. Gustave LeBon, *The Crowd: A Study of the Popular Mind* (New York: The Viking Press, Inc., 1960).
6. Ibid., p. 27.

The organizational characteristics of crowds vary. The participants in a conventionalized crowd—e.g., an audience at a football game (bottom left)—have a common, socially approved goal and impose simple norms and roles on one another. A casual crowd, on the other hand, lacks any form of self-generated social organization; participants follow general societal norms, roles, social controls, and so on. The crowd (opposite) that has gathered to view a building that has exploded is a casual crowd. In an expressive crowd, as at a religious revival meeting (top left), institutionalized expectations cease to be relevant and emotional behavior comes to be normative. An active crowd—like the rioters at a rock music festival (above)—is almost wholly lacking in structure, and members of the active crowd engage in unpredictable and sometimes violent behavior.

This, he felt, permits the individual to be responsive to unconscious motivations. LeBon believed that several factors lead to this change in psychological functioning when the ordinary person becomes a member of a crowd. First, he said, individuals in a crowd acquire a "sentiment of invincible power." This allows them to yield to impulses they would normally resist. Second, the processes of *contagion* aid in spreading sentiments and orientations throughout the crowd; and at the same time members of the crowd become highly suggestible. LeBon saw a close analogy between the participant in an active crowd and the person in the grip of a hypnotic trance:

The individual forming part of a psychological crowd . . . is no longer conscious of his acts. In his case, as in the case of the hypnotized subject, at the same time certain faculties are destroyed, others may be brought to a high degree of exaltation. Under the influence of a suggestion, he will undertake the accomplishment of certain acts with irresistible impetuosity. This impetuosity is the more irresistible in the case of crowds than that of the hypnotized subject, from the fact that the suggestion being the same for all individuals of the crowd, it gains strength by reciprocity.[7]

Thus the key concepts in LeBon's analysis of the social-psychological impact of the crowd on its members are: *anonymity, unconscious motivations, contagion, suggestibility,* and *reciprocal influence.* While many aspects of LeBon's work can be criticized within contemporary perspectives, these concepts recur in analyses of crowd behavior up to the present time.

THE SOCIAL DYNAMICS OF COLLECTIVE BEHAVIOR

It is difficult to generalize about the dynamics of such varied forms of collective behavior as riots, panics, and manias. However, most instances of collective behavior seem to develop around conditions that (1) define existing forms of social organization as inadequate for some substantial number of persons, (2) excite these persons through the reciprocal generation of emotional orientations, and (3) diffuse shared beliefs about the situation, shared rumors of interpretation, and shared patterns of overt response. We will examine each of these concepts in turn.

STRUCTURAL INADEQUACIES

Dramatic forms of collective behavior do not ordinarily develop unless existing patterns of social organization are perceived as being somehow inadequate. The significance of structural inadequacies in precipitating incidents of collective behavior is most readily apparent in crises. On a sinking ship, for example, established norms and roles provide people with few clues about how to behave. Panic in such instances is especially likely if the passengers and crew have not been trained in the use of lifeboats and in procedures for abandoning ship.

Existing patterns of social organization may also prove inadequate for coping with the challenges of everyday life as experienced by different groups or categories of people. In the United States—as in most other large urban-industrial societies—occupational, regional, political, ethnic, racial, and class differences provide fertile ground for social discontent and thus for incidents of collective behavior. The riots that erupted in the black ghettos of most major American cities during the 1960s provide clear illustrations of collective behavior developing out of dissatisfaction with the existing structure of American society.

EMOTIONAL CONTAGION

Perhaps no other interactional process is so important in generating collective action as that by which emotional orientations spread from person to person. It is through this process of "emotional contagion" that the members of a collectivity can become increasingly unified in their psychological outlook and increasingly

---

7. Ibid., pp. 31–32.

committed to given forms of overt action. The usual self-imposed restraints on behavior cease to operate, allowing the individual to be guided by impulse and emotion.

Shared Orientations of Participants

Emotional contagion is more likely to occur among members of crowds that have common characteristics than it is among more heterogeneous aggregations. For example, an audience composed of teen-agers is more likely to experience waves of emotion in response to a popular singer than an audience made up of persons of many different age levels. Similarly, a new craze or fad is more likely to spread among some specific segment of the population than among people from varying walks of life.

Shared mood also facilitates the development of emotional contagion. People who are assembled for a religious service usually have similar feelings of awe, reverence, and humility, and this provides an important basis for psychological unity. People so unified can be led to states of religious exhilaration by an evangelist more easily than can an audience of people whose emotional states are initially mixed.

Distraction from Self

Emotional contagion is most likely to occur in crowd situations where some dramatic event commands undivided attention. Under such circumstances people's normal tendencies to be self-critical may temporarily cease to operate.

In a crowd or similar large aggregate, the individual feels relatively anonymous, and this in itself reduces self-monitoring. Constraints that are normally effective in the presence of friends or acquaintances are less likely to operate among strangers. Self-monitoring is further reduced when attention becomes sharply focused on something that is out of the ordinary—a spellbinding speaker, a street arrest, a theater fire. Absorbed in the situation at hand, individuals become distracted from evaluating the appropriateness of their own reactions and thus subject to emotional contagion.

Fads are more likely to spread among people who have common characteristics than among people from varying walks of life. For example, "streaking" (running naked through a crowded place), a fad that began in 1974, was limited almost exclusively to high-school and college students.

Suggestibility and Reciprocal Stimulation

People who lose awareness of self become especially suggestible. If people around them are exhibiting signs of growing excitement and tension, they are likely to accept these emotional states as appropriate to the situation and develop similar feelings themselves. Reciprocal stimulation can raise emotional levels quickly and sharply. For example, if a large number of people are verging on some strong emotional state such as fear, ecstasy, or anger, an observable manifestation of feeling on the part of one person can call out a similar response on the part of another. This, in turn, can reinforce the emotions of the first person and lead to an even stronger manifestation, which serves to stimulate the other person to a still greater response. Thus an aggregate of persons can mutually reinforce each other's emotional responses and lead each other to emotional states of quickly mounting intensity.

Selective Perception

People tend to see situations within selective frameworks even under the most ordinary circumstances. Their attitudes, needs, values, and other psychological predispositions all influence the meaning they assign to the events around them. This tendency is clearly apparent when people are in the grip of strong emotions. In a state of religious fervor, for example, people are far more likely to read supernatural implications into events than they would in ordinary circumstances.

DIFFUSION PROCESSES

Three forms of diffusion play an important part in generating incidents of collective behavior. One is the spread of beliefs prior to the incident that define its significance for those involved. The second is the exchange and spread of "information" by rumor. The third is rapid diffusion of particular forms of overt behavior. As will be noted, when rumor complements prior conviction, potential participants in collective behavior are often moved to become actual participants.

Beliefs

Before people can respond collectively to a situation, they must share some set of beliefs about what it means to them. They have to become convinced that they are threatened or deprived, that something is wrong, that they are moved by a spirit, or that there is some other call for action on their part. The factual accuracy of their shared interpretation is irrelevant: people respond not to facts per se but rather to *social constructions of reality*. If people are convinced that Martians have landed, or that the Second Coming is at hand, they will behave accordingly.

The Case of the Phantom Anesthetist of Mattoon, Illinois, provides an example of the way in which a spreading belief can provide a new social construction of reality and thus become a guide to collective action.[8] In September 1944 many of the people in this small community became deeply alarmed over a "mad gasser" who, they thought, was prowling their streets at night, spraying a "sweet sickly-smelling gas" into bedrooms. This gas was said to

paralyze its victims for a period of two hours or more but not to harm them permanently. The gas seemed to disappear without a trace once the victims recovered.

The incident got its start when a middle-aged woman called the police to report that she and her daughter had been victimized. The local newspaper ran a front-page story on the event the next day, complete with pictures. That night, several other persons phoned the police to report that they had been similarly attacked. By the second night, dozens of gassings were reported. During several succeeding evenings the mad gasser terrorized the entire community. The state police were called in along with other authorities. Elaborate measures were taken to apprehend the phantom anesthetist, but even though people kept reporting that he had struck, he was never seen. After a few days, no more gassings were reported, and the people of Mattoon stopped talking about the incident.

The tension produced by the war years, with the ever present fear of such dangers as sabotage, secret weapons, and germ warfare was an important element in this case. The role of the press in spreading the interpretive beliefs is clear. Suggestion and rumor also played their part. Finally, thanks to selective perception, any hissing sound heard after dark became the anesthetist's sprayer; any odd smell was the dreaded gas; any dim figure seen on a dark street was the mad gasser making his rounds. The spread of a particular belief, then, provided the basis for an incident of collective behavior.

Rumor

A rumor can be defined as an unverified report that is passed along from person to person, usually by word of mouth. It has no clearly identified source to establish its authenticity, but it answers a felt need for information and is therefore likely to be accepted at face value. Rumors usually develop within a context of ambiguity and stress, as when norms or beliefs are challenged, when physical danger looms, or when our welfare seems to be at stake. Such situations arouse anxieties and concern. It is these

8. Donald M. Johnson, "The Phantom Anesthetist of Mattoon: A Field Study of Mass Hysteria," *Journal of Abnormal and Social Psychology* (April 1945): 145–186.

The "mad gasser" incident began with a single telephone call and spread throughout the community by rumor, suggestion, and extensive news coverage. This front-page headline and story appeared in Mattoon's daily newspaper on September 9, 1944.

feelings that provide the motivation for both listening to and passing on what we hear. Rumors are socially derived interpretations of reality that fill the gap created by a lack of objective definitions.

Social scientists have been studying the rumor process for a long time. One investigative approach has been to study artificially created "rumors" in a controlled laboratory setting, where rumorlike experimental messages are passed from person to person. Typical of such laboratory studies are those of Allport and Postman.[9] One subject, selected as the starter, is presented with a complex story or set of ideas. These stimulus materials are often reinforced with a drawing, photograph, or motion picture. It is the task of the first subject to relate what he or she has seen and heard to the next subject, who has not previously been exposed to the materials. This subject passes the information on to the next, and so on down the line. The version of the story reproduced at each stage is recorded and studied for content changes.

A number of investigations have shown that the general patterns of change a message follows as it moves from person to person through these artificially constructed networks are fairly uniform.[10] The kinds of content distortion that occur in serial retelling have been termed the *embedding pattern*. The key elements in this pattern are leveling, sharpening, and assimilation:

Leveling has been defined as follows: "As rumor travels it tends to grow shorter, more concise, more easily grasped and told. In successive versions, fewer words are used and fewer details are mentioned."[11]

Sharpening has been defined as "the selective perception, retention, and reporting of a limited number of details from a larger context."[12] Through this process certain central details are kept in the story, becoming the dominant theme, while others are dropped.

9. Gordon W. Allport and Leo Postman, *The Psychology of Rumor* (New York: Henry Holt and Company, 1947).

10. T. M. Higham, "The Experimental Study of the Transmission of Rumour," *British Journal of Psychology* (March-May 1951): 42-55.

11. Allport and Postman, *The Psychology of Rumor*, p. 75.

12. Ibid., p. 86.

Assimilation refers to the way in which items in the rumor are leveled, sharpened, or otherwise altered in accordance with shared attitudes, cultural themes, stereotypes, and the like. Assimilation distorts rumor content in the direction of shared habits and conventions.[13]

Researchers are in substantial agreement that experimental messages studied under the conditions described tend to become reduced in length, edited in content to a more concise form, and, finally, fused with a combination of common cultural themes plus the attitudinal and interest biases of the subjects who actually do the retelling.

A second major pattern of content distortion is likely to occur in spontaneously generated rumors as they diffuse through a population. According to field studies of actual rumors in such settings as army camps, small towns, prisons, and college campuses, distortion in content seems to follow a *compounding pattern* when rumor serves to explain an unusual or unexpected situation. Typical are the findings of Peterson and Gist, who investigated the diffusion of rumors in a small community during a period of public concern about the rape and murder of a fifteen-year-old girl.[14] A central theme emerged to the effect that Mr. X (who had employed the girl as a baby-sitter) left the party that he and his wife were attending, returned to his home, raped and murdered the girl, and then, after changing his clothes, went back to the party. Around this central theme there developed a series of infinitely elaborated and distorted interpretive accounts concerning the activities, characteristics, motivations, background, and reactions of Mr. X. Stories were circulated concerning his relationship with his wife, details of the crime, the activities and suspicions of the police, and a multitude of related topics. Despite this accumulation of convincing "evidence," Mr. X had had nothing to do with the crime. He was completely exonerated after thorough police investigation.

The compounding pattern of rumor distortion occurs when people want and need to interpret a situation but have little "official" informa-tion to go on. In such cases, one rumor almost automatically generates another. If people hear that someone has been murdered, the natural questions are "Who did it?" and "What were the circumstances?" Under conditions that create anxiety or distress, any scraps of explanatory information are eagerly sought and quickly transmitted. The fact that their source may have been someone's imagination can easily be overlooked.

Rumor processes have been discussed at some length because they often play a key part in generating collective behavior. In Chapter 5 (pages 137–138) we noted that interpersonal activity of every type is dependent upon communication based upon significant symbols. Collective behavior is no exception. Rumors play a part in mobilizing participants, in orienting them individually to the events they will respond to in a collective manner, and in spreading shared definitions of appropriate action. These functions of rumor in the development of collective behavior will be illustrated in detail in a later section.

Action

Just as emotions and beliefs sometimes diffuse rapidly through a crowd or other collectivity, so also do patterns of overt behavior. Thus normally "sensible" people may suddenly find themselves stampeding for the exit of a theater or sports arena, selling their assets at a loss in a financial panic, or setting buildings afire in a riot.

The social sciences have by no means developed a complete explanation of behavioral diffusion during incidents of collective behavior. In many respects, the phenomenon seems to resemble what Gabriel Tarde and other sociologists of the late nineteenth century referred to as "imitation." As Kurt and Gladys Lang have pointed out, a wide range of societal phenomena were once explained on the basis of pre-

---

13. Ibid., pp. 99–155.
14. Warren A. Peterson and Noel P. Gist, "Rumor and Public Opinion," *The American Journal of Sociology*, 57 (September 1951): 159–161.

sumed instincts for imitation.[15] While we no longer attempt to explain human behavior in terms of instincts, some form of imitation seems to play a part in the spread of behavior patterns from one person to another under a wide variety of circumstances. But imitation does not wholly account for the rapid spread of seemingly irrational forms of action during riots, panics, and the like.

Contemporary explanations of behavioral diffusion during incidents of collective behavior place less emphasis on the factor of imitation than on people's need to know what is expected of them. Individuals who are faced unexpectedly with a stressful situation feel compelled to do *something* — but what action is most appropriate? Prior experience usually provides few socially validated guides to action. If someone suddenly responds to the situation with an overt act — throwing a rock at a police car, bolting for a theater exit, or scrambling to withdraw funds from a bank — this behavior helps create a social definition of what action fits the occasion. If several other individuals take up the behavior of the innovator, it is likely that most of the other people involved will follow suit. Thus the quick transformation of a casual crowd into a violent mob may be explained in part, at least, in terms of the rapid emergence of an *apparent norm*. Although the new norm may later be abandoned as quickly as it was adopted, it serves temporarily as a guide to appropriate action.

In summary, the social dynamics of collective behavior typically involve *structural inadequacies, emotional contagion,* and the *diffusion* of belief, interpretation, and overt response. We will apply these concepts to the analysis of a concrete instance of collective behavior — an urban riot.

THE ANATOMY OF A RIOT

During the late 1960s American society was shaken by a series of riots within black urban ghettos. Because of their scope and because they occurred so close to home for the growing number of urban and suburban dwellers, these riots became a matter of great public concern. There were many attempts to assign blame — to Communist conspirators, Black Power militants, recent migrants, local or imported agitators, the criminal element, the young. Careful analysis, however, failed to indicate that members of any of these categories had either caused or controlled the upheavals.[16]

What triggers a riot and how does it spread? In an attempt to find out how such crises occur and through what stages they progress, we shall examine the riot that occurred in the Watts district of Los Angeles in 1965. This riot attracted international attention, and its details have been painstakingly reported, providing a useful illustration of the anatomy of a riot.[17]

STRUCTURAL INADEQUACIES IN WATTS
Flaws in existing social structure do not in themselves cause riots, but they create discontent that can become aggravated to a point where violence flares. Societal conditions conducive to dissatisfaction and resentment among blacks have always existed in American society. Blacks have traditionally been assigned the most menial roles and the lowest status, and elements in our system of social control have long been aimed at "keeping them in their place." Perhaps the remarkable thing is not that riots erupted in many black ghettos during the 1960s but that such riots did not come sooner and in even more communities. In some ways, conditions for American blacks were better in the sixties than they had been in earlier times.

15. Kurt Lang and Gladys Engel Lang, *Collective Dynamics* (New York: Thomas Y. Crowell Company, 1961), pp. 210–211.

16. See, for example, Anthony Oberschall, "The Los Angeles Riot of August 1965," *Social Problems,* 15, No. 3 (1968): 322–341.

17. See Jerry Cohen and William S. Murphy, *Burn, Baby, Burn* (New York: E. P. Dutton & Co., Inc., 1966); *Violence in the City—An End or a Beginning,* Governor's Commission on the Los Angeles Riots (December 2, 1965); and Oberschall, "The Los Angeles Riot of August 1965."

TOOLS OF SOCIOLOGY
THE CASE STUDY

The sociological case study is a detailed description of an event of theoretical significance, based upon systematic observation carried out within a framework of sociological concepts. Typically, the researcher uses local records, intensive and extensive interviews with informants and others, participant observation, and other techniques.

To illustrate the case study, we may examine briefly the "Leeville Lynching," as summarized by Hadley Cantril in his well-known work *The Psychology of Social Movements*. This event took place during the 1920s in a small Texas community after a black farm laborer was reported to have raped the wife of his white employer. Although some people said the woman had invited the sexual attentions of the black man, she insisted that he had forced his way into her home with a shotgun when her husband was absent and had assaulted her repeatedly. Whatever the true story, sexual activity had indeed occurred.

After attempting flight, the farm hand was apprehended by a deputy sheriff, charged with the crime, lodged in the county jail, and swiftly brought to trial. Local whites were determined that he would "get what was coming to him." On the morning of the trial, many white people came to Leeville to see what would happen. As the trial proceeded, the crowd grew larger and increasingly hostile. Texas Rangers were on hand to keep order, but the crowd was convinced that the Rangers would never shoot to protect the black defendant. Shouting and heckling increased as the day wore on. Many rumors were passed around. The precipitating event, "which changed the huge curious crowd into a vicious mob, was the bringing of the woman from the hospital in an ambulance and carrying her on a stretcher into the courtroom. . . . After that the crowd went wild." Members of the mob stoned the courthouse, tried repeatedly to break in, and eventually set it on fire. "The fire department used its ladders to carry the people from the second floor courtroom. There was some objection to the rescuing of the judge, county attorney, sheriff, and Rangers. 'Let the bastards burn up with the nigger,' was the cry."

The governor of Texas sent a small detachment of the National Guard to reinforce the Rangers, but by this time the mob had grown so belligerent that the troops were no match for them. A violent confrontation ensued, and the defenders were forced to retreat. The would-be lynchers used stolen dynamite to blast their way into the building and get the accused, who was killed by the explosion. When his corpse was brought out, the crowd shouted, "Take him to niggertown." As the case study reports, "the body was fastened behind a Ford roadster. . . . About five thousand howling, yelling people fell into a midnight parade behind the corpse. Someone struck up the strains of 'Happy days are here again,' and soon hundreds joined in. . . ."

The dead man was pulled up onto a tree limb and a nearby drugstore was ransacked for burnable material to place under it. Some claimed that the corpse was desexed before the fire was set. A great cheer went up as the flames engulfed the body. Children danced as they watched it burn.

After burning the corpse, the mob fell to looting the homes and businesses of blacks. Numerous buildings were set on fire after being doused with gasoline and the fire department was not permitted to extinguish any fire if the property was not owned by whites. Meanwhile, the two thousand black citizens of Leeville hid.

The next day, the National Guard arrived in strength and restored order. Civil authorities eventually indicted fourteen persons, but only one man was sentenced (for arson). He got out of prison in a short time by order of the governor.

Clearly, this instance of collective violence has parallels with the upheaval in Watts, though the precipitating events were quite different and the racial characteristics of the participants were reversed. Comparisons of such case studies indicate that the sociological variables shaping crowd action have a similar impact regardless of the exact situation and regardless of who is involved. Case studies of this type constitute an essential part of sociological knowledge and contribute significantly to the development of adequate theories.

Hadley Cantril, *The Psychology of Social Movements* (New York: John Wiley & Sons, Inc., 1963); quotations from pp. 99, 100, and 102. Cantril's summary of the "Leeville Lynching" is based on a case study by Durward Pruden, unpublished M.A. thesis, Southern Methodist University, 1930.

Why, then, did ghetto riots flare up where and when they did? A partial explanation is that chronic problems had become acute under particular local conditions, creating what Smelser has called "structural strain."[18] The black residents of Watts, for example, were mostly relative newcomers to the Los Angeles area; by far the majority of them came from the South. Some came during World War II, drawn by the economic opportunity provided by an aircraft industry that was experiencing a shortage of labor. In the postwar years others arrived from rural regions of the South where the average unskilled black had no better prospect than a lifetime of grinding toil as a poorly paid field hand. They came to Los Angeles because relatives or friends were already there, because they were attracted by the climate or by the idea of moving west to a better life, or for any of a thousand other personal reasons. But whatever their motivation in coming to Watts, the majority anticipated a better way of life where the traditional problems of being black would be minimized.

On the surface, Watts did indeed seem to offer a better environment, at least compared to the sharecropper's shack of the rural South or the urban tenement of the eastern city. The houses were small but neat; there were trees and grass; the streets were wide and free of trash. Population density was high, to be sure, but not nearly so high as in some areas of other cities.

Less apparent were a number of other factors. The area was treated with official apathy and neglect.[19] There was little in the way of economic opportunity for the residents. Stores in Watts, operated for the most part by white owners, charged more than did stores in other areas of the city. Unemployment rates were excessively high, especially for young males. The lack of adequate public transportation aggravated the unemployment problem by making it difficult for those without cars (about half the people in

Watts) to take jobs in many parts of the city. The surrounding white population was indifferent. Watts was an area of excessively low educational levels, heavy dependency on welfare programs, high rates of crime and delinquency — in general, a "problem area" by almost every index of personal and social disorganization. The response of the larger community was mainly to make certain that the area was heavily policed.

Personal responses of bitterness and frustration may become cultural norms of alienation when shared with others who have had similar experiences. Such norms provide collective orientations that help make chronic problems acute. Blacks who had moved to Watts in anticipation of a better life found little improvement in their lot relative to the dominant white majority. New patterns of discrimination had been substituted for more familiar ones; total indifference had replaced more obvious prejudice; and unemployment had taken the place of poorly paid agricultural work.[20]

BELIEFS ABOUT THE POLICE

In areas where people with similar grievances are concentrated, chronic problems tend to be perceived as acute. Before a violent collective response can erupt, however, the situation of strain must be clearly *focused* and made more meaningful to the potential actors by the spread of defining beliefs. Specific targets for hostility must be identified. These must be interpreted as major *sources* of the dissatisfactions and strains impinging upon the potential actors. For the people of Watts, the specific target became the police.

While it is difficult to say with certainty whether or not the police in this urban area were any more abusive in their contacts with black residents than police are in similar areas elsewhere, the limited available evidence suggests that they probably were. The important point is that a belief had built up among the population that white officers were unnecessarily harsh and discriminatory in their enforcement of the law where blacks were concerned. Many

18. Neil Smelser, *Theory of Collective Behavior* (New York: The Free Press, 1962).

19. Raymond J. Murphy, "Postscript on the Los Angeles Riots," in *Problems and Prospects of the Negro Movement*, ed. Raymond J. Murphy and Howard Elinson (Belmont, Calif.: Wadsworth Publishing Co., 1966), pp. 231–234.

20. Oberschall, "The Los Angeles Riot of August 1965," pp. 331–332.

of the black residents of Watts interpreted every act of the police within this framework of selective perception. If a breakdown of social order was to occur it was likely to be precipitated by an incident involving the police.

THE PRECIPITATING INCIDENT

The kinds of incidents that touch off riots are often said to be insignificant in themselves. In Watts any one of a hundred events could have ignited the spark. But careful examination of the kinds of incidents that have in fact incited people to such violence indicates that they may have particular characteristics. Lieberson and Silverman recently studied available accounts and records of seventy-six race riots in the United States between 1913 and 1963 and noted that such riots "almost always involve some confrontation between the groups in which members of one race are deeply 'wronged' in fact or in rumor by members of the other."[21]

Yet confrontations of this sort occur every day *without* touching off a riot. It takes a great deal of provocation for people to engage in burning, looting, and killing, even when all the background elements are present. Apparently incidents of confrontation must have special characteristics before they can touch off widespread violence. The incident that took place on the evening of August 11, 1965, at the corner of 116th Street and Avalon Boulevard in Watts, illustrates how a casual crowd can be transformed into a rampaging mob.

Mobilization of Potential Actors

One of the most significant preconditions for the development of a riot is the state of the weather! Few riots occur in the winter or in a heavy rain simply because most people stay indoors, unaware of the outside events that might otherwise attract their attention and bring them together as onlookers. In the summer, however, especially on hot humid evenings, residents of places like Watts are likely to escape their small, stuffy living quarters by sitting on the front steps and the lawn or strolling in the streets. Such was the case on the evening in question. It had been the hottest day of the summer, and the early evening offered little relief. The yards and streets of the neighborhood were filled with people.

Into this setting drove two young men in an old sedan. A highway patrol motorcycle, with siren screaming and red light blazing, was in close pursuit. The two young blacks had been clocked driving at fifty miles an hour in a thirty-five-mile-per-hour zone. As the two vehicles stopped, the event drew the attention of the curious for several blocks around. The officer approached the car and began to question the occupants. A crowd gathered almost immediately. Within a few moments it was apparent to everyone that the offenders were under the influence of alcohol. The members of the crowd joked good-naturedly. Meanwhile, more and more people gathered just to see what was going on.

The officer was polite but firm. He made the driver try to walk a straight line—a task he was patently unable to perform. The crowd was amused. Relationships between the driver, the officer, and the crowd were cordial; they kidded with each other.

Emotional Contagion

The incident seemed to be coming to a close. A police transport car came to take away the driver, who had been placed under arrest; a wrecker had been summoned to remove the automobile; and the policeman's back-up motorcycle officer had also arrived on the scene. However, as the police wrecker was preparing to haul away the car, the mother of the arrested driver arrived in a state of agitation and sought to persuade the wrecker operator to release the car to her. When it was discovered that the automobile was actually registered in her name, the officer in charge granted her request, and the car was released. It was still only a routine situation. Although a substantial number of onlookers had gathered, they showed no signs of hostility.

21. Stanley Lieberson and Arnold R. Silverman, "The Precipitants and Underlying Conditions of Race Riots," *American Sociological Review*, 30, No. 6 (December 1965): 888.

The Watts riot of 1965 provides a clear example of what can happen to a crowd when emotional and behavioral contagion sets in. An active "hard core" of rioters, mainly younger men, set fires and occasionally shot at police and firemen. Many adults and children joined in the looting of stores. The rioters were drawn from almost all segments of the population, though most were from the lowest socioeconomic stratum.

Then suddenly the mother turned on her son and began to berate him for being drunk and for misbehaving with her automobile. The son pleaded with her for forgiveness. When she rejected his pleas, his mood changed quickly and dramatically. He became angry and shouted that the police would never take him to jail. He declared that they would have to kill him first. He screamed obscenities in a fit of rage, and the officer was unable to calm him. A minor struggle ensued, and the arrested youth attempted to strike the officer. The crowd grew silent.

The officers converged on their prisoner with handcuffs, determined to get him under control. By this time they were surrounded by a huge crowd that was becoming sullen. Quickly radioing for additional help, the transport-car officer removed his (unloaded) shotgun from his car and held it where the onlookers could see it. A wave of tension swept through the crowd. The situation had quickly grown potentially dangerous.

At that moment, the first of the reinforcements arrived. The police had armed themselves with clubs. Meanwhile the arrested driver was still resisting violently and shouting abuse. One officer had had enough. He struck the young man sharply on the head with his club. This succeeded in quieting him down, but it also caused him to begin bleeding as the handcuffs were clamped on.

At this point the crowd began to stir. A few individuals shouted insults at the patrolmen. Suddenly the companion of the man under arrest started fighting the police. The mother grabbed her son and tried to pull him away from the officers, setting off a general pushing and shoving melee as members of the crowd tried to assist her. The situation was deteriorating; the police were losing control. But additional squad cars arrived at that very moment, and the officers succeeded in pushing the crowd back.

Now emotions had heightened considerably. The processes of emotional contagion and reciprocal influence were transforming the onlookers from a passive collection of bystanders into a hostile and aggressive crowd that needed only a little more stimulation to respond with overt action. The usual norms and guides to behavior which restrain even angry individuals from acts of violence were crumbling. Hecklers in the crowd began shouting proposals for retaliatory measures. Yet even at this point a riot had not been touched off; the situation could still have gone either way. But selective perception then gave rise to rumors that further agitated the crowd and finally stirred it to action.

Selective Perception and Rumor

An important detail in the developing situation had been the clubbing of the arrested driver. Perhaps in calmer circumstances the majority of the onlookers would have agreed that, given his behavior, he deserved to be forcibly controlled, but under the charged emotional pressures of the moment this event was selectively perceived, raising the issue of police brutality.

Given this perceptual framework, two additional events supplied further evidence, as far as the crowd was concerned, of intolerable acts of brutality on the part of the police. One of these took place when the arrested driver was being placed in the police transport car. As an officer was pushing the still resisting subject into the vehicle, he had to shove the man's legs in forcefully with his knee and quickly slam the door. Police are taught to do this rapidly so as not to remain long with their backs to a hostile crowd. To onlookers, however, it appeared that the officer had kicked the handcuffed and bleeding youth and then slammed the door on his feet. Those who "saw" this shouted in angry protest, and their interpretation was quickly rumored through the remainder of the crowd.

The crowd became extremely agitated at this apparent evidence of police brutality. Rocks and bottles began to appear in many hands. By this time everyone was milling about and shouting. As new police reinforcements arrived, they were greeted with corrosive verbal abuse by the entire crowd. Yet even in this last moment of boiling anger, no rock or bottle had been thrown.

Meanwhile, a young black woman who worked as a barber in a nearby shop had been attracted to the scene. Swept up in the emotion of the crowd, she found herself face to face with a white officer just as the police were preparing to leave. She stepped forth, with her blue barber's smock flapping loose, and spat on the officer.

Two nearby policemen who saw the act reached into the crowd and dragged her out. Members of the crowd tried to pull her back. The woman screamed abuse and fought to get away. Finally the police succeeded in handcuffing her and half-carried, half-dragged her, still protesting, to a car. This episode spawned a second rumor. The story shot rapidly through the crowd that the police were manhandling a pregnant woman. The blue barber's smock she was wearing was perceived as a maternity dress! This was the straw that broke the camel's back.

The Diffusion of Overt Action

Shouts arose of "Let's get those cops!" "Kill the bastards!" "Smash those white sons-of-bitches!" The officers saw the situation had gotten out of control and ran to their vehicles to get clear of the area. Just as they attempted to leave, the riot broke. A few individuals took the lead and began to throw things at the police, and this pattern of behavior diffused rapidly through the crowd. The last station wagon in the police convoy was deluged with bricks, bottles, and stones. The mob broke loose in a frenzy of destruction.

THE RIOT

The precipitating incident set in motion new frames of reference, definitions of the situation, motivations to action that served as focal points for the mobilization of thousands of additional people. The original active crowd surged out from the site of the precipitating incident, providing stimuli that drew increasing numbers of people into immediate participation in the excitement.

Recruitment of Additional Participants

Perhaps the most significant element in the recruitment of additional participants was the rumors growing out of the original incident. The story of the police mistreating the arrested driver was distorted to a point where the man was said to have been viciously beaten and repeatedly kicked while already bleeding and helplessly manacled. The story of the "pregnant woman" and her brutal manhandling by the police was regarded as an especially ugly affair for which the police deserved punishment. Members of the original crowd, moreover, reported that they "had seen it with their own eyes."

This combination of half-truths based upon selective perception, prior shared beliefs, and distorted rumor was a clear call to action for thousands of Watts residents, especially young men. Accounts of how the police cars were stoned by the crowd provided suggestions for further action. Soon all cars containing white passengers going through the area were stoned. From that point it was an easy step to stopping the cars and dragging out their terrified occupants. This pattern of generalized retaliation against all whites spread swiftly. A bus was stopped, its windows smashed, and its passengers attacked with bricks and two-by-fours. White children were beaten along with their parents, who had happened to drive into the riot area.

During this period many blacks in Watts were horrified by what they saw their fellow residents doing to innocent people. Some tried to intervene to aid the victims of the mob. In a few cases they were successful but often they were unable to help. People were severely bruised by kicks and by blows with bottles and boards. Teeth were knocked out, eyes were gouged, bones were broken.

As more and more automobiles containing whites were stoned and their occupants mistreated, the police tried desperately to seal off and contain the violence. An area of some twenty square blocks was loosely surrounded but rioters spilled out across back alleys and through yards.

The police had largely withdrawn from the main area of the riot. A few probing teams entered from time to time in an attempt to disperse concentrations of people, but they lacked sufficient numbers for any really effective sweeps.

By this time, television cameras had arrived to record and broadcast what was happening. The seeming inability of the police to control the situation or to force the rioters off the streets stimulated the mob to bolder action. The police served as a continuing focus for aggression. They were under a constant barrage of rocks, bottles, and verbal abuse.

During the first night of the riot, the police avoided a total confrontation. It was apparently their strategy to let the rioters blow off steam and then, when things had calmed down, to quietly restore order. But when sunrise came, nineteen policemen had been injured, sixteen other persons were seriously hurt, thirty-four had been arrested, and fifty vehicles, including two fire trucks, had been damaged or burned.

Burning and Looting

The phrase "Burn, baby, burn" was used by "Magnificent Montague," a black disc jockey with a large audience in Los Angeles, to get all his listeners into a receptive mood for the records he played on his program. But as the riot progressed, the phrase became both a rallying cry for participants and a suggestive stimulus to action.

No one knows who set the first building on fire, but as the riot entered its second night the pattern became widespread. At first the rioters continued doing what they had done the night before—stoning and overturning cars and beating motorists. Initially only automobiles were set on fire, but soon neighborhood stores and other buildings were being put to the torch. When firemen responded and attempted to control the flames, they were pelted with rocks and occasionally harassed with sniper fire. The police had the additional duty of trying to protect the firemen who were being attacked.

The area of the riot was expanding block by block. Buildings in a wide area were burning, and authorities began to fear a fire storm of the type that had wrought such terrible damage on cities under bombing attack in World War II. The arson continued for five more days until much of the Watts area looked like the devastated and gutted communities in postwar Europe.

A norm of looting arose at the same time. Windows and storefront barricades were smashed, and blacks entered to carry off whatever they could remove. The most frequent targets were liquor stores and appliance stores. Supermarkets were another favorite; entire families joined in wheeling away carts overflowing with foodstuffs. There was some selectivity in these attacks: stores and businesses known to be owned by blacks were sometimes (but not always) left unscathed.

As has already been suggested, not all the black residents of the area responded to the riot in the same way. Some provided the active hard core. These were mainly younger men, who set the fires, systematically stripped stores, and occasionally sniped at the police and firemen. Others—men, women, and children—were drawn in when free food, clothing, liquor, and appliances were there for the taking. Somehow the fact that these goods belonged to "Whitey" made it seem legitimate to take them. One witness heard a youngster loaded down with booty say, "That don't look like stealing to me. That's just picking up what you need and going."[22] The majority of the residents of the area simply stood on the sidelines and either threw an occasional rock or joined in the general shouting and screaming at the police. Still others refrained from taking any part at all and remained in their homes.

Oberschall has summarized and analyzed the statistics on arrests during the riot. He has concluded that the 3371 adults and 556 juveniles who were arrested did not represent any unusual concentration of the criminal element, brand-new arrivals, school dropouts, or juvenile delinquents. The rioters were apparently drawn from almost all segments of the population of the area, though most were from the lowest socioeconomic stratum.[23]

SOCIAL CONTROL

After much delay, the National Guard was called in to restore order. Doing so was not an easy task. Some ten thousand black rioters had

22. *Time*, August 20, 1965, p. 17.
23. Oberschall, "The Los Angeles Riot of August 1965," pp. 326–329.

In Northern Ireland, tensions between Catholics and Protestants have often erupted into riots. As in the Watts riot, social inequality, frustration, and belief in the brutality of the "powers-that-be" are among the causes of violent collective behavior.

been roaming the streets on a wild rampage for several days. Arriving during the peak of disorders, 13,500 National Guardsmen were required to bring the area under control.

In addition to use of military force, many ordinary citizens in the white community were prepared to take individual action. There was a rush to buy firearms, and those who already had them in their homes brought them out and oiled them "just in case." On the other hand, this riot was quite unlike those in the past in which pitched battles took place between groups of whites and blacks. In Watts (as in the riots that erupted after the murder of Martin Luther King, Jr., in 1968), the main thrust of the violence was against the police and against property in the area, especially that owned by whites. Little or no effort was made to attack white people in other areas of the city.

The riot raged for six days. A total of thirty-four people, most of them black, lost their lives. Thousands were injured. Some $40 million worth of property was destroyed, including six hundred buildings that were burned down or severely damaged. It was the worst civil disorder that had ever taken place in the United States.

The Watts riot illustrates almost every mechanism and concept that sociologists have ever used in attempting to understand collective behavior. Against a configuration of general background conditions, acute local strains developed. These were coupled with shared beliefs in police brutality. When the precipitating incident took place, emotional contagion gradually transformed an assembly of normally law-abiding people into an angry crowd ready to erupt into violence. When rumor concerning police brutality finally touched off the first overt acts of retaliation, rioting behavior diffused quickly through the crowd; ordinary norms became largely ineffective as the newly emerged norms of violence spread rapidly. The riot sustained itself for six full days as a relatively unstructured situation, without institutionalized organization or leadership, in the face of repeated attempts at control.

Although it is possible to view the upheaval in Watts as an isolated incident of collective behavior, it had a significant impact on the nation as a whole. For one thing, it seems to have provided a stimulus to collective violence among blacks in other urban ghettos. During the late 1960s riots very similar to the one in Watts took place in almost every major city of the United States; some were even more devastating than the Watts upheaval in terms of loss of life and property. Together, these separate incidents of collective behavior served to focus the anguished attention of all Americans on the problems inherent in a society in which prejudice and discrimination breed inequality, frustration, and, occasionally, violence.

SOCIAL MOVEMENTS

Social movements share many characteristics with incidents of collective behavior, but they develop and persist over longer periods of time and are relatively more structured. Sometimes they merge into organized group behavior.

A social movement may be defined in a general way as *more-or-less organized collective activity aimed at correcting some perceived inadequacy in existing social arrangements.* Some of the members of society become aware of a shared problem and act collectively over a period of time to solve it. Often incidents of collective behavior and social movements occur simultaneously as different reactions to a particular source of dissatisfaction.

Social movements cover an extremely broad spectrum of human activities. Important social movements in the United States have focused on the abolition of slavery, temperance, unionism, civil rights, resistance to war, feminism, and environmentalism. But there have been literally hundreds of other social movements over the course of American history aimed at solving a wide range of problems. In this section, we will analyze the characteristics of social movements from a sociological perspective and then examine a movement of current significance, the women's movement.[24]

THE SOCIOLOGICAL ANALYSIS OF SOCIAL MOVEMENTS

Although social movements differ greatly from one another, all share certain general characteristics. First, they represent collective attempts to change *unwanted conditions* in society. Judging conditions as unwanted and in need of change implies shared orientations—values, attitudes, beliefs—that serve as a framework for assessment. For example, many Americans collectively define the conditions of sexism in our society as contrary to the American belief in equality and therefore unwanted and in need of change.

Second, those with a given set of convictions about the need for change generally have a *sense of shared identity.* As Lewis M. Killian puts it, "there is a 'we-ness'; a distinction between those who are for and those who are against."[25] When people feel they share a problem, this common bond provides a basis for collective action aimed at solving the problem.[26]

Finally, social movements have many *elements of social organization.* For example, participants in the movement come to share norms and role definitions concerning how they should act or how they should behave toward people who do not share their beliefs. At some point, moreover, organized groups with formally defined goals, norms, and leader-follower roles are likely to emerge. This feature most clearly distinguishes a social movement from collective behavior.

24. For some recent general analyses of social movements, see Joseph R. Gusfield, *Protest, Reform and Revolt: A Reader in Social Movements* (New York: John Wiley & Sons, Inc., 1970); Roberta Ash, *Social Movements in America* (Chicago: Markham Publishing Co., 1972); Anthony Oberschall, *Social Conflict and Social Movements* (Englewood Cliffs, N.J.: Prentice-Hall, Inc., 1973); and John Wilson, *Introduction to Social Movements* (New York: Basic Books, Inc., 1973).

25. Lewis M. Killian, "Social Movements: A Review of the Field," in Robert R. Evans, ed., *Social Movements: A Reader and Source Book* (Chicago: Rand McNally & Co., 1973), p. 16.

26. Hans Toch, *The Social Psychology of Social Movements* (Indianapolis: The Bobbs-Merrill Co., Inc., 1965), p. 5.

VIEWPOINTS THE IMPACT OF THE YOUTH MOVEMENT

■ Only two or three years since what we labeled the "counterculture" indisputably dominated the campus, it has lost social momentum. The counterculture has become an ill-defined thing, increasingly more difficult to discern from what it supposedly "counters." It has gained some concessions and made some, and in this manner its former polar relationship to the old culture is being synthesized, gradually, into a new, single culture.

A wound is healing. Students are more flexible socially than they were a decade ago. Individual freedom is this generation's proclaimed common value, and it has necessitated a general increase in social tolerance. Consequently, society's authority over the individual has decreased and, so too, has the individual's concern with the standards of society. . . .

If we describe what happened during the late '60s as a breakdown in the social contract, then we are presently negotiating a new one. And while I'm certain that the breakdown was not only necessary but inevitable and that our society will be stronger and better for having been through it, I'm not certain what the terms — the values and goals — of the new social contract will be. I do know that they will not be the same as they were. . . .

In any case, property rights, sexual roles, and the social obligations of industry are among some of the major issues that will be resettled in the new social contract. . . .

When today's students are running the world as adults, their present characteristics will no doubt emerge in some recognizable form as the characteristics of established American society.
Doug Campbell
"After the Counterculture, What?"

● At best [the youth movement] was a splendid display of energy, enthusiasm, altruism, and commitment. The Peace Corps, the civil rights movement, the early days of the antiwar protest, the strong vision of the possibilities of a better life — all of these were part of an interlude in American life of which no one need be ashamed.

But at worst the Movement was simplistic, self-righteous, naive, romantic, and inept. It preached relevance and commitment and yet when the going got tough, it abandoned politics. It preached high moral standards and yet decided that stealing was all right when it was called "ripping off," that violence was all right because other people practiced it, that promiscuity was all right because bourgeois marriage was dull, that freedom meant the right to disrupt other men's freedom of speech, that oppression was justified in the name of liberty, and that those who disagreed with the Movement's form of dissent were not to be permitted their own dissent. . . . It denounced virtually everyone else in sight as immoral, but never questioned its own behavior. It wanted to remake the world, but it never had time to formulate clearly its own vision of what the world ought to be, much less to articulately communicate this vision to others. . . .

What, then, has the Movement accomplished? It has justified massive budget cuts for American higher education. It has made "student" a term of opprobrium in many parts of the society. It has messed up some lives with narcotics and embittered, if not a whole generation, at least part of a generation by raising the hope that complex questions could be answered by quick and simple solutions.

In fact, about all it really accomplished in a positive way was to influence the fashions of an era. And while long hair, beards, rock music, marijuana, bell bottom trousers, and nudity are something of a change, they are scarcely a revolution in any sense that the word has ever previously conveyed.
Andrew M. Greeley
"The End of the Movement"

Not all people who share a social movement's broad orientations, goals, and definitions join the formal organizations that develop within it. For example, many who believe that change in the status of women is necessary remain unaffiliated with formal feminist organizations. Such unaffiliated participants are an important part of a movement, for they help determine whether the general public will ultimately accept or reject changes the movement advocates.

Types

Efforts to classify social movements extend well back into the history of sociology, beginning in Europe as early as the 1850s. There are many different classification schemes, most of them rather elaborate. One of the best known is that of Ralph H. Turner and Lewis M. Killian, who distinguished three general types of movements: value-oriented, power-oriented, and participation-oriented.[27] These formulations are not intended to be accurate descriptions of specific movements; rather they are ideal types (page 70) or analytic constructs that attempt to identify clusters of essential characteristics possessed by a variety of movements. An actual social movement may in fact have some characteristics of each type.

According to Turner and Killian, *value-oriented movements* generally focus on seeking changes that will benefit some particular segment of the society. In public statements the changes proposed by such movements are carefully tied to widely approved values, so that attaining the goals of the concerned segment will be seen by the public at large as achieving and supporting values cherished by the society as a whole. For example, the achievement of changes in the status of women is often portrayed by leaders of the women's movement as the attainment of personal freedom and equal rights for every person in our democratic society. Achievement of the goals, therefore, is identified in the movement's program as consistent with significant societal values.

Power-oriented movements are based on a different strategy. The participants have as their primary objective the acquisition of power, recognition, or special status for those leading the movement, and other goals may be sacrificed in the interest of this objective. Tactics may include aggressive actions or violence. Such historical movements as Russian Bolshevism and Nazism are conspicuous examples.

Participation-oriented movements center primarily around the personal satisfactions that come to the individual from the fact of being involved. Messianic cults, for example, await the arrival of a deliverer or some other supernatural intervention. In the late nineteenth century the Ghost Dance cult that spread among certain American Indian tribes promised deliverance from white oppression.

Some social movements seek *reform* within the established social system, whereas others are oriented toward radical modification or overthrow of the system through *revolution*.[28] For example, the movement that sought the adoption of laws prohibiting the manufacture and sale of alcoholic beverages in the United States in the nineteenth and early twentieth centuries was a reform movement, but the social movement that brought Fidel Castro to power in Cuba in 1959 was revolutionary. The civil rights movement of the 1960s had elements of both reform and revolution.

"Life Cycle"

A major problem in defining social movements is that they have quite different characteristics at different stages in their development. At first a social movement may be little more than a diffuse social trend, in which the participants are just beginning to realize that they have common orientations toward a shared problem and may be able to do something about it through collective action. Later, one or more formally organized groups may develop within the movement, and finally the movement may become an institutionalized part of the social order.

27. Ralph H. Turner and Lewis M. Killian, *Collective Behavior* (Englewood Cliffs, N. J.: Prentice-Hall, Inc., 1957) pp. 331–453.
28. Oberschall, *Social Conflict and Social Movements*, pp. 74–84. See also Rex Hopper, "The Revolutionary Process: A Frame of Reference for the Study of Revolutionary Movements," *Social Forces*, 28 (March 1950): 270–279.

Most attempts to describe the typical pattern or "life cycle" of social movements have been modifications or extensions of a scheme first introduced by Carl A. Dawson and Warner E. Gettys in the 1930s.[29] They noted that a social movement first passes through an *incipient* phase, in which its early advocates formulate its essential definitions and orientations. This is followed by a period of *popular excitement* in which the goals and orientations of innovators gradually spread through relevant segments of the population. At some point *coalescence* occurs. One or more groups form around leaders and develop patterns of formal organization, specifying goals, norms, a division of labor, social controls, and so on. As these groups interact with the larger society, *institutionalization* gradually occurs, and the movement becomes a recognized part of society that must somehow be taken into account by the public at large.

Some writers postulate further stages for certain types of movements. Armand Mauss, for example, discusses fragmentation among radical movements and their eventual demise as they are either co-opted or repressed by the larger society.[30] Finally, not every movement passes through all stages. A movement may collapse and vanish at any stage. In fact, a great many do so without ever having exerted a notable effect on the larger society.

Effects

Some social movements have profound effects; others, relatively few. Some accomplish the objectives of their founders; others die before their goals are attained. Many bring about changes in society that were never anticipated by their leaders, their followers, or the public at large.

Few long-term social movements seemed so clearly to have accomplished their objectives as the efforts to establish national prohibition. On January 16, 1919, the Eighteenth Amendment to the Constitution was ratified and the nation entered upon the so-called Noble Experiment. But the unanticipated consequences of prohibition turned out to be much more alarming to most Americans than the conditions it sought to correct. The fourteen years of prohibition were an era of speakeasies and overburdened courts, corrupted public officials, burgeoning organized crime, and growing cynicism among ordinary citizens toward the law, the courts, the police, and hypocrisy in high places. In 1933 the prohibition amendment was repealed.

In general, the changes brought about by social movements tend to be absorbed into the general culture. Whether successful or not, the movements themselves tend to subside after a time, perhaps permanently, perhaps later to revive with new strength. The pacifist movement of the 1930s faded from sight with the outbreak of World War II. Resistance to the Vietnam War "deescalated" along with that conflict. The abolitionist movement saw its goal achieved but left unsolved the moral and social problems that led to the civil rights movement of the 1960s; that movement scored some victories but subsided without achieving its ultimate goals. Often the effects of a social movement go far beyond the showing that it makes at the polling place or even the legislation that it manages to have passed. It plants ideas and influences attitudes, and this effect may lead to renewal and revival, as in the case of the women's movement.

THE WOMEN'S MOVEMENT IN THE UNITED STATES

The current social movement popularly called the women's movement, the feminist movement, the women's liberation movement, or simply women's lib has roots that go well back in history.[31] In 1776 Abigail Adams half-jestingly warned her husband, John, a participant in the Constitutional Convention, that "If perticuliar care and attention is not paid to the Laidies we are determined to foment a Rebelion, and will not hold ourselves bound by any Laws in which we have no voice, or Representation."[32]

29. Carl A. Dawson and Warner E. Gettys, *An Introduction to Sociology*, rev. ed. (New York: The Ronald Press Company, 1935), pp. 689–709.
30. Armond L. Mauss, "On Being Strangled by the Stars and Stripes: The New Left, the Old Left, and the Natural History of American Radical Movements," *Journal of Social Issues*, 27, No. 1 (1971): 183–202.
31. The authors are indebted to Vicki Rose for organizing much of the material that appears in this section.
32. Quoted in Alice S. Rossi, *The Feminist Papers* (New York: Columbia University Press, 1973), Part I.

TOOLS OF SOCIOLOGY
THE STRUCTURED INTERVIEW   S. J. Ball-Rokeach

The structured interview is one of the most widely used sociological measuring techniques. In a structured interview, the interviewer reads the questions, explanations, and probes to the respondent from a printed or mimeographed schedule. The interviewer does not change the wording of the questions or the order in which they are presented. The effect of a structured interview is that the interviewing process is standardized—all interviewers say the same thing, so all respondents hear the same thing. This greatly increases the likelihood that the measuring instrument will be reliable (see page 129).

A researcher who prepares the schedule for a structured interview must construct clear questions and arrange them so that they will not confuse, bore, irritate, or seem threatening to respondents. The questions must be valid (see page 129). Pretesting—that is, conducting trial interviews to check out the quality of the interview schedule—is done. When the schedule is ready, the interviewers are trained to use it and are given specific directions on how to contact the people who will be interviewed. Often interviewers spend as much or more time trying to locate and contact the subjects as they do conducting the interview. A structured interview seldom lasts more than an hour.

A recent study of people's attitudes toward sexual equality made use of the structured interview technique. Following sample design procedures similar to those discussed on page 365, a representative sample of 1429 adult Americans was selected. Questions were designed to measure respondents' attitudes toward some of the issues involved in the women's movement.

The interviewer began by instructing the respondent: "Now I'll read some . . . statements people have made. Please look at this card and tell me which of the answers on the card you would choose for each one." The card given to the respondent had five response categories: Agree Strongly, Agree Somewhat, Disagree Somewhat, Disagree Strongly, and Don't Know.

Statements like the following were read to the respondent, who chose a response category from the card. The interviewer recorded the answers.

1. "A wife should have as much say as her husband in making the important decisions affecting their family."
2. "It would be a good thing if more married couples decided not to have children."
3. "Whether or not to have an abortion is a decision which should be left entirely to the woman involved."
4. "A woman who decides not to get married can be a perfectly normal person and adequate woman."
5. "Women are as capable of being good leaders in industry, politics, education, or science as men."

The majority of the people interviewed held "favorable" attitudes toward sexual equality in that they chose either Strongly Agree or Agree Somewhat for all but the second statement. Men's attitudes were as favorable as women's, and older people's as favorable as younger people's. However, people with high incomes and education expressed more favorable attitudes toward sexual equality than did people with low incomes and education.

The principle disadvantage of the structured interview is its inflexibility. Interviewers may not alter the wording of a question even if they suspect that it is producing invalid responses because respondents find it confusing or interpret it in ways other than that intended. A researcher must weigh this disadvantage against the advantages of precision, reliability, and efficiency.

The study cited above was conducted by S. J. Ball-Rokeach and is being prepared for publication. For an appraisal of the structured interview as a research technique, see Gideon Sjoberg and Roger Nett, *A Methodology for Social Research* (New York: Harper & Row, Inc., 1968), especially p. 193.

During the late nineteenth and early twentieth centuries, some feminists were allied with other social movements, including the temperance, moral reform, and pacifist movements. This photograph is of the Women's Peace Congress at the Hague in 1915.

A movement to improve women's status in England provided stimulus for the rapid growth of feminist sentiment among American women during the early 1800s, and by mid-nineteenth century, feminism had become a full-fledged social movement in the United States. The movement waned after the ratification of the Nineteenth (suffrage) Amendment in 1920 but came back to life again during the late 1960s and is in full development today.

Nineteenth-Century Feminism

As the nineteenth century began, married women in America had almost no legal rights apart from their husbands. They could not sign contracts, have title to their own earnings, vote, hold office, inherit property independently, or have custody of their own children. Divorce was all but impossible to obtain without their husbands' consent. In fact, their legal status was little different from that of indentured servants.[33]

The incipient stage of the original feminist movement began early in the nineteenth century. Feminist ideas were gradually diffused among a growing audience of both sexes through the work of such pioneer advocates of women's rights as Hannah Mather Crocker, who in 1818 published a plea for education for women, and Emma Hart Willard, who established the Troy Female Seminary in 1821.

33. An excellent history and documentation of these issues and the subsequent struggle to change them is contained in Eleanor Flexner, *Century of Struggle: The Women's Rights Movement in the United States* (New York: Atheneum, 1973).

The contemporary women's movement is composed of a variety of organizations, and participants often have somewhat different goals. The reform branch of the movement works through established channels to eradicate sex discrimination. Among the goals of this branch is greater representation of women in politics and government, and one strategy to achieve this goal has been the participation of women in political conventions (above). Radical feminists, by contrast, wish to reshape—rather than reform—societal institutions. They have concentrated on demonstrations (top) and other techniques of highlighting the oppression of women, including consciousness-raising groups (right).

The movement for equal rights began to coalesce in the 1840s. Partly as a result of earlier involvement in the antislavery movement, many women had come to see the necessity of organizing to overcome their own servitude. The beginning of the institutionalized phase of the feminist movement was the first Women's Rights Convention at Seneca Falls, New York, in 1848; the organizers included Lucretia Mott and Elizabeth Cady Stanton. At the convention, they presented a Declaration of Sentiments listing the "repeated injuries and usurpations on the part of man toward woman."[34] The convention adopted a series of resolutions calling for, among other things, economic, legal, and educational equality and the right to vote. These resolutions became the formal goals of the nineteenth-century women's movement.

Various other conventions were held and several groups formed as the movement became nationwide. Radical reformers tried to broaden the goals of the movement to include vast social change; others focused on the problems of the working-class woman; and still others allied themselves with the temperance and moral reform movements that flourished during the late nineteenth and early twentieth centuries. But the main thrust of the movement, under the leadership of such women as Elizabeth Cady Stanton, Susan B. Anthony, and Carrie Chapman Catt, was focused on gaining the vote. Finally in 1918 Congress passed the Nineteenth Amendment. Two years later ratification was achieved.

Although feminism waned with the ratification of the Nineteenth Amendment, it did not disappear entirely. Instead, as Alice Rossi has suggested, women "retreated into private consolidation of the gains made by their mothers."[35]

Rather than pressing for more political and legal rights, women pressed for equality within their marriages, sought the advantages of higher education, and in rising numbers joined the labor force. But it was not until the 1960s that feminism emerged again as a major social movement.

The Current Movement

The revival of feminism in the 1960s was apparently spurred in part by the findings of the President's Commission on the Status of Women, formed in 1961 to review the status of women's legal rights and economic opportunities. The Commission's report, released in 1963, documented numerous inequities and led to the formation of comparable commissions in all fifty states. These commissions, as well as the passage of the Civil Rights Act of 1964, in which discrimination in employment on the basis of sex was outlawed, can be said to have set the stage for revival of the movement to obtain equality for American women.

Also important to that revival was the book *The Feminine Mystique* by Betty Friedan, published in 1963. Friedan wrote about the plight of the middle-class American housewife, cut off from doing anything society considered important and pressured into conforming to the stereotype of the "feminine" homemaker.[36] The book became a best-seller, and once more feminism began to diffuse throughout the country.

The women's movement today includes many types of organizations and participants, representing a variety of goals and strategies for achieving them. There are two main branches to the movement.[37] The *reform* branch has for the most part worked through established political and legal channels to eradicate sex discrimination in all major social institutions. The *radical* branch, by contrast, has aimed most of its activities at making women more conscious of being an oppressed group. In general, members of the radical branch see a need for reshaping societal institutions in fundamental ways rather than merely reforming existing institutions.[38]

34. Reprinted in Rossi, *The Feminist Papers,* Part II.
35. Ibid, Part IV.
36. Betty Friedan, *The Feminine Mystique* (New York: W. W. Norton & Company, Inc., 1963).
37. The distinctions made between these branches are adapted from Judith Hole and Ellen Levine, *Rebirth of Feminism* (New York: Quadrangle Books, Inc., 1971); and Jo Freeman, "The Origins of the Women's Liberation Movement," in *Changing Women in a Changing Society*, ed. Joan Huber (Chicago: The University of Chicago Press, 1973).
38. Anne Koedt, Ellen Levine, Anita Rapone, eds., *Radical Feminism* (New York: Quadrangle Books, Inc., 1973), pp. 271–390.

The coalescence stage of the reform branch of the movement came with the formation of the National Organization for Women (NOW) in 1966 by Betty Friedan and others. The largest of the reform groups, NOW has worked for such goals as ratification of the Equal Rights Amendment (passed by Congress in 1972), development of child-care centers, legalization of abortion, the appointment of more women to positions in government, and the election of more women to political office.

The radical branch of the women's movement has had a distinct history of its own. Its participants have tended to work outside established political and legal channels for effecting change, and they have not attempted to become formally organized on a nationwide scale.

Many of the women identified with the radical branch were involved during the 1960s with the draft resistance, student protest, and civil rights movements, and this fact may help explain not only their strategy but also their concern with making women more conscious that they are oppressed. In working for the liberal and New Left causes of the sixties, women found that they were denied equal status with their male counterparts, even though their causes were oriented toward equal rights and freedom. Many resented the fact that, as "chicks," they were assigned such chores as typing, making coffee, cleaning up, and providing the males with sexual gratification. Many also resented being pushed "up front" during demonstrations so that television cameras could record the brutality of the police to females.

The radical branch of the women's movement has never fully coalesced, but during the late 1960s it provided impetus for the formation of many local and informal feminist groups. The strategy of such groups included highly visible "zap actions," such as disrupting the 1968 Miss America Beauty Contest. Methods learned in the student activists' fights and the civil rights movement were carried over into women's liberation.

The radical branch has continued to concentrate on demonstrations, disruptions of "sexist" events, rallies, teach-ins, boycotts, and other techniques for highlighting the oppression of women.[39]

The long-term effects of the contemporary women's movement remain to be seen. Many of the reforms that NOW and similar women's organizations have been pressing for—equal pay, equal educational and job opportunities, greater political representation, and so on—are slowly taking place. The impact of the radical branch is more difficult to measure. It appears that many women have become conscious of their social subjugation and have readjusted their personal goals as a result of this realization—by seeking better education and better jobs, by continuing to work after marriage, by deciding not to marry, by insisting that their husbands share the work of homemaking and child raising, and, more generally, by demanding to be treated as individuals rather than as "women."

But as earlier chapters of this text have made clear, sex differences remain very important in our society's system of ranking, in its division of labor, and in its system of social relationships more generally. Although our societal institutions will be further modified as a result of the women's movement, traditional patterns probably will not entirely disappear.[40]

39. Barbara B. Polk, "Women's Liberation: Movement for Equality," in Constantina Safilios-Rothschild, ed., *Toward a Sociology of Women* (Lexington, Mass.: Xerox Publishing Co., 1972).
40. For an analysis of some possible long-range effects of the women's movement, especially as they relate to economic and family patterns, see Judith Blake, "The Changing Status of Women in Developed Countries," *Scientific American*, September 1974, esp. pp. 144–147.

SUMMARY

Collective behavior differs from group behavior in being relatively unstructured. Although collective behavior takes many different forms, the study of crowds has been a focus of special interest. Each of the several types of crowds identified by Herbert Blumer — the casual crowd, the conventionalized crowd, the active crowd, and the expressive crowd — has distinctive characteristics. The casual crowd, for example, is almost wholly unstructured, whereas the conventionalized crowd has a loose pattern of norms and roles and also a system of social control.

Gustave LeBon's classic analysis of crowd psychology provided many insights into the dynamics of collective behavior. Contemporary theorists have refined LeBon's explanation and added to it by noting the part played by social as well as psychological factors in the development of riots, panics, and other dramatic instances of collective behavior. In the present chapter, the social dynamics of collective behavior have been examined in terms of structural inadequacies, emotional contagion, and the diffusion of beliefs, interpretations, and actions. These concepts have been illustrated by an analysis of the Watts riot.

Social movements have many elements in common with incidents of collective behavior, representing another form of collective response to some perceived inadequacy in existing social arrangements. However, social movements develop and persist over extended periods of time and often become quite highly structured. Social movements differ greatly from one another, and they also have quite different characteristics at different stages in their "life cycle." The women's movement in the United States illustrates both the general characteristics of social movements and their typical pattern of development.

14
Mass Communication

Societies, like other human groups, are in a very basic sense systems of communication. They depend not only on exchanges of symbols between members in face-to-face situations but also on the use of various communication *media* for encoding, transmitting, and receiving messages. A medium of communication can be as simple as a clay tablet with symbolic marks pressed onto it or as technically complicated as television. Today's *mass* media (e.g., radio, television, newspapers, magazines, and movies) are capable of reaching millions of people very rapidly.

The media of communication available in a society help determine its potentials for social and cultural change.[1] This point becomes clear when we consider the impact of the development of writing. The earliest written symbols beyond mere pictorial representation were in the form of elaborate glyphs, carved on temples and other monuments. The great limitation of this form of communication was that such "documents" were not easily transported; stone had the capacity to endure through *time,* but could not be moved readily across *space.* Clay tablets were somewhat more portable but still left much to be desired. Then, about 2500 years before Christ, the Egyptians discovered how to make a kind of durable paper from papyrus, a reed found growing in the Nile delta. Fresh green stems of the reed were cut and stripped, sliced into thick strips, laid parallel to each other, and pounded into a single mass that was then pressed out and dried. Long rolls could be prepared by joining one sheet to another. The glyphs set down on papyrus with ink and brush were gradually simplified, making writing easier and faster.

With the acquisition of a communications technology based upon a portable medium and a system of symbols that could be quickly set down, the door was opened to great social and cultural changes.[2] By 2000 B.C., papyrus was

1. See Alan Wells, ed., *Mass Communications: A World View* (Palo Alto, Calif.: National Press Books, 1974), esp. pp. 11–17; also Ray E. Heibert, Donald F. Ungurait, and Thomas W. Bohn, *Mass Media: An Introduction to Modern Communication* (New York: David McKay Co., Inc., 1974), esp. pp. 383–398.
2. An excellent discussion of media and change in ancient societies is found in Harold A. Innis, *Empire and Communications* (Toronto: University of Toronto Press, 1972), p. 14.

widely used in Egypt to transmit written orders and to record information of all kinds. The central administration employed an army of scribes, who became a privileged class under the control of the elite. A body of sacred writing was developed. Successful treatments for diseases were recorded, and observations and interpretations of natural phenomena were written down. Gradually, people were freed from the burdensome task of having to remember and pass on by word of mouth the wisdom of the past. Ideas could now be stored, to be drawn upon by subsequent generations.

Paper began to replace papyrus and parchment in the Islamic world during the eighth century, and its use slowly spread to Christian Europe. But written communication remained in the hands of religious, political, and intellectual elites until the invention of the printing press in the fifteenth century. This breakthrough in communication technology made possible the spread of information and ideas to increasing numbers of people and thus opened the way for a growing challenge to established religious, political, and economic institutions. In a very real sense, it marked the beginning of the transformation of medieval into modern society.

In studying the significance of mass communication in contemporary society, sociologists have been concerned with such questions as the following: How are systems of mass media organized, and how have they developed differently in different societal settings? What are the key variables in the process by which mass communication takes place? What kinds of direct and indirect effects do the media have on individuals and on society in general? And how are the media related to the processes by which public opinion is formed? In the following sections we will examine each of these issues in turn.

3. Daniel Lerner, *The Passing of Traditional Society* (New York: The Free Press, 1958).
4. Melvin L. DeFleur and Sandra Ball-Rokeach, *Theories of Mass Communication*, 3rd ed. (New York: David McKay Co., Inc., 1975).

SYSTEMS OF MASS COMMUNICATION

Only during the twentieth century has technology advanced sufficiently to permit the development of mass communication devices that can span great distances and bring the same message to huge numbers of people simultaneously. Today, motion pictures, radio, television, and printed matter—newspapers, books, and magazines—are reaching hundreds of millions of ordinary people. Few societies remain untouched by mass communication.[3]

The mass communication system of a country is made up of the totality of the media through which relatively large audiences are quickly reached with a given message. Each specific medium constitutes a somewhat separate subsystem, and each subsystem is made up of a complicated set of interlocking components.[4] For example, the medium will operate very differently and is likely to produce different content depending upon whether *ownership* is vested in a private corporation, a government bureau, a political party, or some other social organization or individual. Much will also depend on who is responsible for the actual *production* of content. Depending upon the society, this may be a government ministry or some combination of private groups such as broadcasting companies, newspaper syndicates, advertising agencies, and commercial sponsors. Similarly, *control* over content may be in the hands of individual editors, a government regulatory agency, or the management of a privately owned company; content may also be subject to codes and regulations set up by censorship boards, owners, or advertisers. The components that *distribute* content to consumers are another important part of the system. They may have freedom to select or edit material from their sources (e.g., local television stations in the United States can accept or reject particular programs distributed by a national network) or they may be required to transmit content directly from producers without alteration (e.g., newspapers in some countries must print stories provided by the government).

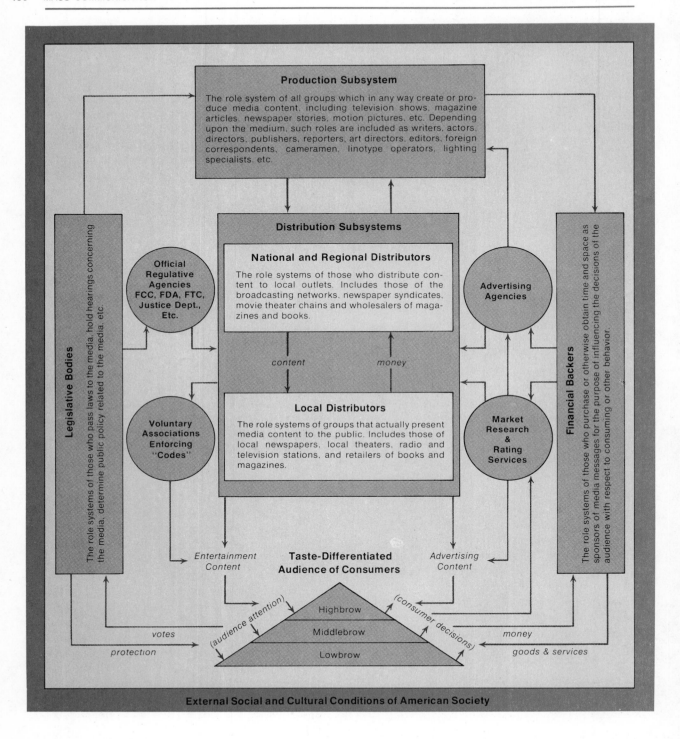

Production Subsystem

The role system of all groups which in any way create or produce media content, including television shows, magazine articles, newspaper stories, motion pictures, etc. Depending upon the medium, such roles are included as writers, actors, directors, publishers, reporters, art directors, editors, foreign correspondents, cameramen, linotype operators, lighting specialists, etc.

Distribution Subsystems

National and Regional Distributors

The role systems of those who distribute content to local outlets. Includes those of the broadcasting networks, newspaper syndicates, movie theater chains and wholesalers of magazines and books.

content   *money*

Local Distributors

The role systems of groups that actually present media content to the public. Includes those of local newspapers, local theaters, radio and television stations, and retailers of books and magazines.

Legislative Bodies

The role systems of those who pass laws to the media, hold hearings concerning the media, determine public policy related to the media, etc.

Official Regulative Agencies FCC, FDA, FTC, Justice Dept., Etc.

Voluntary Associations Enforcing "Codes"

Advertising Agencies

Market Research & Rating Services

Financial Backers

The role systems of those who purchase or otherwise obtain time and space as sponsors of media messages for the purpose of influencing the decisions of the audience with respect to consuming or other behavior.

Entertainment Content

Taste-Differentiated Audience of Consumers

Advertising Content

(audience attention)   *(consumer decisions)*

Highbrow

Middlebrow

Lowbrow

votes   *money*

protection   *goods & services*

External Social and Cultural Conditions of American Society

SOURCE: Melvin L. DeFleur and Sandra Ball-Rokeach, *Theories of Mass Communication*, 3rd ed. (New York: David McKay Co., Inc., 1975).

Figure 14.1. MASS COMMUNICATION IN AMERICAN SOCIETY

Finally, the characteristics of *audiences* make a great difference in the mass communication process. A given audience may be highly educated or largely illiterate, stratified or relatively undifferentiated, affluent or poor. It may be concentrated in urban centers or scattered over a vast territory. An audience may or may not be able to feed information back to the content producers in such a way that its interests and needs can be taken into account (see Figure 14.1). If the characteristics of the audience are ignored, communication is almost certain to break down.

As we have previously noted, the means of communication available within a society help shape its general culture, its principal values, its interests and tastes, and the nature of its social institutions. And a society's culture and patterns of social organization, in turn, help shape its system of communication. Both kinds of relationships can be illustrated by a brief comparison of mass communication systems in two of the world's major societies, the United States and the Soviet Union.

THE MEDIA IN THE UNITED STATES

With the exception of printing, of course, the media that make up the complex mass communication system of the United States are for the most part products of the twentieth century. The daily newspaper reached its peak of circulation around the time of the First World War, when more newspapers were sold per American household than at any time since (see Figure 14.2). Household radio was not a reality until the 1920s, and it did not reach its "golden age" until the 1940s. Television, the newest of our major media, was adopted by the American public as recently as the 1950s.

The Early Press

Our modern newspapers developed out of the Colonial Press, as the papers of the thirteen colonies are collectively called.[5] Small in size and circulation, these papers were written for and read by an educated elite and were devoted

5. Edwin Emery, *The Press and America,* 3rd ed. (New York: Prentice-Hall, Inc., 1972).

more to political commentaries and literary essays than to news as we think of it today. They were also expensive, with subscriptions paid in advance by the year.

One of the most significant heritages of the period of the Colonial Press was the conviction that the government should not have the power to restrict the communication of ideas. For generations, political essayists and pamphleteers in England had been hampered by prior government censorship and fear of government reprisal. Englishmen on both sides of the Atlantic resented this control. In the American colonies a system of licensing and prior censorship was intended to prevent "seditious libel," as unwelcome political criticism in print was officially known. In 1735 an immigrant printer, John Peter Zenger, was put on trial in New York for publishing seditious libel in his weekly journal. Leading citizens rallied to his support, and his lawyer, Andrew Hamilton, argued with consummate skill that speaking and writing the truth was so basic a freedom that the jury should take matters into its own hands, regardless of the existing laws against criticism of the government.

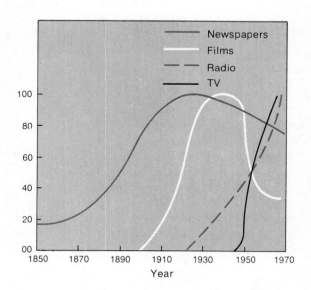

SOURCE: Melvin L. DeFleur, *Theories of Mass Communication,* 2nd ed. (New York: David McKay Co., Inc., 1970). p. 74. The units on the vertical axis have been "standardized" so that 100 percent represents the maximum use each medium has ever achieved. This procedure facilitates comparison among curves

Figure 14.2. DIFFUSION CURVES FOR NEWSPAPERS, FILMS, RADIO, AND TELEVISION

The National Police Gazette *was one of many nineteenth-century American periodicals devoted to sensationalism, muckraking, and melodramatic accounts of events of people's lives. This illustration, which appeared in the periodical in the middle of the nineteenth century, was entitled "Saved by His Sweetheart" and helped tell the story of "The birthday present which protected a Long Island lover's purse and discomfited a desperate footpad."*

SINS OF NEW YORK

The jury did so, and Zenger was acquitted. Although laws against seditious libel remained in force for many years and editors continued to be harassed by colonial governors, the Zenger case is often cited as a turning point in the struggle for freedom of the press.[6]

In 1791 the First Amendment to the Constitution was ratified, prohibiting Congress from abridging the freedom of the press. Thus, almost from the birth of the nation, the press in the United States has developed under the protection of the Bill of Rights.

The Mass Press

In the 1830s a new kind of newspaper appeared on the streets of New York. It sold for a penny, which was less than it cost to produce. The publishers made their profit by selling advertising space. The concept of "news" was redefined.

Less attention was given to complex political and economic issues, and more and more space was devoted to the kinds of things ordinary people liked to read about. High on the list were crimes, accidents, human interest stories, reports of bizarre happenings, and exposés of sin in high places.

By the end of the nineteenth century, newspaper publishing empires had been built up by such men as William Randolph Hearst and Joseph Pulitzer. Huge metropolitan dailies and newspaper chains engaged in bitter circulation wars. Under the impact of this competitive struggle, concern over ethics and responsibility in publishing declined sharply. Yellow journalism came into its own as the century ended.

6. Edwin Emery et al., *Introduction to Mass Communications,* 2nd ed. (New York: Dodd, Mead & Company, 1965).

Theirs was a shrieking, gaudy, sensation-loving, devil-may-care kind of journalism which lured the reader by any possible means. It seized upon the techniques of writing, illustrating, and printing, which were the prides of the new journalism, and turned them to perverted uses. It made the high drama of life a cheap melodrama, and it twisted the facts of each day into whatever form seemed best suited to produce sales for the howling newsboy.[7]

Another splurge of sensationalism marked the 1920s, but the Depression years had a sobering effect on the press. With the passing of decades, business failures and mergers reduced the number of newspapers in America. Competition also decreased: many cities soon had only a single paper or two papers with a single owner. And frequently, thanks to the growth of newspaper chains and wire services, the "local" paper was owned by a corporation based a thousand miles away, and it filled its news columns with material supplied by a syndicate.

The distinguishing characteristics of newspaper publishing in the United States are clearly a product of the societal context within which the system developed—a context based upon American cultural values, which support *private enterprise* and the *profit* motive. These values, plus the heritage of the Colonial Press and the protection of the Constitution, give individual and corporate owners of the press a maximum of freedom from governmental restraint. A newspaper obtains its profit not from its readers but from those who wish to attract the attention of potential customers to their advertising messages. To capture this attention, it gives its readers what it believes they want. In short, newspaper content is aimed at selling newspapers and attracting attention to advertisements in order to make money.

The Broadcast Media

The broadcast media in the United States have had a very different history.[8] The federal government controls the frequencies, transmitting power, and transmitting times of radio and television stations through the Federal Communica-

7. Emery, *The Press and America*, pp. 415–416.
8. Gleason L. Archer, *History of Radio to 1926* (New York: The American Historical Society, Inc., 1938).

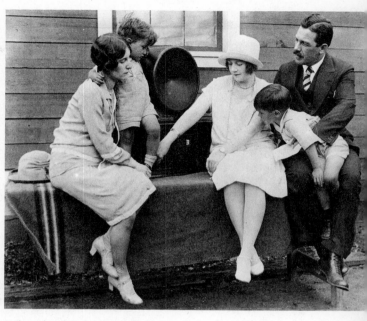

Before the development of television, as this 1927 photograph suggests, the radio provided entertainment—music, drama, comedy—for American families.

tions Commission (FCC). During the 1920s, when the uncontrolled growth of broadcasting produced chaotic conditions, Congress established the principle that the *air waves belong to the people*. Thus a federal agency could issue licenses and control transmitters in the interests of the people. There are also numerous state and local statutes pertaining to broadcasting.

In spite of these controls, however, the parallels between the broadcast media and newspaper publishing are numerous. The FCC is supposed to award a license to broadcast when such action is "in the public interest, convenience, or necessity"; and when frequencies and channels are available, requests for licenses are seldom refused. The FCC is supposed to encourage competition, and it is prohibited from censoring program content. Under certain conditions, broadcasters are required to provide equal time to political parties, and they must agree to offer a certain amount of "public service" broadcasting, to refrain from using obscene material, and to limit the amount of time devoted to commercials.

But like newspapers, radio and television stations are privately owned and make their profits from advertising. (Exceptions are the stations that telecast programs produced by the Public Broadcasting System or that broadcast music and discussions without "commercials," depending on their audiences for financial support.) And generally advertisers have an even greater influence on content in broadcasting than in newspaper publishing. The newspaper publisher sells empty space to the advertiser and provides the news stories, columns, and features that are expected to attract readers. The broadcaster not only sells empty time to the advertiser but allows the advertiser to choose the material—the program—that will expose audiences to the commercials.

One major by-product of this system is that the central emphasis of the broadcast media in the United States is on *entertainment*. Generally, commercial sponsors select program content that seems likely to appeal to a broad spectrum of the population in order to win the attention of the greatest possible number of potential consumers for their products. Thus, the system continually produces a "mass culture" keyed to popular tastes. There has been much controversy and debate both among students of the media and among the public at large concerning the effects of such programming on the tastes and value systems of audience members.

"Freedom of the Press"

Most Americans are more or less aware that the Constitution protects the freedom of the press. But the nature of that freedom has remained rather ambiguous, meaning one thing to one group and something quite different to others. Numerous court actions and controversies have introduced great complexities into the seemingly simple ideas expressed in the First Amendment: "Congress shall make no law . . . abridging the freedom . . . of the press."

Those who pressed for adoption of the First Amendment would no doubt be astonished to learn that in the late twentieth century their principle would be evoked as a legal basis for such matters as public showings of "explicit" sex films. Similarly, they had no way of anticipating the problems that would arise because television advertisers are often less than candid concerning the merits of their products or because "national security" could be used as an argument against the disclosure of governmental information.

In fact, efforts were made very early in our history to silence a hostile press. The Sedition Acts of 1798 threatened fines or imprisonment for anyone who published anything damaging to the reputation of Congress or the President. The excuse given by the Federalist party in power was that pro-French Republicans were threatening internal security. While the chief effects of the Sedition Acts were to hasten the downfall of the Federalists and strengthen popular support for a free press, relations between representatives of the news media and agencies of government—from the police and the courts to the President—have often been strained if not hostile. It is commonly said that the news media in the United States are in an adversary role vis-à-vis government at all levels.

According to this view, representatives of the news media feel it their duty to protect the public's "right to know"—to keep readers and viewers and listeners informed about what government is up to at all times. Representatives of government, on the other hand, seek to control the information that reaches the public, sometimes because it would be embarrassing to the individual or agency or political party involved, sometimes because it could upset delicate negotiations or embarrass the United States internationally or genuinely endanger national security.

As crusaders against government secrecy, dishonesty, and corruption, the news media have in some instances helped make history. During the unpopular war in Vietnam, it was the press that revealed the My Lai massacre. The *New York Times* published the so-called "Pentagon Papers," and the *Washington Post* was largely responsible for preventing the Watergate break-in from being dismissed and forgotten. But by accepting the role of moral watchdogs, the news media accept great responsibility. In some cases, editors and publishers set themselves up as final judges of what is in the best interest of the country. For example the *New York Times* knew of plans for the Bay of Pigs invasion before the action took place. If it had decided to break the story, a near disaster might have been avoided. But suppose that a newspaper knew in advance of plans for the invasion of Normandy in World War II and had decided that this was information the public had a right to know.

Furthermore, the news media do not consistently play an adversary role with respect to government: newspeople and politicians often cooperate in managing the news at its source. Every reporter knows of wrongdoing by government officials that is never printed or broadcast. The reasons for the silence range from personal sympathy to personal corruption, but usually they are in some way related to the fact that political reporters and political officeholders need each other. In return for the news tips on which they depend, media personnel further the interests of government officials not only by remaining silent about wrongdoings but also by passing on as "news" what are actually public-relations handouts designed to aggrandize the accomplishments or increase the popularity of the political figures involved.

Other types of conflict can be seen concerning the questions of freedom and responsibility of the press. With respect to judicial processes, for example, how does the right of the news media to publicize details of a criminal case balance against the right of the accused to a fair trial? And how does the right of reporters to keep confidential their sources of information balance against the right of the courts to subpoena evidence? There is also the broader question of what limits there are, if any, to the public's "right to know," particularly as it concerns the right to know about people who are not in public life. At what point does the "right to know" (to say nothing of "need to know" or even

How explicit must a film be to be classified as "pornographic"? Does "freedom of the press" give theater owners the right to show pornographic movies? Currently, each community can decide for itself whether a film is pornographic and whether it can be shown in the community.

"want to know") violate the individual's right to privacy? Like other fundamental democratic freedoms, freedom of the press in the United States has been threatened by abuse from those who uphold it as well as by attack from those who fear it.

MASS COMMUNICATION IN THE SOVIET UNION

While American culture includes a belief in the right to free communication, such a belief is not a part of the Russian tradition.[9] The autocratic regimes of the czars controlled the press every bit as firmly as the Soviet government does today. However, a modern mass communication system did not begin to develop in Russia much before the Communists took power. It has been shaped, then, largely around Soviet goals and philosophy.

9. The present section is based on: Mark W. Hopkins, "Media, Party and Society in Russia," in Wells, *Mass Communications;* Alex Inkeles, *Public Opinion in Soviet Russia: A Study in Mass Persuasion,* 2nd ed. (Cambridge, Mass.: Harvard University Press, 1950); Gayle O. Hollander, "Recent Developments in Soviet Radio and Television News Reporting," *Public Opinion Quarterly,* 31, No. 3 (Fall 1967): 359–365; Mark W. Hopkins, "Lenin, Stalin, Khrushchev: Three Concepts of the Press," *Journalism Quarterly,* 42, No. 4 (Autumn 1965): 523–531; and Richard R. Fagen, "Mass Media Growth: A Comparison of Communist and Other Countries," *Journalism Quarterly,* 61, No. 4 (Autumn 1964): 563–572.

These photographs point up the fact that the Soviet press functions primarily as an arm of the Communist party. The picture at the top was released in April 1969, by a Czech news agency. It shows the former leader of the Czech republic, Alexander Dubček, standing beside President Ludvik Svoboda, who is holding his hat in his hand. The second photograph was later released in the Soviet Union. Note that buildings have moved and Dubček has disappeared, except for one well-polished toe.

Historical Background

During the period immediately following World War I, the entire Russian social structure underwent violent upheaval. In 1917 the czarist government was overthrown, and the Bolsheviks, led by Nikolai Lenin, seized control. The leaders of the new government set about to consolidate their power and to unify the nation around a new ideological system.

The unification of the Soviet peoples would have been a formidable task under any circumstances. The territory that now makes up the Union of Soviet Socialist Republics constitutes about one sixth of the earth's surface. Here live more than 240 million people, representing about 140 distinct ethnic groups and a great variety of religions, languages, life-styles, and degrees of technological advancement. All of this implies an audience of mass communication that is in some ways unique. The population of the USSR is obviously one of great heterogeneity; it ranges from nomadic illiterates to educated urbanites. Social differentiation was even more pronounced in the 1920s, the first decade of the new regime, and it was this population that Lenin was determined to weld into a nation that would be one the the world's great powers.

The Goals of the Soviet Media

Lenin understood that the Russian people had to be led toward accepting the party's goals and decisions, and he saw clearly that the mass media of communication were an important element in achieving these ends. This meant that the media had to be in the hands of those who were guiding the revolution. "Class consciousness" had to be developed among the people. They also needed education, and they needed to be made selectively aware of the rich cultural traditions of their past. Moreover, communication links had to be established between the leaders and the masses so that political policies and decisions could be communicated and explained to every eye and ear.

From the beginning, then, the party was seen as a kind of teacher whose task was to educate and indoctrinate the masses concerning their political thought, their national directions, and their social destiny. All decisions were to be worked out by party leaders and communicated to the people via the press and later by radio and television in order to obtain compliance and support. To achieve these goals, a governmental agency was established, under the firm control of the top party leaders, to oversee all the mass communication media. Alex Inkeles has described this organization as it operated during the late 1940s:

The Department of Propaganda and Agitation of the Central Committee is charged with general responsibility for molding and mobilizing public opinion in the Soviet Union so that it will effectively support and facilitate the achievement of those long- and short-range ends which the party leadership has defined as the goals of the nation as a whole. It unifies and gives central direction to the vast and multiform activities designed to influence public opinion which are carried on by the party, and the government and public agencies under the party's supervision.[10]

There has been little significant change in this organization or its goals up to the present time.[11]

Private ownership of the media does not exist in the Soviet Union. All of the various facilities for the production and distribution of books, films, radio and television broadcasts, magazines, and newspapers are operated by a complex of governmental bureaus whose task is defined by a mandate from the party.

The Soviet Press

Control of the press has been maintained by three principal means. First, editorial personnel are selected on the basis of their loyalty to the regime. This eliminates the need for an elaborate and cumbersome system of censorship. Second, party directives provide guidelines within which the press must operate. Third, formal supervisory machinery monitors the press and sees that it is carrying out the policies of the party within the system of rules and regulations it is supposed to follow. Such surveillance exists not only at the national level but at regional and even local community levels. This system ensures that the press functions in the manner intended—as an instrument of social control, as a transmitter of political ideology, and as a means for the selective dissemination of information.[12]

10. Inkeles, *Public Opinion in Soviet Russia*, p. 30.
11. Hopkins, "Lenin, Stalin, Khrushchev," pp. 527–531.
12. Ibid.

Broadcasting in Russia

Of all the mass media, none contrasts more sharply with its American counterpart in its pattern of historical development than the Soviet system of broadcasting. This system was developed during the period prior to World War II, when Russian energies were being devoted mainly to the establishment of heavy industry, to the building of a vast military machine, and to the reorganization of agriculture. Little was left in the way of resources for producing consumer goods such as individual radios. Yet it was important for the government to reach the masses with broadcasts as a means of ensuring ideological commitment and compliance. Millions of people had to be reached, and vast distances had to be spanned. The financial, demographic, and geographical difficulties, plus the urgency of the party's political goals, gave rise to a unique system.

Soviet broadcasting was not conceived of as a means of providing entertainment but rather as a channel of communication between the party and the masses. By the 1940s the system consisted of a number of powerful radio transmitting stations in all the principal urban centers and local communities. These formed a tightly controlled network. While some broadcasts originated from regional centers, most originated from Moscow itself, to be rebroadcast within a given region. Local stations originated some material, but they were under careful supervision.

Soviet citizens did not receive these broadcasts in their homes on their own radio sets, at least not during the decade following the Second World War. Instead, a powerful receiver served as a local "radio diffusion exchange." The broadcasts it received were then sent *by wire* into individual homes, apartments, factories, barracks, etc., which were equipped with simple speakers. The radio diffusion exchange served from a few dozen to several hundred subscribers in this manner.

This system had several advantages from the Soviet point of view. First, and most important, it was far cheaper to establish than a system in which each family would be provided with its own receiver. (The average Russian family at that time could barely afford the small subscription fee; to purchase a radio set would have been out of the question.) Second, the system permitted maximum control over what the Soviet people would hear. This was felt to be essential during the authoritarian regime of Joseph Stalin. Broadcasts from foreign lands could be received only on clandestine sets, and the government could partially block such reception by "jamming" the signals. Third, the system permitted broadcasting to large groups over public-address systems, and this encouraged discussion under the direction of local leaders who could interpret and explain the message according to party doctrine.

The system was well adapted to bringing educational and cultural content, as well as political doctrine, to a very wide audience. The technical properties of the broadcasts were excellent: the central receiver was of high quality, and transmission through wires did not lower fidelity appreciably.

In more recent years, the radio system has been greatly expanded, and television broadcasts have become popular. In 1974 there were 125 stations, mainly located in large cities.[13] Foreign broadcasts are now regularly received in the Soviet Union by those who own shortwave receivers. Their number is unknown but is thought to be substantial. After 1963 the jamming of outside broadcasts ceased except in times of crisis, as during the Soviet invasion of Czechoslovakia in 1968.

Politics Versus Profits

The changes in the Russian broadcasting system in the post-Stalin era have had a substantial impact on the handling of news by all Soviet media. As people became able to receive reports from foreign broadcasts, the Soviet approach to reporting had to be "liberalized." News was released faster, and less reliance was placed upon centralized party-line interpretations. But much of the old system persists. The media are still defined by party officials as agencies for furthering the Marxist-Leninist theories

13. Hopkins, "Media, Party and Society," p. 67.

upon which the system was founded. The only group whose members are seen as legitimate interpreters of these theories is the Communist party. The main purpose of the media remains that of supporting the ongoing ideology of the party.

One significant change in the Soviet mass media is the increased use of advertising. In the days of chronic shortages of consumer goods, there was little need to create demands, but in recent times many shortages have ended. The supply of watches, dresses, canned goods, film, and other products often exceeds demand, and advertising has come to be recognized as a necessary marketing tool. At present, not only do more advertisements appear in Soviet newspapers (except *Pravda* and *Izvestia*), but posters, billboards, and handbills also present commercial messages. Even radio and television carry commercials.[14]

But while advertising is used to reduce surpluses, it does not represent private enterprise. Overall, the Soviet system of mass communication is not concerned with private profit. The sharp contrast between the Soviet and American systems can be understood only in terms of differing national values, traditions, and ideologies that are products of distinctive historical developments within societies with very different social and political institutions.

MASS COMMUNICATION AS PROCESS

During the early part of this century, students of the mass communication process saw it as a one-way relationship. They assumed that a message transmitted via one of the mass media would reach large numbers of unrelated individuals; that all members of the audience would receive it more or less uniformly; and that all would act upon it in more or less the same way. But starting in the 1920s discoveries by psychologists concerning individual differences in personal organization and behavior forced mass communication theorists to modify their earlier conceptualizations. It was noted that people's needs, attitudes, values, prior knowledge about a topic, and numerous other factors played a part in determining what media content would attract them and also how they would interpret and react to what they heard, saw, or read.

Considerable progress was made in the development of communication theory during the 1930s and 1940s, as the significance of psychological variables became increasingly understood. But the importance of social variables was still largely overlooked. Communication theorists, like sociologists generally, tended to assume that with the transition to "mass society," individuals had become increasingly isolated from one another, even as they crowded together ever more closely in densely populated cities. Research over the past few decades has shown, however, that interpersonal and intergroup relationships among members of "the mass" moderate the effects of the media in many ways.

Both psychological and social variables are taken into account in contemporary communication theory, which attempts to explain why individuals *select, interpret,* and *respond to* particular kinds of media content in given ways.[15] In the following sections we will examine some of the generalizations that have been developed about the influence of given psychological and social variables as they intervene between communication stimuli and audience response.

THE INFLUENCE OF INDIVIDUAL DIFFERENCES

Every person does not respond in the same way to stimulus events in the environment. The unique pattern of people's needs, attitudes, habits, and values derived through socialization determines what they will selectively attend to, what they will selectively interpret, and what they will selectively act upon. This *principle of selectivity* is well established and has been adequately documented by research.[16]

14. Carter R. Bryan, "Communist Advertising: Its Status and Function," *Journalism Quarterly,* 39, No. 4 (Autumn 1962): 500–506.
15. Wilbur Schramm, ed., *Mass Communications* (Urbana, Ill., University of Illinois Press, 1949), pp. 387–429.
16. See, for example, Douglas Waples et al., *Why They Read* (Chicago: The University of Chicago Press, 1940).

In terms of mass communication, the principle of selectivity means that selective attention, perception, and action enter into the communicative behavior of the audience member. From the great variety of available content in print, on film, and through broadcasts, members of the audience pick out, concentrate upon, and interpret messages. They attend most closely to those messages that are (1) related to their interests, (2) consistent with their attitudes, (3) congruent with their beliefs, and (4) supportive of their values.[17]

For example, research has established that new car owners are much more likely to read advertisements for the car they have just purchased than are owners of the same make but an earlier model.[18] In a study of smokers and nonsmokers, the former were significantly less likely to read articles on the relationship between smoking and health. (Only 32 percent of male smokers read such articles as compared to 60 percent of nonsmoking males.)[19]

The *interpretation* that people place on communications is similarly influenced by their personal attributes. More than twenty-five years ago Kendall and Wolfe reported a study in which a campaign intended to reduce prejudice through the use of cartoons backfired among more prejudiced respondents.[20] Such persons completely misinterpreted the intent of the cartoons and saw them as supporting their own attitudes rather than ridiculing bigotry. This generalization was reaffirmed by research findings in a study by Vidmar and Rokeach of the television program "All in the Family." Studying audience samples in both Canada and the United States, these social scientists determined that members of the audience with strong racial and ethnic prejudices tended to agree with the themes of bigotry expressed by the program's main character, "Archie Bunker." They liked the program because they believed that it supported their own views. This apparently came as something of a surprise to the sponsors and directors of the program, who had maintained that "All in the Family" reduced bigotry by exposing it to ridicule.[21]

Care must be exercised, of course, in drawing causal inferences from research such as these studies of bigotry. There is no basis for assuming that media content can either cause or eliminate prejudiced attitudes and bigoted actions. The conclusion that can be advanced is that personal attitudes, values, and other prior orientations greatly influence the *interpretations* people place on a given television program, movie, or newspaper account. At this point social scientists lack conclusive evidence that media content either modifies attitudes or changes behavior, at least in a direct way.[22]

SOCIAL CATEGORIES AND AUDIENCE BEHAVIOR

Patterns of attention and response to the content of mass communication have been found to be roughly similar for people of the same age, sex, income level, area of residence (rural or urban), occupation, and educational background. This phenomenon can be explained in terms of subcultural similarities among people in various social categories.

The social-categories approach to understanding the mass communication process reflects back on the work of early sociologists who were concerned with analyzing the impact of

17. For a basic discussion of the psychological principles underlying perceptual selectivity, see David Krech and Richard S. Crutchfield, "Perceiving the World," in *The Process and Effects of Mass Communication,* ed. Wilbur Schramm (Urbana, Ill.: University of Illinois Press, 1954), pp. 116–137.

18. Danuta Ehrlich, Isaiah Guttman, Peter Schonbach, and Judson Mills, "Postdecision Exposure to Relevant Information," *Journal of Abnormal and Social Psychology,* 54 (1957): 98–102.

19. Charles F. Cannell and James C. MacDonald, "The Impact of Health News on Attitudes and Behavior," *Journalism Quarterly,* 33 (1956): 315–323.

20. Patricia L. Kendall and Katherine M. Wolfe, "The Analysis of Deviant Cases in Communications Research," in *Communications Research 1948–49,* ed. Paul Lazarsfeld and Frank Stanton (New York: Harper and Brothers, 1949), pp. 152–179.

21. Neil Vidmar and Milton Rokeach, "Archie Bunker's Bigotry: A Study of Selective Perception and Exposure," *Journal of Communication* (January 1974): 36–47.

22. These relationships are thoroughly discussed in Walter Weiss, "Effects of the Mass Media of Communication" in Gardner Lindsey and Elliot Aronson, *The Handbook of Social Psychology,* 2nd ed. (Reading, Mass.: Addison-Wesley Publishing Company, 1969), pp. 77–195. See also, Joseph T. Klapper, "What We Know About the Effects of Mass Communication: The Brink of Hope," *Public Opinion Quarterly,* 21 (1957): 453–474.

societal heterogeneity on patterns of social inter-action. The theories of Durkheim, Tönnies, and Weber all noted that different positions in the social structure tend to produce different patterns of attitudes, values, and beliefs as well as different norms of behavior. In a sense, analyses of the mass communication process in terms of individual differences and in terms of social categories focus on the same point: people relate to the media in terms of their personal needs and orientations.

A modern example of the social-categories approach is the research of Greenberg and Dervin, who studied mass communication behavior among a sample of black and white families in a very low-income urban area.[23] They found that these people owned fewer TV and radio sets, subscribed to fewer newspapers, and read fewer magazines than the general population. Most of them, however, did have one TV set and watched considerably *more* television than the general population—5.2 hours daily as compared to 2.0 hours. The poor also tended to concentrate their viewing more on musical and variety shows and on westerns than on more serious programs. There were also differences in the use of other media. A smaller percentage of the poor than the general population subscribed to a newspaper (65 versus 77 percent), and the poor were more likely to read only headlines. They listened to fewer radio programs, went to fewer movies, and read fewer magazines. Blacks and whites did not differ significantly in any of these patterns. However, poor blacks relied less on the media and more on people for local news than did poor whites. In summary, then, the study showed that the variables of income level and, to a lesser extent, race are related to specific patterns of media use.

23. Bradley Greenberg and Brenda Dervin, "Mass Communications Among the Urban Poor," *Public Opinion Quarterly*, 34, No. 2 (Summer 1970): 224–235.
24. Elihu Katz, "Communications Research and the Image of Society: Convergence of Two Research Traditions," *American Journal of Sociology*, 65, No. 5 (1959): 436.
25. Terry N. Clark, ed., *Gabriel Tarde on Communication and Social Influence* (Chicago: The University of Chicago Press, 1969), pp. 57–58.
26. Paul Lazarsfeld, Bernard Berelson, and Helen Gaudet, *The People's Choice* (New York: Columbia University Press, 1948).

THE INFLUENCE OF INTERPERSONAL RELATIONSHIPS

For many years, systematic investigation of the mass communication process was based upon the assumption that audiences in modern urban societies had mainly impersonal ties. Students of the media, influenced by the conceptualization of society as a *Gesellschaft*, assumed that the responses of "mass" audiences to the content of "mass" communications were relatively individualistic. One well-known scholar of the media stated the issue in this way:

Until very recently, the image of society in the minds of most students of communication was of atomized individuals, connected with the mass media, but not with one another. Society—the "audience"—was conceived as aggregates of age, sex, social class, and the like, but little thought was given to [informal interpersonal relationships].[24]

Almost by accident a major sociological investigation uncovered the significant part informal social relationships play in the mass communication process. Early social theorists such as Gabriel Tarde had suspected that these relationships were important but had lacked evidence.[25] Then, in studying the responses of hundreds of people to a presidential election campaign, it was noted over and over again that for many of the respondents, one of the most significant sources of information about the campaign was *other people*. In other words, not everyone was getting information about the candidates, the issues, etc., directly from the media. Many were getting it from other people who were in direct contact with the media and who were passing on information about the campaign.[26]

This seemingly simple discovery stimulated research aimed at understanding the significance of informal interpersonal relations in the mass communications process. The overall conclusion has been that such relationships often modify the manner in which given individuals will attend to, interpret, and act upon a message transmitted by the mass media. In fact, it has been discovered that there are many persons whose firsthand exposure to particular media is quite limited. Information often moves through two basic stages. First, it goes from a given medium to a set of relatively well-informed individuals who attend directly. Second, it moves from those persons through interpersonal channels to people who depend upon others for their information. Sometimes, it may pass through many steps in this process of "message diffusion."

This diffusional process has been labeled the "two-step flow of communication."[27] The key individuals, who are in direct contact with the media, are generally called "opinion leaders." Such individuals not only pass on information to others but also inevitably play some part in influencing the interpretations and lines of behavior of those to whom they pass on ideas. For this reason, they are said to engage in "personal influence," even though their activities as influencers may be unintended.

Wherever media are used to suggest new courses of action or new ideas, social relationships become important in determining how people will respond. Physicians adopting new drugs may do so because of the personal influence of other physicians who have read about the drugs in medical journals.[28] Similarly, interpersonal influence plays a part when farmers take up new agricultural practices, when homemakers begin using new household products, when college students accept new fashions, when teachers adopt new educational techniques, and so forth. The mechanisms of the two-step flow of communication are widely found wherever there is a flow of ideas from media to audience.

EFFECTS OF THE MEDIA

As we have seen, a number of psychological and social variables influence how audience members select, interpret, and respond to media content. But given this fact, what generalizations can be made about the effects of the media, not only on individuals but on society generally? For example, to what extent—and in what ways—do the news media shape public opinion? Are explicit sex scenes in movies changing standards of sexual morality? Does violence portrayed through the media encourage increased violence in everyday life?

Public concern over such questions is understandable in view of the great amount of time people spend with the mass media. The statistically average American family reads more than one daily newspaper, subscribes to several magazines, owns three or more radios, and has at least one television set.[29] Individual members of that family watch television on an average of two hours a day—12.5 percent of their waking hours.[30] For many people the figure is much

27. Elihu Katz, "The Two Step Flow of Communication: An Up-to-Date Report on an Hypothesis," *Public Opinion Quarterly*, 21, No. 1 (Spring 1957): 61–78. For an excellent summary of the large amount of contemporary work on this formulation, see Everett M. Rogers and F. Floyd Shoemaker, *Communication of Innovations*, 2nd ed. (New York: The Free Press, 1971), esp. pp. 198–225.
28. James S. Coleman, Elihu Katz, and Herbert Menzel, *Medical Innovation: A Diffusion Study* (Indianapolis: The Bobbs-Merrill Co., Inc., 1966).
29. DeFleur and Ball-Rokeach, *Theories of Mass Communication*.
30. L. A. Lo Sciuto, "A National Inventory of Television Viewing Behavior," in E. A. Rubinstein, G. A. Comstock, and J. P. Murray, eds., *Television and Social Behavior, Vol. 4, Television in Day-to-Day Life: Patterns of Use* (Washington, D.C.: U.S. Government Printing Office, 1971).

Table 14.1 COMMUNICATIONS MEDIA PER 1000 POPULATION IN SELECTED AREAS OF THE WORLD

Medium	North America	Europe	South America	Africa	South Asia
Newspaper circulation	299	259	65	11	16
Radio receivers	1,339	280	167	45	33
Television receivers	397	188	54	3	2

SOURCE: UNESCO, *Statistical Yearbook*, 1969, 1970. Figures for Europe exclude the Soviet Union.

In the United States 96 percent of all households have at least one television set, and nearly 30 percent of households have two or more sets. The average American watches television about two hours each day. In the approximately twenty-five years that the television has been widely available, it has become one of the most important sources of information and entertainment for Americans.

higher. In the following sections we will examine the accumulated research regarding the effects of mass media exposure.

THE MEDIA AND SOCIETAL CHANGE

We noted in Chapter 10 that the media serve as important agents of social and cultural change. The impact they have can be great, especially when they are introduced into societies where newspapers, radio, television, etc., have not previously been widely available.

Modernization

Two-thirds of the world's population are only now beginning to experience the mass communications revolution that the industrialized Western nations have gone through during the last fifty years. In the densely populated countries of

South Asia, for example, relatively few media outlets are available to the ordinary person (Table 14.1). Vast populations continue to live traditional lives relatively untouched by the changes that have transformed societal life in other parts of the world. But this situation is unlikely to continue. Already the cheap transistor radio is diffusing information and "modern ideas" to many people who were previously isolated from the rest of the world by their illiteracy.[31]

Daniel Lerner has analyzed the transformation of "traditional" societies into "modern" societies in terms of four principal variables— *urbanization, literacy, mass media exposure,* and *citizen participation.*[32] Urbanization tends to increase literacy by making schools more readily available and by making the ability to read and write a major advantage, if not an absolute necessity. It also facilitates increased exposure to radio and television broadcasts, newspapers, books, and magazines. Together, literacy and increased exposure to the mass media create an informed citizenry that is likely to take

31. Frederick W. Frey, "Communication and Development," in Ithiel de Sola Pool et al., eds., *Handbook of Communication* (Chicago: Rand McNally & Co., 1973).

32. Daniel Lerner, *The Passing of Traditional Society* (New York: The Free Press, 1958).

an active interest in the possibilities for social, political, and economic change. Thus, advances in communication technology can be expected to play a significant part in altering life-styles in the now developing societies, just as they have in the developed world.

Innovation and Mass Culture

In technologically advanced societies, mass communications foster cultural changes that can be observed almost on a day-to-day basis. The media trigger rapid adoption of new clothing styles, household products, speech mannerisms, fads, and other innovations of all kinds.

Considerable attention has been given to the effects of the media in creating, and continuously reshaping, a *mass culture*. Modern communication technology has brought the best in art, music, drama, and literature within the reach of millions of Americans by way of inexpensive reproductions, recordings, films, and books, but it has also created a popular culture based primarily on what people attend to readily and what is commercially successful. This mass culture includes the best-selling books, the Top 40 records, the hit movies, the television shows with the largest audiences, and the sports events with the most publicity. Because of the emphasis on profit, there is a quick turnover in mass culture, with many of its hits and its stars disappearing overnight; but it also produces popular art that becomes a continuing part of our society's cultural heritage.

DIRECT EFFECTS OF MEDIA CONTENT

To date, the most comprehensive survey of research concerning the *direct* effects of the mass media in changing attitudes, opinions, and behavior tendencies is that of Joseph Klapper.[33] Examining hundreds of articles, books, and other sources of research data, Klapper developed a number of generalizations about media influence on individuals. The most important of them can be summarized briefly as follows:

1. Mass communication is usually not in itself a necessary and sufficient cause of audience change; whatever influence it exerts is achieved through a set of *mediating factors*.

2. Because of these mediating factors, mass communication is usually a contributory agent which *reinforces* (rather than changes) audience predispositions (voting intentions, tendencies regarding delinquency, opinions, attitudes, etc.).

3. On those relatively rare occasions where mass communication content *does* seem to have a direct effect in fostering change, either (a) mediating factors will be found to be inoperative, *or* (b) mediating factors that normally favor reinforcement will be found to favor change.

4. The ways in which mass communication achieves effects, either directly or as a contributory agent, depends upon many factors, such as the source of the message, the type of medium used, the nature of the situation in which the communication is received, current trends in public opinion, and so forth.

To illustrate in more concrete terms the effects—and noneffects—of the media on audience members, we will focus on opinions and attitudes, leaving aside for the moment such matters as cultural tastes and buying or voting behavior. In terms of opinions and attitudes, the accumulated mass media research seems to indicate that, depending on various conditions, mass communication can lead to *creative effects, reinforcement, minor change,* or have *no effect* at all.

Creative Effects

Creative effects tend to occur when people have few if any prior attitudes and knowledge about an issue. Where the issue is undefined in terms of existing cultural norms or personal psychological considerations, the treatment given to it by the mass media can weigh heavily in the creation of attitudes and opinions.

A good example of a creative effect can be seen in a classic study by Lang and Lang entitled "The Unique Perspective of Television and Its Effect."[34] The research involved a comparison of the manner in which a public event appeared to persons who actually viewed the event and to another audience that saw it only on television.

33. Klapper, "What We Know About the Effects of Mass Communication."
34. Kurt Lang and Gladys E. Lang, "The Unique Perspective of Television and Its Effect," *American Sociological Review*, 18, No. 1 (1953): 3–12.

VIEWPOINTS CHILDREN AND TELEVISION

■ What had been happening all those years of watching television, I see now [a year after selling the set], was not only an addiction but also, on a deeper level, an adjustment. All of us had become adjusted to living with a stranger in the house. . . . More, the stranger in the house was not there to entertain us . . . . The stranger was present to sell us products. . . .

I was not only paying personally for the stranger-salesman in my house but he was often manipulating or lying to my children. I saw the effects in such places as the supermarket aisles, when the boys would loudly demand a sugared cereal, junk-snack or six pack of soda . . . . My kids had been conditioned well by the sellers on TV . . . . But, someone told me, that's only commercial television, suggesting that programs like "Sesame Street" and its mimics are different. They are, perhaps, but no more worthy.

If the televisers want to teach my children something, I suggest such subjects as obedience to parents, sharing toys with brothers and sisters, kindness to animals, respect for grandparents. These kinds of lessons were strangely missing from the "quality" childrens' shows I looked in on. It is true that these concepts must be taught by the parents but it is insufferable to note the preachings of the "Sesame"-type producers, hearing them blat about how they care for children. I see their programs as a moral hustle, conning parents into thinking it's a high educational experience to dump the kids before the tube. In the end, the yammering about letters, shapes, numbers does not liberate the child's imagination. It captures it, a quick-action lariat that ropes in the child's most precious resource, his creativity.

Colman McCarthy
"Ousting the Stranger from the House"

● I get very annoyed with the assorted educational, psychological and political criticisms of *Sesame Street.* What is this madness that says if children memorize letters and numbers, they have stopped thinking and begun parroting? All they've done is learn their letters and numbers, and that's swell and makes them feel terrific. There are certain rote things, such as memorizing French verbs, that you have to do in order to be able to do certain swell things—like speak French. That's life, and it's not so terrible.

As for being unrealistic, as some critics say *Sesame Street* is, because it fails to show prostitutes and drug addicts—nonsense! Should it also show people urinating in the gutters? And having sex in the doorways? Aren't there acceptable limits for the depiction of reality without calling that reality false?

The year before the Head Start program began, I worked one day a week in a kind of pre-Head Start pilot school. It had a million things wrong with it, but we were trying and we cared, and it was better that the school existed than if it hadn't; and we hoped that with love and nourishment it would improve. But the perfectionists and supercritics in our group almost destroyed it because they believed if it wasn't just right, it was worthless, no good, so good-by!

Sesame Street is not the only answer. But it is an effort—a caring and a valuable one. I'm glad it exists. Let it be!

Judith Viorst
"Is *Sesame Street* Really All That Good?"

The first group made careful notes on a parade honoring a national hero (General Douglas MacArthur), which they watched firsthand as it passed through the streets of Chicago. Another panel of researchers saw only "on-the-spot" reports of the parade on television. Comparisons revealed that the latter group, which saw it only on television, thought the parade was exciting and thrilling, while the group that was actually there found it dull and disappointing. By developing excitement and interest with close-ups, dramatic camera angles, and a constant flow of suggestions from announcers, the medium had literally created impressions in the minds of its viewers that did not occur to eyewitnesses. In a sense, every medium creates a unique perspective by its selection and editing of material.

Reinforcement

The reinforcement of attitudes and opinions by mass communication has been widely documented. People select material from the mass media that interests them, and they interpret it in the light of their existing attitudes and beliefs. Many political speeches at election time appear to be designed around this effect. They are intended more to supply the party faithful with reinforcement for their existing beliefs than to convert opponents.

The best known study of the reinforcement effect is that of Lazarsfeld, Berelson, and Gaudet, *The People's Choice*.[35] In this exhaustive study of the presidential election of 1940, it was found that the majority of voters knew whom they would vote for even before the candidates were officially selected at the national conventions. Those studied paid attention to mass media material consistent with their attitudes and finally voted according to their original predispositions. Some who had not formulated a voting intention by May of the election year were "activated" by mass communications before the election in November, but few were converted from one side to the other.

Only under very unusual conditions is it possible for mass-communicated messages to change people's attitudinal convictions drastically. Completely surrounded by persuasive messages, we tend to build up "mental calluses" that effectively screen out much of their influence. Campaigns aimed at persuading us to stop smoking, drive more safely, quit littering, or otherwise change our patterns of belief and conduct have only a limited chance of success. The people who attend most intensely to such communications are generally those who are already convinced.

Minor Changes

Minor changes in opinions and attitudes are relatively common. This type of influence is often observed in experimental studies in which subjects are exposed to persuasive communications incorporating various types of appeals. For example, in communities where persuasive leaflets were dropped to try to alter attitudes toward donating blood to a visiting bloodmobile, few sweeping changes in opinions or attitudes were noted; but there were many minor shifts in attitude, and the leaflets appear to have kept donation rates from dropping as much between visits of the bloodmobile as they had in prior years.[36]

INDIRECT EFFECTS OF MEDIA CONTENT

Although the effectiveness of the media as vehicles of persuasion is less than is commonly supposed, there are a number of ways in which the media can *indirectly* influence individual audience members and also society as a whole. Most relate to selectivity of content.

Status Conferral

The mass media often perform what Lazarsfeld and Merton have called a *status conferral function*.[37] That is, the media lend a certain amount of prestige to those people they focus on. In the minds of ordinary members of society, people who "count" will be reported on by the media. By the same logic, people who are given attention by the media are assumed to be important.

35. Lazarsfeld, Berelson, and Gaudet, *The People's Choice*.

36. William R. Catton, Jr., unpublished study from "Project Revere," 1960, University of Washington.

37. Paul F. Lazarsfeld and Robert K. Merton, "Mass Communication, Popular Taste and Organized Social Action," in *The Communication of Ideas*, ed. Lyman Bryson (New York: Harper and Brothers, 1948), pp. 95–118.

Many of the "celebrities" whose names appear in the newspapers and whose faces appear on television are celebrated chiefly, or solely, because of these appearances.

Definition of Events and "Pseudo-Events"

In performing their central function of providing their audiences with *information,* the news media not only serve the public's "right to know" but also help determine what it *will* know — and thus what it will become concerned about. Modern audiences are very *dependent* upon information delivered by the mass media.[38] From the multitudinous events that occur daily, newspaper and broadcasting personnel select those they feel various audiences would like information about. Thus they create an ever changing *agenda* for the public, around which people can form opinions, beliefs, and attitudes. The issue of Watergate provides a clear example. Because specific media (such as the *Washington Post*) persisted in putting the Watergate affair "on the agenda," it became defined by the public as a national scandal and an issue of utmost concern. If the media had not focused on Watergate as an issue, in all likelihood the public would have passed it off as just one more example of political shenanigans. In all likelihood, too, President Nixon would not have resigned. One can only speculate on the possible outcome of other events if the news media had — or had not — delivered information about them and placed them on the public's agenda.

The media have sometimes been accused of creating "pseudo-events" — that is, of puffing up the importance of minor incidents simply by giving them extensive coverage.[39] In many cases the charge seems justified: freedom of the press has sometimes been interpreted as freedom to make news where none exists. But in many other cases, as in the Watergate affair, the media

have seemingly served the public well by focusing attention on issues of genuine consequence. As we noted earlier in this chapter, questions concerning freedom and responsibility of the press have no easy answers. Here, the point to be made is that the news media, simply by their selection of events to be reported, indirectly influence audience attitudes and responses.

Other Indirect Effects

By emphasizing certain cultural themes and ignoring others, the media can provide "definitions of the situation" that may eventually come to be seen by a population as *normative.* Various minorities have objected to television advertisements on precisely such grounds. Thomas Martinez has cited two examples of TV advertisements that "defined the situation" regarding Chicanos in American society.[40] One was the *Frito Bandito* series. A particular snack product was advertised on television by a cartoon that portrayed a fat bandit with a Mexican accent who repeatedly "stole" the snack product because it was delicious. Soon, Chicano youngsters in schools all over the country were being called "Frito Bandito" by their Anglo schoolmates. The second objectionable advertisement was a TV commercial advertising an underarm deodorant. It began with a band of horsemen galloping across a desert toward the camera. As they stopped in the foreground it became apparent that they were "Mexican bandits." The leader — a particularly disreputable-looking, grubby, glowering individual — reached in his saddlebag and took out a can of the deodorant. As he squirted it on himself, a male voice said, "If it can work on *him,* think of what it can do for you!"

The implication of these commercials was clear: Mexicans are dirty, untrustworthy, and ridiculous. Although the people who created the advertisements had no such message in mind, that was the way the situation was defined. By simply supplying information selectively, then, the media define numerous situations as real and normative for audience members.

38. Sandra J. Ball-Rokeach and Melvin L. DeFleur, "A Dependency Model of Mass Media Effects," *Communication Research* (forthcoming, 1975).

39. Daniel Boorstin, *The Image: A Guide to Pseudo-Events in America* (New York: Harper & Row, Inc., 1964).

40. Thomas M. Martinez, "How Advertisers Promote Racism," *El Grito* (Summer 1969): 3–13.

The average American child is expected to see 13,000 killings dramatized on television in the ten years between ages five and fifteen. Parents and educators, among others, are concerned that excessive televised violence will lead children to accept violence as a normal, socially approved way of dealing with problems.

THE IMPACT OF MEDIA VIOLENCE

As our preceding discussion makes clear, it is extremely difficult to identify the exact effects of the mass media on audience behavior because of the large number of factors involved. Bernard Berelson summed up the complexity of the problem some years ago when he noted that "Some kinds of *communications,* on some kinds of *issues,* brought to the attention of some kinds of *people,* under some kinds of *conditions,* have some kinds of *effects.*"[41]

The difficulty of isolating cause and effect has been clearly apparent in efforts to determine the impact of media emphasis on violence. This issue has received more attention in recent years than any other problem related to the potential effects of mass communication. During the 1960s, the American public became particularly sensitized to what was perceived as an alarming trend toward higher levels of violence in society. Three public leaders—John Kennedy, Robert Kennedy, and Martin Luther King, Jr.—were assassinated. Riots occurred in urban ghettos and on university campuses. Crimes of physical brutality multiplied, particularly among the young.

Prompted by public concern, Congress appropriated funds for extensive inquiries into a possible causal connection between televised violence and antisocial behavior, especially among the young. Studies have shown that children, overall, spend as many of their waking hours absorbed by television, radio, comics, and the other mass media as by school.[42] What have been the effects of their concentrated exposure to media portrayals of violence?

41. Bernard Berelson, "Communications and Public Opinion," in *Communications in Modern Society,* ed. Wilbur Schramm (Urbana, Ill.: University of Illinois Press, 1948), p. 178.

42. J. P. Robinson, "Television's Impact on Everyday Life: Some Cross-National Evidence," in Rubinstein, Comstock, and Murray, eds., *Television in Day-to-Day Life;* B. S. Greenberg and B. Dervin, eds., *Use of the Mass Media by the Urban Poor* (New York: Praeger Publishers, Inc., 1970); and Wilbur Schramm et al., *Television in the Lives of Our Children* (Stanford, Calif.: Stanford University Press, 1961), p. 27.

Critics have charged that the news media have created "pseudo-events" by giving minor incidents extensive coverage. Evel Knievel's attempt in 1974 to jump the Snake River Canyon on a rocketlike motorcycle (opposite) received weeks of news coverage, and many felt that the news media were responsible for turning Knievel into a "folk hero" and the event into "news." Because the news media sent reporters and camera crews when Christo draped curtains over part of the Australian coastline (above), he quickly became a "famous artist."

In 1971 a report published by the Surgeon General's Advisory Committee offered some very tentative conclusions about the impact of televised violence on young viewers.[43] The report summarized experimental studies carried out under laboratory conditions which showed that children would imitate aggressive adult models, whether they appeared in the flesh or on a movie or television screen. Following exposure to such models, children would engage in acts of violence toward dolls or toys of almost any kind. However, the report noted, the influences of norms and social controls opposing violence were absent in the contrived experimental situations; thus, there is reason to question whether the same subjects would behave similarly outside the laboratory. The report also cited evidence showing that those children most stimulated toward violence were those who were aggressive to start with.

Nonlaboratory studies, conducted by survey techniques, revealed low but statistically meaningful relationships between high exposure to televised violence and aggressive tendencies. The Surgeon General's report pointed out that there were problems of interpretation here also, primarily because both heavy viewing of violent content and aggressive behavior may be brought about by antecedent conditions or factors (e.g., preexisting propensities toward aggression, parental attitudes or behavior, personality traits, etc.). In other words, an interest in viewing televised violence and aggressive behavior may both be products of prior conditioning.

After examining twenty-three special studies conducted for the program, and after reviewing some eight hundred existing studies, the Surgeon General's report concluded that there appear to be *certain categories of children* among whom televised violence is conducive to an increase in aggressive behavior.[44] Overall, the children most influenced are those whose viewing context, prior socialization, and emotional makeup predispose them to imitate or to be incited by violent content on television. There is no simple, straightforward relationship between televised violence and aggressive behavior that affects all children equally. Nevertheless, even

if only a few thousand of the millions of American children who watch television are made more aggressive by witnessing televised portrayals of violence, the problem for the nation is a serious one.

STRATEGIES OF MASS PERSUASION

Persuasion can be defined as an attempt to achieve some form of behavioral change on the part of an audience through communication. The term is a broad one and includes face-to-face communication as well as communication through the mass media. In this section the meaning of the popular term *propaganda* is limited to *message content* that is designed to have persuasive effects. As such, it carries no moral connotation.

Although persuasion through the use of mass-communicated propaganda has become a very important social process, there is little scientific understanding of how the process works. Mass advertising, political campaigning via the media, charity appeals, and other attempts to influence public action through mass communication are in large part carried out without any systematic theoretical basis. Sometimes a clever advertisement or an engaging political appeal will be highly successful, but little is known about *why* particular efforts succeed. In developing a persuasion campaign, however, two general strategies are widely followed. One emphasizes the psychology of the *individual;* the other emphasizes the sociocultural variables that affect the individual as part of a *group.*

PSYCHODYNAMIC STRATEGIES
Rightly or wrongly, it has been assumed that a persuasive media message is one that is capable of altering one or more psychological variables within the individual in such a way that he or

43. U.S. Department of Health, Education and Welfare, *Television and Growing Up: The Impact of Televised Violence* (Washington, D.C.: National Institute of Mental Health, 1971).
44. Ibid., p. 10.

she will respond overtly (by voting or spending more money, for example) in ways desired and suggested by the communicator. It is assumed, in other words, that internal psychological processes dynamically influence overt behavior and that altering the former will lead to predictable correlated changes in the latter in a manner desired by the persuader (Figure 14.3).

In Chapter 5 we noted that personality is often viewed as a "system" that seeks to maintain its equilibrium. Presumably, when its equilibrium is disturbed, the individual experiences some form of discomfort. Thus (according to the theory), if a persuasive message can temporarily create disequilibrium in the personality system, the individual will tend to seek a course of action that will restore equilibrium and thus relieve discomfort. If the persuasive message also includes suggestions as to *how* equilibrium can be restored, presumably the suggested course of action will be followed. If this happens, effective persuasion has been accomplished.

These ideas are illustrated by the common use of fear-threat as a means to persuade with mass communications. For example, if the object of a short-run persuasion campaign is to get people to remove dangerous medicines from the reach of children, the television public-service announcement might show a child gasping for life on the floor beneath an open medicine cabinet. This is presumed to pose a considerable fear-threat for audience members. The communication can then suggest the means by which the threat can be avoided and equilibrium can be restored—namely, by locking dangerous medicines away in a safe place. The fallacy of a fear-arousing approach is that audience members may take a quite different route to avoid the threat that has been created. For example, they may avoid, deliberately misunderstand, or repress the message.[45] Many other psychological

variables besides fear have been used in media propaganda as a basis for the psychodynamic strategy of persuasion—sex urges, status drives, preoccupations with health, vanity, greed, and others.

Propaganda based on a psychodynamic strategy often assumes that *attitudes* are psychological variables directly correlated with particular patterns of *overt behavior*. Thus a media campaign may be undertaken to reduce racial or ethnic prejudice (attitudinal variable) on the grounds that if this can be accomplished, discriminatory behavior (overt action) will be reduced. But as suggested previously, attitudes are by no means the only variables influencing how people behave. For example, social constraints may prevent individuals with prejudiced attitudes from engaging in overt acts of discrimination,[46] and people who want to "keep America beautiful" may themselves throw trash on the highway. Despite such complications, psychodynamic strategies for mass persuasion remain popular.

SOCIOCULTURAL STRATEGIES
Sociocultural strategies of mass persuasion concentrate on defining or redefining, through the use of the media, certain *patterns of expectation* that serve as behavioral guides for members of groups. The task is simplest when the members have no clearly defined expectations with respect to the object of the persuasive appeal. Persuasion is much more difficult to achieve when established patterns of expectations and behavior have to be supplanted with new ones.

Although sociocultural strategies must still take account of the perceptual, cognitive, and attitudinal characteristics of group members as individuals, they are based on the assumption

45. Irving L. Janis and Seymour Feshbach, "Effects of Fear-arousing Communication," *Journal of Abnormal and Social Psychology,* 48 (1953): 78–92.

46. The literature on this issue is summarized in Melvin L. DeFleur and Frank R. Westie, "Attitude as a Scientific Concept," *Social Forces,* 42, No. 1 (1963): 17–31; and Lyle Warner and Melvin L. DeFleur, "Attitude as an Interactional Concept: Social Constraint and Social Distance as Intervening Variables Between Attitudes and Action," *American Sociological Review,* 34, No. 2 (1969): 153–169.

propaganda (persuasive message)

↓

alters internal psychological process

↓

achieves change in overt behavior

Figure 14.3. THE PSYCHODYNAMIC STRATEGY FOR ACHIEVING PERSUASION

that external, group-validated guides to action have a strong impact on shaping behavior, and these become the chief target for manipulation (Figure 14.4).

Many variables are used to provide individuals, through media messages, with what appear to be group-supported modes of conduct toward an object, event, or issue. Social-organizational concepts such as norms, roles, and systems of social control play an important part, for they aid people in interpreting ambiguous situations and defining appropriate modes of action. If individuals can be convinced through mass-media messages that there is *consensus* in the group with respect to a particular pattern of response, then they feel pressure to act in that manner, under the conviction that they are *conforming to expectations*. Actions taken in the belief that they represent conformity to group expectations are not likely to arouse anxieties or otherwise disturb psychological equilibrium. On the contrary, they are likely to be rewarding to the people involved.

To illustrate the achievement of persuasion through the use of the sociocultural strategy, we may examine the tactics commonly used by charity drives. Although the "community fund" type of charity campaign uses elements of both psychodynamic and sociocultural strategies, we will stress the latter for illustrative purposes.

An important step in the campaign is to announce (via the news media) the community *quota*. This is a formulation of an apparent *collective goal,* and it has a certain compelling

propaganda (persuasive message)

↓

defines (or redefines)
sociocultural processes of group(s)

↓

forming or altering definitions
for socially approved behavior
for group members

↓

achieves change in direction
of overt behavior

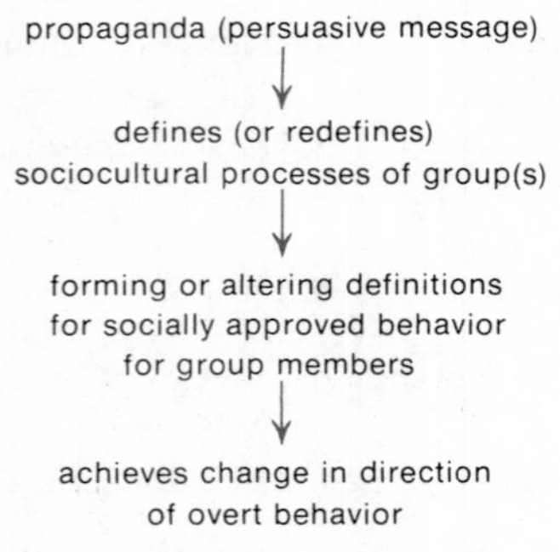

Figure 14.4. THE SOCIOCULTURAL STRATEGY FOR ACHIEVING PERSUASION

quality because it is portrayed as the goal of the whole community. The appearance of widespread approval is often achieved by getting socially prominent persons in the community to participate in the announcement. The news media generally give considerable coverage to these events, thus making them seem important.

Another step is to announce to the members of the community that their *fair share* is some specified portion of their monthly or weekly income. Again, media campaigns assure that this message is understood by all. The concept of a fair share is especially compelling because it has the appearance of a widely approved *norm*. No one wants to be "unfair." If the members of the community can be convinced that others are giving according to this norm, then they feel pressure to perform according to the shared expectations.

Along with mass-communicated propaganda, an equally important part of the campaign is to create as many *roles* and *counter-roles* as possible within the economic groups of the community. Thus every place of business or division within a bureaucracy is asked to have its own "chairman" for the drive. Each member of the group must play a counter-role to this chairman's role. For example, IBM cards are often distributed so that members can "pledge" donations to be collected later. People who do not choose to play this counter-role must make their *deviance* known by signing cards to indicate refusal or by telling the chairman of their group. Thus role and counter-role provide a structure that places considerable social pressure on the individual to make a donation.

Even more compelling is the use of neighborhood collectors. These persons call on the residents of their area and request a donation. The role of "good citizen" and "neighbor" thus includes donating to the cause. It is socially embarrassing to refuse a neighbor a reasonable and socially approved request, and refusal risks informal sanctions. No matter if people have given to other charities, they are unlikely to refuse contributions in this context.

With skillful use of the media, then, plus manipulation of the sociocultural milieu, this strategy of persuasion can be very successful. The variables utilized in the persuasive campaign to give the potential donor a "definition of the situation" include norms, roles, and informal sanctions as well as the deep-seated values that underlie all charitable activities.

PUBLIC OPINION

The significance of the mass media in the formation of public opinion has been a subject of controversy for decades. Those who are generally critical of the media and those disenchanted with contemporary society seem especially prone to attribute to mass communication an overwhelming power to mold and manipulate public opinion. They note that governmental power, even in democratic societies such as the United States, has been increasingly removed from local authority and concentrated in the hands of remote figures at the national level. This tends, they say, to separate average citizens from events and controversies that may affect their destiny. Lacking first-hand information upon which to make up their minds or to take action, they are seen as increasingly at the mercy of those who control the media and can feed the public selected information, predigested opinion, and restricted courses of action. Under such conditions, ordinary citizens (so such critics maintain) are reduced to little more than automatons who parrot the opinions they have been taught and carry out only those programs of action that have been laid out for them.

There seems little basis for attributing such power to the media, especially in societies where they are not under monopolistic control. In a totalitarian regime, there is little doubt that the media can play a prominent role in mobilizing public opinion.[47] But even in the totalitarian system, public opinion is not a simple product of mass communication; it is also created and

manipulated by controlling the educational system, suppressing groups (such as churches) that compete for individual loyalties, using a single tightly organized political party, punishing dissidents, staging mass meetings, parades, and demonstrations, and so on.

In a democratic society, information monopolies seldom exist. The media, under distributed ownership and control, do not represent a single point of view. In addition, a great variety of pressure groups, political factions, and special-interest associations vie with each other for public attention. Still, it cannot be denied that mass communication plays an important part in the formation and crystallization of public opinion even in democracies. In the section that follows, we will examine a theory that attempts to explain the opinion-formation process, including the part played by the media.

A THEORY OF PUBLIC-OPINION FORMATION

Before attempting to analyze the complex process by which public opinion is formed, it is necessary to clarify the meaning of the terms *mass, public,* and *opinion* as they are used in sociology.

The Mass

Perhaps the most helpful way to view the idea of the *mass* is to regard it as a useful abstraction — an "ideal type" — that may have no actual point-by-point correspondence with any specific aspect of social reality. Thus conceptualized, the mass is a large number of individuals who exist within a society but who have no social connections with one another; it exemplifies the *complete absence of social organization.*

While there is probably no aggregate that actually corresponds to the mass, there are certain characteristics that could theoretically be assigned to such a collectivity if it did exist. For example, the members would be drawn from every conceivable social category and stratum; they would be unknown to each other and physically separated from each other. In other words, they would not engage in interaction, would have no sense of belonging to the mass, and would even be unaware of their fellow members.

47. Daniel Lerner, *Propaganda in War and Crisis* (New York: George W. Stewart, 1952); Leonard Doob, "Goebbel's Principles of Propaganda," *Public Opinion Quarterly,* 14 (1950): 419–442; Martin F. Herz, "Some Psychological Lessons from Leaflet Propaganda in World War II," *Public Opinion Quarterly,* 13, No. 3 (1949): 471–486.

TOOLS OF SOCIOLOGY
OPINION POLLING   Arline McCord

Opinion polls are essentially adaptations of the survey technique (see page 195). They make use of samples, interviews, and statistical analyses in an attempt to gauge people's preferences, attitudes, and other predispositions. Polling organizations such as Gallup, Roper, and Nielsen are prominent in the United States.

Business and government depend heavily on opinion polls in order to discover what people think and want. Organizations commission polls—on political party preferences, consumer tastes, use of leisure time, product images—and use the information obtained to alter activities and products to fit the expressed desires of the population polled. To a limited degree, polls make it possible to project future trends. For example, if manufacturers learn that older people tend to like a particular kind of car, and if they also know that the proportion of older people in the population is growing, they can expect to sell more of that kind of car in the future. During times of rapid social change, information from polls may mean the difference between the success or failure of a business enterprise or a government program. Business and political leaders may also base their advertising or campaigning on the results of opinion polls.

To be useful, opinion polls must be valid and reliable (page 129). A carefully developed sample design provides one mode of ensuring accuracy. When proper sampling is not done, the results of a poll are often incorrect. This was the case in the presidential election of 1936 when a poll conducted by the *Literary Digest* erred by 20 percent and predicted that the Republican candidate, Alfred Landon, would win over the Democratic incumbent Franklin D. Roosevelt. Although the sample used in this poll included more than two million people, it was not representative of the voting population as a whole, since it was limited to *Literary Digest* subscribers and to people who had telephones—a relatively affluent group. (Many of the families who had been hardest hit by the Depression, and would thus be inclined to vote for Roosevelt, could not afford the luxury of a telephone.) The sample was further distorted by the fact that polling was done by means of a mailed questionnaire; many people did not take the trouble to respond.

The accuracy of an opinion poll depends not only on how the sample is selected but also on how the questions are framed and administered and how the results are analyzed. The failure of polling organizations to predict President Truman's reelection over Thomas Dewey in 1948 apparently stemmed from inadequate analysis of "undecided" responses and inadequate attention to probable patterns of voter turnout—to the question of how many people, and what *kinds* of people, would actually vote.

Learning from such errors, opinion pollsters have increasingly improved their sampling and interviewing techniques and thus their accuracy. They have been greatly aided by advances in technology. Computers are used to analyze the data, and in some new polls subjects can respond to an event as it is taking place. At a movie opening, for example, viewers may register opinions about scenes in the movie by pushing a button. Some day television sets may be equipped with consoles, so that people can instantly report their feelings about any type of issue or product.

Polls do pose some dangers, particularly in the political system. By showing that a majority of people favor a particular candidate or policy, they may create a bandwagon effect, leading some people who might otherwise not have done so to vote for the "popular" candidate or support the "popular" issue. Polls can also have the opposite effect: in England, for example, polls predicted that the Conservative party could easily win in the 1968 election. Because they assumed that their party would easily defeat the opposition, many Conservatives stayed at home on election day. The Conservative party lost the election.

Advocates of opinion polling see it as a way to extend democracy by making it possible for all citizens to vote on all political issues and to have their desires considered in the development of new products. Opponents consider polling an invasion of privacy; some also fear that the information gained from polls will be used to manipulate people and to destroy individuality in society—if the middle way is followed on all issues, they say, extreme positions will be lost, to the detriment of society. But whatever its ultimate effect, opinion polling appears to be solidly entrenched in American society.

The classic statement on the nature of the mass has been made by Herbert Blumer:

[The] *mass is devoid of the features of a society or community. It has no social organization, no body of custom or tradition, no established set of rules or rituals, no organized group of sentiments, no structure of status roles, and no established leadership. It merely consists of an aggregation of individuals who are separate, detached, anonymous, and thus, homogeneous as far as mass behavior is concerned. It can be seen, further, that the behavior of the mass, just because it is not made by preestablished rule or expectation, is spontaneous, indigenous, and elementary.*[48]

The term *mass* provides a needed abstraction to identify behavior in which large numbers of individuals can potentially act simply on their own, each responding to the environment in terms of private attitudes and needs. If mass behavior becomes organized, if members begin to influence each other and to develop *shared* orientations or expectations of each other, then mass behavior ceases and the actions of the participants may evolve into group behavior.

Individual Versus Public Opinion

Several different behavorial phenomena are often identified as "opinion."[49] First, there are the private opinions of individuals. The concept *private opinion* refers to a given person's verbalized or communicable set of interpretive beliefs concerning some issue or situation. This is the kind of opinion measured by "public opinion" polls (see Tools of Sociology, page 430).

Individuals formulate private opinions in part on the basis of their personal attitudes and values. They may draw upon norms they have internalized. They may also use their interpretations of the views of their reference groups, or other sociocultural sources, to formulate their belief.[50] *Public opinion*, on the other hand, is a

sociological rather than a psychological concept. Its formation, as we shall see, entails elaborate interactional processes.

Publics

The term *public* has been used in a variety of ways by social scientists. As used in connection with public opinion, it refers to much more than simply a large number of people. To begin with, we may think of a number of *potential* publics existing in a given population.

How does a given public emerge and become recognizable? A public becomes defined in a preliminary way when some issue or event captures the attention of a large number of individual members of the mass—say as a response to some significant item presented by the media. This shared attention provides a necessary basis for the formation of a public. But while attention is a necessary condition, it is not a sufficient condition. That is, there must be something about the phenomenon being attended to that is provocative, controversial, or unclear—something that makes the situation "unstructured" for the emerging public. We can say, then, that a public emerges from the mass when the attention of a relatively large number of people is focused upon some issue or event to which they cannot easily respond in terms of inner guides or established cultural norms.

The Formation of Public Opinion

Having reviewed the concepts, we can now bring them together in a theory. An important generalization about human behavior that is relevant to the formation of public opinion is the so-called *reality principle*—the tendency of people to use social sources in order to assign meaning to unstructured events. When human beings are confronted with an ambiguous event and lack adequate information and relevant norms to react to it, they usually try to establish orienting frames of reference through interaction with others.

To illustrate, we may assume that a major news event has been noted by the mass media.

48. Herbert Blumer, "Elementary Collective Behavior," in *New Outline of the Principles of Sociology,* ed. Alfred McClung Lee (New York: Barnes & Noble, Inc., 1951), pp. 185–189.

49. For an analysis of several approaches to this concept, see Daniel Katz et al., eds., *Public Opinion and Propaganda* (New York: Holt, Rinehart, and Winston, Inc., 1954).

50. Ibid., pp. 86–158.

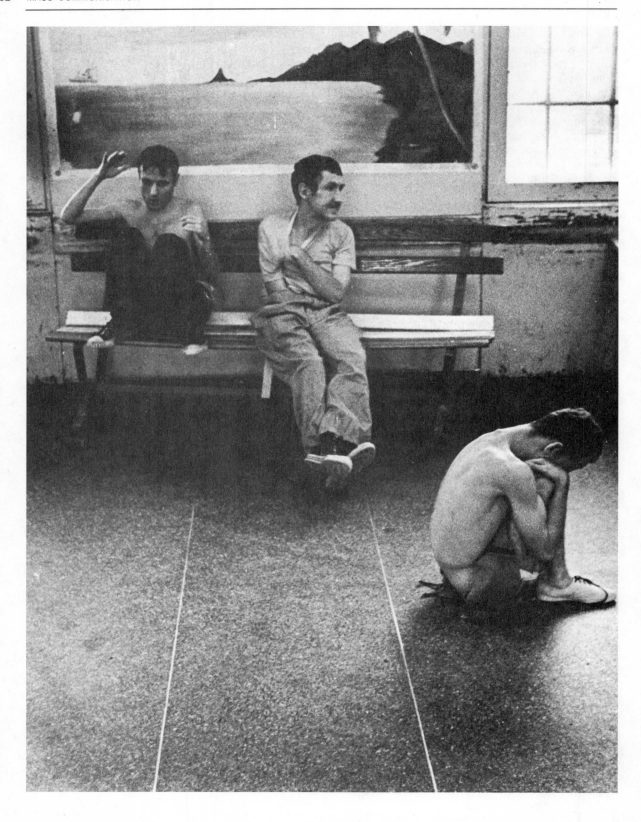

By presenting news information and by publicizing various sides of an ambiguous issue, the mass media play a significant role in the formation of public opinion. The media played a role in changing America's view of its former ally, South Vietnam, by printing pictures of the dead children left in the wake of deserting South Vietnamese forces in April of 1975. Similarly, news exposés of conditions in mental institutions have been influential in arousing public concern over the treatment of patients. In some cases it may be that the mere presence of the mass media clarifies situations that would otherwise be ambiguous. For example, in 1963 there was little doubt in the minds of the American people as to who killed Lee Harvey Oswald, the accused assassin of President John F. Kennedy, because he was shot by Jack Ruby before an audience of millions of television viewers.

If the news event belongs to a familiar category (e.g., an auto crash, an earthquake, a revolution in South America), it may not constitute an unstructured situation that requires the formation of public opinion. Those who attend to the event can follow their personal predispositions or the usual norms. They might comment on the riskiness of automobile travel, feel sorry for the earthquake victims, or deplore the instability of Latin-American governments. After having done so, however, they would probably forget the whole thing. But let us suppose that the news event is both ambiguous and more demanding of orientation and response. For example, through what stages might public opinion develop in an area where electrical blackouts have just occurred for the first time because of an energy shortage? In such a situation we should be able to trace the emergence of public opinion as people seek socially derived definitions with which to interpret an unfamiliar and disturbing event.

Perhaps the initial tendency of some people will be to castigate those in charge of the electric power company. But as it becomes evident that there are many sides to the issue, individuals may find it increasingly difficult to react in clear-cut terms. And the more attention they pay it, the more confusing the situation becomes. Nevertheless, they must formulate appropriate modes of orientation and action. As the attention of many individuals at various points in the population focused on this unstructured event, a *public* would gradually emerge from the *mass,* and the formation of *public opinion* would be well under way.

The process of public-opinion formation would continue as various interpretations of the event were circulated among the members of the emerging public. The final shaping of public opinion would probably hinge upon the attitudes toward those in charge of planning for electrical and energy needs. Some individuals might call for strong reprisals against those in charge, while others might urge sympathy and toleration. Various interest groups and factions might add their voices to the debate. Representatives of the electric company might denounce environmentalists who had prevented them from building a dam or establishing a nuclear power plant, while environmentalists would probably attempt to justify their values and policies and accuse the owners of the company of short-sightedness and greed. Some people might see the situation as a Communist plot. Religious zealots might attribute it to divine punishment. Politicians might blame the whole mess on the other party.

The mass media would play a significant role throughout these developments. Not only would they present factual information about the blackout and the energy shortages behind it, but they would publicize the comments of spokespersons for various sides in the ensuing debate and perhaps note the development of consensus by one segment of the public or another.

The formation of public opinion would thus proceed as an exceedingly complex, even chaotic process of debate, discussion, and exchange—a process involving mass communication, the predispositions of individual members of the public, networks of informal interaction, special-interest groups, public leaders, spokespersons for various associations, and so on.

Out of all of this, a limited number of shared interpretive frameworks would emerge and eventually become dominant. One large segment of the public might develop a consensus, that the environmentalists who had prevented the establishment of the dam or nuclear power plant deserved little consideration, and possibly even deserved negative sanctions, in the future. Another substantial faction might agree that the whole unfortunate incident was a symptom of the failure of bureaucratic government to adapt to changing needs. They might maintain that those responsible for planning should be held accountable for their deeds and removed from office. Thus public opinion would crystalize around two polar positions—anti-environmentalist and anti-government.

As these opposing positions became established, undecided members of the public would be attracted to one side or the other, and public opinion would become increasingly stabilized. In this case, public opinion would be clearly *divided,* but within the opposing factions a considerable amount of consensus and uniformity would have developed. In other cases, public opinion can emerge as a *single* shared interpretation about which considerable consensus exists. But whether one or several shared orientations ultimately emerge, we can identify as *public opinion* the newly formulated and shared convictions of the members of the public concerning the appropriate way to interpret the event or issue under consideration. A "public opinion" poll taken at this point (based on a sampling of individuals) would reveal the extent of the normative consensus existing among the various segments of the population.

The interpretations of those sharing a given view constitute a normative set of convictions for them. Since the interpretations are shared, they have *social validation* — they are seen as legitimate guides for orientation and action. In a sociological sense, therefore, public opinion is a newly established norm that has not been fully institutionalized. If more than one view has stabilized, there will be more than one such norm.

FUNCTIONS OF PUBLIC OPINION

Once formed, public opinion serves as an important means of social control, both over members of a community or society and over those who lead them. It also serves to clarify ambiguous situations to which people must respond, and to promote integration and social solidarity within groups or population segments that share common views.

Cultural Adaptation

If a population has had experience with an unstructured situation of a given type and has created norms of interpretation within which to adapt to it, such a population is in a position to handle more easily another situation or issue of this same type. What was in the first instance a matter of controversy and debate has now become more understandable and routine. For example, in 1940 when selective service legislation took effect, the draft created considerable controversy. There were debates and demonstrations, sometimes of a very stormy nature. But during World War II the necessity for the draft was generally accepted, and for many years after that war new draft calls created little more than a ripple of protest from those immediately involved. The majority of Americans continued to accept the draft and used established norms of orientation to interpret it. But opposition grew both during the Korean war and the much longer and far more unpopular war in Vietnam. Out of the controversies over the draft during the 1960s, a new set of public-opinion norms emerged. Many people now regarded the draft as unnecessary and even immoral. There were protests and draft evasion. Even during the Vietnamese war years, however, more conservative Americans clung to earlier orientations. Public opinion was thus divided into pro-draft and anti-draft blocs. At present, the controversy has subsided as draft calls have been eliminated.

When the norms of public opinion become both widespread and institutionalized, as they were during World War II regarding the draft, they are part of the *culture* of a people. It is in this sense that public opinion serves as an important part of cultural adaptation. Through the process of public-opinion formation, interpretive norms are invented and institutionalized to give structure and cultural organization to what were previously unstructured situations.

Social Control

At least in societies where the ordinary citizen has a voice in the selection of leaders, public opinion concerning the actions of those leaders provides a measure of social control over public policy. But that control is by no means complete. Even in democracies there is seldom a one-to-one correspondence between public opinion and political decisions. If public opinion becomes unified in such a situation, it serves as a means of social control in two ways. First, the actions of leaders may cause strong reactions, controversies, and debate. Public opinion may form against them and their policies, resulting ultimately in their being ousted. The events surrounding Watergate, which eventually led to the resignation of President Nixon, provide a dramatic illustration of this mechanism of social control. Second, the *potential* of outraged public opinion may check leaders and prevent them from acting in unpopular ways, precisely because they anticipate that a public outcry would follow. This is particularly true in a society characterized by intense media surveillance of public officials. This second mechanism of social control was well illustrated by the uproar that followed President Ford's pardon of former President Nixon. When it was reported that President Ford was considering granting pardons to *all* Watergate participants, public expression of disapproval was so strong that he quickly dropped the matter.

Social Solidarity

When public opinion is unified, it helps to integrate a community or a nation behind collective goals. But it is difficult under any circumstances to marshal the support of the diverse and heterogeneous populations of urban-industrial societies. These differentiated populations are not bound together by that "reciprocal, binding sentiment" which provides the basis for the integrated *Gemeinschaft*.

When such societies face great crises, such as war, the need to achieve social solidarity becomes critical. Stronger links must be forged between individuals and the larger society so as to effectively harness the energies of all citizens to the national purpose. It becomes essential to mobilize their sentiments, enlist their loyalties, instill in them a hatred of the enemy, maintain their morale in the face of privations, and direct their energies to making a maximum contribution to the collective effort. An important means of accomplishing these goals is through propaganda intended to achieve uniform public opinion. If the attention of relevant publics can be elicited via mass-communicated propaganda, and if appropriate norms supportive of the national purpose can by such means be developed and maintained, then collective plans of action for meeting the crisis can be more easily implemented.

Social Disunity

Public opinion can make or break such plans of action. Excellent illustrations of this point are provided by comparing the behavior of Americans during World War II with their conduct during the war in Vietnam. Although considerable division of opinion concerning American participation existed in 1939, consensus was gradually developed; and from Pearl Harbor on, public support of the war effort was both widespread and powerful; sacrifices were willingly made in almost all social spheres. Response to the conflict in Vietnam was very different. Dissident segments of the population, openly critical of the conduct of the war and often strongly opposed to the United States participation in it, appeared early and multiplied rapidly. Lack of unified public opinion regarding the essential nature of the war contributed to domestic disunity. Tax increases that were said to be required to meet the costs of the conflict were resisted; the system of selective service was openly criticized. Even the military aspects of the war—how many soldiers should be sent, what weapons should be used, what places should be bombed—became objects of conflicting public opinion. The nation, in short, lacked the consensus of supportive opinion that leads to social solidarity behind a unified national purpose. Indeed, long before American forces were finally withdrawn, the disunity in public opinion had become as great a national concern as the war itself.

SUMMARY

Systems of communication have formed the basis for social processes throughout the course of human history. Before the invention of written symbols, people were limited to face-to-face communication; they were unable to extend their ideas through time or across space. The emergence of systems of written symbols made possible the accumulation and transmission of culture. As the media available for recording and transmitting ideas became increasingly portable, there was a corresponding elaboration of culture and societal organization. The development of mechanical methods capable of duplicating words and pictures was eventually followed by the discovery of electronic methods capable of transmitting sounds and images, thereby bringing millions of people into communication with each other in new ways.

The mass-communication system of a given society is shaped by its general culture. It operates within the society's political and economic institutions and is a product of historical development. The mass-communication systems of the United States and the Soviet Union illustrate these principles and also show the effects of communication systems in reinforcing societal values.

The process of mass communication has been conceptualized by social scientists primarily within a stimulus-response perspective: media messages provide stimuli to which audience members respond. Intervening between stimulus and response, however, are three major classes of factors: psychological variables, social categories, and informal relationships all influence the way an individual will attend to and respond to mass-communicated material.

The media achieve a variety of direct and indirect effects. By their very existence they alter the organizational characteristics and operation of a society. For the individual they may alter beliefs, attitudes, knowledge, or overt forms of behavior. The concept of media responsibility has been much debated, with critics blaming television, the press, and the movies for a variety of social and political ills and with owners and operators of the media rejecting such conclusions. Social scientists attempt to accumulate research findings to settle such debates with objective generalizations.

The media are widely used in attempts to achieve mass persuasion. One common strategy presumes a psychodynamic relationship between personality components and behavior. Another common strategy attempts to alter the definitions people have of the sociocultural structure around them.

The media play a key part in the formation of public opinion. Issues are brought to the attention of potential members of the public by the media, and the media help develop normative interpretations of unstructured situations. Resulting public opinion serves several significant functions for the society. It is a mechanism of cultural adaptation, a means of social control, and, under certain circumstances at least, a basis of social solidarity.

Part VI
SOCIAL INSTITUTIONS

15
Marriage and the Family

We have defined a social institution (page 92) as a complex pattern of norms, values, roles, sanctions, and goals that focuses on a major area of social activity. Each institution is oriented toward a particular task. The primary goal of the economic institution, for example, is the production and distribution of goods, and the primary goal of the familial institution, from a societal perspective, is biological and cultural survival. Of the five basic social institutions—familial, religious, political, economic, and educational—the family has traditionally been the most fundamental. It is probably the oldest form of social organization.

Though anthropological research has revealed a variety of structural forms and patterns for the family, certain activities seem to be universal. In all societies, the family regulates sexual behavior, parental obligations, and property rights to food, clothing, and shelter. It also provides for the adult need for companionship and for the socialization of children. Because human infants mature slowly, the family cares for them over an extended period to ensure their survival. And because they are born into a complex social world, the family teaches them their society's ways and passes on whatever knowledge and wisdom their ancestors may have acquired in the past. Thus the family is the basic agent not only for replenishing a society's population but also for transmitting its culture.

As the primary agent of socialization, the family plays an important part in preparing children for the sex roles they will assume in adult life. The traditional sex roles of marriage partners are complementary: the woman bears and rears the children; the man provides housing and food; the woman keeps the shelter livable, prepares the food, and sees to it that everyone is adequately clothed; the man acquires or manufactures material goods to be passed on to the next generation; and so on. In most societies men have been the principal decision makers in economics, politics, law, religion, and other social institutions, while women have largely been limited to domestic roles. In modern urban-industrial societies, however, the traditional division of labor between males and females has become blurred, and male dominance is no longer accepted as being necessarily "in the natural order of things." There has been an increased emphasis on marriage as a form of companionship and, at the same time, a growing recognition that marriage does not always satisfy the partners' psychological and emotional needs — that it can be a source of conflict as well as harmony.

In this chapter we will attempt to gain a better perspective on marriage and family life by examining some of the different patterns they have taken in our own culture and in other cultures as well. We will also examine changing norms regarding sexual behavior and sex-role relationships more generally.

VARIATIONS IN FAMILY DESIGN

From a societal perspective, as we have noted, the primary goal of the family is to ensure biological and cultural survival. Societies everywhere have provided for this goal to be met through marriage: a contractual agreement between at least one male and at least one female specifying the rights and obligations of the partners with respect to sexual behavior, child rearing, and the provision of such necessities as food, shelter, and clothing. The agreement can be either formal or informal, but always it is sanctioned within community controls. In our own society, for example, marriage includes a formal contract for most people. Couples must meet certain legal requirements (they must be unmarried, above a particular age, etc.) in order to receive a marriage license; they must then mutually affirm before an authorized civil or religious official that they wish to be married. An informal contractual agreement, by contrast, does not directly involve the state: the individuals simply decide to live together. In some states this arrangement is considered after a specified

period of time to be a common-law marriage; the individuals are entitled to the same legal rights as formally married people (for example, inheritance rights), and the law treats their children as legitimate.[1]

Marriage laws and customs may vary widely from culture to culture, but they all seem to work — that is, they ensure that new generations of children will be cared for and trained in the society's ways. The same thing is true of the varying organizational patterns that characterize the family in different societies — determining such things as the allocation of authority between male and female, the transmission of property from one generation to the next, and the place of residence of the newly married couple (whether they will live with one set of parents or the other or in their own home). (For a discussion of family organizational patterns, see pages 442 – 443.)

Since we are all exposed to the organizational patterns of our own culture from infancy, it is not surprising that we develop strong feelings about the "rightness" of those patterns and the "wrongness" of patterns that are unfamiliar to us. It is especially difficult to avoid ethnocentrism — the feeling that the customs of other groups are quaint, queer, unnatural, or immoral — in considering marital and family practices and patterns of sexual behavior.

As we noted in Chapter 4 (page 103) ethnocentrism can be intracultural as well as crosscultural. With respect to sex codes, Kinsey found a quarter of a century ago that college students in the United States defined moral behavior quite differently than did their contemporaries with less education. College students tended to condone a form of heterosexual activity called "petting," whereas the less educated, who condoned premarital coitus for males, defined petting as unnatural and immoral.[2] Class differences can also be discerned in American child-rearing practices and family authority patterns (see page 158).

Clearly, one of the best antidotes to ethnocentrism is learning more about cultures and subcultures different from our own. In the following sections we will examine some widely

1. For more information on the legal aspects of formal and informal marriage agreements, see William M. Kephart, *The Family, Society, and the Individual,* 2nd ed. (Boston: Houghton Mifflin Co., 1966), pp. 376 – 400.

2. A. C. Kinsey et al., *Sexual Behavior in the Human Male* (Philadelphia: W. B. Saunders, 1948); and *Sexual Behavior in the Human Female* (Philadelphia: W. B. Saunders, 1953).

differing patterns of family life—ranging from those in ancient Palestine to those in present-day China—as a means of broadening our perspective on the family as a social institution and of suggesting its relationships to other social institutions.

FAMILY PATTERNS IN THE ANCIENT WORLD

The cultural roots of the contemporary Western family can be traced to ancient Palestine, Greece, and Rome. A brief historical overview may help us recognize these roots, while at the same time demonstrating that the cultural patterns in any society can be understood only with reference to that society and to a given point in time.

The Ancient Hebrews

The typical Hebrew family in Old Testament days was patriarchal, patrilineal, and to a great extent patrilocal. The father or oldest male ruled over his household. He was literally the priest of the home, and this conception of his role made the family into a religious as well as a social and economic unit.

Although the marriage structure was basically monogamous, the patriarch could have several lawful wives, a man could take his female slaves as concubines, and a man was obliged to accept as wife the childless widow of his brother and to "raise up seed" so that his brother's family might not die out. This last rule served a number of important functions, not the least of which was keeping property within the family. It also provided a widow with a home and could spare her the disgrace of being barren, one of the gravest of social shortcomings for a woman of that time.[3]

Divorce among the ancient Hebrews was originally the prerogative of the male. It was a legal affair in that the man was required to give his wife a written "bill of divorcement."[4] A deterrent to divorce was the fact that a husband had to return his wife's dowry if the divorce was without due cause.

FAMILY ORGANIZATIONAL PATTERNS

FORMS OF MARRIAGE

The two basic organizational forms of marriage are *monogamy*, the union of one man and one woman, and *polygamy*, plural marriage. Polygamy may involve either the union of one man with more than one woman *(polygyny)* or the union of one woman with more than one man *(polyandry)*. Monogamy occurs in all societies and is predominant even where polygamy exists. It has prevailed as the only "moral" form of marital relationship wherever Christian influence is dominant.

Polygyny, the most common form of polygamy, is still in evidence throughout much of the world. Often, where polygyny is found, only males with prestige and power can afford to have more than one wife. Aside from the economic problem, polygyny as a general practice would require either a surplus of women or many wifeless men.

Polyandry is much less common. It may develop where there is a shortage of females or where the means of subsistence are so scarce that more than one male is needed to support one woman and her children. When disparities in the sex ratio decrease and means of subsistence improve, societies that permit polyandry tend to move toward monogamy.

TYPES OF FAMILY GROUP

A family can be *nuclear*, consisting only of one set of parents and their children, or *extended*, involving a greater number of familial relationships other than parents, children, and siblings.

The members of the nuclear family are the father, the mother, and their immediate children. For the children, it is the *family of orientation*, and it is also *consanguine*, because they are biologically related to all the other members. For the parents, it is the *family of procreation*. The nuclear family exists in modified form when one of the spouses is missing.

3. Earle B. Cross, "The Hebrew Family in Biblical Times," in *Marriage and the Family*, ed. Jeffrey K. Hadden and Marie L. Borgatta (Itasca, Ill.: F. E. Peacock Publishers, Inc., 1969), p. 71.
4. Ibid., p. 70.

We shall call any family that includes more than mother, father, and their children an extended family. As such, the extended family continues to be found in modern urban societies, including our own. However, more rigidly defined as a family that includes within one household mother, father, children, and married children with their spouses and children, it has not been common at any time in history.

PATTERNS OF RESIDENCE, AUTHORITY, AND DESCENT

Solutions to such problems as who lives where with whom, who makes what decisions, and who inherits whose name and what property have led to a variety of patterns of family life.

In *patrilocal* residence patterns, the norms require that all the father's male children live in or near his house. *Matrilocal* patterns require that the female children live with the mother. These patterns are also called *virilocal* or *uxorilocal* respectively, because the point at issue is whether the young couple lives with his parents or hers. We are most familiar with the *neolocal* pattern, which permits the couple to live away from the parents of both; but the patrilocal pattern predominates in a great many other societies and can be found in American cities among various ethnic groups.

Patriarchy, or rule by the oldest male in the household, is the dominant family pattern in most parts of the world. *Matriarchy,* or rule by the mother, is much less common. When maternal domination does occur, it is usually related to the absence of a male provider—that is, the father is either missing or, if present, unable to provide economic support. In Western society today, the emerging family pattern is increasingly *egalitarian,* with authority shared by husband and wife and to some extent by the children. But to the extent that the husband's occupational role determines the family income, place of residence, and general social standing, the contemporary pattern remains patriarchal.

Descent, family name, inheritance, performance of religious rituals, interaction with relatives, and a host of related activities may be focused on the father's side of the family *(patrilineal),* on the mother's *(matrilineal),* or on both *(bilateral).* In patrilineal societies a person's major kin relations and the greater part of all social relationships are established in the male line. In the matrilineal pattern the major social relations are developed through the female line. In the bilateral pattern—found in American society and in about 30 percent of all other societies—social relationships are developed through both the mother's and the father's line.

The reasons why particular organizational patterns become preferred in a given society are not always clear, though some patterns appear to fit logically with certain others—for example, a patriarchal authority pattern seems consistent with a patrilineal pattern for property transfer and social relationships and a patrilocal pattern for determining place of residence. In contemporary industrial societies, where growing numbers of women have entered the labor force and there is a good deal of geographical and occupational mobility, the trend has been toward an egalitarian authority pattern accompanied by a bilateral pattern of descent and a neolocal pattern of residence. But despite a tendency toward such congruity, patterns are sometimes mixed. Thus in the Hopi family (page 446) the patterns of descent and residence are matrilineal and matrilocal, whereas the authority pattern tends to be patriarchal or egalitarian.

For more information see Michael Gordon, *The Nuclear Family in Crisis* (New York: Harper & Row, Inc., 1972), pp. 2–21; and George P. Murdock, *Social Structure* (New York: Macmillan, Inc., 1949), pp. 15 ff.

This Egyptian funeral stela from the First Intermediate Period (2170–1991 B.C.) illustrates the respective social ranking of men and women in a male-dominated society. The nobleman Uha is depicted as being nearly twice the size of his wife, befitting his rank as a male and a nobleman.

Although marriages were often arranged by the parents, a Hebrew girl was allowed to reject a proposed marriage partner. Once wed, she had more freedom than wives in other societies of that time, and despite her subordinate position, she was not without influence on her husband. The Old Testament offers much evidence of deep love between husbands and wives, a feature of marriage not found as commonly among the early Greeks and Romans or later among the neighboring Muslims. In time, Hebrew wives were allowed to sue for divorce under certain conditions.

The Old Testament is full of injunctions to children to have regard for both their parents. The most famous, of course, is the Fifth Commandment: "Honor thy father and thy mother" (Exodus 20:12). Early laws permitted the death penalty for children who struck their parents, and the Deuteronomic code specified that children who disobeyed or failed to respond to the voice of their parents could be tried by the elders. Yet parental authority obviously did not extinguish affection; over the centuries the closeness and warmth of the Jewish family has been proverbial.

The Ancient Greeks

Families in the Greek city-states were patriarchal and patrilineal. Although not required by formal law, an important feature of Greek marriage was the dowry given by the bride's father to the groom. Like their Hebrew counterparts, Greek parents arranged the marriage, but, unlike the Hebrew bride, the Greek bride had little to say about her marriage partner. Adultery was looked on almost as a violation of a property right and, perhaps for that reason, was punished only when the wife was guilty.[5] While the Greeks were monogamous, both prostitution and concubinage were institutionalized. Divorce existed, but it was not common, apparently because the husband was required to return the dowry to his wife's family. This tradition seems to have served as a mechanism of social control for many peoples.

Accounts of abiding love between husbands and wives can be found in Greek literature, as in Homer's description of Odysseus and Penelope; but the predominant roles of Greek women seem to have been those of childbearer, housekeeper, and overseer of the female slaves. Greek men turned to their own sex for companionship and sometimes for love affairs as well. Male homosexuality was accepted as an alternative form of sexual behavior.

5. Panos D. Bardis, "Family Forms and Variations Historically Considered," in *Handbook of Marriage and the Family,* ed. Harold T. Christensen (Chicago: Rand McNally & Co., 1964), p. 431.

The Romans and Early Christians

The patriarchal family of the early Romans was perhaps the closest to the ideal type of all the progenitors of the modern Western family. The descent pattern was patrilineal, and the extended family system was the ideal. The father had great legal power over his wife and children, though all surviving sons were eligible for inheritance on an equal basis—a normative pattern that tended to break up the extended family system and eventually the power of the family by reducing the dependence of the younger sons on their oldest brother.

The Romans were monogamous, but they accepted concubinage. Marriages were generally arranged, and dowries were customary. Divorce, though strongly proscribed during the early period, became more and more common under the Empire. It appears that if a man divorced his wife without due cause, he was required to return the dowry.[6] Under the Empire, Roman women achieved more freedom and prestige than Greek and Hebrew women ever had.

The decline of the Roman Empire was accompanied by the gradual disintegration of its family system and the gradual development of a new system based on Christian ideals. The early Christians saw the trends toward easy divorce, the emancipation of women, and sexual freedom as mirroring the overall decadence of Roman society. As Leslie notes, the Roman family system, once an unusually strong and stable one, "had become a symbol of social disorganization and personal degeneracy."[7]

Early Christian attitudes toward marriage were shaped partly by traditional cultural values, but these values came gradually to be reshaped around the tenets of a new religious faith. Believing as they did that the day of final judgment was close at hand, followers of the new faith called for spiritual cleansing and for rejection of concerns of the flesh. Asceticism and celibacy were primary ideals in the culture of the early Christians, with the result that the institution of marriage was held in low esteem—

lower, perhaps, than in any other culture before or since.[8] St. Paul, himself a bachelor, recommended marriage only as prevention of sin: "If they cannot contain, let them marry; for it is better to marry than to burn" (that is, be consumed by licentious passions). St. Paul's letter to the Ephesians on the roles of husband and wife helped establish male dominance as a Christian ideal: "Let wives be subject to their husbands as to the Lord; because a husband is head of the wife, just as Christ is head of the Church. . . . But just as the Church is subject to Christ, so also let wives be to their husbands in all things" (Eph. 5:22–24). Although St. Paul and other Christian leaders set forth norms urging husbands and wives to love one another, this emphasis on male dominance and the hierarchical structure of the family sharply restricted the role of women in Christian societies.

The conflict between spirit and flesh was most powerfully expressed in the writings of St. Augustine in the fifth century. He saw sex as basically sinful, excusable only for purposes of procreation. He believed that the sex act, as an act of animal lust, was despiritualizing and that norms had to be developed to discourage couples from performing it. Augustine's theology of marriage and family life dominated Church thinking for over a thousand years.

In the fifth century the Christian Church declared firmly that marriage was permanent and that divorce and remarriage were to be negatively sanctioned by excommunication. This was a sharp break with Hebrew and Roman practices—indeed with the practices of almost all other societies. In addition, marriage to non-Christians was strongly forbidden. Throughout most of Europe during the Middle Ages, and long after the Protestant Reformation challenged the power of the Church, family organization and sexual behavior in the West reflected the beliefs and practices of the early Christians.

THE HOPI FAMILY

The marital and family patterns discussed in the previous sections, of course, are all part of the Western heritage. Although they differ in many ways from patterns in contemporary Western

6. Ibid., p. 438.
7. Gerald L. Leslie, *The Family in Social Context* (New York: Oxford University Press, 1967), p. 176.
8. Ibid., pp. 177 ff.

societies, we can nevertheless recognize elements of continuity. To broaden our perspective on the family as a basic social institution, we must look to societies that have developed independently of the West. Here we will briefly examine one such society, that of the Hopi Indians.

Closely related to the Zuñi (pages 105–107), the Hopi have lived in an isolated desert region of northern Arizona for more than fifteen hundred years.[9] The present population of about four thousand is descended from a society five times as large that inhabited the region at the time of the Spanish conquest. The Hopi kept to themselves then as they do now, and they remain culturally homogeneous. They eke out a precarious living based on farming, with famine a constant danger. Few peoples have faced greater challenges in the struggle to survive.

The Hopi see the universe as an ordered, interrelated system of reciprocal relations which they express in ritual behavior. Although nonhuman forces are acknowledged, it is the will of the human being that counts. Reciprocity is not between individuals but rather between groups, so that in a ceremonial a Hopi acts as a representative of some group. The group protects the individual throughout the life cycle. Hopi norms call for unselfish, modest, nonaggressive behavior. No competing ideologies or contrasting religious doctrines disturb the Hopi way of life.

Family Organization

The Hopi pattern of family organization emphasizes extended kin role relations, but the nuclear family is also important. The nuclear family unit is part of a larger group of related units that form a single household. The Hopi are matrilineal and matrilocal—blood relationships are traced through the female line, and home ownership and performance of major ceremonials are based on this line of descent.

Ceremonials are conducted by the clans, each of which consists of two or more households related through the female line. Clans are grouped in units called *phratries.* Among the important functions of the phratry are social control of marriage (marriage is not allowed within a phratry) and control over important reli-

gious ceremonials. The chief priest is the brother of the formal head of the clan—the ruling matriarch, who keeps the symbol of ownership of the ceremonial in her home.

The village political structure is composed of the chief priests of the ceremonial societies. Their purpose is not to make new laws but rather to affirm the traditional Hopi mores in their decisions. Within the family, the mother and her brother are expected to exercise authority—again by enforcing traditions, not by making new rules.

Courtship and Marriage

Courtship among the Hopi is informal. After boys and girls have endured the *rites de passage,* they are ready for courting. Boys are then considered as men and sleep in the men's ceremonial houses rather than at home. Apparently they are free to visit girls of their choice by night; the girl's parents will not protest if the boy is a good prospect. A girl of marriageable age may have several suitors. If she becomes pregnant, she chooses a husband from among them. (There are ceremonial occasions when a girl can choose a marriage partner, but on these other occasions the boy is permitted to decline the honor.) Despite some dispute on this point, virginity does not seem to be a prime requisite for marriage among the Hopi. Indeed, the lack of shame or guilt about premarital pregnancy suggests one way in which the matrilineal structure supports the status of women.

Marriage to a person within the phratry is prohibited, and marriage to a person within one's father's phratry is usually avoided. Ceremonial preparation for marriage is extensive. The ceremony is completed when the girl brings her new husband into her mother's home. Divorce occurs among the Hopi with little fanfare: the husband simply moves back into his mother's house. The wife always retains custody of the children, and they are cared for by the household group, which, with the mother's brother, fills the gap left by the departed father.

9. This summary is based on Stuart A. Queen et al., *The Family in Various Cultures* (Philadelphia: J. B. Lippincott Co., 1961), Ch. 3; Wayne Dennis, *The Hopi Child* (New York: John Wiley & Sons, Inc., 1940); and Ruth E. Simpson, *The Hopi Indians* (Los Angeles, Calif.: Southwest Museum Leaflets, 1953), No. 25.

The life-style of the Hopi Indians of northern Arizona differs considerably from the life-style of most industrialized societies. Hopi family organization is an interesting combination of the nuclear and extended families. Typically, men work the cornfields and weave clothing, while women make baskets and pottery and take care of cooking and household chores. Because of the matrilineal pattern of family organization, the mother's brother is the primary disciplinarian and educator of his sister's sons. This relationship is probably the most crucial one in the development of the male self, but it also makes possible the development of a warmer and friendlier relationship between a son and his father.

In fact, these people play an important role in a child's upbringing even in a stable marriage. The fact that divorce is permitted does not imply that Hopi marriages are unstable and beset with conflict. Hopi life tends to be peaceful in all respects.

Kin Relationships

The terminology of kin among the Hopi gives an idea of the extensiveness of clan arrangements. The mother's blood brother and all males of this generation in the clan are called "mother's brother." All men and women of one's father's generation are called "father's brother" and "father's sister," respectively. These kinship terms are not just quaint expressions; they are reflections of the roles people are expected to perform and of the attitudes they are expected to have toward one another. For example, the husband is a guest in his wife's home; in many ways his closest ties are with his mother's home, since he is "mother's brother" to his sister's children. And since if necessary he is considered to be mother's brother to all females of his sister's generation in his mother's clan, the possibility of his playing this role is greatly enhanced. Through training, he has been prepared to help his sister(s) discipline her (their) children. Just as he learned his ceremonial and clan roles from an uncle of his mother's family, so will he in turn help his sister's children prepare to take over these roles.

Another aspect of matrilineal structure with matrilocal residence is revealed when a conjugal quarrel occurs: the wife is backed by a solid wall of kin while the husband stands alone. Thus the status of women is relatively high in Hopi society, compared to traditional Western societies.

Despite the matrilineal patterns, the father-son tie among the Hopi is very close, partly because the division of labor allows the father to teach his son about planting and herding. In addition, since the mother's brother has the major responsibility as disciplinarian, the father is free to develop a warm, affectionate relationship with his son. Thus every adult male has some degree of role specialization with reference to the young male. The adult male can be primarily expressive and affectionate with his son and a disciplinarian with his nephew.

In a matrilineal society in its ideal form, the role relationship between a mother's brother and her son is the most crucial one in the development of masculine identity. With some modification, this is true among the Hopi. Mother's brother is the disciplinarian, and to make the boy a reliable worker, the uncle often resorts to drastic measures, putting him through all sorts of trials to prepare him for life. The mother's brother is also the key man in the boy's marriage arrangements and may even act as marriage counselor. Finally, he will eventually teach the boy the ceremonial and clan roles, thus preserving them within the clan for another generation.

A girl is raised by her mother and maternal relatives. From babyhood she is trained to perform household tasks, and when she is old enough, her mother or a particularly skilled neighbor or relative teaches her the handicraft that is practiced by the women of her village. By the time the girl is fifteen or sixteen, she has learned all the skills and knowledge necessary to maintain her own household.

Similarities with the Western Family

When we compare the Hopi way with that of Western societies, we find striking similarities as well as differences. The classic Jewish family also seeks oneness within an extended family pattern, with strong symbolic-religious overtones. No better example of a Christian achievement of unity through an extended pattern is to be found than in Horace Miner's study of the French-Canadian parish, St. Denis.[10] There, as among the Hopi, family, work, and religion were integrated into a yearly cycle.

Although the Hopi vest the authority to make decisions in the female line, the males actually make most of the important decisions, as they have traditionally done in Western societies. If the Hopi courtship, marriage, and divorce patterns differ from our own, we can still see that sexual behavior in their society is regulated, as it is to some extent in all societies.

10. Horace Miner, *St. Denis: A French-Canadian Parish* (Chicago: The University of Chicago Press, 1939).

Hopi society, like ours, has norms to guide the procreation and education of children, the bestowal of status, and daily social interaction. Such organizational forms define interaction with nonfamily members and also the mechanisms of social control.

Perhaps the most significant difference between the Hopi way and the Western way lies not so much in goals as in the different means used to achieve them. In most Western societies, individuals seek self-fulfillment through personal freedom. The Hopi, on the other hand, do not desire personal freedom; self-fulfillment is gained through the achievement of *group* goals. The Hopi way is to be in harmony with the group.

RESTRUCTURING OF THE FAMILY IN CHINA

The close relationship between family patterns and cultural orientations can be further illustrated by the restructuring of family life in China since the Communist Revolution of 1949. In an earlier chapter we cited the traditional Chinese family as a model of the extended patriarchal, patrilineal system based on a clan structure (see pages 318–323). A key feature of the social revolution that has followed the Communists' military victory has been the attempt to restructure marriage and the family.[11] The Marriage Law of 1950 (see inset, page 450) was aimed directly at the heart of the old system.

The law not only abolished the traditional system of marriage; it also set up a new system in which people could choose their own marriage partners and in which women had the same rights as men. However, unlike the family structure of the West, which is highly individualistic, the new system in China is part of a collectivist ideology that puts the group above the individual. Like the Hopi, the Chinese to a large extent

find the meaning of their individual behavior in the contribution it makes to group well-being.

Work Units

Almost all of China is divided into decentralized work units. Some 80 percent of the families live in rural units called people's communes. The population of each commune varies from twenty to sixty thousand. Each commune aims at self-sufficiency; all able-bodied members are expected to contribute to achieving that goal. Women work along with men, and, at least theoretically, all the jobs in each commune can be performed equally well by either sex. Each commune has its own health services and day-care centers and provides schooling for the young, through high school if possible.

Urban areas are divided into factory and neighborhood units, both of which—depending on their size—may provide educational, day-care, and health services. Whatever the nature of the unit within which they live, people are encouraged to develop and maintain a strong sense of group identity.

Male and Female Roles

Not least among the changes being wrought in the new China are those relating to societal roles for men and women and to the liberation of both sexes from traditional ways. Women can and do perform any of the jobs in the factories, and in the production brigades of the agricultural communes they make up roughly half the labor force. But despite government efforts to make women coequal with men, sex-role differentiation has not been completely eliminated. Engineering, for example, is still considered a man's job, while day-care centers and elementary schools are staffed primarily by women. Significantly, too, women are far behind men in positions of political power. In 1973, after the proportion of women in the Central Committee was increased by the Tenth Congress of the Chinese Communist Party, only 10.25 percent of the full membership of the Committee was female. Only two of the twenty-five full and alternate members of the Politburo are women, and there are no women members on the standing committee of the Politburo.[12]

11. Unless otherwise specified, this discussion of the Chinese family is derived from the following sources: Ping-ti Ho, "An Historian's View of the Chinese Family System," in *Man and Civilization,* ed. Seymour Farber et al. (New York: McGraw-Hill Book Company, 1965), pp. 15–30; Leslie, *The Family in Social Context,* pp. 81–123; "Coming of Age in Communist China," *Newsweek,* February 21, 1972, pp. 44–51; and John S. Aird, *Population Policy and Demographic Prospects in the People's Republic of China* (Washington, D.C.: National Institutes of Health, U.S. Department of Health, Education, and Welfare, 1972).

12. *New York Times,* September 16, 1973.

THE CHINESE MARRIAGE LAW OF 1950

CHAPTER ONE: GENERAL PRINCIPLES
ARTICLE 1.

The arbitrary and compulsory feudal marriage system, which is based upon the superiority of man over woman and which ignores the children's interests, is abolished.

The New Democratic marriage system, which is based on free choice of partners, on monogamy, on equal rights for both sexes, and on protection of the lawful interests of women and children, shall be put into effect.
ARTICLE 2.

Polygamy, concubinage, child betrothal, interference with the remarriage of widows and the exaction of money or gifts in connection with marriage shall be prohibited.

CHAPTER TWO: CONTRACTING OF MARRIAGE
ARTICLE 3.

Marriage shall be based upon the complete willingness of the two parties. Neither party shall use compulsion and no third party shall be allowed to interfere.
ARTICLE 4.

A marriage can be contracted only after the man has reached twenty years of age and the woman has reached eighteen years of age.
ARTICLE 5.

No man or woman in any of the following instances shall be allowed to marry:

(a) Where the man and woman are lineal relatives by blood or where the man and woman are brother and sister born of the same parents or where the man and woman are half-brother and half-sister. The question of prohibiting marriage between collateral relatives by blood within the fifth degree of relationship is to be determined by custom.

(b) When one party, because of certain physical defects, is sexually impotent.

(c) Where one party is suffering from venereal disease, mental disorder, leprosy, or any other disease which is regarded by medical science as rendering the person unfit for marriage.
ARTICLE 6.

In order to contract a marriage, both the man and the woman shall register in person with the people's government of the subdistrict or village in which they reside. If the marriage is found to be in conformity with the provisions of this law, the local people's government shall, without delay, issue a marriage certificate. . . .

From C. K. Yang, *The Chinese Family in the Communist Revolution* (Cambridge, Mass.: The Technology Press, Massachusetts Institute of Technology, 1959), pp. 221–222.

Sex and Marriage

Chinese sexual mores are very conservative. Western visitors report seeing young couples showing affection in public, but this type of activity is frowned upon and is certainly not common. Overt sexual provocation seems to be avoided: women use no makeup and wear jackets and trousers that hide rather than reveal the body. Since the promulgation of the Marriage Law in 1950, the government has gradually extended the acceptable age for marriage to twenty-five for women and twenty-eight for men. It appears probable that most young men and women in their early twenties are virgins.

The government seems to have been fairly successful in altering the traditional pattern of early marriage. One of the primary goals has been to slow population growth: increasingly, the norm of family size is two or at most three children.[13] At the same time, the government has added goals other than marriage and parenthood to the period of late adolescence and early adulthood, urging young people to devote these years to studying, to developing their talents, to extending their physical capacities through sports, and to becoming politically aware. Thus they will be better able to serve the country.

13. See the discussion of China in Chapter 11, "Demographic Change," pages 318–323.

Increasingly, young Chinese are choosing their own marriage partners. The most likely place to meet them is on the job, and the degree of success of the government's program to replace old customs with new seems to vary with locality: the closer to cities and modern communes, the more effective the new norms are likely to be.

The Family

The role of the Chinese family as an agent of socialization has been deemphasized. Instead, day-care centers, schools, communes, and factories perform this function. Political indoctrination—in the form of games and songs representing aspects of the thought of Chairman Mao Tse-tung—is begun in day-care centers and kindergartens (see page 146). Socialization for the collectivist ideology is apparent throughout the educational system. Although academic subjects are studied in the schools, students are not graded and competition among pupils has been eliminated. Even the relationship between teacher and pupil has been altered: observers have been impressed by the degree of cooperation and general helpfulness found in the learning process.[14]

Because both parents are actively engaged in the labor force, children spend most of their early years in day-care centers or under the care of grandmothers in a communal setting. Within the communal unit, they work along with their parents in an atmosphere in which cooperation between all members, regardless of age, is stressed. The Chinese proudly proclaim that there is no generation gap in China, and Western observers agree that it is not apparent in the activities they have witnessed.

Between parents and children there is a relaxed, generally happy relationship, which is particularly evident in the evenings after work. The old style patriarchal family is rapidly disappearing; and although the nuclear family in China does not perform as many functions as the nuclear family in the West, it seems to persist as an important affectional group. Ping-ti Ho comments on this enduring feature of family strength:

Today, after more than two thousand years, they have stripped the family of all its functions except one, namely, to procreate, nurture, and educate children with understanding and love, a function which no other human agency can perform. If they have so far succeeded in making this one function work under circumstances many times more difficult than those which confront the Western family, we may perhaps end on a note of guarded optimism: the family will survive.[15]

THE CHANGING AMERICAN FAMILY

In comparing family patterns in several societies, ancient as well as modern, we have attempted to show both similarities and differences. In *all* societies, the cluster of values, norms, roles, sanctions, and so forth that make up "the family" as a social institution provide a means for ensuring biological survival (e.g., by regulating sexual behavior and parental obligations) and also for transmitting the society's culture. But different societies evolve different means for achieving these basic goals. In the sections that follow we will consider how cultural tradition and changing circumstance have combined to shape—and to continuously reshape—family life and sexual morality in the United States.

INFLUENCES FROM COLONIAL DAYS

The colonists from England who settled in the northeastern part of what is now the United States were—or were influenced by—the Puritans, a dissenting religious group that had broken away from the Anglican Church, the national Church of England. The New England environment encouraged the settlement of towns, and the existence of towns enabled the church to be a central force in the daily lives of the people.

14. Personal communication with Dr. Norman Chance, Anthropology Department, University of Connecticut.
15. Ping-ti Ho, "An Historian's View," pp. 27–28.

This marriage certificate, which was used in the United States in the second half of the nineteenth century, illustrates the influence of Christianity on American family patterns. Biblical injunctions require husbands to love and provide for their wives, "giving honor unto them, as unto the weaker vessel," while wives are told: "submit yourselves unto your own husbands, as unto the Lord."

In the South, an agricultural economy discouraged the kind of centralization typical of New England. Under the plantation system, great spreads of land were owned by white planters and worked by black slaves. Although small farmers with few, if any, slaves were much more numerous than owners of large plantations, the big planters dominated the society. They took over a number of traditional church functions, holding weddings and funerals on their own estates and sometimes running the local church.

In both North and South, European patterns of male dominance and patriarchal control of the home remained in evidence. In the South, the household tended to be larger than in New England. On the great plantations, married sons might bring their brides to live in the big house, while slave cabins clustered nearby. In New England, sons might build houses near their father's farm or his place of business, but they were equally likely to move to a new town, set off for the frontier, or go to sea. In both regions, the household was the center of social life, performing as a largely self-sufficient economic unit and providing educational, religious, and protective activities for its members.

Because of strong Puritan influence, the New England colonies had stringent laws on sexual behavior. The Puritans in Massachusetts, like their English counterparts, made adultery a crime punishable by death, though the death penalty was rarely invoked.[16] Fornicators were fined, subjected to corporal punishment, or forced to marry. In Connecticut, adultery, homosexuality, and bestiality could be punished by death. Later, the laws governing sexual behavior became less severe. In 1649 the death penalty for adultery was revoked in Massachusetts; but offenders could still be punished by up to forty blows of the whip, public exposure in the stocks, and perpetual wearing of the letter "A," as described in Nathaniel Hawthorne's novel *The Scarlet Letter*.

In the South, where most of the early colonists were Anglicans rather than Puritans, the laws were somewhat more lenient. In colonial Virginia, for example, prosecutions of free persons for adultery were rare, though indentured servants were regularly called to account.[17] Servant women who bore illegitimate children were punished. The law of 1661 fixed the punishment at two years of extra service, but a year later the preamble of a new law acknowledged that dissolute masters often got their servant maids with child in order to keep them indentured.

Colonial Americans, like their European forebears, embraced a double standard of sexual morality. This was equally true in both the North and the South. In the South, however, the presence of the black slave population led to a special emphasis on defending "the purity of white womanhood." Elsewhere in the country, women labored in the fields beside men; and as New England became industrialized, girls often went to work in mills and factories. But in the South every white family that could afford to do so kept its female members at home. Before the Civil War, the teachers in Southern schools were often Northern women.

The activities of women during the Civil War—as nurses, seamstresses, munitions makers, office workers, and fund raisers—should have exploded the myth of female fragility. However, norms, values, and beliefs continued to support male dominance, and prudishness and prostitution went hand in hand. In the bourgeois home the wife allowed her husband to slake his animal passions upon her so that she might fulfill her calling by bearing and rearing children. The daughters of the family were expected to blush at male compliments and faint at male vulgarity, while the sons were expected to sow their wild oats with "easy" women before marrying virgins of their own social class. Although individual feminists had been calling for legal justice, moral reform, and liberation from domestic confinement for decades, not until the 1920s did American women in considerable numbers rebel against their social and sexual subordination.

INFLUENCES OF INDUSTRIALIZATION AND URBANIZATION

In a classic essay written more than a generation ago, William Ogburn enumerated the activities traditionally performed by the American family: affectional-procreational; economic; educational; religious; protective (political); status-giving; and recreational.[18] The colonial family satisfied many of the needs of its members by performing all of these activities—often with little or no aid from outside agencies. Ogburn saw the dilemma of modern times as the loss of many of the traditional activities of the family. He theorized that industrialization and urbanization had changed the family from a relatively self-sufficient institution to an institution whose main function was the distribution of affection and the formation of personality. Below, we will discuss some of the major changes that have taken place in the structure and activities of the American family and consider their implications.

16. Morris Ploscowe, *Sex and the Law* (Englewood Cliffs, N.J.: Prentice-Hall, Inc., 1951), p. 143.
17. Arthur P. Scott, *Criminal Law in Colonial Virginia* (Chicago: The University of Chicago Press, 1930), p. 280.
18. William F. Ogburn with Clark Tibbitts, "The Family and Its Functions," in *Recent Social Trends,* by the President's Research Committee on Social Trends (New York: McGraw-Hill Book Company, 1934), pp. 661 ff.

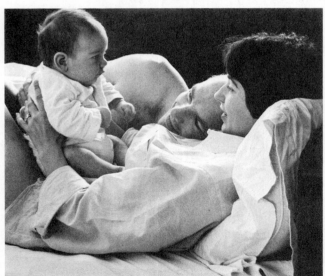

Family patterns in the United States are undergoing rapid change. The dramatic rise in divorce rates, the dissatisfaction of some women with housework and child care, the fact that many families move frequently—never getting a chance to "put down roots"—are all pointed to as signs of the failure of the nuclear family. But some families still maintain close ties among members—as does the family in the photo on the top of the opposite page, which has gotten together annually for Thanksgiving dinner for forty-five years. Elderly people without families can sometimes find new roles—for example, by becoming foster grandparents to disadvantaged children (above). Since many nuclear families appear to meet the needs of their members, it is difficult to know if the nuclear family is "in crisis" or if it is adapting to changing times.

Economic Activities

Murdock reports that family organization always combines the rights of sexual intercourse with norms and roles for a division of labor designed to satisfy the needs for food, shelter, and clothing.[19] In traditional societies, the family is a producing and a consuming unit. In urban-industrial societies, it has become mainly a consuming unit. The wife no longer has to make all the clothes, preserve a large part of the year's supply of food, and help her husband with gardening and caring for the livestock. The husband's labor brings forth not agricultural produce for his family's use but an abstract medium of exchange—money—or, more often than not, an even more abstract check representing the money. Quite likely the wife earns a paycheck of her own. Most children have no economic role at all, although they are often set to doing little chores simply because work is alleged to be good for building "character." Even adolescents, who once would have been putting in full days of labor in the home, the shop, or the fields, often find meaningful work very hard to get.

In an important sense, then, the family has lost the productive activity: it no longer produces its own material goods. But *consumption* of goods and services is very much an activity of the family, and all members are encouraged to participate. Once they worked together; today they shop together—for food, clothing, sporting goods, television sets, and the like. Children learn early the ways of the marketplace.

Socialization and Education

Although the family has lost many of its socialization activities to other societal institutions, it has retained many others. Parsons has argued that the family continues to be the prime agent for a sense of social solidarity for the individual:

In socialization the family is above all the agency for establishing cathexes and identification, for integration into the series of social systems in which the child will function as an adult. Above all, perhaps, it is the primary agency for developing his capacity to integrate with others, to trust and be trusted, to exercise influence, and to accept legitimate influence.[20]

The influence of family socialization is obvious in courtship and mate selection. Early family training puts limits on so-called free choice, contributing to the strong tendency for individuals to marry within their own race, ethnic group, religion, and social class. Parental influences are also strong in other areas of adult life, especially if the family has been harmonious. Lazarsfeld and his colleagues have reported that the family is one of the most important influences on voting behavior;[21] and Davies, in summarizing the literature on political socialization, states:

The family's central role in forming the individual's political personality derives from its role as the main source for the satisfaction of his needs. The child therefore tends to identify with his parents and to adopt their outlook toward politics.[22]

Another important aspect of socialization is the degree of conflict children observe between their parents. Studies show that the factor correlating most consistently with successful marriage is harmony in the parental home—that is, the children of a happy marriage are more likely than others to have happy marriages. Thus the family continues to contribute to education for future family life.

Protecting and Disciplining Family Members

In the past the father of the family was often the sole protector of his wife and children against external dangers. Often, too, he had the power of life and death over them. It was *his* business if his children, or his wife, needed a beating. Now police, city, county, and state organizations handle many of the protective activities the head of the family used to be responsible for, and both law and custom have drastically reduced the father's disciplinary power.

The reciprocal role obligations by which parents looked after their children's needs and

19. George P. Murdock, *Social Structure* (New York: Macmillan, Inc., 1949), pp. 15 ff.

20. Talcott Parsons in *Man and Civilization,* ed. Farber et al., p. 44.

21. Paul F. Lazarsfeld, Bernard Berelson, and Helen Gaudet, *The People's Choice* (New York: Columbia University Press, 1948).

22. James C. Davies, "The Family's Role in Political Socialization," *The Annals of the American Academy of Political and Social Science* (September 1965): 10.

children looked after their parents' needs in old age have also broken down. Just as various governmental and private agencies provide protective services for the children, so also are there extrafamilial agencies to protect the elderly, providing them with retirement pensions, social security benefits, and special housing. However, this reduction of the family's protective function has created many problems for the elderly in our society.

Old age, like youth, is a period of social dependency, but so far at least, we have not given our older people the attention and support we give the young. That is not too difficult to understand, given the fact that the young are looked on as the coming generation, to be nourished and nurtured and trained for the future. But though the elderly may have "had their day," it is not humane to ignore their needs—or wise to overlook their potential contributions to family, community, and society.

Gordon looks to the Israeli kibbutzim as the model for a type of commune that may offer useful roles and new meaning to life for the aged. In the kibbutzim, where baby-sitting and similar chores have become institutionalized for the aged, the elderly are better off, he believes, than the elderly who live alone in urban settings, even though not all problems have been solved.[23]

In the United States today, programs like Foster Grandparents provide new ways to share activities across generations by establishing quasi-family relations between underprivileged children and interested older people. Although such programs are limited in scope and financial support, they indicate that useful roles are available for the elderly in our society.[24] And for many thousands of elder Americans who prefer to be with their own generation, centers for senior citizens provide a place to go, people to talk to, and things to do—from a game of pinochle or cribbage to a lesson in oil painting or transcendental meditation. Making sure that old people living alone can reach such centers is a simple service that many cities are attempting to provide through such means as free public transportation.

Religious Activities

In colonial days, particularly in New England, religion was often central to social life, and the religious training of children was a basic familial activity.[25] But as society has become increasingly secularized, the importance of religion in family life has declined. While such forms of ritual as attending church, saying grace at meals, and being married by a clergyman are still widely observed, many religious practices, such as fasting and observing special days of prayer, have lost some of their significance to the family as a group. A major change has been the secularization of Sunday. Fifty years ago Sunday was still a day when members of most American families got dressed up, went to church, ate a big meal, and spent the rest of the day quietly at home or visiting relatives. Today, even families that attend church each Sunday are likely to devote the rest of "the Lord's Day" to thoroughly secular forms of relaxation—golf, swimming, watching ball games, going to movies, even shopping.

But despite such changes, the home continues to be the source of basic values and beliefs, many of which have a religious basis. The influence of the home on the religious behavior of children can be seen in a study by Greeley and Rossi, who found that religious instruction in Catholic parochial schools appeared to be most effective with students who came from homes with religious parents.[26]

23. Michael Gordon, *The Nuclear Family in Crisis: The Search for an Alternative* (New York: Harper & Row, Inc., 1972), pp. 20–21.

24. Gordon F. Streib, "Older Families and Their Troubles," in *Love—Marriage—Family: A Developmental Approach,* ed. Marcia E. Lasswell and Thomas E. Lasswell (Glenview, Ill.: Scott, Foresman and Company, 1973), pp. 531–540.

25. Bardis, "Family Forms and Variations," p. 455.

26. Andrew Greeley and Peter H. Rossi, *The Education of Catholic Americans* (Chicago: Aldine Publishing Co., 1966).

VIEWPOINTS THE FUTURE OF THE FAMILY

■ Changes of a profound nature are under way in American family life.

Millions of young adults, born in the World War II baby boom and products of the youth revolt and "counter culture" of the 1960s, are settling down to family life.

Most are heading to the altar in the traditional way before setting up housekeeping. Others — disillusioned with conventional marriage — are experimenting with ways of life that are vastly different from those of their parents.

Involved in either case is a strong questioning of values that have shaped life in Western civilization for centuries — lifelong commitment, parental responsibility and distinct roles for man and wife.

Social scientists point out that these young people are coming of age at a time when the extended family already has broken up. The grandparents have retired to Florida, the aunts and uncles have moved away, and the cousins are in college. . . .

This ferment has convinced some social scientists that the "death of the family" is at hand. Ferdinand Lundberg, author of "The Coming World Transformation," says the nuclear family is "near the point of complete extinction." . . .

For growing numbers of disillusioned young couples . . . marriage is becoming a tentative arrangement — often a transitory one. Marriage counselors, clergymen and others dealing with young couples warn that this growing preoccupation with pleasure in marriage could result in a subordination of marital responsibilities once taken for granted, such as child raising.

Child psychologists cite the disproportionate number of delinquents usually originating from homes where the father is absent, or both parents work. . . .

Dr. Amitai Etzioni, a Columbia University sociologist, says that society must face these problems in the coming years.

"Family life has reached a turning point," he says. "It is not falling apart at the seams, but it has serious problems. Some new and positive definitions of what marriage is all about are needed in the 1970s."

U.S. News & World Report
"Is the American Family in Danger?"

● They all tell us that the family is in trouble.

On the right, the professional religious viewers-with-alarm lament the collapse of all family values. . . .

On the left, the professional secularist heralds-of-revolutionary-trends proclaim the dawn of a new era of sexual permissiveness. . . . Both sides agree that the "family" is finished. . . .

The prophets of the New Age of sexual enlightenment [say] look at all the alternative forms that are emerging as substitutes for marriage: sexually open communes, trial marriages among the young, co-marital sex, "swinging," temporary liaisons among singles or divorced people, childless marriages, open marriages, etc., etc. Do not these alternatives spell the doom of the family?

Let us put aside the question of how new they are (as far as I can see, no new forms of sexual behavior have been developed in recorded history) to ask how typical they are.

How many people engage in wife swapping? How many really do go to weekly orgies? How many do draw up elaborate contracts for open marriages? (And how well do the contracts work?) How many are flocking off to sexually permissive communes, and how long do they stay there?

It doesn't matter, say the heralds of revolution, how small in number these innovators may be, they represent the direction of change.

Well maybe, but I wish these sexual revolutionaries appeared a little more joyous and happy and a little less somber and earnest when they appear on the late TV talk shows to preach their gospel of liberation. It doesn't look like they are having much fun. . . .

Instead of being less important, the family is in fact more important than ever before. As a wise anthropologist once put it, in the "Götterdämmerung" being prepared for us by an overwise science and an overfoolish technology, the last man will spend the last hour of his life looking for his wife and child.

Andrew M. Greeley
"Sex and More Sex, But Family Still Here"

THE NUCLEAR FAMILY "IN CRISIS"

The American family has undergone many changes over the past few generations. The pattern of patriarchal authority has diminished in importance as women have attained new roles in society and as children have rejected parental dominance. The schools have assumed an ever greater role in educating and socializing the young, even in such personal areas as sex education. Indeed, the nuclear family has been said to be in crisis—unable to meet the needs of either young people or adults.[27]

Those who consider the family to be in crisis point to men who ignore—or abandon—their families; women who trade child care and housework for outside jobs; the high divorce rate; the thousands of adolescents who run away from home; the elderly who live in loneliness and often in poverty, isolated from their families; and the many young couples who live together without marrying. But it might also be argued that the family was in crisis in the nineteenth century, when sex roles were most radically divided, when divorce was relatively rare but other kinds of marital breakdowns abounded, and when sexual taboos caused fear, worry, and frustration for all family members—both parents and children. Many observers of the current scene find more reasons to be optimistic than pessimistic about the future of the family. If some couples are shunning marriage, most—two million in 1973—are still marrying.[28] And if roles within the family have changed, the movement toward egalitarianism between husband and wife—and between parents and children—may give family members the strength and independence needed to cope with the modern world.

Burgess and Locke, among others, have argued that the family has not been weakened but rather has simply adapted to the challenges posed by urban-industrial society:

The form of the family that appears to be emerging in modern society may be called the companionship family because of its emphasis upon the intimate interpersonal association as its primary function. Other characteristics of the companionship family are: the giving and receiving of affection; the assumption of equality of husband and wife; democracy in family decisions, with a voice and a vote by the children; the personality development of its members as a family objective; freedom of self-expression which is consistent with family unity; and the expectation that the greatest happiness is to be found in the family.[29]

As we noted in Chapter 12 (pages 364–366), empirical studies of urban life do not support the hypothesis that family ties have lost their central importance to individuals. However much the family has changed from earlier times, it is still the most significant source of personal satisfaction and is likely to remain so in the future.

MARRIAGE PATTERNS IN THE UNITED STATES

Though young people in the United States today have a wide choice of potential marriage partners, they continue for the most part to date and marry people who live near them and who share similar social, physical, and perhaps even psychological characteristics.[30] In this section we will examine some of the key factors influencing mate selection and then consider the relationship between love and marital satisfaction. We will also discuss some of the problems associated with the dissolution of marriage, either by death or divorce.

MARRIAGE AND SOCIAL DIFFERENTIATION

Mixed marriages—interclass, interfaith, interethnic, and interracial—have been opposed in all societies throughout history.[31] The main reasons for opposition have been the ethnocentric belief that "we are better than they" and the feeling that it is usually wiser, and safer, to stay with one's own kind.

27. Gordon, *The Nuclear Family in Crisis.*
28. See Marcia Seligson, *The Eternal Bliss Machine: America's Way of Wedding* (New York: William Morrow & Co., Inc., 1973).
29. Ernest W. Burgess and Harvey J. Locke, *The Family: From Institution to Companionship* (New York: American Book Company, 1960), p. 651.
30. F. Ivan Nye and Felix Berardo, *The Family* (New York: Macmillan, Inc., 1973), pp. 116–127.
31. Milton L. Barron, ed., *The Blending American* (New York: Quadrangle Books, Inc., 1972).

The Class Factor

Most marriages in America, as well as in other societies, are intraclass. Teen-age dating patterns are very much class-oriented, so the probability that the young will become deeply involved with persons not of their class-status position is greatly reduced before serious dating occurs.[32] At many colleges and universities, fraternities and sororities and other social groups continue to act as filtering mechanisms that ensure a minimum of cross-class dating and marriage. And in practically all schools, there is a homogeneity of the student body that mitigates against the development of breaks in the class dikes. It should be remembered that children from the lower classes are likely to go to elementary school and high school with other children from the lower classes and that, despite "open admission" policies, they don't get to college as often as middle- and upper-class children do.

Interfaith Marriages

Most religious groups have traditionally opposed interfaith marriage on some or all of the following grounds:

1. Differences in religious beliefs may cause fundamental differences in individual and family value systems, threatening the maintenance and development of conjugal love and family unity.

2. There is likely to be a value conflict centering around the religious training of children. Until recently, for example, the Roman Catholic Church required non-Catholics who married Catholics to agree that the children would be brought up in the Catholic faith. In effect, this forced non-Catholics to say that their religious values were not as significant or valid as those of their mates.

3. Family loyalties and church loyalties may clash.

4. The spiritual aspect of marriage may suffer when each partner has different beliefs and values.[33]

Studies conducted over the past fifty years suggest, on the one hand, that interfaith marriages have become increasingly common and, on the other, that religious endogamy is still a dominant characteristic of marriage patterns in the United States.[34] In a recent study of college graduates, Greeley found that 94 percent of marriages involving Jews, nearly 80 percent involving Protestants, and 75 percent involving Catholics were religiously endogamous.[35] Other studies have similarly found that Jews are most likely and Catholics least likely to marry within their own faith, with Protestants somewhere in between.[36] But among the members of all organized religious groups, intrafaith marriage remains the general rule. Endogamy prevails even within Protestantism—that is, Lutherans are most likely to marry other Lutherans, Baptists to marry other Baptists, and so on.

Among the factors found to influence rates of interfaith marriage are the degree of ethnic cohesiveness, the size and proportion of one religious group relative to others in the community, the socioeconomic and status differences among religious groups, and attitudes of prejudice.[37] In a study of data gathered in midtown Manhattan, Heiss compared matched samples of intrafaith and interfaith marriages and found that those who married within their religion were more likely to have religious parents and to come from harmonious, closely knit families.[38] Some partners in interfaith marriages also had such backgrounds, but they saw the choice of a marriage partner as a purely personal decision

32. For a classic early study on the class factor, see A. B. Hollingshead, *Elmtown's Youth* (New York: John Wiley & Sons, Inc., 1949); see also Betty Yorburg, *The Changing Family* (New York: Columbia University Press, 1973), esp. pp. 153 ff.

33. Barron, *The Blending American*, esp. pp. 52–86.

34. Clark E. Vincent, "Interfaith Marriages: Problem or Symptom," in Barron, *The Blending American*; and Larry D. Barnett, "Research in Interreligious Dating and Marriage," in *Love—Marriage—Family*, ed. Lasswell and Lasswell, pp. 150–154.

35. Andrew M. Greeley, "Religious Intermarriage in a Denominational Society," *American Journal of Sociology*, 75 (May 1970): 949–952.

36. See, for example, Nye and Berardo, *The Family*, p. 145; and Harvey J. Locke and Mary M. Thomas, "Interfaith Marriages," *Social Problems* (April 1957): 329–333.

37. John L. Thomas, "The Factor of Religion in the Selection of Marriage Mates," *American Sociological Review*, 16 (August 1951): 487–492; and Barnett, "Research in Interreligious Dating and Marriage."

38. Jerold S. Heiss, "Premarital Characteristics of the Religiously Intermarried," *American Sociological Review*, 25 (February 1960): 53.

and believed that love and compatibility could more than compensate for differences in religious belief.

As the ecumenical movement has gathered strength, many religious groups have de-emphasized doctrinal differences and removed some of the barriers to interfaith marriage. The Catholic Church, for example, no longer requires that non-Catholics marrying Catholics agree not to use contraceptive birth control or pledge to raise children in the Catholic faith. Although it is not yet clear whether the proportion of interfaith marriages will increase as a result of such changes, it at least seems likely that some of the tensions associated with interfaith marriages will be lessened.

Ethnicity

In American cities during the early years of this century, there were as few mixed marriages among Irish Catholics, Italian Catholics, and Polish Catholics as there were between Catholics and non-Catholics. As one third-generation American put it, "When I was young, 'marrying out' meant marrying someone who was not of the same ethnic group." To a great extent the values, beliefs, and sentiments that held these ethnic groups together have broken down as members have moved into the broader context of American life and as more and more Americans have entered the middle class. However, although interethnic marriages are more common today—approximately 25 to 40 percent of all marriages are interethnic—members of ethnic groups have not "married out" indiscriminately. To a large degree, interethnic marriages have been intrareligious and intraclass.[39]

The major social forces fostering interethnic marriage in the United States have been industrialization and urbanization, which have drawn diverse peoples together in metropolitan areas. The trend toward minimization of ethnic differences has also been supported by a strong ideological commitment to assimilation—to the ideal of American society as a "melting pot." But as we noted in Chapter 9, "Intergroup Relations," ethnic life in the United States has had a continuing vitality that, until recently, has been largely overlooked. Current movements of ethnic independence and assertion seem likely to strengthen existing preferences for in-group marriage.

Race

The most strongly proscribed form of mixed marriage in the United States continues to be interracial marriage, particularly marriage between blacks and whites. It may be hypothesized that much of the resistance by whites to integrated housing and schools is based on the fear that integration in these areas will lead to interracial marriage.

Even though state laws forbidding racially mixed marriage have been declared unconstitutional, the mores against it remain strong, and they are broken very infrequently. In 1960, seven years before the Supreme Court ruled on the issue of interracial marriage, the Census reported only 51,409 black-white marriages, constituting only 0.12 percent of all marriages. During the 1960s the rate fluctuated only slightly: interracial marriages constituted between 0.1 and 0.3 percent of all marriages.

The lack of social contact resulting from prejudice and discrimination has helped minimize interracial marriage. In recent years there has been some broadening of contact—in schools, on the job, in interracial neighborhoods, and through voluntary organizations—and there is some evidence that among those with some college education there are ten to fifteen times as many interracial marriages today as there were a half century ago.[40] Counteracting this trend is the growth of black pride, which strongly supports marriage within the race.[41] Overall, there seems little basis for predicting a rapid increase in racially mixed marriages in the near future.

39. Harold J. Abramson, "Inter-Ethnic Marriage Among Catholic Americans and Changes in Religious Behavior," *Sociological Analysis*, 32, No. 1 (Spring 1971): 31–44; and Joseph P. Fitzpatrick, "Intermarriage of Puerto Ricans in New York City," in Barron, *The Blending American*, pp. 147–163.

40. William B. Furlong, "Interracial Marriage Is a Sometime Thing," in Barron, *The Blending American*, pp. 114–127.

41. Blacks have challenged the assimilationist ideology that interracial marriage is necessarily good for the society and should thus be encouraged. See, for example, William Turner, "Black Men—White Women: A Philosophical View," Paper delivered at the Annual Meeting of the American Sociological Association, New York City, 1973.

Interracial marriage is still extremely rare, and the mores against it remain strong. Although social contact is increasing among blacks and whites, we are unlikely to see a rapid increase in racially mixed marriages in the near future.

MARITAL SATISFACTION

Sociological research supports the generalization that the greater the sociocultural differences between the partners, the less likely the chances for success in marriage. But the evidence also allows a second generalization—namely, that a *majority* of mixed marriages survive as well as other marriages. Perhaps the "mixed" factor helps a couple to be more realistic about the potential for conflict in marriage and the need for working to make marriage a success.

In American society, young people are socialized into the belief that romantic love is the basis for a successful marriage. A young man and young woman are "meant for each other"; for each, the other is the "one person in the world who can bring happiness." Popular songs, novels, movies, soap operas, and advertisements have all contributed to the illusion that romantic love brings the ultimate in personal fulfillment and that love can conquer all.

Romantic love is experienced as an intense emotional state, what Folsom has called "a cardiac-respiratory ailment."[42] But the excited love that characterizes courtship is only a temporary phenomenon. While it is instrumental in propelling couples to the altar, it does not seem to have staying power in marriage. Indeed, a good deal of marital dissatisfaction seems to stem from the refusal of many couples to believe that the emotional excitement of early love will subside. They want perpetual romance. Bell argues that writers of marriage manuals who romanticize sexual union in marriage may make it difficult for couples to adjust to reality by creating unrealistic expectations.[43] The strong emphasis on personal happiness in the "romantic myth" can also easily lead to sexual exploitation by either partner, whether intended or not.

42. Joseph K. Folsom, "The Romantic Complex and Cardiac-Respiratory Love," in *Selected Studies in Marriage and the Family,* ed. R. F. Winch and R. McGinnis (New York: Holt, Rinehart and Winston, Inc., 1953), pp. 354–362.
43. Robert R. Bell, *Premarital Sex in a Changing Society* (Englewood Cliffs, N.J.: Prentice-Hall, Inc., 1966), p. 137.

Studies of marital adjustment do little to support a belief in romantic love as the keystone to a successful marriage. The factor most consistently associated with successful adjustment is that of perceived happiness of parents' marriages. Other factors that have been found to correlate positively with marital happiness include high occupational status, educational level, and income and similarities in age, religion, and desire for sexual satisfaction.[44]

Studies show that the love relationship between happily married couples today reflects the growing emphasis on companionship and egalitarianism that has come to typify family life more generally. As Alice Rossi notes:

Men and women who participate as equals in their parental and occupational and social roles will complement each other sexually in the same way, as essentially equal partners, and not as ascendent male and submissive female. This does not mean, however, that equality in nonsexual roles necessarily de-eroticizes the sexual one. The enlarged base of shared experience can, if anything, heighten the salience of sex qua sex.[45]

According to Foote, love in a companionship marriage is a reciprocal relationship "between one person and another which is most conducive to the optimal development of both."[46] It is not exploitative and can develop only in an atmosphere that is largely free of super-subordinate relations.

Reciprocity implies the recognition of the value of another person's attempts to do something for you. Reciprocity is basic to much if not all of social interaction. What distinguishes love as a reciprocal relation is that doing something for the other person becomes more of an end in itself than in most ordinary interactions. People in love are constantly performing reciprocal acts

Americans have been socialized to believe that marriage means perpetual romance; for many, the realities of marriage have come as an unpleasant surprise. Success in marriage is more likely to be associated with companionship and egalitarianism than it is with emotional and sexual excitement.

for one another as an expression of their love. Where one or the other spouse does not or cannot reciprocate, then a dependency relation tends to develop.

In summary, while the love that helps cement successful marriages may derive from the high emotional states associated with romantic love, it does not remain focused there, nor does it depend on sexuality alone. Rather the relationship involves the whole person: intellectual, spiritual, physical, emotional. What seems to distinguish the companionship marriage from the more traditional marriage is that with couples who pursue a reciprocal relationship, the relationship itself tends to become more central in their lives.[47]

44. Mary W. Hicks and Marilyn Platt, "Marital Happiness and Stability: A Review of Research in the Sixties," *Journal of Marriage and the Family* (November 1970): 553–574; see also Clifford Kirkpatrick, *The Family as Process and Institution,* 2nd ed. (New York: The Ronald Press Company, 1963), pp. 384 ff.

45. Alice Rossi, "Equality Between the Sexes: An Immodest Proposal," *Daedalus,* 93, No. 2 (Spring 1964): 648.

46. Nelson Foote, "Love," *Psychiatry,* 16 (1953): 247.

47. J. Richard Udry, *The Social Context of Marriage* (Philadelphia: J. B. Lippincott Co., 1974), pp. 131 ff.; and Hicks and Platt, "Marital Happiness and Stability," esp. pp. 560–561.

MARITAL DISSOLUTION

All marriages eventually end—the majority through the death of one of the partners, the remainder through divorce, desertion, or annulment. During the fifties the divorce rate in the United States dropped by about 10 percent, but during the sixties it increased by 34 percent and during the early seventies it continued to rise.

Divorce

Most Americans, influenced by the Judeo-Christian tradition, have been inclined to view divorce as something "bad," to be avoided if possible. Even supposedly dispassionate social scientists speak of the "alarmingly" high divorce rate. One reason for this attitude is the assumption that the effect of divorce on children is apt to be negative and that the children of divorced parents are more likely than other children to become delinquent or otherwise fail to "adjust" to society. Recent research casts doubt on these assumptions.[48] Unhappy unbroken homes often seem to cause more problems than broken homes.

There is no wholly satisfactory explanation for the increase in divorces, but certainly part of the explanation is that divorce no longer carries the stigma it formerly did. Couples who at one time might have stayed together unhappily "for the sake of appearances" or because it was the "right" thing to do, especially if there were children involved, are now turning to divorce as an acceptable way out of their difficulties. In the nineteenth century, desertion was a very common alternative to divorce. According to John Demos, the hundreds of thousands of tramps who roamed the nation were largely "men who had run away from their wives."[49]

Changing mores have been reflected in a liberalization of state divorce laws, most of which formerly required that one party be clearly at fault, and some of which accepted only adultery as legitimate grounds for dissolving a marriage. More than a fourth of the states now have no-fault divorce laws, and more than half the remainder grant divorces automatically after a specified period of legal separation.

The following factors have consistently been found to correlate with divorce: youth, alcoholism, economic instability, religious differences, personality maladjustments, and sexual incompatibility. In Idaho, a study showed that financial nonsupport accounted for 20 percent of divorces, adultery for 19 percent, and drunkenness for 18 percent. A number of sociologists have found strong support for the hypothesis that "there is a rough inverse relationship between economic status and the divorce rate."[50] The fact is that in total numbers and by percentage poorer people have more divorces than those who are better off financially, despite the expense of obtaining a divorce. In general, the social setting of the lower-class family is conducive to many forms of tension not found among the more prosperous;[51] and in the lower socioeconomic strata marital strain from whatever source tends to end up as financial nonsupport, which typically leads to divorce.

Death

Today about eleven million persons in the United States have lost their marriage partners through death, and about 80 percent of these are women.[52] The proportion of widows has risen steadily in recent decades and will probably continue to rise because women live longer than men, are usually younger than their husbands, and are less likely to remarry.

Some of the problems created by the death of a marriage partner have traditionally been

48. See, for example, Lee G. Burchinal, "Characteristics of Adolescents from Unbroken, Broken, and Reconstituted Families," *Journal of Marriage and the Family*, 26 (February 1964): 44–51; and F. Ivan Nye, "Child Adjustment in Broken and in Unhappy Unbroken Homes," *Marriage and Family Living*, 19 (November 1957): 356–361.

49. John Demos, "The American Family in Past Time," *The American Scholar*, 43, No. 3 (Summer 1974): 422–446.

50. See A. B. Hollingshead, "Social Class and Family Stability," in Marvin Sussman, ed., *Sourcebook of Marriage and the Family* (Boston: Houghton Mifflin Co., 1968); and William J. Goode, *The Family* (Englewood Cliffs, N.J.: Prentice-Hall, Inc., 1964).

51. For a powerful documentary on these forces and their disruptive consequences, see Elliot Liebow, *Tally's Corner: A Study of Negro Streetcorner Men* (Boston: Little, Brown and Company, 1967).

52. The following discussion draws heavily on Felix M. Berardo, "Widowhood Status in the United States: Perspectives on a Neglected Aspect of the Family Life-Cycle," *The Family Coordinator*, 17 (July 1968): 191–203.

more difficult for women than for men. Income maintenance and employment are the best examples. Although women are reported to be the beneficiaries of 80 percent of all life insurance policies, few of them are "wealthy widows." Three-fourths of the policies, a recent study showed, were for less than $5000, and an additional 20 percent were for less than $10,000. Because the widow has to pay funeral expenses and medical bills and because she is likely to be over sixty-five years of age and unable to earn an adequate income for herself, her economic situation is often precarious.

Some widows of working age are unable (or unwilling) to enter the labor market. Those who have never been previously employed frequently can find work only at low-skill jobs that pay very small wages. Yet even the woman who has no pressing financial need for employment may discover that any kind of job at any wage is preferable to lonely days at home, keeping house only for herself. Greater emphasis on the need to acquire a marketable job skill has been emerging as an important aspect in the socialization of females.

Some of the problems of widowhood are common to both sexes. The survivors tend to be socially isolated. Because much American social life is designed for couples, the widowed are likely to find themselves excluded from most social gatherings as well as being deprived of companionship at home. The isolation brought by death of a partner appears to have physical as well as psychological consequences. The widowed die sooner than nonwidowed of the same age; the tendency toward suicide is increased; and mental illness is more common.

"THE SEXUAL REVOLUTION"

In the preceding sections of this chapter we have discussed some of the changes that have occurred in marriage patterns and family life in the United States. These changes and others have led to much questioning of norms, values,

About 80 percent of the widowed in the United States are women, the majority of whom do not have adequate incomes; often they are socially isolated.

and behavior patterns related to the institution of the family. The questioning has been especially vigorous with regard to issues concerning sexuality.

Throughout its history, American society has paid a great deal of public attention to sexual behavior. From colonial times to the present there has been a tendency to equate sexual indulgence—mental as well as physical—with sin and damnation. In the late nineteenth century, middle-class avoidance of words that could be associated with sexuality—e.g., *bull, leg*—reflected a strong cultural de-emphasis of sex.

Now, having achieved the fullest measure of sexual freedom in their history, Americans argue among themselves whether or not a sexual revolution has been taking place and, if so, what its implications will be for the future of marriage and the family. Of special concern have been the changing norms of sexual behavior among the unmarried.

PREMARITAL SEXUAL BEHAVIOR

When families arranged marriages, the feelings young people had toward one another were considered relatively unimportant as criteria for mate selection. In contemporary America, young people generally arrange their own marriages, and the mechanism whereby they test out their ideas of each other has been called dating. As a form of recreation, dating has become a part of teen-age and young adult culture, consistent with the emphasis on freedom from adult supervision and with the idea that young people should have fun together. At the same time, it has served as an important form of socialization. In a society that values freedom in mate selection, dating has provided a mechanism by which young people can come to know each other, develop interpersonal competency, and see themselves in a variety of adult sex roles. It has also provided them with a means for expressing their sexuality and for testing out their beliefs about romantic love.

The so-called youth movement of the sixties seems to have accelerated significant changes in dating patterns, especially with respect to sexual attitudes and behavior. Marriage and family researchers emphasize that the extent of the sexual revolution of the 1960s has been exaggerated;[53] data suggest that an increase in premarital sexual intimacy has been underway since at least the 1920s. But it has only been quite recently that attitudes, norms, and beliefs have caught up with behavior and that the sexual behavior of females and males has become more congruent.[54]

The double standard whereby premarital coitus for the male was condoned but virginity for the female was expected has been gradually giving way as a norm. The almost universal awareness of and increasing acceptance of contraceptives has removed fear of pregnancy as a major deterrent to premarital coitus. However, the availability of effective contraceptives does not tell the whole story. In China, where the pill and other contraceptives are also widely available, premarital sexual intercourse appears to be relatively uncommon. The cultural norms of that society foster virginity for both males and females until they are in the middle or late twenties. In our own society, by contrast, attitudes have changed in support of increased sexual freedom for the young and unmarried.

A key feature of dating for earlier generations of Americans was the way in which sexual needs and desires were fed but not fulfilled.[55] With virginity still the norm, young couples looked forward to marriage for sexual fulfillment. What happens now that these sexual needs are being increasingly met outside of marriage? We have learned the following facts about the behavior of unmarried young people from research during the past quarter century:

1. Among the poor and the working class, early coital experience by males—with prostitutes, "loose women," and "easy lays"—has long been the expected pattern.[56] Until recently, virginity among the women of these classes was still the norm.

2. In the middle and upper classes, there has been more emphasis on necking, petting, and a variety of ways other than coitus of achieving orgasm. Since World War II male and female college students have increasingly become more liberal and permissive in their sexual attitudes and behavior.[57]

3. Today there is less difference in the coital experience of college and noncollege young people. A majority of males and a near majority of females have had such experience by age twenty-one.[58]

4. Estimates indicate that about half the young people who have premarital intercourse eventually marry each other.

53. Ira Reiss, *The Social Context of Premarital Sexual Permissiveness* (New York: Holt, Rinehart and Winston, Inc., 1967); and Robert Bell, *Social Deviance* (Homewood, Ill.: Dorsey Press, 1971).

54. Christensen, *Handbook of Marriage and the Family*. For a somewhat different view, see Morton Hunt, "Sexual Behavior in the 1970s," *Playboy*, October 1973, pp. 85 ff.

55. Willard Waller, "The Rating and Dating Complex," *American Sociological Review*, 2 (1937): 727–734.

56. See, for example, William F. Whyte, *Street-Corner Society: The Social Structure of an Italian Slum* (Chicago: The University of Chicago Press, 1943); Liebow, *Tally's Corner*; Lee Rainwater and Karol Weinstein, *And the Poor Get Children* (New York: Quadrangle Books, Inc., 1960); and Lee Rainwater, *Family Design* (Chicago: Aldine Publishing Co., 1965).

57. See Kinsey et al., *Sexual Behavior in the Human Male* and *Sexual Behavior in the Human Female*; Bell, *Premarital Sex*; and Reiss, *The Social Context of Premarital Sexual Permissiveness*.

58. Hunt, "Sexual Behavior in the 1970s."

TOOLS OF SOCIOLOGY
THE SELF-ADMINISTERED QUESTIONNAIRE   C. E. Noll

The self-administered questionnaire is especially popular among researchers who want to reach a large number of respondents but have a limited budget and thus cannot afford to pay interviewers. It allows researchers to find out about the knowledge, attitudes, and beliefs of a specific segment of the population—female college graduates, administrators in osteopathic hospitals, etc.—that is scattered over a large geographical area. Respondents often feel a greater sense of confidentiality when filling out a self-administered questionnaire than they would if talking to an interviewer. Some social scientists feel that self-administered questionnaires are better than interviews because the standardized format reduces the problem of experimenter effects (see page 386).

The problems with self-administered questionnaires, however, are also significant. In general, the response rates to mailed questionnaires—the most common form—can be low. But when respondents are extremely interested in the issues involved, high rates of return are common—even on long questionnaires.

Because there is no one to interpret the questions for the respondents, questions must be specific. The best questions are those that offer little opportunity for different interpretations and that can be understood by all respondents. When a specific segment of the population is being studied, the range of interpretation is obviously restricted.

Careful pretesting of questions is necessary. The questions and possible answers are precoded—that is, assigned numbers—to make it easier for respondents to understand and answer questions quickly. The more difficult a survey form is to fill out, the greater the likelihood respondents won't complete and return it. Precoding also makes it easier to transfer the answers to computer systems for analysis.

In the mid-1960s Alice Rossi designed a self-administered questionnaire to study the definitions and possible role conflict felt by women and the developmental patterns that lead to different definitions of roles. She surveyed a sample of women who had graduated from college three years earlier. Because the women were located throughout the country, personal interviews would have been costly and time-consuming. The questionnaire was unusually long (40 pages), but the response rate was very high.

Rossi focused on the interaction of marital and career roles. The following two questions from the study illustrate how relatively complex questions can be stated in a clear way. The numbers on the right are code numbers.

1. Generally speaking, how would you describe your and your husband's response to each other's social and emotional needs?
I respond to my husband's needs more than he does to mine. 0
My husband responds to my needs more than I do to his. 1
We both respond to each other's needs to the same extent. 2

2. A. If you were to take a full-time job (or are now working full time) how would (does) your husband feel about it?
B. At the present time, how would (do) you feel about full-time employment for yourself?

	A. My Husband's Attitude	B. My Attitude
Very positive	5	X
Mildly positive	6	0
Neutral	7	1
Mildly negative	8	2
Very negative	9	3

A letter explaining the project, a copy of the questionnaire, and a self-addressed return envelope are mailed to respondents. The initial mailing is almost always followed by a second mailing to those who have not returned the questionnaire. When the sample is reasonably localized, the questionnaires can be dropped off and picked up in person. This personal contact reinforces the importance of the survey to the respondent, but it increases the cost and may reduce the sense of confidentiality.

Alice S. Rossi, "Family Development in a Changing World," *American Journal of Psychiatry*, 128, No. 9 (March 1972): 1057–1066.

It may be that heterosexual relationships among the unmarried are now serving a broader socialization function than ever before. Simon and Gagnon note that dating provides the opportunity for each sex to train the other about what each wants and expects. Presumably, the more permissive atmosphere of the seventies allows dating couples increased opportunity to discover whether their wants and expectations are compatible before formally committing themselves to marriage.[59]

There is some evidence that as females become less concerned about virginity, males are becoming less exploitative in seeking to satisfy their sexual desires. Thus a new pattern of sexual relationships seems to be emerging. Reiss calls it "permissiveness with affection."[60] Males as well as females now speak of having a "meaningful relationship," while a large number of the females link their willingness to engage in sexual intercourse to being in love with or to feeling deep affection for the other person. However, data still show that women are more interested than men in a relationship that will lead to marriage.

It might be expected that, with their new sexual freedom, young people would tend to postpone marriage. However, the average age at marriage has risen only slightly in recent years (23.3 for males and 20.9 for females in 1972 as compared to 23 for men and 20 for women in 1958), and there has been no significant change since 1950 in the percentage of males (67 percent) and females (68 percent) who are married.[61]

SEX ROLES AND SEXUALITY

We are taught from the earliest moments of life that we are boys or that we are girls. Kohlberg points out that sex gender identity is the most strongly ingrained identity in people.[62] People may lie about their age, pretending to be older when young and younger when old; they may drop their religious affiliation or change it; and they may cease to identify with their ancestral group. But seldom do they question, much less attempt to alter, their sex gender identity.

As children, our sex gender identities are established primarily by the social definitions provided by adults rather than by consciousness of genital differences as such. Indeed, adults traditionally have gone to great lengths to hide genital differences from children. Norms encourage bathing boys and girls separately, separate use of bathroom facilities by males and females, and the like. Sex gender identity has focused instead on patterns of clothing, hair styles and length, toys, attitudes and beliefs, and, gradually, role playing. These social definitions of sex gradually mold our ideas about who we are and what shall be our proper roles as adults.

Increasingly, fundamental questions have been raised not only about the meaning and implications of sex gender identity and the social roles which flow from it, but also about the nature and meaning of human sexuality itself. Perhaps the most important hypothesis to emerge from recent studies of human sexuality is that "the sexual is precisely that realm where the sociocultural forms most completely dominate biological influences."[63] Expression of the sexual drive is socially organized and controlled, just as is all other human behavior.

Contemporary research on human sexuality has destroyed many of the old myths on the naturalness of male dominance and female submission. One of the most startling theories to come out of such research is that at conception and for the first few weeks thereafter, all fetuses are anatomically female. Previously, the fact that basic genetic composition is established at conception by the presence or absence of the Y chromosome was taken to mean that sex gender

59. William Simon and John H. Gagnon, "Psychosexual Development," in *Intimacy, Family, and Society,* ed. Arlene Skolnick and Jerome H. Skolnick (Boston: Little, Brown and Company, 1974), pp. 144–147.

60. Reiss, *The Social Context of Premarital Sexual Permissiveness,* p. 15.

61. Abbott L. Ferris, *Indicators of Change in the American Family* (New York: Russell Sage Foundation, 1970), pp. 8–29.

62. Lawrence Kohlberg, "A Cognitive-Developmental Analysis of Sex-Role Concepts," in Skolnick and Skolnick, *Intimacy, Family and Society,* pp. 134–144.

63. Simon and Gagnon, "Psychosexual Development," p. 145. For a more detailed statement, see William Simon and John H. Gagnon, *The Sexual Scene* (New Brunswick, N. J. : Transaction Press, 1970).

was anatomically established at that time. However, we now know that early anatomical development is always female; and that for a male to emerge, the androgen hormones must be present and working by around the sixth week of pregnancy. If they are, a male fetus will develop by the tenth or eleventh week.[64] Thus the Eve-out-of-Adam myth has suddenly been challenged by a theory that reverses the order of progression.

The research of Masters and Johnson, following the pioneer efforts of Kinsey, has thrown into doubt many other traditional ideas about human sexuality. It is now known, for example, that women have at least as great a capacity for orgasm as do men.[65] Findings such as these, which challenge the long-held belief that women's social subordination to men was supported by biology, have the potential for changing not only patterns of sexual behavior but, in the process, traditional sex roles as well.

SUMMARY

In all known societies, the family serves as a primary agent not only for replenishing the population but also for the transmission of culture through the socialization of children. Marriage defines the responsibilities of the partners in terms of sexual behavior, child rearing, inheritance, and the provision of food and other necessities.

Family organizational patterns vary among societies. In the Hebrew, Greek, Roman, and early Christian societies, families were—to varying degrees—male dominated. The roots of the contemporary Western family can be found in the practices of these societies. The Hopi family, by contrast, is matrilineal and matrilocal. Family life among the Hopi reflects cultural emphases on kinship ties and group goals. The Chinese Communists have attempted to restructure Chinese family life in terms of new cultural orientations, which are reflected in a communal form of family life, sexual puritanism, and equality for the sexes.

The contemporary American family developed out of colonial—especially Puritan—family patterns. The early American family was a producing unit and was responsible for socializing, protecting, and disciplining its members. The religious training of children was also an important family activity. As a result of industrialization and urbanization, the American family has changed from a self-sufficient unit to one whose main activities are giving affection and forming personality. Because of these changes, many observers believe the American family to be in crisis.

Most Americans marry members of their own social class, religion, ethnic group, and race. Although intramarriages have a greater chance of success than do intermarriages, the majority of mixed marriages survive as well as other marriages.

The illusion that romantic love will bring marital happiness is one cause of marital dissatisfaction. Research has indicated that people with high occupational, educational, and income levels and people whose marriages are based on reciprocity are more likely to have successful marriages than those who expect love to "conquer all."

Divorce has become an acceptable means of ending an unhappy marriage. The divorce rate in the United States has increased sharply in recent years, partly because of changing mores. Because American social life is designed for couples, the end of a marriage—through divorce or death—can bring social isolation.

Attitudes toward sex have undergone considerable change in the United States, and the double standard of sexual morality has largely disappeared. Recent research on sex roles and human sexuality presage further changes in attitudes toward sexual behavior.

64. See Mary J. Sherfey, *The Nature and Evolution of Female Sexuality* (New York: Random House, Inc., 1972).
65. William H. Masters and Virginia E. Johnson, *Human Sexual Response* (Boston: Little, Brown and Company, 1966).

16
Religion

Sociologists use an institutional approach in studying religion. They make no attempt to evaluate the merits or validity of one body of beliefs as opposed to another; rather, they attempt to understand religious behavior by identifying the major dimensions of religiosity (religious commitment), the organizations and subcultures of various kinds of religious groups, the role of religion in social integration and social conflict, and the relationships between religion and other areas of social life. The present chapter is organized around these issues.

There is disagreement over what types of human activity can properly be called religious and what constitutes true religious commitment. Some scholars would apply the term *religion* only to convictions about the existence of a god or gods. Others would define as a religion almost any kind of belief system to which people are deeply committed. For example, communism has often been referred to as a religion. Morris Cohen, a well-known American philosopher, argued seriously that baseball could be considered a religion in the United States because it served to integrate American society.[1] But *religion* so broadly defined loses all specific meaning. Most sociologists use the term *religion* in a limited sense, to refer to beliefs and acts that in some way relate people to the supernatural. In his classic work, *The Elementary Forms of Religious Life*, Émile Durkheim approached the problem of definition this way:

All known religious beliefs, whether simple or complex, present one common characteristic; they presuppose a classification of all things, real and ideal, of which men think, into two classes or opposed groups, generally designated to two distinct terms which are translated well enough by the words profane *and* sacred.[2]

To Durkheim, the distinction between the sacred and the profane was absolute; he saw them as two totally distinct classes with nothing

---

1. Morris R. Cohen, *The Faith of a Liberal* (New York: Henry Holt and Company, 1946), pp. 334–336.
2. Émile Durkheim, *The Elementary Forms of Religious Life* (New York: The Macmillan Company, 1926), originally published in 1912, quotation from p. 36.

in common. The sacred consisted of things "set apart, and forbidden"—that is, things and ideas considered worthy of profound respect and honor. The profane was defined as everything else. Durkheim stressed that, to constitute a religion, a body of beliefs has to be shared by an *organized group:* "Religious beliefs are always common to a determined group, which makes a profession of adhering to them and of practicing the rites connected with them."[3] Thus the forms of activity associated with religious beliefs are forms of social conduct.

Although others have been cited, the features of any religion include a group of shared symbols, understandings, and behaviors associated with the supernatural.[4] The proper study of religion for the sociologist, then, includes not only what people *believe* to be true of the supernatural but—more importantly—how they *act,* individually and collectively, upon their convictions.

RELIGION AS INDIVIDUAL BEHAVIOR

Although the more personal or "inner" aspects of religious experience can never be subjected to direct observation, researchers have arrived at a number of objective conclusions about religious behavior. Some of the major *dimensions of religiosity,* or *religious commitment,* have been delineated, and individual and social con-

3. Ibid., p. 41.
4. See, for example, Robert N. Bellah, *Beyond Belief: Essays on Religion in a Post-Traditional World* (New York: Harper and Row, Inc., 1970), p. 21; and J. Paul Williams, "The Nature of Religion," in *Religion's Influence in Contemporary Society: Readings in the Sociology of Religion,* ed. Joseph E. Faulkner (Columbus, Ohio: Charles E. Merrill Publishing Co., 1972), p. 33.
5. Charles Y. Glock and Rodney Stark, *Religion and Society in Tension* (Chicago: Rand McNally & Co., 1965); Glock and Stark, *Christian Beliefs and Anti-Semitism* (New York: Harper and Row, Inc., 1966); and Stark and Glock, *American Piety: The Nature of Religious Commitment* (Berkeley: University of California Press, 1970). An attempt to measure the dimensions identified by Glock and Stark can be found in Joseph E. Faulkner and Gordon F. DeJong, "Religiosity in 5-D: An Empirical Analysis," *Social Forces,* 45 (December 1966): 246–254.
6. Glock and Stark, *American Piety,* pp. 22–56.

sequences of religiosity have been identified. These will be discussed in the sections that follow.

DIMENSIONS OF RELIGIOSITY

On the basis of thousands of interviews and responses to questionnaires about religious behavior in American congregations, Charles Glock and Rodney Stark have identified several basic dimensions of religiosity (see Tools of Sociology, page 472). Though referred to by different names in their work, essentially these dimensions are religious *belief, ritual* (or practice), *knowledge,* and *experience.*[5]

Belief

Every organized religion includes some set of theological tenets to which adherents are expected to subscribe. Theologies vary greatly from one religion to another and may be quite distinct even within a given religious category. Christians, for example, not only hold different beliefs from Moslems and Jews but are divided into denominations and sects that vary substantially from one another.

For sociologists, theology is merely the starting point for analyzing religious beliefs. They are more concerned with what individuals actually believe than with what their religion says they should believe. One of the most comprehensive studies in this area was carried out in four metropolitan counties of northern California.[6] Over three thousand people were asked about some basic Christian doctrines. One of these was the doctrine that God exists. A considerable gap between official doctrines and the actual beliefs of church members was found.

For example, among Congregationalists, only 41 percent of those questioned subscribed without reservation to a belief in the existence of God. For Protestants as a whole, less than three fourths unreservedly accepted it. Even among church members, then, a large number had doubts of one kind or another concerning the existence of the very deity to which their formal doctrines, rituals, and organizations were dedicated.

TOOLS OF SOCIOLOGY
MEASURING RELIGIOSITY Garry W. Hesser

What images are associated with the label *religious*? Does it connote a person who is a pious churchgoer or a conscientious objector, one who has ecstatic experiences or one who simply knows the Bible, an individual whose major motive is neighborly love or one who carefully attends to the prescribed obligations of the denomination? Before classification according to dimensions of religiosity began, single items — such as church membership or attendance — were used as sole indicators of religious commitment. Now, however, researchers can focus on different levels of analysis: individual, institutional, and societal.

1. Individual — Charles Y. Glock identified five dimensions of individual religious commitment within which all the diverse manifestations of religiosity could be ordered: *ritualistic* (attendance, prayer, etc.); *intellectual* (knowledge about basic tenets); *ideological* (belief); *experiential* (feeling); and *consequential* (effect).

2. Institutional — Joseph Fichter classified the members of a Roman Catholic parish with respect to their attachment to the church as an institution. Visualized in concentric circles, *nuclear* (most involved) members are at the core, followed by *modal* (average) members and *marginal* and *dormant* (noninvolved) members.

3. Societal — N. J. Demerath and others focused upon the association between religiosity and socioeconomic factors, suggesting that churchlike and sectlike tendencies are closely related to socioeconomic status.

Following Glock's analysis of individual religious commitment, many researchers began to study the relationships between all five of Glock's individual dimensions. The results of this body of research suggest that no two dimensions of religious commitment overlap by much more than 30 percent. In other words, one cannot predict any dimension of religiosity (e.g., ritual involvement) on the basis of another (e.g., ideological fervor).

Some researchers have subdivided Glock's dimensions. *Orthodoxy,* for instance, is a subdimension of ideology. To measure orthodoxy, sociologists use research questions that usually focus on the certainty of belief in the existence of a personal god, the divinity of Jesus, the authenticity of Biblical miracles, and the existence of the Devil. Critics have charged that this measure is neither theologically nor methodologically valid, for theologically literate individuals cannot correctly respond to questions that force them to choose between extreme and simpleminded positions. Others contend that the questions do not really measure orthodoxy and that they do not focus on authentic Christianity.

Other studies have used several religious dimensions in an attempt to show an individual's total relationship to the religious institution. Thus, when one person scores 5 on ritual and 1 on orthodoxy and another scores 1 on ritual and 5 on orthodoxy, both have average scores of 3 and rank equally as "modal" members.

Overall, the tendency of research on religiosity has been to move in the direction of ever more subtle dimensions. The crucial question is whether or not new refinements and indices lead to increased understanding of religious behavior. The structure and number of such dimensions remains an open issue, but it is clear that researchers will never again be satisfied with a single, convenient indicator of religiosity.

Charles Y. Glock and Rodney Stark, *Christian Beliefs and Anti-Semitism* (New York: Harper & Row, Inc., 1966) and *Religion and Society in Tension* (Chicago: Rand McNally & Co., 1965); Charles Y. Glock, "On the Study of Religious Commitment," *Religious Education*, Research Supplement, 42 (July–August, 1962): 98–110; Joseph Fichter, *Social Relations in the Urban Parish* (Chicago: The University of Chicago Press, 1954); N. J. Demerath, *Social Class in American Protestantism* (Chicago: Rand McNally & Co., 1965).

The system of religious beliefs known as spiritism is still a powerful ideology in some parts of the world. This ceremony in New Guinea, for example, reflects the tribal members' belief in the survival of their ancestors' "spirits." They paint themselves with gray paint and wear frames on their heads, which are plastered with mud and often decorated with teeth. The ceremony commemorates a battle in which their tribal ancestors were forced into a river by a marauding tribe and then emerged covered with mud to frighten off the attackers.

These same people were asked whether they had any doubts that "Jesus is the Divine Son of God." Again, there was a substantial range of responses. Slightly over two-thirds (69 percent) of Protestants as a whole said that their belief was completely firm, and only 40 percent of Congregationalists subscribed to the idea without reservation. Among Catholics, 86 percent were completely certain. Such statements as "The miracles the Bible reports are true," "Jesus walked on water," and "There is a life beyond death" met with substantial skepticism, and there was much hesitation over accepting the biblical account of the birth of Jesus. When asked if it was completely true that "Jesus was born of a virgin," Southern Baptists expressed certain belief in 99 percent of the cases studied, but theirs was the only resoundingly affirmative response. At the other extreme only one-fifth (21 percent) of the Congregationalists accepted the virgin birth literally.

What are the implications of such data? The fact that those surveyed were church members showed that they considered themselves religious to some degree, even though they might be unable to make a full commitment. Belonging to a church apparently satisfies many needs, of which sharing religious beliefs is only one.

Ritual

A variety of behaviors and practices are prescribed by various religious groups for their members. What most religious rituals have in common is the purpose of symbolizing some aspect of the faith, honoring the divinity or divinities worshipped, and reminding participants of their religious duties and responsibilities. Some typical rituals are following diets and routines of prayer, handling sacred objects, wearing distinctive clothing, reading scripture, observing religious holidays, and tithing. Comprehensive data on the extent of such practices among Americans are not readily available.

One form of ritual, church attendance, has been audited by the Gallup organization since 1955. From that year on, there has been a rather steady decline in attendance (see Figure 16.1 and Table 16.1). Catholics, the most frequent churchgoers, have shown the largest drop (from 72 percent attending church weekly in 1955 to 55 percent in 1973). Protestant attendance, which has always been lower, dropped from 40 percent in 1955 to 37 percent in 1973.[7] There were not enough Jews in the Gallup samples to provide reliable estimates.

There is some evidence that the practice of many other forms of ritual has declined sharply. In a recent replication of an earlier study, researchers found that American Catholics had lessened their observance of many religious practices. For example, in the mid-1960s, when the first study was made, 38 percent of Catholics attended monthly confession; by the mid-1970s this figure had fallen to 17 percent. The percentage practicing daily private prayer declined from 72 percent to 60 percent. Other traditional religious practices among Catholics also declined: the percentage making a Day of Recollection had fallen from 22 percent to 9 percent; the percentage reading a spiritual book was down from 58 percent to 33 percent; and those making a mission had declined from 34 percent to 6 percent. On the other hand, in the mid-1960s 13 percent of Catholics received weekly communion; ten years later the proportion had increased to 26 percent.[8]

Percent Attending Church Weekly

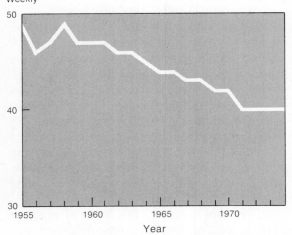

SOURCE: Gallup Poll. "Churchgoing Audits. 1955–1973" (Princeton. N.J.: Gallup International).

Figure 16.1. CHURCHGOING AMONG AMERICAN CHRISTIANS

Descriptive studies of the rituals of the world's religions are numerous.[9] The most conspicuous characteristic of the many systems is their almost incredible variety. Dramatic demonstrations of religiosity include self-mutilation, human sacrifice, and cannibalism.[10] Although it might be thought that such practices are too exotic to throw light on religion in modern America, even here some groups cultivate extreme forms of ritual. Within recent years a number of people have died and others have become seriously ill because of their literal interpretation of this passage from the New Testament:

And these signs shall follow them that believe; In my name they shall cast out devils; they shall speak with new tongues;

They shall take up serpents; and if they drink any deadly thing, it shall not hurt them; they shall lay hands on the sick, and they shall recover. (Mark 16: 17–18)

For example, in 1973 two members of the Holiness Church of God in Jesus Name of Carson Springs, Tennessee, drank mixtures of strychnine and water during services, declaring that "a perfect love casteth out fear." By the next morning both were dead.[11]

Table 16.1. PERCENT OF MEMBERS ATTENDING CHURCH

Year	Catholics	Protestants
1955	72%	40%
1960	74	44
1965	67	38
1970	60	38
1973	55	37

SOURCE: Gallup Poll, "Churchgoing Audits, 1955–1973." Gallup International, Princeton, N.J.

7. Gallup Poll, "Churchgoing Audits, 1955–1973," by George Gallup (Princeton, N.J.: Gallup International).

8. Andrew M. Greeley and Peter Rossi, *The Education of Catholic Americans* (Chicago: Aldine Publishing Co., 1966); and Shirley Saldahna, William McCready, Kathleen McCourt, and Andrew M. Greeley, "American Catholics—Ten Years Later," *The Critic* (January-February 1975): 14–21.

9. For a survey, see William J. Goode, *Religion Among the Primitives* (New York: The Free Press, 1951).

10. See James Frazer, *The Golden Bough* (1890), available in a one-volume abridgment (New York: Macmillan, Inc., 1955); and Arnold van Gennep, *The Rites of Passage* (Chicago: The University of Chicago Press, 1960), originally published in 1909.

11. *Newsweek*, April 23, 1973, p. 23.

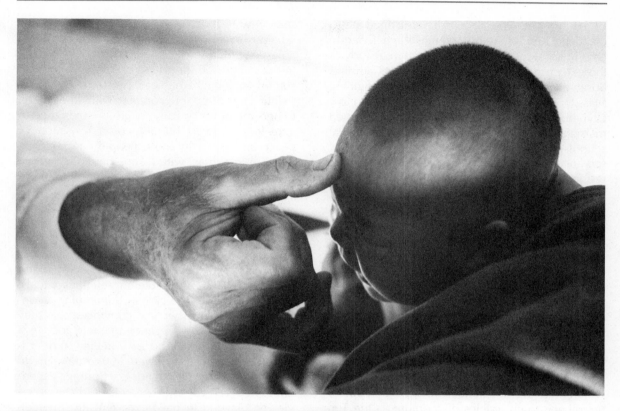

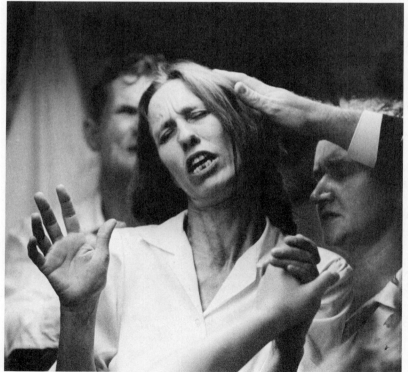

A variety of behaviors and practices are associated with American Christianity. One common form of ritual is baptism, which ranges from a light sprinkling with water to total immersion. Some denominations and sects perform the ritual shortly after birth; others perform it when the person is older. A less common form of ritual is snake handling. At the Church of Jesus in Jolo, West Virginia, handfuls of snakes are placed under clothing or worn as crowns. Overcome by emotion and the Holy Spirit, the woman on the left speaks in tongues.

In most religious groups in the United States the degree of ritual observance varies sharply among different types of members. In a study of the extent to which 8363 white urban Catholics observed such ritual prescriptions as attending Mass, performing Easter duties, taking Holy Communion, accepting only Church-validated marriage, and sending children to parochial schools, Fichter reported that the extent of observance varied according to educational level, residential mobility, sex, age, and income.[12]

Knowledge

To what extent do people in various religious groups understand the sacred writings and the history and traditions of their faith? There is considerable variation. Some Christian denominations stress familiarity with the Bible and operate formal schools, summer camps, and adult classes in which scripture is discussed by church members. In other denominations scripture reaches the congregation chiefly through the clergy, who explain and interpret it.

Glock and Stark probed the extent to which members of major Christian denominations knew such articles of scripture as the Ten Commandments.[13] On this issue, Catholics were best informed, with 34 percent saying that they could give the exact words of the Commandments. Protestants ranged from 1 percent (Congregational) to 27 percent (Missouri Lutheran). These data should not be taken to mean that modern Americans have less formal knowledge about their religions than did Christians in earlier times. In Europe during the Middle Ages, for example, most Christians could not read; and since the printing press had not yet been invented, most did not even own copies of the Bible. The limited formal knowledge of most medieval Christians reached them through the priest and from the illustrations of Bible stories on the stained glass windows of the churches.

Experience

Generally, participants in an organized religion are expected to have some sense of contact with the supernatural, some feelings (perceptions and sensations) that lead them to believe they are somehow in touch with a divine essence. Such religious experiences are shaped to a considerable degree by the individual's beliefs and by the rituals he or she follows. An experience of sublime joy might be seen by some as an authentic indicator of contact with the diety. Others might find a truly religious experience in a feeling of deep humility or a sensation of peace and calm. In short, people can feel that they are in contact with a supernatural power in many ways and with varying degrees of intensity.

Several widespread variations of the experiential dimension of religious commitment have been identified. A *confirming* experience can amount to little more than rather vague and diffuse feelings of reverence or awe that accompany participation in solemn religious rituals. But in other cases individuals undergoing a confirming experience become convinced that they are actually in the presence of their god. In a controversial study, Andrew Greeley and William McCready interviewed 600 Americans to discover how widespread confirming experiences are. About 40 percent of those interviewed claimed to have experienced "the feeling of being very close to a powerful spiritual force that seemed to lift them out of themselves," leading these researchers to wonder if such experiences may be more common than most observers believe.[14]

In the *responsive* type of religious experience individuals not only perceive themselves to be in the presence of the divinity but feel that the divinity has become aware of them. This experience may convince believers that they belong to a "chosen" group or have been spiritually "saved" by conversion to the true faith. They may also become convinced that they have been healed or cured or that their lives have been saved through divine intervention.[15]

12. Joseph H. Fichter, *Dynamics of a City Church: Southern Parish* (Chicago: The University of Chicago Press, 1951).
13. Glock and Stark, *American Piety*, pp. 142–145.
14. Andrew M. Greeley and William C. McCready, "Are We a Nation of Mystics?" *The New York Times Magazine*, January 26, 1975, pp. 12–25.
15. See the examples collected in William James, *The Varieties of Religious Experience* (New York: Macmillan, Inc., 1961), originally published in 1902.

A third kind of religious experience, the *ecstatic,* is often accompanied by violent physical and psychological manifestations, such as an uncontrollable urge to jump, scream, twitch, roll on the floor, or "speak in tongues." Such "visitations" of the supernatural often occur in a group context. The classic American example is the revival meeting.

Another form of experience is *revelation.* Here, individuals not only believe they are in communication with divinity but feel they have received a sacred message of some kind, often through visions and voices. Historically, those receiving such messages have been regarded with wonder and reverence, and special significance has been attached to the sites where their revelations occurred. The divine messages received by the prophets of the Old Testament guided the destiny of the entire Hebrew people. Muhammad, the founder of Islam, and many Christian saints also experienced revelation. Outstanding among religious leaders who have claimed divine inspiration in modern times was Joseph Smith, founder of the Church of Jesus Christ of Latter Day Saints, who by his own account discovered and translated the Book of Mormon at the direction of an angel.[16]

CONSEQUENCES OF RELIGIOSITY

The *functional* aspect of individual religious commitment has been the object of so much sociological inquiry that it deserves separate treatment. Here we are dealing with the question of what consequences religion has for individuals. In what ways do religious people orient themselves to the world differently than the non-religious?

Security and Crises

Most religions provide an ideology that enables individuals to make sense of their lives. Illness, injustice, poverty, death—all may be comprehensible if they are seen as part of a divine plan.

Or they may simply seem unimportant in comparison with the spiritual life.

The lives of most people are periodically touched by crisis. Whatever their sources, these crises create fears and anxieties that must be coped with. Religious beliefs and practices may help the individual manage crises without overwhelming psychological costs. Because rituals often take the form of appeals for divine intervention, they permit the participants to feel they are "doing something"—as indeed they are. If the crisis is averted, the individual feels that the efficacy of the prayers or sacrifices is affirmed. If the catastrophe occurs, it can be regarded as having been divinely ordained, perhaps as just punishment for past transgressions. Either outcome provides believers with an explanation of the crisis, which otherwise might crush them through its seeming senselessness.

Death

Most religions, primitive and modern, have something to say about life after death. Some speak of a miserable hereafter in which the spirits of the dead wander about wailing and moaning; others—including Christianity and Islam—hold forth inviting visions of paradise, at least for the deserving. Belief in personal immortality in a happy setting makes the deaths of loved ones more tolerable and the prospect of one's own death less terrifying. Hope of a happy heareafter can also help reconcile the individual to a life of deprivation in this world, since earthly existence can be looked on as no more than a temporary state leading to eternal bliss. The fact that a belief in immortality is found in nearly all societies has led some writers to suggest that it may fulfill a basic social need.[17]

Social Values

Research tends to show that individuals who are strongly linked through religious commitment to traditional norms and values gain a source of moral strength and behavioral stability.[18] Under such conditions, people are more willing to

16. A standard sociological account of Mormonism is Thomas F. O'Dea, *The Mormons* (Chicago: The University of Chicago Press, 1957).

17. Ashley Montagu, *Immortality* (New York: Grove Press, Inc., 1955), pp. 31–67.

18. Carl G. Jung, *Psychology and Religion* (New Haven, Conn.: Yale University Press, 1938).

Religion serves a variety of functions for individual believers. Some people believe, for example, that exposure to sacred religious artifacts can cure physical suffering. Seeking spiritual and physical relief, pilgrims from all over the world have visited the shrine at Lourdes in southern France, where the Virgin Mary is reported to have revealed herself to a young girl in 1858.

comply with the norms of their society, especially if they interpret the norms as having divine sanction. They are also more likely to interpret social deviance as a form of religious deviance. For centuries, kings and emperors claimed to be God's chosen representatives (or, in some cases, to be divine themselves), thereby making rebellion against the Crown synonymous with defiance of God's will. Belief in sacred kingship helped maintain political and social stability.

Other Consequences

There have been a number of recent attempts to trace ways in which religion influences the daily lives of people in modern urban-industrial society. In an extensive study of white Protestants, black Protestants, white Catholics, and Jews in a large American city, Lenski was able to show that membership in any one of these socioreligious groups was associated with many significant variations in behavior:

Depending upon the socioreligious group to which a person belongs, the probabilities are increased or decreased that he will enjoy his occupation, indulge in installment buying, save to achieve objectives far in the future, believe in the American Dream, vote Republican, favor the welfare state, take a liberal view on the issue of freedom of speech, oppose racial integration in the schools, migrate to another community, maintain close ties with his family, have a large family, complete a given unit of education or rise in the class system. These are only a few of the consequences we have observed to be associated with differences in socioreligious group membership, and the position of individuals in these groups.[19]

Of course, to speak of "consequences" as Lenski does is to assume the presence of a causal relationship. And, as Lenski admits, the

19. Gerhard Lenski, *The Religious Factor* (Garden City, N.Y.: Anchor Books, 1963), p. 320.

nature of this relationship—the intervening group processes and variables, including complex subcultures, socialization practices, and the like—is not at all clear. Nor can we really tell from this kind of evidence which of the supposed "consequences" of religious affiliation are functional and which dysfunctional. (See the discussion of functional analysis in Chapter 2, pages 48–50.) Nevertheless, it is beyond dispute that when Americans are grouped according to their religious affiliations, significant differences in behavior can be observed from one religious category to another.

RELIGION AS GROUP BEHAVIOR

Experimental social psychology clearly indicates that beliefs gain credibility in proportion to the degree in which they are shared.[20] Even such extraordinary beliefs as the conviction that the world is in imminent danger of a cosmic catastrophe can become acceptable to otherwise conventional people if the predictions are supported by a trusted group.

Festinger and his associates report on the case of an American housewife who claimed to be receiving messages predicting a vast catastrophe. These messages, she said, were sent by the inhabitants of another planet. The catastrophe was to take the form of a flood that would completely inundate the west coasts of both North and South America. But she and those who believed her would be rescued by a flying saucer. A number of persons did believe her. As the time predicted for the catastrophe drew near, the prophet and most of her followers began to spend all their time together.

When the time came and there was no flood, the prophet did not abandon her convictions. After a few hours of soul-searching, she announced that God had decided to spare the earth from destruction. Those who were with her were glad to accept this explanation. They believed even more than before in the truth of her messages and made no attempt to conceal the fact. But those who, though they had believed, were not with her when she explained the apparent failure of her prophecies, tended to abandon membership in her group and to keep quiet about their experiences in it.[21]

As we have already noted, Durkheim maintained that "truly religious beliefs are always common to a determined group."[22] Sociologists are interested in finding out what kinds of groups develop and maintain various kinds of religious beliefs and practices. This section will be concerned with some of the major forms of such groups, the ways in which they are organized, and the types of individuals who lead them. Discussion will be based mainly on Christian groups. As one experienced scholar has pointed out, "virtually all attempts to develop a typology of religious groups have been concerned with Christian materials; their applicability to other religions has yet to be tested adequately."[23] This restriction, while limiting, has the advantage of permitting variations in religious organization to be discussed within the context of the same general religious belief.

SOURCES OF RELIGIOUS VARIATION

One problem in studying religion as group behavior is to account for the many different religious bodies that have similar theological doctrines. Each of the major American religions—Christian and Jewish—is characterized by subgroups whose beliefs and practices differ somewhat from those of other subgroups within the same faith. Though some of these differences may seem to be minor, they are considered to be very important by their adherents. The greatest splintering of Christians is among Protestants; literally hundreds of Protestant groups practice some form of Christianity.

20. Solomon E. Asch, "Effects of Group Pressure Upon the Modification and Distortion of Judgments," in *Readings in Social Psychology*, ed. Eleanor E. Maccoby, Theodore M. Newcomb, and Eugene L. Hartley (New York: Holt, Rinehart and Winston, Inc., 1958), pp. 174–183. See also Chapter 6, "Socialization," esp. pages 150–151.

21. Leon Festinger, Henry W. Riecken, Jr., and Stanley Schachter, *When Prophecy Fails* (Minneapolis: University of Minnesota Press, 1956).

22. Durkheim, *Elementary Forms*, p. 41.

23. J. Milton Yinger, *Religion, Society and the Individual* (New York: Macmillan, Inc., 1957), p. 143.

Analysis of this diversity has been undertaken by both European and American scholars. Built upon the work of Max Weber and Ernst Troeltsch, the best-known discussion of the social sources of variation among Christian groups in America is H. Richard Niebuhr's.[24] Niebuhr approached the problem of religious variation in two ways. First, he took account of the conditions under which *sects* develop within an established *church*. This analysis was based largely on the theories of Troeltsch (which will be discussed briefly below). Niebuhr then reviewed the continuous modification of Protestant doctrines in the United States, as influenced by such factors as economic conditions, nationalism, regionalism, immigration, and racial identification. In the following sections these sources of sectarianism and denominationalism will be discussed.

Church and Sect

The German sociologist Ernst Troeltsch contrasted two "ideal types" (page 70) of religious organization as an aid to understanding how new theological doctrines are generated within particular religious bodies.[25] He called these ideal types *church* and *sect*. They are not intended to be accurate descriptions of any specific group but are instead abstractions that attempt to identify the essential characteristics of two different forms of religious social organization and their relationship to each other.

The universal *church* in Troeltsch's theory is an inclusive and deeply institutionalized religious body that is often national in scope. It draws its membership from a broad spectrum and stresses the universalism of its doctrines. During the nineteenth century the Catholic Church in Italy was a universal church, as was the Eastern Orthodox Church in czarist Russia. Universal churches have systems of norms, roles, sanctions, and status hierarchies that are widely accepted and backed by tradition. One important goal is the perpetuation of the faith through education of the young. Another goal is to extend and maintain control over the spiritual life of as many people as possible. The services of the church center around formalized rituals

conducted by a professional clergy. Such services are usually devoid of spontaneous religious expression.

The church sometimes fails to meet the religious needs of some of its members. The highly institutionalized forms of worship may not provide emotional fulfillment or a real sense of religious experience. The abstract theological doctrines produced by church scholars may fail to provide inspiration in daily life. Thus some members may feel a need to return to the more fundamental ethics and life-styles of the founders of the faith.

The universal church is usually allied with power elites in the society and draws protection, recognition, and support from them. Because of this support, the church must be prepared to accommodate its ethical outlook and even its creed to changing conditions in the secular social order, thereby distressing many of its members. When a Christian church disappoints its members, the reform often called for is a return to a more fundamental form of Christianity, closer to the literal teachings of Jesus.

When religious systems fail to satisfy individual or group needs, alternate forms develop.[26] A *sect* may emerge within, or break away from, the established church. Usually a small group to begin with, the sect is likely to demand some definite type of religious experience (e.g., a feeling of "being saved," or of having "seen the light") as a prerequisite to membership. As a rule it rejects official clergy, elaborate or formal rituals, and alliances with secular sources of power.

Important to the sect is a shared rejection of some feature of the larger church or of the larger society. Thus members of the sect develop a strong sense of self-identity and compelling in-group loyalties and identifications. Such characteristics lead members to believe that the sect constitutes an elite:

24. H. Richard Niebuhr, *The Social Sources of Denominationalism* (New York: Henry Holt and Company, 1929).
25. Ernst Troeltsch, *The Social Teaching of the Christian Churches* (New York: The Macmillan Company, 1931). For an excellent survey of contemporary extensions and criticisms of the church-sect typology, see Benton Johnson, "On Church and Sect," in *Religion's Influence in Contemporary Society*, ed. Faulkner, pp. 217–232.
26. Yinger, *Religion, Society and the Individual*, p. 145.

The sect, as the sole possessor of true doctrine, or appropriate ritual and of warranted standards of rectitude in social behavior, regards itself as a people set apart, making claim, if not always to absolutely exclusive salvation, at least to the fullest blessings.[27]

Usually, membership in the sect transcends all other allegiances in importance, and sects develop both formal and informal behavior codes that members are expected to adopt.

At first, the organizational pattern of the sect is very informal. Simply because it is new, its norms, roles, social control, and ranking patterns are not deeply institutionalized. Interaction within the sect is likely to be spontaneous and emotional. Its ranking system generally consists of a leader, with perhaps a few lieutenants, and a group of followers whose power and status remain undifferentiated.

One of the ironies with respect to the development of a sect is that, if it survives, sooner or later it loses its ability to meet the needs of its members as effectively as it did when it was newly formed. Any religious group that persists over time and has more than a handful of members has to cope eventually with the same problems as the church. For example, members expect the sect to solemnize and record births, marriages, and deaths. For these and other purposes, formalized rituals are necessary—rituals usually modeled after those of the rejected church.

Furthermore, later generations of sect members have not experienced the problems that caused the sect to be formed in the first place, and they may not willingly accept the sect's codes of behavior. New forms of social control must therefore be designed in order to retain purity of beliefs and practices. This means increasing formalization. The original leader dies. Others struggle for control, and the winner must consolidate his or her position. These and other difficulties cause the sect to lose its original spontaneity and informality. It becomes increasingly subject to routine. Finally, the origi-

nal sect becomes a church, and some of its members may leave to found a new sect of their own.

In the United States many religious sects have arisen and have subsequently disbanded. A small number of such groups have tried to maintain a social and cultural life that differs greatly from the larger society. Mennonites, Amish, and Hutterites have avoided big cities and settled in various rural areas in order to perpetuate their social, cultural, and religious practices. The Hasidic Jews of New York City, on the other hand, have had remarkable success in perpetuating their way of life in the midst of a complex urban environment.[28]

Hasidism, a very orthodox form of Judaism with highly emotional services, originated in eastern Europe in the eighteenth century. One of the many groups that make up the sect—the Satmar Hasidim—came from Hungary and settled in the Williamsburg section of Brooklyn during World War II. This community has more than twenty thousand members, and its size is increasing. In part, the group is maintained through strong religious teachings that stress procreation. The rabbis provide strong leadership and make many of the decisions concerning everyday life. The men divide their time between religious and economic pursuits, while the women occupy themselves with domestic life and selected religious activities.

Like some of the Christian sects in the United States, the Satmar Hasidim are self-sufficient and therefore limit their contact with the outside world. They have their own businesses, medical facilities, newspapers, banks, and even a bus system. They do not own television sets or radios; they do not go to the movies; and the young people attend private schools and play only with other Hasidim.

According to some researchers, the reason that the Hasidim, in contrast to fundamentalist Protestant groups, are flourishing, is that they have successfully merged their economic and religious institutions.[29] The products of the Hasidic sect—food, clothing, and religious artifacts—are in great demand. Thus, by integrating its religious life with its economic activities and

---

27. Bryan Wilson, *Religious Sects* (New York: McGraw-Hill Book Company, 1970), pp. 26–27.

28. Solomon Poll, *The Hasidic Community of Williamsburg: A Study in the Sociology of Religion,* 2nd ed. (New York: Schocken Books, Inc., 1969).

29. Ibid., pp. 248–266.

The Hasidim, members of a highly orthodox Jewish sect, avoid extensive interaction with outsiders. Males divide their time between religious and economic pursuits. The rabbi is the leader of the Hasidic community, making secular as well as religious decisions.

by avoiding extensive interaction with nonmembers, the sect has been able not only to survive but to grow.

Social Sources of Denominationalism

Denominations are relatively large, well established, and widely accepted as "respectable." The dictionary defines *denomination* as "a religious organization uniting in a single legal and administrative body a number of local congregations." Denominations resemble Troeltsch's concept of "church." Services are conventionalized; emotional conversions are rare. Spontaneous expressions of religious fervor are not common. Examples in American society range from Baptists to Unitarians. Most denominations originated as sectarian movements that split from established churches.

Niebuhr's analysis is still one of the best accounts of the social conditions and factors that made it possible for so many denominations to flourish in American society.[30] He showed that people with distinctive economic, ethnic, regional, and racial backgrounds generally interpret religious doctrines in different ways and may reject, accept, or modify existing religious creeds according to their own needs. The Quakers, Baptists, Methodists, and Salvation Army, for example, were originally "churches of the disinherited"—the religiously neglected poor—who formed sects and split off from older Protestant denominations. The longer they existed, the more these newer religious groups tended to become middle-class. Their members worked hard and lived frugally; this led to prosperity for the sect, which expanded into a denomination, gradually lost its sectarian vigor, and acquired the institutional aspects of an established church.

Ethnic and nationalistic factors have also played an important role as sources of denominationalism. Much of the diversity in Christianity in the United States is due to the variety of national origins of the population. Immigrants brought their own variants of the Christian faith. And as the nation developed, regional factors played a part in shaping the religious makeup of the area.

---

30. Niebuhr, *The Social Sources of Denominationalism*.

Along the frontier, attitudes and ways of life, as well as physical conditions, were different than in settled areas, where towns and villages had developed. Protestant churches established on the frontier depended more on lay preachers; members were less concerned with formal ritual, and few were interested in an intellectualized theology. These conditions led to modified versions of established denominations, especially Methodist and Baptist. Sects also tended to move westward, in search of privacy and freedom to worship as they wished. Among the most successful were the Mormons, who now proselytize at home and abroad from their base in Utah.

The same type of analysis can be made for the influence of different sociocultural conditions in the North and the South. In particular the issue of slavery created schisms in the established denominations, and special forms of Methodist, Baptist, and other churches emerged in each region. Slavery was also the basis for the growth of many black religious groups. Ironically, given their missionary efforts among blacks, white Christians did not welcome black Christians in their churches, either before or after the Civil War. As a result, more or less parallel forms of a given denomination developed within each racial category. There are now four main black denominations—National Baptist Convention, African Methodist Episcopal, African Methodist Episcopal Zion, and Colored Episcopal—plus literally hundreds of smaller black religious groups. Most black people still worship in segregated congregations.

THE CONTEMPORARY JESUS PEOPLE

At the height of the development of dissident and hippie subcultures during the late 1960s, an unusual religious phenomenon—the Jesus Movement—began to assert itself in a number of cities along the West Coast of the United States.

Later it spread elsewhere. Members of the various groups that make up this movement were recruited from young people who had participated in the drug subculture and had become dissatisfied with it. Enroth, Ericson, and Peters studied several groups of the Jesus People, and the following summary draws much of its material from their report.[31]

Although the Jesus People, in part, represent an extension of an older, larger fundamentalist religious movement, some of their practices, beliefs, and orientations are unique. They seek a much more intense form of Christianity than that offered by traditional denominations. They are also rebelling against the secular order and the drug subculture.

Pentecostalism

The Jesus Movement is an outgrowth of the Pentecostal religious movement that began in the United States in the early 1900s. Among Christians, the term *Pentecost* refers to a festival celebrating the descent of the Holy Spirit upon the Apostles, and *Pentecostal* is applied to groups in which members claim to have been "touched by the Spirit," have "been saved," have "known Jesus," and so on.

Pentecostal groups, while differing one from another, typically have stressed a literal interpretation of the Bible, authoritarian (but charismatic) lay preachers, emotional religious services (e.g., those of the "holy rollers" and the snake cults), baptism by total immersion to receive the Holy Spirit, healing by "laying on of hands," glossolalia or "speaking in tongues," and extensive Bible study by all members. The Pentecostal Movement has had a rebirth and is now an important part of religious activity in America, with some impact on traditional Protestant denominations and on the Catholic Church. A number of the founders of the Jesus Movement were Pentecostal preachers who brought along their religious forms and rituals. The modes of religious expression, some of the Christian beliefs, and some practices of the Jesus People are patterned after Pentecostal groups.

31. Ronald M. Enroth, Edward E. Ericson, Jr., and C. Breckinridge Peters, *The Jesus People: Old-Time Religion in the Age of Aquarius* (Grand Rapids, Mich.: William B. Eerdmans Publishing Co., 1972). See also Robert B. Simmonds, James T. Richardson, and Mary W. Harder, "Organization and Structure of a Jesus Movement Community," *Social Compass*, 21, No. 3 (1974): 269–281.

Emotional religious services, the literal interpretation of the Bible, and charismatic preachers are characteristic of Pentecostalism, of which the Jesus Movement is a part. Many Jesus People came to the movement from the drug counterculture. One of the most famous groups of Jesus People is the Children of God (above), members of which frequently hold vigils in public places.

The Jesus Movement

As was discussed in Chapter 13, social movements represent collective responses to unwanted conditions in society and often attract people who share some common problem (see pages 394–402). This is true of the Jesus People. During the 1960s many young people cut their ties with parents and friends and with a number of social institutions, leaving home to experiment with drugs, communal living, and sexual freedom. But many found the new life lonely and frustrating, and others, having made all the "trips," were burnt out and sick of street life. Among these youths the Jesus People found willing converts. Some were brought into the Jesus Movement by enthusiastic recruiters. Others came on their own to seek salvation.

Some of the larger groups published newspapers to aid in recruiting and to spread their message. They used the language of the drug counterculture to appeal to potential converts:

To what can we compare the Kingdom of Heaven? . . . Do you smoke dope? Have you ever smoked bad dope? You know, full of stems, maybe mixed with parsley and catnip. Yeh, you burn your throat, and the only way you can get high is hyperventilating.

Let's say you just bought a lid for fifteen bucks. Bad dope. You're sitting there, puffing away. Maybe you're getting a little high hyperventilating. Maybe you're getting a little bummed out because it's a burn.

I come tripping up to you, and I have a big sack of Acapulco gold. Say it's one of those plastic garbage sacks full. And I say, "Man, if you'll just throw down that lid, I'll give you this Acapulco gold, free. It's already paid for, but the only way you can get it is to throw down your lid."

What would you do?

Well, that's what Jesus is saying to you. He's just saying, "Man, if you're getting a little tired of your trip, of getting burned. If you just give up your trip and accept My life, I'll give it to you free with all the love and all the joy and all the peace that comes with it."

You know, only a fool would smoke parsley when you could have Acapulco gold.[32]

Such recruiting efforts were successful. Having shared the same life-style and experienced similar problems, the new members found a sense of identity with the Jesus People and looked to the movement for guidance and solutions.

Jesus People as Sectarians

The Jesus groups are exceptionally sectarian in organization, practice, and outlook. This intensity may be attributed to the fact that they represent a revolt not only from established religion but also from the counterculture with its drug and sex orientations and from American society in general.

Membership in the small groups that make up the Jesus Movement is voluntary. The groups place strong emphasis on religious experience; they reject formalized services; their leaders are authoritarian, charismatic figures. Their beliefs follow a typical sectarian pattern in that a major portion is developed around the Apocalyptic theme—that the end of the world is near and only those who have seen the light (themselves) will achieve salvation. Their orientations toward established denominations are negative. Institutionalized religion with its ecumenical orientations is often referred to as the "Great Whore of Babylon" (implying that the church as "bride of Christ" has sold out to worldly interests). In addition, Jesus People foster and maintain elitist conceptions of themselves as the only people with the true faith.

Rituals vary somewhat from group to group. Most Jesus People live communally and share all worldly goods in common. They proselytize intensively and hold services several times a day. Some (for example, the Children of God) conduct silent protest gatherings in public places:

As the Spirit leads, the "Prophets of Doom" (their term) don red sackcloth (symbol of repentance), daub their foreheads with ashes (symbol of mourning), place wooden yokes about their neck (symbol of bondage) and wear one earring (symbol of willingness to be a "slave of love" to Christ). Carrying wooden staves (symbol of divine judgment) they stand in protest at public events to denounce the unrepentant.[33]

32. *Truth*, May 1971, p. 14; quoted in Enroth, Ericson, and Peters, *The Jesus People*, p. 125.
33. Enroth, Ericson, and Peters, *The Jesus People*, p. 34.

Such vigils have been held at football games, funerals, trials, and elsewhere. Other rituals among some of the groups include exorcising demons, singing, glossolalia, "witnessing" (aggressive recruiting), and "smiting" (hitting people over the head with a Bible).[34]

Among the Jesus People, religious commitment is measured by knowledge of the Bible. In particular, members are expected to be able to cite scriptural passages from the New Testament. Some participants carry clipboards, worn on chains around the neck, with verses they are trying to memorize. The Jesus People become highly skilled at citing Biblical passages to support their various claims.

Religious experience is central to commitment among the Jesus People. The founders of the groups can and do tell about their personal contacts with God and their calling to their task. Among ordinary members, the conversion experience is an important part of their decisions to join and remain with the group. The experiential basis for conversion may be a vision, a dream, or "good vibes" (feelings that Jesus is with them). Members frequently describe their religious experiences as "being high" or being "on a trip."

The individual consequences of membership in these groups can range from trivial to profound. Members often report that their lives have been dramatically changed. Typically, they say that the movement has brought them out of the despair of their prior life-style—with its spiritual alienation, drug dependency, sexual promiscuity, and loneliness—to the warm fellowship of a religious community where purpose and meaning are restored. For thousands of young people, there is little doubt that some kind of transformation has taken place. There is a question, however, about how long-lasting such conversions really are. Thousands who were initially converted have since left the sects, many to return to life in regular society. And,

like backsliders in other religious groups, at least some have returned to their old ways and blame the sect for failing them:

I'm back on acid. I used to be tripped out on Jesus. I was really zapped by the Spirit. I was really up on Christ. But it was a bummer. Nobody told me about forsaking the crowd—nothing about temptations, about the devil trying to bring me down. Somebody wasn't honest with me.[35]

At the present time, the Jesus Movement appears to be in a state of transition. As Mauss and Peterson point out, the counterculture from which most of the earlier participants were drawn is no longer so widespread.[36] The "flower children" have left Haight-Asbury, and the drug culture no longer attracts large numbers of young people. Perhaps because of this, the Jesus People are starting to develop rapport with more established religious groups.

RELIGIOUS LEADERSHIP

What kind of people lead religious groups? In what ways do they relate to their followers? In the present section, two types of religious leaders will be discussed: religious innovators—those who start new systems of belief—and clergy—leaders of established religious groups. Although roughly the same questions can be asked about both types, each provides a very different style of leadership.

Religious Innovators

Individuals who start religions come from a variety of social backgrounds. Often, they are of humble origin. More important, it seems, are the times in which they live. It is during periods of social unrest, when established systems of values begin to crumble, that founders of new faiths are likely to emerge. In particular, mass migration, rapid urbanization, industrialization, war, and other social upheavals provide conditions conducive to the formation, or attempted formation, of new religions.

Two major types of religious innovators can be discerned: the "prophet" and the "messiah."

34. Ibid.

35. Comment of a former member of the Jesus Movement, recorded by David Wilkerson in his *Jesus Person Maturity Manual,* and quoted in Enroth, Ericson, and Peters, *The Jesus People,* p. 243.

36. Armand L. Mauss and Donald W. Petersen, "Prodigals as Preachers: The 'Jesus Freaks' and the Return to Respectability," *Social Compass,* 21, No. 3 (1974): 283–301.

(The meanings of these terms are not intended to be identical with their usage in established religious groups.) To their followers, both prophets and messiahs appear to have charismatic powers or qualities. In other respects, however, they differ considerably. Vernon has summarized the major behavior patterns associated with the role of prophet in the following terms:

An individual typically comes to believe that he is in communion with his deity or deities and has received divine mandates to perform certain tasks or "missions." He then defines himself as being the mouthpiece or instrument of divine will, having learned his deity's wishes through visions, dreams, trances, direct verbal communication or other means.[37]

The messiah is also a religious innovator who possesses great charisma. But unlike the prophet (who merely claims to speak for a divinity), the messiah claims to *be* a divine being. Furthermore, instead of calling for reform in the existing social or religious system, the messiah predicts the total collapse of the system and the coming of a millennium when the entire world, or at least the society, will be utterly transformed.

Numerous Americans have started successful sectarian groups by playing the role of prophet or messiah. A good example of the prophet is Georgia-born Elijah Poole, who as Elijah Muhammad, the "Messenger of Allah," founded the Black Muslim sect.[38] Another black leader, Father Divine, provides an example of the messiah. Father Divine also came from humble origins in the South, where his name was George Baker. His career began after he migrated to New York and announced that he was a divine being—in fact, God himself! He developed the Peace Mission Movement, which spread to many urban centers.[39]

Clergy

We have already seen how any religious group that persists through time tends to become institutionalized. If the group grows in size, a formal division of labor and a hierarchy of leadership become necessary, and a class of religious specialists develops. While such specialists are variously referred to as priests, rabbis, ministers, or pastors, depending upon which denomination or religion they serve, they are sufficiently alike to be grouped under the general heading of clergy. They perform a considerable variety of roles—teacher, preacher, scholar, master of ritual, counselor, institutional representative, and administrator.

The typical Protestant minister is directly responsible to the members of the congregation, and the democratic power structure leads to an emphasis on service roles, such as counseling and organizing social functions. In some denominations it may also mean adapting the ritualistic and doctrinal aspects of the faith to the interests of particular congregations. Many ministers deal little with theological issues in their sermons, speaking instead on current secular themes.

In contrast, the main responsibility of the Catholic priest has traditionally been to higher church authority. For centuries parishioners had little or no voice in how the church was run. Today there are numerous signs of challenge and change, but the priest is still in charge of the parish.[40]

Like the Protestant minister, the rabbi is directly responsible to the congregation. Traditionally, the rabbi is a religious leader, a teacher, and a scholar. Most contemporary rabbis perform service roles and function as leaders of their congregations.

In terms of formal training, both Jews and Catholics make extensive demands on prospective clergy. The typical Catholic priest must spend several years in advanced study after the equivalent of graduation from college, and the

37. Glenn M. Vernon, *Sociology of Religion* (New York: McGraw-Hill Book Company, 1962), p. 174.
38. E. U. Essien-Udom, *Black Nationalism: The Search for an Identity* (Chicago: The University of Chicago Press, 1962).
39. Robert A. Parker, *The Incredible Messiah: The Deification of Father Divine* (Boston: Little, Brown and Company, 1937).
40. For two recent studies on the Catholic clergy, see Andrew M. Greeley, *Priests in the United States: Reflections on a Survey* (Garden City, N.Y.: Doubleday & Company, Inc., 1972); and Joseph H. Fichter, *America's Forgotten Priests: What Are They Saying?* (New York: Harper & Row, Inc., 1968).

rabbi must spend from four to six years in rabbinical school after completing college. Protestant standards, by contrast, range from no formal educational requirements at all to advanced university training.

Reasons given for entering the clergy vary somewhat among the major religions. In certain Protestant and Catholic groups the individual is expected to have been "called" to the ministry by "a subjective emotional experience which semi-miraculously reveals God's will that one should become a clergyman."[41] Such experiences are not regarded as so important by Jews and are somewhat more typical of sectarian than of denominational Protestant groups. However, in a study of 1704 students from fifty-seven Protestant seminaries, "a definite call of God" was given by more than a third as a reason for entering the ministry.[42]

While the clergy are drawn from every social stratum, there are certain preconditions that seem to increase the probability that an individual will decide to enter the ministry. Some researchers have attempted to trace this decision to psychological factors,[43] but it can also be explained as a product of purely social influences. It is known that homes in which the father is a minister provide twenty-five times as many members of the clergy as other homes. Close friendship with a respected member of the clergy appears to be another important influence. In short, many of the same kinds of factors appear to influence prospective members of the clergy as influence prospective doctors, dentists, lawyers, and other apprentice professionals.[44]

Historically, in Protestant England the Anglican Church offered one of the few careers open to the younger sons of gentry, whose first-born sons inherited the family estates. On the Continent the Catholic Church provided the sole opportunity for advancement for boys of the lower class for centuries. While conditions were very different in nineteenth-century America, here too the priesthood offered poor boys a chance to achieve positions of respect and authority. Home influence also played an important role. For the immigrant mother in particular, having a son become a priest was often a matter of great pride and satisfaction.

RELIGION AND SOCIETY

In trying to relate religion to stability and conflict in society, modern sociologists are following in the footsteps of early social philosophers.[45] For example, in discussing the concept of a *civil* religion as an essential framework upon which a secular political order can be based, Robert Bellah points out that the phrase "civil religion" originated with Jean Jacques Rousseau.[46] In *The Social Contract* (1762), Rousseau outlined the simple precepts of such a religion: affirmation of the existence of God, belief in a life to come, recognition of the merits of virtue and the negative aspects of vice, and emphasis on religious tolerance. Evidence of a civil religion in the United States can be seen in many national symbols and rituals. "In God we trust" appears on our coins; and God's existence is affirmed in our pledge of allegiance, the benedictions that open legislative sessions, the prayers on our national Thanksgiving holiday, the oaths taken in court, and other official rituals and public pronouncements.

RELIGION AND SOCIAL INTEGRATION
Basic religious concepts are important in the maintenance of *all* aspects of the social machinery. Religions define sacred values and prescribe behavioral codes consistent with these values. There is, in short, a direct line of dependence between the powerful sentiments of reverence, awe, and fear that religious beliefs generate and the rules that religions prescribe for leading a life that will assure divine approval.

41. David O. Moberg, *The Church as a Social Institution* (Englewood Cliffs, N.J.: Prentice-Hall, Inc., 1962), p. 484.
42. Ralph A. Felton, *New Ministers* (Madison, N.J.: Drew Theological Seminary, 1949), pp. 15–17.
43. Moberg, *The Church as a Social Institution*, p. 485.
44. Ibid., pp. 482–483.
45. Guy E. Swanson, *Religion and Regime: A Sociological Account of Reformation* (Ann Arbor, Mich.: University of Michigan Press, 1967), p. viii.
46. Robert N. Bellah, "Civil Religion in America," in *Religion in America*, ed. by William McLoughlin and Robert N. Bellah (Boston: Houghton Mifflin Co., 1968), pp. 3–23.

THE TEN COMMANDMENTS

JUDAISM

I the Lord am your God who brought you out of the land of Egypt, the house of bondage. You shall have no other gods beside Me.

You shall not make for yourself a sculptured image, or any likeness of what is in the heavens above, or on the earth below, or in the waters under the earth. You shall not bow down to them or serve them. . . .

You shall not swear falsely by the name of the Lord your God . . . .

Remember the sabbath day and keep it holy. . . .

Honor your father and your mother, that you may long endure on the land which the Lord your God is giving you.

You shall not murder.

You shall not commit adultery.

You shall not steal.

You shall not bear false witness against your neighbor.

You shall not covet your neighbor's house: you shall not covet your neighbor's wife, or his male or female slave, or his ox or his ass, or anything that is your neighbor's.
Exodus 20:2 – 14.

CHRISTIANITY

I am the Lord thy God, which have brought thee out of the land of Egypt, out of the house of bondage.

Thou shalt have no other gods before me.

Thou shalt not make unto thee any graven image, or any likeness of any thing that is in heaven above, or that is in the earth beneath, or that is in the water under the earth:

Thou shalt not bow down thyself to them, nor serve them . . . .

Thou shalt not take the name of the Lord thy God in vain . . . .

Remember the sabbath day, to keep it holy. . . .

Honour thy father and thy mother: that thy days may be long upon the land which the Lord thy God giveth thee.

Thou shalt not kill.

Thou shalt not commit adultery.

Thou shalt not steal.

Thou shalt not bear false witness against thy neighbor.

Thou shalt not covet thy neighbour's house, thou shalt not covet thy neighbour's wife, nor his manservant, nor his maidservant, nor his ox, nor his ass, nor any thing that is thy neighbour's.
Exodus 20:2 – 17.

ISLAM

SAY: Come, I will rehearse what your Lord hath made binding on you – (1) that ye assign not aught to Him as partner: (2) and that ye be good to your parents: (3) and that ye slay not your children, because of poverty; for them and for you will we provide: (4) and that ye come not near to pollutions, outward or inward: (5) and that ye slay not anyone whom God hath forbidden you, unless for a just cause. . . . (6) And come not nigh to the substance of the orphan, but to improve it, until he come of age: (7) and use a full measure, and a just balance: We will not task a soul beyond its ability. (8) And when ye give judgment, observe justice, even though it be the affair of a kinsman, (9) and fulfil the covenant of God. This hath God enjoined you for your monition – And, "this is my right way." Follow it then: (10) and follow not other paths lest ye be scattered from His path. This hath He enjoined you, that ye may fear Him.
Surah vi. 152.

Source: *The Torah: A New Translation of The Holy Scriptures According to the Masoretic Text* (Philadelphia: The Jewish Publication Society of America, 1962); *The Holy Bible,* Authorized King James Version; Thomas Patrick Hughes, *A Dictionary of Islam* (Clifton, N.J.: Reference Book Publishers, Inc., 1965).

These rules in turn become important aspects of societal organization in the form of shared mores. For example, Jews, Christians, and Muslims are expected to follow the codes of conduct set forth in the Ten Commandments which, according to all three religions, were given Moses by God (see type box, page 490). At some point, if social change or other processes threaten to make religious rules ineffective, they may be translated into law. Thus religions define, reinforce, and reaffirm the elementary human responses upon which the social order ultimately rests. The English anthropologist Radcliffe-Brown makes the point that the social utility of a religion is not dependent on its "validity":

The hypothesis we are considering is that the social function of a religion is independent of its truth or falsity, that religions which we think to be erroneous or even absurd and repulsive, such as those of some savage tribes, may be important and effective parts of the social machinery, and without these "false" religions, social evolution and the development of modern civilization would have been impossible.[47]

RELIGION AND SOCIAL CONFLICT

Conflict based on religious differences has been a familiar fact throughout history. At the beginning of the Christian era, followers of Christ were persecuted by the Roman government. Then, after Christianity became the official religion of the Roman Empire, non-Christian groups were no less energetically persecuted. In later centuries "religious" wars wracked both East and West, though often economics and politics had at least as much to do with the struggles as religion. Christians clashed with Muslims, Catholics with Protestants, Protestants with other Protestants.

After World War II, at the time of the partition of India and Pakistan, tens of thousands were killed and millions made refugees in the explosive conflict between Muslims and Hindus. For years, Jews and Arabs have battled in the Middle East. Catholics and Protestants have

turned adjacent neighborhoods in Northern Ireland into warring camps.

In the United States, where freedom of religion is guaranteed by the Constitution, religious conflict is usually nonviolent today, but religious prejudice and discrimination are by no means dead. There are still tensions between believers and nonbelievers, between Christians and Jews, between Protestants and Catholics, among some branches of Protestantism, within some Protestant denominations, and within the Catholic Church. There can also be tension at times between the government and some religious groups, particularly when legislative issues under consideration run counter to the beliefs of these groups—for example, laws concerning prayer in public school, tax exemptions for church property, federal support for parochial schools, abortion, artificial insemination, divorce, and military conscription.[48]

RELIGION IN AMERICA

Because the Constitution of the United States prohibits government interference in religious matters, Congress has always refused to authorize official inquiries into church membership. As a result, the best available data on the religious composition of the American population are only estimates, made at irregular intervals by a variety of agencies. Table 16.2 shows one such estimate, based on a 1972 study by the National Opinion Research Center. An older estimate made by the Bureau of the Census in 1957, based on a sample of 119,333 persons over fourteen years old, showed a very similar distribution (66.2 percent Protestant, 25.7 percent Roman Catholic, and 3.2 percent Jewish).

When America's religious composition is examined in terms of place of residence, certain ecological and geographical patterns emerge. Jews tend to be concentrated in the larger urban centers, particularly in the Northeast. To a lesser extent the same is true of Catholics. Of the Protestants, Baptists are heavily represented in the South; it is much harder to generalize about other denominations.

47. A. R. Radcliffe-Brown, *Structure and Function in Primitive Society* (New York: The Free Press, 1952), p. 154.

48. W. Seward Salisbury, *Religion in American Culture* (Homewood, Ill.: Dorsey Press, 1964), pp. 329–330.

RELIGION AND SOCIAL CLASS

Studies of the relationship between religion and social class fall into two main categories. In the first, statistical indices of social class position, such as years of education or occupational group, are used to give a *quantitative* overview of class variations in religious affiliation. In the second, the same kinds of variations are examined from a *qualitative* viewpoint—that is, in terms of what religious experiences *mean* to the persons in question.

Table 16.2. ESTIMATED RELIGIOUS COMPOSITION OF THE ADULT POPULATION OF THE UNITED STATES

Religious groups	Percent of adult population
Protestants	64%
Baptists	20%
Methodists	14%
Lutherans	9%
Presbyterians	5%
Episcopalians	2%
Other Protestants	14%
Roman Catholics	26%
Jews	3%
Other Religions	2%
No Religion or Religion not reported	5%
Sample Size	1613
U.S. Adult Population, 18 or older (as reported by the 1970 Census)	126.2 million

SOURCE: Tables 16.2, 16.3, and 16.4 were constructed from data obtained in the *National Data Program for the Social Sciences, Spring 1972 General Social Survey, July 1972 Codebook* (Chicago and Williamstown, Mass.: National Opinion Research Center, University of Chicago, Roper PORC, and Williams College, 1972), James A. Davis, Principal Investigator.

The Quantitative Approach

Tabulation of membership by education and occupation reveals substantial class differences among major religious groups. The National Opinion Research Center survey cited above showed that three Protestant denominations—Episcopalian, Presbyterian, and Methodist—had more college-educated members than the others (Table 16.3) and were also more heavily represented in managerial and professional occupations (Table 16.4). Other Protestants, as well as most Roman Catholics, tend to be of the middle or lower-middle class, as measured by either education or occupation. Jews, on the other hand, vary considerably in education but have very strong representation in managerial and professional occupations. Of all the major religious groups, the Baptists appear most frequently at the bottom of the social structure; a large proportion of their members are poorly educated and in low-status jobs. The data from which these generalizations are drawn are reasonably consistent with earlier nationwide surveys of religious identification.[49]

It should not be concluded from these data, however, that religious affiliation is simply a class phenomenon. All groups draw *some* of their members from each social stratum. Anoth-

49. Herbert W. Schneider, *Religion in Twentieth Century America* (Cambridge, Mass.: Harvard University Press, 1952), p. 288; Lenski, *The Religious Factor*, pp. 79–81; Donald O. Cowgill, "The Ecology of Religious Preference in Wichita," *Sociological Quarterly*, 1 (1960): 87–96.

Table 16.3. EDUCATIONAL ATTAINMENT OF ADULTS IDENTIFYING THEMSELVES WITH MAJOR RELIGIOUS GROUPS IN THE UNITED STATES

Religious groups	Sample size	0–8 Grades	Some high school	4 Years high school	1–3 Years college	4 Years or more college	Total
Nation	1613	20%	20%	31%	17%	12%	100%
Protestants	1031	22	20	30	17	11	100
All Baptists	324	30	25	27	10	8	100
Baptists: White	178	21	30	31	9	10	100
Baptists: Blacks	146	41	22	23	11	3	100
Methodists	232	17	16	39	17	11	100
Lutherans	139	25	19	32	15	9	100
Presbyterians	80	8	15	27	30	20	100
Episcopalians	33	6	15	18	34	27	100
Roman Catholics	413	19	18	38	15	10	100
Jews	54	6	15	28	20	31	100

SOURCE: *National Data Program for the Social Sciences* (see Table 16.2).

er statistical generalization that should be interpreted with caution is the finding that upper- and middle-class people are more likely to be formal members of a church and to attend services with some regularity than are lower-class people.[50] This, again, is not a simple or invariant relationship; many lower-class people are ardent churchgoers, while many upper- and middle-class people attend rarely or not at all.

The Qualitative Approach

Figures on church affiliation or attendance tell us nothing about the quality of the experience of those involved. Some clues to the kinds of needs churches fulfill for their members are provided by their different styles of worship. As we have already noted, people attending the services of fundamentalist and Pentecostal sects often exhibit spontaneous forms of emotional behavior. By contrast, in many older denominations services are highly formal, thoroughly institutionalized, and almost completely without spontaneity. In a statistical survey, however, both types of service would be classified simply as "Protestant."

In some religious groups people shake, scream, jump, faint, roll on the floor, and give unsolicited testimony of their religious salvation. Here is a firsthand account:

50. Bernard Lazerwitz, "Some Factors Associated with Variations in Church Attendance," *Social Forces,* 39 (1961): 301–309.
51. Claude Brown, *Manchild in the Promised Land* (New York: Signet Books, 1966), pp. 25–26.

After Mrs. Rogers had been preaching for about fifteen minutes, an old lady got up and started screaming and shouting, "Help me, Lord Jesus!" She was still throwing her arms up and shouting for Jesus to help her when a younger woman jumped up and hollered, "Precious Lord Jesus, save me!" Mrs. Rogers' voice was getting louder all the time. For two hours, she preached—and for two hours, people were getting up, shouting, jumping up and down, calling to Jesus for help and salvation, and falling out exhausted. Some of these "Holy Rollers," as Dad called them, would fall to the floor and start trembling rapidly; some of them even began to slobber on themselves. When I asked Mama what was wrong with those people and what they were doing on the floor, she told me that the "spirit" had hit them. When Carole heard this, she began to cry and wanted to get out of there before the spirit hit us.[51]

The distinctive human needs generated at different levels of the social structure find expression and satisfaction within different types of religious groups. Black Americans, white, rural migrants to the impersonal city, farmers whose means of subsistence have been wiped out by technological change—these are the ready recruits for revivalist and Pentecostal sects, for churches where it is preached that the poor are the chosen people and the meek shall inherit the earth. In these groups people with little social status can find religious status. In addition, the emotional quality of the services makes them feel closer to God.

Table 16.4. OCCUPATIONAL STATUS OF ADULTS IDENTIFYING THEMSELVES WITH MAJOR RELIGIOUS GROUPS IN THE UNITED STATES

Religious groups	Sample size	Without an occupation	Farmers	Unskilled	Semi-skilled	Skilled	Clerical and sales	Owners, managers, and officials	Professions	Total
Nation	1613	10%	3%	13%	19%	12%	20%	10%	13%	100%
Protestants	1031	11	4	14	19	10	20	10	12	100
All Baptists	324	11	4	18	29	10	13	8	7	100
Baptists: White	178	11	5	8	25	15	17	12	7	100
Baptists: Black	146	10	3	31	35	5	8	2	6	100
Methodists	232	10	5	12	15	12	22	9	15	100
Lutherans	139	15	9	16	16	9	18	7	10	100
Presbyterians	80	5	5	4	16	8	29	14	19	100
Episcopalians	33	9	0	3	3	21	18	19	27	100
Roman Catholics	413	7	2	13	18	16	24	6	14	100
Jews	54	11	0	11	6	6	32	14	20	100

SOURCE: *National Data Program for the Social Sciences* (see Table 16.2).

VIEWPOINTS   THE NEW GENERATION OF SEEKERS

■   There is a movement easing across the land, a movement in which individuals are trying to work out personal salvation — a way to proceed through life with harmony and peace, a minimum of tension, and a maximum of fulfillment. What we are witnessing is the flowering of a generation of seekers, a generation whose world boundaries were shattered by . . . rapid social change, and who came to believe in the possibility of an answer, a key that would make life better immediately. . . .

Because of doomsday warnings, which seekers take literally, there is an urgency to reach satori now. . . . Charles Berner, who founded a religion called abilitism and developed an "enlightenment intensive" which produces dramatic results in three to five days, says, "The emphasis everywhere is on technique. Kids are coming by the droves out of the drug experience into the spiritual movement, and they won't tolerate nonsense. They say, your ideas are wonderful but show me what you do. . . . If the kids try your technique and it doesn't do what you say, they drop you. Those teachings which are doing well now are the ones that deliver the goods."

Success has not been limited, though, to groups which teach effective techniques. Virtually any spiritual organization that has outlined a path outside the establishment churches and synagogues has been flooded with seekers. . . .

Those religions which see God as the supreme authority to whom man must bow have failed to inspire interest. The notion of God being experienced and sought now is that of a force within us all, not outside sitting in judgment. . . . Each person comes to his own experience of the truth, and all experiences are valid. . . . Each man is seen as a continuous spirit, with the power to understand everything, if he can just bring that power into consciousness!

Sara Davidson
"The Rush for Instant Salvation"

●   We're all in search of sages — my generation in particular. . . . I long for — capital W — Wisdom. We all do, I think. . . .

We, who so hated school, are in search now of *teachers*. An apricot-robed, lotus-folded guru with a name too long to fit on one line of a poster, an old man on a park bench (with a beard if possible), a plain-talking, no-nonsense Maine farmer with a pitchfork in his hand, the author of any slim volume of austere prose or poetry (the fewer words he writes, the more profound each one must be) — we attend their words so abjectly, sometimes even literally sit at their feet, waiting for any crumbs of what will pass as wisdom to be offered us.

I remember a show-and-tell day when I was in fourth grade. . . . One boy brought his rosary beads and his crucifix and took from his wallet a photograph of his priest and himself beside their church. We were all too stunned to laugh at first, but then the giggling started, until we were all hiccupping and one girl had to run off to the bathroom without waiting for a pass, and even the teacher was smiling . . . . (Going to church was OK, like going to Brownies. But to speak, as Ralphie Leveque did, of loving God and of the blood of Christ, and Mary's tears and thorns and nails — that seemed almost dirty.)

Now, while the fourth graders might still giggle, Jesus has come out of the closet. . . . It is a sign of many things: an attempt to purify the spirit, to be drenched in holy waters after a drug-filled adolescence, a form of the new nostalgia, even — almost *camp*. What's really going on, though, in the Jesus movement is our search for a prophet, for someone who can, for a change, tell us the answers. . . . After so many unprofound facts and so much loose, undisciplined freedom, it's comforting to have a creed to follow and a cross to bear.

Joyce Maynard
"Searching for Sages"

Airplanes are the only contact that these natives in New Guinea have with Western civilization. Since the "strange birds" bring food, medicine, tobacco, and alcohol, they have, in effect, ushered in a millennium—a period of prosperity for the tribe. Not surprisingly, however, this sudden appearance of cargo is also a source of some consternation to the natives. Thus they have developed a cargo cult that explains the arrival of the supplies in terms of their existing beliefs. Because ancestor worship is an important part of their ritual, most members of the tribe believe that the goods are sent by their ancestors.

To the middle class, by contrast, sectarian religious behavior often seems ludicrous. The "pleasant and dignified" atmosphere of the Sunday service held in a building that "looks like" God's house, where there is a chance to socialize with "nice" people afterwards, seems to this class a more appropriate form of worship.

52. For a discussion of the various challenges currently facing the major religious denominations in the United States, see Harvey Cox, *The Secular City,* rev. ed. (New York: Macmillan, Inc., 1966); and Peter Berger, *The Sacred Canopy: Elements of a Sociological Theory of Religion* (Garden City, N.Y.: Doubleday & Company, Inc., 1967).

RELIGION IN A CHANGING SOCIETY

Societies and their religions undergo change together. This does not imply that one is necessarily "determined" by the other; religion may change society and vice versa. At the present time in the United States the traditional beliefs and practices of all major religious denominations are being challenged not only by an increasingly secularized society but also by those within the churches. What does this imply for the future of religion?[52]

Secularization

With scientific and industrial progress, societies tend to become increasingly secular in their basic value orientations. American churches, especially the Protestant ones, have reacted to this situation by becoming less otherworldly. Members of the clergy have become increasingly involved in the nonreligious affairs of their communities. The heavy participation of the clergy in the civil rights movement of the 1960s is one example.[53] Less controversial has been the involvement of virtually all urban churches (and increasingly the suburban ones as well) with such social problems as juvenile delinquency, poverty, and drug addiction.

But the increasing involvement of the clergy in social problems and other secular affairs does not mean that religion is declining in importance. On the contrary, such a trend could be interpreted as marking a shift in emphasis from salvation of the soul to the ways in which religious values can serve as guides in day-to-day living. There are numerous indications that, in spite of the declines in church attendance cited earlier, *interest* in religion remains high. For example, religious coverage by radio and television is extensive, and religious books of an inspirational nature are frequently high on the list of best sellers.

Adaptation

It seems possible to conclude that religion in America is not dying out but is assuming new forms that will assure its survival in a changing society. Religious faiths have often adapted themselves to changing circumstances in the past. For example, there are now three major varieties of Judaism in the United States, representing three general degrees of acculturation to American society. Many Orthodox Jews maintain their religion much as it was in their area of origin—usually eastern Europe—resisting the impact of American culture. Conservative Jews maintain strong ties with traditional Jewish beliefs and traditions but permit numerous modifications of traditional worship, religious organization, and doctrine. Finally, the proponents of Reform Judaism, while continuing to regard themselves as Jews, have abandoned many traditional features of their religion.

The Continuing Conflict with Science

Prior to the emergence of modern science, religion provided accounts of the nature of the cosmos, of the origins of the earth, and of the creation of human life. In recent centuries, science has challenged explanations based on divine revelation and has offered alternate hypotheses based on observation, experiment, physical evidence, and scientific laws.

Although the debates between theologians and scientists that accompanied the growth of science in the nineteenth and early twentieth centuries have subsided, this does not mean that all the differences between religion and science have been settled. There is no longer much organized opposition to the teachings of modern science in the public schools, but conservative denominations and fundamentalist sects continue to insist that the Biblical account of the Creation, for example, be given at least equal standing with the theory of evolution in textbooks. And a number of leading scientists continue to believe that the two systems of explanation—the one based on faith and revelation and the other on empirical evidence and scientific logic—can never achieve real rapprochement.[54]

Science, by its nature, admits of uncertainty, and it makes no attempt to deal with such questions as the ultimate meaning of existence. Thus, whatever the future progress of science, religion will undoubtedly remain relevant to many individuals, helping them come to terms with problems that are beyond empirical investigation.

53. Jeffrey K. Hadden and Raymond R. Rymph, "The Marching Ministers," in *Religion in Radical Transition*, 2nd new ed., ed. Jeffrey K. Hadden (New Brunswick, N.J.: Transaction Books, 1973), pp. 99–109.

54. Glock and Stark, *Religion and Society in Tension*, p. 263.

SUMMARY

Sociologists study religion as an important social institution that is of significance both to individuals and to society. Individual religious behavior can be understood as a complex of beliefs, rituals, knowledge, and personal experience. Individuals look to religion for ideologies that give meaning to life's events. Religion helps people face crises and death, provides a source of social values, and influences individual choices in many aspects of daily life.

Religion is also group behavior. When beliefs, rituals, and knowledge are shared, they gain in credibility and importance. The creeds and composition of religious groups vary greatly. Sectarian groups split from established churches and denominations. Denominations and other religious groups are influenced by the ethnic, regional, economic, and racial characteristics of the populations that support them. An excellent recent example of sectarianism is the Jesus Movement. The Jesus People are in part an extension of the older Pentecostal movement and in part a unique expression of the desires and problems of young people who were dissatisfied with the countercultures of the 1960s.

Religious leaders can be categorized as the innovators—the prophets and messiahs—and the clergy. Prophets see themselves as instruments of divine will, while messiahs present themselves as divine beings. The clergy—religious specialists—of the various faiths receive different amounts of training and have different relationships with the groups they lead. In choosing their profession, prospective members of the clergy appear to be influenced by many of the same kinds of factors that influence those choosing other occupations.

From the perspective of society as a whole, a major consequence of religion is the contribution it makes to social stability and social integration. Many of our beliefs, values, and norms have their origins in religious systems and continue to provide a basis for many types of behavior in contemporary society. However, religion can also be a source of social conflict: from ancient times to the present day, religious groups have clashed. Religious beliefs can also conflict with laws passed by the state, as in the case of conscientious objection to military service.

About 64 percent of all Americans can be described as Protestants, 26 percent as Roman Catholics, and about 3 percent as Jews. The educational and occupational levels of the members vary from denomination to denomination. In general, life circumstances generate distinctive religious needs at different levels of social stratification. Religious services in groups that draw members mainly from lower socioeconomic classes tend to be more spontaneous and emotional. In churches with predominantly middle-class congregations, formal, dignified services meet the different needs of those who attend.

As American society has undergone social change, religious groups and their clergy have become increasingly involved in the problems of the secular world. Religions adapt to changing circumstances and attitudes by modifying their beliefs and practices. While the findings of science pose a continuing challenge to many of the beliefs of religious groups, it seems clear that human beings will continue to turn to religion when they seek to understand the meaning of life.

17
The Political Institution

Political power, as we noted in Chapter 8, is not only one of the rewards of a society's stratification system but may also be a means for determining the distribution of the other rewards, wealth and prestige. Thus *politics* has been defined, not inaccurately, as being concerned with "who gets what, when, and how."[1]

In the United States as in many other countries, existing power arrangements have been vigorously attacked in recent years by groups of citizens demanding—in one way or another—a more active voice in the political process. Radicals here and abroad have charged that the governments of the Western democracies are corrupt and immoral handmaidens of the giant national and multinational corporations. Some black militants have renounced the American system on the grounds that its institutions are carefully designed to keep blacks in economic and psychological chains. And some militants of a very different sort, aggressive defenders of the status quo, have urged that the freedoms guaranteed by the Constitution be put aside at times in order to protect what they call "the American way of life."

A much larger portion of politically active citizens has tried to make its voice heard by working *within* the existing system in an effort to reform it. Many of these concerned Americans have worked through the major parties, but an increasing number have become independents who support reform candidates regardless of party. Also working for political reform within the system are citizens' groups in which Democrats, Republicans, minor party members, and independents are merged. And while some black leaders have rejected "white" politics, many more have worked for black power by building strength at the polls and by running for elective office. Meanwhile, a great many citizens —young and old, black and white—have remained politically apathetic.

The purpose of this chapter is to provide some explanation of the basic forces involved in the political process. First, it examines the problems common to all governments—legitimation,

1. Harold D. Laswell, *Politics: Who Gets What, When, How?* (New York: McGraw-Hill Book Company, 1936).

authority, and influence, the underpinnings of political power. The chapter then looks at the democratic nation-state and considers the question of what makes democracy possible. It next examines power arrangements in the United States at the local and national levels, concluding with a discussion of some of the factors that create political and apolitical attitudes and behavior among a society's members.

THE FOUNDATIONS OF POLITICAL POWER

Max Weber called attention to the concept of power—the ability to make and implement decisions—as central to the political process. Weber defined power as "the probability that one actor within a social relationship will be in a position to carry out his own will despite resistance."[2] Thus conceived, power is a significant part of all social interaction. Individuals whose behavior, or expected behavior, is taken into account by others in a given situation have some degree of power, whether it be the power of parents over their children, professors over their students, or department heads over the people they supervise. The important measure of power is the ability to affect decision making. People have greater or lesser amounts of power, depending on the roles they play in the groups they belong to.

LEGITIMATION OF POWER

According to Weber, political power is first and foremost the kind of power exercised by the state, and it is distinguished by the state's authority to use force or violence, if necessary, as an instrument of policy. In fact, the state only remains a state, Weber maintained, "if and in so far as its administrative staff successfully upholds

a claim to the monopoly of the *legitimate* use of physical force in the enforcement of its order."[3] Weber did not mean that the power of the state is "legitimate" in some absolute sense, only that the state *claims* it is legitimate and is able to make good this claim in the eyes of its people. The perceived legitimacy of the government provides the "inner justification" for what the government does.

The Importance of Shared Norms and Values

The concept of legitimacy is very useful in analyzing political systems, for it links the visible machinery of government—administrative offices, law courts, police, and so forth—to the subjective values responsible for creating that machinery and for keeping it in existence. Ralph Linton has stated this relationship as follows:

The most successful states are those in which the attitudes of the individual toward the state most nearly approximate the attitudes of the uncivilized individual toward his tribe. If the members of a state have common interests and a common culture, with the unity of will which these give, almost any type of formal governmental organization will function efficiently. If the members lack this feeling of unity, no elaboration of formal governmental patterns or multiplication of laws will produce an efficient state or contented citizens. How such unity may be created and maintained in great populations and especially in fluid ones where the individual's close, personal contacts are reduced to a minimum is probably the most important problem which confronts us today.[4]

As Seymour Lipset has noted, any kind of political system can be considered legitimate if it is able "to engender and maintain the belief that existing political institutions are the most appropriate or proper ones for the society."[5] Indeed, this belief may be more important to the stability of the system than its success in performing the basic functions of government. A state may be *effective*, Lipset says, but still suffer a "crisis of legitimacy" if its values are rejected by significant segments of its population. Groups within a society

2. Max Weber, *The Theory of Social and Economic Organization* (New York: The Free Press, 1957), p. 152.
3. Ibid., p. 154
4. Ralph Linton, *The Study of Man* (New York: Appleton-Century-Crofts, Inc., 1936), p. 252.
5. Seymour M. Lipset, "Some Social Requisites of Democracy: Economic Development and Political Legitimacy," *American Political Science Review*, 53 (March 1959): 86–87.

will regard a political system as legitimate or illegitimate according to the way in which its values fit in with their primary values. Important segments of the German army, civil service, and aristocratic classes rejected the Weimar Republic not because it was ineffective, but because its symbolism and basic values negated their own. Legitimacy, in and of itself, may be associated with many forms of political organization, including oppressive ones. Feudal societies, before the advent of industrialism, undoubtedly enjoyed the basic loyalty of most of their members. Crises of legitimacy are primarily a recent historical phenomenon, following the rise of sharp cleavages among groups which have been able, because of mass communication resources, to organize around different values than those previously considered to be the only legitimate ones for the total society.[6]

Legitimacy rests, in the last analysis, on the support of the ruled. There is much debate, however, over how much popular support—or *consensus*—is necessary to keep a political system operating effectively and over how that support can be established and maintained, especially in a large, heterogeneous society. Legitimacy is not something that rulers can give themselves, however much they may try.

Legitimate Power Versus Coercive Power

When individuals, groups, or societies are forced to behave in ways contrary to what they believe right, they are said to be "coerced." In political sociology, the term *coercion* denotes a form of power based on the illegitimate use or threat of force. In other words, the coercive decision maker acts outside the norms established by or with the consent (whether tacit or explicit) of the members of the political community. Thus the Nixon administration, in using agencies of government such as the Justice Department and the Internal Revenue Service to discredit and harass its opponents, may be said to have exerted coercive power in those areas of its activities.

Coercive power should not be confused with the *legitimate* use of force by established governments, as in putting down civil disorders or in punishing criminal acts. Political power is considered coercive only when force is used *arbitrarily*, in a manner inconsistent with the

government's recognized rights and duties. Coercive power is never power by "right" or authority.

Revolution

Revolution, the forceful overthrow of an established government, often has elements of both legitimate and coercive power. During the last two hundred years revolutions have served both to maintain and to change the political and economic structures of nation-states. Some revolutionary governments are seen by the citizens as legitimate; others are considered coercive.

Few revolutions are spontaneous mass uprisings against unpopular regimes; more commonly, a revolution is planned and directed by a small group seeking political control. In many so-called palace revolutions this group may simply oust the head of government and principal assistants and take their places, without attempting to win over the people or to change societal institutions in any basic way. In such cases it is quite possible that the people would consider neither the old nor the new government legitimate. In the absence of popular support, revolutionary regimes of this sort must continue to rely on coercion.

By contrast, revolutions that propose new and different ideologies usually make every effort to win the support of the people and establish legitimacy for the new regime. This was the case during the American Revolution, when the leaders and supporters of colonial independence gained support for the ideology of economic and political freedom from British rule.

Many Marxist revolutions have enlisted public support and thus gained legitimacy. For example, Fidel Castro had gathered a broad base of support when, in 1958, he led a revolution against Fulgencio Batista in Cuba. The upper and middle classes supported Castro because he promised to restore free elections, a free press, and other democratic freedoms, while the lower classes supported his programs for economic and social reform. Castro's government gradually lost legitimacy in the eyes of

6. Ibid.

the middle and upper classes, many of whom fled to the United States, because he did not restore the democratic political processes. But he did institute the promised economic, educational, and health-care reforms, thereby retaining legitimacy in the eyes of the lower classes. In 1961, when Cuban refugees supported by the government of the United States launched an invasion of Cuba, they expected the Cuban people to rise up against Castro; the invasion failed at least in part because the Cuban people continued to support Castro's government.

Occasionally an ideologically based revolution takes place in a political atmosphere that is hostile to the new regime. This was the case in Chile in 1973 when Salvador Allende, who had been elected president in 1970, was deposed in a revolution led by the military. Allende's government was considered legitimate by most citizens, despite the fact that the socialist reforms he had instituted were not supported by the middle class. The military junta intervened in order to bring an end to the reforms; today it rules by coercion and is considered legitimate by only a minority.

TYPES OF AUTHORITY

In a now-classic formulation, Weber delineated three types of authority as bases for the legitimate exercise of power: traditional, charismatic, and legal-rational.[7] In all of them, authority is a group-centered phenomenon; individuals with authority are perceived by others as having the *right* to make and implement decisions. Except in the case of charismatic authority, the right to decide is vested in some organizational role, not in an individual as such. Authority is legitimate by definition; to speak of an organization as "losing authority" means that its legitimacy is being questioned.

Traditional Authority

The oldest known form of power is traditional authority, in which legitimation has been handed down from the past. There is a sacred quality to such authority; it is upheld by the belief that

7. Weber, *Theory of Social and Economic Organization*, pp. 329 ff.

Mao Tse-tung, the charismatic leader of the Chinese revolution, remains a hero to the people of China today. In the late 1960s, when Mao went swimming to disprove a rumor that his health was poor, swimming became the most popular pastime in China. This photograph, taken in 1967, shows some of the fifty thousand soldiers who swam the Yangtze in honor of Mao.

"It is being done this way because this is the way it has always been done." Such control is generally based on a set of unwritten rules or laws. The recruitment of persons or groups of persons to positions of traditional authority is not based so much on technical competence (the basic criterion under a system of legal-rational authority) as on family ties. Commands are legitimized partly by tradition and partly by the fact that the rulers enjoy unquestioning loyalty from their subjects.

What, then, are the limits of traditional authority? What is there to prevent all traditional leaders from acting arbitrarily and coercively? The answer is the tradition itself: because it is considered sacred, it acts as a curb on the leader's power. The challenge to those in authority is not to legislate new rules but to find *precedents* to justify any apparent novelty.

Examples of whole societies ruled entirely by traditional authority are now hard to find anywhere in the world, but the authority on which most so-called modern political systems operate includes a measure of the traditional. For example, the United States Constitution is in one sense a sacred document, accepted as the unquestioned foundation for the American political system. Debates on constitutional issues invariably involve conflicting interpretations of the Constitution; the document itself is rarely overtly attacked. An example of an authority system based almost wholly on tradition is provided by the Hopi Indians, whose family organization was examined in Chapter 15.

Charismatic Authority

The nature of charismatic authority and the important role it plays in social change have been discussed in Chapter 10 (page 283). The charismatic leader's claim to legitimacy lies primarily in his or her own inner perception of personal power. If the individual attracts followers, then the perception is verified. Another characteristic of charismatic authority is that it lacks stable social organization. It has no set of rules, traditional or rational, by which to guide conduct, and there are no tests for competency beyond the "gift of grace" itself. Most important, charismatic authority is *in conflict with routine.*

One of the great challenges to charismatic authority is the problem of developing a stable political system. Charismatic leaders are generally not concerned about routinization, but only if the movements they represent develop some kind of social organization can they persist over the long term. This means that, to survive, charismatic movements must ultimately evolve into either traditional or legal-rational systems of authority.

Legal-Rational Authority

The hallmark of legal-rational systems of authority is bureaucratic organization (pages 71–79). In government, as in business, this pattern of social organization places definite limits on the exercise of power by causing a specified amount of power to inhere in a social role or position rather than in an individual.

Since legal-rational authority must clearly limit and diffuse power, it has the effect of increasing individual freedom. But the creation of such a system of authority is not simple; and often the system will contain seeds of traditional or charismatic authority. For example, in many of the developing nations of the world, systems of legal-rational authority are superimposed on systems of traditional authority. In their study of business and politics in the Mexican border area, D'Antonio and Form found that one of the sources of continuing conflict in Mexico resulted from this mixture of systems.[8] Mexican businessmen who had become acquainted with business and government practices in the United States perceived the American pattern of legal-rational authority as a model to be followed. They believed that if clear-cut rules were set up, people could be counted on to follow them. But the attempt to establish a legal-rational system in Mexico was undercut by the long-standing institution known as the *mordida* ("bite" or "pay-off"). D'Antonio and Form found that not only did government leaders play favorites, but that key political appointments were often made to relatives and friends regardless of competency. The common reaction from the person on the street was "that's what I would do if I had a chance."

INFLUENCE

Influence is a distinct element in the power equation. Roughly defined, influence is the sum of all the resources an individual in a decision-making situation can bring to bear in order to ensure a particular outcome. It is more personal than authority, inhering in the individual more than in the office. Influence may be derived from a position of formal authority, but it may also be derived from wealth, knowledge, personal charm, persuasiveness, and many other sources.

The interplay of influence and authority is the very stuff of political decision making, especially under a democratic form of government. When power is diffused and lines of formal au-

8. W. V. D'Antonio and W. H. Form, *Influentials in Two Border Cities: A Study in Community Decision-Making* (South Bend, Ind.: University of Notre Dame Press, 1965), p. 12.

thority are unclear, a contest for control usually determines who makes the decisions. D'Antonio and Form have described the elements of conflict at the local level:

Conflict over who will control derives from many sources, only a few of which may be identified here. First, the authority of several interrelated positions, agencies or institutions is seldom so clearly defined as to eliminate a struggle over who has the right to decide. Second, and very important in a democracy, people in positions of authority have to justify themselves continually to those who may be affected by their decisions. Thus, the city council's right to levy taxes is restricted by its ability to convince the electorate or specific interest groups that the tax is needed and is reasonable. Failure to do so creates an issue—a question of who will control—for both the council and the people have some authority in this case. Third, the influence of persons or groups may operate either to activate authority or to impede its application. For example, respected citizens or groups may call on the city council to act in a given way. The council has to weigh the consequences of obeying or not obeying. Although such persons of influence do not have legitimate authority over the council, they may, in fact, constitute an informal government. Fourth, and this is the obverse of the third, there is a tendency for persons in authority to extend their control beyond its legitimate limits by acquiring the "influence of office."[9]

The interplay of authority and influence is important in other ways. When people lack legitimate access to positions of authority but use their resources to exert influence, the political system may be seriously undermined. This may be the case, for example, when a city's top police officials are in the pay of the underworld, or when the top officials of a state or nation have been "bought" by wealthy businessmen. In addition to these extremes are the numerous efforts of interested groups and individuals to help shape the decision-making process. Whether such efforts are perceived as legitimate or not is ultimately determined by the society's values.

9. Ibid.
10. For several related views on American political parties, see Ralph M. Goldman, *The Democratic Party in American Politics* (New York: Macmillan, Inc., 1966), p. 2; and Henry A. Turner, ed., *Politics in the United States* (New York: McGraw-Hill Book Company, 1955), esp. the articles by Warren Moscow, Sonya Forthal-Spiesman, and Robert L. Morlan.

Political Parties

Of all the nongovernmental organizations that wield political influence in American society, the Republican and Democratic parties come closest to having authority as well.[10] This is because they appear to have no serious rivals and because their leaders are regularly elected to key political offices.

During the heyday of political "bosses" and city "machines" (corresponding roughly to the period of heavy immigration and rapid urbanization between 1870 and 1925) the local party obtained influence by serving as a kind of informal welfare agency, giving service and jobs in exchange for votes. During the past thirty or forty years, however, the power of political machines—that is, party organizations that tightly control large blocs of votes—has progressively waned. With the conspicuous exception of Chicago, where in 1975 the Democratic machine elected Mayor Richard Daley for a sixth term, urban political machines have all but disappeared. Their loss of power has been the result of such changes as the establishment of the social security system and formal welfare agencies—which have rendered many of the services of the precinct worker unnecessary—and the introduction of civil-service bureaucracies, federal voting laws, and (not least important) electric voting machines. Changes in transportation and communication patterns have further disrupted the influence of the local party organization by reducing the significance of the precinct as a social unit.

At the national level, the major activity of both the Republican and Democratic parties has been nominating candidates for President and Vice-President and then trying to get them elected. All other activities are clearly subordinate. Potential presidential candidates spend time cultivating the state committees, since in some states these groups select the delegates to the national conventions. The entire procedure for nominating presidential candidates has come under severe criticism as both cumbersome and undemocratic, though no alternative has won widespread support.

Richard J. Daley heads one of the last big-city political machines in the United States. The Democratic party in the city of Chicago controls a large number of patronage jobs at the city and county levels. These jobs — as well as help in coping with governmental agencies — are available to citizens who are "loyal" to the party.

Interest Groups

A group that attempts to exert political influence without being either a major political party or a part of government is generally known as an *interest group*. Although interest groups are independent of government control, they must have access to sources of power if they are to be politically useful.

Not all interest groups can be active all the time: "All the conceivable adjustments between all citizens cannot be made simultaneously and openly through the processes of government. The political system would not stand the strain."[11] But a great many organizations actively exert pressure year in and year out through *lobbying,* which usually involves personal contact with legislators.

In 1973 more than $9 million was spent on lobbying activities in the United States (see Table 17.1). While the largest amount of money was spent by the business sector, almost all sectors of society did some lobbying. The twenty-five groups that spent the most money on lobbying in 1973 included labor, professional, farm, and civic action groups as well as business associations (see Table 17.2).

Most Americans are only vaguely aware of lobbyists and the groups they represent. Politicians, however, are very much aware of them. Polls may indicate that the majority of Americans want strict gun-control laws, but when proposals for such laws reach Congress, the people the legislators hear from are the members of the American Rifle Association, expressing strong opposition. Individual lobbyists may offer hospitality and entertainment or more tangible gifts. Organized groups may mean organized votes, for or against. And corporations may be even more persuasive: after the election of 1972, investigations uncovered a long list of illegal contributions to the presidential campaign from corporations and associations that could potentially have benefited from administration decisions.

Of course, not all lobbyists and interest groups work secretly and rely on political deals. Nor do they all represent special interests as such. For example, Common Cause is a citizens' action group with a membership of over 300,000. Its lobbying activities are aimed at making the government more responsive to the needs and interests of individual citizens and at reducing political corruption.[12] It has been active in promoting campaign finance reform, home rule for the District of Columbia, the Equal Rights Amendment, and consumer protection laws, among other legislation. In 1973 Common Cause spent more than $900,000 on lobbying activities making it the top spender that year (Table 17.2). (It should be noted that Common Cause "claims to report all spending on lobbying, including salaries, overhead, newsletter costs, printing,

11. David B. Truman, *The Governmental Process: Political Interests and Public Opinion* (New York: Alfred A. Knopf, Inc., 1959), p. 356.
12. See John W. Gardner, *In Common Cause* (New York: W. W. Norton & Company, Inc., 1972).

Table 17.1. LOBBY SPENDING, BREAKDOWN BY CATEGORY

Category	Amount reported
Business	$3,287,561.89
Professional	732,633.35
Labor	1,886,793.86
Agriculture	672,838.74
Military and Veteran	249,899.74
Miscellaneous	2,634,095.69
Total	**9,463,823.27**

SOURCE: *Congressional Quarterly*, July 27, 1974, p. 1953.

Table 17.2. THE TOP LOBBY SPENDERS

Organization	Amount reported
1. Common Cause	$934,835
2. International Union, United Automobile, Aerospace and Agricultural Implement Workers	460,992
3. American Postal Workers Union (AFL-CIO)	393,399
4. American Federation of Labor-Congress of Industrial Organizations (AFL-CIO)	240,800
5. American Trucking Associations Inc.	226,157
6. American Nurses Association, Inc.	218,354
7. United States Savings and Loan League	204,221
8. Gas Supply Committee	195,537
9. Disabled American Veterans	193,168
10. The Committee of Publicly Owned Companies	180,493
11. American Farm Bureau Federation	170,472
12. National Education Association	162,755
13. National Association of Letter Carriers	160,597
14. National Association of Home Builders of the United States	152,177
15. Recording Industry Association of America Inc.	141,111
16. National Council of Farmer Cooperatives	140,560
17. American Insurance Association	139,395
18. The Farmers' Educational and Co-operative Union of America	138,403
19. Committee of Copyright Owners	135,095
20. National Housing Conference Inc.	125,726
21. American Petroleum Institute	121,276
22. American Medical Association	114,859
23. Citizens for Control of Federal Spending	113,659
24. American Civil Liberties Union	102,595
25. National Association of Insurance Agents Inc.	87,422

SOURCE: *Congressional Quarterly*, July 27, 1974, p. 1948.

13. *The Congressional Quarterly*, July 27, 1974, p. 1953.
14. See Hans Kohn, *Nationalism: Its Meaning and History*, rev. ed. (Princeton, N.J.: D. Van Nostrand Co., Inc., Anvil Books, 1965).

mailing and telephoning."[13] Many lobbies take advantage of legal loopholes to avoid reporting the full extent of their spending.)

TOWARD A THEORY OF DEMOCRACY

Political institutions are common to all societies. But the form of the institution and its importance in the overall social structure differs among societies. For example, political affairs play a small role among Zuñi Indians and positions of leadership are not emphasized (see Chapter 4, page 105). But in most modern and developing societies, the political institution—in the form of the nation-state—is the most inclusive social institution and clearly affects the lives of all citizens. In this section we will examine the nature of the nation-state and the political and ideological structures that undergird Western-style democracy. We will focus mainly, but not exclusively, on democracy in the United States.

THE MODERN NATION-STATE

In ancient and medieval times people's loyalties were to the family, the clan or tribe, the local community, or sometimes to the city-state. People did not think in terms of loyalty to the nation because nations as we know them did not exist.

Beginning in the fifteenth century, a new form of political organization spread gradually throughout Europe. This was the nation, or *nation-state*. With its emergence, centralized authority replaced the fragmented power that had characterized medieval politics. Kings ruled the nation-states, and royal bureaucracies developed to replace the local bureaucracies of barons and dukes, provinces and shires, cities and towns. And loyalties, too, had to be shifted and refocused—from the local leader to the king, from the locality to the nation.[14] Usually, of course, loyalty to locality survived, but in time it came to augment love of nation and pride of nationality.

FASCISM AND COMMUNISM

FASCISM

Fascist governments focus on the maintenance of *order.* Capital, industry, and labor are all enlisted in the service of the state, though they may be directed, at least nominally, by their own representatives, working in cooperation with government officials. Fascist governments base their rule on the assumption that only through direct, total control of the citizenry can order be maintained. Thus the fascist state ordinarily makes use of a paramilitary police force, including secret police. It strictly controls the communication media and uses the educational system to indoctrinate its citizens. Property and the means of production may remain in private hands, but they are strictly controlled to serve the interests of the party or leader in control of the state.

Fascism is generally intensely nationalistic. Benito Mussolini, whose Fascist party came to power in Italy in the 1920s, promised to restore the country to the position of world leadership held by the Roman Empire. In Nazi Germany, Adolf Hitler appealed to the citizenry to suppress "inferior races" and conquer the world. With Germany's military successes, fascism spread through much of Europe; but with Germany's defeat, most fascist governments were overthrown. Fascism did survive, however, in Francisco Franco's Spain; and although the term *fascist* is no longer used as freely as it once was, right-wing totalitarian regimes, often headed by a military dictator or a military junta, are common today in Latin America, Africa, and the Middle East and continue to reappear in parts of Europe.

COMMUNISM

The term *communism* refers to a model of society developed in the nineteenth century by Karl Marx and Friedrich Engels and modified in the twentieth century by Lenin and others. According to the communist ideology, true freedom lies in freeing the workers from exploitation, in making work meaningful and the product of work accessible to all. The first stage in instituting a communist government, according to the ideology, is a "dictatorship of the proletariat" (perhaps "for the proletariat" is more accurate), which controls all institutional sectors in order to cleanse them of capitalism, false individualism, religious superstition, and other forms of exploitation. Once this is done, the dictatorship is expected to eventually wither away, presumably leaving the people free to work and to choose what they want to produce and how they will produce it. In its ideal form, communism implies that power will be totally democratized through collective decision making.

Democracy has a different meaning in countries controlled by the contemporary Communist party than it does in the West. To a member of the Communist party, democracy means the freedom to make decisions regarding jobs and the production process—that is, freedom to make decisions in the *economic* sphere. To a citizen of the West, on the other hand, democracy essentially means free elections and the freedom of dissent—that is, freedom to make decisions in the *political* sphere.

The individual political structures of the Communist bloc countries vary. In the Soviet Union, for instance, the goal of collective decision making is far from an accomplished fact (see page 214). In the People's Republic of China, on the other hand, there is evidence that people are encouraged to participate in the decision-making process regarding work and other activities within the communes.

During the last two centuries most of the nation-states structured as kingdoms have disappeared. In their place have arisen modern nation-states ruled by presidents, parliaments, or dictators. All are characterized by *nationalism,* the ethnocentric belief that one's nation is better than any other. Nationalism provides solidarity within nation-states, but it produces tension and conflict between them.

The modern nation-state is also characterized by its inclusiveness. As Greer and Orleans have described it:

The population of the earth today is entirely included, as citizens, fiefs, or captives of nation-states, and each state is inclusive of both persons and behaviors. One cannot act outside the boundaries of a state, and one's actions must conform to what is permitted by the state under pain of probable sanction. Even birth is a matter of state, an automatic membership. . . . The state has become the chief custodian of overall social order; it is monitor, comptroller, arbitrator.[15]

The nature of this inclusiveness is related to the political and ideological structures of the society. A state can have single-person or single-party rule, or it can have many political parties that vie for power. The government can be controlled by the military or by civilians. The constitution—if there is one—can guarantee political freedom or restrict it in favor of government control. And the political ideology of the state can favor protecting the rights of the individual or restricting them for the "common good."

In the so-called totalitarian states, be they Communist or fascist (see type box, page 506), political control may be close to absolute, while in the western democracies there is greater individual political freedom. Totalitarian states are ruled by a single person or party that cannot be removed without resorting to force; this person or party has the power to control all other institutional sectors—the economy, education, religion, and so on. But probably only fascist governments would consider themselves totalitarian. Most Communist leaders proclaim that their governments are true democracies—or are in the process of becoming true democracies—in that they protect the majority by restricting the rights of individuals. The western democracies, as we will see in the next section, concentrate on protecting the rights of the individual.

THE WESTERN DEMOCRATIC STATE

The key characteristic of the western democratic state is the legitimate existence of effective opposition to those in power. Competing political parties offer the citizen a choice of representatives, who stand for a variety of policies, and the party that controls the government can be voted out of power. Moreover, the losers voluntarily turn over political power to the victors. There are rules limiting the power of those holding office, and everyone is expected to live by these rules.

In principle, democracy implies nothing about the nature of the economic, religious, and other institutional sectors of society. The economic system can be based on socialism, free-enterprise capitalism, or—as is most common—a combination of the two. There can be a universal church or a number of denominations and sects (see Chapter 16, pages 490–491), and individuals are free to belong to the "church of their choice." A single elite does not control all the institutional sectors; instead, various groups may have power in different sectors at different times.

Essential to a democracy are freedom of speech and of the press and two or more political parties that compete in open elections. Unlike the totalitarian form of government, where the party *is* the state, in a democracy the state itself is distinct from whatever political party happens to be in power. The governmental structures of democracies vary: many European countries have parliamentary systems in which the head of the party that controls the legislature becomes the head of the government; in the United States, on the other hand, the President is elected independently of the legislature, and the legislature is not always controlled by the President's party. Some democracies have a great many political parties, each representing a different interest or shade of opinion; others, like

15. Scott Greer and Peter Orleans, "Political Sociology," in *Handbook of Modern Sociology,* ed. Robert E. L. Faris (Chicago: Rand McNally & Co., 1964), pp. 809–810.

Political traditions favoring the democratic process—open, honest elections, freedom of speech, "orderly" dissent—are necessary for the development and maintenance of a democracy.

the United States, Canada, and Great Britain, have a small number of parties, each representing numerous interests and ideologies.

What Makes Democracy Possible?

Having defined *western democracy*, we may ask what conditions are necessary to develop and maintain a democracy. Among the factors that have been found important are a class structure dominated by the middle class, a relatively high level of economic development, political traditions favoring the "democratic way," and the existence of voluntary associations that are independent of the state. All these factors make it possible for citizens to engage in dissent.

Class Structure Aristotle argued in the fourth century B.C. that democracy is not possible when there are great disparities in wealth.[16] On the other hand, he said, when the majority of the people are in the middle class, and neither the rich above nor the poor below are too far removed from them, the broad value consensus necessary to democracy can develop, permitting orderly dissent and conflict in the body politic. Aristotle's reasoning seems to be that a democratic consensus can be achieved only when people are free from hunger and ignorance. Only then will they be free from exploitation so that they can develop the internal restraints that make possible democracy's unique balance between consensus and conflict.

16. Aristotle, *Politics*, Book IV, Chapter 11; see also R. Bendix and S. M. Lipset, eds., *Class, Status and Power: A Reader in Social Stratification* (New York: The Free Press, 1961), pp. 17–18.

A study by Lipset set out to determine exactly what social and economic conditions were associated with stable democratic government.[17] Lipset classified forty-eight countries as stable and unstable democracies and dictatorships and then compared groups of these countries with respect to wealth, industrialization, educational level, and urbanization. He concluded that all these factors could be regarded as aspects of the same thing—namely, economic development. The higher the level of economic development, the more likely that there would be both democracy and political stability. There were very few exceptions to this pattern, and they could be explained in terms that confirmed the author's general thesis.

Political Traditions Modern researchers are quick to point out that general economic betterment does not necessarily build democracy. There is no easy way to transform a traditional society into a western democracy. For instance, it is obvious that democracy cannot develop unless people have experience in democratic processes. But freedom of speech and open, honest elections among competing parties, which Americans take to be major signs of a democratic society, may not be possible or seem important in a developing nation. Indeed, there is little in the socialization process of most underdeveloped countries to prepare their citizens to be voters. Such societies are usually composed of various traditional socioeconomic groupings— tribes, estates, or autonomous villages—with few or no ties to the central government. The autonomy of a traditional village or landed estate does not constitute some form of local democracy but a type of monolithic or oligarchic rule. It is one of the paradoxes of political organization that totally autonomous communities tend to be *less* competitive and *more* monolithic and to provide *less* individual freedom for

their members than do communities that are more dependent on a central government.

Among the traditions that characterize western democracies are freedom of speech and the press, the right to own property, and the right to due process of law. Also important is a shared political culture. In the United States, for example, we recognize many of the same national heroes. Although some segments of the population have cultural heroes that the rest of the country would not recognize as such, admiration for, say, George Washington, Thomas Jefferson, and Abraham Lincoln is nearly universal. In Mexico, on the other hand, the political left has an entirely different pantheon of cultural heroes than the political right. A broadly based democratic consensus has only recently begun to emerge in Mexico.

Democratic tradition also stresses the idea that people have the right to develop their own beliefs and opinions, even if they conflict with those of the majority. While the will of the majority is supposed to prevail in all matters affecting society as a whole, the minority is free to try to influence the majority. And in matters not considered central to societal well-being, people are relatively free to do as they please.

Voluntary Associations Voluntary associations (page 78) appear to serve several important functions in a democratic society:

1. They may be a source of new opinions independent of the state.
2. They may be a means for communicating new ideas to a portion of the citizenry.
3. They may help train people in the skills of politics.
4. They may stimulate their members to take a more active interest in politics.
5. They may serve as bases of opposition to the central authority.[18]

Political parties are one type of voluntary association important to a western democracy. The party has become the instrument by which governmental power is fought for and exercised,

17. Lipset, "Some Social Requisites of Democracy," pp. 86–87.
18. Seymour M. Lipset, Martin Trow, and James S. Coleman, *Union Democracy* (New York: Anchor Books, 1962), pp. 1–17; and Arnold M. Rose, *Theory and Method in the Social Sciences* (Minneapolis: University of Minnesota Press, 1954), pp. 50–72. Rose presents an updated discussion of his ideas in *The Power Structure* (New York: Oxford University Press, 1967), pp. 213–252.

both at the local and national levels. It is generally assumed that, in the United States at least, democratic processes are preserved, individual freedom protected, and power diffused because of the existence of opposing parties.

In the United States, voluntary associations have acted as lobbyists for a variety of causes (see page 504). Sometimes voluntary associations act politically to resolve community issues, as in raising money to build hospitals or day-care centers. Often a voluntary association will apply for and receive government funds to help them achieve a goal, such as the development of a regional health-care system.

Dissent in a Democracy

In the western democracies opposition, and thus political conflict, is considered legitimate. In fact, this may be the feature that most clearly distinguishes democracy from any other type of political system. In the United States the right to dissent is guaranteed by the Constitution and safeguarded by the courts. It is regarded as fundamental in protecting not only the individual citizen but also the political system itself.

Virtually every adult citizen today has the right to vote and has a choice of candidates and parties among which to choose (though, as critics point out, the range of choice may be limited ideologically). Votes are cast in secret, and precautions are taken to assure that they are counted correctly. It is expected that the winner will be allowed to take office without having to use violence. Losers give up office knowing that they can return to power if they win next time. Thus conflict is built into the system, but it is ordered by law and also by a widely accepted system of values.

Conflict can remain orderly only insofar as the contenders in any situation believe that they can achieve their goals by following what D. B. Truman has called "the rules of the game."[19] If out-groups perceive their goals to be permanently blocked, they may begin to question the rules and, in some circumstances, to challenge them by going outside the law. Similarly, if those in power perceive opposing factions as threatening their ability to govern, they may sidestep the rules in an effort to quash or at least limit dissent.

The recent history of the United States provides many examples of the disregard of the rules on the part of out-groups and on the part of those in power. For example, when Daniel Ellsberg made public classified government documents regarding the Vietnamese conflict in 1971, he broke the law because he saw no other way to get the facts to the American people and to end the war. The Nixon administration perceived this action as threatening the power and security of the government and ordered a break-in of Ellsberg's psychiatrist's office in order to find information to discredit Ellsberg. Illegal wiretaps were ordered so that similar "national security leaks" could be prevented in the future. One of President Nixon's aides offered the judge who was trying the Ellsberg case the directorship of the FBI. When information about the illegal government actions became public, the judge dismissed the charges against Ellsberg, thus reaffirming the validity of the "rules of the game."

The Ellsberg case was one of many violations of the law that eventually resulted in the resignation of President Nixon. In a democracy, as "Watergate" made clear, not even the President can step outside the law to limit dissent.

THE STRUCTURE OF POWER IN THE UNITED STATES

To what extent are the principles of democracy operative at the local and national levels in the United States? The power-structure studies that have been carried out over the years have examined and tested democratic theory in order to determine the extent to which local and national power structures are monolithic and elitist or democratic and pluralist. As we shall see, these studies have revealed both patterns as well as points in between.

19. Truman, *The Governmental Process*, pp. 393, 513, and elsewhere.

Decision making on the community level is not entirely the prerogative of a single group, and it is possible for citizens to influence local government. The neighborhood organization shown here successfully resisted a county plan to widen a road and build a bigger bridge. A member of the organization feels: "Community action works if you hire a lawyer."

COMMUNITY POWER STRUCTURES

Most of the research on power structures in the United States has focused on the interplay of authority and influence at the local level.[20] More than 150 cities and towns have been studied in order to provide empirical answers to the question: Who governs, how, and with what consequences?[21] There has been an attempt to find regularized patterns within the community whereby decisions are made and implemented through the exercise of authority, influence, and possibly coercion. These studies have been concerned not only with political parties and governmental bodies but also with *all* groups whose activities affect the community and therefore represent participation in its power structure.

20. For some interesting studies of power structures in other countries see John Porter, *The Vertical Mosaic: An Analysis of Social Class and Power in Canada* (Toronto: University of Toronto Press, 1965); and Delbert C. Miller, *International Community Power Structures* (Bloomington, Ind.: Indiana University Press, 1970).

21. Two recent summaries of findings are Claire Gilbert, "Some Trends in Community Politics," *South-Western Social Science Quarterly*, 48, No. 3 (December 1967): 373–382; and John Walton, "The Vertical Axis of Community Organization and the Structure of Power," in the same edition of the same journal, pp. 353–368. The following discussion draws heavily on these findings and on D'Antonio and Form, *Influentials in Two Border Cities*.

Community power structures have typically been thought of as comprising leaders of business, elected and appointed government officials, professionals (especially lawyers), and possibly the leaders of labor unions, ethnic groups, and political parties. Voluntary associations play a role, as does the electorate. Researchers have studied the extent to which the community power structure reflects the roles community leaders play in their governmental and nongovernmental positions as well as the personal influence that may derive from these roles.

We will first review the politics of local government as they relate to studies of power structures, then we will summarize the findings regarding the relative influence of business on community power structures. Finally, we will examine the implications of the decentralization of community power.

Local Government

There are two major types of municipal government in the United States—the mayor-council system and the council-manager system. In the mayor-council system there are regular political contests for council seats and for key administrative jobs. Mayor-council governments may have either a strong mayor and a weak council (as in some of the largest cities) or a strong council and a mayor who is essentially a ceremonial figure (a more common pattern today, especially in medium-sized and small cities). Under the council-manager system, voters choose a small city council to establish policy, usually in a nonpartisan election, and the council members hire a professional administrator — the city manager — who is responsible to them.

More and more communities are using the council-manager system in an attempt to eliminate party politics from municipal government. They believe that party contests engender conflict and therefore make it difficult to cope with important issues on a reasonable basis. The council-manager system is set up on the model of business efficiency and is designed to eliminate both conflict and political corruption. It is predicated on the belief that, after reasonable discussion, citizens can resolve all issues on the basis of merit. The task of implementing their decisions is left to technical experts — the city manager and staff — who, in principle at least, are not subject to pressures from vested interests.

If minimizing conflict within the community is a prime goal, then council-manager systems of government must clearly be judged more effective than those in which there are regular two-party contests for all positions of power. In one comparative study of sixty-eight cities, for example, Gilbert found that 71 percent of the council-manager governments had low conflict levels, whereas the same proportion of the more political governments had medium-to-high conflict levels.[22] But the question must be raised as to whether conflict is necessarily dysfunctional — and, if so, from whose viewpoint. Is a reduction of conflict consistent with the democratic ideal of the right of dissent?

The available evidence suggests that communities with a high proportion of middle-class business and professional people are the ones most likely to opt for municipal government of the council-manager type. In other words, the people who deplore political conflict as disruptive — "Are we going to have our city run in an efficient manner or settle for politics as usual?" — are likely to be those who already enjoy a comfortable income, relatively high status, and adequate representation in the community power structure. Local governments that have been taken "out of politics" are more likely than others to have business and professional leaders as opinion makers on almost all issues, business and professional leaders as elected community representatives, an increasingly heavy reliance on professional experts such as urban planners, and only minimal representation — either formal or informal — for the working class, minority groups, or the poor.[23] Thus the trend toward deemphasizing political conflict in municipal government would seem to have serious implications for the future of the democratic process at the community level.

The Question of Business Influence

Early studies of community power structures produced some evidence that people known as community leaders, whether inside or outside of political parties, were more likely to have come from the business sector of the community than from any other single sector. Perhaps more time and energy have been devoted to testing this hypothesis (business control of the community) than any other concerned with the study of community power.[24]

22. Gilbert, "Some Trends in Community Politics," pp. 377–378.

23. For instance, a research study in El Paso, Texas, revealed that one consequence of a low conflict level in politics was to drastically restrict the participation of Mexican Americans, the working class, and the poor in local political and governmental activity. El Paso had a weak mayor-council type of government but a competitive one-party primary. Conflict has been minimized because labor unions were weak or nonexistent and, until recently, the Mexican Americans were not organized. See D'Antonio and Form, *Influentials in Two Border Cities.*

24. For example, see Delbert C. Miller, "Industry and Community Power Structure: A Comparative Study of an American and English City," *American Sociological Review,* 23 (February 1958): 9–15; Floyd Hunter, *Community Power Structure* (Chapel Hill, N.C.: University of North Carolina Press, 1953); W. V. D'Antonio and H. J. Ehrlich, eds., *Power and Democracy in America* (South Bend, Ind.: University of Notre Dame Press, 1961); and Terry N. Clark, *Community Power and Policy Outputs* (Beverly Hills, Calif.: Sage Publications, Inc., 1973).

The proposition of predominant business influence has two aspects: first, the assertion that business is the sector of the community that produces most of the decision makers; second, the assertion that the business leaders do in fact act as an oligarchy, a small cohesive group that generally manages to control things. There is considerable evidence to support the first assertion, but its significance remains subject to debate. For example, one simple reason why community leaders are likely to come from the business sector may be that political opportunities at the local level rarely are financially attractive. Local governments are often structured so as to encourage volunteer or part-time effort, and only those who are well-off can afford to handle these jobs. Also, the skills and knowledge of business executives and lawyers are more applicable to local governmental activity than is the skill and knowledge of, say, teachers and doctors. The second assertion, that business leaders form a cohesive, controlling elite, has been challenged by the evidence that they often appear in opposing factions and that, even when they present a united front, they do not always gain their objectives.

The controversy over the question of the extent of business influence in community decision making has stemmed in part from different methodological approaches to the problem of community power. (See Tools of Sociology, pages 514–515.) Some sociologists have analyzed community power in terms of formal *positions* of authority; others have tried to determine which individuals in a community have the greatest *reputation* for power. Still another approach has been to identify the kinds of *issues* that come before a community and to analyze how they are resolved. Common issues of community-wide concern include attracting new sources of jobs, building new hospitals and schools, urban renewal, local elections, and public welfare programs. The numerous studies that have been done on these issues reveal a

number of things: (1) issues are less and less often the concern of only one institutional sector; (2) only a small number of persons are involved in resolving issues; (3) there is some overlap of personnel from issue to issue, but it is not great; (4) the business, political, and legal sectors of the community are the most involved; (5) specialists, technical experts, and other persons not reputed to be influential can and do initiate and help resolve important issues; (6) the working class (through ethnic clubs, labor unions, and political parties) does exert some influence on certain decisions; (7) there is no preordained pattern determining that issues will be settled within either the public or the private domain.

Not surprisingly, different approaches to the study of community power produce different data and lead to contrasting hypotheses and theories. In recent years, many researchers have attempted to combine the positional, reputational, and issues approaches in order to overcome this problem. The most important finding that can be generalized from all studies to date is that no single pyramid of power has been uncovered consistently in American communities. There is increasing evidence of patterns of power wherein fluid coalitions develop over specific issues and leadership is drawn from a moderately large pool of active citizens. At the same time, the decision-making game is clearly not open to everyone on an equal basis.

The Decentralization of Community Power

Urbanization has meant increased contact between diverse peoples, lessened independence for each community, and a broadened range of extracommunity and nonpolitical involvements. With respect to community power structures, one important consequence of these changes seems to be that power at the community level has, in general, become less centralized.[25] The growing number and complexity of issues to be resolved at the community level have rendered simple power arrangements obsolete. In short, neither control by a political boss nor control by a small, cohesive group of community leaders seems to be consistent with the complexity of contemporary urban life.

25. The best documentation in support of this hypothesis can be found in Robert A. Dahl, *Who Governs: Democracy and Power in an American City* (New Haven, Conn.: Yale University Press, 1961).

TOOLS OF SOCIOLOGY
MEASURING COMMUNITY POWER: POSITIONS AND REPUTATIONS

Social scientists have used three distinct approaches in studying community power structures: the identification of those in positions of authority; the identification of those having a reputation for being influential in the community; and the analysis of how decisions are actually made on important community issues. As might be expected, the *positional, reputational,* and *issues* approaches yield different kinds of data and have been partly responsible for conflicting hypotheses and theories about the structure of community power.

The simplest and probably the most objective approach to the study of community power is the positional approach. Here, community decision makers are defined as those persons who occupy the formal positions of authority in the community's institutionalized political, economic, and civic structures. Because they have authority, they are assumed also to have power. This approach makes no provision for the fact that persons not in formal positions of authority may exert influence or coercion on those who are, and thus be the effective decision makers. Furthermore, even if a more perfect correlation existed between authority and control, identifying the persons in the top positions of authority would be only a first step in analyzing community power.

A more sophisticated approach, though a highly controversial one, is the reputational approach first developed by Floyd Hunter in the early 1950s. Here the investigator seeks out some fifteen to twenty-five persons who are presumed to be closely familiar with various aspects of community life. These persons, called "knowledgeables," usually occupy minor positions of authority in the major institutional sectors. They are interviewed about major local issues and problems and about the persons in the community whom they consider to be most influential. The investigator may ask them to compare influential persons within and between institutional sectors or simply to list an overall category of influential persons. Another question often asked in some form is: If you had to select a committee whose objective would be to get community approval on some issue, e.g., a school bond issue, who would you select for that committee in order to ensure its success, regardless of whether you know them personally? The hypothesis is that the names listed for this committee and those selected as generally influential will be highly correlated.

After interviewing the "knowledgeables," the researcher generally proceeds to the reputed "influentials" themselves, asking them similar questions. The influentials may also be asked to rank the persons selected by the knowledgeables. On the basis of the answers given by both knowledgeables and influentials, the researcher attempts to construct a picture of the power structure.

Critics of the reputational approach point out that the reputation for power is not a *demonstration* of power; at most, it represents power *potential.* Although this assertion is true, it is equally true that there has to be some reason why certain people are considered influential, and that generally the reason is their perceived ability to influence decision making. Either they have done so in the past, are doing so at the present time, or are believed to be able to do so whenever they choose.

Another criticism leveled at the reputational approach is that the information gathered from informants is ambiguous because the investigator cannot always be sure that they are thinking in terms of recent or important issues. However, defenders of the approach insist that they can determine the scope of power that a reputed influential actually has through the use of probing questions.

Contemporary researchers using the reputational approach have modified Hunter's original techniques and have become increasingly careful in interpreting the data they obtain. But while recognizing the limitations of the approach, they insist on its continuing usefulness. It is important to know how community leaders *perceive* the power structure, they argue, because people *act* according to their perceptions of reality. Furthermore, the approach has yielded data showing that community power structures are more complex than analyses of formal authority would suggest.

For a detailed critique of the various research approaches to the study of community power, see Arnold M. Rose, *The Power Structure* (New York: Oxford University Press, 1967), pp. 255–280. For an elaboration of the reputational approach, see Floyd Hunter, *Community Power Structure* (Chapel Hill, N.C.: University of North Carolina Press, 1953).

TOOLS OF SOCIOLOGY
MEASURING COMMUNITY POWER: ISSUES

The *positional* approach implies that the power structure of a community is fully reflected in its formal systems of authority. It makes no provision for the fact that a person who has a position of high authority does not always enjoy a like degree of power, nor does it provide a means for measuring the influence of persons who lack formal authority but act as powers behind the throne. Used alone, this approach leads to the depiction of community power structures arranged in terms of simple hierarchies. The *reputational* approach, on the other hand, has been criticized for assuming that a reputation for influence necessarily implies some degree of actual power. For these and other reasons, the positional and reputational approaches have increasingly been combined with the *issues* approach.

The issues (or decision-making) approach, first systematically developed by Robert Dahl and his associates, assumes that power inheres in those persons who successfully carry through— or successfully block—action on community issues. The key in determining the power structure is a detailed analysis of actual issues and the way they are resolved. Dahl used the following operations to judge the relative influence of the actors:

1. Restrict attention to "comparable" respondents who participate in a "single" scope.

2. Examine decisions where the number of direct participants is more or less the same during the period under investigation.

3. Assume that the following collective actions are responses of roughly the same strength or extent: (a) when a proposal initiated by one or more of the participants is adopted despite the opposition of other participants; (b) when a proposal initiated by one or more of the participants is rejected; (c) when a proposal initiated by one or more of the participants is adopted without opposition.

4. Determine the number of successful initiations or vetoes by each participant and the number of failures.

5. Consider participants as more influential than others if the relative frequency of their successes is higher, or if the ratio of their successes to their total attempts is higher.

In his study of the power structure in New Haven, Connecticut, Dahl chose three issue areas that cut across a wide variety of interests and participants: community redevelopment, public education, and nominations in the two major parties. In the area of redevelopment, eight major decisions were carefully examined for the period between 1950 and 1959. In the same time period there were also eight major decisions involving public education. In the political area, the period used for study was 1941 through 1957, when there were nine elections and eighteen important nominations by the two major parties.

The results of Dahl's New Haven study and of other studies using the same basic approach suggest that in most American communities there is little overlap among leaders or influentials from issue to issue. Some sociologists have argued that this demonstrates the pluralism of community power structures; others have argued that it may be an artifact of the number and/or the nature of the issues chosen for study. Critics of the issues approach note that it fails to take account of those participants who lose out in issue contests, and also of important issues that may be settled behind the scenes. Another criticism is that the issues chosen for analysis have usually been political in nature. However, this does not reflect any inherent weakness of the method itself: issues-analysis can be applied effectively to issues that fall outside the political sphere (e.g., establishment of a charity fund or of a private hospital) no less than to those within it. The reputational approach, when used in conjunction with the issues approach, provides one means for identifying key issues of general community concern.

In recent years, studies of community power in the United States have tended to use a combination of the positional, reputational, and issues approaches. Overall, their findings have confirmed some degree of pluralism; a strong middle-class background for the overwhelming majority of influentials; and rather loose coalitions of influentials in the economic, political, and legal spheres of community life.

For Dahl's description of the issues approach as applied to his New Haven study, see Robert A. Dahl, *Who Governs: Democracy and Power in an American City* (New Haven, Conn.: Yale University Press, 1961), esp. pp. 332–333. For a debate on the utility of the various approaches, see W. V. D'Antonio and H. J. Ehrlich, eds., *Power and Democracy in America* (South Bend, Ind.: University of Notre Dame Press, 1961).

Walton points to three trends that have contributed to the decentralization of community power.[26] (1) There is a continual movement toward absentee-owned industry. More and more corporations that originally were locally owned are becoming parts of national and international organizations. Nationally owned industries can threaten to pull out of a community if their wishes are not granted; and their executives may have few ties to the community. (2) There is a tendency on the part of local governments to become more and more involved with the state and federal governments. A community may bring in urban planners and other technical experts who may have stronger ties to the state capitol or to Washington than to the community government. (3) There is a tendency for other groups within the community to have outside ties. For example, local professional and voluntary associations typically are affiliates of national associations, which have national goals. Also, the organized life of the city is closely intertwined with that of its suburbs through regional hospital and health-care planning units, metropolitan councils of government, councils on mass transit, and the like. All these patterns of influence are part of the growth process of the modern metropolis, and all of them point to the decentralization of community power. Whether they also mean an increase in competitive politics and orderly conflict or broader participation by the middle and working classes remains to be seen.

NATIONAL POWER STRUCTURES

The structure of the federal government in the United States as set forth in the Constitution is based on the separation of powers, a principle derived mainly from the writings of the eighteenth-century French historian and jurist, Montesquieu. Briefly, his idea was that kings and emperors were able to rule tyrannically because they exercised many different *kinds* of power. At the very least, Montesquieu argued, the same person should not be allowed to make the laws, carry them out, and judge people accused of breaking them.[27] The first, second, and third articles of the Constitution deal respectively with legislative, executive, and judicial powers and assign these powers to Congress, the president, and the Supreme Court.

In practice, the literal separation of powers has been impossible to sustain. Through its ever increasing size and the vast resources at its command, the executive branch has become by far the most powerful branch of government. At the same time, the giant bureaucracies, civil and military, that have been created as administrative agencies within the executive branch have become policy-making bodies in their own right. Similarly, the judicial branch, as represented by the Supreme Court, has been accused of usurping the authority of both the executive and the legislative branches.[28]

The Power of the Presidency

Since the 1930s the president of the United States has dominated the federal government. The ever expanding executive branch of government now comprises giant military and civil bureaucracies that deal with all major aspects of social life—from war and espionage to agriculture and health.

But if it is true to say that the president dominates the government, it is nevertheless false to say that he controls it. No Congress has wholly followed the lead of the president, and no president has yet been able to rule the courts. Even the agencies that comprise the executive branch of government, of which the president is head, sometimes carry out policy differently than the president would like. In *Presidential Power*, Richard Neustadt suggests one reason for this:

Like our governmental structure as a whole, the executive establishment consists of separated institutions sharing powers. The President heads one of these; Cabinet officers, agency administrators, and military commanders head others. Below the departmental

26. Walton, "Vertical Axis of Community Organization," p. 354.
27. Montesquieu, *The Spirit of Laws* (first published 1748), Book II, Chapter 6.
28. One of the best studies of the Supreme Court is still C. Herman Pritchett, *The Roosevelt Court: A Study in Judicial Politics and Values, 1937–1947* (New York: Quadrangle Books, Inc., 1969). See also Glendon Schubert, *Judicial Policy Making,* rev. ed. (Glenview, Ill.: Scott, Foresman and Company, 1974).

level, virtually independent bureau chiefs head many more. Under mid-century conditions, Federal operations spill across dividing lines on organizational charts; almost every policy entangles many agencies; almost every program calls for interagency collaboration. Everything somehow involves the President. But operating agencies owe their existence least of all to one another—and only in some part to him. Each has a separate statutory base; each has its statutes to administer; each deals with a different set of subcommittees at the Capitol. Each has its own peculiar set of clients, friends, and enemies outside the formal government. Each has a different set of specialized careerists inside its own bailiwick. Our Constitution gives the President the "take-care" clause and the appointive power. Our statutes give him central budgeting and a degree of personnel control. All agency administrators are responsible to Congress, to their clients, to their staffs, and to themselves. In short, they have five masters.[29]

But if presidential power remains limited in some respects, it has greatly increased in others. For example, the Constitution reserves the right to declare war to Congress, but recent presidents have overcome this limitation by fighting undeclared wars, as in Korea and Southeast Asia. The Senate must approve treaties, but the president can substitute executive agreements, which require no Senate approval. Similarly, presidents may bypass government departments in order to keep control in their own hands. For example, President Nixon bypassed the State Department by making Henry Kissinger his personal diplomatic envoy, a position Kissinger held until he became secretary of state in 1973.

The main argument in favor of a president's acting with such independence is that the times no longer allow the luxury of waiting for Congress to act or of coaxing the bureaucracy into line—that the national welfare demands speed and decisiveness. In some cases involving foreign policy, this argument may carry consider-

able weight; but insistence on the superiority of presidential judgment has not always been convincing even in the area of international affairs. The expensive and divisive undeclared war in Southeast Asia led to much debate on the powers of the presidency, as did the Watergate affair, and the principle of maintaining checks and balances in a democratic society has gained renewed support in the 1970s.[30]

The Power of the Federal Bureaucracy

When George Washington was president, the federal civil bureaucracy employed fewer than a hundred people; today it employs nearly three million (see Table 17.3), over a tenth of whom work in the Washington, D.C., area.[31] The majority work within the executive branch of government. There are now eleven departments under the direct control of the president and about fifty independent agencies that are associated in some way with the executive branch.

The federal bureaucracy is a loose federation of organizations ranging in size from the forty-seven-member Council of Economic Advisers to the Department of Defense, which employs more than a million people. Each agency has its own goals, norms, ranking systems, and budget, and each is linked to the executive branch in its own way. Agencies are also linked to various interest groups—labor unions, industries, and so on—in ways that produce an important interplay of influence and authority. For example, some of the people who work for federal agencies previously worked for the industry they are supposed to be regulating. Civil bureaucrats are not directly accountable to the public; the heads of agencies are generally appointed by the president, and the lower-level bureaucrats are hired through the civil service system. Agency workers are supposed to be directed by congressional legislation, but in fact they have acquired significant power in their own right. As Merton puts it, "the governmental personnel are held to be 'servants of the people' but in fact they are often superordinate."[32]

Monsen and Cannon have described the sources of bureaucratic power and its outcome:

29. Richard E. Neustadt, *Presidential Power: The Politics of Leadership* (New York: John Wiley & Sons, Inc., 1960), p. 39.

30. Arthur M. Schlesinger, Jr., *The Imperial Presidency* (Boston: Houghton Mifflin Co., 1973).

31. Ralph M. Goldman, *Behavioral Perspectives on American Politics* (Homewood, Ill.: Dorsey Press, 1973), pp. 11–14.

32. Robert K. Merton, *Social Theory and Social Structure,* rev. ed. (New York: The Free Press, 1957), p. 203.

The power of the civil bureaucracy . . . stems from several sources. First, its members are frequently the initiators of new public policy and are generally able to "shape" legislative programs by making suggestions to the administration concerning the type and details of legislation that should be proposed. As well, they testify and give advice to Congress. For instance where other pressure groups are not resourceful, the civil bureaucracy has almost a monopoly on information in its sphere of interest. By releasing or withholding data, it can have considerable influence. Thus, the civil bureaucracy has definite power and effect upon the type of legislation that is actually proposed. Once

a law is passed, it is the bureaucracy that has to make interpretations of it, to write the rules which make specific the general provisions of the law and its usage. Congress usually only outlines laws in a somewhat general form; consequently from there on, the interpretation is done by the bureaucracy. This of course amounts, in fact, to the legislating of the specific points of the law by the bureaucracy.[33]

33. R. Joseph Monsen, Jr., and Mark W. Cannon, *The Makers of Public Policy* (New York: McGraw-Hill Book Company, 1965), p. 256.

Table 17.3. PAID CIVILIAN EMPLOYMENT IN THE FEDERAL GOVERNMENT, BY AGENCY

Agency	1960	1974	Agency	1960	1974
All agencies	**2,398,704**	**2,835,348**	Equal Employment Opportunity		
Legislative branch	22,886	34,696	Commission		1,968
Judicial branch	4,992	9,300	Export-Import Bank, U.S.	237	401
Executive branch	2,370,826	2,791,352	Farm Credit Administration	245	209
			Federal Aviation Administration*	38,132	
Executive Office of the President			Federal Communications		
White House Office	446	527	Commission	1,403	1,869
Office of Management and Budget	434	642	Federal Deposit Insurance Corp.	1,249	2,642
Council of Economic Advisers	32	47	Federal Home Loan Bank Board	1,000	1,313
Executive Mansion and Grounds	70	71	Federal Maritime Commission		294
National Security Council	65	79	Federal Mediation and Conciliation		
Office of Economic Opportunity		1,143	Service	347	441
Office of Emergency Preparedness	1,833		Federal Power Commission	859	1,255
All other	39	2,121	Federal Trade Commission	782	1,648
Executive departments			General Services Administration	28,211	38,557
Agriculture	98,694	103,621	Information Agency	10,915	8,948
Commerce	49,300	35,359	Interstate Commerce Commission	2,381	1,931
Defense	1,047,120	1,042,090	Nat'l. Aero. and Space Admin.	10,232	26,523
Health, Education, and Welfare	61,641	139,024	Nat'l. Capital Housing Authority	331	
Housing and Urban Development	11,105	16,769	Nat'l. Credit Union Admin.		523
Interior	56,111	69,424	National Foundation on the Arts		
Justice	30,942	49,285	and Humanities		535
Labor	7,096	13,572	National Labor Relations Board	1,750	2,433
State	37,983	33,296	National Mediation Board	129	104
Transportation		70,552	National Science Foundation	734	1,323
Treasury	76,179	126,260	Panama Canal Company	11,436	12,342
Independent agencies			Railroad Retirement Board	2,234	1,723
Action (Peace Corps)		2,050	Renegotiation Board	284	194
American Battle Monuments			St. Lawrence Seaway Development		
Commission	401	390	Corporation*	159	
Arms Control and Disarmament			Securities and Exchange Comm.	980	1,759
Agency		102	Selective Service System	6,230	3,570
Atomic Energy Commission	6,907	7,749	Small Business Administration	2,244	4,454
Board of Governors, Federal			Smithsonian Institution	1,555	3,192
Reserve System	598	1,283	Soldiers' and Airmen's Home	1,041	1,157
Canal Zone Government	2,625	3,539	Tariff Commission	271	335
Civil Aeronautics Board	755	692	Tax Court of the United States*	153	
Civil Service Commission	3,579	7,752	Tennessee Valley Authority	14,993	24,726
Commission on Civil Rights	82	251	U.S. Postal Service*	562,868	704,744
Environmental Protection Agency		10.302	Veterans Administration	172,338	200,303
			All other	1,038	1,884

*The Federal Aviation Administration and the St. Lawrence Seaway Development Corporation were transferred to the Department of Transportation in 1967. The Tax Court of the United States has been included in the Legislative Branch since 1970. The U.S. Postal Service was an executive department until 1971, when it became an independent agency. SOURCE: *Statistical Abstract of the United States, 1974*, pp. 236–237.

Some bureaucratic agencies have much more power than others. Among the most powerful are the Federal Bureau of Investigation (an agency of the Justice Department) and the Internal Revenue Service (an agency of the Treasury Department). The FBI is empowered to investigate American citizens suspected of illegal activities — its duties range from investigating kidnapings and murders to spying on citizens suspected of subversive activities. The duties of the Internal Revenue Service are well known, dealing as they do with the collection of taxes. Both agencies keep detailed records on citizens, and both were used by recent presidents to collect information about their political opponents. Critics have charged that these activities are detrimental to the right of dissent, and various proposals on how to regulate these agencies have been put forth.

The Power of the Military

The military has long been a major force in the political affairs of nation-states, and today many nations are ruled by military governments. In democracies, however, there is a clear-cut distinction between military and civilian roles, and the military is expected to remain outside of civilian affairs.[34] In addition, it is expected that the military will be under civilian control. It is evident that in the United States the military does not exert political power equal to that of elected officials. But it has been charged that the United States is coming under the power of a "military-industrial complex" composed of top military officers and defense-related industries.[35]

The charge of a military-industrial complex is given credibility by the amount of money and the human and material resources the military has been able to command.[36] Since 1960 the military has received anywhere from 26 to 41 percent of the total federal budget, with the larg-

In the United States the socialization of military personnel encourages them to stay out of civilian affairs, to accept civilian decision making, and to avoid exerting political power equal to that of elected government officials.

est proportion being appropriated during the war in Southeast Asia. The Department of Defense employs over a million people, almost 40 percent of those employed by the executive branch of government (see Table 17.3). Another two million serve in the various branches of the armed forces. The military holds land greater in size than Tennessee and has assets greater in value than the combined wealth of the hundred largest United States corporations. The economies of twenty-two states are heavily dependent on military spending. It has been estimated that

34. Morris Janowitz, *Political Conflict* (New York: Quadrangle Books, Inc., 1970), p. 119 ff.

35. Warning about the growing power of a "military-industrial complex" was first given by President Dwight D. Eisenhower. A similar thesis, that of the "power elite," will be discussed on page 521.

36. Monsen and Cannon, *Makers of Public Policy*, pp. 258–307; Seymour Melman, *Pentagon Capitalism: The Political Economy of War* (New York: McGraw-Hill Book Company, 1970); and Seymour Melman, "Pentagon Bourgeoisie," *Trans-action*, March/April 1971, pp. 4–12.

during the 1960s more than half the nation's research talent was working for the military and for defense-related industries.[37]

But despite the evidence that the military exerts considerable influence over civilian affairs, there is no indication that it has enormous power. As Lenski has pointed out, the military has never challenged civilian authority in the United States.[38] When conflict has arisen between a military leader and the government, as in the case of General MacArthur's disregard of President Truman's orders during the Korean War, civilian decisions have won out over military decisions. The military wanted to press for victory in Vietnam, but civilian authority withdrew U.S. forces before either side won. There is little evidence that the United States needs to fear that the military will resort to force in order to increase their power, for the socialization of military personnel encourages them to support the norms, goals, and values of the civilian society.

The Power of the Citizen

Given the sheer size and complexity of government today, what chance has the average citizen — as contrasted with the well-financed pressure groups and giant corporations, all served by professional lobbyists — of influencing policy at any level? "Not much," seems to be a logical response. Nevertheless, the unaffiliated crusader does occasionally succeed in playing the role of giant killer. One modern example is Ralph Nader, who almost single-handedly, through his writing and public appearances, compelled the Congress to pass automobile safety legislation and then went on to expose additional causes for consumer concern and to lead a corps of volunteers in investigations of the federal bureaucracy itself. Earlier, Rachel Carson's *Silent Spring* sounded the first clear warning against DDT and aroused sufficient public dismay to keep the danger from being ignored or forgotten.[39] A century ago, persistent lobbying of state governors and legislatures by Dorothea Dix raised standards of care for the mentally ill all across the nation.

In fact, the chances of an ordinary individual getting the government to act are much better than one might suppose, provided that: (1) there is a growing public awareness of a need for action; (2) the individual forms a pressure group; and (3) the issue is one in which the government possesses some policy-making authority and on which it may be looking for an opportunity to act. Congressional hearings are set up for the very purpose of producing legislation, and, as Nader's experience indicates, the individual who speaks out authoritatively at a hearing may attract powerful support.

The investigations related to the Watergate affair revealed another kind of power held by those citizens who work within the federal government—that of "leaking" information to the press. The various anonymous government employees who contacted reporters with information regarding the misuse of power by the Nixon administration were in a good part responsible for bringing the facts to the attention of the public and thus for the eventual resignation of the president. Many government investigations of other matters were started when a government employee gave information to the press.

The power of the citizen is most generally manifest, of course, when citizens exercise their right to vote for candidates and for referenda. We will examine the degree to which Americans take advantage of this power in the final section of this chapter (pages 524–525).

The Legislator as Broker

In a variety of ways, American legislators act as brokers between the local citizens, to whom they are responsible, and the executive. If they play their roles well, they not only improve their chances of survival with the voters but also increase their influence with the executive—which in turn helps them further increase their influence at home.

Members of the House and Senate thus play an important part in formulating consensus at

37. Melman, "Pentagon Bourgeoisie."
38. Gerhard Lenski, *Power and Privilege* (New York: McGraw-Hill Book Company, 1966), pp. 361–364.
39. Rachel Louise Carson, *Silent Spring* (Boston: Houghton Mifflin Co., 1962).

Citizens in the San Francisco Bay area have been working with the Army Corps of Engineers and the Justice Department to stop the illegal dumping of dirt and garbage in the bay. Filling the bay without a permit has been prohibited by federal law since 1899, but many cities have nevertheless used the bay as a garbage dump. An inspector for the Army Corps has stated: "We absolutely could not do our job without the help of the citizenry in calling our attention to illegal filling."

the national level. But to do this in a society as diversified as ours takes time and debate. Federal aid to education is a case in point. This issue involves racial and religious controversy as well as concern for local autonomy and fear of federal control. From the first unsuccessful attempts to get aid bills passed to the voting of billions of dollars for education during the last two years of the Johnson administration, almost twenty years went by. Congress acts on controversial national issues when it finds a sufficient consensus among the people, not before.

Another vital function of the legislator is to explain federal programs to the people. When no local interests are involved, citizens may have great difficulty in understanding why they

should accept—and particularly why their taxes should support—policies initiated in the nation's capital. This is where members of Congress come in. As one of them has put it: "These activities of explaining, justifying, interpreting, interceding, all help . . . build acceptance for government policy, an essential process in democratic government, and an especially important one, . . . given the circumstances of American social diversity and a decentralized party system."[40]

Is There a Power Elite?

During the 1950s, C. Wright Mills developed the thesis that America's top leadership formed something approaching a power elite—a kind of conspiracy on the part of a few to dominate the majority.[41] Mills's theory depicts a self-conscious elite whose members belong to the upper class and occupy upper-status positions in business, the military, and the executive branch of government. Mills documented his theory with examples of the social intermingling among

40. John Brademas (Congressman, 3rd District, Indiana), "The Emerging Role of the American Congress," *Proceedings of the Indiana Academy of Social Sciences* (1968).

41. C. Wright Mills, *The Power Elite* (New York: Oxford University Press, 1956). For criticism of this thesis, see Robert A. Dahl, "A Critique of the Ruling Elite Model," *American Political Science Review*, 52 (June 1958): 463–469; and Daniel Bell, "The Power Elite Reconsidered," *American Journal of Sociology*, 64 (November 1959): 238–250. Floyd Hunter developed a similar theory at the same time Mills did; see Floyd Hunter, *Top Leadership, U.S.A.* (Chapel Hill, N.C.: University of North Carolina Press, 1959).

Interaction among members of the various elites in the United States is a common occurrence, but there has been no proof that such interaction indicates a unified power elite that runs the country by influence and favoritism.

business, military, and political leaders. He illustrated the movement of leaders from the military to business and from business to top political posts, the domination of the political elite by the military and business elites, and the importance of large campaign contributions by business leaders to political parties and politicians. Although Mills raised challenging questions about the relationship between influence and authority at the national level, the data he presented offer no proof of the existence of a power elite—that is, of a group that can and does get its way on most important national issues. As his critics have pointed out, for every instance Mills presented of an elite controlling a decision, another instance could be cited in which the presumed elite failed.

Perhaps the chief merit of Mills's work was that it challenged others to produce alternative hypotheses about the national power structure. We will look at two of these, the governing-class hypothesis and the multi-influence hypothesis.

The governing-class hypothesis is based on the fact that there is an upper class in the United States, composed of corporate executives, corporate lawyers, members of foundation boards,

university trustees, and high officials in the executive branch of government. The leading proponent of the hypothesis, G. William Domhoff, believes that these people are not so much a cohesive elite, as Mills would have it, as a "governing class." In other words, Domhoff believes that most national leadership positions are held by individuals whose outlook is similar because they have upper-class backgrounds or have been socialized in upper-class institutions.[42] While they may and often do belong to different political parties and different social and economic cliques and factions, their decisions are generally intended to protect and enhance private property and the right to make a profit. According to Domhoff, the United States is ruled by and for these people, and the key political decisions are made in their interest.

A third approach to the national power structure is the multi-influence hypothesis of Arnold Rose. Rose's main thesis, which is not unlike one of the major hypotheses that has emerged from community power studies, is stated as follows:

Segments of the economic elite have violated democratic political and legal processes, with differing degrees of effort and success in the various periods of American history, but in no recent period could they correctly be said to have controlled the elected and appointed political authorities in large measure. The relationship between the economic elite and the political authorities has been a constantly varying one of strong influence, cooperation, division of labor, and conflict, with each influencing the other in changing proportion to some extent and each operating independently of the other to a large extent.[43]

Rose concluded that there are a *number* of power structures in American society and that no unified elite is in control of all or any of them. Within each such structure, however, a small number of persons hold the largest share of power. If business leaders have a disproportionate influence on government, it is because

42. G. William Domhoff, *Who Rules America?* (Englewood Cliffs, N.J.: Prentice-Hall, Inc., 1967), and "Is the American Upper Class a Governing Class?" in *Issues in Social Inequality,* ed. Gerald W. Thielbar and Saul D. Feldman (Boston: Little, Brown and Company, 1972), pp. 315–332.

43. Arnold M. Rose, *The Power Structure: Political Process in American Society* (New York: Oxford University Press, 1967), p. 2.

they enjoy advantages of education, knowledge, and money. But Rose argued that business leaders had been less successful in influencing government since the 1930s than they were prior to that era. He found encouraging, moreover, the resurgence of political activity on the part of voluntary associations, especially those concerned with such issues as civil rights and help for the elderly. Finally, he argued that events of the 1950s and 1960s showed that political authorities controlled the economic elite at least as much as the latter controlled the former.

POLITICAL SOCIALIZATION AND VOTING BEHAVIOR

In all societies—democratic and totalitarian—young people are indoctrinated with the belief that their country is "best of all" and that its institutions are designed to maximize possibilities for a good life. In the United States, as we saw in Chapter 6 (pages 146–173), the family, peer groups, teachers, and civic, business, and political leaders all engage in the process of socialization. Although the family is not always the predominant agent of political socialization, it continues to play an important role. For example, in a study of party affiliation of American high-school seniors, Jennings and Niemi found that some "59 percent of the students fall into the same broad category as their parents and only seven percent cross the sharp divide between Democrats and Republicans."[44] In this final section we will examine the impact of family socialization on political behavior in terms of ethnic origin and social class.

THE IMPACT OF ETHNICITY

Ethnicity has been found to be as important in political socialization as in other kinds of social-

ization. The religious and ethnic values, beliefs, and customs of people, as transmitted through the family's cultural traditions, influence their voting behavior.[45]

The earliest European immigrants to America—English, Scottish, German, Dutch, and Swiss—had as part of their ethnic heritage the Puritan ethic (see page 111), with its emphasis on individuality. These people have long been the backbone of the Republican party, which generally stands for lower taxes, less governmental power, and particularly self-reliance and self-initiative. The strength of the Republican party lies for the most part in rural areas and small towns, where the inheritors of the Puritan ethic have the greatest political strength.

The Democratic party is strongest in the cities, where the later immigrants—mainly Catholic and Jewish—are most numerous. Before coming to the United States these people lived a "collective" life: the Catholics gained religious and social support from the Church, the Jews from the ghetto and the family group. In general, Catholics and Jews tend to have stronger ties to the Democratic party, with its commitment to governmental action on behalf of the people—for example, the creation of welfare legislation and government jobs for the unemployed.

The Democratic party has long recognized the "ethnic factor," as is evidenced by their tendency to put together "balanced tickets," that is, to slate candidates who represent more or less proportionately the ethnic groups in a particular area. Republicans have tended to emphasize assimilation over ethnicity and hence have run fewer "balanced" tickets.

Some social scientists and politicians have suggested that the ethnic factor in politics would disappear as the descendants of immigrants became assimilated into American society. But as we saw in Chapter 9 (pages 260–264), many members of the third and fourth generations have not assimilated. Members of the ethnic groups traditionally affiliated with the Democratic party primarily voted for Democratic candidates in the presidential elections of 1960 through 1972 (see Table 17.4). Only in 1972 did these voters fail to give full support to a Demo-

44. M. Kent Jennings and Richard G. Niemi, "The Transmission of Political Values from Parent to Child," in *Power and Change in the United States,* ed. Kenneth M. Dolbeare (New York: John Wiley & Sons, Inc., 1969), p. 228.

45. Harold J. Abramson, *Ethnic Diversity in Catholic America* (New York: John Wiley & Sons, Inc., 1973); and Andrew M. Greeley, *The Denominational Society* (Glenview, Ill.: Scott, Foresman and Company, 1972).

cratic contender and, according to Levy and Kramer, this was because the nominee, George McGovern, failed to court the ethnic vote. But even in 1972 Catholics and Jews supported the Democratic candidates in senatorial and gubernatorial races.[46]

Ethnicity affects not only the party affiliation of voters but also whether they will exercise their right to vote. Generally, whites are more likely to vote than nonwhites, but there is much variation within these categories. In the 1972

Table 17.4. PERCENTAGE OF MAJOR ETHNIC GROUPS VOTING DEMOCRATIC IN FOUR PRESIDENTIAL ELECTIONS, 1960–1972

	1960	1964	1968	1972
Chicanos	85	90	87	73
Puerto Ricans (In New York City only)	77	86	83	
Blacks	75	97	94	87
Jewish	82	90	83	66
Slavic	82	80	65	—
Irish	75	78	64	47
Italian	75	77	50	42

SOURCE: Mark R. Levy and Michael S. Kramer, *The Ethnic Factor: How America's Minorities Decide Elections* (New York: Simon & Schuster. Inc., 1972), pp. 226–227, 256–259.

Table 17.5. REPORTED VOTER PARTICIPATION AND REGISTRATION OF PERSONS OF VOTING AGE, BY ETHNIC ORIGIN, NOVEMBER 1972

Ethnic origin	Percent reported registered	Percent reported voted
German	79.0	70.8
Italian	77.5	71.5
Irish	76.7	66.6
French	72.7	63.2
Polish	79.8	72.0
Russian	85.7	80.5
English, Scottish, and Welsh	80.1	71.3
Spanish	44.4	37.5
Mexican	46.0	37.5
Puerto Rican	52.7	44.6
Other Spanish	36.8	33.5
Negro	67.5	54.1
Other	74.1	65.9
Do not know	64.9	51.8
Not reported	47.9	42.4

SOURCE: *Current Population Reports, Population Characteristics,* Series P-20, No. 253 (Washington, D.C.: U.S. Department of Commerce, Bureau of the Census, October 1973), p. 27.

presidential election, for example, 63 percent of the registered voters cast ballots. Below the national average were blacks (54.1 percent) and those of Spanish origin (37.5 percent). People of Russian (predominantly Jewish) descent showed the highest participation, with 80.5 percent reporting that they voted (see Table 17.5). The Bureau of the Census summarized voting behavior in the 1972 elections as follows:

Higher levels of registration and voting were associated with persons who were male, white, those in the middle age group (35–64), those persons with at least a high school diploma, those in families with incomes greater than $10,000, and those in white collar occupations. Conversely, females, Negroes, persons of Spanish ethnic origin, the youngest (18–34) and oldest age groups (65 or older), those who did not complete elementary school education, those in families with incomes less than $5000, and those in unskilled occupations, such as laborers and private household workers, were less likely to be registered and to vote.[47]

As this quotation makes clear, other variables interact with ethnicity in influencing political participation. In the next section we will discuss the influence of one such variable—social class—on voting behavior.

THE IMPACT OF SOCIAL CLASS

There appears to be very little we learn in childhood that may not affect our political behavior as adults, for political behavior is not something apart. In effect, we *are* politically as we live and think socially. Thus children are developing political concepts when they learn who "the poor" are and what makes up "a slum," and when they come to recognize the various ethnic and other minority groups in their society. The whole spectrum of class-related values—degree of ability to trust other people, degree of personal autonomy permitted or obedience demanded, degree of ability to plan ahead, and so on—all arise through socialization, and all shape political thinking and perception.

46. Mark R. Levy and Michael S. Kramer, *The Ethnic Factor: How America's Minorities Decide Elections* (New York: Simon & Schuster, Inc., 1972).

47. U.S. Department of Commerce, *Current Population Reports, Population Characteristics,* Washington, D.C., Bureau of the Census, Series P-20, No. 253, October 1973, p. 1.

VIEWPOINTS   CONSERVATIVES AND LIBERALS

■ When a liberal looks into a crowd, he sees stereotypes to fit on computer cards, not individual people. He sees "blue-collar-white ethnic" or "middle-aged black professional" or whatever.

We conservatives see you—John Doe, Joe Doakes, Mary Smith or whoever—as individual people who have individual identities, hopes, aspirations, dreams.

Modern American conservatism is the antithesis of authoritarianism. The conservative would leave as much as possible to popular control in the area of public decision.

Basically, we believe that you have the right to do whatever it is you want to do, provided you do not interfere with any other citizen's God-given rights to life, liberty and property.

We believe in the free enterprise system because we believe that nobody has the right to tell you what kind of work to do or what you can be paid for doing it.

There is no democracy like the democracy of the marketplace. When a consumer spends a dollar he is, in effect, casting a ballot—a ballot that determines what goods and services American business will produce.

We support a strong national defense and vigorous law enforcement because we recognize the basic duty of government is to protect its citizens from predators, at home or abroad.

We favor cutting down the cost of government because we believe that you should decide how the money you have earned should be spent.

Because we believe that government should be your servant and not your master, we favor transferring as many governmental responsibilities as possible to the state and local levels so that you will have more control over them.

Ours is the only political philosophy based on the concept of individual sovereignty—the notion that you, and you alone, have the right to determine your own destiny.

Senator John Tower
"Conservatives Protect Rights of Individuals"

● If I'm a liberal, it is because I've always believed that government can make a positive contribution toward helping each person live a reasonably secure, happy and satisfying life.

This does not mean that government can or should do everything—that's the definition of totalitarianism. But government can be a partner in building a more just society where each person has the freedom to develop his or her abilities to the fullest, whatever they may be.

In today's world, this means a chance for a good education, a safe neighborhood, a decent home, access to medical care and the chance for a job. Figuring out how government can help accomplish these goals is at the heart of contemporary liberalism.

James Madison, the father of our Constitution, once wrote that if all men were angels, no government would be necessary. I often think that some of my conservative friends believe too much in the angelic nature of human beings. Just keep government out of our lives, they say, and everything will be okay.

Well, it will be okay for some people—those who are blessed with great ability or wealth or extraordinary ambition. But most people aren't so lucky. Liberalism believes everyone has a right to justice, to opportunity and to freedom.

A liberal believes that government can be a positive force in lives of people—a working partnership in removing inequities and giving people a chance to make something of their lives.

As a result, liberalism has taken the lead in destroying artificial barriers of racial, ethnic, religious and sex discrimination. Liberalism has sought to develop an economy that provides everyone with a chance for rewarding work, at decent wages and in safe working conditions. . . .

Put most simply, liberals believe in giving people a chance. Liberals have faith that most people will make something of their lives if they have this chance.

Senator Hubert Humphrey
"Liberals Use Government Help"

From what we know of the socialization process, it is not surprising to find data indicating that interest in politics is readily transmitted from parents to children. One study of schoolchildren, for example, revealed that more than twice as many of those with college-educated mothers had taken at least some interest in a presidential election campaign, as compared with those whose mothers had only completed grade school. At the ninth-grade level, three times as many children with low-income parents admitted to showing hardly any interest, as compared with children of high-income parents.[48]

The authors of another study found that lower-class children of all ages had less confidence in their own and other people's ability to influence the government than did children from the classes above them. Consider the attitude of this boy from a working-class home:

> "Richard, if the President did something that people didn't like what could they do?"
> "The people can't do anything. They can't go to the White House and tell him what to do because he makes all the decisions. If the people don't like it, too bad for them."[49]

Political socialization in support of the established political system seems to work most effectively in American society for the middle and upper classes, who benefit most from the system. But even among these dominant segments of the population the level of political apathy appears to be relatively high. For example, the turnout in American presidential elections of those qualified to vote has averaged between 60 and 70 percent in recent years, as compared with regular turnouts of between 70 and 90 percent for most other industrial democracies.[50] If other types of political activity are taken into account, the percentage of the politically active is much lower. In one study, for instance, a representative sample of the American electorate was classified in terms of five different criteria of political participation.[51] Only 10.3 percent were rated "very active" and 16.8 percent as "active"; the remainder—72.9 percent—were either "inactive" or "very inactive."

Significantly, the level of political apathy becomes disproportionately high among those people in American society who are poor and subject to discrimination—although these individuals are precisely the ones who would seem to have the most to gain from making use of the democratic political institutions. In the study just cited, only 12 percent of those at the lowest income level fell into one of the "active" categories, compared with 69 percent of those at the highest income level. Differences in education appeared to reinforce this effect. An individual with a college education was over five times as likely to be "very active" as one with only a grade school education. The same general picture is reflected in many other studies, before and since.[52] In general, it can be said of American society that the more a group is deprived and discriminated against, the lower is its level of political participation. Voter turnout among American blacks, in particular, has been low, even in areas where there has been no attempt to prevent blacks from registering or voting.[53]

During the 1960s and early 1970s it was believed that young people active in various political campaigns and movements—the antiwar movement, the New Left, the 1968 and 1972 presidential campaigns, the movement to change drug-use laws—wanted to participate in the political system via the polls. Indeed, it was predicted that young people would turn out to vote in record numbers when the voting age was lowered to eighteen. But in 1972—the first national election in which eighteen-year-olds

48. From a study by H. H. Remmers, summarized by Herbert H. Hyman in *Political Socialization: A Study in the Psychology of Political Behavior* (New York: The Free Press, 1969), Chapter 3.

49. Robert D. Hess, "Political Attitudes in Children—Do Our Schoolteachers Subvert Solid Social Growth?" *Psychology Today*, 2, No. 8 (January 1969): 28. The data are from Robert D. Hess and Judith V. Torney, *The Development of Political Attitudes in Children* (Chicago: Aldine Publishing Co., 1967).

50. Gabriel Almond and Sidney Verba, *The Civic Culture: Political Attitudes and Democracy in Five Nations* (Princeton, N.J.: Princeton University Press, 1963).

51. R. E. Agger and V. A. Ostrom, "Political Participation in a Small Community," in *Political Behavior*, ed. Heinz Eulau, Samuel Eldersveld, and Morris Janowitz (New York: The Free Press, 1956), pp. 138 ff.

52. See especially Lester W. Milbrath, *Political Participation* (Chicago: Rand McNally & Co., 1965).

53. *President's Commission on Registration and Voting Participation* (Washington, D.C.: U.S. Government Printing Office, 1963). See also Donald R. Matthews and James W. Prothro, *Negroes and the New Southern Politics* (New York: Harcourt Brace Jovanovich, Inc., 1966).

could vote—only 48.3 percent of the more than eleven million people aged eighteen to twenty reported voting. While the full explanation of this apathy is not known, it is certain that social class had some influence. Of those eighteen to twenty year olds not in school—who comprised more than half the members of the age group—fewer than 40 percent reported voting.[54]

Data on political apathy raise some disquieting possibilities. They suggest that, to the poor and deprived, the distribution of power in the United States has become frozen and that this status quo is defended by economic and political interests unresponsive to the have-nots. To the extent that these views are accurate, the consensus basis for American democracy may be eroding.

SUMMARY

The phenomenon of *power*—the ability to make and implement decisions—is basic to the political system. Political power can be classified as legitimate or coercive. *Coercion,* based on the illegitimate threat or use of force, is a sign of political weakness. The power of stable political systems, by contrast, is based on some pattern of legitimate *authority:* traditional, charismatic, or legal-rational. *Influence* is distinct from authority, being the sum of all the resources an individual or group can bring to bear in order to effect a desired outcome in a decision-making situation. Most modern political systems shape policy through an interplay of authority and influence.

Today we live in a world of *nation-states,* characterized by centralized, more or less inclusive authority. Most inclusive is the authority of *totalitarian* states, both of the right—fascist—and of the left—Communist. Less inclusive is the authority of the *democratic* states, which stress individual freedom rather than collective welfare. Democracy is made possible by a class structure in which the middle class predominates and the lower class perceives that it has

access to the middle class. Essential to democracy are shared political traditions and voluntary associations—social organizations free of governmental controls. The hallmark of democracy is the right of dissent.

The structure of political power in the United States demonstrates the society's traditional concern for individual freedom and the diffusion of power. In general, power at the community level has become less centralized and more pluralistic, a trend that is largely the result of growing economic and political interdependence. Studies show that community leadership tends to come from the business sector, especially under the council-manager system, but such studies have failed to disclose evidence of unified power structures.

The formal structure of the federal government, as of American government generally, is based on the separation of executive, legislative, and judicial powers, but often they overlap. Also important in the power equation is the influence of the federal bureaucracy, the military, and the business sector. Although the accumulated evidence from studies of the national power structure suggests that public policy is shaped by multiple influences rather than by a unified "power elite," it also suggests the existence of a "governing class" from which come the most potent influences on national policies. Ordinary citizens, though relatively powerless as individuals, can make their influence felt by joining together to form pressure groups. Congress is the organ of government most responsive to the wishes of the people.

How effectively adults relate themselves to the political system can be shown to stem from their early political socialization, in which the influence of the family is predominant. Ethnicity continues to have a significant influence on voting patterns, particularly among racial and religious minorities. Studies of political socialization in the United States show that it is most effective, in terms of maintaining a political consensus, for members of the middle and upper classes. Low income and low status have been shown to correlate with a lack of interest in politics and feelings of political ineffectiveness.

54. U.S. Department of Commerce, *Current Population Reports, Population Characteristics,* p. 5.

18
The Economic Institution

THE DEVELOPMENT OF MODERN INDUSTRIALISM

The Preindustrial Organization of Work   The Factory System   The Rise of the Corporation   Capitalism as an Economic System

INDUSTRIAL ORGANIZATION: MANAGEMENT

The Formal Bureaucratic Structure   Informal Patterns of Interaction

INDUSTRIAL ORGANIZATION: LABOR

Labor Unions   Human Relations and the Worker

THE WORKER IN INDUSTRIAL SOCIETY

Occupational Choice and Occupational Mobility   Women and Work   Worker Dissatisfaction   The Impact of Unemployment

In the previous chapter we discussed the nature and distribution of power, focusing our attention on the United States. We saw the close relationship between power and wealth in almost every aspect of political life. In this chapter we will examine the social institution concerned with the production and distribution of a nation's wealth. We will begin with a historical overview of the development of the industrial system, which has radically altered economic patterns in modern societies, and then examine industrial organization as represented by both management and labor. Finally, we will turn our attention to the meaning of work for those employed in a rapidly changing economy.

THE DEVELOPMENT OF MODERN INDUSTRIALISM

Although the Industrial Revolution is usually said to date from approximately 1780, the origins of the Western economic institution go back much further. Before the modern union there was the medieval guild; before the medieval guild there was the guild, or *collegium*, of the Roman Empire. Consequential development, however, can be said to stem from the later Middle Ages.

THE PREINDUSTRIAL ORGANIZATION OF WORK

Between the tenth and the thirteenth centuries western Europe experienced a period of remarkable commercial growth. In the south, Italian cities expanded rapidly, while in the north thriving towns developed. Peddlers banded together in merchant guilds to control trade, and urban workers formed craft guilds to shut out competition. Indeed, the towns themselves formed leagues for commercial purposes.

The Guild System
Medieval craft guilds and towns were interdependent. The craft guilds, each representing a specific craft, depended on the urban market for their existence. At the same time, the prosperity

of the town depended on the economic well-being of the guilds, and it was the prosperous town that could purchase and maintain autonomy by paying tribute to the overlord or king.

Fundamental to the development of the guilds was the freedom of the townspeople. Neither slaves nor serfs could legally enter into the contractual relationships upon which these organizations were based. But medieval towns opened the way to personal liberty: "In general, a man who lived in a town for a year and a day was a free man, whatever his previous status."[1]

Although guild members were free in the sense that they were neither slaves nor serfs, they were by no means free to do whatever they wished. In addition to controlling recruitment, guild leadership determined the ranks of its members. After three to twelve years of training, apprentices usually became paid journeymen, working under the supervision of master craftsmen. More years would have to pass before they could hope to become masters themselves. All this was done in the name of upholding standards of craftsmanship. Work methods changed very little over the centuries, partly because guild leaders opposed innovations that might subvert their authority. On the positive side, standards of craftsmanship, fostered by guild examinations and supervision, were very high, as medieval artifacts show, and so too, presumably, was the level of satisfaction that a skilled craftsman could derive from work.

The Domestic or "Putting-Out" System

Under the classic form of the guild system—the form that prevailed, for instance, in late fourteenth century Florence—individual producers took care of the entire production process. They designed the product, obtained the raw materials, and, often with the help of apprentices, worked on every stage of the item until it was completed. They also sold it, usually directly to a purchaser though sometimes to a middleman.

It was this middleman, often a member of a merchants' guild, who eventually undermined the craft guilds' economic and political independence. As markets expanded, craftsmen came to depend increasingly on merchants to sell their goods. Those who simply waited for prospective customers to visit their workshops and look over the finished goods could not sell nearly as much as those who regularly filled orders for shop owners and traders. And the merchants, being continually in touch with consumers, had a clearer idea of what was in demand.

Soon the merchants were telling the craftsmen what to produce. When they also began to supply raw materials and take complete charge of marketing, the craftsmen were well on their way to becoming employees rather than independent artisans. The emphasis in production shifted from all-around quality to unit cost, from finely wrought individual items (a masterpiece was originally the sample of skill that a journeyman produced to gain the rank of master craftsman) to large batches of goods of lower but more uniform quality.

To take advantage of expanding markets and to meet the demands of their customers, merchants also created the domestic or "putting-out" system. Briefly, this meant that several families, working in their own homes, regularly produced work for one merchant, who provided the raw materials or unfinished goods and paid by the piece for finished work. The system appeared in medieval Italy and by the fifteenth century was providing serious competition for the guilds, which tried—on the whole unsuccessfully—to regulate and even to suppress it. By the seventeenth century the putting-out system was the mainstay of the English woolen industry. Rural families supplemented the husbands' meager seasonal earnings as farm laborers by spinning the yarn brought to them in their cottages by clothiers' agents. Hence the term "cottage industries."

Increasing production, spurred by population growth and expanding overseas trade, required increasing specialization. Spinners spun wool into yarn that was passed along to weavers, and so on until the finished, dyed cloth was produced. A man with a "cottage industry" broke his work down into steps so that his wife

1. Norman F. Cantor, *Western Civilization: Its Genesis and Destiny*, Vol. 1 (Glenview, Ill.: Scott, Foresman and Company, 1969), p. 372.

In the United States, as in England, the factory system depended on a large labor pool. This photograph shows women and children working primitive machines at a cotton factory in Alabama in the late 1800s. Early factory owners paid very small wages, and often entire families had to work in order to earn a living.

and children, as well as any apprentices he might have, could help in the production process. Often these steps were simple enough to be performed by workers with very little skill. Thus the division of labor and specialization within the work force grew. Gradually the production process moved completely out of the control of workers, who depended on the entrepreneur for the materials they worked with and for the distribution and sale of what they produced. No longer did the producer deal directly with the consumer; indeed, the two never met. Production had become impersonal.

THE FACTORY SYSTEM

By the middle of the eighteenth century, the idea of craftsmen producing goods for entrepreneurs had become well established throughout most of western Europe. In Great Britain a combination of factors—demographic, economic, political, technological, religious, and social— opened the way for the development of the factory system and the emergence of an entirely new kind of relationship between capital, technology, and labor.[2]

Investment Capital

Manufacturing consumer goods was an unusual way of making money in a society still dominated by landed aristocracy. Those not of noble birth who had succeeded in making money had usually done so in foreign or domestic trade, not

2. Much of the material in this section is based upon Wilbert E. Moore, *Industrial Relations and the Social Order* (New York: Macmillan, Inc., 1951), pp. 17–39.

by investing in *fixed capital,* such as goods, land, buildings, machines, raw materials, and labor. All these things, once acquired, constitute capital that retains the same form over a long period. As Max Weber pointed out, investment by private entrepreneurs in fixed capital really marked the beginning of modern capitalism.[3]

In eighteenth-century Britain, entrepreneurs were able to obtain credit from banks, but they received no help from the government. Their chief source of investment capital was their own profits, which they plowed back into their infant businesses.

Machines and Power

Machines and mechanical tools of various kinds had been in use since prehistoric times. So had water power. But the mechanical devices of the late eighteenth century were vastly superior to anything invented earlier, and the development of steam power made it possible to run mechanical devices with a speed and uniformity impossible for the unaided human hand. By 1780 a succession of mechanical innovations had already revolutionized the British cotton industry. And in 1785 the steam-powered loom was introduced. While decades passed before it was widely adopted, this device freed manufacturers from the necessity of building their mills near running streams in the countryside and opened the way for the development of the factory town.

The Labor Market

The factory system could not have come into existence without a large labor pool. In England, many of those evicted from their farms under the Enclosure Acts were forced to seek work in the new factories and mills. This situation, plus the fact that great numbers of Britain's rural poor were resigned to a hand-to-mouth existence in any case, helps explain why a typical factory worker was prepared to put in a dawn-to-dusk day for wages that would buy little more than bread. Only by having the entire family working was it possible to eke out a living.

There is a temptation to think of the early factory employers as wicked exploiters of women and children as well as of male workers. Though some of them undoubtedly were cruel and callous, it must be remembered that this pattern of employment had never existed before. All previous types of employment, except for the use of slaves in agriculture and mining, had been on a far smaller scale and had involved a more personal association between employer and employee. Seventeenth-century baker's apprentices were not paid, but their master's obligation to them was moral as well as legal. Relations between factory owners and their "hands," by contrast, were legal only. Independent entrepreneurs with large investments to protect felt no moral obligation toward workers they would have to lay off whenever the market took an unfavorable turn.

From the point of view of early industrial capitalism, free labor was much superior to slave labor because in slack periods workers could be dismissed to shift for themselves. On the other hand, with workers coming and going, it was necessary to keep training new employees. Because of this problem, the employer tried to reduce the productive process to a series of steps that did not require a high level of training or skill.

Shop Production

The factory system was a direct result of the economic advantages to be derived from "shop production"—housing each stage of the production process under one roof. During the early industrial period, when transportation was a major problem, it paid manufacturers to locate their plants as close as possible to everything they needed, including labor and the products of other manufacturers. In modern terms, however, "one roof" has organizational rather than physical connotations; it refers to a single system of supervision and control.

By centralizing the production of goods, employers could impose much more effective controls on labor. In the putting-out system, people set their own pace. In the factory system,

3. Max Weber, *General Economic History,* trans. Frank H. Knight (New York: Collier Books, 1961), p. 100.

they worked at the pace set by their supervisor and the machines they operated. The shop concept also made it possible to use capital much more effectively. Concentrating production facilities in one strategically located building made it easy to move goods from step to step in the production process and to exercise control over quality.

With increasingly efficient machines, more dependable sources of power, expanding markets, greater amounts of investment capital, and a rapidly developing technology, the factory system of industrial production was well under way by the early decades of the nineteenth century. As this organization of work continued to grow and spread, it had numerous consequences and implications for the society as a whole.

THE RISE OF THE CORPORATION

Although corporations existed prior to the eighteenth century, this pattern of multiple ownership and risk sharing did not become predominant until industrial capitalism developed around the factory system in the nineteenth century. Corporate ownership—that is, ownership of collective property by the fictitious "person" known as a corporation—tended to replace personal ownership as industrial enterprises increased in size and complexity.

A share of the stock issued by a corporation is, in a sense, a "piece of the company." The general principle of shareholding is that investors own and potentially control a corporation to the extent that they own a proportion of shares in it. For the corporation, issuing such shares is not only a method of raising investment capital; it also limits the risks of ownership. If the business fails, only the assets of the corporation itself fall into the hands of creditors. The personal property of shareholders is protected, as it is if the corporation is sued.

The corporate shareholder is even further removed than the entrepreneur from concern for the worker. Indeed, the investor may not even be sure what the company produces, and the speculator—who buys and sells stocks to make a profit—may hold shares in the company for only a brief time. Both, however, are very much interested in the company balance sheet: a healthy net profit usually means a good stock market price for the speculator and a good dividend for the investor. Thus, to keep the shareholders happy, corporate management must concentrate on keeping profits high. And this means, among other things, resisting the efforts of workers to obtain higher wages.

Ownership and Control

The advantages of corporate ownership over personal ownership were particularly obvious to industrialists in the United States, where the rise of manufacturing was paced by the rise of corporations. The greatest expansion took place after the Civil War, when the country was opened up to commerce by the railroads. Indeed, by the last quarter of the nineteenth century the success of such giant industrial enterprises as Armour and Company, U.S. Steel, and Standard Oil was causing so much public concern that some attempt was made to regulate them, notably through the Sherman Antitrust Act of 1890. This was the classic piece of antitrust legislation that defined "restraint of trade" as a federal offense.

But who is to be held responsible for the offenses of corporations? The stockholders who "own" them? The truth is that the role of the stockholder is an ambiguous one. Between 1965 and 1975 the number of Americans who owned stocks rose from 20 million to more than 35 million; almost one in every six Americans now owns some stock in a corporation. But ownership is very much a sometimes thing for millions of these shareholders, and about 12 to 14 percent of all stocks are sold each year. About half of all stockholders are middle-income Americans, with annual family incomes of $10,000 to $20,000. They own less than 25 percent of all stocks and receive less than 25 percent of all stock dividends.[4] Clearly, they can exercise little practical control over the corporations of which they are legally, if often briefly, part owners. The great majority of stockholders participate in control only by returning proxy forms that allow management a free hand.

4. *Business Week*, March 10, 1975, p. 55; and Kevin P. Philips and Albert E. Sindlinger, "Poll Finds More Americans Seeking to Purchase Stock," *Hartford Courant*, March 17, 1975, p. 7.

Increasingly, too, the owners of stock in American corporations are not individuals but other organizations. One kind of organization is the mutual fund, which typically is a collection of stock holdings in a hundred or more different companies, and which itself is "owned" by shareholders. Other organizations include universities, religious bodies, unions, and foundations. Corporations gain control over other corporations, and these in turn are controlled by still other corporations. Thus it is becoming more and more difficult to specify precisely the structure of industrial ownership.

Power and Influence

In 1970 nearly 50 percent of the total assets of all manufacturing corporations were held by only a hundred corporations. Many of these corporations were conglomerates—corporations that own other corporations, most of which produce unrelated products. The top executives of a conglomerate, who often own 5 percent or less of the stock of the parent company, control the operations of all the corporations in the conglomerate and decide how to use the profits.[5]

Given the great wealth of these corporations, the people who direct them wield enormous power and influence. Some students of American society see this as a growing threat. C. Wright Mills, for example, concluded that major corporation heads, along with top government officials and military brass, formed a "power elite" that controlled national decision making.[6] (For a critical analysis of this thesis, see Chapter 17, pages 521–523.) A growing number of Americans are concerned about the far-reaching effects that corporate policies can have on the national welfare.

For many years American automobile manufacturers promoted the principle, "the bigger the car the better the car." This policy led to increased use of finite natural resources—including not only petroleum products but also land for highways and parking lots. And it fostered the neglect of mass transit systems throughout much of the United States.

For their part, American oil companies were able to obtain crude oil from the Near East and South America, as well as from the United States, at relatively low costs and could therefore make gasoline available to American car owners at well below world market prices. Meanwhile, tax concessions encouraged the oil companies to exploit domestic supplies, and company advertising encouraged unrestrained consumption. In effect, the financial power of the automobile manufacturers and oil companies was being gained in part at least at the cost of the future.

The Multinational Corporation

The power and influence of corporations have been extended by the rise of the multinational corporation. A multinational is a large corporation or conglomerate with substantial business operations in at least six countries. Most multinationals are involved in the extraction of natural resources, in manufacturing, or in technology-producing industries (e.g., production of computers and computer programs). Currently, there are about two hundred multinational corporations, about 75 percent of which are owned and controlled by Americans. Each has annual earnings of at least $100 million.[7] Some well-known multinational corporations are General Motors, International Telephone and Telegraph, International Nickel, and Xerox.

Most multinationals operate in markets dominated by only a few sellers, of which the multinational is often the largest. If their products are in great demand, this limited competition makes it possible for them to control market prices and hence the amount of their profits.[8] In addition, multinational corporations are able to control their sources of raw materials, diversify their risks, and reallocate resources to meet changing market conditions.

5. *Encyclopaedia Britannica,* 15th ed., Vol. 5 (Chicago: Encyclopaedia Britannica, Inc., 1974), p. 184.

6. C. Wright Mills, *The Power Elite* (New York: Oxford University Press, 1956).

7. Irving Louis Horowitz, "Capitalism, Communism, and Multinationalism," *Society,* 11, No. 2 (January-February 1974): 32–44.

8. Ibid. See also P. G. Bock, "The Transnational Corporation and Private Foreign Policy," *Society,* 11, No. 2 (January-February 1974): 44–49.

VIEWPOINTS   BUSINESS AND SOCIAL RESPONSIBILITY

■ Perhaps the most frustrating thing about business, for those who keep trying to shoot it down, is this: Corporations are so tenacious that they will even do good in order to survive. This tenacity goes beyond the old maxim that man, in his greed for profit, often unavoidably serves the public interest. In times of crisis, business will even do good *consciously* and *deliberately*. . . .

Businessmen are pragmatists, and with their daily feedback from the marketplace, they readily abandon dogma whenever their survival instinct tells them to. It has become less and less a question of what they *want* to do or might *like* to do, but of what their common sense and survival instinct tell them they *have* to do. . . .

Because it is keyed so closely to the marketplace and so responsive to it, private business is necessarily the most effective instrument of change. Some would call it revolutionary. Many of those who attack business fail to comprehend its constructive contributions to responsive change. And this sort of change is one of the basic reasons business manages to survive. . . .

While businessmen as a whole are not exactly social reformers, they do respond to criticism and to sustained social pressures. The alert businessman regards such pressures as a useful early warning system. The danger is that criticism can become a mindless reflex action that persists long after the basis for it has been dissipated.

Partly because of its ability to adapt — which is simply another word for responsive change — private business remains the most productive element in our society and on balance the best allocator of resources. If you decide to draw a bead on it, remember you're aiming at a moving target. Because, as we've said here before, business is bound to change.

Mobil Oil Corporation
"Capitalism: Moving Target"

● You don't have to argue that the profit motive itself is bad. Incentives and risks are the energizers of our society . . . . And although there does seem to be a lot of chicanery going on these days, among respectable corporations as well as fly-by-night companies . . . lawless conduct is not the real problem. More to be concerned about is the natural dynamism of corporate growth and conquest, with shrewd and talented men assembled in a cause — the corporation — whose ends are narrower than society itself. Just leave it to business — and who then can quarrel when television broadcasters convert their medium to a money box, auctioning off hours to whatever trivia cheaply gathers the largest audience? Leave it to business — and then do you expect those who junk up the landscape and pollute the rivers to volunteer to clean up after themselves? Leave it to business — and who then is to contest its right to squander our resources as it pleases, and to charge us more for these resources the scarcer they become?

Of course, the "natural right" of business to do as it pleases has been challenged ever since the first Roosevelt . . . . Public agitation often forces reform, only to have legislation weakened by business control of the congressional levers of power . . . .

Oddly enough, I think there are many in business who agree that too much in society has been left to private enterprise, which efficiently does only that part of the assignment in which it can make the most money. . . .

Central to any change is the acceptance of an activist, intervening state . . . . Government is a cumbersome means to achieve what a society cannot otherwise accomplish, yet it is also the best place for individuals to register their common wishes. In recent years, despite its vast size, government has done too little, and too often its interventions have been tilted against the interests of a listless public. It must be used to give us direction, for nothing else can.

Thomas Griffith
The Atlantic Monthly

Because the Western nations do not have international alliances that would make it possible to closely control the multinationals, the corporations have been able to transcend government controls to some extent. For example, taxable profits from operations in one country can often be written off against corporate losses or expenses elsewhere. For American-owned companies, foreign investment is often a way to get around antitrust laws, which make it illegal to restrain trade (for example, by gaining monopolistic control of the market). The economic importance of foreign business to a host country and the skill of corporate management often make it difficult for host nations to influence corporate policy or to limit corporate power.

Many multinationals are able to reduce expenses by maintaining mobility of production. If wages, taxes, duties, or other economic factors are higher in one nation than in another, the multinational corporation may shift its production. For example, when Charles de Gaulle was president of France, General Motors closed one of its Paris plants. President de Gaulle was unhappy with this action, and when he attempted to retaliate against the corporation, General Motors moved its entire French operation to Belgium. It then shipped the finished product back to France—duty free.[9]

Multinational corporations have created a complex array of top executive positions. The executives who occupy these positions interact with political and business leaders in a world setting. Not only are these executives establishing new procedures for the production and distribution of goods, they are also creating new ways of thinking about corporations and about nation-states. In 1970, for example, the top executives of International Telephone and Telegraph attempted to persuade the United States government to interfere in the internal affairs of Chile to try to prevent the election of the socialist candidate for president, Salvador Allende.[10]

The ITT executives apparently felt that their large economic investment in Chile justified the interference.

The multinational is also threatening to upset traditional trade unionism. As Horowitz notes, "auto workers in Western Europe find themselves competing against workers in Latin America producing essentially the same cars."[11] Since Latin American workers receive lower wages than do European workers, and since a multinational can move its operations easily, the European workers face the threat of losing their livelihoods if they apply pressure for higher wages. The established trade unions are trying to restructure themselves on an international level so that large wage differentials will no longer exist.

Horowitz describes the influence of the multinational on the nation-state this way:

Multinationals take precedence over political differences in prosaic but meaningful ways. They serve to rationalize and standardize international economic relationships. They demand perfect interchangeability of parts; a uniform system of weights and measurements; common auditing languages for expression of world trade and commerce; standard codes for aircraft and airports, telephonic and telegraphic communications; and banking rules and regulations that are adhered to by all nations.[12]

In effect, then, multinational corporations are creating new cultural patterns, values, beliefs, goals, and norms, which, for the present at least, transcend the boundaries of nation-states.

CAPITALISM AS AN ECONOMIC SYSTEM

As we have noted elsewhere, a complex series of events overlapped to usher in a new era in world history: improvements in transportation and agriculture, the discovery of new lands, increasing contact between peoples of different cultures, the establishment of the nation-state, the growth of the cities. All these changes helped pave the way for the development of modern capitalism. So too did the Protestant Reformation, with its emphasis on rationality, individualism, and the "work ethic" (see page 282). In this section we will examine capitalism in terms of its organization and its ideology.

9. Reported in Horowitz, "Capitalism, Communism, and Multinationalism," p. 40.
10. Bock, "The Transnational Corporation," pp. 45 ff.
11. Horowitz, "Capitalism, Communism, and Multinationalism," p. 40.
12. Ibid., p. 42.

The Organization of Capitalism

The goal of capitalism is production for profit. The capitalist, who owns the means of production, will produce goods or services only if it is profitable to do so. To provide a profit, the final sale price of the product must be greater than the cost of production. The goods that earn profits are produced through the efforts of laborers, and if there is to be a profit, workers must receive less for their work than the result of their work effort actually earns for their employer. The work effort of sales personnel and managers must also be considered as part of the cost of production, as must the cost of borrowing money for equipment and materials. Profit, then, is the *surplus value* that accrues to a product after all the costs have been accounted for.

Max Weber delineated the prerequisites of a capitalist system as follows:[13]

1. Double-entry bookkeeping, which provides a rational basis for determining income and expenses and thus a means to calculate prices that will ensure profits.

2. The ability of an enterprise to appropriate to itself the physical means of production—that is, to effectively control the land, machinery, tools, etc., necessary to its operation.

3. A free market—that is, a market in which there are no arbitrary limitations on trading.

4. A predictable system of law—that is, a system in which the law will not be arbitrary, whimsical, or subject to change without notice.

5. A free labor force—that is, persons who are legally free but who must offer their labor for sale in the market in order to earn a living. In Weber's words, what is needed is "a class compelled to sell its labor services to live," but also a class that is not bound to slavery.

6. The commercialization of economic life—that is, the invention of stocks, which facilitate the purchase and sale of property, and of state bonds and certificates, which facilitate the creation of credit and of capital formation.

Although much has been made of the differences between capitalist and socialist economies, many features of industrial societies seem more or less universal. For example, such key elements of capitalism as double-entry bookkeeping and a money economy are also found in the Soviet Union, as are at least some degree of competition for skilled jobs and some variation in wages and salaries. And there is probably great similarity in the role expectations and skills displayed by Soviet, Chinese, and American managerial elites.

The Ideology of American Capitalism

Wilensky and Lebeaux have summed up the ideology of American capitalism as follows:[14]

1. The individual should strive to be successful in competition with others, under the rules of the game.

2. These rules involve "fair play": everyone should start with equal opportunity, and no one should take unfair advantage through force, fraud, or "pull."

3. The test of reward should be ability. There should be unequal rewards for unequal talents and unequal contributions.

4. Those who work hard and have ability will be rewarded with success. Success includes wealth, possessions, occupational prestige and power—along with the style of life these permit.

5. Success is a reflection of virtue. Failure (if it is not a temporary way station to success) is a sign of moral weakness.

6. When the lazy, incompetent, and unvirtuous attain success, it is purely a matter of luck; it could happen to anybody. Besides, it does not happen too often.

This focus on individualism in our economic system has its equivalents in other sectors of American life. In the political sector there are the inalienable rights of the individual and local autonomy in government. In the religious sector individuals must work for their own salvation. In

---

13. Weber, *General Economic History*, pp. 207–209.
14. Harold L. Wilensky and Charles N. Lebeaux, *Industrial Society and Social Welfare* (New York: The Free Press, 1965), pp. 34–35.

Our culture places a high value on productivity and success, and Americans are constantly reminded that it is "good" to have money and a job. People who earn little and those who are unemployed or retired feel not only a financial loss but also a loss of self-esteem; they are relegated to a low social position because of their economic situation.

the educational sector the focus is on achievement (high grades), on learning as a competitive enterprise.

Closely related to the emphasis on individualism in American capitalist ideology is the emphasis on private property and a free market.[15] Private property is almost a sacred value among Americans. Most of us strongly believe in the right of ownership and in the right to use our assets in a free market system—that is, one in which supply and demand determine value or price without interference from government or other agencies. The ideal of a free market continues to have strong support despite the fact that markets are often controlled, sometimes by the government (which may either restrict or subsidize corporate activities) and sometimes by corporations themselves (which may use various means to fix prices or restrain trade).

The ideology of American capitalism has made it possible to extol the entrepreneur for individual initiative and the system itself for the

benefits it has brought to many individuals. Although our system focuses on profits for the owners, it has been widely assumed that its benefits will flow out to workers and, indeed, to the country as a whole. As Howard J. Morgens, chairman of the board of Proctor and Gamble, puts it:

The American business system . . . is a competitive system. It is a free enterprise pricing system. It is an incentive system. It is more than all of these, of course, but the profit motive is the key to all of them. It is the mainspring of our economic structure and one of the greatest instruments of public service ever devised.[16]

As we have seen, the ideology does not accurately reflect the realities of economic life: individuals who work hard do not always achieve success, even if they have considerable ability; the market does not always operate freely; the distribution of profits is not always equitable. Yet despite all this, and despite growing challenges to the system, the ideology remains remarkably strong.

15. Ibid., pp. 37–38.
16. Howard J. Morgens, "The Profit Motive and the Public Interest," an address before the Advertising Council on the occasion of his receipt of the Council's Annual Award for Public Service, December 18, 1973.

INDUSTRIAL ORGANIZATION: MANAGEMENT

In recent years sociologists have focused increasingly on what goes on in corporations and other work-related organizations, and a large body of research and writing has accumulated under the general head of "formal organizations." We shall use the distinction between formal and informal organizations that was developed in Chapters 2 and 3 as the main theme in our brief account of people's behavior in modern work settings.

THE FORMAL BUREAUCRATIC STRUCTURE

Nothing could be more rational, in a Weberian sense, than the managerial structure of a corporation—at least on paper. In practice, however, executives and managers depart from their prescribed roles in many ways.

First, what are these prescribed roles? At the top of the managerial pyramid, or hierarchy, is the chief executive, the company president. Just below this command role is a second level consisting of *top managers*—vice-presidents in charge of such divisions and activities as sales, manufacturing, research and development, and so forth. Next come various levels of *middle management*. While policy is formulated at the first two levels, it is implemented at this broad middle level. Here are the assistant vice-presidents, chiefs of sales divisions, and plant managers. Finally, at the lowest level of management, are the *first-line* supervisors: foremen, crew leaders, office managers, etc. Occupants of these roles are in regular face-to-face contact with workers engaged in the actual process of production.

Policy Making

The president of a corporation is usually appointed and indirectly supervised by a board of directors. The central task of a president is coordination in the face of change.[17] To ensure the survival, prosperity, and growth of a business corporation, its chief executive is expected to lead the top managers in the collective formulation of policy. Thus the president works mainly with people, and skill at judging their motives and capabilities may be as important to the corporation's welfare as technical knowledge. Corporation presidents also play a key role in deciding which parts of the organization shall have what share of its resources and in providing solutions for problems their subordinates cannot handle—for instance, emergencies. In so doing, they may have to decide if an exception can be made to policies they themselves have formulated.[18]

Like corporation presidents, top managers also enjoy considerable autonomy, since they have full responsibility for planning, supervising, and coordinating activities for their divisions of the company. Even if the chief executive tells the top managers exactly what to do, they will probably not be told much about how it should be done.

Middle Management

The primary role responsibility of middle managers, who have their own bureaucratic hierarchy, is to implement the policy decisions they receive from above. They are normally not party to these decisions, nor are they in contact with workers to any significant extent. They make routine administrative decisions within the framework of established procedures, prepare reports of a mainly factual nature, and solve a lot of day-to-day problems that top managers do not have the time, the inclination, or the ability to deal with and that foremen are not charged with. The complexity of the middle management hierarchy—and it can become impenetrably complex—depends mainly on the size of the organization.

Line Supervision

The largest single managerial group is made up of foremen, straw bosses, supervisors, office managers, and inspectors. They are the last link

17. Burleigh B. Gardner and David G. Moore, *Human Relations in Industry*, rev. ed. (Homewood, Ill.: Richard D. Irwin, Inc., 1950), p. 62.
18. Delbert G. Miller and William H. Form, *Industrial Society*, 2nd ed. (New York: Harper & Row, Inc., 1964), p. 175.

in the hierarchy of administration—the final interpreters of executive orders. These orders, however, are spelled out to them by middle management in terms of their particular supervisory situation, not in terms of the general policy being implemented.

INFORMAL PATTERNS OF INTERACTION

Presumably the people in management have their places in the hierarchy, know their places, and perform their roles. Superiors direct subordinates, who carry out the instructions they receive. Equals cooperate for the good of all. But in fact, every managerial role has its characteristic problems, tensions, and frictions, some of which have been studied by sociologists.

At the Top

Corporation presidents work most closely with their own top managers. They adjudicate between competitive factions within the managerial group, hoping to maintain the loyalty and enthusiasm of each. They attempt to motivate greater commitment and encourage subordinates to greater effort. And they strive to keep in touch with what is going on at lower levels.

The leadership styles of chief executives vary considerably with the type of economic organization and the historical period. The personal, authoritative style of leadership we associate, for instance, with the "tycoon" or "captain of industry" seems to have given way to leadership by a managerial "team" that operates through consensus.[19] But this may be mainly a difference of manner. The fact that presidents establish policy by conferring with their top lieutenants rather than shouting out orders does not necessarily alter the realities of power.

The Power Struggle

Relationships at the vice-presidential level are in many ways competitive. Change introduced into the operations of one divison of the organization will inevitably have an impact on those of another. If such change makes a top manager's

task more difficult or appears to place that division at a disadvantage, it is likely to be covertly or overtly resisted. Miller and Form maintain that vice-presidents often withhold information from the chief executive:

Fear and distrust may grow as vice-presidents vie for power. Upward communications are likely to be highly filtered. A subordinate's future in an organization is often influenced appreciably by how well he senses and communicates to his boss information which fits the latter's orientation.[20]

Thus the responsibility of vice-presidents to make their divisions of the organization successful, plus their personal ambitions, may cause conflict among them and may lead to a struggle for power. Although these social realities are not consistent with the cherished ideal of smooth teamwork and harmonious relationships, they may benefit the organization—if the competition is kept within bounds.

An important key to understanding relationships between heads of various divisions within an economic organization is the distinction between *line* and *staff* segments of the overall structure. Line divisions are those responsible for producing the things or processing the cases that constitute the organization's product. In a household appliance manufacturing corporation, the refrigerators, washing machines, freezers, stoves, etc., assembled by workers would constitute the product and would be the responsibility of line divisions. Other divisions or departments more or less support or supplement the actual processes of production, and their services are often called staff functions. In principle, these groups serve the line divisions so that a better product can be produced efficiently and marketed in effective ways. In practice, because of limiting perspectives on both sides, relationships between such segments of the organization are sources of considerable conflict.[21] At the center of these conflicts are the vice-presidents in charge of the various divisions.

The kinds of conflicts that can be generated can be illustrated by the case of an actual firm that decided to develop and market a new model of refrigerator. The engineering department

19. Peter M. Blau, *Bureaucracy in Modern Society* (New York: Random House, Inc., 1956), p. 76.

20. Miller and Form, *Industrial Society*, p. 189.

21. Robert K. Merton, "The Machine, the Worker, and the Engineer," *Science*, 105 (January 24, 1947): 79–81.

The problems of the amorphous middle manager are in some ways linked to the differences between Max Weber's ideal bureaucracy and its counterpart in reality. Ideally, the roles in a bureaucratic structure call for specialized skills, and these roles make up a ranking system that is rational and efficient. Middle managers, however, often find that their specialized skills amount to little more than the ability to shuffle papers, attend meetings, write reports, and solve day-to-day crises. The middle manager may become disillusioned because the competent performance of the role seems unrelated to or at odds with the overall rationality and efficiency of the organization.

was asked to work out a design for a moderately priced machine. Market research was given the task of assessing consumer acceptance of the new model. Accounting was instructed to make a cost analysis so that the product could be produced at a competitive price. The sales division had to develop a suitable advertising campaign. The line division—manufacturing—was instructed to retool and add employees in readiness for producing the new refrigerator efficiently. But quarrels among the staff divisions over questions of cost and styling delayed actual production. Finally, when the first refrigerators began to come off the assembly line, the accounting division showed that the cost of production was still

too high for the company to realize the needed margin of profit, and the staff divisions had to repeat the entire process of working out a mutually acceptable design.

Relationships between the heads of divisions, then, are likely to be strained and difficult because of the pressure each is under to make a good showing. The effective accomplishment of the task of one almost invariably interferes with the activities and goals of another. For this reason, the interplay among top managers is potentially one of continuing strain and friction.

The Amorphous Middle

Relations between top management and middle management also involve problems. In large corporations, top managers communicate mainly with people in the upper levels of middle management. Top managers who attempt to find out what is going on at lower levels are likely to be given either a report from which much information has been screened out or, if they make a personal visit, a highly selective guided tour. In either case, middle managers are not going to volunteer information that might be damaging to them. Nor do they like to accept orders as such. One study found that downward communications from senior executives that were intended as "instructions or decisions" were almost invariably classified by subordinate managers as "information or advice"—i.e., as something they could take or leave alone.[22] One possible interpretation of this form of distortion by middle managers is that it represented a rejection of subordinate status and authority.

Nowadays most corporations recruit middle managers directly from college graduating classes. These recruits are fed into the bottom level of the middle-management hierarchy in somewhat larger numbers than the company will eventually need. The hope is that, after a year or two, the less able ones will be weeded out and the others will begin to move up the organizational ladder. One significant result of this system is that capable individuals without college degrees who, in an earlier generation, could have hoped to rise to the top are now barred from doing so.

22. Tom Burns, "The Direction of Activity and Communication in a Department Executive Group," *Human Relations*, 7, No. 1 (February 1954): 73–79.

INDUSTRIAL ORGANIZATION: LABOR

Sociological research into work groups began in 1927 when the management of the Western Electric works at Hawthorne, near Chicago, invited an Australian psychologist named Elton Mayo to come and study the effects of physical work conditions on workers' output.[23] At that time, unions had little or no legal protection, and union organizers were widely persecuted. Sociological research into unions, on the other hand, began in the very different political and social climate of the late 1940s and early 1950s. By that time unions were well established and were under political attack for allegedly misusing their power.

These two traditions of research, then, cannot be approached in precisely the same way, though efforts have been made to combine them. Both throw light on the situation of the ordinary worker but from rather different angles.

LABOR UNIONS

The rise of labor unions was a direct result of the working and living conditions created by the Industrial Revolution. In the United States about 12 percent of the labor force was organized by 1920, but by 1933 that figure had been cut in half.[24] Then union membership began a rapid rise. This could not have happened without federal recognition of the right to organize, as embodied in the National Industrial Recovery Act (1933) and the Wagner Act (1935). From 1936 on, membership soared, largely through the crusading tactics of the newly formed Committee for Industrial Organization, which broke with the parent American Federation of Labor to pursue a philosophy of industrial rather than craft unionism. By the mid-1950s fully 25 percent of

the labor force was unionized, and a third of all nonagricultural workers belonged to unions, including over 75 percent of the workers in transportation and about 50 percent of those in other major industrial areas.[25] In the early 1970s the unionized portion of the nonagricultural labor force comprised about 27 percent (see Table 18.1).

Table 18.1. UNION MEMBERSHIP AS A PROPORTION OF THE LABOR FORCE

Year	Total union membership	Percentage of total labor force	Percentage of nonagricultural labor force
1930	3,401,000	6.8	11.6
1931	3,310,000	6.5	12.4
1932	3,050,000	6.0	12.9
1933	2,689,000	5.2	11.3
1934	3,088,000	5.9	11.9
1935	3,584,000	6.7	13.2
1936	3,989,000	7.4	13.7
1937	7,001,000	12.9	22.6
1938	8,034,000	14.6	27.5
1939	8,763,000	15.8	28.6
1940	8,717,000	15.5	26.9
1941	10,201,000	17.7	27.9
1942	10,380,000	17.2	25.9
1943	13,213,000	20.5	31.1
1944	14,146,000	21.4	33.8
1945	14,322,000	21.9	35.5
1946	14,395,000	23.6	34.5
1947	14,787,000	23.9	33.7
1948	14,319,000	23.1	31.9
1949	14,282,000	22.7	32.6
1950	14,267,000	22.3	31.5
1951	15,946,000	24.5	33.3
1952	15,892,000	24.2	32.5
1953	16,948,000	25.5	33.7
1954	17,022,000	25.4	34.7
1955	16,802,000	24.7	33.2
1956	17,490,000	25.2	33.4
1957	17,369,000	24.9	32.8
1958	17,029,000	24.2	33.2
1959	17,117,000	24.1	32.1
1960	17,049,000	23.6	31.4
1961	16,303,000	22.3	30.2
1962	16,586,000	22.6	29.8
1963	16,524,000	22.2	29.1
1964	16,841,000	22.2	28.9
1965	17,299,000	22.4	28.4
1966	17,940,000	22.7	28.1
1967	18,367,000	22.7	27.9
1968	18,916,000	23.0	27.9
1969	19,036,000	22.6	27.1
1970	19,381,000	22.6	27.5
1971	19,211,000	22.1	27.2
1972	19,435,000	21.8	26.7

Membership figures and percentages include a relatively small number of trade union members in areas outside the United States. All figures are exclusive of Canada.
SOURCE: *Handbook of Labor Statistics,* 1974 (U.S. Department of Labor, Bureau of Labor Statistics), p. 366.

23. See especially Fritz J. Roethlisberger and William J. Dickson, *Management and the Worker* (Cambridge, Mass.: Harvard University Press, 1939), which describes the whole series of experiments initiated by Mayo. One of the Hawthorne studies is summarized on pages 544–545 of this chapter.
24. Arthur M. Schlesinger, Jr., *The Coming of the New Deal* (Boston: Houghton Mifflin Co., 1959), p. 385.
25. H. Gregg Lewis, "Labor Unions: Influence on Wages," *International Encyclopedia of the Social Sciences,* Vol. 8 (New York: Macmillan, Inc., 1968), p. 544.

In recent years the labor movement has failed to grow faster than the labor force, inspiring a great deal of soul-searching among union leaders. Among the reasons cited for the stagnation are alleged loss of idealism and energy among top leaders; federal legislation aimed at curbing labor's recruiting power, especially the Landrum-Griffin Act of 1959; the general change in the character of the American labor force since the 1930s from predominantly blue-collar to predominantly white-collar; and the shift of the economy from manufacturing to service industries.

The labor movement is now making efforts to recruit agricultural and white-collar workers. The retail clerks' union, for example, is one of the fastest growing in the country. And there are some unions of professionals. The American Federation of Teachers has enough strength to bring some local school systems to a halt, and there are strong unions of journalists, performers, airline pilots, and several other highly skilled occupations. But organized labor seems far indeed from recruiting a *majority* of white-collar workers, even in those areas where it has already had some success. Thus it remains a predominantly working-class movement.

Union Organization

In both formal and informal structure, American unions resemble other bureaucratic associations. But as economic organizations they have one differentiating characteristic: they are supposed to be run for the benefit of their members. As a result, the formal structure is always very democratic. Local unions send delegates to state and national conventions, and these delegates elect the executive officers of the national union. All major issues—whether to strike, whether to accept a particular contract, etc.—are decided by membership vote. In union meetings, members may speak on any topic they care to raise.

As a bureaucracy, a local union has a formal structure not unlike that of management. Policy is formulated by the president and the top managers who make up the executive board. Another key role in the union hierarchy is the potentially powerful one of the elected secretary-treasurer, a full-time paid position in many larger unions. In smaller unions the only full-time paid functionary is likely to be the business agent, who represents the union in all disputes concerning the administration of its wage contract. In national unions another full-time employee is the international representative (unions of national scope that include Canadian locals are often called "internationals"), who seeks to ensure that the parent group retains some control over the locals and who takes a leading role in negotiations with top management.

Much of the administration of union policy is handled by committees. Grievances, the formulation of aims, and negotiations with management over contract terms are often committee matters. Members are either appointed or elected, and the roles carry considerable responsibility.

Direct day-to-day contact with lower-level representatives of management is carried on primarily by the union stewards. These are usually elected representatives of workers in a given department of a plant. Union members who have grievances turn first to the steward. If the steward cannot handle the problem, it goes to the grievance committee or perhaps to the business agent. The steward also monitors the activities of the company to make certain that the terms of its contract with the union are not violated.

Union Democracy

In principle, the rank-and-file members of a union hold ultimate power over union policy. They can vote a leader into or out of office, accept or reject the decisions of officers, and otherwise control the union and determine its direction. In fact, however, most union members have come to be content with the gains their leadership wins for them and/or to feel that their collective voice can carry no real weight. Thus, there has been a gradual tendency in labor unions, as in other types of voluntary associations, for the officers to take more and more power into their own hands—a situation that may increase efficiency, but at the expense of democratic participation.[26]

26. William Spinrad, "Correlates of Trade Union Participation," *American Sociological Review*, 25 (1960): 237–244.

As the photograph of the 1919 steelworkers strike (top) indicates, the labor union movement began among blue-collar workers. Only recently has a determined effort been made to unionize agricultural and white-collar workers. The middle photograph shows a union meeting of civil service employees, one of several white-collar occupational groups that have recently formed unions. The bottom photograph shows a demonstration by Mexican Americans in support of the United Farm Workers, the union led by Cesar Chavez.

The difficulty of strengthening the bargaining power and efficiency of unions while also maintaining the tradition of union democracy has been illustrated in a study of union organization among oil workers over an extended period.[27] During the late 1930s, the continually poor state of this union's finances, at a time when other industrial unions were becoming stronger, led to a revolt of the union convention against the administrative officers. This revolt mainly took the form of an amendment to the union constitution, creating an executive council (the body that makes important policy decisions between conventions) consisting of rank-and-file workers to act as a watchdog over the union's elected leadership. This was a most unusual step, since the executive councils of all other large American unions are made up of the union's president and other chief officers.

The oil workers' "nonpolitical" executive council succeeded in reducing the power of the president, but it also created administrative chaos at union headquarters. Only after some of the president's powers had been restored and an international policy committee had been established to centralize collective bargaining policies and procedures did the union begin to make solid economic progress for its members.

It might seem that this progress was achieved at some cost to union democracy, especially since union elections virtually ceased to be contested. However, the study concludes that the problem was—and is—not one of a power-hungry central administration but of a politically apathetic membership at the local level, combined with a union convention that simply does not seem interested in the problems of international organization. Members of local unions who take an active interest in union affairs have a good chance of being chosen by their locals to serve on the executive council, which continues to fulfill its watchdog function. This is a sign that democracy in some sense continues to exist, though the union has not yet solved the problem of what *form* of democracy would best serve its interests.

HUMAN RELATIONS AND THE WORKER

Beginning in 1927, Elton Mayo's team of researchers at Western Electric initiated a whole tradition of research that compelled management to see workers as human beings with human needs and problems. This may not seem a very revolutionary concept today, but at that time all the emphasis was on the workers' physiology and the strictly physical aspects of the operations they had to perform in their jobs. Psychologically, workers were looked on as isolated individuals working for themselves. It was assumed that if they could be shown that working harder was in their own interest, they would automatically do so, provided the work was made physically easy for them. This approach, developed by the American engineer Frederick W. Taylor and his associates, was known as "scientific management" or "Taylorism."

Discovery of the Group

Management at Western Electric's Hawthorne works was trying to find out, by means of systematic experiments, whether such environmental factors as variations in the intensity of illumination could explain variations in workers' productivity and morale. The Mayo team was allowed to experiment with a small group of five experienced women workers, set apart from the rest in a special room so that their conditions of work could be systematically controlled and observed.

The operation selected was that of assembling telephone relays. This consists in "putting together a coil, armature, contact springs, and insulators in a fixture and securing the parts in position by means of four machine screws"; each assembly takes about one minute when the work is going well.[28]

After an initial period of observation to obtain base-line data, the experimenters systematically varied the conditions under which these women worked, retaining each condition for a period of several weeks or even months. The first variation was in method of payment; the women were paid on the basis of the number of relays the group put together. Production went

27. Melvin Rothbaum, *The Government of the Oil, Chemical and Atomic Workers Union* (New York: John Wiley & Sons, Inc., 1962).

28. Elton Mayo, *Human Problems of an Industrial Civilization* (New York: The Viking Press, Inc., 1966), p. 56; first published in 1933.

up. (The experimenters were pleased.) Next, two brief rest pauses were introduced, one in the morning and one in the afternoon. Again, productivity rose. (The experimenters were happy.) Then, refreshments were served during morning and afternoon breaks. Once more, production went up. (The experimenters were delighted.) Additional breaks were instituted; the group stopped working half an hour early, then a full hour early. Each of these variations seemed to produce increased hourly output. (The experimenters were ecstatic.)

However, certain grave doubts had begun to grow in the minds of members of the research staff. They decided to return to the somewhat more repressive conditions of an earlier experimental period to see if productivity would fall. When they did so, hourly output per worker rose to new heights! It seemed that there was little or no relationship between the experimental conditions they had been systematically introducing and the productivity of the group. Further checks indicated that this was indeed the case. There was an "unexpected and continual upward trend in productivity throughout the periods, even . . . when the girls were put on a full forty-eight hour week with no rest periods or lunch . . . ."[29]

In retrospect, it is easy to see what had happened. After working together for months, the women of the relay assembly room had come to know and like each other. They visited each other after working hours and regarded their little group as something special, apart from the common run of workers. Since they had come to believe in the importance of what they were doing, they were determined to do a good job even if rather unfavorable conditions were introduced.

From management's point of view, then, the whole experiment was a failure. Sociologists, however, perceived that what Mayo and his associates had produced was a demonstration of the importance of the primary group in a context where no one had thought to look for it. Individual workers were not social atoms in a lonely crowd of other social isolates. Even in an impersonal bureaucratic setting they were tied to other workers through bonds of friendship.

Overall, studies have shown that employees develop primary group ties within their work groups that make the daily task tolerable if not pleasurable. The informal codes and controls that emerge in work settings do much to modify relationships between worker and supervisor, as well as between workers themselves.[30]

The Human Relations Era

Mayo and his colleagues showed that the behavior of workers on the job could not be explained without reference to the values and structure of work groups and that there were circumstances in which money was not the workers' chief concern. Unfortunately, many sociologists and industrial relations managers jumped to the conclusion that money was never a prime motivating force and that the work group was the only group affecting workers' behavior. Word spread that all management's problems with its production-level employees could be solved by administering large doses of sympathy and understanding, and research by social psychologists unconnected with Mayo's school confirmed this trend by demonstrating that a "permissive" and "democratic" style of leadership was apparently more effective with small work groups than an "authoritarian" one. Foremen were sent to training courses (sardonically referred to by union leaders as "charm schools") in order to unlearn their authoritarian ways.

Some years later, William Foote Whyte reviewed the entire field of "human relations," as this approach had come to be called, and concluded that somehow money had to be brought back into the picture.[31] He also pointed out that

29. G. A. Pennock, "Industrial Research at Hawthorne; an Experimental Investigation of Rest, Working Conditions and Other Influences," *Personnel*, 8, No. 5 (February 1930): 304. For related research and commentary, see Roethlisberger and Dickson, *Management and the Worker*, Part 4; Henry A. Landsberger, *Hawthorne Revisited* (Ithaca, N.Y.: Cornell University Press, 1958); and George Homans, *The Human Group* (New York: Harcourt Brace Jovanovich, Inc., 1950), pp. 48–55.

30. See, for example, the discussion of Peter Blau's study of a state employment agency in Chapter 3 (pages 77–78).

31. William Foote Whyte, "Human Relations—A Progress Report," in *Complex Organizations: A Sociological Reader*, ed. Amitai Etzioni (New York: Holt, Rinehart and Winston, Inc., 1962), pp. 100–112.

even though informal group organization is undoubtedly important, not all groups have the same *kind* of informal organization. Finally, he suggested that if a company wanted the kind of informal organization that would motivate its employees to work hard, it should restructure its formal organization to allow for more delegation of authority. Meanwhile, other researchers had succeeded in discrediting the notion that high morale always involved high productivity. Some groups just enjoyed being lazy, it seemed, while others apparently could be scared into working hard.[32]

These and other criticisms have resulted in a redirection of human relations research. The very term "human relations" is scarcely used anymore. Instead, researchers have attempted to look beyond the primary work group to the whole organization. For example, it has been discovered that workers simply are not fooled by a permissive style of supervision if it is clearly at variance with the company's overall policy,[33] and that democratic first-line supervisors will not have much influence at the shop floor level unless they can make their opinions stick with management.[34]

THE WORKER IN INDUSTRIAL SOCIETY

Only industrial societies have what we ordinarily regard as occupations. Of course, people have always pursued various trades and callings, even in many so-called preliterate societies. But occupations are far more specialized roles and cannot be conceived of as existing apart from a modern type of labor market. In contrast with workers in preliterate, ancient, and medieval societies, modern workers are relatively free to change their occupations and to pursue them for financial gain. They are also increasingly likely to value a job for the income and life-style it makes possible rather than for the work itself.

The Industrial Revolution also gave birth to the concepts of employment and unemploy-

ment. Being employed, in the sense we use the word today, is not just keeping busy. It means actually taking part in the industrial economy as a producer or distributor. In the early eighteenth century, according to a careful inquiry made at that time, the average French peasant spent at least 164 days a year without work.[35] But this should not be labeled "unemployment"; there *was* no other work, and no one expected there to be any. The life of the peasant followed the rhythm of a technologically primitive agriculture. In an industrial economy, on the other hand, most occupations involve year-round work, and most people count on have a steady job. Indeed, in contemporary society, having a steady job seems to be the most important means by which many people acquire a sense of fulfillment.[36]

The governments of industrial societies are interested in measuring levels of employment and unemployment, however they may define these concepts. Nearly all of them have set up statistical agencies for this purpose. In addition, most have national censuses that record, among other facts, the number of people pursuing different occupations. In the United States detailed information on occupations is collected every ten years as part of the Census of Population. Measurement of employment and unemployment is carried out monthly in the Current Population Survey (see Tools of Sociology, page 547). By combining data from these two sources, it is possible to trace some of the important changes that have occurred in the composition of the American labor force. (See, for example, Table 8.5, page 231, showing the percentage of workers in major occupational groups.)

32. See especially Leonard R. Sayles, *Managerial Behavior: Administration in Complex Organizations* (New York: McGraw-Hill Book Company, 1964); Landsberger, *Hawthorne Revisited;* and Richard D. Mann, "A Review of the Relationships Between Personality and Performance in Small Groups," *Psychological Bulletin,* 56 (1959): 241–270.
33. Sayles, *Managerial Behavior.*
34. Donald C. Pelz, "Influence: A Key to Effective Leadership in the First-Line Supervisor," *Personnel,* 29, No. 3 (November 1952): 209–217.
35. The inquirer was the engineer Sabestien Le Prestre de Vauban, whose book was immediately banned.
36. See, for example, Robert Blauner, *Alienation and Freedom* (Chicago: The University of Chicago Press, 1964).

TOOLS OF SOCIOLOGY
MEASURING THE LABOR FORCE

As a result of programs evolved during the 1930s and 1940s, the government of the United States now derives most of its information on employment and unemployment from labor force statistics. These are obtained by the Bureau of Labor Statistics from the monthly Current Population Survey (a sample survey covering fifty thousand households, conducted by the Bureau of the Census).

Contrary to the impression many people have, labor force statistics do *not* divide everyone into the categories of "employed" and "unemployed." In the first place, only persons over fourteen years of age are interviewed and then only if they are living in households. This provision automatically excludes all juveniles, even those who may contribute regularly to the family income (e.g., the children of migrant farm workers); it also excludes members of the armed forces and inmates of hospitals, prisons, and other such institutions. Second, under the procedures used by the Bureau of Labor Statistics, individuals cannot be classed as employed or unemployed unless they *first* qualify for inclusion in the labor force. The minimum qualification for this is whether they looked for work during the previous week. If they did not, and if they did no paid work at all and/or were not just temporarily absent from their jobs, they are classified, not as unemployed, but *as not in the labor force.* On the other hand, even the smallest amount of part-time work during the previous week qualifies people for inclusion in the labor force as "employed."

Criticism of these procedures by labor economists and others, on the grounds that they systematically understate the amount of unemployment, has recently led to certain refinements. Since 1967 additional questions have been used in the survey in order to determine *why* those who are not in the labor force have failed to seek work; the unemployed are asked how they lost their last jobs; part-time employment is more carefully distinguished from full-time employment. But the basic labor force concept remains the same.

The detailed information on occupations collected every ten years as part of the general population census (see page 324) makes use of the following overall classifications:

Professional, technical, and kindred workers

Managers, officials, and proprietors, except farm

Clerical and kindred workers

Sales workers

Craftsmen, foremen, and kindred workers

Operatives and kindred workers

Laborers, except farm and mine

Private household workers

Service workers, except private household

Farmers and farm managers

Farm laborers and foremen

This schema has changed very little since it was first introduced in 1943 by Alba M. Edwards, then director of the Census. At that time, it was rightly considered a great improvement. New occupations are continually being created, however, and the need to fit all of them into the schema can sometimes produce classifications that appear rather peculiar. Why, for instance, should "dietitians and nutritionists" be classified as "professional, technical, and kindred workers," while "officers, pilots, pursers, and engineers, ship," are classified as "managers, officials, and proprietors, except farm"? Nevertheless, the schema has proved adequate for reflecting the major changes that have been taking place in the composition of the American labor force, and it has the advantage of making the censuses from 1950 through 1970 directly comparable with respect to occupational distribution.

For the latest procedures used in gathering information on employment and unemployment, see *Concepts and Methods Used in Manpower Statistics from the Current Population Survey* (Washington, D.C.: U.S. Department of Labor, Bureau of Labor Statistics, June 1967), BLS Report No. 313. The older procedures are described in *Measuring Employment and Unemployment,* President's Commission to Appraise Employment and Unemployment Statistics (Washington, D.C.: U.S. Government Printing Office, 1962). See also *Classified Index of Occupations and Industries* (Washington, D.C.: U.S. Department of Commerce, Bureau of the Census, 1960).

Although sociologists studying labor force participation find such data very useful, they are also concerned with many things statistics can not show—how a society defines and values work, for example, and what impact labor force participation has on individuals as they select their occupational roles, engage in work activity within the labor force, and suffer unemployment. It is to these issues that we now turn.

OCCUPATIONAL CHOICE AND OCCUPATIONAL MOBILITY

American values hold that a person's occupation is a matter of free and rational choice, limited only by natural ability. In fact, however, the choices people make are seldom wholly reasoned or free. Research shows that although youngsters know they will probably be expected to work when they grow up, most of them have only a dim understanding of occupational roles.[37] A child's earliest vocational aspirations are largely fantasies. By adolescence they may be more realistic, but in general the aspirations of young people far exceed what they will eventually achieve. Most of the young people who aspire to professional and managerial roles via higher education will never be college graduates but will find employment in the skilled labor force.[38]

Ignorance of job opportunities is another limiting factor. Most workers' first jobs are the only ones they know about at the time they take them. Moreover, this first step, often casually taken, can set the pattern for a lifetime of employment. Also largely accidental is the range of role models available to an individual; many youngsters enter an occupation in imitation of an older person whom they admire. Cultural and reference group values exert a similar influence. (See Chapter 14, pages 415–418.) Underlying all these factors are variables of class and status that restrict the range within which a free choice of occupation is even conceivable.

As noted in Chapter 8, "Social Stratification," a person's position in the social hierarchy limits not only choice of occupation but also opportunities for advancement. Job changing appears to be more common in the United States than elsewhere. In 1955, 1961, and 1970, three years for which census surveys are available, one in ten American workers changed jobs at least once. Other studies, using different methods, have discovered rates that are even higher. But most of this movement results in horizontal rather than vertical mobility.[39] Movement between jobs in the same major category (using the Bureau of the Census classification of major occupational groups) is far more frequent than vertical movement into the category immediately above. Vertical movement two categories above appears to be rare indeed. In addition, some categories, such as those of "clerical and kindred workers" and "operatives and kindred workers," seem to be especially hard to get out of. The offspring of "managers, officials, and proprietors," however, have a good chance of becoming professionals.[40]

Not many broad generalizations can be made with certainty in the area of intergenerational mobility, partly because of the ambiguity of the occupational categories used by the census and partly because the only way of analyzing occupational mobility through census statistics is to work in terms of age groups. But it appears that the chances of being upwardly mobile relative to one's parents are no better than fifty-fifty. A study made in 1962 that included data on individuals indicated that, in a sample of 20,700 American males, 41 percent of sons had been upwardly mobile relative to their fathers' occupations. Fewer sons were in farming than their fathers, and more sons than fathers were in white-collar occupations. The study also showed that more sons than fathers were in blue-collar occupations, largely as a result of the

37. Walter L. Slocum, *Occupational Careers: A Sociological Perspective* (Chicago: Aldine Publishing Co., 1966), pp. 186–225.

38. John C. Flanagan et al., *The American High School Student* (Pittsburgh: Project Talent Office, University of Pittsburgh, 1964).

39. See, for example, Robert M. Hauser and David L. Featherman, "White-Nonwhite Differentials in Occupational Mobility Among Men in the United States, 1962–1972," Working Paper 73-10, University of Wisconsin at Madison, March 1973.

40. See the comprehensive (but now somewhat outdated) study by Seymour M. Lipset and Reinhard Bendix, *Social Mobility in the Industrial Society* (Berkeley, Calif.: University of California Press, 1959). For more recent information see John Porter, "The Future of Upward Mobility," *American Sociological Review*, 33 (February 1968): 5–19, and Peter M. Blau and Otis D. Duncan, *The American Occupational Structure* (New York: John Wiley & Sons, Inc., 1967).

move away from farming.[41] An earlier study, made in 1957, showed that 42.2 percent of skilled manual workers had fathers who were also skilled manual workers and that much the same father-son relationship appeared among the professionals.[42]

There is some evidence that American workers begin their working lives with unrealistically optimistic expectations about how far they can advance themselves but that, as they grow older, they become resigned to their fate. One study of attitudes among workers in an automobile manufacturing plant found that the older workers tended to define "success" not as moving up in the occupational hierarchy but as acquiring newer and better material goods such as cars and washing machines. Less experienced workers, on the other hand, still had hopes of moving into a higher occupational category. The author of the study concluded that the older workers had come to terms with their lack of upward mobility by compensating for it as consumers. The younger ones still believed in the American Dream.[43]

WOMEN AND WORK

One of the most significant trends in the American economic institution over the past several decades has been the continuing increase in the number of women in the labor force. At the start of this century, only about 20 percent of American women of working age were employed outside the home. This figure rose very slowly, increasing only to about 25 percent over the next forty years. But during World War II, when more than 15 million men were in the armed forces, the need for additional workers drew many women out of their homes and into work roles. Since the mid-1940s, the proportion of women in the labor force has increased markedly, until today almost half of all women in the United

41. Lawrence E. Hazelrigg, "Cross-National Comparisons of Father-to-Son Occupational Mobility," in *Social Stratification: A Reader*, ed. Joseph Lopreato and Lionel S. Lewis (New York: Harper & Row, Inc., 1974), pp. 467–473.

42. Elton F. Jackson and Harry J. Crockett, Jr., "Occupational Mobility in the United States: A Point Estimate and Trend Comparison," *American Sociological Review*, 29 (1964): 7.

43. Ely Chinoy, "The Tradition of Opportunity and the Aspirations of Automobile Workers," *American Journal of Sociology*, 57 (1951–1952): 453–459.

Today nearly ten million women — or a third of all women working outside the home — hold clerical jobs. Some observers charge that clerical jobs constitute a "women's job ghetto," where pay is low and opportunities for advancement are nonexistent.

States between the ages of eighteen and sixty-four work outside the home on either a full-time or part-time basis. Studies show that women seek jobs for much the same reasons that men do: they need or want the income, and often they value the life experiences that their jobs provide.

The attention currently being given to the phenomenon of "working women" should not obscure the fact that most women have *always* worked, both in the United States and in other societies. But most of the jobs women have traditionally performed have been in the home and without pay. These jobs have gradually been devalued in industrial societies, where feelings of worth and accomplishment have become increasingly linked to occupational success in the labor market. When the United States was primarily an agricultural society, few women felt that it was demeaning to be "just a housewife"; husband, wife, and children worked together as an economic unit. But societal life has drastically changed, and today more and more women are seeking both employment at every level and equal pay for equal work.

But despite the growing representation of women in the labor force, and despite recent efforts to end discriminatory employment practices, structured inequality continues to limit job opportunities for women as it does for other minorities. By and large, recognition has been on a token basis — one woman made a corporate vice-president, one woman appointed to a well-publicized government post, one woman allowed to become a commercial airline pilot or a jockey. Such success stories tend to obscure the fact that women usually are still second-class citizens when it comes to jobs. Of nearly thirty million women currently in the labor force, almost a third are employed in clerical jobs, where the pay is generally poor and the work (typing, filing, answering the telephone) allows little room for personal initiative or for job mobility.[44] Even those women who are singled out as "successful" are more often than not the victims of discrimination. As one well-informed observer has noted:

Women at the top are at the bottom of the top, just as they are at the bottom of any stratum in which they happen to be represented. The occupational spread of women is bottom-heavy. As service workers, women cluster in the lowest paying domestic jobs, ranking lower even than porters and janitors (male jobs); as clerical workers, they hold the lowest ranking jobs as file clerks and typists; in the school system, the women teach and the men administrate. Women lawyers still seem to be found primarily in the specialties considered low ranking, such as matrimonial and real estate work; women doctors cluster in the lower-ranking areas of public health and psychiatry. In the university, women are most often found in the ranks of lecturer and assistant professor, and fade into statistical obscurity as one goes to the top.[45]

The average income of women who work on a full-time, year-round basis is still about 40 percent less than that of men despite new federal laws requiring equal pay for equal work (Figure 18.1). This statistic is somewhat misleading, however, since it is difficult to make comparisons of earnings in which all factors but sex are controlled. Some of the differential between men's

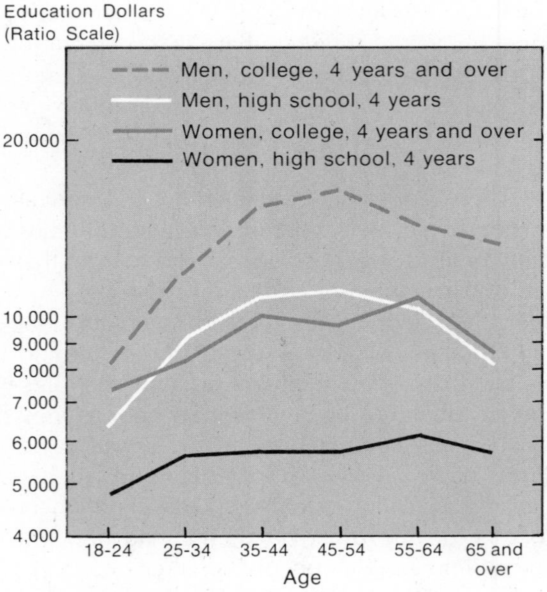

SOURCE: *Economic Report of the President*, U.S. Government Printing Office. January 1973. p. 105.

Figure 18.1. ANNUAL INCOME OF FULL-TIME WORKERS BY AGE, SEX, AND EDUCATION

and women's average earnings must be attributed, for example, to the factor of continuous versus interrupted employment. Whereas about 95 percent of males remain in the labor force continuously from the time they leave school until they retire (except for involuntary unemployment), most women do not follow this pattern. Rather, they enter and leave the labor force, by necessity or choice, at various points in their life cycle. This obviously reduces their earning potential. However, studies show that women, on the average, earn about 20 percent less than men even when their training and work experience is roughly comparable.

Earnings differentials for men and women are partly a matter of subtle sex-role discrimina-

44. *Work in America*, Report of a Special Task Force to the Secretary of Health, Education, and Welfare (Cambridge, Mass.: The M.I.T. Press, 1973), pp. 57–58.

45. Cynthia Fuchs Epstein, "Bringing Women In," in *Women and Success*, ed. Ruth B. Kundsin (New York: William Morrow & Co., Inc., 1974), p. 14. See also Donald J. Treiman and Kermit Terrell, "Sex and the Process of Status Attainment: A Comparison of Working Women and Men," *American Sociological Review*, 40 (April 1975): 174–200.

tions that have resulted in *generally* lower incomes for women. As an *Economic Report of the President* noted:

There is clearly prejudice against women engaging in particular activities. Some patients reject women doctors, some clients reject women lawyers, some customers reject women in sales, and some workers reject women bosses. Employers may also have formulated discriminatory attitudes about women, exaggerating the risk of job instability or client acceptance and therefore excluding women from on-the-job training that could advance their careers.[46]

Today the occupational roles of men and women appear to be moving in the direction of increasing similarity, not only with respect to job opportunities and earning potential but also with respect to the importance attached to work itself. While women have been increasing their involvement with work outside the home, men have gradually been reducing the proportion of their lives spent at a job.[47] They now spend more years in school than they once did, enter the labor force later, work fewer hours per week, have more and longer vacations, and retire earlier. Whether the changing occupational patterns for the two sexes will be accompanied by changes in other aspects of their adult roles (such as allocation of responsibility for child care and homemaking) remains an open question.

WORKER DISSATISFACTION

The question of satisfaction with work and of worker discontent and alienation has been the subject of national polls, government studies, articles in news magazines, and national symposia with participants from business, labor, government, special service organizations, and education.[48] In this section we will discuss Marx's theory of alienation and consider the question of how widespread alienation and discontent are among workers in the United States.

46. *Economic Report of the President* (Washington, D.C.: U.S. Government Printing Office, 1973), p. 106.
47. Ibid., p. 92.
48. See, for example, "The Changing World of Work," Report of the Forty-Third American Assembly, November 1–4, 1973, Arden House, Harriman, New York; and *Work in America.*

Marx's Theory of Alienation

In Chapter 1 we introduced some of the major theories that have guided the direction sociology has taken during the past century. All the major theorists were concerned about the effects of the changing nature of work upon people. Durkheim predicted that a significant increase in anomie or normlessness would result from the increasingly complex division of labor in society; Weber foresaw the dangers of dehumanization rising out of the structures of bureaucratic organization; and Marx maintained that the industrial work situation effectively alienated workers—that is, prevented them from fulfilling themselves in their work situation (see pages 214–216). While research has continued on the theories of all three men, we will here confine ourselves to Marx's theory.

Marx maintained that during the preindustrial period people controlled their work, but that after factories were established, work controlled them. Under the factory system, Marx emphasized, workers did not share in the ownership of the means of production or in the profits from their labor. They suffered misery and poverty at the hands of their employers and could be "locked out" of their means of livelihood. Furthermore, factories increased the division of labor and reduced the level of responsibility and skill required from each worker. These developments, he argued, had two main results for workers: jobs became increasingly *meaningless* to them, and they became more *powerless*. Jobs were meaningless because individual workers were simply links—and mechanical links, at that—in a process they did not need to grasp as a whole. Workers were powerless not only because they could not prevent the profits of their labor from going to the factory owners but because, under the procedures of mass production, they could not even regulate the pace of their own work.

Marx termed the worker's situation "alienation." Workers were alienated from the act of production, from other people in the production process, and even from themselves. For Marx, *alienation* was an abstract philosophical concept, denoting far more than just the worker's feelings of dissatisfaction. Indeed, workers might not even be aware of their own plight.

TOOLS OF SOCIOLOGY
MEASURING ALIENATION IN WORK   William Flanagan

The concept *alienation,* particularly as it relates to work, finds its earliest and most systematic development in the works of Karl Marx (see page 551). Marx described alienation and its social effects, but he did not attempt to validate its existence through the scientific method. Robert Blauner's study of alienation among American factory workers is a classic attempt to scientifically prove and measure the existence of alienation.

Blauner focused on four types of industries: the printing (craft), textile (machine-tending), automobile (automated production line), and chemical (continuous process) industries. He used the comparative approach (page 101) to determine whether different kinds and levels of alienation were produced in different industries. Since the study required a large number of industrial workers, he used the survey technique (page 195), interviewing factory workers selected by a controlled sampling technique (page 365).

Blauner used four dimensions in defining alienation:

1. *Powerlessness:* being controlled by persons or impersonal systems, such as technology; feeling an inability to assert oneself.

2. *Meaninglessness:* being unable to see how one's task contributes to the production process due to the size and complexity of the process and the fragmentation of individual roles through the division of labor.

3. *Social alienation:* being or feeling isolated from other workers; not feeling a sense of place in a work role and in the industrial community.

4. *Self-estrangement:* being detached from rather than engrossed in the work task; being unable to gain identity or acquire a positive self-definition from the role. (This dimension comes closest to Marx's definition of *alienation.*)

In order to measure these dimensions, workers were asked such questions as: *Powerlessness*—Does your job make you work too fast? Does it let you try out your own ideas? *Meaninglessness*—What product do you make? What is it used for? Where does your job fit in? *Social alienation*—For a person in your trade or occupation do you think your company is about as good a place as there is to work? Is your job really essential to the success of the company? *Self-estrangement*—Can you do the work on the job and keep your mind on other things most of the time? Is your job too simple to bring out your best abilities?

This study determined that not all blue-collar workers were alienated. Blauner found that alienation is related to the amount of technology, the division of labor (how much each task was broken down), the social organization (whether work groups existed), and the economic well-being of the industry. Generally, alienation was lower when the level of skill required was high, but in a highly automated plant—where little skill was required—alienation was low because workers felt responsible for the costly equipment they used. Alienation was highest in the automobile industry, while workers in printing, chemical, and textile plants experienced less alienation and greater work satisfaction. Even among auto workers, however, only a minority could be characterized on the basis of this study as alienated.

Blauner's study has been criticized because he did not design the questionnaire or conduct the interviews himself but instead used an old questionnaire prepared by a different researcher and had assistants do most of the interviewing. But the study was successful in achieving its goal. Blauner established empirically that certain kinds of industrial work produce feelings of alienation and that the kind of work—rather than the fact that it is factory work—is the alienating agent.

Robert Blauner, *Alienation and Freedom: The Factory Worker and His Industry* (Chicago: The University of Chicago Press, 1964). Blauner's study is discussed in Joachim Israel, *Alienation: From Marx to Modern Sociology* (Boston: Allyn & Bacon, Inc., 1971). See also Melvin Seeman, "On the Meaning of Alienation," *American Sociological Review,* 24 (1959): 783–791.

Worker Dissatisfaction in American Society

Although worker alienation, as Marx defined it, does not appear to be widespread in the United States (see Tools of Sociology, page 552), there is ample evidence that high levels of worker dissatisfaction exist in some industries. Both popular writers and social scientists have discussed the "blue-collar blues." In the automobile industry younger workers, who make up about a third of the work force in major plants, are having particular difficulty adjusting to the assembly line. They tend to be better educated than workers over thirty and to have higher aspirations and expectations. They are restless, demanding, changeable, and mobile. Often they dislike their jobs intensely, perform them poorly, are absent from work repeatedly, and change jobs frequently.[49]

In the past several years, national studies have reported that there is significant discontent and disaffection among workers.[50] As Tables 18.2 and 18.3 indicate, while professional people seem generally pleased with their jobs, white-collar workers are less so. Among blue-collar workers only skilled printers registered a majority who would choose similar work again.

49. Judson Gooding, "Blue-Collar Blues on the Assembly Line," Fortune, 82 (July 1970): 69–71.
50. "The Changing World of Work," p. 4; and Work in America, pp. xv–xvi.

Table 18.2. PERCENTAGES IN OCCUPATIONAL GROUPS WHO WOULD CHOOSE SIMILAR WORK AGAIN

Professional and lower white-collar occupations	Percent	Working-class occupations	Percent
Urban university professors	93	Skilled printers	52
Mathematicians	91	Paper workers	42
Physicists	89	Skilled autoworkers	41
Biologists	89	Skilled steelworkers	41
Chemists	86	Textile workers	31
Firm lawyers	85	**Blue-collar workers, cross section**	**24**
Lawyers	83	Unskilled steelworkers	21
Journalists (Washington correspondents)	82	Unskilled autoworkers	16
Church university professors	77		
Solo lawyers	75		
White-collar workers, cross section	**43**		

SOURCE: *Work in America,* Report of a Special Task Force to the Secretary of Health, Education, and Welfare (Cambridge, Mass.: The M.I.T. Press, 1973), p. 16.

Table 18.3. PROPORTION OF FACTORY WORKERS DESIRING DIFFERENT OCCUPATIONS, BY INDUSTRY

Industry	Percent			Number of Respondents
	Yes	No	Don't know and depends	
Leather	71	20	9	129
Sawmills and planing	71	24	6	68
Oil refining	71	27	2	51
Automobiles	69	23	8	180
Iron and steel	65	25	10	407
Machinery	65	29	6	293
Furniture	64	29	7	259
Apparel	63	35	2	265
Chemicals	58	29	13	78
Non-ferrous metals	55	36	9	88
Textiles	54	37	9	409
Food	51	34	15	296
Stone, clay, and glass	48	25	27	108
Transportation equipment	48	48	3	93
Paper	37	49	14	102
Printing	36	50	13	107
All factory workers	**59**	**32**	**9**	**2933**

Note: Workers were asked: "If you could go back to the age of 15 and start life over again, would you choose a different trade or occupation?"
SOURCE: Robert Blauner, *Alienation and Freedom: The Factory Worker and His Industry* (Chicago: The University of Chicago Press, 1964), p. 202.

Surveys have indicated that many Americans are dissatisfied with their jobs, finding them dull and pointless. Only 24 percent of blue-collar workers would choose the same job again, though the percentage for certain blue-collar workers, such as printers (above), is considerably higher. Professional people by and large appear satisfied with their jobs, but about a third of business people think they have chosen the wrong career. Job dissatisfaction seems to be related to societal affluence, and though many workers want their jobs to be interesting and meaningful, few would choose unemployment over even the dullest job.

The findings on auto and steel workers are consistent with the attitudes reported in national studies and news articles on work in contemporary society.[51]

Although professional people are in general most satisfied with their jobs, even those at the top report some dissatisfaction. In 1973 a survey of nearly three thousand American businessmen found that half had changed or had considered changing their occupations in the five years preceding the study. About a third believed that they would achieve more satisfaction from a different career. A third also reported that their jobs had adversely affected their health in the preceding five years. More than half reported that their jobs made it necessary for them to compromise their personal principles at least once. This survey also found that top managers were least dissatisfied with their jobs, while nearly 40 percent of middle managers and 52 percent of supervisors found their work unsatisfying.[52]

It appears that worker discontent is related to a general change in the attitudes of Americans:

Dull, repetitive, seemingly meaningless tasks, offering little challenge or autonomy, are causing discontent among workers at all occupational levels. This is not so much because work has greatly changed; indeed, one of the main problems is that work has not changed fast enough to keep up with the rapid and wide scale changes in worker attitudes, aspirations, and values. A general increase in their educational and economic status has placed many American workers in a position where having an interesting job is now as important as having a job that pays well.[53]

Meeting the Problem

Must work in modern factories and corporations cause workers and management to feel that they are powerless, their tasks menial or trivial, and their jobs generally meaningless? Blauner's classic study of alienation (page 552) indicates that job satisfaction is possible, even in highly automated industries. It has been suggested that worker discontent would decrease if jobs — both in factories and in corporations — were redesigned in order to involve all workers in the entire production process.[54]

Plants in Norway, Sweden, France, Australia, and New Zealand that have experimented with job and plant redesign have reported some increase in worker satisfaction.[55] In the United States the General Foods Corporation began experimenting with job and plant redesign in 1968, resulting in the opening of an experimental plant in 1970. Richard Walton has studied this plant, and the following report is based on his study.[56]

A key feature of the General Foods experiment was the creation of autonomous work groups composed of a leader and seven to fourteen members. Each work group was responsible for a large part of the production process, and individual tasks were assigned to group members by a vote of the group. Work groups could reassign tasks to members, select new employees to replace departing members, and counsel members who were not living up to the standards set by the group. The work groups were designed to be large enough to accomplish the production tasks, but small enough to allow for interaction in decision making and coordination.

The jobs in the General Foods plant were designed so that all of them combined both challenging and nonchallenging tasks. For example, group members were expected to care for and conduct regular quality tests on their equipment as well as to share housekeeping tasks. Workers were encouraged to learn the features of all jobs within their work group and then within the entire plant. The more they learned, the higher their salary would be. Since no limit was set on the number of jobs a single worker could learn, and since workers were re-

51. See, for example, "The Job Blahs: Who Wants to Work?" *Newsweek*, March 26, 1973, pp. 79 ff.

52. Dale Tarnowieski, "The Changing Success Ethic: An AMA Survey Report" (New York: AMACOM, a Division of the American Management Association, 1973). The summary findings are taken from pp. 1 and 2.

53. *Work in America*, pp. xv–xvi.

54. Richard E. Walton, "Alienation and Innovation in the Workplace," in *Work and Quality of Life: Resource Papers for Work in America*, ed. James O'Toole (Cambridge, Mass.: The M.I.T. Press, 1974).

55. See, for example, Jan-Peter Norstedt, *Work Organization and Job Design at Saab-Scandia in Sodertalije* (Stockholm: Swedish Employers' Confederation, Technical Department, December 1970).

56. Walton, "Alienation and Innovation," pp. 232–241.

warded for learning, a cooperative work situation evolved, with workers teaching other workers.

The management of the plant did not impose rules on the workers. Instead, the plant community was given self-government, and rules evolved from the experiences of the workers.

According to Walton, during the first two years of operation the plant experienced some problems. A minority of workers was unable to live up to the expectations of the work groups, and occasionally excessive group pressure was exerted to bring about conformity to group norms. Some workers (who were used to taking orders) had difficulty gaining a fair hearing from supervisors (who were used to giving orders). But Walton concluded that the experiment had been successful from the perspective of both management and workers. He reported that "the workers' seriousness, competence and self-confidence usually have earned them respect," that the high initial investment in the plant had been earned back, and that profits for the plant were high. The workers reported themselves very satisfied with the job redesign, commenting: "I never get bored." "I can make my own decisions." "People will help you; even the operations manager will pitch in to help you clean up a mess—he doesn't act like he is better than you are."[57]

57. Ibid, p. 238.
58. *Time*, March 17, 1975, p. 21.

It would appear, then, that dissatisfaction and alienation are not automatic by-products of an industrial economy. When jobs can be made challenging, worker dissatisfaction decreases. So far, however, few American industries have experimented with job redesign.

THE IMPACT OF UNEMPLOYMENT

Despite the high level of worker dissatisfaction, most American workers would agree that it is better to have a job than not to have one. Especially during times of increasing unemployment, any job seems better than none, and rather than hold out for jobs that utilize their abilities to the fullest, people will hide talents they feel are not needed. For example, in 1975, during the economic recession, a microbiologist who had lost her job was reported as saying: "Nobody is going to hire a microbiologist to drive a bus. But I'm prepared to handle that. On job application forms, I can put down that I'm only a high-school graduate. This is called the sin of omission. Everybody does it."[58]

Who are the unemployed? Unemployment is most prevalent among nonwhites, teen-agers, and women (Table 18.4). Blue-collar workers are more likely to lose their jobs than white-collar workers, and within the white-collar occupations, sales and clerical workers have higher rates of unemployment than professionals and managers (Table 18.5). And, as Table 18.6 indicates, a recession tends to intensify these trends rather than to change their direction.

Table 18.4. UNEMPLOYMENT RATES BY RACE, SEX, AND AGE, 1950–1973 (ANNUAL AVERAGES)

| | Males | | | | | | Females | | | | | |
| | White | | | Nonwhite | | | White | | | Nonwhite | | |
Age	1950	1960	1973	1950	1960	1973	1950	1960	1973	1950	1960	1973
Total	4.7	4.8	3.7	9.4	10.7	7.6	5.3	5.3	5.3	8.4	9.4	10.5
16–17	13.4	14.6	15.1	12.1	22.7	34.4	13.8	14.5	15.7	17.6	25.7	36.5
18–19	11.7	13.5	10.0	17.7	25.1	22.1	9.4	11.5	10.9	14.1	24.5	33.3
20–24	7.7	8.3	6.5	12.6	13.1	12.6	6.1	7.2	7.0	13.0	15.3	17.6
25–34	3.9	4.1	3.0	10.0	10.7	5.8	5.2	5.7	5.1	9.1	9.1	9.7
35–44	3.2	3.3	1.8	7.9	8.2	4.0	4.0	4.2	3.7	6.6	8.6	5.3
45–54	3.7	3.0	2.0	7.4	8.5	3.2	4.3	4.0	3.1	5.9	5.7	3.7
55–64	4.7	4.1	2.4	8.0	9.5	3.1	4.3	3.3	2.8	4.8	4.3	3.2
65 and over	4.6	4.0	2.9	7.0	6.3	3.6	3.1	2.8	2.8	5.7	4.1	3.9

SOURCE: U.S. Department of Labor, *Manpower Report of the President*, April 1974, pp. 273–274.

The economic effects of unemployment are felt both by those who have lost their jobs and by those still working. People who lose their jobs must rely on their savings, if they have any, or on unemployment insurance benefits or welfare payments if they are eligible to receive them. A high level of unemployment—as during an economic recession—results in reduced industrial productivity, and the financial burdens of the government are passed on to the employed through higher taxes. Wages are depressed—or at least do not increase quickly—when surplus workers are available. During the recession of the mid-1970s many workers accepted reductions in pay and reduced hours so that their jobs would not be eliminated.

As we have seen, occupational activity defines one's place in society and one's worth within the social structure. The fact of having a job and performing it in a satisfactory manner is essential to an individual's self-image. People who work and who can support themselves and their families see themselves differently than those who cannot find work. As we saw in Chapter 8 (pages 223–226), the unemployed are defined as moral failures, and this sense of failure is reflected in the feelings of depression and guilt that are typical of people who have lost their jobs. The economic impact of unemployment is generally hardest on those at the lower end of the social scale, who generally have less money put away for hard times. But the highly ranked, well-paid white-collar worker may feel the emotional impact of unemployment more strongly.

When enough people lose their jobs in a society geared to high levels of production and consumption, unemployment becomes a threat to the structure of society itself. Traditional values, beliefs, and norms are called into question; solutions are debated; and, most certain of all, there is increasing call for the federal government to use its power to help restore the health of the economy.

Table 18.6. UNEMPLOYMENT AND ECONOMIC RECESSION

Category	Percentage unemployed in February 1975
Black teen-agers	36.7
Teen-agers	19.9
Construction workers	15.9
Nonwhites	13.5
Blue-collar workers	10.9
Vietnam veterans	8.8
Women	8.1
Whites	7.4
Men	6.2
Household heads	5.4
White-collar workers	4.5

SOURCE: Data from *Time*, March 17, 1975, p. 22; and *Newsweek*, March 17, 1975. Ranked from highest to lowest percentage of unemployment.

Table 18.5. UNEMPLOYMENT RATES OF PERSONS 16 YEARS AND OVER BY OCCUPATION GROUP, 1963–1973

	White Collar				Blue Collar		
	Professional	Mgrs.	Sales	Clerical	Craftsmen	Operatives	Nonfarm laborers
1963	1.8	1.5	4.3	4.0	4.8	7.5	12.4
1968	1.2	1.0	2.8	3.0	2.4	4.5	7.2
1973	2.2	1.4	3.7	4.2	3.7	5.7	8.4

SOURCE: U.S. Department of Labor, *Manpower Report of the President*, April 1974, p. 275.

SUMMARY

The historical approach to the study of industrial society traces the growth of the factory system and the beginnings of modern industrialism—developments found to depend on the existence of free labor, investment capital, and machinery driven by a power source more versatile than water. Among the most important accompaniments of the factory system were the rise of the corporation and the concentration of economic power in a relatively few hands.

The modern industrial corporation is a special type of formal bureaucratic organization. On the management side, the supposed rationality of corporate organization—with its division of functions between top management, middle management, and line supervision—is impaired by power struggles, staff-line conflict, and a lack of effective direction and communication at the middle levels. And this lack is compounded by typical corporation recruitment and promotion policies. A particularly unsatisfactory position is that of the first-line supervisor, who is torn between management and labor.

The American labor union movement had its most rapid period of growth during the late 1930s; in recent years it has grown more slowly than the labor force. Today efforts are being made to recruit agricultural and white-collar workers.

The sociological study of labor dates from the classic studies of industrial work groups by Mayo. The principal lesson of these studies was that the informal organization of the work group itself and the satisfaction derived from group membership had more influence on the workers' behavior than individualistic incentives such as money. This discovery initiated a new era in industrial relations. Some of the excesses of the human relations era are now being corrected.

The analysis of labor force and occupational statistics in the United States depends on the technical definitions and procedures of the Bureau of the Census and the Bureau of Labor Statistics. Underlying both is the more general notion of occupation, a form of work role that did not exist before the rise of industrial society. Choice of occupation is for most Americans a rather haphazard procedure, and most young people achieve less than they think they will. Occupational mobility in American society is more often horizontal than vertical.

Growing numbers of American women are joining the labor force, sometimes out of financial need and sometimes in an effort to build more satisfying lives. Despite laws designed to provide equal wages and equal opportunity for women, most women are concentrated in lower-status and lower-paying occupations.

Studies have found high levels of worker dissatisfaction in the United States, especially among blue-collar workers. This, however, should not be mistaken for dissatisfaction with work as a means to an end, since people, given a choice between work and leisure, usually choose work.

Unemployment is highest among blacks, women, young people, and blue-collar workers in the United States. Recessions and depressions intensify these trends while at the same time affecting all other sectors of the labor force. High levels of unemployment can pose a serious threat to the strength and stability of an industrial society.

19
Education and Social Welfare

CHANGE AND CONFLICT IN AMERICAN EDUCATION

Changing Goals of American Education   Sources of Conflict in Education

EDUCATION AND SOCIAL STRATIFICATION

The Advantages of Education   Variations in Educational Opportunity   Unraveling Cause and Effect

SOCIAL WELFARE

Origins of American Orientations Toward Welfare
The Establishment of a National Welfare System   Outlooks for Further Change

This final chapter on social institutions reviews two large and complex formal systems in contemporary society. In one way or another these institutions touch the lives of every citizen. Although our public schools and our national system of social welfare may at first glance seem relatively unrelated, they are in fact the two principal means our society has used to improve the life conditions of its citizens.

Viewed sociologically, public education and social welfare systems are techniques of social intervention in the positivistic traditions of Auguste Comte (page 6) and Lester Ward (page 17). Both represent attempts to achieve what the nineteenth-century sociologists called "progress" and what earlier writers referred to as "social justice." While both the educational and social welfare systems operate in less than perfect ways, they still represent a significant collective effort to improve the lives of large numbers of people.

In this chapter we will trace the development of education in the United States and review the ways that education has influenced the life chances of millions of people in our society. We will then discuss changing American orientations toward social welfare and review the development of a national welfare system in the United States.

CHANGE AND CONFLICT IN AMERICAN EDUCATION

In traditional societies people can acquire the knowledge and skills necessary for the successful performance of adult roles without formal schools. But in complex societies—particularly urban-industrial ones—parents may be unable to pass on to their children the knowledge and skills they will need as adults. As a society becomes more industrialized, there is an ever-increasing demand for general skills—reading, writing, and arithmetic—and for specialized vocational and technical training for specific occupational roles.

There is considerable disagreement over how well the American school system prepares young people for the roles they will later assume. It is clear that the United States offers a tremendous range of educational opportunity, and that this opportunity has been extended to a growing proportion of its citizens. In 1870 about 57 percent of Americans aged five to seventeen were enrolled in school; by 1970 the proportion had increased to nearly 87 percent (see Table 19.1). During the same period the number of people who had received bachelor's degrees increased from about nine thousand to more than eight hundred thousand. But it is also clear that the American school system has not equally benefited all categories of people in our society—as demonstrated by the fact, for example, that illiteracy is higher among nonwhites than among whites (see Figure 19.1). This failure of the educational institution has become an important source of social conflict.

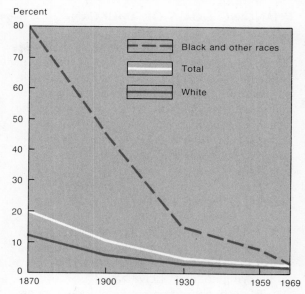

SOURCE: U.S. Department of Commerce. Bureau of the Census. *Current Population Reports*, Series P-20. No. 217. Data for 1870 to 1930 are for the population ten years and over; data for 1959 and 1969 are for the population fourteen years and over. Data for black and other races for 1969 are for blacks only.

Figure 19.1. PERCENT OF ILLITERACY IN THE POPULATION, BY RACE, 1870–1969

Table 19.1 THE GROWTH OF EDUCATION IN THE UNITED STATES, 1869–1970

	1869–1870	1889–1890	1909–1910	1929–1930	1949–1950	1969–1970
Population aged 5–17 years, inclusive	12,055,000	18,543,000	24,009,000	31,417,000	30,168,000	52,490,000
Percent of population aged 5–17 enrolled in elementary and high schools	57.0%	68.6%	74.2%	81.7%	83.2%	86.9%
Percent of enrolled pupils attending daily	59.3%	64.1%	72.1%	82.8%	88.7%	90.4%
Number of high-school graduates		22,000	111,000	592,000	1,063,000	2,589,000
Number of colleges	563	998	951	1,049	1,851	2,528
Number of bachelor's and first professional degrees conferred	9,371	15,539	37,199	122,484	432,058	827,234

SOURCES: Bureau of the Census; U.S. Department of Health, Education and Welfare, *Statistics of State School Systems; Biennial Survey of Education in the United States; Earned Degrees Conferred.*

CHANGING GOALS OF AMERICAN EDUCATION

Over the years, America's schools have replaced old goals with new ones. Changes in educational philosophy and practices have taken place primarily in response to changing social conditions. The following discussion of the history of American education can be reduced, at the risk of some oversimplification, to an account of how one goal gave way to another in successive periods.[1]

Training Elites

The first elementary schools in the United States taught children how to read, write, and do arithmetic. Many parents sent their children to school in fear that otherwise the youngsters might grow up knowing nothing of civilization.

The concept of free public schools supported by taxes with required attendance by all children developed slowly in the United States. Education under colonial rule was compulsory only in the sense that some of the colonies required their towns to provide elementary schools and teachers. It was not until 1834 that a state (Massachusetts) required all of its towns to provide free public schools for all children. Except in New England, education was not free during the early period. By and large, the property-owning class considered free public education a form of welfarism with potentially dangerous consequences.

Interest in education beyond the primary level first developed in the towns and cities of the Northeast. The earliest secondary schools were private institutions that concentrated on subjects useful to the small minority headed for college. At the time of the Revolutionary War there were nine colleges in the colonies. After independence, a number of new colleges were founded, and by 1799 the United States had twenty-five institutions of higher learning, including two state universities. But at this time the function of higher education in America was still similar to that of England—training the elites of the society.

Spreading Equality

American education began to break out of the British mold as the mass of white Americans sought a larger share in democracy. In the troubled atmosphere of the 1820s was born the idea of free public education for all. It was not until the late 1830s that "common schools," as free public elementary schools were called, began to appear in large numbers outside New England, and some states did not provide them until the 1850s or later. The principal reason for the delay was the resistance of the property-owning classes.

There is no doubt that the educational reformers of this period were aiming at greater social equality.

The object of the common school system is to give every child a free, straight, solid pathway by which he can walk directly up from the ignorance of an infant to a knowledge of the primary duties of a man, and can acquire a power and an invincible will to discharge them.[2]

So wrote Horace Mann in his first annual report as secretary of the first state board of education, set up in Massachusetts in 1837. Over great opposition from both teachers and legislators, Mann established the first "normal," or teacher-training, school. Along with the adoption of his system of schooling by grades, this began the movement for the professionalization of teaching. Thus, through the efforts of Mann and other reformers, the groundwork was laid for the American system of education as we know it today. By 1850, the basic principles of American public education had been established: (1) free elementary and secondary schools should be available to *all* children; (2) teachers should be given *professional training;* and (3) all children should be *required* to attend school (or they could go to equivalent private schools).[3] It

1. Henry J. Perkinson, *The Imperfect Panacea: American Faith in Education, 1865 to 1965* (New York: Random House, Inc., 1968) is the main source for the following discussion.
2. Quoted in Alice V. Crow and Lester D. Crow, eds., *Vital Issues in American Education* (New York: Bantam Books, 1964), p. 41.
3. Samuel Eliot Morison, *The Oxford History of the American People* (New York: Oxford University Press, 1965), p. 291.

took some time before these principles were implemented.

Although new colleges sprang up every-where during the 1850s and 1860s, over 80 percent of them closed for lack of pupils. Even so, when the Civil War broke out, colleges out-numbered public high schools.[4] America was not yet ready for universal education beyond the primary level.

Promoting—and Preventing—Integration

Crises over integration of the races in public schools have occurred repeatedly for more than a century. By the end of the Civil War, most southern schools were closed. And the majority of the newly freed blacks had never had any schooling. As northern reformers saw it, the South should become culturally closer to the North, and its black citizens should immediately be "uplifted" so that they could take their right-ful place in society. Both goals, they thought, could be met through education.

The movement to educate the southern black included the idea of racially integrated or "mixed" schools. (The private charitable and religious organizations that financed the flow of teachers to the South were not disturbed by the fact that most northern schools systems were racially segregated.) School buildings were con-structed by the so-called Freedmen's Bureau, a federal agency set up to care for ex-slaves, and were financed from the sale of requisitioned Confederate real estate. By 1869, the peak peri-od, the Bureau had employed 9503 teachers in these schools, including many southern blacks trained by northern whites.[5]

At first, southern whites simply avoided the mixed schools; later they openly harassed and persecuted the teachers. During the Reconstruc-tion Period (1867–1877), Louisiana, Florida, Mississippi, and Arkansas had black educators in charge of their school systems for consider-able periods; but already, during the federally supervised state constitutional conventions of 1867–1868, it had proved impossible to per-suade southern whites to support mixed schools with their taxes. When state assemblies with black majorities voted in favor of integrated schools, white parents withdrew their children from school altogether.

All the southern states had been "recon-structed" by the late 1870s, and all had insti-tuted, or reinstituted, systems of free elementary education. As white conservatives regained con-trol of the legislatures in state after state, how-ever, they began to pass laws establishing segre-gated public school systems. Methods were found to divert public funds so that the schools for blacks received the lesser share. The final blow to black educational hopes was the omis-sion of any provision for integrated schools in the Civil Rights Act of 1875. By 1896, after twenty years of northern indifference and south-ern determination, the political climate was ripe for the Supreme Court's historic decision in *Plessy* v. *Ferguson* that the "separate but equal" fa-cilities in the South were indeed constitutional. The facilities were not equal, and the separation rested on a philosophy of racism. Nevertheless, this legal basis for segregation was not changed until 1954.

Americanizing Immigrants

Curiously enough, it was just as Reconstruction was drawing to a close that compulsory educa-tion laws, which might have saved integrated schools in at least some parts of the South, be-gan to be introduced into the North. (Massachu-setts had had a form of compulsory education since 1852, but at the time the concept was too progressive even for the other New England states.) In 1874 a compulsory education law was passed in the state of New York. The two princi-pal reasons behind this revolutionary measure— and it should be noted that it *was* a revolution in the history of relations between government and the citizen—were that the cities were growing rapidly and that their newest inhabitants were mostly immigrants. In the half-century after 1860, America's population increased by over sixty million. In six of the ten years between 1905 and 1914 the *annual* total of immigration exceeded one million.[6]

4. David M. Potter in Carl N. Degler et al., eds., *The Democratic Experience*, 3rd ed. (Glenview, Ill.: Scott, Fores-man and Company, 1973), p. 267.
5. Perkinson, *The Imperfect Panacea*, p. 15.
6. Morison, *The Oxford History*, p. 813.

Especially after the closing of the western frontier, the tremendous growth in population was most evident in the cities. Urban problems associated with the immigrants were the most pressing domestic issue of the times:

Confronted with the deterioration of their cities, many native urban Americans placed the blame on the newcomers. . . . Their kids were everywhere, especially in the streets. . . . The schoolroom was where these young hoodlums belonged. It was scandalous that many of these "future citizens" could hardly speak English, let alone read or write it. They needed to be civilized and Americanized. . . .[7]

Another reason for keeping immigrant children off the streets was that they formed a pool of cheap labor that depressed wage levels. Urban workers were in no mood to encourage the entry of immigrant children into the labor market, even if employers held the opposite point of view. Thus it came about that by 1900 thirty-one states had enacted compulsory schooling laws. Their purpose was clear: the children of immigrants were to be "Americanized."

Preparing Future Citizens

By the turn of the century, it was clear that large cities were to be a characteristic feature of the American scene, and that they would continue to grow. Recognizing this fact, a number of educators and reformers turned their attention to the quality of urban life and education.

The most influential educator of the period was John Dewey.[8] Dewey argued that, rather than focus on specific academic skills, the schools should take on the task of socializing children for every aspect of life. In particular, he believed that the schools should teach the young the value of cooperation (the basis of democracy) and train them to participate in the democratic community. Dewey's ideas caught on, and providing education for all of life's experiences became a goal of the educational institution.

During the latter part of Dewey's teaching career, drastic changes were wrought in American society by the First World War and the restriction of immigration. Further drastic change came with the Great Depression. But Dewey's influence remained strong, extending to curricula and teaching methods, on the one hand, and to the relationship between school and society, on the other. In Dewey's philosophy, the school was never just the agent of society; it was an independent source of social change. This conception clearly underlay the Social Frontier Movement, a program begun in the early 1930s by some of Dewey's former colleagues at Columbia University. The movement tried to involve both teachers and students more closely with society and simultaneously bring them to a clearer recognition of what they needed to ask of society.[9] The most lasting effect of the Social Frontier Movement was in enlarging school curricula and goals.

Allocating Roles in the Labor Force

When education became compulsory, the schools had to please larger and larger numbers of parents, most of whom wanted their children to find jobs better than their own. At the same time business interests wanted the schools to train new workers. As a result of such pressures, the public schools became involved in the process of *vocational sorting*. Without dropping the older goals of Americanization and equalization, the schools turned to the task of training people for positions in the labor force and aiming them toward specific work roles.

Schools devised arrangements for dividing students into potential vocational categories as soon as they were considered old enough to think about careers. In the last decades of the nineteenth century courses in a variety of work skills and trades began to be offered, and the first vocational high schools were opened. The trend was greatly accelerated in 1917, when vocational education began to receive federal support.

Soon the schools had the major responsibility for selectively preparing, sorting, and allocating people into various occupational roles.

7. Perkinson, *The Imperfect Panacea,* p. 68.
8. John Dewey, *School and Society* (Chicago: The University of Chicago Press, 1915).
9. Ibid., pp. 205–210.

Here in a pleas-ant row we stand,
Of boys and girls a hap-py band;
Some-times we sing, and some-times
     play,
But now our **A B C** we say.

Although the earliest elementary schools were set up to teach the children of the property-owning classes to read, write, and do arithmetic (top left), it was not long before schools were being used to help solve serious social problems. In the South after the Civil War, for example, schools were opened for the freed slaves (top right); and during the period of heavy immigration, northern schools were charged with the task of Americanizing the new immigrants (bottom).

Some children were pointed toward management and the professions; others were sent to typists' desks or the carpentry shop. Special curricula and special schools were devised in order to achieve effective vocational preparation. And, in spite of some problems, the schools played their part well. But the very success of such efforts placed the American education system in a somewhat ambivalent position. Educators who developed systems to prepare students for different types of careers were in fact reinforcing existing patterns of social inequality. By training some for prestigious roles and others for more humble work, they were scarcely providing equal opportunity for all. In sorting and selecting students for different careers and different ways of life, the schools often failed to meet the older goals of education—Americanization and equalization.

Contemporary Challenges to Education

When the Soviet Union put the first satellite into space in 1957, shock waves went through our nation's educational institution. Demands were made that the schools produce more scientists, engineers, and technicians to meet the Russian challenge, and federal funds were provided to make this possible. Even when the U.S. space program surpassed that of the USSR, the goal of producing experts remained. Today, when society wants experts to clean up the environment, develop alternate sources of energy, produce more efficient cars, or whatever, the American educational system is called upon to train people for the task.

Federal support for education was at first limited to projects involving national defense. Then in 1964 funds were allocated for the humanities, and in 1965 federal aid was provided for schools at all levels and for scholarships for needy college students. During the 1970s federal funding has been provided not only for educating gifted students and technical experts but also for instituting educational programs on values clarification, mental health, marriage problems, and so on.

The late 1960s and early 1970s also saw new concern with the issue of equalization. Educational programs were designed to promote equality in education for minorities. The three main strategies used to accomplish this aim were increased aid to schools in areas of heavy minority population, transporting minority students to schools outside their neighborhood, and compensatory education. All three remain quite controversial.[10] The dual challenge of educating the expert society and providing equal education for all students is not easily accomplished. As a result, there is continuing reassessment of the goals of the educational system and the ways in which they can be met.

SOURCES OF CONFLICT IN EDUCATION

In Chapter 2, "Social Organization," we pointed out that conflicting conceptions of goals are frequently responsible for disruptions in group functioning (pages 53–54). This principle is also important in understanding the problem of maintaining stability within a complex social institution such as education. The tax-supported educational system in the United States has at least six major categories of participants who feel that they have a direct stake in defining the goals of schools—students, parents, faculty, administrators, legislators, and the public at large. The individuals in each of these categories are involved in some role relationship with the schools, either as direct participants, supervisors, or taxpayers bearing the costs. Understandably, all want some voice in defining the goals of the system.

Because of their very different orientations, the various categories of participants in the educational system seldom agree entirely on what the schools should accomplish, or how. Thus any attempt to change or redefine educational goals and purposes inevitably introduces some degree of tension—and when the different groups feel strongly that important values are at stake, tension may erupt into open conflict. The specific focus of controversies over educational goals changes from time to time as new ideas ebb and flow in the nation at large. The following examples are representative of recent controversies over what American schools should be doing.

10. See pages 574–576 for a discussion of some of the controversies surrounding these programs.

During the 1960s student strikes occurred at many colleges and universities throughout the United States. Among the conflicts between students and university administrators were the responsibility of the school to the community in which it was situated, student participation in policy making, and an end to restrictions regarding living quarters.

Controversies over Control

Major controversies have been generated in recent years over the issue of the rights of schools to dictate curriculum, rules, discipline, and all the rest. American schools have always taught students to believe that under a representative government all citizens should take part—that they should exercise initiative, exert leadership, and have a share in controlling decision making. However, when college students and even high-school students began to apply these lessons to the schools themselves in the late 1960s, asking for a stronger voice in policy making, most educators as well as most of the general public viewed the development with apprehen-

sion. The goals of the established educational institution clashed with the goals of young people who wanted to implement the democratic principles the schools themselves had championed. While the intensity of this conflict seems to have diminished, it has by no means been fully resolved.

Today, college students have pretty much won their independence from *alma mater* in personal affairs, as evidenced by the virtual ending of restrictions on male-female visiting in dormitory rooms and of requirements to live on campus. Students have also had some influence on the curriculum, hastening the introduction of new courses in black studies, women's studies, environmental problems, and other areas of contemporary concern.[11] And they have won at

11. Riley E. Dunlap and Richard P. Gale, "Politics and Ecology," *Youth and Society,* 3, No. 4 (June 1972): 379–397.

least a small foothold in policy making—gaining seats on boards of regents, boards of trustees, and curriculum, faculty, and admissions committees. However, their power to influence what is taught, how it is taught, and who teaches it remains limited. In the great majority of cases, they either have no vote at all or are so outnumbered that their vote is meaningless. In some cases too, they have gained the right to participate in policy making and then failed to use it.

Teachers have been involved in controversies over control of school matters and their own behavior. They have been subject not only to the positive and negative sanctions that prevail in any bureaucratic structure but also to a great deal of external control. Parents, local administrators, school boards, and special interest groups (for example, ethnic organizations) are deeply concerned about what teachers are doing.

One area of disagreement between some outside groups and teachers concerns what kind of information is to be presented in the classroom. For example, is it proper to assign books containing "dirty words" to elementary students? Some parents, administrators, and church groups think not. A continuing battle has raged for a number of years over how the topic of the origin of human beings should be taught. In some states (e.g., California and Tennessee) laws have been passed that make it necessary for information about evolution to be "balanced" by the Biblical account of the creation.

At the college and university level, educators have long insisted on the principle of academic freedom. The college teacher is expected to be free to choose the content of the course and to teach unpopular doctrines or hold unpopular points of view, without fear of being fired. But at times the exercise of academic freedom has been resisted, especially at colleges and universities supported by public funds. During the 1960s some teachers who opposed the war in Vietnam and counseled draft resistance found themselves embroiled in controversy. Earlier, conflict arose over whether it was acceptable for a teacher to be a Communist.

Other Goal Conflicts

Other examples of conflicting attitudes toward the proper goals of education exist at all levels. Who should be educated, and what should be taught? What teaching methods should be used? Should education be general or specialized? Should it be predominantly humanistic or scientific? At the university level, should instructors place research before teaching or vice versa? In general, should scholars stick to seeking and dispensing truth, or do they also have the responsibility to attempt to solve the critical problems society is facing? Should they remain professionally neutral concerning the political issues of their times, or should they speak out for the causes they believe in? Can they put their talents at the service of government or private industry without accepting some responsibility for the policies and activities of such employers?

Many of these issues are centuries old. But they continue to be debated—especially by scientists and social scientists whose work often has a direct relationship to problem conditions in society.

EDUCATION AND SOCIAL STRATIFICATION

Education is linked to social stratification in two ways: first, position in the social structure helps determine what education individuals receive; and, second, the education they receive helps determine their future position in the social structure. In this section we will discuss the part social ranking plays in educational opportunity, and the part education plays in determining occupation and class membership. Then we will look at some of the controversies over why poor and minority students do not perform well in school.

THE ADVANTAGES OF EDUCATION

Each year our society requires fewer unskilled and semiskilled workers and more professional and technical workers. Young people who terminate their education early—especially those who do not complete high school—face a lessening demand for lower level skills in a labor market that places a high premium on formal education. The importance of educational attainment as a factor in channeling workers into different levels of the labor force can be seen in Table 19.2. People who did not graduate from high school are concentrated in the lower level jobs (operatives, laborers), while college graduates take the higher level jobs (about two-thirds of those in administrative, technical, and professional roles graduated from college).

The economic benefits of education can be seen in other ways. In 1974 the average lifetime income for a male with a college degree was estimated at $758,000, as compared with $479,000 for a male high school graduate and $344,000 for a man who only finished elementary school. These figures break down to annual incomes of $16,200, $10,430, and $6759 respectively.[12]

To graduate from either high school or college, then, is to advance to a new income level; the diploma seems to have commercial value in itself.[13] The reason for this is not always clear.

12. *U.S. News and World Report,* April 1, 1974.
13. For the nonwhite, the commercial value of a diploma is by no means equal to its value for the white. But one study suggests that the benefits of a college education to nonwhites are increasing rapidly. See Melvin Borland and Donald E. Yett, "The Cash Value of College," *Trans-action,* November 1967, pp. 44–49.

While it can be argued that individuals who have the perseverence to finish college are likely to become superior employees and thus deserve higher pay, it is still hard to see why possession of a high school diploma should ensure at least another $1000 a year in brick laying, or why the lack of a college diploma should prevent admission to an executive training program. But employers are free to demand whatever qualifications they may desire, regardless of whether or not these qualifications are necessary for—or even relevant to—performance of the job. The fact is that the number of years of education completed by young, inexperienced job applicants tends to determine not only their chances of obtaining a particular job, but their employability in general. Currently, the number of years of education completed is the single best predictor of an individual's economic performance in the labor force.

VARIATIONS IN EDUCATIONAL OPPORTUNITY

In principle, educational opportunity is equal for all. But in practice, the chances of receiving formal education is not only determined by native potential but also by one's socioeconomic background and by the attitudes of one's family, friends, and teachers.

Table 19.2. EDUCATIONAL LEVEL BY OCCUPATION FOR MALES AND FEMALES

Occupational Category	Not High School Graduate		High School Graduate		1 to 3 Years of College		4 Years of College or More	
	Male	Female	Male	Female	Male	Female	Male	Female
Professional and technical	0.9	1.0	6.3	1.6	17.1	22.5	54.1	71.1
Farmers and farm managers	5.7	0.5	3.2	0.2	1.6	0.3	1.0	0.3
Managers and administrators	5.5	2.9	15.5	5.2	24.2	7.7	26.3	6.8
Clerical workers	2.9	6.5	8.3	19.0	10.0	46.8	3.1	13.5
Sales workers	1.3	3.7	5.9	7.4	10.6	5.0	8.3	3.0
Craft and kindred workers	25.4	2.7	29.4	3.0	18.7	1.2	3.9	0.5
Operatives	29.7	35.1	19.3	27.9	8.9	4.4	1.1	1.3
Service workers	10.6	42.9	7.3	33.0	6.4	11.0	1.6	3.1
Farm laborers and supervisors	4.7	3.5	0.6	1.1	0.4	0.4	0.2	0.2
Laborers, except farm	13.4	1.4	4.2	1.5	2.2	0.7	0.4	0.0

SOURCE: U.S. Bureau of the Census, *Current Population Reports*, Series P-20, No. 274, December 1974, p. 6.

TOOLS OF SOCIOLOGY
STATISTICAL ANALYSIS

Professional sociologists use statistical analysis extensively for describing and comparing groups and social categories. In brief, a set of statistics is a group of numerical measurements arranged in some meaningful way. The numerical values are produced by observation—by counting or measuring some phenomenon. The most important task of statistics, in fact the real meaning of the term *statistics,* is to summarize in a single numerical value some quality, trend, or property of an array of measures. This summarizing number is called an *index* number or a *coefficient* and is computed by applying a mathematical formula to an array of measures.

Statistical coefficients have many uses: some are used to describe a situation for which data is complete; some to make inferences from a sample. As an example of a descriptive coefficient, let us assume that we wanted to describe with precision the *central tendency* of a set of observations. At least three different coefficients can be used for this purpose: the *mode,* the *median,* and the *mean.* The *mode* is the numerical value that occurs most frequently in a given set of measures. Thus, in the set 100, 17, 2, 8, 17, 15, the mode (though not the average) is 17. The *median* is the value above and below which *precisely* half of the entries in a given array will fall. Thus in the above array the median (but, again, not the average) is 16. The *mean* is the coefficient that corresponds to the average. Let us use the mean (symbolized X̄) to determine the central tendency of the sample in the figure below:

Measures	Conventional symbols:
4	X = the numerical value of any
3	measure (4, 3, etc.)
7	n = the number of measures (in
1	this case, n = 11)
4	Σ = "sum up all numerical
2	values"
6	X̄ = the symbol for the mean
3	
5	
4	*Computational formula:*
5	$\bar{X} = \dfrac{\Sigma X}{n}$ or $\dfrac{44}{11}$ or 4
44 = Sum	

What is the mode of the above array? What is the median of the above array?

We can summarize the mathematical formula used to obtain the mean (X̄) as follows: *The mean is obtained by adding up all the values in an array of measures and then dividing the obtained sum by the number of measures in the array.* To define this very simple statistic we have had to use twenty-nine words; many commonly used statistics would require several paragraphs. As indicated by our figure, however, the definition of the mean can be given in conventional statistical notation as: X̄ = ΣX/n, which requires only six symbols.

Another aspect of statistics involves the degree of "scatter" or *variability* that exists in an array of measures. In the array indicated in the column at the left, there is relatively little dispersion or scatter. Note that the lowest and highest entries are only 3 points away from the mean. However, if we included measures as high as 100 or even larger, we would increase the variability greatly (and, of course, change the central tendency).

Statisticians indicate the degree of variability in an array by using an index of scatter. One such index is the *standard deviation,* which is symbolized by the small sigma σ and has the following formula:

$$\sigma = \sqrt{\frac{\Sigma (X - \bar{X})^2}{n}}$$

Prepare a verbal description of this formula and then compute the standard deviation of the array given in the figure at the left. Remember that Σ means to sum up a whole series of individual items and that X means each individual numerical value. Notice also that you are to square *each* term and not the sum of the terms.

Another important statistical problem involves showing the *association* between variables. This requires two measures for every person or object that is to be studied. The goal is to summarize in a single coefficient the degree to which a high or low score on one measure also implies a high or low score on another. There are dozens of these statistical coefficients—which are referred to as coefficients of "correlation"—and some are available for use with multiple sets of measures, such as data from two different experiments or surveys.

TOOLS OF SOCIOLOGY
STATISTICAL CONTROL OF VARIABLES

It is difficult at best to analyze the relationships between the variables commonly studied in sociological research. Human behavior is the most complex of all objects of scientific study, and sociologists are seldom certain that they have taken into account all the factors that can lead people to behave as they do. Often, researchers uncover additional influencing variables, making it necessary to revise their earlier interpretations.

One way that sociologists attempt to understand complex social processes is to control certain variables *statistically* while studying the influence of others. The difficulties one may encounter in this method will be apparent if we examine the problem of explaining why certain types of educational institutions seem to produce so many graduates who go on to take the doctor of philosophy degree. There are innumerable variables from which to construct tentative explanations of this phenomenon. One hypothesis (popular among smaller schools) is that the small liberal arts college provides a rich educational environment that stimulates students to undertake graduate work. In fact, many distinguished scholars did receive their undergraduate degrees from just such schools. But more recent research has suggested that this may merely reflect initial student ability. Indeed, it can be hypothesized that able students, who would do well anywhere, are attracted to small liberal arts schools because of prevailing beliefs about their influence. According to this hypothesis, the number of Ph.D.s who spend their undergraduate years at these colleges merely reflect a "self-fulfilling prophecy."

To study this problem, and to control for the influence of student ability, Astin carried out a large-scale research project on a sample of 265 colleges and universities. He obtained data on selected characteristics of all incoming freshmen. The schools studied included all types of bachelor's programs in the United States (except for certain very small colleges and those with extremely low levels of student ability). From official records on all Ph.D.s granted in the United States during a specific three-year period, he determined how many doctoral recipients earned their undergraduate degrees from each of the 265

institutions. He then obtained data on all bachelor's degrees awarded by each institution during a three-year span just six years earlier. From these data he was able to calculate simple Ph.D. "output rates." Some schools produced no graduates who went on to receive Ph.D.s. As many as 23 percent of the graduates of other schools went on to take the advanced degree.

The problem was to find out whether individual or institutional attributes had resulted in these differences. To do this, the researcher needed to know the influence of a student's individual characteristics on continuing to a Ph.D. Earlier studies gave partial answers. For example, completion of the Ph.D. was clearly related to sex, IQ, and undergraduate major, and males were far more likely to obtain the degree than females. High IQ students had clear advantages over those with lower IQs, and some majors were more likely to continue than others (e.g., psychology versus business).

With these relationships understood, the "student input" factor was controlled statistically to see if the differences in the Ph.D. output rates could be attributed to the type of institution. To do this, Astin devised a way of predicting what output rate a particular institution *should* have, given the characteristics of its entering students. He computed an "expected" Ph.D. output rate for each institution, based upon student intelligence, percent of males, and distribution of majors. He then compared each school's *actual* rate with its *expected* rate to see if it was "overproducing" or "underproducing" Ph.D.s, given its student input.

Astin found that some colleges produced far more Ph.D.s than their expected rates. In general, larger, state-supported, coeducational schools overproduced, while small colleges—especially those with religious affiliations—made a poor showing. The all-male and all-female schools of all sizes tended to underproduce. Among the lowest producers were Harvard, Princeton, and Dartmouth. Among the highest were Brooklyn College, Yeshiva, Brigham Young, Utah, and Utah State. The latter finding pointed to the need for further controls. Socioeconomic, ethnic, and religious factors appeared to be significant variables for further study.

Alexander W. Astin, "'Productivity' of Undergraduate Institutions," *Science* (April 13, 1962): 129–135.

Place of Residence and Income Level

Where one lives—what state, community, neighborhood—determines the quality of educational facilities one will be exposed to, for the amount of public money allocated to education varies considerably from one area to another. In the early 1970s, for example, New York annually spent $1580 per pupil on education, while Alabama spent only $590.[14] Differences also exist between school districts and even among schools within a given district. High-income areas spend more on their schools than do low-income areas, and even when the state provides equalization funds, significant differences remain. Children in higher-income areas are provided with better school buildings, libraries, science equipment, recreation programs, and audiovisual aids than are children in poorer areas. And the teachers in wealthier areas are generally better trained and better paid.

A study of the effect of parental income on education in a large midwestern city found that the school facilities in areas of low family income were definitely inferior, that many teachers were poorly qualified, that science equipment was substandard (or nonexistent), and that the buildings were in poorer condition.[15] Many schools lacked lunchrooms, which meant that the poorest children were often unable to take advantage of the city's free lunch program. The poorer children also received fewer medical examinations and less medical treatment, which interfered with their educational advancement. The study also compared IQ scores and results of scholastic achievement tests and found that scores were notably higher for children in the schools in the upper-income areas.

There is clear evidence that upper- and middle-class children receive the services of the best educated and most experienced public school teachers. For example, in studying Chicago teachers, Havighurst found that 89 percent of the elementary school teachers in upper-income areas had six or more years of experience, whereas only 52 percent of those in lower-income areas had similar qualifications.[16] Attempts to change this situation have met with great resistance. Many teachers do not wish to serve in a "problem" school in a low-income area, and many upper-income parents have placed pressure on the school board to keep the more experienced teachers in their schools.

Although there is considerable evidence that children who attend lower quality schools do more poorly than children in better schools, simple or direct causal relationships between the quality of educational facilities and the level of academic performance among children cannot be assumed. As we will see, achievement in school is the product of many factors operating together.

The Orientations of Significant Others

Families vary greatly in the degree to which they encourage children to perform well in school, yet such encouragement can contribute to success in the classroom. It also helps if a child's friends come from families with positive attitudes toward school. There is considerable evidence that peer subcultures in which an emphasis on scholastic achievement is found influence their members to perform better in school. In fact Jencks maintains that true equality of education is impossible unless all children have the same access to schoolmates who are "advantaged (i.e., white, middle-class, academically talented, or all three)." He states that "equalizing opportunity would mean making the social composition of every school the same. Such a school system would be completely desegregated—racially, economically, academically, and in any other way that seemed relevant."[17]

Teachers' orientations also have a great impact on students. For the most part teachers are middle class. Like other middle-class people, they share a set of values that places stress on achievement, striving, and discipline—orientations in which children of the poor may receive

14. *Statistical Abstract of the United States* (Washington, D.C.: U.S. Government Printing Office, 1973), p. 128.

15. Patricia Sexton, *Education and Income* (New York: Compass Books, 1964). See also Christopher Jencks et al., eds., *Inequality: A Reassessment of the Effect of Family and Schooling in America* (New York: Basic Books, Inc., 1972).

16. Robert J. Havighurst, "Teachers in Chicago Schools," *School Children in the Urban Slum*, ed. Joan I. Roberts (New York: The Free Press, 1967), p. 556.

17. Jencks et al., *Inequality*, p. 30.

little socialization at home. Yet the expectations teachers have concerning the performance of poor children and the values they use in assessing them may greatly affect the childrens' educational experience.[18] If middle-class teachers judge lower-class children by a set of standards that they do not understand and to which they do not subscribe, school can become a punishing experience. On the other hand, middle-class children who understand and share their teachers' values are likely to receive positive reinforcement for approved behavior. School for such children is typically a place of achievement and success.

In a study of high-school students in a small California college town, a questionnaire administered to virtually all the school's sixteen hundred students was analyzed in terms of three criteria of rebellion against the school—receiving flunk notices, skipping school, and being sent out of class by a teacher.[19] It was found that rebellious behavior was not necessarily the result of home influences or such personal attributes as a low IQ score. Instead, rebellion was often caused by "poor articulation between present activity and future status increments"—that is, by the fact that what the students expected to do and learn in school had little or no apparent connection with what the students themselves expected to be doing as adults. The investigator found that most of the rebels were males who expected to be manual workers and females whose main interest was in early marriage. These young people were especially likely to rebel if they had low IQ scores, lived in slums, or were members of ethnic minorities. Male students were also likely to rebel if they saw the labor market they were about to enter as one in which they would not be judged as individuals.

School was hard on these students because they were being judged in terms of achievement-oriented, middle-class values that defined anything less than getting into college as "failure." Finding such values irrelevant to their needs and threatening to their self-esteem, they

Young people who are denied a sense of self-identity and personal worth in school sometimes seek it in rebellious activities such as vandalism.

withdrew into an "expressive alienation" that made itself known by (among other things) claims for the privileges of adults—smoking, drinking, driving fast cars, and "making out." These activities were likely to get them into trouble at school, if not with the police, but they were the means by which these young people sought a sense of self-identity and personal worth that was denied them in school.

UNRAVELING CAUSE AND EFFECT

As we have seen, young people who come from lower-income families generally receive fewer educational opportunities in terms of educational facilities and family, peer-group, and teacher

18. W. W. Charters, Jr., "Consequences of Educators' Social Position on the Teacher-Learning Process," in *Handbook on Teaching,* ed. N. L. Gage (Chicago: Rand McNally & Co., 1963), pp. 722–740.

19. Arthur Stinchcombe, *Rebellion in a High School* (New York: Quadrangle Books, Inc., 1969).

The integration of schools by busing minority children into white neighborhoods has been seen as one means of providing equal educational opportunity. Busing has met with a great deal of opposition from minority parents who do not want their children to travel great distances to school as well as from white parents who feel that their schools will be "ruined" by an influx of minority students. The use of busing to achieve school integration is one of the most explosive political issues of the 1970s.

support. Poor children and, particularly, minority children do more poorly in school than their more affluent contemporaries. Many attempts have been made to understand why this is so, and much controversy has been generated over some of the research findings. In this section we will discuss some controversial studies that attempt to explain the causes of such differences in scholastic performance.

Compensatory Educational Programs

Education, as we have already pointed out, has important relationships to life chances. And, as we have also seen, the schools attended by lower-class children generally have poorer facilities and less experienced teachers than those attended by wealthier students. So it is not surprising that many politicians, educators, and interested citizens came to believe that a national program for improving the schools attended by the poor would upgrade their scholastic attainment. If the poor did better in school, presumably they would be able to get better jobs and

more income, and the next generation of children would be less culturally handicapped and do even better in school. Consequently, in the late 1960s Congress appropriated huge sums of money for compensatory development of curricula, teacher education, physical plants, and other school facilities. Between 1965 and 1969 more than forty important education bills were passed and the federal budget for education was increased from about $2 billion a year to about $10 billion.

Congress also made provision for the commissioner of education to conduct large-scale assessments of the "lack of availability" of "equal educational opportunities for individuals of different races, colors, religions, or national origins." A sociologist, James Coleman, was asked to design and conduct research to assess American educational opportunities for the poor and to make recommendations concerning how they could be improved. In carrying out this research, over 600,000 pupils were studied in approximately 4000 schools staffed by over 60,000 teachers.[20]

20. James S. Coleman, *Equality of Educational Opportunity* (Washington, D.C.: U.S. Government Printing Office, 1966), p. 575.

VIEWPOINTS   EDUCATION AND SOCIAL CHANGE

■ None of the evidence we have reviewed suggests that school reform can be expected to bring about significant social changes outside the schools. . . . Even if we reorganized the schools so that their primary concern was for the students who most needed help, there is no reason to suppose that adults would end up appreciably more equal as a result.

There seem to be three reasons why school reform cannot make adults more equal. First, children seem to be far more influenced by what happens at home than by what happens in school. They may also be more influenced by what happens on the streets and by what they see on television. Second, reformers have very little control over those aspects of school life that affect children. Reallocating resources, reassigning pupils, and rewriting the curriculum seldom change the way teachers and students actually treat each other minute by minute. Third, even when a school exerts an unusual influence on children, the resulting changes are not likely to persist into adulthood. It takes a huge change in elementary school test scores, for example, to alter adult income by a significant amount. . . .

In America, as elsewhere, the general trend over the past 200 years has been toward equality. In the economic realm, however, the contribution of public policy to this drift has been slight. As long as egalitarians assume that public policy cannot contribute to economic equality directly but must proceed by ingenious manipulations of marginal institutions like the schools, progress will remain glacial. If we want to move beyond this tradition, we will have to establish political control over the economic institutions that shape our society. This is what other countries usually call socialism. Anything less will end in the same disappointment as the reforms of the 1960s.
Christopher Jencks
Inequality

● It is now clear that American public education is organized and functions along social and economic class lines. A bi-racial public school system wherein approximately 90 per cent of American children are required to attend segregated schools is one of the clearest manifestations of this basic fact. The difficulties encountered in attempting to desegregate public schools in the South as well as in the North point to the tenacity of the forces seeking to prevent any basic change in the system.

The class and social organization of American public schools is consistently associated with a lower level of educational efficiency in the less privileged schools. This lower efficiency is expressed in terms of the fact that the schools attended by Negro and poor children have less adequate educational facilities than those attended by more privileged children. Teachers tend to resist assignments in Negro and other underprivileged schools and generally function less adequately in these schools. Their morale is generally lower; they are not adequately supervised; they tend to see their students as less capable of learning. The parents of the children in these schools are usually unable to bring about any positive changes in the conditions of these schools. . . .

Given these conditions, American public schools have become significant instruments in the blocking of economic mobility and in the intensification of class distinctions rather than fulfilling their historic function of facilitating such mobility. In effect, the public schools have become captives of a middle class who have failed to use them to aid others to move into the middle class. It might even be possible to interpret the role of the controlling middle class as that of using the public schools to block further mobility.
Kenneth B. Clark
"Alternative Public School Systems"

Coleman had expected to find that the schools attended by nonwhite children were inferior to those attended by white children in terms of physical facilities, curricula, qualifications of teachers, and so on. Many earlier studies had indicated the existence of such differences. Instead, he found that the schools attended by poor blacks were, *on the average,* quite similar to those attended by poor whites. He also found that there were roughly equal numbers of good and bad schools attended by the poor of both races. The study found, too, that minority students, particularly blacks, *on the average* scored lower in educational achievement tests than did white children who attended comparable schools: "With some exceptions—notably in Oriental-Americans—the average minority pupil scores were distinctly lower on these tests at every level than the average white pupil."[21] In other words black children were not performing as well as white children in comparable schools. Furthermore, Coleman noted that the gap between pupils widens with each higher grade. As they grow older, minority students (especially blacks) fall farther and farther behind white students in the development of several skills critical to making a living and participating fully in modern society.[22]

Coleman's study indicated that the quality of schools, as measured by traditional means, does not account for the generally lower scholastic performance of minority students. But, then, what *does?*

The Hypothesis of Genetic Influence

Arthur Jensen, an educational psychologist, touched off a storm when he advanced the proposition that differences in school performance shown in the Coleman study and others may be at least partly due to genetic factors.[23] As he put it:

There is increasing realization among students of the disadvantaged that the discrepancy in their average performance cannot be completely or directly attributed to discrimination or inequalities in education. It seems not unreasonable in view of the fact that intelligence variation has a large genetic component to hypothesize that genetic factors may play a part in this picture.[24]

Thus Jensen reopened the old controversy of "Nature versus Nurture," an issue much debated when it was discovered at the time of World War I that blacks on the average tended to score lower on IQ tests than did whites. (It was also noted at that time that northern blacks had higher scores than did southern whites of equal educational attainment.) The controversy had subsided because a strong case had been made that minorities were denied equal educational facilities, and until Jensen and a few other scholars began to examine the issue again, it was not a subject of scholarly debate.

Jensen's proposition has been strongly criticized by citizens, scientists, and political groups, among others.[25] Some critics have accused Jensen of racism; others attack him for using the IQ score as a measure of "intelligence," claiming that it really measures knowledge of white middle-class culture. Social scientists have generally argued that the differences between minorities and whites can be attributed to sociocultural, rather than genetic, factors. According to this view, differences in such matters as scholastic performance are caused by different socialization processes and subcultural systems, such as those of the neighborhood, peer groups, and family. Very simply, a child from a poor and culturally deprived family cannot do as well in school—even in a "good" school—as a child from a home environment supportive of education.

Self-Fulfilling Prophecies

Another hypothesis that attempts to explain why poor and minority children do not perform well in school is that of the self-fulfilling prophecy. According to this view, slum children do poorly in school because their teachers *expect* them to do poorly—in other words, the teacher's prophecy of poor performance is self-fulfilling. In one of several experiments that they have per-

21. Ibid., p. 21.
22. Ibid.
23. Arthur Jensen, "Reducing the Heredity-Environment Uncertainty: A Reply," *Harvard Educational Review*, 39, No. 3 (1969): 449–483.
24. Arthur Jensen, *Educability and Group Differences* (New York: Harper & Row, Inc., 1973).
25. See, for example, *Psychology Today* (March 1974): 5; *Society* (May–June 1973): 5–7; *Psychology Today* (December 1973): 40–86.

formed on the self-fulfilling prophecy, Rosenthal and Jacobson gave three kinds of IQ tests to 650 students in an elementary school in a lower-class district.[26] They told the teachers that these tests would predict which children were about to "bloom," or "spurt," intellectually. After administering the tests, they randomly selected a certain proportion of names in each class as those of "intellectual bloomers" and gave the names of these "special" children to the teachers. The other children were used as the control group, even though the teachers, of course, did not know this.

Rosenthal and Jacobson retested all the children at regular intervals for two academic years. At the end of the first year, they discovered that the gains in IQ of the special students exceeded the gains of the control group, especially among children in the two lower grades. The difference between the gains of the two groups was too great to be the result of chance. The following year the IQ scores of the younger special students did not increase more than did those of the younger control students, but the older special students gained in IQ more than did the control group. The experimenters interpreted these results as indicating that the expectations of the teacher had a definite effect on the school performance of the students. Because these findings met with vigorous criticism, a large number of additional research projects were carried out. Some of the subsequent studies have confirmed the original findings.[27]

In a recent article, Rosenthal hypothesized that the self-fulfilling prophecy is produced because: (1) When teachers have been led to expect good things from their students, they may create a warmer social-emotional mood for these students. (2) Teachers may give more feedback to "better" students concerning their performance. (3) They also may present these students with more supplementary materials in order to stimulate their intellectual blooming. (4) The teachers may give these special students greater opportunity to pose questions or to respond in other ways.[28] Whether these factors are the main ones that operate to produce a self-fulfilling prophecy can only be confirmed as results from further studies are analyzed.

Obviously, it is important to understand all the factors that operate to deny poor and minority students equal educational opportunity. Only when the advantages of education are available to everyone will the schools be fulfilling the societal goal of improving the life conditions of all citizens.

SOCIAL WELFARE

Unlike the American educational system, which attempts to serve all people, the social welfare system in the United States is directed only toward those in financial need. It is based largely on the view that poverty is produced by social, political, and economic events that are beyond the control—or even the comprehension—of most people. The poor are poor and stay that way because the social and cultural system fails to provide opportunities for them to improve their circumstances. Some social scientists have also seen poverty as part of a deeply established *subculture* from which the participants cannot escape because their socialization experiences do not produce the necessary skills, knowledge, and motivational pressures to get ahead.[29]

The corollary of viewing poverty as the result of impersonal forces is that those who *benefit* from the system do so, in part at least, because of favorable outcomes of the same impersonal forces. Consequently, obligations to help the poor are seen as the legitimate responsibility of the social system that produced their condition.

In the United States, two older views of the origin of poverty remain part of our culture and influence the thinking of many people. The first

26. Robert Rosenthal and Lenore Jacobson, *Pygmalion in the Classroom: Teacher Expectation and Pupil's Intellectual Ability* (New York: Holt, Rinehart and Winston, Inc., 1968).

27. Robert Rosenthal, "The Pygmalion Effect Lives," *Psychology Today* (September 1973): 56–63.

28. Ibid., p. 60.

29. The existence of a subculture of poverty remains a matter of debate; see Joan Huber and Peter Chalfant, eds., *The Sociology of American Poverty* (Cambridge, Mass.: Schenkman Publishing Co., 1974), p. 25.

is the belief that poverty is "God's work." According to this view, God created society according to his design. As a part of this design, the poor will always be with us. To live virtuously, one must do good works by giving alms to the poor in the tradition of Jesus and the Good Samaritan. Offering charity is a Christian act, to be performed as an individual or as a church member. It is not part of one's civic obligations within a secular, political order.

The second older view of the origin of poverty sees the condition of the poor as of their own doing. According to this interpretation, the poor are intemperate and lazy; they lack moral fiber and the will to work; they fail to discipline themselves and thus ruin their own lives. Only the "helpless" poor—e.g., the blind, the very young, the very old, the mentally deranged, and the sick—deserve aid. This aid should be given willingly, but only by individuals; helping the poor should not be a concern of the government. This view is consistent with the orientations of the Protestant Ethic (page 282) and Social Darwinism (page 7).

While our contemporary social welfare system has been built around the view that poverty is a socially caused problem, many Americans still see poverty as God's work or as caused by the personal failings of the poor. Indeed, the three views of the origin of poverty are not mutually exclusive, and it is not uncommon for people who categorize welfare recipients as free-loaders to offer money and other kinds of help to a welfare recipient whose plight is dramatized by the press.

In this section we will briefly trace the development of the American welfare system from its historical background in England, making reference to the changing views of poverty that underlay changes in the system. We will then look at some of the ways in which the welfare system may change in the near future.

ORIGINS OF AMERICAN ORIENTATIONS TOWARD WELFARE

Contemporary welfare policies in America are a unique product of many historical events and conditions. As colonists came to the New World, they brought with them cultural concepts regarding the poor. Developments in the colonies fostered a somewhat different ideological climate and set of values. The American Revolution added still other factors, as did later experiences of the new nation. A brief overview of a number of these developments will help us more fully understand current orientations in welfare policies.[30]

England's Poor Laws

In the early 1500s most of England's population lived on the land, and the common people rented small holdings from the nobility. Most of the common people were able to make a meager living as farmers. Relief to destitute people was usually provided by the local church or landlord.

At that time, England's chief export—raw wool—was sold to the cloth weavers of Flanders (present-day Belgium). When the demand for cloth increased, the price of wool in England also went up. As a result the English landlords turned more and more to raising sheep. Many of them forced their tenants to leave the land, which was converted from farming to grazing. Rents were raised to exorbitant levels; pasture lands that had been used by the common people for centuries were taken over and fenced in; farmhouses, and even whole villages, were torn down to make room for sheep.

All during the 1500s English farm families were dispossessed and forced to look after themselves as best they could. The proportion of England's population that was destitute rose sharply even though the economy of the whole country was becoming more prosperous. By the end of the century many thousands of common people were forced to wander from place to place,

30. The present section is based in part on Sidney Lens, *Poverty: America's Enduring Paradox* (New York: Thomas Y. Crowell Company, 1971).

reduced to begging, stealing, and prostitution. Although such people had neither land nor opportunities for work, idleness and begging were not condoned. The poor who were observably ill, sick, or old were seen as worthy of charity. Those of sound limb and mind who did not work, however, were treated savagely under local laws:

able-bodied idlers were ordered lashed or imprisoned. For their sinfulness, they might be tied to a cart-tail, whipped, or made to pledge under oath that they would return to their birthplaces to find honest labor. The second offense was punished by having an ear cut off; the third, frequently by execution.[31]

Against such a background of rising misery, a national Poor Law was established early in the 1600s during the reign of Queen Elizabeth. The Poor Law of 1601 established almshouses; tried to provide work for the able-bodied poor; arranged apprenticeships for destitute children; and provided money, food, or shelter for the helpless. In earlier times the relief of destitution had been regarded as a moral obligation of individuals or a collective responsibility of the Church. But after the establishment of the Poor Law, such relief activities became an obligation of the state. In part, at least, the new law may have been a political move to prevent armies of the poor from rebelling against the crown.[32]

Exporting the Poor

The success of the Poor Law was spotty; it was well administered in some areas and poorly in others. More important, the Poor Law dealt with the symptoms rather than the underlying causes of poverty. Providing almshouses and giving food to the starving were not an adequate solution to problems caused primarily by forcing people off the land that had once fed them. In an agrarian society, the only real solution

to the problems of the poor would be to resettle them on land where they could again make their own way.

It was during this period — the early 1600s — that charters began to be issued for establishing colonies in the New World. It appeared to many that such ventures might provide an opportunity to solve some of the problems of the English poor. They could be sent to the colonies where people were in short supply and there was much uncultivated land.

Many poor made the dangerous crossing of the ocean; some even sold themselves into years of indentured servitude to pay for their passage. From the beginning, however, the best land went to the rich and powerful rather than to the poor. Some who arrived as indigent eventually achieved affluence in the New World, but many others had merely exchanged one form of poverty for another.

As time went on, some land came into the hands of the less affluent. Groups of religious radicals, for example, took over a number of areas in the New World. In some places people moved in as squatters and later obtained title to the land. In other places indentured servants also ended up with land. But a small elite owned or controlled the largest proportion of the English colonies. Although the poor and almost poor constituted a large segment of the population, few of them were able to obtain substantial land holdings. While conditions for the poor in the colonies were somewhat better than in England — few went hungry, for example — the New World had scarcely turned out to be the promised paradise.

The destitute of colonial America were faced by a system of relief that was essentially the same as the one established under the English Poor Law. Almshouses and workhouses were set up. Those who were truly helpless received grants of money and food, and local taxes were imposed to support such programs. There were also numerous private charities connected with churches. The colonists brought over with them the same attitudes of contempt for "able-bodied idlers" that had existed in England a century earlier.[33]

31. Ibid., p. 17.
32. The thesis that government relief programs have traditionally been little more than techniques to pacify the politically dangerous poor has recently been advanced in Francis Fox Piven and Richard A. Cloward, *Regulating the Poor: The Functions of Public Welfare* (New York: Pantheon Books, 1971).
33. June Axinn and Herman Levin, *Social Welfare: A History of the American Response to Need* (New York: Dodd, Mead & Company, 1975).

Attitudes Toward Poverty in Early America

The American Revolution brought severe financial hardships to great numbers of people. Many of the soldiers' farms failed during the years of turmoil, and their families were reduced to destitution. Rampant inflation followed the war, and a collapse of the new nation's currency created additional hardships. Aid to the poor continued to follow the practices and policies brought over from England and established at an earlier time in the colonies.

The Industrial Revolution raised living standards for many Americans, but it also created poverty for many others. During the 1800s the expansion of industry concentrated production, population, and poverty in nothern cities. Millions of European immigrants joined native-born migrants from rural areas as laborers living in city tenements. Whole families worked under deplorable conditions to eke out a miserable existence. By the late part of the century, huge overcrowded slums had developed in every major northern city.

Relief was offered to the poor only through local systems of charity. Such systems consisted of orphanages, workhouses, and poor farms as well as a variety of private or religious charities. Direct aid was provided to sick and old persons who had no families to look after them, but there was considerable contempt for the "able-bodied" unemployed. In many cities, soup kitchens kept the poor from actually dying in the streets during hard times.

After the Civil War four million former slaves were added to the ranks of the poor. A number of proposals were made to help black Americans become self-supporting. During Reconstruction days one slogan called for giving "forty acres and a mule" to black heads of families, but little or no real progress was made toward land reform. Many blacks had to work as sharecroppers on the lands of their former masters. They had exchanged slavery for a form of peonage, and most of them lived at the same level of privation they had known as slaves. Legally they were free to go where they wanted, but most found few opportunities elsewhere, even if they had the resources to move away.

The Era of Rugged Individualism

From the beginning American culture had fostered a spirit of self-reliance or "rugged individualism." Late in the nineteenth century this spirit led to a widespread acceptance by Americans of an ideology known as Social Darwinism, which had been developed by English philosopher Herbert Spencer. Spencer's ideas were vigorously supported by the American sociologist William Graham Sumner and other scholars. A growing number of American business leaders were receptive to the notion that their economic success was due to their personal superiority. Social Darwinism provided them with a convenient rationale to account for the plight of the poor: those who were unemployed or forced to accept subsistence wages merely reflected a law of nature whereby society weeded out the unfit. Thus the adoption of Spencerian intellectual orientations and the strong belief in rugged individualism effectively prevented the development of cultural bases for the creation of a national system of social welfare.

As the twentieth century began, however, Social Darwinism became less influential. There was a growing recognition that, in a system where most people were a part of a large pool of urban industrial labor, unemployment was not generally due to personal failures of workers but to downturns in economic cycles, technological displacement, and other economic and social factors.

The Concept of "Social Responsibility"

During the early 1900s, new armies of the poor were created as immigration rose sharply, reaching a peak of 1,285,000 in 1907. The majority of the new immigrants were people from southern and eastern Europe who spoke no English; many were illiterate even in their own languages. They tended to resettle among others like themselves in crowded slums.

In the Progressive Era prior to World War I, a number of Americans began looking more closely at poverty.[34] Journalists, editors, social scientists, lawyers, religious leaders, and politi-

34. Clarke A. Chambers, *Seed Time of Reform: American Social Service and Social Action, 1918–1933* (Minneapolis: University of Minnesota Press, 1963).

cians exposed and denounced conditions in slums, factories, prisons, poorhouses, and mental institutions—as well as in the nation's city halls, state houses, and national capital. Under such prodding, more Americans began to take an active interest in reform through the ballot box and the statute book. Meanwhile, as in the past, dedicated individuals took action on their own. Jane Addams' Hull House in Chicago is probably the best known of the "settlement houses" established in big-city slums to help the very poor.

Before the 1930s, however, there was still no national approach to preventing conditions that created poverty or to alleviating the situation of those caught in its grip. Although Congress placed some restrictions on the actions of big business and took a number of steps to improve the lot of workers, it was the national government's policy to leave charity to private hands or to local authorities. Separate municipalities, counties, states, and religious and secular organizations provided a hodgepodge of efforts to relieve the poor. Not all states assumed responsibility in this area; the state governments that did so often followed approaches similar to those of the English Poor Law. State systems of relief continued to focus on such issues as the control of vagrancy and institutional care for the indigent or helpless.

THE ESTABLISHMENT OF A NATIONAL WELFARE SYSTEM

The 1920s were prosperous years for the United States. Only the nation's farmers had tough times because of an overproduction of crops that resulted in cheap food prices. But eight months after Herbert Hoover took office as President, the stock market crashed in October 1929. Without sufficient capital, businesses foundered; banks closed as depositors withdrew their funds in a rush; markets for goods disappeared; factories closed their doors; workers were laid off; mortgages were foreclosed; farms and homes were lost. Many Americans had no money—even to buy food. The nation was close to economic ruin.

Five months after the crash, four million people were out of work. This figure doubled in

Courtesy Chicago Historical Society

Established in 1889 by Jane Addams and Ellen Gates Starr, Hull House was America's first settlement house. According to Addams, Hull House was "to provide a center for higher civic and social life, to institute and maintain educational and philanthropic enterprises, and to investigate and improve conditions in the industrial sections of Chicago."

a year. By 1933—the worst year of the Great Depression—an estimated fifteen million people were unemployed. Many still working suffered substantial cuts in pay.

Recalling the number of jobless Americans provides only a hint of the underlying privation and suffering experienced by many families during the period. Workers who lost their jobs and homes were often reduced to eating garbage and living in makeshift shanties in vacant lots. Desperate people, including hundreds of thousands of children and adolescents, wandered as vagrants seeking some means of support. The nation desperately needed bold new measures to relieve the situation. With the election of Franklin D. Roosevelt in 1932, the ideology of rugged individualism gave way to a new philosophy of government called the *New Deal*.

WORK-IS-WHAT-I-
WANT-AND-NOT-CHARITY
WHO-WILL-HELP-ME-
GET-A-JOB.-7 YearS-
IN-DETROIT. NO-MONEY
SENT-AWAY-FURNISH-
BEST-OF-REFERENCES
PHONE RANDOLPH 8381 ROOM #59.

Caused by complex economic and social forces, the Great Depression put as many as fifteen million Americans out of work. Early in the Depression, charity was distributed by private donors and voluntary organizations like the Red Cross. As this 1930 photograph indicates, receiving monetary aid was looked upon as a demeaning experience by the out-of-work. By the end of 1930, the resources of private donors, voluntary organizations, and local governments were exhausted; it became apparent to many that some form of federal relief was necessary.

The New Deal

The guiding principle of Roosevelt's plan for economic recovery was to use government spending to get economic activity started, to subsidize it to a self-sustaining level, and then to continue to stimulate its growth. New programs and new legislation quickly pumped money into business and agriculture, provided funds to the states for direct relief, and created work for unemployed youth. The number of jobless was reduced in six years from fifteen million to ten million—hardly an unqualified success. But under Roosevelt's programs the nation lost its fear of impending economic disaster. It also accepted—over the strong objections of some—the principle of manipulation of the economy. Resistance to the idea that the national government shared responsibility for the welfare of its citizens was broken.

As a temporary measure to keep millions from starvation, in 1933 Congress hastily allocated an incredible (for the time) half billion dollars for providing grants to relief programs of the states. Shortly later, about 28 million Americans (about 20 percent of the population) were receiving some form of emergency aid from this source. A significant feature of the program was that it represented an abrupt shift in thinking concerning the role of government in welfare. The philosophy developed that the government had an obligation to provide financial assistance to its citizens during times of crisis.

Along with direct cash relief, a large-scale program of "make work" was designed. Newly created agencies found ways to absorb millions of unemployed people into work projects financed by federal funds.

The first phase of the New Deal was composed largely of temporary measures to relieve pressures of the moment. The next stage was the design and implementation of a more permanent and long-range program to meet the welfare needs of American citizens.

The Social Security Act of 1935

The Social Security Act of 1935 is still the basic form of relief for the poor. The first provision of the act is direct public assistance to several categories of people: dependent children, the indigent aged, the blind, the permanently disabled,

One of many "alphabet agencies" set up during the New Deal period, the NRA (National Recovery Administration) had the job of regulating the economy. Public support of the NRA and of other New Deal programs fostered compliance. The NRA was declared unconstitutional in 1935, the same year the Social Security Act passed into law.

and certain categories of unemployed. Grants-in-aid are given to the states, which supplement these funds. Each state then gives assistance to its residents in need. Within prescribed limits, the state operates its own administrative system and sets its own eligibility requirements. Thus the amount and kind of relief available to a given family or person varies considerably from state to state. This feature of public assistance has been a factor in population movement—needy people have moved from where relief is minimal (e.g., the rural South) to where it is more generous (e.g., the urban North).

The second feature of the Social Security Act is its provision of old-age pensions. The Old Age and Survivors and Disability Insurance Program (popularly known as "Social Security") is operated directly by the federal government. A portion of the worker's pay is withheld by the employer. This sum is matched by the employer, and the total is collected by the Internal Revenue Service. From this continuing flow of funds, workers who retire—or their surviving dependents—are able to draw varying monthly amounts.

The third provision of the Social Security Act is unemployment insurance. Again, both the worker and the employer contribute. The money goes into a trust fund, and workers draw benefits when unemployed. This program is complicated because many states also have their own systems of unemployment compensation. In such cases, the federal government and the state work together. The basic idea has been to provide partial support for unemployed people for a specified amount of time while they seek another job. If they remain out of work, individuals become eligible to receive public assistance under the first provision of the Social Security Act.

One federal and state strategy for improving social conditions is the development of housing for low-income people.

Social welfare programs that began in the 1930s did much to stimulate the growth of the professional field of social work. Bureaucracies were formed at the federal, state, and municipal levels. With large amounts of money to be awarded and millions of potential recipients, a corps of social workers was needed to establish eligibility and to monitor assistance programs.

More Recent Social Legislation

Since the 1930s several significant changes have been introduced in the overall approach to social welfare. Under President Harry S. Truman's Fair Deal, the federal government took on such new responsibilities as providing housing for low-income families. Additional categories of workers were brought into the Social Security program, and the GI Bill enabled many war veterans to continue their schooling at government expense.

During the Eisenhower administration, the National Defense Education Act opened college doors to a number of lower-income groups, but little was done to alter the basic welfare system. The Kennedy adminstration sought to alleviate poverty abroad through the Peace Corps and the Alliance for Progress. John F. Kennedy also intended to design new poverty programs for the United States, but he was assassinated before they were fully developed.

Kennedy's successor, Lyndon B. Johnson, had worked under a number of prior presidents, including Franklin Roosevelt. Johnson's program—the so-called Great Society—included medical care for the aged (Medicare and Medicaid), expanded aid for education, and the ambitious "War on Poverty." To conduct this "war," the Economic Opportunity Act set up a number of new agencies to create new jobs, train the unskilled, and help low-income students obtain additional education. A variety of community action programs were also established, some of which—e.g., Head Start and Upward Bound—were particularly aimed at helping underprivileged young people in the inner city.

OUTLOOKS FOR FURTHER CHANGE

As we have seen, American attitudes toward social welfare programs are based on cultural beliefs that are products of earlier societal conditions. Today changes appear to be taking place in American orientations toward poverty and welfare that, to some degree, indicate the possibility of further modifications in the welfare system.

Despite grumbling about welfare and despite the fact that many blame poverty on a lack of initiative on the part of the poor, Americans have shown themselves to be charitable people, willing not only to provide direct assistance to needy individuals and charitable causes but also to support welfare programs with tax money.

Contemporary Orientations Toward Welfare

In 1945 a survey of Americans indicated that the majority believed that poverty was a result of a lack of initiative and character on the part of the poor. In this survey there was little or no mention of the idea that poverty was caused by conditions in society.[35] In a recent investigation of the attitudes of Americans toward the poor and toward various types of welfare programs, Feagin surveyed more than a thousand adults from all parts of the country and all walks of life.[36] He found that the majority of those surveyed held the view that poverty results from personal failure or other personal factors. A considerable proportion, however, now accepts the view that poverty is socially caused. (For a discussion of Feagin's findings, see Chapter 8, page 233.)

35. Joe R. Feagin, "God Helps Those That Help Themselves," *Psychology Today* (November 1972): 103–104.
36. Ibid., pp. 101–129.

Since the welfare system is based on an official view of poverty that is not accepted by a majority of Americans, we can understand why a majority of our citizens regard the system as unsatisfactory (see Table 19.3). But there are other reasons for dissatisfaction. News reports on "welfare cheating," bureaucratic mismanagement, and the continued existence of extreme poverty attest to the fact that the system does not work as well as it should.

Furthermore, the amount of money spent by the federal government on programs to improve conditions of health, education, and welfare has drastically increased during the last decade. Not only is more money being taken out of workers' paychecks for social security but more tax dollars are going to the agency most responsible for welfare-linked programs, the Department of Health, Education and Welfare. In 1965 the department accounted for a fifth of all federal money spent; today it accounts for a third. HEW currently spends about $100 billion a year, or $301 million every day, on its more than 300 major programs and thousands of minor ones. Each month every seventh person in the United States receives a check from the agency. And its programs affect everyone:

The scope of HEW activities virtually defies imagination—hospitals for merchant seamen, Eskimos, American Indians; a college for the deaf; a printing house for the blind; medical assistance for the elderly and the indigent; counseling for teen-agers in trouble; a range of educational programs from prekindergarten through college, and controls in one degree or another over carpet for your floors, paint for your walls, clothing for your children and what you can or cannot eat, drink or smoke.[37]

Despite grumbling about cheating and about the cumbersome and expensive bureaucracy, the public seems to have become committed to the idea that government has a responsibility for alleviating the plight of the poor. Thus, the question is not whether welfare programs will be continued but rather how best they can be reformed.

Proposals for Reform

In the early 1970s President Nixon proposed legislation aimed at widespread reforms of the welfare system. Essentially, the plan was aimed at three categories of the poor: aged, blind, and disabled adults; families with no breadwinner;

and working people whose incomes were very low. It was hoped that the plan would solve problems that have plagued our welfare system since the 1930s. First, it proposed to abolish the "means test"—elaborate investigations by social workers to see if people qualify for assistance. Second, it sought to equalize assistance from one state to another, to make welfare uniform throughout the country. The plan provided for outright money grants plus food stamps and other benefits so that a family's income would not fall below an arbitrarily selected level. Under the existing welfare plan, people who work have the amount of their earnings subtracted from their welfare payments, thus making it impossible, say, for a woman with children to afford a babysitter while she is working. Nixon's plan proposed doing away with this system, making it more rewarding for those able to work to do so.

The welfare reforms proposed by Nixon were essentially shelved by Congress, and most of the ideas were never implemented. But during the Nixon administration, the federal government sponsored a number of studies to evaluate the impact of some of the proposals. Four major experiments were designed to study the

37. *U.S. News and World Report,* April 21, 1975, p. 45.

Table 19.3. AMERICAN ATTITUDES TOWARD WELFARE AND WELFARE RECIPIENTS

Statements presented to respondents	Percent who agreed	Percent who disagreed	Percent who were uncertain
There are too many people receiving welfare money who should be working.	84	11	5
Many people getting welfare are *not* honest about their need.	71	17	12
Many women getting welfare money are having illegitimate babies to increase the money they get.	61	23	16
Generally speaking, we are spending too *little* money on welfare programs in this country.	34	54	13
Most people on welfare who can work try to find jobs so they can support themselves.	43	49	8

SOURCE: Joe R. Feagin, "God Helps Those That Help Themselves," *Psychology Today* (November 1972): 107.

consequences of a guaranteed annual income (variously called "income maintenance," "negative income tax," and "income subsidy") on selected samples of poor families. Preliminary findings indicate that the recipients of a guaranteed income do not stop working when they receive the money, as opponents of the plan assumed they would.[38] The results of the experiments indicate that such an alternative would work better than the current welfare system.[39] Studies on the effectiveness of a guaranteed-income plan continue, and undoubtedly additional proposals will be made—leading ultimately to significant modifications of the present welfare system.

Perhaps the simplest way of gaining a perspective on our society's efforts in this area is to remind ourselves that prior to the 1930s the United States had no national welfare policy at all. Today a billion-dollar welfare system affects the lives of all citizens. As government officials and social scientists bring new research findings and new strategies to the task of fighting poverty, our society may come closer to solving one of its most pressing problems.

SUMMARY

Every society provides for the training of its young. But it is only rather recently—since the impact of urbanization and industrialization—that school systems have become necessary to provide individuals with the knowledge and skills of their society.

Since colonial times American education has had a succession of different goals, depending on the needs of society. Although socializing the young remains fundamental, there are differences of opinion as to just what the schools should be doing. Today the schools have the primary responsibility for training the experts society needs.

Education pays in the United States. Not only does the college graduate earn considerably more than the high-school graduate, but graduation at either level means an appreciably better income than the dropout at that level can expect. The number of years of education completed is now the single best predictor of an individual's economic performance.

Position in the class structure helps determine what education individuals get, and the education they get helps determine whether they rise, sink, or remain at the same level in the class structure. Place of residence, family income, family background, and teachers' expectations and values all have their effects. Race is particularly influential: the child of black parents is less likely than the white child to receive a good education.

Opinion is divided on why some people are more able than others to take advantage of educational opportunity. It appears that social and cultural factors, including the self-fulfilling prophecies of teachers, play a larger role in scholastic achievement than genetic ones.

American society attempts to improve the lives of its citizens not only through the educational system but also through programs of social welfare. The social welfare system is based on the belief that poverty results from impersonal factors rather than from personal defects of the poor or a divine plan.

American orientations toward welfare reach back to seventeenth-century English policy. Not until the 1930s did the United States institute a national welfare system. Basic to this system is the Social Security Act of 1935. Today the welfare system is growing larger and more complex even while it is under increasing attack. Numerous proposals have been made to reform and improve it.

38. Harold W. Watts, "The Graduated Work Incentive Experiments: Current Progress," *American Economic Review: Papers and Proceedings*, 61 (May 1971): 6.
39. Bonny Baker, "Guaranteed Annual Income: A Study of Current Proposals and Experiments," mimeographed paper, Department of Sociology, Washington State University, 1974.

EPILOGUE
THE SOCIOLOGIST IN
CONTEMPORARY SOCIETY

20 The Sociologist in Contemporary Society

SOCIOLOGY AND PUBLIC POLICY

Designing and Evaluating Social Programs   Scientists as Lobbyists

THE RESPONSIBILITIES OF THE SOCIOLOGIST

The Sociologists' Dilemma   Social Reform and Social Science

THE ETHICS OF RESEARCH

Research Methods   Deception and Human Freedom   The Right of Privacy Versus the Right to Know   The Outcome

In the preceding chapters, we have viewed sociology from a number of perspectives. We have found that sociology is more than an accumulation of data, explanations, and generalizations; it is an exciting venture in the history of ideas. Sociology is an attempt to bring scientific objectivity to the study of the ways people relate themselves to each other in group settings and the consequences of such relationships. The founders of sociology somewhat grandiosely hoped to develop a science of society that would quickly provide a guide to solving social problems and achieving a just and harmonious social order. Obviously, sociology has by no means accomplished these goals. The field has many deficiencies. In its development of theory, it is characterized by numerous competing perspectives or orientations—e.g., functionalism, neopositivism, symbolic interactionism, conflict theory. There is no consensus on the merits of its techniques and methods of research. Even the mode of reporting sociological findings—e.g., in humanistic reports, statistical summaries, or mathematical models—remains a topic of debate.

In spite of such problems, however, the discipline has made impressive progress. Sociologists have gradually changed their focus from speculation about the overall structure of societies to a more detailed empirical examination of specific phenomena, such as social stratification, deviance, public opinion, divorce, demographic change, and prejudice. In so doing, they have developed an extensive body of verified findings about social processes. And increasingly, their findings are being applied in governmental and privately sponsored programs aimed at remedying societal ills.

In the sections that follow we will look at the accomplishments of the discipline, particularly with regard to the formation and evaluation of public policy. We will review the responsibilities of sociologists to society, to the discipline, and to their students and conclude with a discussion of ethical problems in contemporary sociological research.

SOCIOLOGY AND PUBLIC POLICY

For many years American sociologists tended to emphasize the goals of social science over those of social reform. Uncertain of sociology's claim to acceptance as a science and uncertain even of the validity of their own findings, most early sociologists avoided confrontations in which they might have been called upon to demonstrate the accomplishments of their field. As the discipline has continued to develop, however, sociologists have become far less hesitant to add their voices to those of other expert witnesses who can aid in the shaping of social policy. Activism, in other words, has become increasingly acceptable to sociologists as the scientific stature of their discipline has become increasingly secure. Today, most sociologists are willing to make their views known on public issues whether or not they wish to become actively involved in seeking social reform.

Some idea of the extent of this involvement can be seen in the increasing application of sociological knowledge to the development of public policy.[1] Between 1955 and 1973 the proportion of the national budget devoted to human welfare resources rose from 21 percent to 45 percent. Increasing amounts of tax money have gone for research and the development of programs in such departments as the National Institutes of Health, the National Institute of Mental Health, and the Department of Health, Education and Welfare; in 1971 these three agencies received almost $1.5 billion for research and development. Several thousand sociologists shared in the use of these funds.[2]

As the amount of money for government programs designed to remedy social problems has increased, so too has the number of sociologists employed in nonprofit private agencies and government. About a third of American sociologists are employed in nonacademic settings (see Table 20.1). Furthermore, between a fourth and a third of sociologists located in colleges and universities received research grants from the federal government. In the field of crime reduction alone, some $70 million was appropriated in fiscal year 1973. Horowitz and Katz have assessed the interest of the federal government in social science research as follows:

This assortment of data adds up to a steadily increasing set of federal expenditures for human resources, public welfare, environmental improvement, education, and other economic and social purposes. This increase takes place against a backdrop of declining federal expenditures for other areas: national security and direct military outlays are being reduced to absorb the new social services. . . . In order to service this changeover properly, manpower resource allocations have shifted from the physical and engineering sciences to the social and behavioral sciences. Thus, we are no longer dealing with the sort of marginal expenditures for social sciences customary in the past, but a new priority that raises profound qualitative considerations by the very fact of the magnitude of expenditures and outlays for the "soft" sciences by federal agencies, private foundations, and a host of other American economic and social institutions.[3]

In the sections that follow we will briefly discuss some of the ways sociologists have become involved in public policy decisions.

Table 20.1 TRENDS IN SOCIOLOGICAL EMPLOYMENT, 1956–1970

Year	Estimated Number of Professional Sociologists Employed		
	By colleges and universities	In nonacademic positions	Total
1956	3750	1250	5000
1958	4500	1500	6000
1960	4875	1625	6500
1962	5525	1875	7500
1965	6000	2000	8000
1967	6750	2250	9000
1968	7500	2500	10,000
1970	9000	3000	12,000

SOURCE: *Occupation Outlook Handbook*, Department of Labor, Bureau of Labor Statistics, editions for 1957, 1959, 1961, 1963–1964, 1966–1967, 1968–1969, 1970–1971, and 1972–1973.

1. Irving L. Horowitz and James E. Katz, *Social Science and Public Policy* (New York: Praeger Publishers, Inc., 1975).
2. Ibid., pp. 7–11.
3. Ibid., p. 21.

In recent years many sociologists have become actively involved in the planning of national policy. The sociologist pictured here, for instance, was particularly involved on May 13, 1970, when a member of the Underground Press Syndicate hurled a cottage cheese pie into his face during a hearing conducted by the President's Commission on Obscenity and Pornography.

DESIGNING AND EVALUATING SOCIAL PROGRAMS

A conference of sociological educators was recently sponsored by the National Institutes of Mental Health. The purpose of the conference was to determine ways in which sociological research and the training of professional sociologists could be made more relevant to national needs. This group of educators was able to identify some eighteen areas in which sociologists could make an important input concerning national policy. Among the areas identified were poverty, community planning, race and ethnic relations, medical care, alcoholism and drug abuse, and mental illness.[4] Sociologists have already made important contributions in some of these areas.

Policy Research

Sociology is essentially a research discipline. One of its goals is to accumulate a scientific base for designing and evaluating procedures for solving problems with social origins. Sociology has other goals as well; for example, it proposes and tests explanatory theories of the ways in which specific social conditions—"good" or "bad"—are brought about. But even this is related to the problem of designing ameliorative programs.

In a direct sense, sociology can play only a limited role in the actual reshaping of society. Legislative decision making is not in the hands of sociologists. Often they serve as consultants or advisors. Sometimes, like other citizens, they form pressure groups with respect to some specific problem. But ameliorative programs and policies are put into law only by elected political leaders acting with the support of their constituencies.

The central role of sociologists remains one of getting the facts together and interpreting them within frameworks that help explain what causes what. From this explanatory base, sociologists can design and propose ameliorative policies and procedures for alleviating unwanted social conditions. They can also evaluate whether the benefits of such procedures outweigh the costs and whether the procedures can be generally successful.

Of course, social policy design and evaluation is not the exclusive domain of sociologists. Much of this activity is done in conjunction with other kinds of social scientists. While the composition of an interdisciplinary team depends on the nature of the problem, sociologists often cooperate with economists, psychologists, social workers, political scientists, and statisticians on a great variety of projects.

Recently social scientists have worked together to test the belief that poor people would lose their motivation to work if they were given a guaranteed annual income (see Chapter 19, page 587). A $5 million project studied 1300 households composed of low-income people in

4. Nicholas J. Demerath et al., *Social Policy and Sociology* (New York: Academic Press, Inc., 1974).

urban New Jersey. These people, who received a guaranteed income determined by a complex formula, did not stop working.[5] Preliminary findings of other experiments, in rural North Carolina and Iowa, in Gary, Indiana, in Seattle, Washington, and in Denver, Colorado, also seem to indicate that some form of guaranteed annual income would be an effective substitute for the existing, often inequitable, welfare system.[6]

Developing Social Indicators

Another significant area of sociological activity lies in the development of indicators of the nation's social well-being. For decades the federal government has made use of economic indicators—for example, the Gross National Product, employment and unemployment trends, new housing starts, imports, exports, department-store sales, and automobile production—in assessing the economic health of the nation and in formulating economic policy. The development of comparable indicators to measure the nation's *social* health is now a realistic possibility. Indeed, steps have already been undertaken by the federal government to develop such a set of indicators.[7] The Department of Health, Education, and Welfare, for example, has assembled

a report that examines trends concerning health and illness, mobility, the quality of the physical environment, income and poverty, public order and safety, learning, science and art, and alienation.[8] Another agency, the Office of Statistical Policy in the Bureau of the Budget, has been assigned the responsibility of assembling and disseminating an even more elaborate and coherent system of social indicators.[9] The utility of such indicators has been summarized in a recent report of the National Academy of Sciences:

Such indicators could serve several purposes. They would be warning signals of dangerous and undesirable trends in the nation, such as increases in crime or poverty, that could call attention to the need for remedial action before the problems reached a critical stage. They could help assess the performance of our social institutions and of special programs or policies established to remedy social ills and to move toward a more ideal society. They could serve as the basis for more informed and enlightened forecasting and action by both public and private agencies.[10]

Needless to say, data derived from sociological research will play a significant part in these new developments.

Sociological Advisers

It has been suggested that the staff of each member of Congress include a social scientist consultant to aid in the formulation of policy. It has also been advocated that sociologists become actively involved in similar roles at local and state levels.[11] More important, there have been numerous proposals from many sources for the establishment of a national council of social advisers, which would be composed of sociologists, anthropologists, psychologists, and political scientists. These professionals would occupy a position in national policy making that would parallel that of the current Council of Economic Advisers. The social advisers would provide the president with a perspective on national and international affairs that is now badly lacking.[12] Finally, many scholars argue that policy-formulating study groups and groups represent-

5. Harold W. Watts "The Graduated Work Incentive Experiments: Current Progress," *American Economic Review: Papers and Proceedings,* 61 (May 1971): 6.

6. Bonny Barker, "Guaranteed Annual Income: A Study of Current Proposals," mimeographed paper, Department of Sociology, Washington State University, 1974.

7. For an introduction to the problem of developing social indicators, see Raymond A. Bauer, ed. *Social Indicators* (Cambridge, Mass.: The M.I.T. Press, 1967); and Eleanor B. Sheldon and Wilbert E. Moore, eds., *Indicators of Social Change: Concepts and Measurements* (New York: Russell Sage Foundation, 1968).

8. U.S. Department of Health, Education and Welfare, *Toward a Social Report* (Washington, D.C.: U.S. Government Printing Office, 1969).

9. *The Behavioral and Social Sciences: Outlook and Needs* (Washington, D.C.: National Academy of Sciences, September 1969), p. 104.

10. Ibid., pp. 101-102.

11. Irving L. Horowitz, *Professing Sociology* (Chicago: Aldine Publishing Co., 1968); Amitai Etzioni makes a similar proposal in "On Public Affairs Statements of Professional Associations," *The American Sociologist,* 3, No. 4 (November 1968).

12. For example, of the eleven commissioners who were members of the National Advisory Commission on Civil Disorders, seven were lawyers, two were businessmen, one was a labor leader, and one, Roy Wilkins, was executive director of the N.A.A.C.P. For more extensive discussion of this issue, see Scott Greer, *The Logic of Social Inquiry* (Chicago: Aldine Publishing Co., 1969), esp. Ch. 16, "Social Science and Social Policy," pp. 186–195.

ing divergent viewpoints are urgently needed within the formal structure of the American Sociological Association and perhaps even within its regional affiliates.

Only the future will show what impact the expert knowledge of sociologists will have on national and local policy making. But as sociology continues to develop a more complete understanding of social causation, ameliorative technology, and social policy evaluation, it promises to make valuable contributions to the improvement of society.

SCIENTISTS AS LOBBYISTS

In recent years sociologists and other scientists have become more willing to take stands regarding political and social issues and to take responsibility for the uses to which their research is put. Not too many years ago, one of the major developers of the hydrogen bomb, Dr. Robert Oppenheimer, was ostracized from governmental research because of his critical questioning of the use of his discovery. Today the Federation of American Scientists, a public-service oriented scientific lobby, is working to make certain scientists will be heard.

The National Council of the Federation of American Scientists consists of thirty-four Nobel laureates as well as scientists from all fields, including sociology.[13] During the past four years, the FAS has appeared before congressional committees in opposition to the development of the antiballistic missile and the supersonic transport plane, organized and sent the first delegation of American scientists to the People's Republic of China, circulated a petition opposing cutbacks in biomedical research, and objected to policies developed by the Environmental Protection Agency.

The organization and activities of the FAS make clear that as scientists have become more involved in doing research for government and business so too have they become more active in lobbying for and against public policy. Despite the inherent dangers in becoming partisans for one cause or another, scientists have decided that their responsibility cannot end with research and theory.

THE RESPONSIBILITIES OF THE SOCIOLOGIST

The increasing involvement of sociologists in the formation and evaluation of public policy has led to heightened debate on their responsibility. Should there be any limits on the kinds of research sociologists perform? Should sociologists be held responsible for the uses to which their research is put? Should they attempt to remain neutral and objective; or is a value-free science of society an impossibility? (For a brief history of this issue in sociology, see Chapter 1, pages 2–21.)

These and other issues came to a head in 1964 with the advent of Project Camelot, a government-sponsored study of insurgency and potential revolution.[14] Sponsored by the Army Research Office of the Department of Defense, this project was an attempt to "make it possible to predict and influence politically significant aspects of social change in the developing nations of the world." In particular, Project Camelot was designed to measure and forecast "the causes of revolutions and insurgency in underdeveloped areas of the world" and to try to find ways to eliminate or cope with these revolutions and insurgencies.[15]

The Department of Defense offered social scientists, among them sociologists, a contract to design and carry out the study under the general outline developed by the Army Research Office. (Typically, social scientists request grants from research sponsors for projects of their own choosing.) But before the project could get under way, controversy broke out. A Chilean scholar denounced it in public; Amercian public officials expressed horror over the implications of the project and its potential effect on American foreign policy; and the project was cancelled.

Sociologists and other social scientists debated the propriety of the research contract, concentrating on such issues as whether the project was scientifically feasible, whether the mili-

13. *Newsletter of the Federation of American Scientists,* Washington, D.C., 1975.

14. Irving L. Horowitz, ed., *The Rise and Fall of Project Camelot* (Cambridge, Mass.: The M.I.T. Press, 1967).

15. Horowitz and Katz, *Social Science and Public Policy,* p. 102.

tary had too much influence over the direction the research would take, and whether the project was ethical, given its political implications. Among the by-products of this debate was the development of a Code of Ethics by the American Sociological Association (see Tools of Sociology, page 596). The code covers a variety of ethical issues, some rising out of the controversy over Project Camelot (for example, rules 10 and 11), others relating more generally to objectivity and integrity in research. Formally adopted in 1971, this code was the first systematic attempt to provide sociologists with guidelines for their research. It will undoubtedly undergo modification as its virtues and flaws become more obvious. In the remaining sections of this chapter, we will briefly look at other ethical issues that confront sociologists today.

THE SOCIOLOGIST'S DILEMMA

As we have seen, there is growing recognition by the federal government and other groups that sociological knowledge may have considerable utility for those whose task it is to formulate new social policies. Although such groups are aware of sociology's limitations, they see the social and behavioral sciences as a better guide to understanding social behavior than such alternatives as folk wisdom or undisciplined observation. A report of the National Academy of Sciences stated the matter as follows:

Behavioral science knowledge is a source of understanding about social and individual behavior that has been confirmed by as careful observation, testing, or statistical analysis as possible. Much of the knowledge of the behavioral sciences is fragmented, much is based on limited verification, and many propositions are only approximate explanations of complex social and behavioral phenomena. The behavioral sciences are, nonetheless, an important source of information, analysis and explanation about group and individual behavior, and thus an essential and increasingly relevant instrument of modern government. At the same time there is a need to be concerned as much with the development of the behavioral sciences as with their use; indeed, to see both the development and the use of the behavioral sciences as parts of a total and continuing problem.[16]

The growing utility of sociological knowledge would seem to demand that sociologists devote an increasing amount of their efforts to research geared to programs aimed at reforming society. Yet if the field is to move forward as a science, a major effort must be directed toward developing a better understanding of basic social processes and formulating more abstract sociological theory. Must a sociologist choose between these alternatives? What are the consequences of such a choice?

If sociologists choose to be analysts who assemble knowledge but never take part in deciding how it will be used, they isolate themselves from the society of which they are a part. On the other hand, if sociologists actively enter the struggle to change society, they may lose their scientific identity and become merely partisans — committed to some kinds of changes and not to others. While partisanship may have an altruistic intent, it is dictated by personal values and not by the logic and rules of the scientific method. Individuals who attempt to persuade others to adopt social innovations dictated by ideological premises — whatever their merits — are difficult to perceive as disinterested investigators. Their value as "expert witnesses" — as suppliers of trustworthy knowledge — may become subject to question. But it can also be argued that those who call themselves objective actually support the establishment by their so-called neutrality. They may be no more objective or neutral than those who openly advocate specific changes. Thus all sociologists may be partisan in some sense.

These considerations have led some sociologists to argue that they are caught on the horns of a dilemma. If they choose the scientific role, they may be shirking their social responsibility, deluding themselves about their neutrality, or both. If they choose to take an active part in rearranging the social order, they may lose credibility as scientists. Although this dilemma has no perfect solution, there are, as we shall see, several different ways in which contemporary sociologists have attempted to resolve it.

16. *The Behavioral Sciences and the Federal Government* (Washington, D.C.: National Academy of Sciences, 1968), p. 2.

TOOLS OF SOCIOLOGY
CODE OF ETHICS OF THE AMERICAN SOCIOLOGICAL ASSOCIATION

Recently the American Sociological Association formulated a set of ethical principles covering both the research process and the applications of research findings. This code, which has been officially adopted by the membership of the ASA, establishes the following guidelines:

1. *Objectivity in Research.* In his research the sociologist must maintain scientific objectivity.

2. *Integrity in Research.* The sociologist should recognize his own limitations and, when appropriate, seek more expert assistance or decline to undertake research beyond his competence. . . .

3. *Respect of the Research Subject's Rights to Privacy and Dignity.* Every person is entitled to the right of privacy and dignity of treatment. The sociologist must respect these rights.

4. *Protection of Subjects from Personal Harm.* All research should avoid causing personal harm to subjects used in research.

5. *Preservation of Confidentiality of Research Data.* Confidental information provided by a research subject must be treated as such by the sociologist. . . . Even though research information is not a privileged communication under the law, the sociologist must, as far as possible, protect subjects and informants. . . . The obligation of the sociologist includes the use and storage of original data to which a subject's name is attached. When requested, the identity of an organization or subject must be adequately disguised in publication.

6. *Presentation of Research Findings.* The sociologist must present his findings honestly and without distortion. There should be no omission of data from a research report which might significantly modify the interpretation of findings.

7. *Misuse of Research Role.* The sociologist must not use his role as a cover to obtain information for other than professional purposes.

8. *Acknowledgement of Research Collaboration and Assistance.* The sociologist must acknowledge the professional contributions or assistance of all persons who collaborated in the research.

9. *Disclosure of the Sources of Financial Support.* The sociologist must report fully all sources of financial support in his research publications and any special relations to the sponsor that might affect the interpretation of the findings.

10. *Distortion of Findings by Sponsor.* The sociologist is obliged to clarify publicly any distortion by a sponsor or client of the findings of a research project in which he has participated.

11. *Disassociation from Unethical Research Arrangements.* The sociologist must not accept such grants, contracts, or research assignments as appear likely to require violation of the principles above, and must publicly terminate the work or formally disassociate himself from the research if he discovers such a violation and is unable to achieve its correction.

12. *Interpretation of Ethical Principles.* When the meaning and application of these principles are unclear, the sociologist should seek the judgment of the relevant agency or committee designated by the American Sociological Association. Such consulation, however, does not free the sociologist from his individual responsibility for decisions or from his accountability to the profession.

13. *Applicability of Principles.* In the conduct of research the principles enunciated above should apply to research in any area either within or outside the United States of America.

Source: *Code of Ethics of the American Sociological Association,* Washington, D.C.

SOCIAL REFORM AND SOCIAL SCIENCE

Sociologists have a long history of trying to apply the basic principles generated within the field to the specific problems of people. For example, rural sociologists have worked for many decades with farm populations to help them take advantage of changes and improvements in agricultural technology.[17] They have been successful in their work because tested theories are available concerning the processes by which innovations spread when people adopt new ideas. Demographic sociologists have taken part in efforts to promote the development of family-planning clinics for the poor, not only in the United States but also in developing countries, because of their hypothesis that large families perpetuate poverty and illness. Medical sociologists have applied basic principles of formal and informal social organization to many aspects of health care, thereby helping make the lot of the patient more tolerable.[18] These and other types of social engineering are as much within the traditions of science as the application of well-tested biological theories to the practice of medicine.[19]

A second way in which socially responsible but scientifically oriented sociologists have been able to resolve the sociologist's dilemma is through their selection of research problems. It would be impossible to list all the societal concerns that have become better understood through the research efforts of sociologists, but among them are racial prejudice and discrimination, drug addiction, the impact of our prison system, problems of the aged and of the bereaved, homosexuality, juvenile delinquency, marital discord, the effects of poverty, sexual discrimination, problems of the unemployed, the effects of televised violence, worker alienation and discontent, and the causes of riots and panics. Thus it can scarcely be said that even

basic sociological research has been conducted in the isolation of some ivory tower. A glance through the professional journals in which sociologists publish their findings shows that, while some research is relatively abstract, the overwhelming number of research-oriented sociologists have chosen to address themselves to achieving a better understanding of specific societal problems. The greater the effort going into such research, sociologists believe, the more reliable the knowledge that will be developed to serve as a basis for social reform.

In recent years a third position has developed with respect to the sociologist's dilemma: some sociologists have elected to de-emphasize, or even abandon, their scientific pursuits in order to join in an attempt to achieve immediate social reforms on a broad scale. The means these sociologists have proposed for changing society vary greatly according to their particular ideological persuasions and value commitments, ranging all the way from the moderate strategy of persuading legislators and the public to improve the existing social system to the extreme strategy, advocated by a small minority, of overthrowing the society through revolution.

Finally, some sociologists resolve the dilemma in their roles as teachers. It has been suggested that sociology courses have a dual purpose: to teach students to see their social worlds more objectively, and to transform the "unformed and uninformed [students] into decision-making persons. In short, to transform a passive mass into an active public."[20] Scholars who subscribe to the second view of their teaching activities are very much activists, even if they limit their efforts to the classroom.

THE ETHICS OF RESEARCH

Ethical problems are common to all disciplines that have a significant impact on our lives. Following the development of the nuclear bomb in World War II, physicists found themselves in the

17. C. Arnold Anderson, "Trends in Rural Sociology," in *Sociology Today*, ed. Robert K. Merton et al. (New York: Basic Books, Inc., 1959), pp. 360–375.
18. See Irene B. Taeuber, "Population and Society," in *Handbook of Modern Sociology*, ed. Robert E. L. Faris (Chicago: Rand McNally & Co., 1964), pp. 83–126; and Saxon Graham, "Sociological Aspects of Health and Illness," in Faris, ed., *Handbook of Modern Sociology*, pp. 310–347.
19. Philip M. Hauser, "Social Science and Social Engineering," *Philosophy of Science* 16 (July 1949): 209–218.
20. Horowitz, *Professing Sociology*, p. 134.

midst of a heated debate concerning the ethical implications of their work. More recently, medical and biological researchers have been involved in controversy over the ethical implications of organ transplants, chemical and germ warfare, the use of insecticides, the meaning of abortion, the use of prisoners in medical research, and the prolongation of human life through "heroic measures."

Like other disciplines, sociology has had its share of controversy over the ethical implications of research. In the mid-1960s, for example, sociologists were involved in the long debate over Project Camelot (page 594). Research studies by individual sociologists and sociological teams have also created ethical controversies. In this section we will illustrate such ethical issues by a close look at one such controversy — the debate over Laud Humphreys's study of male homosexuality, *Tearoom Trade,* first published in 1970.

RESEARCH METHODS

For the purposes of his study, Humphreys chose a specific subpopulation of male homosexuals — those men who seek impersonal sex in the public restrooms of parks.[21] The majority of the men Humphreys studied were not part of the homosexual subculture; indeed, many did not perceive themselves as homosexuals. Most were married and had children. The "tearoom trade" cuts across social class lines; among the participants Humphreys studied there were semiskilled workers, truck drivers, teachers, salesmen, and executives.

Humphreys's objective in doing this research study was to learn about the social origins and social behavior of the men who engaged in the "tearoom trade" and to combine this knowledge with existing findings to gain a better understanding of the homosexual world. He hoped, too, that his findings would lead to greater social acceptance of homosexuality.

The research was carried out in two stages. First, by performing the role of lookout (or "watchqueen"), whose job it is to signal the participants when an outsider approaches, Hum-

phreys was able to observe the activities of the persons engaged in impersonal sex in park restrooms. During this stage, he wrote down the license numbers of their automobiles. Later on, he posed as a market researcher in order to gain access to the license registers from the police. He was thus able to attach names and addresses to the license numbers. A year after the first stage, having first changed his way of dressing, hair style, and car, he interviewed a sample of fifty tearoom participants. So as not to embarrass his subjects or cause them trouble, he added their names to a different survey he was involved in, did the interviewing himself, and did not notify these men about the real object of his questions.

Humphreys took elaborate precautions to ensure that the information he collected would not be used against the research subjects. As far as anyone knows, none of the men studied recognized Humphreys or suffered because of his research. But some social scientists have charged that Humphreys violated at least two of the rules of the Code of Ethics (page 596) — the rule dealing with respect for privacy and dignity of subjects and, potentially, the rule dealing with the protection of subjects from personal harm, in this case through the possibility of disclosure of information.

DECEPTION AND HUMAN FREEDOM

The ethical problems involved in the Humphreys study center around the issue of deception. Humphreys has been accused of deceiving the tearoom participants when he posed as a "watchqueen," the police when he posed as a market researcher in order to obtain access to their files, and the fifty interview subjects, who were unaware of his real purpose in interviewing them.[22] In his postscript to *Tearoom Trade,*

21. Laud Humphreys, *Tearoom Trade: Impersonal Sex in Public Places* (Chicago: Aldine Publishing Co., 1970). In homosexual jargon, public restrooms in which homosexual activity takes place are known as "tearooms."

22. This section is based on Donald P. Warwick, "Tearoom Trade: Means and Ends in Social Research," *The Hastings Center Studies,* 1, No. 1 (1973): 27–38. For other criticisms of Humphreys's study, see Nicholas von Hoffman, "The Sociological Snoopers," *Washington Post,* January 30, 1970; and Myron Glazer, *The Research Adventure: Promise and Problems of Field Work* (New York: Random House, Inc., 1972), pp. 107–124.

Humphreys justified this deception on the grounds that it was the only way to study tearoom behavior without exposing the subjects to personal harm.

According to sociologist Donald Warwick, Humphreys's deception violated human freedom. First, Humphreys misled the subjects and the police about who he was, what he was doing, and why he wanted particular information, thus receiving information that might have been unavailable to him had he told the truth. Second, by spying on them, he infringed upon the privacy of the subjects in that they were unable to refrain from revealing things about themselves they did not want to reveal. Third, if Humphreys had been unable to keep the data secret, great harm could have been done to the research subjects—by the police, their families, or their employers, or more subtly in that the realization that someone knew or that they had been studied without their consent could cause them anxiety. Finally, Humphreys violated the freedom of other researchers in that his research methods might cause other research subjects and the public as a whole to distrust social scientists. As Warwick points out, at least 250 communities have already passed legislation restricting the activities of survey interviewers or prohibiting surveys entirely.

The goals of Humphreys's study were knowledge about the family life and general behavior of tearoom participants—that is, their nonhomosexual as well as homosexual behavior—and the use of this knowledge to change the current repressive laws against homosexuals. Essentially, Humphreys claimed that these goals justified the deception. But though Warwick agrees that scientists have an obligation to do research on controversial and politically sensitive subjects, he insists that they do not have the right to use unethical means—that is, to deceive or manipulate research subjects—in order to do this important research. For who is to decide which research goals are important and which causes are good? Is it any more ethical for a so-

cial scientist to spy on homosexuals in order to relieve the plight of homosexuals than for the FBI or CIA to spy on American citizens to protect the United States from internal subversion? Do the ends justify the means? Warwick thinks not.

THE RIGHT OF PRIVACY VERSUS THE RIGHT TO KNOW

The defense of Laud Humphreys's research methods is based on the contention that the right of individuals to privacy must be balanced against the right of society to know about and understand human social behavior.[23] As Irving Louis Horowitz and Lee Rainwater, Humphreys's principal advisers, put it, social science research "demystifies" human life and culture, making it possible for people to "understand themselves and each other in an existential sense."[24]

Horowitz and Rainwater note that Humphreys did the first part of his research in public restrooms in public parks and that he had as much right to be there as the tearoom participants he studied. By choosing a public location for their acts, the research subjects had sacrificed their own privacy and were aware that they were running the risk of being discovered.

Horowitz and Rainwater also question the contention that Humphreys deceived the subjects and violated their rights by not telling them who he was and what his purpose was. Why, they ask, did Humphreys have an obligation to tell? Virtually no conversation goes on in tearooms; it is an accepted convention for participants to reveal nothing about themselves to each other. Rather than attempting to deceive, Horowitz and Rainwater argue, Humphreys was exercising tact.

According to Horowitz and Rainwater, the most significant violation of individual privacy lay in the act of writing down and tracing license numbers and interviewing the subjects in their own homes. They note that Humphreys used extreme tact and skill, ensuring that the persons involved could in no way be identified by anyone other than the researcher himself. Thus a tremendous burden of trust was placed on Humphreys in this situation, a burden that he proved himself equal to.

23. This section is based on Irving Louis Horowitz and Lee Rainwater, "Journalistic Moralizers," *Trans-action*, 7, No. 7 (May 1970): 5–8.

24. Ibid., p. 5.

VIEWPOINTS   PRIVACY AND SOCIAL RESEARCH

■ It is certainly not that sociologists should deliberately violate any laws of the land, only that they should leave to the courtrooms and to the legislatures just what interpretations of these laws governing the protection of private citizens are to be made. Would the refusal of a family to disclose information to the Census Bureau on the grounds of the right to privacy take precedence over the United States government's right to knowledge in order to make budgetary allocations and legislation concerning these people? The really tough moral problem is that the idea of an inviolable right of privacy may move counter to the belief that society is obligated to secure the other rights and welfare of its citizenry. Indeed one might say that this is a key contradiction in the contemporary position of the liberal: he wants to protect the rights of private citizens, but at the same time he wants to develop a welfare system that could hardly function without at least some knowledge about these citizens. . . .

Laud Humphreys has gone beyond the existing literature in sexual behavior and has proven once again, if indeed proof were ever needed, that ethnographic research is a powerful tool for social understanding and policymaking. And these are the criteria by which the research should finally be evaluated professionally. If the nonprofessional has other measurements of this type of research, let him present these objections in legal brief and do so explicitly. No such attempt to intimidate Humphreys for wrongdoing in any legal sense has been made, and none is forthcoming. The only indictment seems to be among those who are less concerned with the right to know than they are with the sublime desire to remain in ignorance. In other words, the issue is not liberalism vs. conservatism or privacy vs. publicity, but much more simply and to the point, the right of scientists to conduct their work as against the right of [others] to defend social mystery and private agony.
Irving Louis Horowitz and **Lee Rainwater**
"On Journalistic Moralizers"

● Nearly every moral code in human history has condemned lying as evil and destructive of mutual trust. Yet deception is common in social science research and, in some areas, virtually the norm. In order to facilitate the collection of data, or to advance man's knowledge, or to help the oppressed, researchers condone deception in the laboratory, on the streets, and in our social institutions. They deliberately misrepresent the intent of their experiments, assume false appearances, and use other subterfuges as dubious means to questionable ends. These tactics are unethical and unjustified. They are also dangerous, because they may spread to other segments of society. . . .

The scientist insists that he only uses deception to advance man's understanding of himself and society, and thus to promote human welfare. . . .

First of all, it is highly doubtful that any study involving deception ultimately promotes human welfare. . . . As Cicero put it: "Knowledge that is divorced from justice should be called cunning rather than wisdom."

Secondly, if it is all right to use deceit to advance knowledge, then why not for reasons of national security, for maintaining the Presidency, or to save one's own hide? Who is to decide which gods merit a sacrifice of the truth? . . .

At the present we too often dispose of ethical questions quickly so that we can get on with the real business of theory and research. The time has come to examine not only the techniques, but the moral implications of social research. . . . In the social sciences, as in politics, the truth is often sacrificed on the altar of some higher principle. The cumulative results are a pervasive suspicion of Government and an increasing wariness in dealing with our fellow man. These are the natural fruits of a deceiving society. Social scientists . . . are too quick to shrug off their own complicity in this moral decay. We should now put our own house in order with a permanent moratorium on deceptive research.
Donald P. Warwick
"Social Scientists Ought to Stop Lying"

Furthermore, Horowitz and Rainwater insist that the methods used by Humphreys cannot be equated with those used by the police, the FBI, or the CIA to catch lawbreakers or subversives. The latter spy on people to catch them in wrongdoing and to put them in prison if possible. Sociological research is not designed to catch people in wrongdoing, nor is it focused on individuals as such. Sociologists do not intend to have a direct effect on the lives of the particular people they study. Rather their interest in people lies in seeing them as part of some larger social process. Since no purpose would be served by identifying particular individuals, "sociologists uphold the right to know in a context of the surest protection for the integrity of the subject matter and the private rights of the people studied."[25]

With regard to the tearoom study, the right to know is predicated on the larger social good expected to ensue from careful research and the fact that scientific knowledge can be used to overcome long held stereotypes about homosexuals and help change public—especially police—behavior toward them. In sum, Horowitz and Rainwater argue that social research into all areas of human life is needed and that it should and can be carried out in such a way to protect the anonymity of the individuals being studied.

THE OUTCOME

As we have seen, the reception of *Tearoom Trade* by sociologists varied. Some condemned it; others defended it. In 1970 the book received the C. Wright Mills Award of the Society for the Study of Social Problems. It was well received by homosexual groups, and Humphreys was elected to the National Committee for Sexual Civil Liberties.

Looking back over the controversy surrounding the study, Humphreys has had second thoughts about the research techniques he used:

Since then, although I remain convinced that it is ethical to observe interaction in public places and to interview willing and informed respondents, I direct my students to inform research subjects before interviewing them. Were I to repeat the tearoom study, I would spend another year or so in cultivating and expanding the category of willing respondents.[26]

The ethical and moral problems involved in the debate over research techniques have no simple solutions. Do people now fear that they will be spied upon by sociologists? Has Humphreys added to the public image of the social scientist as a manipulator and deceiver who is not to be trusted? Or does his research show that social scientists can do sensitive work in such a way that research subjects can put full confidence in them? Was the right to privacy violated in this case? Was freedom enhanced or restricted? For the present, at least, there are no definitive answers for these questions.

As the pace of social research quickens, sociologists will find themselves faced with more—and more complex—responsibilities. Because our lives can be influenced by their research, sociologists will be called upon to conduct research according to principles that provide maximum protection for the groups and individuals they study. And at the same time, sociologists will be expected to "dig out the facts" about important societal concerns. The authors of this text hope that many of their readers will join them in this challenging venture.

25. Ibid., p. 6.
26. Laud Humphreys, "Retrospect: Ethical Issues in Social Research," in *Tearoom Trade*, Enlarged Edition (Chicago: Aldine-Publishing Co., 1975), p. 231.

PICTURE CREDITS

COVER Werner H. Müller from Peter Arnold.

PROLOGUE

Opening photograph: p. xvi George Malave from STOCK, BOSTON.

Chapter 1. *p. 4* The Bettmann Archive. *p. 12 top left:* Library of Congress; *top right:* Brown Brothers; *bottom:* Brown Brothers. *p. 13 top left:* Photograph by Jacob A. Riis, The Jacob A. Riis Collection, Courtesy of the Museum of the City of New York; *top right:* Lewis Hine, International Museum of Photography at George Eastman House, Rochester, N.Y.; *bottom:* Culver Pictures. *p. 18 top:* © 1975 Robert D' Alessandro; *bottom:* Bruce Davidson from MAGNUM PHOTOS. *p. 19 top left:* Jean-Claude Lejeune; *top right:* Harvey Stein; *bottom:* Donald Dietz from STOCK, BOSTON. *p. 25* Ernest Harburg, Ann Arbor, Michigan.

PART ONE

Opening photograph: p. 30 Burk Uzzle from MAGNUM PHOTOS.

Chapter 2. *p. 38* Patricia Hollander Gross from STOCK, BOSTON. *p. 44 top:* Jack Prelutsky from STOCK, BOSTON; *bottom:* UPI. *p. 45 top:* Jeffrey Blankfort from BBM Associates; *bottom:* Virginia Hamilton. *p. 51* Jeffrey Blankfort from BBM Associates. *p. 53* © 1975 Fred W. McDarrah. *p. 56* Reproduced with permission from the *Chicago Daily News*. Photograph by Perry C. Riddle.

Chapter 3. *p. 64 top:* Warren D. Jorgensen; *bottom:* Hella Hammid from Rapho/Photo Researchers. *p. 69* Michael Marienthal. *p. 74* Christopher Morrow from STOCK, BOSTON. *p. 82* Allan L. Price from Rapho/Photo Researchers. *p. 86* Harvey Stein. *p. 89* Rene Burri from MAGNUM PHOTOS. *p. 93 top:* The Bettmann Archive; *bottom:* Paul S. Conklin.

Chapter 4. *p. 98 top:* The American Museum of Natural History; *bottom:* © 1964 Charles Harbutt from MAGNUM PHOTOS. *p. 104* Ben Fernandez from Black Star. *p. 108* Courtesy, International Correspondence Schools. *p. 114 top:* Stephen J. Potter from STOCK, BOSTON; *bottom left:* Sally Bordwell; *bottom right:* Bruce Davidson from MAGNUM PHOTOS. *p. 115 top:* Mike Tappin; *bottom:* Roy Zalesky from Black Star.

PART TWO

Opening Photograph: p. 122 David Capps.

Chapter 5. *p. 128* Hal A. Franklin. *p. 131* Reproduced with permission from the *Chicago Daily News*. Photograph by Perry C. Riddle. *p. 139 top left:* Jean-Claude Lejeune from STOCK, BOSTON; *top right:* Charles Gatewood; *middle:* Jean-Claude Lejeune; *bottom:* Daniel S. Brody from STOCK, BOSTON. *p. 140* Bob Adelman. *p. 142* © 1970 United Artists. *p. 143* John Launois from Black Star.

Chapter 6. *p. 151* Jay King. *p. 152* J. Berndt from STOCK, BOSTON. *p. 156* Bob Adelman. *p. 166 top left:* Richard Lawrence Stack from Black Star; *top right:* Burk Uzzle from MAGNUM PHOTOS; *bottom:* © Thomas Hopker from Woodfin Camp. *p. 167* Burk Uzzle from MAGNUM PHOTOS. *p. 169* Bill Owens from BBM Associates. *p. 170 left:* © Norman Hurst from STOCK, BOSTON; *right:* Reproduced with permission from the *Chicago Daily News*. *p. 171* Harvey Stein.

Chapter 7. *p. 177* Donald Dietz from STOCK, BOSTON. *p. 179* The Bettmann Archive. *p. 183* Joel Gordon from DPI. *p. 189 top:* David Powers from Jeroboam; *bottom left:* Susan Ylvisaker from Jeroboam; *bottom right:* Michael Abramson from Black Star. *p. 202* Danny Lyon from MAGNUM PHOTOS.

PART THREE

Opening photograph: p. 204 George Malave from STOCK, BOSTON.

Chapter 8. *p. 208* Henri Cartier-Bresson from MAGNUM PHOTOS. *p. 209* © Radio Times Hulton Picture Library. *p. 216* © 1975 Him Anderson fom Nancy Palmer Photo Agency. *p. 220 top left:* Bill Owens from BBM Associates; *top right:* Bob Adelman from MAGNUM PHOTOS; *bottom:* Herb Goro. *p. 221 top left:* Roger Malloch from MAGNUM PHOTOS; *top right:* Bill Owens from BBM Associates; *middle:* David Glaubinger from Jeroboam; *bottom:* Bill Owens from BBM Associates. *p. 224* Stephen L. Feldman.

Chapter 9. *p. 239* Courtesy, Anti-Defamation League. *p. 248 top:* Bob Adelman from MAGNUM PHOTOS; *bottom left:* Harvey Stein; *bottom right:* Howard Simmons from Plus Four, Inc. *p. 249 top:* Charles Moore from Black Star. *bottom:* Owen Franken from STOCK, BOSTON. *p. 255* John Echave/Echave Assoc. *p. 256* The Bettmann Archive. *p. 257* Hansel Mieth, LIFE Magazine © 1972 TIME INC. *p. 259* Bob Adelman from MAGNUM PHOTOS. *p. 263* © 1974 Jac Stafford. *p. 264 left* and *right:* Jay King. *p. 265* UPI. *p. 269* George Gardner.

PART FOUR

Opening photograph: p. 272 Peter Vilms from Jeroboam.

Chapter 10. p. 275 Alain Nogues from SYGMA. p. 278 Alain Nogues from SYGMA. pp. 286 & 287 © John Nance/Panamin from MAGNUM PHOTOS. p. 296 *top left:* Courtesy Chicago Historical Society; *bottom left:* Alfred W. Mueller. p. 302 © 1973–74 Robert D'Alessandro from *GLORY*.

Chapter 11. p. 306 Courtesy, Metropolitan Museum of Art. p. 309 Piedrabuena O'Sullivan from MAGNUM PHOTOS. p. 320 *top:* Richard Balzer from STOCK, BOSTON; *bottom:* Wide World Photos. p. 321 *top left:* Marc Riboud from *MAGNUM PHOTOS; top right;* Georg Gerster from Rapho/Photo Researchers; *bottom:* Richard Balzer from STOCK, BOSTON. p. 329 Palo Koch from Rapho/Photo Researchers. p. 331 Tom Broderick. p. 335 Bernard Pierre Wolff from Photo Researchers.

Chapter 12. p. 340 Courtesy, Historical Society of Pennsylvania. p. 343 William E. Sauro, The *New York Times.* p. 346 Spence Air Photos. p. 348 Jerry Frank from DPI. p. 351 Burk Uzzle from MAGNUM PHOTOS. p. 356 *top left:* Tem Horwitz; *top right:* Michael Weisbrot from Black Star; *bottom:* Burk Uzzle from MAGNUM PHOTOS. p. 357 *top:* Bob Henriques from MAGNUM PHOTOS; *bottom:* Bobbe Wolf. p. 358 Catherine Ursillo. p. 363 William A. Graham. p. 369 Stephen L. Feldman.

PART FIVE

Opening photograph: p. 372 Paul Sequira.

Chapter 13. p. 378 *top:* Tim Eagan from Woodfin Camp; *bottom:* Ellis Herwig from STOCK, BOSTON. p. 379 *top:* Michael Budrys, The *Chicago Tribune; bottom:* Guy Gillette from Photo Researchers. p. 381 Photo Trends, Syndication International. p. 383 Courtesy, *Daily Journal-Gazette*, Mattoon, Illinois. p. 389 *top:* UPI; *bottom: Los Angeles Times.* p. 393 Jim Anderson from Woodfin Camp. p. 399 Courtesy, Sophia Smith Collection, Smith College. p. 400 *top:* Ginger Chih; *bottom left:* The *New York Times; bottom right:* Suzanne Arms from Jeroboam.

Chapter 14. p. 408 Collection of J. Lochridge. p. 409 The Bettmann Archive. p. 411 Charles Gatewood. p. 412 a European news service. p. 419 Reproduced with permission from the *Chicago Daily News.* Photograph by Perry C. Riddle. p. 424 Arnold Zann. p. 425 *top:* David Moore from Black Star; *bottom:* Rene Burri from MAGNUM PHOTOS. p. 432 Bob Adelman. p. 433 *top:* Jean Claude Francolon from Gamma; *bottom:* © 1963 Bob Jackson.

PART SIX

Opening photograph: p. 438 Mears Studios from Photo Researchers.

Chapter 15. p. 444 Courtesy of the Oriental Institute. p. 447 Courtesy of the Museum of Northern Arizona. p. 452 Library of Congress. p. 454 *top:* Bill Owens from BBM Associates; *bottom left:* Joanne Leonard from Woodfin Camp; *bottom right:* Jay King. p. 455 *top:* Paul Sequira; *bottom:* Bill Owens from BBM Associates. p. 462 Dave Bellak from Jeroboam. p. 463 Andy Mercado fom Jeroboam. p. 465 Burk Uzzle from MAGNUM PHOTOS.

Chapter 16. p. 473 Camera Press, Transworld Feature Syndicate. p. 475 *top:* Charles Harbutt from MAGNUM PHOTOS; *bottom:* James Holland from Black Star. p. 478 H. W. Silvester from Rapho/Photo Researchers. p. 482 Cary Wolinsky from STOCK, BOSTON. p. 484 *top:* Dave Bellak from Jeroboam; *bottom:* Gary Freedman from Jeroboam. p. 485 *top:* Peter L. Gould; *bottom:* Patricia Hollander Gross from STOCK, BOSTON. p. 495 S. Toth, New Guinea.

Chapter 17. p. 501 A. F. P. from Pictorial Parade. p. 504 Courtesy of the Mayor's Office of Public Information. p. 508 Karen R. Preuss from Jeroboam. p. 511 Bill Owens from BBM Associates. p. 519 Burk Uzzle from MAGNUM PHOTOS. p. 521 Teresa Zabala, The *New York Times.* p. 522 Stephen L. Feldman.

Chapter 18. p. 530 Courtesy, Smithsonian Institution. p. 537 *INSIGHT* from University of Notre Dame. p. 540 © The *Daily Telegraph Magazine* from Woodfin Camp. p. 543 *top:* UPI; *middle:* Peeter Vilms from Jeroboam; *bottom:* Bobbe Wolf. p. 549 Burk Uzzle from MAGNUM PHOTOS. p. 554 *top:* Ken Graves from Jeroboam; *bottom:* Cary Wolinsky from STOCK, BOSTON. p. 555 Torkel Korling.

Chapter 19. p. 565 *top left:* Courtesy of the New York Public Library; *top right: Harpers Weekly,* June 23, 1866; *bottom:* Photograph by Jacob A. Riis, The Jacob A. Riis Collection, Courtesy of the Museum of the City of New York. p. 567 Constantine Manos from MAGNUM PHOTOS. p. 573 Jay King. p. 574 Patricia Hollander Gross from STOCK, BOSTON. p. 581 Courtesy Chicago Historical Society. p. 582 The *Detroit News.* p. 583 UPI. p. 584 Mike Mazzaschi from STOCK, BOSTON. p. 585 Stephen L. Feldman.

EPILOGUE

Chapter 20. p. 592 President's Commission on Obscenity and Pornography.

GLOSSARY

ACCULTURATION (p. 496) Process by which people adopt traits of a culture not their own. The term is also used to refer to the results of this process.

ACHIEVED STATUS (p. 209) Social prestige assigned on the basis of individual ability and accomplishment. *See also* Ascribed Status.

ACQUIRED PREDISPOSITIONS (p. 126) Learned response patterns resulting in a tendency to regularly accept or reject a particular type of object, situation, or event. Most predispositions fall into the class of preferences, attitudes, or values.

ACTIVE CROWD (pp. 376–377) An aggregate of people who are motivated by some unexpected turn of events to engage in volatile and often violent forms of behavior, as in a riot.

AGGRESSION (p. 261) Pattern of intergroup relations characterized by overt or covert hostility. Typically, aggression by either a dominant or a minority group is not fully open or direct. For example, intergroup antagonisms are often expressed through *symbolic* aggression: derogatory jokes, epithets, etc.

ALIENATION (pp. 551–552) Feelings of self-estrangement stemming from the perception of one's work role as meaningless and of oneself as powerless. Marx considered alienation to be an inevitable by-product of the factory system.

ALTRUISTIC SUICIDE (p. 10) One of three types of suicide identified by Durkheim, in which people feel such strong ties to a group that they place its welfare above their own and willingly accept self-destruction in its behalf. *See also* Anomic Suicide; Egoistic Suicide.

ANOMIC SUICIDE (p. 10) One of three types of suicide identified by Durkheim, in which self-destruction is related to disruption of group stability and consequent loss of social constraints on the individual. *See also* Altruistic Suicide; Egoistic Suicide.

ANOMIE (p. 10) Condition of normative confusion in which the individual has few socially validated guides to behavior.

ANOMIE THEORY OF DEVIANCE (p. 181) Theory developed by Merton stating that when people reject society's goals or the institutionalized means of attaining them (or both), they experience anomie (normlessness) and may adapt to this condition with behavior that society terms "deviant." *See also* the specific modes of deviant adaptation conceptualized by Merton: Innovation, Rebellion, Retreatism, and Ritualism.

ANTICIPATORY SOCIALIZATION (p. 152) Any type of activity that helps, either directly or indirectly, to prepare an individual for the assumption of future roles.

APTITUDE (p. 135) Ability or talent for a certain activity. Like intelligence, aptitudes are thought to be partly determined by heredity, which seems to set an upper limit on the development of certain complex skills.

AREA SAMPLE (p. 365) A study of a population taken from certain units, e.g., city blocks, census tracts, counties, or other spatial configurations. These units are selected by random sampling, and those living or working in them then become the subjects for study.

ARGOT (p. 118) Specialized vocabulary or set of words and phrases used by a particular group or collectivity.

ASCRIBED STATUS (pp. 209, 239) Social prestige assigned on the basis of characteristics an individual can do nothing about (e.g., race, ethnicity, sex, age). *See also* Achieved Status.

ASSIMILATION (p. 262) Process whereby members of a minority group acquire the sociocultural patterns of a dominant group and gradually become absorbed by it.

ASSOCIATION (p. 71) Large, formally organized group typified by bureaucratic structure. *See also* Bureaucracy.

ASSOCIATIVE vs. COMMUNAL RELATIONSHIPS (p. 87) The associative relationship, as defined by Weber, is "one resting upon a rational motivated adjustment of interests or a similarly motivated agreement [arranged] by mutual consent." This kind of relationship typifies bureaucratically organized groups. The communal relationship, in contrast, rests upon subjective feelings derived from personal ties, feelings that "we belong together."

ATTITUDE (p. 127) A configuration of evaluative beliefs that predispose an individual to accept or reject certain broad classes of stimuli, such as minority groups, economic policies, religions, and so on.

ATTRIBUTES (p. 130) The qualities of an object or event that, taken together, enable us to assign it a meaning.

AUTHORITY (pp. 74, 501) The perceived right of an individual to make decisions and to expect that they will be implemented. Power based on authority usually resides in a position rather than in an individual as such, and (unlike power based on coercion) it rests on the consent of the group's members rather than on the threat or use of force. *See also* Charismatic Authority; Legal-Rational Authority; Traditional Authority.

BALANCE THEORY (p. 131)   Hypothesis that individuals seek consistency or balance in trying to interpret how various elements of their environment interrelate; the theory assumes that people try to interpret both physical and social phenomena in terms of invariant properties underlying changing surface conditions. *See also* Dissonance Theory.

BILATERAL FAMILY PATTERN (p. 443)   Family organizational pattern in which descent, inheritance of goods, interaction with relatives, etc., involve both the mother's and father's sides of the family, as is common in the U.S.

BIRTH RATE (p. 307)   Number of persons born to a given population in a given year; generally figured on the basis of every 1000 persons. Thus a birth rate of 20 means that there were 20 births, on the average, for every 1000 persons in the total population.

BLACK POWER (p. 250)   Movement among black Americans to achieve full equality in economic, political, and social life without sacrificing their separate identity.

BUREAUCRACY (p. 71)   Type of social organization characteristic of large, formally organized groups *(associations)* and geared to the achievement of complex goals. Typified by an elaborate division of labor, clearly defined rules for role performance, and routinization of activity.

CASE STUDY (p. 386)   Detailed description and analysis of an event of sociological significance, based upon systematic observation carried out within a framework of theoretical concepts.

CASTE (p. 208)   Most extreme form of the closed status group, usually part of the most rigid form of social stratification, based on such ascribed criteria as family membership, religion, or race. Patterns of stratification in a caste system are deeply institutionalized and are supported by religious beliefs, custom, and law. In essence, all forms of social interaction are narrowly prescribed by the particular style of life of the caste to which individuals belong by birth.

CASUAL CROWD (p. 376)   An aggregate of people who come together spontaneously for brief periods when their attention is drawn to some commonly perceived event.

CENTRAL TENDENCY (p. 570)   The mean, median, or mode of an array of numerical values. These are expressed by separate, numerically computed coefficients, each indicating in a somewhat different way the most likely or commonly found value in the array.

CHANGE   *See* Cultural Change; Social Change.

CHARACTER TRAIT (p. 126)   A cluster of habitual response tendencies which together add up to some characteristic way of behaving.

CHARISMATIC AUTHORITY (pp. 283, 502)   Authority residing in an individual by virtue of exceptional personality characteristics that set him or her apart from ordinary people. Unlike traditional and legal-rational authority, charismatic authority lacks stable social organization.

CHICANOS (p. 253)   The largest category of Spanish-surnamed Americans, composed of citizens of Mexican birth or descent.

CLAN (p. 319)   Association of families sharing a common ancestry.

CLASS (p. 210)   Stratum or aggregate of persons who share more or less the same economic privileges in a society. In the United States these privileges derive largely but not exclusively from the occupational role or roles of the household breadwinner(s). Inherited wealth is the other major source.

CLASS CONSCIOUSNESS (pp. 210, 215)   Collective recognition by members of a given social stratum that they constitute a specific class, plus a feeling of identification and loyalty to that class. The idea of class consciousness is a key element in the Marxian theory of social stratification.

COERCION (p. 500)   Arbitrary, illegitimate use of power to achieve one's will (or a group's will), as by force or threat of force.

COGNITION (p. 130)   The complex psychological processes by which individuals interpret objects and events in their environment and determine appropriate ways of responding to them.

COHESION (pp. 21–22)   Degree to which group members share common beliefs, practices, and values and thus act "like one."

COLLECTIVE BEHAVIOR (p. 374)   Social behavior that does not follow an organized pattern of conventions and expectations. Essentially, collective behavior differs from group behavior in that it is relatively unstructured and therefore relatively unpredictable. Those involved do not know what they can expect of others or what is expected of them. As a result, their behavior often takes unexpected turns.

COMMUNAL *vs.* ASSOCIATIVE RELATIONSHIPS   *See* Associative *vs.* Communal Relationships.

COMMUNICATION (p. 137)   The exchange of meaning and mutual influence. Communication among humans is based on the use of significant symbols—arbitrarily chosen stimuli (e.g., words, gestures, etc.) that have become conventionally associated with a given meaning. *See also* Symbolic Interaction.

COMMUNITY (pp. 79–80)   Aggregate of people living together in a particular geographical area and bound together politically, economically, and socially. Also (p. 86), a term used to identify the feeling of "oneness" characteristic of *Gemeinschaft* relationships.

COMPANIONSHIP FAMILY (p. 459) Pattern of family life emphasizing close interpersonal association, personal satisfaction and development, and egalitarian relationships among family members.

COMPARATIVE STUDY (p. 101) Research technique that contrasts specific sociological patterns in one group or society with those of another.

COMPLEX ORGANIZATION See Association.

CONCENTRIC ZONE THEORY (p. 351) Hypothesis that the impersonal process of land-use competition in cities leads to the development of a series of concentric units spreading out from the city's center, each reserved for particular activities and for occupancy by particular segments of the population. See also Multiple Nuclei Theory; Sector Theory.

CONCEPT (pp. 21, 130) A system of meaning that identifies a given object, event, or idea as belonging to a particular class of phenomena. Because all members of a class share certain properties or attributes, a concept serves as a guide for understanding a particular segment of reality.

CONFLICT THEORY (pp. 16, 214–215) A theoretical perspective which assumes that social behavior can best be understood in terms of tension and conflict between groups and individuals. Marx maintained that the crucial area of conflict is in the economic sphere—in an inevitable struggle between those who control the means of production and those who do not.

CONFORMITY (p. 182) Acceptance of the goals and of the approved means to achieve these goals in a particular group or society.

CONSANGUINE RELATIONSHIP (p. 442) Family relationship based on blood ties.

CONSENSUS (pp. 39, 500) Widely shared agreement among a group's members concerning preferred values, beliefs, norms, goals, etc. An important basis of group stability and cohesion.

CONTROL GROUP (p. 149) Group of subjects in an experiment who are not exposed to changes in the independent variable.

CONTROL VARIABLES (pp. 26, 149) In scientific research, extraneous variables that must be held constant, measured, or otherwise taken into account so that the researcher can rule out their effect on the phenomenon being observed. See also Dependent Variable; Independent Variable.

CONVENTIONALIZED CROWD (p. 376) Collectivity of persons assembled for a specific purpose, such as a religious service or sports event. Its behavior is essentially like that of the casual crowd except that it is usually expressed in established ways.

CORPORATION (p. 532) A group of persons who have been granted a charter legally permitting them to act as a single person, with rights, privileges, and liabilities distinct from those of individual members. See also Enterpreneur.

CORRELATION (p. 570) In statistical usage, degree to which two or more variables are found to be related.

CRAZE (p. 289) Behavior pattern that appears and disappears quickly. It generally involves limited segments of society and typically is regarded by the majority as extreme, outlandish, or foolish. See also Fashion; Fad.

CROWD (p. 375) Aggregate of people in close proximity who share some common interest. Its relatively unstructured nature makes it a potentially disruptive force at times. See also Active Crowd; Casual Crowd; Conventionalized Crowd; Expressive Crowd.

CULTURAL CHANGE (p. 275) Process by which new traits, trait complexes, ideas, beliefs, and other aspects of culture emerge in and become part of a society. See also Social Change.

CULTURAL DIFFUSION See Diffusion.

CULTURAL LAG (p. 295) Cultural incongruities resulting from the tendency of material and technological aspects of culture to change more rapidly than norms, values, and beliefs.

CULTURAL RELATIVITY (p. 102) Principle that the standards societies use for making judgments and evaluations concerning truth, beauty, morality, and the ''correctness'' of particular patterns of behavior vary and can only be judged within the context of a given culture.

CULTURAL VARIABILITY (p. 100) Principle that different societies develop different cultural solutions for the problems of life and that all cultures seem to ''work.''

CULTURE (p. 96) In sociological usage, the total of all material, social, and symbolic creations that a society's members have incorporated into their overall design for living. See also Subculture.

CULTURE COMPLEX (p. 110) Cluster of related culture traits around which people organize some aspect of their lives.

CULTURE TRAIT (p. 109) Smallest meaningful unit of cultural content. There is no standard procedure for either defining or classifying traits. However, as used for the analysis of culture, the term usually refers to some specific item or element, such as a particular tool, weapon, folkway, law, shared belief, hairstyle, or dance.

DEATH (MORTALITY) RATE (p. 307) Number of persons who die in a given year figured on the basis of every 1000 persons in a given population. Thus a death rate of 20 means that there were twenty deaths, on the average, for every 1000 persons in the population in the particular year. Often specific mortality rates are calculated for particular categories of the population (e.g., infants, the two sexes, members of different races).

DECRIMINALIZATION (p. 201) The removal of "victimless offenses" such as public drunkenness and homosexuality from the criminal justice system.

DEDUCTION (p. 26) Process of reasoning which proceeds from the general to the specific, or from a series of general principles to a specific consequence. *See also* Induction.

DELINQUENCY Violations of law by persons younger than a specified legal age, which varies in different jurisdictions. When defined by statute, it may include acts (such as running away) that are not considered criminal when committed by adults.

DEMOGRAPHIC TRANSITION (p. 307) Demographic pattern in countries undergoing industrialization and modernization whereby population begins to grow rapidly as the death rate drops while the birth rate remains high, then gradually levels off as the birth rate also drops.

DEMOGRAPHY (p. 307) The statistical study of populations, their size, distribution, and composition. It is concerned with such matters as the changes over time in fertility, mortality, and migration and with the factors related to these changes.

DENOMINATION (p. 482) An organized religious group that has gained widespread acceptance in a society.

DEPENDENT VARIABLE (p. 149) That element in a scientific study which changes when another element (the independent variable) is altered; it is the *effect* in a cause-effect situation. *See also* Control Variables.

DETERRENCE (p. 199) Efforts to prevent certain forms of deviant behavior through threats of negative sanctions.

DEVIANCE (p. 175) Conduct of any kind that fails to meet shared behavioral expectations of the particular group in which it occurs.

DIFFERENTIAL ASSOCIATION (p. 186) Theory first developed by Sutherland which states that "conforming" and "deviant" behavior are functions of the particular norms an individual internalizes as the result of varying associations with different groups. Commitment to the norms of one's primary groups (which may or may not be consistent with those of society as a whole) is usually greater than commitment to the norms of more impersonal groups. Thus, an individual who is socialized in a deviant subculture is likely to internalize values and standards of conduct that are contrary to those of conventional society.

DIFFERENTIAL FERTILITY (p. 232) Differences between categories of the population in total number of offspring ever born, as, for example, between the members of the lower classes and those of the upper and middle classes.

DIFFUSION (p. 288) Transfer of cultural and social elements (traits or configurations of traits) from one society to another; also, the spread of cultural and social elements *within* a society.

DISCRIMINATION (pp. 270–271) Overt act of denying to individuals or groups equal access to the valued goods and services of a society, or in other ways treating them as inferiors, on the basis of arbitrary grounds.

DISSONANCE THEORY (pp. 131–132) Prediction that lack of harmony between the way we interpret our environment and the way we behave will motivate us to change either our interpretations or our behavior. *See also* Balance Theory.

DIVERSION (p. 201) Strategy for controlling crime and delinquency by placing some offenders in special programs rather than letting the law run its full course; examples of diversion include pretrial release, parole, and referral to treatment programs.

DIVISION OF LABOR (p. 40) Separation of the work process into a series of distinct and interdependent roles, such that the end result is a coordinated effort toward group goal achievement.

DOMINANCE (p. 241) With reference to minority groups in a society, the term refers to the control exercised upon them by a more privileged group.

DRIVES (p. 125) Basic motivational patterns, closely tied to biological needs, which help ensure an individual's survival.

DYSFUNCTION (p. 50) In functional analysis, consequence of any role activity which hampers the achievement of group goals or disrupts the group's equilibrium.

ECOLOGY, SPATIAL (p. 350) Study of the way in which human groups (communities and societies) relate to their physical environment, especially in their land-use patterns.

EGALITARIAN FAMILY (p. 443) Emerging family pattern in U.S. and many other industrial societies, in which authority is more-or-less equally shared by the husband and wife and is also shared to a degree by the children.

EGOISTIC SUICIDE (p. 9) One of three types of suicide identified by Durkheim, in which self-destruction is related to the absence of effective social constraints on an individual. *See also* Altruistic Suicide; Anomic Suicide.

ELITE Those who occupy the highest level in some system of social ranking.

EMOTIONAL CONTAGION (p. 380) Process found in certain crowd situations whereby people seem to "infect" one another with emotional feelings that incite the crowd toward some action.

ENTREPRENEUR (p. 530) Person who individually organizes, operates, and assumes the risks associated with a business or industrial enterprise. *See also* Corporation.

EQUILIBRIUM ASSUMPTION (p. 48) A theoretical perspective which assumes that social groups tend naturally toward order and balance, and that conflict and disequilibrium are forms of deviance or abnormality. *See also* Functional Analysis.

ESTEEM (p. 43)   Value accorded to individuals for their personal qualities and the manner in which they perform their roles, as opposed to prestige, which is the status derived from a role regardless of how it is performed. *See also* Status.

ETHICAL NEUTRALITY (pp. 17, 595)   Thesis that social scientists must not make value judgments in the performance of their roles as scientists. Current debate centers around whether such neutrality is truly possible.

ETHNIC GROUP (pp. 243–244)   Human collectivity whose members are bound together by common cultural ties, regardless of their current national, political, or social identity. Members feel a ''consciousness of kind'' which differentiates them in varying degrees from groups around them.

ETHNICITY (pp. 243–244)   Quality of perceiving oneself as identified with an ethnic group. *See* Ethnic Group.

ETHNOCENTRISM (p. 103)   Tendency of a group's members to regard their own culture as superior and to look down upon the cultures of other groups.

ETHNOMETHODOLOGY (pp. 101, 130)   Social research aimed at understanding ''everyday'' behavior, especially the meanings of social interaction for the persons involved.

ETHOS (p. 112)   Sum of the characteristic usages, ideas, standards, and codes by which a group is differentiated and individualized in character from other groups.

EXCLUSION (p. 261)   Form of behavior (e.g., segregation or avoidance) which prevents certain individuals or groups from interacting with others; a common pattern of discrimination against minority group members.

EXPLANATION (p. 23)   Statement, often in the form of a theory or a generalization, which accounts for an event by ascertaining all the factors in the situation existing prior to the event.

EXPONENTIAL PRINCIPLE (p. 290)   In the analysis of cultural change, the principle that items of culture are being added at an ever ascending rate.

EXPRESSIVE CROWD (p. 377)   Aggregation of people in which the subjective (emotional) experiences of the members themselves are the principal feature of attention.

EXTENDED FAMILY (p. 442)   Large family structure composed of several nuclear families that are related by blood or marriage. A primary social and economic unit in many traditional societies. *See also* Nuclear Family.

FAD (p. 289)   Cultural pattern or form of behavior such as a dance or a mode of dress which is adopted for only a brief period of time and usually by only a small segment of society. *See also* Craze; Fashion.

FAMILY OF ORIENTATION (p. 442)   The nuclear family one grows up in as a child.

FAMILY OF PROCREATION (p. 442)   The nuclear family of which one is a parent.

FASHION (p. 289)   Cultural pattern or form of behavior that becomes generally accepted but is periodically subject to change. *See also* Craze; Fad.

FECUNDITY (p. 307)   Biological capacity for producing offspring—in human females about twenty-five or thirty at the most—but a capacity which is seldom if ever approached.

FEMINISM (p. 399)   Part of the national movement to achieve equality of status for women in society.

FERTILITY RATE (p. 307)   Number of births in a particular population figured on the basis of every 1000 women of childbearing age (usually defined as women from fifteen to forty-five).

FOLK SOCIETY (p. 349)   Concept developed by Redfield as an ideal type; such a society is characterized as small, isolated, nonliterate, homogeneous, spontaneous, having a high degree of group solidarity, traditionalism, informal social control, and an uncritical acceptance of events as being in the natural order of things.

FOLKWAYS (p. 87)   Norms that do not specifically apply to any particular group within a society but are simply established as common practices. They specify modes of dress, etiquette, language usage, and other routine matters not regarded as having much moral significance.

FORMAL ORGANIZATION (p. 71)   Group interaction in which tasks and rules are clearly and formally prescribed. Often used synonymously with *association* and *bureaucracy*.

FUNCTION (p. 50)   In functional analysis, consequences of a system of social relationships that contribute to the maintenance of the equilibrium of the group or social system. *See also* Equilibrium Assumption.

FUNCTIONAL ANALYSIS (p. 48)   Research aimed at discovering the features of a social system whose consequences help maintain the stability of the group and enable it to operate effectively.

GEMEINSCHAFT *vs.* GESELLSCHAFT (p. 84)   Concepts developed by Tönnies as part of his analysis of the change from traditional to industrial, bureaucratic relationships. Very broadly, the term *Gemeinschaft* is used to refer to communal, traditional, emotional, family-oriented relationships. The term *Gesellschaft* defines social relationships of an impersonal, contractual, bureaucratic nature.

GENERALIZATION (p. 22)   Combination of concepts into a statement that sets forth some meaningful relationship between them, for example, that if one variable changes in some regular fashion, predictable changes will take place in another.

GENERALIZED OTHER (p. 138)   Concept developed by Mead to refer to the fact that as young people mature, they learn to understand and incorporate into their own makeup the attitudes and expectations of others with whom they interact. Thus, as the individual mentally assumes the roles of other people, their attitudes organize into a sort of unit, and it is that organization which controls the response of the individual.

GENOCIDE   As an extreme form of aggression, the mass, planned destruction of a race or ethnic group.

GEOGRAPHICAL MOBILITY (p. 232)   Generally, movement from one place to another within a community or society; often an important factor in social mobility.

GESELLSCHAFT vs. GEMEINSCHAFT   See Gemeinschaft vs. Gesellschaft.

GHETTO (p. 359)   Historically, an area of a city into which some specific group was segregated and confined by law. In contemporary terms, an ecological area—usually of a city—in which a minority group is concentrated for a variety of social, cultural, and economic reasons.

GOAL (p. 36)   Common end or objective shared by the members of a group. See also Latent vs. Manifest Goals.

GRATIFICATION (p. 154)   Feeling of pleasure or satisfaction experienced by an individual when rewarded or sustained by the treatment of others. According to learning theory, positive gratification has the effect of reinforcing the behavior that elicited the reward, increasing the probability that the individual will behave in a similar way in future similar circumstances.

GROUP (p. 33)   A number of individuals who interact recurrently according to some pattern of social organization. The pattern includes norms, roles, social control, and social ranking.

GUILD (p. 528)   In medieval times, an association of persons sharing the same trade, pursuits, or interests, formed for their mutual aid or protection.

HABIT (p. 125)   Any regularly patterned way of acting, feeling, or thinking that an individual has acquired through learning.

HISPANOS (p. 253)   The oldest Spanish-surnamed minority in the United States, located in the Southwest, especially New Mexico; descendants of the people of Spanish origin who occupied that region before New England was first settled.

HISTORICAL-STATISTICAL ANALYSIS (p. 294)   Assembling data to describe and measure an event as it existed at previous times and as it exists currently.

HORIZONTAL MOBILITY (p. 231)   Movement from one job to another involving little or no change in social rank; often an important precondition for achieving upward mobility.

HYPOTHESIS (p. 23)   Generalization that has not yet been adequately confirmed by empirical evidence.

"I" and "ME" (p. 138)   Two complementary elements of personality as identified by Mead. The I encompasses that which is personal, distinct, and creative about the individual. The Me, on the other hand, is the predictable reflection of the social group; it is the product of socialization.

ID (p. 133)   According to Freud, the aspect of personality that motivates the individual toward seeking physically pleasurable gratification.

IDEAL TYPE (p. 70)   A mental construct used as a methodological tool in making a comparative analysis of two or more social phenomena. Examples of ideal types are "bureaucratic organization," as developed by Weber, and "folk society," as developed by Redfield. An ideal type exaggerates observed characteristics and is not intended to be an accurate description of reality. Also, it is "ideal" only in the sense of being a pure type, not in the sense of representing a desired or preferred pattern.

IDEOLOGY (p. 281)   Complex of beliefs and values providing an overall rationale for a society in being or for one that is envisaged.

INDEPENDENT VARIABLE (p. 149)   In studies of cause-effect relationships, that element which is manipulated by the experimenter in order to determine its effect on another element (the dependent variable). See also Control Variables.

INDUCTION (p. 26)   Process of reasoning in which the individual moves from the particular to the general. Thus, a general statement is arrived at on the basis of a series of specific instances. See also Deduction.

INFLUENCE (p. 502)   Sum of all the resources a participant in a decision-making situation can bring to bear in order to ensure a desired outcome.

IN-GROUP (p. 63)   Any social unit with which the individual identifies and feels a consciousness of kind. See also Out-group.

INNER-DIRECTED PERSONALITY (p. 160)   Ideal type developed by Riesman, identifying a personality type that acts on the basis of norms and goals that have been internalized and derived from a clearly defined ethical system. Presumably, an individual with such a personality is almost immune to social pressures to conform to changing norms, values, and goals. See also Other-Directed Personality; Tradition-Directed Personality.

INNOVATION (p. 182)   As used by Merton, a deviant mode of adaptation in which the individual accepts the goals of society but uses disapproved means to attain them, e.g., stealing to obtain money and other symbols of success which seem inaccessible by legitimate means. See Anomie Theory.

INSTINCT (p. 133)   A complex behavior pattern that is inherited through genetic transmission and is universal in every member of the species. Scientists have abandoned instinct theories as general explanations of human behavior.

INSTITUTION   *See* Social Institution.

INSTITUTIONALIZATION (p. 36)   Process whereby orderly, stable, and increasingly predictable forms of interaction are developed, as individuals come to accept the norms and role expectations of their several groups as binding upon them.

INTEGRATION   *See* Social Solidarity.

INTERACTION (p. 34)   Behavior of two or more persons toward each other which is in some way meaningful to them and which makes them to some degree at least mutually dependent.

INTEREST GROUP (p. 504)   People organized to influence decision making by exerting pressure on some agent or agency of government.

INTERNALIZATION (p. 148)   Acceptance as one's own of a behavioral norm to which one's group is collectively committed.

INVENTION (p. 290)   Creation of a thing, idea, object, or social form that has not previously been part of a culture or society.

LABELING THEORY (p. 184)   A perspective on deviance that attempts to understand how societal definitions of deviance are formed and what the consequences of being labeled a deviant may be for the individual. One hypothesis is that a person who becomes officially labeled as a "criminal" or other type of deviant is in effect assigned a new social role and is likely to behave accordingly.

LATENT FUNCTION (p. 50)   In functional analysis, the unintentional and often unrecognized consequences of a specific pattern of social relationships.

LATENT *vs.* MANIFEST GOALS (p. 36)   Latent goals are aims or purposes which are not consciously recognized by the members of a group (e.g., enjoying the companionship provided by group membership). Manifest goals are specified aims or purposes that group members can state explicitly (e.g., improving community services, helping the handicapped, building a successful business).

LEGAL-RATIONAL AUTHORITY (p. 502)   Pattern of authority in which power to make and implement decisions is specifically delimited by rules and sanctions and is vested in positions (roles) rather than in individuals.

LEGITIMATION (p. 499)   Process whereby the power of a ruling group becomes valid in the eyes of both rulers and ruled. More generally, process by which actions become approved or by which norms arise granting them approval.

LIFE CYCLE (p. 168)   The successive and interrelated stages through which individuals pass during the course of a lifetime, each involving special demands and expectations.

LOBBYING (p. 504)   In politics, the process by which individuals or groups try to influence legislators to work for the passage (or defeat) of laws related to their special interests.

LOOKING-GLASS SELF (pp. 135–137)   Cooley's term for the social processes by which we gain our images of self. Through social interaction, we develop a sense of how we are perceived by others; and by interpreting the perceived reactions of others we develop our own sense of identity.

MALTHUSIAN THEORY (pp. 305–306)   A set of assumptions developed by Malthus in the late nineteenth century maintaining that human populations have the potential for growing geometrically, whereas food production can increase only arithmetically. Malthus predicted that societal efforts to improve living standards were ultimately destined to fail since the benefit of any increase in the food supply would be quickly wiped out by an increase in population size.

MANIFEST *vs.* LATENT GOALS   *See* Latent *vs.* Manifest Goals.

MASS COMMUNICATION (p. 404)   The transmission of ideas, information, entertainment, etc., to a large and dispersed audience by means of mechanical and electronic devices. *See also* Communication.

MASS MEDIA (pp. 162, 404)   Communication devices (such as newspapers, magazines, radio, and television) capable of reaching millions of people very rapidly.

MATRIARCHY (p. 443)   Family organizational pattern in which authority resides in the mother of the household.

MATRILINEAL FAMILY PATTERN (p. 443)   Family organizational pattern in which descent, inheritance of goods, interaction with relatives, etc., are focused on the mother's side of the family, as in the Hopi and Zuñi societies.

MATRILOCAL FAMILY PATTERN (p. 443)   Family residence pattern in which a married couple resides in or near the wife's mother's household.

MEAN, MEDIAN, MODE   *See* Central Tendency.

MECHANICAL *vs.* ORGANIC SOLIDARITY (p. 90)   Durkheim's terms for two different types of social solidarity, both of them based on the division of labor in a society. *Mechanical* solidarity, as found in traditional and small agricultural societies, is social cohesiveness based on *role similarities,* which lead people to identify with each other and to share the same values and beliefs. *Organic* solidarity, as found in urban-industrial societies, is based on *role specialization,* which separates people in terms of beliefs, values, etc., but makes them dependent on one another for goods and services.

METHODOLOGY   Broad design of social research which includes the logic of scientific inquiry as well as the body of techniques that can be used in such research.

METROPOLIS (p. 342)   A large central city and the area immediately surrounding it, including communities that were once largely self-sufficient. *See also* Standard Metropolitan Statistical Area.

MINORITY GROUP (p. 239)   A subdivision of a society's population that is assigned to a low level in the system of social ranking. The criteria most often used for designating categories of people as minorities are race and ethnicity.

MOBILITY   *See* Social Mobility.

MONOGAMY (p. 442)   The most common form of marriage, involving the union of one man and one woman.

MONOLITHIC RULE (p. 510)   Control of government (or other group) by one person or by a small coalition acting in concert.

MORES (p. 88)   Societal norms associated with intense feelings of right and wrong. Mores come down to us from the past and define basic rules of conduct; an individual who violates them is severely sanctioned by society.

MORTALITY RATE   *See* Death Rate.

MOTIVATION (p. 125)   Energies, urges, or pressures – perceived or unperceived – that impel an individual to action. *See also* Need.

MULTINATIONAL CORPORATION (p. 533)   Large business organization with substantial operations in several countries; typically involved in the extraction of natural resources, manufacturing, or technology-producing industries.

MULTIPLE NUCLEI THEORY (p. 353)   Hypothesis that land use within a city is organized around a number of distinct foundations (units), each distinguished by its own special functions and requirements. *See also* Concentric Zone Theory; Sector Theory.

NATIONALISM (p. 507)   The ethnocentric belief that one's own nation is better than any others; promotes solidarity within nation-states, but produces tension and conflict between them.

NEED (p. 125)   Condition that must be satisfied in order for the individual to experience well-being. Needs may be innate (as the biological need for food) or acquired (as a need for social approval).

NEOLOCAL FAMILY PATTERN (p. 443)   Family residence pattern in which a married couple establishes a new residence apart from both sets of parents and with no preference shown for either.

NEOPOSITIVISM (p. 16)   Scientific position held by certain scholars who believe that propositions can have scientific significance only if the concepts comprising the propositions have empirical referents that can be measured in some way. *See also* Positivism.

NORMS (p. 37)   Shared convictions about the patterns of behavior that are appropriate or inappropriate for the members of a group; what group members agree they can, should, might, must, cannot, should not, ought not, or must not do in any given situation.

NUCLEAR FAMILY (p. 442)   Family structure composed of only the father, mother, and children as the primary social unit. *See also* Extended Family.

OBSOLESCENCE (p. 289)   Abandonment of previously established modes of conduct toward some cultural item.

OCCUPATIONAL MOBILITY (pp. 231–232)   Movement horizontally or vertically from one job category to another. If the move involves no change in class or status, it is horizontal; if it involves change in one or both, it is vertical.

OPINION (p. 431)   A person's verbalized or communicable set of interpretive beliefs concerning some issue or situation. *See also* Public Opinion.

ORGANIC *vs*. MECHANICAL SOLIDARITY   *See* Mechanical *vs*. Organic Solidarity.

ORGANIC THEORY OF SOCIETY (p. 6)   As developed by Comte, the notion that society is like a living organism: it has a structure, its parts function interdependently, and it has evolved from simpler to more complex forms.

OTHER-DIRECTED PERSONALITY (p. 160)   Ideal type developed by Riesman, identifying an individual who lacks strong internalized convictions about how to behave. Other-directed individuals have a particular sensitivity to the probable approval or disapproval of their peers, which they use as a guide to action in a wide variety of life situations. *See also* Inner-Directed Personality; Tradition-Directed Personality.

OUT-GROUP (p. 63)   Any social unit with which the individual feels no sense of identity – a group associated with feelings of "they" rather than "we." *See also* In-group.

PARTICIPANT OBSERVATION (p. 49)   Research method in which the sociologist actually participates in a particular group in order to closely observe its social organization and the patterns of interaction among its members.

PATRIARCHY (p. 443)   Family organizational pattern in which authority resides in a male, often the oldest, on the father's side of the family. Dominant pattern of family organization in many parts of the world.

PATRILINEAL FAMILY PATTERN (p. 443)   Family organizational pattern in which descent, inheritance of goods, interaction with relatives, etc., are focused on the father's side of the family.

PATRILOCAL FAMILY PATTERN (p. 443) Family residence pattern in which a married couple resides in or near the husband's father's household.

PEER GROUP (p. 65) A primary group composed of people who are closely alike in age and interests.

PENTECOSTALISM (p. 483) Religious movement that was started in the U.S. around 1900 stressing literal interpretation of the Bible, lay preachers, emotional services, faith healing, "speaking in tongues," etc.

PERCEPTION (p. 128) Process through which the individual assigns meaning to sensory data.

PERSONALITY (PERSONAL ORGANIZATION) (p. 124) The motivational patterns, habit patterns, acquired predispositions, etc., that underlie an individual's behavior and account for its consistency.

PERSONALITY TRAIT See Character Trait.

PERSUASION (p. 426) An attempt to achieve some type of behavioral change on the part of an audience through communication.

PHRATRY (p. 446) Association of two or more clans responsible for performing certain social functions, e.g., marital and religious functions in Hopi society.

PLURAL MARRIAGE See Polygamy.

PLURALISM (pp. 263–264) Pattern of intergroup relations that permits a minority group with a distinct cultural background to retain differences in customs and traditions while enjoying equal access to societal privileges.

POLITICAL INSTITUTION (p. 498) Pattern of structural relationships that underlies a system of government and helps determine the distribution of societal rewards (status, wealth, and power).

POLYANDRY (p. 443) Type of polygamy (plural marriage) involving the union of one woman with two or more men. Very rare.

POLYGAMY (p. 443) Form of marriage in which a person has more than one mate at a time; sometimes called plural marriage. See also Polyandry; Polygyny.

POLYGYNY (p. 443) Most common type of polygamy (plural marriage), involving the union of one man with two or more women.

POPULATION The inhabitants of a given territory or area, such as a city or country. Statistically (p. 365), a defined set of units from which a sample is to be drawn, such as people (e.g., registered voters), acts (e.g., crimes), or events (e.g., court trials).

POSITIVISM (p. 6) Scientific approach that uses observation and experimentation to understand natural phenomena. See also Neopositivism.

POWER (p. 212) Ability of an individual or group to control the process of decision making, even against resistance. See also Authority; Coercion.

POWER ELITE (pp. 521–522) Hypothesis that the national power structure in the U.S. is controlled by a relatively small number of political, business, and military leaders acting regularly in concert and in effect forming an oligarchy.

POWER STRUCTURE (p. 511) Pattern of role relationships, involving an interplay of authority and influence, that guides decision making at the community or national level.

PREDICTION, THEORETICAL (p. 26) Testable generalization that is a logical consequence of propositions in a theory.

PREDISPOSITIONS See Acquired Predispositions.

PREJUDICE (p. 264) Emotional and relatively inflexible antipathy toward the members of some group or social category, individually and collectively.

PRESTIGE See Status.

PRIMARY vs. SECONDARY GROUPS (p. 63) Primary groups (as defined by Cooley) are small intimate groups that are especially important to the individual as a source of emotional satisfaction. Secondary groups are those in which interaction patterns are relatively impersonal; such groups are not necessarily "secondary," however, in terms of their effects on the individual's life.

PROFANE See Sacred vs. Profane.

PROTESTANT (PURITAN) ETHIC (p. 107) Complex of beliefs, ideas, and norms which stress the value of hard work, frugality in life-style, and rational use of time. Weber advanced the thesis that the Protestant Ethic provided a set of value orientations which became an important motivating force in the development of rational capitalism in Western Europe.

PSYCHODYNAMIC PERSUASION (pp. 426–427) A persuasive strategy based on manipulation of psychological variables through communication. See also Persuasion.

PUBLIC OPINION (p. 431) The shared convictions of the members of a public concerning the appropriate way to interpret and respond to a given issue or situation. See also Opinion.

PUTTING-OUT SYSTEM (p. 529) A system of production, also called "cottage industry," in which workers produce products in their homes for a merchant who provides them with their raw materials and then buys the finished items back by the piece.

QUESTIONNAIRE (p. 467) A printed list of carefully designed questions which research subjects fill out under controlled conditions.

RACE (p. 243) Defined scientifically as a subdivision of the human species that is biologically distinguishable in terms of such characteristics as skin color, blood type, gene frequency, head measurement, and facial structure. The criteria used in cultural definitions of race are much less precise and sometimes are extremely arbitrary.

REBELLION (p. 183)   As used by Merton, a deviant mode of adaptation in which the individual attempts to replace conventionally accepted goals and means with new ones (e.g., by participating actively in a social movement). *See* Anomie Theory.

RECIPROCAL STIMULATION (p. 381)   In active and expressive crowds, the process by which people mutually reinforce each other's emotional responses and thus lead each other to emotional states of quickly mounting intensity.

REFERENCE GROUP (p. 63)   Any group that serves as a guide in the formation of attitudes and values, whether or not one is actually a member.

REHABILITATION (p. 199)   Attempts to help deviant persons develop behavior patterns, attitudes, and skills that will be consistent with societal norms.

REINFORCEMENT (p. 154)   Process whereby a particular pattern of behavior becomes firmly established through repeated association with rewards.

RELIABILITY (p. 129)   The degree to which a given measurement procedure yields comparable results when used with different subjects or by different investigators.

RETREATISM (p. 182)   As used by Merton, a deviant mode of adaptation in which the individual abandons both cultural goals and the institutionalized means for attaining them. *See* Anomie Theory.

REVELATION (p. 477)   Knowledge that is claimed to have been received from a divine source.

REVOLUTION (p. 500)   A challenge to the legitimacy of an established system, especially political, usually involving violent conflict.

RITE OF PASSAGE (p. 446)   Act or event that marks the transition of an individual from one general position in society to another. For example, the transition from adolescent to adult position is marked by significant ceremonies in some societies.

RITUAL (p. 540)   A practice prescribed for members of a religious group for the purpose of symbolizing, honoring, and reinforcing some aspect of the members' faith.

RITUALISM (p. 182)   As used by Merton, a deviant mode of adaptation in which the individual abandons or rejects cultural goals but nevertheless follows institutionalized means for achieving them (e.g., a bureaucrat who concentrates on enforcing petty rules). Not ordinarily regarded as seriously deviant behavior. *See* Anomie Theory.

ROLE (p. 40)   Group expectations concerning the rights, duties, and obligations of any member who performs a specialized function within the group.

ROLE ALLOCATION (p. 40)   The development of specialized behavioral expectations for different members of a group.

ROLE CONFLICT (p. 55)   Incompatible demands or expectations associated with a given role; also, incompatible demands imposed on an individual who must play or choose between two or more different roles at the same time.

RUMOR (p. 382)   Unverified report that is passed along from person to person, usually by word of mouth. Rumors often play a key part in generating incidents of collective behavior.

SACRED *vs.* PROFANE (pp. 470–471)   Concepts introduced by Durkheim to describe the "classification of all things, real and ideal, of which men think into two classes or opposed groups." The *sacred* includes those things and ideas that people set apart as being worthy of profound respect and unquestioning acceptance. The *profane* encompasses everything else.

SAMPLING (p. 365)   A procedure for studying a particular population by systematically selecting a relatively small segment of that population and using that sample in making inferences about the whole. A sample is said to be representative, or unbiased, to the extent that it accurately reflects the characteristics of the entire population, or at least those characteristics that are relevant to the research problem.

SAMPLING FRAME (p. 365)   Complete list of elements of a population from which a sample is to be drawn.

SANCTIONS (pp. 41–42)   Actions taken to help maintain social control; may be either positive or negative. Negative sanctions are meted out as punishment or threat of punishment to members who violate norms or fail to perform their roles adequately; their purpose is to check deviation. Positive sanctions are used to reward members who meet or exceed the group's expectations; thus they serve to reinforce approved patterns of behavior.

SCIENTIFIC METHOD (p. 24)   Procedure for formulating research questions, designing appropriate studies, measuring variables, analyzing results, and forming conclusions within a system of technique and logic that is accepted by other scientists in a discipline.

SECONDARY GROUP   *See* Primary *vs.* Secondary Groups.

SECT (p. 480)   A distinct religious unit that has broken away from an established group because of certain refinements or distinctions of belief.

SECTOR THEORY (p. 353)   Hypothesis developed by Hoyt stating that transportation arteries are crucial in determining the spatial organization of a city and produce a series of unequal spokes radiating from the center. *See also* Concentric Zone Theory; Multiple Nuclei Theory.

SECULARIZATION (p. 496)   Process that removes established social patterns and institutions from the classification of "sacred" (i.e., set apart as worthy of profound respect and unquestioning acceptance) and subjects them to critical scrutiny and/or skepticism.

SEGREGATION (pp. 261–262)   Spatial and/or social separation of a minority group from the dominant sector(s) of society.

SELECTIVE PERCEPTION (pp. 415–416)   Selective response of an individual to stimuli in the environment, reflecting his or her unique pattern of needs, habits, attitudes, values, etc., which results in the individual's focusing on certain aspects of reality while ignoring others.

SELF (p. 138)   Beliefs and evaluations that an individual holds concerning his or her own body, abilities, appearance, circumstances, etc.; sometimes termed "self-concept." Such beliefs and evaluations develop through social experience. See also Looking-Glass Self.

SELF-FULFILLING PROPHECY (pp. 282, 576)   A proposition, stating that people behave so as to bring about the results that others have expected of them or that they have expected of themselves.

SIGNIFICANT SYMBOL (p. 137)   Concept developed by Mead in his analysis of human communication. A symbol (e.g., a word or phrase) is a significant symbol if it evokes essentially the same meaning (internal response) in the interacting parties. See also Symbolic Interaction.

SMSA   See Standard Metropolitan Statistical Area.

SOCIAL BONDS PERSPECTIVE (pp. 185–186)   An explanation of deviance which maintains that lack or loss of attachments and commitments to conventional groups makes an individual more likely to perform deviant acts or to assume deviant roles.

SOCIAL CATEGORY (p. 33)   A number of individuals who can be classified together on the basis of a common characteristic or cluster of characteristics.

SOCIAL CHANGE (p. 275)   Alteration in the patterns of social organization of a group or society. See also Cultural Change.

SOCIAL CLASS   See Class.

SOCIAL COHESION (pp. 21–22)   Degree to which group members share common beliefs, practices, and values and thus act "like one."

SOCIAL CONFLICT   See Conflict Theory.

SOCIAL CONTRACT THEORY (p. 5)   Theory of the origins of the state as a system of government, first stated systematically by Hobbes and elaborated later by Rousseau. Assumes that the state originated in an agreement among people (social contract) to surrender to a sovereign power some of their freedoms in order to have rules enforced that would assure a more harmonious and stable form of social life.

SOCIAL CONTROL (p. 41)   Application of positive and negative sanctions (rewards and punishments) by a group to encourage members to (1) abide by the group's norms, (2) perform required roles in the expected manner, and (3) coordinate their activities in such a way that group goals can be achieved.

SOCIAL DARWINISM (p. 7)   Spencer's interpretation of society in terms of evolution and natural selection—survival of the fittest.

SOCIAL DIFFERENTIATION (p. 112)   Differences in values, beliefs, attitudes, etc., among members of a community or society, reflecting their different positions in the social structure and different patterns of experience. Social differentiation provides the basis for the development of subcultures.

SOCIAL DISTANCE (p. 267)   Degree to which individuals are willing to interact with people from different social or ethnic backgrounds.

SOCIAL INSTITUTION (pp. 92, 440)   A complex pattern of established social and cultural forms within a given society—groups, norms, roles, customs, traditions, shared attitudes, values, etc.—that pertain to some important goal-oriented activity. All societies have several basic social institutions: familial, religious, economic, political, and educational. Urban-industrial societies have many others, e.g., scientific, legal, military, recreational.

SOCIAL INTEGRATION   See Social Solidarity.

SOCIAL INTERACTION   See Interaction.

SOCIAL MOBILITY (pp. 228–232)   Movement up or down in a system of social stratification; sometimes referred to as vertical mobility. See also Geographical Mobility; Horizontal Mobility; Occupational Mobility.

SOCIAL MOVEMENT (p. 394)   Collective activity aimed at correcting some perceived inadequacy in existing social arrangements (e.g., in the political or economic institution). In their early stages, social movements are relatively unstructured, but if they persist over time they tend to become increasingly organized and to merge into group activity.

SOCIAL ORGANIZATION (p. 33)   Relatively stable pattern of interaction among members of a group who relate themselves to each other through norms, roles, social control procedures, and a system of social ranking.

SOCIAL RANKING (p. 43)   Differential evaluation of roles in a group and thus of the individuals who fill them. See also Stratification.

SOCIAL ROLE   See Role.

SOCIAL SCHEMATA (p. 130)   In the analysis of cognition, a term used to describe the subjective "theories" of behavior individuals use in everyday life to predict how other people will behave.

SOCIAL SOLIDARITY (p. 90)   Condition of a social system in which the parts or members are so intermeshed or interdependent as to form a more-or-less unified whole; social integration or cohesion. See also Mechanical vs. Organic Solidarity.

SOCIAL STATUS   See Status.

SOCIAL STRATIFICATION   See Stratification.

SOCIAL STRUCTURE   See Social Organization.

SOCIAL SYSTEM (p. 47)   Term used by social scientists in conceptualizing a group as a configuration of interrelated parts that function together as an ongoing whole. Like other types of systems, each social system is composed of subsystems and is itself part of a larger system, or field.

SOCIAL VALIDATION (p. 435) The process by which a given view, idea, or belief comes to be perceived as valid by virtue of the fact that it is shared by other people.

SOCIALIZATION (p. 146) Complex process of social learning whereby individuals come to internalize, or accept as their own, cultural and subcultural behavior patterns.

SOCIETY (p. 83) The most complex type of human group, composed of many subgroups; the largest group with which most people feel a sense of personal identity, and in some ways the most important in its effects on their lives.

SOCIOCULTURAL PERSUASION (p. 427) A persuasive strategy that attempts to manipulate behavior by using communication to define or redefine the patterns of expectation on which the behavior of group's members is based. *See also* Persuasion.

SOCIOGRAM (p. 46) Method of representing symbolically the existing patterns of interpersonal attraction, indifference, and rejection among the various members of a group.

SOCIOLOGY (pp. 2–29) Organized inquiry into the fundamental nature of social life: an attempt to examine human social behavior systematically—within the scientific perspective—to understand it, to predict it, and, in some cases, to do something about it.

SOCIOMETRY (p. 46) Objective measurement technique for assessing patterns of interpersonal relationship among the members of a specific group. *See also* Sociogram.

SOLIDARITY *See* Social Solidarity.

STANDARD DEVIATION (p. 570) A coefficient indicating scatter (variability or dispersion) in an array of numbers.

STANDARD METROPOLITAN STATISTICAL AREA (SMSA) (p. 342) As defined by the Bureau of the Census, "a county or group of contiguous counties which contains at least one city of 50,000 inhabitants or more or 'twin cities' with a combined population of at least 50,000. In addition to the county or counties containing such a city or cities, contiguous counties are included in an SMSA if, according to certain criteria, they are essentially metropolitan in character and are socially and economically integrated with the central city."

STATISTICAL ANALYSIS (p. 570) Numerical procedures used in many sciences for describing trends, differences, relationships, and probabilities in categories of phenomena under study; widely used in sociology for both descriptive purposes and for making decisions about the probable validity of research findings.

STATISTICS Numerical measurements arranged in some meaningful way. The most important task of statistics (in fact, the literal meaning of the term) is to summarize in a single numerical value some quality, trend, or property of an array of measures.

STATUS (pp. 43, 46) As used in the present text, the levels of prestige accorded to particular group members as a result of the differential value placed on the roles they play. *Status* is thus distinguished from *esteem*, which is the level of value accorded to a group member as a result of personal qualities, including (but not limited to) the quality of role performance.

STATUS CONFERRAL FUNCTION (p. 422) The effect the mass media have of conferring prestige on persons simply by focusing attention on them.

STEREOTYPE (p. 267) Cluster of beliefs and attitudes used to characterize a whole category or group of people without regard for individual differences.

STRATIFICATION (pp. 83, 206) In communities and societies, the ranking of individuals and families into levels (strata) that share unequally in the distribution of status, wealth, and power.

SUBCULTURE (p. 112) Somewhat distinctive pattern of norms, beliefs, attitudes, values, and other cultural elements that characterize a particular group, type of group, or subsegment of a society.

SUBORDINATE Belonging to lower class or rank.

SUCCESSION (p. 350) In urban ecology, process by which one pattern of land use becomes predominant and replaces another which in turn re-creates itself in a different (usually adjoining) locality.

SYMBOL (pp. 98, 137) Gesture, object, utterance, or written mark with an agreed-upon meaning; the basis of human communication.

SYMBOLIC INTERACTION (pp. 34, 137) The fundamental form of social interaction, in which a group's members use arbitrary and conventionalized signs (e.g., language symbols) to communicate with one another. Symbolic interaction is essential to the development and maintenance of personal organization as well as to the development and maintenance of social organization.

TECHNOLOGY Means available to a group or society for the production and distribution of goods and services, usually consisting of machines, tools, and other equipment, as well as knowledge.

TEMPERAMENT (p. 135) Characteristic manner in which an individual responds to the environment, depending on such general traits as energy level, degree of sensitivity to stimulation, adaptability, etc. Such reaction tendencies are thought to have a constitutional basis, but the evidence is inconclusive.

THEORY (p. 23) A set of interrelated propositions or generalizations combined in such a way as to provide a logical and verifiable system of explanation of a set of events.

TOLERANCE LIMIT (p. 42)   Range of behavior that a group accepts as being in general conformity with its "rules." Tolerance limits are seldom precisely defined, but the members of a group soon learn from experience how much leeway they have in interpreting particular norms and roles.

TRADITIONAL AUTHORITY (p. 501)   Pattern of authority in which power to make and implement decisions is based on unwritten rules or laws that have been handed down from the past and that are often felt to be sacred.

TRADITIONAL SOCIETY (p. 349)   Broad term used in contrasting the social characteristics of urban-industrial societies with those of earlier and/or seemingly simpler forms of societal organization; a "folk society" or "primitive society" that is characterized by a predominance of communal rather than associative relationships.

TRADITION-DIRECTED PERSONALITY (p. 160)   An ideal type developed by Riesman, identifying an individual who looks to society's established ways for guidance in personal conduct. See also Inner-Directed Personality; Other-Directed Personality.

TRAIT   In the social and behavioral sciences, any characteristic of an individual or group that can be observed and measured.

TWO-STEP FLOW OF COMMUNICATION (p. 418)   Mass communication process whereby information passes from the media to a relatively small number of well-informed people, who in turn transmit it to others.

UNIFORM CRIME REPORTS (p. 193)   Annual publication of the FBI containing a number of indices of various types of crimes for different cities and sections of the country.

UNIVERSAL CHURCH (p. 480)   A religious group that has no serious competitors in the society in which it exists, e.g., the Catholic Church in thirteenth-century Europe.

URBAN (p. 342)   Term used to denote localities in which economic activities are predominantly non-agricultural. The U.S. Bureau of the Census arbitrarily designates as *urban* any locality with a population of 2500 or more people; in other countries, the term is generally restricted to localities with populations of 20,000 or more. See also Urbanized Area.

URBAN REGION (p. 342)   An area having a population of a million or more people in a continuous zone of metropolitan areas.

URBANISM (p. 350)   Patterns of social organization and culture that have developed as a consequence of urbanization.

URBANIZATION (p. 341)   The progressive movement of people from rural areas to cities, resulting in city growth and a shift in the relative proportions of rural *vs.* urban population.

URBANIZED AREA (p. 342)   Term developed by the U.S. Bureau of the Census to provide a meaningful distinction between urban and rural populations. An urbanized area includes at least one city of 50,000 people or more plus all closely settled territory around it. See also Urban.

VALIDATION (p. 24)   Formulation and verification of a hypothesis or explanatory theory. Most theories remain in a state of partial validation for substantial periods of time, as scientists continue to test them against empirical data. Strictly speaking, no theory or hypothesis is ever finally proved; it is valid only in the sense that it has been supported by a substantial amount of empirical evidence.

VALIDITY (p. 129)   The degree to which a measuring procedure is actually capable of assessing the variable that it has been designed to assess, (e.g., if a particular IQ test actually measures "intelligence").

VALUES (p. 161)   Basic sentiments or standards by which people orient themselves toward goals and ideals.

VARIABLES (p. 21)   Concept whose properties can vary—that is, come in different amounts—either quantitatively or qualitatively.

VERSTEHEN APPROACH (p. 15)   Approach to the study of social interaction first proposed by Weber in which the observer attempts to assume the perspective of the interacting parties. The word *Verstehen* in German means "understanding" or "insight."

VERTICAL MOBILITY   See Social Mobility.

VICTIMIZATION STUDIES (p. 196)   Surveys of households used to obtain more reliable indicators of the actual incidence of crime than those provided by police files and other official records.

VOCATIONAL SORTING (p. 564)   Educational process of channeling students into particular occupations or types of occupations according to their interests and abilities.

VOLUNTARY ASSOCIATION (p. 79)   Group of people banded together voluntarily in order to meet a specific need or to solve personal, community, or societal problems.

WHITE-COLLAR CRIME (p. 198)   Crime committed by people of relatively high social ranking and generally related to their occupation, e.g., tax evasion by a self-employed professional or embezzlement by a banker.

ZONAL THEORY   See Concentric Zone Theory.

NAME INDEX

SUBJECT INDEX